Usborne
Illustrated
English
Dictionary
&Thesaurus

Edited by
Jane Bingham and Fiona Chandler

Designed by
Susie McCaffrey, Matthew Hart
and Stephanie Jones

Illustrated by
Sean Wilkinson, Gerald Wood, Nicholas Hewetson,
Ian Jackson, Peter Dennis, Michelle Ross, David Cuzik,
Ann Johns and Gary Bines

D1323849

COVER DESIGN: Michael Hill

PHOTOGRAPHY: MMStudios

MANAGING EDITOR: Chris Rawson

EDITORIAL DIRECTOR: Felicity Brooks

DEFINITIONS BY John McIlwain, Sheila Dignen,
Jessica Feinstein, Andrew Delahunty

ADDITIONAL EDITORIAL WORK: Rachel Wardley, Alex Frith, Rachel Firth,
Rachel Tranter, Alice Primmer and Hannah Wood

ADDITIONAL DESIGN WORK: Sue Grobecker

ADVISORS: Shelley Harris, Colin Hope, Susan Hitch, George Phillipson,
Richard Hatton, John Rostron, Margaret Rostron,
Anne Rooney, Bill Chambers, Anne Millard, Michael Reiss

Internet links

There are lots of great websites on the internet to help with English writing, grammar, spelling, and punctuation. At the Usborne Quicklinks Website, you can search online dictionaries, use handy thesauruses and find help with homework. There are also writing activities, quizzes, word searches, puzzles and games to build skills and understanding.

To visit the recommended websites for this book, go to the Usborne Quicklinks Website at **www.usborne.com/quicklinks** and type the keyword "**dictionary**".

When using the internet, please follow the internet safety guidelines shown on the Usborne Quicklinks Website. The recommended websites in Usborne Quicklinks are regularly reviewed and updated, but Usborne Publishing Ltd. is not responsible and does not accept liability for the content or availability of any website other than its own. We recommend that children are supervised while using the internet.

THE PUBLISHERS ARE GRATEFUL TO THE FOLLOWING: Benetton Formula Ltd. (196); Boss Trucks Ltd. (102); Corporation of Trinity House (144); Douglas MacKenzie, Visitor Services Manager, HMS Victory, Portsmouth (222-223); Flight International (14-15); Ford Motor Company Ltd. (46); Massey Ferguson (259); Minolta Cameras (179); Mitsui Machinery Sales (UK) Ltd. (158); New Holland Ford Sales Promotion & Product Support Department (117); Renault UK Ltd. (192); Rolls Royce plc (135); Shell UK Exploration and Production (167); Stephen Bateman (164); Thames Barrier Visitor's Centre (28); Vickers PLC, Defence Systems (21); Yamaha-Kemble Music (UK) Ltd. (200). The picture on page 203 is based on the drawing "Study for the Head of Leda" by Leonardo da Vinci, The Royal Collection, Windsor.

This edition first published in 2015 by Usborne Publishing Ltd, 83-85 Saffron Hill, London EC1N 8RT, England. **www.usborne.com**
Copyright © 2015, 2012, 2007, 1994 Usborne Publishing Ltd. The name Usborne and the devices ♀☺ are Trade Marks of Usborne Publishing Ltd. All rights reserved. No part of this publication may be reproduced, stored in a retrieval system, or transmitted in any form or by any means, electronic, mechanical, photocopy, recording or otherwise, without the prior permission of the publishers. UKE. Printed in Dubai, UAE.

Usborne

Illustrated English Dictionary

Contents

YOUR DICTIONARY: A USER'S GUIDE

This dictionary contains over ten thousand entries and over a thousand pictures, many of them surrounded by picture labels. Here is the entry for "satellite" with its labelled picture.

Finding a word

Entries are listed in alphabetical order. Make a guess at the first few letters of your word, for example, for "satellite", find "sat", then try different ways of spelling the next part.

If you can't find a word

- You may have chosen the wrong first letters. Try some alternative spellings and look out for **spelling guides** at the bottom of the page.

- You may be able to find a related word. For example, you would find the word "slothful" under "sloth".

- The word you want may be a **picture label**. Look for it in the **Index of picture labels** at the back of the dictionary.

horn cluster (receives and sends signals to and from reflector)

control antenna

reflector (receives signals and focuses signals back to Earth)

infra-red Earth sensor (keeps satellite facing Earth)

heat pipes (keep equipment cool)

mirrored radiator wall (keeps equipment cool)

thruster nozzle (adjusts position of satellite in orbit)

rocket motor (blasts satellite into circular orbit)

fuel tank

solar sailing flap (helps control satellite's position)

solar array drive mechanism (rotates solar panels to face Sun)

thermal blanket cover (layers of protective foil)

solar array panel (generates electricity from Sun)

communications satellite

satellite *(n)*
1 a machine that is sent into orbit around the Earth. *The picture shows the main parts of a communications satellite, which receives and sends television and telephone signals.*
2 a moon or other natural object that moves in orbit around a planet. *See* **Moon**.

Looking at pages

Guide words help you to find the right page.

Guide letters help you to find the right letter section.

Spelling guides help you to find tricky words by suggesting other spellings.

Looking at entries

Headwords show how a word is spelt.

Pronunciation guides show how a word is said.

Definitions explain what a word means.

sloth *(rhymes with both)*
1 *(n)* a very slow-moving South American mammal with a shaggy coat.
2 *(n)* laziness. **slothful** *(adj)*.
slouch slouches slouching slouched
1 *(v)* to sit, stand, or walk in a lazy way, with your shoulders and head drooping.
2 *(n)* *(slang)* a slow and lazy person. *Dan's no slouch at football.*

Parts of speech identify what a word does in a sentence (see page 3).

Related words introduce words from the same family.

Changing forms show how words change their spelling when they are used in different ways.

Numbers indicate a separate sense of a word.

Usage guides show that a word is old-fashioned, poetic, informal or slang. Informal words are used in everyday speech, but not in formal or official writing. Slang is usually only spoken.

Example sentences show how a word is used.

Weights, measures, numbers, days, months, countries and nationalities are listed on page 284.

PARTS OF SPEECH: THE PARTS THAT WORDS PLAY

Each word plays a different part in a sentence, depending on its part of speech. If you know a word's part of speech, you can work out how to use it. This sentence contains all eight parts of speech.

interjection **"Crumbs!"**

verb *cried*

adjective *the[1] cowardly*

noun *knight*

conjunction *as*

pronoun *he*

verb *saw a[2]*

noun *dragon*

verb *swoop*

adverb *swiftly*

preposition *to*

noun *earth.*

[1] "The" is a special adjective called **the definite article**.

[2] "A" is **the indefinite article**.

noun (n) Nouns give the name of a person, animal, or thing. They tell you who or what a sentence is about.

Bobo is juggling.

Practice is essential.

pronoun (pronoun) Pronouns refer to a person or thing without naming it. They act like nouns.

(Annie is very good at skiing.)
She is very good at skiing.

(The weather is extremely cold.)
It is extremely cold.

adjective (adj) Adjectives are descriptive words which tell you more about a person or thing. They are used with nouns and pronouns.

Toucans have enormous beaks.

They are very bright.

verb (v) Verbs are action words. They say what someone or something does, thinks, or feels. All sentences need verbs to tell you what is happening.

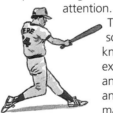

Spike loves his motorbike.

It goes really fast.

adverb (adv) Adverbs tell you how, when, where, or why something happens. They are used with verbs.

The horse is bucking wildly.

Its rider may soon fall off.

conjunction (conj) Conjunctions are linking words. They join parts of sentences.

Penguins have wings, but cannot fly.

They breed on land and hunt in water.

preposition (prep) Prepositions show where people or things are, or what relation they have to each other.

A Chinese dragon weaves through the streets.

People are dancing under the dragon.

interjection (interject) Interjections are used to show surprise, delight or pain, or to get attention.

They are sometimes known as exclamations and often have an exclamation mark.

"Wow!" cried the crowd as the baseball player hit the ball.

"Yippee!" yelled the fielder as he caught it.

Note – Some words in the dictionary are not given a part of speech. This is because they are used with other words or in a phrase.

WRITING ENGLISH: SOME HINTS AND GUIDELINES

These two pages give some help with spelling and punctuation. You should find them useful to refer to when you are writing.

Spelling English

It is sometimes hard to spell English correctly because it is a mixture of so many languages (see pages 6-7). Here are some patterns to follow and spellings to remember, but watch out for exceptions and use a dictionary to check your spelling.

Making plurals

Most nouns simply gain an **s** to become plural.

dinosaur

dinosaur - dinosaurs
book - books
garden - gardens
apple - apples

zoo - zoos
day - days
house - houses
bicycle - bicycles

dinosaurs

Some words, however, change differently. Here are some word groups for you to remember.

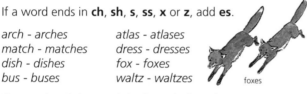

If a word ends in **ch**, **sh**, **s**, **ss**, **x** or **z**, add **es**.

arch - arches
match - matches
dish - dishes
bus - buses

atlas - atlases
dress - dresses
fox - foxes
waltz - waltzes

fox

foxes

If a word ends in **y** and the letter before the y is not a, e, i, o or u, replace the y with **ies**.

berry - berries
baby - babies
party - parties
pony - ponies

country - countries
city - cities
puppy - puppies
library - libraries

berry

berries

Many words ending in **f** drop their final f and gain **ves**.

leaf - leaves
half - halves
loaf - loaves
shelf - shelves

wife - wives
thief - thieves
dwarf - dwarves
wolf - wolves

leaf

leaves

Many words ending in **o** gain **es**.

buffalo - buffaloes
cargo - cargoes
tomato - tomatoes

potato - potatoes
echo - echoes
hero - heroes

buffalo

buffaloes

Odd plurals

Some words change their spelling dramatically when they become plural. These plurals need to be learnt.

woman - women
child - children

man - men
mouse - mice

foot - feet
tooth - teeth

Letter pairs

qu
q is always followed by **u**.

queen   request
quit   squad

queen

gh
When **g** and **h** are written together, **g** always comes before **h**.

sleigh
right
ghost
although

sleigh

i and e
It is very easy to get these two letters the wrong way round, but this rule should help you.

"i before e, except after c, when the sound is ee."

i before **e**   **e** before **i**
shield   ceiling
believe   receive
thief   conceited
field   receipt

Note - there are some exceptions to this rule, such as *seize, weir, weird*.

Doubling up

Watch out for the double letters in these words.

accommodate   disappoint
accurate   embarrass
address   necessary
beginning   occasion
communicate   parallel

One word or two?

Here are some common words and phrases that are often spelt wrongly.

two words	one word
thank you	cannot
no one	someone
all right	altogether

Double or single l?

It is sometimes hard to know whether words have a single or a double l. The following words have only one l.

already	careful
always	until
awful	welcome

Remember - when full is added to a word, it drops its final l.

Whenever I see a spider, I am <u>full</u> of fear.

Whenever I see a spider, I am fear<u>ful</u>.

Tricky endings

-le or -el

Most words end in **-le**.

battle	bubble
trouble	table
able	Bible

but watch out for:
travel barrel label quarrel

-ic or -ick

Words with two or more sounds (syllables) end in **-ic**. Words with one sound end in **-ick**.

comic	stick
fantastic	lick
artistic	trick

Learning spellings

Follow the four steps below when you are learning to spell a word.
1 LOOK at the word carefully and memorize the order of letters.
2 COVER the word.
3 WRITE it down from memory.
4 CHECK that it is right.

Punctuation

Without punctuation to break them up, your sentences would be impossible to read. These guidelines will help you to use some tricky punctuation marks.

Apostrophes

Apostrophes show the owner of something *(The hat that belongs to Ben = Ben's hat)* or mark missing letters *(I am hungry = I'm hungry)*.

Apostrophe s

If the owner is singular, add an **apostrophe s**
Ben<u>'s</u> hat
Charles<u>'s</u> hat

If the owner is plural and ends in s, add an **apostrophe only**
The boys' hats

If the owner is plural, but does not end in s, add an **apostrophe s**
The children<u>'s</u> hats

Never use an apostrophe s to make a plural.

Missing letters

Usually, an apostrophe shows that one letter has been dropped, but sometimes more than one letter is missing:
I'd = I would or I had
shan't = shall not
won't = will not

it's and its

it's is only used to show that a letter has been missed out from **it is**.

I'm glad <u>it's</u> a sunny day.

The kangaroo carries <u>its</u> baby in <u>its</u> pouch.

Colons and semi-colons

You can manage without colons and semi-colons in your writing, but they can be very useful. Here are some ways to use them.

Colons can be used to introduce a statement or a list.

At last Harry revealed the secret of his success: three raw carrots every day.

For this trick you need: a pack of cards, a silk scarf and a wand.

Semi-colons are useful for breaking up lists when the items in the list are long and complicated.

We visited the zoo and saw: two giraffes; an elephant with a baby; some performing seals; and a very mischievous monkey.

Inverted commas

You use inverted commas, or speech marks, to show that someone is speaking. Always start someone's spoken words with a capital letter and use a comma to separate speech from the rest of the sentence.

"The view is amazing," said the astronaut.

The astronaut said, "The view is amazing."

"The view," said the astronaut, "is amazing."

THE STORY OF ENGLISH: A HISTORY OF OUR LANGUAGE

People first spoke English fifteen hundred years ago. Since then, our language has changed enormously, both in the way it is spoken and written, and in its range of words. These two pages show how English grew and changed as the British were invaded, visited, and influenced by people from other countries.

Old English: 5th-11th century

Three main groups of people created Old English: the Anglo-Saxon tribes who settled in England, Christian missionaries from Rome, and Viking and Danish invaders and settlers.

Anglo-Saxons
5th-6th century: Tribes of Angles, Saxons and Jutes from mainland Europe and Scandinavia invaded the British Isles and created a new kingdom of England. People in England spoke Anglo-Saxon, the earliest form of English.

Anglo-Saxon helmet

--- ANGLO-SAXON WORDS ---
fire	day	book
man	what	and
house	earth	you

Missionaries from Rome
5th-7th century: Christian missionaries travelled to Britain and founded monasteries. The monks held services in Latin and copied Latin manuscripts.

6th-century monk

--- LATIN WORDS ---
verse	altar
angel	candle
demon	school
pope	hymn

Vikings and Danes
8th-11th century: Vikings and Danes from Scandinavia attacked Britain. During the 10th and 11th centuries the Danes ruled over north-east England.

Viking invaders

--- SCANDINAVIAN WORDS ---
leg	knife	skin
want	sky	egg
dirt	get	bull

Beowulf - an Old English poem
Written in the 8th century, and over 3,000 lines long, *Beowulf* tells the story of a courageous warrior who fights against monsters to save his people.

"Wiht unhælo, grim ond
The unholy creature, grim and

grædig, gearo sona wæs,
greedy, was soon ready,

reoc ond repe, ond on
savage and cruel, and from

ræste genam pritig pegna.
their rest seized thirty thanes.

Middle English: Late 11th-15th century

In this period, the Normans added French words to the language, some spellings changed, and borrowing from Latin continued.

Normans
1066-1300: In 1066, William of Normandy conquered England. French was spoken by the upper classes and used in parliament and the law courts.

William the Conqueror

--- FRENCH WORDS ---
court	crime	feast
royal	fashion	music
attorney	beauty	story

Spelling changes
12th-15th century: Old English letters were abandoned. French scribes introduced "qu", "gh", "ch" and "ng" spellings.

The Canterbury Tales - a Middle English poem
Geoffrey Chaucer began writing the *Canterbury Tales* around 1387. The poem presents 23 tales, told by pilgrims.

"Thanne longen folk to goon
Then people long to go

on pilgrimages...And specially
on pilgrimages... And specially

from every shires ende of
from the end of every county of

Engelond to Caunterbury
England to Canterbury

they wende."
they travel.

The birth of modern English: Late 15th-18th century

In this period, English gradually became recognizable as the language that we use today.

Caxton and the rise of printing

1476: William Caxton began printing books in English. This led to a great increase in reading and writing.

15th-century printing press

William Shakespeare

1590-1612: William Shakespeare used the English language in new and exciting ways in his plays and poetry.

Shakespeare

PHRASES FROM SHAKESPEARE

good riddance
a blinking-idiot
high time
foul play
a laughing stock
an eyesore

The King James Bible

1611: An English version of the Bible was printed. This version, which was authorized by King James I, was used throughout the country.

PHRASES FROM THE KING JAMES BIBLE

in the twinkling of an eye
the skin of my teeth
a wolf in sheep's clothing
the salt of the earth
the apple of my eye
an eye for an eye

THE GOSPEL ACCORDING to S. Matthew

The Renaissance

1475-1650: People became interested in Ancient Greek and Roman writings, and developed new ideas in science and the arts. To express these ideas, they borrowed words from Greek, Latin, French and Italian.

17th-century astronomical sphere

RENAISSANCE WORDS

SCIENTIFIC WORDS
temperature (Latin)
skeleton (Greek)
pneumonia (Greek)
gravity (Latin)
muscle (Latin)
virus (Latin)

MUSICAL WORDS
violin (Italian)
madrigal (Italian)
soprano (Italian)
opera (Italian)
ballet (French)
fugue (French)

ARCHITECTURAL WORDS
cupola (Italian)
balcony (Italian)
grotto (Italian)
dome (French)
portico (Italian)
stucco (Italian)

Dr Johnson's dictionary

1755: Dr Samuel Johnson published his *Dictionary of the English Language*. By this time, English spelling was almost standardized.

Dr Johnson

Traders and explorers

16th-18th century: explorers discovered new countries and merchants traded with them, bringing back new words.

yam

apricot

maize

TRADING WORDS

coffee (Turkish)
banana (Spanish)
yam (Portuguese)
apricot (Portuguese)
maize (Spanish)
potato (Spanish)

coffee

potatoes

bananas

Gulliver's Travels - an 18th-century novel

Jonathan Swift wrote *Gulliver's Travels* in 1726, using words and spellings that are very close to modern English. In this passage, Gulliver has been captured by tiny Lilliputians.

"I attempted to rise, but was not able to stir...I could only look upwards; the Sun began to grow hot, and the Light offended mine eyes."

Modern English: 19th century onward

No major changes took place in the language after 1800, but English spread around the world and gained thousands of new words.

ENGLISH TODAY: ITS RANGE AND VARIETY

English is now a world language, spoken by over 350 million people, with at least 750 million more using it as a second language. Here are some words used by English speakers in different parts of the world.

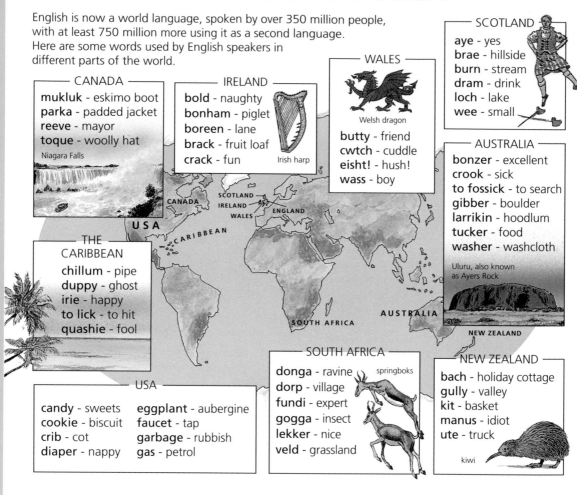

SCOTLAND
aye - yes
brae - hillside
burn - stream
dram - drink
loch - lake
wee - small

CANADA
mukluk - eskimo boot
parka - padded jacket
reeve - mayor
toque - woolly hat

Niagara Falls

IRELAND
bold - naughty
bonham - piglet
boreen - lane
brack - fruit loaf
crack - fun

Irish harp

WALES

Welsh dragon

butty - friend
cwtch - cuddle
eisht! - hush!
wass - boy

AUSTRALIA
bonzer - excellent
crook - sick
to fossick - to search
gibber - boulder
larrikin - hoodlum
tucker - food
washer - washcloth

Uluru, also known as Ayers Rock

THE CARIBBEAN
chillum - pipe
duppy - ghost
irie - happy
to lick - to hit
quashie - fool

USA
candy - sweets
cookie - biscuit
crib - cot
diaper - nappy
eggplant - aubergine
faucet - tap
garbage - rubbish
gas - petrol

SOUTH AFRICA
donga - ravine
dorp - village
fundi - expert
gogga - insect
lekker - nice
veld - grassland

springboks

NEW ZEALAND
bach - holiday cottage
gully - valley
kit - basket
manus - idiot
ute - truck

kiwi

New words

English speakers today continue to borrow words from other languages as well as creating new words. "Karaoke" is a borrowing from Japanese, while the words listed here are all new arrivals in our language.

COMPUTERS
byte
e-book
email
internet
laptop
online
PC
software
blog
website

SPORTS
bungee jumping
hang glider
mountain bike
skateboard
windsurfing

windsurfer

TECHNOLOGY
DVD
mobile phone
texting
touchscreen
satellite TV

communications satellite

SCIENCE AND MEDICINE
acid rain
AIDS
carbon footprint
fiber optics
pacemaker

AIDS virus (magnified)

FASHION AND POP
break dance
grunge
heavy metal
hip hop
jeggings
rap

electric guitar

Aa

aardvark *(n)* an African mammal with a long, sticky tongue, that it uses to search for insects.

aardvark

abacus abacuses *or* abaci *(n)* a frame with sliding beads on wires, used for counting.

abandon abandoning abandoned *(v)*
1 to leave forever. *Abandon ship!*
2 to give up. *As night fell, we abandoned hope of being rescued.*

abattoir *(ab-er-twar) (n)* a place where animals are killed for meat.

abbey *(n)* a group of buildings where monks or nuns live and work.

abbreviation *(n)*
a short way of writing a word. *CD is an abbreviation of "compact disc".* **abbreviated** *(adj).*

abdicate abdicating abdicated *(v)* to give up being king or queen. **abdication** *(n).*

abdomen *(n)*
1 the part of your body between your chest and hips.
2 the back section of an insect's body. *See* **beetle**.

abduct abducting abducted *(v)* to kidnap someone. **abduction** *(n).*

abhor abhorring abhorred *(v)* to hate someone or something. **abhorrent** *(adj).*

abide abiding abode *or* abided *(v)*
1 *(old-fashioned)* to stay or live somewhere.
2 If you **cannot abide** something, you cannot put up with it.

ability abilities *(n)*
1 the power to do something. *I know I have the ability to do better.*
2 skill. *Paul has great ability in art.*

abject *(adj)* miserable and without dignity. *The refugees lived in abject poverty. An abject apology.*

ablaze *(adj)* on fire.

able abler ablest *(adj)*
1 If you are **able** to do something, you can do it.
2 skilful or clever. *Our team has many able players.* **ably** *(adv).*

able-bodied *(adj)*
Someone who is **able-bodied** has no injuries or disabilities.

abnormal *(adj)* unusual or not normal. **abnormality** *(n).*

aboard *(prep)* on or into a train, ship, or aircraft. **aboard** *(adv).*

abode *(n) (old-fashioned)* a home. *Welcome to my humble abode.*

abolish abolishes abolishing abolished *(v)* to put an end to something officially. *We voted to abolish school uniform.* **abolition** *(n).*

abominable *(adj)*
horrible or disgusting. *An abominable mess.* **abominably** *(adv).*

Aborigine *(ab-or-ij in-ee) (n)* one of the native people of Australia who lived there before Europeans arrived. **Aboriginal** *(adj).*

abort aborting aborted *(v)*
1 to remove a fetus from its mother's womb so that the pregnancy ends. **abortion** *(n).*
2 to stop something from happening. **abortive** *(adj).*

abound abounding abounded *(v)* to have a large amount of something. *The forest abounds with wildlife.*

about
1 *(prep)* on a particular subject. *Tell me about your holiday.*
2 *(adv)* almost, or more or less. *My dad is about 40.*

above *(prep)*
1 higher up, or over. *Above the clouds.*
2 more than. *Above average.*

above board *(adj)*
If something that you do is **above board**, it is completely honest and legal.

abrasive *(adj)*
1 rough and grinding, like sandpaper. *An abrasive surface.*
2 rude. *Simon has a terribly abrasive manner.*

abreast *(adv)* side by side. *We walked three abreast.*

abridged *(adj)* shortened. *An abridged novel.* **abridge** *(v).*

abroad *(adv)*
in or to another country. *We are going abroad this summer.*

abrupt *(adj)*
1 sudden and unexpected. *The car came to an abrupt halt.* **abruptly** *(adv).*
2 rude and short-tempered. *An abrupt reply.* **abruptly** *(adv).*

abscess *(ab-sess)* abscesses *(n)* a painful swelling, full of a yellow substance called pus.

abscond absconding absconded *(v)* to go away suddenly and secretly, usually after doing something wrong.

abseil *(ab-sail)* abseiling abseiled *(v)* to lower yourself down a steep cliff or mountain face by holding on to a rope. **abseiler** *(n).*

absent *(adj)* not present. **absence** *(n),* **absentee** *(n),* **absenteeism** *(n).*

absent-minded *(adj)*
If you are **absent-minded**, you are forgetful and do not think about what you are doing. **absent-mindedly** *(adv).*

absolute *(adj)*
1 complete or total. *Ben looks an absolute idiot in that hat.* **absolutely** *(adv).*
2 without any limit. *The dictator had absolute power.*

absolve absolving absolved *(v)* to pardon someone or free them from blame. **absolution** *(n).*

absorb absorbing absorbed *(v)*
1 to soak up liquid. *The sponge absorbed the juice.* **absorbent** *(adj).*
2 to take in information. *The students absorbed all the facts.*
3 If something **absorbs** you, it takes up all your attention.

abstain abstaining abstained *(v)* to stop yourself from doing something. *The prisoners abstained from eating until their demands were met.* **abstention** *(n).*

abstract *(adj)*
based on ideas rather than things. *Abstract artists paint shapes rather than people or objects.*

absurd absurder absurdest *(adj)* silly or ridiculous. **absurdity** *(n),* **absurdly** *(adv).*

abundant *(adj)*
If there is an **abundant** supply of something, there is plenty of it. **abundance** *(n),* **abundantly** *(adv).*

abuse abusing abused
1 *(ab-yuce) (n)* rude or unkind words. **abuse** *(ab-yooze) (v),* **abusive** *(adj).*
2 *(ab-yooze) (v)* to treat a person or creature cruelly. **abuse** *(ab-yuce) (n).*
3 *(ab-yuce) (n)* wrong or harmful use of something. *Alcohol abuse.* **abuse** *(ab-yooze) (v).*

abysmal *(ab-iz-mal) (adj)*
very bad, or terrible. **abysmally** *(adv)*.

abyss *(ab-iss)* **abysses** *(n)* a very deep hole that seems to have no bottom.

academic
1 *(adj)* to do with study and learning. *Eileen loves sport, but hates academic work.* **academically** *(adv)*.
2 *(n)* someone who teaches in a university or college or someone who does research.

accelerate accelerating accelerated *(v)* to get faster and faster. **acceleration** *(n)*.

accent *(n)*
1 the way you pronounce words. *Helmut speaks with a German accent.*
2 a mark put over a letter in some languages to show how it is pronounced, for example, *'café'*.

accentuate accentuating accentuated *(v)* to emphasize or draw attention to something.

accept accepting accepted *(v)*
1 to take something that you are offered. **acceptance** *(n)*.
2 to agree to something. *Kerry won't accept our plan.* acceptance *(n)*, acceptable *(adj)*.

access accesses accessing accessed
1 *(n)* an entrance or approach to a place. **accessible** *(adj)*.
2 *(n)* the right to see someone. *Lucy lives with her mother, but her father has access at weekends.*
3 *(v)* to open up a document, program or website on a computer.

accessory accessories *(n)*
1 an extra part for something. *Car accessories.*
2 something, such as a belt or a scarf, that goes with your clothes.
3 An **accessory** to a crime is someone who helps another person to commit a crime.

accident *(n)* something that takes place unexpectedly, and which often involves people being hurt. **accidental** *(adj)*, **accidentally** *(adv)*.

acclimatize *or* **acclimatise** acclimatizing acclimatized *(v)* to get used to a different climate or to new surroundings. **acclimatization** *(n)*.

accommodation *(n)* a place where people live. **accommodate** *(v)*.

accompany accompanies accompanying accompanied *(v)*
1 to go somewhere with someone.
2 to support a musician or singer by playing a musical instrument. **accompaniment** *(n)*, **accompanist** *(n)*.

accomplice *(ak-um-pliss) (n)* someone who helps another person to commit a crime.

accomplish accomplishes accomplishing accomplished *(v)* to do something successfully. **accomplishment** *(n)*.

accomplished *(adj)* skilful.

accord
1 *(n)* peaceful agreement.
2 If you do something **of your own accord**, you do it without being asked.

according to *(prep)*
1 as someone has said or written. *According to Amy, all boys are stupid!*
2 in a way that is suitable. *You'll be paid according to the amount of work that you do.* **accordingly** *(adv)*.

accordion *(n)* a musical instrument that you squeeze to make sound, and play by pressing keys and buttons. *See* **instrument**.

accost accosting accosted *(v)* to approach someone and talk to them, usually in an insulting way.

account accounting accounted
1 *(n)* a description of something that has happened.
2 *(n)* a sum of money in a bank that you can add to or take from, when needed.
3 **accounts** *(plural n)* records of money earned and spent.
4 *(v)* If you **account for** something, you explain it. **accountable** *(adj)*.

accountant *(n)* an expert in finance and keeping accounts.

accumulate accumulating accumulated *(v)* to collect things or let them pile up. **accumulation** *(n)*.

accurate *(adj)* exactly correct. **accuracy** *(n)*, **accurately** *(adv)*.

accuse accusing accused *(v)* to say that someone has done something wrong. **accusation** *(n)*, **accuser** *(n)*.

accustomed *(adj)*
1 usual. *My accustomed seat.*
2 When you are **accustomed to** something, you are used to it.

ace *(n)*
1 a playing card with only one symbol on it.
2 a serve in tennis that is impossible to return.

ache *(rhymes with take) (n)* a dull pain that goes on and on. **ache** *(v)*.

achieve *(uh-cheev)* achieving achieved *(v)* to do something successfully, especially after a lot of effort. **achievement** *(n)*.

acid
1 *(n)* a substance that turns blue litmus paper red. Strong acids can burn your skin. **acidic** *(adj)*.
2 *(adj)* sour or bitter.

acid rain *(n)* rain that is polluted by acid in the atmosphere and damages the environment. *The diagram below shows how fumes containing acids from factories, car exhaust, etc. travel until they meet damp air, then fall as acid rain.*

fumes
acid cloud
acid rain
acid soil
polluted water
damaged trees
acid rain

acknowledge acknowledging acknowledged *(v)*
1 to admit to something. *I acknowledged my mistake.*
2 to show that you have seen and recognized somebody. *Toby walked past without acknowledging me.*
3 to let the sender know that you have received a letter or parcel. **acknowledgement** *(n)*.

acne *(ak-nee) (n)* lots of red pimples on the skin, especially on the face.

acorn *(n)* the seed of an oak tree.

acoustic *(a-koo-stik)*
1 *(adj)* to do with sound or hearing.
2 **acoustics** *(plural n)* If a place has good **acoustics**, you can hear sounds and music very clearly inside it.

acoustic guitar *(n)* a guitar which does not need an amplifier.

acoustic guitar (cutaway)
string
sound-hole
fret fingerboard
tuning-head
neck
rosette
soundboard
bridge
bridge pins
saddle
x-bracing
strut
lining

acquaintance *(n)*
someone you have met, but
you do not know very well.

acquire acquiring acquired
1 *(v)* to obtain or get something.
2 *(n)* If something is an **acquired**
taste, you grow to like it slowly.

acquit acquitting acquitted *(v)*
to find someone not guilty
of a crime. **acquittal** *(n)*.

acrobatics *(plural n)* difficult and
exciting gymnastic acts, often
performed in the air or on a high
wire. **acrobat** *(n)*, **acrobatic** *(adj)*.

acronym *(n)* a word made from the
first or first few letters of the words
of a phrase. Radar is an acronym
for RAdio Detecting And Ranging.

across *(prep)*
1 from one side to the other.
We ran across the field.
2 on the other side. *Emma lives
across the street from me.*

acrylic *(ak-rill-ik) (n)*
a chemical substance used
to make fibres and paints.

act acting acted
1 *(v)* to do something. *We must act
now to save the rainforests.* **act** *(n)*.
2 *(v)* to perform in a play, film, etc.
3 *(v)* to have an effect.
This drug acts very quickly.
4 *(n)* a short performance.
A comedy act.
5 *(n)* one of the parts of a play.
6 *(n)* a law made by Parliament.

action *(n)*
1 something that you do to
achieve a result. *Kamran's rapid
action prevented a serious accident.*
2 When you **take action**, you
do something for a purpose.

active *(adj)*
1 energetic and busy.
2 An **active** verb is one where the
verb's subject does the action, rather
than having something done to it.
*In the sentence, "I kicked the ball",
the verb is active, but in, "The ball
was kicked", the verb is passive.*

activity activities *(n)*
1 action or movement. *The
playground was full of activity.*
2 something that you do for
pleasure. *Leisure activities.*

actor *(n)* someone who performs
in the theatre, films, television, etc.

actual *(adj)*
real or true. **actually** *(adv)*.

acupuncture *(ak-yoo-punk-cher)*
(n) a way of treating illness by pricking
parts of the body with small needles.

acute acuter acutest *(adj)*
1 sharp or severe. *Acute pain.*
2 able to detect things easily.
Dogs have an acute sense of smell.
acuteness *(n)*, **acutely** *(adv)*.
3 An **acute** angle is an
angle of less than 90°.

AD the initials of the Latin phrase
Anno Domini, which means "In the
year of the Lord". AD is used to
show that a date comes after
the birth of Christ. *Columbus
discovered America in AD1492.*

adapt adapting adapted *(v)*
1 to make something suitable for a
different purpose. *We have adapted
our garage into a games room.*
2 to change because you are
in a new situation. *It can be
hard to adapt to life in a foreign
country.* **adaptable** *(adj)*.

adapter *or* **adaptor** *(n)* a type of
electrical plug that you use to connect
two or more plugs to one socket.

add adding added *(v)*
1 to put one thing with another.
Add the eggs to the flour.
2 to put numbers together
to make a total. **addition** *(n)*.

adder *(n)* a small, venomous
snake, sometimes called a viper.
*The illustration to the right shows
a common adder, which
can be found in Britain.*

addict *(n)* someone who
cannot give up doing
or using something.
A drug addict.
addiction *(n)*,
addicted *(adj)*.

**common
adder**
(male)

addictive *(adj)*
If something, such
as a drug, is **addictive**,
people find it very hard to
give it up. *Tobacco is addictive.*

additive *(n)*
something added to a substance
to change it in some way. *Jon tries
not to eat food with additives.*

address
addresses addressing addressed
1 *(n)* the details of the place where
someone lives. *What's your address?*
2 *(v)* to write an address on
a letter, card, or package.
3 *(n)* the series of letters (and
sometimes numbers) that you type
into a computer to enable a browser
to find a particular website or page.
What's the address for that website?

adenoids *(ad-en-oyds) (plural n)*
spongy lumps of flesh at
the back of your nose.

adequate *(adj)*
just enough or good
enough. **adequately** *(adv)*.

adhesive *(n)*
a substance, such as glue, that makes
things stick together. **adhesive** *(adj)*.

adjacent *(adj)* close or next
to something or someone. *Our
families live in adjacent streets.*

adjective *(n)*
a word that describes someone or
something. *In the phrase, "A tall,
handsome stranger", "tall" and
"handsome" are adjectives.*
adjectival *(adj)*. *See page 3.*

adjudicate
adjudicating adjudicated *(v)*
to judge something, for
example, a competition.
adjudication *(n)*, **adjudicator** *(n)*.

adjust adjusting adjusted *(v)*
1 to move or change
something slightly.
adjustment *(n)*, **adjustable** *(adj)*.
2 to get used to something new
and different. **adjustment** *(n)*.

ad-lib ad-libbing ad-libbed *(v)*
to speak in public without
preparing first. **ad-lib** *(adj)*,
ad lib *(adv)*.

administer
administering administered *(v)*
1 to govern or control something.
Nat administers the team funds.
administration *(n)*.
2 to give something to someone.
The nurse administered the medicine.

administrate administrating
administrated *(v)* to manage
and control an organization.
administration *(n)*,
administrator *(n)*.

admiral *(n)*
an officer who holds a very
high rank in the British navy.
*The picture shows a statue
of Admiral Nelson.*

admire
admiring admired *(v)*
1 to like and respect
someone. **admiration** *(n)*.
2 to look at something
and enjoy it. **Admiral
Nelson**

admit

admit admitting admitted *(v)*
1 to confess to something, or
to agree that something is true,
often reluctantly. **admission** *(n)*.
2 to allow someone
or something to enter.
admission *(n)*, **admittance** *(n)*.

admonish admonishes
admonishing admonished *(v)*
to tell someone off or to warn
someone. **admonishment** *(n)*.

adolescent *(n)* a young person
who is more grown-up than
a child, but is not yet an adult.
adolescence *(n)*, **adolescent** *(adj)*.

adopt adopting adopted *(v)*
1 When someone **adopts** a child, they
take it into their family and become
its legal parents. **adoption** *(n)*.
2 to accept an idea or a way of
doing things. *The government is
adopting a tough approach to crime.*

adorable *(adj)*
very sweet and lovable.

adore adoring adored *(v)*
to love someone or something
very much. **adoration** *(n)*.

adorned *(adj)* decorated. **adorn** *(v)*.

adrenaline *(n)*
a chemical produced by your
body when you are excited,
frightened, or angry.

adult *(n)* a fully-grown person or
animal. **adulthood** *(n)*, **adult** *(adj)*.

adulterate adulterating
adulterated *(v)* to spoil something by
adding something less good to it.

adultery *(n)*
If someone commits **adultery**,
they are unfaithful to their
husband or wife by having sexual
intercourse with somebody else.
adulterer *(n)*, **adulterous** *(adj)*.

advance advancing advanced
1 *(v)* to move forward or to make
progress. **advancement** *(n)*.
2 *(adj)* happening before something
else. *Advance warning.*
3 *(v)* to lend money. **advance** *(n)*.
4 *(n)* a movement forward
by a group of soldiers.

advanced *(adj)*
1 If something has reached an
advanced stage, it is nearly finished.
2 **Advanced** work is not elementary
or easy. *Advanced level science.*

advantage
1 *(n)* something that helps you or is
useful to you. **advantageous** *(adj)*.
2 *(n)* the first point in
a tennis game after
the score of deuce.

3 If you **take advantage of**
a person or situation, you use
them for your own benefit.

advent *(n)*
1 the beginning of something
important. *The advent of
the computer age.*
2 **Advent** the weeks leading
up to Christmas in the
Christian Church's year.

adventure *(n)*
an exciting or dangerous experience.
adventurous *(adj)*.

adverb *(n)* a word usually used to
describe a verb. Adverbs tell how,
when, where, how often, or how
much something happens. *"Slowly",
"late", and "soon" are all adverbs.*
adverbial *(adj)*. See page 3.

adversary adversaries *(n)* someone
who fights or argues against you.

adverse *(adj)*
unfavourable or difficult. *Adverse
weather conditions.* **adversely** *(adj)*.

advertise advertising advertised
(v) to give information about
something that you want to sell.
advertisement *(n)*, **advertiser** *(n)*.

advice *(n)* suggestions about what
someone should do. *Shahid gave me
good advice on how to mend my bike.*

advisable *(adj)*
If something is **advisable**, it is sensible
and worth doing. **advisably** *(n)*.

advise advising advised *(v)*
to give someone information or
suggestions, so that they can decide
what to do. *Tom advised me to
stay at home until the rush hour
was over.* **adviser** *(n)*, **advisory** *(adj)*.

advocate advocating advocated
1 *(ad-voh-kate) (v)*
to support an idea or plan.
I would never advocate violence.
2 *(ad-voh-kut) (n)* a lawyer who
defends someone during their trial.

aerial *(air-ee-ul)*
1 *(n)* a piece of wire that receives
television or radio signals.
2 *(adj)* happening in the
air. *Aerial refuelling.*

aerobatics *(plural n)* skilful or
dangerous movements made by
aircraft in the sky. *The picture shows a
plane performing the positive flick roll,
an example of aerobatics.*
aerobatic *(adj)*.

aerodynamic *(adj)*
designed to move through the air very
easily and quickly. *The streamlined
shape of this Suzuki Nuda motorcycle
makes it very aerodynamic.*

aerodynamic motorbike — streamlined windscreen

fairing
(streamlined bodywork) — angled headlights

aeronautics *(singular n)*
the science and practice of
designing and building aircraft.
aeronautical *(adj)*.

aeroplane *(n)*
a machine with wings and
an engine, that flies through
the air. See **aircraft**.

aerosol *(n)*
a can containing liquid which
is forced out in a fine spray.
*When you press
the button on
an aerosol,
propellant
gas pushes
liquid up
a tube
and out
through
a nozzle.*

button
nozzle
spray
stem
spring

aerosol
(cross-section)

propellant gas

dip tube

air freshener
with liquid
propellant

aestivate *(ee-stiv-ate)*
aestivating aestivated *(v)*
When animals or insects **aestivate**,
they spend the summer in a deep
sleep. Their heartbeat, temperature,
and breathing rates become very
low, so that they can survive heat
and drought. **aestivation** *(n)*.

affair *(n)*
1 a special event.
The wedding was a grand affair.
2 **affairs** *(plural n)* business connected
with private or public life. *Personal
affairs. Business affairs.*

aerobatics

affect affecting affected *(v)*
to influence or change someone
or something. *Lance's accident
affected him badly.*

affected *(adj)*
false and unnatural. *Gloria
has an affected voice.*

affection *(n)*
a fondness for someone or something.

affectionate *(adj)*
loving. **affectionately** *(adv).*

affinity affinities *(n)*
If you have an **affinity** with
someone or something, you like
them and feel close to them.

affliction *(n)*
illness or suffering. **afflict** *(v).*

affluent *(adj)*
If you are **affluent**, you have
plenty of money. **affluence** *(n).*

afford affording afforded *(v)*
1 If you can **afford** something,
you have enough money to buy it.
2 to have enough time or ability
to do something. *I'm so far
ahead, I can afford to relax.*

afloat *(adj)* floating on water.

afraid *(adj)*
1 frightened or worried.
2 sorry. *I'm afraid I can't
come to your party.*

afresh *(adv)*
When you start **afresh**, you
begin something again.

after *(prep)*
1 later than. *After lunch.*
2 following. *The puppy ran after her.*
3 trying to catch someone or
something. *The police are after him.*

afternoon *(n)*
the time of day between midday and
about five o'clock in the evening.

afterwards *(adv)* later.

again *(adv)*
one more time. *Say it again, Leo.*

against *(prep)*
1 next to and touching.
Put your ear against the wall.
2 competing with. *It's Manchester
United against Liverpool tonight.*
3 opposed to. *I'm against
killing whales.*

agate *(n)* a hard, semi-precious stone
with bands of colour.
*The picture shows
a piece of agate
that has been
cut in half
and polished.*

agate
(cross-section)

age ageing *or* aging aged
1 *(n)* the number of years
that someone has lived or
that something has existed.
2 *(n)* a period of time in
history. *The Stone Age.*
3 *(v)* to become or seem older.

aged *(adj)*
1 *(rhymes with caged)* being a
particular number of years old.
Anyone aged 12 can join our club.
2 *(ay-jid)* Someone who
is **aged** is very old.

ageism *or* **agism** *(n)*
prejudice or discrimination because
of age. **ageist** *or* **agist** *(adj).*

agenda *(aj-en-der)* *(n)*
a list of things that need
to be done or discussed.

agent *(n)*
1 someone who arranges
things for other people.
Travel agent. **agency** *(n).*
2 a spy. *Secret agent.*

aggravate
aggravating aggravated *(v)*
1 to make a difficult
situation even worse.
2 *(informal)* to annoy someone.
aggravation *(n),* **aggravating** *(adj).*

aggregate *(ag-rig-ut)* *(n)*
a total created by adding together
lots of smaller amounts. *The
aggregate of our scores was 25.*

aggression *(n)*
fierce or threatening behaviour.
aggressive *(adj),* **aggressively** *(adv).*

aghast *(uh-gast)* *(adj)*
shocked or dismayed.

agile *(adj)*
1 If you are **agile**, you can
move quickly and easily. **agility** *(n).*
2 Someone with an **agile**
mind can think quickly
and cleverly. **agility** *(n).*

agism *see* **ageism**.

agitate agitating agitated *(v)*
1 to make someone nervous and
worried. **agitation** *(n),* **agitated** *(adj).*
2 to stir up a liquid.

agnostic *(n)*
someone who believes that
you cannot know whether God
exists or not. **agnostic** *(adj).*

ago *(adv)* before now or
in the past. *Three days ago.*

agony agonies *(n)*
great pain or suffering. *David was
screaming in agony.* **agonizing** *(adj).*

agree agreeing agreed *(v)*
1 to say yes to something. *I agreed
to his plan.* **agreement** *(n).*

air-conditioning

2 to share the same opinions.
Dan and I always agree on politics.
3 If something **agrees** with you,
it suits you, or is good for you.

agreement *(n)*
1 the same way of thinking. *Bill and
I are in agreement over that book.*
2 an arrangement. *We've
made an agreement to
share the cost of the party.*

agriculture *(n)* farming.
*This picture of agriculture in the
Middle Ages shows labourers
using scythes to mow a field.*
agricultural *(adj). Also see* **farm**.

medieval farming

aground *(adv)*
If a boat runs **aground**, it gets stuck
on the bottom in shallow water.

ahead *(adv)*
1 in front. *Go on ahead.*
2 in the future. *You must think ahead.*

A.I. *(n)*
short for **Artificial Intelligence**.

aid aiding aided
1 *(v)* to help someone. **aid** *(n).*
2 *(n)* money or
equipment for
people in need.
Foreign aid.

AIDS *(n)*
an illness in which
the body's ability to
protect itself against
disease is destroyed.
AIDS stands for
Acquired Immune
Deficiency Syndrome.

AIDS virus
(magnified)

aileron *(ay-ler-on)* *(n)*
a hinged piece on an aircraft wing,
used to control balance. *See* **aircraft**.

ailment *(n)* an illness, though
not usually a serious one.

aim aiming aimed *(v)*
1 to hit, throw, or shoot something in
a particular direction. **aim** *(n).*
2 to intend to achieve something.
I aim to become a chef. **aim** *(n).*

air airing aired
1 *(n)* the invisible mixture of gases
around you that you need to breathe.
2 *(v)* to let air into a room.
3 *(n)* an appearance or manner.
Wanda has an air of mystery.

air-conditioning *(n)* a system
for keeping the air in a building cool.

a
b
c
d
e
f
g
h
i
j
k
l
m
n
o
p
q
r
s
t
u
v
w
x
y
z

aircraft *(n)*

a vehicle that can fly. *The picture shows a Boeing 747-400 aircraft, known as a jumbo jet because of its enormous size. It can carry more than 500 passengers and cruises at around 920km (570 miles) per hour.*

long-haul passenger aircraft
(cutaway)

flight deck
crew escape hatch
upper deck escape door
toughened glass and plastic windscreen
crew's sleeping area and toilet
anti-collision light
first-class passenger cabin
nose cone
radar equipment
tyres (filled with nitrogen gas)
nose landing gear
electronic equipment bay
luggage hold
staircase to upper deck
front galley (kitchen)
multi-glazed window
passenger entry door
first-class seating
communications antenna
fuselage (main body)
outboard aileron
spoiler (air brake)
flaps
undercarriage bay
undercarriage (main landing gear)
turbofan jet engine
light aluminium alloy frame strengthened with girders and hoops
overhead luggage locker
economy class seating
rear galley (kitchen)
air-conditioning duct
luggage hold
toilet
inboard aileron
fuel tanks
engine mounting pylon
engine cowling

aircraft carrier *(n)*

a warship with a large, flat deck where aircraft take off and land.

air force *(n)*

part of a country's fighting force that can attack or defend from the air.

airline *(n)* a company that

owns and flies aircraft, carrying passengers and goods by air.

airmail *(n)* a postal service by

which letters, packages, etc. are carried abroad by aircraft.

airport *(n)* a place where aircraft

take off and land and where people get on and off them.

airship *(n)*

a large air balloon with engines and a passenger compartment hanging underneath it. *The airship below is a Zeppelin, built in Germany in 1910.*

airship
(cutaway)
metal frame
fabric skin
bag containing helium gas
rudder
engine
walkway
gondola (passenger and crew compartment)

airtight *(adj)*

If a container is **airtight**, it is so well sealed that no air can get in or out.

airy airier airiest *(adj)*

1 An **airy** room is not stuffy.
2 lighthearted or casual. *Camilla gave an airy wave.* **airily** *(adv).*

aisle *(rhymes with pile) (n)*

the passage that runs between the rows of seats in a church, cinema, aircraft, etc.

ajar *(adj)* If a door is **ajar**,

it is partly open. **ajar** *(adv).*

alarm alarming alarmed

1 *(n)* a device containing a bell, buzzer, or siren that wakes someone or warns them of danger.
2 *(n)* a sudden fear that something bad will happen. *Don't worry, there's no cause for alarm.*
3 *(v)* to make someone afraid that something bad might happen. *I don't want to alarm you, but I can smell smoke.* **alarming** *(adj),* **alarmingly** *(adv).*

alas *(interject)* unfortunately or sadly.

I'd love to come but, alas, I can't.

albino *(al-bee-no) (n)* a person or

animal born without any natural colouring in their skin, hair, or eyes.

album *(n)*

1 a book or folder in which you keep photographs, stamps, etc.
2 a collection of pieces of music recorded on a CD or music player.

alcohol *(n)* a colourless liquid found

in drinks such as wine, whisky, and beer, which can make people drunk.

alcoholic

1 *(adj)* containing alcohol.
2 *(n)* If someone is an **alcoholic**, they are addicted to alcohol. **alcoholism** *(n).*

alcove *(n)* a part of a room that

is set back from the main area.

alert alerting alerted

1 *(adj)* If you are **alert**, you pay attention to what is happening and are ready for action.
2 *(v)* to warn someone that there might be danger. *Alert the fire brigade!*
3 *(n)* a warning of danger.

algae *(al-jee) (plural n)*

small plants that grow without roots or stems in water or on damp surfaces. See **seaweed**.

algebra *(al-jer-bra) (n)*

a type of mathematics in which signs and letters are used to represent numbers, for example, $2x + y = 7$.

alias *(ay-lee-uss) aliases (n)*

a false name, especially one used by a criminal.

alibi *(al-ee-bye) (n)*

a claim that a person accused of a crime was somewhere else when the crime was committed.

alien

1 *(n)* a creature from another planet.
2 *(adj)* different and strange. *Poppy found her new school very alien.*
3 *(n)* a foreigner.

tail fin

rudder

tail cone

elevator

auxiliary power unit

tailplane

fuselage (cross-section)

soundproof insulation

overhead luggage locker

passenger seats

passenger compartment floor

luggage hold

wing tip

leading edge flap

navigation light

winglet

alike
1 *(adj)* looking or acting the same.
2 *(adv)* in a similar way. *All the children were treated alike.*

alive *(adj)*
1 living.
2 full of life.

alkali *(al-ka-lye) (n)* a substance which turns red litmus paper blue. Strong alkalis can burn your skin. *Toothpaste is an alkali.* **alkaline** *(adj)*.

Allah *(n)* the Muslim name for God.

allegiance *(a-lee-jens) (n)* loyal support for someone or something, for example, a sports club.

allergic *(adj)* If you are **allergic** to something, it makes you ill. *Ned is allergic to cats.* **allergy** *(n)*.

alliance *(n)* a friendly agreement to work together.

alligator *(n)* a large reptile similar to a crocodile, with strong jaws and very sharp teeth. *Alligators live in parts of North and South America and China.*

alligator

alliteration *(n)* repeated use of the same sound at the beginning of a group of words, for example, "*The gruesome ghost gave a ghastly groan.*" **alliterative** *(adj)*.

allocate allocating allocated *(v)* to decide that something should be used for a particular purpose. *We allocated half the money to charity.* **allocation** *(n)*.

allotment *(n)* a small piece of land that people can rent and use to grow vegetables, fruit, or flowers.

allow allowing allowed *(v)* to let someone have or do something.

allowance *(n)* money given to someone regularly.

alloy *(n)* a mixture of two or more metals.

all right
1 *(adj)* good enough or acceptable.
2 *(adj)* not hurt or not ill. *Helena fell off her horse, but she's all right now.*
3 *(interject)* You say **all right** when you agree to do something.

ally *(al-eye)* allies *(n)* a person or a country that gives support to another.

almighty *(adj)*
1 very big. *An almighty crash.*
2 possessing total power.

almost *(adv)* very nearly.

alone *(adj)* by yourself. **alone** *(adv)*.

along
1 *(prep)* from one end to the other. *We drove along the street.*
2 all along *(adv)* all the time. *I knew all along that Hal was lying.*

aloud *(adv)* in a voice that other people can hear. *Reading aloud.*

alphabet *(n)* all the letters of a language arranged in order. *The first six letters of the Greek alphabet are shown below.* **alphabetical** *(adj)*.

Greek alphabet

$$\alpha \quad \beta \quad \gamma \quad \delta \quad \epsilon \quad \zeta$$

alpha   beta   gamma   delta   epsilon   zeta

already *(adv)* before now. *I've seen that film already.*

also *(adv)* as well.

altar *(n)* a large table in a church or a temple, used for religious ceremonies.

alter altering altered *(v)* to change something. *We've altered our plans.* **alteration** *(n)*.

alternate *(ol-ter-nat) (adj)* If something happens on **alternate** days, it happens every second day. **alternate** *(ol-ter-nate) (v)*.

alternative
1 *(n)* something you can choose to have or do instead of something else. **alternative** *(adj)*, **alternatively** *(adv)*.
2 *(adj)* different from what is usual. *Alternative medicine.*

although *(conj)*
1 in spite of something. *Although it was wet, we had fun.*
2 but. *Natalie is only nine, although she seems much older.*

altitude *(n)* the height of something above the ground. *This plane can fly at very high altitudes.*

alto *(n)*
1 a singing voice that is quite high for a man and quite low for a woman.
2 a singer with an alto voice.

altogether *(adv)*
1 in total. *Pippa has seven hats altogether.*
2 completely or entirely. *What I told you wasn't altogether true.*
3 on the whole. *Altogether, it was a very good party.*

aluminium *(n)* a light, silver-coloured metal.

always *(adv)* If something is always happening, it happens all the time or very many times.

Alzheimer's disease *(alts-hi-merz diz-eez) (n)* a disease that affects a person's brain, making it gradually harder for them to think clearly or remember things. Alzheimer's disease usually only affects people in old age.

a.m. the initials of the Latin phrase *ante meridiem*, which means "before midday". *I get up at 7 a.m.*

amateur *(n)* someone who takes part in a sport or other activity for pleasure rather than for money.

amaze amazing amazed *(v)* to make someone feel very surprised. **amazement** *(n)*, **amazing** *(adj)*, **amazingly** *(adv)*.

amber *(n)*
1 an orangey-yellow colour. **amber** *(adj)*.
2 a yellowish substance, formed from fossilized tree sap, and used for making ornaments and jewellery. *This piece of amber contains an insect that was trapped in the sap before it hardened and fossilized.*

amber

ambidextrous *(adj)* If you are **ambidextrous**, you can use both hands equally well, especially for writing.

ambiguous *(am-big-yoo-us) (adj)* If something is **ambiguous**, it can be understood in more than one way. *Conrad gave an ambiguous answer.* **ambiguity** *(am-big-you-it-ee) (n)*.

a b c d e f g h i j k l m n o p q r s t u v w x y z

b c d e f g h i j k l m n o p q r s t u v w x y z

ambition (n)
1 something that you really want to do. *My ambition is to be a film star.*
2 a strong wish to be successful. *Jean is driven by ambition.* **ambitious** (adj).

ambivalent (adj) If you feel ambivalent about something, you have two different opinions about it at the same time. **ambivalence** (n).

amble ambling ambled (v) to walk slowly because you are not in a hurry.

ambulance (n) a vehicle that takes people to hospital when they are ill.

ambush ambushes ambushing ambushed (v) to hide and then attack someone. **ambush** (n).

amenity amenities (n) something that is available for everyone to use and enjoy, such as a sports centre.

ammonia (n) a gas or solution with a strong smell. Some cleaning liquids contain ammonia.

ammunition (n)
1 things that can be fired from weapons, such as bullets or arrows.
2 information that you can use against someone else.

amnesty amnesties (n)
1 an official promise by a government to release prisoners or pardon crimes.
2 a chance to hand in something you should not possess, without being punished.

amoeba (am-ee-ber)
amoebas or amoebae (n)
a microscopic creature made of only one cell. *The diagram below shows the parts of an amoeba.*

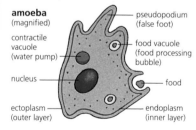

amoeba
(magnified)

pseudopodium
(false foot)

contractile
vacuole
(water pump)

food vacuole
(food processing
bubble)

nucleus

food

ectoplasm
(outer layer)

endoplasm
(inner layer)

among or **amongst** (prep)
1 surrounded by other people or things.
2 If you share something among several people, you divide it between them.

amount amounting amounted
1 (n) how much of something there is.
2 (v) If something amounts to a total, it adds up to it.

amp (n)
a unit which measures the strength of an electrical current. Amp is short for ampere.

amphibian (n)
1 an animal that lives on land, but breeds in water. *Frogs, toads, and newts are amphibians.* **amphibious** (adj).
2 a vehicle that can travel on land and in water. **amphibious** (adj).

amphitheatre (n) a large, open-air building, built in Roman times, with rows of seats in a high circle around an arena. Amphitheatres were used for public entertainments, such as gladiator and animal fights. *The picture shows a famous amphitheatre.*

The Colosseum, Rome, Italy
(cutaway)

velarium
(canvas awning)

mast

staircase

marble pillar

standing area
for slaves

marble seats

Emperor's box

arena
(stage)

underground
rooms for gladiators
and animals

statue

corridor

foundations

public entrance

ample ampler amplest (adj)
1 more than enough. *There was ample food for everyone.* **amply** (adv).
2 large. *Moira has an ample figure.*

amplifier (n) a piece of equipment that makes sound louder. **amplification** (n), **amplify** (v).

amputate amputating amputated (v) to cut off someone's arm or leg because it is damaged or diseased. **amputation** (n).

amuse amusing amused (v)
1 to make someone laugh or smile. **amusing** (adj).
2 to keep someone happy and stop them from being bored. *Dad's new camera kept him amused for hours.* **amusement** (n).

anaemic (a-nee-mik) (adj)
If you are anaemic, you become easily tired and weak because your blood does not contain enough iron. **anaemia** (n).

anaesthetic (an-iss-thet-ik) (n)
a drug or gas given to someone before an operation to prevent them from feeling pain. **anaesthetist** (an-ees-the-tist) (n).

anagram (n) a word or phrase made by changing the order of letters in another word or phrase. *"Stop" is an anagram of "post".*

analyse analysing analysed (v) to examine something carefully in order to understand it. *Let's analyse the problem before we do anything.* **analysis** (n), **analytical** (adj).

anarchy (n) a situation with no order and no one in control. **anarchist** (n).

anatomy (n)
1 The **anatomy** of a person or an animal is the structure of their body.
2 the study of how the bodies of people and animals fit together. **anatomical** (adj).

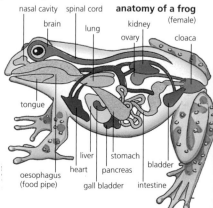

anatomy of a frog
(female)

nasal cavity

spinal cord

brain

lung

kidney

ovary

cloaca

tongue

liver

stomach

bladder

oesophagus
(food pipe)

heart

pancreas

gall bladder

intestine

ancestor *(n)*
Your **ancestors** are members of your family who lived a long time ago. **ancestry** *(n)*, **ancestral** *(adj)*.

anchor *(n)*
a heavy metal hook which is lowered from a ship or boat to stop it drifting. **anchorage** *(n)*, **anchor** *(v)*. See **ship**.

anchovy anchovies *(n)*
a small, edible fish. Anchovies have a salty taste.

ancient *(ayn-shent) (adj)*
1 very old.
2 belonging to a time long ago. *Ancient Rome.*

android *(n)* a robot that acts and looks like a human being.

anecdote *(n)*
a short, funny story about something that has happened. **anecdotal** *(adj)*.

anemometer *(n)*
a scientific instrument used to measure the wind's speed.

anemone *(n)*
a small flower, shaped like a cup.

angel *(n)*
1 a messenger of God. **angelic** *(adj)*.
2 a very kind, gentle person. **angelic** *(adj)*.

anger *(n)* the feeling of being very annoyed.

angle *(n)*
1 the space between two lines at the point where they touch. *Angles are measured in degrees, for example, 90°.*
2 a way of looking at something. *Danny approached the problem from a different angle.*
3 If something is **at an angle**, it is sloping and not straight.

angling *(n)*
the sport of fishing with a fishing rod rather than a net. *The picture shows equipment used for freshwater angling.* **angler** *(n)*, **angle** *(v)*.

line
rod ring
carbon fibre rod
float ring
grayling float
split shot
drag nut setting
spool
reel fitting
cork handle
bale arm
reel handle
float fishing rod
fixed spool reel
bait on hook

angora *(n)*
1 a long-haired variety of rabbit, goat, or cat.
2 fluffy wool made from the hair of angora rabbits, mixed with sheep's wool.

angora rabbits

angry angrier angriest *(adj)*
If you are **angry**, you feel that you want to argue or fight with someone. **angrily** *(adv)*.

anguish *(ang-wish) (n)*
a strong feeling of misery or distress. **anguished** *(adj)*.

angular *(adj)*
Something that is **angular** has a lot of straight lines and sharp corners. *Cara had a thin, angular face.*

animal *(n)* any living creature that can breathe and move about.

animated *(adj)*
1 lively. *An animated conversation.* **animation** *(n)*, **animatedly** *(adv)*.
2 An **animated film** is made by showing a series of still images in sequence, very rapidly, to create the illusion of movement. Animated films can be made using hand drawings, models and computer generated images. **animation** *(n)*, **animate** *(v)*.

animation sequence

animosity animosities *(n)*
a strong dislike for someone.

aniseed *(n)* a strong-smelling seed used in sweets and drinks.

ankle *(n)* the joint that connects your foot to your leg.

annex annexes annexing annexed *(v)* When one country **annexes** another, it takes control of it by force.

annexe *(n)* an extra building joined on to or placed near a main building.

annihilate *(an-eye-ill-ate)* annihilating annihilated *(v)* to destroy something completely. **annihilation** *(n)*.

anniversary anniversaries *(n)* a date which people remember because something important happened on that date in the past.

annotate annotating annotated *(v)* to write notes explaining a piece of writing. **annotated** *(adj)*.

announce announcing announced *(v)* to say something officially or publicly. **announcement** *(n)*.

announcer *(n)*
someone who introduces programmes on television or radio.

annoy annoying annoyed *(v)*
to make someone feel angry. *Harry really annoys me when he puts on that stupid voice.* **annoyance** *(n)*, **annoying** *(adj)*, **annoyingly** *(adv)*.

annual
1 *(adj)* happening once every year or over a period of one year. *The annual writing competition. An annual subscription.* **annually** *(adv)*.
2 *(n)* a book published once a year.
3 *(n)* a plant or insect that only lives for one year. *Sunflowers are annuals.*

anon
1 *(adj)* short for anonymous.
2 *(old-fashioned)* See you anon means "see you soon".

anonymous *(adj)*
written, done, or given by a person whose name and identity is not known. *An anonymous letter.* **anonymity** *(n)*, **anonymously** *(adv)*.

anorak *(n)*
a waterproof jacket with a hood.

anorexia *(n)*
If someone suffers from **anorexia**, they think that they are too fat and so they eat very little and become dangerously thin. Anorexia is short for *anorexia nervosa*. **anorexic** *(n)*, **anorexic** *(adj)*.

another
1 *(adj)* one more of the same kind. *Have another sweet.*
2 *(pronoun)* a different one. *I didn't like the red dress, so I chose another.*

answer answering answered
1 *(v)* to say or write something as a reply to a question. **answer** *(n)*.
2 *(n)* the solution to a problem. *Is there an answer to world poverty?*
3 *(v)* If you **answer back**, you make a rude or cheeky reply.
4 If someone has **a lot to answer for**, they have caused a lot of trouble.

answerable *(adj)*
responsible. *Each leader is answerable for the safety of her group.*

ant *(n)* a small insect often with no wings that lives in a group called a colony. See **desert**, **insect**.

antagonize or **antagonise** antagonizing antagonized *(v)* If you **antagonize** someone, you make them feel very angry with you. **antagonism** *(n)*, **antagonist** *(n)*.

Antarctic *(n)* the area around the South Pole. **Antarctic** *(adj)*. See **polar**.

anteater

anteater (n)
a South American mammal with a very long tongue that it uses to search for ants and other small insects.

giant anteater

antelope (n) a large animal like a deer that runs very fast. Antelopes are found in Africa and parts of Asia.

antenna antennas or antennae (n)
1 a feeler on the head of an insect. See **beetle**.
2 a piece of wire that receives radio and television signals.

anthem (n) a religious or national song, sometimes sung by a choir.

anthology anthologies (n)
a collection of poems or stories by different writers which are all printed in the same book.

anthropology (n)
the study of the beliefs and ways of life of different people around the world. **anthropologist** (n).

antibiotic (n) a drug, such as penicillin, that kills bacteria and is used to cure infections.

antibody antibodies (n)
Your blood makes **antibodies** to fight against infection.

anticipate anticipating anticipated (v) to expect something to happen and be prepared for it. The police anticipate trouble after the match. **anticipation** (n).

anticlimax anticlimaxes (n)
If something is an **anticlimax**, it is not as exciting as you had expected.

anticlockwise (adv) in the opposite direction from that of the hands of a clock. **anticlockwise** (adj).

anticyclone (n) an area of high pressure in the atmosphere that causes settled weather. In summer, an anticyclone brings clear skies and warm weather.

antidote (n) something that stops a poison from working.

antiperspirant (n) a substance which you put on your skin to stop you sweating too much.

antique (an-teek)
1 (n) a very old object that is valuable because it is rare or beautiful.
2 (adj) very old.

antiseptic (n) a substance that kills germs and prevents infection.

antisocial (adj)
1 When someone behaves in an **antisocial** way, they do something that upsets or harms other people.
2 If somebody is **antisocial**, they do not enjoy being with other people.

antler (n) one of the two large, branching, bony structures on a stag's head. Stags grow and shed new antlers each year. The diagram shows a new antler. See **stag**.

velvet (skin)
antler bone
tine (branch)
pedicel (antler base)
skull bone

stag's antler
(cross-section)

anxiety (ang-zye-it-ee) anxieties (n)
a feeling of worry or fear.

anxious (ank-shuss) (adj)
1 worried. Mum gets anxious when I'm late. **anxiously** (adv).
2 very keen to do something. Sid is anxious to do well in his exams.

anybody (pronoun) any person.

anyhow (adv)
1 in any case. I didn't want to come anyhow.
2 carelessly. Her clothes were thrown down just anyhow!

anyone (pronoun) any person.

anything (pronoun) any thing. I'm not fussy, I'll eat anything.

anyway (adv) in any case. I never liked him anyway.

anywhere (adv) in or to any place. I'd follow Jade anywhere.

apart (adv) If two people or things are **apart**, they are separated from each other.

apartheid (a-part-ate) (n)
a political system in which people of different races are kept apart from each other.

apartment (n)
a set of rooms for living in, usually on one floor of a building.

apathetic (adj) If you are **apathetic**, you do not care about anything or want to do anything. **apathy** (n).

ape aping aped
1 (n) a large animal like a monkey, but with no tail. Gorillas, gibbons, and chimpanzees are kinds of apes. The picture shows a type of ape called a chimpanzee.
2 (v) to copy the way another person behaves or speaks.

apex apexes (n) the highest point of something.

ape

apologize or **apologise**
apologizing apologized (v) to say that you are sorry about something. **apology** (n), **apologetic** (adj).

Apostle (n)
one of the twelve men chosen by Christ to spread his teaching. This picture of the Apostle Matthew is taken from the 7th-century Lindisfarne Gospels.

apostrophe
(a-poss-truh-fee) (n)
the punctuation mark (') used to show ownership, for example, "Jane's bag", or to show that letters have been missed out, for example, "can't". See page 5.

Apostle

app (n) (informal)
a program or game you can download onto your phone, tablet or computer. App is short for application.

appalling (adj) horrifying and shocking. **appallingly** (adv).

apparatus (n)
1 equipment used for performing sports, especially gymnastics.
2 equipment or machines used to do a job or laboratory experiment.

laboratory apparatus

pipeclay triangle
gauze
test tube rack
tripod
Bunsen burner
flat-bottomed flask
conical flask
gas jar
filter paper
filter funnel
test tube holder
test tube
measuring cylinder
evaporating dish
dropping pipette
beaker
spatula
spirit thermometer

Arabic

apparent *(adj)*
1 obvious or clear. *Bruce's guilt was apparent to us all.*
2 seeming real or true. *Claudia's apparent confidence is really a sham.* **apparently** *(adv).*

appeal appealing appealed *(v)*
1 to ask for something urgently.
2 to ask for a decision made by a court to be changed.
3 If something **appeals** to you, you like it or find it interesting.

appear appearing appeared *(v)*
1 to come into sight. **appearance** *(n).*
2 to seem. *Paul appears to be happy.* **appearance** *(n).*

appendicitis *(n)*
If someone has **appendicitis**, their appendix is infected and very painful.

appendix
appendices *or* appendixes *(n)*
1 a small, closed tube leading from your bowel. *See* **digestion**.
2 extra information at the end of a book.

appetite *(n)*
1 desire for food.
2 great enjoyment of something. *Sadjit has a real appetite for work.*

appetizing *or* **appetising** *(adj)*
Food that is **appetizing** looks and smells good to eat.

applaud applauding applauded *(v)*
to show that you like something by clapping your hands. **applause** *(n).*

apple *(n)*
a round, usually crispy, fruit. *See* **fruit**.

appliance *(n)* a machine designed to do a particular job. *Our kitchen is full of modern appliances.*

applicant *(n)*
someone who has written formally, asking for something, like a job or a place on a course.

application *(n)*
1 a written request for something, such as a job. *A job application.*
2 a way of using something. *There are various applications for this new piece of technology.*
3 a computer program.
4 *See* **app**.

apply applies applying applied *(v)*
1 to ask for something in writing.
2 to be relevant. *These rules don't apply to us.*
3 If you **apply yourself** to something, you work hard at it.

appoint appointing appointed *(v)*
1 to choose someone for a job.
2 to arrange something officially. *We've already appointed a date for the match.*

appointment *(n)*
1 an arrangement to meet someone at a certain time.
2 a job.

appreciable *(adj)* important enough to be noticed. *The company has lost an appreciable amount of money.*

appreciate
appreciating appreciated *(v)*
1 to enjoy or value somebody or something. **appreciation** *(n),* **appreciative** *(adj),* **appreciatively** *(adv).*
2 to understand something. *I appreciate your point of view.*
3 to increase in value. **appreciation** *(n).*

apprehensive *(adj)* worried and slightly afraid. *Louisa was apprehensive about making her speech.* **apprehension** *(n),* **apprehensively** *(adv).*

apprentice *(n)*
someone who learns a trade, craft or profession by working with a professional person. **apprenticeship** *(n).*

approach approaches approaching approached *(v)*
1 to move nearer. **approach** *(n).*
2 If you **approach** somebody, you go up to them and talk to them.
3 When you **approach** a problem, you think of ways of tackling it. **approach** *(n).*

approachable *(adj)*
If someone is **approachable**, they are friendly and easy to talk to.

appropriate
appropriating appropriated
1 *(ap-ro-pree-at) (adj)* suitable or right. **appropriately** *(adv).*
2 *(ap-ro-pree-ate) (v)* to take something that is not yours.

approve approving approved *(v)*
1 If you **approve of** someone or something, you think that they are acceptable or good. **approval** *(n).*
2 to accept a plan or an idea. **approval** *(n).*

approximate *(adj)*
more or less accurate or correct. *An approximate price.* **approximation** *(n),* **approximately** *(adv).*

apricot *(n)* a small, soft fruit with an orange skin. *See* **fruit**.

apron *(n)*
1 a piece of clothing that you wear to protect your clothes when you are cooking, painting, etc.
2 the part of a stage in front of the curtain.

apt *(adj)*
1 very suitable. *An apt reply.*
2 quick to learn things.
3 If you are **apt to** do something, you are likely to do it.

aptitude *(n)*
a natural ability to do something well.

aqualung *(n)* breathing apparatus for diving. An aqualung consists of an air tank with a tube leading to a mouthpiece. *See* **scuba diving**.

aquarium aquariums *or* aquaria *(n)* a glass tank in which you can keep fish. *The picture shows an aquarium for tropical freshwater fish.*

hood   fluorescent tube   **aquarium**
(hood cutaway)
glass cover
gravel
aquatic plant
lead to power supply
combined heater and thermostat   glass tank   internal power filter
spirit thermometer   clean water outlet

aquatic *(adj)*
1 living or growing in water. *Aquatic plants.*
2 performed in or on water. *Aquatic sports.*

aqueduct *(n)* a large bridge built to carry water across a valley. *The Roman aqueduct shown below was built in France in AD14.*

aqueduct

Arabic *(n)*
1 a language spoken by many people in the Middle East and North Africa.
2 **Arabic numerals** are the sort of figures, such as 1, 2, 3, that we use today. *Arabic numerals are easier to use than Roman numerals.*

arable *(adj)* Arable land is used for growing crops.

arbitrate
arbitrating arbitrated *(v)* to help two sides to reach an agreement. **arbitration** *(n)*.

arc *(n)*
1 a curved line.
2 An **arc** is part of the circumference of a circle. *See* **circle**.

arcade *(n)*
1 a row of arches in a building.
2 a covered area housing a collection of places to visit.
A shopping arcade. A video arcade.

arch
arches arching arched
1 *(n)* a curved structure. Arches often help to support a building or bridge. *The picture below shows four different types of arch.*
2 *(v)* to curve. *The cat arched its back and spat.* **arched** *(adj)*.
3 *(adj)* chief. *Joe is my arch-enemy.*

arches

Roman   Islamic horseshoe

Gothic pointed   Gothic ogee

archaeology *or* **archeology**
(ar-kee-ol-oh-jee) (n) If you study **archaeology**, you learn about the past by digging up old buildings and objects and examining them carefully. **archaeologist** *(n)*, **archaeological** *(adj)*.

archaic *(ar-kay-ik) (adj)* very old-fashioned and not used any more.

archbishop *(n)*
one of the most important leaders in the Christian Church.

archeology *see* **archaeology**.

archery *(n)*
the sport of shooting at targets, using a bow and arrow. **archer** *(n)*.

archipelago *(ar-kee-pel-ag-o) (n)* a group of small islands.

architect *(ar-ki-tekt) (n)*
someone who designs buildings and checks that they are built correctly.

architecture *(n)*
1 the activity of designing buildings.
2 the style in which buildings are designed.
The selection of buildings on this page shows how different styles of architecture have been used for places of worship throughout the world, and for modern buildings. **architectural** *(adj)*.
Also see **building**.

pyramid
(The Great Pyramids, Giza, Egypt)

Greek temple
(The Parthenon, Athens, Greece)

Byzantine cathedral
(St Basil's, Moscow, Russia)

pagoda
(Soochow Lake, China)

Gothic cathedral
(Salisbury, England)

mosque
(The Blue Mosque, Istanbul, Turkey)

Shinto shrine
(Izumo, Japan)

Hindu temple
(Khajuraho, India)

communications tower
(CN Tower, Toronto, Canada)

opera house
(Sydney, Australia)

museum entrance
(Louvre Museum, Paris, France)

skyscraper
(Hong Kong and Shanghai Bank, Hong Kong)

external maintenance crane

helipad

internal staircase

terrace

steel support mast

steel hanger

hanging glass curtain wall

10-storey atrium

steel suspension truss

aluminium cladding panel

glass typhoon screen

arctic
1 **The Arctic** (n) the frozen area around the North Pole. **Arctic** (adj). See **polar**.
2 (adj) extremely cold and wintry. *Arctic weather conditions.*

ardent (adj) If you are **ardent** about something, you feel very strongly about it. **ardently** (adv).

arduous (ard-yoo-uss) (adj) very difficult and demanding a lot of effort. *An arduous journey.*

area (n)
1 the size of a surface. To work out the area of a surface, you multiply its length by its width.
2 part of a place. *A poor area of the country.*

arena (n) a large area, used for sports or entertainment. See **amphitheatre**, **track and field**.

argue arguing argued (v)
1 to disagree with someone angrily. **argument** (n), **argumentative** (adj).
2 to give your opinion about something. *Sean argued that hunting was cruel.* **argument** (n).

arid (adj)
Land that is **arid** is extremely dry because very little rain has fallen on it.

arise arising arose arisen (v)
1 If something, such as a problem, **arises**, it comes into being.
2 (old-fashioned) to stand up. *Arise, Sir Francis!*

aristocrat (n) a member of the highest social rank, or nobility. **aristocracy** (n), **aristocratic** (adj).

arithmetic (n)
calculations with numbers. Addition, subtraction, multiplication, and division are all types of arithmetic.

arm arming armed
1 (n) the part of your body between your shoulder and your hand.
2 (v) If a country or a person **arms** itself, it gets ready for war.
3 **arms** (plural n) weapons.

armadillo (n) a mammal covered by hard, bony plates. *The nine-banded armadillo, shown below, is found in North and South America.*

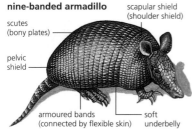

nine-banded armadillo — scapular shield (shoulder shield)
scutes (bony plates)
pelvic shield
armoured bands (connected by flexible skin) — soft underbelly

armaments (plural n) weapons and other equipment used for fighting wars.

armchair (n) a comfortable chair with supports for your arms.

armistice (n)
an agreement to stop fighting a war.

armour (n)
1 metal covering worn by soldiers to protect them in battle. See **knight**.
2 protective scales, spines, or shells that cover some animals, such as an armadillo. See **armadillo**.

armoured vehicle (n) a tank or other military vehicle with a strong metal covering. *This armoured vehicle is used for carrying troops.*

searchlight   machine gun   water tank cap   container for stores   compartment for diesel engine
bulletproof windscreen   driver   armoured steel casing
escape hatch
air vents   exhaust pipe
radio aerial
wing mirror
folded sand mat   commander
wire mesh container   cupola (gun turret)   sliding firing port
soldier in camouflage uniform

armoured personnel carrier (APC)   puncture-proof tyre   spare fuel can

armpit (n) the area under your arm where it joins to your shoulder.

army armies (n) a large group of people trained to fight on land.

aroma (n)
a pleasant smell. **aromatic** (adj).

around
1 (prep) surrounding, or in a circle. *He tied a rope around the tree.*
2 (adv) in many different parts of a place. *We travelled around Spain.*
3 (adv) more or less. *There were around 30 of us.*

arouse arousing aroused (v)
1 to wake someone.
2 to stir up a feeling. *Milo's strange behaviour aroused my curiosity.* **arousal** (n).

arrange arranging arranged (v)
1 to make plans for something to happen. **arrangement** (n).
2 to place things so that they look attractive. **arrangement** (n).

3 to change a piece of music slightly, so that it can be played on different instruments. **arrangement** (n).
4 If someone has an **arranged marriage**, their parents have chosen a husband or wife for them.

arrest
arresting arrested (v)
1 to take someone prisoner. **arrest** (n).
2 to stop something from developing or happening any more.

arrive arriving arrived (v)
1 to reach a place. *We arrived home early.* **arrival** (n).
2 to come. *At last, the great day arrived.* **arrival** (n).

arrogant (adj) conceited and proud. **arrogance** (n), **arrogantly** (adv).

arrow (n)
1 a pointed stick, shot from a bow.
2 a sign showing a direction.

arson (n) If someone commits **arson**, they deliberately and wrongly set fire to something.

art (n)
1 the skill of creating something by drawing, painting, or making things with your hands.
2 something that requires a lot of skill. *The art of Chinese cookery.*
3 **the arts** (plural n) forms of entertainment, such as music, theatre, and film.

artery arteries (n) one of the tubes that carry blood from your heart to all the other parts of your body. **arterial** (adj). See **circulation**.

arthritis (n) a disease which makes people's joints swollen and painful.

article (n)
1 an object or a thing.
2 a piece of writing published in a newspaper, magazine, or online.
3 a word, such as "a", "the", or "some", that goes in front of a noun.

articulate (adj) If you are **articulate**, you can express yourself clearly and well in words. **articulately** (adv).

articulated truck (n)
a truck with a cab and a trailer linked by a flexible joint so that the truck can turn round corners easily. See **truck**.

artificial (adj)
false, not real, or not natural. *Artificial flowers.* **artificially** (adv).

artificial intelligence (n)
the use of computers to do things that previously needed human intelligence, such as understanding language.

artillery (n)
1 large, powerful guns.
2 the part of an army that uses large guns.

artist (n) someone very skilled at painting, drawing, or making things. *This picture shows a range of tools and materials used by artists.* **artistic** (adj), **artistically** (adv).

artists' equipment

watercolour box
cartridge paper
putty rubber
watercolour paper
cotton canvas
sponge
sable brush
oil paint
linseed oil (keeps oil colours bright)
double clipper (clips onto palette)
turpentine (thins oil paints)
hog bristle brush
palette knife
wooden palette
dropper
ink bottle
charcoal
acrylic paint
gouache paint
pastel

ascend (uh-send)
ascending ascended (v)
to move upwards. **ascent** (n).

ash ashes (n)
1 the powder that remains after something has been burnt.
2 a tree with long, thin leaves.

ashamed (adj) If you are **ashamed**, you feel embarrassed and guilty.

aside
1 (adv) to one side, or out of the way. *Sarah pushed her brothers aside.*
2 (n) a remark made quietly so that not everyone can hear it.

ask asking asked (v)
1 to make a request or put a question to someone.
2 to invite someone to do something. *I've asked Tim to lunch.*

askew (uh-skyoo) (adj) crooked.

asleep (adj)
sleeping. *The baby soon fell asleep.*

aspect (n) one feature or characteristic of something. *Robbie enjoys most aspects of school life.*

asphyxiate (uh-sfix-ee-ate)
asphyxiating asphyxiated (v)
to suffocate. **asphyxiation** (n).

aspiration (n) a strong desire to do something great or important. *In order to succeed, you need to have aspirations.* **aspire** (v).

aspirin (n) a drug that relieves pain and reduces fever.

ass asses (n)
1 a donkey.
2 (informal) a stupid person.

assassinate assassinating assassinated (v) to murder an important person, such as a president. **assassin** (n), **assassination** (n).

assault assaulting assaulted (v) to attack someone or something violently. **assault** (n).

assemble assembling assembled
1 (v) to gather together in one place. *All the school assembled in the hall.*

2 (v) to put all the parts of something together. *Follow the instructions to assemble this model.*

assembly (n)
1 a meeting of lots of people.
2 **assembly line** (n) a series of machines and workers in a factory that each do a job in turn.

assent assenting assented (v) to agree to something. **assent** (n).

assert asserting asserted (v) If you **assert yourself**, you behave in a strong, confident way.

assertive (adj)
able to stand up for yourself and tell other people what you think or want. **assertiveness** (n), **assertively** (adv).

assess assesses assessing assessed (v) to judge how good or bad a thing is. **assessment** (n), **assessor** (n).

asset (n) something or someone who is helpful or useful. *Imran is a great asset to our team.*

assignment (n) a special job that is given to somebody. **assign** (v).

assistance (n)
If someone gives you **assistance**, they do something to help you or to make things easier for you. **assist** (v).

assistant (n) a person who helps someone else to do a task or job.

association (n)
1 an organization, club, or society.
2 a connection that you make in your mind between different things. *Our holiday house has many happy associations for me.* **associate** (v).

assonance (n)
repeated use of the same vowel sound in words that are close together, for example, "How now brown cow?".

assortment (n) a mixture of different things. **assorted** (adj).

assume assuming assumed (v)
1 to suppose that something is true, without checking it. *I assume that you're right.* **assumption** (n).
2 If you **assume** responsibility for something, you agree to look after it.
3 An **assumed name** is a false name.

assurance (n)
1 a firm promise.
2 confidence in yourself and in what you can do. *Self-assurance.*

assure assuring assured (v)
1 to promise something or say something positively. *Alicia assured me of her support.*
2 If you **assure yourself** of something, you make certain of it.

asterisk (n) a mark (*) used in printing and writing.

asteroid *(n)*
an object in space that is smaller than a planet and orbits around a star.

asthma *(ass-muh) (n)* If you have **asthma**, you sometimes wheeze and find it hard to breathe. **asthmatic** *(n),* **asthmatic** *(adj).*

astonish astonishes astonishing astonished *(v)*
to make someone feel very surprised. **astonishment** *(n),* **astonishing** *(adj),* **astonishingly** *(adv).*

astray
1 *(adv)* If something has gone **astray**, it has been lost.
2 If someone **leads you astray**, they encourage you to do something wrong.

astride *(prep)* If you sit **astride** something, such as a horse, you sit with one leg on either side of it.

astrology *(n)* the study of stars and planets and the ways in which they might affect people's lives. **astrologer** *(n),* **astrological** *(adj).*

astronaut *(n)* someone who travels in space. *The picture shows an astronaut operating a manned manoeuvring unit (MMU), which is used for moving around outside of a spaceship.*

astronomical sphere

astronomical *(adj)*
1 to do with astronomy. *The astronomical instrument shown here dates from the 16th century and was used to work out the positions of the stars.*
2 very large. *An astronomical amount of money.*
astronomically *(adv).*

astronomy *(n)* the study of stars, planets, and space. **astronomer** *(n).*

astute *(uh-styoot) (adj)*
If someone is **astute**, they understand situations and people clearly and quickly.

asunder *(adv) (old-fashioned)* in or into pieces. *The veil was torn asunder.*

asylum *(uh-sy-lum) (n)*
1 protection given by a country to someone escaping from danger in their own country.
2 *(old-fashioned)* a hospital for people who are mentally ill.

asymmetrical *(adj)*
A shape that is **asymmetrical** cannot be divided into two equal halves.

atheist *(ay-thee-ist) (n)*
someone who does not believe that there is a God. **atheism** *(n).*

astronaut with manned manoeuvring unit (MMU)
(spacesuit cutaway)

athlete *(n)*
1 someone who takes part in sports that require physical skill or strength, such as running, jumping, and throwing.
2 someone who is very good at physical sports. **athletic** *(adj).*

athletics *(n)*
competitive sports that involve running, jumping, or throwing. **athletic** *(adj). See* **track and field**.

atlas *(n)* a book of maps.

atmosphere *(at-muss-fear) (n)*
1 the mixture of gases that surround a planet. *The layers of the Earth's atmosphere are shown in this diagram.*
2 the air in a particular place. *The atmosphere in some of our cities is very polluted.* **atmospheric** *(adj).*
3 a mood or feeling created by a place or a work of art. *I didn't like the atmosphere in Uncle Colin's house.* **atmospheric** *(adj).*

layers of the atmosphere

atom *(n)*
the smallest part of a substance. Everything is made up of atoms. *The diagram shows the main parts of an atom.*

atomic *(adj)*
1 to do with atoms. *Atomic structure.*
2 using the power created when atoms are split. *Atomic energy.*

atone atoning atoned *(v)*
If you **atone** for something, you make up for it. *Kayleigh atoned for her lateness by working extra hard.*

atrocious *(at-roh-shuss) (adj)*
disgusting or terrible.

atrocity atrocities *(n)* a very wicked or cruel act, often involving killing.

attach
attaches attaching attached (v)
1 to join or fix one thing to
another. attachment (n).
2 If you are attached to
someone, you are very fond
of them. attachment (n).

attack attacking attacked
1 (v) to try to hurt someone or
something. attack (n), attacker (n).
2 (v) to criticize someone
strongly. attack (n).
3 (v) to try to defeat an enemy
or capture a place where the
enemy is. *The troops attacked
the castle.* attack (n).
4 (n) a sudden period of
illness. *A bad attack of flu.*

attainment (n) an achievement.
attain (v), attainable (adj).

attempt attempting attempted (v)
to try to do something. attempt (n).

attend attending attended (v)
1 to be present in a place or at
an event. *Thousands of people
attended the concert.* attendance (n).
2 If you attend to something,
you deal with it.

attendant (n) someone who
looks after an important person
or place. *A museum attendant.*

attention (n)
1 concentration and careful
thought. *Attention to detail.*
2 If you pay attention, you
concentrate on something.
3 When soldiers stand to attention,
they stand up straight, with their feet
together and their arms by their sides.

attic (n)
a room in the roof of a building.

attitude (n)
1 your opinions and feelings about
someone or something. *Aidan has
a positive attitude towards his work.*
2 the position in which
you are standing or sitting.

attract attracting attracted (v)
1 If something attracts you, you
are interested in it. attraction (n).
2 If a person attracts you,
you like them. attraction (n).
3 If something attracts objects
or people to itself, it pulls them
towards itself. *Magnets attract
iron and steel.* attraction (n).

attractive (adj)
1 pleasant or pretty to look at.
attractiveness (n), attractively (adv).
2 interesting or exciting. *An
attractive plan.* attractiveness (n).

auburn (or-burn) (n)
a reddish-brown colour. auburn (adj).

auction (n) a sale where goods are
sold to the person who offers the
most money for them. auctioneer (n).

audience (n)
1 the people who watch or listen
to a performance, speech, or show.
2 a formal meeting with an
important or powerful person.

audio-visual (adj) Audio-visual
equipment uses sound and pictures,
often to teach people something.

audition (n) a short performance
by an actor, singer, etc. to see
whether they are suitable for a
part in a play, concert, etc.

aunt (n) the sister of either of your
parents, or the wife of your uncle.

au pair (oh-pair) (n)
a young person from another country
who lives with a family and helps
them, in order to learn a language.

aural (or-al) (adj)
to do with listening. *My piano
exam includes an aural test.*

author (n) the writer of a book,
play, or poem. authorship (n).

authority authorities (n)
1 the right to do something
or to tell other people what
to do. *The detectives have the
authority to search our house.*
2 a group of people with power
in a certain area. *A local authority.*
3 someone who knows a lot
about a particular subject. *Sam
is an authority on computers.*

authorize or **authorise**
authorizing authorized (v)
to give permission for something
to happen. authorization (n).

autistic (adj)
Someone who is autistic has
a condition that can cause
problems with social interaction
and language skills. autism (n).

autobiography autobiographies
(n) a book that tells the story of the
writer's life. autobiographical (adj).

autograph (n)
a famous person's signature.

automatic (adj)
1 An automatic machine can
perform some actions without anyone
operating it. automatically (adv).
2 An automatic action happens
without your thinking about it.
automatically (adv).

automation (n) the use of machines
rather than people to do jobs,
especially in factories. automate (v).

automobile a type of passenger
motor vehicle. *See car.*

autumn (n) the season between
summer and winter, when it gets
colder and the leaves fall from
the trees. autumnal (adj).

available (adj)
1 ready to be used or
bought. availability (n).
2 not busy and so free to
talk to people. availability (n).

avalanche (av-er-larnsh) (n) a large
mass of snow and ice that suddenly
moves down the side of a mountain.

avenue (n) a road in a town or
city, often with trees on either side.

average (n)
1 In maths, you find an average by
adding a group of figures together
and then dividing the total by the
number of figures you have added.
The average of 2, 4, and 6 is 4.
2 usual, or ordinary.

aviary aviaries (n)
a large cage for birds.

aviation (n) the science of building
and flying aircraft. *The great age of
aviation began in 1903, when Orville
Wright first left the ground in the
Flyer, shown below.* aviator (n).

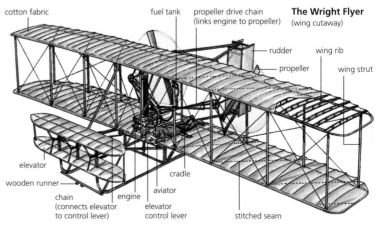

cotton fabric — fuel tank — propeller drive chain (links engine to propeller) — **The Wright Flyer** (wing cutaway)
rudder — wing rib
propeller — wing strut
elevator
cradle
wooden runner
aviator
chain (connects elevator to control lever) — engine — elevator control lever — stitched seam

avoid avoiding avoided *(v)*
1 to keep away from a person
or place. **avoidance** *(n)*.
2 to try to prevent something
from happening. *We must
avoid making that mistake again.*
avoidance *(n)*, **avoidable** *(adj)*.

await awaiting awaited *(v)* to wait
for or expect someone or something.

awake awaking awoke awoken
1 *(adj)* not asleep. *I'm wide awake.*
2 *(v)* to wake up. **awakening** *(n)*.

award awarding awarded *(v)*
to give something to someone
officially, often as a prize. **award** *(n)*.

aware *(adj)*
If you are **aware** of something, you
know that it exists. **awareness** *(n)*.

away
1 *(adv)* moving from a place, person,
or thing. *Rosie ran away from me.*
2 *(adv)* distant from a place.
We live three miles away.
3 *(adv)* not at home, or not present.
4 *(adv)* in a safe place.
Put your money away.
5 *(adj)* An **away** sports match is
played at your opponent's ground.

awe *(n)* a feeling of admiration
and respect, mixed with a little
fear. **awesome** *(adj)*.

awful *(adj)*
1 terrible or horrible.
2 *(informal)* very great. *I spent an
awful lot of money.* **awfully** *(adv)*.

awkward *(adj)*
1 causing difficulties. *An awkward
catch.* **awkwardness** *(n)*,
awkwardly *(adv)*.
2 not able to relax and talk to
people easily. **awkwardness** *(n)*,
awkwardly *(adv)*.

axe axing axed
1 *(n)* a tool with a sharp blade
on the end of a long handle,
used for chopping wood.
2 *(v)* to bring something to an
end, usually in order to save
money. *200 jobs will be axed.*

axis axes *(n)*
1 an imaginary line through the
middle of an object, around which
that object spins. *The Earth's axis.*
2 a line at the side or
the bottom of a graph.

axle *(n)* a rod in the centre of
a wheel, around which it turns.

Aztec *(n)*
a member of a Mexican Native
American people, who had
a great civilization before the
conquest of Mexico in the
16th century. **Aztec** *(adj)*.

Bb

babble babbling babbled *(v)*
1 to talk in an excited way,
without making any sense.
2 to make sounds like a baby.

baboon *(n)* a large
monkey that lives in
Africa. Baboons
have long,
dog-like
snouts and
large teeth.

**olive
baboons**

baby babies *(n)* a newly-born or very
young child or animal. **babyish** *(adj)*.

baby-sitter *(n)* someone who is paid
to stay in the house and look after
children while their parents are out.

bachelor *(n)*
a man who has never been married.

back backing backed
1 *(n)* the rear part of your body
between your neck and your bottom.
2 *(n)* the opposite end or side
from the front. **back** *(adj)*.
3 *(adv)* to where someone or
something was before. *Ed came back.*
4 *(v)* to support someone.
5 **back down** *(v)* to admit
that you were wrong.
6 **back out** *(v)* to decide not to do
something that you had agreed to do.

backfire backfiring backfired *(v)*
1 If a car **backfires**, there is a small
explosion inside its exhaust pipe.
2 If an action **backfires**, it does
not work out as you planned it.

background *(n)*
1 the part of a picture that
is behind the main subject.
2 the facts or events that
surround something and help
to explain why it happened.

backhand *(n)* a stroke in
tennis that you play with
the back of your hand facing
outwards and your arm across your
body. *The sequence below shows
how to play a backhand.*

backpack
1 *(n)* a large bag that you
carry on your back when
you are walking or climbing.
2 *(v)* If you **go backpacking**,
you go on a long walk or hike.

backstroke *(n)* a style of swimming
in which you swim lying on your back.

backwards *(adv)*
1 in the direction that your back
is facing. *Jill stepped backwards.*
2 in the opposite to the usual
way. *Say the alphabet backwards.*

bacon *(n)* smoked or salted meat
from the back or sides of a pig.

bacteria *(plural n)* microscopic living
things which exist all around you and
inside you. Many bacteria are useful,
but some cause disease. *The diagram
shows a simplified bacteria cell,
magnified millions of times.*

bacteria cell chromosome cytoplasm
(magnified) (contains DNA)

flagellum
(moves cell)

jelly-like
coat

cell membrane cell wall

bad worse worst *(adj)*
1 not good.
2 serious. *A bad mistake.*
3 not fit to eat. *The fish has gone bad.*

badge *(n)*
a small sign with a picture or message
on it that you pin to your clothes.

badger badgering badgered
1 *(n)* a mammal with a grey body
and a black and white head, that
lives in a sett under the ground
and comes out at night to feed.
2 *(v)* to keep asking someone to do
something. *Fran kept badgering
me to let her come with us.*

**European
badger's sett**

sow
(female
badger) (cutaway)

cubs on bedding
of dry grass
and leaves

sett
entrance

tunnel chamber

badly
(adv)
1 not
well or
not skilfully.
2 urgently.
I want it badly.

backhand drive

badminton (n)
a game like tennis, in which players use rackets to hit a shuttlecock over a high net.

badminton racket and shuttlecocks

frame
string
shaft
plastic shuttlecock
feather shuttlecock

baffle baffling baffled (v)
to puzzle or confuse someone. **baffling** (adj).

bag (n) a container used for carrying things.

baggage (n) suitcases and bags.

baggy baggier baggiest (adj)
hanging in loose folds. *Baggy shorts.*

bagpipes (plural n) a musical instrument. To play the bagpipes, you blow air through the blowstick into a bag, and squeeze it out through the drones and the chanter.

Scottish bagpipes
tenor drones
bass drone
cords
chanter
bag covered in tartan cloth
blowstick
mouthpiece

bail (n)
1 a sum of money paid to a court to allow someone accused of a crime to be set free until their trial.
2 one of the two small pieces of wood that are placed across the top of cricket stumps.

bailiff (n) a law officer who makes sure that a court's decision is carried out, especially by taking someone's property when they owe money.

bail out see **bale out**.

bait (n) a small amount of food used to attract a fish or an animal, so that you can catch it. See **angling**.

baize (n) a green felt-like material, used for covering card tables, snooker tables, etc.

bake baking baked (v)
1 to cook food in an oven, especially bread or cakes. **baker** (n), **bakery** (n).
2 to heat something in order to make it hard. *Bake the clay in a kiln before glazing it.*

balaclava (n)
a woolly hat that covers your head and neck, like a helmet.

balance
balancing balanced
1 (n) an instrument used for weighing things.
2 (v) When two things **balance** in a pair of scales, they weigh the same and do not tip the scales either way.
3 (n) Your **balance** is your ability to keep steady and not fall over.
4 (v) If you **balance** something, you keep it steady and do not let it fall.
5 (n) When you subtract an amount from another amount, what you have left is the **balance**.

balcony (n)
1 a platform with railings on the outside of a building, usually on an upper level.
2 the upstairs seating in a theatre.

bald (borld) balder baldest (adj)
1 Someone who is **bald** has very little or no hair on their head. **baldness** (n), **balding** (adj).
2 A **bald** fact or statement is stated simply, without any attempt to make it more pleasant. **baldly** (adv).

bale out baling out baled out (v)
1 to jump out of an aircraft, using a parachute.
2 If you **bale someone out**, you help them out of a difficult situation.

ball (n)
1 a round object, used in games.
2 something made into a round shape. *A ball of wool.*
3 a very formal party where people dance.
4 (informal) If you **have a ball**, you really enjoy yourself.

ballad (n)
a song or a poem that tells a story.

ballast
1 (n) heavy material, such as water or sand, that is carried by a ship to make it more stable.
2 **ballast tank** (n) a large tank in a submarine that is filled with water to make the submarine sink, and with air to make it come to the surface.

ball bearings (n) small, metal balls used to help parts of machinery move more smoothly against each other.

ballerina (n) a female ballet dancer.

ballet (bal-ay) (n)
1 a style of dance with set movements.
2 a performance using dance and music, often to tell a story.

grand jeté
arabesque
pirouette
ballet movements

ballistics (singular n)
the science and study of missiles that are fired from guns. **ballistic** (adj).

balloon (n)
1 a small bag made of thin rubber that is blown up and used as a decoration.
2 See **hot-air balloon**.

ballot
1 (n) a secret way of voting for something.
2 **ballot box** (n) a box with a slit in the top into which votes are put.
3 **ballot paper** (n) a special piece of paper used for marking a vote.

ballpoint (n) a pen with a tiny ball at its tip that lets ink flow as you write.

balsa (n) a very light wood, used for making models.

bamboo (n) a tropical plant with a hard, hollow stem, often used for making furniture.

ban banning banned (v)
to forbid something. *Ball games are banned in this park.* **ban** (n).

banana (n) a tropical fruit that is long, curved, and yellow.

banana tree
unripe bananas
flower

band
banding banded
1 (n) a narrow ring of rubber, paper, or other material, that is put around something to hold it together.
2 (n) a group of people who play music together.
3 (n) a group of people who do something together. *A band of robbers.*
4 (v) When people **band together**, they join together in a group in order to do something.

barracks

bandage (n) a long piece of cloth that is wrapped around an injured part of the body in order to protect it. **bandage** (v).

bandit (n)
an armed robber, usually one of a gang, who attacks travellers.

bang banging banged
1 (n) a sudden loud noise.
2 (v) to knock hard against something. **bang** (n).

banger (n)
1 a firework that makes a loud noise.
2 (informal) an old, battered car.
3 (slang) a sausage.

bangle (n)
a band of metal, plastic, etc. worn around the wrist.

banish
banishes banishing banished (v)
to send someone away from a place and order them not to return. **banishment** (n).

banister or **bannister** (n)
a rail that runs along the side of a flight of stairs.

banjo (n)
a musical instrument like a small, round guitar with a long neck.

banjo

arm rest

tuning peg

headstock

fifth tuning peg

string

fingerboard

neck

velum (thin membrane)

tone ring

bridge

tailpiece

wooden rim

bank banking banked
1 (n) a place where people keep their money or can borrow money.
2 (n) the land along a river or a canal.
3 (n) a place where something is stored and collected. *A bottle bank.*
4 **bank holiday** (n) a public holiday when banks and businesses are closed.
5 (v) If you **bank on** something, you rely on it.

banknote (n)
a piece of paper money.

bankrupt (adj)
If a person or company is **bankrupt**, they cannot pay their debts. **bankruptcy** (n), **bankrupt** (v).

banner (n) a long piece of material with writing on it, often carried in sports crowds and processions.

bannister see **banister**.

banns (plural n) an announcement of a wedding made in a church.

banquet (n)
a formal meal for a large number of people, usually on a special occasion.

banter (n) conversation that sounds mean-spirited but is actually good-natured. **banter** (v).

bap (n) a soft bread roll.

baptize or **baptise**
baptizing baptized (v)
to pour water on someone's head, or to immerse someone in water, as a sign that they have become a Christian. **baptism** (n).

bar (n)
1 a long stick of metal. *An iron bar.*
2 a long, flat block of something hard. *A chocolate bar. A bar of gold.*
3 a place where drinks, especially alcoholic drinks, are sold.
4 one of the groups of notes into which a piece of music is divided.

barbarian (n)
a member of a wild and uncivilized tribe that lived in the past.

barbaric (adj) very cruel. *The animals were kept in barbaric conditions.*

barbecue (n)
1 a charcoal or gas grill used for cooking meat and other food out of doors. **barbecue** (v).
2 an outdoor meal or party in which food is cooked using a barbecue.

barbed wire (n) wire with small spikes along it, used for fences.

barber (n) someone who cuts men's and boys' hair.

bar code (n) a band of thick and thin lines printed on goods sold in shops which gives information about the goods.

bare
baring bared; barer barest
1 (adj) wearing no clothes.
2 (adj) empty. *The room was bare.*
3 (adj) plain and simple. *Just give me the bare facts.*
4 (v) to uncover or reveal something. *The dog bared its teeth. Verity bared her secret thoughts.*

bareback (adv) If you ride a horse **bareback**, you do not use a saddle.

barefaced (adj) open and undisguised. *Barefaced cheek.*

barely (adv) only just. *Scarlett was so scared, she could barely speak.*

bargain bargaining bargained
1 (n) something that you buy for less than the usual price.
2 (v) When you **bargain** with someone, you agree to do or give something if they will do or give something else in exchange. **bargain** (n).

barge barging barged
1 (n) a long, flat-bottomed boat, used on canals.
2 (v) If you **barge** into someone, you knock against them roughly or push them out of the way.

baritone (n)
1 the second-lowest singing voice for a man. **baritone** (adj).
2 a singer with a baritone voice.

bark barking barked
1 (v) When a dog **barks**, it makes a loud sound in its throat. **bark** (n).
2 (v) to shout at someone gruffly. *"Attention!" barked the sergeant.*
3 (n) the hard covering on the outside of a tree.

barley (n)
a common cereal plant. *See* **grain**.

bar mitzvah (n)
a celebration that takes place on a Jewish boy's 13th birthday, after which they can take part in their religion as an adult.

barn (n) a farm building where crops or animals are kept. *See* **thresh**.

barnacle (n) a small shellfish that sticks itself firmly to the sides of boats, rocks, and other shellfish. *See* **scallop**.

barometer (n) an instrument that measures changes in air pressure and shows how the weather is going to change. *In the simple barometer shown here, liquid rises in the spout for stormy weather and falls for good weather.*

19th-century barometer

baron (n) a nobleman. In Britain, a baron is a male peer of the lowest rank. **baronial** (adj).

baroness baronesses (n)
a noblewoman. In Britain, a baroness is a female peer of the lowest rank, or the wife of a baron.

barracks (plural n)
the buildings where soldiers live.

barrage

barrage (n)
1 a dam built across a river to control the level of the water.
2 a large amount of something that all comes at the same time. *A barrage of complaints.*

barrel (n)
1 a container for liquids, such as water or beer, which has curved sides and a flat top and bottom.
2 the long part of a gun that looks like a tube. *See* **blunderbuss**.
3 the part of a dart that you hold.
4 If someone has you **over a barrel**, they have made you powerless.

barren (adj)
1 If land is **barren**, farmers cannot grow crops on it.
2 (old-fashioned) A woman who is **barren** is not able to have children.

barricade barricading barricaded
1 (n) a wall built in a hurry to stop people from getting past.
2 (v) If people **barricade** themselves into a place, they build walls to stop other people reaching them.

barrier (n)
1 a bar, fence, or wall that prevents people, traffic, water, etc. from going past it. *The Thames Barrier is made up of a series of linked gates across the River Thames which can be opened to let water through, or closed to prevent flooding. The picture below shows a gate in the closed position.*
2 something that prevents you from communicating properly with someone else. *A language barrier.*

barring
(prep) except for. *We'll be there, barring an emergency.*

barrister (n) a lawyer who works in the higher law courts in Britain.

barrow (n)
1 a small cart used for carrying things.
2 a mound of earth made to cover a grave in prehistoric times.

bartender (n) someone who serves behind the bar in a pub.

barter bartering bartered (v) to trade by exchanging food and other goods, rather than by using money. **barter** (n).

base basing based; baser basest
1 (n) the lowest part of something, or the part that it stands on.
2 (v) to use something as the starting point for something else. *I based my story on a real event.* **basis** (n).
3 (n) the place from which a business, army, etc. is controlled. **base** (v).
4 (n) In baseball or rounders, a **base** is one of the four points to which you have to run in order to score a run or rounder. *See* **baseball**.
5 (n) In chemistry, a **base** is a substance that will neutralize an acid. Bases react with acids to form salts.
6 (n) In maths, a **base** is the starting point for a counting system. For example, ten is the base of the decimal system.
7 (adj) selfish or mean. *A base trick.*

baseball (n) an American game, played with a bat, ball, and two teams of nine players. *The picture shows the batting area of a baseball field, beyond which is the centre field, a large fielding area. Some baseball equipment is also shown.*

basement (n) an area or room in a building below ground level.

bash bashes bashing bashed
1 (v) (informal) to hit something hard.
2 (informal) If you **have a bash** at something, you try it.

bashful (adj) shy. **bashfully** (adv).

basic
1 (adj) simple and straightforward.
2 **basics** (plural n) the most important things to know about a subject.

basin (n)
1 a large bowl used for washing, usually fixed to a wall.
2 a deep bowl, often used for mixing food.
3 an area of land around a river from which water drains into the river.

basis (n) the idea or reason behind something. *The basis of a plan.*

bask basking basked (v)
1 to lie or sit in the sunshine and enjoy it.
2 If you **bask in** someone's praise, admiration, etc., you enjoy it.

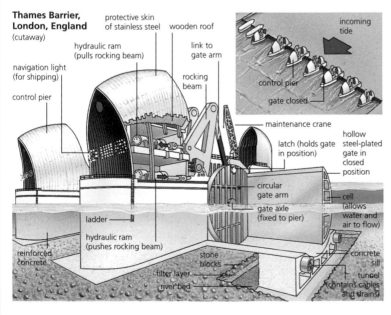

outfield — infield
second base
pitcher's mound
diamond — first base
third base — home plate
batter's box
aircraft aluminium — catcher's box
baseball field
webbed catching pocket — fingers laced together
rubber grip
leather ball with cork centre
flexible leather
hand stitching
baseball bat — **fielder's glove and baseball**

Thames Barrier, London, England (cutaway)
protective skin of stainless steel — wooden roof
hydraulic ram (pulls rocking beam)
link to gate arm
navigation light (for shipping)
rocking beam
control pier
incoming tide
control pier
gate closed
maintenance crane
latch (holds gate in position)
hollow steel-plated gate in closed position
circular gate arm
gate axle (fixed to pier)
cell (allows water and air to flow)
ladder
hydraulic ram (pushes rocking beam)
reinforced concrete
stone blocks
concrete sill
filter layer
tunnel (contains cables and drains)
river bed

bean

basket *(n)* a container, usually with handles, made of cane, wire, etc.

basketball *(n)* a game played by two teams who try to score points by throwing a ball into a high net at the end of a court. *The picture sequence shows a goal being shot in basketball.*

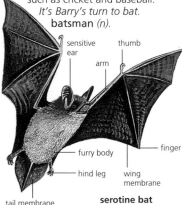

basketball.

bass *(rhymes with lace)* **basses** *(n)*
1 the lowest singing voice for a man.
2 a musical instrument that makes a low sound, for example, a double bass or a bass guitar.

bat batting batted
1 *(n)* a small, flying mammal that comes out at night to feed. Bats find their way around by making high-pitched squeaks which send back echoes that are picked up by their sensitive ears.
2 *(n)* a piece of wood used for hitting the ball in games such as cricket, baseball, and table tennis. *See* **baseball**.
3 *(v)* to take a turn at hitting the ball and scoring runs in games such as cricket and baseball. *It's Barry's turn to bat.* **batsman** *(n)*.

sensitive ear
thumb
arm
furry body
finger
hind leg
wing membrane
tail membrane

serotine bat

bat mitzvah *(n)*
a celebration that takes place on a Jewish girl's 13th birthday, after which they can take part in their religion as an adult.

batch batches *(n)* a group of things that arrive together or are made together. *A batch of cakes.*

bath
1 *(n)* a large, open container for water in which you sit and wash your whole body.
2 **baths** *(plural n)* a public swimming pool.

bathe bathes bathing bathed *(v)*
1 to go swimming in the sea or in a stream. **bather** *(n)*.
2 If you **bathe** part of your body that is sore, you wash it gently in water or antiseptic.

bathroom *(n)*
a room that contains a bath or a shower, and often a basin and toilet.

batik *(bat-eek)* *(n)* an Eastern method of printing designs on cloth.

baton *(n)*
1 a short, thin stick used by a conductor to beat time for an orchestra.
2 a short stick passed from one runner to another in a relay race.

batsman batsmen *(n)* the person who is batting in games such as cricket.

battalion *(n)*
a large number of soldiers.

batten *(n)* a light strip of wood, used to support or strengthen something.

batter battering battered
1 *(v)* to hit someone or something many times. **battering** *(n)*.
2 *(v)* If someone **batters down** a door, they break through it by hitting it many times.
3 *(n)* a mixture of milk, eggs, and flour that can be cooked to make pancakes, or used to coat food which you fry.

battering ram *(n)* a heavy, wooden beam, that is rammed against an enemy's walls or gates.

medieval battering ram

battery batteries *(n)*
1 a group of machines or heavy guns that are all used together.
2 a container that stores chemicals which produce electrical power. *Also see* **car**.

battery (cutaway)
metal cap (positive terminal)
carbon rod
chemical mixture
electrolyte layer in paper
plastic case
zinc case
base (negative terminal)

battery farming *(n)* a system for breeding and rearing poultry or cattle or for producing eggs, in which a large number of animals are kept in small cages or pens.

battle *(n)*
1 a fight between two armies.
2 a struggle with someone.

battleship *(n)*
a warship armed with powerful guns.

bawl bawling bawled *(v)*
1 to cry loudly like a baby.
2 to shout loudly in a harsh voice. *"Get off my roses!" bawled Mr Jones.*

bay
1 *(n)* a part of the coast that curves inwards.
2 If you keep something or someone at bay, you fight them off. *Abbie managed to keep her fears at bay.*
3 **bay window** *(n)* a window that sticks out from the wall of a house. *See* **building**.

bayonet *(n)* a long knife that can be fitted to the end of a rifle to make a weapon.

bazaar *(n)*
1 a street market, especially one held in Middle Eastern countries.
2 a sale held to raise money for charity, usually by selling second-hand items or handmade craft.

BC the initials of the phrase "before Christ". BC is used to show that a date comes before the birth of Jesus Christ. *Julius Caesar died in 44BC.*

beach beaches *(n)* a strip of sand or pebbles where land meets water.

beacon *(n)* a light or fire used as a signal or warning.

bead *(n)*
1 a small piece of glass, wood, or plastic with a hole through the middle that can be threaded on to a string.
2 a drop of liquid.

beak *(n)* the hard, horn-like part of a bird's mouth. *See* **bird**.

beaker *(n)* a plastic or glass jar used in chemistry. *See* **apparatus**.

beam beaming beamed
1 *(n)* a thick ray of light from a torch, car headlight, etc. **beam** *(v)*.
2 *(n)* a long, thick piece of wood, concrete, or metal, used to support the roof or floors of a building.
3 *(v)* to smile widely. **beam** *(n)*.

bean *(n)*
1 **Beans** are large seeds that you can eat or that can be used to make a drink. *Baked beans. Coffee beans.*
2 *(informal)* If you are **full of beans**, you are very lively.

bear bearing bore borne
1 (v) to support or carry
something. *Is the ice thick
enough to bear my weight?*
2 (v) When a tree or plant **bears** fruit,
flowers, or leaves, it produces them.
3 (v) If you cannot **bear** something,
you cannot put up with it, either
because it upsets you or because
you do not like it at all. *My mum
can't bear rap music.* **bearable** (adj).
4 (n) a large, heavy mammal with
thick fur. *The picture shows a young
male grizzly bear catching a salmon.*

grizzly bear

beard (n)
the hair on a man's chin.
beast (n)
1 (old-fashioned) a wild animal.
2 (informal) a horrible or unkind
person. **beastliness** (n), **beastly** (adj).
beat beating beat beaten
1 (v) to hit someone or something
many times. **beating** (n).
2 (v) to defeat someone in a game or
contest. *Jonathan beat me at chess.*
3 (n) the regular rhythm of a
piece of music or of your heart.
4 (v) If you **beat** a mixture, you stir
it up quickly with a whisk or fork.
beautiful (adj) very pleasing
to the senses. **beauty** (n),
beautify (v), **beautifully** (adv).
beaver beavering beavered
1 (n) an animal like a large rat
with a wide, flat tail. Beavers
build dams across streams to
create safe areas for their lodges.
2 (v) If you **beaver away** at
something, you work very hard at it.

beaver's dam and lodge
(cutaway)

lowered
water level
dam
entrance
tunnel
moat
beaver
ventilation
shaft
lodge
kit
(young
beaver)
living chamber
above water level

because (conj) for the reason that.
I came because I wanted to see you.
beckon beckoning beckoned (v)
to make a sign to someone,
asking them to come. *Jack
beckoned for us to follow him.*
become becoming became (v)
to start to be. *When did you
first become suspicious?*
bed (n)
1 a piece of furniture
that you sleep on.
2 a place in a garden
where flowers are planted.
3 the bottom of
an ocean or river.
bedclothes (n)
sheets, duvets, blankets, etc.
bedridden (adj) If you are
bedridden, you are so ill that
you cannot get out of bed.
bedroom (n)
a room used for sleeping.
bedsitter (n) a rented room
that someone lives and sleeps in.
bee (n) a flying insect with yellow
and black stripes that makes honey.
*A bee lets other bees know where
food is by performing a "dance",
in which it waggles its abdomen
a certain number of times. Also see*
hive, **honeycomb**, **insect**.

bee dance

watching bee
dance
direction
dancing bee
waggling
abdomen

beech beeches (n)
a tree with a smooth, grey bark
and leaves that spread outwards.

beef (n)
the meat from a cow, a bull, or an ox.
beefy beefier beefiest (adj)
(informal) big and muscular.
beehive (n) a nest or house
where bees live. *See* **hive**.
beer (n) an alcoholic drink made
from malt, barley, and hops.
beetle (n) a flying insect with hard
wing covers. *The goliath
beetle, pictured here,
weighs as much
as a sparrow.*

claw
antenna
compound eye
head
thorax
abdomen
elytron
(wing cover)
**goliath
beetle**

beetroot (n)
a purplish-red root vegetable.
See **vegetable**.
before
1 (prep) sooner or earlier
than. *The time before last.*
2 (adv) earlier. *I've been here before.*
beg begging begged (v)
1 to ask someone in the street for
help, especially for money. **beggar** (n).
2 to plead with someone
to do something.
begin beginning began begun (v)
to start. **beginner** (n), **beginning** (n).
begrudge begrudging begrudged
(v) to be jealous or resentful.
behalf If you do something
on **behalf** of someone else, you
do it for them, or in their place.
behave behaving behaved (v)
1 to do and say things in a
particular way. *Matthew behaved
very strangely.* **behaviour** (n).
2 to act properly and avoid
being noisy or causing trouble.
behind
1 (prep) on the other side, or towards
the back of a thing. *Get behind me!*
2 (prep) further back or in
a lower position. *Joshua
finished the race behind me.*
3 (adv) not making good progress.
I'm behind with my work.
beige (bayjh) (n)
a pale brown colour. **beige** (adj).

being (n) a living thing.

belch belches
belching belched (v)
1 to let out gases from your stomach through your mouth with a loud noise. **belch** (n).
2 to send out fire and smoke.

believe believing believed (v)
1 to feel that something is true. **belief** (n), **believer** (n).
2 to support someone or something. *I believe in rights for children.* **believer** (n).

bell (n)
1 an instrument which makes a ringing sound. Bells are often tapered cup shapes and have a clapper hanging down inside them.
2 (informal) If something **rings a bell**, you think you have heard it somewhere before.
3 a bell-shaped object, especially on a musical instrument.
See **brass**.

crown **bell**
(cutaway)
shoulder
waist
lip
mouth — clapper

bellow bellowing bellowed
1 (v) to shout or roar. **bellow** (n).
2 **bellows** (plural n)
an instrument used for pumping air into something like an organ or a fire.

belly bellies
1 (n) the stomach, or the part of a human's or animal's body that contains their stomach and bowels.
2 **belly flop** (n) an awkward dive into water in which you hit the water horizontally instead of vertically.
3 **belly button** (n) see **navel**.

belong belonging belonged (v)
1 If something **belongs** to you, you own it. **belongings** (plural n).
2 If you **belong** to a group, you are a member of it.
3 If something **belongs** somewhere, that is its proper place.

below (prep)
1 lower than. *The temperature is below freezing point.*
2 at or to a lower place. *The captain of the ship went below deck.*

belt belting belted
1 (n) a strip of leather, cord, etc. that you wear around your waist.
2 (n) a moving band of rubber, used for transporting objects or for driving machinery. *Conveyor belt.*
3 (v) (informal) to hit someone hard.
4 (v) (informal) to travel very fast.
5 (n) an area or a strip.
Commuter belt. A belt of rain.

bench benches (n)
1 a long, narrow seat for several people, usually made of wood.
2 a work table in a workshop or laboratory.
3 The **bench** is the word used collectively for a group of judges or magistrates in British courts.

bend bending bent (v)
1 If you **bend, bend down,** or **bend over,** you lean forward from your waist.
2 If something **bends,** it changes direction by turning to one side. *The road bends to the left.* **bend** (n).
3 to change the shape of something so that it is no longer straight.

beneath (prep)
1 underneath. *We hid beneath the bedclothes.*
2 lower than or not worthy. *It's beneath my dignity to talk to her.*

beneficial (adj) Something that is **beneficial** is good for you.

benefit benefiting benefited
1 (v) If you **benefit** from something, you gain an advantage from it or are helped by it. *We really benefited from our holiday.* **benefit** (n).
2 (n) money paid by the government to people who need it, such as people who are poor, ill, disabled, or unemployed.

Bengali (ben-gor-lee) (n)
a language spoken in Bangladesh and the Indian state of West Bengal.

benign (adj) harmless. *The tests showed that the lump was benign.*

bent (adj)
1 crooked or curved.
2 (slang) dishonest.

bequeath
bequeathing bequeathed (v)
to leave something to somebody in a will. **bequest** (n).

bereaved (adj) A person is **bereaved** if a friend or relative of theirs has died. **bereavement** (n).

berry berries (n)
a small, often brightly-coloured fruit, found on bushes or trees.

berth berthing berthed
1 (n) a bed in a ship, train, or caravan.
2 (n) a place in a harbour where a boat is tied up.
3 (v) When a boat **berths,** it comes into harbour and is tied up.

beside
1 (prep) next to.
2 If you are **beside yourself,** you are overcome with emotion. *Jamie is beside himself with rage.*

besides
1 (prep) as well as or apart from. *Who went to the match besides Jim?*
2 (adv) also or in addition to this. *I hate boats and, besides, I can't swim.*

besiege besieging besieged (v)
to surround a place in order to make it surrender. *Enemy troops are besieging the castle!*

best
1 (adj) better than everything else.
2 When you **do your best,** you try as hard as you can to do something.
3 **best man** (n) the friend of the bridegroom who helps him at his wedding.

bet betting bet (v)
1 to risk a sum of money on the result of something, such as a horse race. If you guess the result correctly, you win some money; if not, you lose money. **betting** (n).
2 If you **bet** someone that they cannot do something, you dare them to do it. *I bet you can't climb that tree!*
3 (informal) If you **bet** that someone does something, you predict that they will do it. *I bet Mona trips over that cat.*

betray betraying betrayed (v)
1 If you **betray** someone, you deliberately let them down or do something to hurt them when you said that you would not. **betrayal** (n).
2 If you **betray** your feelings, you are not able to keep them hidden.

better (adj)
1 more suitable or higher in quality.
2 no longer ill or hurting.
3 **better off** richer.

between (prep)
1 If something is **between** two things, it has them on either side of it. *Dale stood between two trees.*
2 from one to the other. *We threw the ball between us.*
3 somewhere within two limits. *Nadia left between three and four o'clock.*

beverage (n) a drink.

beware (v) (no past tense)
If a person or sign tells you to **beware of** something, they warn you to look out for something dangerous or harmful.

bewilder
bewildering bewildered (v)
to confuse or muddle someone. **bewilderment** (n), **bewildered** (adj).

beyond (prep)
1 on the far side of something. *We couldn't see beyond the bushes.*
2 If something is **beyond you,** you cannot understand it.

biased

biased (by-ursd) (adj) prejudiced or favouring one person or point of view more than another. *Tim thinks that the referee is biased against our team.* **bias** (n).

Bible (n)
the holy book of the Christian religion.

bibliography bibliographies (n)
a list of books on a subject. **bibliographical** (adj).

bicycle (n) a two-wheeled vehicle which you ride by steering with handlebars, and pedalling. *The mountain bike shown below is a type of bicycle that has been specially developed for off-road cycling.*

bid bidding bid
1 (v) to offer to buy something at an auction for a certain amount of money. **bid** (n), **bidder** (n).
2 (v) (old-fashioned) to order someone to do something. *Bid the prince to come here!*
3 (n) an attempt to do or win something. *Mark made a bid for fame.*

bidet (bee-day) (n)
a low bowl in some bathrooms, in which you sit and wash yourself.

biennial (by-en-ee-ul)
1 (adj) happening every two years or over a period of two years.
2 (n) a plant that lives for two years.

big bigger biggest (adj)
large or important.

bigot (n) someone who has a strong and unreasonable dislike of certain other people, especially people of a different race, nationality, or religion. **bigotry** (n), **bigoted** (adj).

bike biking biked
1 (n) a bicycle or a motorcycle.
2 (v) to ride a bicycle or motorcycle. **biker** (n).

bikini (n) a two-piece swimming costume worn by women and girls.

bile (n) a greenish-coloured liquid that is made by the liver and which helps to digest food.

mountain bike, tools, and accessories

bilingual *(adj)*
If someone is **bilingual**, they can speak two languages very well.

bill *(n)*
1 a piece of paper telling you how much money you owe for something that you have bought.
2 a written plan for a new law, to be discussed in Parliament.
3 the beak of a bird, especially a duck's beak.

billiards *(singular n)* a game, similar to snooker, in which you use a stick, called a cue, to hit balls around a table and into pockets.

billow billowing billowed
1 *(v)* When a curtain, sail, sheet, etc. **billows**, it is pushed outwards by the wind.
2 *(v)* If smoke or fog **billows**, it rises up in large clouds.
3 *(n)* an ocean wave.

binary *(adj)*
1 made up of two parts or units.
2 Binary arithmetic uses only two digits, 1 and 0. **binary** *(n)*.

bind binding bound *(v)*
1 to tie something up.
2 to wrap a piece of material tightly around something.
3 to fasten the pages of a book together and put a cover on them.

binder *(n)*
a hard folder with metal rings inside it, used for holding papers.

bingo *(n)* a game in which you cross out numbers on a card as they are called out.

binoculars *(plural n)*
an instrument that you look through with both eyes to make distant things seem nearer.

biodegradable *(adj)*
Something that is **biodegradable** can be destroyed naturally by bacteria.
Biodegradable packaging helps to reduce waste and pollution.

biography
biographies *(n)*
a book that tells someone's life story. **biographer** *(n)*, **biographical** *(adj)*.

biology *(n)*
the scientific study of living things. **biologist** *(n)*, **biological** *(adj)*, **biologically** *(adv)*.

biplane *(n)*
an aeroplane with two sets of wings, one above the other. See **aviation**.

bird *(n)*
a two-legged creature with wings, feathers, and a beak. Birds lay eggs, and most birds can fly.
The picture of an orange chat on the right shows the main parts of a bird's body. Birds can be grouped into orders, or types. Examples of birds in some orders are shown below.

orange chat

ear coverts · crown · beak
nape
secondary feathers
throat
wing
breast
belly
primary feathers
claw
flank
toe
undertail coverts
scaly leg
tail
thigh

birds

short-eared owl

greater roadrunner

Indian hornbill

whooping crane

waxwing

turtle dove

white-cheeked turaco

sooty-capped puffbird

scarlet macaw

king penguin

red-and-yellow barbet

sparkling violet-eared hummingbird

swift

red-throated bee-eater

white-backed mousebird

red-bellied trogon

hoopoe

Canada goose

ostrich

painted buttonquail

red grouse

spotted tinamou

mallee fowl

Some words that begin with a "bi" sound are spelt "by".

birth

birth *(n)*
1 the event of being born.
2 the beginning of something.
The birth of the internet.
3 When a woman **gives**
birth, she has a baby.

birth control *(n)*
the methods used to prevent
women from becoming pregnant.

birthday *(n)* a yearly celebration
of the day that someone was born.

biscuit *(n)*
a small, flat cake, which has
been baked until it is hard.

bisect bisecting bisected *(v)*
to divide a line, angle, or
shape into two equal parts.

bishop *(n)*
1 a senior priest in the
Christian Church who
is in charge of priests
and churches in a large
area called a diocese.
2 a chesspiece that
can move diagonally
across the board.
*The picture shows
a bishop from a
12th-century
Viking chess set.
Also see* **chess**.

bishop
chesspiece

bison bison *(n)*
an American buffalo.

bit *(n)*
1 a small piece or
amount of something.
2 the smallest unit of information
in a computer's memory.
3 the metal bar that goes
in a horse's mouth and is
attached to the reins. *See* **tack**.
4 the end part of a drill. *See* **drill**.

bitch bitches bitching bitched
1 *(n)* a female dog.
2 *(v)* If you **bitch about**
someone, you say unkind
or untrue things about them.

bite biting bit bitten *(v)*
1 to close your teeth around
something. *Lindsay bit into the
apple and found a maggot!* bite *(n)*.
2 If an insect or snake **bites** you,
it pricks your skin and injects
venom into your body. bite *(n)*.

bitter bitterest
1 *(adj)* tasting sharp and slightly
sour, often in an unpleasant way.
2 *(adj)* If you feel **bitter**, you are
upset and angry about something.
3 *(adj)* If the weather is
bitter, it is very cold indeed.
4 *(n)* a British beer with
a slightly bitter taste.

black
1 *(n)* the colour of coal or
of the sky at night. **black** *(adj)*.
2 *(adj)* **Black** people have naturally
dark skin or are descended from
people with naturally dark skin.

blackberry blackberries *(n)*
a small, black fruit that grows
on brambles. *See* **fruit**.

blackboard *(n)* a dark surface
that teachers write on with chalk.

black hole *(n)* the area in space
around a collapsed star that sucks
in everything around it, even light.

blackmail *(n)*
the crime of threatening to reveal a
secret about someone unless they
pay a sum of money. **blackmail** *(v)*.

blackout *(n)* a short period of
unconsciousness. **black out** *(v)*.

blacksmith *(n)* someone who
makes and fits horseshoes and
mends things made of iron.

bladder *(n)* the organ in your body
where waste liquid is stored before
it leaves your body. *See* **organ**.

blade *(n)*
1 a sharp edge on a knife,
sword, dagger, etc.
2 the long, flat part
of an oar or propeller.
3 a single piece of grass.

blame blaming blamed *(v)* If you
blame someone for something, you
say that it is their fault. **blame** *(n)*.

bland blander blandest *(adj)*
mild and rather dull. *Bland food.*

blank blanker blankest
1 *(adj)* If something is **blank,** it
has nothing on it. *A blank page.*
2 *(n)* a cartridge for a gun that makes
a noise but does not fire a bullet.
3 **blank verse** *(n)* a type of poetry
that does not rhyme and usually
has ten syllables in each line.

blanket *(n)*
1 a thick cover for a bed.
2 a thick covering of something,
such as snow or flowers.

blare blaring blared *(v)* to make
a very loud and unpleasant noise.
His radio has been blaring out all day.

blaspheme blaspheming
blasphemed *(v)* to say offensive
things about God or a religion.
blasphemy *(n)*, blasphemous *(adj)*.

blast blasting blasted
1 *(n)* a loud noise or explosion.
2 *(n)* a sudden rush of air.
3 *(v)* to fire a gun.
4 *(v)* When a rocket or a spaceship
blasts off, it leaves the ground.

blatant *(adj)* obvious and
shameless. *Hayden grinned as he
told a blatant lie.* **blatantly** *(adv)*.

blaze blazing blazed
1 *(v)* to burn fiercely.
2 *(n)* a large fire.

blazer *(n)* a smart jacket, often
worn as part of a school uniform.

bleach
bleaches bleaching bleached
1 *(n)* a chemical substance used to
kill germs or to make things white.
2 *(v)* to make something white or very
light. *The sun had bleached Ian's hair.*

bleak bleaker bleakest *(adj)*
1 A **bleak** place is cold,
empty, and depressing.
2 depressing and without hope.
The future looks really bleak.

bleat *(n)* the cry made by
a sheep or goat. **bleat** *(v)*.

bleed bleeding bled *(v)*
to lose blood. **bleeding** *(adj)*.

bleep bleeping bleeped *(v)* to
make a short, high sound. **bleep** *(n)*.

blend blending blended *(v)*
to mix two or more things
together. **blend** *(n)*.

blender *(n)* an electrical machine
that chops and mixes food.

bless blesses blessing blessed *(v)*
1 to ask God to look after someone
or something. **blessing** *(n)*.
2 You say **bless you** when
a person sneezes or as a
way of thanking someone.

blind
1 *(adj)* Someone who is
blind cannot see. **blindness** *(n)*.
2 *(adj)* A **blind** bend or corner is so
sharp that drivers cannot see round it.
3 *(n)* a covering for a window
that can be pulled over it.
4 **blind spot** *(n)* the area
slightly behind a driver that
they cannot see in the rear-view
mirror or in the wing mirror.

blink blinking blinked *(v)*
to move your eyelids down and
then up very quickly. *You blink all the
time without realizing it.* **blink** *(n)*.

blinkers *(plural n)*
leather flaps worn by racehorses
on each side of their head so that
they can only see straight ahead.

bliss *(n)* great happiness. *Our
holiday to the Caribbean was
bliss.* **blissful** *(adj)*, **blissfully** *(adv)*.

blister *(n)* a sore bubble of
skin, filled with liquid, that is
caused by something burning
your skin or rubbing against it.

Some words that begin with a "bi" sound are spelt "by".

blitz *(n)*
1 a sudden attack in which bombs are dropped from the air.
2 If you **have a blitz** on something, you tackle it energetically.

blizzard *(n)* a heavy snowstorm.

bloated *(adj)* fat and swollen, often as a result of eating too much.

block blocking blocked
1 *(n)* a large lump of something hard. *A block of wood.*
2 *(v)* to stop something from getting past or from happening. **block** *(n)*.
3 *(n)* A **block** of flats is a tall building where a lot of people live.
4 **block capitals** *(n)* capital letters.

blond *or* **blonde**
blonder blondest *(adj)*
Blond men and boys or **blonde** women and girls have pale yellow hair.

blood
1 *(n)* the red liquid that is pumped around your body by your heart.

Blood is made up of red cells, white cells, and platelets, all floating in plasma. **bloody** *(adj)*.

red blood cell

white blood cell

plasma

nucleus   platelet

human blood (magnified)

2 **blood donor** *(n)* someone who allows some blood to be taken out of their body to be stored and given to someone else.
3 **blood vessel** *(n)* one of the narrow tubes in your body through which your blood flows.

bloodshed *(n)* all the killing that happens in a battle or war.

bloodthirsty *(adj)* Someone who is **bloodthirsty** really enjoys violence and killing. **bloodthirstiness** *(n)*, **bloodthirstily** *(adv)*.

bloom blooming bloomed
1 *(n)* a flower on a plant.
2 *(v)* When a plant **blooms**, its flowers come out.
3 *(adj)* If someone is **blooming**, they look very healthy.

blossom blossoming blossomed
1 *(n)* the small flowers that appear on trees in the spring.
2 *(v)* to grow or improve. *Francesca has blossomed into a first-rate dancer.*

blot blotting blotted
1 *(n)* a stain caused by spilled ink or paint.
2 *(v)* to dry ink on a page using a piece of soft paper.

blotch blotches *(n)*
an area of reddened skin or a stain. **blotchy** *(adj)*.

blouse *(n)* a piece of clothing, like a loose shirt, worn by women and girls.

blow blowing blew blown
1 *(v)* to make air come out of your mouth.
2 *(v)* to move in the wind. *The leaves were blowing around.*
3 *(n)* a punch or hit on the body.
4 *(n)* a disappointment.
5 **blow up** *(v)* to destroy something with an explosion.

blubber blubbering blubbered
1 *(n)* the fat under the skin of a whale or seal.
2 *(v)* to cry noisily.

blue bluer bluest
1 *(n)* the colour of the sky on a sunny day. **blue** *(adj)*.
2 *(adj)* sad and depressed.
3 **out of the blue** suddenly.

blueprint *(n)* a detailed plan for a project or an idea.

blues *(singular n)*
a type of slow, sad, jazz music, first sung by black Americans.

bluff bluffing bluffed
1 *(v)* to pretend to be in a stronger position than you really are or, to know more about something than you really do. *Nat says he's going to win, but I think he's bluffing.* **bluff** *(n)*.
2 If you **call someone's bluff**, you challenge them to do what they say they can do, because you think that they are bluffing.

blunder blundering blundered
1 *(n)* a stupid mistake. **blunder** *(v)*.
2 *(v)* to move in an awkward and clumsy way, usually because you cannot see where you are going.

blunderbuss blunderbusses *(n)*
an old-fashioned gun with a wide-mouthed barrel that fires several lead balls at once. *The picture below shows the parts of a blunderbuss. When the trigger is released, the flint strikes against the frizzen, making the gunpowder explode and shoot the lead balls out of the barrel.*

blunt blunter bluntest *(adj)*
1 not sharp.
2 direct and straightforward in what you say. **bluntly** *(adv)*.

blur blurring blurred
1 *(v)* to make something smeared and unclear.
2 *(n)* a shape that is unclear because it has no outline or is moving too fast. **blurred** *(adj)*.

blurb *(n)* writing on a product, usually a book, which aims to get people interested in it.

blurt blurting blurted *(v)*
If you **blurt** something out, you say it suddenly, without thinking.

blush blushes blushing blushed *(v)*
When you **blush**, your face turns red because you are embarrassed or ashamed. **blush** *(n)*.

bluster blustering blustered *(v)*
1 to blow in gusts. *The wind blustered round the chimney pots.* **blustery** *(adj)*.
2 to act or speak in an aggressive and over-confident way.

boar *(n)*
1 a male pig.
2 a type of wild pig.

wild boar

board
boarding boarded
1 *(n)* a flat piece of wood or stiff card. *A chess board.*
2 *(v)* to get on to a train, an aeroplane, or a ship.
3 *(n)* The **board** of a company is the group of people who manage it.

boarder *(n)* a student who lives at school during the term.

boarding school *(n)* a school which students live in during the term.

boast boasting boasted *(v)*
1 to talk proudly about what you can do or what you own, in order to impress people. **boast** *(n)*, **boastful** *(adj)*, **boastfully** *(adv)*.
2 If a place **boasts** something good, it possesses it. *Paris boasts many fine restaurants.*

18th-century blunderbuss

flint-lock (in "half-cock" safety position)

flint

frizzen

frizzen spring

brass barrel

wide muzzle

brass butt cap

wooden stock

side plate

priming pan (contains gunpowder)

ramrod (pushes gunpowder and lead balls into barrel)

trigger guard   trigger

boat

motorboat (cutaway)
chain locker
sleeping accommodation
bathroom
wraparound windscreen
electronic chart plotter
helm control panel
radio aerial
deck light
cabin door
satellite-linked navigation system
helm seat
television aerial
extending crane (lowers life-raft)
steering wheel
mast head light
light mast
life raft
trim tab (controls boat's angle)
navigation aerial
cockpit settee
bathing platform
pulpit rail
anchor winch locker
wardrobe
porthole
cockpit side window
radar arch
dining area
turbo-charged engine
propeller
rudder
reinforced fibreglass hull
galley (kitchen)
scuppers (drainage holes)
folding bathing ladder
engine exhaust outlet
fixing for gangplank

boat (n)
1 a vehicle used for travelling on water. *The boat shown here is a motor cruiser.*
2 If people are **in the same boat**, they are all in the same situation.

bob bobbing bobbed
1 (v) to keep moving up and down on water.
2 (n) a short hairstyle in which the hair is all one length.

bobsleigh (*bob-slay*) (n)
a sledge with mechanical steering and brakes, used for racing down a steep, ice-covered run. *A bobsleigh team consists of a driver, at the front, and a brakeman, at the back. Four-person bobsleighs also have two pushers to help build up speed.*

four-person bobsleigh
handle for push-start
driver
fibreglass hood
steel runner
pushers
brakeman
driver's handle

body bodies (n)
1 all the parts that a person or an animal is made of. *The human body.*
2 the main part of something, especially a car or an aircraft.
3 a dead person. *The detectives have found another body.*

bodyguard (n)
someone who protects an important person from attacks.

bodywork (n) the outer covering of a car or other motor vehicle.

bog (n) an area of wet, spongy land. **boggy** (adj).

bogus (adj) false. *Basil gave a bogus name to the police.*

boil boiling boiled
1 (v) to heat a liquid until it starts to bubble and give off vapour. **boiling** (adj).
2 (v) to cook something in boiling water.
3 (n) an infected lump under the skin.

boiler (n) a tank that heats water for a house or other building.

boiling point (n)
the temperature at which a liquid that has been heated turns to gas.

boisterous (adj) If you are boisterous, you behave in a rough and noisy way. **boisterousness** (n), **boisterously** (adv).

bold bolder boldest (adj)
1 Someone who is **bold** is very confident and shows no fear of danger. **boldness** (n), **boldly** (adv).
2 Bold colours stand out clearly.

bollard (n) a short post placed in a road to stop traffic from going in a particular direction.

bolster bolstering bolstered
1 (v) to support someone or something.
2 (n) (old-fashioned) a long pillow.

bolt bolting bolted
1 (n) a metal bar that slides into place and locks something. **bolt** (v).
2 (n) a strong metal pin, used with a metal nut to hold things together.
3 (v) to run away suddenly.

bomb bombing bombed
1 (n) a container filled with explosives, used in war or to blow up buildings, vehicles, etc.
2 (v) to attack a place with bombs.

bombard bombarding bombarded (v)
1 to attack a place with heavy gunfire. **bombardment** (n).
2 If you **bombard** someone with questions, you ask them lots of questions in a short time.

bombshell (n)
1 a bomb.
2 something shocking and surprising.

bond bonding bonded
1 (n) a close friendship or connection with someone. *A special bond developed between the boys.*
2 (v) When two things **bond**, they stick together. **bond** (n).
3 **bonds** (plural n) ropes, chains, etc. used to tie someone up.

bone (n) one of the hard, white parts that make up the skeleton of a person or an animal.

human thighbone or femur (cutaway)

head
soft, spongy bone
bone marrow
hard, compact bone
periosteum (tough outer layer)
shaft

boundary

bonfire (n) a large, outdoor fire, often used to burn garden rubbish.

bonnet (n)
1 the cover for a car's engine. *See* **car**.
2 a baby's or woman's hat, tied with strings under the chin.

bonsai *(bonz-eye)*
bonsai (n) a miniature tree or shrub, often grown in a pot for decoration.

bonsai
(needle juniper)

bonus bonuses (n)
1 an extra reward that you get for doing something well. **bonus** (adj).
2 a good thing that is more than you expected. *It's a bonus to have a cinema so close to our new house.*

booby trap (n) a hidden trap or trick which is set off when someone or something touches it.

book booking booked
1 (n) a set of pages that are bound together in a cover.
2 (v) to arrange for something to be kept for you to have or use later. *We've booked a holiday in Crete.*

hardback book
(cutaway)

endpaper — fore edge
back board — flyleaf
head band — head
paper signatures or sections — front board
spine lining — front board cover
spine —
joint — tail

book-keeper (n)
someone who keeps financial records for a business. **bookkeeping** (n).

booklet (n) a book with a paper cover and a small number of pages.

bookmaker (n) someone who takes money for bets and pays out money to people who win. **bookmaking** (n).

bookworm (n)
someone who loves reading books.

boom booming boomed
1 (n) a very loud, deep sound, like an explosion. **boom** (v).
2 (v) to speak in a loud, deep voice. *"Sit down!" the guard boomed at us.*
3 (n) a rapid increase in something. *A spending boom.*
4 (n) a long pole, used to control the angle of a sail. *See* **dinghy**, **sail**.

boomerang (n)
a curved stick that is thrown through the air and returns to the thrower if it misses its target. *Boomerangs were used by Aboriginal hunters in Australia.*

Aboriginal boomerang

boon (n) (old-fashioned)
something that makes life easier. *Our dishwasher is a real boon.*

boost boosting boosted
1 (v) to increase the power or amount of something. **boost** (n).
2 (n) If something gives you a **boost**, it cheers you up.

booster (n)
1 a rocket that gives extra power to a spacecraft.
2 an injection of a vaccine, given to increase the effect of an earlier injection.

boot booting booted
1 (n) a heavy shoe that covers your ankle and sometimes part of your leg.
2 (n) the place, usually at the back of a car, where luggage can be carried. *See* **car**.
3 (v) When you **boot up** a computer, you turn it on.
4 (v) (informal) to kick something hard.

booty (singular n)
valuable objects that are taken away by pirates or an army after a battle.

booze (n) (informal)
alcoholic drink.
boozer (n), **boozy** (adj).

border bordering bordered
1 (n) the dividing line between one country or region and another.
2 (v) If one country **borders** another, their boundaries meet.
3 (n) a decorative strip around the edge of something.
4 (n) a long flowerbed.

bore boring bored
1 (v) If something or someone **bores** you, you find them very dull and uninteresting. **boredom** (n), **bore** (n), **boring** (adj), **bored** (adj).
2 (v) to make a hole in something with a drill. *This machine can bore into solid rock.*
3 (n) the hole inside a gun barrel.

borough (buh-ruh) (n)
1 a town, or an area of a town, that has its own local government.
2 an area in Britain that has its own Member of Parliament.

borrow borrowing borrowed (v)
to use someone else's belongings for a short time, with their permission.

bosom (n)
1 a woman's breasts.
2 (old-fashioned) a person's chest.

boss bosses bossing bossed
1 (n) someone in charge of a company or someone who people work for.
2 (v) If you **boss** someone about, you keep telling them what to do.

bossy bossier bossiest (adj) A bossy person likes telling other people what to do. **bossiness** (n).

botany (n)
the study of plants. *The picture shows a watercolour painting of a Christmas rose, from an 18th-century book on botany.*
botanist (n), **botanical** (adj).

bother bothering bothered (v)

botanical drawing

1 If something **bothers** you, it makes you feel uncomfortable.
2 to interrupt someone who is busy. *Luke keeps bothering me.*
3 to make an effort to do something. *At least Caroline bothered to come to the meeting.*

bottle bottling bottled
1 (n) a glass or plastic container in which liquids are stored.
2 (v) to put things into bottles.
3 (v) If you **bottle up** your feelings, you keep them to yourself.
4 (n) (slang) courage or spirit.

bottleneck (n) a narrow part of a road that causes traffic jams.

bottom (n)
1 the lowest part of something. *The bottom of the sea.* **bottom** (adj).
2 the part of your body you sit on.
3 the most basic part of something. *He'll get to the bottom of this.*

bough (rhymes with now) (n)
a thick branch on a tree.

boulder (n) a large rock.

bounce bouncing bounced
1 (v) to spring back after hitting something. **bounce** (n), **bouncy** (adj).
2 (n) If someone has lots of **bounce**, they are very cheerful. **bouncy** (adj).

bound bounding bounded
1 (v) to move forward quickly with leaps and jumps. **bound** (n).
2 (adj) If something is **bound** to happen, it will definitely take place.
3 If a place is **out of bounds**, you are not allowed to go there.

boundary boundaries (n) the line that separates one area from another.

bouquet (boh-**kay** or boo-**kay**) (n)
a bunch of flowers given
to someone as a present.

bow bowing bowed
1 (rhymes with cow) (v) to bend
low as a sign of respect or to
accept applause. **bow** (n).
2 (rhymes with low) (n)
a knot with loops.
3 **bow** or **bows** (rhymes with cow) (n)
the front of a ship.
4 (rhymes with low) (n) a long flat
piece of wood with strings stretched
along it, used for playing stringed
instruments. See **strings**.
5 (rhymes with low)
(n) a curved piece
of wood with a
stretched string
attached to it,
used for shooting
arrows. *This archer
from the Bayeux
tapestry draws
his bow, ready to
shoot, and holds
some spare arrows
in his hand.*

medieval
archer

bowels (plural n) the part of
your body that carries solids
away from your stomach.

bowl bowling bowled
1 (n) a deep dish. *This porcelain
dragon bowl was made in China
in the 16th century.*
2 (v) When you
bowl in a
game like
cricket or
rounders, you
throw a ball
for someone to hit
with a bat. **bowl** (n), **bowler** (n).

Chinese
dragon bowl

bowls (singlular n) a game played
with heavy, wooden balls called bowls.

box boxes boxing boxed
1 (n) a container, especially
one with four flat sides.
2 (v) to fight with your fists as
a sport. **boxer** (n), **boxing** (n).
3 **box in** (v) If you **box someone
in**, you surround them so that
they cannot escape.

box office (n) the place in a theatre
or cinema where you buy tickets.

boy (n) a male child. **boyish** (adj).

boycott boycotting boycotted (v)
to refuse to take part in something
or buy something as a way of
making a protest. **boycott** (n).

boyfriend (n)
the man or boy with whom someone
is having a romantic relationship.

bra (n)
a piece of underwear that
supports a woman's breasts.
Bra is short for brassière.

brace bracing braced
1 (n) an object that supports another
object or holds it in place. **brace** (v).
2 (n) a wire device worn inside your
mouth to straighten your teeth.
3 **braces** (plural n) two elastic
straps worn over the shoulders
to hold up a pair of trousers.
4 (v) If you **brace yourself**, you
prepare yourself for a shock or for
the force of something hitting you.

bracelet (n)
a band worn around the
wrist as a piece of jewellery.

bracket (n)
1 a support, made of metal or wood,
used to hold up a shelf or cupboard.
2 one of a pair of round marks
( ) used to separate an extra
phrase or explanation. **bracket** (v).
3 a grouping. *This game is
intended for your age bracket
and is in my price bracket.*

brag bragging bragged (v)
to talk in a boastful way about
how good you are at something.

braid (n) a piece of hair that
has been twisted together with
decorative ribbon or string.

Braille (brayl) (n)
a system of printing for blind people.
Braille uses raised dots that are read
by feeling with the fingertips. *This
picture shows what the word "Braille"
looks like when it is printed in Braille.*

B   R   A   I   L   L   E

brain (n)
1 the organ inside your head that
controls your body and allows
you to think and have feelings.
2 your mind or intelligence.

brainstorm
brainstorming brainstormed
1 (v) If people **brainstorm**, they
get together to share ideas on
a topic or to solve a problem.
2 (n) a sudden idea.

brainwash brainwashes
brainwashing brainwashed (v)
to make someone accept and
believe something by saying it
to them over and over again.
brainwashing (n).

brainwave (n) a sudden good idea.

brainy brainier brainiest (adj)
(informal) clever or intelligent.

brake braking braked
1 (n) You use **brakes** to slow down
or stop a vehicle. The brakes press
against a wheel and stop it turning.
2 (v) to slow down or
stop by using brakes.

bramble (n) a thorny bush
that blackberries grow on.

bran (n) the outer covering of
wheat or other grains that is sifted
out when flour is made. Bran is
used in baked goods and cereals.

branch
branches branching branched
1 (n) a part of a tree that grows
out of its trunk like an arm.
2 (v) When a road, river, etc.
branches, it splits into two parts that
go in different directions. **branch** (n).
3 (n) A **branch** of a company or
organization is one of its shops,
offices, etc. in a particular area.

brand branding branded
1 (n) a particular make of
product. *A brand of toothpaste.*
2 (v) If someone **brands** an
animal, they burn a mark on
to its skin to show that the
animal belongs to them. **brand** (n).
3 (v) to call by a shameful name.
The soldier was branded a coward.

brandy brandies (n) a strong
alcoholic drink made from wine.

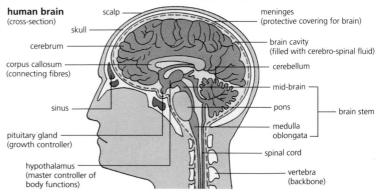

human brain
(cross-section)

scalp

skull

cerebrum

corpus callosum
(connecting fibres)

sinus

pituitary gland
(growth controller)

hypothalamus
(master controller of
body functions)

meninges
(protective covering for brain)

brain cavity
(filled with cerebro-spinal fluid)

cerebellum

mid-brain

pons

medulla
oblongata

spinal cord

vertebra
(backbone)

brain stem

breeze

brass

1 *(n)* a yellow metal made from copper and zinc.
2 *(adj)* The **brass** section in an orchestra contains musical instruments that are made of brass and usually have a funnel-shaped mouthpiece. *The picture shows the main instruments in an orchestra's brass section.*

cornet

tuba

first valve
valve casing
second valve
third valve
coiled tubing
French horn
finger hook
mouthpiece
stay
first valve slide
second valve slide
finger ring
trombone
weight (balances slide)
third valve slide
water key
bell
tuning slide
trumpet
slide

brassière *see* bra.

brass rubbing *(n)*
a copy of a picture carved on a brass plate. Brass rubbings are made by rubbing with a wax crayon on a piece of paper placed over the plate. *This brass rubbing is taken from the tomb of a 15th-century knight.*

bravado *(n)* If you
are full of **bravado**, you pretend to be braver and more confident than you really are.

brave
braving braved; braver bravest
1 *(adj)* If you are **brave**, you show courage and are willing to do difficult things. **bravery** *(n)*, **bravely** *(adv)*.
2 *(v)* If you **brave** something difficult, you face it deliberately.

brass rubbing

brawl *(n)* a rough fight. **brawl** *(v)*.

bray braying brayed *(v)*
1 When a donkey **brays**, it makes a loud, harsh noise in its throat. **bray** *(n)*.
2 When a person **brays**, they make a harsh noise like a donkey.

brazen *(adj)*
1 shameless. **brazenly** *(adv)*.
2 made of brass.

brazier *(bray-zee-er) (n)*
a container for burning coals, used to keep people warm out of doors.

bread *(n)*
a baked food made from flour, water, and often yeast.

breadline
If people are **on the breadline**, they have only just enough money to live.

breadth *(n)*
1 the distance from one side of something to the other.
2 a wide range. *Julian has a breadth of experience in caring for animals.*

breadwinner *(n)* someone
who earns money for a family.

break breaking broke broken
1 *(v)* to damage something so that it is in pieces or it no longer works. **breakage** *(n)*, **breakable** *(adj)*.
2 *(n)* a rest from working or studying.
3 *(v)* If someone **breaks** the rules or the law, they do something that is not allowed.
4 **break in** *(v)* to get into a building by force.
5 **break out** *(v)* to begin suddenly. *Fighting broke out on the streets.*

break dance *(n)* a very energetic
and acrobatic form of dance.

breakdown *(n)*
1 If you have a **breakdown** while you are travelling, your vehicle stops moving because its engine has stopped working. **break down** *(v)*.
2 If someone has a **breakdown**, they are so worried or depressed that they become ill. **break down** *(v)*.

breaker *(n)* a big sea wave.

breakfast *(n)*
the first meal of the day.

breakthrough *(n)* an important
step towards achieving something.

breakwater *(n)*
1 a wall built in the sea to protect a harbour from the force of the waves.
2 a barrier built on a beach to reduce the force of the waves.

breast *(n)*
1 A woman's **breasts** are the two round fleshy parts on her chest that can produce milk to feed a baby.
2 *(old-fashioned)* a person's chest.

breaststroke *(n)*
a style of swimming on your front in which you move your arms forwards and out from your chest and kick your legs like a frog.

breath *(n)*
1 the air that you take into your lungs and breathe out again.
2 If you are **out of breath**, you have difficulty breathing.
3 When you say something **under your breath**, you say it very quietly.

breathalyze *or* breathalyse
breathalyzing breathalyzed *(v)*
When drivers are **breathalyzed**, they have to blow into a special machine, called a breathalyzer, which shows whether they have drunk too much alcohol to drive safely.

breathe breathing breathed *(v)*
to take air in and out of your lungs.

breather *(n) (informal)* a short rest.

breathtaking *(adj)*
very beautiful or impressive. *The view from the cliff was breathtaking.* **breathtakingly** *(adv)*.

breed breeding bred
1 *(v)* to keep animals or plants so that you can produce more of them and control their quality. **breeder** *(n)*.
2 *(v)* When animals **breed**, they mate and produce babies.
3 *(n)* a particular type of animal. *Labrador retrievers are the most popular breed of dog in the UK.*

breeze *(n)*
a gentle wind. **breezy** *(adj)*.

a b c d e f g h i j k l m n o p q r s t u v w x y z

brew brewing brewed *(v)*
1 to make beer.
2 to make tea or coffee.
3 If something is **brewing**, it is about to start. *There's trouble brewing at home.*

brewery breweries *(n)*
a place where beer is made.

bribe bribing bribed
1 *(n)* money or a gift that you offer to someone to persuade them to do something for you, especially something wrong.
2 *(v)* to offer someone a bribe. **bribery** *(n)*.

bric-a-brac *(n)*
various objects, such as ornaments, that are not worth very much.

brick *(n)* a block of hard, baked clay, used for building.

bride *(n)* a woman who is about to be married or has just been married.

bridegroom *(n)*
a man who is about to be married or has just been married.

bridesmaid *(n)*
a girl or a woman who helps a bride on her wedding day.

bridge bridging bridged
1 *(n)* a structure built over a river, railway, etc. so that people or vehicles can get to the other side.
2 *(n)* a card game for four players.
3 *(n)* an upright piece of wood on a guitar, violin, etc. over which the strings are stretched. *See* **guitar**, **strings**.
4 *(v)* If something **bridges a gap**, it provides a connection between two different things.

bridges

suspension bridge

cantilever bridge

beam bridge

arch bridge

bridle *(n)* the straps that fit around a horse's head and mouth, and that are used to control it. *See* **tack**.

bridle path *(n)* a track or path for horse riders or walkers.

brief
briefing briefed; briefer briefest
1 *(adj)* lasting only a short time. *A brief visit.* **briefly** *(adv)*.
2 *(adj)* using only a few words. *Be as brief as you can.* **briefly** *(adv)*.
3 *(v)* to give someone information so they can carry out a task. **brief** *(n)*.
4 briefs *(plural n)* underpants.

briefcase *(n)* a bag with a handle, used for carrying papers.

brigade *(n)*
1 a unit of an army.
2 an organized group of workers. *The fire brigade.*

bright brighter brightest *(adj)*
1 A **bright** light or colour is strong and can be seen clearly. **brightness** *(n)*, **brightly** *(adv)*.
2 cheerful. **brightly** *(adv)*.
3 *(informal)* clever.

brilliant *(adj)*
1 shining very brightly. *A brilliant diamond.* **brilliance** *(n)*.
2 very clever. **brilliance** *(n)*, **brilliantly** *(adv)*.
3 very good. *It was a brilliant party.* **brilliantly** *(adv)*.

brim *(n)* the wide part that sticks out around the bottom of a hat.

brine *(n)* salty water.

bring bringing brought *(v)*
1 to take something or someone with you. *Bring a friend.*
2 to make something happen or appear. *Vandals bring trouble.*
3 If a company **brings out** a product, it starts selling it.
4 **bring up** to look after and guide a child as it grows up.
5 **bring in** If you **bring something in**, you introduce it. *The government is bringing in new employment laws.*

brink *(n)*
1 the edge of something, such as a cliff or a river bank.
2 If you are **on the brink** of something, you are just about to do it. *Jake is on the brink of leaving.*

brisk brisker briskest *(adj)*
1 quick and energetic. *A brisk walk.* **briskly** *(adv)*.
2 fresh and invigorating. *Brisk weather.*

bristle
1 *(n)* one of the long, wiry hairs used to make brushes. **bristly** *(adj)*.

2 bristles *(plural n)* the short, stiff hairs that start to grow on a man's chin if he does not shave. **bristly** *(adj)*.
3 *(v)* to show anger.

brittle *(adj)* easily snapped or broken. *Dried flowers can be very brittle.*

broach broaches broaching broached *(v)* When you **broach** a subject with someone, you start to talk or ask about it.

broad broader broadest *(adj)*
1 wide. **broaden** *(v)*.
2 covering the most important points, but not the details. *Give me a broad outline of the story.* **broadly** *(adv)*.

broadcast broadcasting broadcast *or* broadcasted
1 *(v)* to send out a programme on television, radio, the internet, etc. **broadcaster** *(n)*, **broadcasting** *(n)*.
2 *(n)* a television or radio programme.

broccoli *(n)*
a green vegetable with rounded heads on stalks. *See* **vegetable**.

brochure (bro-shur) *(n)*
a booklet, usually with pictures, that gives information about a product or service. *A holiday brochure.*

brogue (brohg) *(n)*
1 a strong, usually Irish, accent.
2 a strong walking shoe.

broke *(adj)* *(informal)* If you are **broke**, you have no money.

broken *(adj)*
1 cracked, smashed or in pieces. *A broken bone.*
2 not working. *My phone is broken.*

bronchitis (bron-ky-tiss) *(n)*
an illness of the throat and lungs that makes you cough a lot.

bronze *(n)*
1 a hard, reddish-brown metal that is a mixture of copper and tin.
2 a reddish-brown colour.

brooch (rhymes with coach) brooches *(n)*
a piece of jewellery that can be pinned to your clothes. *The Tara brooch, shown here, was made in 10th-century Ireland.*

Tara brooch

brood
brooding brooded
1 *(n)* a family of young birds.
2 *(v)* to keep worrying or thinking about something. *Don't brood about your problems.*

brook *(n)* a small stream.

broom *(n)*
a large brush with a long handle, used for sweeping floors.

brother *(n)*
a boy or man with the same parents as you. **brotherly** *(adj)*.

brow *(n)*
1 forehead. *A wrinkled brow.*
2 the top of a hill.

brown *(n)* the colour of wood, leather, and coffee. **brown** *(adj)*.

brownie *(n)* a small and chewy chocolate cake, often with nuts in it.

browse browsing browsed *(v)*
to look casually at something, often on a computer or a phone. *Max browsed the internet.*

browser *(n)*
a program on a computer or a phone that allows you to use the internet.

bruise *(brewz)* *(n)*
a dark, painful mark that you get on your skin when you fall or are hit by something. **bruise** *(v)*.

brush brushes brushing brushed
1 *(n)* an object with bristles and a handle, used for sweeping, painting, or smoothing hair. *See* **artist**, **stencil**.
2 *(v)* to use a brush. *Brush your hair before you go out.*
3 *(v)* to touch something lightly. *Her coat brushed my hand.*

brutal *(adj)*
cruel and violent. *A brutal act.* **brutally** *(adv)*.

brute
1 *(n)* a rough and violent person. **brutish** *(adj)*.
2 If you do something by **brute force**, you use a lot of strength instead of skill or intelligence.

bubble bubbling bubbled
1 *(n)* one of the tiny balls of gas in fizzy drinks, boiling water, etc.
2 *(v)* to make bubbles. *The water bubbled in the saucepan.*

bubbly *(adj)*
1 If a liquid is **bubbly**, it is full of balls of gas.
2 If a person is **bubbly**, they are very lively and talkative.

buccaneer *(n)*
(old-fashioned)
a pirate.

buck
bucking
bucked
1 *(n)*
a male deer, kangaroo, etc.

2 *(v)* If a horse **bucks**, it jumps in the air with all four feet off the ground.
3 *(n)* *(slang)* a dollar.
4 If you **pass the buck**, you pass the responsibility for something on to someone else.

bucket *(n)*
a plastic or metal container with a handle, used for carrying liquids.

buckle buckling buckled
1 *(n)* a metal fastening on shoes, belts, or straps. *The elaborate buckle shown here was made by Anglo-Saxon craftsmen in the 7th century AD.* **buckle** *(v)*.
2 *(v)* to crumple. *Hugh's legs buckled under him and he fell.*

bud *(n)* a small shoot on a plant that grows into a leaf or flower. *See* **plant**.

buckle

Buddha *(n)*
1 the name given to Siddhartha Gautama, the teacher who founded the religion of Buddhism.
2 a statue or picture of Buddha.

Buddha

Buddhism *(n)*
a religion based on the teachings of Buddha and practised mainly in eastern and central Asia. Buddhists believe that you should not become too attached to material things and that you live many lives in different bodies.
Buddhist *(n)*, Buddhist *(adj)*.

budge budging budged *(v)*
If you cannot **budge** something, you are not able to move it.

budgerigar *(n)* a brightly-coloured Australian bird, often kept as a pet. *Budgerigars are also called budgies.*

budget budgeting budgeted
1 *(n)* a plan for how money will be earned and spent. **budgetary** *(adj)*.
2 *(v)* If you **budget** for something, you plan how to spend your money so that you can afford it.

buff *(n)*
1 a pale, yellow-brown colour. **buff** *(adj)*.
2 *(informal)* someone who knows a lot about a particular subject. *Billy is a great film buff.*

buffalo buffaloes *(n)*
a type of ox with heavy horns.

buffer *(n)* something that softens a blow, especially the springs fixed to the front and back of a train carriage. *See* **steam locomotive**.

buffet buffeting buffeted
1 *(buff-et)* *(v)* to strike and shake something or someone. *The wind buffeted the trees.*
2 *(boo-fay)* *(n)* a meal in which many cold dishes are laid on a table and people serve themselves.
3 **buffet car** *(boo-fay)* *(n)* a railway carriage containing a snack bar.

bug bugging bugged
1 *(n)* an insect.
2 *(n)* *(informal)* a minor illness caused by germs. *A stomach bug.*
3 *(n)* *(informal)* an error in a computer program or system that prevents it from working properly.
4 *(adj)* *(informal)* If a room is **bugged**, someone has hidden microphones there so that they can listen to what people are saying. **bug** *(n)*.
5 *(v)* *(informal)* If someone or something **bugs** you, they annoy you.

buggy buggies *(n)*
1 a chair on wheels, in which you push young children.
2 *(old-fashioned)* a light, two-wheeled carriage, pulled by a horse. *This buggy dates from the 1800s and has seats for three passengers.*

hooded
buggy

folding hood

hood window

rest for reins

suspended body

lamp

open seat

shafts for horse

step

step

rubber tyre

bugle *(n)* a musical instrument like a small trumpet, often used in the army to send signals to the troops. *The picture shows a 19th-century British army bugle.*

bugle

build building built
1 *(v)* to make something by putting different parts together.
2 *(n)* the size and shape of a person's body. *Nick has quite a large build.*
3 **build up** *(v)* to increase or make stronger. *The traffic has built up. You must build yourself up for the race.*

buccaneer

a b c d e f g h i j k l m n o p q r s t u v w x y z

building

building (n)
a structure with walls
and a roof. *This cutaway
picture of a house shows
the different parts
of a building.*

house (cutaway)

Labels: ridge board · roofing felt · ridge tile · chimney stack · glass fibre insulation · rafter · flashing · roof tie · skylight · timber studding · roof tile · plaster-skim · batten · plasterboard · gutter · ceiling joist · fascia board · weatherboard · brick · vertical batten · foam insulation · cavity wall · felt · building block · floor joist · floorboards · downpipe · hipped roof · partition wall · window pane · porch · window frame · gully · window sill · letter box · transom · plaster · mullion · cement screed · doorstep · bay window · plastic foam insulation · paving slab · damp-proof membrane · top-hung window · concrete floor slab · casement window · lintel · hardcore base · foundations · soil · concrete footing

---

building society
building societies (n)
an organization with which
you can save money and
which lends money to
people to buy houses.

bulb (n)
1 the onion-shaped
root of some plants.
2 the glass part of an electric
light or torch that lights
up when you switch it on.

bulge **bulging** **bulged** (v)
to swell out like a lump.
*Hannah's bag bulged
with presents.* **bulge** (n).

bulk
1 (n) The **bulk** of something
is the main part of it.
2 When you buy **in bulk**, you
buy in large quantities.

bulky **bulkier** **bulkiest** (adj)
1 large and difficult to handle.
2 very filling. *Bulky food.*

bull (n)
1 the male of the cattle family.
2 a male elephant, seal, or whale.

bulldozer (n) a powerful tractor
with a wide blade at the front,
used for moving earth and rocks.

bullet (n) a small, pointed metal
object fired from a gun.

bulletin (n)
a short news report
on television
or radio.

bulldozer

Labels: exhaust pipe · air-cleaning filter · cab · windscreen wiper · blade lift cylinder · ripper · diesel engine · radiator grill · steel blade · blade tilt cylinder · cutting edge · push frame · metal track · sprocket wheel · track roller · ripper tooth

bulletproof (adj) Something that is
bulletproof is made to protect people
from bullets. *Bulletproof glass.*

bullfight (n) a public entertainment
in which people fight against bulls.

bullion (n) bars of gold or silver.

bullock (n) a castrated bull.

bully bullies bullying bullied *(v)* to frighten or hurt people who are weaker than you. **bully** *(n)*.

bump bumping bumped
1 *(v)* to knock into something by accident. **bump** *(n)*.
2 *(n)* the sound of one thing hitting something else.
3 *(n)* a round lump or swelling.
4 *(v)* *(informal)* If you **bump into** someone, you meet them by chance.
5 *(slang)* If someone has been **bumped off**, they have been killed.
6 **speed bump** *(n)* a ridge across a road designed to reduce the speed of vehicles.

bumptious *(adj)* loud and conceited.

bumpy bumpier bumpiest *(adj)* very uneven. *A bumpy road.*

bun *(n)*
1 a small, round cake or bread roll.
2 hair fastened in a round shape at the back of the head.

bunch bunches
1 *(n)* a group of something. **bunch** *(v)*.
2 **bunches** *(plural n)* a hairstyle in which hair is tied into two sections.

bundle bundling bundled *(v)*
1 to tie or wrap things together loosely. **bundle** *(n)*.
2 to handle someone quickly and carelessly.

bung bunging bunged
1 *(n)* a piece of cork, rubber, or wood used to close up the opening in a bottle or other container.
2 *(v)* *(slang)* to throw something roughly and carelessly.

bungalow *(n)*
a house with only one storey.

bungee jumping *(n)* an extreme sport in which someone jumps from a high place and is stopped from hitting the ground by a long piece of elastic attached to their legs.

bungle bungling bungled *(v)* to do something badly or clumsily.

bunk
1 *(n)* a narrow bed.
2 **bunk beds** *(plural n)* two beds stacked one above the other.
3 **bunk off** *(v)* *(slang)* to miss something, such as a lesson, on purpose.

bunker *(n)*
1 a place for storing coal.
2 a large, sand-filled hollow on a golf course.
3 an underground shelter from bomb attacks and gunfire.

bunting *(n)* small flags joined by a string and used for decoration.

buoy *(boy)* *(n)*
a floating marker in the sea or in a river.

buoyant *(adj)*
1 able to keep afloat. **buoyancy** *(n)*.
2 cheerful. **buoyantly** *(adv)*.

burden burdening burdened
1 *(n)* a heavy load that someone has to carry.
2 *(v)* to weigh someone down with heavy things.
3 *(n)* a serious task or responsibility.

— top mark
— lantern
— radar reflector
— water line
— float
— shackle for mooring line
— tail
buoy

bureau *(byoor-oh)* bureaus or bureaux *(n)*
1 a writing desk with drawers.
2 an office that provides information or some other service.

burger *(n)*
a round, flat piece of cooked meat, usually served in a bread roll.

burglar *(n)* someone who breaks into a house and steals things. **burglary** *(n)*, **burgle** *(v)*.

burn burning burnt or burned
1 *(v)* to hurt or damage someone or something with heat or fire.
2 *(n)* a sore area on the skin or a mark on something, caused by heat.

burp burping burped *(v)* to make a noise because gases have been forced up from your stomach, usually after eating or drinking. **burp** *(n)*.

burrow burrowing burrowed
1 *(n)* a tunnel or hole in the ground where a rabbit or other animal lives.
2 *(v)* to move along under the ground by digging.

bursar *(n)* the person in a college or school whose job is to look after the money and the buildings.

burst bursting burst
1 *(v)* to split or break apart suddenly. *The balloon burst.*
2 *(n)* a short, concentrated outbreak of something, such as speed, gunfire, or applause.
3 *(v)* to start doing something suddenly. *Riley burst into tears.*

bury buries burying buried *(v)*
1 to put a dead body into a grave. **burial** *(n)*.
2 to hide something in the ground or under a pile of things.

bus buses *(n)* a large vehicle, used for carrying passengers.

bush bushes *(n)*
1 a large plant with many branches.
2 **the bush** *(n)* the wild areas of Australia and Africa.

bushy bushier bushiest *(adj)* growing thickly. *Bushy eyebrows.*

business businesses *(n)*
1 the type of work that someone does. *Jerry's in the music business.*
2 the buying and selling of goods and services. *Our company does a lot of business with Japan.*
3 a company or shop that makes or sells things, or provides a service.
4 If something is **none of your business**, it is nothing to do with you.

businesslike *(adj)* efficient and practical.

busker *(n)*
someone who sings or plays music in the street, in order to earn money. **busking** *(n)*.

bust
busting busted or bust
1 *(n)* a statue of a person's head and shoulders. *The marble bust on the right is of the Ancient Greek scientist, Galen.*
2 *(n)* a woman's breasts.
3 *(v)* *(informal)* to break something. **bust** *(adj)*.

bustle
bustling bustled *(v)* to rush around being busy. **bustle** *(n)*.

marble bust

busy busier busiest *(adj)*
1 If you are **busy**, you have a lot of things to do. **busily** *(adv)*.
2 A **busy** place has a lot of people in it and is full of activity.

butcher *(n)* someone who sells meat.

butler *(n)*
the chief servant in a house, who is usually in charge of serving food.

butt butting butted
1 *(n)* a large barrel for water.
2 *(v)* to hit with the head or horns.
3 *(n)* the handle of a gun.

butter *(n)* a yellow fat made from cream, used in cooking and for spreading on bread. *This picture shows a 19th-century dairymaid using a plunger churn to turn cream into butter.*

buttercup *(n)*
a small, yellow wild flower. See **plant**.

butter-making

butterfly

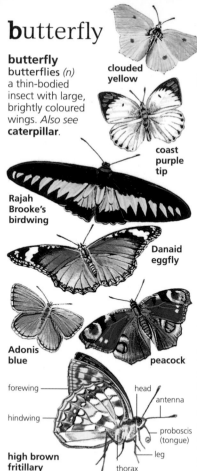

butterfly
butterflies *(n)*
a thin-bodied
insect with large,
brightly coloured
wings. *Also see*
caterpillar.

clouded
yellow

coast
purple
tip

Rajah
Brooke's
birdwing

Danaid
eggfly

Adonis
blue

peacock

forewing
head
antenna
hindwing
proboscis
(tongue)
leg
**high brown
fritillary**
thorax

buttocks *(plural n)*
the two fleshy parts of your bottom.

button *(n)*
1 a round piece of plastic, metal,
etc. that is sewn on to clothing
and used as a fastener. **button** *(v)*.
2 a small knob on a machine that
you press to switch it on or off.

buy buying bought *(v)* to get
something by paying money for it.

buzz buzzes buzzing
buzzed *(v)* to make a noise
like a bee or a wasp. **buzz** *(n)*.

bypass
bypasses bypassing bypassed
1 *(n)* a main road that goes around
a town or city rather than through it.
2 *(v)* to avoid something by
going around it. **bypass** *(adj)*.

byte *(n)* a unit of information that
is contained in a computer's memory.

Byzantine *(adj)*
1 to do with Byzantium, the
ancient eastern Roman empire.
2 in the style of art or architecture
used in the Byzantine empire.
*Byzantine buildings have large domes
and rounded arches, and are highly
decorated, often with mosaics.*

Cc

cabbage *(n)* a large, leafy
vegetable. *See* **vegetable**.

cabin *(n)*
1 the driver's section of a vehicle.
2 a room for passengers
on a ship or plane.
3 a small, wooden house.

cabinet *(n)*
1 a cupboard with
shelves or drawers.
2 a group of top members of a
government who advise the leader.

cable *(n)*
1 a thick wire or rope.
2 a tight bundle of wires
used for carrying electricity,
television signals, etc.
3 **cable car** *(n)* a vehicle pulled
along by a moving cable, used
for carrying people up mountains.
4 **cable television** *(n)* a television
service received by cable or fibre-optic
cable, with a wide choice of channels.

cactus cacti *or*
cactuses *(n)*
a spiky plant
that grows
in hot, dry
countries.

prickly pear cactus

barrel
cactus

cacti

cadet *(n)*
a young person
who is training
to become a
member of the
army, navy, air
force, or police force.

café *(kaf-ay) (n)* a small restaurant
that serves snacks and hot drinks.

cafeteria *(n)* a self-service restaurant.

caffeine *(kaf-een) (n)* a chemical
found in tea and coffee which makes
your brain and body more active.

caftan *or* **kaftan** *(n)* a long, loose
piece of clothing with long sleeves,
worn by people in Arab countries.

cage *(n)* a container in which
animals or birds are kept, made of
wires or bars. **cage** *(v)*, **caged** *(adj)*.

cajole cajoling cajoled *(v)*
to persuade someone to do
something by flattering them.

cake caking caked
1 *(n)* a sweet food made
by baking flour, butter,
eggs, and sugar together.
2 *(v)* If you are **caked** in
something, you are covered in it.

calamity calamities *(n)*
a terrible disaster. **calamitous** *(adj)*.

calcium *(n)* a soft, white element
found in teeth and bones.

calculate calculating calculated *(v)*
to work something out, especially
a sum. *Andy calculated that it
would take two hours to get
there by car.* calculation *(n)*.

calculating *(adj)* A calculating
person makes clever plans so that
things work out the way they want.

calculator *(n)* a small electronic
machine, used for working out sums.
*This picture shows the face, the circuit
board, and the case of a pocket
calculator.*

power switch
calculator
display screen
number key
function key
switch
contact

liquid-crystal
display panel
sliding switch
contacts
plastic
casing
printed circuit
board
copper
track
button
battery

calendar *(n)*
a chart containing all the days
in a year, usually showing one
month at a time.

calf calves *(n)*
1 a young cow, seal, elephant,
giraffe, or whale.
2 the fleshy part at the back
of your leg, below your knee.

call
calling called *(v)*
1 to shout something out,
especially someone's name.
2 to give someone
or something a name.
3 to phone someone. **call** *(n)*.
4 If you **call on** someone,
you visit them. **caller** *(n)*.
5 If you **call something off**, you
cancel it. *We had to call off the
party because of the bad weather.*

calligraphy *(n)* the art of beautiful
handwriting. *The picture shows a
dip pen and the word "calligraphy",
written in the Foundational style.*

calligraphy

Some words that begin with a "c" sound are spelt with a "k".

callous *(adj)*
hard-hearted and cruel.
callousness *(n)*, **callously** *(adv)*.

calm
calming calmed;
calmer calmest
1 *(adj)* peaceful and untroubled.
calmness *(n)*, **calmly** *(adv)*.
2 *(v)* to soothe an animal or a person.
3 *(n)* peacefulness.

calorie *(n)*
a measurement of the amount
of energy that a food gives you.

calypso *(n)*
a West Indian song with a strong
rhythm and often improvised lyrics.

camel *(n)* a mammal with one
or two humps on its back that is
used for carrying people and
goods across the desert. *The two
types of camel are shown here.*

camels

Bactrian
camel

Arabian camel
or dromedary

cameo *(kam-ee-oh) (n)*
1 a small medallion with
a carved portrait on it.
2 a small character part
in a play or film, usually
played by a famous actor.

camera *(n)*
a machine for taking
photographs or making
videos.

cameo

camouflage *(kam-er-flarj)*
camouflaging camouflaged
1 *(n)* colouring or covering
that makes animals, people,
and objects look like
their surroundings.
2 *(v)* to disguise something
so that it blends in with its
surroundings. *The picture
shows a Stonefish, a sea
creature that disguises
itself as a stone to hide
on the sea bed.*

Stonefish

camp camping camped
1 *(v)* to have a holiday
in a tent. **camping** *(n)*.
2 *(n)* a group of tents together.

campaign *(n)*
a series of actions organized over a
period of time in order to achieve or
win something. *An election campaign.*

camper *(n)*
1 someone who has
a holiday in a tent.
2 a large vehicle in which you
can sleep and cook meals.

can could
1 *(v)* to be able to. *Natalie
can speak fluent French.*
2 *(v) (informal)* to be allowed
to do something. *You can
stay out until dark.*
3 *(n)* a metal container. **canned** *(adj)*.

canal *(n)* a man-made waterway
used by barges and narrow boats.

cancel cancelling cancelled *(v)*
1 If someone **cancels** something
that has been arranged, they say
that it is not going to happen
anymore. **cancellation** *(n)*.
2 **cancel out** *(v)* If two things
cancel each other out, they stop
the effect of one another. *If you eat
all day, it will cancel out the benefit
of all the exercise you've done.*

cancer *(n)*
a serious disease in which some
cells in the body produce harmful
growths. **cancerous** *(adj)*.

candid *(adj)*
honest and open in what you
are saying. **candidly** *(adv)*.

candidate *(n)*
someone taking an examination,
applying for a job, or standing
in an election. **candidacy** *(n)*.

candle *(n)* a stick of wax with a string
or wick running through it, which you
burn to produce light. **candlelight** *(n)*.

candy candies *(n) (US)*
a small piece of food, made with
sugar or chocolate (sweet, *UK*).

cane caning caned
1 *(n)* the hollow stem of a plant
such as bamboo,
used to make
furniture.

2 *(n)* a stick, especially a walking stick
or a stick used for beating someone.
3 *(v) (old-fashioned)* to beat someone
with a cane as a punishment.

canine
1 *(adj)* to do with dogs.
2 *(n)* the pointed tooth on
each side of your upper
and lower jaw. See **teeth**.

cannabis *(n)* a drug that people
smoke to give them a feeling of
pleasure. Cannabis is illegal in
Britain and in many other countries.

cannibal *(n)* someone who eats
human flesh. **cannibalism** *(n)*.

cannon *(n)*
a heavy gun which fires large
metal balls. *The picture shows
an 18th-century cannon.*

cannon
(cutaway)
trunnion
(supports barrel)
shot pricker
wad cascabel
gun barrel
rammer
muzzle
carriage
wheel
powder
charge
towing eye
worm
or reamer
cannonballs
sponge

canoe *(n)*
a small boat that you move
through the water by paddling.

canopy canopies *(n)*
1 a piece of cloth used as a
cover over a doorway, bed, etc.
2 a shelter over something.
*Tree tops formed a canopy
over the forest floor.*
3 a cover over a cockpit.
See **glider**, **helicopter**.

canteen *(n)*
an area in an office, school,
etc. where you can eat meals.

Some words that begin with a "c" sound are spelt with a "k".

canter cantering cantered *(v)*
When a horse **canters**, it
runs at a speed between a
trot and a gallop. **canter** *(n)*.

canvas canvases *(n)*
1 a type of coarse, strong cloth
used for tents, sails, and clothing.
2 a surface for painting, made
from canvas cloth stretched
over a wooden frame.
Artists paint on canvases.

canvass canvasses
canvassing canvassed *(v)*
to ask people for their opinions
or votes. **canvasser** *(n)*.

canyon *(n)*
a deep, narrow river valley.

cap capping capped
1 *(n)* a soft, flat hat with
a peak at the front.
2 *(n)* the top of a bottle, jar, or pen.
3 *(v)* If you **cap** someone's story,
you tell an even better one.
4 *(n)* a maximum limit set on
prices, spending, wages, etc.

capable *(adj)*
1 If you are **capable** of doing
something, you are able to do it.
*Ingrid is capable of winning the
competition.* **capability** *(n)*.
2 able to do something well
and skilfully. *Derek is a capable
tennis player.* **capably** *(adv)*.

capacity capacities *(n)*
1 the amount a container can hold.
2 an ability to do something.
*Christopher has the capacity
to absorb facts very fast.*

cape *(n)*
1 a sleeveless coat that you wear
over your shoulders.
2 a part of the
coastline that sticks
out into the sea. *The
picture shows Cape
Cod, on the east coast
of North America.*

cape

capillary capillaries *(n)*
1 a small tube in your
body which carries blood
between arteries and veins.
2 **capillary tube** *(n)* a very thin tube,
made out of glass. *See* **thermometer**.

capital *(n)*
1 the main city of a country,
where the government is based.
2 an upper-case letter. *You
begin a sentence with a capital.*
3 an amount of money
used to start a business.
4 **capital punishment** *(n)*
punishment by death.

capitalism *(n)* a way of organizing
a country so that all the land, houses,
factories, etc. belong to private
individuals rather than the state.
capitalist *(n)*, **capitalist** *(adj)*.

cappuccino *(kap-er-cheen-oh)* *(n)*
coffee made with frothy milk.

capricious *(adj)* Someone who
is **capricious** is unpredictable
and tends to change their mind
without any obvious reason.

capsize capsizing capsized *(v)*
If a boat or ship **capsizes**,
it turns over in the water.

capsule *(n)*
1 a small container of medicine
that you can swallow.
2 the part of a rocket or spacecraft
in which the crew travel.

captain *(n)*
1 the person in charge
of a ship or an aircraft.
2 the leader of a sports team.
3 an army officer.

caption *(n)* a short title or
description printed below a
cartoon, drawing, or photograph.

captivate
captivating captivated *(v)*
to delight someone. *Clara
captivated us with her singing.*

captive *(n)* a prisoner.
captivity *(n)*, **captive** *(adj)*.

capture capturing captured *(v)*
to take a person or a place by force.

car *(n)* a type of passenger motor
vehicle. *The picture shows a cutaway
view of a Ford Mondeo saloon car.*

petrol flap · boot · heated rear window · radio aerial · electrically-operated sunroof · **saloon car** (cutaway) · seat belt · electrically-operated passenger window · rear-view mirror · adjustable seat · wing mirror · brake fluid reservoir · windscreen wiper · cowl top grille · air cleaner · heated, tinted windscreen · battery · shielded door lock · wheel cover · steel safety cage · head rest · steel door beam · power steering fluid reservoir · front suspension (supports car body) · shock absorber · electronic anti-lock brake · drive shaft (transmits power from engine to wheels) · engine coolant reservoir · 16-valve petrol engine · directional indicator · oil dipstick · front towing eye · resonator (reduces noise) · number plate · bonnet · headlight · bumper · radiator grille

caramel (n)
1 burnt sugar.
2 a sweet made from burnt sugar, butter, and milk.
3 a light brown colour. **caramel** (adj).

carat (n) a unit for measuring the weight of precious metals. *24-carat gold is the purest form of gold.*

caravan (n)
1 a small home on wheels which can be towed by a car and is used by people on holiday.
2 a group of people and camels that travel together across a desert.

caravan

carbohydrate (n)
a substance in foods such as bread and potatoes that gives you energy.

carbon (n)
1 an element found in diamonds, coal, and in all plants and animals.
2 **carbon dioxide** (n)
a gas that is breathed out by people and animals, and is also used to make drinks fizzy.
3 **carbon fibre** (n) a light, strong material made from threads of carbon and used for fishing rods, racing car bodies, etc.
4 **carbon footprint** (n) the amount of greenhouse gases generated by a person's or organization's energy use.

carburettor (n) the part of a car's engine where air and fuel mix.

carcass carcasses (n)
the body of a dead animal.

card (n)
1 stiff paper.
2 a folded piece of card sent on birthdays and special occasions.
3 one of a set of rectangular pieces of card, used in games such as rummy and bridge.
The cards shown here were made in France in the 18th century.

playing cards

cardboard (n) very thick card, used for making boxes.

cardiac (adj)
to do with the heart.

cardigan (n) a knitted jacket which fastens down the front.

care caring cared
1 (v) If you **care** about someone or something, you are very concerned about what happens to them. **caring** (adj).
2 If you **take care of** someone, you look after them.
3 If you do something **with care**, you pay attention to what you are doing.

career (n)
the series of jobs that a person has in their life, usually in the same profession. *A career in teaching.*

carefree (adj) Someone who is **carefree** has no worries.

careful (adj) Someone who is **careful** takes trouble over what they are doing and does not take risks. **carefully** (adv).

careless (adj)
Someone who is **careless** does not take much trouble or care over things. **carelessness** (n), **carelessly** (adv).

caress
caresses caressing caressed (v)
to touch gently. **caress** (n).

caretaker (n)
someone whose job is to look after a school or some other public building.

cargo cargoes (n) goods that are carried by ship or aircraft.

caricature (n)
an exaggerated picture of someone.

carnival (n)
a public celebration. *People often wear colourful costumes, walk in processions, and dance in the streets at carnival time.*

carnivore (n) an animal that only eats meat. **carnivorous** (adj).

carob (n)
1 an evergreen tree whose beans are used to make a food similar to chocolate.
2 a chocolate-like food.

carol (n) a religious song that people sing at Christmas. **carol** (v).

carpenter (n) someone who makes or repairs the wooden parts of buildings or wooden furniture. **carpentry** (n).

carpet (n)
1 a thick floor covering. **carpet** (v).
2 a thick layer of something. *A carpet of flowers.* **carpet** (v).

carriage (n)
1 one of the parts of a train in which passengers travel.
2 a vehicle that is pulled by horses.

carriageway (n)
Motorways and major roads are divided into two **carriageways**, for traffic travelling in opposite directions.

carrot (n)
1 a long root vegetable.
See **vegetable**.
2 If someone offers you a **carrot**, they promise you something nice in order to persuade you to do something.

carry carries carrying carried (v)
1 to hold on to something and take it somewhere. *Please carry this tray.*
2 If a sound **carries**, it can be heard some distance away.
3 If you **carry out** a plan or idea, you put it into practice.

cartilage (n) a strong, stretchy substance found around your joints.

cartography (n) the art of drawing maps. **cartographer** (n).

carton (n) a cardboard or plastic box, usually containing food or drink.

cartoon (n)
1 a short, animated film.
2 a funny drawing or series of drawings. **cartoonist** (n).

cartridge (n)
1 a tube of ink used in a fountain pen.
2 a container that holds a bullet or pellets and the explosive that fires them.

cartwheel (n)
a circular, sideways handstand.

carve carving carved (v)
1 to cut slices from a piece of meat.
2 to cut a shape out of a piece of wood, stone, etc. **carver** (n), **carving** (n).

case (n)
1 a container for carrying clothes when you travel.
2 an example of something. *This is a case of deliberate disobedience!*
3 a trial in a court of law.
4 a crime that the police are investigating.
5 The **case** of a noun or pronoun is the form that it takes, depending on its relationship with other words in a sentence. *"I" is the nominative case, "me" is the accusative case, and "my" is the possessive case.*

cash cashes cashing cashed
1 (n) money in the form of notes and coins.
2 (v) If you **cash in** on something, you take advantage of it.

Some words that begin with a "c" sound are spelt with a "k".

cash-and-carry
cash-and-carry
cash-and-carries (n)
a warehouse where you can buy things in large quantities at low prices.

cashier (n) someone who takes or pays out money in a shop or bank.

cashpoint (n) a machine from which people can take out money from their bank accounts, by using a bank card. Also called an **ATM**, which stands for Automated Teller Machine.

casino (n) a place where people play gambling games such as roulette.

casket (n) (poetic) a jewellery box.

casserole (n)
1 a stew that is cooked slowly.
2 a dish with a lid that is used for cooking casseroles.

cast casting cast
1 (n) the actors in a play, musical, or film. **cast** (v).
2 (n) a hard plaster covering that supports a broken arm or leg.
3 (v) to throw a fishing net or line into the water.
4 (v) to form something by pouring soft material into a mould.

castaway (n) someone left on a deserted island after a shipwreck.

caster sugar or **castor sugar** (n) finely ground white sugar.

castle (n)
1 a large, strong building, often surrounded by a wall and a moat. In the Middle Ages, noble families stayed in castles and soldiers defended them from attack. *The picture shows a cutaway view of a medieval castle's keep or tower and a ground plan of the castle. Also see* **portcullis**.
2 a chesspiece, also known as a rook, that moves in straight lines across a chessboard. *See* **chess**.

castle keep (cutaway)

man-at-arms
lord's bedchamber
four-poster bed
parapet
solar (private room for lord's family)

turret
arrow loop (slit for shooting arrows through)
crenellation
merlon crenel
stables
garderobe (toilet)
forge
toilet chute
blacksmith
knife grinder
storeroom
inner bailey
entrance
great hall
kitchen
spiral staircase

castle (ground plan)
moat
inner bailey
tower
inner bailey wall
keep
outer bailey
outer bailey wall
drawbridge
gatehouse
barbican (watch tower)

chapel
oven
baker
guard room
falcon
main entrance
well
travelling pedlars
dungeon
minstrel
dovecote
falconers

castor sugar *see* **caster sugar**.

castrate castrating castrated *(v)*
to remove the sex organs of a male
animal so that it cannot breed.

casual *(adj)*
1 not planned. *A casual
meeting.* **casually** *(adv)*.
2 not formal. *Casual
dress.* **casually** *(adv)*.

casualty casualties *(n)*
1 someone who is injured or killed
in an accident, disaster, or war.
2 the department in a hospital that
handles accidents and emergencies.

cat *(n)*
1 any
member of
the cat family,
including
lions, tigers,
and cheetahs.
2 a small,
furry mammal,
often kept
as a pet. *The
picture shows
a range of
domestic
cats.*

cats silver Classic tabby

Chinchilla

brown Abyssinian

red Devon Rex

seal point Siamese

catalogue *(n)*
1 a book listing things you can buy
from a company, or works of art on
show in an exhibition. **catalogue** *(v)*.
2 a list of all the books in a library.

catalyst *(n)*
1 a substance that causes or
speeds up a chemical reaction,
without changing itself.
2 a person or thing that
causes something to happen.

catamaran *(n)*
a boat with two hulls joined together.

catapult *(n)*
1 a simple, Y-shaped weapon,
with elastic stretched over it,
used for shooting small stones.
2 a large weapon used in the past
for firing rocks over castle walls.

cataract *(n)*
1 a large waterfall.
2 an eye disease in which
the lens becomes cloudy
and vision becomes blurred.

catarrh *(kat-arh) (n)* the thick
liquid that blocks up your nose
and throat when you have a cold.

catastrophe *(kat-ass-trof-ee) (n)*
a sudden disaster.
catastrophic *(kat-ass-trof-ik) (adj)*.

catch catches catching caught
1 *(v)* to grab hold of something
moving through the air. **catch** *(n)*.
2 *(v)* to get someone whom you are
chasing. *The police caught the thieves.*
3 *(v)* If you **catch** a bus
or train, you get on it.
4 *(v)* If you **catch** someone
doing something wrong,
you see them doing it.
5 *(n)* a fastening on a door, box, etc.
6 *(v)* If something **catches on**,
it becomes very popular.

categorical *(adj)* clear and plain.
Henry's reply was a categorical "No".
categorically *(adv)*.

category categories *(n)*
a class or group of things that
have something in common.

cater catering catered *(v)*
1 to provide food for a lot of
people. **caterer** *(n)*, **catering** *(n)*.
2 to provide people with the
things that they need. *This
restaurant caters for vegetarians.*

caterpillar *(n)* a worm-like larva
that changes into a butterfly or moth.
*The pictures show the life cycle
of a swallowtail butterfly,
including the main parts of
a swallowtail caterpillar.*

1 egg
or ovum

head with
simple
eyes
thoracic leg

thorax

spiracle
(breathing hole)

abdomen

mandible (jaw)

2 caterpillar
or larva
proleg

anal proleg

3 chrysalis
or pupa

4 butterfly
or imago

tower

spire

lead
roof

flying
buttress

pinnacle

rose window

west entrance

buttress

porch

lancet window

cathedral *(n)* a large
and important church
with a bishop or an
archbishop as its main
priest. *The picture
shows Chartres
cathedral in France.*

cathedral

Catholic *(n)* a member of
the Roman Catholic Church.
Catholicism *(n)*, **Catholic** *(adj)*.

cattle *(plural n)* cows and bulls.

cauldron *(n)*
a large, round cooking pot.

cauliflower *(n)*
a vegetable with a large, round,
white centre, surrounded by
leaves. *See* **vegetable**.

cause causing caused
1 *(v)* to make something happen.
2 *(n)* the reason that
something happens.
3 *(n)* an aim or principle
for which people fight.

cautious *(adj)*
If you are **cautious**, you try hard
to avoid mistakes or danger.
caution *(n)*, **cautiously** *(adv)*.

cavalry *(plural n)*
1 soldiers who fight on horseback.
2 soldiers who fight
in armoured vehicles.

cave *(n)*
a large hole underground or
in the side of a hill or cliff.

caveman cavemen *(n)*
someone who lived in
caves in prehistoric times.

cave painting *(n)*
a picture painted
on a cave wall
in prehistoric times.
*This cave painting
of a bison was
discovered in
northern Spain.*

cave painting

cavern (n) a large cave.

caviar (n) the salted eggs of a sturgeon, usually served before a meal.

caving (n) If you **go caving**, you explore caves. **caver** (n).

cavity cavities (n) a hole or hollow space in something solid, such as a tooth.

CCTV short for **closed-circuit television**.

CD short for **compact disc**.

cease ceasing ceased (v) to stop.

cease-fire (n) a period during a war when both sides agree to stop fighting.

ceaseless (adj) without stopping. **ceaselessly** (adv).

cedar (n) a large, evergreen tree with needle-like leaves.

ceiling (n)
1 the upper surface inside a room.
2 the upper limit that something can reach. A price ceiling.

celebrate celebrating celebrated (v) to do something fun on a special occasion, such as having a party. **celebration** (n), **celebratory** (adj).

celebrated (adj) famous.

celebrity celebrities (n) a famous person, especially a singer or actor.

celery (n) a vegetable with crisp white or green stalks, often eaten raw in salads. See **vegetable**.

celestial (adj) to do with heaven. **celestially** (adv).

cell (n)
1 a room in a prison or a police station where someone is locked up.
2 a basic, microscopic part of an animal or a plant.

plant cell (magnified)

nucleus

chloroplast (traps light and energy)

cell membrane

large vacuole (contains cell sap)

starch grain

cell wall

cytoplasm

cellar (n) a room below ground level in a house, often used for storage.

cellular (adj) made out of, or to do with cells. Cellular tissue.

celluloid (n) a type of plastic, once used to capture very early films.

cellulose (n) the substance from which the cell walls of plants are made.

Celsius (adj) measured on a temperature scale on which water boils at 100° and freezes at 0°. Celsius is also called centigrade. See **thermometer**.

cement (n)
1 a grey powder, used in building, that becomes hard when you mix it with water and let it dry.
2 a substance that joins two things together. See **tooth**.

cemetery cemeteries (n) a place where bodies are buried.

censor censoring censored
1 (v) to remove parts of a book, film, play, etc. that are thought to be harmful to the public. **censorship** (n).
2 (n) someone whose job is to censor books, films, plays, etc.

census (n) an official count of all the people living in a country.

cent (n) a unit of money in the USA, Canada, Australia, parts of Europe, etc. One hundred cents make one Euro.

centaur (n) a creature found in Greek and Roman myths which had the body and legs of a horse but the chest, arms, and head of a man.

centenary centenaries (n) the hundredth anniversary of something.

centigrade see **Celsius**.

centipede (n) a small creature with a very long body and lots of legs. Centipedes can measure more than 25cm and have over 300 legs.

central (adj)
1 in the middle. **centrally** (adv).
2 most important. The central position.
3 **central heating** (n) a system for heating a building in which water or air is heated in one place and then carried in pipes all over the building.

centre centring centred
1 (n) the middle of something.
2 (n) a place where people go to do a particular activity. A sports centre.
3 (v) to concentrate on something. The campaign centres on the problems of the elderly.
4 **centre of gravity** (n) the point on an object at which it can balance.

centrifugal (adj) pulling away from the centre. You can feel the centrifugal effect when you swing an object in a circle.

centripetal (adj) pulling towards the centre. When you swing an object in a circle, you pull it inwards and exert a centripetal force.

centurion (n) an officer in the Roman army who was in command of a company of soldiers.

century centuries (n) a period of 100 years.

ceramics
1 (singular n) the craft of making objects out of clay.
2 (plural n) objects made of clay. **ceramic** (adj).

centurion

plumed helmet
woollen cloak
chain mail corselet
decorated belt
dagger
sword
double pleated kilt
twisted vine rod
bronze greave (shin plate)

cereal (n)
1 a grain crop grown for food, such as wheat, oats, or maize.
2 a breakfast food usually made from grain and eaten with milk.

ceremony ceremonies (n) formal actions, words, and often music, performed to mark an important occasion. A wedding ceremony. **ceremonial** (adj), **ceremonially** (adv).

certain (adj)
1 If you are **certain** about something, you are sure about it. Alex was certain he had posted the letter. **certainty** (n), **certainly** (adv).
2 particular. The shop is closed at certain times of the day.

certificate (n) a piece of paper given to someone to prove that they have done something. An examination certificate.

chain (n)
1 a line of metal rings, called links, joined together.
2 a series of connected things. A chain of events.
3 **chain store** (n) one of a group of shops in different towns that are owned by the same company and sell similar goods.

chair chairing chaired
1 (n) a piece of furniture that you sit on, with four legs and a back.
2 (n) the person in charge of a meeting, also called the chairman, chairwoman, or chairperson.
3 (v) to take charge of a meeting.

Some words that begin with a "c" sound are spelt with a "k".

chauffeur

chairlift (n) a line of chairs attached to a moving cable, used for carrying people up mountains.

chalet (shall-ay) (n) a small, wooden house with a sloping roof.

chalk (n)
1 a soft, white rock.
2 a stick of soft rock that can be used for writing and drawing. **chalk** (v).

challenge challenging challenged
1 (n) something difficult that you try to do. **challenging** (adj).
2 (v) If you **challenge** someone, you invite them to try to do something, or to fight. **challenge** (n).
3 (v) If you **challenge** something, you question whether it is right or not.

chamber (n)
1 a large room.
2 a hollow place in something.
3 **chamber music** (n) classical music for a small number of instruments.

chameleon (kam-ee-lee-un) (n) a lizard that can change colour to match its surroundings.

chameleon

champagne (n) an expensive, sparkling white wine, usually drunk on special occasions.

champion
championing championed
1 (n) the winner of a competition or a tournament. **championship** (n).
2 (v) If someone **champions** a cause, they support it. **champion** (n).

chance (n)
1 the possibility of something happening. *We have a chance of winning the cup.*
2 an opportunity to do something. *Warren has the chance to learn to ski.*
3 If you **take a chance**, you try something, even though it is risky.
4 If something happens **by chance**, it happens accidentally.

chancellor (n)
1 a name for the leader of an organization or a country. *The Chancellor of Germany is its elected leader.*
2 **Chancellor of the Exchequer** (n) the minister in charge of finance and taxes in the British Government.

change changing changed
1 (v) to become different or to make something different. **change** (n).
2 (n) If you pay more money than something costs, the money you get back is called **change**.
3 (n) coins rather than banknotes.

channel (n)
1 a narrow stretch of sea between two areas of land.
2 a television or radio station.

chant chanting chanted (v) to say or sing a phrase over and over again. **chant** (n).

Chanukah see **Hanukkah**.

chaos (kay-oss) (n) total confusion. **chaotic** (adj), **chaotically** (adv).

chapel (n)
1 a small church.
2 a side section of a large church.
3 a place in a school, prison, etc. where Christian services are held.

chapter (n) one of the parts into which a book is divided.

character (n)
1 Your **character** is what sort of person you are.
2 one of the people in a story, book, film, or play.
3 a letter, figure, or other mark used in printing.

characteristic
1 (n) a typical quality or feature. *Stubbornness is a characteristic of our family.* **characteristically** (adv).
2 (adj) typical. *Sophie worked with characteristic efficiency.* **characteristically** (adv).

charcoal (n) a form of carbon made from burnt wood. Charcoal is used for drawing and as a fuel for barbecues.

charge charging charged (v)
1 to ask someone to pay a particular price for something. **charge** (n).
2 to rush at someone in order to attack them. **charge** (n).
3 When you **charge** a battery, you pass an electric current through it so that it stores electricity.
4 If someone is **in charge** of something, they have to deal with it or take control of it.

chariot (n) a small, horse-drawn vehicle, used in ancient times in battles or for racing. *The picture shows a Roman chariot.*

Roman chariot

charity charities (n)
1 money or other help given to people or animals in need.
2 an organization which raises money for people or animals in need.

charm charming charmed
1 (n) If someone has **charm**, they behave in a pleasing and attractive way. **charmer** (n), **charming** (adj).
2 (v) to please someone and make them like you.
3 (n) a small object that some people believe will bring them good luck. *This Ancient Egyptian charm represents a sacred eye.*

Egyptian charm

chart charting charted
1 (n) a drawing showing information in the form of a table or picture.
2 (n) a map of the stars or the sea.
3 (v) to show information in the form of a chart.

chase chasing chased (v) to run after someone in order to catch them or make them go away. **chase** (n).

chasm (kaz-um) (n) a deep crack in the surface of the earth.

chassis (sha-see) chassis (n) the frame onto which the body of a vehicle is built.

chat chatting chatted (v)
1 to talk to someone in a friendly and informal way. **chat** (n).
2 to communicate with other people through a website on the internet by typing messages on a computer or phone. **chat** (n).
3 **chat room** (n) a website on the internet where people can communicate by typing messages to each other.
4 **chat up** (v) If you **chat someone up**, you talk in a friendly way to them because you find them attractive.

château (shat-oh) **châteaux** (n) a castle or large country house in France. *The picture shows the Azay-le-Rideau château in the Loire valley in France.*

château

chatter chattering chattered (v)
1 to talk about unimportant things. **chatter** (n).
2 When your teeth **chatter**, they knock together because you are cold.

chauffeur (show-fur) (n) someone whose job is to drive a car for somebody else. **chauffeur** (v).

chauvinist *(show-vin-ist) (n)*
1 a man who believes that women are inferior to men. **chauvinism** *(n)*, **chauvinistic** *(adj)*.
2 someone who believes that no other country is as good or as important as their own. **chauvinism** *(n)*, **chauvinistic** *(adj)*.

cheap cheaper cheapest *(adj)*
1 not costing very much. **cheapness** *(n)*, **cheaply** *(adv)*.
2 unkind and mean. *That was a cheap trick you played on me!*

cheat cheating cheated *(v)* to act dishonestly in order to win a game or get what you want. **cheat** *(n)*.

check
checking checked
1 *(v)* to look at something in order to make sure that it is all right. **check** *(n)*.
2 *(v)* to stop something from moving or growing. *We must check inflation.*
3 *(n)* a pattern of different coloured squares. **checked** *(adj)*.

checkout *(n)*
the place in a supermarket where you pay for your goods.

checkup *(n)*
a medical examination to make sure that there is nothing wrong with you.

cheek *(n)*
1 the side of your face below your eyes.
2 rude and disrespectful behaviour or speech. **cheeky** *(adj)*, **cheekily** *(adv)*.

cheer
cheering cheered *(v)*
1 to shout encouragement or approval. **cheer** *(n)*.
2 If you **cheer up**, you begin to feel better.

cheerful *(adj)* happy and lively. **cheerfulness** *(n)*, **cheerfully** *(adv)*.

cheese *(n)*
a food made from the solid parts of milk after it has turned sour.

cheetah *(n)*
a wild cat with a spotted coat that is found in Africa and the Middle East. *Cheetahs can run at 120km (75 miles) per hour, faster than any other land animal.*

cheetah

chef *(sheff) (n)*
the chief cook in a restaurant.

chemical
1 *(n)* a substance used in chemistry.
2 *(adj)* to do with, or made by chemistry. *A chemical reaction. Chemical fertilizers.* **chemically** *(adv)*.

chemist *(n)*
1 a shop where you can buy drugs and medicines.
2 someone trained in chemistry.

chemistry *(n)* the scientific study of substances and the ways in which they react with each other.

cheque *(n)*
a printed piece of paper on which someone writes to tell their bank to pay money from their account.

cherish
cherishes cherishing cherished *(v)*
to care for someone or something in a kind and loving way.

cherry cherries *(n)*
a small red or black fruit with a stone at its centre. *See* **fruit**.

chess *(n)* a game for two people with sixteen pieces each, played on a black and white board.

chessboard and pieces

rook or castle
knight
bishop
king
pawn
queen

chest *(n)*
1 the front part of your body between your neck and waist.
2 a large, strong, often wooden box.

chestnut *(n)*
1 a large, reddish-brown nut that grows in a prickly case.
2 a tree which produces chestnuts.
3 a reddish-brown colour. **chestnut** *(adj)*.

chest of drawers
chests of drawers *(n)*
a piece of furniture with drawers, used for storing clothes.

chew chewing chewed *(v)*
to crush food in your teeth.

chewing gum *(n)* a kind of sweet that you chew but do not swallow.

chick *(n)* a very young bird, especially a very young hen.

chicken *(n)*
1 a hen, usually a young one.
2 the meat from a young hen. *Roast chicken.*
3 *(slang)* someone who is too scared to do something.

chicken
(cross-section)
developing egg
oesophagus
liver
caecum
gall bladder
oviduct
ovary
vent
crop (food store)
cloaca
gizzard (second stomach for grinding food)
egg travelling to vent
pancreas
intestine   duodenum

chickenpox *(n)*
a common disease that gives you red, itchy spots on your skin.

chief
1 *(n)* the leader of a group of people.
2 *(adj)* main or most important. **chiefly** *(adv)*.

child children *(n)*
1 a young person who is not yet grown up.
2 a son or daughter.

childhood *(n)*
the time when you are a child. *Marcus had a happy childhood.*

childish *(adj)* immature and thoughtless. *Childish behaviour.* **childishness** *(n)*, **childishly** *(adv)*.

childminder *(n)*
someone who looks after children while their parents are at work.

chill chilling chilled
1 *(v)* to make something cold.
2 *(n)* a feeling of slight coldness. *There is a chill in the air.* **chilly** *(adj)*.
3 *(n)* a feeling of fear. **chilling** *(adj)*.
4 **chill out** *(v)* relax, especially after energetic activity.

chilli chillies *(n)*
a small, hot-tasting red or green seed pod used to flavour food.

chime chiming chimed *(v)*
When a bell or clock **chimes**, it makes a ringing sound. **chime** *(n)*.

chimney *(n)*
a vertical pipe through which smoke escapes from a fire. *See* **building**.

chubby

chimpanzee *(n)*
a large ape with dark fur, that comes from Africa. *See* **ape**.

chin *(n)* the part of your face below your mouth.

china *(n)*
1 very thin, delicate pottery.
2 cups, plates, and dishes made out of china. *See* **bowl**.

chink *(n)*
1 a narrow opening.
2 a gentle, jingling sound. **chink** *(v)*.

chip chipping chipped
1 *(v)* to break a small piece off something by accident. **chip** *(n)*.
2 *(n)* a long, thin piece of potato, cooked in oil.
3 If you have a **chip on your shoulder**, you feel angry because you think you have been treated unfairly.
4 *(n)* a minute piece of silicon, with electronic circuits printed on it, used in computers and electronic equipment.

silicon chip
(magnified)

The magnified silicon chip shown here is small enough to fit on your fingernail.

chiropractor *(ky-ro-prak-tor)* *(n)*
someone who treats back pain and other illnesses by adjusting the spine.

chivalry *(shiv-ul-ree)* *(n)*
1 very polite and helpful behaviour, especially by a man towards a woman. **chivalrous** *(adj)*.
2 a way of behaving that a medieval knight was meant to practise. **chivalrous** *(adj)*.

chlorine *(klor-een)* *(n)*
a strong-smelling gas which is added to water to kill harmful germs. **chlorinate** *(v)*.

chlorophyll *(klor-oh-fill)* *(n)*
the green substance in plants that allows them to use the Sun's energy.

chocolate *(n)* a sweet food made from beans that grow on the tropical cacao tree. *The picture shows a cacao pod and some dried and roasted beans that can be ground up to make chocolate.* **chocolaty** *(adj)*.

cacao pod and beans
raw beans in pulp
roasted beans

choice
1 *(n)* the thing or person that you have selected. *Jeremy was a good choice as team captain.*
2 *(n)* all the things that you can choose from. *This menu offers a very wide choice.*
3 *(adj)* of very good quality. *Choice fruit and vegetables.*

choir *(kwire)* *(n)*
a group of people who sing together.

choke choking choked *(v)*
1 to struggle to breathe because something is blocking your breathing passages.
2 to kill someone by squeezing their neck until they stop breathing.
3 to block something. *Leaves had choked the stream.*

cholera *(kol-er-ah)* *(n)*
a dangerous disease which causes severe sickness and diarrhoea.

cholesterol *(kol-est-er-ol)* *(n)*
a substance found in foods such as butter and cheese, that is used to carry fats around your body.

choose
choosing chose chosen *(v)*
1 to pick out one person or thing from several.
2 If you **choose** to do something, you decide to do it.

chop chopping chopped
1 *(v)* to cut something with a knife or an axe. **chop** *(n)*.
2 *(n)* a small piece of lamb or pork on a bone.
3 *(v)* If you **chop and change**, you keep changing your mind.

choppy choppier choppiest *(adj)*
When the sea is **choppy**, it is quite rough.

chopstick *(n)*
one of a pair of thin sticks for eating food, used by people in Far Eastern countries.

choral *(korr-al)* *(adj)*
sung by a choir. *Choral music.*

chord *(kord)* *(n)*
1 a combination of musical notes played at the same time. *See* **notation**.
2 a straight line that joins two points on a curve. *See* **circle**.

chore *(chaw)* *(n)*
a job that has to be done many times, such as washing dishes or cleaning.

choreographer
(kor-ee-og-raf-er) *(n)*
someone who arranges dance steps and movements for a ballet or show. **choreography** *(n)*.

chorus *(kor-uss)*
choruses chorusing chorused
1 *(n)* the part of a song that is repeated after each verse.
2 *(n)* a large group of people who sing or speak together.
3 *(v)* to say something all together.

Christ *(n)* the name given to Jesus, the man whom Christians believe is the Son of God and the Saviour. *This mosaic of Christ was made in the 12th century.*

Christ

christening *(n)* a Christian ceremony in which a person is accepted into the Christian Church and is given a name. **christen** *(v)*.

Christianity *(n)*
the religion based on the life and teachings of Jesus Christ. Christians believe that they will live with God after they die if they believe in Jesus and follow his teachings. **Christian** *(n)*, **Christian** *(adj)*.

Christmas Christmases *(n)*
the Christian festival which celebrates the birth of Jesus Christ.

chromatography *(n)*
the process of separating parts of a mixture by letting it travel through a material that absorbs each part at a different rate. *You can use chromatography to separate the different coloured chemicals in ink.*

chromosome *(n)*
the part of a cell that carries the genes that give living things their special characteristics. You inherit your chromosomes from your parents.

chronic *(adj)*
1 *(informal)* very bad. **chronically** *(adv)*.
2 If something is **chronic**, it lasts for a long time. *Chronic bronchitis.* **chronically** *(adv)*.

chronicle chronicling chronicled *(v)*
to record historical events in a careful, detailed way. **chronicle** *(n)*.

chronological *(adj)*
arranged in the order in which events happened. **chronology** *(n)*, **chronologically** *(adv)*.

chrysalis *(kriss-er-liss)* chrysalises *(n)* a moth or butterfly at the stage of development between a caterpillar and an adult. A chrysalis is covered by a hard outer shell. *See* **caterpillar**.

chubby chubbier chubbiest *(adj)*
slightly fat or plump.

a b c d e f g h i j k l m n o p q r s t u v w x y z

chuck chucking chucked *(v)*
(informal) to throw something carelessly.

chuckle chuckling chuckled *(v)*
to laugh quietly. **chuckle** *(n).*

chug chugging chugged *(v)*
to make a heavy, regular, thumping sound while moving along. *The truck chugged slowly up the hill.*

chunk *(n)* a thick piece of something.

chunky chunkier chunkiest *(adj)*
1 thick and short.
2 containing thick pieces.
Chunky dog food.

church churches *(n)*
1 a building used by Christians for worship.
2 **Church** a group of Christians.

churn churning churned
1 *(n)* a large metal container for milk.
2 *(n)* a machine in which milk is made into butter. *See* **butter**.
3 *(v)* to move around roughly.
The tractor churned through the mud.

chutney *(n)* a mixture of vegetables, fruit, and spices, often eaten with meat or cheese.

cider *(sy-der) (n)* a fizzy alcoholic drink made from apples.

cigar *(n)* a thick, brown roll of tobacco which people smoke.

cigarette *(n)*
a thin roll of tobacco, covered with white paper, which people smoke.

cinder *(n)* a small piece of wood or coal that has been partly burned.

cinema *(n)* a large building where people go to watch films.

circa *(prep)*
the Latin word for "about". You can also write circa as "c". *Geoffrey Chaucer was born circa 1340.*

circle circling circled
1 *(n)* a flat, perfectly round shape. *The diagrams below show parts of a circle and other geometric terms connected with circles.* **circular** *(adj).*
2 *(v)* to draw or make a circle around something.
3 *(n)* a group of people who all know each other.
4 *(n)* a curved, upper area of seating in a theatre.

parts of a circle

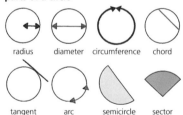

radius   diameter   circumference   chord

tangent   arc   semicircle   sector

circuit *(sir-kit) (n)*
1 a circular route. *A race circuit.*
2 the complete path that an electrical current can flow around.
3 **circuit diagram** *(n)* a diagram that shows an electrical circuit, using symbols recognized throughout the world. *The picture shows some symbols used in circuit diagrams.*

circuit symbols

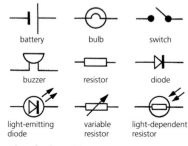

battery   bulb   switch

buzzer   resistor   diode

light-emitting diode   variable resistor   light-dependent resistor

circulation *(n)*
1 the number of copies of a newspaper, magazine, etc. that are bought each day, week, etc.
2 the movement of blood in blood vessels around the body. *Blood travels from the heart in arteries, and returns to the heart in veins. It then travels to the lungs to collect oxygen, before being pumped round again.* **circulatory** *(adj).*

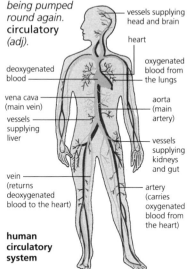

vessels supplying head and brain
heart
oxygenated blood from the lungs
deoxygenated blood
vena cava (main vein)
vessels supplying liver
aorta (main artery)
vessels supplying kidneys and gut
vein (returns deoxygenated blood to the heart)
artery (carries oxygenated blood from the heart)

human circulatory system

circumcision *(n)*
the removal of the foreskin at the end of a boy's or a man's penis, usually for religious reasons. **circumcise** *(v).*

circumference *(n)*
1 the outer edge of a circle. *See* **circle**.
2 the distance around the edge of a circle.

circumspect *(adj)* cautious or careful. **circumspectly** *(adv).*

circumstance *(n)*
The **circumstances** of an event are the things which affect the way that it happens. *Laura took her exam under very difficult circumstances.*

circus circuses *(n)*
a travelling show in which clowns and acrobats perform.

cistern *(n)*
a container for storing water, especially one in the roof of a house or attached to a toilet.

citizen *(n)*
1 a member of a particular country who has the right to live there. *A British citizen.*
2 a person who lives in a particular town or city. *A citizen of London.*

citrus fruit *(n)*
a sharp-tasting, juicy fruit with a thick skin, such as an orange, a lemon, or a grapefruit.

city cities *(n)*
a very large or important town.

civic *(adj)*
to do with a city or the people who live in it. *Civic centre.*

civil *(adj)*
1 to do with the government or people of a country, rather than its army or religion. *The civil service.*
2 polite. *Please try to be civil to your great aunt!* **civility** *(n).*
3 **civil rights** *(plural n)* the claims that all members of a society have to equal treatment and freedom.
4 **civil servant** *(n)* someone who works in a government department, such as a tax office.
5 **civil war** *(n)* a war between different groups of people within the same country.

civilian *(n)* someone who is not a member of the armed forces.

civilization *or* **civilisation** *(n)*
1 a highly developed and organized society, especially one in the past. *The ancient civilizations of Greece and Rome.*
2 an advanced stage of human development, organization, and culture.

civilize *or* **civilise** civilizing civilized *(v)*
1 to improve a society, so that it is better organized and its people have a higher standard of living. **civilized** *or* **civilised** *(adj).*
2 to improve someone's manners and education.
civilized *or* **civilised** *(adj).*

Some words that begin with a "c" sound are spelt with a "k".
Some words that begin with a "ci" sound are spelt "sci", "psy", "si", or "scy".

claim claiming claimed (v)
1 to say that something belongs to you, or that you have a right to have it. *My dad claims unemployment benefit.* **claim** (n).
2 to say that something is true. *Ned claims he can beat me.* **claim** (n).

clam (n) a large shellfish with two shells that can close tightly.

clamber clambering clambered (v) to climb up or over something with difficulty.

clammy clammier clammiest (adj) unpleasantly damp. *Clammy hands.*

clamour clamouring clamoured (v) to demand something noisily. *The children all clamoured for food.* **clamour** (n).

clamp clamping clamped
1 (n) a tool for holding things firmly in place.
2 (v) to fasten something with a clamp.
3 (v) When you **clamp down** on something, you control it more firmly. *The police have clamped down on illegal parking.*

clan (n) a group of related families, especially in Scotland and Ireland.

clap clapping clapped
1 (v) to hit your hands together in order to show that you have enjoyed something. **clap** (n).
2 (n) a loud bang of thunder.

clarify clarifies clarifying clarified (v) to make something clear. **clarification** (n).

clarity (n) clearness. *Ellie writes with great clarity.*

clash clashes clashing clashed (v)
1 to fight or argue violently. **clash** (n).
2 If colours **clash**, they look unpleasant together.
3 to make a loud, crashing noise.

clasp clasping clasped
1 (v) to hold on to something firmly and tightly. *Daisy clasped Gary's hand as they approached the cave.*
2 (n) a small fastener, for example on a purse.

class classes (n)
1 a group of people or things that are similar.
2 a group of people who are taught together.
3 a group of people in society. *The middle class.*
4 (informal) attractiveness and stylishness. *That bike has class!* **classy** (adj).

classic (adj)
1 of very good quality and likely to remain popular for a long time. *A classic film.*
2 typical. *A classic example.*
3 **classics** (plural n) the languages and literature of Ancient Greece or Rome.

classical (adj)
1 in the style of Ancient Greece or Rome. *Classical architecture.*
2 traditional or accepted.
3 **classical music** (n) serious music, such as that performed by orchestras.

classify classifies classifying classified (v) to put things into groups according to their characteristics. **classification** (n).

clatter clattering clattered (v) When things **clatter**, they bang together noisily. **clatter** (n).

clause (n)
1 a group of words which contain a verb and form one part of a sentence. *The sentence, "She ran away when she saw the alien" is made up of two clauses: "She ran away" and, "when she saw the alien".*
2 one section of a formal document.

claustrophobia (klos-tro-**foh**-bee-yuh) (n) the fear of being in small, enclosed places. **claustrophobic** (adj).

claw clawing clawed
1 (n) a hard, curved nail on the foot of an animal or a bird.
2 (v) If a person, animal, or bird **claws** something or someone, they scratch at them with their nails or claws.

clay (n) a kind of earth that is baked to make bricks or pottery.

clean cleaning cleaned; cleaner cleanest
1 (adj) not dirty or not messy. **cleanly** (adv).
2 (v) to remove the dirt from something. **cleaner** (n).

cleanse cleansing cleansed (v) to make something clean or pure.

clear clearing cleared; clearer clearest
1 (adj) easy to see through. **clearly** (adv).
2 (adj) easy to understand. **clearly** (adv).
3 (v) to remove things that are covering or blocking a place. *Clear the table.* **clear** (adj).
4 (v) to jump over something without touching it. *The horse cleared all the jumps.* **clearance** (n).
5 (v) to declare that someone is not guilty of a crime.

clearing (n) an area of a forest or a wood that has been cleared of trees.

clef (n) a symbol written at the beginning of a line of music, to show the pitch of the notes. *Bass clef. Treble clef. See **notation**.

cleft (n) a split or a division.

clench clenches clenching clenched (v) to hold or squeeze something tightly.

clergy (plural n) priests in the Christian Church.

clerical (adj)
1 Clerical work is general office work, for example, filing.
2 to do with the clergy.

clerk (rhymes with dark) (n) someone who keeps records in an office, a bank, or a law court.

clever cleverer cleverest (adj)
1 able to understand things or to do things quickly and easily. **cleverness** (n), **cleverly** (adv).
2 intelligently and carefully thought out. *A clever plan.* **cleverly** (adv).

cliché (klee-shay) (n) a phrase that is used so often that it no longer has very much meaning. *"Over the moon" is a cliché.*

click clicking clicked (v)
1 to make a short, sharp sound, often with your fingers. **click** (n).
2 (informal) If an idea **clicks**, it suddenly becomes clear to you.

client (n) someone who uses the services of a professional person, such as a lawyer or an accountant.

cliff (n) a high, steep rock face on a coast.

cliffhanger (n) a story, film, etc. that is exciting because you do not know what is going to happen next.

climate (n)
1 the usual weather in a place. *A warm climate.* **climatic** (adj).
2 the general situation or mood at a particular time. *A positive economic climate.*

climax climaxes (n) the most exciting part of a story or an event, which usually happens near the end.

climb climbing climbed
1 (v) to move upwards. **climber** (n).
2 (n) an upwards movement or slope.
3 (v) to get on or off something using your hands to support and help you.

cling clinging clung (v) to hold on to something very tightly.

clinic

Left margin: a b **c** d e f g h i j k l m n o p q r s t u v w x y z

clinic *(n)* a room or building where people can go for specialist medical treatment or advice. *A health clinic.*

clip clipping clipped
1 *(v)* to trim something. *Clip the hedge.*
2 *(v)* to attach things together with a small fastener.
3 *(n)* a small metal or plastic fastener.
4 *(n)* a short piece of a film shown by itself.
5 *(v) (old-fashioned)* to hit someone. *Sid clipped me round the ear.* **clip** *(n).*

clipboard *(n)*
a board with a clip at the top, for holding papers.

clique *(rhymes with beak) (n)*
a small group of people who are very friendly with each other and do not easily accept others into their group. **cliquey** *(adj).*

cloak *(n)* a loose coat with no sleeves that you wrap around your shoulders and do up at the neck.

cloakroom *(n)*
1 a room where you can hang coats.
2 *(old-fashioned)* a bathroom.

clobber clobbering clobbered *(v) (slang)* to hit someone.

clock *(n)* an instrument that tells the time. *The picture shows the main working parts of a spring-driven clock. When you wind the clock, you tighten the mainspring which unwinds very slowly. Energy from the mainspring is transferred to the hour and minute hands by a series of wheels. The escape wheel keeps the clock ticking regularly.*

spring-driven clock

balance · hairspring · escape wheel · platform · contrate wheel · minute hand · minute hand square · intermediate wheel · hour hand · hour wheel · great wheel · centre post · barrel · mainspring

clockwise *(adv)*
in the direction that the hands of a clock move. *We ran clockwise round the track.* **clockwise** *(adj).*

clockwork *(n)*
1 a mechanism that makes things like clocks and toys work when they are wound up with a key. **clockwork** *(adj).*
2 If things go **like clockwork**, there are no problems.

clod *(n)* a lump of earth or clay.

clog clogging clogged
1 *(v)* to block something. *Some leaves had clogged the drain.*
2 *(n)* a heavy, slip-on shoe, traditionally made of wood.

wooden clogs

clone cloning cloned *(v)* to grow a plant or animal from the cells of a parent plant or animal so that it is identical to the parent. **clone** *(n).*

close closing closed; closer closest
1 *(rhymes with nose) (v)* to shut something.
2 *(rhymes with nose) (v)* to end something. *The enquiry is closed.* **close** *(n).*
3 *(rhymes with dose) (adv)* near. *Stay close to me!* **close** *(adj).*
4 *(rhymes with dose) (adj)* careful. *Keep a close watch on the children.* **closely** *(adv).*

closed-circuit television *or* **CCTV**
(n) a television system that shows things happening nearby. It is often used to watch shoppers or people in banks.

closet *(n)* a piece of furniture or a small room, used for storing things, especially clothes. *A closet can also be called a wardrobe.*

close-up *(n)* a very detailed view of something, especially a photograph taken from close to a person or thing. **close-up** *(adj).*

clot clotting clotted
1 *(v)* When a liquid, such as blood, **clots**, it becomes thicker and forms lumps. **clot** *(n).*
2 *(n) (informal)* a stupid person.

cloth *(n)*
1 material made from wool, cotton, etc.
2 a small piece of material used for cleaning.

clothes *(plural n)*
things that you wear, for example, shirts and trousers.
clothe *(v),* **clothed** *(adj).*

cloud clouding clouded
1 *(n)* a white or grey mass of water drops or ice crystals suspended in the air. *The picture shows different types of clouds and their approximate levels in the sky.* **cloudy** *(adj).*
2 *(n)* a mass of smoke or dust. **cloudy** *(adj).*
3 *(v)* If something **clouds over**, it becomes less easy to see through.

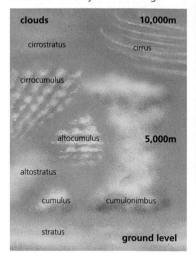

clouds — 10,000m
cirrostratus — cirrus
cirrocumulus
altocumulus — 5,000m
altostratus
cumulus — cumulonimbus
stratus
ground level

clover *(n)*
a small plant with pink or white flowers and leaves divided into three parts. *Four-leaf clovers are rare and are believed to be lucky.*

clown clowning clowned
1 *(n)* an entertainer who wears funny clothes, has a painted face, and tries to make people laugh.
2 *(v)* to do silly or foolish things in order to make people laugh. *Bart is always clowning around.* **clown** *(n).*

club *(n)*
1 a group of people who meet regularly to enjoy a common interest.
2 a place where people go late at night to drink and dance.
3 a stick with a metal head used in the game of golf. *See* **golf.**
4 a thick, heavy stick used as a weapon. **club** *(v).*
5 **clubs** *(plural n)* one of the four suits in a pack of cards, with a black three-leaf symbol.

clue *(n)*
something that helps you to find an answer to a question or a mystery.

clump clumping clumped
1 *(n)* a group of trees or other plants growing together.
2 *(v)* to walk slowly with clumsy, noisy footsteps. *Eddie clumped up the stairs and woke everyone up.*

cold

clumsy clumsier clumsiest *(adj)* careless and awkward in the way that you move or behave. **clumsiness** *(n)*, **clumsily** *(adv)*.

cluster clustering clustered *(v)* to stand or grow close together. *The flowers clustered around the tree.* **cluster** *(n)*.

clutch clutches clutching clutched
1 *(v)* to hold on to something tightly.
2 *(n)* the pedal of a car or motorcycle that you press to change gear.
3 *(n)* a number of eggs laid by a bird.

clutter cluttering cluttered *(v)* to fill up a place and make it messy. **clutter** *(n)*.

co. short for **company**.

coach coaches coaching coached
1 *(n)* a bus used for long journeys.
2 *(n)* a large carriage pulled by horses. *See* **stagecoach**.
3 *(v)* to train someone in a subject or sport. **coach** *(n)*.

coal *(n)*
1 a black rock formed from the remains of ancient plants. *Coal is mined from under the ground and burned as a fuel.*
2 **coals** *(plural n)* small pieces of burning coal.

coalfield *(n)*
an area where there is coal under the ground and where coal is mined.

coalition *(ko-al-ish-un)* *(n)*
When two or more groups, especially political parties, form a **coalition**, they join together for a common purpose.

coarse coarser coarsest *(adj)*
1 If something is **coarse**, it has a rough texture or surface. **coarseness** *(n)*, **coarsely** *(adv)*.
2 If a person is **coarse**, they are rude and have bad manners. **coarseness** *(n)*, **coarsely** *(adv)*.

coast coasting coasted
1 *(n)* the land that is next to the sea. **coastal** *(adj)*.
2 *(v)* to move along in a car or other vehicle without using any power.
3 *(v)* to make progress without much effort. *Eva coasted through her exams.*

coastguard *(n)* someone who watches the sea for ships in danger and who looks out for smugglers.

coat coating coated
1 *(n)* a piece of clothing that you wear over other clothes to keep you warm.
2 *(n)* an animal's fur or wool.
3 *(v)* to cover a surface with a thin layer of something. **coat** *(n)*.

coating *(n)* a covering of something. *The cake had a coating of chocolate.*

coat of arms coats of arms *(n)* a design in the shape of a shield that is used as the sign of a family, city, or organization.

crest
crown
mantling
helmet
supporter
arms
Royal coat of arms
motto
DIEU ET MON DROIT

coax *(kokes)* coaxes coaxing coaxed
(v) to persuade someone gently and patiently to do something.

cobbles *(plural n)* small, round stones, used in the past for making road surfaces. **cobbled** *(adj)*.

cobra *(n)* a snake with a venomous bite. Cobras can spread the skin of their neck so that it looks like a hood.

cobweb *(n)* a very fine net of sticky threads, made by a spider to catch flies and other insects.

cocaine *(n)* a powerful drug used by doctors to prevent pain. *Cocaine is strongly addictive and is used illegally by some people.*

cock *(n)*
a male bird, especially a chicken.

cockpit *(n)* the area in the front of a plane where the pilot sits.

cockroach cockroaches *(n)* a large insect which lives in warm, dark places, especially where food is stored. *See* **insect**.

cocktail *(n)*
a drink made by mixing several different kinds of drink together. Cocktails are usually alcoholic.

cocoa *(n)*
1 a brown powder made from the roasted beans of the cacao tree, used to make chocolate.
2 a hot, milky drink made with cocoa powder.

coconut *(n)* a very large nut with a hard, hairy shell and sweet, white flesh.

cocoon *(n)*
a covering made from threads or mucus, produced by some animals to protect themselves or their eggs.

lynx spider *(female)*
cocoon (contains eggs)

cod cod *(n)*
a fish that is found in the Atlantic and Arctic oceans, which has white flesh that you can eat.

code *(n)*
1 a system of words, letters, or numbers used to send secret messages. **code** *(v)*, **coded** *(adj)*.
2 a set of numbers or letters used to give information briefly.
3 a set of rules. *A safety code.*
4 special instructions to a computer that make it work in a certain way.

coeducation *(n)* the system of teaching boys and girls together in the same school. **coeducational** *(adj)*.

coerce *(ko-erss)* coercing coerced *(v)* to force someone to do something. **coercion** *(n)*.

coffee *(n)*
1 a brown powder made from the roasted and ground beans of the coffee shrub.
2 a hot drink made with coffee powder.

coffin *(n)* a box which contains the body of a dead person.

cog *(n)*
1 one of the teeth on the edge of a wheel that turns machinery.
2 **cogwheel** *(n)* a wheel with teeth that turns machinery. *See* **gear**.

coherent *(ko-hear-unt)* *(adj)* clear and logical. *A coherent argument.*

coil coiling coiled *(v)*
1 to wind something round and round into a series of loops. *The sailor coiled the rope neatly.* **coil** *(n)*.
2 to form loops. *The snake coiled around Penny's leg.*

coin coining coined
1 *(n)* a piece of money in the form of a metal disc. **coinage** *(n)*.
2 *(v)* to invent a new word or a new meaning of a word. **coinage** *(n)*.

Ancient Chinese coins

coincide *(ko-in-side)* coinciding coincided *(v)* If two things **coincide**, they happen at the same time.

coincidence *(ko-in-sid-enss)* *(n)* a chance happening or meeting. **coincidental** *(adj)*, **coincidentally** *(adv)*.

colander *(n)* a bowl with holes in it, used for draining liquid off food, such as vegetables or pasta.

cold colder coldest
1 *(adj)* having a low temperature. **cold** *(n)*, **coldness** *(n)*.
2 *(adj)* unfriendly. **coldly** *(adv)*.
3 *(n)* a common, mild illness that causes sneezing, a sore throat, and sometimes a slight fever.

Some words that begin with a "c" sound are spelt with a "k".

cold-blooded (adj)
1 Cold-blooded animals have body temperatures that change according to the temperature of their surroundings. *Reptiles and fish are cold-blooded.*
2 A **cold-blooded** act is done deliberately and cruelly.

collaborate
collaborating collaborated (v)
to work with someone and help them to do something. collaboration (n), collaborator (n).

collage (kol-*arj*) (n)
a picture made by sticking different things on to a surface, for example sticking pieces of cloth onto paper.

collapse collapsing collapsed (v)
1 to fall down suddenly from weakness or illness. collapse (n).
2 to fail suddenly and completely. *The company collapsed after only six months.* collapse (n).

collar collaring collared
1 (n) the part of a shirt, blouse, coat, etc. which fits round your neck and is usually folded down.
2 (n) a thin band of leather worn round the neck of a dog or a cat.
3 (v) (informal) to catch someone, because you want to talk to them.

colleague (n)
someone who works with you.

collect collecting collected (v)
1 to gather things together.
2 to fetch someone or something from another place.

collection (n)
1 a group of things gathered over a long time. *A shell collection.*
2 If you hold a **collection** for something, you take money for it.

college (n)
a place where students can continue to study after they have left school.

collide colliding collided (v)
to crash into something violently, often at high speed. collision (n).

colloquial (kol-oh-kwee-al) (adj)
Colloquial language is used in everyday conversation, but not usually in written English.

colon (n)
1 the punctuation mark (:) used to introduce a list of things. *See page 5.*
2 the part of your large intestine where remaining food is broken down by bacteria and has water removed from it.

colonel (n)
an army officer in command of a regiment of soldiers.

colony colonies (n)
1 a country that has been settled in by people from another country and is controlled by that country. colonial (adj).
2 a large group of insects that live together. *A colony of ants.*

colossal (adj) extremely large.

colour colouring coloured
1 (n) When you say what **colour** something is, you say whether it is red, yellow, black, etc. colourful (adj), colourless (adj).
2 (v) to make something a certain colour using pens, paint, dye, etc.
3 (v) to influence your opinion about something. *Mum's hatred of noise colours her view of parties.*
4 (adj) If you are colour-blind, you are unable to see the difference between certain colours. *You may not be able to see the number in this pattern if you are colour-blind.*

colour blindness test

colt (n) a young male horse.

column (n)
1 a tall, upright pillar that helps to support a building or a statue. *The picture below shows three styles of Roman column.*
2 a row of figures or words running down a page.
3 a piece of writing by the same person, or on the same subject, that appears regularly in a newspaper or magazine. columnist (n).

Roman columns

Doric   Ionic   Corinthian

coma (n)
a state of deep unconsciousness from which it is very hard to wake up.

comb combing combed
1 (n) a flat piece of metal or plastic with a row of teeth used for making you hair smooth and tidy.
2 (v) to use a comb to make your hair smooth and tidy.
3 (v) to search a place thoroughly.

combat combating combated
1 (v) to fight against something. *Regular brushing helps combat tooth decay.*
2 (n) fighting between people or armies. combatant (n).

combine
combining combined (v)
1 to join or mix two or more things together. combination (n)
2 combine harvester (n) see **harvest**.

combustion (n)
the process of catching fire and burning. combust (v).

come coming came come (v)
1 to move towards a place. *Louise came into the garden.*
2 to arrive. *Barney was waiting for his friends to come.*
3 If you **come from** a particular place, you were born in that place.
4 If something **comes about**, it happens.
5 If you **come across** something, you find it by chance.
6 If you **come round**, you become conscious again, or you start to accept someone else's ideas.

comedian (n)
an entertainer who tells jokes and funny stories to make people laugh.

comedy comedies (n)
1 a funny play or film.
2 anything that makes people laugh. *Marty's first attempt at skating was pure comedy!*

comet (n)
an object that travels around the Sun and leaves a trail of light behind it.

comfort comforting comforted
1 (v) to make someone feel less worried or upset. *We comforted the lost child.* comforting (adj), comfortingly (adv).
2 (n) the feeling of being relaxed and free from pain or worries.
3 (n) a luxury that makes your life more pleasant and enjoyable. *Home comforts.*

comfortable (adj)
1 If you are **comfortable**, you feel relaxed in your body or your mind. comfortably (adv).
2 If something is **comfortable**, it allows you to relax and feel pleasure. *A comfortable chair.*

comic
1 (n) a magazine containing stories told with pictures.
2 (n) someone who tells jokes and funny stories.
3 (adj) funny or amusing. comical (adj).

comma (n) the punctuation mark (,) used for separating different parts of a sentence or different words in a list. *See page 5.*

a b **c** d e f g h i j k l m n o p q r s t u v w x y z

command
commanding commanded
1 *(v)* to order someone to do something. command *(n)*.
2 *(v)* to have control over a group of people. commander *(n)*.
3 *(n)* Your command of something is your knowledge of it and your skill in using it.

commemorate commemorating commemorated *(v)* to do something special to remember an important person or event. commemoration *(n)*, commemorative *(adj)*.

commence commencing commenced *(v)* to begin something. commencement *(n)*.

commend commending commended *(v)* to say that someone has done something very well. *The mayor commended our courage.* commendation *(n)*, commendable *(adj)*.

comment commenting commented *(v)* If you comment on something, you give an explanation or an opinion about it. comment *(n)*.

commentary commentaries *(n)*
1 a description and comments about an event. *Political commentary.* commentator *(n)*, commentate *(v)*.
2 a description of an event as it is happening, often broadcast on television or radio. *A race commentary.* commentator *(n)*, commentate *(v)*.

commerce *(n)* the buying and selling of goods in order to make money.

commercial
1 *(adj)* to do with buying and selling goods. *Commercial activities.*
2 *(adj)* having profit as a main aim. *A commercial scheme.*
3 *(n)* a television or radio advertisement.

commercialized or
commercialised *(adj)*
If something is commercialized, it has been changed, usually for the worse, in order to make a profit. commercialization *(n)*.

commiserate commiserating commiserated *(v)* to share someone else's sadness or disappointment. *We commiserated with Alan over his bad luck.* commiserations *(plural n)*.

commit committing committed *(v)*
1 to do something wrong or illegal. *To commit murder.*
2 If you commit yourself to something, you promise that you will do it or support it. commitment *(n)*, committed *(adj)*.

committee *(n)* a group of people chosen to discuss things and make decisions for a larger group.

commodity commodities *(n)* a product that is bought and sold.

common
commoner commonest
1 *(adj)* existing in large numbers.
2 *(adj)* happening often. *Migraines are a common occurance.*
3 *(adj)* ordinary and not special.
4 *(adj)* shared by two or more people or things. *This feature is common to both cars.*
5 common sense *(n)* the ability to think and behave sensibly.
6 The Commons *(plural n)* the House of Commons, the lower house of the British Parliament, whose members are elected.

commonplace *(adj)*
If something is commonplace, it happens frequently. *Traffic jams in city centres are commonplace events.*

Commonwealth *(n)*
1 The Commonwealth
an association of countries all over the world that used to be ruled by Britain.
2 a country made up of several self-governing states that are controlled by a central government. *The Commonwealth of Australia.*

commotion *(n)*
a lot of noisy, excited activity.

communal *(adj)*
shared by several people. *A communal bathroom.* communally *(adv)*.

commune *(n)*
a group of people who live together and share things with each other.

communicate
communicating communicated *(v)* to share information, ideas, or feelings with another person by talking, writing, etc. communication *(n)*, communicative *(adj)*.

Communion *(n)* a Christian service in which people eat bread and drink wine in memory of the death and resurrection of Jesus Christ.

communiqué *(kom-yoon-ee-kay)* *(n)* an official report or statement.

communism *(n)*
a way of organizing a country so that all the land, houses, factories, etc. belong to the state, and the profits are shared among everyone. communist *(n)*, communist *(adj)*.

community communities *(n)* a group of people who live in the same area or who have something in common with each other.

commuter *(n)* someone who travels to work each day, usually by car or train. commute *(v)*.

compact
1 *(kom-pakt)* *(adj)* cleverly designed to take up very little space.
2 *(kom-pakt)* *(n)* a small, flat case containing face powder and a mirror.

compact disc or **CD** *(n)*
a disc with music or information stored on it. *The picture below shows the thin metal layer inside the plastic disc, with its pattern of pits and lands, which is read by a laser beam as the disc rotates.*

compact disc

compact disc
(magnified view from below)

land
pit
laser beam
aluminium layer

companion *(n)* someone you spend time with, either through friendship or by chance.

company companies *(n)*
1 a group of people who work together to produce or sell goods or services.
2 a group of actors or dancers who work together.
3 one or more guests. *We have company this weekend.*
4 companionship. *I enjoyed her company yesterday.*
5 an army unit, usually under the command of a captain.

comparative *(adj)*
1 judged against other similar things. *This year's play was a comparative success.* comparatively *(adv)*.
2 Comparative adjectives and adverbs are used when you compare two things or actions. *"Older" is the comparative of "old"; "more quickly" is the comparative of "quickly".* comparative *(n)*.

compare comparing compared *(v)*
1 to judge one thing against another and notice similarities and differences. comparison *(n)*.
2 to be as good as something or somebody else. *Our team compares with any in the area.*

compartment *(n)*
1 one of the small areas into which a railway carriage is divided.
2 a separate part of a container, used for keeping certain things.

a b c d e f k l m n o p q r s t u v w x y z

compass

compass compasses *(n)*
1 an instrument for finding directions, with a magnetic needle that always points north. *You can use a compass like the one shown below to follow a route on a map.*
2 **compasses** *(plural n)* an instrument used for drawing circles, which has two legs connected by a flexible joint. *See* **geometry**.

compass

liquid-filled housing
bezel (movable ring)
orienteering lines
base plate
magnifying lens

lanyard (carrying cord)
magnetic needle
centimetre measure
inch measure

direction-of-travel arrow

compassion *(n)* a deep feeling of sympathy for people who are suffering. **compassionate** *(adj)*, **compassionately** *(adv)*.

compatible *(adj)* If people or objects are **compatible**, they can live together or be used together without difficulty. **compatibility** *(n)*.

compel compelling compelled *(v)* to make someone do something by giving them orders or by using force.

compensate compensating compensated *(v)* to make up for something. *Nothing can compensate for my suffering.* **compensation** *(n)*.

competent *(adj)* If you are **competent** at something, you have the skill or ability to do it well. **competence** *(n)*, **competently** *(adv)*.

competition *(n)*
1 an event in which two or more people try to do something as well as they can, to see who is the best. **competitor** *(n)*, **compete** *(v)*.
2 a situation in which two or more people are trying to get the same thing. *There was a lot of competition for places at the school.* **compete** *(v)*.

competitive *(adj)*
1 A **competitive** sport or game is one where the players try to win.
2 very eager to win.
3 If a shop offers **competitive** prices, its prices are at least as low as in most other shops.

compile compiling compiled *(v)* to write a book or a report by bringing together many different pieces of information. **compilation** *(n)*.

complain complaining complained *(v)* to say that you are unhappy about something.

complaint *(n)*
1 a statement saying that you are unhappy about something.
2 an illness. *A heart complaint.*

complete completing completed
1 *(adj)* If something is **complete**, it has all the parts that are needed or wanted. *A complete pack of cards.*
2 *(v)* to finish something. **completion** *(n)*.
3 *(adj)* in every way. *The news was a complete surprise.* **completely** *(adv)*.

complex complexes
1 *(adj)* very complicated. **complexity** *(n)*.
2 *(n)* a set of strong feelings that you cannot control or forget about, and that causes problems for you. *Nathan has a complex about being short.*
3 *(n)* a group of buildings that are close together and are used for a particular purpose. *A leisure complex.*

complexion *(n)* the colour and look of the skin on your face.

complicated *(adj)* Something that is **complicated** contains lots of different parts or ideas and so can be difficult to use or understand. **complication** *(n)*, **complicate** *(v)*.

compliment complimenting complimented *(v)* When you **compliment** someone, you tell them that you admire them or think that they have done something well. **compliment** *(n)*.

complimentary *(adj)*
1 If someone is **complimentary** about a person or thing, they praise them.
2 free, or without cost. *Complimentary tickets.*

component *(n)* a part of a machine or system.

compose composing composed
1 *(v)* to write a piece of music, a poem, etc. **composer** *(n)*.

2 *(v)* If something is **composed of** certain things, it is made from those things.

compost *(n)* a mixture of rotted plants that is added to soil to make it richer.

comprehension *(n)*
1 understanding. **comprehend** *(v)*.
2 a test in which you read or listen to a text and then answer questions about it, to show how well you have understood it.

comprehensive
1 *(n)* In Britain, a **comprehensive** is a secondary school where pupils of all abilities are taught together.
2 *(adj)* including everything that is necessary. *A comprehensive list.* **comprehensively** *(adv)*.

compress compresses compressing compressed *(v)* to press or squeeze something so that it will fit into a small space. **compression** *(n)*.

compromise compromising compromised
1 *(v)* to agree to accept something that is not exactly what you wanted. **compromise** *(n)*.
2 *(n)* an agreement that is half way between two opposite views.

compulsory *(adj)* If something is **compulsory**, there is a law or rule that says you must do it.

computer *(n)* a machine that can store large amounts of information and do very quick and complicated calculations. **computing** *(n)*.

computer-aided design or **CAD** *(n)* plans and drawings made using a computer, especially product designs or architectural drawings.

Wolfgang Amadeus Mozart (1756-1791) *began composing music at the age of five. He is shown here playing the piano.*

comrade (n)
1 (old-fashioned) a good
friend. **comradeship** (n).
2 a companion in battle.
3 a member of the same trade
union or left-wing political group.

concave (adj)
curved inwards, like the inside
surface of a dish. See **lens**.

conceal
concealing concealed (v)
to hide something. **concealment** (n).

concede
conceding conceded (v)
to admit something unwillingly.
*Eventually, Natalie conceded
that she was wrong.*

conceited (adj)
If you are **conceited**, you are
too proud of yourself and of
what you can do. **conceit** (n).

conceive
conceiving conceived (v)
1 to form an idea in your mind.
Charlie conceived a cunning plan.
2 to become pregnant.

concentrate
concentrating concentrated (v)
1 to focus your thoughts or attention
on something. **concentration** (n).
2 to make a liquid thicker and
stronger by removing water from it.
concentrate (n), **concentration** (n),
concentrated (adj).

concentric (adj)
Concentric circles all have
their centres at the same point.

concept (n)
a general idea or understanding of
something. *Lea has a very vague
concept of history.* **conceptual** (adj).

conception (n)
1 a general idea that you have
formed in your mind.
2 the act of becoming pregnant.

concern
concerning concerned (v)
1 to involve you or to be
of interest to you. *These
plans concern you.* **concern** (n).
2 to be about a particular
subject. *This project concerns
local history.* **concerning** (prep).

concerned (adj)
If you are **concerned** about
something, you are anxious and
worried about it. **concern** (n).

concert
1 (n) a performance given
by musicians or singers.
2 (adj) used for concerts.
A concert hall.

concerto concertos or concerti (n)
a piece of music for one or more solo
instruments playing with an orchestra.

concession (n)
1 an agreement to allow something
that would not normally be permitted.
2 a reduction in price for particular
types of people. *The theatre
offers concessions to students.*

concise (adj) saying a lot in
a few words. **concisely** (adv).

conclude
concluding concluded (v)
1 to decide that something is true
because of the facts that you
have. *I concluded that Boris must have
stolen the jewels.* **conclusion** (n).
2 to finish or end something.
conclusion (n).

concoct
concocting concocted (v)
1 to create something by
mixing several different things
together. **concoction** (n).
2 If you **concoct** an excuse
or an plan, you invent it.

concrete
1 (n) a building material made from
a mixture of sand, small stones,
cement, and water. **concrete** (v).
2 (adj) real or definite. *The detectives
need some concrete evidence.*

concussion (n)
unconsciousness, dizziness, or
sickness caused by a heavy blow
to your head. **concussed** (adj).

condemn
condemning condemned (v)
1 to say very strongly that you
do not approve of something.
*Mahatma Gandhi condemned
all violence.* **condemnation** (n).
2 to force someone to suffer
something unpleasant. *The
murderer was condemned to death.*

condense
condensing condensed (v)
1 When a gas **condenses**, it turns
into a liquid, usually as a result
of cooling. **condensation** (n).
2 to make a piece of writing shorter
by taking out unnecessary parts.

condescending (adj)
If you are **condescending**, you
behave as though you are better or
more important than other people.
condescension (n), **condescend** (v).

condition
conditioning conditioned
1 (n) the general state of a
person, an animal, or a thing.
My house is in good condition.

2 (n) a medical problem that
continues over a long period
of time. *A heart condition.*
3 (n) something that is needed
before another thing can
happen or be allowed. *One
condition of having a bike
is that you always lock it up.*
4 (v) to train someone to believe
certain things or to behave in
certain ways. **conditioning** (n).

conditional (adj)
depending on something else.
*I have a conditional place on
the course.* **conditionally** (adv).

conditioner (n) a thick liquid that
you rub into your hair after washing
it, to make it strong and shiny.

condolence (n)
an expression of sympathy for
a person who is upset because
a friend or relative has just died.

condom (n)
a thin rubber covering that a man
wears on his penis as a contraceptive.

conduct conducting conducted
1 (kon-dukt) (v) to organize
something and carry it out.
*The police conducted an
enquiry into the robbery.*
2 (kon-dukt) (v) to stand in front of
a group of musicians, especially an
orchestra, and direct their playing.
3 (kon-dukt) (v) If something
conducts heat, electricity, or
sound, it allows them to pass
through it. *Copper conducts
electricity.* **conduction** (n).
4 (kon-dukt) (n) behaviour.

conductor (n)
1 someone who stands in
front of a group of musicians
and directs their playing.
2 a substance that allows heat,
electricity, or sound to travel through
it. *Metal is a good conductor of heat.*
3 (old-fashioned) someone
who collects bus or train fares.

cone (n)
1 an object or shape with a
round base and a point at the
top. **conical** (adj). See **shape**.
2 the hard, woody fruit
of a pine or fir tree.

confectionery (n) sweets and
chocolates. **confectioner** (n).

conference (n) a formal meeting
for discussing ideas and opinions.

confess confesses
confessing confessed (v)
to admit that you have done
something wrong. **confession** (n).

confetti

confetti *(plural n)* small pieces of coloured paper that are thrown over the bride and groom after a wedding.

confide confiding confided *(v)* If you **confide in** someone, you tell them a secret because you can trust them not to tell anyone else.

confident *(adj)*
1 having a strong belief in your own abilities. *Ella is a confident swimmer.* **confidence** *(n)*, **confidently** *(adv)*.
2 certain that things will happen in the way you want. **confidence** *(n)*, **confidently** *(adv)*.

confidential *(adj)* secret. **confidentially** *(adv)*.

confirm confirming confirmed *(v)*
1 to say that something is definitely true or will definitely happen. **confirmation** *(n)*.
2 When someone is **confirmed**, they are accepted as a full member of the Christian Church in a special ceremony. **confirmation** *(n)*.

confiscate confiscating confiscated *(v)* to take something away from someone as a punishment or because that thing is not allowed. **confiscation** *(n)*.

conflict *(kon-flikt)* conflicting conflicted *(n)*
1 a serious disagreement or difference. **conflict** *(kon-flikt)* *(v)*
2 a war or time of fighting.

conform conforming conformed *(v)*
1 If you **conform**, you behave in the same way as everyone else, or in a way that is expected of you. **conformist** *(n)*, **conformity** *(n)*.
2 If something **conforms** to a rule or law, it does what the rule or law requires. *All these machines conform to strict safety regulations.*

confront confronting confronted *(v)*
1 to meet or face someone in a threatening or accusing way. **confrontation** *(n)*.
2 If a problem **confronts** you, you have to deal with it.

confuse confusing confused *(v)*
1 If someone or something **confuses** you, you do not understand them or know what to do. **confusion** *(n)*, **confusing** *(adj)*.
2 to mistake one thing for another. *I confused Alexis with his twin brother.* **confusion** *(n)*, **confused** *(adj)*.

congeal congealing congealed *(v)* When a liquid **congeals**, it becomes thick or solid.

congested *(adj)* blocked up and not allowing movement. *Congested roads. Congested sinuses.* **congestion** *(n)*.

congratulate congratulating congratulated *(v)* to tell someone that you are pleased because something good has happened to them or they have done something well. **congratulations** *(plural n)*.

congregation *(n)* a group of people gathered together for worship.

Congress *(n)* the law-making body of a country, such as the USA. **Congressional** *(adj)*.

conifer *(n)* an evergreen tree that produces cones. **coniferous** *(adj)*.

conjunction *(n)* a word that connects two parts of a sentence or phrase. *"And", "but", and "if" are all conjunctions.* See page 3.

conjurer or **conjuror** *(n)* someone who performs magic tricks to entertain people. **conjuring** *(n)*.

conker *(n)* a hard and shiny brown nut from the horse chestnut tree.

connect connecting connected *(v)* to join together two or more things.

connection *(n)*
1 a link between objects or ideas.
2 a train or bus arranged so that people getting off other trains or buses can use it to continue their journey.

connoisseur *(kon-er-ser)* *(n)* someone who knows a lot about a subject and appreciates things that are of good quality.

conquer conquering conquered *(v)* to defeat an enemy and take control of them by force. **conqueror** *(n)*.

conscience *(kon-shenss)* *(n)* your knowledge of what is right and wrong, which makes you feel guilty when you do something wrong.

conscientious *(con-shee-en-shuss)* *(adj)*
1 If you are **conscientious**, you make sure that you do things well and thoroughly. **conscientiously** *(adv)*.
2 **conscientious objector** *(n)* someone who refuses to fight in a war because they believe that it is wrong to fight and kill.

conscious *(adj)*
1 awake and able to see, hear, think, etc. **consciousness** *(n)*.
2 aware of something. *I slowly became conscious that everyone was looking at me.* **consciousness** *(n)*.
3 deliberate. *I've made a conscious effort to improve.* **consciously** *(adv)*.

consecutive *(adj)* happening or following one after the other. *Marcia was away for four consecutive days.* **consecutively** *(adv)*.

consent consenting consented *(v)* If you **consent** to something, you agree to it. **consent** *(n)*.

consequence *(n)* the result of an action. **consequent** *(adj)*, **consequently** *(adv)*.

conservation *(n)* the protection of nature, wildlife, art, and other valuable things. **conservationist** *(n)*.

conservative
1 *(adj)* moderate, cautious, and not extreme. *Adam has a conservative dress sense.* **conservatively** *(adv)*.
2 **Conservative Party** *(n)* one of the main political parties in Britain, promoting private enterprise and competition.

conservatory conservatories *(n)* a glass room attached to a house, used for growing plants.

consider considering considered *(v)*
1 to think about something carefully before deciding what to do.
2 to believe that something is true. *Darrell considers school to be a waste of time!*
3 to take something into account. *We must consider Celia's feelings.*

considerable *(adj)* fairly large. *A considerable amount of money.* **considerably** *(adv)*.

considerate *(adj)* If you are **considerate**, you think about other people's needs and feelings. **considerately** *(adv)*.

consideration *(n)*
1 careful thought that you give to something before making a decision.
2 a fact that needs to be taken into account before a decision can be made.
3 If you **show consideration**, you care about other people's needs and feelings. **considerate** *(adj)*.

considering *(conj)* taking into account certain things. *You got here very quickly, considering the weather.* **considering** *(prep)*.

consignment *(n)* a number of things that are delivered together.

consist consisting consisted *(v)* If something **consists** of different things, it is made up of those things.

consistent *(adj)* always behaving in the same way or supporting the same principles. **consistency** *(n)*, **consistently** *(adv)*.

console consoling consoled
1 (*kon-sole*) (*v*) to comfort someone in a time of loss, grief, or sadness. **consolation** (*kon-sol-ay-shun*) (*n*).
2 (*kon-sole*) (*n*) an electronic device connected to a television, on which you can play games.
3 **handheld games console** (*n*) a battery-powered, portable games device with its own screen.

consonant (*n*) any of the letters in the alphabet except the five vowels.

conspicuous (*adj*) Something that is **conspicuous** stands out and can be seen easily. **conspicuously** (*adv*).

conspiracy conspiracies (*n*) a secret, illegal plan made by two or more people. **conspirator** (*n*), **conspire** (*v*), **conspiratorial** (*adj*).

constable (*n*) a British police officer of the lowest rank.

constant (*adj*)
1 happening all the time and never stopping. *The traffic creates a constant noise.* **constantly** (*adv*).
2 staying at the same rate or level all the time. *A constant speed.*
3 If someone is **constant**, they continue to support a person or an idea without ever changing their mind. **constancy** (*n*).

constellation (*n*) a group of stars that form a shape or pattern.

constipated (*adj*)
If you are **constipated**, you find it hard to pass solids from your body frequently or easily. **constipation** (*n*).

constituency constituencies (*n*) an area of a country represented by a Member of Parliament.

constitution (*n*)
1 the written or unwritten system of laws in a country that states the rights of the people and the powers of the government. **constitutional** (*adj*).
2 your general health and strength.

constraint (*n*)
something that limits what you are able or allowed to do. **constrain** (*v*).

construct
constructing constructed (*v*) to build or make something. **construction** (*n*).

constructive (*adj*)
helpful and useful. *Constructive criticism.* **constructively** (*adv*).

consult consulting consulted (*v*)
1 to go to a person for advice. *If you feel ill, you should consult a doctor.* **consultation** (*n*).
2 If you **consult** a book or a map, you use it to find information.

consultant (*n*)
1 a senior doctor with specialist knowledge in one area of medicine.
2 a person with a lot of knowledge and experience of something, who gives professional advice to others.

consume consuming consumed (*v*)
1 to eat or drink something.
2 to use something up. **consumption** (*n*).
3 If a fire **consumes** something, it destroys it.

consumer (*n*) someone who buys goods, eats food, or uses services.

contact contacting contacted
1 (*n*) When things are in **contact**, they touch each other.
2 (*n*) If you are in **contact with** someone, you write or talk to them.
3 (*v*) to get in touch with someone.

contact lens contact lenses (*n*) a small plastic lens that fits closely over your eyeball to improve your eyesight.

contagious (*adj*)
A **contagious** disease can be caught by being near someone or something already infected with it.

contain
containing contained (*v*)
1 When an object **contains** something, it holds that thing inside itself or that thing forms a part of it. *The chest contained the treasure. This book contains many stories.* **container** (*n*).
2 to keep an emotion or reaction under control. *I tried to contain my laughter.*

contaminated (*adj*) If something is **contaminated**, it has been made dirty or impure. *Contaminated drinking water.* **contamination** (*n*).

contemplate
contemplating contemplated (*v*)
1 to think seriously about something. *Mohammed contemplated leaving college.* **contemplation** (*n*).
2 to look at something thoughtfully. *Annabelle contemplated the view.* **contemplation** (*n*).

contemporary contemporaries
1 (*adj*) up-to-date or modern.
2 (*adj*) If something is **contemporary** with something else, they both occurred at around the same time.
3 (*n*) a person of about the same age as you. *A contemporary of mine from school.*

contempt (*n*) a total lack of respect. **contemptuous** (*adj*).

contend contending contended (*v*)
1 to compete. *The two teams contended for the cup.* **contender** (*n*).

2 to try to deal with a difficulty. *Lois has had a lot to contend with since her parents split up.*

content
contenting contented
1 (*adj*) happy and satisfied. **contented** (*adj*), **contentedly** (*adv*).
2 (*v*) If you **content yourself** with something, you are satisfied with it.

contents (*plural n*)
the things that are inside something or form part of something.

contest contesting contested
1 (*kon-test*) (*n*) a competition.
2 (*kon-test*) (*v*) to compete or fight for something. **contestant** (*n*).
3 (*kon-test*) (*v*) to claim that something is wrong. *Thomas contested the judges' decision.*

context (*n*)
1 The **context** of a word, phrase, or text is the information around it which helps you to understand its meaning.
2 If you put an event or an action in **context**, you take into account all the things that affect it.

continent (*n*)
1 one of the seven large land masses of the Earth. **continental** (*adj*).
2 **the Continent** the mainland of Europe. **continental** (*adj*).

continents

continual (*adj*) happening again and again. **continually** (*adv*).

continue continuing continued (*v*) to go on doing something. **continuation** (*n*).

continuous (*adj*) When something is **continuous,** it does not stop. *A continuous line.* **continuously** (*adv*).

contort contorting contorted (*v*) to twist something out of its usual shape. **contortion** (*n*), **contorted** (*adj*).

contour (*n*)
1 an outline.
2 a line joining points of equal height on a map.

contraceptive (*n*)
a device or drug that prevents a woman from becoming pregnant. **contraception** (*n*).

a b c d e f g h i j k l m n o p q r s t u v w x y z

contract contracting contracted
1 (kon-*trakt*) (v) to become smaller.
2 (kon-*trakt*) (n) a legal agreement between people or companies, stating the terms on which one will work for the other or sell to the other.

contradict
contradicting contradicted (v) to say the opposite of what someone else has said. **contradiction** (n).

contraption (n) a strange and complicated-looking machine.

contrary (adj)
1 (kon-*truh-ree*) opposite.
2 (kon-*trair-ee*) awkward and difficult.

contrast (kon-*trast*)
contrasting contrasted (v)
1 to be very different from something else. **contrast** (kon-*trast*) (n).
2 to identify the difference between things.

contribute
contributing contributed (v)
1 to give help or money to a person or an organization. **contribution** (n), **contributor** (n).
2 to write for a magazine or newspaper. **contribution** (n), **contributor** (n).

control controlling controlled
1 (v) to make something or someone do what you want. **control** (n).
2 (plural n) The **controls** of a machine are the levers and switches which make it work.

controversial (adj) If something is controversial, it causes a lot of argument. **controversy** (n).

convalescence (n) a time during which someone recovers from an illness. **convalesce** (v), **convalescent** (adj), **convalescent** (n).

convection (n) the movement of heat through liquids and gases. *The diagram shows how convection currents are created when a liquid is heated.*

convection currents warm water expands and rises

cool water contracts and falls — heat

convenience
1 (n) something which is useful and easy to use. *This house has been fitted with modern conveniences.*
2 **convenience foods** (plural n) foods that are quick and easy to prepare, such as frozen meals.
3 **public conveniences** (plural n) public toilets.

convenient (adj) If something is **convenient**, it is useful or easy to use. **conveniently** (adv).

convent (n)
1 a building where nuns live and work.
2 a school for girls, run by nuns.

conventional (adj) A conventional person does things in a traditional or accepted way. **conventionally** (adv).

conversation (n) If you hold a conversation with someone, you talk with them for a while. **converse** (v).

convert converting converted (v) to make something into something else. *We've converted our loft into a bedroom.* **conversion** (n).

convex (adj) curving outwards, like the side of a ball. *See* **lens**.

conveyor belt (n) a moving belt that carries objects in a factory.

convict convicting convicted
1 (kon-*vikt*) (v) to prove that someone is guilty of a crime.
2 (kon-*vikt*) (n) someone who is in prison because they have committed a crime.

conviction (n)
1 a strong belief in something.
2 If you have a **conviction** for a crime, you have been found guilty of committing it.

convince
convincing convinced (v) If you convince somebody, you make them believe you. **convincing** (adj), **convincingly** (adv).

convoy (n) a group of trucks or other vehicles travelling together.

cook cooking cooked
1 (v) to prepare and heat food for a meal. **cooking** (n).
2 (n) someone whose job is to prepare food.

cookie (n)
1 a biscuit that is round and often has chocolate chips in it.
2 a piece of information left on your computer after you have been using a website. Cookies are usually used to store information about the choices you have made.

cool
cooling cooled; cooler coolest
1 (adj) quite cold. **coolness** (n).
2 (adj) (informal) great, interesting, or fashionable. *Cool clothes.*
3 (v) to lower the temperature of something.
4 (adj) unfriendly and distant. **coolly** (adv).

co-operate
co-operating co-operated (v) to work together. **co-operation** (n).

co-operative (adj) If you are co-operative, you work well with other people. **co-operativeness** (n).

co-ordinate
co-ordinating co-ordinated
1 (v) to organize activities or people so that they all work together. **co-ordination** (n), **co-ordinator** (n).
2 (n) a number used to show the position of a point on a line or map.

co-ordinated (adj)
1 If you are **well co-ordinated**, you have good control over how you move your arms and legs.
2 Co-ordinated clothes go well together.

cop (n) (informal) a policeman.

cope coping coped (v) to deal with something successfully.

copper (n)
1 a reddish-brown metal. *See* **mineral**.
2 a reddish-brown colour. **copper** (adj), **coppery** (adj).

copy copies copying copied
1 (v) to do the same as someone else.
2 (n) A **copy** is made to look or sound exactly the same as something else.
3 (v) to make a copy of something.

copyright (n) If someone owns the **copyright** in a book, song, etc., people must ask for their permission before they copy or perform them.

coral (singular n) sea creatures, closely related to sea anemones, whose skeletons remain after they die. Coral can be hard or soft. *The picture shows two kinds of soft coral.*

coral
sea fan
brain coral

cord (n) a length of string or rope.

cordial
1 (n) a sweet, fruit drink. *Lime cordial.*
2 (adj) friendly. **cordially** (adv).

cordon (n) a line of people or objects used to control crowds. *A police cordon blocked the street.*

core (n) the centre of something, such as the Earth or an apple.

cork (n) soft bark used as a stopper in bottles or to make mats, tiles, etc.

corkscrew
1 (n) a tool used for pulling corks out of bottles.
2 (adj) spiralling or turning in circles. *Corkscrew curls.*

Some words that begin with a "c" sound are spelt with a "k".

count

corn (n)
1 the grain of crops such as wheat or barley.
2 a small patch of hard skin on your foot.

corner cornering cornered
1 (n) the place where two sides of something meet. *A square has four corners.*
2 (v) to get a person or animal into a situation where they are trapped.

cornet (n)
1 a brass musical instrument similar to a trumpet. *See* **brass**.
2 a cone-shaped wafer with a scoop of ice-cream on top.

corn on the cob (n)
a stalk of juicy, yellow seeds eaten as a vegetable. *See* **vegetable**.

coronary coronaries
1 (adj) to do with the heart.
2 (n) a heart attack.

coronation (n) the ceremony when a king or queen is crowned.

coroner (n) If someone dies suddenly or in an unnatural way, a **coroner** investigates their death.

corporal (n)
a soldier of fairly low rank.

corporal punishment (n)
physical punishment, such as beating.

corporation (n)
a group of people who work together to run a company or town council.

corpse (n) a dead body.

corpuscle (kor-puss-ul) (n) a red or white blood cell. *See* **blood**.

correct correcting corrected
1 (adj) true, or right. **correctly** (adv).
2 (v) to make something right. **correction** (n).

correspond corresponding corresponded (v)
1 If two things **correspond**, they match in some way. **correspondence** (n).
2 When you **correspond** with someone, you write messages to each other. **correspondence** (n).

correspondent (n)
1 someone who writes messages.
2 someone who reports for television, radio, or newspapers about a special subject or place.

corridor (n)
a long passage in a building or train.

corrode corroding corroded (v)
to eat away at something. *Water corrodes metal and makes it rust.* **corrosion** (n), **corrosive** (adj).

corrugated (adj)
ridged or rippled. *Corrugated iron.*

corrupt corrupting corrupted
1 (v) to make someone bad or dishonest. **corrupt** (adj).
2 (adj) If computer data is **corrupt**, it contains errors which make it useless. **corrupt** (v).

cosmetic
1 **cosmetics** (plural n) beauty products such as lipstick or mascara.
2 (adj) changing the way that a person or a thing looks. *Cosmetic surgery.*

cosmic (adj) to do with the universe. *Cosmic laws.* **cosmically** (adv).

cosmopolitan (adj)
1 If you are **cosmopolitan,** you feel at home in more than one country.
2 containing elements of cultures from all around the world. *London is a cosmopolitan city.*

cosmos (n) the universe.

cost costing cost (v)
1 to have a certain price. **cost** (n).
2 to make someone give up or lose something. *The battle cost many lives.* **cost** (n).

co-star (n) an actor who appears in a film with another actor of equal importance. **co-star** (v).

costly costlier costliest (adj)
expensive. *Costly gifts.*

costume (n)
1 clothes worn by actors.
2 clothes worn by people at a particular time in history. *This shows a selection of European costumes from the 15th to 19th centuries.*

European costumes

| 1450s | 1550s | 1630s | 1750s | 1850s |

cosy cosier cosiest (adj) comfortable or snug. *The house was small but cosy.* **cosiness** (n), **cosily** (adv).

cot (n) a small bed for a baby, with high sides.

cottage (n) a small house, usually in the country. *See* **thatch**.

cottage cheese (n) cheese made from curdled skimmed milk.

cotton (n)
1 soft, thin material made from the cotton plant and used to make clothes. **cotton** (adj).
2 thread used for sewing.

cotton plant — raw cotton — boll

cotton wool (n)
soft, raw cotton which you use to put cosmetics on your skin.

couch couches (n)
1 a long, soft seat with arms and a back, and room for two or more people.
2 **couch potato** (n) (slang) someone who spends most of their time watching television rather than being active.

cough (koff) coughing coughed
1 (v) to make a sudden, harsh noise as you force air out of your lungs. **cough** (n).
2 (n) an illness that makes you cough.

council (n) a group of people chosen to look after the interests of a town, county, or organization.

council tax (n) a British tax that pays for local services.

counsel counselling counselled (v)
to listen to people's problems and give them helpful advice. **counselling** (n), **counsellor** (n).

count counting counted (v)
1 to say numbers in order.
2 to work out how many there are of something. *I counted the planes as they took off.*
3 If you can **count on** something or someone, you can rely on them.

Some words that begin with a "c" sound are spelt with a "k".

a b c d e f g h i j k l m n o p q r s t u v w x y z

counter (n)
1 a small, flat, round playing piece used in some board games.
2 a long, flat surface. *A shop counter.*

counteract counteracting counteracted (v)
to act against something so that it is less effective. *You should take some exercise to counteract the effects of overeating.*

counterfeit (n)
a fake that has been made to look like the real thing.

countless (adj)
so many that you cannot count them.

country countries (n)
1 a part of the world with its own borders and government.
2 undeveloped land away from towns or cities. **country** (adj).

countryside (n) undeveloped land away from towns or cities.

county counties (n)
an area in some countries, such as Britain, with its own local government.

couple (n)
1 two of something.
2 two people. *A married couple.*

coupon (n)
a small piece of paper which gives you a discount on something.

courage (n)
bravery or fearlessness. **courageous** (adj), **courageously** (adv).

courgette (kor-jhet) (n)
a green, fleshy vegetable like a small marrow. *See* **vegetable**.

courier (kur-ee-er) (n)
1 someone who carries messages or parcels for somebody else.
2 someone who looks after a group of people on holiday.

course (n)
1 a series of lessons.
2 a part of a meal.
3 a piece of ground where a sport is played. *A golf course.*

court (n)
1 a place where legal cases are heard.
2 a place where games such as tennis or squash are played.
3 a place where a king or queen meets visitors and advisors.

courteous (kur-tee-us) (adj)
polite and respectful. **courtesy** (n), **courteously** (adv).

courtship (n)
1 attempts by an animal to attract a mate.
2 (old-fashioned) attempts by a man to persuade a woman to become his wife.

cousin (n) Your **cousin** is the child of your uncle or aunt.

cover covering covered (v)
1 to put something over something else. *Cover the table with a cloth.* **cover** (n).
2 to teach or study something thoroughly. *Have you covered that topic?* **coverage** (n).
3 to travel a certain distance. *We covered twenty miles before nightfall.*
4 to include or provide for. *Does your insurance cover storm damage?*

cow (n)
1 an adult female farm animal that produces milk. *See* **cud**.
2 an adult female seal or whale.

coward (n) someone who is easily scared and keeps away from frightening situations. **cowardice** (n), **cowardly** (adj).

cowboy (n) a man who rears cattle, especially in the USA. *See* **rodeo**.

cox coxes (n)
someone who steers a rowing boat and gives orders to its crew. **cox** (v).

crab (n) a creature with a hard shell, eight legs, and two pincers.

furrowed crab — carapace (shell), eye on stalk, pincer, walking leg, abdomen, mouth

crack cracking cracked
1 (v) to break or split, often with a loud, sharp noise. **crack** (n).
2 (n) (slang) a form of the drug cocaine.

3 (v) to find the answer to something. *At last, we cracked the problem.*
4 (informal) When you **have a crack at something,** you try to do it.

cracker (n)
1 a thin, plain biscuit, usually eaten with cheese.
2 a paper-covered tube that contains presents, and bangs when you pull it apart. *A Christmas cracker.*

crackle crackling crackled (v)
to make a noise like lots of small bangs. *The dry leaves crackled.*

cradle cradling cradled
1 (n) a wooden bed for a young baby.
2 (v) to hold something or someone in your arms very gently. *Rachel cradled the kitten in her arms.*
3 (n) a protective platform or box for workmen. *A window-cleaning cradle.*

craft (n)
1 work or a hobby where you make things with your hands. *Woodwork, pottery, and needlework are all crafts.*
2 a vehicle, such as a boat or plane.

craftsman craftsmen (n)
someone skilled at making things with their hands. **craftsmanship** (n).

crafty craftier craftiest (adj)
A **crafty** person is clever at tricking other people. **craftily** (adv).

crag (n)
a steep, sharp rock. **craggy** (adj).

cram cramming crammed (v)
to fit things into a small space. *I crammed all my clothes into a backpack.*

cramp cramping cramped
1 (n) pain caused by a muscle tightening suddenly.
2 (v) (informal) If someone or something **cramps your style,** they do not allow you to express yourself freely.

cramped (adj)
If a place is **cramped,** there is not enough room in it for everyone or everything.

crane craning craned
1 (n) a machine used for lifting heavy objects.
2 (n) a large wading bird.
3 (v) to stretch your neck so you can see better.

trolley-jib tower crane

trolley travel gear, trolley, hoisting rope, hoisting block, hook, load, trolley cable, main jib, latticed metal structure, operator's cab, slewing gear (turns cab and jibs), tower mast, counter-jib, counterweight, hoist cable, concrete, hoisting gear

crank cranking cranked
1 *(n)* a bent rod used for winding or lifting something. *See* **bicycle**.
2 *(v)* to wind something with a crank.

cranky crankier crankiest *(adj)* irritable.

crash
crashes crashing crashed
1 *(v)* to make a loud noise like thunder.
2 *(n)* an accident in which a vehicle hits something at high speed. **crash** *(v)*.
3 *(v)* When a computer system or program **crashes**, it fails completely.

crate *(n)* a large, usually wooden, box. *A crate of oranges.*

crater *(n)*
1 a large hole in the ground, caused by something, such as a bomb or a meteorite, falling on it.
2 the mouth of a volcano.
See **volcano**.

crave craving craved *(v)*
to long for something desperately. **craving** *(n)*.

crawl crawling crawled
1 *(v)* to move on your hands and knees.
2 *(n)* a style of swimming on your front in which you use your arms in turn while kicking your legs.

crayon crayoning crayoned
1 *(n)* a coloured pencil or wax stick used for drawing and colouring.
2 *(v)* to draw or colour with a crayon.

craze *(n)*
a fashion that does not last very long.

crazy crazier craziest *(adj)*
1 mad or foolish.
craziness *(n)*, **crazily** *(adv)*.
2 *(informal)* very enthusiastic.
Josh is crazy about football.
craziness *(n)*, **crazily** *(adv)*.

creak creaking creaked *(v)*
to make a squeaky, grating noise.
creak *(n)*, **creaky** *(adj)*, **creakily** *(adv)*.

cream *(n)*
1 a thick liquid taken from the top of the milk. You eat cream with food. **creamy** *(adj)*.
2 a thick, smooth substance like cream that you put on your skin. *Hand cream.*
3 a yellowy-white colour, or the colour of cream. **cream** *(adj)*.

crease creasing creased *(v)*
to make lines or folds in something, especially material or paper. **crease** *(n)*.

create creating created *(v)* to make or design something. **creator** *(n)*.

creation *(n)*
something that has been made.

creative *(adj)* If you are **creative**, you use your imagination and are good at thinking of new ideas.
creativity *(n)*, **creatively** *(adv)*.

creature *(n)*
an animal, bird, or insect.

crèche *(rhymes with fresh)* *(n)*
a place where babies and young children can be looked after safely while their parents are busy.

credible *(adj)* If something or someone is **credible**, you can believe in them or trust them. **credibility** *(n)*.

credit *(n)*
1 If you buy something **on credit**, you pay for it later.
2 If you or your bank account are **in credit**, you have money.
3 praise or acknowledgement.
4 *(plural n)* The **credits** at the end of a film or television programme tell you who acted in it and made it.

creek *(n)*
1 a narrow inlet where the sea flows inland for a long way.
2 a small stream.

creep creeping crept
1 *(v)* to move very slowly and quietly.
2 *(v)* to crawl along the ground.
3 *(n)* *(slang)* an unpleasant person.
4 *(informal)* If something or someone **gives you the creeps**, they are unpleasant and frightening. **creepy** *(adj)*.

cremate
cremating cremated *(v)*
to burn a dead body.
cremation *(n)*, **crematorium** *(n)*.

crescent *(n)*
1 a curved shape.
2 a row of houses, built in a curve.

cress *(n)* a green plant with tiny leaves which you can eat in sandwiches and salads.

crest *(n)*
1 a comb or tuft of feathers on a bird's head. **crested** *(adj)*.
2 the top of something, such as a wave or a hill.
3 a design that represents a noble family, a town, or an organization.
4 part of a coat of arms.
See **coat of arms**.

crevice *(n)* a crack or split in a rock.

crew *(n)* a team of people who work together, especially on a ship.

crib cribbing cribbed
1 *(n)* a small bed for a baby.
2 *(v)* *(informal)* to copy someone else's work and pretend it is your own.

cricket *(n)*

crickets

1 a game played by two teams of eleven players, with two bats, a ball, and two sets of stumps.
cricketer *(n)*.
2 a jumping insect similar to a grasshopper.

house cricket

speckled bush cricket

oak bush cricket

crime *(n)*
something that is against the law.

criminal
1 *(n)* someone who commits a crime. **criminally** *(adv)*.
2 *(adj)* to do with crime.
A criminal investigation.

crimson *(n)*
a deep red colour. **crimson** *(adj)*.

cripple
crippling crippled
1 *(n)* *(old fashioned)* someone who is lame or disabled. **crippled** *(adj)*.
2 *(v)* to stop someone or something from moving or working properly.
The company was crippled by strikes.

crisis crises *(n)*
1 a time of danger and difficulty.
2 a turning point or decision point.

crisp crisper crispest
1 *(n)* a very thin slice of fried potato, with salt or other flavours added.
2 *(adj)* hard and easily broken.
A crisp piece of toast. **crispy** *(adj)*.
3 *(adj)* fresh, dry, and cool. *A crisp winter morning.* **crisply** *(adv)*.

critical *(adj)*
1 If you are **critical** of someone or something, you find faults in them. **critically** *(adv)*.
2 important or serious. *A critical operation.* **critically** *(adv)*.

criticize *or* **criticise**
criticizing criticized *(v)*
1 to tell someone that they have done something wrong. **criticism** *(n)*.
2 to point out the good and bad parts in a book, film, etc.
critic *(n)*, **criticism** *(n)*.

a b c d e f g h i j k l m n o p q r s t u v w x y z

croak

croak croaking croaked *(v)*
1 When a frog **croaks**, it makes a deep, hoarse sound. **croak** *(n)*.
2 If you **croak**, you speak with a deep, hoarse voice. **croaky** *(adj)*.

crochet crocheting crocheted *(cro-shay) (v)* to make a kind of lace from cotton thread or wool, using a hooked needle. **crochet** *(n)*.

crockery *(n)*
pottery or china that you use at home, such as plates, cups, and saucers.

crocodile *(n)*
a large, scaly reptile with short legs and strong jaws.

crocodile

crook *(n)*
1 a dishonest person or a criminal.
2 a long stick with a hook at one end, used by shepherds.

crooked *(cru-kid) (adj)*
1 bent. *A crooked path.*
2 *(informal)* dishonest. *A crooked deal.*

crop cropping cropped
1 *(n)* a plant grown in large amounts, usually for food. *Potatoes and wheat are crops.*
2 *(v)* If an animal **crops** grass, it eats it.
3 *(v)* If something **crops up**, it happens unexpectedly.
4 *(n)* the pouch in a bird's gullet where food is stored and softened before being digested. *See* **chicken**.

cross
crosses crossing crossed
1 *(v)* to go from one side to the other. *Columbus crossed the ocean.*
2 *(adj)* angry or not pleased.
3 *(n)* The shapes "x" and "+" are **crosses**.
4 *(n)* a wooden structure in the shape of a cross, on which criminals used to be crucified.
5 *(v)* If someone **crosses** you, they block your plans.

cross-country *(adj)*
A **cross-country** race is run through the countryside.

cross-examine
cross-examining cross-examined *(v)* to question somebody very closely. **cross-examination** *(n)*.

crossroads *(plural n)* a place where one road crosses another.

cross-section *(n)*
1 a diagram which shows the inside of something, by cutting through it.
2 A **cross-section** of the public is a selection of different types of people.

crossword *(n)*
a puzzle in which you answer clues in order to fill blank spaces with words.

crouch
crouches crouching crouched *(v)*
When you **crouch**, you bend your legs and lower your body.

crow crowing crowed
1 *(n)* a large, black bird.
2 *(v)* When a cockerel **crows**, it makes a loud, crying noise.
3 *(v)* to boast about something.

crowd crowding crowded
1 *(n)* a lot of people packed together. **crowded** *(adj)*.
2 *(v)* If you **crowd** someone, you do not allow them enough room.

crown *(n)*
1 a headdress worn by a king or queen, made from precious metal and jewels.
2 the top of something. *At last, we reached the crown of the hill.*

crucial *(adj)* vital or extremely important. **crucially** *(adv)*.

crucify crucifies crucifying crucified *(v)* to put someone to death by fastening them to a cross and leaving them to die. **crucifixion** *(n)*.

crude cruder crudest *(adj)*
1 rough and poorly made. **crudely** *(adv)*.
2 A **crude** joke is rude and not very funny. **crudity** *(n)*, **crudely** *(adv)*.

cruel crueller cruellest *(adj)*
A **cruel** person deliberately causes pain to others or is happy to see them suffer. **cruelty** *(n)*, **cruelly** *(adv)*.

cruise cruising cruised
1 *(n)* If you go on a **cruise**, you take a holiday on a ship which calls at several places.
2 *(v)* to travel smoothly and easily. *We cruised down the river.*

cruiser *(n)*
1 a motorboat with a cabin. *See* **boat**.
2 a large warship.

crumb *(n)*
a tiny piece of bread or cake.

crumble crumbling crumbled *(v)* to break into small pieces. **crumbly** *(adj)*.

crumple crumpling crumpled *(v)*
1 If you **crumple up** a piece of paper, you screw it into a ball.
2 to collapse. **crumpled** *(adj)*.

crunch crunches crunching crunched *(v)* If you **crunch** something, you crush it noisily. *Ali crunched her carrot.* **crunchy** *(adj)*.

crush crushes crushing crushed
1 *(v)* to squash something under a heavy weight.
2 *(n) (slang)* If you have a **crush** on someone, you like them very much, but usually only for a short time.

crust *(n)*
1 the crisp, outer case of bread or pastry. **crusty** *(adj)*.
2 The Earth's **crust** is its thin, outer layer of land and sea. *See* **Earth**.

crutch crutches *(n)*
one of two long sticks used to help support someone with injured legs.

cry cries crying cried *(v)*
1 to weep tears. **cry** *(n)*.
2 to shout out. **cry** *(n)*.

crystal *(n)* a hard, glassy piece of rock with many sides. Crystals are formed when minerals boil, then cool and solidify. **crystallize** *(v)*, **crystalline** *(adj)*. *See* **quartz**.

cub *(n)* a young lion, wolf, bear, etc.

cube cubing cubed
1 *(n)* a three-dimensional shape with six square faces. *A dice is a cube.* **cubic** *(adj)*. *See* **shape**.
2 *(v)* to multiply a number by itself twice. *3 cubed is 3 x 3 x 3 = 27.*

cubicle *(n)* a small, private area in a changing room or public toilet.

cucumber *(n)*
a long, green vegetable with a watery centre. *See* **vegetable**.

cud *(n)* undigested food that cows bring up from the first part of their stomachs to chew again. *Grass is formed into cud balls in the rumen, returned to the mouth for chewing and passed into the reticulum where any stones are trapped. The pulp can then be digested.*

digestive system of a cow

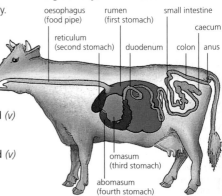

oesophagus (food pipe)
rumen (first stomach)
small intestine
caecum
reticulum (second stomach)
duodenum
colon
anus
omasum (third stomach)
abomasum (fourth stomach)

cuddle cuddling cuddled *(v)*
to hold someone closely in your arms.

cue *(kyoo)* *(n)*
1 a long stick used to hit the ball
in games like snooker and pool.
2 the signal to say some lines
or take an action in a play.
Don't miss your cue!

cuff
1 *(n)* the end part of a shirt or blouse
that goes round your wrist.
2 *(informal)* If you speak **off the
cuff**, you give a speech or an
answer without preparing it first.

cul-de-sac *(n)*
a road that is closed at one end.

culprit *(n)* someone who
has done something wrong.

cult *(n)*
1 a religion with a small following.
2 a strong, almost religious
devotion to a person, an idea,
or a way of life. *The hippie cult.*
3 A **cult hero** is someone who is
very popular with his or her followers.

cultivate
cultivating cultivated *(v)*
If you **cultivate** land, you grow
crops on it. **cultivation** *(n)*.

culture *(n)*
1 the arts, such as music, literature,
painting, etc. **cultural** *(adj)*.
2 The **culture** of a group of people is
their way of life, ideas, and traditions.

cultured *(adj)* well-educated.

cunning *(adj)* A **cunning** person
is clever at tricking people.
cunning *(n)*, cunningly *(adv)*.

cupboard *(n)*
a piece of furniture or a built-in
space, used for storing things.

curator *(n)* the person in charge
of a museum or art gallery.

curb curbing curbed *(v)*
to control and hold back something.
I curbed my desire for another cake.

curdle
curdling curdled *(v)*
When milk **curdles**, it goes sour
and breaks up into curds and whey.

curds *(plural n)*
the solid part of sour milk,
often used to make cheese.

cure curing cured *(v)*
1 *(v)* to make someone better
when they have been ill.
2 *(n)* a drug or course of treatment
that makes someone better.

curfew *(n)* a law which prevents
people from travelling around
freely, especially after dark.

curious *(adj)*
1 eager to find out.
curiosity *(n)*, curiously *(adv)*.
2 strange. *A curious creature.*
curiosity *(n)*, curiously *(adv)*.

curl curling curled
1 *(n)* a curved lock of hair. **curly** *(adj)*.
2 *(v)* to bend into a spiral shape.

currant *(n)* a dried grape.

currency *(n)*
the money used in a country.

current
1 *(adj)* happening now.
currently *(adv)*.
2 *(n)* the movement of water
in a river or an ocean, or of
electricity through a wire.

current affairs *(plural n)* important
events that are happening now and
are often discussed on television,
in newspapers or on the internet.

curriculum
curricula or curriculums *(n)*
a programme of study
for a school or college.

curry curries *(n)* a spicy meal of
meat or vegetables, served with rice.

curse cursing cursed
1 *(n)* an evil spell intended
to harm someone.
2 *(v)* to swear.

cursor *(n)*
a small indicator which shows your
position on a computer screen.

curtain *(n)*
a piece of material that is pulled across
a window or a stage to cover it.

curtsy or **curtsey**
curtsies curtsying curtsied *(v)*
to bend slightly at the knee, with one
leg crossed behind the other. Women
and girls curtsy to show respect
or to accept applause. **curtsy** *(n)*.

curve curving curved
1 *(v)* to bend or turn gently.
2 *(n)* a bend in something.
curved *(adj)*, curvy *(adj)*.

cushion cushioning cushioned
1 *(n)* a type of pillow used to make
chairs or sofas more comfortable.
2 *(v)* to soften the effect of something.
The mattress cushioned her fall.

custard *(n)* a sweet, yellow sauce
made from milk, eggs, and sugar, or
from milk, sugar, and custard powder.

custody *(n)*
1 If someone has **custody** of a
child, they have the legal right to
look after that child. **custodial** *(adj)*.
2 If someone is **taken into
custody**, they are arrested
by the police. **custodial** *(adj)*.

custom *(n)*
1 a tradition. **customary** *(adj)*.
2 something that you do regularly.
A family custom. **customary** *(adj)*.
3 **customs** *(plural n)* a checkpoint
at country borders, ports, or airports
where officials make sure that you
are not carrying anything illegal.

customer *(n)* A shop's **customers**
are the people who buy things from it.

customize or **customise**
customizing customized *(v)*
to change something to suit
your needs and to make it look
different. *Gareth customized his car.*

cut cutting cut
1 *(v)* to use a sharp instrument,
such as scissors or a knife, to
divide, shorten, or shape something.
2 *(n)* a skin wound.
3 *(v)* to reduce something. *The
shop is cutting its prices.* **cut** *(n)*.
4 *(v)* If you are **cut off** from other
people, you cannot contact them.
5 *(v)* If you **cut down** on something,
like eating sweets, you do it less often.
6 *(v)* If a person or an organization
cuts back, they reduce the amount of
money that they spend. **cutback** *(n)*.

cute cuter cutest *(adj)*
charming and attractive.

cutlery *(singular n)*
knives, forks, and spoons.

cutting
1 *(n)* something cut off or cut
out of something else. *A plant
cutting. A newspaper cutting.*
2 *(adj)* If you make a **cutting**
remark, you say something hurtful.

cycle *(sy-kul)* cycling cycled
1 *(n)* a series of events which are
repeated over and over again.
2 *(n)* a bicycle. *See* **bicycle**.
3 *(v)* to ride a bicycle. **cyclist** *(n)*.

cyclone *(sy-klone)* *(n)* a very
strong wind that blows in a spiral.

cygnet *(sig-net)* *(n)*
a young swan. *See* **swan**.

cylinder *(sill-in-der)* *(n)*
1 a shape with circular ends and
curved walls. *Most drink cans are
cylinders.* **cylindrical** *(adj)*. *See* **shape**.
2 a tube-shaped container
in an engine. *See* **engine**.

cynical *(sin-ik-al)* *(adj)* Someone who
is **cynical** always expects the worst to
happen and sees the worst in others.
cynic *(n)*, cynicism *(n)*, cynically *(adv)*.

cytoplasm *(n)* the contents of a
cell, apart from its nucleus. *See* **cell**.

czar or **tsar** *(zar)* *(n)* a Russian king.
The last czar was murdered in 1918.

Some words that begin with a "cy" sound are spelt "ci", "psy", "si", or "scy".

a b c d e f g h i j k l m n o p q r s t u v w x y z

Dd

dab dabbing dabbed *(v)*
to touch a surface gently with
something soft. *Liz dabbed some
ointment on the wound.* **dab** *(n).*

dabble dabbling dabbled *(v)*
1 to dip something into water
and splash it about. *Michael
dabbled his fingers in the stream.*
2 If you **dabble** in something,
you do it, but not very seriously
or very well. **dabbler** *(n).*

dad *or* **daddy** *(n)*
an informal name for your father.

daffodil *(n)* a spring plant
with yellow, bell-like flowers.

daft dafter daftest *(adj) (informal)*
silly or foolish. *A daft idea.*

dagger *(n)*
1 a short, pointed knife, used
as a weapon. *The dagger shown
below was made by the ancient
Sumerians around 4,000BC.*
2 If you **look daggers** at someone,
you look at them in
an angry way.

dagger
and sheath

daily *(adj)* produced or happening
every day. *A daily newspaper.*

dainty daintier daintiest *(adj)*
small and delicate.
daintiness *(n),* **daintily** *(adj).*

dairy dairies *(n)* a place where milk
is bottled and milk products, such
as cheese and yogurt, are made.

dais *(day-us) (n)*
a raised platform at the end of a hall.

daisy daisies *(n)* a wild flower with
white petals and a yellow centre.

dam *(n)* a strong barrier built across a
river to hold back water. *See* **beaver**.

damage damaging damaged
1 *(n)* the harm that something does.
Flood damage. **damaging** *(adj).*
2 *(v)* to harm something or someone.
3 **damages** *(plural n)* money
given to someone by a law court
to try to make up for an injury
or loss that they have suffered.

damn *(dam)* damning damned *(v)*
1 to say that something or
someone is very bad. *The critics
damned the play.* **damning** *(adj).*
2 to curse someone or
something. **damn!** *(interject).*

damp damper dampest *(adj)*
slightly wet or moist. **dampness** *(n).*

damsel *(n) (old-fashioned)*
a young woman. *A damsel in distress.*

dance dancing danced
1 *(v)* to move in time to music.
dancer *(n),* **dancing** *(n).*
2 *(n)* a ball or disco.
3 *(n)* the movements that
go with a particular kind
of music. *Country dance.*

dandruff *(n)*
small, white flakes of dead skin
found in some people's hair.

danger
1 *(n)* a situation that is not safe.
The children are in danger.
2 *(n)* something or someone
that is not safe. *George's
motorbike is a danger on the road.*
dangerous *(adj),* **dangerously** *(adv).*
3 **danger!** *(interject)*
a warning word.

dangle
dangling dangled *(v)*
to swing or hang down. *Maurice
dangled from the drainpipe.*

dank danker dankest *(adj)*
unpleasantly wet or damp.
The cellar was cold and dank.

dappled *(adj)*
marked with spots or with
patches of light and dark.
A dappled pony. **dapple** *(v).*

dare daring dared *(v)*
1 to challenge someone
to do something. **dare** *(n).*
2 to be brave enough to do
something. *Do you dare to dive into
the river?* **daring** *(adj),* **daringly** *(adv).*

daredevil *(n)*
someone who takes risks and does
unnecessarily dangerous things.

dark darker darkest
1 *(adj)* without light. *A dark room.*
2 *(adj)* containing more black
than white. *Dark blue.*
3 *(n)* a place without light.
I can't see in the dark.
4 *(n)* sunset. *I'm not
allowed out after dark.*

darn darning darned *(v)*
to mend a hole in a piece of clothing
by sewing across it. **darning** *(n).*

dart darting darted
1 *(n)* a pointed object that you
throw in the game of darts.
2 *(v)* to move forward suddenly.
Stefan darted out into the traffic.
3 **darts** *(singular n)* a game
in which players score points
by throwing darts at a
board with numbers on it.

dash dashes dashing dashed
1 *(n)* a small line (–) used as a
punctuation mark or in Morse code.
2 *(v)* to move quickly. *I dashed
to the shop before it shut.*

data *(n)* information or facts.
The scientists examined all the data.

database *(n)* a store of
information held on a computer.

date dating dated
1 *(n)* a particular day, month, or year.
2 *(n)* an appointment to
meet someone, especially
a girlfriend or boyfriend.
3 *(v)* to go out with your
boyfriend or girlfriend regularly.
4 *(v)* If something **dates from**
a certain time, it was made then.
5 *(n)* a sweet fruit with a
long thin stone inside it.
6 If something is **dated** or **out
of date**, it is no longer fashionable.
7 If something is **up to date**,
it is modern or contains
the newest information.

daughter *(n)* Someone's
daughter is their female child.

daunt daunting daunted *(v)*
If something **daunts** you, it frightens
and discourages you. *We were a little
daunted by the long climb ahead.*

dawdle dawdling dawdled *(v)*
1 to walk slowly. *The boys dawdled on
their way to school.* **dawdler** *(n).*
2 to do something slowly.
Jen dawdled over her breakfast.

dawn dawning dawned
1 *(n)* sunrise or the beginning
of the day. **dawn** *(v).*
2 *(n)* the start of something new.
The dawn of a new age. **dawn** *(v).*
3 *(v)* If something **dawns on**
you, you begin to understand it.

day *(n)*
1 a 24-hour period, from
midnight to midnight.
2 the light part of the day.

daydream
daydreaming daydreamed
1 *(n)* a dream that you
have while you are awake.
2 *(v)* to let your mind
wander. **daydreamer** *(n).*

daze *(n)* If you are **in a daze**,
you are stunned and unable
to think clearly. **dazed** *(adj).*

dazzle dazzling dazzled *(v)*
1 to blind someone for a short time
with a bright light. **dazzling** *(adj).*
2 to amaze someone. *Tanya
dazzled the audience with
her playing.* **dazzling** *(adj).*

dead *(adj)* no longer alive.

dead end
1 *(n)* a street that is closed
to traffic at one end.
2 dead-end *(adj)* leading nowhere.
Pete had a dead-end job.

deadline *(n)*
a time by which a piece of
work or a job must be finished.

deadlock *(n)* a situation
where nothing can be agreed.

deadly deadlier deadliest *(adj)*
capable of killing or likely to kill.

deaf deafer deafest *(adj)*
1 If someone is **deaf**, they
cannot hear anything or they
can hear very little. **deafness** *(n)*.
2 If you are **deaf** to something,
you choose not to hear it.

deafening *(adj)* very loud.
A deafening crash. **deafeningly** *(adv)*.

deal dealing dealt
1 *(v)* to do business. *Hugo
deals in antiques.* **dealer** *(n)*.
2 *(n)* a business agreement.
3 *(v)* When you **deal with**
something, you sort it out.
4 *(v)* to give out cards to people
playing a game. **dealer** *(n)*.
5 *(v)* to cover a subject or an area.
Does that book deal with dogs?

dear dearer dearest
1 *(adj)* highly valued or much
loved. *A dear friend.* **dearly** *(adv)*.
2 *(adj)* You use the word
Dear when you write
to someone. *Dear Sir.*
3 *(n)* a kind or sweet person.
4 *(adj)* expensive.

death *(n)* the end of life.

deathly *(adj)*
very pale or very quiet. *His
face turned deathly white.
There was a deathly hush.*

deathtrap *(n)* a place or
vehicle that is very dangerous.

debate
debating debated
1 *(n)* a discussion between
sides with different views,
usually held in public.
2 *(v)* to consider or discuss something.
*The family debated where to
go on holiday.* **debatable** *(adj)*.

debit debiting debited
1 *(n)* money that you owe. *My
account shows a small debit.*
2 *(v)* If a bank account is **debited**
with a sum of money, that money
is taken out of the account.

debris *(deb-ree) (n)*
the scattered remains of something.

debt *(rhymes with pet) (n)*
1 an amount of money that you owe.
2 If you are **in debt** to
someone, you owe them
money or a favour. **debtor** *(n)*.

debug debugging debugged *(v)*
1 to remove the faults
in a computer program.
2 to remove secret listening
devices from a place.

debut *(day-byoo) (n)* a first public
appearance. *An acting debut.*

decade *(n)* a period of ten years.

decaffeinated *(adj)* If a drink, such
as coffee, is **decaffeinated**, it has
had most of its caffeine removed.

decapitate decapitating
decapitated *(v)* to remove the
head of a person or creature.

decathlon *(n)* a competition
made up of ten athletic events.

decay decaying decayed *(v)*
to rot or break up. **decay** *(n)*.

deceased *(adj)* dead.

deceive deceiving deceived *(v)*
If someone **deceives** you, they
trick you into believing something
that is not true. **deceit** *(n)*,
deceitful *(adj)*, **deceitfully** *(adv)*.

decent *(adj)*
1 good or satisfactory.
Decent quality. **decently** *(adv)*.
2 respectable and proper.
Decent behaviour. **decency** *(n)*,
decently *(adv)*.

deception *(n)*
a trick that makes people believe
something that is not true.
deceptive *(adj)*, **deceptively** *(adv)*.

decibel *(n)* a unit for measuring
the volume of sound.

decide deciding decided *(v)*
1 to make up your
mind about something.
2 to settle something. *The vote
was decided by a show of hands.*

deciduous *(adj)*
Trees that are **deciduous**
shed their leaves every year.

decimal
1 *(adj)* A **decimal** system
uses units of tens, hundreds,
thousands, etc. *Decimal currency.*
2 decimal point *(n)* a dot separating
whole numbers from tenths,
hundredths, thousandths, etc.
*The numbers 2.5, 3.75, and
4.624 all use decimal points.*
3 *(n)* a fraction, or a whole
number and a fraction, written
with a decimal point. *0.5, 6.37,
and 82.54 are all decimals.*

decipher deciphering deciphered
(v) to work out something that
is written in code or is hard to
understand. **decipherable** *(adj)*.

decision *(n)* If you make a
decision, you make up your mind.

decisive *(adj)*
If you are **decisive**, you make choices
quickly and easily. **decisively** *(adv)*.

deck *(n)*
1 the floor of a boat or ship. *See* **ship**.
2 a wooden platform outside
a house or other building.
3 a pack of playing cards.

declare declaring declared *(v)*
1 to say something firmly. *Justin
declared that he would never
eat meat again.* **declaration** *(n)*.
2 to announce something formally.
*The government declared that
the war was over.* **declaration** *(n)*.
3 When you **declare** in a cricket
match, you end your team's innings.

decline declining declined *(v)*
1 to turn something down,
or to refuse something.
2 to get worse or to get smaller.
*The population of our village
is declining.* **decline** *(n)*.

decode decoding decoded *(v)*
to turn something that is written
in code into ordinary language.

decompose decomposing
decomposed *(v)* to rot or to
decay. **decomposition** *(n)*.

decongestant *(n)* a drug that
unblocks your nose, chest, etc. when
you have a cold. **decongestion** *(n)*.

decontaminate
decontaminating decontaminated
(v) to remove radioactive or other
harmful substances from something
or somewhere. **decontamination** *(n)*.

decorate decorating decorated *(v)*
1 If you **decorate** something, you
add things to it to make it look nicer.
decoration *(n)*, **decorative** *(adj)*.
2 If you **decorate** a room or house,
you paint it or put up wallpaper.
decoration *(n)*, **decorator** *(n)*.

decrease decreasing decreased
1 *(v)* to become less, smaller, or
fewer. *Enthusiasm for this project
is decreasing.* **decreasing** *(adj)*,
decreasingly *(adv)*.
2 *(n)* a loss or the amount
by which something lessens.

decree decreeing decreed *(v)*
to give an order that must
be obeyed. **decree** *(n)*.

decrepit *(adj)* old and feeble.

a b c d e f g h i j k l m n o p q r s t u v w x y z

dedicate

dedicate dedicating dedicated *(v)*
1 If you **dedicate** yourself to
something, you give lots of time
and energy to it. **dedication** *(n)*.
2 If you **dedicate** a book to
someone, you put their name
at the front of it to thank them
or to show that you like and
admire them. **dedication** *(n)*.

deduce deducing deduced *(v)*
to work out something from clues
or from what you know already.

deduct deducting deducted *(v)*
to take away or subtract something,
especially money. **deductible** *(adj)*.

deduction *(n)*
1 something that is
worked out from clues.
2 an amount that is taken away
or subtracted from a larger amount.

deed *(n)*
1 something that is
done. *A good deed.*
2 a legal document saying who
owns a house or a piece of land.

deep deeper deepest *(adj)*
1 going a long way down.
A deep well. **deepen** *(v)*.
2 very intense and strong. *Deep
sorrow.* **deepen** *(v)*, **deeply** *(adv)*.

deep-sea *(adj)* living or
happening in the deeper
part of an ocean. *Some
deep-sea creatures, like this
viper fish, make their own
light from luminous cells.*

viper fish

deer deer *(n)* a fast-running wild
animal with four legs. Male deer
grow bony antlers. *See* **antler**, **stag**.

deface defacing defaced *(v)*
to spoil the way something looks.

defeat defeating defeated
1 *(v)* to beat someone
in a war or competition.
2 *(n)* If you suffer a
defeat, you are beaten.

defect defecting defected
1 *(dee-fect) (n)* a fault or
weakness in something
or someone. **defective** *(adj)*.
2 *(dif-ect) (v)* to leave your country
or political party and join another one.

defend defending defended *(v)*
1 to protect something or
someone from harm. **defence** *(n)*.
2 to support someone or some
idea by arguing. *The strikers
defended their action.* **defence** *(n)*.

3 *(v)* to try to stop goals being scored
in football, hockey, netball, etc.
defence *(n)*, **defender** *(n)*.

defendant *(n)*
the person in a court case who
has been accused of a crime.

defensive *(adj)*
1 to do with defending
yourself or others. *The
players took defensive action.*
2 If you are **defensive**, you
feel and act as if someone
is attacking or criticizing you.
defensiveness *(n)*, **defensively** *(adv)*.

defer deferring deferred *(v)*
to put something off until later. *The
outing will be deferred until next term.*

defiant *(adj)* If you are **defiant**,
you stand up to someone or to
some organization and refuse to obey
them. **defiance** *(n)*, **defiantly** *(adv)*.

deficient *(adj)*
lacking something. *My diet is
deficient in vitamin C.* **deficiency** *(n)*.

deficit *(def-er-sit) (n)* If an account
shows a **deficit**, more money
has been spent than has come in.

define defining defined *(v)*
to explain or describe
something exactly.

definite *(adj)*
1 certain. *Do we have a definite
date for the trip?* **definitely** *(adv)*.
2 clear. *These drawings
have a very definite outline.*
3 **definite article** *(n)* the grammatical
term for "the". *See page 3.*

definition *(n)* an explanation
of what a word or an idea means.
This dictionary has 20,000 definitions.

deflate deflating deflated *(v)*
1 to let the air out of something such
as a tyre or balloon. **deflation** *(n)*.
2 to make someone feel less
confident and important. *The
teacher's comments deflated Don.*

deflect deflecting deflected *(v)*
to make something go in a different
direction. *The ball was deflected off
the post into the goal.* **deflection** *(n)*.

deforestation *(n)*
the cutting down of forests.

deformed *(adj)* If something is
deformed, it is a strange shape.
A deformed carrot. **deformity** *(n)*.

defraud
defrauding defrauded *(v)*
to cheat someone out
of money, property, etc.

defrost defrosting defrosted *(v)*
1 to allow frozen food
to thaw out completely.
2 to remove ice from
a refrigerator or freezer.

deft defter deftest *(adj)*
skilful, quick, and neat. *Deft
footwork.* **deftness** *(n)*, **deftly** *(adv)*.

defuse defusing defused *(v)*
1 When someone **defuses** a bomb,
they make it safe so it cannot explode.
2 If a situation is **defused**,
it is made calmer.

defy defies defying defied *(v)*
1 If you **defy** a person or a
rule, you stand up to them
and refuse to obey them.
2 to challenge someone or to
dare them to do something.
I defy you to eat all that cake!

degenerate degenerating
degenerated *(v)* to become worse.
The lesson degenerated into a riot.

degrading *(adj)* If a situation or
an activity is **degrading**, it makes
you feel worthless or disgraced.
degradation *(n)*, **degrade** *(v)*.

degree *(n)*
1 a unit for measuring temperature
or angles. The symbol for a degree is °.
*The temperature yesterday reached
20° Celsius. A 90° angle.*
2 a qualification given by a university
or other institute of higher education.

dehydrated *(adj)*
1 If you are **dehydrated**, you do
not have enough water in your body.
dehydration *(n)*, **dehydrate** *(v)*.
2 **Dehydrated** food has had
the water removed from it.
dehydration *(n)*, **dehydrate** *(v)*.

deign *(rhymes with pain)* deigning
deigned *(v)* If you **deign** to do
something, you lower yourself
to do it. *The princess deigned
to let the peasant kiss her hand.*

deity *(day-it-ee)* deities *(n)*
a god or goddess.

dejected *(adj)* sad and depressed.
dejection *(n)*, **dejectedly** *(adv)*.

delay delaying delayed *(v)*
1 to be late. *Don't delay or
we'll miss the bus!* **delay** *(n)*.
2 to make someone late.
The accident delayed me.
3 to put something off until
later. *Sarah delayed doing her
homework until the last minute.*

delegate delegating delegated
1 (*del-er-gate*) (*v*) to give someone responsibility for doing a part of your job.
2 (*del-er-gurt*) (*n*) someone who represents other people at a meeting.

delete deleting deleted (*v*) to remove something from a piece of writing or text. **deletion** (*n*).

deliberate
deliberating deliberated
1 (*der-lib-er-ut*) (*adj*) planned or intended. **deliberately** (*adv*).
2 (*der-lib-er-ate*) (*v*) to consider something carefully. **deliberation** (*n*).

delicate (*adj*)
1 finely made, or sensitive. *A delicate instrument.* **delicately** (*adv*).
2 If a person is **delicate**, they are not very strong and easily become ill.

delicatessen (*n*) a shop that sells a variety of foods already prepared.

delicious (*adj*) very pleasing to taste or smell. **deliciously** (*adv*).

delight delighting delighted
1 (*n*) great pleasure. **delightful** (*adj*).
2 (*v*) If something **delights** you, it pleases you very much. **delighted** (*adj*).

delinquent (*n*) a young person who is often in trouble with the police. **delinquency** (*n*), **delinquent** (*adj*).

delirious (*adj*) If you are **delirious**, you cannot think straight because you have a fever or you are extremely happy. **deliriously** (*adv*).

deliver delivering delivered (*v*)
1 to take something to someone. **delivery** (*n*).
2 If someone **delivers** a baby, they help it to be born. **delivery** (*n*).
3 (*old-fashioned*) to rescue someone from something. *Deliver us from evil.* **deliverance** (*n*).

delta (*n*)
1 the fourth letter of the Greek alphabet. See **alphabet**.
2 an area of land where a river deposits its sediment as it enters the sea, causing it to split into channels. See **river**.

deluge deluging deluged
1 (*n*) heavy rain, or a flood.
2 (*v*) If a river or a storm **deluges** a place, it floods it.
3 (*v*) If people **deluge** you with letters, presents, etc., they send you lots of them. **deluge** (*n*).

demand
demanding demanded
1 (*v*) to claim something or to ask for something firmly. *We demand justice!*

2 (*n*) If there is a **demand** for something, many people want it.

demanding (*adj*)
1 If somebody is **demanding**, they are always wanting things and are hard to please.
2 A **demanding** job requires a lot of effort.

demeanour (*n*) the way that you behave.

demo (*n*) (*informal*) a meeting or march to protest about something. Demo is short for demonstration.

democracy democracies (*n*)
1 a way of governing a country, in which the people choose their leaders in elections.
2 a country that has an elected government.

democrat (*n*)
1 someone who agrees with the system of democracy.
2 Democrat a supporter of the Democratic Party in the USA.

democratic (*adj*)
1 A **democratic** system is one where all people have equal rights. **democratically** (*adv*).
2 Democratic Party (*n*) the name of one of the main political parties in the USA.

demolish demolishes demolishing demolished (*v*)
1 to knock something down and break it up. *The builders demolished the old school.* **demolition** (*n*).
2 (*informal*) to eat something quickly. *Will demolished his lunch in five minutes.*

demon (*n*) a devil or an evil spirit. **demonic** (*adj*).

demonstrate
demonstrating demonstrated (*v*)
1 to show other people how to do something or how to use something. *Alanna demonstrated how to use the computer.* **demonstration** (*n*).
2 to join together with other people to protest against something. **demonstration** (*n*), **demonstrator** (*n*).
3 to show something clearly. *Adrian demonstrated his anger by shouting loudly.* **demonstrative** (*adj*).

demoralized or **demoralised** (*adj*) If you are **demoralized**, you feel depressed and hopeless.

den (*n*)
1 the home of a wild animal, such as a lion.
2 a private place where you can work or play.

denim (*n*) strong, cotton material used for making jeans. **denim** (*adj*).

denominator (*n*) In fractions, the **denominator** is the number under the line which shows how many equal parts the whole number can be divided into. *In the fraction $7/8$, 8 is the denominator.*

denounce denouncing denounced (*v*) to say in public that someone has done something wrong.

dense denser densest (*adj*)
1 thick or crowded. *Dense fog.* **denseness** (*n*), **densely** (*adv*).
2 (*informal*) slow to understand. **denseness** (*n*), **densely** (*adv*).

density (*n*) The **density** of an object is how heavy or light it is for its size. Density is measured by dividing an object's mass by its volume.

dent denting dented (*v*) to damage something by making a hollow in it. **dent** (*n*).

dental (*adj*) to do with your teeth. *Dental hygiene.*

dentist (*n*) someone who is trained to check and treat teeth.

denture (*n*)
1 a plate that fits into your mouth, with a false tooth or false teeth attached to it.
2 dentures (*plural n*) a set of false teeth.

deny denies denying denied (*v*)
1 to say that something is not true. *Laura denied that she had taken the pens.* **denial** (*n*).
2 to stop someone having something or going somewhere. *The guards denied us entry to the hall.*

deodorant (*n*) a substance used to cover up or get rid of unpleasant smells.

depart departing departed (*v*) to leave, especially to go on a journey. **departure** (*n*).

department (*n*) a part of a shop, hospital, university, etc. **departmental** (*adj*).

depend depending depended (*v*)
1 If something **depends on** something else, it is related to it or influenced by it in some way. *The result depends on the skill of our team.* **dependent** (*adj*).
2 to rely on someone or something. *We're depending on your help.* **dependence** (*n*), **dependable** (*adj*), **dependent** (*adj*).

dependant (*n*) someone who is looked after and supported by somebody else.

depict depicting depicted *(v)*
to show something in a picture,
or by using words. *Paul's painting
depicts a group of purple aliens.*

deplorable *(adj)*
shockingly bad. *Louis has
deplorable taste in clothes.*
deplore *(v)*, deplorably *(adv)*.

deport deporting deported *(v)*
to send someone back to their own
country. *The terrorists were deported
to face trial at home.* deportation *(n)*.

depose deposing deposed *(v)*
If a king or queen is **deposed**,
they have their power taken
from them. deposition *(n)*.

deposit depositing deposited
1 *(n)* a sum of money given as the first
part of a payment or as a promise
to pay for something. deposit *(v)*.
2 *(n)* a natural layer of rock,
sand, or mineral found in
the ground. deposit *(v)*.
3 *(v)* to place or to lay down. *Dad
deposited the shopping on the table.*

depot *(dep-oh) (n)*
a warehouse or a bus station.

depreciate
depreciating depreciated *(v)*
to lose value. depreciation *(n)*.

depressed *(adj)* sad and gloomy.
depress *(v)*, depressing *(adj)*.

depression *(n)*
1 a mental illness that makes someone
feel very sad and unmotivated.
2 an area of air at low pressure
which may bring rain.
3 a time when businesses do
badly and many people are poor.
4 a shallow dip in the ground.

deprive depriving deprived *(v)*
to prevent someone from
having something or to take
something away from someone.
deprivation *(n)*, deprived *(adj)*.

depth *(n)*
1 deepness, or a measurement
of deepness.
2 If you study something **in
depth**, you study it thoroughly.
3 If you are **out of your depth**, you
cannot understand what is going on.

deputy deputies *(n)*
someone who helps somebody else in
their job and takes their place when
they are ill or absent. deputize *(v)*.

deranged *(adj)* insane.

derelict *(adj)* neglected and in ruins.

derive deriving derived *(v)*
1 to take or receive something.
*Eleanor derives a lot of
pleasure from her work.*

2 If a word is **derived** from another
word, it has developed from it.
*The word dictionary is derived from
the Latin word "dictio", meaning
word or phrase.* derivation *(n)*.

descant *(n)* a tune that is played
or sung above the main tune.

descend descending descended *(v)*
1 to climb down or go down
to a lower level. descent *(n)*.
2 If you are **descended** from
someone, you belong to a
later generation of their
family. descendant *(n)*

describe describing described *(v)*
to say or write what someone or
something is like. *Describe your house.*
description *(n)*, descriptive *(adj)*.

desert deserting deserted
1 *(dez-ut) (n)* a sandy or stony
area where hardly any plants grow
because there is so little rain. *The
map shows the main deserts of the
world and is surrounded by examples
of desert wildlife.* desert *(adj)*.
2 *(de-zert) (v)* to abandon
someone, or to run away
from the army. deserter *(n)*.

deserve deserving deserved *(v)*
to earn something because of the
way that you behave. *Katherine
deserves a reward for her hard work.*

design designing designed
1 *(v)* to draw something that could
be built or made. designer *(n)*.
2 *(n)* the shape or style of something.

desire *(n)* a strong wish or
need for something or someone.
desire *(v)*, desirable *(adj)*.

desk *(n)* a table, often with drawers,
used for working at or writing on.

desktop *(n)*
the main screen display on a
computer, from which you can
run programs and open files.

desolate *(adj)*
1 deserted or uninhabited.
A desolate village. desolation *(n)*.
2 sad and lonely. *After my
friend left, I felt really desolate.*
desolation *(n)*, desolately *(adv)*.

**deserts and
desert wildlife**

desert

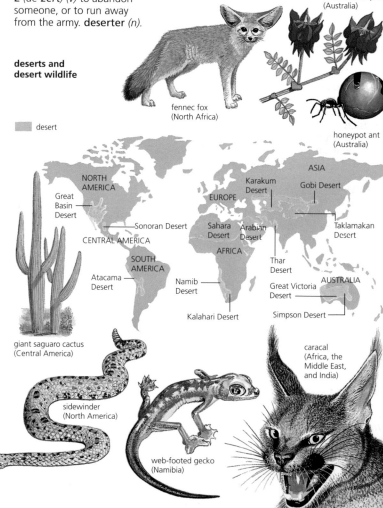

Sturt's desert pea
(Australia)

fennec fox
(North Africa)

honeypot ant
(Australia)

NORTH
AMERICA

Great
Basin
Desert

Sonoran Desert

CENTRAL AMERICA

SOUTH
AMERICA

Atacama
Desert

EUROPE

ASIA

Karakum
Desert

Gobi Desert

Sahara
Desert

Arabian
Desert

Taklamakan
Desert

AFRICA

Thar
Desert

Namib
Desert

Great Victoria
Desert

AUSTRALIA

Kalahari Desert

Simpson Desert

giant saguaro cactus
(Central America)

caracal
(Africa, the
Middle East,
and India)

sidewinder
(North America)

web-footed gecko
(Namibia)

diabolical

despair
despairing despaired *(v)*
to lose hope completely. *Aiden despaired of getting home on time.* despair *(n),* despairing *(adj).*

despatch see **dispatch**.

desperate *(adj)*
1 If you are **desperate**, you will do anything to change your situation. desperation *(n),* desperately *(adv).*
2 dangerous or difficult. *A desperate shortage of medicine.* desperately *(adv).*

despise despising despised *(v)*
If you **despise** someone, you dislike them and have no respect for them.

despite *(prep)* in spite of. *Rob won the race, despite falling off his bike.*

dessert *(de-zert) (n)*
the sweet course of a meal.

destination *(n)* the place that someone or something is travelling to.

destiny destinies *(n)*
Your **destiny** is your fate or the future events in your life. *Cinderella's destiny was to marry a handsome prince.*

destitute *(adj)* A **destitute** person has no money to live on.

destroy destroying destroyed *(v)*
to ruin something or someone completely. destruction *(n).*

destructive *(adj)*
causing lots of damage and unhappiness. destructively *(adv).*

detach
detaches detaching detached *(v)*
to separate one part of something from the rest of it. detachable *(adj).*

detached *(adj)*
1 A **detached** house stands by itself.
2 If you are **detached**, you are able to stand back from a situation and not get too involved in it. detachment *(n).*

detail *(n)*
1 a small part of something larger.
2 delicate work. *Lara's paintings are full of detail.* detailed *(adj).*
3 *(plural n)* If you ask for **details** about something, you want information about it.

detain detaining detained *(v)*
to keep somebody back when they want to go. *The police detained two men for questioning.*

detect detecting detected *(v)*
to notice or discover something. *I detected a strange smell in the house.* detection *(n).*

detective *(n)*
someone who investigates crimes, usually for the police.

detention *(n)*
1 a punishment in which a pupil has to stay in school when other pupils are free.
2 If someone is held in **detention**, they are kept prisoner.
3 **detention centre** *(n)* a type of prison for young offenders.

deter deterring deterred *(v)*
to prevent or discourage someone from doing something.

detergent *(n)*
a liquid or powder used for cleaning things, especially clothes.

deteriorate
deteriorating deteriorated *(v)*
to get worse. deterioration *(n).*

determined *(adj)*
If you are **determined** to do something, you have made a firm decision to do it. determination *(n).*

deterrent *(n)*
something that stops you doing something because you are afraid of the consequences. *Burglar alarms are effective deterrents against crime.*

detest detesting detested *(v)*
If you **detest** someone or something, you dislike them very much. detestable *(adj).*

detonate
detonating detonated *(v)*
to set off an explosion. detonator *(n),* detonation *(n).*

detour *(n)* a longer, alternative route to somewhere, usually taken to avoid an obstacle, such as roadworks.

detract detracting detracted *(v)*
to make something less enjoyable or valuable. *The rain detracted from the pleasure of our walk.*

detrimental *(adj)* harmful. *Smoking is detrimental to your health.*

deuce *(jooss) (n)*
In tennis, the score of **deuce** means that both players have 40 points.

devalue
devaluing devalued *(v)*
1 to reduce the value of a currency in relation to another currency or to gold. devaluation *(n).*
2 to make something worth less than it was. *Why do you always devalue my efforts?*

devastated *(adj)*
1 very badly damaged or destroyed. *The area was devastated by the floods.* devastation *(n),* devastate *(v).*
2 shocked and distressed. *I was devastated by the dreadful news.* devastating *(adj).*

develop
developing developed *(v)*
1 to grow. *The boys' friendship developed slowly.* development *(n).*
2 to build on something or make something grow. *The farmer is developing the field as a campsite.* developer *(n),* development *(n).*

deviate deviating deviated *(v)*
to do something different from what is normal or acceptable. *The cyclist deviated from his usual route.* deviation *(n),* deviant *(adj).*

device *(n)*
1 a piece of equipment which does a particular job. *This is a useful device for taking the tops off bottles.*
2 If you are **left to your own devices,** you can do what you want.

devil *(n)*
1 In Christianity and Judaism, **the Devil** is the spirit of evil.
2 If you call someone a **devil,** you mean that they are naughty or wicked.

devious *(adj)*
1 A **devious** person keeps their thoughts and actions secret, and cannot be trusted. deviousness *(n),* deviously *(adv).*
2 complicated and indirect. *We took a devious route back home.*

devise devising devised *(v)* to think something up or invent something. *Let's devise a way to escape.*

devoid *(adj)* without something or empty of something. *The house was devoid of furniture.*

devolution *(n)* the handing over of some power from a central government to a local government.

devoted *(adj)* loyal and loving. devotion *(n),* devotedly *(adv).*

devour devouring devoured *(v)* to eat something quickly and greedily.

devout *(adj)* deeply religious. devoutness *(n),* devoutly *(adv).*

dew *(n)* small drops of moisture which form overnight on cool surfaces outside. dewy *(adj).*

dexterity *(n)* skill, especially in using your hands. *Simon showed great dexterity in modelling the clay.* dexterous *(adj).*

diabetes *(dye-a-bee-tees) (n)*
a disease in which you have too much sugar in your blood. diabetic *(dye-a-bet-ik) (adj).*

diabolical *(adj)*
1 extremely wicked. *A diabolical villain.* diabolically *(adv).*
2 *(informal)* awful or terrible. *A diabolical essay.* diabolically *(adv).*

a b c d e f g h i j k l m n o p q r s t u v w x y z

diagnose
diagnosing diagnosed (v)
to work out what disease a patient
has or what the cause of a problem is.
diagnosis (n), **diagnostics** (plural n).

diagonal (adj)
A **diagonal** line is a straight line
joining opposite corners of a
square or rectangle. **diagonally** (adv).

diagram (n)
a drawing or plan that explains
something simply. A diagram of
an engine. **diagrammatic** (adj).

dial dialling dialled
1 (n) the face on a clock, watch,
or measuring instrument.
2 (v) to enter a phone number
by pressing buttons on a phone.
3 **dialling tone** (n) the sound
you hear when you pick up a
landline telephone.

dialect (n)
a way of speaking that
belongs to a particular place.

dialogue (n)
conversation, especially
in a play, film, or book.

diameter (dye-am-it-er) (n)
a straight line through the
centre of a circle, from one
side to another. See **circle**.

diamond (n)
1 a very hard, clear, precious
stone. See **mineral**.
2 a shape with four equal
sides, like a square standing
on one of its corners.
3 **diamonds** (plural n) one of
the four suits in a pack of cards.

diaphragm (dye-a-fram) (n)
1 the wall of muscle between
your chest and your stomach.
See **respiration**.
2 the thin disc in a phone
or microphone that vibrates
to change voice signals into
electrical signals.

diarrhoea (dye-er-ree-a) (n)
a stomach illness which causes
normally solid waste to become runny.

diary diaries (n)
a book in which people write down
things that happen each day, either
to use as a record or to plan ahead.

dice dicing diced
1 (plural n) six-sided cubes with
a different number of spots on
each face, used in games.
The singular of dice is die,
although most people say dice.
2 (v) to cut something, such as
vegetables, into small cubes.
Dice the carrots. **diced** (adj).

dictate dictating dictated (v)
1 to talk aloud so that
someone can write down
what you say. **dictation** (n).
2 to control something.
Mum dictates our bedtimes.

dictator (n) someone who
has complete personal control
of a country. **dictatorship** (n).

dictionary dictionaries (n)
a book like this one that explains
what words mean and shows
you how to spell them.

didgeridoo or **didjeridu**
(dij-er-ree-doo) (n)
a long, decorated tube,
made from a hollowed-
out branch or tree trunk,
which is played as a
musical instrument
by Aborigines.

didgeridoo

die dying died
1 (v) to stop living, or come to an end.
2 (v) If you are **dying** to do
something, you really want to do it.
Lauren was dying to go skiing.
3 (n) the singular form
of the word dice.

diesel (dee-zull)
1 **diesel engine** (n) a type of engine
used in trains and motor vehicles.
In a diesel engine, fuel is ignited
by heat from compressed air,
rather than by a sparking plug.
2 (n) a fuel used in diesel engines
that is heavier than petrol.

diet dieting dieted
1 (n) Your **diet** is what
you eat. **dietary** (adj).
2 (v) When you **diet**, you
choose what you eat in order
to lose or gain weight.
3 (n) a controlled eating plan.

difference (n)
1 the way in which one thing
is not like another thing. **differ** (v),
different (adj), **differently** (adv).
2 The **difference** between two
numbers is the amount by which
one is less or more than the other.
The difference between 5 and 2 is 3.

difficult (adj)
1 not easy. A difficult exam.
2 A **difficult** person is
not easy to get on with.

difficulty difficulties (n) a problem.

dig digging dug
1 (v) to use a spade to move earth.
2 (n) a push or a poke.
3 (n) an unkind remark.
4 (n) an archaeological excavation.

digestion (n)
the process of breaking down food
in the stomach, so that it can be
absorbed into the blood. This diagram
shows the main organs used in human
digestion. **digest** (v), **digestive** (adj).

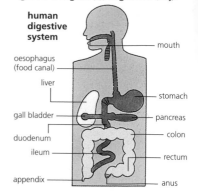

human
digestive
system

mouth

oesophagus
(food canal)

liver

stomach

gall bladder

pancreas

duodenum

colon

ileum

rectum

appendix

anus

digger (n) a large machine,
used for moving earth.

digit (dij-it) (n)
1 a finger or toe.
2 a single figure. 625 is
a three-digit number.

digital (adj)
1 represented as a series of ones
and zeros. Digital information.
digitize (v), **digitally** (adv).
2 **Digital** equipment works by using
digital information. A digital camera.
3 A **digital** display shows
time, speed, etc. in numbers.

dignified (adj) calm, serious,
and in control. **dignity** (n).

dilapidated (adj) shabby and
falling to pieces. **dilapidation** (n).

dilemma (n) If you are in
a dilemma, you have to
choose between alternatives.

diligent (adj) hard-working.
diligence (n), **diligently** (adv).

dilute diluting diluted (v)
If you **dilute** a liquid, you make it
weaker by adding water. **dilution** (n).

dimension (n)
The **dimensions** of an object
are its measurements or its size.
Objects have three dimensions:
length, width, and height.

diminish diminishes diminishing
diminished (v) If something
diminishes, it becomes smaller
or weaker. A diminishing flame.

dimple (n) a small dent in a person's
cheek or chin. **dimpled** (adj).

dine dining dined (v) to have a
meal in a formal way. Lord and Lady
Fortescue dined at eight. **diner** (n).

Some words that begin with a "di" sound are spelt "dy".

disabled

dinghy dinghies *(n)*
a small, open boat.

mast
kicker (or vang)
mast step
mainsheet (controls the sail)
boom
centre board
thwart (seat)
toe strap
tiller
mainsheet traveller
rudder
tiller extension
transom

sailing dinghy

dingy *(din-jee)* dingier dingiest *(adj)* dull and shabby. *A dingy room.*

dinner *(n)*
1 the main meal of the day, eaten at midday or in the evening.
2 a formal banquet.

dinosaur *(n)* the general name for the large, land-living reptiles that existed in prehistoric times. *The picture shows a range of dinosaurs and the periods when they existed.*

dip dipping dipped
1 *(v)* to put something briefly into something, usually a liquid. *Dip your brush in the water.*
2 *(v)* to slope downwards. **dip** *(n).*
3 *(v)* If you **dip** a vehicle's headlights, you lower its beams.
4 *(n)* a short swim.
5 *(n)* a savoury sauce into which you dip raw vegetables, crisps, etc.

diploma *(n)* a certificate showing that you have gained a qualification in a particular subject area.

diplomat *(n)* a person who represents their country's government in a foreign country. **diplomacy** *(n).*

diplomatic *(adj)*
1 If you are **diplomatic**, you are tactful and good at dealing with people. **diplomacy** *(n).*
2 to do with being a diplomat. *The diplomatic service.*

dire direr direst *(adj)* disastrous. *Dire consequences.*

direct directing directed
1 *(adj)* in a straight line or by the shortest route. **directly** *(adv).*
2 *(v)* to supervise people, especially in a play or film.

3 *(v)* to tell someone the way to go. *Please direct me to the hotel.*
4 *(adj)* If someone is **direct**, they have a very straightforward manner. **directly** *(adv).*

direction *(n)*
1 the way that someone or something is moving or pointing. *We travelled in a westerly direction.*
2 **directions** *(plural n)* instructions. *Follow the directions carefully.*

director *(n)*
1 one of the senior people in charge of a company.
2 the person in charge of making a film or television programme.

directory directories *(n)* a book which gives addresses, phone numbers, etc. in alphabetical order.

dirty dirtier dirtiest *(adj)*
1 not clean. **dirt** *(n).*
2 unfair. *A dirty trick.*
3 rude. *Dirty jokes may offend some people.*

disabled *(adj)*
People who are **disabled** are restricted in what they can do, usually because of an illness or injury. **disability** *(n).*

dinosaurs

- ■ Triassic 250-200 million years ago
- ■ Jurassic 200-145 million years ago
- ■ Cretaceous 145-65 million years ago

■ staurikosaurus

■ plateosaurus

■ velociraptor

■ kentrosaurus

■ triceratops

■ parasaurolophus

■ brachiosaurus

■ deinonychus

■ stegosaurus

■ pachycephalosaurus

■ tyrannosaurus rex

■ spinosaurus

disadvantage

disadvantage *(n)* something which causes a problem or makes life more difficult. **disadvantaged** *(adj)*.

disagree disagreeing disagreed *(v)* If you **disagree** with someone, you do not think the same way as they do. **disagreement** *(n)*.

disappear disappearing disappeared *(v)* to go out of sight. **disappearance** *(n)*.

disappoint disappointing disappointed *(v)* to let someone down by failing to do what they expected. **disappointment** *(n)*, **disappointed** *(adj)*.

disapprove disapproving disapproved *(v)* If you **disapprove** of something, you do not think it is a good thing. **disapproval** *(n)*.

disarm disarming disarmed *(v)*
1 to take weapons from someone.
2 If a country **disarms**, it gives up its weapons. **disarmament** *(n)*.
3 If someone **disarms** you, they stop you feeling angry.

disaster *(n)*
1 a very serious accident, earthquake, etc. in which many die.
2 If something is a **disaster**, it goes completely wrong. **disastrous** *(adj)*, **disastrously** *(adv)*.

disbelief *(n)* refusal to believe something. *My story was greeted with total disbelief.* **disbelieve** *(v)*.

disc *or* **disk** *(n)*
1 a flat, circular shape.
2 a piece of plastic, used for recording music or information. *See* **compact disc**.

discard discarding discarded *(v)* to throw something away.

discharge *(diss-charge)* discharging discharged *(v)*
1 to tell someone officially that they can go, especially from prison.
2 to release a substance into the open. *The factory discharged chemicals into the river.* **discharge** *(diss-charge) (n)*.

disciple *(n)* someone who follows the teachings of a leader or a set of ideas.

discipline *(n)* control over the way that you or other people behave. **discipline** *(v)*, **disciplinary** *(adj)*.

disc jockey *or* **DJ** *(n)* someone who introduces and plays pop music on the radio, at a disco, etc.

disco *(n)*
1 an event at which music is played for dancing.
2 a type of music that is sometimes played at clubs.

disconnect disconnecting disconnected *(v)*
1 to separate things that are joined together. **disconnection** *(n)*.
2 If something, such as an electricity supply or an internet connection, is **disconnected**, it is cut off.

discontented *(adj)* not satisfied. **discontent** *(n)*, **discontentedly** *(adv)*.

discontinue discontinuing discontinued *(v)* to stop doing something that you have been doing regularly.

discord *(n)*
1 disagreement between two or more people.
2 a mixture of musical notes which sounds unpleasant. **discordant** *(adj)*.

discount *(n)* a price cut.

discourage discouraging discouraged *(v)* If you **discourage** someone from doing something, you persuade them not to do it. **discouragement** *(n)*.

discouraged *(adj)* If you are **discouraged**, you lose your enthusiasm or confidence.

discover discovering discovered *(v)*
1 to find something. **discovery** *(n)*.
2 to find out about something. *I soon discovered that Abigail was lying.* **discovery** *(n)*.

discreet *(adj)* If you are **discreet**, you know the right thing to say, and can be trusted to keep a secret. **discretion** *(n)*, **discreetly** *(adv)*.

discrete *(adj)* distinctly separate.

discriminate discriminating discriminated
1 *(v)* If you **discriminate** against someone, you are prejudiced against them and treat them unfairly. **discrimination** *(n)*.
2 *(adj)* A **discriminating** person knows the difference between things of good and bad quality. **discrimination** *(n)*.

discus *(disk-uss)* discuses *or* disci *(n)* a large, weighted disc that is thrown in athletics events. *This statue shows an ancient Greek athlete throwing the discus. Also see* **track and field**.

discus thrower

discuss *(disk-uss)* discusses discussing discussed *(v)* to talk something over. *Can we meet to discuss the new plans?* **discussion** *(n)*.

disease *(n)*
1 an illness. *Measles is an infectious disease.*
2 sickness. *Disease spread throughout the city.* **diseased** *(adj)*.

disgrace disgracing disgraced
1 *(v)* If you **disgrace yourself**, you do something which other people disapprove of and which makes you feel ashamed.
2 *(n)* If something is a **disgrace**, it is very bad indeed. **disgraceful** *(adj)*.

disguise disguising disguised
1 *(v)* to hide something. *Sebastian tried to disguise his boredom.*
2 *(n)* If you put on a **disguise**, you dress up to look like someone else or to hide your identity.

disgusting *(adj)* very unpleasant and offensive to others. **disgust** *(n)*, **disgustingly** *(adv)*.

dish dishes dishing dished
1 *(n)* a bowl used for cooking or for serving food.
2 *(n)* one course of a meal. *A chicken dish.*
3 **dish out** *(v)* If you **dish something out**, you give portions of it to several people.

dishevelled *(adj)* very untidy.

dishonest *(adj)* not truthful. **dishonesty** *(n)*, **dishonestly** *(adv)*.

disillusion disillusioning disillusioned *(v)* If you **disillusion** someone, you destroy their ideas about something.

disinfectant *(n)* a chemical used to kill germs. **disinfect** *(v)*.

disintegrate disintegrating disintegrated *(v)*
1 to break into small pieces. *The chair disintegrated when Oli sat on it.* **disintegration** *(n)*.
2 to break up. *Elana is sad because her parents' marriage is disintegrating.*

disjointed *(adj)* unconnected or not flowing smoothly.

disk *see* **disc**.

dislike disliking disliked *(v)* If you **dislike** something or someone, you do not like them. **dislike** *(n)*.

dislocate dislocating dislocated *(v)* If you **dislocate** a bone, it comes out of its usual place. **dislocation** *(n)*.

dismal *(adj)*
1 gloomy and sad. *Dismal weather.*
2 dreadful. *A dismal failure.*

dismantle dismantling dismantled *(v)* to take something to pieces.

Some words that begin with a "dis" sound are spelt "dys".

dismayed *(adj)* If you are **dismayed**, you are upset and worried by something. **dismay** *(n)*.

dismiss dismisses dismissing dismissed *(v)*
1 to allow people to leave. *Our teacher dismissed us early.*
2 to sack someone from their job. **dismissal** *(n)*.
3 to put something out of your mind. *I've dismissed the idea of having a party.*

disobedient *(adj)*
If you are **disobedient**, you do not do as you are told. **disobedience** *(n)*, **disobediently** *(adv)*.

disorderly *(adj)*
1 untidy and disorganized. *A disorderly desk.*
2 A **disorderly** person is uncontrolled and possibly violent.

disorganized or **disorganised** *(adj)* muddled and not in order. **disorganization** *(n)*.

disown disowning disowned *(v)*
If you **disown** someone, you act as though you do not know them.

dispatch or **despatch** dispatches dispatching dispatched
1 *(v)* to send someone or something off. *We dispatched Uncle Albert to catch his train.*
2 *(n)* a message or a report.

dispensary dispensaries *(n)* a place where medicines are prepared and given out. **dispense** *(v)*.

disperse dispersing dispersed *(v)* to scatter. *The crowd dispersed.* **dispersal** *(n)*.

displace displacing displaced *(v)*
1 to take the place of someone or something else. *When you sit in the bath, you displace some water.* **displacement** *(n)*.
2 to move someone or something from their usual place.

display displaying displayed
1 *(v)* to show something. *Jo displayed no emotion as she read my note.*
2 *(n)* a public show or exhibition.
3 *(n)* special behaviour by an animal to attract a mate. *This picture shows part of the courtship display of a bird of paradise.*
4 *(n)* a screen or panel on electronic equipment, showing information.

courtship display

disposable *(adj)* suitable for throwing away after use. *Disposable plates.* **dispose** *(v)*.

disprove disproving disproved *(v)* If you **disprove** something, you show that it cannot be true.

dispute disputing disputed
1 *(n)* a disagreement.
2 *(v)* If you **dispute** what someone says, you say that you think they are wrong.

disqualify disqualifies disqualifying disqualified *(v)* to prevent someone from taking part in an activity, often because they have broken a rule. **disqualification** *(n)*.

disregard disregarding disregarded *(v)* to take no notice of someone or something. **disregard** *(n)*.

disreputable *(adj)*
If someone or something is **disreputable**, they are known for being bad in some way. **disrepute** *(n)*.

disrespect *(n)* lack of respect, or rudeness. **disrespectful** *(adj)*, **disrespectfully** *(adv)*.

disrupt disrupting disrupted *(v)* to disturb or break up something which is happening. *Owen disrupted the class by shouting loudly.* **disruption** *(n)*, **disruptive** *(adj)*.

dissatisfied *(adj)* unhappy or discontented. **dissatisfaction** *(n)*.

dissect dissecting dissected *(v)* to cut something up and examine it. **dissection** *(n)*.

dissident *(n)* someone who disagrees with the laws of a country or other organization. *A political dissident.* **dissidence** *(n)*.

dissolve dissolving dissolved *(v)*
1 to mix into liquid. *Does this tablet dissolve in water?*
2 If parliament is **dissolved**, it is officially ended and an election takes place. **dissolution** *(n)*.

distance *(n)*
1 the amount of space between two places.
2 If you see something in the distance, it is a long way off. **distant** *(adj)*.

distil distilling distilled *(v)* to purify a liquid by heating it until it turns into a gas, and then letting it cool to form a liquid again. **distillation** *(n)*.

distinct *(adj)*
1 very clear. *Pascale has a distinct French accent.* **distinctly** *(adv)*.
2 clearly different. *The original recording is quite distinct from the cheap copies.* **distinctive** *(adj)*.

distinction *(n)*
1 a clear difference.
2 the highest grade in some exams.

distinguish distinguishes distinguishing distinguished *(v)* to tell the difference between things. *Can you distinguish between a frog and a toad?* **distinguishable** *(adj)*.

distinguished *(adj)*
A **distinguished** person is famous for the important things they have done.

distort distorting distorted *(v)*
1 to twist something out of shape. **distortion** *(n)*, **distorted** *(adj)*.
2 to try to twist the truth.

distract distracting distracted *(v)* If something or someone **distracts** you, they put you off what you are doing. **distraction** *(n)*.

distress *(n)*
1 a feeling of great pain or sadness. **distressed** *(adj)*, **distressing** *(adj)*.
2 **distress signal** a radio message, flare, etc. from a ship or aircraft to show that it is in trouble.

distribute distributing distributed *(v)*
1 to give things out. *Nicole distributed the sweets among her friends.* **distribution** *(n)*.
2 to deliver products to various places. **distribution** *(n)*.

distributor *(n)*
1 a person or company that delivers products to various places.
2 the part of a car engine which revolves, sending electricity from the ignition system to the cylinders.

district *(n)* an area or region.

distrust distrusting distrusted *(v)* If you **distrust** someone, you think that they cannot be trusted. **distrust** *(n)*, **distrustful** *(adj)*, **distrustfully** *(adv)*.

disturb disturbing disturbed *(v)*
1 to interrupt someone when they are doing something.
2 to worry someone. *His news disturbed me.*

disturbed *(adj)* unstable and uncontrolled. *A disturbed personality.*

ditch ditches ditching ditched
1 *(n)* a long, narrow channel that drains water away.
2 *(v)* If a pilot **ditches** his plane, he makes an emergency landing in water.
3 *(v) (slang)* If one person **ditches** another, they leave them suddenly. *Jodie ditched her boyfriend last week.*
4 *(slang)* A **last-ditch** attempt is a final effort made in desperation.

ditto

ditto
1 (n) the same thing as something already said.
2 Ditto marks (") are used in lists to show that what is written is repeated on the line below.

dive diving dived (v)
1 to plunge headfirst into water with your arms in front of you. **dive** (n).
2 to drop down suddenly. *The kite dived to the ground.* **dive** (n).

diver (n)
someone who uses breathing apparatus to work or explore underwater. *See* **scuba diving**.

diverse (adj) varied or assorted.

diversion (n)
1 When a road is closed, a **diversion** takes you on a different route.
2 something that takes your mind off other things.

divert diverting diverted (v)
1 If someone **diverts** the traffic, they make it take a different route.
2 When you **divert** someone's attention from something, you stop them from thinking about it.

divide dividing divided (v)
1 to split into parts.
2 In maths, if you **divide** one number by a second number, you work out how many times the second number will go into the first. *12 divided by 4 is 3, or 12 ÷ 4 = 3.*
3 to share something out. *Let's divide the food between us.*

divine divining divined
1 (adj) to do with God, or like a god.
2 (v) to discover something by instinct, magic, or guesswork. **divination** (n).
3 (adj) (informal) wonderful.

division (n)
1 the act of dividing one number by another.
2 one of the parts into which something large has been divided. *The research division of the company.*

divorce (n)
the ending of a marriage by a court of law. **divorce** (v), **divorced** (adj).

Diwali (n) a festival of light, celebrated by Hindus and Sikhs in the autumn. *At Diwali, Hindus decorate their doorsteps with rangoli patterns like the one shown here.*

rangoli

DIY (n) home improvements, repairs, and decorations that you do yourself. DIY stands for do-it-yourself.

dizzy dizzier dizziest (adj) If you feel **dizzy**, you feel giddy and confused.

DJ short for **disc jockey**.

DNA (n) the molecule that carries information which gives living things their special characteristics. The letters stand for deoxyribonucleic acid. *The diagram shows the linked strands of DNA which separate, as a cell divides, to produce two identical new cells.*

DNA

do does doing did done (v)
1 to perform an action. *Dad was doing the washing up.*
2 to fix or arrange something. *Have you done your hair today?*
3 to be acceptable or suitable. *This bread will do until tomorrow.*
4 to get on. *Philippa is doing well at college.*

dock docking docked (n)
1 a place where ships load and unload their cargo. **dock** (v).
2 In a court of law, the **dock** is where the accused person stands.

doctor (n)
someone trained to treat sick people.

document
documenting documented
1 (n) a piece of paper containing important or useful information.
2 (n) a file on a computer.
3 (v) to write down the facts about something.

documentary documentaries (n) a film or television programme made about real situations and people.

dodge dodging dodged (v)
to avoid someone or something by moving quickly. *Kirsty dodged the ball.*

doe (n) the female of animals such as rabbits, deer, or kangaroos.

dog dogging dogged
1 (n) a four-legged mammal that is often kept as a pet.
2 (v) to follow someone closely.

breeds of dog

golden labrador

withers
stop
flews
muzzle
shoulder
buttocks loins flank
tail
elbow
hock
brisket
sheath
pastern
stifle
dew claw

dole doling doled
1 (n) (informal) money paid by the government to unemployed people.
2 (v) If you **dole out** something, such as food or money, you give it out.

dollar (n)
the main unit of money in the USA, Canada, Australia, New Zealand, etc.

dolphin (n) an intelligent water mammal with a long snout.

bottlenose dolphin
melon (forehead)
rostrum (beak)
dorsal fin
gape (lower jaw)
pectoral fin (flipper)
tail fluke

dome (n)
a rounded roof.

domestic (adj)
1 to do with the home. *Domestic chores.*
2 Domestic animals are kept by people in their homes as pets. **domesticated** (adj).
3 to do with your own or a specific country. *A domestic flight.*

dominate
dominating dominated (v)
1 to control very powerfully. **domination** (n), **dominant** (adj).
2 to be the main feature of a situation. *The castle dominates the view.* **dominant** (adj).

donate donating donated (v)
to give something as a present. **donation** (n).

dalmatian
collie
greyhound
chihuahua
West Highland white terrier

donkey *(n)*
a long-eared mammal,
related to the horse.

donor *(n)*
1 someone who gives something,
usually to an organization or a charity.
2 someone who gives part of their
body, usually after they are dead,
to help sick people. *A kidney donor.*

doodle doodling doodled *(v)*
to draw absent-mindedly while
concentrating on something else.

doom *(n)*
Your **doom** is your fate or
destiny, usually a terrible or
deadly one. **doomed** *(adj)*.

door *(n)*
1 a barrier that opens and closes at
the entrance of a building, room, etc.
2 a house or a building. *My
friend lives three doors away.*

dormant *(adj)*
1 Animals become **dormant** when
they hibernate. They show no signs
of action as if they were asleep.
2 A **dormant** volcano is not active
at present, but could still erupt.
3 When plants or seeds are **dormant**,
they are alive, but not growing.

dormitory dormitories *(n)*
a bedroom for several people, usually
in a boarding school or youth hostel.

dose *(n)*
1 a measured amount of medicine.
2 a brief experience of something
unpleasant. *A dose of flu.*

dot dotting dotted
1 *(n)* a small, round point.
2 *(v)* If you **dot** things around,
you scatter them in various places.

dotty *(adj)* *(informal)* slightly crazy.

double doubling doubled
1 *(v)* If you **double** something, you
make it twice as big. **double** *(adj)*.
2 *(n)* If you have a **double**, there is
someone who looks just like you.
3 *(n)* When you play **doubles** in
tennis, badminton, etc. there
are two players on each side.
4 If someone is a **double agent**,
they work for two opposing sides.

doubt *(dowt)* doubting doubted
1 *(v)* If you **doubt** something, you are
uncertain about it. **doubtful** *(adj)*.
2 *(n)* uncertainty.

dough *(doh)* *(n)*
a thick, sticky mixture of flour,
water, etc., used to make bread
and other things.

doughnut *(doh-nut)* *(n)*
a small cake made from dough
and covered with sugar.

dove *(n)* a bird that makes a
gentle, cooing sound. *The dove is
often used as a symbol of peace.*

down
1 *(prep)* from a higher to a lower
place. *Eliza ran down the hill.*
downward *(adj)*, **down** *(adv)*.
2 *(n)* the soft feathers
of a bird. **downy** *(adj)*.
3 *(adj)* If you feel **down**,
you feel sad or depressed.

download
downloading downloaded *(v)*
to copy information or pictures onto
your computer or phone over the
internet. **downloadable** *(adj)*.

dowry dowries *(n)*
the money, possessions, or property
that women in some cultures
bring with them when they marry.

doze dozing dozed *(v)*
to sleep lightly for a short time. *Uncle
Arthur has dozed off again.* **doze** *(n)*.

dozen *(n)* a group of twelve.

Dr short for **doctor**.

drab *(adj)* very dull and dreary. *Abby
wore a drab, grey dress.* **drabness** *(n)*.

draft drafting drafted *(v)*
1 When you **draft** something,
such as a letter, you make a
first rough copy of it. **draft** *(n)*.
2 If someone is **drafted**,
they are made to join the
armed forces. **draft** *(n)*.

drag dragging dragged
1 *(v)* to pull something
heavy along the ground.
2 *(v)* If something **drags**, it seems to
go slowly. *The lesson really dragged.*
3 *(n)* *(informal)* If something
is **a drag**, it is very boring.

dragon *(n)* a fire-breathing monster
that appears in stories and
legends. *In China, people
create colourful dragons
which dance in their
New Year processions.*

Chinese dragon

drain draining drained
1 *(v)* to remove the
liquid from something.
2 *(n)* a pipe or channel that takes
away water or sewage. **drainage** *(n)*.

drained *(adj)* If you feel **drained**,
you have no energy left.

drama *(n)*
1 a play.
2 If you study **drama**, you learn
about acting and the theatre.
3 something which
affects people seriously.

dramatic *(adj)*
1 to do with acting and the theatre.
2 very noticeable. *A dramatic
change.* **dramatically** *(adv)*.
3 If someone is being **dramatic**,
they are making too much
fuss about something.

dramatize or **dramatise**
dramatizing dramatized *(v)*
1 to adapt a story into a play
or film. **dramatization** *(n)*.
2 If you **dramatize** an event,
you make it seem more exciting
than it really was.

drastic *(adj)*
If you do something **drastic**,
you take action suddenly and
violently. **drastically** *(adv)*.

draught *(draft)* *(n)*
a flow of cold air. **draughty** *(adj)*.

draughts *(drafts)* *(plural n)*
a game played by two people
with black and white counters
on a squared board.

draw drawing drew drawn
1 *(v)* to make a picture with
a pencil, pen, etc. **drawing** *(n)*.
2 *(v)* to pull something. *The
carriage was drawn by horses.*
3 *(v)* to attract. *The band drew
a huge crowd.*
4 *(n)* If a competition ends in
a **draw**, both sides are level.
5 *(n)* a competition where something
is picked out. *A lucky draw.*

drawback *(n)*
a problem or a disadvantage.

drawer *(n)* a sliding box in a piece
of furniture, used for storing things.

drawing pin *(n)*
a small pin with a flat, round
head, used for fastening paper
on noticeboards, walls, etc.

drawing room *(old-fashioned)* *(n)*
a formal room where guests
are entertained.

dread dreading dreaded *(v)*
If you **dread** something, you are very
afraid of it. **dread** *(n)*, **dreaded** *(adj)*.

dreadful *(adj)*
1 very unpleasant. *A dreadful
accident.* **dreadfully** *(adv)*.
2 very bad. *A dreadful film.*

dreadlocks *(plural n)* a West Indian
hairstyle, where the hair is grown long
and twisted into strands.

dream
dreaming dreamed or dreamt (v)
1 to imagine events while you are asleep. dream (n), dreamer (n).
2 If you dream of doing something, you really want to do it. dream (n), dreamer (n).

Aboriginal bark painting

dreamtime
(n) Aborigines believe that life began in the dreamtime, when the world was created by animal, plant, and human ancestors. This painting shows the Rainbow Serpent giving birth to the Aboriginal people in the dreamtime.

dreamy
dreamier dreamiest (adj)
If you are dreamy, you are always day-dreaming and imagining things. dreamily (adv).

dreary drearier dreariest (adj)
dull and miserable. drearily (adv).

dredge dredging dredged (v)
to scrape sand, mud, etc. from the bed of a river or harbour. dredger (n).

drench drenches
drenching drenched (v)
to make something completely wet.

dress dresses dressing dressed
1 (v) to put clothes on.
2 (n) a single piece of clothing, which consists of a top joined to a skirt. A wedding dress.
3 (n) a general name for clothes. Formal dress.
4 (v) If you dress a wound, you clean it, put ointment on it, and cover it.

dresser (n)
a tall piece of kitchen furniture with shelves and cupboards.

dressing (n)
1 a covering for a wound.
2 a type of sauce for salads. French dressing. Caesar dressing.

dressing gown (n) a loose robe
that is worn over your nightclothes.

dressing table (n)
an item of bedroom furniture, often with a mirror and drawers.

dress rehearsal (n)
the last rehearsal of a play or musical, in full costume.

dribble dribbling dribbled (v)
1 to let saliva trickle from your mouth.
2 When you dribble in football, hockey, basketball, etc. you run with the ball, touching it often and keeping it close to you.

drift drifting drifted
1 (v) When something drifts, it moves wherever the water or wind takes it.
2 (n) a pile of sand or snow, created by the wind.
3 (v) to move or act without any sense of purpose. Ollie spent the whole day just drifting about. drifter (n).

drill drilling drilled
1 (n) a tool used for making holes.
2 (v) to use a drill.
3 (n) a strict and methodical exercise or way of doing something. Fire drill.

electric drill
(cutaway)

chuck | gears | electric motor | housing | commutator (regulates electric current)

bit

jaw | drive shaft | cooling fan | trigger switch | handle | air vents | lock-on switch

drink drinking drank drunk
1 (n) a liquid that you swallow.
2 (v) to swallow liquid.
3 (n) an alcoholic liquid. drinker (n).

drip dripping dripped
1 (v) When a liquid drips, it falls down slowly, drop by drop. drip (n).
2 (n) (informal) a silly and rather boring person.

dripping (n) fat that drips
from meat while it is cooking.

drive driving drove driven
1 (v) to control a vehicle. driver (n), driving (n).
2 (v) to force someone into a desperate state. Losing his passport drove Marc to despair.
3 (n) a private road leading to a house.
4 (n) energy. Jenny will succeed, because she has a lot of drive.

drivel (n) If someone talks
drivel, what they say is rubbish.

drizzle (n) light rain. drizzle (v).

drone droning droned
1 (v) to make a steady, dull sound.
2 (v) to talk in a dull and monotonous way. Joseph droned on about cricket.
3 (n) a male bee which does not make honey and has no sting. See honeycomb.
4 (n) a pilotless aircraft.
5 (n) a pipe attached to a bagpipe. See bagpipes.

drool drooling drooled (v)
1 to let saliva trickle from your mouth.
2 If you drool over something, you really like and want it.

droop drooping drooped (v)
1 to hang down or to sag. droopy (adj).
2 When people droop, they run out of energy.

drop dropping dropped
1 (v) to let something fall. Nancy dropped her bag on the sofa.
2 (v) to go downwards. The acrobat dropped to the floor. drop (n).
3 (n) a small quantity of liquid.
4 (v) If you drop out, you stop doing something. dropout (n).
5 (v) When players are dropped, they are left out of a team.

drought
(rhymes with shout)
(n) a long spell of very dry weather.

cable sleeve

cable

drown
drowning drowned (v)
1 When someone drowns, they die because their lungs fill with water.
2 to make a louder noise than something else. The noise of the drill drowned out my singing.

drowsy
drowsier drowsiest (adj)
sleepy. This medicine may make you feel drowsy. drowsiness (n), drowse (v), drowsily (adv).

drug
1 (n) a chemical substance used to treat illness.
2 (n) a substance that people take because of its effect on them. Drugs are dangerous and usually cause addiction.
3 (v) to make someone unconscious by giving them a drug. drugged (adj).
4 drug addict (n) someone who cannot give up using drugs.

dyslexia

drum drumming drummed
1 *(n)* a musical instrument, with a hollow body covered with a stretched skin, that makes a loud noise when you hit it.
2 *(v)* to beat a drum or other surface with drumsticks or your fingers. *Jez drummed his fingers on the table.* drummer *(n)*.

drum kit
tom-tom holder
snare drum
tom-tom
crash cymbal
cymbal stand
ride cymbal
hi-hat
snare drum stand
bass drum
hi-hat pedal
bass drum pedal
floor tom-tom

drumstick *(n)*
1 a stick used to hit a drum.
2 the cooked leg of a bird, such as a chicken or turkey.

drunk
1 *(adj)* If a person is **drunk**, they have had too much alcohol to drink, and cannot control themselves.
2 *(n)* a person who often gets drunk. drunkard *(n)*.

dry dries drying dried; drier driest
1 *(v)* to take the moisture out of something.
2 *(adj)* not wet.
3 *(adj)* dull or boring. *A dry speech.*

dry-clean
dry-cleaning dry-cleaned *(v)* to clean clothes with special chemicals to remove stains. dry-cleaner *(n)*.

dual *(adj)*
1 double.
2 dual carriageway *(n)* a road with a dividing strip between traffic travelling in opposite directions.

dubious *(dyoo-bee-us) (adj)* If you are **dubious** about something, you are not sure about it. dubiously *(adv)*.

duchess *(n)* the wife or widow of a duke, or a woman with the rank which is equal to a duke.

duck ducking ducked
1 *(n)* a water bird.
2 *(v)* to bend low to avoid something.

wood ducks
male
female

due
1 *(adj)* If something is **due**, it is expected to arrive or happen. duly *(adv)*.
2 *(adj)* suitable. *Due care.* duly *(adv)*.

3 If something happens **due to** something else, it happens because of it.

duel *(old-fashioned) (n)* a sword or gun fight between two people, fought according to strict rules.

duet *(n)* a piece of music or a song performed by two people.

duke *(n)* a nobleman. In Britain, a duke is the highest rank of male peer.

dull duller dullest *(adj)*
1 not bright. *Dull metal.*
2 not clever.
3 boring. *A dull speech.*

dumb dumber dumbest *(adj)*
1 not able to speak.
2 *(informal)* stupid. *A dumb film.*

dummy dummies *(n)*
1 a rubber teat given to a baby to suck.
2 an imitation person or object.

dump dumping dumped
1 *(v)* to leave something thoughtlessly or roughly. *Don't dump your bag there!*
2 *(n)* a place where unwanted things can be left. *A rubbish dump.*
3 *(v)* to finish a relationship with someone in an unkind way.

dune *(n)* a sand hill made by the wind, near the sea, or in a desert.

dung *(n)* the solid waste products of large animals.

dungeon *(n)* a prison, usually underground. *See* **castle**.

duplicate duplicating duplicated *(v)* to make an exact copy of something. duplicate *(n)*.

during *(prep)* within a particular time. *Please call during the morning.*

dusk *(n)* the time of day after sunset when it is nearly dark.

dust dusting dusted
1 *(n)* particles of dirt, fluff, etc. that gather on surfaces. dusty *(adj)*
2 *(v)* to remove dust from surfaces with a cloth. duster *(n)*.

duty *(joo-tee)* duties *(n)*
1 the things a person must do or ought to do. *A soldier's duty.*
2 tax charged on goods brought into a country.
3 If you are **on duty**, you are at work.

duvet *(doo-vay) (n)*
a thick, padded cover for a bed, filled with feathers or other light material.

DVD *(n)* a disc that looks like a CD and stores sound, information and moving pictures. The initials DVD stand for digital versatile disc. DVD player *(n)*.

dwarf dwarves or dwarfs dwarfing dwarfed
1 *(n)* a very small person, animal, or plant. dwarf *(adj)*.
2 *(v)* to make something seem small.

dwell dwelling dwelt or dwelled *(v) (old-fashioned)* to live in a place.

dwindle dwindling dwindled *(v)* to become smaller or less.

dye dyeing dyed
1 *(n)* a substance used to change the colour of something.
2 *(v)* If someone **dyes** something, they change its colour by soaking it in dye.

dynamic *(adj)* energetic and good at getting things done. dynamism *(n)*.

dynamite *(n)* an explosive.

dynamo *(n)* a machine for converting the power of a turning wheel into electricity. Some bicycle lights are powered by a dynamo. *As the bicycle wheel turns, the roller makes the magnet inside the dynamo rotate, creating a moving magnetic field. Electricity is produced as the magnetic field sweeps over the wire coil.*

bicycle dynamo
(cutaway)
tyre
roller
iron casing
rotating magnet
wire coil
cable to back lamp
cable to front lamp
release trigger

dyslexia *(dis-lex-ee-a) (n)* If you have **dyslexia**, you find reading and spelling difficult because you confuse the order of letters. dyslexic *(adj)*.

a b c d e f g h i j k l m n o p q r s t u v w x y z

eager

Ee

eager (adj) keen and enthusiastic. **eagerness** (n), **eagerly** (adv).

eagle (n) a large bird of prey which often nests in mountainous areas.

Philippine eagle

ear (n) the part of the body used for hearing. *Sound waves travel down the ear canal and hit the eardrum, making it vibrate. These vibrations are transferred to the cochlea where they are changed to electrical signals and sent to the brain.*

human ear
- nerves leading to the brain
- oval window
- ossicles (small bones)
- cochlea
- ear canal
- eardrum
- outer ear
- middle ear
- inner ear

earl (n) a nobleman. In Britain, an earl is a male peer of middle rank.

early earlier earliest (adj)
1 before the usual time. *An early start.* **earliness** (n), **early** (adv).
2 near the beginning of a period of time. *An early 20th-century house.*

earn earning earned (v)
1 to receive money for working. **earner** (n), **earnings** (plural n).
2 to work to achieve a result. *You have earned your reward.*

earnest (adj)
serious and keen. **earnestly** (adv).

earth (n)
1 Earth the planet on which we live. *The diagram shows the different layers of the Earth.* **earthly** (adj).
2 soil. **earthy** (adj).
3 the hole where a fox lives.
4 a wire through which electricity can pass into the ground. **earth** (v).

Earth (cutaway)
- solid inner core
- liquid outer core
- mantle
- crust

earthquake (n)
a violent shaking of the Earth, caused by a movement of rock plates at the Earth's surface. *See* **fault**.

easel (n) a folding, often wooden, stand for a painting.

east
1 (n) one of the four main points of the compass, the direction from which the Sun rises. **east** (adj), **east** (adv).
2 (adj) An **east wind** blows from the east. **easterly** (adj).
3 (adj) to do with or existing in the east. *The east coast.* **eastern** (adj).

Easter (n) the Christian festival in which people celebrate the resurrection of Jesus Christ.

easy easier easiest (adj)
1 If something is **easy**, it does not require much effort or ability. **easiness** (n), **easily** (adv).
2 comfortable and relaxing. *An easy chair.* **ease** (n).

eat eating ate eaten (v)
1 to take in food through your mouth.
2 If something is being **eaten away**, it is being destroyed slowly.

eavesdrop
eavesdropping eavesdropped (v)
to listen in secret to someone's conversation.

ebb ebbing ebbed (v)
1 When the tide **ebbs**, it goes out and the sea level goes down. **ebb** (n).
2 to get weaker. *The wounded tiger's strength ebbed away.*

ebony (n)
1 a very hard, black wood.
2 a deep black colour. **ebony** (adj).

e-book (n) a book in electronic form.

eccentric (ek-sen-trik) (adj)
odd or strange. **eccentric** (n), **eccentrically** (adv).

echo echoes echoing echoed (v)
When a sound **echoes**, it repeats several times, because its sound waves have met a large surface and bounced back. **echo** (n).

éclair (ek-lair) (n)
a finger-shaped cake made from sweet pastry, filled with cream and usually covered with chocolate.

eclipse
1 (n) In an **eclipse of the Moon**, the Earth comes between the Sun and the Moon, so that all or part of the Moon's light is blocked out.
2 (n) In an **eclipse of the Sun**, the Moon comes between the Sun and the Earth, so that all or part of the Sun's light is blocked out.

3 (v) to do much better than someone else. *They eclipsed all the other teams.*

ecological (adj)
causing little or no damage to the environment. *An ecological detergent.*

ecology (n)
1 the study of the relationship between plants, animals, and their environment. **ecologist** (n).
2 the study of how human activity affects the Earth. This is also known as human ecology. **ecologist** (n), **ecological** (adj), **ecologically** (adv).

e-commerce (ee-kom-urs) (n)
e-commerce is the general name for business carried out on the internet.

economical (adj) not wasteful. *Our car is very economical on petrol.*

economics (singular n)
the study of the way money is made and used in a society. **economist** (n).

economize or **economise**
economizing economized (v)
to reduce the amount of money you spend.

economy economies (n)
the way that a country runs its industry, trade, and finance.

ecosystem (ee-koh-sis-tem) (n)
a self-contained community of creatures, plants, and their environment. *If part of an ecosystem is destroyed, other parts may be affected.*

ecstasy ecstasies (n)
1 a feeling of great happiness. **ecstatic** (adj), **ecstatically** (adv).
2 a drug which creates a short-term effect of pleasure and extreme energy, followed by exhaustion.

eczema (ex-ma) (n)
a skin condition that makes the skin dry, rough, and itchy.

eddy eddies (n) a circular current in a liquid. **eddy** (v), **eddying** (adj).

edge edging edged
1 (n) a boundary.
2 (v) to move very slowly and carefully. *We edged our way along the ledge.*
3 If you are **on edge**, you are nervous or anxious. **edgy** (adj).

edgeways (adv)
1 sideways.
2 If you cannot **get a word in edgeways** in a discussion, people do not give you a chance to speak.

edible (adj) fit or safe to be eaten.

edit editing edited (v)
1 to check a piece of writing for errors and cut it down if it is too long.
2 to select, cut and arrange material for a film, television programme, etc.

edition (n) a version of a book or newspaper, published at a particular time. *A new e-book edition.*

editor (n)
1 the person in charge of the content of a newspaper, magazine, television programme, etc.
2 someone who checks the contents of a book, newspaper article, etc. and gets it ready to be published.

educate educating educated (v) to give people knowledge or a skill.

education (n)
the process of gaining knowledge and skills. **educational** (adj).

eel (n) a long, thin, snake-like fish. *The picture to the right shows an electric eel.*

electric eel

eerie eerier eeriest (adj) strange and frightening. **eerily** (adv).

effect (n) the result or consequences of something.

effective (adj) If someone or something is **effective**, they do their job very well. **effectively** (adv).

effervescent (adj)
1 fizzy or bubbly. **effervescence** (n).
2 lively. **effervescence** (n).

efficient (eff-ish-ent) (adj)
If someone or something is **efficient**, they work very well and do not waste time or energy. **efficiency** (n), **efficiently** (adv).

effluent (eff-loo-ent) (n) waste water and sewage.

effort (n)
If you make an **effort**, you try hard.

effortless (adj)
easy to do or needing little effort.

e.g. the initials of the Latin phrase *exempli gratia*, meaning "for example".

egg (n)
1 an oval or rounded object produced by female birds, reptiles, and fish, in which their young develop. *Also see* **chicken**.
2 a cell created within a woman's body which, when fertilized, grows into a baby.

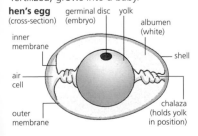

hen's egg
(cross-section)
germinal disc (embryo)
yolk
albumen (white)
inner membrane
shell
air cell
chalaza (holds yolk in position)
outer membrane

egocentric (adj)
If you are **egocentric**, you are far more interested in yourself than in others. **egocentricity** (n).

eiderdown (eye-der-down) (n) a warm bed cover filled with feathers or some other stuffing.

Eid-ul-Adha (n)
the Muslim festival during the last month of the Islamic year when many Muslims make a pilgrimage to Mecca. Some Muslims celebrate the festival by sacrificing animals.

Eid-ul-Fitr (n)
the Muslim festival to celebrate the end of the Ramadan period of fasting.

either
1 (conj) **Either** can be used to indicate a choice. *You can either stay or go.*
2 (pronoun) one of two. *Take either of them.* **either** (adj).
3 (adv) also or similarly. *If Tom's not going to the party, I won't either.*

eject ejecting ejected (v)
1 to push something out. *Press this button to eject the DVD.*
2 to throw someone out. *We ejected the troublemakers from the meeting.*
3 When pilots **eject** from their planes, they are thrown out of the cockpit by a special seat.

spur (breaks through plane canopy)
protective helmet with safety visor
oxygen mask
quick-release harness
lightweight seat (contains rocket motors, parachutes, and survival pack)
leg restraint line

ejector seat
life raft (inflates on contact with water)

elaborate elaborating elaborated
1 (el-ab-or-ut) (adj) complicated and detailed. *An elaborate pattern.* **elaborately** (adv).
2 (el-ab-or-ate) (v) to give more details. *Please elaborate on your plans.*

elapse elapsing elapsed (v)
When time **elapses**, it passes.

elastic (n)
a rubbery material which stretches. **elasticity** (n).

elated (adj) very pleased and excited. **elation** (n).

elbow (n) the joint that connects the upper and lower parts of your arm.

elder
1 (adj) older. *My elder sister.*
2 (n) an older person. *Respect your elders!*

elderly (adj) old.

elect electing elected (v)
to choose someone or decide something by voting. **election** (n).

electrician (n) someone who installs electrical systems and mends electrical machines.

electricity (n)
a form of energy caused by moving electrons, that is used for lighting, heating, and making machines work. **electric** (adj), **electrical** (adj).

electrocute electrocuting electrocuted (v) to kill or injure someone by giving them a severe electric shock. **electrocution** (n).

electrode (n)
a conductor through which an electric current can flow into or out of a gas or liquid. *See* **spark plug**.

electrolyte (n) a soluble substance that conducts electricity.

electromagnet (n)
a magnet which works by electricity.

electron (n) one of the microscopic parts of an atom. Electrons carry electrical energy. *See* **atom**.

electronic (adj) **Electronic** machines contain transistors or silicon chips that control an electric current which makes the machine work. *Computers, televisions, and radios are all electronic.* **electronically** (adv).

electronics (singular n)
1 the study of minute electrical currents, by creating circuits with electronic components.
2 the technology that makes electronic machines work.

elegant (adj) graceful and stylish. **elegance** (n), **elegantly** (adv).

element (n)
1 In chemistry, an **element** is a substance that cannot be split into a simpler substance. *Oxygen, copper, and carbon are elements.*
2 one of the simple, basic parts of something. *Claude taught me the elements of cooking.*
3 a wire or coil in an electrical heater, toaster, etc. that heats up when electricity passes through it. *See* **iron**.
4 **the elements** (plural n) the weather.

a b c d e f g h i j k l m n o p q r s t u v w x y z

elementary *(adj)* simple or basic.

elephant *(n)* a large mammal with a long trunk and ivory tusks, that lives in Africa or southern Asia.

elephants

African elephant Indian elephant

elevate elevating elevated *(v)*
1 to lift something up.
2 to promote someone to an important job or status. **elevation** *(n)*, **elevated** *(adj)*.

elevator *(n)*
1 *(US)* a machine that carries people or goods between different levels of a building (lift, *UK*).
2 the moveable part of a tailplane, used to alter the angle of flight of an aircraft. *See* **aircraft**.

elf elves *(n)* a small, magical, mischievous person described in legends and fairy stories. **elfin** *(adj)*.

eligible *(adj)*
1 If you are **eligible** for something, such as a job, you have the right qualifications for it. **eligibility** *(n)*.
2 An **eligible** man or woman is a suitable person for someone to marry.

eliminate eliminating eliminated *(v)*
1 to get rid of someone or something. **elimination** *(n)*.
2 When a person or a team is **eliminated** from a competition, they cannot take part in it any more. **elimination** *(n)*.

elite *(el-eet)* *(n)* a group of people who have special advantages and privileges. **elitism** *(n)*, **elite** *(adj)*.

ellipse *(n)*
an oval shape. **elliptical** *(adj)*.

elocution *(n)*
the art of speaking clearly.

elongate elongating elongated *(v)*
to make something longer or stretch it out.

elongated *(adj)* long and thin.

elope eloping eloped *(v)*
When a young man and woman **elope**, they run away from their homes to get married. **elopement** *(n)*.

eloquent *(el-oh-kwent)* *(adj)*
An **eloquent** person speaks easily and interestingly. **eloquence** *(n)*.

else *(adv)*
1 other or different. *They have gone somewhere else.*
2 more. *Tell me if you need anything else.*

elsewhere *(adv)* somewhere else.

elusive *(adj)* very hard to find or catch. **elusiveness** *(n)*, **elusively** *(adv)*.

email *(n)*
a message sent electronically. **email** *(v)*.

embankment *(n)*
1 a long, low, earth bank, built to carry a railway, road, etc.
2 a high bank at the sides of a river, built to stop it from flooding.

embargo embargoes *(n)*
an official order forbidding something from happening.

embark embarking embarked *(v)*
1 to go on board a ship or aeroplane, ready for a journey.
2 to start something that will take a long time to finish. *Tanya has embarked on a massive art project.*

embarrass embarrasses embarrassing embarrassed *(v)*
If something **embarrasses** you, it makes you feel awkward and uncomfortable. *Ron blushes when he is embarrassed.* **embarrassment** *(n)*.

embezzle embezzling embezzled *(v)* to steal money secretly from the organization that you work for. **embezzlement** *(n)*.

emblem *(n)* a symbol or a sign.

embrace embracing embraced *(v)*
to hug someone. **embrace** *(n)*.

embroider embroidering embroidered *(v)* to sew a picture or a design on to cloth. **embroidery** *(n)*.

embroidery stitches

backstitch

running stitch

cross-stitch

blanket stitch

double cross-stitch

French knots

feather stitch chain stitch

satin stitch

embryo *(em-bree-oh)* *(n)*
an unborn baby in the very early stage of development in its mother's womb.

emerald *(n)*
1 a bright green precious stone.
2 a bright green colour. **emerald** *(adj)*.

emerge emerging emerged *(v)*
1 If you **emerge** from somewhere, you come out into the open. **emergence** *(n)*.
2 to become known. *News is emerging of a serious road accident.*

emergency emergencies *(n)*
a sudden and dangerous situation that must be dealt with quickly.

emigrate emigrating emigrated *(v)*
to leave your own country in order to live in another one. **emigrant** *(n)*, **emigration** *(n)*.

eminent *(adj)* well-known and respected. *An eminent surgeon.* **eminence** *(n)*, **eminently** *(adv)*.

emir *(n)* a ruler in some Muslim countries, known as emirates.

emission *(n)* the release of something, like chemicals, into the air. **emissions** *(plural n)*.

emit emitting emitted *(v)*
to release or send out something, such as heat, light, or sound. *The spaceship emitted a strange beeping sound.*

emotion *(n)* a strong feeling, such as happiness, love, anger, or grief.

emotional *(adj)*
1 to do with your feelings. *Emotional problems.*
2 If someone becomes **emotional**, they show their feelings, especially by crying. **emotionally** *(adv)*.

emperor *(n)*
the male ruler of an empire.

emphasize or **emphasise** emphasizing emphasized *(v)*
If you **emphasize** something, you make it stand out clearly because you think it is important. **emphasis** *(n)*, **emphatic** *(adj)*.

empire *(n)*
1 a group of countries that all have the same ruler. *The Roman Empire.*
2 a large group of companies controlled by one person.

employ employing employed *(v)*
1 to pay someone to work for you. **employer** *(n)*, **employment** *(n)*.
2 to use something. *You can employ an electric whisk to beat the eggs.*

employee *(n)* a person who works for someone or for an organization and is paid by them.

empress empresses *(n)*
the female ruler of an empire, or the wife of an emperor.

engine

empty empties emptying emptied; emptier emptiest
1 *(adj)* If a container is **empty**, there is nothing inside it.
2 *(v)* to take the contents out of a container.
3 *(adj)* without meaning or purpose. *An empty promise.* **emptiness** *(n)*.

emulsion *(n)*
1 a mixture of two liquids in which the particles of one liquid spread out in the other liquid, but do not dissolve. *When oil and vinegar are mixed, they form an emulsion.*
2 a type of paint, used on inside walls.

enable enabling enabled *(v)*
to make it possible for someone to do something. *Telescopes enable people to see the stars more clearly.*

enamel *(n)*
1 a shiny, glass-like substance that is used to coat and protect metal, pottery, and glass. **enamelled** *(adj)*.
2 the hard, white surface of your teeth. *See* **tooth**.

enchant enchanting enchanted *(v)*
1 to captivate and delight. *I was enchanted by the view.*
2 to put under a magic spell. *An enchanted forest.* enchanted *(adj)*.

enchanting *(adj)* delightful and lovely. *An enchanting cottage.* enchanted *(adj)*, enchantingly *(adv)*.

enclose enclosing enclosed *(v)*
1 to put a fence or wall around an area. **enclosure** *(n)*.
2 to put something in an envelope or package along with a message. **enclosure** *(n)*.

encore *(on-kor)* *(n)*
an extra performance at the end of a show because the audience is applauding so much.

encounter *(n)* an unexpected or difficult meeting. **encounter** *(v)*.

encourage encouraging encouraged *(v)* to give someone confidence by praising or supporting them. **encouragement** *(n)*, encouraging *(adj)*.

encyclopedia or **encyclopaedia** *(en-sy-klo-pee-dee-a)* *(n)* a book or online collection of information about many different subjects. **encyclopedic** *(adj)*.

end ending ended
1 *(n)* the last part of something.
2 *(n)* one of the two points furthest from the middle of an object.
3 *(v)* to finish something.

endanger endangering endangered *(v)* to be dangerous to someone or something. *Pollution can endanger wildlife.* **endangered** *(adj)*.

endangered species *(n)* a type of animal that is in danger of becoming extinct. *The blue whale is an endangered species.*

endless *(adj)*
Something **endless** has no end or seems to have no end.

endure *(v)*
1 If you **endure** something unpleasant or painful, you put up with it. **endurance** *(n)*.
2 If something **endures**, it lasts for a long time. **enduring** *(adj)*.

enemy enemies *(n)*
1 someone who hates you and wants to harm you.
2 the country or army that you are fighting against in a war.

energetic *(adj)* strong and active. **energetically** *(adv)*.

energy energies *(n)*
1 the strength to do active things without getting tired.

2 power from gas, electricity, and other sources which makes machines work and produces heat.
3 In physics, **energy** is the ability of something to do work. It is measured in joules.

engaged *(adj)*
1 If two people are **engaged**, they have decided that they will get married. **engagement** *(n)*.
2 If a phone number or public toilet is **engaged**, it is in use.
3 If someone is **engaged** in doing something, they are busy doing it.

engine *(n)*
1 a machine that changes an energy source, such as petrol, into movement. *In the petrol engine shown here, electrical sparks from the sparking plugs ignite the compressed petrol and air mixture in the cylinders which burns rapidly and pushes the pistons down in turn. The fast-moving pistons turn the crankshaft which produces a twisting effect that turns the wheels. Also see* **jet engine**.
2 the front part of a train that pulls all the carriages. *See* **steam locomotive**.

cambelt
cambelt tensioner
camshaft pulley
cambelt cover
alternator in here (charges battery)
inlet valve (allows petrol and air mixture in)
exhaust valve (sends exhaust gases out)
oil filler cap
four-cylinder-in-line petrol engine (cutaway)
camshaft
cam follower
spark plug lead
spark plug
piston
flywheel
crankshaft
connecting rod
drive belt for alternator
crankshaft pulley
oil sump
oil filter
cylinder filled with petrol and air mixture

engineer engineering engineered
1 *(n)* someone who is trained to design and build machines, vehicles, bridges, roads, etc. **engineering** *(n)*.
2 *(v)* to make something happen by using a clever plan. *Darryl engineered a meeting between the two rivals.*

English
1 *(adj)* from England or to do with England.
2 *(n)* the main language spoken in Britain, the USA, Australia, etc.

engrave engraving engraved *(v)* to cut a design or letters into a metal or glass surface. **engraver** *(n)*, **engraving** *(n)*.

engrossed *(adj)* If you are **engrossed** in something, you give it all your attention. **engrossing** *(adj)*.

engulf engulfing engulfed *(v)* to cover or swallow up someone or something. *A huge wave engulfed the swimmers.*

enigma *(n)* a mystery or a puzzle. **enigmatic** *(adj)*.

enjoy enjoying enjoyed *(v)* to get pleasure from doing something. **enjoyment** *(n)*, **enjoyable** *(adj)*, **enjoyably** *(adv)*.

enlarge enlarging enlarged *(v)* to make something bigger. *We want to enlarge this photo.* **enlargement** *(n)*.

enlist enlisting enlisted *(v)*
1 to join the army, navy, or air force.
2 If you **enlist** someone's help, you get them to help you.

enormity *(n)* a great evil or very wicked thing.

enormous *(adj)* extremely large. **enormousness** *(n)*, **enormously** *(adv)*.

enough *(n)* as much as is needed. **enough** *(adv)*.

enquire see **inquire**.

enquiry see **inquiry**.

enrage enraging enraged *(v)* to make someone angry. *Lacey's unhelpful comments enrage me!*

enrich enriches enriching enriched *(v)* to improve the quality of something by adding good things to it. *You can enrich soil with fertilizer.* **enrichment** *(n)*, **enriching** *(adj)*.

enrol enrolling enrolled *(v)* When you **enrol** in a club, class, or school, you put your name on a list because you want to join. **enrolment** *(n)*.

ensemble *(on-som-bul) (n)* a group of musicians or actors who often perform together.

ensue ensuing ensued *(v)* to happen next. *A furious argument ensued.* **ensuing** *(adj)*.

ensure ensuring ensured *(v)* to make certain that something happens. *Please ensure that you lock the door.*

enter entering entered *(v)*
1 to go into a place.
2 to say that you want to take part in a competition, race, or exam.
3 to type a small amount of information into a computer, or write it in a book. *Enter your name here.*

enterprise *(n)* something that you try to do that is new and difficult.

enterprising *(adj)* Someone who is **enterprising** has lots of good ideas and is brave enough to try things that are new and difficult.

entertain entertaining entertained *(v)*
1 to amuse and interest someone. **entertainer** *(n)*, **entertainment** *(n)*, **entertaining** *(adj)*.
2 to invite people to your home for a meal. *We're entertaining friends tonight.*

enthusiastic *(adj)* If you are **enthusiastic** about something, you are very keen to do it or like it very much. **enthusiasm** *(n)*, **enthusiast** *(n)*.

entice enticing enticed *(v)* to tempt someone to do something. **enticement** *(n)*, **enticing** *(adj)*.

entire *(adj)* whole. **entirely** *(adv)*.

entrance entrancing entranced
1 *(en-trunss) (n)* the way into a place.
2 *(en-transs) (v)* to give someone a feeling of wonder and pleasure. **entrancing** *(adj)*.

entrant *(n)* someone who takes part in a competition, race, or exam.

entrepreneur *(n)* someone who starts businesses and is good at finding new ways to make money. **entrepreneurial** *(adj)*.

entrust entrusting entrusted *(v)* If you **entrust** someone with something valuable or important, you give it to them to look after for you.

entry entries *(n)*
1 a way into a place.
2 a picture, story, answer, etc. that you send into a competition.
3 a small piece of information in a dictionary, diary, computer, etc.

envelop *(en-vel-up)* enveloping enveloped *(v)* to cover or surround something completely. *The house was soon enveloped in flames.*

envelope *(en-ve-lope or on-ve-lope) (n)* a paper cover for a letter or card.

enviable *(adj)* If someone has something **enviable**, you would like to have it yourself.

envious *(adj)* If you are **envious**, you wish that you could have something that someone else has. **enviously** *(adv)*.

environment *(n)*
1 the natural world of the land, sea, and air. *We must protect the environment.* **environmentalist** *(n)*, **environmental** *(adj)*, **environmentally** *(adv)*.
2 all the things that influence your life, such as the area where you live, your family, and the things that happen to you. *Some children never have a secure home environment.*

environmentally friendly *(adj)* Products are **environmentally friendly** if they are made of substances that do not damage the natural environment.

envy envies envying envied *(v)* to wish that you could have something that someone else has. **envy** *(n)*.

enzyme *(n)* a protein in the bodies of humans and animals which speeds up chemical reactions, without being changed itself. *Enzymes help to digest food.*

epic
1 *(n)* a long story, poem, or film about heroic adventures and great battles. **epic** *(adj)*.
2 *(adj)* heroic or impressive. *An epic voyage of exploration.*

epidemic *(n)* When there is an **epidemic**, an infectious disease spreads quickly to many people.

epigram *(n)* a short, witty saying. **epigrammatic** *(adj)*.

epilepsy *(n)* a disorder that causes a person to have sudden blackouts or fits. **epileptic** *(n)*, **epileptic** *(adj)*.

epilogue *(n)* a short speech or piece of writing added to the end of a play, story, or poem.

episode *(n)*
1 one of the programmes in a television or radio series.
2 an event or set of events in your life. *I don't want to talk about that embarrassing episode!*

epitaph *(n)* a short description of someone who has died, written on their gravestone.

equal equalling equalled
1 *(adj)* to be the same as something else in size, value, or amount. **equally** *(adv)*.
2 *(v)* If you **equal** what someone else has done, you do as well as them.

equality *(n)* the same rights for everyone. *Racial equality.*

equation *(n)* a mathematical statement that one set of numbers or values is equal to another set of numbers or values, for example, $4 \times 4 = 16.$ $3x + 2y = 13.$

equator *(n)* an imaginary line around the middle of the Earth, halfway between the North and South Poles. *The equator is marked by a red line in this picture.* **equatorial** *(adj)*.

equator

equestrian *(adj)* to do with horse riding. *Equestrian events.*

equilateral *(adj)*
An **equilateral** triangle has sides of equal length. *See* **shape**.

equilibrium *(n)* balance.

equinox equinoxes *(n)* one of the two days in the year when day and night last exactly the same length of time all over the world.

equip equipping equipped *(v)* to provide someone with all the things that they need.

equipment *(n)* the tools and machines that you need for a particular purpose.

equivalent *(adj)* If one thing is **equivalent** to another, it is the same as the other in amount, value, or importance. **equivalent** *(n)*.

era *(n)* a period of time in history.

eradicate eradicating eradicated *(v)* to get rid of something completely, especially something bad such as disease, poverty, etc. **eradication** *(n)*.

erase erasing erased *(v)*
1 to rub something out with a rubber.
2 to wipe out something stored in a computer, recorded on a DVD, etc.

eraser *(n)* a small piece of rubber used for removing pencil mistakes.

e-reader *(n)* an electronic device used for reading e-books.

erect erecting erected
1 *(adj)* standing upright. **erection** *(n)*, **erectly** *(adv)*.
2 *(v)* to put up a structure. *This building was erected in 2012.* **erection** *(n)*.

erode eroding eroded *(v)* When something is **eroded**, it is gradually worn away by water or wind.

erosion *(n)* the gradual wearing away of a substance by water or wind. *Soil erosion.*

erotic *(adj)* to do with sexual love.

errand *(n)* If someone sends you on an **errand**, they ask you to go somewhere nearby to take a message, or to deliver or collect something.

erratic *(adj)* If something is **erratic**, it does not follow a regular pattern. *Erratic behaviour.* **erratically** *(adv)*.

error *(n)* a mistake.

erupt erupting erupted *(v)*
1 When a volcano **erupts**, it throws out rocks, hot ash, and lava with great force. **eruption** *(n)*. *See* **volcano**.
2 to start happening suddenly. *Fighting erupted on the streets.*
3 If someone **erupts**, they suddenly become very angry.

escalator *(n)* a moving staircase. *This diagram of an escalator shows how a moving belt of steps is controlled by a drive wheel.*

drive wheel for handrail

belt (links drive wheels)

drive wheel for steps

upper track

returning steps

rising steps

lower track (supports wheels)

moving handrail

escalator (cutaway)   wheel (runs along track)

escape escaping escaped *(v)*
1 to break free from a place where you have been kept by force. **escape** *(n)*.
2 to avoid something. *We escaped the rush hour traffic.*
3 to leak out of a crack or hole in something. *Gas was escaping from the pipe.* **escape** *(n)*.

escort escorting escorted *(v)* to go somewhere with someone, especially to protect them. **escort** *(n)*.

especially *(adv)* specially or mainly. *Carrie is especially good at singing. Aaron loves sport, especially tennis.* **especial** *(adj)*.

Esperanto *(n)* an artificial language invented in the 19th century and intended to be a world language.

espionage *(es-pee-on-arj)* *(n)* spying.

essay *(n)* a piece of writing about a particular subject.

essential
1 *(adj)* vital and important. *It is essential that you read the instructions before you begin.* **essentially** *(adv)*.
2 *(n)* something you really need and cannot do without. *Make sure that you bring the essentials listed below.*

establish establishes establishing established *(v)*
1 to set up a business, society, or organization. **establishment** *(n)*.
2 to settle somewhere. *We established ourselves in Paris.*
3 to confirm that something is true or correct. *The detectives established that the crime took place at night.*

estate *(n)*
1 a large area of land owned by one person.
2 an area of land with houses, factories, or offices on it.
3 all the money, property, and other assets that someone leaves behind when they die.

estate agent *(n)* someone whose job is selling houses or land for people.

esteem *(n)* If you hold someone in **esteem**, you respect and admire them. **esteem** *(v)*, **esteemed** *(adj)*.

estimate estimating estimated
1 *(ess-tim-ate)* *(v)* to work something out roughly.
2 *(ess-tim-ut)* *(n)* a rough guess or calculation about an amount, distance, cost, etc.

a b c d e f g h i j k l m n o p q r s t u v w x y z

estuary *(est-yur-ee)* **estuaries** *(n)* the wide part of a river where it joins the sea. *See* **river**.

etc. an abbreviated form of the Latin phrase *et cetera*, which means "and the rest". Etc. is used at the end of lists.

eternal *(adj)* lasting for ever. **eternally** *(adv)*.

ethnic *(adj)* to do with different racial groups. **ethnically** *(adv)*.

EU *(n)* a group of countries in Europe which have special trade and political agreements with each other. EU stands for European Union.

euro *(yoor-oh)* *(n)* the currency of some of the countries in the EU.

European *(adj)* from Europe or to do with Europe. **European** *(n)*.

euthanasia *(yooth-an-ay-zee-a)* *(n)* the painless killing of someone who is suffering from an incurable or painful disease, or who is very old. Euthanasia is against the law in Britain.

evacuate evacuating evacuated *(v)* to move away from an area because it is dangerous. *Please evacuate the building!* **evacuation** *(n)*.

evade evading evaded *(v)*
1 to keep away from someone, or to keep out of their way.
2 to avoid something you should do or respond to. **evasive** *(adj)*.

evaluate evaluating evaluated *(v)* to decide how good or how valuable something is, after thinking carefully about it. **evaluation** *(n)*.

evangelical *(adj)* An **evangelical** Christian tells people about the Christian gospel.

evaporate evaporating evaporated *(v)*
1 When a liquid **evaporates**, it changes into a vapour. **evaporation** *(n)*.
2 to become less and then completely disappear. *Matt's confidence evaporated.*

eve *(n)* the evening or day before an event or festival.

even evening evened
1 *(adj)* An **even** number can be divided exactly by two.
2 *(adj)* equal. **evenly** *(adv)*.
3 *(adj)* smooth and level. *An even surface.*
4 *(adv)* in spite of. *Even if it takes all day, I'll complete the course.*

5 *(adv)* surprisingly. *We all enjoyed the film, even Claire.*
6 **even out** *(v)* If you **even things out**, you make them more equal.

evening *(n)* the time of day between the late afternoon and the early part of the night.

event *(n)*
1 something that happens, especially something interesting or important. **eventful** *(adj)*.
2 one of the activities, such as a race, that is held during a sports competition.

eventually *(adv)* finally or at last. **eventual** *(adj)*.

ever *(adv)*
1 at any time. *Have you ever tried hang-gliding?*
2 all the time. *Ever grateful.*

evergreen *(n)* a bush or tree which has green leaves all the year round. **evergreen** *(adj)*.

everlasting *(adj)* never-ending.

every *(adj)* all the people or things in a group. *Every day of the week.*

everybody *(pronoun)* all people.

everyday *(adj)* usual or normal. *An everyday event.*

everyone *(pronoun)* all people.

everything *(pronoun)* all things.

everywhere *(adv)* in all places.

evict evicting evicted *(v)* to force someone to move out of their home. **eviction** *(n)*.

evidence *(n)* information and facts that help to prove something or make you believe that something is true.

evident *(adj)* clear and obvious. **evidently** *(adv)*.

evil *(adj)* wicked and cruel. **evil** *(n)*.

evolution *(n)*
1 the gradual development of animals and plants over millions of years in order to fit in better with their environment. **evolve** *(v)*, **evolutionary** *(adj)*.
2 a gradual change into a different form. **evolve** *(v)*.

ewe *(n)* a female sheep.

exact *(adj)* perfectly correct and accurate. **exactness** *(n)*, **exactly** *(adv)*.

exaggerate exaggerating exaggerated *(v)* to make something seem bigger, better, more important, etc. than it really is. **exaggeration** *(n)*, **exaggerated** *(adj)*.

exam *(n)* an official test that you take to show how much you know about a subject. Exam is short for examination.

examination *(n)*
1 *See* **exam**.
2 a careful check or inspection. *A medical examination.*

examine examining examined *(v)*
1 to look carefully at something. *The detectives examined the evidence.*
2 When doctors **examine** you, they check your body carefully to see what is wrong with you.
3 to test someone in an exam. **examiner** *(n)*.

example *(n)*
1 something typical of a larger group of things. *The wallaby is an example of a marsupial.*
2 a model for others to follow. *Felicity is an example to the rest of the class.*
3 If you **make an example** of someone, you punish them as a warning to other people.

exasperate exasperating exasperated *(v)* If someone or something **exasperates** you, they make you very annoyed. **exasperation** *(n)*, **exasperating** *(adj)*.

excavate excavating excavated *(v)* to dig in the earth, either in order to put up a building or to discover ancient remains. **excavation** *(n)*, **excavator** *(n)*.

exceed exceeding exceeded *(v)*
1 to be greater or better than something else. *The holiday exceeded my wildest dreams.*
2 to do more than is allowed or expected. *Drivers who exceed the speed limit will be fined.*

excel *(ex-sel)* excelling excelled *(v)* If you **excel** at something, you do it extremely well. *Kate excels at ice-skating.*

excellent *(adj)* very good indeed. **excellence** *(n)*, **excellently** *(adv)*.

except *(prep)* apart from. *Everyone except Hannah went home.* **except** *(conj)*.

exception *(n)*
1 something that is not included in a general rule or statement. *Jasper hates girls, with just a few exceptions.*
2 If someone **takes exception** to something, they are offended or annoyed by it.

exceptional *(adj)* outstanding or rare. *Alexandra has an exceptional talent for drawing.*

excerpt *(n)* a short piece taken from a longer book, film, or piece of music.

excess excesses
1 (n) too much of something. **excess** (adj).
2 **in excess of** more than.
3 If you do something **to excess**, you do it too much.

excessive (adj) too much. *Adam always eats an excessive amount.* **excessively** (adv).

exchange exchanging exchanged
1 (v) to give one thing and receive another. *They exchanged presents. We exchanged glances.* **exchange** (n).
2 (n) a place where people meet to buy and sell things. *The Stock Exchange.*
3 **exchange rate** (n) a comparison of currencies throughout the world. You use the exchange rate to calculate how much money you will receive when you exchange one currency for another.

Exchequer (n) the British government department in charge of collecting taxes and paying out public money.

excite exciting excited (v) If something **excites** you, it makes you eager and interested. **excitement** (n), **excited** (adj), **exciting** (adj).

exclaim exclaiming exclaimed (v) to say something loudly, especially because you are surprised or excited. **exclamation** (n).

exclamation mark (n) the punctuation mark (!) used after an expression of surprise, excitement, or other strong feeling.

exclude excluding excluded (v)
1 If you **exclude** something, you leave it out. *The list excludes prices.* **excluding** (prep).
2 to stop someone joining or taking part in something. **exclusion** (n).

excrete excreting excreted (v) to pass solid waste matter out of your body. **excretion** (n), **excretory** (adj).

excruciating (adj) extremely painful. **excruciatingly** (adv).

excursion (n) a short journey, often to a place of interest.

excuse excusing excused
1 (ex-kuze) (v) If you **excuse** someone for doing something, you forgive them. **excusable** (adj).
2 (ex-kuse) (n) a reason you give to explain why you have done something wrong.
3 (ex-kuze) (v) to give someone permission not to do something. *The instructor excused Lydia from playing because of her injured toe.*

execute executing executed (v)
1 to kill someone as a punishment for a crime. **execution** (n).
2 If you **execute** a plan or order, you put it into action.

executive (n) someone who has a senior job in a company and is involved in planning its future.

exempt (adj) If you are **exempt** from something, you do not have to take part in it. **exemption** (n), **exempt** (v).

exercise exercising exercised
1 (n) physical activity that you do to keep fit and healthy.
2 (v) to make your body work hard, for example, by playing sport, in order to keep fit and healthy.
3 (n) a piece of work that you do in order to practise a skill. *Piano exercises.*

exhale exhaling exhaled (v) to breathe out. **exhalation** (n).

exhaust exhausting exhausted
1 (v) If something **exhausts** you, it makes you very tired. **exhaustion** (n), **exhausted** (adj), **exhausting** (adj).
2 (v) to use something up completely. *The explorers had almost exhausted their food supplies.*
3 (n) the waste gases produced by the engine of a motor vehicle.
4 (n) the pipe at the back of a motor vehicle from which waste gases from the engine are sent out.

exhibit exhibiting exhibited (v) to show something to the public. **exhibit** (n), **exhibitor** (n).

exhibition (n) a public display of works of art, historical objects, etc.

exhilarating (adj) very exciting and thrilling. **exhilaration** (n).

exile exiling exiled (v) to send someone away from their own country and order them not to return. **exile** (n).

exist existing existed (v)
1 to live or to be real. *Did King Arthur exist?* **existence** (n).
2 to have just enough food to stay alive. *We existed on berries and water.*

exit exiting exited
1 (v) to leave or to go out. **exit** (n).
2 (n) the way out of a place.

exorcize or **exorcise** exorcizing exorcized (v) to make an evil spirit leave a person or a place. **exorcism** (n), **exorcist** (n).

exotic (adj)
1 from a foreign, tropical country. *An exotic plant.*
2 strange and fascinating. *An exotic perfume.*

expand expanding expanded (v) to increase in size. **expansion** (n).

expanse (n) a very large area. *A vast expanse of desert stretched ahead.*

expect expecting expected (v)
1 to think that something will happen. *I expect it will rain.*
2 to wait for someone to arrive. *We're expecting visitors.*
3 to think that something ought to happen. *Aunt Alice expects you to behave perfectly.* **expectation** (n).
4 (informal) If a woman is **expecting**, she is pregnant.

expedition (n)
1 a long journey for a special purpose, such as exploring.
2 a short trip to do something enjoyable. *A shopping expedition.*

expel expelling expelled (v)
1 If someone is **expelled** from a school, they have to leave because they have behaved badly. **expulsion** (n).
2 to send or force something out. *You expel air from your lungs.*

expenditure (n) the amount of money that a person, a company, or a country spends.

expense (n)
1 the spending of money, time, energy, etc. *Never mind the expense!*
2 **expenses** (plural n) money spent on something to do with a job, which is paid back later. *Travelling expenses.*

expensive (adj) costing a lot of money. **expensively** (adv).

experience experiencing experienced
1 (v) If you **experience** something, it happens to you.
2 (n) something that happens to you.
3 (n) the knowledge and skill that you gain by doing something. *Do you have any experience of sailing?* **experienced** (adj).

experiment experimenting experimented
1 (n) a scientific test to try out a theory or to see the effect of something. **experiment** (v).
2 (v) to try something new. **experiment** (n).

expert (n) someone who is very skilled at something or knows a lot about a particular subject. **expertise** (n), **expert** (adj).

expire expiring expired (v)
1 When a ticket, licence, etc. **expires**, it reaches the end of the time when it can be used. **expiry** (n).
2 to die.

explain

explain explaining explained (v)
1 to make something clear so
that it is easier to understand.
explanation (n), **explanatory** (adj).
2 to give a reason for something.
*Please explain why you are
so late.* **explanation** (n).

explode exploding exploded (v)
If something **explodes**, it blows apart
with a loud bang and great force.

exploit exploiting exploited
1 (*ex-ployt*) (v) to treat someone
unfairly, usually by not paying
them enough for their work.
exploitation (n).
2 (*ex-ployt*) (n) a brave or daring deed.

explore exploring explored (v)
1 to travel around a place
to discover what it is like.
exploration (n), **explorer** (n).
2 If you **explore** an idea or
possibility, you discuss it or think
about it carefully. **exploratory** (adj).

explosion (n)
1 a sudden and noisy
release of energy.
2 a sudden increase or growth.
A population explosion.

explosive
1 (n) a substance that can blow up.
2 (adj) able or likely to
explode. **explosively** (adv).
3 (adj) If a situation is **explosive**,
it is very dangerous.

export exporting exported (v)
to send goods to another country
to be sold there. **export** (n).

expose
exposing exposed (v)
1 to uncover something
so that people can see it.
2 to reveal the truth about
someone or something.
3 (old-fashioned) to let light
fall on to a photographic film.

exposure (n)
1 the harmful effect of very cold
weather or water on someone's body.
*The survivors from the shipwreck
were suffering from exposure.*
2 (old-fashioned) the length
of time that a photographic
film is exposed to light.
A long exposure.

express expresses
expressing expressed
1 (v) to show what you feel or
think by saying, doing, or writing
something. *Harriet expressed
her happiness in a little dance.*
2 (n) a fast train that stops
at only a few stations.
3 (adj) very fast. *Express delivery.*

expression (n)
1 the act of showing your feelings.
2 the look on someone's
face. *A puzzled expression.*
3 a phrase that has a particular
meaning. *Where does the expression
"lock, stock, and barrel" come from?*

exquisite (adj) very beautiful
and delicate. *An exquisite piece
of embroidery.* **exquisitely** (adv).

extend extending extended (v)
1 to make something longer or
bigger. *We are going to extend our
house at the back.* **extension** (n).
2 to stretch out. *Our garden
extends right down to the stream.*

extensive (adj)
1 spreading over a wide area.
2 including a lot of things.
An extensive choice of desserts.
extensively (adv).

extent (n)
the size, level, or scale of something.
What is the extent of the damage?

exterior (n)
the outside of something,
especially a building. **exterior** (adj).

exterminate
exterminating exterminated (v)
to kill large numbers of people
or animals. **extermination** (n).

external (adj)
on the outside. **externally** (adv).

extinct (adj)
1 If a type of animal
or flower is **extinct**, it
has died out. *The dodo
was a large, flightless
bird that lived on the
island of Mauritius and
became extinct in the
17th century.* **extinction** (n).
2 If a volcano is **extinct**,
it has stopped erupting.

dodo

extinguish extinguishes
extinguishing extinguished (v)
1 to put out a flame, fire, or light.
2 to put an end to a feeling or
belief. *Nothing could extinguish
Romeo's love for Juliet.*

extra
1 (adj) more than the usual amount.
An extra helping of chips. **extra** (adv).
2 (n) someone with a very small part
in a film, usually in a crowd scene.

extract extracting extracted
1 (*ex-trakt*) (v) to take or pull
something out. **extraction** (n).
2 (*ex-trakt*) (n) a short section taken
from a book, piece of music, etc.

extraordinary (adj) very unusual
or remarkable. **extraordinarily** (adv).

extraterrestrial
1 (adj) to do with or coming from
outer space. *Extraterrestrial messages.*
2 (n) a creature from outer space.

extravagant (adj)
If you are **extravagant**, you spend too
much money, or are wasteful in the
way you use things. **extravagance**
(n), **extravagantly** (adv).

extreme (adj)
1 very great. *Extreme
happiness.* **extremely** (adv).
2 furthest or outermost. *We
reached the extreme edge
of the wood.* **extremity** (n).

extrovert (n) someone who enjoys
being with other people and is
lively and talkative. **extrovert** (adj).

exuberant (*ex-yoo-ber-ent*) (adj)
very cheerful and lively.
exuberance (n), **exuberantly** (adv).

eye eyeing eyed
1 (n) one of the two organs in
your head that you use for seeing.
2 (n) the small hole in a needle.
3 (v) to look carefully at
someone or something. *Bert
eyed the parrot suspiciously.*
4 If you have an **eye for something**,
you can judge how good it is.
Sue has an eye for a bargain.

human eye
(cross-section)

ciliary muscles
(used to focus)

sclera
(outer covering)

conjunctiva
(protective layer)

optic nerve
(leads to
brain)

cornea

iris

pupil

vitreous
humour
(jelly-like
substance)

aqueous
humour
(watery
liquid)

lens

suspensory
ligament

retina
(light
sensitive cells)

eyebrow (n) the line of hair that
grows above each of your eyes.

eyelash eyelashes (n)
one of the short, curved hairs that
grow on the edge of your eyelids.

eyelid (n)
the upper or lower fold of skin that
covers your eye when it is closed.

eyesight (n) the ability to see.

eyewitness eyewitnesses (n)
someone who has seen
something take place and
can describe what happened.

eyrie (*ear-ee*) (n) the nest of an
eagle or other bird of prey, built
high on trees, mountains, or cliffs.

a b c d e f g h i j k l m n o p q r s t u v w x y z

Ff

fable *(n)* a story that teaches
a lesson. Fables are often
about animals. *Aesop's fables.*

fabric *(n)* cloth or material.

fabulous *(adj)*
1 wonderful or marvellous.
2 existing only in stories and legends.
Fabulous creatures. **fabulously** *(adv).*

face facing faced
1 *(n)* the front of your head, from your
forehead to your chin. **facial** *(adj).*
2 *(n)* a side or surface of something.
A mountain face. A clock face.
3 *(v)* to look towards something.
Our flat faces the park. **facing** *(adj).*
4 *(v)* to meet or tackle something.
Robin faced many dangers.

facility facilities *(n)*
1 a service provided for people
to use and enjoy, such as
a sports centre, park, etc.
2 the ability to do something easily.
Danielle has a facility for drawing.

fact
1 *(n)* a piece of information that is
true. **factual** *(adj),* **factually** *(adv).*
2 in fact *(adv)* actually.

factor *(n)*
1 one of the things that helps
to produce a result. *Malcolm's
speed was a factor in his success.*
2 a whole number that can be
divided exactly into a larger number.
2, 3, 4, and 6 are factors of 12.

factory factories *(n)*
a building where things are made
in large numbers, using machines.

fad *(n) (informal)*
a temporary fashion or interest.

fade fading faded *(v)*
1 to become paler in colour.
2 to become gradually weaker.
Hope is fading among the survivors.

faeces (*fee-sees*) *(plural n)*
the solid waste matter that people
and animals pass out of their bodies.

Fahrenheit *(adj)*
measured on a temperature scale
on which water boils at 212° and
freezes at 32°. *See* **thermometer.**

fail failing failed
1 *(v)* If you **fail** an exam or
test, you do not pass it. **fail** *(n).*
2 *(v)* If you **fail** to do something,
you do not do it. **failure** *(n).*
3 **without fail** *(adv)*
definitely or every single time.

failing *(n)*
a fault or weakness in
someone or something.

faint fainting fainted;
fainter faintest
1 *(adj)* weak. *A faint sound.*
faintness *(n),* **faintly** *(adv).*
2 *(v)* to become dizzy and lose
consciousness for a short time.
3 *(adj)* A **faint** chance or
idea is a very slight one.
4 **faint-hearted** *(adj)*
timid and not at all confident.

fair fairer fairest
1 *(adj)* reasonable and equal. *Fair
treatment.* **fairness** *(n),* **fairly** *(adv).*
2 *(adj)* **Fair** hair is light yellow.
3 *(adj)* quite good. **fairly** *(adv).*
4 *(n)* an outdoor entertainment
with rides, amusements, and
stalls. **fairground** *(n).*

fairy fairies
1 *(n)* a magical creature
like a tiny person with
wings, found in fairy stories.
2 **fairy lights** *(n)* small
lights that are used to
decorate Christmas trees.
3 **fairy story** or **fairy tale** *(n)*
a children's story about magic,
fairies, giants, witches, etc.

faith *(n)*
1 trust and confidence in
someone or something. *Our
coach has faith in our team.*
2 a religion.

faithful *(adj)*
loyal and trustworthy.
faithfulness *(n),* **faithfully** *(adv).*

fake faking faked
1 *(v)* to make a copy of something
and pretend that it is genuine.
Mia faked her boss's signature.
2 *(n)* a copy of something that is
made to fool people. *This painting
is not by Raphael, but it's a clever
fake.* **fake** *(adj).*

falcon *(n)*
a bird of prey that
has long, tapered
wings and hooked
claws that catches
small birds in flight.
Traditionally, falcons
are trained to return
with their prey to their
owner, or falconer.

falcon

fall falling fell fallen
1 *(v)* to decrease or to become lower.
The temperature has fallen. **fall** *(n).*
2 *(v)* to drop downwards
to the ground. **fall** *(n).*

3 *(v)* to become.
After a while, Eve fell asleep.
4 *(v)* to happen. *Night fell.*
5 *(n) (US)* the season between summer
and winter, when it gets colder, the
days get shorter, and the leaves fall
from the trees (autumn, *UK).*
6 *(v)* If two people **fall out,**
they quarrel with each other.
7 *(v)* If something **falls
through,** it fails to happen.

fallow *(adj)*
Land that is **fallow** has been
ploughed but not planted with crops,
so that it can improve in quality.

false *(adj)*
1 not true or not correct.
False information. **falsely** *(adv).*
2 not real. *False eyelashes.*

fame *(n)* being famous. *Terry
longs for fame.* **famed** *(adj).*

familiar *(adj)*
1 If something is **familiar,**
it is well known or easily
recognized. *A familiar saying.*
2 If you are **familiar** with
something, you know it well.
*Stuart is familiar with all of
Shakespeare's plays.* **familiarity** *(n).*

family families *(n)*
1 a group of people related
to each other, especially
parents and their children.
2 a group of related animals or
plants. *The leopard and the jaguar
are members of the cat family.*
3 **family tree** a chart that shows how
the members of a family are related
over many generations.

famine *(n)* a serious shortage
of food in a country.

famished *(adj)* If you are
famished, you are very hungry.

famous *(adj)* If someone
is **famous,** they are well
known to many people.

fan *(n)*
1 an enthusiastic
supporter of a sport,
pop group, etc.
2 a machine or
an object that
you use to
blow or wave
air on to you,
so that you can
keep cool. **fan** *(v).*

leaf or
mount

stick

guard

Japanese fan

fanatic *(n)*
someone who is
wildly enthusiastic about
a belief, a cause, or an
interest. *Lee is a football fanatic.*
fanatical *(adj),* **fanatically** *(adv).*

fancy

fancy fancies fancying
fancied; fancier fanciest
1 *(adj)* highly decorated or elaborate.
2 *(v) (informal)* If you **fancy**
something, you would like to do
it or have it. *I fancy some lunch.*
3 *(v) (informal)* If you **fancy** someone,
you are attracted to them.

fancy dress *(n)*
If you wear **fancy dress**, you dress up
as someone else, usually for a party.

fang *(n)* a long, pointed tooth.

fantastic *(adj)*
1 too strange to be believable.
fantastically *(adv).*
2 extremely good. **fantastically** *(adv).*

fantasy fantasies *(n)*
1 something that you imagine
happening, but which is not likely
to happen in real life. **fantasize** *(v).*
2 a very imaginative story, often
including magic and fantastic creatures.

far farther farthest
or further furthest
1 *(adv)* at or to a great distance.
Have you travelled far?
2 *(adv)* very much. *I far
prefer cycling to walking.*
3 *(adj)* opposite or distant. *Kim was
waving on the far side of the river.*

farce *(n)*
1 a funny play in which there
are many silly misunderstandings.
2 a ridiculous situation. **farcical** *(adj).*

fare *(n)*
1 the cost of travelling on
a bus, train, plane, etc.
2 *(old-fashioned)* food and drink.

Far East *(n)* the countries of eastern
Asia such as China and Japan.

farewell *(interject) (old-fashioned)*
goodbye. **farewell** *(n).*

far-fetched *(adj)* hard to believe.

farm farming farmed
1 *(v)* to grow crops and rear
animals. **farmer** *(n),* **farming** *(n).*
2 *(n)* land and buildings used
for growing crops or rearing
animals. *The pictures below
show a range of machinery
used on a farm.* **farm** *(adj).*

fascinate fascinating fascinated *(v)*
If someone or something **fascinates**
you, you are really interested and
excited by them. **fascination** *(n).*

fascism *(fash-izm) (n)*
a way of organizing a country
according to extreme right-wing
and nationalist principles, with
a powerful dictator and only
one political party. **fascist** *(n).*

fashion *(n)*
1 a style of clothing that is popular
at a certain time. **fashionable** *(adj).*
2 a way of doing things.

**20th-century
fashions**

1900s 1910s 1920s 1930s 1940s 1950s 1960s

fast fasting fasted; faster fastest
1 *(adj)* quick. **fast** *(adv).*
2 *(v)* to give up eating food
for a time. *Muslims fast
during Ramadan.* **fast** *(n).*
3 *(adv)* firmly or tightly. *Kitty's head
was stuck fast between the railings.*
4 *(adj)* ahead of the right time.
My watch is five minutes fast.
5 *(adj)* **Fast** colours or dyes do not
run or fade when you wash them.

fasten fastening fastened *(v)*
to tie or join something firmly.
fastener *(n),* **fastening** *(n).*

fast food *(n)* food, such as burgers
and pizzas, that is prepared and
served quickly by restaurants.

fat fatter fattest
1 *(adj)* overweight or plump.
fatness *(n),* **fatten** *(v).*
2 *(n)* the soft substance in the body
of a person or animal that helps
to keep them warm. **fatty** *(adj).*
3 *(n)* **Fats** are found in foods such
as meat, milk, and cheese. They
give you energy and are stored
in your body to keep you warm.
4 *(adj)* big or thick. *A fat dictionary.*

fatal *(adj)*
1 causing death. *A fatal
accident.* **fatally** *(adv).*
2 likely to have important, and
usually bad, results. *A fatal decision.*

fatality fatalities *(n)*
a death caused by an accident,
a war, or another form of violence.

fate *(n)*
1 the force that some people
believe controls events and
decides what happens to people.
2 Your **fate** is what will
happen to you in the future.

seed drill

baler

tail
gate

bale chamber

hopper
(seed box)

bale

belts

muck spreader

vertical beater

plough

disc coulter
(vertical blade)

mouldboard
(curved blade)

ploughshare
(horizontal blade)

Some words that begin with an "f" sound are spelt "ph".

fateful *(adj)* important because it has a strong, usually unpleasant, effect on future events. *I remember the fateful day I first met Anna.* **fatefully** *(adv).*

father *(n)*
a male parent. **fatherhood** *(n)*, **fatherly** *(adj).*

fathom fathoming fathomed
1 *(v)* If you cannot **fathom** something, you cannot understand it.
2 *(n)* a unit for measuring the depth of water. 1 fathom = 1.8m or 6ft.

fatigue *(fuh-teeg) (n)*
extreme tiredness.

fault faulting faulted
1 *(n)* something wrong. *A mechanical fault.* **faulty** *(adj).*
2 *(n)* a weakness in someone's character. *Everyone has some faults.*
3 *(n)* If something is your **fault**, you are to blame for it.
4 *(v)* to criticize or to find a mistake in something. *I can't fault your plan.*
5 *(n)* a large crack in the Earth's surface that can cause earthquakes. *The picture shows a tear fault, like the San Andreas fault in California, USA, where parts of the Earth's crust have pulled in opposite directions.*

layers of the Earth's crust   **tear fault**

fauna *(n)* the animal life of a particular area. *Woodland fauna.*

favour favouring favoured
1 *(n)* something helpful or kind that you do for someone.
2 *(v)* to like one thing or person best. *Dad always favours Johnny!*
3 If you are **in favour of** something, you agree with it or support it.

favourite *(n)*
1 the person or thing that you like best. **favourite** *(adj).*
2 the person, team, or animal that is expected to win a race.

favouritism *(n)*
unfair kindness shown to one person more than others.

fawn *(n)*
1 a young deer.
2 a light brown colour. **fawn** *(adj).*

faze fazing fazed *(v)*
to worry or disturb. *Nothing seems to faze her.*

fear fearing feared
1 *(n)* the feeling you have when you are in danger or you expect something bad to happen. **fearful** *(adj).*
2 *(v)* to be afraid of something or someone.
3 *(v)* to be worried about something. *I fear we're going to be late again.*

fearless *(adj)* very brave and not afraid. **fearlessly** *(adv).*

fearsome *(adj)*
frightening. *A fearsome monster.*

feasible *(adj)* If something is feasible, it can be done. **feasibility** *(n)*, **feasibly** *(adv).*

feast *(n)* a large meal for a lot of people on a special occasion. **feast** *(v).*

feat *(n)* an amazing achievement.

feather *(n)* one of the light, fluffy parts that cover a bird's body. **feathered** *(adj).* *Also see* **bird.**

feather

shaft

shaft

barb

hooked barbule

quill   vane
(flat part of feather)   **feather vane**
(magnified)

feature featuring featured
1 *(n)* Your **features** are the different parts of your face.
2 *(n)* an important part or quality of something. *My new laptop has several useful features.* **feature** *(v).*
3 *(v)* to use someone as one of the main stars in a film.
4 *(n)* a newspaper article or part of a television programme that deals with a particular subject. *A music feature.*

federal *(adj)* If a country has a federal government, it is made up of several states which are controlled by a central government but also have their own governments and their own laws. **federalism** *(n)*, **federalist** *(n).*

fed up *(adj) (informal)*
If you are **fed up**, you are bored, or unhappy about something.

fee *(n)* the amount of money that someone charges for a service.

feeble feebler feeblest *(adj)*
very weak. **feebly** *(adv).*

feed feeding fed
1 *(v)* to give food to a person or an animal.
2 *(v)* When babies or animals **feed**, they eat.

3 *(n)* food for animals.
4 *(v)* to put something, for example coins or information, into a machine. *Jan fed all the data into her computer.*

feedback *(n)*
1 comments and reactions to something. *I'd like some feedback on these ideas.*
2 the loud, piercing noise made when the sound produced by an amplifier goes back into it.

feel feeling felt *(v)*
1 to touch something with your fingers, or to experience something touching you. *Jess felt the sun on her face.*
2 to have a certain emotion or sensation. *Maddy felt angry.* **feeling** *(n).*
3 to think, or to have an opinion. *Blaine felt that he had been badly treated.* **feeling** *(n).*

feign *(rhymes with pain)* feigning feigned *(v)* to pretend. *Sam feigned illness so that he could miss the test.*

feisty *(fy-stee) (adj) (informal)*
If you are **feisty**, you are lively and able to stand up for yourself.

feline *(adj)* to do with cats.

fell felling felled *(v)* to cut something down or make something fall. *The gardener felled the tree.*

fellow
1 *(n) (old-fashioned)* a man or a boy.
2 *(adj)* belonging to the same class or group. *I like my fellow students.*

felon *(n) (old-fashioned)*
someone who has committed a serious crime. **felony** *(n).*

felt *(n)*
1 a thick cloth made of wool or other fibres pressed together.
2 **felt-tip** *(n)* a colouring pen with a felt nib.

female *(n)* a person or animal of the sex that can give birth to babies or lay eggs. **female** *(adj).*

feminine *(adj)*
1 to do with women.
2 Someone who is **feminine** has qualities that are supposed to be typical of women. **femininity** *(n).*
3 belonging to one of the main classes or genders of nouns in French, Latin, and other languages.

feminist *(n)*
someone who believes strongly that women ought to have the same opportunities and rights that men have. **feminism** *(n)*, **feminist** *(adj).*

fen *(n)*
an area of flat, low, marshy land.

Some words that begin with an "f" sound are spelt "ph".

fence

fence fencing fenced
1 (n) a wooden or wire barrier built to separate two areas of land. **fencing** (n), **fence** (v).
2 (v) to fight with long, thin swords or foils, as a sport. **fencer** (n), **fencing** (n).
3 If you **sit on the fence**, you are undecided and so avoid taking either side in an argument.

fencing

mask

foil

fend fending fended (v)
1 If you **fend for yourself**, you take care of yourself.
2 If you **fend off** someone who is attacking you, you defend yourself.

fender (n)
a low guard put around a fireplace to stop coal, etc. falling into the room.

ferment fermenting fermented (v)
When a drink, such as beer or wine, **ferments**, a chemical change takes place which makes the sugar in it turn into alcohol. **fermentation** (n).

fern (n) a plant with feathery leaves, or fronds, and no flowers, that usually grows in damp places.

fern frond

spore cases on underside of frond

ferocious (adj)
very fierce and savage. **ferocity** (n), **ferociously** (adv).

ferret (n)
a small, fierce mammal, often used for catching rabbits.

ferry ferries ferrying ferried
1 (n) a boat or ship that regularly carries people across a stretch of water.
2 (v) to carry people or things from one place to another.

fertile (adj)
1 able to have babies. **fertility** (n).
2 Land that is **fertile** is good for growing lots of crops and plants. **fertility** (n).

fertilize or **fertilise**
fertilizing fertilized (v)
1 When an egg or a plant is **fertilized**, sperm joins with the egg, or pollen comes into contact with the reproductive part of the plant, so that reproduction begins. **fertilization** (n).

2 to put a substance, such as manure, on land to make it richer and to make crops grow better. **fertilizer** (n).

fervent (adj) If someone is **fervent** about something, they believe in it passionately. **fervently** (adv).

festival (n)
1 a time when people celebrate something, such as a holy day.
2 an organized set of events, often held at the same time each year. A food festival. A beer festival.

festive (adj) cheerful and lively because there is something to celebrate. A festive mood.

festoon festooning festooned (v)
to cover something with decorations.

fetch fetches fetching fetched (v)
1 to get something or somebody.
2 to be sold for a particular price. That lamp should fetch a good price.

fetching (adj) attractive or pretty.

fête (rhymes with late) (n)
an outdoor event with games, stalls, and things for sale, usually held to raise money for charity.

fetus or **foetus**
(feet-uss) fetuses (n)
a baby or animal before it is born, at the stage when it is developing in its mother's womb. See **pregnant**.

feud (rhymes with chewed) (n)
a bitter quarrel between two people or families that lasts for a long time. **feud** (v).

feudalism (n)
the medieval system in which people were given land and protection by the landowner and, in return, worked and fought for him. This diagram shows how feudalism worked, with the king at the head of the system, and people at every level of society owing loyalty to the lord above them. **feudal** (adj).

feudal system

king

nobles

knights

peasants (freemen and serfs or villeins)

fever (n)
1 If someone has a **fever**, they have a high temperature. **feverish** (adj).
2 great excitement or agitation. **feverish** (adj).

few fewer fewest (adj)
not many. **few** (n).

fez fezzes (n) a round, flat-topped, red hat, worn by some Muslim men.

fiancé (fee-on-say) (n)
If a man and woman are engaged to be married, he is her **fiancé**.

fiancée (fee-on-say) (n)
If a man and woman are engaged to be married, she is his **fiancée**.

fiasco (n) a complete failure.

fib fibbing fibbed (v)
to tell a small lie. **fib** (n), **fibber** (n).

fibre (n)
1 a fine thread of cloth.
2 a part of foods such as cereals and vegetables, which passes through the body, but is not digested. Fibre helps you to digest food. **fibrous** (adj).

fibreglass (n) material made from fine threads of glass, used in buildings, cars, boats, etc.

fibre optics (singular n)
the passing of light through extremely thin glass or plastic tubes, or fibres. Fibre optics is used in operations and for sending communications signals.

fickle (adj)
Someone who is **fickle** changes their mind very often. **fickleness** (n).

fiction (n) stories that are made up. **fictional** (adj).

fiddle fiddling fiddled
1 (v) to keep touching or playing about with something.
2 (v) (informal) to cheat. Nora fiddled her expenses. **fiddle** (n).
3 (n) (informal) a violin. **fiddler** (n).

fiddly (adj) If something is **fiddly**, it is awkward to do because it is very small or very complicated.

fidget fidgeting fidgeted (v)
to keep moving because you are bored or uneasy. **fidgety** (adj).

field
fielding fielded
1 (n) a piece of land, sometimes used for growing crops or playing sports.
2 (v) In games like cricket and baseball, the team that is **fielding** tries to catch the ball and get the batting team out.
3 (n) an area of study or interest.

fielder (n) someone who fetches or catches the ball in games such as cricket and baseball.

Some words that begin with a "f" sound are spelt "ph".

field trip *(n)* If you go on a **field trip**, you travel somewhere to study something in its natural environment.

fiend (rhymes with leaned) *(n)* a wicked person or a devil. **fiendish** *(adj)*, **fiendishly** *(adv)*.

fierce fiercer fiercest *(adj)* violent or aggressive. **fierceness** *(n)*, **fiercely** *(adv)*.

fiery fierier fieriest *(adj)*
1 like fire or to do with fire.
2 very emotional. *A fiery temper.*

fiesta (fee-est-a) *(n)* a holiday or religious festival, especially in Spain and Latin America.

fight fighting fought
1 *(v)* to attack someone and try to hurt them. **fight** *(n)*.
2 *(v)* to have an argument. **fight** *(n)*.
3 *(n)* a determined attempt to achieve something. *The speaker invited us to join the fight against poverty.*

fighter *(n)*
1 someone who fights, such as a boxer or soldier.
2 an aeroplane used in a war.

figure figuring figured
1 *(n)* a written number.
2 *(n)* a person's shape. *Mary has a wonderful figure.*
3 *(n)* a person. *A well-known figure.*
4 *(v)* If you **figure something out**, you understand or solve it.

file filing filed
1 *(n)* a set of data held in a computer.
2 *(n)* a box or folder for papers or documents.
3 *(v)* to put data or documents in a file.
4 *(n)* a tool used to make things smooth. **file** *(v)*.
5 **single file** *(n)* a line of people one behind the other.

fill filling filled *(v)*
1 to make something full.
2 If you **fill in a form**, you answer all the questions on it.
3 If you **fill in** for someone, you do their job while they are away.

fillet *(n)* a piece of meat or fish with the bones taken out. **fillet** *(v)*.

filling *(n)*
1 a substance that a dentist puts into holes in your teeth to prevent more decay.
2 the food inside a sandwich, pie, cake, etc.

filling station *(n)* a garage where you can buy petrol.

filly fillies *(n)* a young female horse.

film filming filmed
1 *(n)* a story shown through moving pictures and sound, which can be viewed on a screen.
2 *(n)* a roll of light-sensitive material that was used in a camera to take photographs.
3 *(v)* to record something with a camera or phone.
4 *(n)* a very thin layer of something. *A film of dirt.*

filter filtering filtered
1 *(n)* a device that cleans liquids or gases as they pass through it. See **aquarium**.
2 *(v)* to put something through a filter.

filth *(n)*
1 dirt. **filthiness** *(n)*, **filthy** *(adj)*.
2 rudeness. *Don't talk filth!* **filthiness** *(n)*, **filthy** *(adj)*.

fin *(n)*
1 a flap-like shape on the body of a fish, used for steering it through the water. See **fish**.
2 a small, triangular-shaped structure on an aircraft, boat, etc., used to help with steering. See **aircraft**.
3 **fins** *(plural n)* long, flat attachments that you fit on your feet to help you swim underwater, also called flippers. See **scuba diving**.

final *(adj)* last. **finally** *(adv)*.

finalize *or* **finalise** finalizing finalized *(v)* to finish making arrangements. *Have you finalized the dates for your trip?*

finance financing financed
1 *(n)* money or the management of money. *An expert in finance.* **financial** *(adj)*, **financially** *(adv)*.
2 *(v)* to provide money for something.
3 **finances** *(plural n)* the amount of money that an individual or a company has. *Our finances are rather low at the moment.*

find finding found
1 *(v)* to discover or to come across something.
2 **find out** *(v)* to learn about something or someone.
3 *(n)* a valuable or important discovery. *This restaurant is a real find!*

findings *(plural n)* the results of an inquiry or a court case.

fine fining fined; finer finest
1 *(adj)* very good or excellent. *A fine painting.*
2 *(adj)* okay or all right.
3 *(adj)* not rainy. *A fine day.*
4 *(adj)* thin or delicate.
5 *(v)* to demand some money as a punishment for doing something wrong. **fine** *(n)*.

finger fingering fingered
1 *(n)* one of the long parts of your hand that you can move.
2 *(n)* an object shaped like a finger. *A chocolate finger.*
3 *(v)* to touch something with your fingers. *Don't finger the food!*

fingerprint *(n)* the print made by the pattern of curved lines on your fingertip.

finicky *(adj)* fussy, especially about food. *A finicky eater.*

finish finishes finishing finished
1 *(v)* to end or complete something.
2 *(n)* the end of something, such as a race.

finite (fy-nyte) *(adj)* limited or with an end. **finitely** *(adv)*.

fiord *see* **fjord**.

fir *(n)* a pointed, evergreen tree with cones and needle-like leaves.

fire firing fired
1 *(n)* flames, heat, and light produced by burning.
2 *(v)* to shoot a gun or other weapon.
3 *(v)* to sack someone from their job.

fire-extinguisher *(n)* a metal case containing water, chemicals, gas, etc. that you use to put out a fire. *When you squeeze the handle of a foam and water fire-extinguisher, the piercer punctures the canister which releases carbon dioxide gas. The gas pushes on the surface of the water and detergent mixture, forcing it up the tube, through the hose and out of the spray nozzle, in a jet of foam and water.*

handle — control spring for hose valve — **foam and water fire-extinguisher** (cross-section) — hose valve — piercer — hose — gas escape drillings — carbon dioxide gas — gas canister — clip for hose — spray nozzle — dip tube — foam and water jet — water mixed with detergent

Some words that begin with a "f" sound are spelt "ph".

a b c d e f g h i j k l m n o p q r s t u v w x y z

fireproof (adj)
If something is **fireproof**, it is made from materials that will not catch fire.

firetrap (n) a building that would be hard to escape from if it caught fire.

fireworks (plural n)
containers, filled with gunpowder and other chemicals, that make bangs and coloured sparks when they are lit.

firm firmer firmest
1 (adj) strong and solid. *A firm bed.*
2 (adj) definite and not easily altered. *A firm manner.* **firmly** (adv).
3 (n) a business or a company.

first
1 (n) a person or thing that acts or happens earliest. *Alfie was the first to leave the party.*
2 (adj) earliest in time. *Michaela took the first bus.*
3 (adv) before something else. *Guy always gets to school first.*
4 (adj) most important. *The first team.* **firstly** (adv).

first aid (n)
medical help that is given to someone immediately after an accident.

fish fish or fishes; fishes fishing fished
1 (n) an animal that lives in water and has scales, fins, and gills. *The fish shown below is a female perch. Also see **gill**.*
2 (v) to try to catch fish. **fishing** (n). See **angling**.
3 (v) If you **fish** for information, you try to discover something in an indirect way.

fist (n) a tightly closed hand.

fit fitting fitted; fitter fittest
1 (adj) healthy and strong. **fitness** (n).
2 (v) to be the right size or shape. *This skirt doesn't fit.*
3 (n) a sudden, uncontrollable attack of something. *A fit of giggles.*
4 (adj) good enough. *Fit for the job.*
5 (adj) (slang) attractive and good-looking.
6 (n) If someone has an **epileptic fit**, they suddenly become unconscious and their muscles become tense.

fitting
1 (adj) right or suitable.
2 **fittings** (plural n) furnishings, such as carpets, curtains, and equipment.

fix fixes fixing fixed
1 (v) to mend something.
2 (v) to decide on something. *Shall we fix a date for the party?*
3 (v) to attach something to another thing. *Fix the photograph to the wall.*
4 (n) (informal) If you are **in a fix**, you are in an awkward situation.

fixation (n)
an obsession or something that you think about a great deal. *Jonathan has a fixation about his height.*

fixture (n)
1 a sports match or event.
2 an object that is fitted into a house, such as a bath or cupboard.

fizz fizzes fizzing fizzed (v)
to bubble and hiss. **fizzy** (adj).

fizzle fizzling fizzled (v) (informal)
If something **fizzles out**, it gradually gives up after a promising start.

flag (n) a piece of cloth with a pattern on it, that is a symbol of a country, organization, etc.

international flags

United Nations

Olympic Games

International Red Cross

European Union

flair (n) natural skill or ability. *Jamie has a flair for cooking.*

flak (n)
1 anti-aircraft fire.
2 (informal) opposition and criticism.

flake flaking flaked
1 (n) a small, thin piece of something. *Large flakes of paint fell off the door.*
2 (v) If something **flakes**, small, thin pieces of it peel off. **flaky** (adj).
3 **flake out** (v) (informal) to fall asleep or collapse.

flaky (adj) (informal) eccentric.

flamboyant (adj)
bold, showy, and brightly coloured.

flame
1 (n) a tongue of fire. **flaming** (adj).
2 **flame-coloured** (adj) deep orangey-red.

flamingo
flamingos or flamingoes (n) a long-legged bird with webbed feet.

flammable (adj) likely to catch fire. *Flammable material.*

flamingos with young

flank flanking flanked
1 (n) the side of an animal, between its ribs and hips.
2 (v) to be at the side of someone or something. *The king was flanked by attendants.*

flannel (n)
1 woven, woollen fabric.
2 a small square of cloth, used to wash your face.

flap flapping flapped
1 (v) to move up and down. *The bird flapped its wings.*
2 (v) to swing loosely. *The sail flapped in the breeze.*

perch (cutaway)

brain — spinal cord — dorsal fin — second dorsal fin — lateral line (for sensing movement) — scales — eye — tongue — kidney — swim bladder — gill — stomach — liver — heart — pelvic fin — spleen — intestine — ovary — vent — urinary bladder — anal fin — caudal fin (tail)

fisherman fishermen (n)
someone who catches fish for a job or as a sport.

fishy fishier fishiest (adj)
1 tasting or smelling of fish.
2 (informal) strange and suspicious. *A fishy story.*

fission (n) nuclear fission
the process of splitting atoms to release energy.

fjord or **fiord** (fee-ord) (n)
a narrow channel of sea that runs inland between high cliffs. Fjords were formed in the Ice Age by glaciers.

flab (n) extra fat on your body. **flabbiness** (n), **flabby** (adj).

flabbergasted (adj) (informal)
stunned and surprised.

flaccid (flass-id) (adj) soft and limp.

Some words that begin with a "f" sound are spelt "ph".

3 *(n)* something attached on one side only. *The flap of an envelope.*

4 *(n)* a hinged part on an aircraft wing, used to control the way that the aircraft rises and falls. *See* **aircraft**.

5 *(n) (informal)* If someone is **in a flap**, they are in a state of panic.

flapjack *(n)* a sweet, sticky cake made from oats and syrup.

flare flaring flared

1 *(n)* a bright flame used as an emergency signal.

2 *(v)* If something **flares up**, it suddenly becomes stronger or more violent.

flash flashes flashing flashed

1 *(n)* a short burst of light.

2 *(v)* to shine brightly, in bursts.

3 *(n)* a short burst of something. *A flash of inspiration. A newsflash.*

4 *(v)* to show something briefly. *Erin flashed a smile at Andrew.*

flashback *(n)*
a part of a book or film that tells you what happened earlier.

flashy flashier flashiest *(adj)*
If something is **flashy**, it is showy and expensive. *Todd wears very flashy clothes.*

flask *(n)*

1 a narrow-necked bottle, used in a science laboratory. *See* **apparatus**.

2 a container which is insulated so that it keeps liquids hot or cold. *See* **vacuum flask**.

flat flatter flattest

1 *(adj)* level or smooth. *A flat surface.*

2 *(adj)* not high. *Flat shoes.*

3 *(adj)* emptied of air. *A flat tyre.*

4 *(adj)* very definite. *A flat refusal.*

5 *(n)* a set of rooms for living in, usually on one floor of a building.

6 *(adj)* In music, a **flat** note is lower in pitch than the usual note. *B flat is a semitone lower than B.*

7 *(n)* In a musical score, a **flat** sign shows that the next note is flat. *See* **notation**.

flatter flattering flattered *(v)*
to praise someone, especially when you want a favour. flatterer *(n)*, flattery *(n)*.

flattering *(adj)*
If something, like a piece of clothing, is **flattering**, it makes you look good.

flaunt flaunting flaunted *(v)*
to show something off confidently. *The duchess flaunted her diamonds.*

flavour flavouring flavoured

1 *(n)* taste. flavoured *(adj)*, flavourless *(adj)*.

2 *(v)* to add taste to food. flavouring *(n)*.

flaw *(n)* a fault or a weakness. flawed *(adj)*, flawless *(adj)*.

flea *(n)*

1 a small, jumping and biting insect that lives on the blood of people or animals.

2 **flea market**
a street market selling old clothes and other second-hand items.

flea
(magnified)

fleck *(n)*
a spot or a tiny patch of something. *A fleck of soot landed on Carl's white shirt.* flecked *(adj)*.

fledgling *(n)*
a young bird.

flee fleeing fled *(v)*
to run away from danger.

fleece *(n)*
a sheep's woolly coat. fleecy *(adj)*.

fleet *(n)* a group of vehicles, such as ships or trucks.

fleeting *(adj)* not lasting long. *A fleeting glance.* fleetingly *(adv)*.

flesh *(n)*

1 the soft part of your body, made up of fat and muscle. fleshy *(adj)*.

2 the meat of an animal, or the part of a fruit or vegetable that you can eat.

flex flexes flexing flexed

1 *(n)* the wire that joins a piece of electrical equipment to the plug.

2 *(v)* to bend or stretch something. *Tarzan flexed his muscles.*

flexible *(adj)*
able to bend or change. *A flexible plastic ruler. Evan is flexible about Saturday's arrangements.* flexibility *(n)*, flexibly *(adv)*.

flick flicking flicked *(v)*
to move with a quick, sudden movement. *Peter flicked a pea off the table.* flick *(n)*.

flicker flickering flickered *(v)*
If something **flickers**, it moves unsteadily. *The flame flickered in the wind.* flicker *(n)*.

flight *(n)*

1 flying or the ability to fly.

2 a journey by aircraft.

3 If you **take flight**, you run away.

flimsy flimsier flimsiest *(adj)*
thin or weak. *Flimsy material.* flimsiness *(n)*, flimsily *(adv)*.

flinch flinches flinching flinched *(v)*
to make a quick movement away from a source of pain. *Diana flinched as the nurse approached with a needle.*

fling flinging flung *(v)*
to throw something violently.

flint *(n)*
a hard, grey stone, used in prehistoric times for making tools and weapons.

flip flipping flipped

1 *(v)* to turn over or move something quickly. *Edward flipped the pancakes.*

2 *(v) (informal)* If someone **flips**, they suddenly become angry or excited.

3 *(n)* a somersault. *A backflip.*

flippant *(adj)* careless and not serious. *A flippant comment.* flippancy *(n)*, flippantly *(adv)*.

flipper *(n)*

1 one of the broad, flat limbs of a sea creature, such as a seal or dolphin, that help it to swim. *See* **dolphin**.

2 one of the long, flat attachments that you fit on your feet to help you swim, also called fins.

flirt flirting flirted *(v)*

1 If you **flirt** with someone, you talk to them in a teasing, sexy way. flirt *(n)*, flirtatious *(adj)*.

2 If you **flirt** with an idea, you consider it, but not very seriously.

float floating floated

1 *(v)* to rest on water or air.

2 *(v)* to move lightly and easily.

3 *(n)* a small object attached to the end of a fishing line, which shows when the fish is biting. *See* **angling**.

4 *(n)* a decorated truck that forms part of a procession.

flock flocking flocked

1 *(n)* a group of animals or birds. *A flock of sheep.*

2 *(v)* to gather in a crowd. *Hundreds of fans flocked to see the band.*

flog flogging flogged *(v)*

1 to beat someone with a whip or stick. flogging *(n)*.

2 *(slang)* to sell something.

flood flooding flooded *(v)*

1 When something, such as a river, **floods**, it overflows with liquid beyond its normal limits. flood *(n)*.

2 to fill or be covered with water. *The road has flooded.*

3 to overwhelm or come in large amounts.

floodlight *(n)*
a strong light, used to light up buildings or sports grounds.

floor *(n)*

1 the flat surface that you walk on inside a building.

2 a storey in a building. *The skyscraper has over 40 floors.*

flop flopping flopped

1 *(v)* to fall limply. floppy *(adj)*.

2 *(n) (informal)* a failure. *The show was a total flop.*

Some words that begin with a "f" sound are spelt "ph".

a b c d e **f** g h i j k l m n o p q r s t u v w x y z

flora (n) the plant life of a particular area. *Woodland flora.*

floral (adj) flowery. *Floral curtains.*

florist (n) someone who sells flowers.

flotsam (n) objects from a shipwreck found floating in the sea or washed up on the shore.

flounder floundering floundered
1 (v) to struggle through water, snow, mud, etc.
2 (v) to have difficulties in coping with something. *Laurence is floundering with his maths.*
3 (n) a flat fish.

flour (n) powder made from ground wheat, corn, etc., that is used for cooking and baking. **floury** (adj).

flourish flourishes flourishing flourished (v)
1 to grow and succeed. *Our new baking club is flourishing.*
2 to wave something around in order to show it off. **flourish** (n).

flout flouting flouted (v)
If you **flout** the rules, you break them deliberately.

flow flowing flowed (v) to move along smoothly like a river. **flow** (n).

flow chart (n)
a diagram that shows how something develops, stage by stage.

flower flowering flowered
1 (n) the coloured part of a plant which produces seeds or fruit.
2 (v) to blossom or produce flowers.
3 (n) a plant which has flowers.

wild rose (cross-section)

anther
petal
filament
stigma
style
ovule
sepal
receptacle
ovary
stalk

flu (n) an illness that gives you a high temperature and makes you feel weak. Flu is short for influenza.

fluctuate fluctuating fluctuated (v) to change all the time. *Petrol prices keep fluctuating.* **fluctuation** (n).

fluent (adj) able to speak smoothly and clearly, especially in another language. **fluency** (n), **fluently** (adv).

fluff fluffing fluffed
1 (n) small, soft clumps of material that come off carpets, clothes, etc.
2 (v) When a bird **fluffs** its feathers, it shakes them out.

fluid
1 (n) a flowing substance, either a liquid or gas.
2 (adj) flowing or liquid. **fluidity** (n).

fluke (n)
1 a lucky accident.
2 part of the tail of a sea creature, such as a whale or dolphin. *See* **dolphin**.

fluorescent (adj)
1 giving out a bright light. *Fluorescent lighting.* **fluorescence** (n).
2 A **fluorescent** colour is so bright that it seems to give out light when a light is shone on it.

fluoride (n) a chemical that can be put in toothpaste and water to prevent tooth decay.

flush flushes flushing flushed (v) to flood something with water as a way of cleaning it. **flush** (n).

flushed (adj) If you are **flushed**, your face has become red. **flush** (n).

flustered (adj) If you are **flustered**, you are confused or rushed. **fluster** (v).

flutter fluttering fluttered
1 (v) to wave or flap rapidly. *The flag fluttered in the breeze.*
2 (n) If you are **in a flutter** about something, you are excited and nervous about it.

fly flies flying flew flown
1 (v) to travel through the air.
2 (n) an insect with wings. *See* **insect**.
3 **flies** (plural n) a flap on trousers which covers a zip or buttons.
4 (v) to move fast or to do something fast. *Time just flew by.*

fly-fishing (n) a type of fishing using artificial flies made from fur, feathers, etc. that are attached to a hook which the fish swallows. *The picture shows examples of four types of fly used in fly-fishing for trout: a dry fly represents an adult fly; a wet fly imitates a hatching fly; a nymph represents a fly larva; and a lure attracts the trout by its colour or brightness.*

trout-fishing flies

Greenwell's glory (nymph)

French partridge mayfly (dry fly)

Peter Ross (wet fly)

black ghost (lure)

flying saucer (n) a saucer-shaped flying object, believed by some to be a spacecraft from another planet.

flyover (n) a bridge that carries one road over another.

foal foaling foaled
1 (n) a young horse.
2 (v) to give birth to a young horse.

foam foaming foamed
1 (n) a mass of small bubbles.
2 (v) to make bubbles.
3 (n) a soft, spongy material, often used to stuff toys or furniture.

focus focuses or foci; focuses focusing focused
1 (v) to adjust your eyes or a camera lens so that you can see something clearly. *I focused my camera carefully before I took the picture.*
2 (v) to concentrate on someone or something. *Let's focus on your problems.*
3 (n) the centre of a picture or the centre of attention. **focal** (adj).

fodder (n) food for cows and horses.

foe (n) an enemy.

foetus *see* **fetus**.

fog (n) a very thick mist of water droplets in the air. **foggy** (adj).

foghorn (n) a loud siren used to warn ships in foggy weather.

foil foiling foiled
1 (n) thin, silvery sheets of metal.
2 (v) to prevent someone from carrying out a plan. *The police foiled the robbers' plot.*
3 (n) a sword used in fencing. *See* **fence**.

fold folding folded
1 (v) to bend something over on itself. *Alison folded the sheets.*
2 (n) a small, fenced area for sheep.
3 (v) If a company **folds**, it collapses and stops trading.

folder (n)
1 a cardboard or plastic cover used for keeping papers.
2 a file for computer documents.

foliage (n) leaves.

folk folk or folks
1 (n) people, especially your family.
2 (adj) traditional and belonging to the ordinary people. *Folk music.*

folklore (n) the stories, customs, and knowledge of ordinary people, that are passed down to their children.

follow following followed (v)
1 to go behind someone.
2 to come after. *August follows July.*
3 to be guided by someone or something. *Harvey always follows the latest trends.* **follower** (n).

Some words that begin with a "f" sound are spelt "ph".

forgive

following
1 *(prep)* coming after something. *Following dinner, there is a short talk.*
2 *(adj)* next or after. *The following year.*
3 *(n)* If someone has a **following**, they are very popular. **follower** *(n)*.

folly follies *(n)*

folly
1 foolishness.
2 a foolish act.
3 a building with no real purpose. *The folly in the picture is on the Isle of Wight, England.*

fond fonder fondest *(adj)* If you are **fond** of someone or something, you like them. **fondness** *(n)*, **fondly** *(adv)*.

fondle fondling fondled *(v)*
to touch or stroke gently. *Nancy fondled the kitten.*

font *(n)*
1 a style of typeface.
2 a large, stone bowl used in a church to hold the water for baptisms.

food *(n)*
substances that people, animals, and plants take in to stay alive and grow.

food chain *(n)* a group of animals and plants which are dependent on each other, since each one feeds on the one below them in the chain. *The food chain shown here has one producer and several consumers.*

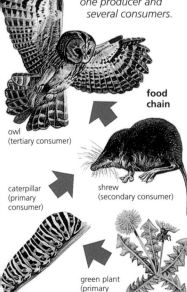

food chain

owl (tertiary consumer)

caterpillar (primary consumer)

shrew (secondary consumer)

green plant (primary producer)

food web *(n)* the complex network of food chains in an ecosystem.

fool fooling fooled
1 *(n)* a silly person. **foolishness** *(n)*, **foolish** *(adj)*, **foolishly** *(adv)*.
2 *(v)* to trick someone. *The dealer fooled Jackie into buying a fake watch.*

foolproof *(adj)* Something that is **foolproof** is very simple to use, and cannot easily go wrong.

foot feet *(n)*
1 one of the two parts of your body that you walk on.
2 the bottom or the lower end of something. *The foot of the bed.*
3 a unit of length equalling 12 inches.

football *(n)*
1 an outdoor ball game played by two teams who try to score goals. Soccer, rugby football, and American football are all types of football. *The picture shows an American football player with part of his clothing cut away.* **footballer** *(n)*.
2 the ball used to play football.

leather football
shoulder pad
helmet
face mask
chin strap
chest plate
jersey
hip pad
towel
girdle shell
knee-length trousers
thigh pad
knee pad
elastic tape (protects ankles)
sock
cleat (studded shoe)

American football player

footnote *(n)*
a note at the bottom of a page.

footprint *(n)*
1 the shape left by the foot of a person or animal.
2 the amount of space something occupies.
3 impact on the environment. *See* **carbon footprint**.

forage foraging foraged *(v)*
to go in search of food. *We foraged for wild mushrooms.*

forbid forbidding forbade forbidden *(v)* to tell someone not to do something. **forbidden** *(adj)*.

forbidding *(adj)* unfriendly or off-putting. **forbiddingly** *(adv)*.

force forcing forced
1 *(v)* If you **force** someone to do something, you make them do it. **forceful** *(adj)*, **forcefully** *(adv)*.
2 *(n)* strength or power.
3 *(n)* In physics, a **force** is any action that alters the shape or the movement of an object.
4 *(n)* an army or other team of people. *The police force.*

forceps *(plural n)* an instrument, similar to tongs, used for holding or lifting, especially in operations.

forecast forecasting forecast *or* forecasted *(v)* to say what you think will happen in the future. *The weatherman forecasts rain for tomorrow.* **forecast** *(n)*, **forecaster** *(n)*.

foreground *(n)*
the part of a picture that is in front of the main subject.

forehead *(n)* the top part of your face between your hair and your eyes.

foreign *(adj)*
1 to do with or coming from another country. **foreigner** *(n)*.
2 If something is **foreign** to you, it is strange or unnatural.

forensic *(adj)* A forensic investigation uses scientific information such as fingerprints, blood tests, etc. to help investigate or solve crimes. **forensically** *(adv)*.

foresee foreseeing foresaw foreseen *(v)* to expect or predict that something will happen. **foresight** *(n)*, **foreseeable** *(adj)*.

forest *(n)* a large area thickly covered with trees. **forested** *(adj)*.

forever *(adv)* always or continually. *Matt is forever asking questions.*

forfeit forfeiting forfeited
1 *(n)* a penalty.
2 *(v)* to give up the right to something.

forge forging forged
1 *(v)* to make illegal copies of paintings, money, etc. **forger** *(n)*, **forgery** *(n)*.
2 *(v)* If you **forge ahead**, you move forward or make progress.
3 *(n)* a blacksmith's workshop.

forget forgetting forgot forgotten *(v)* If you **forget** something, you do not remember it. **forgetfulness** *(n)*, **forgetful** *(adj)*.

forgive forgiving forgave forgiven *(v)* to pardon someone or to stop blaming them for something. **forgiveness** *(n)*, **forgiving** *(adj)*.

Some words that begin with a "f" sound are spelt "ph".

a b c d e **f** g h i j k l m n o p q r s t u v w x y z

fork

fork forking forked
1 (n) an instrument with prongs, used for eating or for working in a garden.
2 (n) a place where a road, river, tree, etc. branches in two or more directions. **fork** (v), **forked** (adj).
3 (v) If you **fork out** for something, you pay for it reluctantly.

fork-lift truck (n) a vehicle with two prongs, or forks, at the front, used for lifting and carrying loads. *When the driver operates the controls on this fork-lift truck, the cylinder rises and chains pull up the carriage and the forks, which carry the load.*

fork-lift truck
(cutaway)

driver's carriage
suspension seat
steering wheel
exhaust pipe
steering axle
wide tyre
high-capacity batteries
counterweight
diesel engine
drum brake
carriage
load
fork
lift chain pulley
mast
lift cylinder (rises to pull up carriage and fork)
hydraulic controls
adjustable steering column
scuttle
hydraulic control valve
lift chain

forlorn (adj)
sad or lonely. **forlornly** (adv).

form forming formed
1 (n) shape. *The monster took on a human form.* **formless** (adj).
2 (n) a type or a kind. *Which form of travel do you prefer?*
3 (v) to make up or create something. *The lines formed a rectangle.*
4 (n) a class at school.
5 (n) a piece of paper with questions to be filled in.
6 If you are **in good form**, you are fit and cheerful.

formal (adj)
1 official. *We're waiting for formal permission before we make any plans.* **formally** (adv).
2 proper and not casual. *Formal clothes.* **formally** (adv).

format formatting formatted
1 (v) to change the structure or style of a document, disc or book.
2 (n) the shape or style of something. *The new magazine has a bolder, larger format than the old one.*

formation (n)
1 the process of making something. *We are studying the formation of crystals.*
2 a pattern or a shape. *Look at that wonderful cloud formation!*

former
1 (n) the first of two things just mentioned. *I am fond of spiders and snakes, but I really prefer the former.*
2 (adj) previous or earlier. *Our former house.* **formerly** (adv).

formidable (adj)
difficult or frightening. *A formidable challenge.* **formidably** (adv).

formula formulas or formulae (n)
1 a rule in science or maths that is written with numbers and symbols.
2 a suggested set of actions. *What's your formula for success?*

formulate
formulating formulated (v)
If you **formulate** a theory, you work out an idea and then state it clearly.

forsake
forsaking forsook forsaken (v)
to abandon or give up someone or something.

fort (n)
1 a building similar to a castle, which is strongly built to survive attacks.
2 If you **hold the fort**, you look after things for someone else while they are away.

forte (for-tay)
1 (n) Your **forte** is your strong point.
2 (adv) loudly. **Forte** is an Italian word, used as an instruction in music.

forthcoming (adj)
1 coming soon. *Forthcoming attractions.*
2 If someone is not very **forthcoming**, they do not say much.

fortify fortifies
fortifying fortified (v)
1 to make a place stronger against attack. *The soldiers fortified the castle's defences.* **fortification** (n).
2 If you **fortify** yourself, you make yourself feel better and stronger.

fortnight (n) a two-week period. **fortnightly** (adj), **fortnightly** (adv).

fortress fortresses (n)
a castle or town that is strengthened against attack.

fortunate (adj)
lucky. **fortunately** (adv).

fortune (n)
1 chance or good luck.
2 a large amount of money.
3 fate or destiny.

forward
1 forward or forwards (adv) toward the front or ahead. *We crept forward cautiously.* **forward** (adj).
2 (adv) toward the future. *I am looking forward to the holidays.*
3 (n) a player in football, hockey, etc. who plays in an attacking position and tries to score goals.

fossil (n) the remains or trace of an animal or a plant from millions of years ago, preserved as rock. *Examples of different types of fossils are shown in this picture.* **fossilized** (adj).

fossils

echinoderm

gastropod

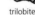

ammonite
brachiopod
trilobite

foster fostering fostered *(v)*
1 to encourage or develop
something. *The new club
fostered a sense of community.*
2 to look after a child who
is not your own, without
becoming its legal parent.

foul fouling fouled; fouler foulest
1 *(adj)* very dirty or disgusting.
2 *(v)* to make something
dirty or unpleasant.
3 *(n)* an action in sport that
is against the rules. **foul** *(v).*

found founding founded *(v)*
to set up or start something,
such as a school. **founder** *(n).*

foundation *(n)*
1 the base or basis of something.
2 foundations *(plural n)*
solid structures on which a
building is built. *See* **building**.

foundry foundries *(n)* a workshop
for melting and shaping metal.

fountain *(n)* a shower of water,
pumped up into a pool, sometimes
through an ornament or statue.

fountain pen *(n)*
a pen with a nib that is supplied with
ink from a container inside the pen.

fowl fowl *or* fowls *(n)* a bird, such
as a chicken or duck, that is kept
for its eggs or meat.

fox foxes *(n)*
a kind of wild
dog, with
large,
pointed
ears, and
a bushy tail.

foyer *(foy-ay) (n)*
the entrance hall of
a cinema, theatre, or hotel.

red fox

fractal *(n)*
a mathematically-produced pattern
whose parts, when magnified,
exactly resemble the whole.

fraction *(n)*
1 a part of a whole number.
$1/2$, $3/4$, *and* $7/8$ *are all fractions.*
2 a small amount. *Polly bought the
painting for a fraction of its real value.*
fractional *(adj),* **fractionally** *(adv).*

fracture fracturing fractured *(v)*
to break or crack something,
especially a bone. **fracture** *(n).*

fragile *(adj)*
delicate or easily broken.

fragment *(frag-ment) (n)*
a small piece of something.
fragment *(frag-ment) (v).*

fragrant *(adj)*
sweet-smelling. **fragrance** *(n).*

frail frailer frailest *(adj)*
feeble and weak. **frailty** *(n).*

frame framing framed
1 *(n)* a basic structure over
which something is built.
Our house has a timber frame.
2 *(n)* a border that surrounds
something. *A picture frame.*
3 *(v)* to put something in a frame.
4 *(v) (informal)* If someone **frames**
an innocent person, they make
them seem guilty by giving
false information about them.

framework *(n)* the structure
of a building or other object.

frank franker frankest *(adj)*
open and honest.
frankness *(n),* **frankly** *(adv).*

frantic *(adj)* wildly anxious
or wildly excited. **frantically** *(adv).*

fraud *(n)*
1 If you practise **fraud**, you
gain money by tricking people.
fraudulent *(adj),* **fraudulently** *(adv).*
2 If someone is a **fraud**, they pretend
to be something they are not.

freak
1 *(adj)* very unusual.
Freak weather conditions.
2 *(n)* an unnatural or
strange person or animal.
3 *(n) (informal)* someone who
is very enthusiastic about
something. *A health freak.*

freckle *(n)*
a small, light brown spot on your
skin, caused by exposure to the sun.
freckled *(adj),* **freckly** *(adj).*

free freeing freed; freer freest
1 *(adj)* If a person or animal is **free**,
they can do whatever they like and
go wherever they like. **freely** *(adv).*
2 *(v)* If you **free** a person or animal,
you let them go from a prison or cage.
3 *(adj)* If something is **free**,
it does not cost anything.

freedom *(n)*
the right to do and say what you like.

freelance *(adj)*
If you are a **freelance** worker, you
do not earn a salary, but are paid for
each job that you do. **freelancer** *(n).*

free-range *(adj)*
Free-range animals are allowed
to feed and wander freely.

freeze
freezing froze frozen *(v)*
1 to become solid or icy at a
very low temperature. *Water
freezes at 0°C.* **freezing** *(adj).*
2 to stop still because
you are frightened.

freezer *(n)* a large refrigerator
which is kept very cold so that you
can store food in it for several months.

freight *(frate) (n)* goods or cargo
carried by trains, ships, planes, etc.

freighter *(fray-ter) (n)*
a plane or ship that carries goods.

frenzy frenzies *(n)* If you are in a
frenzy, you are wildly excited or angry
about something. **frenzied** *(adj).*

frequency frequencies *(n)*
1 the number of times that
something happens. *The frequency
of road accidents has decreased.*
2 the number of radio waves
per second of a radio signal.
High frequency radio signals.

frequent frequenting frequented
1 *(free-kwent) (adj)* common or
happening often. **frequently** *(adv).*
2 *(free-kwent) (v)* to visit
somewhere often or regularly.
Mike frequents the local park.

fresco frescos *or* frescoes *(n)*
a painting made on a wall or
ceiling while the plaster is still
wet. *This ancient Minoan fresco
shows a bull-leaping ritual.*

fresco

fresh fresher freshest *(adj)*
1 clean or new. **freshly** *(adv).*
2 not frozen, tinned, dried,
etc. *Fresh fruit.*
3 cool. *A fresh sea breeze.*

freshwater *(adj)* to do with or
living in water that does not contain
salt. *Freshwater fish.*

fret fretting fretted
1 *(v)* to worry or get annoyed
about something. **fretfulness** *(n),*
fretful *(adj),* **fretfully** *(adv).*
2 *(n)* one of the bars on the
fingerboard of a stringed
musical instrument, such
as a guitar. *See* **guitar**.

friction *(n)*
1 the force which slows objects down
when they rub against each other.
2 disagreement or arguing.

fridge *short for* **refrigerator**.

friend *(n)*
someone you enjoy being
with and know well. **friendship** *(n).*

friendly
friendlier friendliest *(adj)*
kind and helpful. **friendliness** *(n).*

Some words that begin with a "f" sound are spelt "ph".

frieze *(freez) (n)* a decorated strip, usually along the top of a wall.

fright *(n)*
1 a sudden feeling of fear. *I had a fright when you jumped out on me.*
2 *(informal)* If someone **looks a fright**, they look messy or shocking.

frighten frightening frightened *(v)* to scare someone. **frightening** *(adj)*.

frightful *(adj)* terrible or shocking. **frightfully** *(adv)*.

frill *(n)* a ruffled strip of material or paper, used as decoration. **frilly** *(adj)*.

fringe fringing fringed
1 *(n)* the hair that hangs over your forehead.
2 *(v)* to form an edge or border. *Bluebells fringed the path.* **fringe** *(n)*.
3 *(adj)* unconventional or not mainstream. *A fringe festival.*

frisk frisking frisked *(v)*
1 to play in a lively way. **frisky** *(adj)*, **friskily** *(adv)*.
2 *(informal)* to search someone for weapons, drugs, etc.

frivolous *(adj)* silly and light-hearted. **frivolously** *(adv)*.

frog *(n)* a small amphibian with long back legs for jumping. Frogs live on land, but lay their eggs in water. *The pictures below show the life cycle of the common frog. Also see* **anatomy**, **rainforest**.

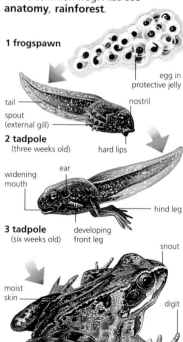

1 frogspawn

egg in protective jelly

tail
spout (external gill)
nostril

2 tadpole
(three weeks old)
hard lips

widening mouth
ear

hind leg

3 tadpole
(six weeks old)
developing front leg

snout

moist skin

digit

4 frog
(adult male)
webbed foot

frolic frolicking frolicked *(v)* to play happily. **frolic** *(n)*.

from *(prep)*
1 You use **from** to show the starting point, origin, or source of something. *The journey from home to school. A few miles from here. From 2010 to 2012. It's made from clay.*
2 because of. *I'm tired from running. We got sick from eating bad fish.*

frond *(n)* a large, divided leaf on a plant such as a fern or palm. *See* **fern**.

front *(n)*
1 the part of something that faces forwards. **front** *(adj)*.
2 the place where armies are fighting.
3 the edge of a mass of cold or warm air.
4 If you **put up a front**, you pretend to feel or think something.

frontier *(n)* the border between two countries.

frost frosting frosted
1 *(n)* powdery ice that forms on things in freezing weather.
2 *(v)* If something **frosts up**, it becomes covered with frost. *The windscreen frosted up overnight.*
3 *(n)* weather with a temperature below freezing point.

frostbite *(n)* If someone suffers from **frostbite**, parts of their body, such as their fingers, toes, or ears, are damaged by extreme cold. **frostbitten** *(adj)*.

frosty frostier frostiest *(adj)*
1 covered with frost.
2 very cold because there is a frost. *Frosty weather.*
3 If someone is **frosty**, they are unfriendly.
frostiness *(n)*, **frostily** *(adv)*.

froth *(n)* lots of small bubbles on top of a liquid. **froth** *(v)*, **frothy** *(adj)*.

frown frowning frowned *(v)* to move your eyebrows together and wrinkle your forehead, usually as a sign that you are annoyed. *Dad frowned when he saw the broken window.* **frown** *(n)*.

frozen *(adj)*
1 If something, such as food, is **frozen**, it has been made so cold that all the water in it has turned into ice.
2 extremely cold. *My hands are frozen.*

frugal *(adj)* If you are **frugal**, you are very careful not to waste anything. **frugality** *(n)*, **frugally** *(adv)*.

fruit fruit *or* fruits *(n)*
1 an edible part of a plant or tree, containing seeds. **fruity** *(adj)*.
2 the result of something. *This book is the fruit of many years' hard work.*

fruit

melon
pear
peach
apple
nectarine
apricot
plum
grapes
cherries
grapefruit
orange
lemon
lime
kumquat
strawberry
raspberry
cranberries
blackberry
gooseberry
redcurrants
elderberries
blackcurrants
pineapple
bananas
mango
fig
papaya
guava
prickly pear
plum tomato
lychee
kiwi fruit
star fruit
passion fruit
pomegranate

fruitful *(adj)* successful or useful. **fruitfulness** *(n)*, **fruitfully** *(adv)*.

fruitless *(adj)* unsuccessful or useless. **fruitlessly** *(adv)*.

fruit machine *(n)* a gambling machine that people operate to try to win money.

frustrate frustrating frustrated *(v)*
1 to prevent someone from doing something. **frustration** *(n)*.
2 to annoy someone. **frustration** *(n)*, **frustrated** *(adj)*, **frustrating** *(adj)*.

fry fries frying fried *(v)* to cook food in hot oil. **frying pan** *(n)*.

fudge *(n)* a rich sweet made with butter, sugar and milk.

fuel *(n)* something that is used as a source of energy, such as coal, petrol, or gas. **fuel** *(v)*.

fugitive *(n)* someone who is running away. **fugitive** *(adj)*.

fulcrum fulcrums *or* fulcra *(n)* the point at which something balances or turns.

fulfil fulfilling fulfilled *(v)*
1 to carry out something. *Toni fulfilled her promise by paying back all the money.* **fulfilment** *(n)*.
2 If you **fulfil** a need, a wish, or an ambition, you satisfy it. *The club fulfils a need for after-school activities.* **fulfilment** *(n)*.

full fuller fullest *(adj)*
1 If something is **full**, there is no room left inside it.
2 whole or complete. *I want a full explanation.* **fully** *(adv)*.

full stop *(n)* the punctuation mark (.) used to show that a sentence has ended or a word has been shortened.

fumble fumbling fumbled *(v)* to handle something uncertainly or clumsily.

fume fuming fumed
1 *(v)* to be very angry. *Harry was fuming at Olivia's rudeness.*
2 **fumes** *(plural n)* strong-smelling or poisonous gas, smoke, or vapour given off by something burning or by chemicals.

function functioning functioned
1 *(v)* If something **functions**, it works.
2 *(n)* a purpose, role, or job.

functional *(adj)* If something is **functional**, it is designed to work well, rather than to look beautiful.

fund funding funded
1 *(n)* a store of money or other things. *A fund of jokes.*
2 *(v)* If someone **funds** something, they give money to support it.

fundamental *(adj)* basic and necessary. **fundamentally** *(adv)*.

funeral *(n)* the ceremony held after someone has died, at which the body is buried or cremated.

funfair *(n)* an outdoor entertainment with rides, amusements, and stalls.

fungus fungi *or* funguses *(n)* a type of plant that has no leaves, flowers, or roots. Mushrooms and toadstools are both fungi. *Some fungi are extremely poisonous.*

fungi

sulphur tuft

chanterelle

amethyst deceiver

Coriolus versicolor

fly agaric

ink cap

orange peel fungus

Russula atropurpurea

funnel funnelling funnelled
1 *(n)* an open cone that narrows to a tube, used for pouring liquids and powders into narrow-necked containers. *See* **apparatus**.
2 *(v)* to pour liquids and powders through a funnel.
3 *(n)* a chimney on a ship.

funny funnier funniest *(adj)*
1 amusing. **funnily** *(adv)*.
2 strange. *There's a funny smell in the kitchen.* **funnily** *(adv)*.

fur *(n)* the soft, hairy coat of an animal. **furry** *(adj)*.

furious *(adj)* extremely angry. **furiously** *(adv)*.

furlong *(n)* (old-fashioned) a distance of 201m, or 220yds.

furnace *(n)* an extremely hot oven, used to melt metal, glass, etc. *The picture shows how pure iron is created from iron ore in a furnace. Blasts of hot air and burning coke raise the temperature of the iron mixture to melting point, when it separates into pure iron and waste products, or slag.*

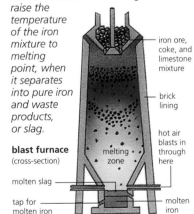

blast furnace (cross-section)

iron ore, coke, and limestone mixture

brick lining

hot air blasts in through here

melting zone

molten slag

tap for molten iron

molten iron

furnish furnishes furnishing furnished *(v)*
1 to equip a room or house with carpets, curtains, and furniture. **furnishings** *(plural n)*.
2 to supply. *Can you furnish any proof of your age?*

furniture *(n)* large, movable things such as chairs, tables, and beds, which are needed in a home.

furrow *(n)* the groove cut by a plough when it turns over the soil.

further education *(n)* education for people who have left school but who are not at university.

furthermore *(adv)* in addition.

furtive *(adj)* sly and cautious. *A furtive glance.* **furtiveness** *(n)*.

fury furies *(n)* violent anger.

fuse fusing fused
1 *(v)* to join two pieces of metal, plastic, etc. by heating them.
2 *(n)* a safety device in electrical equipment which cuts off the power in an emergency. If too much current is flowing in the circuit, the wire in the fuse melts, or blows, and the circuit is broken.
3 *(v)* If a piece of electrical equipment **fuses**, the fuse blows.
4 *(n)* a string or wick leading from a bomb, which is lit to make the bomb explode.

fuselage *(fyoo-zil-arj)* *(n)* the body of an aircraft. *See* **aircraft**, **glider**.

fusion *(n)*
1 the joining together of two pieces of metal, plastic, etc., caused by heating.
2 **nuclear fusion** the process of combining atoms to release energy.

fuss fusses fussing fussed
1 *(v)* to be unnecessarily worried or excited about something. **fussy** *(adj)*.
2 *(n)* more talk or activity than is necessary. *Carla always makes a fuss about having visitors.*

futile *(adj)* useless and a waste of time. **futility** *(n)*.

future *(n)* the time to come. **future** *(adj)*.

fuzz *(n)*
1 short, soft hair. **fuzzy** *(adj)*.
2 **the fuzz** (slang) the police.

a b c d e f g h i j k l m n o p q r s t u v w x y z

Gg

gabble gabbling gabbled (v)
If you **gabble**, you talk so fast that it is hard for people to understand you.

gadget (n) a small machine that does a particular job. *We have a gadget for slicing hard-boiled eggs.*

Gaelic (gay-lik or gal-ik)
1 (n) the name of the traditional languages spoken by some people in Scotland, Ireland, and the Isle of Man.
2 gaelic (adj) having to do with Gaelic language and culture.

gag gagging gagged
1 (v) to tie something around someone's mouth in order to stop them from talking. **gag** (n).
2 (v) to retch or feel like vomiting.
3 (n) (informal) a joke.

gain gaining gained
1 (v) to get or win something.
2 (n) a profit or an increase.
3 (v) If you **gain on** someone, you start to catch up with them.

gala (n) a special event or entertainment. *A swimming gala.*

galaxy galaxies (n) a group of stars and planets. **galactic** (adj).

gale (n) a very strong wind.

gallant (adj)
brave and courteous. *A gallant knight.* **gallantly** (adv).

gall bladder (n) the organ in your body that stores bile from the liver. *See* **anatomy, chicken, digestion**.

galleon (n)
a sailing ship with three masts built from the 16th to 18th century.

gallery galleries (n)
1 a place where exhibitions of paintings, sculptures, photographs, etc. are displayed.
2 an upstairs seating area, especially in large halls and theatres.

galley (n)
1 the kitchen on a boat or aircraft. *See* **aircraft, boat**.
2 a long boat with oars, used in ancient times.

gallop galloping galloped (v)
When a horse **gallops**, it runs as fast as it can. **gallop** (n).

gallows gallows (n)
a wooden frame used in the past for hanging criminals.

galore (adj) in large numbers.
There were rides galore at the fair.

galoshes (plural n) waterproof shoes that fit over your ordinary shoes to protect them.

galvanize or **galvanise** galvanizing galvanized (v)
1 to coat steel or iron with zinc to stop it rusting.
2 If you **galvanize** someone into action, you shock them into doing something.

gamble gambling gambled (v)
1 to bet money on a race, game, or something that might happen. **gambler** (n).
2 to take a risk. *We gambled on the weather staying fine all day.*

game
1 (n) an activity with rules that can be played by one or more people. *A game of tennis. A computer game.*
2 (n) wild animals, including birds, that are hunted for sport and for food.
3 (adj) willing to try something new or adventurous.

gamekeeper (n)
someone whose job is to protect game, especially from poachers.

gamesmanship (n)
If you practise **gamesmanship**, you try to beat your opponent by using methods that are not against the rules, but are tricky and surprising.

gaming (singular n)
1 playing video games. *Do you like gaming?* **gamer** (n), **gaming** (adj).
2 gambling. **gaming** (adj).

gammon (n) meat from the side or back leg of a pig.

gander (n)
a male goose.

gang ganging ganged
1 (n) a group of people, usually with a leader.
2 (n) an organized group of criminals.
3 (v) If several people **gang up** on you, they all turn against you.

gangplank (n)
a short bridge or piece of wood, used for walking on and off a boat.

gangrene (n) If someone has **gangrene**, their flesh rots, because the blood supply has been cut off.

gangster (n)
a member of a criminal gang.

gangway (n)
1 a clear pathway between rows of seats, for people to walk down.
2 a gangplank.

gaol see **jail**.

gap (n)
a space between things.

gape gaping gaped
1 (v) to open your mouth wide, usually with surprise. *The children gaped at all the presents.*
2 (v) to split or hang open. *My shirt is gaping at the seams.*
3 (n) the part of a beak that opens. *See* **dolphin**.

garage (n)
1 a small building for storing vehicles.
2 a place where petrol is sold and vehicles are repaired.

garbage (n) (US) rubbish.

garbled (adj)
If you receive a **garbled** message, it is mixed up and does not make sense.

garden (n)
a place where flowers, vegetables, shrubs, etc. are grown. **gardener** (n), **gardening** (n), **garden** (v).

gargle gargling gargled (v)
to move a liquid around your throat without swallowing it.

gargoyle (n)
a grotesque stone head or figure, carved below the roof of old buildings, such as churches. Gargoyles were often used as waterspouts.

gargoyle

garish (gair-ish) (adj)
brightly coloured and over-decorated. **garishly** (adv).

garland (n) a ring of flowers, often worn around the neck or on the head.

garlic (n)
1 a strong-smelling plant similar to an onion.
2 the strong-tasting bulb of the garlic plant, used in cooking to add flavour to food.

garment (n) a piece of clothing.

garnish garnishes garnishing garnished (v)
to decorate food with small amounts of other food or herbs. **garnish** (n).

garrison (n)
a group of soldiers based in a town and ready to defend it. **garrison** (v).

garter (n) (old-fashioned)
a piece of elastic worn around the top of socks or stockings to stop them slipping down.

gas gases or gasses (n)
1 an air-like substance that will spread to fill any space that contains it. *Hydrogen gas.* **gaseous** (adj). *See* **molecule**.
2 a gas that is used as a fuel. Gas can be made from coal and can also be found underground.

gash gashes (n) a long, deep cut. I've got a nasty gash on my knee.

gasp gasping gasped (v) to take in breath suddenly because you are surprised or in pain. **gasp** (n).

gastric (adj) to do with the stomach. Gastric juices.

gate (n)
1 a frame or barrier that can be opened and closed.
2 the number of people entering a sports ground for a match or event.

gateau (gat-oh) gateaux (n) a rich cake, usually containing cream.

gatecrash gatecrashes gatecrashing gatecrashed (v) to go to an event when you have not been invited. **gatecrasher** (n).

gather gathering gathered
1 (v) to collect or pick things. We gathered blackberries from the bushes beside the road.
2 (v) to come together in a group. A large crowd gathered. **gathering** (n).
3 (v) to discover or learn something. I gather we're not welcome here.
4 gathers (plural n) small folds in material. **gather** (v), **gathered** (adj).

gaudy (gaw-dee) gaudier gaudiest (adj) very brightly coloured and vulgar.

gauge (rhymes with page) gauging gauged
1 (v) to judge something or make a guess about it. We've tried to gauge people's reaction to the plan.
2 (n) an instrument for measuring something. A pressure gauge.
3 (n) the distance between the two rails of a railway track.

gaunt (adj) unnaturally thin and bony.

gauntlet (n) a long, protective glove. In the past, gauntlets were worn by soldiers to prevent injury from weapons. This pair of leather gauntlets was worn by a cavalryman in the 17th century.

gauntlets

gauze (gawz) (n)
1 a very thin woven cloth, used as a bandage.
2 a thin mesh of wire. See **apparatus**.

gay gayer gayest (adj)
1 homosexual or lesbian.
2 (old-fashioned) happy and lively. **gaily** (adv).

gaze gazing gazed (v) to stare at something steadily. **gaze** (n).

gazetteer (n) an index of places at the back of a map or atlas.

gear (n)
1 gears (plural n) a set of toothed wheels which fit together and pass on or change the movement of a machine. The diagram shows how gears work. The arrows show the direction of movement.
2 equipment or clothing.

gears

cogwheel
axle
tooth

geek (n) someone who is very knowledgeable and enthusiastic about a particular subject. **geeky** (adj).

gel (jel) (n) a jelly-like substance.

gelatine (n) a clear, tasteless substance that you add to liquids to make them become solid.

gem (n) a precious stone, such as a diamond, ruby, or emerald.

gender (n)
1 the sex of a person or creature.
2 All nouns have genders. The four genders are masculine, feminine, neuter (neither masculine nor feminine), and common (either masculine or feminine). In some languages, such as French and German, the **gender** of a noun changes the way that it is used.

gene (n) one of the parts of the cells of all living things. Genes are passed from parents to children and control how you look and grow. **genetic** (adj).

genealogy genealogies (n)
1 the study of family history. genealogist (n).
2 the history of a family.

general
1 (adj) to do with everybody or everything. **generally** (adv).
2 (adj) not detailed or not specialized.
3 (n) a very high-ranking army officer.

generation (n) all the people born around the same time.

generator (n) a machine which produces electricity.

generous (adj) People who are **generous** are happy to use their time and money to help others. generosity (n), generously (adv).

genetics (singular n) the study of the ways that personal characteristics are passed from one generation to another through genes. genetic (adj), genetically (adv).

genitals (plural n) the sex organs on the outside of the body.

genius (jee-nee-us) geniuses (n) an unusually clever or talented person.

genome (jee-nome) (n) all the DNA making up a living plant or animal. Scientists are studying the human genome to help them learn more about human diseases.

gentle gentler gentlest (adj)
1 not rough. gentleness (n), gently (adv).
2 kind and sensitive. gentleness (n), gently (adv).
3 not extreme. A gentle slope.

gentleman gentlemen (n)
1 a polite name for a man.
2 a man with good manners.

genuine (jen-yoo-in) (adj)
1 real and not fake.
2 If someone is **genuine**, they behave in a natural way and do not pretend. genuinely (adv).

geography (n) the study of the Earth, including its people, resources, climate, and physical features. geographer (n), geographical (adj).

geology (n) the study of the Earth's layers of soil and rock. geologist (n), geological (adj).

geometric (adj)
1 to do with geometry.
2 A **geometric** shape is a regular shape, such as a circle, triangle, rectangle, or square.

geometry (n) the branch of mathematics which deals with lines, angles, shapes, etc. The picture below shows a range of instruments used in geometry.

geometry instruments

ruler
shape template
set square
compasses
protractor

Some words that begin with a "g" sound are spelt "gh".

geranium

geranium *(n)* a common garden plant with thick stems and red, pink, white, or purple flowers.

gerbil *(n)* a small, furry rodent with long feet and a long, tufted tail. Gerbils are often kept as pets.

gerbil with babies

geriatric *(adj)* to do with very old people. *A geriatric ward.*

germ *(n)* a very small living organism that can cause disease.

German measles *(singular n)* a contagious illness which gives you a rash and a slight fever. It is not usually serious, except for pregnant women.

germinate germinating germinated *(v)* When seeds or beans **germinate**, they start to grow shoots and roots.

germinating bean

plumule (young shoot)

seed containing cotyledons (food stores)

radicle (young root)

1 radicle grows down

2 plumule breaks above ground

testa (seed case)

leaf

cotyledon

shoot

root

root hairs

3 testa is discarded

4 shoot sprouts leaves

gesticulate *(jes-tik-yoo-late)* gesticulating gesticulated *(v)* to indicate something by waving your hands in an excited or angry way. *The chef was gesticulating wildly from the kitchen.* **gesticulation** *(n)*.

gesture gesturing gestured
1 *(v)* to move your head or hands in order to communicate a feeling. *The teacher gestured to Nikki that she should sit down.* **gesture** *(n)*.
2 *(n)* an action which shows a feeling. *I sent her flowers as a gesture of friendship.*

get getting got *(v)*
1 to obtain something. *Please get me a paper.*
2 to own something. *Have you got a pet?*

3 to become. *The pond got bigger.*
4 to arrive somewhere. *At last, we got home.*
5 get by to manage with very little money.
6 get at to attack or annoy someone.
7 get off with *(informal)* to kiss someone passionately.
8 get over to recover from something.

getaway *(n)* a fast escape from a situation, especially a crime.

geyser *(gee-zer)* *(n)* a hole in the ground through which hot water and steam shoots up in bursts. *Geysers are found in volcanic areas, where water is heated to boiling point underground and then forced upwards.*

geyser

hot spring

geyser

crater-shaped nozzle

collecting chamber

narrow passageway

hot, cracked rocks

ghastly ghastlier ghastliest *(adj)*
1 *(informal)* very bad or unpleasant. *A ghastly mistake.*
2 If you feel or look **ghastly**, you feel or look very ill.

ghetto ghettos *or* ghettoes *(n)* an area of a city where a group of poor people of the same minority group live together.

ghost *(n)* a spirit of a dead person, believed to haunt people or places. **ghostly** *(adj)*.

GI *(n)* *(US)* an American soldier. GI is short for government issue.

giant
1 *(n)* In stories, a **giant** is a very large and strong creature.
2 *(adj)* very large. *Giant size.*

giddy giddier giddiest *(adj)* If you feel **giddy**, you feel dizzy and unsteady, because you are ill or excited. **giddiness** *(n)*, **giddily** *(adv)*.

gift *(n)*
1 a present.
2 a special talent. *Vincent has a gift for painting.* **gifted** *(adj)*.

gig *(n)* *(informal)* a booking for a musician or band to play in public.

gigabyte *(n)* a unit used to measure the capacity of a computer's memory.

gigantic *(jy-gan-tik)* *(adj)* huge or enormous. **gigantically** *(adv)*.

giggle giggling giggled *(v)* to laugh in a silly, high-pitched way. **giggle** *(n)*, **giggly** *(adj)*.

gill *(n)* one of the two organs on the sides of a fish, through which the fish breathes. *The gill filaments are filled with blood. As water flows over them, oxygen from the water passes into the blood and carbon dioxide from the blood passes into the water.* Also see **fish**.

fish's gill

water sucked in through mouth

gill bar

gill filament

gill opening

water pushed out

gilt *(adj)* A **gilt** object is decorated with a thin coating of gold leaf or gold paint. **gild** *(v)*.

gimmick *(n)* something unusual, used to get people's attention. *The entertainer's gimmick was a flashing bow tie.* **gimmicky** *(adj)*.

gin *(n)* a strong alcoholic drink made from grain and juniper berries.

ginger *(n)*
1 a plant root used to give a hot, spicy flavour to food and drink.
2 a reddish-brown colour. **ginger** *(adj)*, **gingery** *(adj)*.

gingerly *(adv)* cautiously and carefully.

gingham *(n)* checked cotton cloth.

Gipsy *see* **Gypsy**.

giraffe *(n)* an African mammal with a very long neck and legs, and dark patches on its skin. The giraffe is the tallest animal in the world.

giraffes

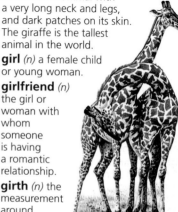

girl *(n)* a female child or young woman.

girlfriend *(n)* the girl or woman with whom someone is having a romantic relationship.

girth *(n)* the measurement around something.

Some words that begin with a "g" sound are spelt "gh".
Some words that begin with a "gi" sound are spelt "gy" or "gui".

glucose

give giving gave given (v)
1 to hand over something to another person. *Give me that book!*
2 to pay. *What will you give me for this beautiful vase?*
3 give way to let someone else go in front of you.
4 give in *or* **give up** to surrender or stop trying.

glacier (*glass-ee-er* or *glays-ee-er*) (n) a huge mass of ice that flows down a mountain valley. As the glacier moves, it erodes rocks and deposits moraine.

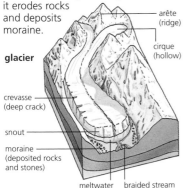

glacier

arête (ridge)
cirque (hollow)
crevasse (deep crack)
snout
moraine (deposited rocks and stones)
meltwater   braided stream

glad gladder gladdest (adj)
1 pleased or happy. **gladness** (n), **gladden** (v), **gladly** (adv).
2 If you are **glad** of something, you are grateful for it.

gladiator (n) an ancient Roman warrior who fought against other gladiators or fierce animals in order to entertain the public. *The picture shows a fight between two types of gladiator: a retiarius, armed with a net and trident, and a murmillo, fighting with a dagger and shield. Also see* **amphitheatre**.

gladiators

glamorous (adj)
attractive and exciting. **glamour** (n).

glance glancing glanced (v)
1 to look at something very briefly. **glance** (n).
2 to hit something and slide off at an angle. *The ball glanced off the goalpost into the net.* **glancing** (adj).

gland (n) an organ in the body which either produces natural chemicals or allows substances to leave the body. *Sweat glands.* **glandular** (adj).

glandular fever (n)
an infectious illness which gives you a sore throat, swollen glands, and a high temperature.

glare glaring glared
1 (v) to look at someone in a very angry way. **glare** (n).
2 (n) very bright light which dazzles.

glaring (adj) very obvious. *A glaring error.* **glaringly** (adv).

glass glasses (n)
1 a transparent material used in windows, bottles, etc. *The picture shows two 16th-century craftsmen blowing glass.*
2 a container for drinking, made from glass. *A wineglass.*

glass-blowing

glasses (plural n)
lenses set in frames, worn to improve your eyesight.

glaze glazing glazed (v)
1 to fit glass into a window.
2 to apply a thin coat of liquid to pottery or pasty before it is heated, to give it a shiny finish. **glaze** (n).
3 If your eyes **glaze over**, they look fixed and glass-like because you are tired or bored. **glazed** (adj).

glazier (n)
a person who fits glass into windows.

gleam gleaming gleamed (v)
to shine. **gleam** (n).

glee (n) enjoyment and delight. **gleeful** (adj), **gleefully** (adv).

glen (n) a narrow mountain valley.

glide gliding glided (v)
to move smoothly and easily. *The swan glided down the stream.*

glider (n) a very light aircraft, which flies by floating and rising on air currents instead of by engine power.

glider

tailplane
tail unit
hinged rudder
fibreglass fuselage
air brake
lightweight wing
tail skid
side-opening canopy
pitot head (measures airspeed)
tail wheel
aileron
landing gear
towing hook under here

glimmer glimmering glimmered (v) to shine faintly. **glimmer** (n).

glimpse glimpsing glimpsed (v)
to see something briefly. **glimpse** (n).

glint glinting glinted (v)
to sparkle or to flash. **glint** (n).

glisten glistening glistened (v)
to shine in a sparkling way.

glitter glittering glittered (v)
to sparkle with many tiny lights or reflections.

gloat gloating gloated (v)
to delight in your own good luck, or in someone else's bad luck.

global warming (n)
a gradual rise in the temperature of the Earth's atmosphere, caused by an increase in the greenhouse effect. *See* **greenhouse effect**.

globe (n)
1 a round model of the world.
2 the world. **global** (adj).
3 anything shaped like a round ball. **globular** (adj).

gloomy gloomier gloomiest (adj)
1 dull and dark. *A gloomy dungeon.* **gloom** (n).
2 If you are **gloomy**, you feel sad and pessimistic. **gloom** (n).

glory glories (n)
1 fame and admiration. *After the victory, the team enjoyed their glory.* **glorious** (adj).
2 a beautiful and impressive sight. *The glories of Venice.* **glorious** (adj).

gloss (n)
a shine on a surface. **glossy** (adj).

glossary glossaries (n) A **glossary** explains the meaning of technical words and phrases used in a book.

glove (n)
a warm or protective hand covering.

glow glowing glowed (v)
If something **glows**, it gives off a steady light, often because it is hot. **glow** (n), **glowing** (adj).

glow-worm (n) a small beetle whose tail gives off a green glow in the dark. *See* **insect**.

glucose (n) a natural sugar found in plants which gives energy to living things.

glue *(n)* a substance used to make one surface stick to another. **glue** *(v)*.

glum glummer glummest *(adj)* gloomy and miserable. **glumly** *(adv)*.

glut *(n)* a very large amount that exceeds demand.

glutton *(n)* a very greedy person. **gluttony** *(n)*, **gluttonous** *(adj)*.

GM *(adj)* The initials **GM** stand for genetically modified. When plants or food are **genetically modified**, some of their genes are treated by scientists to change them in some way, such as making crops more resistant to pests.

gnarled *(narld) (adj)* twisted and lumpy with age. *A gnarled oak tree.*

gnash *(nash)* gnashing gnashed *(v)* If you **gnash** your teeth, you grind them together in anger or grief.

gnat *(nat) (n)* a small, winged insect which bites.

gnaw *(naw)* gnawing gnawed *or* gnawn *(v)* to keep biting something.

gnome *(nome) (n)* In folk and fairy stories, **gnomes** are dwarf-like old men.

go goes going went gone
1 *(v)* to move away from or towards a place. *I'm going home.*
2 *(v)* to work properly. *This machine won't go.*
3 *(v)* to become. *The class went quiet.*
4 *(v)* If you are **going** to do something, you will do it in the future.
5 *(v)* to have a place or to belong. *Where do the plates go?*
6 *(n)* a turn. *It's my go at batting.*

goal *(n)*
1 something that you aim for. *Shelagh's goal is to run for Ireland.*
2 a frame with a net into which you aim a ball in sports such as soccer and lacrosse.
3 When you score a **goal** in a game, you send the ball into or through a net, and win points.

goalkeeper *(n)* a player who defends the goal in various sports. *See* **ice hockey**, **soccer**.

goat *(n)* a farm animal with horns and a beard, reared mainly for its milk.

gobble gobbling gobbled *(v)* to eat food quickly and greedily.

goblet *(n)* an old-fashioned drinking container with a stem and a base.

goblin *(n)* In fairy stories, **goblins** are small, unpleasant, ugly creatures.

God *(n)* In Christianity, Judaism, and Islam, **God** is the creator and ruler of the universe.

god *(n)* a supernatural being that is worshipped.

goddess goddesses *(n)* a female supernatural being that is worshipped. *This picture shows some Ancient Egyptian gods and goddesses.*

Egyptian gods and goddesses

Ma'at

Ra

Amun

Osiris   Isis

Horus   Hathor   Anubis

godparent *(n)* someone who promises their support for a child when the child is baptized into the Christian religion.

goggles *(plural n)* special glasses that fit tightly round your eyes to protect them. *Swimming goggles.*

go-kart *(n)* a very low, small, open vehicle, built for racing.

gold *(n)*
1 a precious metal used for jewellery and sometimes money. *See* **mineral**.
2 a warm, yellow colour.
gold *(adj)*, **golden** *(adj)*.

goldfish goldfish *or* goldfishes *(n)* an orange-coloured fish, often kept in ponds and aquariums.

golf *(n)* a game in which players use clubs to hit a small, white ball round a special course. *The picture shows four types of clubs used for playing golf: a wood for striking the ball long distances; an iron for medium to short-range shots; a wedge for lifting the ball high in the air; and a putter for tapping the ball into the hole on the green.* **golfer** *(n)*, **golfing** *(n)*.

wood

golf ball

iron

wedge

tee

putter

face   toe
heel
neck
shaft

gondola *(n)* a light boat with high pointed ends, used on the canals of Venice. Gondolas are moved through the water by a gondolier using a single oar.

gong *(n)*
1 a disc of metal that makes a hollow, echoing sound when it is hit with a hammer.
2 *(slang)* a medal.

gondola

good better best *(adj)*
1 of high quality or deserving praise. *A good teacher. A good book.*
2 kind or virtuous. *A good deed.*
3 suitable. *A good fit.*
4 well-behaved. *Maddy is such a good girl!*
5 fit and well. *I'm feeling good.*
6 If something is **good** for you, it improves your health or behaviour.

goodbye *(interject)* a word said to someone who is leaving.

goods *(plural n)* a general name for things which are sold or things which someone owns. *Leather goods.*

gooey gooier gooiest *(adj)* *(informal)* sticky. **gooeyness** *(n)*.

goose geese *(n)* a large, long-necked bird with webbed feet. *See* **bird**.

goose bumps *or* **goose pimples** *(plural n)* tiny lumps on your skin which appear when you are cold or frightened.

gore goring gored
1 *(n)* *(old-fashioned)* blood that flows from a wound.
2 *(v)* If someone is **gored** by a bull, they are pierced by its horns.

gorge gorging gorged
1 (n) a deep valley with steep, rocky sides. See **river**.
2 (v) If you **gorge** yourself, you stuff yourself with food.

gorgeous (adj)
really beautiful or attractive.

gorilla (n) a very large, strong ape with dark fur, that lives in Africa.

gorse (n) a prickly, evergreen shrub with bright yellow flowers.

gory gorier goriest (adj)
If something is **gory**, it involves a lot of blood. A gory film.

gospel (n)
1 one of the first four books in the New Testament of the Bible. The gospels describe the life and teachings of Jesus Christ.
2 If you take something as **gospel**, you believe it to be completely true.

gossip gossiping gossiped (v)
to talk with enjoyment about other people's personal lives. gossip (n), gossipy (adj).

Gothic (adj) in the style of art or architecture used in Western Europe between the 12th and 16th centuries. Gothic buildings have pointed arches and windows. See **arch**.

govern governing governed (v)
to control a country, organization, etc. using laws or rules. governor (n).

government (n)
1 the people who rule or govern a country or state.
2 the control and administration of a country, state, or organization. governmental (adj), governmentally (adv).

gown (n)
1 (old-fashioned) a woman's dress.
2 a loose robe worn by judges, lawyers, university teachers, etc.

GP (n) a family doctor, who treats common illnesses and refers patients to specialist doctors if necessary. GP is short for general practitioner.

grab grabbing grabbed (v)
to take hold of something suddenly and roughly.

grace (n)
1 an elegant way of moving.
2 pleasant behaviour. Ashley accepted my apology with grace. gracious (adj), graciously (adv).
3 a short prayer of thanks before or after a meal.
4 divine mercy. By the grace of God.

graceful (adj)
moving in an elegant or beautiful way. A graceful ballerina. gracefully (adv).

grade (n)
1 a mark given for work done in school, college, etc. I got grade A for maths. grade (v).
2 quality. Top grade eggs.

gradient (n)
a slope or the steepness of a slope.

gradual (adj)
If something is **gradual**, it takes place slowly but steadily. gradually (adv).

graffiti (singular or plural n)
things that people write or draw on the walls of public buildings.

graft grafting grafted (v)
1 to plant a shoot from one plant into a slit in another, so that they grow as one. graft (n).
2 to take the skin from one part of the body to help repair an injury to another part. graft (n).
3 (informal) to work hard.

grain (n)
1 the seed of a cereal plant.
2 a general name for the product of cereal crops.
3 a very small particle of salt, sand, sugar, etc.

barley

rye

grain crops

wheat

oats

grammar (n) the rules of writing or speaking a language. grammatical (adj), grammatically (adv.)

grand grander grandest (adj)
large and impressive. grandly (adv).

grandchild grandchildren (n)
You are the **grandchild** of your parents' parents.

grandparent (n) Your **grandparent** is the parent of one of your parents.

grandstand (n)
a covered structure at a sports ground with seats for spectators.

grant granting granted
1 (v) to give something or allow something. We were granted permission to leave.
2 (n) a sum of money given by the government or other organizations for a special purpose. A study grant.
3 If you take something for **granted**, you do not appreciate it, or you assume that you will get it.

granulated sugar (n)
coarsely ground white sugar.

grape (n) a small fruit that grows on a vine which can be eaten as it is, dried to make currants, raisins, etc., or crushed to make wine. See **fruit**.

grapefruit
grapefruit or grapefruits (n) a large yellow or pink citrus fruit. See **fruit**.

grapevine (n)
1 a climbing plant on which grapes grow.
2 If you hear something **on the grapevine**, you hear news before most other people hear about it.

graph (rhymes with laugh) (n)
a diagram which shows how two sets of numbers are related.

graphic (adj)
1 very realistic. Sonia told the story in graphic detail.
2 to do with art and design.

graphics (plural n)
1 the layout and pictures of a book or magazine.
2 the pictures in a computer game. This game has terrible graphics.

grapple grappling grappled (v)
1 to wrestle with someone.
2 If you **grapple** with a problem, you think hard about all the ways that it could be solved.

grasp grasping grasped (v)
1 to seize something and hold it tightly. grasp (n).
2 to understand something. Have you grasped what I'm telling you? grasp (n).

grass grasses (n)
1 a green plant with long, thin, leaves that grows wild and is used for lawns. grassy (adj).
2 (slang) marijuana.

grasshopper (n)
a jumping insect with long back legs. A grasshopper sings to other grasshoppers by rubbing the hard veins on its front wings over the tiny teeth inside its back legs.

European grasshopper

hard vein

pronotum (protective shield)

teeth

wing

antenna

thorax

compound eye

ear on side of body

abdomen

grassland (n)
a large, open area of grass, often used for animals to graze on.

Some words that begin with a "g" sound are spelt "gh".

grate grating grated
1 (v) to shred food, such as cheese, into small, thin pieces.
2 (v) If something **grates** on you, it annoys you.
3 (n) a grid of metal bars in a fireplace.

grateful (adj)
If you are **grateful** for something that you are given, you appreciate it and are thankful for it. **gratefully** (adv).

gratitude (n)
a feeling of being glad and thankful.

grave graver gravest
1 (n) a place where a dead person or animal is buried.
2 (adj) very serious. *Grave danger.* **gravely** (adv).

gravestone (n) a piece of carved stone that marks someone's grave.

graveyard (n)
a piece of land, often near a church, where dead people are buried.

gravel (n) small, loose stones used for paths and roads.

gravity (n)
1 the force that pulls things down towards the surface of the Earth and stops them from floating away into space.
2 seriousness.

gravy (n)
a hot, savoury sauce, served with meat and usually made from the juices of cooked meat.

graze grazing grazed (v)
1 to scrape the surface off your skin. **graze** (n).
2 When animals **graze**, they eat grass and other plants.

grease (n)
1 an oily substance found in animal fat, and in hair and skin. **greasy** (adj).
2 a thick, oily substance used on machines to help the parts move easily. **grease** (v), **greasy** (adj).

great greater greatest (adj)
1 very big or large. **greatly** (adv).
2 very important and famous. *A great man.* **greatness** (n).
3 very good or wonderful. *We had a great time.*

greedy greedier greediest (adj)
If you are **greedy**, you want more of something than you need. **greed** (n), **greedily** (adv).

green greener greenest
1 (n) the colour of grass or leaves. **green** (adj).
2 (adj) to do with protecting the environment. *Green issues.*
3 (n) an area of grass in a public place. *The village green.*

4 (n) an area of ground used for an activity or sport. *A bowling green.*

greenhouse (n) a glass building used for growing plants.

greenhouse effect (n)
the warming of the atmosphere around the Earth, caused by gases such as carbon dioxide, which collect in the atmosphere and prevent the Sun's heat from escaping.

greenhouse effect

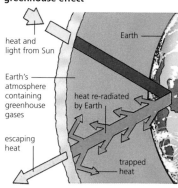

heat and light from Sun

Earth

Earth's atmosphere containing greenhouse gases

heat re-radiated by Earth

escaping heat

trapped heat

greenhouse gases (plural n)
gases such as carbon dioxide and methane that are found in the Earth's atmosphere and help to hold heat in.

greet greeting greeted (v)
1 to say something friendly or welcoming to someone when you meet them. **greeting** (n).
2 to react to something in a particular way. *Alexander greeted the news with horror.*

grenade (n)
a small bomb that is thrown by hand or fired from a rifle.

grey (n)
the colour between black and white, like the colour of the sky on a rainy day. **grey** (adj).

grid (n)
1 a set of straight lines that cross each other at right angles to form a regular pattern of squares.
2 **national grid** the network of wires and cables through which electricity is supplied to all parts of the country.

grief (n)
a feeling of great sadness.

grievance (n)
If you have a **grievance**, you have a real or imagined reason to feel angry or annoyed about something.

grieve grieving grieved (v)
to feel very sad, usually because someone whom you love has died.

grill grilling grilled
1 (n) the part of a cooker that heats food from above.
2 (v) to cook food under a grill.
3 (v) (informal) to ask someone lots of detailed questions to find out information.

grim grimmer grimmest (adj)
gloomy, stern, and unpleasant. *A grim expression.* **grimly** (adv).

grime (n) thick dirt. **grimy** (adj).

grin grinning grinned (v) to give a large, cheerful smile. **grin** (n).

grind grinding ground (v) to crush something into a powder.

grip gripping gripped (v)
1 to hold something very tightly. **grip** (n).
2 If something **grips** you, it holds your attention completely because it is so exciting. **gripping** (adj).

gristle (n) a tough substance, sometimes found in meat.

grizzle grizzling grizzled (v) to whine and complain constantly.

groan groaning groaned (v) to make a long, low sound, showing that you are in pain or are unhappy. **groan** (n).

grocer (n)
someone who owns a shop selling food and household goods.

groin (n) the area between the top of your leg and your stomach.

groom grooming groomed
1 (n) someone who looks after horses.
2 (v) to brush and clean an animal, such as a horse. **grooming** (n).
3 (n) a man who is about to get married or has just been married.

grooming kit for horses

hoof oil

dandy brush

sponges

body brush

currycomb

mane comb

sweat scraper

stable rubber

hoof pick

water brush

groove (n)
a long cut in the surface of something.

grope groping groped (v)
to feel about with your hands for something that you cannot see.

gross grosser grossest
1 (adj) (informal) unpleasant and ugly. *That's gross!*
2 (adj) The **gross** amount is the total amount, with nothing taken away. *Gross income.* **gross** (n).
3 (adj) very rude and bad-mannered.
4 (adj) very bad. *A gross error.* **grossly** (adv).
5 (singular or plural n) a group of 144 things.

grotesque (grow-tesk) (adj)
unnatural and horrible.
grotesquely (adv).

grotty grottier grottiest (adj)
(slang) unpleasant and unattractive.

ground
1 (n) the surface of the Earth.
2 (n) a piece of land used for playing a game or sport.
3 **grounds** (plural n)
reason or cause. *What grounds do you have for accusing me?*
4 **grounds** (plural n)
the land surrounding a large building or group of buildings.

grounded (adj)
1 If an aircraft is **grounded**, it cannot fly.
2 (informal) If you are **grounded**, you are not allowed to go out.

group grouping grouped
1 (n) a number of things that go together or are similar in some way.
2 (v) to put things into groups or to make a group.
3 (n) a number of musicians who play or sing together.

grove (n) a small group of trees.

grovel grovelling grovelled (v)
to be unnaturally humble and polite to someone because you are afraid of them or because you think that they are very important.

grow growing grew grown (v)
1 to increase in size, length, or amount. *The tree grew quickly.*
2 to plant something and look after it so that it lives and gets bigger.
3 to become. *Simon grew lazier and lazier.*
4 If something **grows on you**, you gradually start to like it.

growl growling growled (v)
When an animal **growls**, it makes a low, deep noise, usually because it is angry.

grown-up (n)
an adult. **grown-up** (adj).

growth (n)
1 the process of growing. *Here's a chart to measure your growth.*
2 a lump of body tissue either on or inside someone's body.

grub (n)
1 the young form of some insects, that looks like a short, white worm.
2 (slang) food.

grubby grubbier grubbiest (adj)
dirty. **grubbiness** (n).

grudge (n)
a feeling of anger towards someone who has hurt or insulted you in the past. *Jon bore a grudge against Daniel for months.*

gruelling (adj) very demanding and tiring. *A gruelling job.*

gruesome (adj) Something that is **gruesome** is disgusting and horrible.

gruff gruffer gruffest (adj)
rough and bad-tempered.
A gruff voice. **gruffly** (adv).

grumble grumbling grumbled (v)
to complain about something in a bad-tempered way.

grumpy grumpier grumpiest (adj)
bad-tempered. **grumpily** (adv).

grunge (adj)
Grunge music features loud guitar playing, and is influenced by heavy metal and punk.

grungy (adj) (slang)
scruffy and dirty. *Grungy old jeans.*

grunt grunting grunted (v)
to make a deep, gruff sound, like a pig. **grunt** (n).

guarantee (n)
1 a promise made by the makers of something that if it breaks or goes wrong within a certain time, they will mend or replace it for you. **guarantee** (v).
2 a promise that something will definitely happen. **guarantee** (v).

guard guarding guarded
1 (v) to protect a person or place from attack.
2 (v) to watch a person carefully to prevent them from escaping.
3 (n) someone who protects or keeps watch over a person or place.
4 (n) a railway official who travels on a train and is in charge of passengers and goods.
5 (n) an object placed near another object to provide protection.
6 (v) If you **guard against** something, you try to stop it happening.

guardian (n)
1 someone who is not the parent of a child but who has the legal responsibility to look after them.
2 someone who guards or protects something. **guardian** (adj).

guard's van (n)
the last compartment on a train, kept for railway officials in charge of the train.

guerrilla (ger-il-er) (n)
a member of a small army that fights an official army by launching surprise attacks. **guerrilla** (adj).

guess (gess) guesses guessing guessed (v)
1 to give an answer that may be right but which you cannot be sure about. *I guessed at the answer instead of working it out.* **guess** (n).
2 to admit something reluctantly. *I guess you're right.*

guest (n)
1 someone who has been invited to visit you or to stay in your home.
2 someone staying in a hotel.

guide guiding guided
1 (v) to help someone, usually by showing them around a place, or by leading them across difficult country. **guide** (n).
2 (n) a book containing maps and information about a place. **guidebook** (n).
3 **guide-dog** (n) a dog trained to lead a blind person.
4 **Guide** (n) a member of the Guide Association.

guillotine (gil-oh-teen) (n)
1 a large machine with a sharp blade, used in the past to behead criminals.
2 an instrument with a sharp blade, used for cutting paper.

guilty guiltier guiltiest (adj)
1 If you are **guilty**, you have committed a crime or done something wrong. **guilt** (n).
2 If you feel **guilty**, you feel bad because you have done something wrong or have failed to do something. **guilt** (n), **guiltily** (adv).

guinea pig (gin-ee-pig) (n)
1 a small mammal with smooth fur, short ears, and a very short tail. Guinea pigs are often kept as pets.
2 a person who is used in an experiment.

guinea pig

guitar (n) a musical instrument with strings, which you pluck or strum with your fingers or a plectrum. *The vibrations of the strings on this electric guitar are transformed by the pick-ups into electrical impulses which are then amplified through a loudspeaker.* Also see **acoustic guitar**.

electric guitar

tuning peg

head

neck

fret

fret marker

fingerboard

scratchplate or pickguard

magnetic pickup

string

tremolo (whammy bar)

pickup selector switch

volume control

tone control

output jack (leads to loudspeaker)

solid body

bridge

Gujarati (goo-jer-ar-tee) (n) a language spoken in Gujarat, a state in Western India.

gulf (n)
1 a large area of sea that is partly surrounded by land. *The Persian Gulf.*
2 a serious difference or disagreement between people.

gull short for **seagull**.

gullible (adj) If you are **gullible**, you believe anything that you are told and are easily tricked.

gully gullies (n)
a long, narrow valley or ditch.

gulp gulping gulped
1 (v) to swallow something quickly and noisily.
2 (n) a large mouthful of drink.

gum (n)
1 Your **gums** are the areas of firm, pink flesh around the base of your teeth. See **tooth**.
2 glue. **gum** (v), **gummy** (adj).
3 See **chewing gum**.

gun gunning gunned
1 (n) a weapon that fires bullets through a long metal tube.
2 **gun down** (v) to shoot someone with a gun. *The sheriff gunned down the bandits.*

gunfire (n) the firing of guns.

gunpowder (n) a powder that explodes easily, used in fireworks and to fire some guns.

gunsmith (n) someone who makes and repairs guns.

gurgle gurgling gurgled (v)
1 When water **gurgles**, it makes a low, bubbling sound. **gurgle** (n).
2 to make a low, bubbling sound like gurgling water. *The baby gurgled happily.* **gurgle** (n).

gush gushes gushing gushed (v)
1 When liquid **gushes**, it flows quickly in large amounts. **gush** (n).
2 When a person **gushes**, they talk in an overly sentimental or emotional way. **gushing** (adj).

gust (n) a sudden, strong blast of wind. **gusty** (adj).

gut gutting gutted
1 (plural n) Your **guts** are the organs inside your body, especially your stomach and intestines.
2 (v) If a fire **guts** a building, it destroys the inside of it.
3 guts (plural n) (informal) courage.

gutter (n)
a channel or length of tubing through which rain is drained away from a road or from the roof of a building. See **building**.

guzzle guzzling guzzled (v) to eat or drink something quickly and noisily.

gym (jim) (n)
1 a large room with special equipment for doing exercises and physical training. Gym is short for gymnasium or gymnastics.
2 a course of physical exercise.

gymkhana (jim-kah-nuh) (n) a sporting event at which horses and their riders take part in competitions.

gymnasium see **gym**.

gymnastics (n)
physical exercises, often on bars or ropes, which involve difficult and carefully controlled body movements. **gymnast** (n), **gymnastic** (adj).

Gypsy or **Gipsy**
(jip-see) gypsies (n)
a term sometimes used for the Romany people.

gyrate (jy-rate) gyrating gyrated (v) to move round and round in a circle. **gyratory** (adj).

gyroscope (n)
a wheel which spins inside a frame and causes the frame to balance in any position. Gyroscopes are used to help keep ships and aircraft steady.

gyroscope

Hh

habit (n)
1 something that you do regularly, often without thinking about it.
2 a piece of clothing, like a long loose dress, worn by monks and nuns.

habitable (adj)
If a building is **habitable**, it is safe, warm, and clean enough to live in.

habitat (n)
the place and conditions in which a plant or an animal lives naturally.

habitually (adv)
usually or normally. *Annie is habitually optimistic.* **habitual** (adj).

hack hacking hacked
1 (v) to chop or cut something roughly.
2 (v) If you **hack** into a computer system, you manage to get information from it illegally. **hacker** (n), **hacking** (n).
3 (n) a long, steady ride on horseback.

haemoglobin or **hemoglobin**
(hee-muh-glow-bin) (n)
a substance found in your red blood cells, which contains iron and carries oxygen around your body.

haemophilia or **hemophilia**
(hee-muh-fil-ee-a) (n)
If someone suffers from **haemophilia**, their blood does not clot, so they bleed severely when they cut themselves. **haemophiliac** (n).

haemorrhage or **hemorrhage**
(hem-er-ij) (n) severe bleeding, usually inside someone's body.

haggard (adj)
Someone who is **haggard** looks thin, tired, and worried.

haggis (n) a Scottish food made from the chopped heart, liver, kidneys, etc. of a sheep, mixed with oatmeal and boiled in a bag made from a sheep's stomach.

haggle haggling haggled (v)
to bargain with someone, usually about the price of something.

haiku (hy-koo) (n)
a short Japanese poem in three parts.

hail hailing hailed (v)
1 When it **hails**, small pieces of frozen rain fall from the sky. **hail** (n).
2 to attract someone's attention. *Travis hailed a taxi.*

hair (n) the mass of fine, soft strands that grow on your head or body, or on the body of an animal.

hanger

haircut *(n)*
When you have a **haircut**,
someone cuts and styles your hair.

hairdresser *(n)* someone who
cuts and styles people's hair.

hairdryer *or* **hairdrier** *(n)*
a small electrical machine that blows
out hor air and is used to dry hair.

hair-raising *(adj)* very frightening.

hairy hairier hairiest *(adj)*
1 covered in hair.
2 *(slang)* dangerous and frightening.

halal *(n)*
meat that has been produced and
prepared according to the rules of
the Muslim religion. **halal** *(adj)*.

half halves
1 *(n)* one of two equal
parts of something.
2 *(adv)* partly or not completely.
The meal was only half-cooked.

half-brother *(n)* a boy who shares
only one parent with someone else.

half-sister *(n)* a girl who shares
only one parent with someone else.

half term *(n)* a short holiday
in the middle of a school term.

half-time *(n)* a short break in the
middle of a game, such as football.

hall *(n)*
1 an area of a house just
inside the front door.
2 a large room used for meetings
or other public events.

hallelujah *(hal-ay-loo-ya)*
(interject) a word used to
express relief, especially joy
and thanks to God.

Halloween *or* **Hallowe'en** *(n)*
the evening of 31st October, believed
in the past to be the night when
witches and ghosts were active.

hallucinate *(hal-oo-sin-ate)*
hallucinating hallucinated *(v)*
to see something in your mind that
is not really there. **hallucination** *(n)*.

halo *(hay-low)* **haloes** *(n)*
a circle of light, around the heads of
angels and holy people in paintings.

halt halting halted *(v)*
to stop. **halt** *(n)*.

halve halving halved *(v)*
1 to cut or divide something
into two equal parts.
2 to reduce something so that
there is only half as much as
there was. *We have halved
the cast for our school play.*

ham *(n)* the meat from the upper
part of a pig's leg, that has been
salted and sometimes smoked.

hamburger *(n)*
a round, flat piece of minced meat,
usually served in a bread roll.

hamlet *(n)* a very small village.

hammer hammering hammered
1 *(n)* a tool with a metal head
on a handle, used for hitting
things, such as nails. **hammer** *(v)*.
2 *(v)* to hit something hard.
Elsa hammered at the door.

hammock *(n)* a piece of strong
cloth or net that is hung up by
each end and used as a bed.

hamper
hampering hampered
1 *(n)* a large box or
basket used for
carrying food,
especially on a picnic.
2 *(v)* to make it difficult
for someone to do
something. *Nina's
high-heeled shoes
hampered her running.*

hamster *(n)* a small
animal like a mouse,
with a tiny tail, often kept
as a pet. *Hamsters have pouches
in their cheeks for storing food.*

hamster

hand handing handed
1 *(n)* the part of your body on the
end of your arm that you use for
picking things up, writing, eating, etc.
2 *(v)* to pass or give something
to someone. *Hand me the salt.*
3 *(n)* a set of cards that you hold in
your hand during a game of cards.
4 *(n)* one of the pointers on
a clock. *The minute hand.*
5 If you **give someone
a hand**, you help them.

handbag *(n)*
a bag in which people carry their
money and other small things.

handbook *(n)* a book that
gives you information or advice.

handcuffs *(plural n)* metal rings
joined by a chain, that are fixed
around prisoners' wrists to prevent
them from escaping. **handcuff** *(v)*.

handful *(n)*
1 the amount of something
that you can hold in your hand.
2 a small number of things.
3 *(informal)* If someone is a **handful**,
they are difficult to cope with.

handicap *(n)*
1 If someone has a **handicap**,
they are disabled in some way.
handicapped *(adj)*.
2 something that makes it difficult
for you to do something. *Laurie's
injury was a handicap in the race.*

3 a disadvantage given to the more
skilful competitors in a sport, in
order to make the competition
more equal. *A golf handicap.*

handicraft *(n)* a skill, such as
pottery or sewing, that involves
making things with your hands.

handkerchief *(n)*
a small square of cloth that
you use for blowing your nose.

handle handling handled
1 *(n)* the part of an object that
you use to carry, move, or hold
that object. *A door handle.*
2 *(v)* to pick something up and
hold it in your hands in order
to look at it carefully. *Please
handle the goods with care.*
3 *(v)* to deal with someone or
something. *Katy is very good
at handling tricky situations.*

handlebars *(plural n)* the bar at
the front of a bicycle or motorcycle
that you use to steer. *See* **bicycle**.

handshake *(n)*
a way of greeting someone by
taking their hand and shaking it.

handsome *(adj)*
attractive or good looking.

handstand *(n)*
When you do a **handstand**,
you balance on your hands,
with your feet up in the air.

handwriting *(n)*
the style you use for forming
letters and words when you write.
Arnie has very neat handwriting.

handy handier handiest *(adj)*
1 useful and easy to use.
2 skilful. *Sasha is handy
with a power drill.*
3 close by. *Is there a cloth handy?*

hang
hanging hung *or* hanged *(v)*
1 to fix something somewhere
by attaching the top of it
and leaving the bottom free.
Hang your coat on this hook.
2 to kill someone by putting a rope
around their neck and then taking
the support from under their feet.
The past tense and past participle of
this sense of the verb is "hanged".
3 **hang up** to end a
telephone conversation.
4 **hang out** *(informal)* to spend a lot
of time in a place or with someone.

hangar *(n)* a large building
where aircraft are kept.

hanger *(n)* a piece of specially
shaped wood, metal, or plastic
used for hanging up clothes.

hang-glider

- anti-luff line (keeps glider stable)
- king post
- keel
- harness
- tension adjustment cord
- batten
- polyester sail
- parachute
- leading edge
- nylon hang loop
- flying wire
- instrument cluster (includes variometer, altimeter, and airspeed indicator)
- hang-glider
- control frame
- control bar

hang-glider *(n)*
an aircraft like a giant kite, with a harness for a pilot hanging below it. *The pilot controls the hang-glider by moving his body.* **hang-gliding** *(n)*.

hangover *(n)* a headache and a feeling of sickness that you get after drinking too much alcohol.

hang-up *(n) (informal)* If you have a **hang-up** about something, you worry about it all the time.

hanker hankering hankered *(v)* to wish or long for something. **hankering** *(n)*.

Hanukkah or **Chanukah**
(hah-ner-ker) (n)
the Jewish festival of lights, when Jews remember the purification of the Temple. *At Hanukkah, Jews light candles on a menorah, or branched candlestick.*

menorah

haphazard *(adj)* disorganized and random. *The papers were scattered over the floor in a haphazard manner.* **haphazardly** *(adv)*.

happen happening happened *(v)*
1 to take place or to occur.
2 If you **happen** to do something, you have the chance or luck to do it. *Ned happened to arrive just as the bus was leaving.*

happy happier happiest *(adj)*
1 pleased and contented. **happiness** *(n)*, **happily** *(adv)*.
2 lucky or fortunate. *Meeting Bob in town was a happy coincidence.*

harangue *(huh-rang)* haranguing harangued *(v)* to talk loudly or crossly to someone. **harangue** *(n)*.

harass harasses
harassing harassed *(v)* to pester or annoy someone. **harassment** *(n)*.

harbour harbouring harboured
1 *(n)* a place where ships shelter or unload their cargo.
2 *(v)* to look after someone secretly.

hard harder hardest *(adj)*
1 firm and solid.
A hard bed. **hardness** *(n)*.
2 difficult. *A hard exam.* **hardness** *(n)*.
3 strong or powerful. *Hard drugs.*
4 *(informal)* tough and brave.

hardboard *(n)* stiff board made from pressed wood pulp.

hard copy *(n)* a printed version of a document created by a computer.

hard disk *(n)*
a disk inside a computer, used for storing large amounts of data. You can also get portable hard disks, which allow you to store more data.

harden hardening hardened *(v)*
1 to become harder or to make something harder.
2 to become tough and unfeeling. *The emperor hardened himself against the complaints of his subjects.* **hardened** *(adj)*.

hardly *(adv)* scarcely or only just. *I could hardly wait to open my gifts.*

hardship *(n)* difficulty or suffering.

hardware *(n)*
1 tools and other household equipment.
2 computer equipment, such as a printer or a monitor.

hardwood *(n)*
strong, hard wood from deciduous trees, such as oak, beech, or ash.

hardy hardier hardiest *(adj)*
If a person, an animal, or a plant is **hardy**, they are tough and can survive in very difficult conditions.

hare *(n)* a mammal similar to a large rabbit, with long, strong back legs. *Hares often box together before they mate.*

hares boxing

harm harming harmed *(v)*
to injure or hurt someone or something. **harm** *(n)*, **harmful** *(adj)*.

harmonica *(n)* a small type of mouth organ, played by blowing out and drawing in your breath through the mouthpiece. *Harmonicas contain two sets of reeds fixed to reed plates above and below the mouthpiece. The reeds are left free at one end so that they can vibrate and produce notes when air passes over them.*

harmonica
- cover plate
- metal reed (fixed below plate)
- metal reed (fixed above plate)
- box
- hole mouthpiece
- lower reed plate inside here
- upper reed plate
- slide (changes notes)

harmony harmonies *(n)*
1 agreement. **harmonious** *(adj)*.
2 a pleasant-sounding set of musical notes played at the same time. **harmonious** *(adj)*.

harness harnesses
harnessing harnessed
1 *(n)* a set of straps used to attach an animal, such as a horse, to a vehicle.
2 *(n)* an arrangement of straps, used to keep someone safe. *A climbing harness.* See **rock climbing**.
3 *(v)* to control and use something. *We can now create electricity by harnessing the Sun's energy.*

harp harping harped
1 *(n)*
a large, triangular musical instrument with strings that you play by plucking. **harpist** *(n)*.
2 *(v)*
If you **harp** on about something, you keep talking about it.

harp
- neck
- tuning pins
- metal plate
- strings
- pillar
- body
- soundboard
- pedal
- foot

harsh harsher harshest *(adj)*
1 unpleasant or cruel. *A harsh punishment.* **harshly** *(adv)*.
2 A **harsh** noise sounds rough and loud. **harshly** *(adv)*.

hazard

harvest harvesting harvested *(v)* to collect or gather up crops. *The picture shows the main parts of a combine harvester, which is used to harvest crops such as wheat, barley, and peas. Wheat is gathered and cut by the header, and carried to the threshing drum and beater to separate the grain from the straw. The straw then travels along straw walkers, where more grain is collected and the waste is unloaded. The grain is cleaned in the cleaning shoe and stored in the grain tank, ready for unloading.* **harvest** *(n)*.

hatch
hatches
hatching
hatched
1 *(v)* When an egg **hatches**, a baby animal such as a bird, fish, or insect breaks out of it.
2 *(n)* a covered hole in a floor, door, wall, or ceiling. *A serving hatch.*

turtles hatching

hatchback *(n)* a car with a rear door that opens upwards.

2 *(v)* If something **haunts** you, you keep worrying about it. *Libby was haunted by the memory of the child's face.* **haunting** *(adj)*.
3 *(n)* a place you have visited often.

have having had *(v)*
1 to own or possess something. *I have a new bicycle.*
2 to experience or enjoy something. *Let's have some fun!*
3 to receive or get something. *Did you have some lunch?*

combine harvester (cutaway)

threshing drum (separates grain and chaff from straw)

bubble-up auger (delivers grain to grain tank)

beater

grain tank

unloading auger (empties grain tank)

straw walker (separates remaining grain and chaff from straw)

wide view cab

control panel

removable header

header auger (carries crops to elevator)

crop elevator

tail light

revolving reel

blade (cuts crops)

tine (lifts crops)

steel skid

side sheet

steps to driver's cab

cleaning shoe (separates grain from chaff)

chute for grain and chaff

sieve

grain collecting area (grain sent from here up to grain tank)

straw hood (straw unloaded here)

hash hashes *(n)*
1 small pieces of meat and vegetables cooked together.
2 *(informal)* a mess. *Brad made a hash of his exams.*
3 *(slang)* a form of the drug cannabis. Hash is short for hashish.

hassle hassling hassled
1 *(v)* *(informal)* If someone **hassles** you, they annoy you by going on about something.
2 *(n)* *(informal)* a nuisance. *It was a real hassle having to get up so early.*

hasty hastier hastiest *(adj)* quick or hurried. *A hasty decision.* **haste** *(n)*, **hasten** *(v)*, **hastily** *(adv)*.

hat *(n)*
1 an item of clothing that you wear on top of your head.
2 **hat trick** three successes in a row, such as three goals in the same football match.

hatchet *(n)* a small axe.

hate hating hated *(v)* to dislike or detest someone or something. **hate** *(n)*, **hatred** *(n)*.

hateful *(adj)* horrible.

haughty haughtier haughtiest *(adj)* If you are **haughty**, you are very proud and look down on other people. **haughtily** *(adv)*.

haul hauling hauled
1 *(v)* to pull something with difficulty. *Madeleine hauled the sack of potatoes into the shed.*
2 *(n)* a distance to be travelled. *The flight between London and Sydney is a long haul.*
3 *(n)* a quantity of something that is caught. *A big haul of fish.*

haunt haunting haunted
1 *(v)* If a ghost **haunts** a place, it visits it often. **haunted** *(adj)*.

haven *(n)*
1 a harbour.
2 a safe place.

havoc *(n)* great damage and chaos. *The floods have wreaked havoc.*

hawk *(n)* a bird of prey, with a hooked beak and sharp claws, that eats other birds and small animals.

hay *(n)* grass which is dried and fed to farm animals.

hay fever *(n)* an allergy to pollen or grass that makes you sneeze, makes your eyes water, and can make you wheeze.

haystack *(n)* a large pile of hay.

hazard hazarding hazarded
1 *(n)* a danger or a risk. *A fire hazard.* **hazardous** *(adj)*.
2 *(v)* to risk or take a chance on something. *I'll hazard a guess at the answer.*

a b c d e f g h i j k l m n o p q r s t u v w x y z

haze

haze *(n)* tiny specks of smoke, dust, or moisture in the air that prevent you from seeing a long way.

hazel *(n)*
1 a tree that produces hazelnuts.
2 a greenish-brown colour. **hazel** *(adj)*.

hazy hazier haziest *(adj)*
1 misty. **hazily** *(adv)*.
2 If you have a **hazy** memory of something, it is vague and unclear.

head heading headed
1 *(n)* the top part of your body where your brain, eyes, and mouth are.
2 *(n)* the person in charge. **head** *(adj)*.
3 *(n)* the top or the front of something. *The head of the queue.*
4 *(v)* to lead something. *Isaac headed the expedition.*
5 *(v)* to move towards something. *We headed for the exit.*

headache *(n)* a pain in your head.

headdress headdresses *(n)* a head covering. *This headdress was worn by Native Americans as a sign of their bravery in wars and raids.*

Native American headdress — tufts of dyed horsehair, brow band, ermine strip, eagle feathers, downy feathers, skullcap of buffalo skin

heading *(n)* words written as a title above a section of writing.

headlice *(plural n)* tiny insects that live and breed in human hair.

headline *(n)*
1 the title of a newspaper article, printed in large type.
2 **headlines** *(plural n)* the most important items in a news broadcast.

headphones *(plural n)* small speakers that you wear in or over your ears.

headquarters *or* **HQ** headquarters *(n)* the place from which an organization is run.

head teacher *(n)* the teacher who is responsible for running a school.

headway *(n)* If you make **headway**, you go forwards or make progress.

heal healing healed *(v)* to cure someone or make them healthy. **healer** *(n)*, **healing** *(n)*.

health *(n)*
1 strength and fitness.
2 the state or condition of your body. *Aunt Agnes is in poor health.*

health food *(n)* food that is natural and good for you.

healthy healthier healthiest *(adj)*
1 If you are **healthy**, you are fit and well. **healthiness** *(n)*.
2 Something that is **healthy** keeps you well. *A healthy diet.*

heap heaping heaped
1 *(n)* a pile. **heaped** *(adj)*.
2 *(v)* to pile up.
3 *(n)* *(informal)* something that is old and broken-down.

hear hearing heard *(v)* to sense sounds through your ears. **hearing** *(n)*.

hearing aid *(n)* a small piece of equipment that people wear in or behind their ears to help them hear.

hearsay *(n)* things you are told but have not actually seen or experienced.

hearse *(rhymes with curse)* *(n)* a car that carries a coffin to a funeral.

heart *(n)*
1 the organ in your chest that pumps blood around your body.
2 courage or enthusiasm.
3 love and affection. *You have won my heart.*
4 the centre of something. *The heart of the city.*
5 If you learn something **off by heart**, you memorize it.
6 **hearts** *(plural n)* one of the four suits in a pack of cards, with a red heart-shaped symbol. *See* **card**.

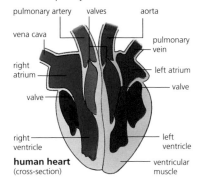

human heart (cross-section) — pulmonary artery, valves, aorta, vena cava, pulmonary vein, right atrium, left atrium, valve, valve, right ventricle, left ventricle, ventricular muscle

heart attack *(n)* If someone has a **heart attack**, they collapse because their heart has started to beat irregularly.

heartbroken *(adj)* If you are heartbroken, you are extremely sad.

hearth *(n)* the area in front of a fireplace.

heartless *(adj)* cruel and unkind. **heartlessness** *(n)*, **heartlessly** *(adv)*.

hearty heartier heartiest *(adj)*
1 cheerful and enthusiastic. **heartiness** *(n)*, **heartily** *(adv)*.
2 A **hearty** meal is large and filling. *A hearty breakfast.*

heat heating heated
1 *(n)* great warmth.
2 *(v)* to warm or cook something.
3 *(n)* passion. *In the heat of the argument, I lost my self-control.* **heated** *(adj)*, **heatedly** *(adv)*.
4 *(n)* a stage in a competition. *Callum got through to the third heat.*
5 **heat wave** *(n)* unusually hot weather that lasts for a few days.

heath *(n)* a large, wild area of grasses, ferns, and heather.

heathen *(old-fashioned)* *(n)*
1 someone who does not believe in any religion.
2 someone who is uncivilized.

heather *(n)* a small, spiky bush with pink, purple, or white flowers.

heave heaving heaved *(v)*
1 to lift, pull, push, or throw something with great effort.
2 to go up and down. *Beth's chest heaved with emotion.*

heaven *(n)*
1 a wonderful place where God is believed to live and where some people believe they will go after they die.
2 a marvellous place, thing, or state. *It was heaven to be on holiday.* **heavenly** *(adj)*.
3 the **heavens** *(plural n)* the sky.

heavy heavier heaviest *(adj)*
1 weighing a lot. **heaviness** *(n)*, **heavily** *(adv)*.
2 great in amount or force. *Heavy fighting. Heavy rain.* **heaviness** *(n)*, **heavily** *(adv)*.
3 *(slang)* serious and hard to cope with. *A heavy film.*

heavy metal *(n)* a type of music with a strong beat, featuring loud electric guitars and drums.

heckle heckling heckled *(v)* to interrupt a speaker by making rude comments. **heckler** *(n)*.

hectic *(adj)* very busy. **hectically** *(adv)*.

hedge *(n)* a border made from bushes.

hedgehog *(n)*
a small mammal, covered with spikes, that comes out at night.

hedgerow *(n)* a row of bushes.

heel *(n)*
1 the back part of your foot.
2 something that supports the back part of your foot.
Suki loves shoes with high heels.

hefty heftier heftiest *(adj)*
(informal) large or powerful.
Neil used to be slim, but now he's really hefty. **heftily** *(adv)*.

heifer *(heff-er) (n)*
a young cow that has not had a calf.

height *(n)*
1 a measurement of how high something is.
2 the most important or greatest point of something.
Sadie thinks that her new hat is the height of fashion.

heighten
heightening heightened *(v)*
to make something higher or stronger.
The painting looked wonderful after Paddy had heightened its colours.

heir *(air) (n)* someone who has been, or will be, left money, property, or a title. *The heir to the throne.*

heiress *(air-ess)* heiresses *(n)*
a girl or woman who has been, or will be, left money, property, or a title.

heirloom *(air-loom) (n)*
something precious that is owned by a family and handed down from one generation to the next.

helicopter *(n)*
an aircraft with large, rotating blades on top, which can take off and land vertically. *The picture shows a Schweizer 300C helicopter.*

hell *(n)*
1 a place of suffering and misery, where some people believe evil people go after they die.
2 a very unpleasant place, thing, or state. *It was hell having to work such long hours.* **hellish** *(adj)*.

hello *(interject)* a word said to someone when you meet them.

helm *(n)*
1 the wheel or handle used to steer a boat. **helmsman** *(n)*.
2 If someone is **at the helm** of something, they are in charge of it.

helmet *(n)*
a hard hat that protects your head.

help helping helped
1 *(v)* to assist.
2 *(n)* assistance. **helper** *(n)*.

helpful *(adj)* friendly and willing to help. **helpfulness** *(n)*, **helpfully** *(adv)*.

helping *(n)* a portion of food.

helpless *(adj)* If you are **helpless**, you cannot look after yourself.
helplessness *(n)*, **helplessly** *(adv)*.

hem hemming hemmed *(v)*
1 to fold over an edge of material and sew it down. **hem** *(n)*.
2 If you are **hemmed in**, you are surrounded and cannot get out.

hemisphere *(n)* one half of a sphere, especially of the Earth. *France is in the northern hemisphere.*

hemoglobin *see* **haemoglobin**.
hemophilia *see* **haemophilia**.
hemorrhage *see* **haemorrhage**.

hemp *(n)* a plant whose fibres are used to make rope and sacks.

hen *(n)*
1 a bird kept for its eggs and its meat. *See* **chicken**.
2 a female bird.

hence *(adv)*
1 for this reason.
2 *(old-fashioned)* from this place.

heptathlon *(n)*
a competition for women, made up of seven athletic events.

heraldry *(n)*
the study of coats of arms and family histories. *The picture shows some patterns and symbols used in heraldry.*

heraldry

cross   chevron   bend

fleur-de-lys   lion rampant   lion passant

herb *(n)* a plant used in cooking or medicine. **herbalist** *(n)*, **herbal** *(adj)*.

herbs

rosemary

bay

dill

sage

mint

basil   thyme   parsley

herbivore *(n)* an animal that eats plants rather than meat. *Rabbits are herbivores.* **herbivorous** *(adj)*.

herd herding herded
1 *(n)* a large group of animals.
2 *(v)* to make people or animals move together as a group. *We were all herded into a tiny room.*

here *(adv)*
1 to, at, or in this place.
Please come here.
2 at this point in time.
Here the music gets louder.

helicopter

rotor blade

rotor hub

fin

tubular steel tail boom

air deflector

tailplane

bumper (stops tail rotor hitting ground)

fuel tank

safety harness

tail rotor (stops helicopter from spinning)

instrument panel

battery

tinted canopy

shock absorber (softens impact of heavy landing)

landing skid

control stick

hereditary

hereditary (adj) If something is **hereditary**, it is passed from parent to child. *A hereditary disease.*

heretic (n) someone whose views are unacceptable to religious leaders or to people in authority. **heresy** (n).

heritage (n) valuable or important traditions, buildings, etc. that belong to a country or a family.

hermit (n) someone who has chosen to live totally alone.

hero heroes (n)
1 a brave or good person. **heroism** (n), **heroic** (adj).
2 the main character in a book, play, film, etc.

heroin (n)
a very powerful drug. Heroin is dangerously addictive and illegal.

heroine (n)
1 a brave or good girl or woman.
2 the main female character in a book, play, film, etc.

heron (n) a long-legged bird, with a long, thin beak, that lives near water.

herself (pronoun) her and nobody else. *Elizabeth has hurt herself.*

hesitate hesitating hesitated (v) to pause before you do something. *Zoë hesitated before diving into the river.* **hesitation** (n), **hesitant** (adj).

hessian (n) thick, rough cloth, used for making sacks or covering walls.

hexagon (n)
a shape with six straight sides. **hexagonal** (adj). See **shape**.

heyday (n)
Someone's **heyday** is the best or most successful period in their life.

hibernate hibernating hibernated (v) When animals **hibernate**, they spend the winter in a deep sleep in which their heartbeat, temperature, and breathing rate become very low. Animals hibernate to survive low temperatures and lack of food. **hibernation** (n).

hiccup or **hiccough** (hik-up) (n)
1 a sudden sound in your throat, caused by a spasm in your chest.
2 (informal) a small delay or problem. *A technical hiccup.*

hide hiding hid hidden
1 (v) to go where you cannot be seen.
2 (v) to keep something secret or concealed. *Julia managed to hide her disappointment.*
3 (n) an animal's skin that is used to make leather.

hideous (adj) ugly or horrible. **hideousness** (n), **hideously** (adv).

hieroglyphics (hi-ra-glif-iks)
(plural n) writing used by ancient Egyptians, made up of pictures and symbols. *The hieroglyphics shown below were used to represent both objects and letters or sounds.*

hieroglyphics

D hand	T loaf	W quail chick
F viper	B foot	Y flowering reed
N water		
H room	M owl	K basket

high higher highest (adj)
1 Something that is **high** is a great distance from the ground. *A high mountain.* **high** (adv).
2 measuring from top to bottom. *The tree was 30m high.*
3 more than the normal level or amount. *High prices.* **highly** (adv).
4 (informal) If you feel **high** or are **on a high**, you are very excited.
5 **high tide** the time when the sea is furthest up the beach.

higher education (n)
education at college or university.

highlands (plural n) areas with mountains or hills. **highland** (adj).

highlight highlighting highlighted
1 (v) to draw attention to something.
2 (n) the best or most interesting part of something.
3 (v) to mark important words using a pen with brightly coloured ink.
4 **highlights** (plural n)
light streaks in your hair.

highwayman highwaymen (n)
a robber, usually on horseback, who used to stop travellers on the road and steal from them.

hijack hijacking hijacked (v)
If someone **hijacks** a plane or other vehicle, they take control of it and force its pilot or driver to go somewhere. **hijacker** (n), **hijacking** (n).

hike (n)
a long walk in the country. **hiker** (n), **hiking** (n), **hike** (v).

hiker

rucksack

woollen hat (prevents heat loss)

scarf

waterproof jacket

map case

overtrousers

thermal glove

hiking boot

gaiter

hilarious (adj) very funny. **hilarity** (n).

hill (n)
a raised area of land that is smaller than a mountain. **hilly** (adj).

himself (pronoun) him and no one else. *Justin has hurt himself.*

hinder hindering hindered (v) If someone or something **hinders** you, they make things difficult for you. **hindrance** (n).

Hindi (n)
a language spoken in northern India.

Hinduism (n)
the main religion of India. Hindus have lots of gods, and believe that they live many lives in different bodies. *This is a statue of Shiva, one of the main gods in Hinduism.* **Hindu** (n), **Hindu** (adj).

Shiva

hinge hingeing hinged
1 (n) a movable metal joint on a window or door. **hinged** (adj).
2 (v) to depend on something. *My future hinges on your decision.*

hint
1 a clue or a helpful tip. **hint** (v).
2 a trace or a tiny amount. *There's a hint of garlic in this soup.*

hip (n) the area at the side of your body between your thighs and waist.

hip-hop (n) a style of dancing, art, and music that originated in urban areas and became popular through break dancing, graffiti, and rap music.

hippie or **hippy** hippies (n) someone who does not live or dress in a conventional way. Hippies often live in groups.

hippopotamus hippopotamuses or **hippopotami** (n) a large African mammal with short legs and thick skin, that lives near water.

Some words that begin with a "hi" sound are spelt "hy".

a b c d e f g h i j k l m n o p q r s t u v w x y z

honey

hire hiring hired (v) to employ someone, or to rent something for a short time. *We hired a car for the day.*

Hispanic (adj) coming from or to do with Spanish or Portuguese-speaking countries. **Hispanic** (n).

hiss hisses hissing hissed (v) to make a "ssss" noise like a snake, especially to show that you do not like something or someone. *We hissed at the villains in the play.* **hiss** (n).

hissy fit (n) (informal) a childish temper tantrum.

historic (adj) important in history.

history histories (n)
1 the study of past events. **historian** (n), **historical** (adj), **historically** (adv).
2 a description of past events. *I'm reading a history of the Wild West.*

histrionic (adj) excessively dramatic or artificial. **histrionically** (adv).

hit hitting hit
1 (v) to smack or strike someone or something with your hand, a bat, etc. **hit** (n).
2 (v) to knock or bump into someone or something.
3 (v) to have a bad effect on someone or something. *The factory was hit by the recession.*
4 (n) a successful song, play, etc.
5 (v) (informal) If you **hit it off** with someone, you get on well with them.

hitch hitches hitching hitched
1 (v) to join something to a vehicle. *They hitched the trailer to the van.*
2 (n) a problem. *There's been a hitch in our plans, so we can't come.*
3 (n) a kind of knot. See **knot**.
4 (slang) If you **get hitched**, you marry someone.

hitchhike hitchhiking hitchhiked (v) to travel by getting lifts in other people's vehicles for free. *It can be very dangerous to hitchhike.* **hitchhiker** (n).

hi-tech or **high-tech** (adj) If something is **hi-tech**, it is very sophisticated and uses the latest technology. Hi-tech is short for high-technology.

hither
1 (adv) (old-fashioned) to or towards this place. *Come hither!*
2 If you run **hither and thither**, you run in lots of different directions.

HIV
1 (n) a virus that can lead to AIDS. HIV stands for Human Immunodeficiency Virus.
2 (adj) If someone is **HIV positive**, they have the HIV virus.

hive (n) a box for keeping bees so that their honey can be collected. The queen bee lays her eggs in the brood box and honey is stored in the supers. The honey-filled supers are collected from the hive by beekeepers. Also see **honeycomb**.

hive
(cutaway)

non-slip roof
ventilator
feeding hole
glass quilt (used for viewing bees)
empty super
honey super
frame
queen excluder
brood box (contains queen bee)
floor
entrance
bottom board
entrance block
hive stand

hoard hoarding hoarded (v) to collect and store things. **hoard** (n), **hoarder** (n).

hoarse hoarser hoarsest (adj) A **hoarse** voice is rough or croaky.

hoax (rhymes with pokes) hoaxes (n) a trick or a practical joke.

hobble hobbling hobbled (v) to walk with difficulty because you are in pain or injured.

hobby hobbies (n) something that you enjoy doing in your spare time.

hockey (n) a game played with sticks and a ball, by two teams aiming to score goals.

hoe (n) a gardening tool with a long handle and a thin blade, used for weeding and loosening earth. **hoe** (v).

hoist hoisting hoisted
1 (v) to lift something heavy, usually with a piece of equipment.
2 (n) a piece of equipment used for lifting heavy objects.

hold holding held
1 (v) to carry, support, or keep something. *Hold this cup.* **holder** (n).
2 (v) to contain something or be able to contain it. *This mug holds a pint.*
3 (v) to organize or arrange something. *We are holding a party.*
4 (n) the part of a ship where the cargo is stored.

hole (n)
1 a hollow place or a gap.
2 an animal's burrow.
3 (informal) an unpleasant or dirty place. *Sidney's flat is a hole.*

holiday (n) time away from school or work, especially a trip away from home.

hollow hollowing hollowed
1 (adj) If something is **hollow**, it has an empty space inside it. **hollow** (n).
2 (v) If you **hollow something out**, you take its insides out.

holly (n) an evergreen tree or bush with prickly leaves and red berries.

hologram (n) an image made by laser beams that looks three-dimensional.

holster (n) a holder for a pistol, worn on a belt.

holy holier holiest (adj) to do with or belonging to God or a god.

Holy Communion (n) a Christian service in which people eat bread and drink wine in memory of the death and resurrection of Jesus Christ.

home
1 (n) Your **home** is where you live or feel like you belong.
2 (n) a place where people who cannot look after themselves are cared for. *A foster home. A retirement home.*
3 If you are **at home**, you are in the place you live. *She's not at home today.*
4 (adj) A **home** game is a sports match that is played at your team's usual training ground.

homesick (adj) If you are **homesick**, you miss your home and family.

homicide (n) murder.

homoeopathy (home-ee-op-ath-ee) (n) a way of treating illness by giving people very small amounts of drugs that produce the same symptoms as the illness. **homoeopath** (n), **homoeopathic** (adj).

homosexual (adj) having sexual feelings for a person of the same sex. **homosexual** (n), **homosexuality** (n).

honest (adj) An **honest** person is truthful and will not lie or steal. **honesty** (n), **honestly** (adv).

honey (n) a sweet, sticky, golden-brown substance made by bees. See **hive**, **honeycomb**.

Some words that begin with a "hi" sound are spelt "hy".
Some words that begin with a "h" sound are spelt "wh".

a b c d e f g **h** i j k l m n o p q r s t u v w x y z

honeycomb

honeycomb *(n)*
a wax structure made by bees and used by them to store honey, pollen, and eggs. A honeycomb consists of many rows of six-sided cells. *The picture shows the different functions of the cells in a honeycomb. For the first six days, the brood cells are unsealed so the worker bees can feed the growing larvae. Then the bees seal the cells and the larvae change into pupae which develop into bees. Also see* **hive**.

unsealed honey cell

worker bee sealing cell with wax

worker bee filling cell with pollen

sealed honey cell

queen bee (lays eggs)

egg

unsealed brood cell containing larva

queen pupa

sealed queen cell

drone (mates with queen)

sealed queen cell (cutaway)

honeycomb

honeymoon *(n)*
a holiday that a husband and wife take together after their wedding.

honour honouring honoured
1 *(n)* Someone's **honour** is their good reputation and the respect that other people have for them.
2 *(v)* to give praise or an award. *The mayor honoured Kimberley for her bravery.*
3 *(v)* to keep an agreement. *Both parties must honour the contract.*

honourable *(adj)*
1 An **honourable** action is good and deserves praise.
2 If someone is **honourable**, they keep their promises.

hood *(n)*
1 the part of a jacket or coat that goes over your head. **hooded** *(adj)*.
2 the folding roof or cover of a car, pram, etc.
3 *(US)* the cover for a car's engine. (bonnet, *UK*).

hoof hooves *or* hoofs *(n)*
the hard covering over the foot of a horse, deer, etc. *See* **horse**.

hook *(n)*
1 a curved piece of metal or plastic, used to catch or hold something.
2 a punch in boxing, made with the elbow bent. *A right hook.*

hooked *(adj)*
1 curved. *A hooked nose.*
2 *(slang)* If you are **hooked** on something, you like it a lot, or are addicted to it.

hooligan *(n)* a noisy, violent person who makes trouble. **hooliganism** *(n)*.

hoop *(n)* a large ring. **hooped** *(adj)*.

hooray *see* **hurray**.

hoot hooting hooted *(v)* to make a sound like an owl or a car horn.

hop hopping hopped
1 *(v)* to jump, especially on one leg. **hop** *(n)*.
2 *(v)* *(informal)* to get into or out of a vehicle. *Hop in the car!*
3 **hops** *(plural n)*
the dried seed cases of hop plants, that are used to flavour beer.

hope hoping hoped
1 *(v)* to wish for or expect something. **hopeful** *(adj)*, **hopefully** *(adv)*.
2 *(n)* a feeling of expectation or confidence. *I have plenty of hope for the future.* **hopefulness** *(n)*, **hopeful** *(adj)*, **hopefully** *(adv)*.

hopeless *(adj)*
1 without hope. *A hopeless case.* **hopelessness** *(n)*, **hopelessly** *(adv)*.
2 bad or lacking in skill. *You're hopeless at map reading!* **hopelessness** *(n)*, **hopelessly** *(adv)*.

horde *(n)* a large, noisy, moving crowd of people.

horizon *(n)*
1 the line where the sky and the Earth or sea seem to meet.
2 the limit of your experience or opportunities. *Travel broadens your horizons.*

horizontal *(adj)*
flat and parallel to the ground. *A horizontal line.* **horizontally** *(adv)*.

hormone *(n)* Your **hormones** are chemicals made in your body that affect the way that you grow and develop. **hormonal** *(adj)*.

horn *(n)*
1 a hard, bony growth on the head of some animals. **horned** *(adj)*.
2 the hard, bony substance that horns and hooves are made from.
3 a musical instrument that you blow. *A French horn.* See **brass**.
4 a machine that gives a signal by making a hooting sound. *A car horn.*

horoscope *(n)*
a prediction about your life, based on the position of the stars and planets when you were born.

horrible *(adj)*
very unpleasant. **horribly** *(adv)*.

horrid *(adj)* nasty or unkind.

horrific *(adj)* horrible and shocking.

horrify horrifies horrifying horrified *(v)*
If something **horrifies** you, you are shocked and disgusted by it. **horrifying** *(adj)*, **horrifyingly** *(adv)*.

horse *(n)*
1 a large, strong animal with hooves, that people ride or use to pull coaches, carriages, ploughs, etc. *The picture shows a male Anglo-Arabian horse.*
2 a piece of gymnastics apparatus that you jump over.

mane   shoulder

forelock

muzzle

withers

cheek

nostril   neck

chin groove

chest

hoof
(underside)

elbow

frog (rubbery pad)

forearm

sole

knee

nail

cannon

iron horseshoe

hoof

back   loin   croup   dock

horse
(male)

tail

thigh

barrel (belly)

flank

sheath

stifle

gaskin

pastern

fetlock

heel

Some words that begin with a "h" sound are spelt "wh".

human

gore
(nylon panel)

burning
propane
gas

scoop
(protects
flame
from wind)

coil

burner

blast valve

flying
wire

parachute valve
cord (deflates
envelope)

load frame

padded edge

envelope

covered
support
pole

flight
instruments

mouth

crown line
(stabilizes
envelope)

mini-burner

cane and
willow basket

fuel cylinder
with padded
cover

rope handle

fuel
cylinder

**hopper
balloon**
(one-person
balloon)

pilot in
adjustable seat

leather
securing strap

hot-air balloon
(basket cutaway)

horsepower (n) an old-fashioned
unit for measuring engine power.

horticulture (n)
the growing of fruit, vegetables,
and flowers. **horticultural** (adj).

hose hosing hosed
1 (n) a long rubber or plastic tube
through which liquids or gases travel.
2 (v) to wash or water something
or someone with a hose.
Stop hosing your brother!

hospice (n)
a hospital that provides special
care for people who are dying.

hospitable (adj) friendly and
welcoming. **hospitality** (n).

hospital (n)
a place where you can receive
medical treatment and are looked
after when you are injured or ill.

host (n)
1 an organizer of an event. **host** (v).
2 a large number. *The audience
asked a host of questions.*

hostage (n)
someone held prisoner and threatened
by an enemy, as a way of demanding
money or other conditions.

hostel (n)
a building where people can
stay, usually at low cost.

hostile (adj) unfriendly or angry.
A hostile crowd. **hostility** (n).

hot hotter hottest (adj)
1 having a high temperature.
2 very spicy and strong-tasting.
3 recent or exciting. *Hot news.*

hot-air balloon (n)
an aircraft that consists of a giant
bag filled with hot air or gas, and
a basket for carrying passengers.

hot dog (n)
a sausage in a long bread roll.

hotel (n)
a place where you pay to stay
overnight and have meals.

hotline (n)
1 a telephone line used for a
special purpose, such as ordering
goods. *A customer hotline.*
2 a direct telephone link
between heads of government,
to be used in an emergency.

hot-water bottle (n) a container
for hot water, used to warm a bed.

hound hounding hounded
1 (n) a dog. *A foxhound.*
2 (v) to chase or pester someone.
Ziggy was hounded by journalists.

hour (n) a unit of time equal
to 60 minutes. **hourly** (adv).

house housing housed
1 (n) a building where people live.
2 (v) If you **house** someone
or something, you find a place
for them to live or to be.
3 If something in a restaurant or
bar is **on the house**, it is free.

houseboat (n)
a boat that people live on, with
cooking and sleeping areas.

household
1 (n) all the people who live together
in a house. **householder** (n).

2 (adj) belonging to or to do
with a house or family. *We all
share the household chores.*

housework (n) work done
to keep a house clean and tidy.

hovel (n)
a small, dirty house or hut.

hover hovering hovered (v)
1 to stay in one place in the air.
2 to linger or be uncertain.
Horace hovered in the doorway.

hovercraft hovercraft (n)
a vehicle that can travel over land and
water, supported by a cushion of air.

however
1 (adv) in whatever way or to
whatever extent. *You have to
go, however much you hate it.*
2 (adv and conj) on the other hand.
*We can't come on Friday. However,
we could manage Saturday.*

howl howling howled (v) to cry
like a dog or wolf in pain. **howl** (n).

HQ short for **headquarters**.

hub (n)
1 the centre of a wheel. See **bicycle**.
2 the centre of an organization
or activity. *London was the
hub of the British Empire.*

huddle huddling huddled (v)
to crowd together in a tight group.
We huddled together against the cold.

hue (n)
a colour, or a shade of a colour.

huff (n)
If you are **in a huff**, you show that
you are upset in a childish, sulky way.

hug hugging hugged (v)
to hold someone tightly in a
loving or caring way. **hug** (n).

huge huger hugest (adj)
very large. *A huge amount of money.*

hulk (n)
1 the remains of a wrecked ship.
2 a large, clumsy person.
hulking (adj).

hum humming hummed (v)
1 to sing with your mouth
closed. **hum** (n).
2 to make a steady, buzzing
noise. **hum** (n).

human
1 **human** or **human being** (n)
a person. **human** (adj).
2 (adj) natural and understandable.
*It was only human for Ada to get
angry when her bike was stolen.*
3 (plural n) When people campaign
for **human rights**, they fight for
everyone's right to have justice,
fair treatment, and free speech.

a b c d e f g h i j k l m n o p q r s t u v w x y z

humane

humane (adj)
kind and merciful. **humanely** (adv).

humanitarian (adj) to do with
helping people and relieving suffering.
Humanitarian aid for refugees.

humanities (plural n)
non-science subjects, such
as literature, history, and art.

humanity (n)
1 all human beings.
2 kindness and sympathy.

humble humbler humblest (adj)
modest and not proud. **humbly** (adv).

humdrum (adj) A humdrum life
is dull and filled with routine events.

humid (adj)
warm and damp. **humidity** (n).

humiliate
humiliating humiliated (v)
to make someone look or feel foolish
and undignified. **humiliation** (n).

humility (n) If you show
humility, you are not proud
and you recognize your own faults.

hummingbird
(n) a very small,
brightly coloured
tropical bird that makes
a humming sound when
it flaps its wings rapidly.
*This Green Violetear
hummingbird is sticking
its long beak into a
flower so that it can
suck up nectar through
its hollow tongue.*

hummingbird

humour humouring humoured
1 (n) the general name for
things that make people
laugh or smile. **humorous** (adj).
2 (n) If you have a good **sense of
humour**, you are quick to appreciate
the funny side of life. **humorous** (adj).
3 (v) If you **humour** someone, you
keep them happy by agreeing with
them or doing what they want.

hump (n)
1 a small hill or a large lump.
2 **the hump** (informal) a bad
mood or sulk. *You've had the
hump all day!*

humus (n) rich earth made from
rotting vegetable and animal matter.

hunch hunches hunching hunched
1 (v) to lower your head into
your shoulders and lean forward.
2 (n) an idea that is not backed by
much reason or proof. *I had a hunch
that I would hear some good news.*

hungry hungrier hungriest (adj)
wanting food. **hunger** (n),
hungrily (adv).

hunk (n)
1 a large piece of something,
such as bread, cheese, meat, etc.
2 (slang) an attractive man.

hunt hunting hunted (v)
1 to search for something.
Lisa hunted for her watch.
2 to chase deer or other wild
animals for sport. **hunt** (n),
hunter (n), **hunting** (n).

hurdle hurdling hurdled
1 (n) a small fence that you jump over
in a running event. *The sequence
below shows a hurdler clearing a
hurdle.* **hurdler** (n), **hurdling** (n).
2 (v) to jump over something.
3 (n) an obstacle.

hurdling

hurl hurling hurled (v)
to throw something very strongly.

hurray or **hooray**
or **hurrah** (interject)
a word used when people cheer.

hurricane (n) a violent storm.

hurry hurries hurrying hurried
1 (v) to do things as fast as possible.
2 When you are **in a hurry**, you
do everything very quickly and
often impatiently. **hurried** (adj).

hurt hurting hurt (v)
1 to cause pain.
2 to be in pain.
3 to upset someone by
doing or saying something
unkind. **hurtful** (adj).

hurtle hurtling hurtled (v)
to move at great speed.

husband (n)
the male partner in a marriage.

hush hushes hushing hushed
1 (n) a sudden period of quietness.
*A hush fell on the audience
as the curtain went up.*
2 (interject) be quiet! *Hush!*
3 **hush up** (v) to keep
something secret.
4 **hush-hush** (adj) (informal)
very secret and confidential.

husk (n)
the outer casing of seeds or grains.

husky huskies; huskier huskiest
1 (adj) A husky voice sounds low and
hoarse. **huskiness** (n), **huskily** (adv).
2 (n) a strong dog with
a furry coat, bred to pull
sledges in arctic conditions.

hustle hustling hustled (v)
to push someone roughly in order to
make them move. *The guard hustled
the prisoners out of the room.*

hut (n)
1 a small, primitive house.
2 a wooden shed.

hutch hutches (n) a wooden cage
for rabbits or other small pets.

hybrid (n)
a plant or an animal that has been
bred from two different species.

hydrant (n) an outdoor water
tap for use in emergencies.

hydraulic (hi-drol-ik) (adj)
Hydraulic machines work using
power that is created by liquid
being forced through pipes under
pressure. **hydraulics** (singular n).

hydroelectricity (n) electricity that
is made from energy produced by
running water. **hydroelectric** (adj).

hydrofoil (n) a boat with ski-like
attachments at the front and back,
which lift the hull out of the
water once the boat is
travelling fast.

hydrofoil

radio
aerial

flash light

radar
antenna

exhaust

control bridge

passenger area

hull
(lifted out
of water)

water forced
out of engine

front steering
flap

front strut

water sucked
into engine

rear foil   jet engine

front foil

hydrogen *(n)*
a colourless gas that is lighter than air and catches fire easily.

hydrometer *(n)* an instrument used to measure the density of a liquid.

hyena *(n)*
a wild animal, similar to a dog, that eats the flesh of dead animals and has a shrieking howl.

hygienic *(hi-jee-nik) (adj)*
clean and free enough from germs not to be a health risk. hygiene *(n)*, hygienically *(adv)*.

hymn *(him) (n)*
a song of praise to God.

hype *(n)* extravagant claims made about something in order to promote it. hype *(v)*.

hyperactive *(adj)*
If someone is **hyperactive**, they are abnormally restless and lively. hyperactivity *(n)*.

hyphen *(hi-fern) (n)*
the punctuation mark (-) used to separate the parts of a word made from two or more parts, for example, "easy-going" and "full-time". hyphenation *(n)*, hyphenate *(v)*.

hypnotize *or* **hypnotise**
hypnotizing hypnotized *(v)*
to put someone into a trance. hypnotism *(n)*, hypnotist *(n)*.

hypochondriac
(hi-per-kon-dree-ak) (n)
someone who continually thinks that they are ill or will become ill. hypochondria *(n)*.

hypocrite *(hip-oh-krit) (n)*
someone who pretends to believe or feel something that is different from their true beliefs or feelings. hypocrisy *(n)*, hypocritical *(adj)*, hypocritically *(adv)*.

hypodermic *(n)* a hollow needle used for giving injections.

hypotenuse *(hi-pot-en-ooz) (n)*
the side opposite the right angle of a right-angled triangle.

hypothermia *(n)* If someone is suffering from **hypothermia**, they have become dangerously cold.

hypothesis hypotheses *(n)*
an idea about the way that a scientific investigation or experiment will turn out.

hysterical *(adj)*
If someone is **hysterical**, they are very emotional and out of control, because they are very excited, frightened, or angry. hysteria *(n)*, hysterically *(adv)*.

Ii

ice icing iced
1 *(n)* frozen water. ice *(v)*, icy *(adj)*.
2 *(v)* If someone **ices** a cake, they cover it with a sweet coating.

ice age *(n)* a very early period of time when a large part of the world was covered with ice.

iceberg *(n)* a huge mass of ice floating in the sea.

ice cream *(n)* a sweet, frozen food made from milk or cream.

ice hockey *(n)* a team game played with sticks and a flat disc called a puck, by skaters aiming to score goals.

ice hockey goalkeeper — helmet — mask — team shirt (left side cutaway) — arm and chest protector with built-in shoulder floater — catcher (catching glove) — blocker (stick glove) — goal stick — puck — strap-on goal pad — skate

ice rink *(n)* a place where people skate on a prepared surface of ice.

ice-skate ice-skating ice-skated *(v)*
to move around on ice, wearing boots with blades on the bottom. ice skate *(n)*.

ice-skating movements — bunny jump — stag jump — death spiral — revolutions in the air

icicle *(n)*
a long, thin stem of ice, formed from dripping water which has frozen.

icing *(n)* a sugar coating used to decorate cakes.

icon *or* **ikon** *(n)*
1 a picture of Jesus or a saint found in some Eastern churches such as the Greek and Russian Orthodox churches. *This icon was painted by a Russian artist in the early 13th century.*
2 one of several small pictures on a computer screen, phone, etc., representing programs or functions that you can use.

icon

icy icier iciest *(adj)*
1 very cold or covered with ice.
2 unfriendly. *An icy stare.*

ID *short for* **identification**.

idea *(n)* a thought or a plan.

ideal
1 *(adj)* very suitable or perfect. *Hamsters make ideal pets.*
2 *(n)* the situation you would most like to see. *My ideal is world peace.* idealistic *(adj)*.

identical *(adj)*
exactly alike. identically *(adv)*.

identification *(n)* something that proves who you are. *A driving licence is often used for identification.*

identify identifies
identifying identified *(v)*
to recognize something or someone.

identity identities *(n)*
Your **identity** is who you are.

idiom *(n)* a commonly used expression or phrase that means something different from what it appears to mean. For example, if you catch someone "red-handed", it does not mean that their hands are red.

idiot *(n)* a foolish person. idiotic *(adj)*, idiotically *(adv)*.

idle idler idlest *(adj)*
1 lazy. idleness *(n)*, idly *(adv)*.
2 not active. *The factory stood idle during the strike.*

idol *(n)*
1 someone or something that is worshipped as a god.
2 someone whom other people love and admire. *A pop idol.*

i.e. an abbreviation of the Latin phrase *id est*, which means "that is", and is used to explain something further. *It's the penultimate shop, i.e. the one before last.*

a b c d e f g h i j k l m n o p q r s t u v w x y z

if *(conj)*
a word used to show that something will happen on the condition that another thing happens first.
I will pay you if you work hard.

igloo *(n)* the traditional, dome-shaped shelter of the Inuit people, made of blocks of ice or hard snow.

ignite igniting ignited *(v)* to set fire to something, or to start burning.

ignition *(n)* the electrical system of a vehicle which uses power from a battery to start the engine.

ignorant *(adj)*
1 uneducated or not knowledgeable about many things. **ignorance** *(n)*, **ignorantly** *(adv)*.
2 not knowing about something. *I was completely ignorant of Bruno's intentions.* **ignorance** *(n)*.

ignore ignoring ignored *(v)* to take no notice of something. *Jessica ignored their rude comments.*

ikon *see* **icon**.

ill *(adj)*
1 sick. **illness** *(n)*.
2 bad. *Did you suffer any ill effects after your accident?*

illegal *(adj)*
against the law. **illegally** *(adv)*.

illegible *(adj)* If your handwriting is illegible, it is very difficult to read.

illegitimate *(adj)*
1 An **illegitimate** child is born to parents who are not married. **illegitimacy** *(n)*.
2 against the law or unacceptable.

illiterate *(adj)* not able to read and write. **illiteracy** *(n)*.

illogical *(adj)*
Something **illogical** is not reasonable and does not make sense. **illogically** *(adv)*.

illuminate
illuminating illuminated *(v)*
1 to light up something, such as a building. **illuminated** *(adj)*.
2 to make something clearer and easier to understand. **illuminating** *(adj)*.
3 In the Middle Ages, manuscripts were **illuminated** by adding pictures and decoration to the text. *The letter* *"L", shown here, comes from a manuscript which was illuminated by monks.* **illumination** *(n)*, **illuminated** *(adj)*.

illusion *(n)* something which appears to exist, but does not. **illusory** *(adj)*.

illustration *(n)*
1 a picture in a book, magazine, etc. **illustrator** *(n)*, **illustrate** *(v)*, **illustrative** *(adj)*.
2 an example. *Keri gave lots of illustrations of her brother's stupidity.* **illustrate** *(v)*.

image *(n)*
1 a picture in a book, on a screen, etc.
2 a picture that you have in your mind of something or someone. *I have an image of my ideal house.*
3 Your **image** is the way that you appear to other people.
4 When writers use an **image**, they describe something in terms of something else, for example, "The dragon's eyes were like pits of fire".

imagery *(n)*
descriptive language used by writers in poems, stories, etc. *Similes and metaphors are both types of imagery.*

imagine imagining imagined *(v)*
to picture something in your mind. **imagination** *(n)*, **imaginary** *(adj)*.

imbecile *(im-ber-seel)* *(n)* an idiot.

imitate imitating imitated *(v)*
to copy or mimic someone or something. **imitation** *(n)*.

immature *(adj)*
1 young and not fully developed. **immaturity** *(n)*.
2 If someone is **immature**, they behave in a silly, childish way. **immaturity** *(n)*, **immaturely** *(adv)*.

immediately *(adv)*
now or at once. **immediate** *(adj)*.

immense *(adj)* huge or enormous. **immensity** *(n)*, **immensely** *(adv)*.

immerse immersing immersed *(v)*
1 to cover something completely in a liquid. **immersion** *(n)*.
2 If you are immersed in something, you are completely involved in it. **immersion** *(n)*.

immigrant *(n)*
someone who comes from abroad to live permanently in a country. **immigration** *(n)*, **immigrate** *(v)*.

imminent *(adj)* about to happen.

immobile *(adj)*
1 not moving.
2 unable to move. *Steve's accident left him immobile.*

immobilize *or* **immobilise**
immobilizing immobilized *(v)*
to make it impossible for someone or something to move. *The accident immobilized Emilia for weeks.*

immoral *(adj)* unfair, wrong, or wicked. **immorality** *(n)*.

immune *(adj)*
protected against a disease. **immunity** *(n)*, **immunize** *(v)*.

impact *(n)*
1 the action of one thing hitting another with a lot of force.
2 the effect that something has on people. *Our first visit to the theatre had a great impact on me.*

impair impairing impaired *(v)*
to damage something or to make something less effective. *The constant gunfire impaired the soldiers' hearing.* **impairment** *(n)*.

impartial *(adj)*
fair or not favouring one person or point of view over another. **impartiality** *(n)*, **impartially** *(adv)*.

impatient *(adj)*
1 in a hurry or unable to wait. **impatience** *(n)*, **impatiently** *(adv)*.
2 easily annoyed. *Dad gets very impatient with quarrelling children.* **impatience** *(n)*, **impatiently** *(adv)*.

imperfect *(adj)*
1 faulty or not perfect. **imperfection** *(n)*, **imperfectly** *(adv)*.
2 The **imperfect** form of a verb is used to describe actions which continue, for example, *"I was running, I am running, I will be running".*

imperial *(adj)*
1 to do with an empire. *In the 19th century, Britain had strong imperial ambitions.*
2 The **imperial** system of measurement is the non-metric system which uses such units as feet, pints, and ounces. *See page 284.*

impersonal *(adj)*
1 lacking in warmth and feeling. *The captain had a cold, impersonal manner.*
2 to do with people generally, rather than with one particular person.

impersonate
impersonating impersonated *(v)*
to pretend to be someone else, either seriously or for fun. **impersonation** *(n)*, **impersonator** *(n)*.

impertinent *(adj)*
rude and cheeky. **impertinence** *(n)*.

impetuous *(adj)*
Someone who is **impetuous** does things suddenly, without thinking first. **impetuously** *(adv)*.

implement
implementing implemented
1 *(n)* a tool or utensil.
2 *(v)* to put something, such as a plan or an idea, into action. **implementation** *(n)*.

incredible

implication *(n)*
1 something that happens as a result of something else, and which is sometimes not foreseen. *Having girls on the team has many implications.*
2 something suggested, but not actually said. *Mum has not said "Yes", but the implication is that we can go.*

imply implies implying implied *(v)* to suggest or mean something without actually saying it.

impolite *(adj)* If someone is impolite, they are rude and have bad manners. **impolitely** *(adv)*.

import *(im-port)* importing imported *(v)* to bring foreign goods into your own country to be sold. **import** *(im-port) (n)*.

important *(adj)*
1 Something important is worth taking seriously and can have a great effect. *An important choice.* importance *(n)*, importantly *(adv)*.
2 An important person is powerful and holds a high position.

impossible *(adj)*
If something is impossible, it cannot be done or cannot happen. **impossibility** *(n)*, **impossibly** *(adv)*.

impostor *(n)* someone who pretends to be someone that they are not.

impractical *(adj)* not sensible or not useful. *An impractical plan.*

impress impresses impressing impressed *(v)*
1 to make people think highly of you. **impressive** *(adj)*.
2 If you impress something on someone, you make it very clear to them.

impression *(n)*
1 an idea or a feeling. *I got the impression that Sid didn't like me.*
2 an imitation of someone or something. *Tom did his impression of a seal.*
3 If something or someone makes an impression on you, they have a strong effect on you.

impressionable *(adj)* easily influenced by other people.

imprison imprisoning imprisoned *(v)* to put someone in prison or lock them up. **imprisonment** *(n)*.

improve improving improved *(v)* to get better or to make something better. **improvement** *(n)*.

improvise improvising improvised *(v)*
1 to do the best you can with what is available. *We improvised a shelter from some old blankets.*

2 *(v)* When actors or musicians improvise, they make up words or music as they perform. **improvisation** *(n)*.

impudent *(adj)* rude, cheeky, and outspoken. *An impudent remark.* **impudence** *(n)*, **impudently** *(adv)*.

impulse *(n)*
a sudden desire to do something. **impulsive** *(adj)*, **impulsively** *(adv)*.

inaccurate *(adj)*
not very precise or not correct. **inaccuracy** *(n)*, **inaccurately** *(adv)*.

inadequate *(adj)* not enough or not good enough. **inadequately** *(adv)*.

inappropriate *(adj)*
unsuitable for the time, place, etc. *Sara's shoes are inappropriate for hiking.* **inappropriately** *(adv)*.

inarticulate *(adj)* not able to express yourself very clearly in words.

inaudible *(adj)*
not loud enough to be heard. **inaudibility** *(n)*, **inaudibly** *(adv)*.

inborn *(adj)* If a skill or quality is inborn, you inherit it from your parents and it is natural to you.

Inc. *(US)*
short for **incorporated company**. An incorporated company is one where, if the company goes bankrupt, the people who own shares in it only lose the value of those shares.

incapable *(adj)*
If you are incapable of doing something, you are unable to do it.

incense *(n)* a substance which is burnt to give off a fragrant smell.

incentive *(n)* something that encourages you to make an effort. *The prospect of winning a prize was an incentive to work hard.*

incessant *(adj)*
nonstop or continuous. *Incessant noise.* **incessantly** *(adv)*.

incident *(n)* an event or something which happens.

incidentally *(adv)*
by the way. **incidental** *(adj)*.

incision *(n)*
a neat cut made by a knife or blade.

incite inciting incited *(v)* If you incite someone to do something, you provoke them or urge them to do it.

incline inclining inclined *(v)*
1 *(in-kline) (v)* to lean or to slope. **incline** *(in-kline) (n)*.
2 If you are inclined to do something, you like to do it, or you tend to do it. *Ramona is inclined to avoid exercise.* **inclination** *(n)*.

include including included *(v)* to contain something or someone as part of something else. *The shopping list includes food for supper. We included Andrea in our plans.*

inclusive *(adj)*
including everything or everyone. *The rent is inclusive of bills.*

incoherent *(adj)* unclear or not logical. **incoherently** *(adv)*.

income
1 *(n)* the money that someone earns or receives regularly.
2 income tax *(n)* the portion of your earnings that is paid to the government to help run the country.

incompatible *(adj)* If people or objects are incompatible, they cannot live together or be used together. **incompatibility** *(n)*.

incompetent *(adj)*
If you are incompetent at something, you cannot do it very well or effectively. **incompetence** *(n)*, **incompetently** *(adv)*.

incomplete *(adj)* not finished or not complete. **incompletely** *(adv)*.

incomprehensible *(adj)*
impossible to understand. **incomprehensibly** *(adv)*.

inconceivable *(adj)* impossible to believe or imagine. **inconceivably** *(adv)*.

inconclusive *(adj)*
not clear or not certain. *Inconclusive results.* **inconclusively** *(adv)*.

inconsiderate *(adj)*
Someone who is inconsiderate does not think about other people's needs and feelings. **inconsiderately** *(adv)*.

inconspicuous *(adj)* Something that is inconspicuous cannot be seen easily. **inconspicuously** *(adv)*.

inconvenient *(adj)* If something is inconvenient, it is awkward and causes difficulties. **inconvenience** *(n)*, **inconveniently** *(adv)*.

incorporate incorporating incorporated *(v)* When you incorporate something into another thing, you make it a part of that thing. *We've incorporated a new song into our show.* **incorporation** *(n)*.

incorrect *(adj)*
wrong. **incorrectly** *(adv)*.

increase *(in-crease)* increasing increased *(v)* to grow in size or number. **increase** *(in-crease) (n)*, **increasingly** *(adv)*.

incredible *(adj)* unbelievable or amazing. *The beanstalk grew to an incredible height.* **incredibly** *(adv)*.

a b c d e f g h i j k l m n o p q r s t u v w x y z

incriminate
incriminating incriminated *(v)*
to show that someone is guilty
of a crime or other wrong action.

incubator *(n)*
1 a container in which premature
babies are kept safe and warm
while they grow larger and stronger.
2 a container in which eggs are
kept warm until they hatch.
incubation *(n)*, incubate *(v)*.

incurable *(adj)*
A person with an **incurable**
disease cannot be made better.

indecent *(adj)* rude or shocking.
indecency *(n)*, indecently *(adv)*.

indeed *(adv)* certainly.

indefinite
1 *(adj)* not clear.
2 The **indefinite article** is the
grammatical term for "a", "an",
or "some", used before a noun.

indent *(in-dent)* indenting
indented *(v)* to start a line of
writing or typing a few spaces in
from the margin. indent *(in-dent) (n)*.

independent *(adj)*
1 free from the control of other
people or things. independence *(n)*,
independently *(adv)*.
2 If someone is **independent**, they
do not want or need much help
from other people. independence
(n), independently *(adv)*.

indestructible *(adj)* If something
is **indestructible**, it cannot be
destroyed. indestructibly *(adv)*.

index indexes *or* indices *(n)*
1 an alphabetical list that shows
you where to find words or
pictures, for example, in a book.
2 Your **index finger** is the
one nearest to your thumb.

indicate indicating indicated *(v)*
1 to show or to prove something.
*The report indicates that the company
is losing money at a rapid rate.*
indication *(n)*, indicative *(adj)*.
2 to signal. *Drivers should
always indicate before turning.*
indication *(n)*, indicator *(n)*.

indifferent *(adj)*
1 If someone is **indifferent** to
something, they are not interested
in it. *Amelia was indifferent to
where we went.* indifference *(n)*.
2 poor in quality. *Toby produced
an indifferent piece of work.*

indigestion *(n)*
If you have **indigestion**, your
stomach hurts because you are
having difficulty in digesting food.

indignant *(adj)*
If you are **indignant**, you are
upset and annoyed because you
feel that something is not fair.
indignation *(n)*, indignantly *(adv)*.

indirect *(adj)* not straightforward.
An indirect route. indirectly *(adv)*.

indispensable *(adj)* If someone
or something is **indispensable**,
they are essential and cannot be
replaced. indispensably *(adv)*.

indistinguishable *(adj)* When two
things are **indistinguishable**, you
cannot tell them apart. *The twins
are virtually indistinguishable.*

individual
1 *(adj)* single and separate. *Slowly,
I got to know the individual members
of the group.* individually *(adv)*.
2 *(n)* a person. *A strange individual.*
3 *(adj)* unusual or different.
*Ricky has a very individual
hairstyle.* individually *(adv)*.

indoors *(adv)* inside a building.

indulge indulging indulged *(v)*
1 to let someone have their own
way. *Nathan's grandparents indulge
him dreadfully.* indulgence *(n)*,
indulgent *(adj)*, indulgently *(adv)*.
2 If you **indulge** in something,
you allow yourself to enjoy it.

industrial *(adj)* to do with businesses
and factories. *The industrial area
of the city.* industrially *(adv)*.

industry industries *(n)* the business
of making things or providing
services in order to earn money.

inefficient *(adj)*
If someone or something is
inefficient, they do not work very
well and they waste time and energy.
inefficiency *(n)*, inefficiently *(adv)*.

inequality inequalities *(n)*
the treatment of people or things
in an unequal or unfair way.

inert
1 lifeless and unmoving.
2 An **inert** gas does not
react with other chemicals.

inertia *(n)*
1 a lazy, tired feeling.
2 The **inertia** of an object is
its resistance to any change in
motion. Inertia makes it hard to
get something moving when it is
still and hard to make something
stop when it is moving.

inevitable *(adj)* If something is
inevitable, it will certainly happen.
inevitability *(n)*, inevitably *(adv)*.

inexpensive *(adj)*
cheap. inexpensively *(adv)*.

inexperienced *(adj)*
An **inexperienced** person has had
little practice in doing something.

inexplicable *(adj)*
If something is **inexplicable**, it cannot
be explained. inexplicably *(adv)*.

infamous *(in-fer-muss) (adj)*
If someone or something is **infamous**,
they have a very bad reputation.

infant *(n)*
1 a young child or baby. infancy *(n)*.
2 In England and Wales, an **infant
school** is for children aged between
four and seven years.

infantry infantries *(n)* the part
of an army that fights on foot.

infatuated *(adj)*
If you are **infatuated** with someone,
you like them so much that you stop
thinking clearly and sensibly about
your relationship. infatuation *(n)*.

infection *(n)*
an illness caused by germs. infect *(v)*.

infectious *(adj)*
1 An **infectious** disease is
spread from one person or
animal to another by germs.
2 If a mood is **infectious**, it spreads
easily. *Infectious laughter.*

infer inferring inferred *(v)*
to draw a conclusion from something
that someone says or does. *I inferred
from Tim's tone of voice that he was
joking.* inference *(n)*.

inferior *(adj)*
If something is **inferior** to something
else, it is not as good. inferiority *(n)*.

infertile *(adj)*
1 unable to have babies.
infertility *(n)*.
2 Land that is **infertile** is useless for
growing crops. infertility *(n)*.

infested *(adj)*
If an object or a building is **infested**,
it is full of animal or insect pests.
infestation *(n)*, infest *(v)*.

infiltrate
infiltrating infiltrated *(v)*
to join an organization secretly,
in order to spy on it or damage
it in some way. infiltration *(n)*.

infinite *(in-fin-it) (adj)* endless.
Infinite possibilities. infinitely *(adv)*.

infinitive *(n)*
the basic form of a verb, for example,
"to run", "to be", "to write".

infirm *(adj)*
weak or ill. infirmity *(n)*.

infirmary infirmaries *(n)* a hospital.

inflammable *(adj)* An **inflammable**
substance can catch fire easily.

innocent

inflatable *(adj)* An **inflatable** object can be filled with air or blown up. *The picture shows an inflatable life raft with its safety equipment.* **inflatable** *(n)*.

inflatable life raft and safety equipment

pressure relief valve

battery-operated light

tie tapes

pull-over canopy

canopy arch

outer envelope

double floor

inner bracing line

outer lifeline

extending boarding ladder

stabilizing pocket

twin buoyancy tubes

drogue (inflation canister)

hand-held flares

chemical light sticks

instruction manual

leak stoppers

pump and hose

floating anchor (rolled up)

waterproof torch

spare batteries

first aid kit

raft repair kit (glue and patches)

bailer

throw ring and line

paddles with handles

inflate inflating inflated *(v)* to make something expand by blowing air into it.

inflation *(n)* a widespread rise in prices. **inflationary** *(adj)*.

inflexible *(adj)* not able to bend or not able to change. **inflexibility** *(n)*, **inflexibly** *(adv)*.

inflict inflicting inflicted *(v)* to cause suffering to someone or something. *The bombing inflicted severe damage on the town.*

influence influencing influenced *(v)* to have an effect on someone or something. **influence** *(n)*.

influenza see **flu**.

inform informing informed *(v)*
1 to tell someone something. *Lyn informed me that she was leaving.*
2 If you **inform on** a criminal, you give the police information about them. **informer** *(n)*.

informal *(adj)* relaxed, easy-going, and casual. *An informal party.* **informality** *(n)*, **informally** *(adv)*.

information *(n)* facts and knowledge.

information technology *(n)* the use of computers and other electronic equipment to produce, store, or communicate information.

informative *(adj)* If something or someone is **informative**, they provide useful information.

infrequent *(adj)* not happening very often. **infrequently** *(adv)*.

infuriate infuriating infuriated *(v)* If someone or something infuriates you, they make you very angry. **infuriating** *(adj)*, **infuriatingly** *(adv)*.

ingenious *(in-jee-nee-us)* *(adj)* clever and original. *An ingenious plan.* **ingenuity** *(n)*, **ingeniously** *(adv)*.

ingredient *(n)* one of the items that something is made from, especially an item of food in a recipe.

inhabit inhabiting inhabited *(v)* If you **inhabit** a place, you live there. **inhabitant** *(n)*.

inhale inhaling inhaled *(v)* to breathe in. **inhalation** *(n)*.

inhaler *(n)* a container from which you take medicine by breathing it in through your mouth.

inherit inheriting inherited *(v)*
1 to receive money, property, or a title from someone who has just died. **inheritance** *(n)*.
2 If you **inherit** a particular characteristic, it is passed down to you from one of your parents.

inhuman *(adj)* cruel and brutal. **inhumanity** *(n)*.

initial
1 *(adj)* first, or at the beginning. *My initial reaction to seeing the ghost was to scream.* **initially** *(adv)*.
2 *(n)* the first letter of a name.

initiative *(in-ish-er-tiv)* *(n)* If you use your **initiative**, you do what is necessary without other people telling you what to do. **initiate** *(v)*.

inject injecting injected *(v)*
1 to use a needle and syringe to put medicine into a person's or animal's body. **injection** *(n)*.
2 to add. *Please inject some humour into your writing.* **injection** *(n)*.

injure injuring injured *(v)* to hurt or harm someone.

injury injuries *(n)* damage or harm.

injustice *(n)*
1 unfairness.
2 an unfair situation or action.

ink *(n)* a coloured liquid used for writing and printing. **inky** *(adj)*.

inland *(adj)* away from the sea. *The hotel is five miles inland.*

inmate *(n)* someone who has to live in a prison or other institution.

inn *(n)* a pub or a small hotel.

inner *(adj)*
1 inside, or nearest the centre. *A bicycle tyre has an inner tube.*
2 private. *Nobody can know your inner thoughts.*

innings *(singular n)* a team's or a player's turn to bat in cricket.

innocent *(adj)*
1 not guilty. **innocence** *(n)*, **innocently** *(adv)*.
2 not knowing about something. *Ellen was innocent of her aunt's plans.* **innocence** *(n)*, **innocently** *(adv)*.

a b c d e f g h i j k l m n o p q r s t u v w x y z

innovation

innovation *(n)*
a new idea or an invention.
innovate *(v)*, **innovative** *(adj)*.

inoculate
inoculating inoculated *(v)*
to inject a weak form of a disease into someone's body, so that they become protected against it. **inoculation** *(n)*.

inpatient *(n)* someone who stays in hospital while being treated.

input *(n)*
1 something that is contributed or put into something else. *Our team has really benefited from Graeme's input.*
2 information fed into a computer. **input** *(v)*.

inquest *(n)*
an official investigation to find out why someone has died. *The police held an inquest after the accident.*

inquire *or* **enquire** inquiring inquired *(v)* to ask about someone or something. *Oliver inquired about the times of the trains.* **inquiring** *(adj)*, **inquiringly** *(adv)*.

inquiry *or* **enquiry** inquiries *(n)* a study or an investigation, especially an official one.

inquisitive *(adj)* questioning or curious. **inquisitiveness** *(n)*, **inquisitively** *(adv)*.

insane *(adj)* mad or crazy. **insanity** *(n)*, **insanely** *(adv)*.

insanitary *(adj)*
dirty and likely to cause disease.

inscribe inscribing inscribed *(v)*
1 to carve or engrave letters on a surface. **inscribed** *(adj)*.
2 to write a special message or dedication in a book.

inscription *(n)*
a carved, engraved, or specially written message. *There are inscriptions under most statues.*

insect *(n)* a small creature, usually with three pairs of legs, two pairs of wings, three main sections to its body, and no backbone. *The picture below shows a selection of insects.*

insecticide *(n)*
a chemical used to kill insects.

insecure *(adj)*
1 unsafe or not fastened properly. *These door locks are very insecure.* **insecurely** *(adv)*.
2 anxious and not confident. *Polly felt very insecure among so many strangers.* **insecurity** *(n)*.

insensitive *(adj)*
thoughtless and unsympathetic to other people's feelings. **insensitivity** *(n)*, **insensitively** *(adv)*.

insert inserting inserted
1 *(v)* (in-sert) to put something carefully inside something else. *Insert a coin in the slot.* **insertion** *(n)*.
2 *(n)* (in-sert) something that is put inside something else. *This magazine has an insert on mountain bikes.*

inside
1 *(n)* the interior or inner part of something. **inside** *(adj)*.
2 *(prep)* in less than. *We were back home inside an hour.*
3 *(prep)* within. *Put it inside the bag.*
4 *(adv)* in or into the inner part. *Look inside.*

insight *(n)*
If you have **insight** into something or someone, you understand something about them that is not obvious.

insignificant *(adj)*
not important. **insignificance** *(n)*, **insignificantly** *(adv)*.

insincere *(adj)*
Someone who is **insincere** is not genuine, or not honest. **insincerity** *(n)*, **insincerely** *(adv)*.

insipid *(adj)* dull or tasteless.

insist insisting insisted *(v)*
If you **insist** on something, you demand it very firmly. *Sally insisted on wearing her jeans.* **insistence** *(n)*, **insistent** *(adj)*.

insolent *(adj)* insulting and rude. **insolence** *(n)*, **insolently** *(adv)*.

insoluble *(adj)*
1 A substance that is **insoluble** will not dissolve.
2 A problem that is **insoluble** cannot be solved.

insomnia *(n)*
If you have **insomnia**, you often find it very hard to sleep. **insomniac** *(n)*.

inspect inspecting inspected *(v)* to look at something very carefully. **inspection** *(n)*.

inspector *(n)*
1 someone who checks or examines things. *A ticket inspector.*
2 a senior police officer.

insects

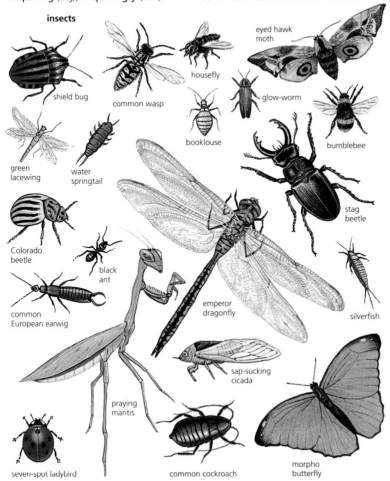

shield bug

common wasp

housefly

eyed hawk moth

glow-worm

booklouse

bumblebee

green lacewing

water springtail

Colorado beetle

black ant

stag beetle

common European earwig

emperor dragonfly

silverfish

praying mantis

sap-sucking cicada

seven-spot ladybird

common cockroach

morpho butterfly

inspire inspiring inspired *(v)*
to influence and encourage someone to do something. *The concert inspired me to take guitar lessons.*
inspiration *(n)*, inspiring *(adj)*.

install installing installed *(v)*
to put something in place, ready to be used. *We have had a new computer installed in our classroom.* installation *(n)*.

instalment *(n)*
1 If you pay for something by **instalments**, you pay for it in regular, small amounts over a period of time.
2 one part of a serialized story.

instance *(n)*
an example. *Nancy gave me several instances of when I had offended her.*

instant
1 *(n)* a moment. *It was over in an instant.* instantaneous *(adj)*, instantaneously *(adv)*.
2 *(adj)* happening straightaway. *Instant results.* instantly *(adv)*.

instead *(adv)* in place of another person or thing. *Bernard couldn't go to the party, so I went instead.*

instep *(n)* the top of your foot, between your toes and your ankle.

instinct *(n)*
1 behaviour that is natural rather than learnt. *Ducks swim by instinct.*
2 If you have an **instinct** about something, you know or feel something without being told about it. *I had an instinct that she was not telling the truth.*
instinctive *(adj)*, instinctively *(adv)*.

institute instituting instituted
1 *(v)* to begin, set up, or found. *The headteacher instituted an inquiry into the missing money.*
2 *(n)* an organization set up to promote or represent the interests of a particular cause or group of people.

institution *(n)*
1 a large organization where people live or work together, such as a hospital or college. institutional *(adj)*.
2 a well-established custom or tradition. *Weekend barbecues have become an institution in our family.*

instruct instructing instructed *(v)*
1 to give an order. *The captain of the ship instructed her crew to set sail.* instruction *(n)*.
2 to teach a subject or skill. *Gina instructed me in tap-dancing.* instruction *(n)*, instructor *(n)*.

instructions *(plural n)*
written or spoken words telling you what to do or how to do something.

instrument *(n)*
1 a tool used for delicate or scientific work. *Surgical instruments.*
2 an object that you use to make music. *The picture shows a range of musical instruments from around the world.* instrumentalist *(n)*.

musical instruments

Spanish castanets

West African talking drum

Indian sitar

Ethiopian bowl lyre

Caribbean steel pan

Russian accordion

Mexican guiro

Korean kayagum

insufficient *(adj)* not enough or not adequate. insufficiently *(adv)*.

insulate insulating insulated *(v)*
to cover or fill something with material in order to stop heat or electricity escaping.
insulation *(n)*, insulating *(adj)*.

insulin *(n)* a hormone produced in your pancreas which regulates the amount of sugar that you have in your body. People who have diabetes may need to be given insulin.

insult insulting insulted *(v)* to say or do something rude and upsetting to someone. insult *(n)*, insulting *(adj)*.

insurance *(n)* When you take out **insurance**, you pay money to a company which agrees to pay you in the event of sickness, fire, accident, etc. insure *(v)*, insured *(adj)*.

intact *(adj)*
unharmed or complete. *Fortunately, our books survived the flood intact.*

intake *(n)*
1 the amount of people or things that are taken in. *Our college has a high intake of music students.*
2 the act of taking something in. *A sharp intake of breath.*

integrate
integrating integrated *(v)*
to combine several things or people into one whole. *People of many nationalities have been integrated into our community.* integration *(n)*.

integrity *(n)*
If someone has **integrity**, they are honest and stick to their principles.

intellectual
1 *(adj)* involving thought and reason. *Bethany enjoys intellectual puzzles.*
2 *(n)* someone who spends most of their time thinking and studying.

intelligent *(adj)*
Someone who is **intelligent** is clever and quick to understand, think, and learn. intelligence *(n)*, intelligently *(adv)*.

intelligible *(adj)*
If something is **intelligible**, it can be understood. intelligibly *(adv)*.

intend intending intended *(v)*
If you **intend** to do something, you mean to do it.

intense *(adj)* very strong. *Intense heat. Intense happiness.* intensity *(n)*, intensely *(adv)*.

intensify intensifies intensifying intensified *(v)*
to make something more powerful or concentrated. *The police intensified their search.* intensification *(n)*.

intent
1 *(adj)* If you are **intent** on doing something, you are determined to do it. *Lloyd is intent on going to college.*
2 *(n)* an aim or a purpose.

intention *(n)* the thing that you mean to do. *It's my intention to win this race.* intentional *(adj)*.

a b c d e f g h i j k l m n o p q r s t u v w x y z

interactive *(adj)* If something such as a book or computer program is **interactive**, it allows users to make choices in order to control and change it in some ways. **interact** *(v)*.

intercept
intercepting intercepted *(v)* to stop the movement of something or someone from one place to another. *The goalkeeper intercepted the ball.* **interception** *(n)*.

intercom *(n)*
a microphone and speaker system which allows you to listen and talk to someone in another room or building.

interest interesting interested
1 *(v)* If something **interests** you, you want to know more about it. **interest** *(n)*, **interesting** *(adj)*.
2 *(n)* an additional amount of money paid by someone who borrows money, or paid to someone who invests money. Interest is usually an agreed percentage of the amount borrowed or invested.

interfere interfering interfered *(v)* to involve yourself in a situation that has nothing to do with you. **interfering** *(adj)*.

interference *(n)*
1 involvement in something that has nothing to do with you. *I can't stand any more interference from our neighbours!*
2 When you get **interference** on your television or radio, something interrupts the signal, so you cannot see or hear the programme properly.

intergalactic *(adj)* between galaxies. *Intergalactic space travel.*

interior *(n)* the inside of something, especially a building. **interior** *(adj)*.

interjection *(n)* a word used as a greeting, or to express surprise, pain, or delight. *"Ah!", "Oh!", and "Hello!" are all interjections. See page 3.*

intermediate *(adj)* in between two things or in the middle. *There are three swimming classes: beginners, intermediate, and advanced.*

intermission *(n)*
a short break in a film.

intermittent *(adj)*
stopping and starting. *Intermittent rain.* **intermittently** *(adv)*.

internal *(adj)*
happening or existing inside someone or something. **internally** *(adv)*.

international *(adj)* involving different countries. *International trade.* **internationally** *(adv)*.

internet *(n)*
a network that connects billions of computers around the world.

interpret
interpreting interpreted *(v)*
1 to decide what something means. *I interpreted Iain's wave as a sign of friendship.* **interpretation** *(n)*.
2 to translate for two or more people who do not speak the same language. **interpreter** *(n)*.

interrogate interrogating interrogated *(v)* to question someone thoroughly. **interrogation** *(n)*.

interrupt
interrupting interrupted *(v)*
1 to stop something happening for a short time. **interruption** *(n)*.
2 to start talking before someone else has finished talking. *Don't interrupt me!* **interruption** *(n)*.

interval *(n)*
1 a time between events or parts of a play, concert, show, etc.
2 a space between two things.

intervene
intervening intervened *(v)*
1 If you **intervene** in a situation, you get involved in it in order to change what is happening. *Bobby intervened in the fight.* **intervention** *(n)*.
2 If a period of time **intervenes** between events, it comes between them. **intervening** *(adj)*.

interview *(n)* a meeting where someone is asked questions. *A job interview.* **interview** *(v)*.

intestines *(plural n)*
the very long tube through which food passes when it is digested, after it leaves your stomach. **intestinal** *(adj)*. See **digestion**.

intimate *(adj)* Friends who are **intimate** are very close and share their feelings with one another. **intimacy** *(n)*, **intimately** *(adv)*.

intimidate
intimidating intimidated *(v)* to frighten someone into doing something. **intimidation** *(n)*.

intolerable *(adj)*
If something is **intolerable**, you cannot bear it. **intolerably** *(adv)*.

intolerant *(adj)* People who are **intolerant** get unreasonably angry when other people think or behave in a different way from them. **intolerance** *(n)*, **intolerantly** *(adv)*.

intransitive *(adj)* Intransitive verbs stand on their own and do not need an object. *The verbs "to laugh" and "to frown" are intransitive.*

intrepid *(adj)* courageous and bold. *An intrepid explorer.*

intricate *(adj)* detailed and complicated. *An intricate pattern.* **intricacy** *(n)*, **intricately** *(adv)*.

intrigue intriguing intrigued
1 *(v)* to fascinate or puzzle someone. *Angelica's story intrigued me.* **intriguing** *(adj)*.
2 *(n)* a secret plot.

introduce
introducing introduced *(v)*
1 to bring people together for the first time and tell each one the other's name.
2 to bring in something new. *The company are introducing a new product.*

introduction *(n)*
1 Your **introduction** to something is your first experience of it. *I can still remember my introduction to ballet.*
2 the act of introducing one person to another.
3 the opening words of a book, speech, etc. **introductory** *(adj)*.

introvert *(n)*
someone who keeps their thoughts and feelings to themselves and is quite shy. **introverted** *(adj)*.

intrude intruding intruded *(v)* to force your way into a place or situation where you are not wanted or invited. **intruder** *(n)*, **intrusion** *(n)*.

intuition *(n)* a feeling about something that cannot be explained logically. *My intuition tells me that you will win this race.* **intuitive** *(adj)*.

Inuit *(plural n)*
a group of peoples from the Arctic regions of Canada, Alaska, Russia, and Greenland. *This Inuit man is fishing through a hole in the ice.* **Inuit** *(adj)*.

Inuit

inundate
inundating inundated *(v)*
1 to flood. *The village was inundated by flood water.*
2 to overwhelm someone with a large quantity of something. *We were inundated with presents.*

invade invading invaded *(v)* to send armed forces into another country in order to take it over. **invader** *(n)*, **invasion** *(n)*.

irritable

invalid

1 *(in-va-lid) (n)* someone who is disabled or who is seriously ill.
2 *(in-val-id) (adj)* If a ticket, library card, etc. is **invalid**, it cannot be used for some reason.

invaluable *(adj)* extremely useful.

invent inventing invented *(v)*
1 to think of an original machine, device, idea, etc. **invention** *(n)*, **inventor** *(n)*, **inventive** *(adj)*.
2 to make something up. *Leon invented a story to explain why he was soaking wet.* **invention** *(n)*.

invertebrate *(n)* a creature without a backbone. **invertebrate** *(adj)*.

inverted commas *(n)*
signs, (") or ('), used in writing to show that someone is speaking. Inverted commas are sometimes called speech marks or quotation marks.

invest investing invested *(v)*
1 to give or lend money to something, such as a company, in the belief that you will be rewarded in the future. **investment** *(n)*, **investor** *(n)*.
2 to give time or effort to something. *I've invested a lot of time in practising the trumpet.*

investigate investigating investigated *(v)* If you **investigate** something, such as a crime, you find out as much as possible about it. **investigation** *(n)*, **investigative** *(adj)*.

invincible *(adj)* unbeatable.

invisible *(adj)*
Something that is **invisible** cannot be seen. **invisibility** *(n)*, **invisibly** *(adv)*.

invite inviting invited *(v)*
to ask someone to do something, or to go somewhere. *We've invited Hattie home for tea.* **invitation** *(n)*.

invoice *(n)* a written request for payment after you have done a job or sold something.

involve involving involved *(v)*
to include something as a necessary part. *The project involves field work.*

involved *(adj)*
1 If you are **involved** in something, you take a part in it. *I was one of the people involved in the play.*
2 complicated. *Involved work.*

inward or **inwards** *(adv)*
towards the inside.

ion *(n)*
an electrically-charged atomic particle.

IQ *(n)* a measure of a person's intelligence. The initials IQ stand for intelligence quotient.

irate *(adj)* angry or very annoyed.

iron *(n)*

1 a strong, hard metal used to make things such as gates and railings. Iron is also found in some foods and is used by your body to make blood.
2 a piece of electrical equipment with a handle and a heated surface, used to smooth creases out of clothing. *This picture shows the main parts inside a steam iron.* **iron** *(v)*.

steam
spray iron

steam switch
(attached to steam
control needle)

electrical
cord

spray button

temperature control knob
(attached to thermostat)

spray
nozzle

temperature
indicator
light

steam
chamber

water
tank

hole for steam
control needle

element

thermostat
(controls temperature
of element)

electrical
connector

sole plate
with steam-release
holes under here

Iron Age *(n)*

a period of history which began about 1,000BC, when iron was first used to make tools and weapons. *In the Iron Age, most people in Western Europe were farmers living in small settlements, like the one reconstructed in this picture.*

**Iron Age
settlement**

thatched roof

hut
(for storage
or cooking)

living quarters

animal
enclosure

look-out
platform

granary
on
stilts

fencing

bank for
defence

ditch for
defence

gateway

ironic *(adj)*

1 If a situation is **ironic**, the opposite happens to what you would expect. *It was ironic that the clumsiest boy in the class should become a famous ballet dancer.* **irony** *(n)*, **ironically** *(adv)*.
2 mildly sarcastic. *"A fine job you made of that!" said Rosa, with an ironic smile.* **irony** *(n)*.

irrational *(adj)*
1 not sensible or not logical. **irrationally** *(adv)*.
2 unreasonable or insane. **irrationally** *(adv)*.

irregular *(adj)*
1 not regular in shape, timing, or size, etc. *An irregular hexagon. An irregular bus service.* **irregularly** *(adv)*.
2 not following the normal pattern. *It's quite irregular to come to school in slippers!* **irregularity** *(n)*.

irrelevant *(adj)* If something is **irrelevant**, it has nothing to do with a particular subject. *The story contained many irrelevant details.* **irrelevance** *(n)*, **irrelevantly** *(adv)*.

irresistible *(adj)*
too tempting to resist. *The fudge cake was irresistible.* **irresistibly** *(adv)*.

irresponsible *(adj)*
reckless and not capable of taking responsibility. **irresponsibly** *(adv)*.

irrigate irrigating irrigated *(v)*
to supply water to crops by digging channels and laying pipes. **irrigation** *(n)*.

irritable *(adj)*
Someone who is **irritable** is bad-tempered and grumpy. **irritably** *(adv)*.

a b c d e f g h i j k l m n o p q r s

irritate

irritate irritating irritated *(v)*
If something or someone **irritates** you, they make you annoyed. **irritation** *(n)*, **irritating** *(adj)*, **irritatingly** *(adv)*.

Islam *(n)* the religion based on the teachings of Mohammed. Muslims believe that Allah is God and that Mohammed is his prophet. Islam is based on prayer, fasting, charity, and pilgrimage. **Islamic** *(adj)*.

island *(n)*
land surrounded on all sides by water.

isolate isolating isolated *(v)*
1 to keep someone or something separate or on their own. *Polly was isolated because she had a highly infectious illness.* **isolation** *(n)*.
2 to discover and identify something. *We've isolated the fault in your computer program.*

isosceles *(eye-soss-il-eez) (adj)*
An **isosceles** triangle has two sides that are the same length. See **shape**.

ISP *(n)* An ISP is a company that provides a service linking individual computers to the internet. The initials ISP stand for Internet Service Provider.

issue issuing issued
1 *(v)* to send out or to give out. *Our group has issued a leaflet.*
2 *(n)* an edition of a newspaper or magazine.
3 *(n)* the main topic for decision.
4 *(n)* a problem or concern.

IT *short for* **information technology**.

italic *(n)* a sloping form of print, used to emphasize certain words or to make them stand out. The word *italic* is printed in italic. **italic** *(adj)*.

itch itches itching itched *(v)*
If your skin **itches**, it is uncomfortable and you want to scratch it. **itch** *(n)*, **itchy** *(adj)*.

item *(n)* one of a number of things. *An item of clothing.*

itinerary itineraries *(n)*
a detailed plan of a journey.

itself *(pronoun)* it and nothing else. *This machine works by itself.*

ivory *(n)*
1 the natural substance from which elephants' tusks are made.
2 a creamy-white colour. **ivory** *(adj)*.

ivy ivies *(n)* an evergreen climbing or trailing plant, which has pointed leaves.

ivy

Jj

jab jabbing jabbed
1 *(v)* to poke someone with something sharp. *Beverley jabbed her elbow into my ribs.*
2 *(n)* (informal) an injection. *A flu jab.*

jabber jabbering jabbered *(v)*
to talk in a fast and excitable way that is hard to understand.

jack *(n)*
1 a tool used to raise a vehicle off the ground for repair.
2 a picture playing card with a value between that of a ten and a queen. The jack is sometimes called the knave.

jackal *(n)* a kind of wild dog, found in Africa and Asia, that feeds off the dead bodies of other animals.

jacket *(n)*
1 a piece of clothing worn on the top half of your body, with a front opening and long sleeves.
2 a covering. *A book jacket.*

jackknife jackknifing jackknifed *(v)* When an articulated truck **jackknifes**, the trailer swings around at right angles to the direction of travel and the driver loses control.

Jacuzzi *(ja-koo-zee) (n)*
a large bath with underwater jets of water which massage your skin.

jade *(n)*
1 a green, semiprecious stone, used for making ornaments and jewellery. *The picture shows a jade death mask, made by the Maya, an ancient civilization of Central America.*
2 a bluish-green colour. **jade** *(adj)*.

jade death mask

jaded *(adj)* If you are **jaded**, you are tired, bored and lacking in enthusiasm.

jagged *(jag-ed) (adj)*
uneven and sharp. *A jagged edge.*

jaguar *(n)* a large wild cat, similar to a leopard, found in South and Central America.

jaguar

jail *or* **gaol**
1 *(n)* a prison. **jailer** *(n)*.
2 **jailbird** *(n)* a prisoner, or a criminal who often breaks the law.

jam jamming jammed
1 *(n)* a sweet, sticky food, made from boiled fruit and sugar.
2 *(n)* a situation in which things cannot move. *A traffic jam.*
3 *(v)* to squeeze or wedge something into place. *Alvin jammed his bag into the locker.*
4 *(n)* (informal) a difficult situation.
5 *(v)* (informal) When musicians jam, they make up music as they play together. **jam** *(n)*.

jangle jangling jangled *(v)*
to make a loud, unpleasant, ringing sound.

janitor *(n)* (US)
someone whose job is to look after a school or some other public building. (caretaker, *UK*).

jar jarring jarred
1 *(n)* a small, glass container with an airtight lid.
2 *(v)* to jolt or shake something or someone. *The fall jarred my knee.*
3 *(v)* If something **jars on** you, it makes you feel uncomfortable or annoyed.

jargon *(n)*
words used by people in a particular business or activity, that other people cannot easily understand. *Computer jargon.*

jaundice *(n)*
If you have **jaundice**, your skin turns yellow, often due to liver problems.

jaunt *(n)*
a short pleasure trip or outing.

jaunty jauntier jauntiest *(adj)*
giving a carefree and self-confident impression. *Sophia wore her cap at a jaunty angle.* **jauntily** *(adv)*.

javelin *(n)* a pointed, light, metal spear, thrown in an athletics event. See **track and field**.

jaw jawing jawed
1 *(n)* one of the two bones that hold a person's or animal's teeth. See **skeleton**.
2 *(n)* the lower part of your face.
3 *(v)* (slang) to talk for a long time in a boring way.

jaywalk jaywalking jaywalked *(v)* to cross a street carelessly, taking no notice of traffic or signals. **jaywalker** *(n)*.

jazz *(n)* a lively, rhythmical type of music in which players often make up their own tunes.

joiner

jazzy jazzier jazziest *(adj) (informal)*
Something that is **jazzy** is very noticeable, and often has bright colours and a strong pattern. *Jeff wore a very jazzy shirt.*

jealous *(adj)* If you are **jealous** of someone, you want what they have. **jealousy** *(n)*, **jealously** *(adv)*.

jeans *(plural n)* casual trousers made of denim or similar strong cloth.

Jeep *(n)* an open vehicle, used for driving over rough country.

jeer jeering jeered *(v)* to make fun of someone in a loud, unpleasant way. **jeeringly** *(adv)*.

Jehovah *(n)*
a name for God in the Old Testament.

jelly jellies *(n)*
1 a fruit-flavoured dessert, made with gelatine, that is boiled and then allowed to set.
2 a clear, semi-solid substance found, for example, surrounding the eggs in frogspawn. *See* **frog**.

jellyfish jellyfish *or* jellyfishes *(n)*
a sea creature with a jelly-like body and trailing tentacles. *The picture shows how a jellyfish has its mouth in the centre, with feelers or arms stretching out from it.*

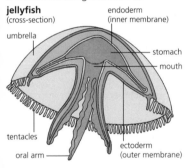

jellyfish
(cross-section)

umbrella

endoderm (inner membrane)

stomach

mouth

tentacles

ectoderm (outer membrane)

oral arm

jeopardy *(jep-er-dee) (n)*
If someone's job or life is **in jeopardy**, it is in danger or is threatened in some way. **jeopardize** *(v)*.

jerk jerking jerked *(v)* to move suddenly, or to pull something suddenly and sharply. **jerky** *(adj)*.

jersey *(n)*
a knitted piece of clothing that you wear on the top half of your body.

jest *(n)* a joke or something said in fun. **jest** *(v)*.

jester *(n)* an entertainer at a court in the Middle Ages.

jet *(n)*
1 a high-pressure stream of liquid or gas.
2 an aircraft powered by jet engines.

jet engine *(n)* an engine that creates the forward thrust needed to move an aircraft, boat, etc. by sucking in air or water, and forcing it out at the rear. *The picture shows a jet turbofan engine, which is used on many aircraft. Air is sucked in by the fan, squeezed by the compressors, then mixed with fuel and burnt in the combustion chamber. The gases produced in the chamber are forced out through a series of turbines which drive the compressors and the fan. Also see* **hydrofoil**.

jet turbofan engine
(cutaway)

combustion chamber

outlet guide vanes

nose cone

fan

fan case

high pressure compressor

turbines driving fan

turbines driving compressors

intermediate pressure compressor

jet lag *(n)* a feeling of tiredness and confusion after a long flight from a different time zone.

jetsam *(n)* part of a ship's cargo that is thrown or lost overboard.

jettison jettisoning jettisoned *(v)* to throw overboard or to throw out something which you no longer need.

jetty jetties *(n)*
a structure built out into the sea to give shelter from the waves. Boats moor and unload beside jetties.

Jew *(n)*
1 someone who belongs to the race of people descended from the ancient tribes of Israel.
2 someone who practises the religion of Judaism.

jewel *(n)* a precious stone, such as a diamond, ruby, or emerald.

jewellery *(n)* ornaments that you wear, such as rings, bracelets, and necklaces, made of jewels, gold, etc.

Jewish *(adj)* to do with Jews or with the religion of Judaism.

jigsaw *(n)* a wooden or cardboard puzzle made up of pieces of a picture that have been cut up and have to be put back together.

jingle
1 *(n)* a tinkling sound made by the movement of small bells, keys, etc. **jingle** *(v)*.

2 *(n)* a simple song used to advertise a product.

jinx jinxing jinxed *(v)*
to bring or attract bad luck. *This project seems to be jinxed.* **jinx** *(n)*.

job *(n)*
1 a task.
2 work that someone does for a living.

jockey jockeying jockeyed
1 *(n)* someone who rides horses in races.
2 *(v)* If you **jockey for position** with someone, you try to beat them at something, often by unfair actions.

jocular *(adj)* cheerful and amusing.

jodhpurs *(jod-pers) (plural n)* trousers that can be worn for horse riding. Jodhpurs are loose around the top part of the leg and tight below the knee.

joey *(n) (Australian) (informal)* a young kangaroo that is carried in its mother's pouch.

jog jogging jogged *(v)*
1 to run at a slow, steady pace. **jogger** *(n)*, **jogging** *(n)*.
2 to knock something by accident.
3 If something **jogs your memory**, it reminds you of something.

join joining joined *(v)*
1 to fasten or tie two things together. **join** *(n)*.
2 to come together with something or someone. *Please join us for supper.*
3 to become a member of a club or group.
4 **join up** to become a member of the army, navy, or air force.

joiner *(n)* someone who makes wooden furniture and house fittings, such as door frames. **joinery** *(n)*.

Some words that begin with a "j" sound are spelt with a "g".

joint

joint
1 *(adj)* done or shared by two or more people. *A joint effort.* **jointly** *(adv)*.
2 *(n)* a large piece of meat.
3 *(n)* a place where two bones meet, for example, your knee or elbow. There are four main types of joint in your body: pivot, gliding, hinge, and ball-and-socket. *This diagram of a human hip joint shows how the ball at the top of the femur fits into the socket of the pelvis.*

human hip joint
(ball-and-socket joint)
pelvis (hip bone)
synovial fluid (lubricates bones)
femur (thigh bone)
ball
socket
ligament (joins bones together)

joke
joking joked *(v)*
to say funny things or play tricks on people to make them laugh. **joke** *(n)*.

jolly jollier jolliest
1 *(adj)* happy and cheerful.
2 *(adv)* very. *Jolly good!*

jolt jolting jolted *(v)*
1 to move roughly. *The cart jolted along the track.* **jolt** *(n)*.
2 to bump into or knock someone or something. **jolt** *(n)*.

jot jotting jotted *(v)*
to write something down quickly. *I've jotted down some ideas.*

joule (rhymes with fool) *(n)* a unit for measuring energy or work done.

journal *(n)*
1 a diary in which you write what you have done each day.
2 a serious magazine.

journalist *(n)* someone who collects information and writes articles for newspapers and magazines. **journalism** *(n)*, **journalistic** *(adj)*.

journey *(n)* a trip from one place to another. **journey** *(v)*.

joust *(n)* a contest between two knights, riding horses and armed with lances. *The picture shows a medieval joust.* **joust** *(v)*.

jousting knights
caparison (saddle cloth)
triple-pronged lance
helmet
shield with heraldic crest
chanfron

jovial *(adj)*
Someone who is **jovial** is cheerful and enjoys talking and laughing with other people. **jovially** *(adv)*.

joy *(n)*
1 a feeling of great happiness.
2 *(informal)* good luck or success. *I asked my dad for some money, but I didn't have any joy.*

joyful *(adj)* very happy. **joyfulness** *(n)*, **joyfully** *(adv)*.

joyride *(n)*
a ride in a stolen car for the thrill of it. **joyrider** *(n)*, **joyriding** *(n)*.

joystick *(n)*
a lever used to control movement in a computer game or in an aircraft.

jubilant *(adj)*
very happy and delighted. *Ellie was jubilant about winning the race.* **jubilation** *(n)*, **jubilantly** *(adv)*.

jubilee *(n)* a big celebration to mark the anniversary of a special event.

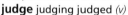

Judaism *(n)* the religion of the Jewish people, based on the law of Moses. Jews believe that they are God's chosen people. *The picture shows the symbol of Judaism, the six-pointed Star of David.*

Star of David

judge judging judged *(v)*
1 to hear cases in a law court and decide how a guilty person should be punished. **judge** *(n)*.
2 to decide who the winner of a competition is. **judge** *(n)*.
3 to form an opinion about someone or something. *After meeting Nat, I judged him to be honest.*

judgment or **judgement** *(n)*
1 the ability to decide or judge something.
2 a decision made by a judge.
3 an opinion of something or someone.

judicial *(joo-dish-al)* *(adj)*
to do with a court of law or a judge.

judicious *(joo-dish-us)* *(adj)*
sensible and wise. *A judicious investment.* **judiciously** *(adv)*.

judo *(n)* a sport in which two people fight each other using controlled movements, and each tries to throw the other to the ground. *This sequence shows a basic forward throw in judo, called Harai goshi.*

judo
(forward throw)

jug *(n)* a container with a lip for pouring liquids.

juggernaut *(n)* a very large lorry.

juggle juggling juggled *(v)*
to keep a set of balls, clubs, or other objects moving through the air by repeatedly throwing them up and catching them again, one after another. **juggler** *(n)*.

juggling equipment
balls
clubs

juice *(n)*
liquid that comes out of fruit, vegetables, or meat. **juicy** *(adj)*.

jukebox jukeboxes *(n)*
a machine that plays songs when you put coins into it.

jumble jumbling jumbled
1 *(v)* to mix things up so that they are untidy and not well organized. **jumble** *(n)*.
2 *(n)* second-hand clothes and other objects that are sold at a jumble sale.
3 **jumble sale** *(n)* a sale of second-hand clothes and other objects, usually to raise money for charity or other good causes.

jumbo
1 *(adj)* very large. *A jumbo packet.*
2 **jumbo jet** *(n)* *(informal)* a very large jet aircraft that can carry hundreds of passengers. See **aircraft**.

jump jumping jumped
1 *(v)* to leap or to spring. **jump** *(n)*.
2 *(n)* an object that you jump over. *The horse fell at the last jump.*
3 *(v)* If you **jump at** something, you accept it eagerly.

keep

jumper *(n)* a knitted piece of clothing that you wear on the top half of your body to keep you warm.

jump jet *(n)*
a jet aircraft that takes off and lands by going straight up and down, instead of using a runway.

jump leads *(plural n)*
a set of wires that are used to connect the batteries of two cars so that one can be started using the other's battery.

junction *(n)*
a place where roads or railway lines meet or join each other.

jungle *(n)* a thick, tropical forest.

junior
1 *(adj)* not very important in rank or position. *A junior manager.*
2 *(n)* someone who is younger than someone else.
3 *(adj)* for young children. *A junior encyclopedia.*
4 *(n)* In Britain, a **junior school** is for children aged between eight and eleven years.

junk *(n)*
1 things that are worthless or useless. *My room is full of junk!*
2 **junk food**
food that is not good for you because it contains a lot of fat, sugar, and chemical additives.
3 **junk mail**
advertising leaflets and letters that you receive without having asked for them.
4 a Chinese sailing boat with square sails and a flat bottom. *Junks have been used for trading for hundreds of years.*

junkie *(n) (informal)* a drug addict.

jury juries *(n)*
a group of people at a trial who decide whether the person accused of a crime is innocent or guilty.

just
1 *(adj)* fair and right. *A just decision.* **justly** *(adv).*
2 *(adv)* exactly. *I'm sure I put the book just there.*
3 *(adv)* very recently. *Ruth just left.*

justice *(n)*
1 fairness and rightness.
2 the system of laws and punishments in a country.
3 **Justice of the Peace**
someone who gives judgments in local British courts of law. Justices of the Peace are also known as JPs.

justify justifies
justifying justified *(v)*
1 If you **justify** an action, you explain why it is acceptable. **justification** *(n).*
2 If you **justify** a point of view, you explain why it is reasonable.

jut jutting jutted *(v)* to stick out. *The cliff jutted into the sea.*

juvenile
1 *(n)* a young person who is not yet an adult, according to the law.
2 *(adj)* involving or concerning young people who are not yet adults, according to the law.
3 *(adj)* childish. *Juvenile behaviour.*
4 **juvenile delinquent** *(n)*
a young person who breaks the law. **juvenile delinquency** *(n).*

juxtapose
juxtaposing juxtaposed *(v)*
to place things side by side, especially to contrast them. **juxtaposition** *(n).*

Kk

kaleidoscope *(n)*
a tube through which you see changing patterns made by mirrors and pieces of coloured glass. **kaleidoscopic** *(adj).*

kangaroo *(n)*
a large Australian marsupial that carries its young in a pouch.

karaoke *(ka-ree-yoh-kee) (n)*
an entertainment in which people sing the words of popular songs while a machine plays the backing music.

karate *(ka-rah-tee) (n)*
a sport in which two people fight each other using controlled movements, especially kicking with their feet and chopping with their hands.

kayak *(ky-ak) (n)* a covered boat in which you sit and move through the water by paddling with a double-bladed paddle.

curved paddle blade
safety helmet
buoyancy aid
kayak
shaft
coaming (keeps water out)
deck

kebab *(n)*
small pieces of meat or vegetables, cooked on a skewer.

keel keeling keeled
1 *(n)* a long bar along the bottom of a boat that holds it together. *See* **ship**.
2 **keel over** *(v) (informal)* to fall over in one smooth, steady movement.

keen keener keenest *(adj)*
1 enthusiastic and eager. *Kelly is keen to join the team.* **keenness** *(n).*
2 If you are **keen on** someone or something, you like them very much.
3 able to notice things easily. *A keen sense of smell.*

keep keeping kept
1 *(v)* to have something and not get rid of it. *Let's keep these books.*
2 *(v)* to stay the same. *We ran around to keep warm.*
3 *(v)* to continue doing something. *Dorothy kept laughing at me.*
4 *(n)* a strong tower in a castle. *See* **castle**.

Chinese junk
main mast
sail (made from linen or matting)
rigging
mizzenmast
foremast
lug sail
sail batten (stiffens sail)
poop deck
transom
rudder
watertight cargo compartments inside hull
cabin porthole
oar

Some words that begin with a "k" sound are spelt with a "c".

keeper

---

keeper *(n)*
someone who looks after an animal, a park, or a museum collection.

keg *(n)* a small barrel.

kennel
1 *(n)* a small hut for a dog to sleep in.
2 **kennels** *(plural n)* a place where dogs are looked after while their owners are away.

kerb *(n)*
the line of stones or concrete along the edge of a pavement. *See* **road**.

ketchup *(n)* a thick, puréed sauce, usually made from tomatoes.

kettle *(n)*
a container with a handle and a spout, used for boiling water.

key *(n)*
1 a shaped piece of metal used for opening a lock, starting a car, etc.
2 one of the buttons on a computer or typewriter.
3 one of the black or white bars that you press on a piano.
4 a scale of musical notes based around one particular note.
A tune in the key of F.

keyboard *(n)*
1 the set of keys on a computer, typewriter, piano, etc.
2 An **electronic keyboard** has keys like a piano, and controls to produce other sounds, and is worked by electricity.

khaki *(kah-kee) (n)* a yellowish-brown colour, used especially for soldiers' uniforms. **khaki** *(adj)*.

kibbutz *(kib-ootz)* **kibbutzim** *(n)*
a small community in Israel in which all the people live and work together.

kick kicking kicked
1 *(v)* to hit something with your foot. *Freddie kicked the ball.* **kick** *(n)*.
2 *(n) (informal)* a feeling of excitement. *Jennifer gets a kick out of driving fast.*
3 **kick off** *(v)* to start a football match by kicking the ball. **kick-off** *(n)*.

kid kidding kidded
1 *(n)* a young goat.
2 *(n) (informal)* a child.
3 *(v) (informal)* to tell someone something untrue, as a joke.

kidnap kidnapping kidnapped *(v)*
to capture someone and keep them as a prisoner until certain demands are met. **kidnapper** *(n)*.

kidney *(n)*
Your **kidneys** are the organs in your body that remove waste matter from your blood and turn it into urine. *See* **organ**.

kill killing killed *(v)* to end the life of a person or animal.

kiln *(n)* a very hot oven, used to bake objects made of clay until they are hard and dry.

kilogram *(n)* a unit for measuring weight. 1 kilogram = 1,000 grams.

kilojoule *(kil-uh-jool) (n)* a unit for measuring energy or work done. 1 kilojoule = 1,000 joules.

kilowatt *(n)*
a unit for measuring electrical power. 1 kilowatt = 1,000 watts.

kilt *(n)* a pleated, tartan skirt worn especially by Scottish men as part of a traditional costume.

kimono *(n)*
a long, loose dress with wide sleeves and a sash, worn by Japanese women.

kimono

- tomoeri (over-collar)
- eri (collar)
- obijime (cord)
- obi (sash)
- kimono
- tabi (split-toed socks)
- zori (sandals)

kin
(plural n)
people related to you.

kind kinder kindest
1 *(adj)* friendly, helpful, and generous. **kindness** *(n)*, **kindly** *(adv)*.
2 *(n)* a type or a sort. *What kind of food is your favourite?*

kindergarten *(n)* a school or class for preschool children.

kindle kindling kindled *(v)*
1 to make something start to burn. *The campers quickly kindled a fire.*
2 to get something started. *Our visit to the castle kindled my interest in history.*

kindling *(n)* small, thin pieces of wood used for starting fires.

kinetic *(adj)* to do with movement, or caused by movement. *Kinetic energy.* **kinetically** *(adv)*.

king *(n)*
1 a man from a royal family who is the ruler of his country.
2 a chesspiece that can move one square in any direction. *See* **chess**.
3 a playing card with a picture of a king on it.

kingdom *(n)*
1 a country that has a king or queen as its ruler.
2 a part of the natural world. *The animal kingdom.*

kingfisher *(n)* a small, brightly-coloured bird which lives near water and catches fish for food. Kingfishers have a shrill whistle.

kingfisher

kiosk *(n)*
a small stall from which sweets, newspapers, magazines, etc. are sold.

kip *(n) (slang)* If you have a **kip**, you have a short sleep. **kip** *(v)*.

kiss kisses kissing kissed *(v)*
to touch someone with your lips to greet them or to show that you like or love them. **kiss** *(n)*.

kit *(n)*
1 the clothes and equipment that you need to play a sport. *Football kit.*
2 a collection of things that you fix together or use to make something. *A cupcake kit.*

kitchen *(n)* a room in which food is prepared and cooked.

kite *(n)* a frame covered with paper or material which is flown in the wind, attached to a long piece of string. *The picture shows a stunt kite, which can be made to perform turns, dips, and loops.*

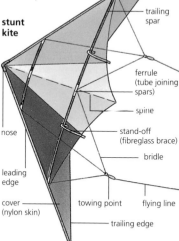

- trailing spar
- ferrule (tube joining spars)
- spine
- stand-off (fibreglass brace)
- bridle
- **stunt kite**
- nose
- leading edge
- cover (nylon skin)
- towing point
- flying line
- trailing edge

kitten *(n)* a young cat.

kitty kitties *(n)*
1 an amount of money contributed by everyone in a group and then used to buy something.
2 an affectionate name for a cat.

kiwi *(kee-wee) (n)*
1 a bird from New Zealand that cannot fly.
2 *(informal)* a name for someone who comes from New Zealand.

Some words that begin with a "k" sound are spelt with a "c".

lacrosse

knack *(nak)* *(n)* an ability to do something difficult or tricky.

knave *(nave)* *(n)* one of the three picture playing cards, with a value between that of a ten and a queen. The knave is sometimes called the jack.

knead *(need)* kneading kneaded *(v)* When you **knead** dough, you punch it and stretch it to make it smooth.

knee *(nee)* *(n)* the joint between your upper and lower leg, which you bend when you walk.

kneel *(neel)* kneeling knelt *or* kneeled *(v)* to bend your legs and put your knees on the ground.

knickers *(nik-ers)* *(plural n)* underwear worn by women and girls.

knife *(nife)* knives; knifing knifed
1 *(n)* a tool with a sharp blade, used for cutting things.
2 *(v)* to stab someone with a knife.

knight *(nite)*
1 *(n)* In medieval times, a **knight** was a warrior who fought on horseback. A king or noble would give a knight land and in return the knight would fight for him. **knightly** *(adj)*. *Also see* **feudalism**, **joust**.
2 *(n)* a man who has been given the title "Sir" as a reward for service to his country. **knighthood** *(n)*, **knight** *(v)*.
3 *(n)* a chesspiece with a horse's head that can move in an L-shape, three squares at a time. *See* **chess**.

plume (ostrich feathers)
chanfron
helmet
visor
sword
gorget
pauldron
breastplate
skirt
vambrace
gauntlet
cuisse
poleyn
greave
sabaton
mounted knight
barding
caparison
coat of arms

knit *(nit)* knitting knitted *(v)*
1 to make a piece of clothing out of wool, using a pair of long, pointed needles. **knitting** *(n)*.
2 When a bone **knits**, it heals after it has been broken.

knob *(nob)* *(n)*
1 a small, round handle on a drawer or door.
2 a control button on a machine.

knock *(nok)* knocking knocked
1 *(v)* to bang or hit something. *Knock the nails into the wall with a hammer.* **knock** *(n)*.
2 **knock out** *(v)* to make someone unconscious.

knocker *(nok-er)* *(n)* a piece of metal attached to a door that you use to knock on the door.

knot *(not)* knotting knotted
1 *(n)* a fastening made by looping and twisting string or rope together.
2 *(v)* to make a knot in a piece of string or rope.
3 *(n)* a hard spot in a piece of wood where a branch joined the main trunk.
4 *(n)* a unit for measuring the speed of a ship or aircraft.

knots
overhand knot or half-hitch
figure-eight knot
reef knot or square knot
double carrick bend
sheet bend

know *(noh)* knowing knew known *(v)* to be familiar with a person, place, or piece of information.

knowledge *(nol-ij)* *(singular n)* the things that someone or everyone knows. *General knowledge.*

knowledgeable *or* **knowledgable** *(nol-ij-ab-ul)* *(adj)* If you are **knowledgeable**, you know a lot. *Al is knowledgeable about art.*

knuckle *(nuk-el)* *(n)* one of the joints where your fingers join your hand.

koala *(n)* an Australian mammal that looks like a small bear and lives in trees.

kookaburra *(n)* an Australian bird that makes a loud sound, similar to sound of someone laughing.

Koran *or* **Qur'an** *(n)* the holy book of Islam.

kosher *(adj)* **Kosher** food is food that has been prepared according to the laws of the Jewish religion.

Ll

label labelling labelled
1 *(n)* a piece of paper, cloth, plastic, etc. that is attached to something and gives information about it.
2 *(n)* a word or phrase explaining something. *Picture labels.*
3 *(v)* to attach a label to something, or give something a label.

laboratory laboratories *(n)* a room containing special equipment for use in scientific experiments.

labour labouring laboured
1 *(v)* to work hard. **labour** *(n)*.
2 *(n)* people employed to do work, especially physical work. *Part-time labour.*
3 *(n)* the work of giving birth to a baby.
4 **Labour Party** *(n)* one of the main political parties in Britain, which believes in social equality and the importance of the welfare state.

lace lacing laced
1 *(n)* thin material made from cotton or silk, with a pattern of small holes and delicate stitches. *This picture shows the equipment used to make lace.* **lacy** *(adj)*.
2 **laces** *(plural n)* long pieces of thin cord to tie shoes.
3 *(v)* to tie something together with a lace. *Lace up your shoes.*

lace-making
pillow
lace
pins
bobbin
pricking (pattern)
threads

lack lacking lacked
1 *(v)* to be without something that you need. *The refugees lack food.*
2 *(n)* If there is a **lack** of something, people do not have enough of it.

lacrosse *(n)* a ball game for two teams, in which each player has a long stick with a small net on the end. The players run with the ball, pass it to each other, and aim to score goals.

lacrosse stick
rubber ball
frame
shooting string
cordbag
side wall
ball stop
leather lace
lightweight aluminium handle

Some words that begin with a "k" sound are spelt with a "c".

a b c d e f g h i j k **l** m n o p q r s t u v w x y z

lad

lad (n) a boy or young man.

ladder (n)
1 a metal, wooden, or rope structure that you use to climb up and down. Ladders are made from two long side pieces linked by a series of cross-pieces, called rungs.
2 (n) a long tear in a pair of tights or stockings. **ladder** (v).

laden (adj) carrying a lot of things. *Miles arrived laden with presents.*

ladle (n) a large, deep spoon with a long handle, used for serving soup, casseroles, etc. **ladle** (v).

lady ladies (n)
1 a polite name for a woman.
2 Lady a title used by a woman who has either earned the title herself, as a reward for service to her country, or who is married to a Lord or a man with the title "Sir".

ladybird (n) a small, round beetle which has colourful wings, often with spots on them. *See* **insect**.

lag lagging lagged (v)
1 to cover water pipes with a thick material to stop them from freezing in cold weather. **lagging** (n).
2 If you **lag behind** other people, you do not keep up with them.

lager (lar-ger)
1 (n) a kind of light, pale beer.
2 lager lout (n) (slang) a young man who gets drunk and then behaves in a noisy, violent way.

lagoon (n)
a large pool of seawater separated from the sea by a bank of sand.

laid-back (adj) (informal) very relaxed and calm.

lair (n) a place where a wild animal rests and sleeps.

lake (n) a large area of fresh water surrounded by land.

lamb (n)
1 a young sheep.
2 meat from a young sheep.

lame lamer lamest (adj)
1 Someone who is **lame** has an injured leg and so is unable to walk properly. **lameness** (n), **lamely** (adv).
2 weak or unconvincing. *A lame excuse.* **lamely** (adv).

lament lamenting lamented
1 (n) a sad song, especially one about someone's death.
2 (v) to feel or show great sadness.

lamp (n)
a light that uses gas, oil or electricity.

lance (n)
a long spear used in the past by soldiers riding horses. *See* **joust**.

land landing landed
1 (n) the part of the Earth's surface that is not covered by water.
2 (v) to come down from the air to the ground. *The plane landed safely.*
3 (v) (informal) to succeed in getting something. *I've landed a place in the team.*
4 (informal) If you are **landed with** something, you have been given something difficult or unpleasant to deal with.

landfill (n) rubbish and waste that is buried under the ground.

landing
1 (n) an area of floor at the top of a staircase.
2 landing strip (n) a strip of ground which aircraft use for taking off and landing.

landlady landladies (n)
1 a woman who rents out a room, house, or flat.
2 a woman who owns or runs a pub.

landlord (n)
1 a man who rents out a room, house, or flat.
2 a man who owns or runs a pub.

landmark (n)
1 an object in a landscape that can be seen from a long way away.
2 an important event in someone or something's development. *Leaving home was a landmark in Finn's life.*

landscape
1 (n) a large area of land that you can view from one place.
2 landscape gardening (n) the designing, shaping, and planting of a garden in an attractive way.

landslide (n)
1 a sudden fall of earth and rocks down the side of a mountain or hill.
2 an election victory in which the winner gains many more votes than anyone else.

lane (n)
1 a narrow road or street.
2 one of the strips marked on a main road, that is wide enough for a single line of vehicles.
3 one of the strips, each wide enough for one person, into which a racetrack, swimming pool, etc. is divided.

language (n)
1 the words that people use to talk and write to each other.
2 a set of signs, symbols, or movements used to express meaning. *Sign language.*

lanky lankier lankiest (adj)
Someone who is **lanky** is very tall and thin. **lankiness** (n).

lantern (n)
a candle with a protective frame around it. *Lanterns can be made from paper, like the ones shown here, or from glass and metal.*

Japanese lanterns

lanyard (n) a cord worn around your neck to which you can attach a whistle, compass, etc. *See* **compass**.

lap lapping lapped
1 (n) the flat area formed by the top part of your legs when you are sitting down. *Why don't you sit on my lap?*
2 (n) the distance around a racetrack. *I can run a lap in under a minute!*
3 (v) When water **laps** against something, it moves gently against it.
4 (v) When an animal **laps up** a drink, it flicks the liquid up into its mouth with its tongue.

lapel (n)
part of the collar of a coat or jacket, that folds back over your chest.

lapse (n)
1 a small mistake or failure. *Kay has been dieting hard, with a slight lapse over Christmas.* **lapse** (v).
2 the passing of time. *After a lapse of two years, Annemarie returned.*

laptop (n)
a portable computer that is so small and light you can use it on your lap.

lard (n)
solid, white fat used in cooking.

larder (n) a cupboard or small room in which food is stored.

large larger largest
1 (adj) big. **largeness** (n).
2 If a person or an animal is **at large**, they are free and dangerous. *There's a tiger at large in the town.*

largely (adv) mostly.

lark (n)
1 a small, brown bird that flies very high in the sky and has an attractive song.
2 (informal) something silly that you do for fun or as a joke. **lark** (v).

larva larvae (n) an insect at the stage of development between an egg and a pupa. *See* **caterpillar**.

laryngitis (la-rin-jy-tuss) (n) a swelling of the throat caused by an infection.

larynx larynxes *or* laryngnes (la-rinx) (n) the top of your windpipe, which holds your vocal cords.

lasagna *or* **lasagne** (laz-an-ya) (n) an Italian dish made from layers of pasta and meat or vegetables, covered with a cheese sauce.

laser
1 (n) a machine that makes a very narrow, powerful beam of light which can be used for light shows, for cutting things, or for medical operations. The word laser stands for "light amplification by stimulated emission of radiation".
2 **laser beam** (n) a concentrated beam of light, made by a laser. Laser beams are used to read compact discs. *See* **compact disc**.

lash lashes lashing lashed
1 (n) a stroke with a whip.
2 (v) to tie things together very firmly using rope. **lash** (v).
3 (n) one of the small hairs growing around your eyes.
4 **lash out** (v) to hit someone suddenly and angrily.

lass lasses (n) a girl or young woman.

lasso (lass-oo) lassos or lassoes (n) a length of rope with a large loop at one end, which can be thrown over an animal to catch it. **lasso** (v).

last lasting lasted
1 (adj) coming at the end or after everything else. *Jane was the last one to leave.* **lastly** (adv).
2 (adj) most recent. *I saw Douglas last week.*
3 (v) to go on for a particular length of time. *The film will last for 90 minutes.*
4 **last straw** (n) the final event in a series that leads to a loss of patience, or to a disaster.
5 (n) If someone **has the last word**, they have put an end to an argument or discussion.

lasting (adj) Something that is lasting keeps going for a long time.

latch latches latching latched
1 (n) a lock or fastening for a door. **latch** (v).
2 If you leave a door **on the latch**, you close it, but do not lock it.
3 (v) If you **latch on** to someone or something, you become very attached to them and dependent on them.

latchkey (n) a key that opens a door with a latch.

late later latest (adj)
1 When someone or something is **late**, they come after the expected time. **lateness** (n).
2 near the end of a period of time. *The late 20th century.*
3 no longer alive. *The late Elvis Presley.*

latecomer (n) someone who arrives late.

lately (adv) recently.

latent (adj) existing, but not yet very obvious or very strong. *A latent talent.*

lateral
1 (adj) on or towards the side. *A lateral root.* **laterally** (adv).
2 **lateral thinking** (n) the ability to think about problems in an unusual and not obvious way.

lather (n) a mass of bubbles formed when soap is mixed with water.

Latin (n) the language of the Ancient Romans.

latitude (n) the position of a place, measured in degrees north or south of the equator. **latitudinal** (adj).

latter
1 (n) the second of two things just mentioned. *I like oranges and bananas, but I prefer the latter.*
2 (adj) later. *It snowed during the latter part of our holiday.*

lattice (n) a pattern of crossed lines, with diamond-shaped spaces in between them. **latticed** (adj).

laugh laughing laughed (v) When you **laugh**, you make a sound to show that you think that something is funny. **laugh** (n), **laughter** (n).

laughable (adj) If something is **laughable**, it is ridiculous and cannot be taken seriously.

launch launches launching launched
1 (v) to put a large ship into the water for the first time. **launch** (n).
2 (v) to send a rocket up into space. **launch** (n).
3 (v) to start or introduce something new. *The charity launched a new fundraising campaign.* **launch** (n).
4 **launch pad** (n) a place where rockets leave the ground to go into space.

launderette (n) a place where you pay to use washing machines and spin-dryers.

laundry laundries (n)
1 clothes, towels, and sheets that are being or will be washed.
2 a place where clothes are washed.

laurel (n)
1 an evergreen bush with smooth, shiny leaves.
2 a wreath made from bay or laurel leaves, given to heroes and poets in Ancient Greece and Rome.
3 If you **rest on your laurels**, you rely on your past achievements and do not try any more.

lava (n) the hot liquid that pours out of a volcano when it erupts. *See* **volcano**.

lavatory lavatories (n) a toilet.

lavender (n)
1 a plant, usually with purple flowers that have a pleasant smell.
2 a pale purple colour, the colour of lavender flowers. **lavender** (adj).

lavish lavishes lavishing lavished
1 (adj) generous or extravagant. *Lavish gifts.* **lavishly** (adv).
2 (v) If you **lavish** attention, money, care, etc. on someone, you give them a lot of it.

law (n)
1 a rule made by the government that must be obeyed.
2 a statement or principle in science, maths, etc. *The law of gravity.*

law-abiding (adj) If you are **law-abiding**, you obey the laws of a country.

law court (n) a place where it is decided whether someone is guilty or innocent of a crime.

lawful (adj) permitted by the law. **lawfulness** (n), **lawfully** (adv).

lawn (n) a piece of grass, usually next to a house.

lawn mower (n) a machine that people use to cut grass.

lawyer (n) someone who advises people about the law and speaks for them in court.

lax (adj) relaxed or not strict.

laxative (n) a medicine or food that you eat to help you pass solids from your body. **laxative** (adj).

lay laying laid
1 (v) to put or to place. *Lay the clothes on the bed.*
2 (v) to produce an egg.
3 (adj) A **lay** person is not a priest.
4 **lay the table** (v) to prepare a table for a meal, by putting on a tablecloth, setting out cutlery, etc.

layabout (n) (informal) a lazy person.

lay-by (n) In Britain, a **lay-by** is a place by the side of the road where drivers can park.

layer (n) a thickness of something. *Layers of paint.* **layered** (adj).

lay-off (n) a situation in which people are temporarily sent home from work because there is not enough for them to do.

layout (n) the pattern or design of something. *The layout of a book.*

lazy lazier laziest (adj) If you are **lazy**, you do not want to work or exercise. **laziness** (n), **laze** (v), **lazily** (adv).

a b c d e f g h i j k l m n o p q r s t u v w x y z

lead

lead leading led
1 *(rhymes with bead) (v)* to show someone the way, usually by going in front of them. **leader** *(n)*.
2 *(rhymes with bead) (v)* to be in charge. **leader** *(n)*, **leadership** *(n)*.
3 *(rhymes with bed) (n)* a soft, grey metal.
4 *(rhymes with bead) (n)* a suggestion or a clue. *The police have been given several new leads.*
5 *(rhymes with bead) (n)* a long strip attached to a collar, that you use to hold and control a dog.

leaf leaves *(n)*
1 a flat and usually green part of a plant or tree, that grows out from a stem, twig, branch, etc. *The cross-section of a leaf, below, shows the palisade cells, where light is converted to food in a process called photosynthesis, and the mesophyll cells, where respiration takes place.* **leafy** *(adj)*.
2 a page of a book.

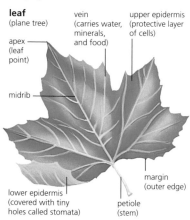

leaf
(plane tree)

apex (leaf point)

midrib

vein (carries water, minerals, and food)

upper epidermis (protective layer of cells)

lower epidermis (covered with tiny holes called stomata)

petiole (stem)

margin (outer edge)

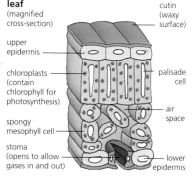

leaf
(magnified cross-section)

upper epidermis

chloroplasts (contain chlorophyll for photosynthesis)

spongy mesophyll cell

stoma (opens to allow gases in and out)

cutin (waxy surface)

palisade cell

air space

lower epidermis

leaflet *(n)*
a printed, and usually folded, piece of paper that gives information or advertises something. **leaflet** *(v)*.

league *(leeg) (n)* a group of people, countries, or teams who have a shared interest or activity. *A football league.*

leak leaking leaked *(v)*
1 If a container **leaks**, it lets liquid or gas escape from it. **leak** *(n)*, **leaky** *(adj)*.
2 If a liquid or gas **leaks**, it escapes through a hole or crack in a container. **leak** *(n)*.
3 If a story or information is **leaked**, someone tells it to someone else who is not meant to know it. **leak** *(n)*.

lean leaning leant *or* leaned; leaner leanest
1 *(v)* to bend towards or over something. *The mother leant over her baby.*
2 *(v)* to slope. *Look how that wall leans!*
3 *(v)* to rest your body against something for support.
4 *(adj)* slim and muscular.
5 *(adj)* If meat is **lean**, it has very little or no fat.

leaning *(n)* If you have a **leaning** towards something, you are interested in it or good at it.

leap leaping leapt *or* leaped *(v)* to jump, or to jump over something. **leap** *(n)*.

leap year *(n)*
a year that has 366 days, caused by adding an extra day in February. A leap year comes every fourth year.

learn
learning learnt *or* learned *(v)*
1 to gain knowledge or a skill.
2 to discover some news. *I learnt that Abdul was going away.*

lease *(n)*
an agreement that you sign when you rent a flat, land, etc.

leash leashes *(n)*
a long strip attached to a collar, that you use to hold and control a dog.

least
1 *(n)* the smallest amount. *Of all the children, Sue eats the least.* **least** *(adj)*.
2 *(adv)* less than anything else. *Turnip is my least favourite vegetable.*
3 at least as a minimum. *We need at least another week's holiday.*

leather *(n)* animal skin that is treated and used to make shoes, bags, and other goods. **leathery** *(adj)*.

leave leaving left
1 *(v)* to go away. *We're leaving for France tomorrow.*
2 *(v)* to let something stay or remain. *Leave the dishes, I'll do them later.*
3 *(n)* time away from work.
4 *(v)* If you **leave something behind**, you forget to bring it.
5 *(v)* If you **leave something out**, you do not include it.

lecture *(n)*
1 a talk given to a class or an audience in order to teach them something. **lecturer** *(n)*, **lecture** *(v)*.
2 a telling-off that lasts a long time. **lecture** *(v)*.

ledge *(n)* a narrow shelf. *A window ledge. A mountain ledge.*

leek *(n)* a long, white vegetable with green leaves at one end. *See* **vegetable**.

leer *(n)* an unpleasant grin. **leer** *(v)*.

left
1 *(adj)* This page is on the **left** side of the book. **left** *(n)*, **left** *(adv)*.
2 In politics, people **on the left** support the equal distribution of wealth and workers' rights.

left-handed *(adj)* If you are **left-handed**, you use your left hand to write, draw, etc. **left-hander** *(n)*.

leftovers *(plural n)*
food that has not been eaten, and can be used for another meal.

left-wing *(adj)* If you are **left-wing**, you believe in the equal distribution of wealth and in workers' rights. **left wing** *(n)*, **left-winger** *(n)*.

leg *(n)*
1 the part of your body between your hip and foot.
2 one of the parts that supports a chair, table, etc.
3 A **leg** of a journey is one part or stage of it.
4 *(informal)* If you **pull someone's leg**, you make fun of them by telling them something untrue.

legacy legacies *(n)*
money or property that has been left to someone in a will.

legal *(adj)*
1 to do with the law. *Legal documents.*
2 lawful or allowed by law. **legally** *(adv)*.

legend *(n)*
1 an old, well-known story. **legendary** *(adj)*.
2 If someone is a **legend**, they are very famous. **legendary** *(adj)*.

leggings *(plural n)*
close-fitting, stretchy trousers.

legible *(adj)* If handwriting or print is **legible**, it can be read easily. **legibility** *(n)*, **legibly** *(adv)*.

legion
1 *(n)* part of the Roman army.
2 *(n)* a large body of soldiers or ex-soldiers. *The foreign legion.*
3 *(adj)* very many or numerous. *Melissa's faults are legion.*

license

legislation *(singular n)* laws. *New traffic legislation.* legislate *(v)*, legislative *(adj)*.

legitimate *(adj)*
1 lawful or acceptable. legitimately *(adv)*.
2 A **legitimate** child is born to parents who are married.

leisure
1 *(n)* free time when you do not have to work. leisure *(adj)*.
2 **leisurewear** *(n)* clothing for relaxing in or for sport.
3 **leisure centre** *(n)* a building where you can take part in enjoyable activities such as swimming, badminton, etc.

leisurely *(adj)* unhurried. *We enjoyed a long, leisurely breakfast.*

lemon *(n)* a yellow citrus fruit with a thick skin. *See* **fruit**.

lemonade *(n)* a sweet, lemon-flavoured drink that is often fizzy.

lend lending lent *(v)* to let someone have something for a short time.

length *(n)*
1 the distance from one end of something to the other.
2 the time that something lasts. *Do you know the length of this film?* lengthy *(adj)*.

lengthen lengthening lengthened *(v)* to make something longer.

lengthways *(adv)* in the direction of the longest side. *Fold the paper lengthways.*

lenient *(lee-nee-ent) (adj)* gentle and not strict. leniently *(adv)*.

lens lenses *(n)*
1 the part of your eye that focuses light. *See* **eye**.
2 a piece of curved glass or plastic in a camera, telescope, pair of glasses, etc. Lenses bend light rays so that you can focus a camera or see things magnified through a telescope. *The diagram shows how concave and convex lenses make light rays bend in different ways. Also see* **telescope**.

lenses

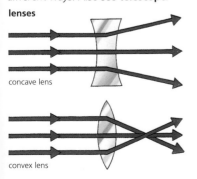

concave lens

convex lens

Lent *(n)* the 40 days before Easter in the Christian Church's year. *Some people give up certain luxuries for Lent.*

lentil *(n)* a small, dried seed that can be cooked and eaten. Lentils can be green, orange, or brown.

leopard *(lep-erd) (n)* a large wild cat with a spotted coat, found in Africa and Asia.

leopard

leprechaun *(lep-ruh-korn) (n)* a mischievous elf in Irish stories, who has a pot of gold.

leotard *(lee-oh-tard) (n)* a tight, one-piece garment worn for dancing or exercise.

lesbian *(adj)* Women who are lesbian have sexual feelings for other women. lesbian *(n)*, lesbianism *(n)*.

less
1 *(adj)* smaller, or in smaller quantities. *There is less fat in margarine than in butter.* less *(adv)*.
2 *(prep)* minus. *We bought it for the sale price, less ten per cent discount.*

lessen lessening lessened *(v)* to get smaller in size, strength, importance, etc.

lesson *(n)*
1 a set period in school when pupils are taught, or a session when a skill is taught.
2 an experience that teaches you something. *Juggling with peaches turned out to be a messy lesson.*

let letting let *(v)*
1 to allow or to permit something.
2 to rent out a house, land, etc.
3 If you **let someone down**, you disappoint them by not doing something that you promised.
4 If you are **let off** a punishment or duty, you no longer have to undergo it or do it.

lethal *(adj)* If something is **lethal**, it can kill. lethally *(adv)*.

letter *(n)*
1 a sign that is part of an alphabet and is used in writing. *The letter "A".*
2 a message that you write to or receive from someone.

lettering *(n)* letters written in a certain style. *Italic lettering.*

lettuce *(n)* a green, leafy salad vegetable. *See* **vegetable**.

leukaemia *(loo-kee-mee-a) (n)* a serious disease in which the blood makes too many white cells.

level levelling levelled
1 *(adj)* flat and smooth. level *(v)*.
2 *(adj)* equal. *The scores are level.*
3 *(n)* a height. *Eye level. Sea level.*
4 *(n)* a standard or a grade. *Level one.*
5 *(v)* If something **levels out**, it stops rising or falling and stays the same.

level crossing *(n)* In Britain, a **level crossing** is a place where a road and railway cross at the same level.

lever *(lee-ver) (n)*
1 a bar that you use to lift an object, by placing one end under the object and pushing down on the other end. leverage *(n)*, lever *(v)*.
2 a handle that you use to make a machine work.

liable *(adj)*
1 likely. *Judy is liable to get angry when she hears the news.*
2 If you are **liable** for something that you have done, you are responsible for it by law. liability *(n)*.

liar *(n)* someone who tells lies.

libel *(n)* an untrue written statement about another person that is damaging to them. libellous *(adj)*.

liberal *(adj)*
1 tolerant, especially of other people's ideas. liberalism *(n)*.
2 generous. *A liberal helping of pie.*

Liberal Democrats *(n)* one of the main political parties in Britain, who believe in following a middle way between the policies of the Conservative and Labour Parties.

liberate liberating liberated *(v)* to set someone free. liberation *(n)*.

liberated *(adj)* Someone who is **liberated** has been set free, or feels free. liberation *(n)*.

liberty liberties *(n)* freedom.

library libraries *(n)* a place where you can go to read or borrow books. librarian *(n)*.

lice *(plural n)* small insects without wings, that live on animals or people.

licence *(n)* a document giving permission for you to do something or own something. *A driving licence.*

license licensing licensed *(v)* If someone is **licensed** to do something, such as sell alcohol, they have official permission to do it.

a b c d e f g h i j k l m n o p q r s t u v w x y z

lichen

lichen *(lye-ken or lit-chen) (n)* a flat, moss-like plant that grows on stones, trees, etc.

Himalayan lichen

lick licking licked *(v)*
1 to pass your tongue over something. **lick** *(n)*.
2 to touch something lightly. *Small waves licked the shore.*

lid *(n)* a top or a cover.

lie lying lied
1 *(v)* to say something that is not true.
2 *(n)* a statement that is untrue.

lie lying lay lain *(v)*
1 to get into or to be in a flat, outstretched position.
2 to be or to be placed somewhere. *The village lies in a deep valley.*

lieutenant *(lef-ten-ent or loo-ten-ent) (n)* a junior officer in the army or navy.

life lives *(n)*
1 Your **life** is the time from your birth until your death.
2 liveliness and cheerfulness. *I feel full of life today!*

lifeguard *(n)* someone who is trained to save swimmers in danger.

life jacket *(n)* a jacket that will keep you afloat if you fall into water.

life jacket

back strap
collar
nylon-covered PVC foam
inflation tube
inflation chamber
band (reflects light)
waist belt
whistle

lifestyle *(n)* a way of living. *Jonah has a very glamorous lifestyle.*

lift lifting lifted
1 *(v)* to raise someone or something.
2 *(n)* a machine that carries people or goods between floors of a building.
3 *(n)* a ride, especially in a car.

light lighting lighted *or* lit; lighter lightest
1 *(v)* to start something burning.
2 *(v)* to make something bright and visible.

3 *(n)* brightness, such as from the Sun or a lamp.
4 *(adj)* not dark. *Light blue.*
5 *(n)* an object that gives out light, such as a torch or lamp.
6 *(adj)* weighing little. **lightness** *(n)*.
7 *(adj)* gentle. **lightly** *(adv)*.
8 **light up** *(v)* to make something bright. *A smile lit up Becca's face.*

lighthouse *(n)* a tower, in or near the sea, with a flashing light that guides ships or warns them of danger.

lighthouse (cutaway)

helicopter
racon (radar beacon)
helipad
emergency light
main light
fog signal
upper engine room
engine control switchboards
bedroom
banana bunk
battery-charging system, radio link, and mobile phones
subsidiary light
kitchen and living area
batteries
jib (hoists up supplies)
storage cupboard
winch
unloading door
fuel storage tank
supplies
lower engine room
entrance room
door
rung ladder

lightning *(n)* flashes of electricity in the sky, usually with thunder.

lightweight *(adj)*
1 not heavy. *A lightweight coat.*
2 not important or not serious.

light year *(n)* a unit for measuring distance in space. A light year is the distance that light travels in one year.

like liking liked
1 *(v)* to enjoy or be pleased by someone or something. **liking** *(n)*.
2 *(prep)* similar to.
3 *(prep)* typical of. *It's just like Linda to be late.*
4 *(adj)* similar. *The twins are as like as two peas.*

likely likelier likeliest *(adj)* probable. **likelihood** *(n)*.

likewise *(adv)* also, or in the same way. *I'll dance if you do likewise.*

lilac *(n)*
1 a tree with sweet-smelling purple or white flowers.
2 a blueish-purple colour. **lilac** *(adj)*.

limb *(n)*
1 an arm or a leg.
2 a branch of a tree.

limber limbering limbered *(v)* When you **limber up**, you stretch your muscles before exercising.

lime *(n)*
1 a round green citrus fruit. *See fruit.*
2 a white substance or powder, used to make cement and as a fertilizer on fields.

limelight *(n)* If you are **in the limelight**, you are the centre of attention.

limerick *(n)* a nonsense verse made up of five lines that rhyme in a particular way.

limestone *(n)* a rock that contains calcium carbonate and from which lime is made.

limit limiting limited
1 *(n)* an edge or a boundary. **limitless** *(adj)*, **limitlessly** *(adv)*.
2 *(v)* to keep within a certain area or amount. *I've limited myself to three cups of tea a day.* **limitation** *(n)*.

limited
1 *(adj)* small and unable to increase.
2 *(n)* A **limited edition** of a book, picture, etc. may be valuable because it is one of only a small number.
3 *(n)* A **limited company** is one where people who own shares in it lose only the value of those shares if the company goes bankrupt.

lizard

limp limping limped; limper limpest
1 *(v)* to walk in an uneven way, usually because of an injury. **limp** *(n)*.
2 *(adj)* floppy and not firm.
A limp handshake. **limply** *(adv)*.

line *(n)*
1 a long, narrow mark.
2 a row of people or words.
3 a piece of string, rope, etc.
4 an attitude or an approach.

linen *(n)* cloth made from the flax plant, used to make clothes and household items, such as tablecloths.

linesman linesmen *(n)*
an official who decides if the ball has gone over the line, in games such as football and tennis. *See* **soccer**.

linger lingering lingered *(v)* to stay or to wait around. *The fans lingered outside the theatre.* **lingering** *(adj)*.

linguist *(n)* someone who studies foreign languages, or speaks them well.

lining *(n)* a piece of material sewn inside something. *A silk lining.* **line** *(v)*.

link linking linked
1 *(n)* one of the separate rings that make up a chain.
2 *(n)* a connection between things or people.
3 *(v)* to join objects, ideas, or people together.
4 *(n)* a picture or piece of text on the internet that you can click on to go to a different webpage. **link** *(v)*.

lino *(n)* short for linoleum. Linoleum is a smooth, shiny material used as a floor covering.

linocut *(n)*
a print made from a block of lino with a pattern or picture cut into it.

lint *(n)* soft material used for covering wounds.

lion *(n)* a large wild cat with a mane, found in Africa and Asia.

lip *(n)*
1 Your **lips** are the pink edges of your mouth.
2 the edge or rim of a cup or hole.
3 *(slang)* cheek, or rude talk.

lip-read lip-reading lip-read *(v)*
When deaf people **lip-read**, they watch someone's lips while they are talking in order to understand what they are saying. **lip-reading** *(n)*.

liquid *(n)* a wet substance that you can pour. **liquid** *(adj)*.

liquid-crystal display *(n)* a way of showing numbers and letters on clocks, calculators, etc. Different parts of a grid of liquid crystals reflect light as electronic signals are sent to them. Often called LCD. *See* **calculator**.

liquidize *or* **liquidise** liquidizing liquidized *(v)* to make solid food into a liquid. **liquidizer** *(n)*.

liquor *(lik-er) (n)* a strong alcoholic drink, such as whisky, gin, or vodka.

liquorice *(lik-er-iss or lik-er-ish) (n)* a black substance that comes from a plant root, and is used to make sweets.

lira *(leer-a)* lire *(n)* the main unit of money in Turkey, and formerly in Italy.

lisp *(n)* a way of talking in which you say "th" instead of "s". **lisp** *(v)*.

list listing listed *(v)*
1 to set down words, numbers, etc. in a line. **list** *(n)*.
2 When a ship **lists**, it leans to one side.

listen listening listened *(v)* to pay attention so that you can hear something. **listener** *(n)*.

literacy *(n)* the ability to read and write. **literate** *(adj)*.

literally *(adv)*
If you take someone **literally**, you believe their exact words.

literature *(n)*
books, especially novels, plays, and poems. **literary** *(adj)*.

litmus *(n)* a substance that turns red when touched by an acid, and blue when touched by an alkali. Litmus comes in paper or liquid form. *See* **pH**.

litter
1 *(n)* rubbish that is left scattered around. **litter** *(v)*.
2 *(n)* a group of kittens, piglets, puppies, etc. born at the same time to one mother.
3 litter tray *(n)* an indoor toilet for a cat or other pet.

little littler littlest
1 *(adj)* small in size. *A little girl.*
2 *(n)* a small amount of something. *I'll have just a little.*
3 *(adj)* not much. *We have little time.*

live living lived
1 *(rhymes with give) (v)* to be alive. *Some cats live for 20 years.*
2 *(rhymes with five) (adj)* alive or living. *You can buy live chickens in the market.*
3 *(rhymes with give) (v)* to have your home somewhere. *Josie lives in Durham.*
4 *(rhymes with five) (adj)* broadcast as it is happening.
5 *(rhymes with five) (adj)* If an electrical wire is **live**, it is carrying electricity which can give you a shock.
6 *(rhymes with five) (adj)* unexploded. *A live cartridge.*

livelihood *(n)* the way that you make money to support yourself.

lively livelier liveliest *(adj)* active and full of life. **liveliness** *(n)*.

liver *(n)*
1 the organ in your body that cleans your blood. Your liver also produces bile which helps to digest food. *See* **digestion**, **organ**.
2 You can eat the **liver** of some animals, such as pigs.

livestock *(n)* animals kept on a farm, such as horses, sheep, and cows.

living
1 *(adj)* alive now.
2 *(n)* money to live. *Jasmine earns her living by painting.*

living room *(n)*
a lounge or a sitting room.

lizard *(n)* a small reptile with a long body and a tail. *The picture shows parts of a lizard and a range of different lizards.*

common iguana

nostril
mouth cavity
gum
nuchal crest
dorsal crest
claw   toe   dewlap

horned lizard

collared lizard

frilled lizard

skink

Some words that begin with a "li" sound are spelt "ly".

llama

llama *(n)* a South American mammal, kept for its wool and meat.

load loading loaded
1 *(n)* something that is carried, especially something heavy.
2 *(v)* to put things onto or into something. *Megan loaded the car with camping equipment.*
3 *(v)* to put a bullet into a gun.
4 *(v)* If a computer program, game, or document is **loading**, it is starting up or opening.
5 *(plural n) (informal)* If you have **loads** of something, you have a lot of it.

loaf loaves; loafing loafed
1 *(n)* bread baked in an oblong shape.
2 *(n)* food that has been cooked in a loaf-shaped tin. *Meat loaf.*
3 *(v)* If you **loaf around**, you are lazy and do very little.

loafer *(n)*
1 someone who is lazy and does not do much.
2 a flat, slip-on, leather shoe.

loam *(n)* loose, rich soil made of sand, clay, and rotted vegetable and animal material. **loamy** *(adj)*.

loan loaning loaned
1 *(v)* to lend something to someone.
2 *(n)* an amount of money that you borrow. *A bank loan.*

loathe loathing loathed *(v)* to hate or dislike someone or something. **loathing** *(n)*.

loathsome *(adj)* very unpleasant or disgusting. *A loathsome monster.*

lob lobbing lobbed *(v)* to throw or hit a ball high into the air. **lob** *(n)*.

lobby lobbies *(n)*
1 a hall in a large building.
2 a group of people who try to persuade politicians to act or vote in a certain way. **lobby** *(v)*.

lobster *(n)* a sea creature with a shell, ten legs, and a long body. Lobsters can be eaten, and turn red or orange when they are cooked.

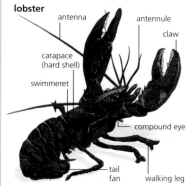

lobster
antenna
antennule
claw
carapace
(hard shell)
swimmeret
compound eye
tail
fan
walking leg

local
1 *(adj)* near your house, or to do with the area where you live. *A local newspaper.* **locally** *(adv)*.
2 *(n) (informal)* Someone's **local** is a pub where they often go to drink.
3 *(adj)* affecting only one part of the body. *Local anaesthetic.*

locality localities *(n)* an area or a neighbourhood.

locate locating located *(v)*
1 to find out where something is.
2 If something is **located** in a particular place, you will find it there.

location *(n)*
1 the place or position where someone or something is.
2 If a film or television programme is made **on location**, it is filmed out of the studio.

loch *(n)* a Scottish lake.

lock locking locked
1 *(n)* a part of a door, box, etc. that you can open and shut with a key.
2 *(v)* to fasten something with a key.
3 *(n)* a part of a canal with gates at each end, where boats are raised or lowered to different water levels.
4 **locks** *(plural n) (poetic)* hair.

locker *(n)* a small cupboard that can be locked.

locket *(n)* a piece of jewellery which is worn on a chain around the neck, and which often contains a photograph.

locksmith *(n)* someone who makes and mends locks and keys.

locomotive *(n)* a railway engine. *See* **steam locomotive**.

locust *(n)* an insect similar to a grasshopper, which eats and destroys crops. Locusts fly in swarms of up to 2,000 million.

locust

lodge lodging lodged
1 *(n)* a small house or place where you can stay.
2 *(v)* If you **lodge** with someone, you stay in their house and usually pay them money.
3 *(v)* If something **lodges** somewhere, it gets stuck there.
4 *(n)* a beaver's home. *See* **beaver**.

lodger *(n)* someone who pays to live in a room in someone else's house. **lodgings** *(plural n)*.

loft *(n)* a room in the roof of a building.

lofty loftier loftiest *(adj)*
1 very high and imposing. *A lofty building.*
2 distant and haughty. **loftily** *(adv)*.

log logging logged
1 *(n)* a part of a tree that has been chopped down or has fallen down.
2 *(n)* a record kept by the captain of a ship. **log** *(v)*.
3 *(n)* a written record of something. *Liza kept a log of her progress.* **log** *(v)*.
4 *(v)* When you **log on** or **log in** to a computer or website, you begin to use it by entering a name or a password.
5 *(v)* When you have finished using a computer or website, you **log off** or **log out**.

logic *(n)* careful and correct reasoning. **logical** *(adj)*, **logically** *(adv)*.

logo (loh-go) *(n)* a symbol that represents a particular company or organization.

loiter (loy-ter) loitering loitered *(v)* to stand around, usually because you have nothing to do.

loll lolling lolled *(v)*
1 to sit or stand in a lazy, sloppy way. *Wayne lolled on the sofa.*
2 to hang loosely. *The wolf's tongue lolled out of its mouth.*

lollipop *(n)* a sweet on a stick.

lolly lollies *(n)* an iced sweet on a stick.

lone *(adj)* single or isolated.

lonely lonelier loneliest *(adj)*
1 If you are **lonely**, you are sad because you are by yourself. **loneliness** *(n)*.
2 far from other people or things. *A lonely farmhouse.*

long longing longed; longer longest
1 *(adj)* more than the average length, distance, time, etc. *A long walk. A long shower.* **long** *(adv)*.
2 *(adj)* from one end to the other. *The footpath was about two miles long.*
3 *(adj)* taking a lot of time. *Is the film very long?*
4 *(v)* If you **long for** something, you want it very much. **longing** *(n)*.

longitude *(n)* the position of a place, measured in degrees east or west of a line that runs through the Greenwich Observatory in London, England. **longitudinal** *(adj)*.

long-range *(adj)*
1 to do with the future. *I don't have any long-range plans.*
2 designed to travel a long way. *Long-range missiles.*

Viking longship

- yard
- mast
- sea chest (containing sailors' belongings)
- mast rest
- deck (made from loose planks with storage room beneath)
- sail rest
- stern head
- storage sacks
- shield
- steerboard (oar for steering)
- overlapping oak planks (sealed with sheep's wool and tar)
- coarse woollen sail
- rigging
- wooden oar

longship (n) a long, narrow ship, with many oars and a sail, used especially by the Vikings. *The Vikings used longships like the one shown above to carry warriors to new lands.*

long-sighted (adj) If you are **long-sighted**, you can see things more clearly when they are far away.

long-term (adj) to do with a long period of time. *Long-term plans.*

long-winded (adj) long and boring.

loo (n) (informal) a toilet.

loofah (n) a rough sponge that you wash yourself with in the bath.

look looking looked
1 (v) to use your eyes to see things.
2 (v) to seem or to appear. *It looks as if the weather will be bad all week.*
3 (n) a glance or expression on someone's face. *An angry look.*
4 (v) If you **look after** someone or something, you take care of them.
5 (v) If you **look down on** someone, you think that you are better than they are.
6 (v) If you **look forward** to something, you wait for it eagerly.
7 (v) If you **look up** something, you try to find out about it in a book or on the internet.

lookout (n) someone who keeps watch for something. *We posted a lookout outside our den.*

loom looming loomed
1 (v) to appear in a sudden or frightening way. *Suddenly, a tall figure loomed out of the shadows.*
2 (n) a machine used for weaving cloth. *The picture shows a woman working on a traditional Bangladeshi backstrap loom.*

loom

loop (n) a curve or circle in a piece of string, rope, etc. **loop** (v).

loose looser loosest (adj)
1 not fitting tightly. *Loose trousers.* **loosely** (adv).
2 not firm. *A loose tooth.* **loosely** (adv).
3 not contained, or not bound together. *Loose papers.* **loosely** (adv).

loosen loosening loosened (v)
1 to make something less tight.
2 If you **loosen up**, you become less shy and more relaxed.

loot looting looted
1 (v) to steal from shops or houses in a riot or war. **looter** (n).
2 (n) stolen money or valuables.

lopsided (adj) unbalanced or with one side heavier than the other.

lord (n)
1 a nobleman. **lordly** (adj).
2 **Lord** a title used by a man who is a member of the aristocracy or who has earned the title as a reward for service to his country.
3 **Lord** a title for God or Jesus.

lorry lorries (n)
a large motor vehicle used for carrying goods by road. *See* **truck**.

lose (looz) losing lost (v)
1 If you **lose** something, you do not have it any more.
2 to be beaten or defeated in a game, argument, etc.

loss losses (n)
1 the losing of something. *The loss of a friend.*
2 something that is lost.

lot
1 (n) a large number or amount.
2 (n) a group of objects that are sold together at an auction.
3 (v) If you **draw lots**, a group of you pick objects, such as straws, to decide who will do something.

lotion (n) a cream that you put on your skin or hair.

lottery lotteries (n)
a competition in which you buy tickets aiming to win a prize.

loud louder loudest (adj)
1 noisy or producing a lot of sound. **loud** (adv), **loudly** (adv).
2 very bright and colourful.

loudspeaker (n)
a machine that turns electrical signals into sounds. *See* **speaker**.

lounge lounging lounged
1 (v) to sit around lazily.
2 (n) a comfortable room for sitting in.

love loving loved
1 (v) to like someone or something very much. **love** (n).
2 If you are **in love** with someone, you are passionately fond of them.
3 If you **make love**, you have sexual intercourse with someone. **lover** (n).
4 (n) in tennis, a score of no points.

lovely lovelier loveliest (adj)
1 If someone is **lovely**, they are beautiful to look at or have a very attractive personality. **loveliness** (n).
2 enjoyable. *We had a lovely day.*

low lower lowest
1 (adj) not high. *A low table.*
2 (adj) A **low** sound is quiet and soft, or deep in pitch.
3 (adj) If someone feels **low**, they are depressed or ill.
4 **low tide** (n) the time when the sea is furthest down the beach.

lower lowering lowered
1 (v) to move something down.
2 (adj) not as high as something else.
3 (adj) **Lower case** letters are small, and not capital, letters.

loyal (adj)
Someone who is **loyal** supports their friends and does not betray or desert them. **loyalty** (n), **loyally** (adv).

LSD (n) a strong drug that makes people see frightening, dream-like things. LSD is illegal in Britain and in many other countries.

Ltd short for **limited**.

lubricate
lubricating lubricated (v)
to add oil or grease to the parts of a machine, so that it runs more smoothly. **lubricant** (n), **lubrication** (n).

luck (n)
1 something that happens to someone by chance. Bingo is a game of luck.
2 good fortune, or good things that happen to you that have not been planned. Wish me luck!

lucky luckier luckiest (adj)
1 Someone who is **lucky** is fortunate and good things seem to happen to them.
2 Something that is **lucky** happens by chance and is fortunate. **luckily** (adv).
3 A **lucky** number, charm, etc. is one that you think will bring you luck.

ludicrous (loo-dik-russ) (adj)
ridiculous or foolish. **ludicrously** (adv).

lug lugging lugged (v)
to move something heavy.

luggage (n) cases and bags that you take with you when you travel.

lukewarm (adj)
1 slightly warm.
2 not keen or not enthusiastic.

lull lulling lulled
1 (n) a short pause or break during a period of fighting or activity.
2 (v) to make someone feel peaceful, safe, or sleepy. The sound of the waves on the shore lulled Fay to sleep.

lullaby lullabies (n) a gentle song sung to send a baby to sleep.

lumber
lumbering lumbered
1 (v) to move around heavily and clumsily. We could hear Terry lumbering about upstairs.
2 (n) sawn-up wood or timber.
3 If you are **lumbered** with an unpleasant job or duty, you have been left to deal with it.

luminous (adj) shining or glowing in the dark. **luminously** (adv).

lump (n)
1 a mass of solid matter. A lump of pastry.
2 a swelling. Look at this lump on my head!

lunar (adj)
to do with the Moon. A lunar eclipse.

lunatic (n) (informal)
a foolish and annoying person. **lunacy** (n), **lunatic** (adj).

lunch lunches (n) the meal that you eat in the middle of the day. **lunch** (v).

lung (n)
Your **lungs** are the two organs inside your chest that you use to breathe. See **organ, respiration**.

lunge lunging lunged (v)
to move forward quickly and suddenly. **lunge** (n).

lurch lurches lurching lurched
1 (v) to move in an unsteady, jerky way. The train lurched to a halt.
2 If someone **leaves you in the lurch**, they leave you in a difficult situation, without any help.

lure luring lured
1 (v) to attract a person or an animal, often with the aim of leading them into a trap.
2 (n) something that attracts you to a particular place. I can never resist the lure of the sea.

lurid (adj)
1 vivid and glowing. A lurid yellow.
2 sensational and shocking. Lurid newspaper stories.

lurk lurking lurked (v)
to wait around secretly. The robbers lurked behind the house.

luscious (lush-uss) (adj) delicious and attractive. **lusciously** (adv).

lush (adj) growing thickly and healthily. Lush vegetation.

lust lusting lusted (v)
If you **lust after** someone or something, you want or desire them very strongly. Dave has always lusted after power. **lust** (n), **lustful** (adj).

luxury luxuries (n)
1 something expensive which you do not really need, but which is enjoyable to have. **luxury** (adj).
2 If you live **in luxury**, you are surrounded by expensive and beautiful things that make your life very comfortable and pleasant. **luxurious** (adj).

lyric
1 (n) a short poem that expresses strong feelings, especially love. **lyrical** (adj).
2 **lyrics** (plural n) the words of a song.

Mm

macabre (mak-ah-ber) (adj)
gruesome and frightening.

macaroni or **maccaroni** (n)
short tubes of pasta. See **pasta**.

Mach (mak) (n)
a unit for measuring an aircraft's speed. Mach 1 is the speed of sound.

machete (ma-shett-ee) (n)
a heavy knife with a broad blade.

machine
1 (n) a piece of equipment made up of moving parts, that is used to do a job.
2 **machine gun** (n) a gun that can fire bullets very quickly without needing to be reloaded.

machinery (singular n) a group of machines, or the parts of a machine.

macho (mat-cho) (adj) (slang)
If men or boys are **macho**, they act in an exaggeratedly masculine way.

mackerel
mackerel or mackerels (n) a shiny, blueish, sea fish that can be eaten.

mackintosh mackintoshes (n)
a coat that keeps you dry in the rain.

mad madder maddest (adj)
1 insane. **madness** (n).
2 very foolish.
3 (informal) very angry.
4 (informal) If you are **mad about** someone or something, you like them very much. **madly** (adv).

madam (n)
a formal name for a woman, used in speaking and writing. Can I help you, madam? Dear Madam.

Mafia (n)
a criminal organization, founded in Sicily, and responsible for many illegal activities worldwide.

magazine (n)
1 a thin book, which is published regularly, and contains news, articles, photographs, advertisements, etc.
2 the part of a gun that holds the cartridges.

maggot (n)
the larva of certain flies, such as the bluebottle and the housefly.

magic (n)
1 In stories, **magic** is the power to make impossible things happen. **magical** (adj), **magically** (adv).
2 clever tricks done to entertain people. **magician** (n).

magistrate (n) someone who acts as a judge in less serious law cases.

mammoth

magnet *(n)* a piece of metal that attracts iron or steel. Magnets have two ends, or poles, a north pole and a south pole. *The diagram illustrates a law of magnetism: the like poles of two magnets repel each other, while the unlike poles attract each other.* **magnetism** *(n)*, **magnetic** *(adj)*.

magnets

like poles repel

unlike poles attract

magnificent *(adj)* very impressive or beautiful. **magnificently** *(adv)*.

magnify magnifies magnifying magnified *(v)*
1 to make something appear larger so that it can be seen more easily. **magnification** *(n)*, **magnified** *(adj)*.
2 to make something seem greater or more important than it really is. *Sabrina always magnifies her problems.*

magnifying glass *(n)* a glass lens that makes things look bigger.

magnitude *(n)* the size or importance of something. *Once she had seen the mess, Tara realized the magnitude of her task.*

magpie *(n)* a black and white bird with a large beak. Magpies often collect shiny objects.

mahogany *(n)* a hard, dark, reddish-brown wood.

maid *(n)*
1 a female servant.
2 *(poetic)* a young, unmarried woman.

maiden
1 *(n)* *(poetic)* a young, unmarried woman.
2 *(n)* A woman's **maiden name** is the surname that she had before she married, if she decided to take her husband's name.
3 *(adj)* A **maiden** voyage or flight is the first one made by a particular ship or plane.

mail *(n)*
1 letters and parcels sent by post. **mail** *(v)*.
2 armour made by joining together small metal rings. *See* **centurion**.
3 If you buy something by **mail order**, you order it and pay for it and then the item is posted to you.

maim maiming maimed *(v)* to injure someone so badly that part of their body is damaged for life.

main
1 *(adj)* largest or most important.
2 **mains** *(plural n)* the large pipes or wires that supply water, gas, or electricity to a building.

mainframe *(n)* a large and very powerful computer to which other smaller computers are connected.

mainly *(adv)*
1 most importantly. *I mainly like swimming.*
2 almost completely. *The film was mainly rubbish.*
3 usually. *Mainly, I go straight home after school.*

maintain maintaining maintained *(v)*
1 to keep a machine or building in good condition. **maintenance** *(n)*.
2 to continue to say that something is so. *Theo maintains that he is innocent.*
3 to continue something and not let it come to an end. *We have always maintained a close friendship.*
4 to give money to support someone. **maintenance** *(n)*.

maize *(n)* a crop plant that produces sweetcorn.

majesty majesties *(n)*
1 dignity and grandeur. **majestic** *(adj)*, **majestically** *(adv)*.
2 The formal title for a king or queen is **His Majesty** or **Her Majesty**.

major
1 *(adj)* important or serious. *A major disaster.*
2 *(n)* an army officer.
3 *(n)* In music, a **major scale** has a semitone between the third and fourth and the seventh and eighth notes.

majority majorities *(n)*
1 more than half of a group of people or things. *The majority of students came by bike.*
2 the number of votes by which someone wins an election.
3 When someone reaches their **majority**, they become an adult by law.

make making made
1 *(v)* to build or produce something.
2 *(v)* to do something. *Wallis made two phone calls.*
3 *(v)* to cause something to happen. *The view made Jules feel dizzy.*
4 *(v)* to add up to. *Six and five make eleven.*
5 *(v)* to earn. *He makes good money.*
6 *(n)* the name of the company that makes a particular type of product. *What make is your bicycle?*

makeshift *(adj)* A **makeshift** object is made from whatever is available and is only meant to be used for a short time.

make-up *(n)* the coloured powders, creams, etc. that women and actors put on their faces. *The picture shows the dramatic make-up used in Japanese Kabuki theatre.*

Kabuki make-up

malaria *(mal-air-ee-a)* *(n)* a tropical disease that people get from mosquito bites. **malarial** *(adj)*.

male *(n)* a person or animal of the sex that fertilizes the female. **male** *(adj)*.

malicious *(mal-ish-uss)* *(adj)* hurting other people deliberately. *Malicious gossip.* **malice** *(n)*, **maliciously** *(adv)*.

malignant *(adj)*
1 nasty and evil. *The villain gave a malignant grin.* **malignantly** *(adv)*.
2 *(adj)* A **malignant** growth or disease is dangerous because it tends to spread very fast.

mall *(rhymes with all)* *(n)* *(US)* a large, covered shopping centre.

malleable *(mal-ee-ab-ul)* *(adj)* If a substance is **malleable**, it is easily moulded into different shapes.

malnutrition *(n)* illness caused by not having enough food or by eating the wrong kind of food.

malt *(n)* dried grain, usually barley, used for making whisky and milky drinks. **malted** *(adj)*.

maltreat maltreating maltreated *(v)* to treat a person or an animal cruelly. **maltreatment** *(n)*.

mammal *(n)* an animal that feeds its young on its own milk. *Humans, cows, mice, and dolphins are all examples of mammals.*

mammoth
1 *(n)* an extinct animal, that lived in the Ice Age and looked similar to a large elephant, with long, curved tusks.
2 *(adj)* very large. *This is a mammoth task!*

woolly mammoth

a b c d e f g h i j k l m n o p q r s t u v w x y z

man men; manning manned
1 (n) an adult male human being.
manhood (n), **manly** (adj).
2 (n) the human race.
3 (v) to be in charge of
equipment. *We need some
people to man the phones.*

manage managing managed (v)
1 to be in charge of a shop, business,
etc. *Timmy manages a small electrical
company.* **management** (n).
2 to be able to do something that
is difficult or awkward. *Can you
manage to carry all those bags?*

manager (n)
1 someone in charge of a shop,
business, etc. or in charge of a group
of people at work. **managerial** (adj).
2 someone who handles the
business affairs of a band, singer,
film star, football team, etc.

mane (n)
the long, thick hair on the head and
neck of a lion or horse. *See* **horse**.

manger (n) a container from
which cattle and horses eat.

mangle mangling mangled
1 (v) to crush and twist something.
*The car was completely mangled
in the crash.* **mangled** (adj).
2 (n) an instrument used in
the past for squeezing the
water out of wet clothes.

manhole (n)
a covered hole in the ground, leading
to sewers or underground pipes.

maniac (may-nee-ak) (n) someone
who is mad, or someone who acts in
a wild or violent way. **maniacal** (adj).

manicure (n) a treatment
for your hands and fingernails.

manipulate
manipulating manipulated (v)
1 to use your hands in a skilful
way. *Karen manipulated the
plane's controls expertly.*
2 to influence people in a clever
way so that they do what you want
them to do. **manipulation** (n),
manipulative (adj).

mankind (n) the human race.

man-made (adj)
Something that is **man-made** is
made by people and not produced
naturally. *Nylon is a man-made fibre.*

manner (n)
1 the way in which you do
something. *Look at the manner in
which Garth uses his paintbrush.*
2 the way that someone behaves.
Kirsty has a very gentle manner.
3 **manners** (plural n) polite behavior.

manoeuvre (mun-oo-ver)
manoeuvring manoeuvred
1 (n) a difficult movement that
needs skill. *The pilots performed
a series of breathtaking manoeuvres.*
2 (v) to move something carefully
into a particular position.
3 When an army is **on manoeuvres**,
a large number of soldiers, tanks,
etc. are moved around an area
to train them for battle.

manor (n)
a lord's estate in the Middle Ages.

mansion (n) a large, grand house.

manslaughter (n)
the crime of killing someone,
without planning it in advance.

mantelpiece (n) a wooden
or stone shelf above a fireplace.

manual
1 (adj) worked by hand. *A manual
sewing machine.* **manually** (adv).
2 (n) an instruction book that
tells you how to do something.
3 **manual work** (n) physical work.

manufacture
manufacturing manufactured (v)
1 to make something with machines
in a factory. **manufacture** (n),
manufacturer (n).
2 to invent something or make
something up. *Eric manufactured
a reason for his strange appearance.*

manure (n) animal waste put on
land to improve the quality of the
soil and to make crops grow better.

manuscript
1 (n) the original
handwritten or
typed pages of
a book, poem,
piece of music,
etc., before
it is printed.
2 (n)
a handwritten
document.
*A medieval
manuscript.*

**part of a page from a
medieval manuscript**

many more most
1 (adj) numerous. **many** (pronoun).
2 **How many?** what number?

Maori (mauw-ree) Maori or Maoris
(n) one of the native people of New
Zealand who lived there before
the Europeans arrived. **Maori** (adj).

map mapping mapped
1 (n) a detailed plan of an area,
showing features such as towns,
roads, rivers, mountains, etc.
2 (v) to make a map of a place.
3 (v) If you **map out**
something, you plan it.

maple (n)
a tree with large, five-pointed leaves.
*Maples are grown for their wood and
their sap, which is used to make syrup.*

marathon (n)
1 a running race of approximately 26
miles (42km), that is run along roads.
2 something that lasts for a long time.
The final tennis set was a marathon!

marble (n)
1 a hard stone with coloured
patterns in it, used for building
and making sculptures.
2 a small glass ball used in games.

march marches marching marched
1 (v) When soldiers **march**, they
walk together with regular steps.
2 (n) a piece of music to
which you can march.
3 (v) to walk somewhere quickly
and in a determined way.
4 (n) a large group of people
walking together in order to
protest or express their opinion
about something. **march** (v).

mare (n) an adult female horse.

margarine (n)
a yellow spread, similar to butter, that
is usually made from vegetable oil.

margin (n)
1 the long, blank space that
runs down the edge of a page.
2 a difference between two
amounts, especially a small one.
*Artie won the election by a very
narrow margin.* **marginal** (adj).

marijuana (ma-roo-whah-nah) (n)
a form of the drug cannabis that
people smoke to give them a feeling
of pleasure. *Marijuana is illegal in
Britain and many other countries.*

marina (n) a small harbour where
boats, yachts, etc. are kept.

marine
1 (adj) to do with the sea. *Marine life.*
2 (n) a soldier trained to serve
both at sea and on land.

mark marking marked
1 (n) a small scratch or stain
on something. **mark** (v).
2 (v) to put a mark on something,
especially to show who something
belongs to or where things are.
3 (n) a number or letter put
on a piece of work to show
how good it is. **mark** (v).
4 (n) something that shows
clearly. *A mark of good
manners is saying "please".*
5 (v) to keep very close to an opposing
player, in a game such as football
or hockey, to prevent them
from getting the ball or from scoring.

material

market
1 (n) a group of stalls, usually in the open air, where things are sold.
2 If a product is **on the market**, it is available and can be bought.

market research (n) When a person or company does **market research**, they collect information about the products that people buy and what people want and need.

marksman marksmen (n) someone who is an expert at shooting guns.

marmalade (n) a jam made from oranges or other citrus fruit and usually eaten on toast for breakfast.

maroon marooning marooned
1 (v) If someone is **marooned** somewhere, they are stuck and cannot leave. *The sailors were marooned on a desert island.*
2 (n) a dark, reddish-brown colour. **maroon** (adj).

marquee (mar-kee) (n) a large tent with open sides.

marriage (n) the relationship between a husband and wife.

married (adj) Someone who is **married** has a husband or wife.

marrow (n)
1 the soft substance inside your bones. See **bone**.
2 a large, long, green vegetable. See **vegetable**.

marry marries marrying married (v)
1 When people **marry**, they go through a ceremony in which they promise to spend their lives together.
2 to perform a marriage ceremony.

marsh marshes (n) an area of wet, low-lying land. **marshy** (adj).

marshal marshalling marshalled
1 (n) an official who helps to organize a public event, such as a concert.
2 (v) to gather together a group of people or things and arrange them in a sensible order. *The general marshalled his troops.*

marshmallow (n) a soft, spongy sweet.

marsupial (mar-soo-pee-ul) (n) a kind of mammal. Female marsupials carry their young in their pouches. *Kangaroos and koalas are marsupials.*

martial (mar-shall)
1 (adj) to do with war or soldiers.
2 **martial arts** (plural n) styles of fighting or self-defence that come from the Far East, for example, judo and karate. See **judo**.
3 **martial law** (n) government by the army.

martyr (mar-ter) (n) someone who is killed or made to suffer because of their beliefs. **martyrdom** (n).

marvel marvelling marvelled (v) If you **marvel** at something, you are filled with surprise and wonder.

marvellous (adj) very good indeed. **marvellously** (adv).

marzipan (n) a sweet, almond-flavoured paste, used on cakes such as Christmas cake.

mascara (n) a substance put on eyelashes to colour them and make them look thicker.

mascot (n) something that is supposed to bring good luck, such as an animal or a toy, especially one to give luck to a sport's team.

masculine (adj)
1 to do with men.
2 Someone who is **masculine** has qualities that are supposed to be typical of men. **masculinity** (n).
3 belonging to one of the main classes or genders of nouns in French, Latin, and other languages.

mash mashes mashing mashed (v) to crush food after it has been cooked.

mask masking masked
1 (n) a covering worn over the face to hide, protect, or disguise it, or as a costume or decoration. *This mask, made in the Tami Islands, New Guinea, would have been worn by a boy at a special ceremony to celebrate his adulthood.* **masked** (adj).
2 (v) to cover something up or disguise it.

mason (n) someone who cuts and carves stone for buildings, gravestones, etc.

masonry (n)
1 the work of a mason.
2 stone used in a building.

mask

mass masses
1 (n) a large number of people or things together.
2 (n) In physics, the **mass** of an object is the amount of physical matter that it contains. *Mass is measured in grams.*
3 **the masses** (plural n) ordinary people. *This show is designed to appeal to the masses.*
4 (adj) **Mass-produced** things are made in very large quantities, usually by machine.

massacre (mass-er-ker) (n) the killing of a very large number of people, often in battle. **massacre** (v).

massage (mass-arj) massaging massaged (v) to rub someone's body with your fingers or with stones, in order to loosen their muscles or to help them relax. **massage** (n).

massive (adj) huge and bulky. **massively** (adv).

mass media (plural n) a general word for different forms of communication that reach a large number of people. Television, radio, and newspapers are all mass media.

mast (n) a tall pole that stands on the deck of a boat and supports its sails. See **dinghy**, **junk**, **ship**.

master mastering mastered
1 (v) If you **master** a subject or skill, you become very good at it.
2 (n) a name for a male teacher, especially in a private school.

mastermind masterminding masterminded (v) If you **mastermind** a course of action, you plan it and control the way that it is carried out.

masterpiece (n) a brilliant piece of art, literature, music, etc.

mat (n) a thick pad of material, used for covering a floor, wiping your feet, protecting a table, etc.

matador (n) a bullfighter.

match matches matching matched
1 (n) a sports game in which one person or team plays another.
2 (v) If two things **match**, they go well together. **matching** (adj).
3 (n) a small, thin stick of wood with a chemical tip which is struck to produce a flame.
4 (v) to put two people or teams in opposition to each other. *The brothers are matched in the first round.*

mate mating mated
1 (v) When male and female animals **mate**, they have sexual intercourse to reproduce. **mating** (n).
2 (n) the male or female partner of a couple or pair.
3 (n) (informal) a friend.

material
1 (n) the substances from which something is made. *What materials do you need to build a house?*
2 (n) cloth or fabric.
3 (adj) made from or to do with matter. *The material world.*
4 (adj) to do with the well-being of the body. *Good food and warm clothes are material needs.*

a b c d e f g h i j k l m n o p q r s t u v w x y z

materialistic *(adj)*
People who are **materialistic** are only concerned with money and possessions. **materialism** *(n)*.

maternal *(adj)* to do with being a mother. *Maternal feelings.*

maternity
1 *(n)* motherhood.
2 **maternity leave** *(n)* time that a woman is allowed away from her job to have a baby.
3 **maternity ward** *(n)* a large room in a hospital for women who have just had or are about to have a baby.

mathematics *(singular n)* the study of numbers, quantities, and shapes. **mathematical** *(adj)*.

maths *short for* **mathematics**.

matinée *(mat-in-ay) (n)* an afternoon performance of a play or showing of a film.

matrimony *(n)* a general name for marriage. **matrimonial** *(adj)*.

matrix *(may-trix)* **matrices** *(n)* In maths, a **matrix** is a rectangular chart with figures set out in columns and rows.

matt *(adj)* not shiny. *Matt paint.*

matter mattering mattered
1 *(n)* things or materials. *Undigested matter. Printed matter.*
2 *(n)* something that needs to be dealt with. *Let's sort this matter out now.*
3 *(v)* If something **matters**, it is important.

mattress mattresses *(n)* a soft, thick pad, usually containing springs, that you put on the base of a bed to sleep on.

mature maturer maturest *(adj)*
1 adult or fully grown. **maturity** *(n)*, **mature** *(v)*.
2 behaving in a sensible, adult way. *Edmund is very mature for his age.* **maturity** *(n)*, **maturely** *(adv)*.
3 ripe. *A mature cheese.* **mature** *(v)*.

maul mauling mauled *(v)* to handle someone or something in a rough and possibly damaging way.

mausoleum *(maw-za-lee-um) (n)* a large tomb.

mauve *(rhymes with stove) (n)* a light purple colour. **mauve** *(adj)*.

maximum *(n)* the greatest possible amount or the upper limit. *Two hours is the maximum allowed for the test.* **maximum** *(adj)*.

maybe *(adv)* perhaps.

mayhem *(n)* a situation of confusion or violent destruction.

mayonnaise *(n)* a creamy sauce made from egg yolks, oil, and vinegar.

mayor *(n)* the leader of a town, city, or district council.

maze *(n)* a complicated network of paths or lines, made as a puzzle to find your way through. *The picture shows the maze at Colonial Williamsburg, Virginia, USA, which is based on a 17th-century maze at Hampton Court, England.*

maze
(aerial view)

meadow *(n)* a field of grass, often used for animals to graze in.

meal *(n)* food which is served and eaten, usually at a particular time of day. Breakfast and lunch are meals.

mean meaning meant; meaner meanest
1 *(v)* to intend to do something. *I mean to go skating tomorrow.*
2 *(v)* to try to convey a message. *What does this poem mean?*
3 *(adj)* not generous. **meanness** *(n)*, **meanly** *(adv)*.
4 *(adj)* unkind or unfair. *A mean trick.* **meanness** *(n)*, **meanly** *(adv)*.
5 *(n)* an average. *The mean of 3, 5, and 10 is 6.*

meaning *(n)*
1 the idea behind something.
2 the importance or significance of something. *What is the meaning of life?* **meaningful** *(adj)*.

meantime *(n)* the time in between. *We leave early tomorrow morning. In the meantime, let's get some sleep!*

meanwhile *(adv)* at the same time.

measles *(n)* an infectious disease causing a fever and a rash.

measure measuring measured
1 *(v)* to find out the size, capacity, weight, etc. of something. **measurement** *(n)*.
2 *(n)* an action intended to achieve a result. *What measures can we take to fight crime?*

meat *(n)* the edible flesh of an animal. **meaty** *(adj)*.

mechanic *(n)* someone who is skilled at operating or mending machinery.

mechanical *(adj)* operated by machinery. *A mechanical toy.* **mechanically** *(adv)*.

mechanics *(singular n)* a part of physics which deals with the way that forces affect still or moving objects.

mechanism *(n)* the system of moving parts inside a machine.

medal *(n)* a piece of metal, shaped like a coin, star, cross, etc, which is given to someone for being brave, for service to their country, or as a prize for a sporting achievement.

media *(plural n)* a general name for different forms of communication with people, such as television, radio, and newspapers.

mediaeval *see* **medieval**.

medical
1 *(adj)* to do with health treatment. *Medical advice.* **medically** *(adv)*.
2 *(n) (informal)* short for medical examination. A **medical examination** is an examination by a doctor.

medicine *(n)*
1 a substance, usually liquid, used in treating illness. **medicinal** *(adj)*.
2 the treatment of illness. *You must study medicine in order to become a doctor.*

medieval *or* **mediaeval** *(adj)* to do with the Middle Ages, the period of history between approximately AD500 and AD1450.

mediocre *(mee-dee-oh-ker) (adj)* of average or less than average quality. **mediocrity** *(n)*.

meditate
meditating meditated *(v)*
1 to think very deeply about something. *Felix meditated on the meaning of life.* **meditation** *(n)*.
2 to relax the mind and body by a regular programme of mental exercise. **meditation** *(n)*.

medium media *or* mediums
1 *(adj)* average or middle. *Kevin is of medium height.*
2 *(n)* the method by which something is communicated. *This art course will teach you to use a variety of media.*
3 *(n)* **Mediums** claim to make contact with the spirits of the dead.

meek meeker meekest *(adj)* quiet, humble, and obedient. **meekly** *(adv)*.

a b c d e f g h i j k l m n o p q r s t u v w x y z

meet meeting met (v)
1 to come face-to-face with someone or something.
2 to come together. *The paths met.*

meeting (n) an arranged event in which people come together, often to discuss something.

megabyte (n) a unit used to measure the capacity of a computer's memory or the size of a computer file.

melancholy (adj) very sad. melancholy (n), melancholic (adj).

mellow mellowing mellowed; mellower mellowest
1 (adj) soft, warm, and gentle. *Mellow colours.*
2 (v) If someone **mellows**, they become gentler and more relaxed.

melodramatic (adj)
If someone is **melodramatic**, they talk and behave in an exaggerated way and make a fuss about small things.

melody melodies (n)
a tune. melodic (adj).

melon (n)
a large, rounded, juicy fruit. *See* **fruit**.

melt melting melted (v)
When a substance **melts**, it changes from a solid to a liquid because it has become hotter.

member
1 (n) someone who belongs to a club, group, family, etc. membership (n).
2 Member of Parliament (n) someone elected by the members of a constituency to represent them in Parliament.

membrane (n) a very thin layer of tissue or skin, that lines or covers certain organs or cells. *See* **cell**, **egg**.

memo (n) short for memorandum. A **memorandum** is a brief message sent by one person to another person in the same organization.

memorable (adj) easily remembered or worth remembering.

memorize or **memorise**
memorizing memorized (v)
to learn something off by heart.

memory memories (n)
1 the ability to remember things.
2 something that you remember from the past. *Happy memories.*
3 the part of a computer in which information is stored.

menace (n)
1 a threat or a danger. menacing (adj).
2 (informal) a nuisance.

mend mending mended (v)
to repair something which is broken.

meningitis (men-in-jy-tiss) (n)
a serious disease that causes the membranes surrounding the brain to become very swollen.

menstruate
menstruating menstruated (v)
When a woman or girl **menstruates**, blood comes from her womb, about once a month. menstruation (n).

mental (adj) to do with the mind. *Mental arithmetic.* mentally (adv).

mention mentioning mentioned (v) to speak briefly about something. mention (n).

menu (n)
1 a list of drinks and dishes served in a café, restaurant, etc.
2 a list of choices shown on a computer screen.

mercenary mercenaries
1 (n) a soldier who is paid to fight for a foreign army.
2 (adj) If someone is **mercenary**, they are mainly interested in making money.

merchandise (n) a general name for goods which are bought or sold, usually in large quantities.

merchant (n)
1 someone who sells goods for profit, especially someone who trades with foreign countries.
2 A country's **merchant navy** is made up of the ships and crew that carry cargo for that country.

mercury (n) a poisonous, silvery, liquid metal. Mercury is used in some thermometers. *See* **thermometer**.

mercy mercies (n) If you show **mercy** to someone, you are kind to them and do not punish them. merciful (adj), mercifully (adv).

merely (adv)
only or simply. *Don't blame me, I'm merely the messenger.* mere (adj).

merge merging merged (v)
When two things **merge**, they join together to form a whole.

merger (n) the act of making two businesses, teams, etc. into one.

merit (n)
1 If something has **merit** it is good. merit (v).
2 a good point or quality of a person or thing.

mermaid (n) In stories, a **mermaid** is a sea creature with the upper body of a women and the tail of a fish.

merry merrier merriest (adj)
1 cheerful or joyful.
2 (informal) slightly drunk.

mesh meshes (n)
a network of wire, rope, etc.

mess messes messing messed
1 (n) a dirty or untidy state or thing. messy (adj), messily (adv).
2 (n) a confused and disorganized state or thing. *My life is a mess!*
3 (v) If you **mess something up**, you make it dirty or untidy, or you make it go wrong.
4 (v) If you **mess around**, you spend time doing something that is unimportant.

message (n)
1 information sent to someone else. *A secret message.*
2 the meaning of something, such as a book or film.

messenger (n)
someone who carries a message.

metal (n)
a chemical substance, such as iron, copper, or silver, which is usually hard and shiny, is a good conductor of heat and electricity, and can be melted and formed into shapes. metallic (adj).

metaphor (n)
a way of describing something as though it were something else, for example, *"She is a shining star"*.

meteorite (n) a remaining part of a meteoroid which falls to Earth.

meteoroid (n) a small piece of rock from space which enters the Earth's atmosphere and burns up, giving a "shooting star" effect.

meteorology (n) the study of the Earth's atmosphere and, in particular, its climate and weather. meteorologist (n), meteorological (adj).

meter (n)
an instrument for measuring the quantity of something, especially the amount of something that has been used. *An electricity meter.* meter (v).

method (n)
a way of doing something.

methodical (adj)
careful, logical, and well-organized. methodically (adv).

meticulous (adj) very careful and precise. meticulously (adv).

metre (n) a unit of length equalling 39.37 inches, or about 3 feet.

metric (adj) The **metric** system of measurement is based on units of ten. Metres, litres, and kilograms are all metric measurements. *See* page 284.

metronome (n) a device that produces a regular beat which helps musicians keep time as they play.

microbe (n)
a germ or other living thing that is too small to be seen without a microscope.

microchip (n)
a minute piece of silicon with electronic circuits printed on it, used in computers and other electronic equipment. See **chip**.

microcomputer (n)
a very small computer, usually without an internal memory.

microorganism (n)
a living thing that is too small to be seen without a microscope. *Bacteria and viruses are examples of microorganisms. The illustration below shows groups of microorganisms known as plankton. These tiny plants and animals are found in water.*

microorganisms
phytoplankton (plants)

zooplankton (animals)

microphone (n)
an instrument that changes sound into an electric current, to make the sound louder, record it, or transmit it to radio or television stations.

microprocessor (n)
the central processing unit of a microcomputer.

microscope (n)
an instrument with powerful lenses that magnifies very small things so that they look large enough to be seen and studied. *The illustration on the right shows a microscope with a revolving triple nosepiece. Each part of the nosepiece provides a different level of magnification. The eyepiece can be adjusted to focus the image seen through the nosepiece.*

microscopic (adj)
too small to be seen without a microscope.

microwave
1 (n) a high frequency electromagnetic wave.
2 **microwave oven** (n)
an oven which cooks food very quickly by beaming microwaves into it. *The microwaves make the moisture in the food vibrate and become hot, and this heat is passed through the food so that it cooks.*

fan
microwave oven (cutaway)
microwave generator tube

midday (n) noon, or 12 o'clock in the middle of the day. **midday** (adj).

middle
1 (adj) central, or halfway between two extremes. **middle** (n).
2 If you are **in the middle** of doing something, you are involved in doing it. *I'm in the middle of watching this programme.*

middle-aged (adj)
Someone who is **middle-aged** is between 40 and 60 years old.

Middle Ages (plural n)
the period of history covering the 5th to the 15th centuries.

eyepiece (magnifies image from objective lens)
fine focusing control
coarse focusing control
body tube
revolving triple nosepiece
objective lens (magnifies object)
stage clip
glass slide
stage
foot
mirror (directs light through object)
microscope

Middle East (n)
the countries of Western Asia between the eastern end of the Mediterranean Sea and India. Israel, Iraq, and Iran are all in the Middle East. **Middle Eastern** (adj).

midge (n)
a tiny, winged insect that bites.

midnight (n) 12 o'clock in the middle of the night. **midnight** (adj).

midway (adv)
halfway. *The car broke down midway between Sydney and Canberra.*

midwife midwives (n)
a nurse trained to help when a baby is being born. **midwifery** (n).

might (n) strength or force. **mighty** (adj), **mightily** (adv).

migraine (n) a very bad headache which makes you feel sick.

migrate migrating migrated (v)
When birds **migrate**, they fly at a particular time of year to live in another region. **migration** (n), **migratory** (adj).

mild milder mildest (adj)
1 gentle and not aggressive. **mildness** (n), **mildly** (adv).
2 moderate and not too harsh. *Mild weather.* **mildness** (n), **mildly** (adv).
3 If food has a **mild** flavour, it is not strong or spicy. **mildness** (n).

mildew (n)
a thin coating of mould that can grow on damp cloth, paper, etc. **mildewed** (adj).

mile (n)
a unit of length equalling 1,760 yards. See page 284.

mileage (n)
the average number of miles a vehicle travels on a gallon of petrol.

militant (adj)
Someone who is **militant** is prepared to fight or to be very aggressive in support of a belief. **militancy** (n), **militantly** (adv).

military (adj)
to do with soldiers and the armed forces. *A military hospital.*

militia (mil-ish-a) (n) a group of soldiers recruited in an emergency.

milk milking milked
1 (n) the liquid produced by female mammals to feed their young. **milky** (adj).
2 (n) a milk-like drink. *Soy milk.*
3 (v) to take milk from a cow or other animal.
4 **milk tooth** (n) one of your first teeth that falls out and is replaced by a permanent tooth.

mill (n)
1 a building containing machinery for grinding grain into flour. **mill** (v). See **windmill**.
2 a large factory with machinery for processing textiles, wood, paper, etc. *A cotton mill.*
3 a small machine used for grinding something into powder. *A pepper mill.* **mill** (v).

millennium millenniums *or* millennia (n) a period of a thousand years. **millennial** (adj).

millimetre (n)
one thousandth of a metre.

million (n)
1 a thousand thousands (1,000,000).
2 (informal) a great many.

millionaire (n) someone whose money and property is worth at least a million pounds or dollars.

mime (n)
a form of acting in which actions are used instead of words. **mime** (v).

mimic mimicking mimicked (v) to imitate someone else's speech or actions. **mimic** (n).

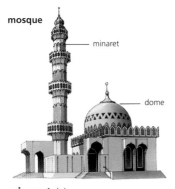

mosque

minaret

dome

minaret (n)
the tall, thin tower of a mosque, from which Muslims are called to prayer.

mince mincing minced
1 (v) to cut or chop meat or similar substances into very small pieces.
2 (n) finely chopped meat.
3 **mince pie** (n) a sweet, pastry tart made from mincemeat.

mincemeat (n) a sweet mixture of finely chopped dried fruit, spices, etc.

mind minding minded
1 (n) the part of you that thinks, remembers, dreams, etc.
2 (v) to care or to be bothered about something. *Do you mind what she says about you?*
3 (v) to look after something or someone. **minder** (n).
4 (v) to watch out for something.

mine mining mined
1 (adj) belonging to me.
2 (v) to dig up minerals from below the ground. **mine** (n), **miner** (n).
3 (n) a bomb placed in the ground or in the sea.

mineral
1 (n) a substance found in the ground, that can be obtained by mining. Iron, salt, and diamonds are all minerals. **mineral** (adj).
2 **mineral water** (n) water that has mineral salts and gases dissolved in it. Mineral water can be still or fizzy.

minerals

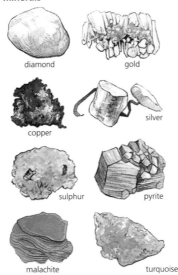

diamond
gold

copper
silver

sulphur
pyrite

malachite
turquoise

mingle mingling mingled (v) to mix together. *The guests mingled happily.*

miniature (min-it-cher) (adj) a small version of something bigger. *A miniature radio.* **miniaturize** (v).

minibus minibuses (n) a small bus that can usually carry between eight and sixteen passengers.

minim (n) a musical note representing two beats. See **notation**.

minimize *or* **minimise** minimizing minimized (v)
1 to make something as small as possible. *Charlotte minimized the risk of getting lost by taking a map.*
2 to make something seem as unimportant or insignificant as possible. *When we told Mum what had happened, we minimized the danger we had been in.*

minimum (n) the smallest possible amount, or the lowest limit. *We need a minimum of six people to play this game.* **minimum** (adj).

miniskirt (n) a very short skirt.

minister
1 (n) a clergyman. **ministry** (n).
2 (n) someone in charge of a government department. *The Minister for Health.* **ministry** (n), **ministerial** (adj).
3 (n) someone sent by the government to represent it overseas. **ministerial** (adj).
4 (v) to help or serve someone.

mink (n) a small animal with dark brown fur, often bred for its pelt.

minnow (n) a tiny freshwater fish.

minor
1 (adj) less important or less serious. *We will deal with minor matters after the main issues have been discussed.*
2 (n) someone under adult age.
3 (n) In music, a **minor scale** has a semitone between the second and third notes.

minority minorities (n)
1 a small number or part within a bigger group. *Only a minority were against the proposal.*
2 (n) a group of people of a particular race or religion living among a larger group of a different race or religion.

minstrel (n)
a medieval musician and poet.

mint (n)
1 a strongly-scented plant with leaves that are used for flavouring. See **herb**.
2 a peppermint-flavoured sweet.
3 a place where coins are manufactured. **mint** (v).
4 (informal) a very large amount of money. *His car must have cost a mint!*

minus (prep)
1 In maths, a **minus** sign (-) is used in a subtraction sum. *6 minus 4, or 6 - 4 = 2.*
2 (informal) without. *I went to school minus my sandwiches.*

minute minuter minutest
1 (min-it) (n) a unit of time equal to 60 seconds.
2 (my-newt) (adj) very small indeed. **minutely** (adv).
3 **minutes** (min-its) (plural n) the written record of what was said at a meeting.

miracle (mir-ak-ul) (n)
1 a supernatural event. **miraculous** (adj), **miraculously** (adv).
2 a remarkable and unexpected event. **miraculous** (adj), **miraculously** (adv).

mirage

mirage (mir-ahj) (n)
something that you think you see in the distance, such as water, which is not really there. Mirages are caused by light refracting off hot surfaces.

mirror (n) a very shiny surface which reflects the image of whatever is in front of it. **mirror** (v).

misbehave misbehaving misbehaved (v) to behave badly.

miscalculate
miscalculating miscalculated (v) to work something out incorrectly, or to judge a situation wrongly. **miscalculation** (n).

miscarriage
1 (n) When a pregnant woman has a **miscarriage**, the baby dies in her womb, usually early in the pregnancy. **miscarry** (v).
2 miscarriage of justice (n) a failure of the legal system to come to the right decision or verdict.

miscellaneous (miss-el-ay-nee-uss) (adj) assorted or of different types. *The drawer was full of miscellaneous socks, but I couldn't find a pair.* **miscellany** (n).

mischief (n)
playful, mildly naughty behaviour that may cause annoyance to others. **mischievous** (adj), **mischievously** (adv).

misconduct (n)
dishonest, irresponsible, or immoral action by someone in a position of responsibility.

miser (my-zer) (n) a very mean person who spends as little as possible in order to hoard money. **miserly** (adj).

miserable (adj) sad, unhappy, or dejected. **misery** (n), **miserably** (adv).

misfit (n)
someone or something not suited to the people or situation around them.

misfortune (n)
1 an unlucky event.
2 bad luck.

misguided (adj) If you are misguided, you have the wrong idea about something. **misguidedly** (adv).

mishap (n) an unfortunate accident.

mislay mislaying mislaid (v) to lose something for a short while, because you have put it in a place where you cannot find it.

mislead misleading misled (v) to give someone the wrong idea about something. **misleading** (adj), **misleadingly** (adv).

misprint (n) a mistake in a book, newspaper, etc. where the letters have been printed incorrectly.

miss misses missing missed
1 (v) to fail to hit something.
2 (v) to fail to catch, see, do, etc. *Gurdit missed the train by seconds.*
3 (v) to be unhappy because someone or something is not with you. *I missed my brother when he went away.*
4 Miss (n) a title given to a girl or an unmarried woman.

missile (n)
a weapon which is thrown or shot at a target. *An atomic missile.*

misspell misspelling misspelled *or* misspelt (v) to spell something incorrectly.

mist (n) a cloud of water droplets in the air. **misty** (adj).

mistake mistaking mistook mistaken
1 (n) an error or a misunderstanding.
2 (v) to believe that someone is somebody different. *I always mistake Tracey for her sister.*

mistletoe (n)
an evergreen plant that grows as a parasite on trees. Mistletoe has white berries and is often used as a Christmas decoration.

mistreat mistreating mistreated (v) to treat something or someone roughly or badly. **mistreatment** (n).

mistress mistresses (n) a name for a female teacher in some schools.

mistrust mistrusting mistrusted (v) to be suspicious of someone. **mistrust** (n).

misunderstanding (n)
1 a failure to understand. **misunderstand** (v).
2 a disagreement between two people.

misuse (miss-yooze) misusing misused (v) to use something in the wrong way. **misuse** (miss-yuce) (n).

mix mixes mixing mixed (v) to combine or blend different things. *Mix all the ingredients together.*

mixture (n) something made from things mixed together.

moan moaning moaned (v)
1 to complain in a dreary way.
2 to make a low, sad sound, usually because you are in pain or are unhappy. **moan** (n).

mob (n) a large and dangerous crowd of people.

mobile
1 (adj) able to move or be moved. *A mobile crane.* **mobility** (n).
2 (n) a decoration made of several things balanced at different heights and hanging from a central thread.
3 (n) short for **mobile phone.**

mobile phone (n) a telephone that you can carry around with you.

mock mocking mocked
1 (v) to make fun of someone in an unpleasant way. **mockery** (n).
2 (adj) false or imitation. *A mock battle.*
3 (n) a practice examination.

model
1 (n) a small version of a real-life object, made to scale. *A model railway.*
2 (adj) perfect or ideal. *A model child.*
3 (n) someone who poses for an artist or a photographer. **model** (v).
4 (n) a particular type of product. *This car is the very latest model.*

moderate (adj)
1 not extreme. *Moderate speed.* **moderation** (n), **moderately** (adv).
2 of average or below average quality.

modern (adj) up-to-date or new in style. *Modern architecture.*

modernize *or* **modernise**
modernizing modernized (v) to make something more modern or up-to-date. **modernization** (n).

modest (adj) People who are modest are not boastful about their abilities or achievements. **modesty** (n), **modestly** (adv).

modify modifies modifying modified (v) to alter something slightly. **modification** (n).

module (n) a separate, independent section that can be linked to other parts to make something larger.

Mohammed *or* **Muhammad** (n) the founder of the Islamic religion. Muslims believe that Mohammed is God's main prophet.

moist (adj) damp and slightly wet. *This cake is lovely and moist!* **moisture** (n), **moisten** (v).

mole (n)
1 a small, furry mammal that digs tunnels and lives underground.
2 a small, dark, growth on the skin.

European mole

Some words that begin with a "mi" sound are spelt "my".

molecule *(n)* the smallest part of a substance that can exist on its own. Molecules are made of two or more atoms bonded together. *The diagrams show how molecules are tightly packed in solids, loosely linked in liquids, and widely spaced in gases. This means that solids usually keep their shape, liquids can flow, and gases can spread out easily.* **molecular** *(adj)*.

molecules

molecules in a solid

molecules in a liquid

molecules in a gas

molest molesting molested *(v)*
1 to disturb, annoy, or interfere with someone.
2 to abuse or attack someone sexually. **molester** *(n)*.

mollusc *(n)* a creature with a soft body and no spine, usually protected by a shell. *Snails, clams, and oysters are all molluscs.*

mollycoddle mollycoddling mollycoddled *(v)* to look after someone too carefully. **mollycoddled** *(adj)*.

molten *(adj)*
Molten metal is so hot that it has melted to become a liquid.

moment
1 *(n)* a very brief period of time. *I only saw the rocket for a moment.* **momentary** *(adj)*, **momentarily** *(adv)*.
2 If something is happening **at the moment**, it is happening now.

monarch *(n)*
a ruler, such as a king or queen, who has usually inherited his or her position. **monarchy** *(n)*.

monastery monasteries *(n)*
a group of buildings where monks live and work. **monastic** *(adj)*.

money monies *(n)*
the coins and notes which people use to buy things. **monetary** *(adj)*.

mongrel *(n)* a dog of mixed breed.

monitor monitoring monitored
1 *(v)* to keep a check on something over a period of time.
2 *(n)* the visual display unit of a computer or television.

monk *(n)* a man who lives in a religious community and has promised to devote his life to God.

monkey *(n)* an animal like a small ape, usually with a tail.

monocle *(n)* a glass lens worn to improve the eyesight of one eye.

monogram *(n)* a design made from two or more letters, usually someone's initials. **monogrammed** *(adj)*.

monologue *(mon-oh-log) (n)* a long speech by one person.

monopolize or **monopolise**
monopolizing monopolized *(v)*
to keep something all to yourself. *Cedric monopolized the conversation so we couldn't get a word in edgeways.*

monopoly monopolies *(n)*
the complete control of something, especially a service or the supply of a product.

monorail *(n)* a railway that runs on one rail, usually high off the ground.

monotonous *(adj)*
If something is **monotonous**, it goes on and on in a dull and boring way. **monotony** *(n)*, **monotonously** *(adv)*.

monsoon *(n)* a season of torrential rain and strong winds in India and other Asian countries.

monster
1 *(n)* In stories, a **monster** is a large, fierce, or horrible creature.
2 *(n)* a very wicked person.
3 *(adj) (informal)* huge. *A monster packet of cereal.*

monstrous *(adj)*
1 extremely large, terrible, or strange. *A monstrous creature.* **monstrosity** *(n)*, **monstrously** *(adv)*.
2 wrong and wicked. *Monstrous behaviour.* **monstrously** *(adv)*.

month *(n)* one of the twelve parts that make up a year. **monthly** *(adj)*, **monthly** *(adv)*.

monument *(n)*
1 an old, important statue, building, etc. *An ancient monument.*
2 a statue, building, etc. that is meant to remind people of an event or a person. *A war monument.*

monumental *(adj)* very large or very important. **monumentally** *(adv)*.

mood *(n)*
1 Your **mood** is the way that you are feeling.
2 If you are **in a mood**, you feel sulky or bad-tempered.

moody moodier moodiest *(adj)*
1 cross or unhappy. **moodily** *(adv)*.
2 A **moody** person has frequent changes of mood or feelings. **moodiness** *(n)*.

moon *(n)*
1 a satellite of a planet. *Mars has two moons.*
2 the Moon the natural satellite that moves around the Earth once each month and reflects light from the Sun. *The first diagram below shows how the Moon moves around the Earth, while the second identifies the different phases of the Moon as they are seen from the Earth during the course of a month.*

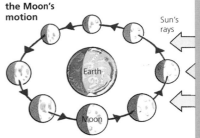
the Moon's motion

Sun's rays

Earth

Moon

phases of the Moon

new moon (invisible)

crescent moon (waxing)

half-moon (first quarter)

gibbous moon (waxing)

full moon

gibbous moon (waning)

half-moon (last quarter)

crescent moon (old moon)

moonlight moonlighting moonlit
1 *(n)* the light of the Moon that you can see at night. **moonlit** *(adj)*.
2 *(v) (informal)* to work at a second job, usually at night, and often secretly.

moor mooring moored
1 *(n)* an open, grassy area, often covered with heather. **moorland** *(n)*.
2 *(v)* If you **moor** a boat, you tie it up or anchor it. **moorings** *(n)*.

mop mopping mopped
1 *(n)* a long stick with a sponge or a bundle of cloth or string at one end, used to clean floors.
2 *(v)* to clean a floor, or soak up liquid with a mop, cloth, or sponge.

mope moping moped *(v)*
1 to be miserable and depressed.
2 to move around in an aimless, gloomy manner.

moral
1 *(adj)* to do with right and wrong. *Paul faced the moral dilemma of saying nothing or telling the truth.* **morality** *(n)*, **morally** *(adv)*.
2 *(plural n)* Your **morals** are your standards of behaviour.
3 *(n)* the lesson taught by a story.

a b c d e f g h i j k l m n o p q r s t u v w x y z

morale (*mor-ahl*) (*n*)
hope or confidence. *The prisoners kept up their morale by telling jokes.*

morbid (*adj*) to do with death and gruesome things. *A morbid sense of humour.* **morbidly** (*adv*).

more most
1 (*adj*) greater in number, size, etc. **more** (*n*), **more** (*adv*).
2 **more or less** roughly or nearly.

moreish (*adj*) (*slang*) If a food is **moreish**, you want more of it.

morning (*n*) the time of day between dawn and midday.

morose (*adj*)
gloomy and bad-tempered.

Morse code (*n*) a way of sending messages that uses light or sound in a pattern of dots and dashes to represent letters. *This picture shows the word "morse" in Morse code.*

M O R S E

morsel (*n*) a small piece of food.

mortal
1 (*adj*) unable to live forever. *All humans are mortal.* **mortality** (*n*).
2 (*n*) a human being.
3 (*adj*) deadly or causing death. *A mortal wound.* **mortally** (*adv*).

mortar (*n*)
1 a mixture of sand, water, and cement or lime that is used for building.
2 a deep bowl, used with a pestle for crushing things.

mortgage (*n*) a loan from a building society or bank to buy a house.

mortuary mortuaries (*n*) a room or building where dead bodies are kept until their funerals.

mosaic
(*moh-zay-ik*) (*n*)
a pattern or picture made up of small pieces of coloured stone or glass. *This Ancient Roman mosaic represents a Byzantine empress.*

mosaic

Moslem *see* **Muslim**.

mosque (*mosk*) (*n*)
a building used by Muslims for worship. *See* **architecture**, **minaret**.

mosquito (*moss-kee-toe*)
mosquitoes *or* mosquitos (*n*)
a small insect which sucks blood from animals and humans. Mosquitoes can spread diseases such as malaria.

sucking tube

mosquito

moss mosses (*n*) a small, furry, green plant that grows on wet soil or stone. Mosses do not have roots, flowers, or fruit, but reproduce by producing spores. **mossy** (*adj*). *See* **spore**.

mostly (*adv*) mainly or usually.

motel (*n*)
a roadside hotel for motorists.

emperor moth
(male)

moth (*n*)
an insect similar to a butterfly, that usually flies at night. *The emperor moth is found in Europe and Asia.*

mother (*n*) a female parent. **motherhood** (*n*), **motherly** (*adj*).

motion motioning motioned
1 (*n*) movement. *The motion of the boat made me feel sick.*
2 (*v*) to tell someone something through movement. *The teacher motioned for Stan to sit down.*
3 (*n*) a suggestion made at a meeting.

motivate motivating motivated (*v*) to encourage someone to do something. *The coach tried to motivate his team to win.* **motivation** (*n*), **motivated** (*adj*).

motive (*n*)
a reason for doing something.

motocross (*n*)
cross-country motorcycle racing.

motor motoring motored
1 (*n*) a machine that changes electrical energy into mechanical energy to produce movement. *See* **engine**.
2 (*adj*) to do with cars or engines. *Motor mechanics.*
3 (*v*) to drive. **motoring** (*n*).

motorbike (*n*) (*informal*)
a motorcycle.

motorcycle (*n*) a two-wheeled vehicle with an engine. *The picture shows a Yamaha TDM850 motorcycle.*

motorcycle

tail cover
pillion (passenger seat)
pillion footrest (folded-up)
fuel tank
speedometer
windscreen
rear direction indicator
twist-grip throttle
rear mudquard
rider's seat
grab bar
shock absorber
cowl (covering)
brake light
headlight
front direction indicator
radiator
brake cable
front mudguard
front fork (contains spring)
front brake calliper
rear fender
lightweight, three-spoke wheel
exhaust pipe
brake pedal
crank case
exhaust down pipe
swingarm
exhaust silencer
rider's footrest
clutch and gearbox
twin-cylinder engine
disc brake

Some words that begin with a "mor" sound are spelt "mau".

multiple

motorist *(n)* a car driver.

motorway *(n)*
a wide road with several lanes
for fast, long-distance traffic.

mottled *(adj)*
If something is **mottled**, it is covered
with patches of different colours.

motto mottos *or* mottoes *(n)*
a short sentence that is meant to
guide your behaviour. Some families
have a motto as part of their coat
of arms. *See* **coat of arms**.

mould moulding moulded
1 *(v)* to model or shape something.
Mould the clay into a cat shape.
2 *(n)* a hollow container that you
can pour liquid into, so that it
sets in that shape. *A jelly mould.*
3 *(n)* a furry fungus that grows
on old food or damp walls.
mouldiness *(n)*, **mouldy** *(adj)*.

moult moulting moulted *(v)*
When a bird or animal **moults**,
its outer covering of fur,
feathers, or skin comes off
so that a new one can grow.

mound *(n)* a hill or a pile.

mount mounting mounted
1 *(v)* to get on or to climb up.
Sheryl mounted her horse. **mount** *(n)*.
2 *(v)* to rise or to increase. *Excitement
mounted as the great day drew near.*
3 *(v)* to put a picture or photograph
in a frame. **mount** *(n)*.
4 *(n)* a mountain. *Mount Everest.*

mountain *(n)*
1 a very high piece of
land, higher than a hill.
2 a large amount of something.
A mountain of work.

mountain bike *(n)* a strong bicycle
with many gears that can be ridden
on rough or hilly ground. *See* **bicycle**.

mountaineer *(n)*
someone who climbs mountains.
mountaineering *(n)*.

mourn mourning mourned *(v)*
to be very sad and grieve for
someone who has died.
mourner *(n)*, **mourning** *(n)*.

mournful *(adj)*
sad and miserable.
mournfully *(adv)*.

mouse mice *(n)*
1 a small, furry animal
with a long tail.
2 a small
control box
that you use
to move the
cursor on a
computer
screen.

**harvest
mouse**

mousse *(rhymes with goose) (n)*
1 a light, chilled food made with
beaten egg whites. *Chocolate mousse.*
2 a substance that you
use to style your hair.

moustache *(n)*
the hair on a man's top lip.

mousy *or* **mousey** *(adj)*
1 Mousy hair is light brown.
2 quiet and shy. **mousily** *(adv)*.

mouth mouthing mouthed
1 *(n)* the part of your face that
you use for eating and talking.
2 *(n)* the entrance to a cave or river.
3 *(v)* If you **mouth** words, you move
your lips but do not make any sound.

mouth organ *(n)*
a small musical instrument that you
play by blowing out and drawing
in your breath. *See* **harmonica**.

move moving moved
1 *(v)* to change place or position.
2 *(n)* a step or a movement.
3 *(v)* to put or keep in motion.
4 *(v)* to make someone do something.
His speech moved me into action.
5 *(n)* an action planned to bring
about a result. *What's our next move?*
6 *(v)* If you are **moved** by something,
such as a film or song, it makes you
feel emotional. **moving** *(adj)*.

movement *(n)*
1 a change from one place
or position to another.
2 a group of people who have
joined together to support a
cause. *The peace movement.*
3 one of the main parts of
a long piece of classical music.

movie *(n) (informal)* a film.

mow mowing mowed mown *(v)*
to cut grass, corn, etc. **mower** *(n)*.

MP *(n)* someone elected by the
people of a constituency to represent
them in Parliament. The initials MP
stand for Member of Parliament.

mph
The initials **mph** stand for miles per
hour. *This car's top speed is 130mph.*

Mr *(miss-ter) (n)* a title put in front
of a man's name. *Mr Roland Brown.*

Mrs *(miss-iz) (n)*
a title put in front of a married
woman's name. *Mrs Justina White.*

Ms *(miz) (n)* a title put in front of
a woman's name which does not
indicate whether she is married
or unmarried. *Ms Julie Black.*

much
1 *(adv)* greatly. *Much to my surprise,
Ralph turned up for work.* **much** *(adj)*.
2 *(n)* a large amount of something.

muck mucking mucked
1 *(n)* dirt or mess. **mucky** *(adj)*.
2 **muck out** *(v)* to clean
out an animal's home.
3 **muck about** *(v) (slang)*
to act in a silly way.
4 **muck up** *(v) (slang)* to spoil
something, or to make a mess of it.

mucus *(myoo-kuss) (n)*
a slimy substance made in some
parts of your body, such as your
nose. **mucous** *(myoo-kuss) (adj)*.

mud *(n)* earth that is wet and
sticky. **muddy** *(v)*, **muddy** *(adj)*.

muddle muddling muddled
1 *(v)* to mix things up or to
confuse them. **muddled** *(adj)*.
2 *(n)* a mess or confusion.

muesli *(myooz-lee) (n)*
a breakfast cereal made from
grain, dried fruit, and nuts.

muffin *(n)*
1 a round, flat bun,
usually eaten toasted.
2 a round, sweet cake.

muffle muffling muffled *(v)*
to make a sound quieter or duller.
*Cassie put her hand over her
mouth to muffle her laughter.*

mug mugging mugged
1 *(n)* a large cup with a handle.
Mugs often have straight sides.
2 *(v) (informal)* to attack someone and
try to steal their money. **mugger** *(n)*.

muggy muggier muggiest *(adj)*
If the weather is **muggy**, it is
warm and damp. **mugginess** *(n)*.

Muhammad *see* **Mohammed**.

mule *(n)*
an animal produced by mating a
female horse with a male donkey.

multicultural *(adj)* involving or
made up of people from different
races or religions. *A multicultural
community.* **multiculturally** *(adv)*.

multilingual *(adj)* using several
different languages. *A multilingual
guidebook.* **multilingually** *(adv)*.

multimedia *(adj)* combining
different media, such as sound,
pictures, and text. *A multimedia
presentation.* **multimedia** *(n)*.

multiple
1 *(adj)* made up of many
parts or things. *Theresa
suffered multiple injuries.*
2 *(n)* a number into which a smaller
number can go an exact number of
times. *10 and 15 are multiples of 5.*
3 *(adj)* If something is **multiple-
choice**, it gives a number of answers,
from which you have to choose one.

a b c d e f g h i j k l **m** n o p q r s t u v w x y z

multiple sclerosis

multiple sclerosis (n)
a serious disease which causes loss
of feeling in parts of the body.

multiply multiplies
multiplying multiplied (v)
1 to grow in number or amount.
The weeds keep multiplying.
2 to add the same number to itself
several times. *If you multiply 3 by 4,
you get 12.* multiplication (n).

multiracial (adj)
involving people of different races. *A
multiracial school.* multiracially (adv).

multistorey (adj) A multistorey
building has several floors.

multitude (n)
1 a crowd of people.
2 a large number of things. *The
new club offers a multitude of
activities.* multitudinous (adj).

mum (n)
an informal name for your mother.

mummy mummies (n)
1 an informal name
for your mother.
2 a dead body that has been
preserved with special salts and resins
and wrapped in cloth so that it will
last for a very long time. The Ancient
Egyptians placed the mummies of
their rulers in elaborate coffins. *The
picture below shows Tutankhamun's
mummy and the three coffins that
surrounded it. The large picture shows
the second coffin in more detail.*
mummify (v), mummified (adj).

mumps (n)
an infectious illness that makes
the glands in your neck swell up.

munch munches munching
munched (v) to chew or crunch food.

mundane (adj) boring and ordinary.

mural (n) a wall painting.

murder murdering murdered (v)
to intentionally kill someone.
murder (n), murderer (n).

murky murkier murkiest (adj)
dark, dirty, and gloomy.

murmur murmuring murmured (v)
1 to talk very quietly. murmur (n).
2 to make a quiet, low, continuous
sound. *The wind murmured
in the trees.* murmur (n).

muscle (n)
1 one of the parts of your body that
causes movement. Your muscles are
attached to your skeleton and
pull on your
bones to make
them move.
*The diagram
shows the
muscles that
move your arm.*
2 strength
or power.
*This job
needs
muscle.*

**upper arm
muscles**
biceps
(contract to
bend arm)
tendons
(attach
muscle to
bone)
triceps
(contract to
straighten arm)

museum (n)
a place where interesting objects
are displayed for people to look at.

mushroom
mushrooming mushroomed
1 (n) a type of plant that has
no leaves, flowers, or roots.
Many mushrooms can be eaten.
2 (v) to grow quickly or to spread.
*New housing estates have
mushroomed around the village.*

music (n)
1 a pleasant arrangement of sounds,
played on instruments or sung.
2 printed or written signs or notes
that represent musical sounds.
Can you read music? See **notation**.

musical
1 (adj) If you are **musical**, you are very
interested in music, or you can play
an instrument well. musically (adv).
2 (adj) to do with music.
Musical instruments. musically (adv).
3 (n) a play or film which
includes singing and dancing.

musical instrument (n)
an instrument on which you can
play music. See **brass**, **instrument**,
percussion, **strings**, **woodwind**.

musician (n) someone who
plays or composes music.

musk (n)
a strong scent used in perfume.

musket (n)
an old-fashioned gun. musketeer (n).

Muslim or **Moslem** (n)
someone who follows the
religion of Islam. **Muslim** (adj).

mussel (n) a type of shellfish
that you can eat. Mussels have
hinged shells and soft,
orangey-coloured
bodies. *In order
to feed, mussels
pump seawater
through their
bodies.*

mussel
shell
or valve
hinge
water
passed
out here
water
drawn in here

must
1 (v) to
have to do
something.
I must go before the rain starts.
2 (v) to be definitely doing
something. *He must be lying.*
3 (n) something that you
need. *This book is a must.*

mustard (n)
a hot and spicy food flavouring,
usually eaten with meat.

muster mustering mustered (v)
1 to assemble in a group. *The
passengers mustered on deck.*
2 to gather something together.
*Fatima mustered all her
strength for the final lap.*

**mummy and coffins of
Tutankhamun**

cobra goddess
vulture
goddess
gold inlaid with
coloured glass
striped
royal
headdress
flail
crook
outer coffin
(wood covered
with plaster
and gold foil)
second coffin
(wood covered
with plaster
and gold foil)
third coffin
(solid gold)
mummy
with solid
gold portrait
mask
layers of
linen sheet
soaked in
preserving
resins
coffin bases

naughty

musty mustier mustiest *(adj)*
If something or somewhere
is **musty**, it smells of damp
and mould. **mustiness** *(n)*.

mutant *(n)* a living thing that has
developed different characteristics
because of a change in its parents'
genes. **mutation** *(n)*, **mutate** *(v)*.

mute
1 *(adj)* silent or unable
to speak. **mutely** *(adv)*.
2 *(n)* someone who cannot speak.
3 *(n)* something that can be
fitted to a musical instrument
to make it play less loudly.

mutilate *(myoo-til-ate)*
mutilating mutilated *(v)*
to injure or damage someone
or something. **mutilation** *(n)*.

mutiny mutinies *(n)* a revolt
against someone in charge, especially
in the army or navy. **mutineer** *(n)*,
mutiny *(v)*, **mutinous** *(adj)*.

mutter muttering muttered *(v)*
to say something quietly so that
people cannot hear you properly.

mutton *(n)* meat from a sheep.

mutual *(adj)* shared or joint.
A mutual friend. **mutually** *(adv)*.

muzzle *(n)*
1 an animal's nose and
mouth. *See* **dog, reindeer**.
2 a cover for an animal's mouth
which stops it biting. **muzzle** *(v)*.
3 the open end of a gun's
barrel. *See* **blunderbuss**.

myriad *(mir-ee-ad) (n)* a large
number. *As we entered the hall, we
were dazzled by a myriad of lights.*

myself *(pronoun)* me and
nobody else. *I have hurt myself.*

mysterious *(adj)*
puzzling and intriguing. *A mysterious
stranger.* **mysteriously** *(adv)*.

mystery mysteries *(n)*
1 something that is puzzling
or hard to understand.
2 a story containing a puzzle which
has to be solved. *A murder mystery.*

mystify mystifies mystifying
mystified *(v)* to puzzle or confuse
someone. **mystification** *(n)*.

myth *(n)*
1 an old story or legend, especially
one about gods and heroes.
mythology *(n)*, **mythical** *(adj)*.
2 a false idea that many
people believe.

mythology mythologies *(n)*
a set of stories that have been made
up about subjects such as ancient
gods and heroes. **mythological** *(adj)*.

Nn

nag nagging nagged *(v)*
to try to persuade someone
to do something by speaking
about it constantly. **nag** *(n)*.

nail
1 *(n)* the hard covering at the
end of your fingers and toes.
2 *(n)* a small piece of pointed metal
that you hammer into something.
3 *(v)* If you **nail** things together,
you attach them together with nails.

naïve *(ny-eve) (adj)* If you are **naïve**,
you are not very experienced, and
may believe or trust people too
much. **naïvety** *(n)*, **naïvely** *(adv)*.

naked *(adj)* bare or uncovered.
nakedness *(n)*, **nakedly** *(adv)*.

name *(n)*
1 what a person or a thing is called.
What is your name? **name** *(v)*.
2 a reputation. *Wesley made
his name as a singer.*

nanny nannies
1 *(n)* someone trained to look after
young children in their home.
2 *(n)* an informal name
for your grandmother.
3 **nanny goat** *(n)* a female goat.

nap napping napped *(v)*
to sleep for a short time. **nap** *(n)*.

nape *(n)* the back of your neck.

napkin *(n)* a square piece of
cloth or paper that you use to
protect your clothes at mealtimes.

nappy nappies *(n)*
paper tissue, padding or cloth
put around a baby's bottom.

narcotic *(n)* a drug which makes
you sleepy or unable to feel pain.

narrate narrating narrated *(v)*
to tell a story. **narration** *(n)*,
narrator *(n)*.

narrative
1 *(n)* a story, or an account of
something that has happened.
2 *(adj)* telling a story. *Narrative verse.*

narrow narrower narrowest
1 *(adj)* thin or not wide. **narrowness**
(n), **narrow** *(v)*, **narrowly** *(adv)*.
2 *(adj)* If you have a **narrow**
escape, you only just get away.
narrowly *(adv)*.
3 *(adj)* If you are **narrow-minded**,
you stick to your own ideas and
do not want to listen to new ones.

narrow boat *(n)* a canal boat.

nasal *(adj)* to do with your nose.

nasty nastier nastiest *(adj)*
1 disgusting or unpleasant.
A nasty taste.
2 cruel or unkind. **nastily** *(adv)*.

nation *(n)*
a large group of people who live in
the same part of the world and often
share the same language, customs,
etc. **national** *(adj)*, **nationally** *(adv)*.

nationalist *(n)*
someone who is proud of their country,
or who fights for its independence.
nationalism *(n)*, **nationalistic** *(adj)*.

nationality nationalities *(n)*
Your **nationality** is the nation
or country to which you belong.
Scott has American nationality.

nationalize *or* **nationalise**
nationalizing nationalized *(v)*
If an industry is **nationalized**,
its ownership is transferred
from a private company to the
government. **nationalization** *(n)*.

native
1 *(n)* someone born in a
particular place. *Craig is a
native of Australia.* **native** *(adj)*.
2 **native country** *(n)* the country
where you were born.

Nativity
1 *(n)* the birth of Jesus Christ.
2 **nativity play** *(n)* a play telling
the story of the birth of Jesus Christ.

NATO *(n)*
a group of countries, including Britain
and the USA, which help each other
to defend themselves. NATO stands
for North Atlantic Treaty Organization.

natural *(adj)*
1 found in nature or to do
with nature. **naturally** *(adv)*.
2 normal or usual. *It's only
natural to need a rest after
a long run.* **naturally** *(adv)*.
3 In music, a **natural** note is one
that is not sharp or flat. The natural
notes on a piano are the white ones.
4 In a musical score, a **natural**
sign shows that the next note
is natural. *See* **notation**.

natural history *(n)*
the study of animals and plants.

naturalist *(n)* someone who
studies animals and plants.

nature *(n)*
1 everything in the world that is
not made by people, such as
plants, animals, the weather, etc.
2 Your **nature** is your character.

naughty naughtier naughtiest
(adj) badly-behaved or disobedient.
naughtiness *(n)*, **naughtily** *(adv)*.

Some words that begin with a "na" sound are spelt "kna" or "gna".

nausea

nausea *(nor-zee-uh) (n)*
a feeling of sickness. **nauseous** *(adj)*.

nautical
1 *(adj)* to do with ships and sailing.
2 **nautical mile** *(n)* a unit for measuring distance at sea.
1 nautical mile = 1853m.

naval *(adj)*
to do with a navy or warships.

navel *(n)*
the small, round hollow in your stomach, where your umbilical cord was attached when you were born.

navigate navigating navigated *(v)*
to travel in a vehicle, using maps, satellites, compasses, etc. to guide you. *The sextant was used to navigate at sea in the 18th and 19th centuries. It helped the navigator to work out his position on a map by measuring the angle between the sun and the horizon, or the angle between stars.* **navigation** *(n)*, **navigator** *(n)*.

sextant

dark glass lens
mirror
telescope
index bar (movable arm)
viewing window
handle
horizon and sun viewing window
vernier scale
magnifying glass

navy navies *(n)*
1 the ships and sailors that defend a country at sea.
2 a very dark blue colour. **navy** *(adj)*.

nb
the initials of the Latin phrase *nota bene*, which means "note well". The initials nb are used to make people take notice of something important.

near nearing neared
1 *(prep)* close to. *Alec lives near me.* **nearness** *(n)*, **near** *(adj)*, **near** *(adv)*.
2 *(v)* to come closer to something. *The train neared the station.*

nearby *(adj)*
near or close by. *The nearby shops sell most basic items.* **nearby** *(adv)*.

nearly *(adv)*
almost or not quite. *Are we nearly there yet?*

neat neater neatest *(adj)*
1 tidy and orderly. *A neat bedroom.* **neatness** *(n)*, **neatly** *(adv)*.
2 *(adj)* simple and pleasing. *A neat solution.* **neatly** *(adv)*.
3 *(adj)* A **neat** drink is not mixed with anything else.

necessary *(adj)* If something is **necessary**, you have to do it or have it. **necessity** *(n)*, **necessarily** *(adv)*.

neck *(n)*
1 the part of your body that joins your head to your shoulders.
2 a narrow part of something. *The neck of the bottle.*

necklace *(n)* a piece of jewellery worn around your neck.

nectar *(n)*
a sweet liquid that bees collect from flowers and turn into honey.

need needing needed
1 *(v)* to want something urgently. *The refugees need food and shelter.*
2 *(n)* something that you have to have. *I have few needs.*
3 *(v)* to have to do something. *I need to practise for the concert tomorrow.*

needle needling needled
1 *(n)* a thin, pointed piece of metal, with a hole for thread at one end, used for sewing.
2 *(n)* a long, thin, pointed rod, used for knitting.
3 *(n)* a thin, hollow tube with a sharp end that doctors and nurses use for giving injections or taking blood.
4 *(n)* a pointer on an instrument such as a compass. *See* **compass**.
5 *(v)* *(informal)* If someone **needles** you, they annoy you.

needless *(adj)*
If something is **needless**, it is not necessary. **needlessly** *(adv)*.

negative
1 *(adj)* giving the answer "no". *I asked James if he wanted to come, but his reply was negative.*
2 *(adj)* If someone is **negative**, they are against lots of things and are unhelpful. **negatively** *(adv)*.
3 *(n)* exposed film from an old-fashioned camera that shows light areas as dark and dark areas as light.
4 *(adj)* A **negative** number is less than zero.

neglect neglecting neglected
1 *(v)* to fail to look after someone or something. **neglectful** *(adj)*.
2 *(n)* If a person, building, etc. is suffering from **neglect**, they have not been looked after properly.

negotiate
negotiating negotiated *(v)*
to bargain or discuss something, so that you can come to an agreement. **negotiation** *(n)*, **negotiator** *(n)*.

neigh *(nay)* neighing neighed *(v)*
to make the sound that a horse makes. **neigh** *(n)*.

neighbour *(n)* someone who lives next door to you or near to you.

neighbourhood *(n)*
Your **neighbourhood** is the local area around your house.

neither *(adj)*
none of two. *Neither of my brothers likes custard.* **neither** *(pronoun)*.

neon *(n)* a gas which glows when an electric current is passed through it. Neon is used in lights and signs.

nephew *(n)*
Someone's **nephew** is their brother's or sister's son.

nerve
1 *(n)* Your **nerves** are the thin fibres that send messages between your brain and other parts of your body, so that you can move and feel.
2 *(n)* courage and calmness. *You need lots of nerve to be a lion tamer.*
3 *(n)* *(informal)* rudeness or cheek. *Brandon's got some nerve, answering back like that!*
4 *(informal)* If someone **gets on your nerves**, they annoy you.
5 *(plural n)* *(informal)* If someone suffers from **nerves**, they are easily worried or frightened.

nervous
1 *(adj)* easily upset or frightened. **nervousness** *(n)*, **nervously** *(adv)*.
2 *(adj)* to do with the nerves. *The human nervous system.*
3 *(n)* If someone has a **nervous breakdown**, they become very depressed and feel that they cannot cope with their problems.

nest nesting nested
1 *(n)* a place built by birds and many other animals to lay their eggs and bring up their young. *Wasps' nests are built by a queen wasp from chewed-up wood mixed with saliva. The queen lays her eggs in the cells and the eggs develop into worker wasps that enlarge and strengthen the nest.*
2 *(v)* to make a nest or home.

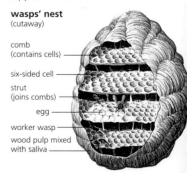

wasps' nest
(cutaway)

comb (contains cells)
six-sided cell
strut (joins combs)
egg
worker wasp
wood pulp mixed with saliva

Some words that begin with a "n" sound are spelt "kn" or "gn".

nomad

nestle nestling nestled (v) to settle into a comfortable position.

net (n)
1 material made from fine threads or ropes that are knotted together with holes between them.
2 a bag made from net material and attached to a pole, that you use to catch fish, butterflies, etc.
3 A **net amount** of money is the amount left after everything necessary, such as tax, has been taken away.
4 The **net weight** of something is its weight without packaging.
5 **the net** short for the internet.

netball (n) a game played by two teams, in which goals are scored by throwing a ball through a high net.

nettle (n) a weed that stings you if you touch it.

network (n)
1 a large number of lines, forming a criss-cross pattern.
2 a system of things that are connected to each other. *A computer network.* network (v).
3 a group of people who exchange professional or social information with each other. **networking** (n).
4 **social network** a website where people can share information, pictures, etc. about themselves.

neurotic (adj) If someone is neurotic, they are very scared or worried, usually about something imaginary. **neurotically** (adv).

neuter neutering neutered
1 (adj) neither masculine nor feminine.
2 (adj) In some languages, such as German, nouns that are neither masculine nor feminine are neuter.
3 (v) If you neuter an animal, you remove its sex organs so that it cannot reproduce. **neutered** (adj).

neutral
1 (adj) If a country or a person is neutral in a war or an argument, they do not support either side. **neutrality** (n), **neutrally** (adv).
2 When a car is in neutral, the gears are not transmitting any power.
3 (adj) Neutral colours are pale and not bright. *Beige is a neutral colour.*
4 (adj) In chemistry, a neutral substance, such as water, is neither an acid nor an alkali.

neutralize or **neutralise**
neutralizing neutralized (v) to stop something from working or from having an effect. *The medicine quickly neutralized the poison.*

neutron (n) one of the extremely small parts of an atom that has no electrical charge. See **atom**.

never (adv) at no time or not ever.

nevertheless (adv) in spite of that, or yet. *Tabitha was cold and hungry. Nevertheless, she kept on walking.*

new newer newest (adj)
1 just made or just begun.
2 different or strange. *New ideas.*
3 **new age** to do with spiritual and mystical ideas and beliefs.

news (singular n) fresh or recent information or facts.

newsagent (n) a person or shop that sells newspapers, magazines, etc.

newspaper (n) several sheets of folded paper containing news reports, articles, letters, etc. Newspapers are usually published daily.

newt (n) a small creature with short legs and a long tail that lives on land but lays its eggs in water.

marbled newt

New Testament (n) the last twenty-seven books of the Christian Bible.

newton (n) a unit for measuring force.

next (adj)
1 immediately following. *We'll catch the next train.* next (adv).
2 beside. *Stand next to me.* next (adv).
3 **next door** in or at the nearest house, building, room, etc.

nib (n) the part of a pen through which ink flows. See **quill**.

nibble nibbling nibbled (v) to bite something gently, or to take small bites of something. **nibble** (n).

nice nicer nicest (adj) pleasant or good. **nicely** (adv).

niche (neesh) (n)
1 a hollow place in a wall.
2 the environment to which an animal or a plant has adapted, or to which it belongs.

nickname (n) a name that you give to a friend. **nickname** (v).

nicotine (n) a poisonous and addictive substance found in tobacco.

niece (n) Someone's niece is their brother's or sister's daughter.

night (n) the time between sunset and sunrise, when it is dark.

nightdress or **nightie** (n) a loose dress that girls or women wear in bed.

nightingale (n) a small songbird.

nightly (adv) happening every night. *The doctor visits nightly.* nightly (adj).

nightmare (n) a frightening or unpleasant dream or situation.

nil (n) nothing or zero.

nimble nimbler nimblest (adj) quick and light. **nimbly** (adv).

nip nipping nipped (v) to pinch someone sharply. **nip** (n).

nipple (n) one of the two small, raised parts on a person's chest.

nitrogen (n) a colourless gas which makes up the majority of the Earth's air.

nits (plural n) eggs laid by lice.

no
1 (interject) a word used to refuse something. *"No, I won't!"*
2 (adj) not any. *There was no hope.*

no. short for **number**.

noble nobler noblest (adj)
1 A noble family is aristocratic and of high rank. **nobility** (n), **nobleman** (n), **noblewoman** (n).
2 good and unselfish. **nobility** (n), **nobly** (adv).

nobody nobodies
1 (pronoun) not a single person. *There was nobody there.*
2 (n) If a person is described as a nobody, they are not considered to be important.

nocturnal (adj)
1 to do with the night, or happening at night. *A nocturnal journey.* nocturnally (adv).
2 A nocturnal animal is active at night. *Badgers and owls are nocturnal animals.*

nod nodding nodded (v)
1 to move your head up and down, especially to say yes. nod (n).
2 If you nod off, you fall asleep.

noise (n) a sound, especially a loud or unpleasant one. **noisiness** (n).

noisy noisier noisiest (adj) loud. **noisily** (adv).

nomad (n) a member of a tribe that moves from place to place. *The picture shows the camp of some Bedouin nomads.* nomadic (adj).

nomads

Some words that begin with a "n" sound are spelt "kn", "gn", or "pn".
Some words that begin with a "ni" sound are spelt "ny".

a b c d e f g h i j k l m **n** o p q r s t u v w x y z

nominate nominating nominated
(v) to suggest that someone would
be the right person to do a job or win
a prize. *I nominate Gordon as our
team leader.* **nomination** *(n)*.

none *(pronoun)*
not one or not any. **none** *(adv)*.

nonetheless *(adv)* in spite of that.
*Hayley fell off her horse three times.
Nonetheless, she completed the
course.* **nonetheless** *(conj)*.

nonfiction *(n)* writing that gives
information about real things,
people, and events, rather than
made-up stories. **nonfiction** *(adj)*.

nonsense *(n)* If something is
nonsense, it is silly or has no
meaning. **nonsensical** *(adj)*.

nonstop *(adj)* without any
stops or breaks. *A nonstop flight
to Los Angeles.* **nonstop** *(adv)*.

noodles *(plural n)*
very thin pasta in long pieces that can
be put in soups, Chinese dishes, etc.

noon *(n)* twelve o'clock
in the middle of the day.

no one or **no-one** *(pronoun)*
not a single person. *There
was no one in the park.*

noose *(n)* a large loop at the
end of a piece of rope, which
closes up as the rope is pulled.

normal *(adj)* usual and ordinary.
normality *(n)*, **normally** *(adv)*.

north
1 *(n)* one of the four main points of
the compass, the direction on your
right when you face the setting sun in
the northern hemisphere. **north** *(adj)*,
northern *(adj)*, **north** *(adv)*.
2 *(adj)* A **north** wind blows
from the north. **northerly** *(adv)*.
3 **North Pole** *(n)* the very cold
part of the Earth in the far north.

nose nosing nosed
1 *(n)* the part of your face that you
use when you smell and breathe.
2 *(n)* the pointed part at the front
of some aircraft. *See* **aircraft**.
3 *(v)* If a ship, car, etc. **noses**
forwards, it moves very slowly.

nostalgic *(adj)* People who are
nostalgic like to think about the
past and are sad because things have
changed since then. **nostalgia** *(n)*.

nostril *(n)* Your **nostrils** are the
two holes in your nose through
which you breathe and smell.

nosy nosier nosiest *(adj)* *(informal)*
Someone who is **nosy** is too
interested in things that do
not concern them. **nosily** *(adv)*.

notation *(n)*
a series of signs or symbols used to
represent elements in a system, such
as music or maths. *An example of
music notation is shown below.*

music notation
flat sign
treble clef
semibreve (four crotchet beats)
dotted minim (three crotchet beats)
quaver (half a crotchet beat)
grace note (short, decorative note)
slur (links notes smoothly)
minim rest
minim (two crotchet beats)
quaver rest
semi-quaver (half a quaver beat)
sharp sign
natural sign (cancels flat sign)
semibreve rest
time signature
key signature
crotchet (one beat)
crotchet rest
chord (three or more notes played together)
tie (joins two notes to make one longer note)
bass clef
bar line
ledger line
repeat sign
double bar line

note noting noted
1 *(n)* a short letter or message.
2 *(n)* a piece of paper money.
3 *(n)* a musical sound or the symbol
that represents it. *See* **notation**.
4 *(v)* to notice a fact and pay attention
to it. *Please note the price increase.*
5 *(v)* to write something down.
I've noted your name in my book.

notebook *(n)*
1 a small pad or book of paper,
used for writing notes.
2 a small, portable computer.

nothing *(pronoun)*
1 not anything at all. *There
was nothing in the cupboard.*
2 not anything important.
I did nothing all weekend.

notice noticing noticed
1 *(v)* to see or become aware of
something. *Did you notice the smell?*
noticeable *(adj)*, **noticeably** *(adv)*.
2 *(n)* a written message put in a public
place to tell people about something.
3 If someone **hands in their
notice**, they tell their employer
that they will be leaving their job.

notify notifies notifying notified
(v) to tell someone about something
officially or formally. **notification** *(n)*.

notorious *(adj)* If someone or
something is **notorious**, they are
well known for something bad.
The school is notorious for bullying.

nought *(rhymes with sort)* *(n)*
the number 0, or zero.

noun *(n)*
a word that refers to a person, place,
or thing. *"Dog", "happiness", and
"France" are all nouns. See* page 3.

nourish *(nuh-rish)* nourishes
nourishing nourished *(v)* to give
a person, animal, or plant enough
food to keep them strong and healthy.
nourishment *(n)*, **nourishing** *(adj)*.

novel
1 *(n)* a book that tells
a story. **novelist** *(n)*.
2 *(adj)* new and interesting.
A novel idea.

novelty novelties *(n)*
something new, interesting,
and unusual. **novelty** *(adj)*.

novice *(n)* a beginner or someone
who is not very experienced.

nowhere *(adv)* not any place.
There was nowhere to hide.

nuclear *(new-klee-ur)*
1 *(adj)* to do with the splitting
of atoms. *Nuclear physics.*
2 **nuclear power** *(n)* energy
released by the splitting of atoms.
3 **nuclear weapon** *(n)*
a weapon which uses the energy
released by splitting atoms.
4 **nuclear reactor** *(n)*
a large machine that produces
nuclear power in a power station.

nucleus nuclei *(n)*
1 the central part of an atom,
made up of neutrons and
protons. *See* **atom**.
2 the central part of a cell, that
contains the chromosomes. *See* **cell**.

nude
1 *(adj)* naked. **nudist** *(n)*, **nudity** *(n)*.
2 *(n)* a naked human figure, especially
one in a painting or sculpture.

nudge nudging nudged *(v)*
to give someone or something
a small push, often with your
elbow. **nudge** *(n)*.

nuisance *(new-sunss)* *(n)*
someone or something that annoys
you and causes problems for you.

Some words that begin with a "no" sound are spelt "kno" or "gno".

numb (num) (adj) unable to feel anything. **numbness** (n), **numb** (v).

number numbering numbered
1 (n) a word or sign used for counting and doing sums.
2 (v) to give a number to something. *Isla numbered the cards from 1 to 10.*
3 (v) to amount to a number. *The crowd numbered at least 300.*

numeral (n) a written sign that represents a number. *Roman numerals. Arabic numerals.*

numerate (adj) If you are numerate, you can understand basic arithmetic. **numeracy** (n).

numerator (n) In fractions, the numerator is the number above the line, which shows how many parts of the denominator are taken.

numerical (adj) to do with numbers. *Numerical order.* **numerically** (adv).

numerous (adj) many. *Tiffany's DVDs are too numerous to count.*

nun (n) a woman who lives in a religious community and has promised to devote her life to God.

nurse nursing nursed
1 (n) someone who looks after people who are ill, usually in a hospital.
2 (v) to look after someone who is ill.

nursery nurseries
1 (n) a room where very young children sleep and play.
2 (n) a place where babies and very young children are looked after while their parents are at work.
3 (n) a place where you can buy plants and seeds.
4 nursery rhyme (n) a short poem for very young children.
5 nursery school (n) a school for children aged three to five years old.

nut (n)
1 a fruit with a hard shell that grows on trees. **nutty** (adj).
2 a small piece of metal with a hole in the middle that screws on to a bolt and holds it in place.

nutritious (nyoo-trish-uss) (adj) Food that is nutritious contains substances that your body can use to help you stay healthy and strong. **nutrition** (n), **nutritiously** (adv).

nylon (n) a light, man-made fibre, used to make tights, fishing line, etc.

nymph (n)
1 In Ancient Greek and Roman stories, a **nymph** is a spirit of nature.
2 a young form of an insect, such as a grasshopper, which changes into an adult by repeatedly shedding its skin.

Oo

oaf (n) a clumsy and rude person.

oak (n) a large, hardwood tree that produces acorns.

OAP (n) an old person who receives a pension. The initials OAP stand for Old Age Pensioner.

oar (n)
a wooden pole with a flat blade at one end, used for rowing a boat.

oasis (oh-ay-siss) oases (n) a place in a desert where there is water, and where plants and trees grow.

oat (n) a cereal plant that is used to make porridge. *See* **grain**.

oath (n)
1 a serious, formal promise.
2 a swear word.

obedient (adj) If you are **obedient**, you do what you are told to do. **obedience** (n), **obediently** (adv).

obese (adj) very fat. **obesity** (n).

obey obeying obeyed (v) to do what someone tells you to do.

object objecting objected
1 (ob-jekt) (n) something that you can see and touch, but is not alive.
2 (ob-jekt) (n) the thing that you are trying to achieve. *The object of this game is to get the ball into the net.*
3 (ob-jekt) (n) The **object** of a verb is the noun that receives the action of the verb and usually comes after it. *In the sentence "Jemima hugged Blake", Blake is the object of the verb "to hug".*
4 (ob-jekt) (v) If you **object** to something, you dislike it or disagree with it. **objection** (n), **objector** (n).

objectionable (adj) unpleasant and likely to offend people.

objective
1 (adj) based on facts, not on feelings or opinions. *An objective report.* **objectivity** (n), **objectively** (adv).
2 (n) an aim that you are working towards. *Our objective is to produce a pollution-free car.*

obligation (n) something that it is your duty to do. *There's no obligation to stay.* **obligatory** (adj).

oblige obliging obliged (v)
1 If you are **obliged** to do something, you have to do it.
2 to do someone a favour. *We needed transport, so Mum obliged by driving us there.* **obliging** (adj), **obligingly** (adv).

obliterate obliterating obliterated (v) to destroy something completely.

oblong (n) a shape with four straight sides and four right angles, that is longer than it is wide.

obnoxious (adj) very unpleasant and annoying. **obnoxiously** (adv).

obscene obscener obscenest (adj) indecent and shocking. **obscenity** (n), **obscenely** (adv).

obscure obscuring obscured; obscurer obscurest
1 (adj) not well known. **obscurity** (n).
2 (adj) not easy to understand.
3 (v) to make it difficult to see something. *The pillar obscured our view of the stage.*

observant (adj)
If you are **observant**, you are good at noticing things. **observantly** (adv).

observatory observatories (n) a building containing telescopes and other scientific instruments for studying the sky and the stars.

observe observing observed (v)
1 to watch someone or something carefully. *The police have been observing the house all week.* **observation** (n).
2 to notice something by looking or watching. *I observed that Holly had torn her trousers.* **observation** (n).
3 to make a remark. *Warren observed that the train was late again.* **observation** (n).

obsess obsesses obsessing obsessed (v) If you are **obsessed** with something, you think about it all the time. **obsession** (n), **obsessive** (adj).

obsolete (adj)
out of date and no longer used.

obstacle (n)
something that gets in your way or prevents you from doing something.

obstinate (adj) If someone is obstinate, they are stubborn and unwilling to change their mind. **obstinacy** (n), **obstinately** (adv).

obstreperous (adj) If someone is obstreperous, they resist in a rough and noisy way. **obstreperously** (adv).

obstruct obstructing obstructed (v)
1 to block a road or path. *Fallen trees obstructed the road.* **obstruction** (n), **obstructive** (adj).
2 to prevent something from happening, or to make something difficult. *Mickey obstructed all attempts to make him tidy his room.* **obstruction** (n), **obstructive** (adj).

obtain obtaining obtained (v) to get or to be given something.

obtuse (adj)
1 If someone is **obtuse**, they are slow to understand things.
2 An **obtuse** angle is an angle of between 90° and 180°.

obvious (adj) If something is **obvious**, it is easy to see or understand. **obviously** (adv).

occasion (n)
1 a time when something happens. *Luke had been to London on several occasions.*
2 a special or important event.

occasional (adj)
happening sometimes. *Occasional visits.* **occasionally** (adv).

occupation (n)
1 a job. **occupational** (adj).
2 something that you enjoy doing in your free time. *Texting is Gabe's favourite occupation.*
3 the taking over and controlling of a country or an area by an army.

occupy occupies occupying occupied (v)
1 to live in a building, room, etc. *Who occupies this house?* **occupant** (n), **occupier** (n).
2 to keep someone busy and happy. *The boys were occupied for hours on the computer.*
3 If an army **occupies** a country or an area, it captures it and takes control of it.

occur occurring occurred (v)
1 to happen. *When did the accident occur?* **occurrence** (n).
2 If something **occurs to you**, you suddenly think of it.

ocean (oh-shun) (n)
one of the large areas of water on the Earth's surface. *This map shows the five main oceans of the world.*

o'clock (adv) a word you use when saying what the time is. O'clock is short for "of the clock". *It's 3 o'clock.*

octagon (n)
a shape with eight straight sides. **octagonal** (adj). See **shape**.

octahedron (n)
a solid shape with eight, usually triangular, faces. See **shape**.

octave (n)
the eight note gap in a musical scale between a note and the next note of the same name above or below it.

octopus octopuses (n)
a sea creature with a soft body and eight long arms that it uses for catching its prey.

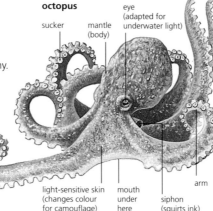

octopus
sucker — mantle (body) — eye (adapted for underwater light)
light-sensitive skin (changes colour for camouflage) — mouth under here — siphon (squirts ink) — arm

odd odder oddest (adj)
1 strange and difficult to explain or understand. **oddly** (adv).
2 An **odd** number cannot be divided exactly by two. *1, 13, 47, and 895 are all odd numbers.*
3 not matching. *Odd socks.*

odds (plural n) the probability of something happening. *The odds are that Tina will win the race.*

ode (n) a poem praising something, such as Keats' Ode to a Nightingale.

odour (oh-der) (n) a smell.

oesophagus
(uh-sof-uh-guss) oesophagi (n)
the tube in your body that carries food from your throat into your stomach. See **anatomy**, **digestion**.

off
1 (prep) away from a place. *Take your shoes off.* **off** (adv).
2 (adv) not switched on. *Someone has turned off the computer.*
3 If food has **gone off**, it has gone bad and can no longer be eaten.

offence (n)
1 a crime.
2 If you **cause offence**, you upset someone.
3 If you **take offence**, you feel upset by something that someone has done or said.

offend offending offended (v)
1 to upset someone.
2 to commit a crime. **offender** (n).

offensive
1 (adj) If someone or something is **offensive**, they are unpleasant and upset people. **offensively** (adv).
2 (n) an attack, usually a military one.
3 (adj) attacking. *The army took offensive action.*

offer offering offered (v)
1 to ask someone if they would like something. **offer** (n).
2 to say that you are willing to do something for someone. *I offered to take the message.* **offer** (n).

offering (n) something that is offered to God or to a god.

offhand (adj)
1 abrupt or casual. *An offhand remark.*
2 without preparation. *I don't know the answer offhand.*

office (n)
1 a room or building in which people work, usually sitting at desks.
2 an important, powerful position. *The office of Prime Minister.*

officer (n) someone who is in charge of other people, especially in the armed forces or the police.

official
1 (adj) approved by someone in authority. *An official inquiry.* **officially** (adv).
2 (n) someone who holds an important position in an organization. *A government official.*

off-licence (n)
In Britain, an **off-licence** is a shop which sells alcoholic drinks.

ARCTIC OCEAN
North America
Asia
Europe
Africa
ATLANTIC OCEAN
PACIFIC OCEAN
PACIFIC OCEAN
South America
INDIAN OCEAN
Australia
N W E S
SOUTHERN OCEAN
Antarctica

off-peak *(adj)*
happening when there is less activity or demand. *Off-peak travel.*

off-putting *(adj)* *(informal)*
discouraging or disturbing.

offside *(adj)*
If a player is **offside** in a game such as football, they have broken the rules of the game by moving too far forward, ahead of the ball. **offside** *(adv)*.

offspring *(plural n)* an animal's young or a human's children.

often *(adv)* many times.

ogre *(oh-ger)* *(n)*
a fierce, cruel giant in fairy stories.

oh *(interject)* a word used to express surprise, disappointment, or pain.

ohm *(rhymes with dome)* *(n)*
a unit for measuring how much resistance a substance gives to the flow of electricity through it.

oil oiling oiled
1 *(n)* a thick, smooth liquid. Different types of oil are used for heating buildings, for cooking, and for making machines run smoothly. **oily** *(adj)*.
2 *(v)* to cover something with oil. *Oil your bicycle chain regularly.*
3 **oils** *(plural n)* artists' paints containing oil. See **artist**.

oil platform *(n)*
a large platform used as a base for drilling for oil under the sea or under the ground. *The picture shows an oil platform in the North Sea.*

okay *or* **OK**
1 *(adj)* *(informal)* all right.
2 *(interject)* *(informal)* When you say **okay**, you mean that you agree.

old older oldest *(adj)*
1 Someone who is **old** has lived for a long time.
2 Something that is **old** has existed or been used for a long time.
3 from an earlier time. *A meeting of old pupils of the school.*

old age *(n)*
the time when a person is old.

old-fashioned *(adj)*
no longer fashionable or popular.

Old Testament *(n)* the first thirty-nine books of the Christian Bible.

olive *(n)*
a small black or green savoury fruit that is eaten whole or crushed for its oil.

omelette *(n)* a dish made of fried, beaten egg, often together with other ingredients such as cheese or ham.

omen *(n)*
a sign or warning about something that will happen in the future.

ominous *(adj)* If something is **ominous**, it makes you feel that something bad is going to happen. *An ominous silence.* **ominously** *(adv)*.

omit omitting omitted *(v)*
1 to leave something out. *Harry omitted a line from the song.* **omission** *(n)*.
2 If you **omit** to do something, you do not do it. *Jack omitted to eat his breakfast.* **omission** *(n)*.

omnivore *(n)* an animal that eats plants and meat. **omnivorous** *(adj)*.

once
1 *(adv)* one time. *I've only been to London once.*
2 *(adv)* in the past. *This country was once covered by ice.*
3 *(conj)* after something has happened. *I'll tell you all about it once we get home.*
4 **at once** immediately. *Come here at once!*

one-way *(adj)*
1 Traffic can only travel in one direction down a **one-way** street.
2 A **one-way** ticket allows you to travel to a place but not back again.

onion *(n)*
a round vegetable with a strong smell and taste. See **vegetable**.

online *(adj)*
1 If you are **online**, you are connected to the internet.
2 to do with the internet. *Online shopping.*

oil platform

seabed
(cross-section)

— platform
— sea
— seabed

— drill pipe

— oil pocket

derrick
(drilling tower)

monkey board
(for drilling crew)

crew's living quarters

helideck

satellite communication equipment

pipe rack   casing for drilled well

control centre

loading crane   storage area

drilling deck

flare
(burns excess gas)

flare stack

mezzanine deck

production deck

flare knock-out drum
(removes liquids from flare gas)

cellar deck

air intake tube for turbines

oil cooler

lifeboat

crane pedestal and diesel storage

steel girder

drill pipe

support leg in steel jacket

only
1 *(adv)* not more than, or just. *There were only three people in the shop.*
2 *(adj)* with nothing or no one else. *Maria was the only person there.*
3 *(conj)* but. *We would have got here earlier, only the car broke down.*
4 *(n)* An **only child** has no brothers or sisters.

onomatopoeia
(on-oh-mat-er-pee-uh) (n)
the use of a word that sounds like the thing it describes. *"Pop" and "sizzle" are examples of onomatopoeia.* **onomatopoeiac** *(adj).*

onward or **onwards** *(adv)* forward. *We've lived there from 2011 onward.*

ooze oozing oozed *(v)* to flow out slowly. *Mud oozed from my shoes.*

opaque *(oh-pake) (adj)* not clear enough to see through. *The water in the stream was muddy and opaque.*

open opening opened
1 *(adj)* not shut. **open** *(v).*
2 *(adj)* not covered or not enclosed. *Open land. Open air.*
3 *(adj)* If you are **open** about something, you are honest about it. **openness** *(n),* **openly** *(adv).*
4 *(v)* to start or to begin. *The story opens in a wild wood.*
5 *(n)* If you have an **open mind**, you are able to accept new ideas.

opening
1 *(n)* a hole or a space in something. *A small opening in the hedge.*
2 *(adj)* coming at the beginning. *The opening lines of a play.* **opening** *(n).*
3 *(n)* a chance. *This part could give you an opening into show business.*

opera *(n)* a play in which the words are sung. **operatic** *(adj).*

operate operating operated *(v)*
1 to make something work. *Damian soon learnt how to operate the machine.*
2 to cut open someone's body in order to repair a damaged part or to remove a diseased part.
3 to work. *Thieves operate in this area. I can't be expected to operate under these conditions!*

operation
1 *(n)* an event that has been carefully planned and involves a lot of people. *A massive security operation.*
2 *(n)* the cutting open of someone's body in order to repair a damaged part or to remove a diseased part.
3 If something is **in operation**, it is working.

operator *(n)*
someone who works a machine.

opinion
1 *(n)* the ideas and beliefs that you have about something. *What's your opinion of our new teacher?*
2 **opinion poll** *(n)* a way of finding out what people in general think about something, by questioning a selection of people.

opponent *(n)* someone who is against you in a fight or a game.

opportunity opportunities *(n)* a chance to do something. *Carol's job gives her the opportunity to travel.*

oppose opposing opposed *(v)* to be against something and try to prevent it from happening.

opposite
1 *(prep)* If something is **opposite** you, it is facing you. **opposite** *(adj).*
2 *(adj)* completely different. *Sue ran in the opposite direction.* **opposite** *(n).*

opposition *(n)*
1 When there is **opposition** to something, people are against it. *There was a lot of opposition to the plans for a new supermarket.*
2 the person or team that you play against in a match or competition.
3 the **Opposition** the main political party that is not in power.

oppress oppresses oppressing oppressed *(v)*
1 to treat people in a cruel, unjust, and hard way. **oppression** *(n),* **oppressor** *(n),* **oppressive** *(adj).*
2 If something **oppresses** you, it makes you feel worried or weighed down. **oppressive** *(adj).*

opt opting opted *(v)*
1 to choose to have or do something. *Lindsey opted to learn German.*
2 **opt out** to choose not to take part in something.

symphony orchestra

optical
1 *(adj)* to do with eyes or eyesight.
2 **optical illusion** *(n)* something that you think you see which is not really there.

optician *(op-tish-un) (n)* someone who tests your eyesight and supplies glasses and contact lenses.

optimistic *(adj)* People who are optimistic always believe that things will turn out well and successfully. **optimism** *(n),* **optimist** *(n).*

option *(n)* something that you can choose to do.

optional *(adj)* If something is **optional**, you can choose whether or not to have it or do it.

oral
1 *(adj)* to do with your mouth. *Oral hygiene.* **orally** *(adv).*
2 *(n)* a spoken exam or test. *A French oral.*
3 *(adj)* to do with speaking. **orally** *(adv).*

orange *(n)*
1 a mixture of red and yellow, or the colour of most carrots. **orange** *(adj).*
2 a round fruit with a thick, orange skin and sweet, juicy flesh. *See* **fruit.**

orbit orbiting orbited
1 *(n)* the invisible path followed by an object circling a planet or the sun. **orbital** *(adj).*
2 *(v)* to travel around a planet or the sun.

orchard *(n)* an area of land where fruit trees are grown.

orchestra *(n)*
a large group of musicians who play their instruments together. *The diagram below shows the positions of the main instruments in a symphony orchestra, which usually plays classical music.*

orchid (or-kid) (n)
a plant with colourful and often unusually shaped flowers. *The Vanda tricolor orchid shown here grows in Southeast Asia.*

orchid

ordeal (n) a very difficult and testing experience.

order ordering ordered
1 (v) to tell someone that they have to do something. **order** (n).
2 (v) to ask for something in a restaurant. **order** (n).
3 (v) to ask a manufacturer, website or shop to get you something. *I've ordered a new television.*
4 (n) neatness. *Phoebe loves order.* **orderly** (adv).
5 (n) good behaviour. *Can we have some order in this classroom?*
6 If you put things **in order**, you arrange them so that each thing is in the right place.
7 If an object is **out of order**, it is broken and does not work.
8 (informal) If a person is **out of order**, they are behaving badly.

ordinary (adj)
normal or usual. **ordinarily** (adv).

ore (n)
a rock which contains metal. *Iron ore.*

organ (n)
1 a large musical instrument with one or more keyboards and pipes of different lengths. **organist** (n).
2 a part of the body that does a particular job. *The diagram shows the main human organs used for breathing, and for digesting and excreting food. The kidneys are shown separately because they are positioned behind the intestines.*

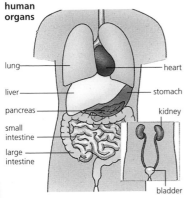

human organs

lung
heart
liver
stomach
pancreas
kidney
small intestine
large intestine
bladder

organic (adj)
1 using only natural products and no chemicals, pesticides, etc. *Organic farming.* **organically** (adv).

2 (adj) to do with living things and their organs.

organism (n)
a living plant or animal.

organization or **organisation** (n)
1 a large company, charity, or other group.
2 the task of planning and running something. *We left the organization of the party to Jeffrey.*

organize or **organise**
organizing organized (v)
1 to plan and run an event. **organizer** (n).
2 to arrange things neatly and in order. *Look how well Connie has organized the books on her shelves!*

orgy (or-jee) orgies (n) a wild party, with too much eating, drinking, etc.

oriental (adj)
belonging to, or coming from the countries of the Far East, especially Japan and China. **Orient** (n).

orienteering (n) a sport in which people have to find their way across rough country as fast as they can, using a map and compass.

origami (n)
the Japanese art of paper folding. *The picture shows an example of origami.*

origami bird

origin (n)
the point where something began. *What was the origin of this argument?*

original
1 (adj) first or earliest. *Who were the original settlers in Australia?* **originally** (adv).
2 (adj) new and imaginative. *What an original idea!* **originality** (n).
3 (n) a work of art that is not a copy. **original** (adj).

originate originating originated (v) to begin from somewhere or something. **origination** (n).

ornament (n) a small, attractive object that you use to decorate a room. **ornamental** (adj).

ornate (adj)
richly decorated. **ornately** (adv).

ornithology (n)
the study of birds. **ornithologist** (n).

orphan (n) a child whose parents are both dead. **orphaned** (adj).

orphanage (n) a place where orphans live and are looked after.

orthodontist (n) someone who straightens uneven teeth.

orthodox (adj)
1 Orthodox views and beliefs are ones that are accepted by most people. **orthodoxy** (n).
2 Members of a religion are described as **orthodox** if they believe in its older, more traditional teachings.

orthopaedic (or-thoh-pee-dik) (adj) to do with the branch of medicine that deals with bones.

osmosis (oz-moh-sis) (n)
the process by which a solvent passes through a membrane from a less concentrated solution to a more concentrated solution, until they reach the same level of concentration.

ostrich ostriches (n) a large African bird that cannot fly. *See* **bird**.

other
1 (adj) not the one that you have just mentioned. **other** (pronoun).
2 others (pronoun) the rest. *Where are the others?*

otherwise
1 (conj) or if not. *Catch a bus from the station. Otherwise, take a taxi.*
2 (adv) apart from that. *We didn't have very good seats, but otherwise the performance was excellent.*

otter (n) a furry mammal that lives in or near water and eats fish.

otter

ouch (owtch) (interject)
a cry of pain.

ought (ort) (v)
If you **ought** to do something, you should do it.

our (pronoun)
belonging to us.

ourselves (pronoun)
us and no one else.

oust (owst) ousting ousted (v) to force someone out of a position or job. *Hamish has been ousted as captain of the team.*

out
1 (adj) not in. *I called round but you were out.*
2 (adv) no longer burning or no longer alight. *The fire went out.*
3 (adj) no longer taking part in a game. *You will be out if you get a question wrong.*
4 (adv) aloud. *Patricia called out for help.*
5 (adj) not correct. *My calculations were wildly out.*

a b c d e f g h i j k l m n o p q r s t u v w x y z

outback (n) the remote areas of Australia, away from the cities.

outbreak (n) a sudden start of something, such as disease or war.

outburst (n) a sudden pouring out of strong emotion. *An outburst of anger.*

outcast (n) someone who is not accepted by other people.

outcome (n) the result of something. *The outcome of the vote is hard to predict.*

outcry outcries (n) If there is an outcry about something, a lot of people complain loudly about it.

outdo outdoes outdoing outdid outdone (v) If you **outdo** someone, you do something better than they do.

outdoors (adv) outside or in the open air. **outdoor** (adj).

outer
1 (adj) on the outside, or furthest from the middle. *The outer edge.*
2 **outer space** (n) space beyond the Earth's atmosphere.

outfit (n)
1 a set of clothes.
2 (informal) a group, company, or organization. *A printing outfit.*

outgoing (adj) Someone who is **outgoing** is very sociable and friendly.

outgrow outgrowing outgrew outgrown (v) to grow too big or too old for something.

outing (n) a short trip.

outlaw outlawing outlawed
1 (n) (old-fashioned) a criminal, especially in the Wild West.
2 (v) to forbid something by law.

outlay (n) money spent on something.

outlet (n)
1 a pipe or hole that lets out liquid or gas.
2 a shop where a company's products can be bought.
3 an activity that lets you express your feelings.

outline (n)
1 the line which shows the edge of something.
2 the basic points or ideas about something. *Give me an outline of the film's plot.* **outline** (v).

outlook (n)
1 your general attitude to things. *Yasmin has a very positive outlook.*
2 the way that something is likely to develop. *The weather outlook.*

outnumber
outnumbering outnumbered (v) to be larger in number than another group. *Girls outnumber boys on this course by four to one.*

outpatient (n) someone who goes to a hospital for treatment, but does not stay there.

outpost (n) a remote fort or settlement.

output (n)
1 the amount produced by a person, machine, or business.
2 information produced by a computer. **output** (v).

outrageous (adj) very shocking or offensive. **outrage** (n), **outrageously** (adv).

outright
1 (adj) total or complete. *The outright winner.*
2 (adv) instantly. *Stanley was dismissed outright for stealing.*

outset (n) the start or the beginning. *I knew from the outset that the show would be a success.*

outside
1 (adv) out of a building or in the open air. **outside** (prep).
2 (n) the surface of something or the part that surrounds the rest of it. *The outside of the box was painted pink.* **outside** (adj).
3 **outside chance** (n) a very small chance.

outskirts (plural n) the outer edges of a town or city.

outspoken (adj) If you are **outspoken**, you express your views strongly and clearly, especially when you are criticizing someone.

outstanding (adj)
1 extremely good. *An outstanding performance.*
2 not yet paid or not yet dealt with. *An outstanding bill.*

outward
1 (adj) appearing on the surface. *Philip's outward appearance was calm, but really he was very nervous.* **outwardly** (adv).
2 (adj) going away from a place. *An outward journey.*
3 **outwards** (adv) towards the outside. *Stand facing outwards.*

outwit outwitting outwitted (v) to gain an advantage over someone by being cleverer than them.

oval (n) a shape like an egg. **oval** (adj).

ovary ovaries (n) the female organ that produces eggs.

ovation (n) loud applause and cheering.

oven (n) an enclosed space where you cook food.

over
1 (prep) above or on top of something. *The shelf over the bed.*
2 (prep) across. *Robin stepped over the line.*
3 (prep) more than. *Over 12 years old.*
4 (adv) leaning or falling down. *John fell over the cat.*
5 (adj) finished. *The match was over in two hours.*
6 (adv) remaining. *I shared out the sweets, and still had three left over.*
7 If you **get over** an illness or an experience, you recover from it and are no longer ill or upset.

overall (adv) generally, or considering everything. *Overall, I think the party was a success.* **overall** (adj).

overalls (plural n) a piece of clothing worn over your clothes to protect them when you are doing a dirty job.

overarm (adv) throwing or hitting with your arm above your shoulder. *Sam served overarm.* **overarm** (adj).

overbearing (adj) very dominating or bossy.

overboard (adv) over the side of a boat. *The pirate fell overboard.*

overcast (adj) An **overcast** sky has dark clouds.

overcome overcoming overcame overcome (v)
1 to defeat or deal with something, such as a feeling or problem. *I must overcome my fear of spiders.*
2 If someone is **overcome** by smoke, emotion, guilt, etc. they are so strongly affected by it that they are made unconscious or helpless.

overdose (n) a quantity of a drug that is large enough to kill you or make you seriously ill.

overdraft (n) an amount of money that someone is able to take out of their bank when they do not have any money in their account. **overdrawn** (adj).

overdue (adj) late. *My library books are overdue.*

overflow
overflowing overflowed
1 (v) to flow over the edges of something. *The bath overflowed.*
2 (n) a pipe or hole through which water can flow out of a bath, sink, etc. when it becomes too full.

ozone

overgrown (adj) An overgrown garden is covered with weeds because it has not been looked after.

overhaul **overhauling overhauled** (v) to examine carefully all the parts of a piece of equipment and make any repairs that are needed. **overhaul** (n).

overhead
1 (adj) above your head. *Overhead lighting.* **overhead** (adv).
2 **overheads** (plural n) regular business costs, such as wages, rent, telephone bills, heating, and lighting.

overhear **overhearing overheard** (v) to hear what someone else is saying when they do not know that you are listening.

overjoyed (adj) extremely happy.

overlap **overlapping overlapped** (v) to cover part of something else. *Arrange the roof tiles so that they overlap. Our holiday dates overlap.*

overleaf (adv) on the next page.

overload **overloading overloaded** (v)
1 to give something or someone too much to carry or too much work to do. **overload** (n).
2 to send too much electricity through something so that it breaks down. **overload** (n).

overlook **overlooking overlooked** (v)
1 to fail to notice something. *Debbie overlooked the extra costs.*
2 to offer a view of something from above. *Our room overlooked the beach.*
3 to choose to ignore something wrong that someone has done. *I overlooked Jude's rude remarks.*

overly (adv) very or excessively. *Oliver is always overly cautious.*

overnight
1 (adv) during the night. *We stayed there overnight.* **overnight** (adj).
2 (adj) done or happening during the night. *An overnight train.*
3 (adv) suddenly. *Timothy's fortunes changed overnight.*

overpower **overpowering overpowered** (v)
1 to defeat someone.
2 If something **overpowers** you, it affects you very strongly. *I was overpowered by the disgusting smell.*

overrated (adj)
If something is **overrated**, it is not really as good as many people say it is.

overrule **overruling overruled** (v)
If someone in authority **overrules** a decision, they say that the decision was wrong and has to be changed.

overrun **overrunning overran overrun** (v)
1 to spread all over a place in large numbers. *The town was overrun with rats.*
2 If something **overruns**, it goes on for longer than it was meant to.

overseas (adj)
to or from other countries. *Overseas visitors.* **overseas** (adv).

oversleep **oversleeping overslept** (v) to sleep for longer than you intended.

overtake **overtaking overtook overtaken** (v) to go past another moving person or thing to get in front of it.

overthrow **overthrowing overthrew overthrown** (v) to defeat a leader or ruler and remove them from power by force. **overthrow** (n).

overtime (n) time spent working beyond normal working hours.

overture (n) a piece of music played at the start of a musical, opera, etc.

overturn **overturning overturned** (v)
1 to turn something over so that it is upside down or on its side.
2 to reverse a decision that someone else has made.

overweight (adj) too fat or heavy.

overwhelm **overwhelming overwhelmed** (v)
1 to defeat someone completely.
2 to have a very strong effect. *I was overwhelmed by the applause.* **overwhelming** (adj).

overwork **overworking overworked** (v) to work too hard.

ovulation (n) the production of eggs from the ovaries.

owe **owing owed**
1 (v) to have to pay money to someone, especially money that you have borrowed.
2 (v) to have a duty to do something for someone in return for something that they have done for you. *I owe you a favour.*
3 (v) to be grateful to someone for giving you something. *My sister owes her life to the brave firefighters.*
4 **owing to** because of. *The bus was late owing to roadworks.*

owl (n) a bird with large eyes, that hunts at night. *The tawny owl, shown below, is found throughout Europe.*

swivelling neck

tawny owl

forward-facing eyes

hooked beak

talon

own **owning owned**
1 (adj) belonging to you. *My own pen.*
2 (v) to possess or to have something. **owner** (n).
3 (v) If you **own up** to something, you confess that you have done something wrong.
4 **on your own** (adj) by yourself.

ox **oxen** (n) a large, horned mammal, often used for carrying things or for pulling carts. See **plough**.

oxygen (n) a colourless gas found in the air, that humans and animals need in order to breathe.

oxymoron (n) a short phrase in which the words seem to contradict each other, for example, "a wise fool".

oyster (n) a flat, edible shellfish that occasionally contains a pearl. See **pearl**.

ozone
1 (n) a form of oxygen that can be poisonous in large quantities.
2 **ozone layer** (n) a layer of ozone high above the Earth's surface that blocks out some of the sun's harmful rays. *In 1985, scientists discovered a hole in the ozone layer above Antarctica. Chemicals thought to have caused the hole have been banned, and the hole has begun to shrink. In this satellite picture, the ozone hole is coloured orange. Also see* **atmosphere**.

hole **ozone layer**

Antarctica

Pp

pace pacing paced
1 (n) a step or a stride.
2 (n) a rate of speed. *A rapid pace.*
3 (v) to walk backwards and forwards. *Archie paced up and down the hall.*

pacemaker (n) a machine put
into someone's body to help their heart beat more regularly.

pacifist (n)
someone who strongly believes that war and violence are wrong, and who will not fight. **pacifism** (n).

pacify pacifies
pacifying pacified (v)
If you **pacify** someone, you make them feel calmer.

pack packing packed
1 (v) to put objects into a box, case, bag, etc. **packing** (n).
2 (v) to fill a space tightly. *A vast crowd packed the stadium.*
3 (n) a collection of objects. *A pack of cards.*
4 (n) a group of wild animals. *A pack of wolves.*
5 (n) a bundle or a load.

package
1 (n) a parcel.
2 (n) a computer program that can do several related things. *A desktop publishing package.*
3 **package deal** (n) an offer which includes several things that must all be taken together.
4 **package holiday** (n) a holiday where everything is included in the price and is arranged for you.

packaging (n) the wrapping
on things that you buy.

packet (n) a small container
or package. *A packet of seeds.*

pact (n) an agreement,
often between two countries.

pad padding padded
1 (n) a wad of soft material, used to absorb liquid, give protection, etc. See **football**.
2 (v) to cover something with soft material.
3 (v) to walk around softly. *Bryan padded along the corridor.*
4 (n) sheets of paper fastened together.

padding (n)
1 stuffing.
2 extra words put into a speech or piece of writing to make it longer.

paddle paddling paddled
1 (v) to walk in shallow water.
2 (n) a short, wide oar, used to propel some boats. **paddle** (v). See **inflatable**, **kayak**.

paddle steamer (n)
a boat which is propelled by large, revolving paddle wheels that are powered by a steam engine.

paddle steamer

paddock (n) a small field
where horses can be kept.

paddy field (n)
a wet field where rice is grown.

paddy field

padlock
(n) a lock with a curved metal bar that you can fix on to things.

paediatrician
(*pee-dee-a-trish-un*) (n)
a doctor who is trained to treat children's illnesses. **paediatrics** (n).

page paging paged
1 (n) a sheet of paper in a book, newspaper, etc.
2 (n) (old-fashioned) a young boy servant.
3 (n) a boy attendant at a wedding.
4 (v) to call someone using a pager.

pageant (*paj-ent*) (n)
a public show where people walk in processions or act out historical scenes. **pageantry** (n).

pager (n) a small, electronic machine
that people such as doctors carry, so that they can be contacted easily.

pail (n) a bucket.

pain
1 (n) a feeling of physical hurt or of great unhappiness.
2 **pains** (plural n) effort or trouble.

painful (adj) If something is **painful**,
it hurts you physically or makes you very unhappy. **painfully** (adv).

painkiller (n) a pill or medicine
that you take to stop pain.

painstaking (adj) careful and
thorough. **painstakingly** (adv).

paint painting painted
1 (n) a liquid that you use to colour surfaces. See **artist**.
2 (v) to use paint to make a picture or cover a surface. **painter** (n), **painting** (n).

pair (n) two things that
match or go together. **pair** (v).

palace (n)
a large, splendid house or building. **palatial** (adj).

palate (n)
1 the roof of your mouth.
2 a person's sense of taste.

pale paler palest (adj)
light or whitish in colour. **paleness** (n).

palette (n)
1 a flat board that you use to mix paints on, with a hole for your thumb. See **artist**.
2 **palette knife** a thin, rounded, flexible knife, used for painting or cooking. See **artist**.

palindrome (n)
a word or sentence that reads the same backwards as forwards. *The names Hannah, Bob and Otto are palindromes.*

pallid (adj) If you are **pallid**,
your skin or face is pale.

palm (n)
1 the flat surface on the inside of your hand.
2 a tall, tropical tree with large leaves at the top.

palmistry (n) the practice of
telling people's fortunes from the lines on their palms. **palmist** (n).

pampas (n)
1 a huge, treeless plain in South America.
2 **pampas grass** a type of tall, feathery grass.

pamper
pampering pampered (v)
to spoil yourself or someone else with food, kindness, etc. **pampering** (n).

pamphlet (n) a small, thin booklet.

pan panning panned
1 (n) a round, metal container, used for cooking.
2 (v) to look for gold by washing earth in a pan or sieve.
3 (v) to move a camera, in order to follow an action. *The cameraman panned in on the speeding car.*

pancake (n)
a thin, flat cake, made from milk, eggs, and flour and cooked in a pan.

paraphernalia

pancreas *(n)*
a gland near your stomach which makes a fluid that helps you to digest food. *See* **digestion**, **organ**.

giant panda

panda *(n)*
a bear that lives in China. *The picture shows a giant panda eating a bamboo shoot.*

pane *(n)*
a sheet of glass in a window or door.

panel *(n)*
1 a flat piece of wood or other material. **panelling** *(n)*.
2 a board with controls or instruments on it.
3 a group of people chosen to do something, such as judge a competition. **panellist** *(n)*.

pang *(n)* a brief pain or feeling of emotion. *A pang of regret.*

panic
1 *(n)* a feeling of terror or fright. **panic** *(v)*, **panicky** *(adj)*.
2 *(adj)* If you are **panic-stricken**, you are struck with a sudden fear.

pannier *(n)*
1 a basket hung on an animal, such as a donkey.
2 a bag hung beside the rear wheel of a bicycle.

panorama *(n)*
a wide view of an area. **panoramic** *(adj)*.

pansy pansies *(n)*
a small garden flower, usually coloured purple, yellow, or white.

pant panting panted *(v)*
to breathe in a quick and laboured way because you are out of breath.

panther *(n)*
a leopard, especially the black leopard.

pantomime *(n)*
a traditional Christmas play, often based on a fairy tale or a children's story, with songs and jokes.

pantry pantries *(n)*
a small room in or near a kitchen, where food or crockery is kept.

pants *(plural n)*
underwear that covers your bottom.

paper papering papered
1 *(n)* thin material usually made from wood pulp.

2 *(n)* a newspaper.
3 *(n)* one part of an exam.
4 *(v)* to put wallpaper up or to cover something with paper.

paperback *(n)*
a book with a paper cover.

paperweight *(n)*
a heavy, often decorative object, used for holding down papers.

paperwork *(n)* writing, such as reports, that is part of someone's job.

papier mâché
(pap-ee-ay mash-ay) (n)
the art of making models, pots, etc. out of pieces of paper that have been soaked in glue.

papyrus *(pa-pye-russ)* papyri *(n)*
paper made from the papyrus plant, which grows in northern Africa and southern Europe.

parable *(n)* a fable or story that has a moral or religious lesson. *The parable of the Good Samaritan.*

parachute *(pah-ruh-shoot) (n)*
a large piece of cloth fastened to thin ropes, that is used to drop people or loads safely from aeroplanes. **parachutist** *(n)*, **parachute** *(v)*.

paradise *(n)*
a wonderful place, or heaven.

paradox paradoxes *(n)*
a statement that seems to contradict itself, but is true. **paradoxical** *(adj)*.

paraffin *(n)* a liquid that is burnt to give light or heat in a lamp or stove.

paragliding *(n)* the sport of cross-country parachuting, using a special parachute shaped like flexible wings. **paraglider** *(n)*, **paraglide** *(v)*.

paragraph *(n)*
a short passage in a piece of writing which begins on a new line.

parallel
1 *(adj)* If two lines are **parallel**, they stay the same distance from each other.
2 *(n)* If a situation has a **parallel**, there is another situation very similar to it. **parallel** *(v)*.
3 If electrical parts are connected **in parallel**, each one can receive power even when the others are not being used.

parallelogram *(n)* a flat, four-sided shape with opposite sides that are equal and parallel. *See* **shape**.

parachute
(ram-air canopy)

suspension line

cell
(holds air)

nylon canopy

steering line

nylon slider
(controls speed of parachute opening)

safety helmet

steering line control

nylon webbing harness

jump suit

goggles

pilot chute
(pulls main parachute from container)

steering line
(controls speed by altering shape of parachute)

canopy container
(hanging open)

reserve parachute in here

training parachute
(aeroconical canopy)

parade parading paraded
1 *(n)* a procession of people, decorated trucks, and musicians.
2 *(v)* If you **parade** something, you show it off.
3 *(n)* a row of shops.

paralyse paralysing paralysed *(v)*
to make someone or something lose power, feeling, or movement. **paralysis** *(n)*.

paraphernalia *(n)* numerous pieces of equipment, belongings, etc.

paraphrase

paraphrase
paraphrasing paraphrased *(v)*
If you **paraphrase** speech or writing,
you say or write it again in a different
way to make it clearer. **paraphrase** *(n)*.

paraplegic *(pa-ruh-plee-jik) (n)*
someone who has no feeling or
movement in the lower part of
their body. **paraplegic** *(adj)*.

parasite *(n)*
1 an animal or plant that gets its
food by living on or inside another
animal or plant. *Leeches are parasites
that use suckers to attach themselves
to people or animals, and then
feed on their blood.* **parasitic** *(adj)*.
2 someone who lives on other
people's money without
doing anything to earn it.

leech

sucker
under
here

muscular body
(contracts and expands
to make the leech move)

parasol *(n)* a type of umbrella
that shades you from the sun.

paratroops *(plural n)* soldiers who
are carried by aeroplane and dropped
by parachute. **paratrooper** *(n)*.

parcel *(n)* a package, or something
wrapped up in paper. **parcel** *(v)*.

parched *(adj)* very dry or thirsty.

parchment *(n)*
1 a material, made from animal
skin, and used for writing on.
2 very good quality
writing paper.

pardon
pardoning pardoned
1 *(v)* to forgive or excuse
someone, or to release
them from punishment.
2 *(interject)* You say **pardon** as a
polite way of asking someone to
repeat what they have said.
3 *(interject)* You say **pardon me** after
you have done something rude, such
as burping, as a way of saying sorry.

parent parenting parented
1 *(n)* a mother or father.
2 *(v)* to be a mother or father.
parenting *(n)*, **parenthood** *(n)*,
parental *(adj)*.

parenthesis parentheses *(n)*
1 an extra phrase or
explanation in brackets.
2 one of a pair of round brackets ( )
used to separate an extra phrase
or explanation. **parenthesize** *(v)*.

parish parishes *(n)*
1 an area that has its own church.

2 **parish council** a group of people
who look after village affairs.

parishioner *(n)*
someone who lives in a parish.

park parking parked
1 *(n)* a large garden or a piece
of ground for public use.
2 *(v)* to leave a car in a parking place
or on the side of a street. **parking** *(n)*.

parking meter *(n)*
a machine that you put money into, in
order to pay for parking on the street.

Parliament *(n)* the group of people
who have been elected to make the
laws of a country. **parliamentary** *(adj)*.

parody parodies *(n)*
a funny imitation of a piece of writing,
song, speech, etc. **parody** *(v)*.

parole *(n)* the early release of
a prisoner on the condition that
they behave well. **parole** *(v)*.

paroxysm *(par-ox-ism) (n)* a sudden
violent fit of something. *A paroxysm
of laughter. A paroxysm of pain.*

parrot
1 *(n)* a tropical bird with a curved
beak and brightly coloured
feathers. Parrots can
learn to repeat things
that are said to
them. *The kind of
parrot shown here
comes from the
South American
rainforest.*
2 *(v)* to repeat
or imitate words
without understanding
what they mean. **parrot** *(n)*.

**scarlet
macaw**

parse parsing parsed *(v)* When you
parse a sentence, you identify its
subject and object, and, sometimes,
the parts of speech it contains.

parsnip *(n)* a sweet, pale yellow
root vegetable. *See* **vegetable**.

parson *(n)*
a priest or a vicar. **parsonage** *(n)*.

part parting parted
1 *(n)* a portion or a piece.
2 *(n)* a character or role in a play or
film. *Ethan played the part of Hamlet.*
3 *(v)* to separate or to divide.
4 *(n)* an expected share
of responsibility or work.
*If everyone does their part,
the show will be a success!*
5 *(v)* If you **part with** something,
you give it away.

part exchange *(n)* If you buy
something by **part exchange**, you
give something you own as part of
the payment. **part exchange** *(v)*.

partial *(par-shal) (adj)*
1 Someone who is **partial**
favours one person or side
more than another. **partiality** *(n)*.
2 not complete. *The holiday was only
a partial success.* **partially** *(adv)*.
3 If you are **partial to** a particular
food or drink, you are especially
fond of it. **partiality** *(n)*.

participate
participating participated *(v)*
to join in or share in an activity or event.
participant *(n)*, **participation** *(n)*.

participle *(n)* a form of a verb. *The
English language has two participles:
the present, for example, "playing",
and the past, for example, "played".
Participles can sometimes be used
as adjectives, for example, "shining",
"crumpled", "swollen".*

particle
1 *(n)* an extremely small
thing or part of something.
2 **particle physics** *(singular n)*
the study of the behaviour of
the minute parts of atoms.

particular
1 *(adj)* individual or special.
2 *(adj)* Someone who is **particular**
is very fussy about small things.
3 *(plural n)* facts or details. *Please send
me some particulars about the course.*
4 **in particular** especially. *All the rides
are fun, but there's one in particular
that you must try.* **particularly** *(adv)*.

parting *(n)*
1 a separation. *An emotional parting.*
2 a line in your hair where it
is combed in two directions.

partly *(adv)* not completely.

partner *(n)*
1 one of two or more people who do
something together. *Business partners.
Dancing partners.* **partnership** *(n)*.
2 a husband, wife, or
permanent companion.

part of speech parts of speech *(n)*
a term, such as noun, verb, adjective,
etc., that describes a word's type
and function. *See page 3.*

part-time *(adj)*
If you have a **part-time** job, you work
for a few hours or a few days each
week. **part-timer** *(n)*, **part time** *(adv)*.

party parties *(n)*
1 an organized occasion with music,
games, etc. when people enjoy
themselves in a group. **party** *(v)*.
2 a group of people working
together. *A search party.*
3 an organized group of people
with similar political beliefs, who try
to win elections. *The Green Party.*

patriot

pass passes passing passed
1 (v) to go past someone or something. *Pass the park and then turn left.*
2 (v) to give something to someone. *Pass the pepper, please.*
3 (v) to kick, throw, or hit a ball to someone in your team in a sport or game. **pass** (n).
4 (v) to succeed in a test or exam. **pass** (n).
5 (n) a crossing-place over a mountain.
6 pass away (v) to die.
7 pass out (v) to faint.

passage (n)
1 a corridor.
2 a short section in a book or piece of music.
3 a journey by ship or aeroplane.

passenger (n)
someone who travels in a car or other vehicle and is not the driver.

passer-by passers-by (n) someone who happens to be going past.

passion (n) a very strong feeling of anger, love, hatred, etc.

passionate (adj) If you are passionate about something or someone, you have strong feelings about them. **passionately** (adv).

passive
1 (adj) If you are passive, you let things happen to you and do not react when you are attacked. **passively** (adv).
2 (adj) A passive verb is one where the verb's subject has something done to it rather than doing the action itself. *In the sentence, "The ball was kicked", the verb is passive, but in "I kicked the ball", the verb is active.*
3 passive smoking (n) breathing in smoke from other people's cigarettes.

Passover (n) an important Jewish festival in the spring, in memory of the way that God rescued the Israelites from slavery in Egypt.

passport (n) an official booklet which proves who you are, and allows you to travel abroad.

password (n) a secret combination of letters, numbers, or symbols that you need to know to get into a building or computer system.

past
1 (n) the period of time before the present. **past** (adj).
2 (adj) finished or ended.
3 (adj) previous. *I've drawn on my past experience in my new job.*
4 (prep) by, after, or beyond. *She went past us.* **past** (adv).

5 (n) The past **participle** is the form of a verb used to show that something happened before the present. For example, "bought" is the past participle of "buy", and "played" is the past participle of "play".

pasta (n) a food made from flour, eggs, and water, that is made into shapes. *The picture shows a selection of different types of pasta.*

spaghetti

pasta

tagliatelle (ribbons)

farfalle (bows)

macaroni

rigatoni (tubes)

fusilli (twists)

conchiglie (shells)

paste pasting pasted
1 (n) a soft, sticky mixture that you can spread. *Fish paste. Wallpaper paste.*
2 (v) to stick with glue.

pastel
1 (n) a chalky crayon.
2 (adj) soft and light in colour.

pasteurized or **pasteurised** (adj) Milk that is pasteurized has been heated to kill bacteria. **pasteurize** (v).

pastor (n) a church minister or priest in charge of a congregation.

pastoral (adj)
1 to do with the countryside.
2 Pastoral care is help with religious or personal matters.

pastry pastries (n)
1 a dough that is rolled out and used for pies, tarts, etc.
2 a small cake made from pastry.

pasture (n) grazing land for animals.

pasty pasties; pastier pastiest
1 (pas-tee) (n) a small pie, usually filled with meat and vegetables.
2 (pay-stee) (adj) If you look pasty, you have a pale or dull complexion.

pat patting patted
1 (v) to tap or stroke something gently with your hand. *Caroline patted the baby donkey.* **pat** (n).
2 If you give someone a **pat on the back**, you praise them and say that they have done well.

patch patches patching patched
1 (v) to put a piece of material on something in order to mend it. **patch** (n).
2 (n) a small, odd-shaped part of something, such as an area of white fur on a black dog.
3 (n) a piece of ground. *A vegetable patch.*
4 (n) a short period of time. *Raisa is going through a bad patch.*

patchwork (n) patterned fabric, made by sewing small patches of different material together.

patchy patchier patchiest (adj) uneven. *Patchy fog made the road dangerous.*

pâté (pa-tay) (n) a soft paste, usually made of meat or fish, that is spread on toast, crackers, etc.

patent patenting patented
1 (v) If you invent something, you can patent it to stop other people copying your idea. **patent** (n).
2 (adj) obvious or open. *Louis told a patent lie.* **patently** (adv).
3 patent leather (n) very shiny leather used for shoes, bags, etc.

paternal (adj) to do with being a father. **paternally** (adv).

path (n)
a track or a route. **pathway** (n).

pathetic (adj)
feeble or useless. **pathetically** (adv).

patience (n)
1 If you have patience, you can put up with difficult things and are able to wait calmly.
2 a card game for one player.

patient
1 (adj) If you are patient, you are good at putting up with things and can wait calmly. **patiently** (adv).
2 (n) someone who is receiving medical treatment.

patio (n)
1 a paved area next to a house, used for sitting outside.
2 patio doors (plural n) glass doors which open out on to a patio.

patisserie (n) a shop where you can buy cakes and pastries.

patriot (n) someone who loves their country and is prepared to fight for it. **patriotism** (n), **patriotic** (adj).

a b c d e f g h i j k l m n o p q r s t u v w x y z

patrol patrolling patrolled
1 (v) to walk or travel around an area in order to protect it or to keep watch on people. *Police are patrolling the neighbourhood.*
2 (n) a group of soldiers, ships, etc. that protect and watch an area.

patron *(pay-tron)* (n)
1 a customer of a shop, or someone who supports a theatre, artist, writer, etc. patronage *(pat-ron-ij)* (n).
2 **patron saint** a saint who is believed to look after a particular country or group of people.

patronize or **patronise** patronizing patronized (v)
1 to talk down to someone or act as though you are better than them.
2 If you **patronize** a shop, restaurant, etc. you go there regularly.

patter pattering pattered
1 (v) to make light, quick, patting sounds. *The rain pattered on my umbrella.* patter (n).
2 (n) fast, insincere talk. *A salesman's patter.*

pattern (n)
1 an arrangement of colours, shapes, etc. on paper or material.
2 a model that you can copy from. *A dress pattern.*
3 If things follow a **pattern**, they happen in a similar way.

pause pausing paused (v)
to stop for a short time. pause (n).

pavement (n)
a raised path beside a street.

pavilion (n) a building at a sports ground where players can get changed, rest, wash, eat, etc.

paw (n) the foot of an animal, such as a dog or cat.

pawn pawning pawned
1 (v) to leave a valuable item at a shop called a pawnbroker's, in return for money. The item is returned to you if you repay your debt, or is sold if you fail to do so.
2 (n) the smallest piece on a chessboard, which can only move one square at a time. *See* **chess**.

pay paying paid
1 (v) to give money for something. payment (n).
2 (v) to be worthwhile or to be advantageous. *It pays to be polite.*
3 (v) to give or offer something. *Carol paid me a compliment.*
4 (v) to suffer. *Ben paid for his mistake.*
5 (n) wages or salary.

PC
1 (n) the initials for Personal Computer.
2 (n) the initials for Police Constable.
3 (adj) (informal) Someone who is **PC** makes a great effort not to offend minority groups, women, etc. The initials PC stand for Politically Correct.

PE (n) a lesson at school in which you do sports, gymnastics, etc. The initials PE stand for Physical Education.

pea (n) a small, green vegetable which grows in a pod. *See* **vegetable**.

peace (n)
1 calm and quiet. peaceful (adj), peacefully (adv).
2 a period without war. peacetime (n).

peach peaches (n)
a soft fruit with a furry skin and a stone at its centre. *See* **fruit**.

peacock (n) a large, blue and green bird with long tail-feathers.

peacock

peak (n)
1 the top of something, such as a mountain.
2 the highest or best point. *Cameron reached the peak of his career when he won the gold medal.* peak (v).
3 the curved, front part of a cap.

peal pealing pealed (v)
When bells **peal**, they ring.

pear (n) a juicy fruit that gets narrower towards its stalk. *See* **fruit**.

pearl (n)
a small, round, whitish object that grows inside oysters and other shellfish, and is used to make jewellery.

mother-of-pearl lining   pearl   oyster shell

oyster

peasant (n)
1 someone who works on a small piece of land.
2 In medieval times, **peasants** were agricultural labourers who worked for their local lord.

peat (n) dark brown, partly decayed vegetable matter that can be used as fuel or compost.

pebble (n)
a small, round stone. pebbly (adj).

peck pecking pecked
1 (v) When a bird **pecks** at something, it strikes it or picks it up with its beak.
2 (n) (informal) a quick kiss. *Aunt Doris gave me a peck on the cheek.* peck (v).

peckish (adj) (informal) hungry.

peculiar
1 (adj) strange or odd. peculiarity (n), peculiarly (adv).
2 **peculiar to** belonging to, or exclusive to. *Koalas are peculiar to Australia.* peculiarity (n), peculiarly (adv).

pedal pedalling pedalled
1 (n) a lever on a bicycle, car, piano, etc. that you push with your foot.
2 (v) to make something work or move by using a pedal or pedals.

peddle peddling peddled (v)
to travel around selling things, often illegally. peddler (n).

pedestal (n) a base for a statue.

pedestrian
1 (n) someone who travels on foot.
2 **pedestrian crossing** (n) a place for people to cross the road safely.
3 **pedestrian zone** (n) a shopping area which cars are not allowed to enter.

pedlar (n) (old-fashioned) In the past, **pedlars** travelled around selling things. *See* **castle**.

peel peeling peeled
1 (n) the tough outer skin of a fruit.
2 (v) to remove the peel of a fruit.
3 (v) to come off. *I got so sunburnt that the skin on my back peeled.*

peep peeping peeped (v)
to glance or look secretly at something. peep (n).

peer peering peered
1 (v) to look hard at something which is difficult to see.
2 (n) a nobleman. peerage (n).
3 (plural n) Your **peers** are people of similar age and type to you.

peg (n) a thin piece of wood, metal, or plastic, used to hold things down or hang things up. peg (v).

pelican (n) a large water bird with a pouch below its beak where it holds the fish that it catches.

pelican

percussion

pellet *(n)*
1 a small, rounded piece of something, such as food or screwed-up paper.
2 a small lead ball fired from a gun.
3 Many birds make **pellets**, which are parcels of things that they cannot digest. *Pellets are made in the bird's stomach and then regurgitated, or coughed up.*

herring gull's pellet

bone

foil

plastic

string

pelt pelting pelted
1 *(v)* to throw something very hard.
2 *(v)* to rain very hard. *It's pelting down outside.*
3 *(n)* an animal's skin or fur.

pen *(n)*
1 an instrument used for writing with ink.
2 a small, fenced area for sheep, cattle, etc.

penalize *or* **penalise** penalizing penalized *(v)*
to make someone suffer a punishment for something that they have done wrong.

penalty penalties *(n)*
1 a punishment.
2 an advantage won in a game when the opposing side breaks a rule.

pence *(n)* Pence is a plural of penny. *This costs 50 pence.*

pencil *(n)* an instrument used for drawing and writing, made from a stick of graphite in a wood casing.

pendant *(n)* a piece of jewellery that hangs on a chain around the neck.

pendulum *(n)*
a weight in some clocks which moves from side to side and helps to keep the clock ticking regularly.

penetrate penetrating penetrated *(v)*
to go inside something or through something. *The nail penetrated Nicola's shoe.* **penetration** *(n)*.

pen friend *(n)*
someone, usually from abroad, who exchanges letters with you.

penguin *(n)*
a large seabird that cannot fly, and which uses its wings as flippers for underwater swimming. *See* **polar**.

penicillin *(n)*
a drug that kills bacteria and helps to treat some diseases.

peninsula *(n)* a piece of land that sticks out into the sea, and is surrounded on three sides by water. *The map shows the North American state of Florida, which is a peninsula.* **peninsular** *(adj)*.

Florida

peninsula

penis penises *(n)*
the male organ used for urinating and for sexual intercourse.

penitent *(adj)*
extremely sorry. **penitence** *(n)*.

penknife penknives *(n)* a small knife with blades that fold into a case.

pen name *(n)*
a public name used by a writer.

penniless *(adj)* If you are **penniless**, you have absolutely no money.

penny pennies *or* pence *(n)*
the smallest unit of money in Britain.

pension *(n)*
an amount of money paid regularly to someone who has retired from work. **pensioner** *(n)*.

pentagon *(n)* a five-sided shape. **pentagonal** *(adj)*. *See* **shape**.

penultimate *(adj)*
next to last. *"This" is the penultimate word in this sentence.*

people *(plural n)* human beings.

pepper *(n)*
1 a spicy powder used to flavour food. **peppery** *(adj)*.
2 a hollow vegetable, usually red, green, or yellow. *See* **vegetable**.

peppermint *(n)*
1 a herb often used in flavouring.
2 a peppermint-flavoured sweet.

per
1 *(prep)* in each, or for each. *There's enough for three sweets per person.*
2 per annum *(adv)* each year.
3 per capita *(adj)* for each person.

perceive perceiving perceived *(v)*
to notice something, or to understand a situation.

percent *(n)* one in every hundred. *Ten percent of a hundred is ten.*

percentage *(n)* a fraction or proportion of something, expressed as a number out of a hundred. The symbol for percentage is %.

perceptive *(adj)*
If you are **perceptive**, you are quick to notice things or understand situations and feelings.

perch perches perching perched
1 *(n)* a place where a bird stands.
2 *(v)* to sit or stand on the edge of something, often high up.
3 *(n)* an edible, freshwater fish. *See* **fish**.

percussion *(n)* musical instruments which are played by being hit or shaken. *The picture shows some small percussion instruments.* **percussionist** *(n)*.

percussion instruments

chime bars

tambourine

maracas

triangle

sleigh bells

cymbals

wood block

perennial
1 (n) a flower which
blooms every year.
2 (adj) happening repeatedly. *A
perennial problem.* **perennially** (adv).

perfect perfecting perfected
1 (*pur-fect*) (adj) without any faults.
perfection (n), perfectly (adv).
2 (*pur-fect*) (v) to succeed, with
effort, in making something
work well. *After much practice,
Elliot perfected his juggling act.*

perforated (adj)
Perforated paper has many
small holes punched in it,
usually so that a section can
be torn off easily. **perforation** (n).

perform
performing performed (v)
1 to do something or to
carry something out. *He
performed his duty well.*
2 to give a show in public.

performance (n) the public acting
of a play, showing of a film, etc.

perfume (n)
a liquid put on your skin to
make you smell pleasant.

perhaps (adv) possibly.

peril (n) serious danger.
perilous (adj), perilously (adv).

perimeter (n)
1 the outside edge of an area.
2 the distance around the
edge of a shape or an area.

period (n)
1 a length of time. *Ewan left
the room for a short period.*
2 the monthly flow of blood from
the womb of a girl or woman.

periodical
1 (adj) happening at intervals.
periodically (adv).
2 (n) a journal or magazine
that is published regularly.

periphery peripheries (n)
the outside edge of something.

periscope (n)
a vertical tube with
prisms at each end
that allows you
to see something
from a position
a long way below
it. Periscopes
are used in
submarines.
*The diagram
shows inside a
periscope works.*

light from
image

prism
(tilts up or
down)

line of sight

lens
(enlarges
and sharpens
image)

prism

eyepiece

periscope

perish perishes
perishing perished (v)
1 to die.
2 If a substance, such as food or
rubber, **perishes**, it becomes rotten.

perk perking perked
1 (n) (informal) an extra advantage
that comes from doing a particular
job. *One of the perks of working
in this café is the free food.*
2 (v) If you **perk up**, you become
more cheerful. **perky** (adj).

perm (n) Perm is short for permanent
wave. This is a process in which hair is
treated with chemicals to give it curls
or waves which last for several months.

permanent (adj)
lasting for a long time or forever.
permanence (n), permanently (adv).

permeate permeating permeated
(v) to spread or pass through
something. *A delicious smell
permeated the house.*

permissible (adj) If something
is **permissible**, it is allowed.

permission (n)
If you give **permission** for something,
you say that it can happen.

permissive (adj) Someone who is
permissive is very tolerant and allows
freedom where others would not.
permissiveness (n), permissively (adv).

permit permitting permitted
1 (*pur-mit*) (v) to allow something.
2 (*pur-mit*) (n) a written statement
giving permission for something.

permutation (n) one of the
ways in which a series of things
can be arranged or put in order.
*There are six permutations of
the numbers 1, 2, and 3: 123,
132, 213, 231, 312, and 321.*

perpendicular (n) a line at right
angles to another line, or vertical to
the ground. **perpendicular** (adj).

perpetual (adj) never-ending or
unchanging. **perpetually** (adv),
perpetuity (n).

perplex perplexes perplexing
perplexed (v) to make someone
puzzled and slightly worried.
perplexity (n), perplexed (adj).

persecute
persecuting persecuted (v)
to treat someone cruelly and unfairly
because you are prejudiced against
them. **persecution** (n).

persevere
persevering persevered (v)
If you **persevere** at something,
you keep on trying and do not
give up. **perseverance** (n).

persist persisting persisted (v)
to keep on doing something.
persistence (n), persistent (adj).

person people
1 (n) an individual human being.
2 If you do something **in
person**, you do it yourself.
3 In grammar, the **first person** refers
to "I" or "we"; the **second person**
refers to "you"; the **third person**
refers to "he", "she", "it", or "they".

personal (adj) to do with one
person only. *This letter is personal
and private.* **personally** (adv).

personality personalities (n)
1 the type of character that
someone has. *Fiona has
a very outgoing personality.*
2 a famous person.
A show business personality.

perspective
1 (n) a particular way of looking at a
situation. *I enjoyed the trip, but from
Gus's perspective, it was a disaster.*
2 If a picture is **in perspective**,
distant objects are drawn smaller
than nearer ones so that the
view looks exactly as someone
would see it in real life.

perspire perspiring perspired (v)
to sweat. **perspiration** (n).

persuade
persuading persuaded (v)
to make someone do something,
by telling them reasons why they
should do it. **persuasion** (n),
persuasive (adj).

perturb perturbing perturbed (v)
to worry or confuse someone.
Tina's questions perturbed me.

perverse (adj)
deliberately unreasonable and
stubborn. **perversity** (n).

pervert (*per-vert*) (n)
someone who behaves in an
unacceptable, disgusting, or harmful
way, particularly in sexual matters.
perverted (*per-ver-ted*) (adj).

peso (*peh-soh*) (n) the main unit of
money in many countries, including
Mexico, Argentina, and the Philippines.

pessimistic (adj)
People who are **pessimistic** are
gloomy and always think that the
worst will happen. **pessimism** (n),
pessimist (n), pessimistically (adv).

pest (n)
1 an insect that destroys or damages
flowers, fruit, or vegetables.
2 any creature that causes serious
interference with human activity.
3 a persistently annoying person.

pester pestering pestered (v) to keep annoying other people, often by asking or telling them something again and again.

pesticide (n) a chemical used to kill animal or insect pests.

pestle (pess-ul) (n) a short stick with a thick, rounded end, used to crush things in a bowl called a mortar.

pet petting petted
1 (n) a tame animal kept for company or pleasure.
2 (n) someone's favourite person or thing. Teacher's pet.
3 (v) to stroke or pat an animal in a gentle, loving way.

petal (n) one of the coloured, outer parts of a flower head. See **flower**.

petition (n) a letter, signed by many people, asking those in power to change their policy or actions.

petrified (adj) If you are **petrified**, you are unable to move because you are so frightened.

petrol (n) a liquid fuel used in many vehicles.

petticoat (n) (old fashioned) a thin garment worn underneath a skirt or dress. See **underclothes**.

petty pettier pettiest (adj) trivial and unimportant. Petty criticisms.

pH (n) a measure of how acidic or alkaline a substance is. The initials pH stand for potential of hydrogen. Acids have pH values under seven and alkalis have pH values over seven. The picture below shows strips of indicator paper. An indicator is a substance that changes color when it is placed in an acid or an alkali.

phantom (n) a ghost.
Pharaoh (fair-oh) (n) one of the kings of Ancient Egypt.

Pharaoh

pharmacist (n) a trained person who prepares and sells drugs and medicines. **pharmacy** (n).

phase phasing phased
1 (n) a stage in someone or something's growth or development. Alex is going through a quarrelsome phase.
2 **phase in** (v) to start something gradually.
3 **phase out** (v) to stop something gradually.

pheasant (fez-ant) (n) a large bird with a long tail that is shot for sport and for food.

pheasant

phenomenal (fuh-nom-in-al) (adj) amazing or astonishing. The group's album was a phenomenal success. **phenomenally** (adv).

phenomenon (fuh-nom-in-on) phenomena (n) something very unusual and remarkable.

philosophical (fil-oss-off-ik-al) (adj)
1 to do with philosophy.
2 able to accept difficulties and problems calmly. **philosophically** (adv).

philosophy (fil-oss-off-ee) (n)
1 the study of ideas about human life. **philosopher** (n).
2 A person's **philosophy** is their set of basic ideas and beliefs on how life should be lived.

phlegm (flem) (n) the thick substance that you cough up when you have a cold.

phobia (n) an overpowering fear of something. **phobic** (adj).

phone short for **telephone**.

phonetically (adv) If something is spelt **phonetically**, it is spelt out as it sounds.

phonetics (singular n) the study of the sounds used in speaking.

phonics (singular n) a method of teaching reading and writing by focusing on sounds.

photo short for **photograph**.

photocopier (n) a machine that copies documents instantly.

photocopy photocopies (n) a copy of a document made by a photocopier. **photocopy** (v).

photo finish photo finishes (n) a very close end to a race, where a photograph has to be studied to decide who has won.

photogenic (foh-toh-jen-ik) (adj) If someone is **photogenic**, they look very good in photographs. **photogenically** (adv).

photograph (n) an image recorded by a camera, and then printed or developed on paper, or stored digitally.

photography (n) the creation of pictures using a camera. **photographer** (n), **photographic** (adj).

strips of indicator paper

photosynthesis *(n)*
a chemical process by which green plants make their food. *Plants use energy from the sun to turn water and carbon dioxide into food, and give off oxygen as a by-product.* **photosynthesize** *(v)*.

phrase *(n)* a group of words that has a meaning, but is not a sentence.

physical *(adj)*
1 to do with the body. *Physical education.* **physically** *(adv)*.
2 to do with the shape and appearance of things. *Physical geography.* **physically** *(adv)*.

physics *(singular n)* the scientific study of energy, movement, heat, sound, light, etc. **physicist** *(n)*.

physiotherapy *(n)*
treatment for damaged muscles and joints, using exercise and massage. **physiotherapist** *(n)*.

piano
1 *(n)* a large keyboard instrument which produces musical sounds when padded hammers strike tuned strings. **pianist** *(n)*.
2 *(adv)* softly. "Piano" is an Italian word, used as an instruction in music.

pick picking picked
1 *(v)* to choose or to select. *Pick a number.*
2 *(v)* to collect or to gather. *Have you picked all the strawberries?*
3 *(n)* a tool with pointed metal ends, used for breaking up earth or stones.

4 *(v)* If you **pick at** something, you take little bits off it.
5 *(v)* If someone **picks on** you, they keep criticizing you.

picket picketing picketed *(v)*
to stand outside a place of work, making a protest and sometimes trying to prevent people from entering. **picket** *(n)*, **picketer** *(n)*.

pickle pickling pickled
1 *(v)* to preserve food in vinegar or in salt water.
2 *(n)* a mixture of chopped, cooked vegetables and spices, often eaten with cold meals.
3 *(n)* *(informal)* a difficult situation.

pickpocket *(n)* someone who steals from people's pockets or bags.

pick-up *(n)*
a small truck with an open back.

picky pickier pickiest *(adj)* *(informal)* fussy or choosy. *A picky eater.*

picnic picnicking picnicked
1 *(n)* a packed meal taken away from home to be eaten outside.
2 *(v)* to eat a picnic. **picnicker** *(n)*.

pictorial *(adj)* using pictures. *A pictorial guide.* **pictorially** *(adv)*.

picture picturing pictured
1 *(n)* an image of something, for example, a painting, photograph, or sketch.
2 *(v)* to imagine something. *I pictured Jimmy as tall, dark, and handsome.* **picture** *(n)*.

picturesque *(pik-chur-esk) (adj)*
If a place or view is **picturesque**, it is beautiful to look at.

pie *(n)* a pastry case filled with meat, fruit, etc. and baked in an oven.

piece piecing pieced
1 *(n)* a bit or section of something.
2 *(n)* something written or made. *A piece of embroidery.*
3 **piece together** *(v)* to put pieces together, or to put facts together.

pier *(n)*
1 a platform of metal and wood extending over the sea. Piers often have entertainments on them.
2 a pillar supporting a bridge.

pierce piercing pierced *(v)*
to make a hole in something. *John has had his ear pierced.*

piercing
1 *(adj)* very loud and shrill. *A piercing scream.*
2 *(n)* a hole in the body to slot a piece of jewellery through. *A nose piercing.*

pig *(n)*
1 a farm animal with a blunt snout, which is kept for its meat.
2 *(informal)* a greedy and disgusting person.

pigeon

pigeon *(n)*
a common, grey bird, sometimes used for racing or for carrying messages.

piggyback *(n)* If someone gives you a **piggyback**, they carry you on their shoulders or on their back.

piggy bank *(n)* a container, often in the shape of a pig, used for saving coins.

pigment *(n)* a substance that gives colour to something.

pigsty pigsties *(n)*
1 a shelter where pigs are kept.
2 a very untidy and often dirty place.

pigtail *(n)* one of two bunches of hair that are tied with bands on either side of the head.

pile *(n)*
1 a heap or mound. **pile** *(v)*.
2 **pile-up** *(informal)* a serious road crash involving several vehicles.

pilfer pilfering pilfered *(v)*
to steal small things. **pilferer** *(n)*.

pilgrim *(n)* someone who goes on a journey to worship at a holy place. **pilgrimage** *(n)*.

pill *(n)*
1 a small, solid tablet of medicine.
2 **the Pill** *(informal)* a pill that women take daily to prevent them from becoming pregnant.

grand piano (lid removed)

bass bridge (transmits vibrations of strings to soundboard)

wooden soundboard (amplifies sound)

overstringing

iron frame

hitch pins

treble strings

bass strings

dampers

bearing bar

wrest plank

keyboard

grand piano and pianist

lid

music rack

pedal

piano case

treble bridge (transmits vibrations of strings to soundboard)

tuning pins or wrest pins

Some words that begin with a "pi" sound are spelt "py".

place

pillar (n) a column which supports part of a building. See **column**.

pillow (n)
a large, soft cushion on which you rest your head when you are lying in bed.

pillowcase (n) a fabric cover that you put over a pillow to keep it clean.

pilot piloting piloted
1 (n) someone who flies an aircraft.
2 (n) someone who steers a ship in and out of port.
3 (v) to control or guide something.
4 (adj) done as an experiment. A pilot television programme. **pilot** (n).

pimple (n) a small, raised spot on the skin. **pimply** (adj).

pin pinning pinned
1 (n) a thin, pointed piece of metal, usually used to join material together.
2 (v) to join things together with a pin. Please can you pin up the hem of my dress?
3 (v) to hold something or someone firmly in position. I pinned a notice on the board. Alfie pinned me against the wall.

pinafore (n)
1 a piece of clothing that you wear to protect your clothes when you are cooking, painting, etc.
2 pinafore dress
a sleeveless dress, usually worn over a shirt or sweater.

pinball (n)
a game in which you shoot small balls around a number of obstacles on a table.

pincer (pin-ser)
1 (n) the pinching claw of a shellfish, such as a crab. See **crab**.
2 pincers (plural n) a tool for gripping and pulling things, especially for pulling out nails.

pinch pinches pinching pinched
1 (v) to squeeze someone's skin painfully between your thumb and index finger. **pinch** (n).
2 (n) a small amount of something. A pinch of salt.
3 (v) (informal) to steal something. Someone's pinched my bike!

pine pining pined
1 (n) a tall, straight, evergreen tree, with cones and needles rather than leaves.
2 (v) If you pine for someone, you feel very sad because you are separated from them.

pineapple (n)
a large, tropical fruit with yellow flesh and a tough skin. See **fruit**.

ping pong see **table tennis**.

pink (n) a pale red colour. pink (adj).

pins and needles
(singular n) (informal)
a pricking, tingling feeling that you get when some of the blood supply to part of your body has been cut off.

pinstripe (n)
a fabric with a very narrow stripe.

pioneer (n)
1 someone who explores unknown territory and settles there.
2 one of the first people to work in a new and unknown area. The Wright brothers were pioneers of flight. **pioneer** (v).

pious (py-uss) (adj)
Someone who is pious practises their religion faithfully and seriously. **piety** (n), **piously** (adv).

pip (n)
the small, hard seed of a fruit.

pipe piping piped
1 (n) a tube, usually used to carry liquids.
2 (v) to send something along pipes, tubes, or wires.
3 (n) a tube with a bowl on the end of it, used for smoking tobacco. Pipes are usually wooden.
4 (n) a tube with holes in it, used as a musical instrument or as part of an instrument. The picture above shows some panpipes from Peru.
5 piped music (n) music that is played all over a building.

panpipes

pipeline
1 (n) a large pipe that carries water, gas, oil, etc. over long distances.
2 If something is in the pipeline, it is being planned.

piping
1 (n) a system of pipes.
2 (n) a thin, pipe-like line of decoration on a cake, chair, etc.
3 (adj) very high or shrill. A piping voice.
4 (adj) If food is piping hot, it is very hot.

pirate pirating pirated
1 (n) someone who attacks and steals from ships at sea. **piracy** (n).
2 (v) If someone pirates a song, computer game, etc., they make illegal copies of the original version and sell them. **pirated** (adj).

pistol (n) a small handgun.

pit pitting pitted
1 (n) a hole in the ground.
2 (n) a small dip.
3 (n) a coal mine.
4 (v) If two people are pitted against each other, they are made to compete with each other.
5 the pits (n) the place where racing cars pull in for fuel and repairs during a race.
6 the pits (adj) the worst example of something. This party is the pits.

pitch pitches pitching pitched
1 (n) an area of grass on which a sport is played.
2 (n) the level of a musical note.
3 (v) If you pitch in, you help do something as part of a team.
4 (v) When you pitch a tent, you put it up.
5 (v) to throw something, especially a baseball.

pitcher (n) an open-topped water container like a large jug.

pitchfork (n) a long-handled fork with two prongs, used for lifting hay.

pitfall (n) a hidden danger.

pitiful (adj)
1 causing or deserving pity. The lost children were in a pitiful state. **pitifully** (adv).
2 useless or worthless. This essay is a pitiful effort! **pitifully** (adv).

pitiless (adj)
If someone is pitiless, they show no pity or mercy. **pitilessly** (adv).

pity pities pitying pitied (v)
If you pity someone, you feel sorry for them. **pity** (n), **pityingly** (adv).

pivot (n) the central point on which something turns or balances. **pivot** (v).

pixel (n) one of the tiny dots on a screen making up the visual image.

pixie or **pixy** (n) a small elf or fairy in legends and fairy stories.

pizza (n) a flat, round base of dough, baked with toppings of cheese, tomato sauce, and other foods.

placard (n)
a poster, nameplate, or notice.

placate placating placated (v)
to make someone calm or happy, often by giving them something they want.

place placing placed
1 (n) a particular area or position.
2 (v) to put something somewhere, deliberately and carefully.
3 (v) to identify by linking with somewhere. I know I've met you before, but I can't place you.
4 If something is in place, it is in its proper position.

Some words that begin with a "pi" sound are spelt "py".

placid

placid *(plass-id) (adj)*
Someone who is **placid** is calm and even-tempered. **placidly** *(adv)*.

plague *(playg)* **plaguing plagued**
1 *(n)* a serious disease which spreads quickly to many people.
2 *(v)* If something **plagues** you, you are troubled and annoyed by it. *The explorers were plagued by flies.*

plaice plaice *(n)*
a flat sea fish that can be eaten.

plaid *(rhymes with bad) (n)*
cloth with a pattern of checks of different colours and sizes, usually made in Scotland.

plain plainer plainest
1 *(adj)* ordinary in appearance, and not fancy or beautiful.
2 *(n)* a large, level area of land.
3 *(adj)* simple and straightforward. *Just give me the plain facts.*
4 **plain clothes** *(n)* ordinary clothes, rather than uniform. *The police wore plain clothes.* **plain-clothes** *(adj)*.

plaintive *(adj)* sad and mournful. *A plaintive cry.* **plaintively** *(adv)*.

plait *(rhymes with bat) (n)*
a length of hair that has been divided into sections and woven together. **plait** *(v)*, **plaited** *(adj)*.

plan planning planned
1 *(v)* to work out how you will do something. **plan** *(n)*.
2 *(v)* If you **plan** to do something, you intend to do it. *I planned to go shopping today.*
3 *(n)* a diagram used in the construction of something.
4 *(n)* a map of a room, building, or small area.

plane *(n)*
1 a machine with wings and an engine, that flies through the air. Plane is short for aeroplane. *See* **aircraft**.
2 a tool used for smoothing wood. **plane** *(v)*. *See* **woodwork**.
3 a flat surface. *A dice has six planes.*

planet *(n)*
one of the large, round objects circling the Sun. *This picture shows the planets of the solar system in their correct order, but not drawn to scale.* **planetary** *(adj)*.

plank *(n)* a long, flat strip of wood used, for example, for floorboards.

plankton *(n)* a general name for the minute animals and plants which live in water. *See* **microorganism**.

plant
planting
planted
1 *(n)* a living organism that often contains a green pigment called chlorophyll, which allows it to capture energy from the Sun. Many land plants have stems, roots, and leaves. *Also see* **flower**.
2 *(v)* to put plants or seeds in the ground so that they can grow.
3 *(v)* to put something in a secret place. *They planted a spy in the factory.*
4 *(n)* a factory, laboratory, or power station. *A chemical plant.*
5 *(n)* large industrial machinery or buildings.

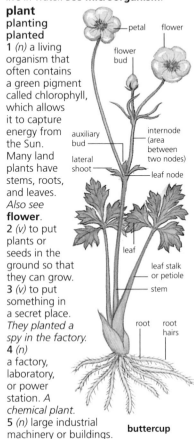

petal — flower
flower bud
auxiliary bud
lateral shoot
internode (area between two nodes)
leaf node
leaf
leaf stalk or petiole
stem
root — root hairs

buttercup

plantation *(n)*
1 a farm in a hot country where coffee, tea, rubber, etc. are grown.
2 a place where a large number of trees or bushes have been planted.

plaque *(plak or plahk) (n)*
1 a plate with words inscribed on it, usually on a wall in a public place.
2 the coating made from food, bacteria, and saliva that forms on your teeth and can cause tooth decay.

plaster plastering plastered
1 *(n)* a substance made of lime, sand, and water, used by builders to put a smooth finish on walls.
2 *(n)* a sticky bandage that you put on a skin wound.
3 *(v)* to spread something thickly on a surface. *Clive plastered his hair with gel.*
4 **plaster cast** *(n)* a hard case that holds the parts of a broken bone together until it mends.

plastic *(n)* a man-made substance that is light and strong and can be moulded into different shapes.

plastic surgery *(n)* an operation on skin and body tissue. Plastic surgery can be used to repair damage or to alter someone's appearance.

plate *(n)*
1 a flat dish for food.
2 a flat sheet of glass or metal.
3 an illustration in a book.
4 one of the sheets of rock which make up the Earth's outer crust. *The map shows the eight main plates that make up the Earth's surface, sometimes known as continental or tectonic plates.*

continental plates

- ■ Eurasian plate
- ■ African plate
- □ American plate
- ■ Caribbean plate
- □ Nazca plate
- □ Pacific plate
- □ Antarctic plate
- ■ Indo-Australian plate

plateau *(plat-oh)*
plateaus or **plateaux** *(n)*
an area of high, flat land.

platform *(n)* a flat, raised structure on which people or things can stand. *A station platform.*

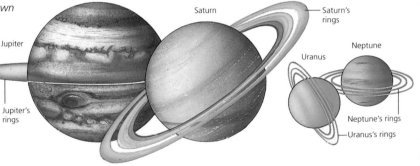

planets

Mercury Venus Earth Mars
Sun
Jupiter
Jupiter's rings
Saturn
Saturn's rings
Uranus
Neptune
Neptune's rings
Uranus's rings

platinum (n)
a very valuable, silvery-white metal.

platypus platypuses (n)
an Australian mammal with
webbed feet and a broad bill.

platypus

plausible
(*plaw-zib-ul*) (adj)
believable. *Frank gave
a plausible reason for being
so late.* **plausibly** (adv).

play playing played
1 (v) to take part in a game
or other enjoyable activity.
2 (n) a story that is acted,
usually in the theatre.
3 (v) to make music on an instrument.
Lesley plays the saxophone.
4 (v) to take part in a sport.
5 (v) to act a part in a play.

playground (n) a surfaced, fenced,
outdoor area, often with swings,
slides, etc. where children can play.

playroom (n)
a room in which children can play.

playtime (n) a time between lessons
when schoolchildren can play.

playwright (n)
someone who writes plays.

plc (n) the initials for public limited
company. A **public limited company**
is one whose shares can be bought by
members of the public. If the company
goes bankrupt, the shareholders
lose only the value of their shares.

plea (n) a strongly felt, emotional
request. *A plea for mercy.*

plead pleading pleaded (v)
1 If you **plead** with someone,
you beg them to do something.
2 to say whether you are guilty
or not guilty in a court. *I plead guilty.*

pleasant pleasanter pleasantest
(adj) enjoyable and likable.
*We spent a pleasant afternoon
by the river.* **pleasantly** (adv).

please pleasing pleased
1 (v) to satisfy or to give pleasure.
I was pleased with the match result.
2 (adv) You say **please** when you ask
for something politely. *Please may I
have some cake?* **please** (interject).

pleasure (n) a feeling of enjoyment
or satisfaction. **pleasurable** (adj).

pleat (n) one of a series of parallel
folds in a piece of clothing, such
as a skirt. **pleated** (adj).

plectrum plectra or plectrums (n)
a small piece of metal or plastic used
to pluck the strings of guitars, etc.

pledge pledging pledged (v)
to make a firm promise. **pledge** (n).

plentiful (adj) existing in large
amounts. **plentifully** (adv).

plenty (n) a great number or a large
amount. *There's plenty of space.*

pliable (*ply-ab-ul*) (adj)
1 able to be bent easily.
2 If a person is **pliable**, they
can be influenced easily.

plight (n) a situation of
great danger or hardship.

plimsoll or **plimsole**
1 (n) a soft, canvas shoe with a rubber
sole, often worn for sports or PE.
2 **Plimsoll line** (n) a line on the
side of a ship that indicates how
heavily loaded it is permitted to be.

plod plodding plodded (v) to walk
or work in a slow and deliberate way.

plot plotting plotted
1 (v) to make a secret plan. **plot** (n).
2 (n) a small area of land.
A building plot.
3 (n) the story of a novel,
film, play, etc.
4 (v) to mark out something, like
a graph, or a route on a map.

plough (*rhymes with cow*)
ploughing ploughed
1 (n) a piece of farm equipment
pulled by an animal or a tractor
and used to turn over soil before
seeds are sown. *The picture below
shows a wooden model of an Ancient
Egyptian plough. Also see* **farm**.
2 (v) to turn over soil using a plough.
3 (v) If you **plough through**
something, you work hard
to get through it.

Egyptian plough

plough   yoke

ox

ploughman's (n)
a lunch of cheese, bread, and pickle.

pluck plucking plucked
1 (v) to pick fruit or flowers.
2 (v) to play notes on a stringed
instrument, by pulling on the strings
with your fingers or with a plectrum.
3 (v) to pull feathers out of a dead bird.
4 (n) courage and bravery.
plucky (adj), **pluckily** (adv).

plug plugging plugged
1 (n) an object pushed into a hole
to block it. *A bath plug.* **plug** (v).
2 (n) an electrical connector.
3 (v) (informal) to gain publicity
for something by talking about
it, usually on radio or television.

plum (n)
a small, soft fruit with a purple,
yellow, or red skin. *See* **fruit**.

plumage (*plew-mij*) (n)
a bird's feathers.

plumbing (*plum-ing*) (n)
the system of water pipes
in a building. **plumber** (n).

plump plumper plumpest
1 (adj) slightly fat, or
rounded in shape.
2 (v) If you **plump up** something,
such as cushions or pillows, you
hit them so that they get bigger.
3 (v) If you **plump for** someone
or something, you support or
favour them.

plunder plundering plundered (v)
to use violence in order to steal things,
usually during a battle. **plunder** (n).

plunge plunging plunged (v)
1 to dive into water. **plunge** (n).
2 to push something into water.
Plunge the lettuce into ice-cold water.
3 to slope steeply. *The
cliffs plunged to the sea.*
4 to do something suddenly.
We plunged into action.

plural (n) the form of a word that is
used for two or more of something.
The plural of 'child' is 'children'.

plus
1 In maths, a **plus** sign (+)
is used in an addition sum.
6 plus 4 equals 10, or 6 + 4 = 10.
2 (prep) in addition to. *Gwen has a
husband plus three children to feed.*

plywood (n) board made from
thin sheets of wood glued together.

p.m. the initials of the Latin phrase
post meridiem which means "after
midday". *School finishes at 4 p.m.*

pneumatic (*new-mat-ik*) (adj)
1 filled with air. *Pneumatic tyres.*
2 operated by compressed
air. *A pneumatic drill.*

pneumonia (*new-moan-ee-a*) (n)
a serious lung disease which
makes breathing very difficult.

poach poaches
poaching poached (v)
1 to catch animals illegally on
someone else's land. **poacher** (n).
2 to cook eggs, fish, etc. by
heating them gently in liquid.

pocket

pocket pocketing pocketed
1 *(n)* a pouch sewn on to or into clothing and used for carrying things.
2 *(v)* to take something secretly. *Baz pocketed the money and ran.*
3 *(n)* a small area. *The army met pockets of resistance on their way.*

pocket money *(n)* spending money that parents give to their children.

pod *(n)* a long case that holds the seeds of certain plants. *A pea pod.*

podgy podgier podgiest *(adj)* slightly fat.

poem *(n)* a piece of writing set out in short lines, often with a noticeable rhythm and some words that rhyme.

poetry *(n)* a general word for poems. *Do you write poetry?* **poet** *(n)*.

point pointing pointed
1 *(v)* to show where something is, especially by using your index finger.
2 *(n)* the sharp end of something. *A pencil point.*
3 *(n)* the main purpose behind something that is said or done. *What is the point of all this?*
4 *(n)* a specific place or stage. *Don't go beyond this point.*
5 *(n)* a unit for scoring in a game.
6 *(v)* to aim at someone or something. *Don't point your finger at me!*
7 *(v)* If you **point out** something, you draw attention to it or explain it.
8 **points** *(plural n)* railway lines which can be moved to send a train on to a different track.

point-blank *(adj)* very close indeed. *They shot at point-blank range.*

pointless *(adj)* If something is **pointless**, it has no realistic purpose. *It's pointless to take your bikini on an Arctic expedition.* **pointlessly** *(adv)*.

poise (rhymes with boys) poising poised *(v)*
1 to balance. *The glass was poised on the edge of the table.*
2 If you are **poised** to do something, you are about to do it.

poised *(adj)* If you are **poised**, you are self-confident and carry yourself in a dignified manner. **poise** *(n)*.

poison *(n)* a substance that can kill or harm someone or something if it is swallowed or breathed in. **poison** *(v)*, **poisonous** *(adj)*.

poke poking poked *(v)* to prod sharply with a finger or pointed object. **poke** *(n)*.

poker *(n)* a long, metal tool used for stirring up a fire.

poky or **pokey** pokier pokiest *(adj)* (informal) very small and cramped.

polar *(adj)* belonging to the icy regions, known as the Arctic and the Antarctic, around the North and South Poles.

polar regions and polar wildlife

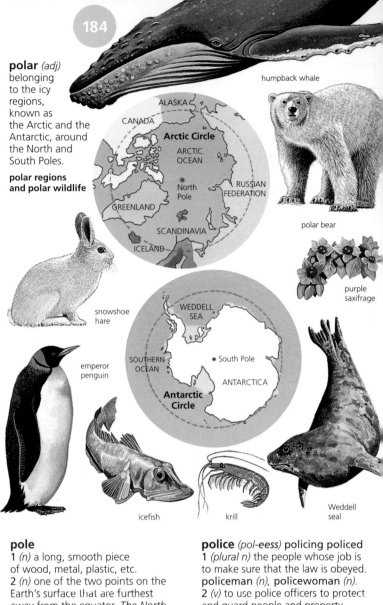

humpback whale

ALASKA
CANADA
Arctic Circle
ARCTIC OCEAN
North Pole
RUSSIAN FEDERATION
GREENLAND
SCANDINAVIA
ICELAND

polar bear

purple saxifrage

snowshoe hare

WEDDELL SEA
SOUTHERN OCEAN
South Pole
ANTARCTICA
Antarctic Circle

emperor penguin

icefish

krill

Weddell seal

pole
1 *(n)* a long, smooth piece of wood, metal, plastic, etc.
2 *(n)* one of the two points on the Earth's surface that are furthest away from the equator. *The North Pole. The South Pole. See **polar**.*
3 *(n)* one of the two opposite ends of a magnet. *See **magnet**.*
4 If two people or things are **poles apart**, they are very different.

pole vault *(n)* a jump over a high bar, using a flexible pole. *The picture sequence shows an athlete performing a pole vault.* **pole-vault** *(v)*.

pole vault

fibreglass pole

vaulting box

police *(pol-eess)* policing policed
1 *(plural n)* the people whose job is to make sure that the law is obeyed. **policeman** *(n)*, **policewoman** *(n)*.
2 *(v)* to use police officers to protect and guard people and property.

bar

policy policies (n) a general plan of action. *A traffic policy.*

polio (n) an infectious virus which affects the brain and spine and which can cause paralysis. Polio is short for poliomyelitis.

polish polishes polishing polished
1 (v) to rub something in order to make it shine. **polish** (n).
2 (n) a cleaning substance used to make things shine.

polished (adj) If you give a **polished** performance, you are well rehearsed and perform confidently.

polite politer politest (adj) well-behaved and courteous to other people. **politeness** (n), **politely** (adv).

politician (n) someone involved in the government of a country, such as an MP or a congressman.

politics (n) the debate and activity involved in governing a country. **political** (adj), **politically** (adv).

poll (n)
1 a counting of votes in an election.
2 a place where people go to vote in an election. *The polls are closed.*
3 a survey of people's opinions.

pollen
1 (n) fine grains found inside flowers. Pollen contains fertilizing cells and is transferred to other plants by the wind or by insects.
2 **pollen count** (n) a measurement of the level of pollen in the air, which indicates how badly people with hay fever may be affected.

willow

water lily

yarrow

pollen grains
(magnified)

pollinate pollinating pollinated (v) to transfer pollen from one flower to another in order to fertilize the flower. **pollination** (n).

polling station (n) a building where people go to vote in elections.

pollution (n) damage to the environment caused by human activities. Pollution includes the harmful effects of noise and light. **pollute** (v).

polo (n) a game played on horseback by two teams of three or four players who try to hit a small ball through goal posts using long, wooden mallets.

polyester (n) a man-made substance used to make plastic products and fabric for clothes.

polygamy (n) If someone practises polygamy, they have several wives or husbands at once. **polygamous** (adj).

polygon (n) a flat shape with many sides.

polystyrene (n) a light, stiff plastic often used to make disposable cups and packing materials.

polythene (n) a light, flexible plastic used to make bags.

polyunsaturates (plural n) soft animal and vegetable fats and oils, thought to be healthier for you than other fats. **polyunsaturated** (adj).

pomegranate (n) a round, red or yellow fruit with tough skin, red flesh and many seeds. *See* **fruit**.

pomp (n) an elaborate and stately display or ceremony.

pompous (adj) full of self-importance. **pompously** (adv), **pomposity** (n).

pond (n) a small, enclosed pool of fresh water.

ponder pondering pondered (v) to think about things carefully.

pond-skater (n) an insect with a long, narrow body and very long, thin legs that it uses to walk on the surface of ponds.

pondweed (n) a general name for plants that grow in freshwater ponds and slow streams.

pong (n) (informal) an unpleasant smell. **pong** (v).

pony ponies (n) a small horse.

ponytail (n) a bunch of hair that is tied with a band and hangs behind the head.

poodle (n) a breed of dog with long, curly hair.

pool pooling pooled
1 (n) a small area of still water.
2 (n) a swimming pool.
3 (n) a game in which you use a stick, called a cue, to hit coloured balls into pockets on a table.
4 (v) If people **pool** their money, ideas, etc. they put them together to be shared.

pools (n) a competition in which people bet on the results of football matches.

poor poorer poorest (adj)
1 If you are **poor**, you do not have very much money.
2 low in quality or standard. *Poor eyesight.*
3 unfortunate, and provoking sympathy. *Poor Alexa!*

poorly
1 (adv) badly. *The room was poorly lit.*
2 (adj) ill. *Cheryl is poorly today.*

pop popping popped
1 (v) to make a small bang or bursting sound. **pop** (n).
2 (n) (informal) a sweet, fizzy drink such as lemonade.
3 **pop music** (n) modern, popular music with a strong, and often fast, beat. **pop** (n).
4 (v) (informal) to go somewhere or put something somewhere quickly. *Graham has just popped out. Lena popped a mint into her mouth.*

popcorn (n) grains of maize that are heated until they swell up and burst open with a popping sound.

Pope (n) the head of the Roman Catholic Church.

poplar (n) a tall tree with wide leaves.

poppadom or **poppadum** (n) a large, round, crispy disc, made from flour and spices, and served with Indian meals.

poppy poppies (n) a flower with large, colourful petals. Poppies have seedcases with tiny holes for the seeds to escape from when they are shaken by the wind.

common poppy

flower

seeds dried seedcase

popular (adj) liked or enjoyed by many people. **popularity** (n), **popularly** (adv).

populated (adj) If a place is populated, it has people living there.

population (n)
1 the people who live in a place.
2 the number of people who live in a place.

porcelain (por-ser-lin) (n) very fine china, often used to make ornaments or cups and saucers. *This 18th-century figure of Madame de Pompadour was made in porcelain at the Meissen factory in Germany.*

porcelain figure

porch

porch porches
(n) a covered
area around
a doorway.
See **building**.

quills

porcupine *(n)*
a rodent covered
with long, sharp
spines, or quills.

pore *(n)*
one of the tiny holes in
your skin through which
you sweat. *See* **skin**.

**Malaysian
porcupine**

pork *(n)* the meat from a pig.

pornography *(n)*
magazines, videos, etc. that are
intended to be sexually exciting in a
way that many people find obscene
and offensive. **pornographic** *(adj)*.

porous *(adj)* Something that is
porous lets liquid or gas through it.

porridge *(n)* a breakfast food made
by cooking oats in milk or water.

port *(n)*
1 a town with a harbour.
2 the left side of a ship
or aircraft. **port** *(adj)*.
3 a strong, sweet dessert wine.

portable *(adj)*
able to be carried easily.

portcullis portcullises *(n)*
a heavy grating in the entrance
to a castle that was used as an
extra defence. *This cutaway view
of a castle gatehouse shows how
the portcullis and drawbridge
were raised and lowered.*

man-at-arms

castle gatehouse
(cutaway)

battlements

gatehouse
tower

guard
room

arrow loop

winch for portcullis

chain

portcullis

winch for
drawbridge

drawbridge

gateway
to castle

stone sill

moat

porter *(n)* (old-fashioned)
someone who carries luggage for
people at a railway station or hotel.

portion *(n)* a part or a piece.

portrait *(n)*
1 a drawing, painting, or
photograph of a person.
2 a description of something.

portray portraying portrayed *(v)*
1 to show or describe someone
or something in a certain way.
*The author portrays Henrietta
as an eccentric.* **portrayal** *(n)*.
2 to act a part in a play
or film. **portrayal** *(n)*.

pose posing posed *(v)*
1 to keep your body in
a particular position so that
you can be photographed,
painted, or drawn. **pose** *(n)*.
2 to pretend to be someone
else in order to deceive people.
The thieves posed as policemen.
3 If you **pose a question**, you ask it.

posh posher poshest *(adj)* (informal)
1 upper-class. *A posh accent.*
2 very smart and expensive.
A posh hotel.

position positioning positioned
1 *(n)* the place where something is.
2 *(v)* to put something in
a particular place. *Position
the pictures carefully.*
3 *(n)* the way in which someone
is standing, sitting, or lying.
4 *(n)* point of view. *What's
your position on this issue?*
5 *(n)* a particular job. *I'm applying
for the position of editor.*

positive *(adj)*
1 sure or certain. *I'm positive
that I left my pencil case here.*
positively *(adv)*.
2 hopeful and optimistic. *Julie
has a positive approach to life.*
3 A **positive** number
is more than zero.

possession
1 *(n)* something that you own.
possess *(v)*.
2 If something is **in your possession**,
you own it or have it.

possessive
1 *(adj)* If someone is **possessive**,
they want to keep someone
or something for themselves
and do not want to share
them with other people.
2 *(n)* the form of a noun or pronoun
that shows that something belongs to
it. *In "This ball is mine" and "Tom's
bat", "mine" and "Tom's" are
possessives.* **possessive** *(adj)*.

possible *(adj)* If something is
possible, it might happen or might
be true. **possibility** *(n)*, **possibly** *(adv)*.

post posting posted
1 *(n)* a long, thick piece of
wood, concrete, or metal
that is fixed in the ground.
2 *(n)* a particular job that
someone has. *Mr Jarvis holds
the post of head teacher.*
3 *(v)* to send a letter or parcel
from one place to another.
4 *(singular n)* the letters and
parcels that you send or receive.

postage *(n)* the cost of sending
a letter or parcel by post.

postcard *(n)* a card, usually with a
picture on one side and writing on the
opposite side, that you send by post.

postcode *(n)* the set of numbers
and letters at the end of an address,
used to help sort letters, parcels, etc.

poster *(n)* a large, printed picture or
notice that can be put up on a wall.

postman postmen *(n)* a man
who delivers letters and parcels.

postmark *(n)*
an official mark on a letter to show
when and where it was posted.

post office *(n)* the place where
people go to buy stamps, send
parcels, receive pensions, etc.

postpone
postponing postponed *(v)*
to put something off until later.
*We postponed the match because
of rain.* **postponement** *(n)*.

postscript *(n)* a short message,
beginning "ps.", which you add to the
end of a letter, after your signature.

posture *(n)*
the position of your body when you
stand, sit, or walk. **postural** *(adj)*.

postwoman postwomen *(n)*
a woman who delivers
letters and parcels.

posy posies *(n)*
a small bunch of flowers.

pot potting potted
1 *(n)* a round container used
for cooking or storing food.
2 *(n)* a container made
of clay, especially one
used for growing plants.
3 *(n)* (slang) marijuana.
4 *(v)* to hit a ball into a pocket
in snooker, pool, or billiards.

potato potatoes *(n)* a round or
oval root vegetable. *See* **vegetable**.

potent *(adj)* powerful or strong.
potency *(n)*, **potently** *(adv)*.

potential (n)
1 Your **potential** is what you are capable of achieving in the future. **potential** (adj), **potentially** (adv).
2 If an idea, place, etc. has **potential**, you think that you can develop it into something better.

pothole (n)
1 a deep hole that leads to underground caves.
2 a hole in the surface of a road.

potholing (n) the sport of climbing down potholes and exploring underground caves. **potholer** (n).

potter pottering pottered
1 (n) someone who makes objects out of clay, such as bowls, plates, vases, etc. *The picture shows a potter working at her wheel.*
2 (v) to be occupied in a leisurely way. *Christy pottered around the house all day.*

potter — electric wheel — worktop shelf — wheel tray — clay tool — wooden cabinet — foot pedal (controls speed) — bin for clay — foot rest — hand controls

pottery potteries (n)
1 objects made of baked clay, such as bowls, plates, vases, etc.
2 the craft or business of making clay objects.
3 a place where clay objects are made.

potty potties; pottier pottiest
1 (n) a type of bowl that very young children use instead of a toilet.
2 (adj) (informal) slightly mad.

pouch pouches (n)
1 a small leather or fabric bag.
2 a flap of skin in which kangaroos and other marsupials carry their young.

poultry (plural n)
farmyard birds kept for their eggs and meat. Chicken, turkeys, ducks, and geese are poultry.

pounce pouncing pounced (v)
to jump on something suddenly and grab hold of it. *The lion pounced on the antelope.*

pound pounding pounded
1 (n) the main unit of money in Britain.
2 (n) a unit of weight, equal to 0.454kgs. *See page 284.*
3 (v) to keep hitting something noisily and with force. *The rain pounded on the roof.*
4 (n) an enclosure, especially one for lost bicycles or stray dogs.
5 (v) to beat quickly or heavily. *My heart was pounding.*

pour pouring poured (v)
1 to make liquid flow out of a jug, bottle, etc.
2 to rain heavily.
3 to move somewhere quickly and in large numbers. *People poured out of the stadium on to the street.*

pout pouting pouted (v)
to push out your lips because you are cross or disappointed about something. **pout** (n).

poverty (n) the state of being poor.

powder powdering powdered
1 (n) tiny grains of a solid substance. **powdery** (adj).
2 (v) to cover something with powder.

power (n)
1 control over other people or things. **powerful** (adj), **powerless** (adj).
2 the ability or authority to do something.
3 great force or great strength. **powerful** (adj), **powerfully** (adv).
4 electricity or other forms of energy.
5 **power cut** a temporary stoppage in the electricity supply.
6 **power station** a place where electricity is produced.

practicable (adj) able to be done successfully. *Is it practicable to do all this work today?* **practicably** (adv).

practical
1 (adj) to do with experience or action rather than with theory and ideas. *Do you have any practical experience of teaching?*
2 (adj) If someone is **practical**, they are good at making and doing things with their hands.
3 (adj) sensible and useful. *Brown is a practical colour for a carpet.*
4 (n) a lesson or exam in which you do something, rather than reading or writing about it. *A chemistry practical.*

practical joke (n)
a humorous trick played on someone.

practically (adv)
1 almost. *It's practically impossible to get there by public transport.*
2 in a sensible way. *Adele tackled the job very practically.*

practice
1 (n) the regular repetition of an action in order to improve it. *Piano practice.*
2 (n) a custom or habit. *How old is the practice of sending birthday cards?*
3 (n) the business of a doctor or lawyer.
4 **in practice** (adv) what really happens when you do something, rather than what is meant to happen.

practise practising practised (v)
1 to do something over and over again so that you improve.
2 If someone **practises** a religion, they follow its teachings and attend its services or ceremonies.
3 to work as a doctor or lawyer. *Giles practises medicine in Glasgow.*
4 to put something into action. *Practise what you preach.*

prairie (n) a large area of grassland in North America.

praise praising praised (v)
1 to say good things about someone because you admire them or think that they have done something well. **praise** (n).
2 to thank and worship God, or a god or goddess. **praise** (n).

pram (n) a four-wheeled vehicle for a baby that you push along.

prance prancing pranced (v)
1 to leap in a lively way.
2 When horses **prance**, they walk quickly with high steps.

prank (n) a trick played on someone.

prawn (n) a small shellfish that you can cook and eat. Prawns are pale pink when cooked.

pray praying prayed (v)
1 to talk to God, or a god or goddess, either out loud or silently. **prayer** (n).
2 to hope very much that something happens. *We're praying that it will be sunny tomorrow.*

preach preaches preaching preached (v)
1 to give a religious talk to people, especially during a church service. **preacher** (n).
2 to tell other people what they should do. *I wish my mum would stop preaching at me!*

precarious (adj) unsafe and risky. *The glass was perched in a precarious position on the edge of the table.* **precariously** (adv).

precaution (n) something that you do in order to prevent something dangerous or unpleasant from happening. *Let's take a first aid kit as a precaution.* **precautionary** (adj).

precede *(pree-seed)*
preceding preceded *(v)*
If one thing **precedes** another thing, it comes before it. *A short cartoon preceded the main film.* **preceding** *(adj)*.

precinct *(pree-sinkt)* *(n)* a shopping area in a town, where traffic is not allowed.

precious *(presh-uss)*
1 *(adj)* rare and valuable.
2 *(adj)* very special to you. *Precious memories.*
3 **precious stone** *(n)* a valuable mineral, often used in jewellery.

precipice *(n)* a steep cliff face.

precis *(pray-see)* **precis** *(n)* a short summary of a longer piece of writing.

precise *(adj)* exact, accurate, and neat. **precision** *(n)*, **precisely** *(adv)*.

precocious *(prek-oh-shuss)* *(adj)* **Precocious** children are very advanced for their age.

predator *(n)* an animal that hunts and kills other animals. **predatory** *(adj)*.

predecessor *(n)*
1 someone who had your job or position before you.
2 an ancestor.

predicament *(n)* an awkward or difficult situation.

predict **predicting predicted** *(v)* to say what you think will happen in the future. **prediction** *(n)*.

predominate
predominating predominated *(v)* to be greater in power or number than others. *Girls predominate in our class.* **predominance** *(n)*, **predominant** *(adj)*, **predominately** *(adv)*.

preen **preening preened** *(v)* When birds **preen** themselves, they clean and arrange their feathers with their beaks.

preface *(pref-uss)* *(n)* an introduction at the front of a book.

prefect *(n)* a school pupil who has special duties and responsibilities.

prefer **preferring preferred** *(v)* to like one thing better than another. *I prefer oranges to apples.* **preference** *(n)*.

prefix **prefixes** *(n)* a part of a word added at its beginning that changes the word's meaning. "Sub", "un", and "re" are all prefixes. *The prefix "pre", which means "before", is used in "prehistoric" and "premeditated".*

pregnant *(adj)* A woman who is **pregnant** has a baby growing in her womb. *This diagram of a pregnant woman's womb shows a baby ready to be born.* **pregnancy** *(n)*.

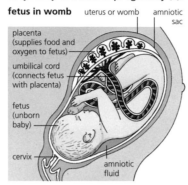

fetus in womb   uterus or womb   amniotic sac

placenta (supplies food and oxygen to fetus)
umbilical cord (connects fetus with placenta)
fetus (unborn baby)
cervix
amniotic fluid

prehistoric *(adj)* belonging to a time very long ago before history was written. **prehistory** *(n)*.

prejudice *(n)*
1 a fixed and unreasonable opinion. **prejudiced** *(adj)*.
2 unfair behaviour that results from having fixed opinions about something or some people. *Racial prejudice.*

preliminary *(adj)* preparing the way for what comes later. *A preliminary talk.* **preliminary** *(n)*.

premature *(adj)* happening or coming early. *A premature baby.* **prematurely** *(adv)*.

premeditated *(adj)* planned in advance. *A premeditated attack.*

premier *(prem-ee-er)*
1 *(adj)* leading, top, or principal. *America's premier rock group.*
2 *(n)* the leader of a government.

premiere *(prem-ee-air)* *(n)* the first public performance of a film or play.

premises *(plural n)* a building and the land that belongs to it.

premium
1 *(n)* money that is paid to take out an insurance policy.
2 If something is **at a premium**, it is rare and valued very highly.

premonition *(n)* a feeling that something bad is going to happen.

preoccupied *(adj)* If you are **preoccupied**, your thoughts are completely taken up with something. **preoccupation** *(n)*.

prep *(n)*
1 *(informal)* homework. Prep is short for preparation.
2 **prep school** a private school for pupils up to the age of thirteen. Prep school is short for preparatory school.

prepare **preparing prepared** *(v)* to get ready. **preparation** *(n)*.

preposition *(n)* a word showing the position of things or people in relation to each other. *"On", "beside", and "with" are prepositions. See page 3.*

preposterous *(adj)* ridiculous and absurd. **preposterously** *(adv)*.

preschool
1 *(n)* a school, for example a nursery school, for children who are too young to go to primary school.
2 *(adj)* to do with children who are too young to go to primary school. *Preschool education.*

prescribe **prescribing prescribed** *(v)*
1 to say what should be done. *Mum prescribed a trip to the cinema to make us feel better.*
2 When doctors **prescribe** medicine for a patient, they decide what drugs they should take and write an order, or prescription, to a pharmacist.

prescription *(n)* an order for drugs written by a doctor to a pharmacist.

presence *(n)* being in a place. *We would appreciate your presence at our party.*

present **presenting presented**
1 *(prez-ent)* *(adj)* If someone is **present** in a place, they are there.
2 *(prez-ent)* *(n)* the time now.
3 *(priz-ent)* *(v)* to give someone a gift or prize in a formal way.
4 *(prez-ent)* *(n)* something that you buy or make to give to someone.
5 *(priz-ent)* *(v)* to introduce something, such as a television programme. **presenter** *(n)*.
6 *(n)* The **present participle** of a verb ends with "ing" and is used to form some tenses, for example, "I am cooking" and "Howard will be cooking tomorrow". It can also be used as an adjective, as in "a thriving business", or as a noun, as in "Their singing gave me a headache".

presentation *(n)*
1 the formal giving of a prize or present. *At the end of term, we had a presentation for our teacher.*
2 the way that something is produced and the way that it looks. *Your work is good but your presentation is atrocious!*

presently *(adv)* soon or shortly.

preserve **preserving preserved**
1 *(v)* to protect something so that it stays in its original state. **preservation** *(n)*.
2 *(v)* to treat food so that it does not go bad. **preservative** *(n)*.
3 *(n)* jam. *Apricot preserve.*

principle

preside presiding presided *(v)* to be in charge of something.

president *(n)*
1 the elected head of state of a republic. *These portraits of American presidents are carved out of rock at Mount Rushmore in the USA.* **presidency** *(n)*, **presidential** *(adj)*.
2 the head of a society or organization.

Mount Rushmore, USA

George Washington · Thomas Jefferson · Theodore Roosevelt · Abraham Lincoln

press presses pressing pressed
1 *(v)* to push firmly. *Press the button to open the door.* **pressure** *(n)*.
2 *(v)* to persuade strongly. *We pressed Anthony into taking a role in the play.*
3 *(v)* to smooth out the creases in clothes with an iron.
4 *(n)* a machine for printing.
5 **the press** *(n)* a general name for newspapers and the people who produce them.

pressing *(adj)* urgent, or needing immediate attention. *I must dash, I have a pressing appointment.*

press-up or **push-up** *(n)* an exercise in which you lie on the floor and raise your body off it by pushing with your arms.

pressure *(n)*
1 the force with which you press on something. *Apply pressure here.*
2 the force with which a liquid or gas pushes against something. *Water pressure.*
3 strong influence. *Erica is under pressure to finish her work.*

pressurize or **pressurise** pressurizing pressurized *(v)*
1 to make someone do something. *Mimi pressurized me into staying.*
2 to seal off an aircraft cabin, diving chamber, etc. so that the air pressure inside stays the same as the pressure at the Earth's surface.

prestige *(press-teej)* *(n)* the good reputation and high status that comes from being successful, powerful, rich, etc. **prestigious** *(adj)*.

presumably *(adv)* probably.

presume presuming presumed *(v)*
1 to think that something is true without being certain.

2 to dare. *Don't presume to tell me what to do!* **presumption** *(n)*.

pretend pretending pretended *(v)*
1 to make believe. *The children pretended they were superheroes.*
2 to claim falsely. *Bridget pretended to know her way around town.*
3 to give a false show to trick or deceive someone. *Otto pretended to be asleep.* **pretence** *(n)*.

pretentious *(adj)* If someone or something is **pretentious**, they claim to be better or more important than they really are. *A pretentious poem.*

pretext *(n)* a false reason or excuse. *Steve went to the pub on the pretext of taking the dog for a walk.*

pretty prettier prettiest
1 *(adj)* attractive and pleasing to look at. **prettiness** *(n)*, **prettily** *(adv)*.
2 *(adv)* *(informal)* quite. *Pretty bad.*

prevail prevailing prevailed *(v)*
1 to succeed despite difficulties.
2 to be common or usual. *Poverty and crime prevail in many inner cities.* **prevalent** *(adj)*.

prevent preventing prevented *(v)* to stop something from happening. **prevention** *(n)*.

preventative
1 *(plural n)* If you take **preventative measures**, you take action to try and stop something from happening.
2 **preventative medicine** *(n)* health education or treatment that is intended to stop people developing disease and illness.

preview *(n)* a showing of a play or film before it is released for the public.

previous *(adj)* former, or happening before. *I like this school more than my previous one.* **previously** *(adv)*.

prey *(rhymes with tray)* prey; preying preyed
1 *(n)* a creature that is hunted and eaten by other animals.
2 *(v)* When an animal **preys on** another animal, it hunts it and then eats it.

price pricing priced
1 *(n)* the amount that you have to pay for something.
2 *(v)* to give something a price.

priceless *(adj)* If something is **priceless**, it is too valuable for anyone to say how much it is worth.

prick pricking pricked *(v)* to make a small hole in something with a sharp point. **prick** *(n)*.

prickle *(n)* a sharp point, for example, on the stalk of a rose. **prickly** *(adj)*.

pricey or **pricy** pricier priciest *(adj)* *(informal)* expensive.

pride *(n)*
1 a feeling of satisfaction in something that you do. *Zara takes pride in her work.*
2 a too high opinion of your own importance and cleverness.

priest *(n)* a religious leader who takes services in a church, temple, etc.

prim primmer primmest *(adj)* Someone who is **prim** is very formal and hates anything rough or rude.

prima donna *(n)*
1 a female opera star.
2 *(informal)* someone who is demanding and often bad-tempered.

primarily *(adv)* chiefly or mainly.

primary *(adj)*
1 most important, chief, or main.
2 first or earliest. *Primary education.*

primary colours *(n)* In painting, the **primary colours** are red, yellow, and blue, which can be mixed to make all the other colours.

primary school *(n)* In Britain, a **primary school** is a school for children aged five to eleven, or five to nine.

primate *(n)*
1 any member of the group of intelligent mammals that includes humans, apes, and monkeys.
2 an archbishop.

prime *(adj)* of first importance or quality. *Prime Minister. Prime beef.*

Prime Minister *(n)* the leader of a government in some countries.

prime number *(n)* a number that can be divided by itself or by 1. *7, 13, and 29 are all prime numbers.*

primeval *(pry-mee-vul)* *(adj)* belonging to the earliest period of the Earth. *Primeval life.*

primitive *(adj)* uncivilized, basic, and crude. *Conditions were very primitive.*

prince *(n)* the son of a king or queen, or the husband of a queen.

princess princesses *(n)* the daughter of a king or queen, or the wife of a prince.

principal
1 *(adj)* most important, chief, or main. **principally** *(adv)*.
2 *(n)* the head of a college or other organization.

principle
1 *(n)* a scientific rule or truth.
2 *(n)* a basic rule which governs your behaviour. *It's against Roy's principles to eat meat.*
3 If you agree to something **in principle**, you are happy with the general idea, but not necessarily with the details.

print

print printing printed
1 (v) to produce words or pictures on a page with a machine that uses ink. *Colour pictures are usually printed by combining four colours of ink on white paper. This is called four-colour printing. The picture below has been magnified so that you can see how it is made up of millions of overlapping dots of black, yellow, cyan (blue), and magenta (red).* **printer** (n).
2 (v) to write using letters that do not join up.
3 (n) a photograph, or a printed copy of a painting.

printed picture

magnified section

print-out (n) a printed copy of information stored in a computer.

prior (adj) earlier. *Paul can't come because of a prior engagement.*

priority priorities (n) something that is more important than other things.

prise prising prised (v) to force something open, using a lever.

prism (n) a clear glass or plastic shape that bends light or breaks it up into the colours of the spectrum. Prisms usually have triangular ends. *See* **periscope**, **shape**, **spectrum**.

prison (n) a building where people are forced to stay, usually as punishment for a crime.

private
1 (adj) If something is **private**, it belongs to or concerns one person, organization, etc. and no one else. *Private possessions.* **privacy** (n).
2 (adj) secret. *Private thoughts.* **privately** (adv).
3 (n) a soldier of the lowest rank.

private school (n) a school where parents pay for their children's education.

privatize or **privatise** privatizing privatized (v) to sell or hand over a government-funded public industry or organization to private individuals or companies. **privatization** (n).

privilege (n) a special advantage given to a person or a group of people. **privileged** (adj).

prize prizing prized
1 (n) a reward for winning a game or competition.
2 (v) to value something very much. *I prize my freedom.* **prized** (adj).

pro
1 (adj) If you are **pro** something, you are in favour of it.
2 (n) a shortened form of the word **professional**, often used in sport.
3 (plural n) **pros and cons** advantages and disadvantages.

probable (adj) likely, or expected to happen. *It's probable that Dawn will win.* **probability** (n), **probably** (adv).

probation (n)
1 If someone is **on probation** at work, they are having a trial period. **probationary** (adj).
2 If an offender is put **on probation** for a crime that they have committed, they are supervised for a certain time by a probation officer.

probe probing probed (v) to examine or explore something very carefully. **probe** (n).

problem (n)
1 a difficult situation that needs to be sorted out or overcome. **problematic** (adj).
2 a puzzle or question to be solved. *A maths problem.*

procedure (pro-see-dure) (n) a way of doing something.

proceed proceeding proceeded
1 (v) to move forward, or to carry on.
2 (plural n) The **proceeds** of an event are the sums of money that it raises.

process processes processing processed
1 (pro-sess) (n) an organized series of actions that produce a result. *We studied the process of making rubber.* **processing** (n).
2 (pro-sess) (v) When food is **processed**, it is treated and changed from its original state. **processing** (n), **processed** (adj).
3 (pro-sess) (v) to take part in a procession.

procession (n) a number of people walking or driving along a route as part of a public festival, religious service, etc.

proclaim proclaiming proclaimed (v) If someone **proclaims** something, they announce it publicly. **proclamation** (n).

procrastinate procrastinating procrastinated (v) to put off something that you have to do. **procrastination** (n).

prod prodding prodded (v) to poke someone or something. **prod** (n).

prodigy (prod-ij-ee) prodigies (n) Child **prodigies** are extraordinarily clever or talented for their age.

produce producing produced
1 (prod-yuce) (v) to make something. *This factory produces cars.*
2 (prod-yuce) (n) things that are produced or grown for eating. *Dairy produce.*
3 (prod-yuce) (v) to bring something out for people to see. *Samantha produced a mouse from her pocket.*
4 (prod-yuce) (v) to be in charge of putting on a play or making a film. **producer** (n).

product (n)
1 something that is manufactured or made by a natural process.
2 the result that you get when you multiply two numbers. *15 is the product of 3 and 5.*

production (n)
1 the process of manufacturing or growing something.
2 a play, opera, show, etc.
3 **production line** a system of manufacturing in which the product moves along while different things are added or done to it.

productive (adj) making a lot of products, or producing good results. *A productive meeting.* **productivity** (n).

profession (n)
1 a job for which you need special training or study. *Medicine, teaching, and law are all professions.*
2 something that you state openly. *A profession of love.*

professional
1 (n) a member of a profession, for example, a lawyer. **professional** (adj).
2 (n) someone who is paid for doing something that many others do as amateurs. *A football professional.* **professional** (adj).
3 (adj) If somebody is **professional** at something, they are expert at it. **professionally** (adv).

professor (n) the head and principal teacher of a university department.

proficient (prof-ish-ent) (adj) If you are **proficient** at doing something, you are able to do it properly and skilfully. **proficiency** (n), **proficiently** (adv).

profile (n)
1 the outline of someone's face, seen from the side.
2 a brief account of someone's life or progress. *Pupil profiles.* **profile** (v).

proportion

profit (n)
the money made by selling something, after the cost of making it or buying it has been taken away.
profit (v), **profitable** (adj).

profound (adj)
very deeply felt or thought. *Profound sadness*. **profoundly** (adv).

program
programming programmed
1 (n) a series of instructions written in a special code that controls the way that a computer works.
2 (v) to give computers or other machines instructions to make them work. **programming** (n).

programme (n)
1 a television or radio show.
2 a schedule, or a list of events.
3 a theatre or concert **programme** is a pamphlet that gives you information about the performance.

programmer (n) someone whose job is to program a computer.

progress progresses
progressing progressed
1 (v) to move forward, or to improve slowly. *How are you progressing with your fitness programme?*
progress (n), **progression** (n).
2 If something is **in progress**, it is happening. *Roadworks are in progress all this week.*

prohibit prohibiting prohibited
(v) to stop or ban something officially.
prohibition (n).

project (proj-ekt)
projecting projected
1 (n) a scheme, or a plan.
2 (n) a study of something, worked on over a period of time. *We are starting a project on the Romans.*
3 (v) to stick out. *The branch projected into the road.* **projecting** (adj).
4 (v) to show an image on a screen. **projector** (n).
5 (v) to throw something forwards. **projectile** (n).
6 (v) to look ahead, or to forecast. *The company has projected a loss for next year.*
7 (v) If you **project** your voice, you make it carry a long way.

projection (n)
1 something that sticks out. *We noticed a strange projection behind the curtain.*
2 a forecast, or a prediction.
3 A **map projection** is a way of representing the globe on a flat page. *Mercator's projection.*

projector (n) a piece of equipment which shows slides or film on a screen.

prolific (adj)
very productive, or producing a large quantity. *A prolific writer.*

prologue (pro-log) (n) a short speech or piece of writing which introduces a play, story, or poem.

prolong prolonging prolonged (v)
to make something last longer.

promenade (n)
a paved road or path that runs beside the beach at a seaside resort.

prominent (adj)
1 very easily seen. *The windmill is a prominent landmark.*
2 famous, or important. *A prominent politician.*
prominence (n).

promise promising promised
1 (v) to say definitely that you will do something. **promise** (n).
2 (n) Someone who shows **promise** seems likely to do well in the future. **promising** (adj).

promote promoting promoted (v)
1 to move someone to a more important job. **promotion** (n).
2 If a sports team is **promoted**, it moves to a higher league.
promotion (n).
3 to make the public aware of someone or something. *Gordon is busy promoting his latest book.* **promotion** (n).

prompt prompting prompted;
prompter promptest
1 (adj) very quick and without delay. *A prompt answer.* **promptly** (adv).
2 (v) to remind actors of their lines when they have forgotten them during a play. **prompt** (n).

prone (adj)
1 vulnerable, or easily affected by something harmful. *Susie is prone to colds in the winter.*
2 lying flat or face-down.

prong (n)
one of the sharp points of a fork.

pronoun (n) a word that is used in place of a noun. "I", "me", "her", and "it" are all pronouns. *See page 3.*

pronounce
pronouncing pronounced (v)
1 to say words in a particular way. *How do you pronounce "psychic"?*
2 to make a formal announcement. *The mayor pronounced the fair open.*

pronunciation
(pro-nun-see-ay-shun) (n) the way in which a word is pronounced.

proof (n)
evidence that something is true. *Do you have proof of your age?*

prop propping propped
1 (v) to support something that would otherwise fall down. *Bob propped the ladder against the wall.* **prop** (n).
2 (n) In theatre, films, etc. a **prop** is any item that the actors need to carry or use. Prop is short for property. *Sam used a wooden sword as a prop.*

propaganda (singular n)
biased information, used to present a certain viewpoint.

propel propelling propelled (v)
to drive or push something forward. *The aircraft was propelled by twin jet engines.* **propulsion** (n).

propellant (n) a chemical or fuel that propels something. See **aerosol**.

propeller (n) a set of rotating blades which provide force to move a vehicle through water or air.

proper (adj)
1 accepted, or right. *Is this the proper way to sit?* **properly** (adv).
2 real. *I want a proper explanation, not a made-up story.*
3 correct in behaviour. *Claudia is very prim and proper.* **properly** (adv).

proper noun (n) A proper noun is the name of a particular person, place, time, etc., such as "Jane", "New York", "Wednesday". Proper nouns start with a capital letter.

property properties (n)
1 the things that someone owns. *Lost property.*
2 buildings and land belonging to someone. *Two fierce dogs guarded the property.*

prophesy (prof-ess-eye) prophesies
prophesying prophesied (v)
to predict that something will happen in the future.
prophecy (prof-ess-ee) (n).

prophet (prof-it) (n)
someone who predicts what will happen in the future.

proportion
1 (n) a part of something. *A large proportion of the class supported me.*
2 (n) the amount of something in relation to other things. *The proportion of boys to girls in the school is growing.* **proportional** (adj),
proportionally (adv).
3 If something is **in proportion** to something else, it is the correct size in relation to it. *Edna has a large nose, but it is in proportion to the rest of her features.*
4 (plural n) The **proportions** of something are its measurements. *The room's proportions were 3 metres by 8 metres.*

a b c d e f g h i j k l m n o p q r s t u v w x y z

propose

propose proposing proposed (v)
1 to suggest a plan or an
idea. *Andy proposed that we
all went swimming.* **proposal** (n).
2 to ask someone to
marry you. **proposal** (n).

propulsion (n)
the force by which a plane, rocket,
etc. is pushed along. *Jet propulsion.*

prose (n) writing that is in
ordinary lines, not in verse.

prosecute prosecuting prosecuted
(v) to accuse someone in a
court of law. **prosecution** (n).

prospect (n)
1 something in the future that
you look forward to or dread.
2 a view, or a scene.

prospectus prospectuses (n)
a brochure giving information
about a school, company, etc.

prosper prospering prospered
(v) to be successful, or to thrive.
prosperity (n), **prosperous** (adj).

protect protecting protected (v)
to guard or shelter something.
protection (n), **protective** (adj).

protein (pro-teen) (n) a substance
found in foods such as meat, cheese,
eggs, and lentils. Humans and animals
need protein in their diet.

protest protesting protested
1 (pro-test) (v) to object to something
strongly and publicly.
2 (pro-test) (n) a demonstration or a
statement against something.

Protestant (prot-iss-tant) (n)
a Christian who does not
belong to the Roman Catholic
or Orthodox church.

proton (n) one of the microscopic
parts of an atom that carries a
positive electrical charge. *See* **atom**.

protoplasm (n)
a jelly-like substance that makes
up the living matter of all cells.

prototype (n)
the first version of a new
invention, used for experiment
and development. **prototype** (adj).

protractor (n) a semicircular
instrument used for measuring angles
and usually made of transparent
plastic. *See* **geometry**.

protrude protruding protruded (v)
to stick out, or to jut out.
The rocks protruded into the sea.

proud prouder proudest (adj)
1 pleased with what you or someone
else has achieved. **proudly** (adv).
2 A **proud** person thinks too highly of
their own importance or abilities.

prove proving proved
or **proven** (v) to show that
something is true.*The experiment
proved our hypothesis.*

proverb (n) a wise, old
saying or piece of advice.

provide providing provided
1 (v) to supply the things that
someone needs. **provision** (n).
2 **provided** (conj) on condition that,
or as long as. *I will go swimming
provided that you come too.*

province (n)
a district, or a region of a country.

provision
1 (n) the act of providing something.
2 **provisions** (plural n) groceries
and other household goods.

provisional (adj) If something
is **provisional**, it is temporary or
not yet definite. *A provisional
driving licence.* **provisionally** (adv).

provoke provoking provoked (v)
to annoy someone and make
them angry. **provocation** (n),
provocative (adj).

prowess (n) skill, or bravery.
*Laura's prowess on the ski
slopes is legendary.*

prowl prowling prowled (v)
to move around secretly, like
an animal looking for food.

proximity (n) nearness.

prudent (adj) If you are **prudent**,
you are cautious and think carefully
before you do something.
prudence (n), **prudently** (adv).

prune pruning pruned
1 (n) a dried plum.
2 (v) to cut off branches from
a tree or bush, in order to make
it grow more strongly.

pry pries prying pried (v)
If you **pry**, you look into other
people's business in a nosy way.

PS short for **postscript**.

psalm (sahm) (n)
a sacred song or poem, especially one
from the Book of Psalms in the Bible.

pseudonym (syoo-doh-nim) (n)
a name that you use which is not your
own. Some writers use pseudonyms.

psychiatrist (sy-ky-a-trist) (n)
a doctor who is trained
to treat mental illness.
psychiatry (n), **psychiatric** (adj).

psychic (sy-kik) (adj)
Someone who is **psychic** claims to be
able to use their mind in an unusual
way, for example, to tell what people
are thinking. **psychic** (n).

psychologist (sy-kol-oj-ist) (n)
someone who studies people's
minds and the ways that
people behave. **psychology** (n),
psychological (adj).

psychopath (sy-koh-path) (n)
someone who has something
wrong with their character,
so that they are violent or
dangerous. **psychopathic** (adj).

PTO
The letters **PTO**, written at the bottom
of a page, stand for Please Turn Over.

pub (n) a place where adults
can go to drink alcohol. Pub
is short for public house.

puberty (pew-ber-tee) (n)
the time when your body changes
from a child's to an adult's.

public
1 (adj) to do with people.
Public opinion.
2 (adj) If something is **public**,
it belongs to, or can be used by,
everybody. *Public transport.*
publicly (adv).
3 the public (n) people in general.

publican (n)
someone who runs a pub.

publication (n)
1 The **publication** of a book
or magazine is the production
and distribution of it, so that
people can buy it.
2 a book, or a magazine.

publicity (n)
information that tells you about a
person or an event. *The film received
a lot of publicity in the newspapers.*

publicize or **publicise**
publicizing publicized (v)
If you **publicize** an event, you
make it known to as many people
as possible. **publicist** (n).

public opinion (singular n) the
views or beliefs of people in general.

public school (n)
a school where parents pay
for their children's education.

publish publishes
publishing published (v)
to produce and distribute a book,
magazine, etc., so that people can
buy it. **publisher** (n), **publishing** (n).

pucker puckering puckered (v)
to wrinkle, or to fold. **pucker** (n).

pudding (n)
1 a sweet food served at
the end of a meal.
2 a sponge or suet mixture
cooked with fruit or meat.
A treacle pudding.

puddle *(n)* a small pool of rainwater or other liquid.

puff puffing puffed
1 *(v)* to blow or breathe out something, such as smoke or steam. **puff** *(n)*.
2 **puff up** *(v)* to swell up. **puffy** *(adj)*.
3 **puff pastry** *(n)* pastry made in thin layers, which puffs up when it is cooked.

puffin *(n)*
a black and white sea bird whose beak becomes brightly coloured in the mating season.

pugnacious *(adj)*
If someone is **pugnacious**, they are fond of fighting or quarrelling. **pugnaciously** *(adv)*.

pull pulling pulled *(v)*
1 to move something towards you. **pull** *(n)*.
2 If you **pull out** of something, you stop doing it. *Adam pulled out of the team because of an injured knee.*
3 **pull up** to stop a vehicle.

puffin

pulley *(n)*
1 a wheel with a grooved rim in which a rope or chain can run, used to lift loads more easily.
2 a lifting machine made from a rope or chain and a set of linked pulleys. *The diagram below shows how a pulley is used to lift a heavy load.*

pullover *(n)* a knitted piece of clothing that you wear on the top half of your body.

pulp *(n)* a soft, crushed mass of something, such as fruit, vegetables, or wood. **pulp** *(v)*.

pulpit *(n)*
a raised, enclosed platform in a church where a priest stands to preach.

pulsate pulsating pulsated *(v)*
to beat or vibrate regularly. *Rock music pulsated through the house.*

pulse *(n)*
1 a bean, pea, or lentil seed.
2 a steady beat or throb, especially the pumping of blood through your body. **pulse** *(v)*.

pulley
— wheel
— rope
— load

puma *(pyoo-ma) (n)*
a large, wild cat found in America. Also known as a cougar.

pumice stone *(n)*
a piece of light, greyish rock, used for rubbing away hard skin.

pummel pummelling pummelled *(v)* to punch someone or something repeatedly.

pump pumping pumped
1 *(n)* a machine that forces liquids or gases from one container into another. *A bicycle pump. A water pump.*
2 *(v)* to empty or fill a container using a pump.
3 **pumps** *(plural n)* flat, slip-on shoes, often made of canvas.
4 *(v)* If you **pump** someone for information, you keep asking them questions.

pumpkin *(n)* a very big, round, orange fruit that grows on the ground. People often carve faces in pumpkins at Halloween.

pun *(n)* a joke based on a word that has two meanings. **pun** *(v)*.

punch punches punching punched
1 *(v)* to hit someone or something with your fist. **punch** *(n)*.
2 *(n)* a drink made from fruit juice, spices, and usually alcohol.
3 *(n)* a metal tool used for making holes. **punch** *(v)*.
4 **punch line** *(n)* the last line of a joke or story, which makes it funny or surprising.

pumpkin

punctual *(adj)* If you are **punctual**, you arrive at the right time. **punctuality** *(n)*, **punctually** *(adv)*.

punctuation
1 *(singular n)* marks that you use in writing to divide up sentences, to show that someone is speaking, or to show questions, etc. **punctuate** *(v)*.
2 **punctuation mark** *(n)* a written mark such as a comma, exclamation mark, full stop, etc.

puncture *(n)*
a hole in a ball, tyre, etc., made by a sharp object. **puncture** *(v)*.

pungent *(adj)* If something is **pungent**, it tastes or smells strong or sharp. *A pungent drink.*

punish punishes punishing punished *(v)* If you **punish** someone, you make them suffer for committing a crime, or for behaving badly. **punishment** *(n)*.

Punjabi *(poon-jah-bee) (n)*
a language spoken in the Punjab, a state of India.

punk *(n)*
1 a style of music and dress that was popular in the 1970s. Punks often used razor blades and safety pins for decoration, and had brightly coloured hair.
2 **punk rock** loud, fast music played by punk bands, often with an anti-authoritarian message.

punt *(n)*
a boat with a flat bottom, which you push along with a long pole. **punt** *(v)*.

puny punier puniest *(adj)* small and feeble. **puniness** *(n)*, **punily** *(adv)*.

pupa pupae *or* pupas *(n)*
an insect at the stage of development between a larva and an adult. *See* **caterpillar**.

pupil *(n)*
1 someone who is being taught, especially a schoolchild.
2 the round, black part of your eye, that lets light travel through it. *See* **eye**.

puppet *(n)*
a toy in the shape of a person or an animal that you control by pulling strings that are attached to it, or by moving your hand inside it.

puppy puppies *(n)*
1 a young dog.
2 **puppy fat** extra weight which children lose as they grow older.

purchase purchasing purchased
1 *(v)* to buy something. **purchaser** *(n)*.
2 *(n)* something that has been bought.

pure purer purest *(adj)*
clean and not mixed with anything else. *Pure gold.* **purity** *(n)*.

purée *(pyoor-ay) (n)*
liquidized or sieved food. **purée** *(v)*, **puréed** *(adj)*.

purge purging purged *(v)*
to clean something out by getting rid of unwanted things. **purge** *(n)*.

purify purifies purifying purified *(v)* to make someone or something pure. *Edward had to purify the water before he could drink it.* **purification** *(n)*.

purple *(n)* the colour of blackcurrant juice. **purple** *(adj)*.

purpose
1 *(n)* a reason, or an intention. **purposeful** *(adj)*, **purposely** *(adv)*.
2 **on purpose** deliberately.

purr purring purred *(v)*
1 When a cat **purrs**, it makes a low sound in its throat to show pleasure. **purr** *(n)*.
2 to make a low sound similar to a cat. *The limousine purred up the drive.*

purse pursing pursed
1 *(n)* a small container in which people keep their money.
2 *(v)* If you **purse your lips**, you press them together.

pursue *(per-syoo)* pursuing pursued *(v)*
1 to follow or chase something.
2 to continue something. *We'll pursue this argument later.*

pursuit *(per-syoot)*
1 *(n)* an activity or an occupation.
2 If you are **in pursuit of** someone, you are trying to catch them.

pus *(n)* a thick, yellowish liquid that comes out of an infected wound.

push pushes pushing pushed *(v)*
1 to move something away from you. **push** *(n)*.
2 to press yourself forward.
3 to try to force someone to do something. *Morgan's father pushed him into a medical career.*

push-up *see* **press-up**.

put putting put *(v)*
1 to place, lay, or move something.
2 to express in words. *How can I put this so that you'll understand?*
3 If you **put down** an animal, you kill it because it is very old or ill.
4 If you **put something off**, you delay doing it.

5 If you **put someone off** something, you stop them liking it.
6 If you **put someone up**, you let them sleep overnight at your house.
7 If you **put up with** something, you allow it even though it annoys you.
8 If you **put someone through** something, you make them endure it.

putrid *(pyoo-trid)* *(adj)* decaying and foul-smelling.

putt *(rhymes with but)* putting putted *(v)* to tap a golf ball into the hole on a green. **putt** *(n)*, **putter** *(n)*.

putty putties *(n)* a paste that sets hard, used to fix windows into frames.

puzzle puzzling puzzled
1 *(n)* a game or activity for which you have to think hard in order to solve problems. *A crossword puzzle.*
2 *(n)* someone or something that is hard to understand.
3 *(v)* to make someone confused or unsure. **puzzled** *(adj)*.

pyjamas *(plural n)* a top and trousers that you wear in bed.

pylon *(n)* a tall, metal tower that supports electricity cables.

pyramid *(n)*
1 a solid shape with triangular sides that meet at the top. Most pyramids have a square base and four sides. *See* **shape**.
2 an Ancient Egyptian stone monument where Pharaohs and their treasure were buried. *The picture shows a reconstruction of how a pyramid was built and a cutaway view of the Great Pyramid at Giza in Egypt.*

Qq

quack quacking quacked *(v)* When ducks **quack**, they make a sharp, loud sound. **quack** *(n)*.

quad *(n)* an open square with buildings around it, in a school or college. Quad is short for quadrangle.

quadrant *(n)* a quarter of a circle, or a quarter of the circumference of a circle.

quadrilateral *(n)* a flat shape with four straight sides. **quadrilateral** *(adj)*.

quadruped *(n)* a four-footed animal.

quadruple quadrupling quadrupled
1 *(v)* to multiply something by four.
2 *(adj)* four times as big, or four times as many.

quadruplet *(n)* one of four children born at almost the same time to one mother.

quagmire *(n)* a wet and boggy area.

quail quailing quailed
1 *(n)* a small bird that is hunted for sport and for food.
2 *(v)* If you **quail**, you feel or look afraid. *Kylie quailed as the monster drew nearer.*

quaint quainter quaintest *(adj)* charming and old-fashioned. *A quaint little fishing village.* **quaintness** *(n)*, **quaintly** *(adv)*.

quake quaking quaked
1 *(v)* to shake and tremble with fear.
2 *(n)* *(informal)* an earthquake.

qualification *(n)*
1 a skill or ability that makes you able to do something.
2 a certificate which shows that you have certain skills or abilities.

qualify qualifies qualifying qualified *(v)*
1 to reach a level or standard that allows you to do something. *Winning the match qualified us to play in the final.*
2 to change or limit the meaning of something. *Victoria qualified the statement, "Boys are stupid", by adding the word "most".*

quality qualities *(n)*
1 The **quality** of something is how good or bad it is. *A poor quality suit.*
2 a special characteristic of someone or something. *Clare has all the right qualities to be a nurse.*

Mediterranean sea

Giza

EGYPT

Nile

capstone (made from solid limestone)

white limestone casing

Great Pyramid, Giza, Egypt (cutaway)

local limestone

Pharaoh's burial chamber

Queen's burial chamber

grand gallery

limestone packing blocks (built in a step structure)

tree trunk (used as roller under sledge)

stone block on wooden sledge

underground burial chamber

descending corridor

ascending corridor

ramp (made of brick and rubble)

Qur'an

qualm *(rhymes with arm) (n)*
a feeling of worry or uneasiness.
I had serious qualms about flying.

quandary *(kwon-dree)*
quandaries *(n)*
If you are **in a quandary** about
something, you are confused, and
do not know what to do about it.

quantity quantities *(n)*
an amount or number.

quarantine *(n)* When an animal
is put **in quarantine**, it is kept
away from other animals in case
it has a disease. **quarantine** *(v).*

quarrel quarrelling quarrelled
1 *(v)* to argue or to disagree.
quarrelsome *(adj).*
2 *(n)* an argument.

quarry quarries *(n)*
1 a place where stone, slate, etc.,
is dug from the ground. **quarry** *(v).*
2 a person or an animal that
is being chased or hunted.

quarter *(n)*
1 one of four equal parts. **quarter** *(v).*
2 a part of a town. *The Latin quarter
in Paris is famous for its artists.*
3 **quarters** *(plural n)* lodgings
or rooms where people live.

quartet *(n)* a piece of music that
is played or sung by four people.

quartz *(n)* a hard mineral that comes
in many different forms and colours.
*Quartz is used to make very accurate
clocks, watches,
and electronic
equipment.*

quash quashes
quashing
quashed *(v)*
1 to put down
a rebellion.
2 to reject an idea
or a decision. *The appeal
court quashed the conviction.*

quaver quavering quavered
1 *(v)* to shake, or to tremble.
*Nicky's voice quavered
because she was so nervous.*
2 *(n)* a musical note representing
half of one beat. *See* **notation**.

quay *(key) (n)* a place where
boats can stop to load or unload.

queasy queasier queasiest *(adj)*
If you feel **queasy**, you feel sick
and uneasy. **queasiness** *(n).*

queen *(n)*
1 a woman from a royal family,
who is the ruler of her country.
2 the wife of a king.
3 a large bee, wasp, or ant, which
can lay eggs. *See* **honeycomb**.

4 a playing card with a
picture of a queen on it.
5 the most powerful
chesspiece, which can move
in any direction. *See* **chess**.

queer queerer queerest *(adj)*
odd or strange. **queerly** *(adv).*

quell quelling quelled *(v)* to stop,
or to become calm. *My fears were
quelled when I saw someone I knew.*

quench quenches
quenching quenched *(v)*
1 If you **quench** a fire, you put it out.
2 If you **quench** your thirst, you
drink until you are no longer thirsty.

query *(kweer-ee)* queries
querying queried
1 *(n)* a question or doubt
about something.
2 *(v)* to ask questions about
something because you think
there has been some mistake.
May I query that statement?

quest *(n)* a long search.

question questioning questioned
1 *(n)* a sentence that asks something.
2 *(n)* a problem, or something that
needs to be talked about. *We need
to tackle the question of bullying.*
3 *(v)* to ask questions.
4 *(v)* to be doubtful about something.
I question the truth of that claim.

question mark *(n)* the punctuation
mark (?), used in writing to show
that a sentence is a question.

questionnaire *(n)* a list of
questions that someone asks you
in order to find out your opinions.

queue *(kyoo)* queueing queued
1 *(n)* a line of people
waiting for something.
2 *(v)* to wait in a line of people.

quibble quibbling quibbled *(v)*
to argue about unimportant
things. **quibble** *(n).*

quiche *(keesh) (n)* a savoury dish
made of pastry and filled with
eggs, cheese, vegetables, etc.

quick quicker quickest
1 *(adj)* fast. **quicken** *(v),*
quick *(adv),* **quickly** *(adv).*
2 *(adj)* clever and lively.
3 *(n)* the skin under your nails.

quicksand *(n)*
loose, wet sand that you can sink into.

quiet quieter quietest *(adj)*
1 not loud. *Everyone spoke
in quiet voices.* **quietness** *(n),*
quieten *(v),* **quietly** *(adv).*
2 peaceful and calm. *We spent
a quiet afternoon by the river.*
quietness *(n),* **quietly** *(adv).*

quill *(n)*
1 the long, hollow, central
part of a bird's feather.
2 one of the long, pointed
spines on a porcupine or
hedgehog. *See* **porcupine**.
3 **quill pen** a pen made
from a bird's feather, with
its quill cut to form a nib.

quilt *(n)* a warm,
usually padded
covering for a bed.

quilted *(adj)*
If material is **quilted**,
it is padded and sewn in lines.

quintet *(n)* a piece of music that
is played or sung by five people.

quip *(n)* a witty or clever remark.

quit quitting
quit *or* quitted *(v)*
1 to stop doing something.
Dad has promised to quit smoking.
2 to leave something.
Pat decided to quit his job.

quite *(adv)*
1 rather or fairly. *The
concert was quite good.*
2 completely. *Have you quite finished?*

quiver quivering quivered
1 *(v)* to tremble or vibrate. **quiver** *(n).*
2 *(n)* a case for arrows.

quiz quizzes
quizzing quizzed
1 *(n)* a test or game where
you have to answer questions.
2 *(v)* to question someone closely.

quota *(n)*
a fixed amount or share of
something. *Our class already
has its quota of books.*

quotation *(n)*
1 a sentence or short passage
from a book, play, speech, etc.
which is repeated by someone else.
2 a written estimate of
how much a job will cost.

quotation mark *(n)*
the punctuation mark (") or (')
used in writing to show where
speech begins and ends or used
to highlight certain words.

quote quoting quoted *(v)*
1 to repeat words that
were spoken or written
by someone else. **quote** *(n).*
2 to estimate or guess how
much a job will cost. **quote** *(n).*

quotient *(kwo-shent) (n)*
the number that you get when
you divide one number by another.
3 is the quotient of 12 and 4.

Qur'an *see* **Koran**.

nib — **quill
pen**

**quartz
crystal**

a
b
c
d
e
f
g
h
i
j
k
l
m
n
o
p
q
r
s
t
u
v
w
x
y
z

Rr

rabbi *(rab-eye)* *(n)*
a Jewish religious leader.

rabbit *(n)*
a small, long-eared, furry mammal
that lives in a burrow. *See* **angora**.

rabble *(n)* a noisy crowd of people.

rabies *(ray-beez)* *(n)* an often fatal
disease that affects dogs, humans,
and other animals. **rabid** *(rab-id)* *(adj)*.

raccoon or **racoon** *(n)*
a mammal with a black and
white face and a ringed tail,
which lives in North America.

race racing raced
1 *(n)* a test of speed.
A running race. **race** *(v)*.
2 *(n)* one of the major groups
into which human beings can be
divided. People of the same race
come from the same part of the
world and share the same physical
characteristics, such as skin colour.
3 *(v)* to run or move very fast.

race relations *(plural n)*
the way that people of different
races get on together when they
live in the same community.

racial *(adj)*
1 to do with a person's race.
2 to do with different races.
Racial harmony.

racist *(ray-sist)* *(adj)* Someone
who is **racist** thinks that some races
are better than others, and treats
people of other races unfairly or
cruelly. **racism** *(n)*, **racist** *(n)*.

rack racking racked
1 *(n)* a framework for holding
things or for hanging things from.
A plate rack. A clothes rack.
2 *(n)* a medieval instrument of torture,
used to stretch the body of a victim.
3 *(v)* If you **rack your brains**,
you think very hard. *I racked my
brains to remember his name.*

racket *(n)*
1 **racket** or **racquet** a stringed bat
that you use in tennis, squash, and
badminton. *See* **badminton**.
2 a very loud noise. *Frankie was
making a racket in the kitchen.*
3 a dishonest activity. *The police
exposed a drugs racket.*

racoon *see* **raccoon**.

racquet *see* **racket**.

radar *(n)* Planes and ships use **radar**
to find solid objects by reflecting
radio waves off them. Radar stands
for RAdio Detecting And Ranging.

radial *(adj)*
spreading out from the centre.

radiant *(adj)*
1 bright and shining. **radiance** *(n)*.
2 Someone who is **radiant**
looks very healthy and happy.

radiate radiating radiated *(v)*
1 to spread out
from the centre.
2 to send out
something strongly.

radiation *(n)*
1 the sending out of rays
of light, heat, etc.
2 particles that are sent out
from a radioactive substance.

radiator *(n)*
1 a metal container through
which hot water or steam circulates,
sending out heat into a room.
2 a metal device through which
water circulates to cool a vehicle's
engine. *See* **car**, **racing car**.

radical *(adj)*
1 If a change is **radical**, it is
thorough and has important and
far-reaching effects. *Eva made
a radical change in her attitude
towards her homework.* **radically** *(adv)*.
2 Someone who is **radical** believes in
extreme political change. **radical** *(n)*.

radio radioing radioed
1 *(n)* a piece of equipment that
you use to listen to sounds sent
by electrical waves. **radio** *(adj)*.
2 *(v)* to send a message using a
radio. *Gareth had to radio for help.*

radioactive *(adj)*
If an object is **radioactive**,
it gives off strong, usually
harmful rays. **radioactivity** *(n)*.

radiography *(n)*
the process of taking X-ray
photographs of people's bones,
organs, etc. **radiographer** *(n)*.

radish radishes *(n)*
a small, red and white vegetable that
you eat in salads. *See* **vegetable**.

radium *(n)*
a radioactive element sometimes
used to treat cancer.

racing car *(cutaway)* — nose cone — driver's pedals — fuel tank in here — rear view mirror — roll hoop (protects driver) — V8 engine — engine oil cooler — wide "slick" tyre — adjustable fins (give car down force)

front wing (gives car down force)

car body (made from carbon fibres soaked in resin)

front wing endplate

carbon fibre disc brake — front wing vortex generator (channels air past wheels) — fireproof racing suit — rain light — rear jack point

brake callipers — suspension wishbone — steering wheel with gear levers — full-harness seat belt — undertray

racing car *(n)* a car designed to race
at high speeds. *The picture shows a
cutaway view of a Benetton Ford
B193B Formula One car from 1993.*

telemetry aerial (transmits information from car to pits) — water radiator — exhaust pipes — rear suspension

radius (ray-dee-uss)
radiuses or **radii** (n)
1 a straight line drawn from the centre of a circle to its outer edge. See **circle**.
2 a bone in your lower arm. See **skeleton**.
3 a circular area around a thing or a place. Most of my friends live within a radius of a mile from my house.

raffle (n) a way of raising money by selling tickets and then giving prizes to people with winning tickets. **raffle** (v).

raft rafting rafted
1 (n) a floating platform, often made from logs tied together.
2 (v) to travel by raft. **rafting** (n).
3 (n) an inflatable rubber craft with a flat bottom. The picture shows an inflatable raft travelling through fast-moving water.

inflatable raft

rag
1 (n) a piece of old cloth.
2 rags (plural n) very old, torn clothing. The beggar was dressed in rags.

rage raging raged
1 (n) If you are **in a rage**, you are very angry. David was in a rage about his parking ticket.
2 (v) to be violent or noisy. The bull raged through the town.

ragged (rag-ed) (adj)
old, torn, and scruffy. **raggedly** (adv).

raid (n)
1 a sudden attack on a place. **raider** (n), **raid** (v).
2 a sudden visit by the police to search for criminals, drugs, etc. **raid** (v).

rail (n)
1 a fixed bar or metal track.
2 the railway. Thomas loves travelling by rail. **rail** (adj).

railing (n)
a metal bar that is a part of a fence.

railway (n)
1 a train track.
2 a system of transport using trains.

rain raining rained
1 (n) water that falls from clouds. **rain** (v), **rainy** (adj).
2 (v) to fall like rain.

rainbow (n)
an arch of different colours caused by sunlight shining through raindrops. See **spectrum**.

rainfall (n) the amount of rain that falls in one place in a certain time.

rainforest (n) a thick, tropical forest where a lot of rain falls. The picture shows the main rainforests of the world, and some examples of rainforest wildlife. **rainforest** (adj).

rainforests and rainforest wildlife

orchid

ruffed lemur (Madagascar)

carpenter bee (South East Asia)

hyacinth macaw (South America)

■ rainforest

NORTH AMERICA

EUROPE

ASIA

Central America

AFRICA

Amazonia

Congo

Borneo

India

Papua New Guinea

palm weevil (Africa)

SOUTH AMERICA

Sumatra

AUSTRALIA

Madagascar

pangolin (Africa)

golden cock-of-the-rock (South America)

poison dart frog (South America)

raise raising raised (v)
1 to lift something up. Raise your glasses for a toast.
2 If you **raise** money, you collect it for a particular cause or charity.
3 to look after children or young animals until they are adults. Martha has raised five sons.

raisin (n) a dried grape.

rake raking raked
1 (n) a garden tool with metal teeth, used to level soil or to collect leaves, grass cuttings, etc.
2 (v) to use a rake. Bernard is raking up leaves.
3 (v) (informal) If you **rake it in**, you make a lot of money.

rally rallies (n)
1 a large meeting. A political rally.
2 In racket games, such as tennis, a **rally** is a long exchange of shots.

ram ramming rammed
1 (n) a male sheep.
2 (v) to crash into something deliberately.
3 (v) to push something into a space. Kitty rammed her clothes into the bag.
4 ram raid (v) to drive a vehicle into a shop front in order to steal from that shop. **ram raider** (n), **ram raiding** (n).

RAM (n) the part of a computer's memory which is lost when you switch the computer off. The initials RAM stand for Random Access Memory.

Ramadan (n)
the ninth month of the Islamic year when Muslims must not eat between sunrise and sunset.

Some words that begin with a "r" sound are spelt "wr".

ramble

ramble rambling rambled *(v)*
1 to go on a long country walk for pleasure. **ramble** *(n)*, **rambler** *(n)*.
2 to speak for a long time in a way that is hard to follow.

rambling *(adj)*
badly planned, or out of control. *A rambling house. A rambling speech.*

ramp *(n)* a man-made slope linking one level with another.

rampage *(n)* If you go **on the rampage**, you rush about in a noisy and destructive way. **rampage** *(v)*.

rampant *(adj)*
wild and unrestrained. *Rampant weeds.*

rampart *(n)* the surrounding wall or embankment of a fort or castle.

ramshackle *(adj)* rickety, or likely to fall apart. *A ramshackle cottage.*

ranch ranches *(n)*
a large farm for cattle, usually in North America. **rancher** *(n)*.

rancid *(adj)* Rancid food tastes unpleasant because it has gone bad.

rand *(n)*
the main unit of money in South Africa.

random
1 *(adj)* without any fixed plan or order. *Julian grabbed a random selection of clothes.* **randomly** *(adv)*.
2 If you do something **at random**, you do it without any plan or purpose.

range ranging ranged
1 *(n)* a collection or number of things.
2 *(v)* to vary between one extreme and the other. *The dogs ranged in size from tiny Chihuahuas to enormous wolfhounds.* **range** *(n)*.
3 *(n)* the distance that a bullet or rocket can travel.
4 *(n)* an area of open land used for a special purpose. *A cattle range.*
5 *(n)* a long chain of mountains.
6 *(v)* to wander over a large area. *Cattle ranged over the plains.*
7 *(n)* a cooking stove.

ranger *(n)* someone in charge of a wildlife park or forest.

rank *(n)*
1 an official position or job level. *Nick rose to the rank of colonel.*
2 a line of people or things. *A taxi rank.*
3 social class.

ransack
ransacking ransacked *(v)* to search a place wildly, usually looking for things to steal.

ransom *(n)*
money that is demanded before someone can be set free.

rant ranting ranted *(v)* to talk or shout in a loud and angry manner.

rap rapping rapped
1 *(v)* to hit something sharply and quickly. *The teacher had to rap the table to get their attention.* **rap** *(n)*.
2 *(n)* a type of music where words are spoken in a rhythmical way with a musical backing. **rap** *(v)*.

rape raping raped
1 *(v)* to force someone to have sexual intercourse. **rapist** *(n)*.
2 *(n)* a bright yellow plant, used for cattle feed and oil.

rapid *(adj)* quick and speedy. **rapidity** *(n)*, **rapidly** *(adv)*.

rapier *(n)* a long, double-edged sword, often used in duels in the 16th and 17th centuries. *This rapier was made in Italy in the 16th century.*

rapier

knuckle guard

double-edged steel blade

hilt   steel inlaid with gold

guard for thumb and forefinger

rare rarer rarest *(adj)*
1 not often seen, or unusual. **rarity** *(n)*, **rarely** *(adv)*.
2 Rare meat is very lightly cooked.

rascal *(n)* a usually friendly name for someone who is very mischievous.

rash rashes; rasher rashest
1 *(n)* spots or red patches on the skin, caused by an allergy or illness.
2 *(adj)* If you are **rash**, you act quickly, without thinking first. **rashly** *(adv)*.

rasher *(n)* a thin slice of bacon.

rasp rasping rasped
1 *(n)* a coarse file used for smoothing metal or wood. *See* **woodwork.**
2 *(v)* to speak in a harsh voice.

raspberry raspberries *(n)*
a small, red, soft fruit. *See* **fruit.**

rat *(n)*
1 a long-tailed rodent, similar to a large mouse. Rats sometimes spread disease.
2 *(informal)* a disloyal or treacherous person.
3 **rat race** very stressful competition for success at work.

rat

rate rating rated
1 *(n)* the speed at which something happens. *Catherine spends money at an alarming rate.*
2 *(n)* a charge or a fee. *William charges very high rates for his work.*
3 *(n)* standard, or quality. *Sasha gave a first-rate performance.*
4 *(v)* to value someone or something. *Dominic's fellow runners rate him highly.* **rating** *(n)*.

rather *(adv)*
1 fairly, or quite. *It's rather a long way to walk.*
2 more willingly. *I'd rather be at the seaside than at school.*

ratio *(ray-shee-oh)* *(n)* the proportion of one thing to another, expressed in its simplest terms. *In a group with 15 girls and 5 boys, the ratio of girls to boys is 3 to 1.*

ration *(n)* a limited amount, or a share. *No more chocolate for you today, you've already had your ration!* **rationing** *(n)*, **ration** *(v)*.

rational *(adj)*
1 sensible and logical. *We made a rational decision to turn the two small shops into one.* **rationally** *(adv)*.
2 calm, reasonable, and sane. *Rational behaviour.* **rationally** *(adv)*.

rattle rattling rattled
1 *(v)* to make a rapid series of short, sharp noises. **rattle** *(n)*.
2 *(n)* a baby's toy.

rattlesnake *(n)* a venomous snake from North and South America with a tail that rattles as it vibrates.

rattlesnake

rattle

raucous *(raw-kus)* *(adj)*
harsh, or loud. **raucously** *(adv)*.

rave raving raved
1 *(v)* to speak in a wild, uncontrolled way. *Jennifer ranted and raved about the bad traffic.*
2 *(v)* *(informal)* to be very enthusiastic about something.
3 *(n)* a type of party with fast, rhythmic, electronic music and flashing lights.

raven *(n)*
a large, black bird of the crow family.

raven

Some words that begin with a "r" sound are spelt "wr".

reception

ravenous (adj) very hungry.

ravine (n)
a deep, narrow valley with steep sides.

raw rawer rawest
1 (adj) Food that is **raw** has not been cooked or processed.
2 **raw materials** (n) the basic things used to make something.

ray (n)
1 a strong line of light, radiation, etc.
2 a type of fish with a flat body, large wing-like fins, and a long tail.

poisonous spine

gill arches (used to strain plankton)

pectoral fin   eye

open mouth

giant devil ray

razor (n) an instrument with a blade, used to shave hair from the skin.

reach reaches reaching reached (v)
1 to stretch out to something with your hand. *Can you reach the top shelf?*
2 to extend, or to go as far as. *Our garden reaches down to the river.*
3 to arrive somewhere. *We eventually reached the summit.*

react reacting reacted (v)
1 to respond to something that happens. *The firefighters reacted quickly to the alarm.* **reaction** (n).
2 If one substance **reacts** with another, a chemical change takes place in one or both of the substances as they are mixed together. **reaction** (n).

reactionary (adj)
If someone is **reactionary**, they are against change and want to keep things as they are. **reactionary** (n).

reactor (n) a large machine in which nuclear energy is produced.

read reading read (v)
1 to look at written or printed words and understand what they mean.
2 to understand some form of communication. *Hilary can read my mind.*

readily (adv)
easily, or willingly. *Connie was always readily able to work overtime.*

ready readier readiest (adj)
If you are **ready**, you are prepared, or you are in a position to start.

real (adj)
1 true and not imaginary. *The real story isn't quite so dramatic.* **reality** (n).
2 genuine and not artificial. *A real diamond.*

realistic (adj)
1 very like the real thing. *A realistic model.* **realism** (n), **realistically** (adv).
2 sensible, practical, or correct. *I will only pay a realistic price for the bike.* **realistically** (adv).
3 If you are **realistic**, you view things as they really are. *Annie is realistic about her chances of winning.* **realistically** (adv).

reality realities (n)
1 truth, or the actual situation. *Being a model looks glamorous, but the reality is not much fun.*
2 a fact of life that must be faced. *After the holiday, we must return to the reality of work.*

realize or **realise**
realizing realized (v) to become aware that something is true. *Kevin realized that he hadn't been working hard enough.* **realization** (n).

really (adv)
1 actually, or in reality. *Are the rumours really true?*
2 very. *I'm really happy.*

reap reaping reaped (v)
1 to cut a crop for harvest.
2 If you **reap the reward** for something you have done, you experience the results of it.

reappear reappearing reappeared (v) to come into sight again. **reappearance** (n).

rear rearing reared
1 (v) to breed and bring up young animals.
2 (v) to care for and educate children.
3 (n) the back of something. **rear** (adj).
4 (v) If a horse **rears**, it rises up on its back legs.

rearrange rearranging rearranged (v) to arrange things differently.

reason reasoning reasoned
1 (n) the motive behind someone's action, or the cause of something.
2 (v) to think in a logical way. *Aaron reasoned that it would be quicker to walk.* **reason** (n).
3 (v) If you **reason** with someone, you try to persuade them that what you suggest is sensible.

reasonable (adj)
1 fair. *Your offer seems reasonable to me.* **reasonably** (adv).
2 sensible. *Hal won't make a fuss, he's always very reasonable.* **reasonably** (adv).
3 moderate, or quite good. *The weather was reasonable.* **reasonably** (adv).

reassure reassuring reassured (v) to calm someone and give them confidence. **reassurance** (n).

rebel (reb-ul) (n) someone who fights against a government or people in authority. **rebel** (rib-ell) (v), **rebellious** (rib-ell-ee-uss) (adj).

rebellion (n)
1 armed resistance against a government.
2 an organized protest against people in authority.

rebuke rebuking rebuked (v) to tell someone off. **rebuke** (n).

recall recalling recalled (v)
1 to remember something. *I can still recall the day I met you.*
2 to order someone to return. *The witness was recalled to the stand.*

recap recapping recapped (v) (informal) to repeat the main points of what has been said. Recap is short for recapitulate. **recap** (n).

recede receding receded (v)
1 to go back. *The tide receded.* **receding** (adj).
2 to fade gradually. *Hopes of rescue receded as night fell.*
3 When a man's hair **recedes**, he becomes more and more bald at the front. **receding** (adj).

receipt (re-seet) (n) a piece of paper acknowledging that money or goods have been received.

receive receiving received (v) to get or to accept something.

receiver (n)
1 the part of a telephone that you hold in your hand.
2 a piece of equipment for receiving radio or television signals.

recent (adj) happening, made, or done a short time ago. **recently** (adv).

reception (n)
1 the way in which someone or something is received. *The play was given a frosty reception. The reception on our television is very bad.*
2 a formal party.
3 the place in a building where people go as they arrive and where inquiries are answered. **receptionist** (n).

Some words that begin with a "r" sound are spelt "wr".

recess recesses *(n)*
1 a break from work for rest or relaxation.
2 a part of a room set back from the main area.

recession *(n)* a time when a country produces fewer goods and more people become unemployed.

recipe *(ress-ip-ee) (n)*
a set of instructions for preparing and cooking food.

recipient *(n)* a person who receives something. *The recipient of the first prize wins a holiday in Barbados.*

recital *(n)* a musical performance by a single performer or by a small group of musicians.

recite reciting recited *(v)*
to say aloud something that you have learned by heart. **recitation** *(n)*.

reckless *(adj)* If you are reckless, you are careless about your own and other people's safety. **recklessly** *(adv)*.

reckon reckoning reckoned *(v)*
1 to calculate or count up. **reckoning** *(n)*.
2 to think or to have an opinion. *I reckon that our team will win.*

reclaim reclaiming reclaimed *(v)*
1 to get back something that is yours. *Sue reclaimed her jewels from the safe.*
2 to make land suitable for farming, etc., by clearing it or draining it. **reclamation** *(n)*.

recline reclining reclined *(v)*
to lean or lie back.

recognize *or* **recognise** recognizing recognized *(v)*
to see someone and know who they are. **recognition** *(n)*, **recognizable** *(adj)*, **recognizably** *(adv)*.

recollect recollecting recollected *(v)*
to remember or to recall. **recollection** *(n)*.

recommend recommending recommended *(v)*
to suggest someone or something because you think that they are good. *My uncle recommended my piano teacher.* **recommendation** *(n)*.

reconcile reconciling reconciled *(v)*
1 to become friendly again after an argument or fight. *Jack was able to reconcile the squabbling brothers.* **reconciliation** *(n)*.
2 to decide to put up with something. *I reconciled myself to working over the holidays.*

reconsider reconsidering reconsidered *(v)* to think again about a previous decision.

reconstruction *(n)*
1 the rebuilding of something that has been destroyed. **reconstruct** *(v)*.
2 the careful piecing together of past events. **reconstruct** *(v)*.

record recording recorded
1 *(rik-ord) (v)* to write down information so that it can be kept. **record** *(rek-ord) (n)*.
2 *(rik-ord) (v)* to put music or other sounds on to a tape or disc. **recording** *(n)*.
3 *(rek-ord) (n)* If you set a **record** in something like a sport, you do it better than anyone has ever done before.

recorder
1 a machine for recording sounds.
2 a woodwind musical instrument. You play the recorder by blowing into the mouthpiece and covering holes with your fingers to make different notes.

mouthpiece

window

ramp

head joint

descant recorder

fingerhole

middle joint or barrel

double hole

foot joint

recover recovering recovered *(v)*
1 to get better after an illness or difficulty. **recovery** *(n)*.
2 to get back something that has been lost or stolen. **recovery** *(n)*.

recreation *(rek-ree-ay-shun) (singular n)*
the games, sports, hobbies, etc. that people do for pleasure in their spare time. *What do you do as recreation?* **recreational** *(adj)*.

recruit *(re-kroot) (n)* someone who has recently joined a business, or an organization such as the armed forces. **recruitment** *(n)*, **recruit** *(v)*.

rectangle *(n)*
a four-sided shape with two pairs of equal, parallel sides and four right angles. **rectangular** *(adj)*. *See* **shape**.

rectify rectifies rectifying rectified *(v)*
to put something right.

recuperate recuperating recuperated *(v)*
to recover slowly from an illness or injury. **recuperation** *(n)*.

recur recurring recurred *(v)*
1 to happen again. *The same problem recurs every time I use the computer.* **recurrence** *(n)*, **recurrent** *(adj)*.
2 In a division sum, if a number in the answer **recurs**, it keeps occurring. For example, 10 ÷ 3 = 3.33333... or 3.3 recurring.

recycle recycling recycled *(v)*
to process used items, such as glass bottles, newspapers, and aluminium cans, so that they can be reused to make new products. **recyclable** *(adj)*.

red *(n)* the colour of blood. **red** *(adj)*.

redeem redeeming redeemed *(v)*
1 to save or to rescue. *Glen redeemed our reputation by scoring three goals.* **redemption** *(n)*.
2 to claim back or exchange something. *Caroline redeemed her tokens for a set of drinking glasses.*

red herring *(n)*
something that diverts people unnecessarily from what they should be doing.

red tape *(n)*
rules, regulations, and paperwork that make it difficult to get things done.

reduce reducing reduced *(v)*
to make something smaller or less. *During the sale, all prices were reduced.* **reduction** *(n)*.

redundant *(adj)*
no longer needed, especially for a job. *When the pit closed, the miners were made redundant.* **redundancy** *(n)*.

reed *(n)*
1 a plant with long, thin, hollow stems, that grows in or near water.
2 a piece of thin cane or metal in the mouthpiece of some musical instruments, such as a clarinet, oboe, or saxophone. When you blow over or through the reed, it vibrates and makes a sound. *See* **woodwind**.

reef *(n)*
1 a line of rocks or coral close to the surface of the sea. *The picture shows part of the Great Barrier Reef near Queensland, Australia.*
2 **reef knot** a strong, double knot. *See* **knot**.

reef

reek reeking reeked *(v)* to smell strongly of something unpleasant. *The room reeked of tobacco smoke.*

reel reeling reeled
1 *(n)* a cylinder on which thread, film, etc. is wound. *See* **angling**.
2 *(v)* to stagger around unsteadily. *The drunk man reeled into a lamppost.*
3 *(n)* a type of folk dance.
4 *(v)* If you **reel off** something, you say it very fast. *Alex reeled off a list of reasons why he should get the job.*

ref *short for* **referee**.

refectory refectories *(n)* a communal dining hall. *A college refectory.*

refer referring referred *(v)*
1 If you **refer to** a book, you look in it for information.
2 If you **refer to** something while talking or writing, you mention it.
3 to pass a question or a problem on to someone else. *My doctor has referred me to a specialist.*

referee *(n)*
1 someone who supervises a sports match or game and makes sure that the players obey the rules.
2 someone who provides a statement about a person's character and abilities.

reference *(n)*
1 a mention of someone or something. *There was a reference to you in the speech.*
2 a written statement about someone's character and abilities. *You will need references for this job.*
3 a book, magazine, etc. that you use to produce a piece of work. *Please list your references at the end of your essay.*

reference book *(n)* a book that you use to find information. *Encyclopedias and dictionaries are reference books.*

referendum referendums *or* referenda *(n)* a vote by the people of a country on a very important question.

refill refilling refilled *(v)* to fill something again. **refill** *(n).*

refine refining refined *(v)* to purify something, such as sugar or oil.

refined *(adj)* A **refined** person is very polite and has elegant manners and tastes.

refinery refineries *(n)* a factory where raw materials are purified. *Oil refineries turn crude oil into petrol and other products.*

refit refitting refitted *(v)* to repair something, or to supply it with new parts or equipment.

reflect reflecting reflected *(v)*
1 to show an image of something on a shiny surface. **reflection** *(n).*
2 When rays of light or heat are **reflected**, they bounce off an object. *The diagram below shows how a light ray is reflected when it hits a mirror.*
3 to think carefully. *Margaret reflected on the meaning of life.* **reflection** *(n).*

reflection

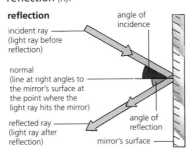

angle of incidence
incident ray (light ray before reflection)
normal (line at right angles to the mirror's surface at the point where the light ray hits the mirror)
reflected ray (light ray after reflection)
angle of reflection
mirror's surface

reflective *(adj)*
1 acting like a mirror.
2 thoughtful. **reflectively** *(adv).*

reflex reflexes
1 *(n)* an automatic and instinctive action. *Blinking is a reflex.* **reflex** *(adj).*
2 *(adj)* A **reflex** angle is an angle between 180° and 360°.

reform reforming reformed *(v)* to improve something that is unsatisfactory. *Andrew is trying to reform his behaviour.* **reform** *(n).*

refract refracting refracted *(v)* When a light ray or sound wave is **refracted**, it changes direction because it has travelled from one medium into another. *The diagram shows how a light ray is refracted as it moves from air into glass and then back into the air.* **refraction** *(n).*

refraction

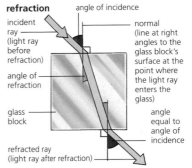

angle of incidence
incident ray (light ray before refraction)
normal (line at right angles to the glass block's surface at the point where the light ray enters the glass)
angle of refraction
glass block
angle equal to angle of incidence
refracted ray (light ray after refraction)

refrain refraining refrained
1 *(v)* to stop yourself from doing something. *Please refrain from standing on the seats.*
2 *(n)* a regularly repeated chorus or song.

refresh refreshes refreshing refreshed *(v)* If something **refreshes** you, it makes you feel fresh and strong again. **refreshing** *(adj).*

refreshments *(plural n)* drink and small amounts of food.

refrigerator *(n)* a very cold cabinet used for storing food and drink. *Refrigerators are kept cool by a special substance called refrigerant that circulates constantly. The diagram shows how refrigerant evaporates inside the refrigerator, drawing heat away from the food, and condenses outside it, sending out the heat that it has gained.*

evaporator (turns refrigerant liquid into vapour which draws heat from freezer compartment)
rubber seal
freezer compartment
expansion valve (decreases pressure of refrigerant)
condenser coil (turns refrigerant vapour into liquid which sends out heat)
cooling fin
compressor (increases pressure of refrigerant and pumps it around the condenser and evaporator)
thermostat (controls compressor)
expanded polystyrene (insulates refrigerator)
plastic inner case
metal outer case
electrical lead
refrigerator (cutaway)

refuel

refuel refuelling refuelled *(v)*
to take on more fuel.

refuge *(n)*
a place of shelter and safety.

refugee *(n)*
a homeless person who has been
forced to leave their home because of
war, persecution, or natural disaster.

refund refunding refunded *(v)*
to give money back to the person
who paid it. **refund** *(n)*.

refuse refusing refused
1 *(rif-yooz)* *(v)* to say you will
not do something or accept
something. **refusal** *(n)*.
2 *(ref-yuce)* *(n)* rubbish or waste.

regal *(adj)* to do with or fit for
a king or queen. **regally** *(adv)*.

regard regarding regarded
1 *(v)* to have an opinion about
something. *Joel regards politicians
with contempt.* **regard** *(n)*.
2 *(plural n)* If someone sends
you their **regards**, they send
you their best wishes.

regarding *(prep)*
about or concerning.

regardless *(adj)*
without considering anything or
anyone else. *Nina drove at high
speed, regardless of the other
drivers.* **regardlessly** *(adv)*.

regatta *(n)* a series of races
for rowing or sailing boats.

reggae *(reg-ay)* *(n)*
a type of rhythmic pop music
which came from the West Indies.

regiment *(n)* a large army unit
under the command of a colonel.

region *(n)* a large area or district.
regional *(adj)*, **regionally** *(adv)*.

register registering registered
1 *(n)* a book in which names or
official records are kept. *A class
register.* **registration** *(n)*.
2 *(v)* to enter something on
an official list. *All cars must be
registered.* **registration** *(n)*.
3 *(n)* the range of notes produced
by a musical instrument or a voice.
4 *(v)* to show an emotion.
Vera's face registered dismay.

register office or **registry office**
(n) a place where births and
deaths are recorded, and where
people can get married.

regret regretting regretted *(v)*
to be sad or sorry about something.
regret *(n)*, **regretful** *(adj)*.

regrettable *(adj)* If something is
regrettable, it is unfortunate and
you wish that it had not happened.

regular *(adj)*
1 usual or normal. *This is my
regular route home.* **regularly** *(adv)*.
2 happening at predictable
times. *Regular meals.*
regularity *(n)*, **regularly** *(adv)*.
3 even or steady. *A regular heartbeat.*
regularity *(n)*, **regularly** *(adv)*.

regulate regulating regulated *(v)*
to control or adjust something.
A thermostat regulates temperature.

regulation *(n)*
1 an official rule.
2 the act of controlling
or adjusting something.

regurgitate *(re-gurj-it-ate)*
regurgitating regurgitated *(v)*
to bring food from the stomach
back into the mouth. *Many birds
regurgitate food and feed it to
their young.*

rehearse *(re-herss)*
rehearsing rehearsed *(v)*
to practise for a public
performance. **rehearsal** *(n)*.

reign *(rain)* reigning reigned *(v)*
to rule as a king or queen. **reign** *(n)*.

reimburse *(re-im-burss)*
reimbursing reimbursed *(v)*
to pay someone back the money
they have had to spend on your
behalf. *The company will reimburse
your train fare.* **reimbursement** *(n)*.

reindeer reindeer *(n)*
a deer that lives in Arctic areas.
*Both the male and
female reindeer
have large,
branching antlers.*

reindeer
(male)

— antler

muzzle

pouch

reinforce reinforcing reinforced
(v) to strengthen something. *Concrete
bridges are reinforced by metal rods.*

reinforcement
1 *(n)* something that strengthens.
2 **reinforcements** *(plural n)*
extra troops sent to strengthen
a fighting force.

reject rejecting rejected
1 *(re-jekt)* *(v)* to refuse to accept
something. *Annie rejected all offers
of help.* **rejection** *(n)*.

2 *(ree-jekt)* *(n)* someone or something
that is not wanted or accepted.
*I've sorted out my collection of toys
and thrown all the rejects away.*

rejoice rejoicing rejoiced *(v)*
to be very happy about something.

relapse relapsing relapsed *(v)*
to fall back or return to the position
that you were in before. *Megan gave
up chocolate for a month, but now
she's relapsed.* **relapse** *(n)*.

relate relating related *(v)*
1 If things **relate** to each other,
there is a connection between them.
2 If people **relate** to each other,
they get on well together.
3 to tell a story.

related *(adj)* If you are **related** to
someone, you are part of their family.

relation *(n)*
1 a connection between things.
2 a member of your family.

relationship *(n)*
1 the way in which two
people get on together.
2 the way in which things
are connected.
3 If you are **in a relationship**
with someone, it means you are
romantically involved with them.

relative
1 *(n)* a member of your family.
2 *(adj)* compared with others.
*Poor people in the West live in
relative luxury compared with
people in the Third World.*

relatively *(adv)* compared with
others. *A 50 year old seems relatively
young in a room full of pensioners.*

relax relaxes relaxing relaxed *(v)*
1 to rest and take things
easy. **relaxation** *(n)*.
2 to become less tense and
anxious. **relaxation** *(n)*.
3 to make something less strict.
*The new headmaster has relaxed
the discipline at our school.*

relay relaying relayed
1 *(ree-lay)* *(n)* a team race in
which members of the team take
it in turn to run, passing a baton.
2 *(re-lay)* *(v)* to pass a message
on to someone else.

release releasing released *(v)*
1 to free someone or something.
release *(n)*.
2 If a record, film, etc. is
released, it is issued for
the first time. **release** *(n)*.

relegate relegating relegated *(v)*
If a sports team is **relegated**, it
is moved to a lower league.

a b c d e f g h i j k l m n o p q r s t u v w x y z

relent relenting relented *(v)*
to become less strict or more merciful.
*I was meant to stay in all day, but
in the end Mum relented.*

relentless *(adj)*
unceasing and determined. *Aled
practises the trumpet with relentless
enthusiasm.* **relentlessly** *(adv).*

relevant *(adj)* If something is
relevant, it is directly concerned
with what is being discussed or
dealt with. **relevance** *(n).*

reliable *(adj)*
trustworthy or dependable.
Shirley's car was old but reliable.
reliability *(n),* **reliably** *(adv).*

relic *(n)* something that has
survived from the distant past.

relief *(n)*
1 a feeling of freedom from
pain or worry. *It's such a relief
to know that you're safe!*
2 aid given to people in special
need. *Famine relief.*
3 **relief map** a map which shows
areas of high and low ground
by shades of colour.

relieve relieving relieved *(v)*
1 to ease someone's trouble or pain.
2 If you **relieve** someone, you
take over a duty from them.

religion *(n)*
1 belief in God or gods. **religious** *(adj).*
2 the practice of your belief
through worship, obedience,
and prayer. **religious** *(adj).*

relish relishes relishing relished
1 *(v)* to enjoy something greatly.
2 *(n)* a sauce. *Tomato relish.*

reluctant *(adj)* If you are **reluctant**,
you do not want to do something.
reluctance *(n),* **reluctantly** *(adv).*

rely relies relying relied *(v)*
If you **rely on** someone or
something, you need and trust
them. *I had to rely on my friends
to help me.* **reliant** *(adj).*

remain remaining remained *(v)*
to be left behind or left over.

remainder *(n)* the amount left over.

remains *(plural n)*
1 things left over. *What shall I do
with the remains of my lunch?*
2 a body after death.
3 the ruins of ancient buildings. *Have
you seen the Roman remains at Bath?*

remark remarking remarked *(v)*
to make a comment about
something. **remark** *(n).*

remarkable *(adj)* unusual and
worth noticing. **remarkably** *(adv).*

remedial *(adj)* intended to help
someone with a learning problem
or physical difficulty. *Remedial maths.*

remedy
remedies remedying remedied
1 *(n)* a cure for an illness.
2 *(n)* the answer to a problem.
3 *(v)* to put something right. *Danny
remedied the problem with the radio.*

remember
remembering remembered *(v)*
1 to keep something in your mind.
I'll always remember Marcus.
2 to bring something to mind.
Try to remember the answer.

remind reminding reminded *(v)*
to make someone remember
something. *Please remind me
to lock the door.* **reminder** *(n).*

reminisce *(rem-in-iss)*
reminiscing reminisced *(v)* to think
or talk about the past and things that
you remember. **reminiscence** *(n).*

remnant *(n)*
a piece or part of something that
is left over. *A remnant of material.*

remorse *(n)*
a strong feeling of guilt and regret
about something that you have done.
remorseful *(adj),* **remorsefully** *(adv).*

remote remoter remotest *(adj)*
far away, isolated, or distant.
remoteness *(n),* **remotely** *(adv).*

remote control *(n)*
a system by which machines can
be operated from a distance, usually
by radio signals or by an infra-red
beam. **remote-controlled** *(adj).*

remove removing removed *(v)*
to take something away. **removal** *(n).*

Renaissance *(n)* the flowering of art
and learning in Europe between the
14th and 17th centuries, inspired by a
revival of interest in
the Ancient Greeks
and Romans. *This
picture is based on
the pen and ink
"Study for the
Head of Leda", by
Leonardo da Vinci,
one of the leading
artists of the
Italian Renaissance.*

**Italian Renaissance
drawing**

rendezvous *(ron-day-voo)*
rendezvous *(n)* an arranged
place and time for a meeting.
rendezvous *(v).*

renew renewing renewed *(v)*
1 to replace something old with
something new. **renewal** *(n).*
2 to start something again.

3 to extend the period of a library
loan, club membership, etc.
renewal *(n).*

renewable energy *(n)* power from
sources, such as wind, waves, and the
Sun, that can never be used up.

renovate renovating renovated
(v) to restore something to good
condition, or to make it more
modern. *Gillian planned to renovate
the old farmhouse.* **renovation** *(n).*

renowned *(adj)*
famous or well known. **renown** *(n).*

rent *(n)* money paid by a tenant
to the owner of a property in
return for using it. **rent** *(v).*

rental *(n)* the hiring of equipment,
such as televisions, cars, or machinery.

repair repairing repaired *(v)*
to make something work again,
or to put back together something
that is broken. **repair** *(n).*

repay repaying repaid *(v)*
to pay back money or something
else. *Please repay the money you
owe. I repaid her visit.* **repayment** *(n).*

repeat repeating repeated *(v)*
to say or do something again.
repeat *(n),* **repetition** *(n).*

repel repelling repelled *(v)*
1 to drive away. *The army repelled
the enemy forces.*
2 to disgust someone.

repellent
1 *(adj)* disgusting. *A repellent smell.*
2 *(n)* a chemical that keeps insects
and other pests away.

repent repenting repented *(v)*
to be deeply sorry for the bad
things that you have done.
repentance *(n),* **repentant** *(adj).*

repertoire *(rep-er-twar) (n)*
the collection of songs, jokes,
stories, etc. that an entertainer
performs in public.

repetition *(n)*
the repeating of words or actions.
repetitious *(adj),* **repetitive** *(adj).*

replace replacing replaced *(v)*
1 to put one person or thing in place
of another. **replacement** *(n).*
2 to put something back where it was.

replay replaying replayed
1 *(re-play) (n)* a second match
between two teams or players,
when the first match has ended
in a draw. **replay** *(re-play) (v).*
2 *(re-play) (v)* to play back a
recording to see or hear something
again. **replay** *(re-play) (n).*

replica *(n)* an exact copy
of something. **replicate** *(v).*

Some words that begin with a "r" sound are spelt "wr".

reply replies replying replied (v)
to give an answer or
a response. **reply** (n).

report reporting reported (v)
1 to give a written or spoken account
of things that have happened. *Rose
reported on the rugby match for
the local paper.* **report** (n).
2 If you **report** someone, you make
an official complaint about them.
3 to appear for duty. *Please report
for work on Monday morning.*

reporter (n)
someone who reports the news for
radio, television, or a newspaper.

represent
representing represented (v)
1 to act on behalf of someone else.
2 to stand for something. *On a map,
water is usually represented by the
colour blue.* **representation** (n).

representative (n)
someone who is sent on behalf of
someone else. *A sales representative.*

repress
represses repressing repressed (v)
1 If you **repress** an emotion, such
as anger, you keep it under
control and do not show
it. **repressed** (adj).

2 to keep people under very strict
control. *The Emperor repressed his
people.* **repression** (n), **repressed** (adj).

reprieve (rip-reeve)
reprieving reprieved (v) to postpone
or cancel a punishment, especially a
death sentence. **reprieve** (n).

reprimand
reprimanding reprimanded (v)
to tell someone off formally.
reprimand (n).

reprisal (n) an act of revenge.

reproach
reproaches reproaching reproached
(v) to blame someone, or to show that
you disapprove of them. **reproach** (n).

reproduce
reproducing reproduced (v)
1 to make a copy of something.
reproduction (n).
2 When animals **reproduce**,
they breed and produce babies.
reproduction (n).

reptile (n) a cold-blooded animal
with a scaly skin, that lays eggs.
Lizards, crocodiles, snakes, turtles,
and tortoises are all reptiles. *The
picture shows a range of reptiles
from around the world.*
reptilian (adj).

republic (n) a country or state that
elects its government and does not
have a king or queen. *The leader of
a republic is the president.*

republican
1 (adj) to do with a republic,
or in favour of a republic.
2 Republican Party (n) the name
of one of the two main political
parties in the USA.

repugnant (adj) very unpleasant
and disgusting. *Melissa found the
job of cleaning out the pigsties
totally repugnant.* **repugnance** (n).

repulse repulsing repulsed (v)
1 to drive or to force back. *The
crew repulsed the alien's attack.*
2 to reject something. *Martha
repulsed my offer of help.*

repulsive (adj)
very ugly or disgusting. *A repulsive
monster.* **repulsively** (adv).

reputable (adj)
reliable and trustworthy. *Always
buy electrical equipment from a
reputable dealer.* **reputably** (adv).

reputation (n) the opinion that
other people have of you. *Abdul
has a reputation for hard work.*

repute (n) fame.

reputed (adj)
supposed to be or thought to be.
*Dominic is reputed to be very good
at chess.* **reputedly** (adv).

request requesting requested
1 (v) to ask for something politely.
*Visitors are requested not to
take photographs.*
2 (n) something that you ask for.
That's a very strange request!
3 request stop (n) a bus stop
where people have to ask the
driver to stop or have to hold out
their arm as the bus approaches.

requiem (rek-wee-em) (n)
1 a church service where prayers
are said for someone who has died.
2 a piece of music composed in
memory of a dead person, often a
musical setting of the requiem service.

require requiring required (v)
1 to need something. *Do you
require anything to eat?*
2 If someone **requires** you to
do something, you must do it.

requirement (n)
something that you need to do or
have. *The ability to swim 50m is a
requirement of this sailing course.*

reread rereading reread (v)
to read something again. *Kerry
reread the train timetable anxiously.*

reptiles

corn snake
(North America)

**dotted
racerunner lizard**
(Central and
South America)

**Indian starred
tortoise**
(India and
Sri Lanka)

snake-necked turtle
(Australia)

Nile crocodile
(Africa)

respectable

rescue helicopter

- radar scanner
- hydraulic rescue winch
- winch operator
- cabin door
- rotor hub
- rotor blade
- tail rotor
- horizontal stabiliser
- engine under here
- engine air intake duct
- viewing window
- tail wheel
- waterproof floor
- footstep
- crash-resistant fuel system
- dual pilot cockpit
- steel lifeline
- exhaust
- landing lights
- winchman
- sponson
- undercarriage
- stretcher
- flotation bag (used for water landing)
- boat-shaped hull
- immersion suit

rescue
rescuing rescued
1 *(v)* to save someone who is in danger or is trapped somewhere. **rescue** *(n)*, **rescuer** *(n)*.
2 **rescue helicopter** *(n)* a specially equipped helicopter used to rescue people on land and at sea. *The picture shows a Sea King rescue helicopter.*

research
researches researching researched
(v) to study and find out about a subject, usually by reading about it, or by doing experiments. **research** *(n)*.

resemble **resembling resembled**
(v) to be or to look like someone or something. *Lucy resembles her Aunt Matilda.* **resemblance** *(n)*.

resent **resenting resented** *(v)*
to feel hurt or angry about something that has been done or said to you. *I resent being treated like an idiot.* **resentment** *(n)*, **resentful** *(adj)*.

reservation
1 *(n)* a booking. *Do you have a reservation for this flight?*
2 *(plural n)* If you have **reservations** about something, you feel doubtful about it. *Roy had reservations about learning to drive.*
3 *(n)* an area of land set aside for native people. *A Native American reservation.*

reserve **reserving reserved**
1 *(v)* to arrange for something to be kept for you. *Harvey reserved a seat on the train.*
2 *(n)* an extra member of a team who plays if one of the team is injured or cannot play.
3 *(n)* a protected place where animals can live and breed safely. *A nature reserve.*

reserved *(adj)*
1 If a seat, table, or room is **reserved**, it is kept for someone to use later.
2 Someone who is **reserved** behaves in a quiet, shy way and does not show their feelings much.

reservoir *(rez-er-vwar) (n)*
a natural or artificial lake used for storing a large amount of water.

residence *(n)* the place where
someone lives, especially someone important or wealthy.

resident *(n)* someone who lives
in a particular place. *The village residents.* **residential** *(adj)*.

residue *(n)*
1 remains or leftovers. **residual** *(adj)*.
2 a substance that is left after combustion or evaporation.

resign *(riz-ine)*
resigning resigned *(v)*
1 to give up a job.
resignation *(rez-ig-nay-shun) (n)*.
2 If you **resign yourself** to something, you accept it without complaining or worrying about it. *I've resigned myself to losing.* **resignation** *(n)*, **resigned** *(adj)*.

resist **resisting resisted** *(v)*
1 to refuse to accept something. *Jessie resisted all offers of help.*
2 to fight back. *The villagers resisted the advancing army.*
3 to stop yourself doing something that you would like to do. *I resisted the temptation to tickle Theo's feet.*

resistance *(n)*
1 fighting back. *Resistance is useless. We must surrender!*
2 the ability of a substance or an electrical circuit to oppose an electrical current passing through it. Resistance is measured in ohms.

resolution *(n)* a promise
to yourself that you will try hard to do something. *New Year's resolutions.*

resolve **resolving resolved** *(v)*
1 to decide that you will try hard to do something. *Shane resolved to find a part-time job.* **resolve** *(n)*.
2 to deal with a problem or difficulty successfully. *We need to resolve this misunderstanding quickly.*

resort **resorting resorted**
1 *(n)* a place where people go on holiday. *A skiing resort.*
2 *(v)* If you **resort to** something, you turn to it because you do not have any other choices.
3 *(n)* If you do something **as a last resort**, you do it because everything else has failed to work.

resource *(n)* something valuable
or useful to a place or person. *North Sea oil is one of Britain's most valuable resources.* **resourceful** *(adj)*.

respect **respecting respected**
1 *(v)* to admire and have a high opinion of someone. **respectful** *(adj)*.
2 *(n)* a feeling of admiration or consideration for someone that makes you take them seriously.
3 *(n)* a detail or particular part of something. *I liked Guy's plan in many respects.*

respectable *(adj)*
1 If someone is **respectable**, they behave in a decent way that does not offend anyone. **respectably** *(adv)*.
2 reasonably good. *Donna got a respectable score.*

Some words that begin with a "r" sound are spelt "wr".

respiration

respiration (n)
breathing, or the process of taking in oxygen and sending out carbon dioxide. *The diagram shows the main organs used in respiration. Air is drawn into the lungs and travels to the alveoli where oxygen from the air passes into the blood. Carbon dioxide from the blood passes into the alveoli and is breathed out.*

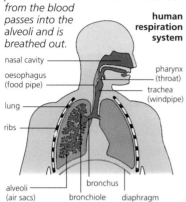

human respiration system

nasal cavity

oesophagus (food pipe)

pharynx (throat)

trachea (windpipe)

lung

ribs

alveoli (air sacs)

bronchus

bronchiole

diaphragm

respond responding responded (v)
1 to reply. **response** (n).
2 to react to something. *Rosie did not respond to her brother's taunts.*

responsibility responsibilities
1 (n) a duty. *It's my responsibility to provide tea.*
2 If you **take responsibility** for something bad that has happened, you agree that you are to blame for it.

responsible (adj)
1 If someone is **responsible** for something, they have to do it and it is their fault if it goes wrong.
2 If a person is **responsible**, they are sensible and can be trusted. **responsibly** (adv).

rest resting rested
1 (v) to relax or to sleep. **rest** (n).
2 (n) the others, or the remaining part of something. *I came first and beat all the rest.*
3 (v) to lean on something. *Rest your rackets against the wall.*
4 (v) to stop and stay in one place. *The spotlight rested on his face.*
5 (n) a period of silence in a piece of music. See **notation**.

restaurant (n) a place where people pay to eat meals.

restless (adj) If someone is **restless**, they find it hard to keep still or to concentrate on anything. **restlessness** (n), **restlessly** (adv).

restore restoring restored (v)
1 to repair something that has been damaged. **restoration** (n).
2 to give or bring something back. *Please restore the pen to its owner.*

restrain restraining restrained (v)
to prevent someone from doing something. *We managed to restrain Harry from eating another ice cream.* **restraint** (n).

restrained (adj)
If someone is **restrained**, they are very quiet and controlled.

restrict restricting restricted (v)
to keep something within limits. *Please restrict yourselves to one cake each.* **restriction** (n), **restricted** (adj).

result resulting resulted
1 (n) something that happens because of something else. *The result of our efforts was a delicious meal.*
2 (v) If one thing **results in** something else, it causes it.
3 (n) a final score or mark. *Football results.*

resume resuming resumed (v)
to start doing something again after a break. *We will resume our discussion after lunch.*

Resurrection (n)
In the Christian religion, the **Resurrection** is Christ's coming back to life three days after his death.

resuscitate (re-suss-it-ate) resuscitating resuscitated (v)
to make someone conscious again after they have stopped breathing. **resuscitation** (n).

retail retailing retailed
1 (v) to sell goods to the public.
2 **retail price** (n) the price at which goods are sold in the shops.

retailer (n) someone who sells goods to the public, usually through a shop. *An online retailer.*

retain retaining retained (v)
to keep something. *Please retain your receipt.* **retention** (n).

retainer (n) a removable metal and plastic device designed to hold a person's teeth in a certain position.

retaliate retaliating retaliated (v) to do something unpleasant to someone because they have done something unpleasant to you. **retaliation** (n), **retaliatory** (adj).

retard retarding retarded (v)
to slow down. *The children's poor diet retarded their growth.* **retarded** (adj).

retch retches retching retched (v)
When you **retch**, you feel your throat and stomach move as if you are going to be sick. **retch** (n).

reticent (ret-i-sent) (adj)
If someone is **reticent**, they are unwilling to tell people what they know or feel. **reticence** (n).

retire retiring retired (v)
1 to give up work, usually because of your age. **retirement** (n), **retired** (adj).
2 to leave a sports competition, usually because of injury.
3 to go to a quieter place. *The jury has retired to consider its verdict.*
4 (old-fashioned) to go to bed.

retort retorting retorted
1 (v) to answer someone quickly and sharply. **retort** (n).
2 (n) a glass container with a round body and a long neck, used in a laboratory.

retrace retracing retraced (v)
to go back over something. *I retraced my steps to see if I had missed the turning.*

retreat retreating retreated
1 (v) to move back or withdraw from a difficult situation. **retreat** (n).
2 (n) a quiet place where you can go to think or be alone.

retrieve retrieving retrieved (v)
to get or bring something back. *Lizzie retrieved her umbrella from the lost property office.* **retrieval** (n).

return returning returned
1 (v) to go back. *It's time to return home.* **return** (n).
2 (v) to give or send something back. *Please return my book.* **return** (n).
3 **in return** in exchange for something, or as a payment for something. *Matt washed the car in return for his pocket money.*
4 **return match** (n) a second match between two teams who have already played each other once.
5 **return ticket** (n) a ticket that allows you to travel to a place and back again.

reunion (n)
a meeting between people who have not seen each other for a long time.

reusable (adj) If something is **reusable**, it can be used again rather than being thrown away.

rev revving revved (informal)
1 (v) to make an engine run quickly and noisily.
2 **revs** (plural n) the speed at which an engine turns. Revs is short for revolutions per minute.

reveal revealing revealed (v)
to allow something to be seen or known. *Carmen would not reveal the whereabouts of her secret hiding place.* **revealing** (adj).

revel revelling revelled (v)
If you **revel in** something, you enjoy it very much.

Some words that begin with a "r" sound are spelt "wr".

ridiculous

revelation *(n)* a very surprising fact that is made known to people.

revenge *(n)* action that you take to pay someone back for harm that they have done to you or to your friends.

revenue *(n)*
1 the money that a government makes from taxes.
2 the money that is made from investments.

reverberate reverberating reverberated *(v)* to echo loudly and repeatedly. *Jo's screams reverberated around the cave.* **reverberation** *(n)*.

reverence *(n)* great respect and admiration. **reverent** *(adj)*, **reverently** *(adv)*.

reverse reversing reversed
1 *(n)* the opposite. *You may think this is fun, but in fact it's quite the reverse.*
2 *(v)* to turn something round or inside out. *You can reverse this jacket.* **reversible** *(adj)*.
3 *(v)* to move a vehicle backwards. *Reverse the car into the parking space.*
4 *(v)* to cancel something. *The verdict was reversed.* **reversal** *(adj)*.

revert reverting reverted *(v)* to go back to the way things were. *Despite her resolutions, Gina soon reverted to her old habits.* **reversion** *(n)*.

review reviewing reviewed
1 *(n)* a piece of writing that gives an opinion about a new book, play, film, etc. **reviewer** *(n)*, **review** *(v)*.
2 *(v)* to study something carefully to see whether changes are necessary. *We will review the budget each year.* **review** *(n)*.

revise revising revised *(v)*
1 to look at your school work and try to learn it before an exam. **revision** *(n)*.
2 to change and correct something, usually in order to bring it up to date. *The new city guide has been thoroughly revised.* **revision** *(n)*.

revive reviving revived *(v)*
1 to bring someone back to consciousness after they have been unconscious.
2 to bring something back into use. *We've revived a play from the 1980s.* **revival** *(n)*.
3 to refresh or strengthen. *The hot drinks revived us.*

revolt revolting revolted *(v)*
1 to fight against authority. **revolt** *(n)*.
2 If something **revolts** you, you find it horrible and disgusting.
revolting *(adj)* disgusting.

revolution *(n)*
1 a violent uprising by the people of a country, intended to change its political system. **revolutionary** *(n)*, **revolutionary** *(adj)*.
2 a very large, important change. **revolutionary** *(adj)*.
3 one complete turn of a wheel.

revolutionize or **revolutionise** revolutionizing revolutionized *(v)* to change something totally. *The introduction of the printing press revolutionized communication.*

revolve revolving revolved *(v)*
1 to turn round and round in a circle.
2 If something **revolves around** a person or thing, that person or thing is the most important part of it. *Clara's life revolves around television.*

revolver *(n)* a small handgun that can fire several shots before it needs to be reloaded.

reward *(n)* something that you receive as a present for doing something good or useful. **reward** *(v)*.

rewarding *(adj)* If something is **rewarding**, it gives you pleasure and satisfaction. *A rewarding job.*

rheumatism *(room-at-izm)* *(n)* a condition that causes the joints and muscles to become stiff and painful. **rheumatic** *(room-at-ik)* *(adj)*.

rhinoceros rhinoceroses or rhinoceros *(n)* a large, heavy mammal that comes from Africa and Asia and has one or two large horns on its nose. *The picture shows a rhinoceros with a cattle egret and two oxpeckers on its back.*

rhinoceros

rhizome *(rye-zome)* *(n)* the thick stem of some plants that grows just under the ground, and from which roots and leaves grow.

rhombus *(rom-buss)* rhombuses or rhombi *(n)* a shape that has four straight sides of equal length but does not have right angles. *See* **shape**.

rhubarb *(roo-barb)* *(n)* a plant with long red or green stems that can be cooked and eaten.

rhyme *(rime)* rhyming rhymed
1 *(v)* If words **rhyme**, they end with the same sound. *Seat rhymes with beat and feet.* **rhyme** *(n)*.
2 *(n)* a short poem.

rhythm *(rith-um)* *(n)* a regular beat in music, poetry, or dance. **rhythmic** *(adj)*, **rhythmical** *(adj)*, **rhythmically** *(adv)*.

rib *(n)*
1 one of the curved bones which protect your lungs. *See* **skeleton**.
2 the main vein of a leaf. *See* **leaf**.

ribbon *(n)* a long, thin piece of material used for tying up hair, or for decorating a present, for example.

rice *(n)* a kind of tall grass that is grown in flooded fields and whose seeds can be cooked and eaten. *See* **paddy field**.

rich riches; richer richest
1 *(adj)* Someone who is **rich** has a lot of money and possessions.
2 *(adj)* If something is **rich in** a particular thing, it contains a lot of it. *Milk is rich in calcium.* **richly** *(adv)*.
3 *(adj)* Food that is **rich** contains a lot of fat or sugar and makes you feel full very quickly.
4 riches *(plural n)* great wealth.

rickety *(adj)* old, weak, and likely to break. *A rickety chair.*

ricochet *(rick-oh-shay)* ricocheting ricocheted *(v)* If a stone or bullet **ricochets**, it hits a wall or other hard surface and flies off in a different direction.

rid ridding rid *(v)*
1 to remove something that is unwanted. *I must rid myself of this ridiculous costume.*
2 If you **get rid of** something, you throw it away.

riddle *(n)* a question that seems to make no sense, but which has a clever answer.

ride riding rode ridden
1 *(v)* to sit on a horse, bicycle, or motorcycle and travel along on it. **rider** *(n)*.
2 *(n)* a journey on a horse, bicycle, or motorcycle, or in a car or other vehicle.

ridge *(n)*
1 a narrow, raised piece of land.
2 a narrow, raised strip on something. **ridged** *(adj)*.

ridicule ridiculing ridiculed *(v)* to make fun of someone or something. **ridicule** *(n)*.

ridiculous *(adj)* extremely silly or foolish. **ridiculously** *(adv)*.

a b c d e f g h i j k l m n o p q r s t u v w x y z

riding hat

riding hat *(n)*
a hard hat that you wear to protect
your head when riding a horse.

rifle *(n)*
a long-barrelled gun that you hold
against your shoulder as you fire it.

rig rigging rigged
1 *(n)* a large structure on land or in
the sea, used to drill for oil or gas
under the ground. *See* **oil rig**.
2 *(v)* to control something dishonestly.
*Natalie rigged the competition so
that she came first.*
3 *(v)* If you **rig up** something,
you make it quickly from whatever
you can find. *We rigged up
a tent from broom
handles and sheets.*

rigging *(n)*
the ropes
on a boat or
ship which
support and
control the
sails.

right
1 *(adj)* This
page faces
the **right**
of the book.
right *(n)*,
right *(adv)*.
2 *(adj)*
correct. *I got the answers right.*
3 *(adj)* good, fair, and acceptable.
It's not right to be cruel to animals.
4 *(adv)* exactly. *We managed to
park right outside the cinema.*
5 *(n)* something that the law
allows you to have or do.
*Suffragettes campaigned
for the right to vote.*
6 In politics, people **on the
right** support capitalism, free
enterprise, and firm law and order.

right angle *(n)*
an angle of 90°, like one
of the angles of a square.

righteous *(adj)*
1 Someone who is **righteous**
does not do anything that is bad
or against the law. **righteousness** *(n)*.
2 with good reason. *When I saw
the mess in my room, I was
filled with righteous indignation.*

right-handed *(adj)*
If you are **right-handed**, you
use your right hand to write.
right-hander *(n)*.

right-wing *(adj)*
If you are **right-wing**, you
believe in free enterprise
and firm law and order.

rigid *(rij-id) (adj)*
1 stiff and difficult to bend.
rigidity *(n)*, **rigidly** *(adv)*.
2 very strict and difficult to
change. *A rigid rule.* **rigidly** *(adv)*.

rim *(n)* the outside or top edge of
something. *The jug has a blue rim.*

rind *(n)* the outer layer on cheese,
bacon, and some fruits. *Lemon rind.*

ring ringing rang rung
1 *(n)* a circle. *Put a ring around
the correct answer.* **ring** *(v)*.
2 *(n)* a thin band worn on your
finger as a piece of jewellery.
3 *(v)* When a bell **rings**, it
makes a musical sound.
4 *(v)* to telephone someone. **ring** *(n)*.
5 *(n)* the area in which a boxing
or wrestling match takes place.

ringleader *(n)* the leader of
a group of people who commit
crimes or do things that are wrong.

ringlet *(n)* a long, tight curl of hair.

rink *(n)* an indoor area with a
specially prepared surface that is
used for ice-skating or roller-skating.

rinse rinsing rinsed
1 *(v)* to wash something in clean water
without using any soap. **rinse** *(n)*.
2 *(n)* a special liquid that you can
put on your hair to colour it slightly.

riot rioting rioted *(v)*
If people **riot**, they behave in a noisy,
violent, and usually uncontrollable
way. **riot** *(n)*, **riotous** *(adj)*.

rip ripping ripped *(v)*
1 to tear something. **rip** *(n)*.
2 **rip off** *(slang)* If someone **rips**
you **off**, they sell you a faulty product
or charge you an unfair amount of
money for something. **rip-off** *(n)*.

ripe riper ripest *(adj)* ready to
be harvested, picked, or eaten.
Ripe fruit. **ripeness** *(n)*, **ripen** *(v)*.

ripple *(n)*
1 a very small wave
on the surface of
a lake, pond, etc.
ripple *(v)*.
2 a small wave
of sound. *A ripple
of laughter.*

rise rising rose risen
1 *(v)* to go or move
upwards. *The balloon
rose slowly into the air.*
2 *(v)* to stand up.
3 *(v)* to increase. *Prices rose
dramatically last year.* **rise** *(n)*.
4 *(n)* the process by which a person,
country, etc. becomes more powerful.
The rise of the British Empire.

risk risking risked *(v)*
to do something that might cause
something unpleasant to happen.
*Joel risked his life to rescue the
kitten.* **risk** *(n)*, **risky** *(adj)*.

ritual *(n)* a set of actions that are
always performed in the same way as
part of a religious ceremony or social
custom. **ritual** *(adj)*, **ritually** *(adv)*.

rival rivalling rivalled
1 *(n)* someone whom you
are competing against.
rivalry *(n)*, **rival** *(adj)*.
2 *(v)* to be as good as
someone or something else.
No team can rival us at ice hockey.

river *(n)* a large stream of fresh
water that flows into a lake or
sea. *The picture shows how a river
develops and changes as it flows
from its source to its mouth.*

sailing
dinghy

rigging

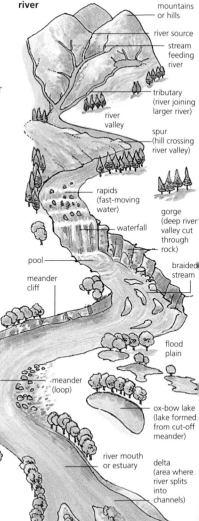

river

mountains
or hills

river source

stream
feeding
river

tributary
(river joining
larger river)

river
valley

spur
(hill crossing
river valley)

rapids
(fast-moving
water)

gorge
(deep river
valley cut
through
rock)

waterfall

pool

braided
stream

meander
cliff

flood
plain

meander
(loop)

ox-bow lake
(lake formed
from cut-off
meander)

river mouth
or estuary

delta
(area where
river splits
into
channels)

Some words that begin with a "r" sound are spelt "wr".

a b c d e f g h i j k l m n o p q **r** s t u v w x y z

roller

rivet riveting riveted
1 (n) a strong metal bolt that is used to fasten pieces of metal together. **rivet** (v).
2 (v) If you are **riveted** by something, you find it so interesting that you cannot stop watching it or listening to it. **riveting** (adj).

road (n) a wide path with a smooth surface on which vehicles travel.

road (cross-section)
wearing course
precast concrete kerb
verge
concrete backing
capping layer
sub-base
roadbase
basecourse
concrete foundation

roadworks (plural n) repair work being done to a road.

roadworthy (adj)
A car that is **roadworthy** is in good enough condition to be driven on the roads. **roadworthiness** (n).

roam roaming roamed (v) to wander around without any particular purpose. I roamed the streets until dark. **roam** (n).

roar roaring roared (v) to make a loud, deep noise. The lion roared. The crowd roared. **roar** (n).

roaring (adj) (informal) If you do a **roaring** trade, you sell a lot of things.

roast roasting roasted
1 (v) to cook meat or vegetables in a hot oven. **roast** (adj).
2 (n) a joint of meat that has been cooked in a hot oven.
3 (v) to be very hot. We were roasted by the sun. **roasting** (adj).

rob robbing robbed (v) to steal something from someone. **robber** (n).

robbery robberies (n) the crime of stealing money or goods.

robe (n) a piece of clothing similar to a long, loose coat.

robin (n) a bird with a red breast. The American robin is much larger than the European robin.

European robin

American robin

robot (n) a machine that is programmed to do jobs that are usually performed by a person. **robotic** (adj).

robotic arm (n) an electronically-controlled mechanical arm that can use tools and work like a human arm. The arrows on this picture of a robotic arm show the six directions in which it can move. Also see **underwater**.

waist
shoulder
elbow
wrist
welding tool

robotic arm

robotics (singular n) the science and study of making and using robots.

robust (adj) strong. A robust child. **robustly** (adv).

rock rocking rocked
1 (n) the very hard substance of which the Earth is made.
2 (n) a large stone.
3 (v) to move gently backwards and forwards or from side to side.
4 (n) a hard sweet, shaped like a long stick, usually sold at the seaside.
5 **rock music** (n) pop music with a very strong beat and a simple tune.

rock climbing (n) the sport of climbing steep rock faces, usually with the help of ropes and other equipment. The picture shows a climber with various pieces of equipment that are used in rock climbing.

rock climbing
helmet
sit harness
chocks on ropes (for inserting in cracks)
rope (attached to fellow climber)
rock boot
chock inserted in crack
carabiner
nylon tape

rockery rockeries (n) an area of a garden where small plants are grown among rocks and stones.

rocket rocketing rocketed
1 (v) to increase very quickly. The price of oil has rocketed.
2 (n) a firework, which shoots high into the air and then explodes.

3 (n) a vehicle shaped like a long tube with a pointed end, which can travel very fast through the air. Rockets are used for space travel and for carrying missiles.

rock'n'roll (n) a kind of dance music with a strong beat and a simple tune. Rock'n'roll is short for rock and roll. **rock'n'roll** (adj).

rod (n) a long, thin pole.

rodent (n) a mammal with large, sharp front teeth that it uses for gnawing things. Rats, beavers, and squirrels are all rodents.

rodeo (n) an entertainment in which cowboys show off their skills, such as riding untamed horses and catching cattle with lassos.

rodeo rider

roe (n)
1 a type of small deer.
2 a mass of eggs or sperm found inside a fish and often eaten as food.

rogue (rohg) (n) a dishonest person.

role (n)
1 the job or purpose of a person or thing.
2 the part that a person acts in a play. Julian played the role of Hamlet.

roll rolling rolled
1 (v) to move along by turning over and over. The ball rolled down the hill.
2 (v) to make something into the shape of a ball or tube.
3 (n) something that has been made into the shape of a tube. A roll of wallpaper. A Swiss roll.
4 (v) to flatten something by pushing a rounded object over it. Roll the pastry.
5 (n) a small, round loaf of bread to be eaten by one person.
6 (n) a continuous, deep, vibrating sound. A roll of thunder.
7 **roll up** (v) (informal) to come along. A large crowd rolled up for the match.

roller (n)
1 an object shaped like a tube, that can turn round and round and is used in machines. An ink roller.
2 a small plastic tube that you wind hair around to make it curl.

Rollerblade

Rollerblade (n) a trademarked name for an ankle-length boot with a row of wheels on its base, that you skate around on. Rollerblades are also known as in-line skates. **rollerblading** (n), **rollerblader** (n).

roller coaster (n) a fairground ride consisting of a train of carriages that travels fast over a track that rises, falls, and curves.

roller-skating (n) the sport of moving about on shoes or boots with wheels attached to them. **roller skate** (n), **roller-skate** (v).

ROM (n) permanent computer memory that can be read but not changed. The initials ROM stand for read-only memory.

romance (n)
1 a love affair.
2 an exciting story, usually about love.
3 mystery and excitement. *The romance of the East.*

Roman numerals (n) letters used by the Ancient Romans to represent figures. Roman numerals are sometimes used today, for example, on some clocks.

Roman numerals

I	II	III	IV	V	X
one	two	three	four	five	ten

XL	L	XC	C	D	M
40	50	90	100	500	1,000

romantic (adj)
1 like a love story. *How romantic of Peter to send you roses!*
2 like a fairy story. *A romantic castle.*

romp romping romped (v) to play in a noisy and energetic way. *The boys love romping in the sea.* **romp** (n).

roof (n)
1 the covering on the top of a building.
2 the top part of something. *The roof of your mouth. The roof of a car.*

roof rack (n) a frame placed on top of a car for carrying luggage.

rook (n)
1 a large, black bird like a crow that lives in a big group called a rookery.
2 a chesspiece, also known as a castle, that can move in straight lines across the board but not diagonally. *See* **chess**.

room (n)
1 one of the separate parts of a house or building, with its own door and walls.
2 enough space for something. *Is there room for us all to go in your car?* **roomy** (adj).

roost roosting roosted
1 (n) a place where birds rest or build their nests.
2 (v) When birds **roost**, they settle somewhere for the night.

rooster (n) a fully-grown male chicken.

root rooting rooted
1 (n) the part of a plant that grows under the ground. *Water and dissolved foods are absorbed from the soil through root hairs and travel up the roots to the plant's stem through xylem and phloem vessels.*
2 (v) to form roots. *I took some plant cuttings, but they didn't root.*
3 (plural n) Your **roots** are where your family comes from, where you grew up, and where you feel that you belong.

phloem (carries dissolved foods)

root hair

xylem (carries water)

cortex (root tissue)

root cap

plant root (cutaway)

rope (n) a strong, thick cord, made from twisted fibres.

rose (n)
1 a garden flower that usually has a sweet smell and grows on bushes with thorns.
2 a light pink colour. **rose** (adj).

rosette (n) a large, round badge with ribbons attached to it, worn to show that you have won something, or that you support a particular person, team, or political party.

Rosh Hashanah or **Rosh Hashana** (n) the Jewish New Year.

rostrum (n) a raised platform for a speaker or conductor.

rosy rosier rosiest (adj)
1 pink. *Rosy cheeks.*
2 hopeful. *A rosy future.*

rot rotting rotted (v) When something **rots**, it becomes weak and starts to break up because it is old or damp. **rot** (n).

rota (n) a list of people who take it in turns to do a job.

rotary (adj) turning round and round or rotating. *This lawn mower has a rotary action.*

rotate rotating rotated (v)
1 to turn round and round like a wheel. **rotation** (n).
2 to do things or use things in a fixed order, one after the other. **rotation** (n).

rotten (adj)
1 Food that is **rotten** has gone bad and cannot be eaten.
2 If floorboards, furniture, etc. are **rotten**, they have become weak and have started to break up.
3 (informal) very bad or unpleasant. *A rotten trick.*

rough (ruff) roughing roughed; rougher roughest
1 (adj) A **rough** surface is not smooth, but has dents or bumps in it.
2 (adj) Someone who is **rough** is not gentle or polite and may fight with people. **roughly** (adv).
3 (adj) (informal) difficult and unpleasant. *Moira had a rough time in her last job.*
4 (adj) vague or not exact. *I've got a rough idea of where Rupert lives.* **roughly** (adv).
5 (adj) **Rough** work is work that you do as preparation for the final version.
6 (v) (informal) If you **rough it**, you manage without the usual comforts of home.

roughage (ruff-ij) (n) the fibre found in foods such as cereals and vegetables, which passes through the body but is not digested. Roughage helps you to digest food.

round rounder roundest
1 (adj) shaped like a circle or ball.
2 (prep) on all sides of something. *We have a fence round our garden.*
3 (prep) going in a circle. *We circled round the tree.*
4 (adj) returning to a place. *A round trip from London to New York.*
5 (n) a series of visits made by a postman, milkman, doctor, etc.
6 (n) a set of matches or games in a competition.
7 (n) a simple song in which people start singing one after another, so that they are singing different parts of the song at the same time.

roundabout
1 (n) a road junction where vehicles must go round in a circle to join the road that they want.
2 (n) a round, revolving platform in a playground, that children can ride on.
3 (adj) indirect in travel, thought, or conversation. *Charles told me the facts in a roundabout sort of way.*

run

rounders *(singular n)*
a ball game in which players score points by hitting a ball and then running round four posts called bases.

rouse rousing roused *(v)*
1 to wake someone up. *I was roused far too early this morning.*
2 to make someone feel interested or excited. *The football coach gave a great speech to rouse his team.* rousing *(adj)*.

route *(root) (n)*
the set of roads or paths that you follow to get from one place to another. *Jenna had to admit that she had forgotten the route home.*

routine *(root een)*
1 *(n)* a regular way of doing things.
2 *(adj)* Something that is **routine** is normal and not at all difficult or unusual. *The doctors prepared for the routine operation.*

row rowing rowed
1 *(rhymes with low) (n)* a line of people or things, side by side. *A row of ornaments.*
2 *(rhymes with low) (v)* to use oars in order to move a boat through water. **row** *(n)*.
3 *(rhymes with cow) (n)* an angry argument or quarrel. *Alice had frequent rows with her sister.* **row** *(v)*.
4 *(rhymes with cow) (n)* a dreadful noise. *The row from the building site was driving Will mad.*

rowdy rowdier rowdiest *(adj)*
wild and noisy. *Don't play such rowdy games!* rowdiness *(n)*, rowdily *(adv)*.

royal *(adj)*
to do with a king or queen, or a member of their family. royalty *(n)*.

RSVP the initials of the French phrase *Répondez s'il vous plaît*, which means "please reply". RSVP is often written at the bottom of an invitation.

rub rubbing rubbed *(v)*
1 to press one thing against another and move them backwards and forwards. *Daniel rubbed his chin thoughtfully.*
2 If you **rub out** pencil marks, you use a rubber to remove them from the paper.
3 *(informal)* If you **rub it in**, you keep telling someone about their mistakes. *Lea couldn't stop rubbing it in that she beat Tim at chess.*

rubber *(n)*
1 a substance made from the juice of a rubber tree, or produced artificially. Rubber is strong, elastic, and waterproof, and is used for making things like tyres, balls, and boots. *The picture shows liquid rubber, or latex, being collected by a method called tapping.*
2 a small piece of rubber used for rubbing out pencil marks.

rubber tapping

area of removed bark

diagonal cut

trunk of rubber tree

funnel

latex (rubber particles in liquid)

cup

rubbish *(n)*
1 things that you throw away because they are not useful or valuable.
2 nonsense. *Don't talk rubbish!*

rubble *(n)* broken bricks and stones. *All that was left of the house was a pile of rubble.*

ruby rubies *(n)*
a dark red precious stone.

rucksack *(n)* a large bag that you carry on your back when you are walking or climbing. See **hike**.

rudder *(n)* a hinged plate, attached to the back of a boat or aeroplane, and used for steering. See **aircraft**, **dinghy**, **ship**.

rude ruder rudest *(adj)*
not polite. rudeness *(n)*, rudely *(adv)*.

rue ruing rued *(v) (old-fashioned)* to regret something. rueful *(adj)*.

ruffle ruffling ruffled *(v)*
1 to disturb something that was smooth so that it becomes uneven or messy. *She ruffled his hair.*
2 to make someone feel annoyed or worried. *Carl's questioning really ruffled me.*

rug *(n)*
1 a thick mat made from wool or other fibres.
2 a small blanket.

rugby or **rugger** *(n)* a game played by two teams with an oval-shaped ball which they can kick, pass, or carry.

rugged *(rug-id) (adj)*
1 wild and rocky. *Rugged countryside.*
2 tough and strong. *I have always admired Kirk's rugged good looks.*

rugger see **rugby**.

ruin ruining ruined
1 *(v)* to spoil something completely. **ruin** *(n)*.
2 *(n)* a building that has been destroyed or very badly damaged.
3 *(v)* to make someone lose all their money. *Geoffrey was almost ruined by the legal costs of the case.*

rule ruling ruled
1 *(n)* an official instruction that tells you what you must or must not do.
2 *(v)* to govern a country, or to have power over it.
3 *(n)* the time during which a person rules a country.
4 *(v)* to make an official decision or judgement. *The judge ruled that the woman was not guilty of the crime.* ruling *(n)*.
5 If you do something as **a rule**, you usually do it.
6 **rule out** *(v)* If you **rule something out**, you decide that it is not possible.

ruler *(n)*
1 a long, flat piece of wood, plastic, or metal that you use for measuring and drawing straight lines.
2 someone who rules a country.

rum *(n)* a strong alcoholic drink made from sugar cane.

rumble rumbling rumbled *(v)*
to make a low, rolling noise similar to the sound of thunder. **rumble** *(n)*.

rummage *(rum-ij)*
rummaging rummaged *(v)*
to look for something by moving things around in an untidy or careless way. *Ned rummaged in his backpack for his phone.*

rumour *(n)*
something that lots of people are saying, although it may not be true.

rump *(n)* the back part of an animal, above its hind legs.

run running ran run
1 *(v)* to move quickly, using your legs. **run** *(n)*.
2 *(v)* to take someone somewhere in a car. *Shall I run you home?*
3 *(v)* to function, or to work. *Most lorries run on diesel.*
4 *(v)* to be in charge of something. *Olivia runs a small business.*
5 *(n)* a point in a game of cricket.
6 *(n)* a small enclosure for animals.
7 *(v)* If you **run away**, you escape from a place or leave it secretly.
8 *(v)* If you have **run out** of something, you have used it all and have none left.
9 If someone is **run over**, they are hit by a car or other vehicle.

runaway

runaway
1 (n) someone who has run away from home.
2 (adj) out of control. *A runaway train.*
3 (adj) very easy. *A runaway victory.*

rung (n)
one of the horizontal bars on a ladder.

runner (n)
1 someone who runs in a race.
2 a rod or bar on which something slides.

runner-up runners-up (n)
the person or team that comes second in a race or competition.

runny
runnier runniest (adj)
1 If something is **runny**, it flows or moves like a liquid. *Runny paint.*
2 If you have a **runny** nose, mucus is dripping from it.

runway (n)
a strip of land that aircraft use for taking off and landing.

rural (adj) to do with the countryside or farming. *Bill is very interested in rural issues.*

rush rushes rushing rushed
1 (v) to go somewhere quickly, or to do something quickly. *Eddie rushed to the shop before it shut.* **rush** (n).
2 **rushes** (plural n) tall plants with rounded stems that grow in damp places.

rust rusting rusted
1 (n) the red-brown substance that can form on iron and steel when they get wet. **rusty** (adj).
2 (v) to become covered with rust. *The door hinges have rusted.*

rustle rustling rustled (v)
1 When leaves, papers, etc. **rustle**, they make a soft, crackling sound as they move together gently.
2 to steal horses or cattle. **rustler** (n), **rustling** (n).
3 (informal) If you **rustle up** something, you provide it quickly. *Ruby rustled up some supper.*

rut (n)
1 a deep, narrow track made in the ground by wheels.
2 If someone is **in a rut**, they do the same sort of thing all the time.

ruthless (adj) Someone who is **ruthless** is cruel and has no pity. **ruthlessness** (n), **ruthlessly** (adv).

rye (n)
a cereal grown in cold countries and used to make flour and whisky.

Ss

Sabbath (n) the weekly day of rest in some religions. The Jewish Sabbath is Saturday, while the Christian Sabbath is Sunday.

sabotage (sab-er-tahj) (n) deliberate damage intended to cause difficulties for an enemy, employer, etc. **saboteur** (n), **sabotage** (v).

sabre (say-bur) (n)
1 a heavy sword with a curved blade.
2 **sabre-toothed tiger** an extinct big cat with very long, sabre-shaped fangs.

sabre-toothed tiger

sack
sacking sacked
1 (n) a large bag made from strong cloth, used for carrying coal, potatoes, flour, etc.
2 (v) If an employer **sacks** someone, the employer tells them that they no longer have a job and must leave. **sack** (n).

sacred (say-krid) (adj) holy or connected with religion. *Sacred music.*

sacrifice sacrificing sacrificed
1 (n) the killing of an animal or person as an offering to a god. **sacrifice** (v), **sacrificial** (adj).
2 (v) to give up something important or enjoyable for a good reason. *June sacrificed her career for her children.* **sacrifice** (n).

sacrilege (sak-ril-ij) (n) disrespect for something holy or very important. **sacrilegious** (adj).

sad sadder saddest (adj)
1 unhappy. **sadness** (n), **sadden** (v), **sadly** (adv).
2 Something which is **sad** makes you feel unhappy. *Sad news.*

saddle saddling saddled
1 (n) a leather seat on the back of a horse on which a rider sits. See **tack**.
2 (n) a seat for a bicycle. See **bicycle**.

3 (v) If someone **saddles** you with an unpleasant job or responsibility, they leave you to deal with it.

safari (n) an expedition to see or to hunt large, wild animals.

safe safer safest
1 (adj) If something is **safe**, it is not in danger of being harmed or stolen. **safety** (n), **safely** (adv).
2 (adj) not dangerous or not risky. *Is this ladder safe?*
3 (n) a strong box in which you can lock away money or valuables.

safeguard
safeguarding safeguarded
1 (v) to protect something.
2 (n) a law or regulation that is meant to protect something.

sag sagging sagged (v)
to hang down or sink down. *The bed sagged in the middle.*

sage
1 (n) a herb whose leaves are often used in cooking. See **herb**.
2 (adj) wise. *A sage remark.*
3 (n) (old-fashioned) a wise person.

sail sailing sailed
1 (n) a large sheet of strong cloth, such as canvas, that makes a boat or ship move when it catches the wind. *The picture below shows the main parts of the sails on a sailing dinghy. Also see* **ship**.
2 (v) to travel in a boat or ship. **sailing** (n).
3 (v) When a boat or ship **sails**, it starts out on a voyage.
4 (n) an arm of a windmill. See **windmill**.

sails
(sailing dinghy)

head
batten
leech (outside edge)
luff (inside edge)
mainsail
spinnaker
jib
window
boom
clew (rear corner)
tack (forward corner)
spinnaker pole

sailboard (n) a flat board with a mast and sail fixed to it, used for windsurfing. See **windsurfing**.

sailor (n) someone who works on a ship as a member of the crew.

saint (n)
1 a man or woman honoured by the Christian Church because of their very holy life. The short form of Saint is St. *The picture shows a painting of Saint Peter from a 13th-century manuscript.*
2 a very good and kind person. **saintly** (adj).

Saint Peter

sake (n)
If you do something for someone else's **sake**, you do it in order to help or please them.

salad (n)
1 a mixture of raw vegetables.
2 a mixture of cold foods. *Rice salad. Fruit salad.*

salamander (n)
1 an amphibian, similar to a newt, which lives on land but breeds in water.
2 In myths and legends, a **salamander** is a newt-like creature that lives in fire.

poison-secreting skin

salamander

salary salaries (n)
the money someone is paid for their work, usually once a month.

sale
1 (n) a time when goods are sold at cheaper than usual prices.
2 (n) the act of selling something.
3 for sale (adj) available for people to buy.
4 on sale (adj) available in the shops.

saliva (n) the liquid in your mouth that keeps it moist and helps you to swallow and begin to digest food.

salmon salmon (n) a large fish with a silvery skin and pink flesh. *Salmon can leap up to three metres in order to jump a waterfall.*

Atlantic salmon

salsa (n)
1 a spicy tomato sauce.
2 a lively Latin American dance.

salt
1 (n) a common white substance, found in sea water and under the ground, used for adding flavour to food. **salty** (adj).
2 (n) a chemical compound formed from an acid and a metal.
3 If you take something with **a pinch of salt**, you do not believe that it is really true.

salute saluting saluted (v)
1 When soldiers **salute**, they raise their hand to their forehead as a sign of respect. **salute** (n).
2 to praise or honour someone for something that they have done. *The school saluted Jill for her bravery.*

salvage salvaging salvaged (v)
to rescue something from a shipwreck, fire, etc. *The firefighters salvaged Duncan's belongings from the building.*

salvation (n)
the state of being saved from evil, harm, or destruction.

same (adj)
exactly alike, or not different.

sample sampling sampled
1 (n) a small amount of something that shows what the whole of it is like. *A blood sample.*
2 (v) to try a small amount of something to see if you like it. *Greg sampled the cheese before buying it.*

samurai (sam-yoo-rye) samurai (n)
a Japanese warrior. *This samurai is defending himself from attack with his naginata, a long rod with a curved blade at the end.*

iron helmet
neck guard
enemy arrow
katana (long, curved sword)
armour of leather scales
wakizashi (short sword)
naginata

samurai warrior

sanction sanctioning sanctioned
1 (v) to allow something or to give approval to something.
2 sanctions (plural n) punishment for breaking the law or for unacceptable behaviour. *One country can apply sanctions against another country by refusing to trade with them.*

sanctuary sanctuaries (n)
1 a holy place.
2 a place where someone who is being hunted can be safe.
3 a place where birds or animals are protected.

sand sanding sanded
1 (n) the tiny grains of rock which make up beaches and deserts. **sandy** (adj).
2 (v) to smooth or polish a surface with sandpaper or a sanding machine.

sandal (n) a light, open shoe with straps that go over your foot.

sandbag (n) a sack filled with sand, used as protection against flood water, bullets, or explosions.

sandpaper (n) paper with grains of sand stuck to it that you rub over surfaces to make them smooth.

sandwich sandwiches (n)
pieces of bread around a filling of cheese, meat, or some other food.

sandwich course (n) a programme of study which includes a period of work in business or industry.

sane saner sanest (adj)
1 Someone who is **sane** has a healthy mind. **sanity** (n), **sanely** (adv).
2 sensible or not at all crazy. **sanity** (n), **sanely** (adv).

sanitary
1 (adj) clean and free from germs.
2 sanitary towel (n) a pad of soft material that some women and girls wear during their periods.

sanitation (n) a system for protecting people from dirt and disease, for example, by a clean water supply and sewage disposal.

sap sapping sapped
1 (n) the liquid in the stems of plants.
2 (v) to weaken something gradually.

sapling (n) a young tree.

sapphire (saf-fire) (n)
a bright blue precious stone.

sarcastic (adj) If you are sarcastic, you say the opposite of what you really mean as a way of criticizing or mocking someone. **sarcasm** (n), **sarcastically** (adv).

sardine (n) a small sea fish, often sold in tins as food.

a b c d e f g h i j k l m n o p q r **s** t u v w x y z

sari

sari *(sah-ree)* *(n)*
a long piece of light
material, worn draped
around the body.
Saris are worn mainly
by Indian women and
girls. *The picture
shows an Indian
woman wearing a sari.*

sari

sarong *(sa-rong)* *(n)*
a piece of cloth wrapped
around the the body like
a skirt or dress, originally
worn by Malaysian
men and women.

sash sashes
1 *(n)* a strip of material
worn around the waist or
diagonally across the chest.
2 **sash window** *(n)* a window with
two frames that can slide up or down.

satchel *(n)*
a leather bag for school books carried
over the shoulder or on the back.

satellite *(n)*
1 a machine that is sent into orbit
around the Earth. *The picture shows
the main parts of a communications
satellite which receives and sends
television and telephone signals.*
2 a moon or other natural object
that moves in orbit around
a planet. *See* **moon**.

satire *(n)* a type of clever, mocking
humour that points out the faults in
certain people or ideas. **satirical** *(adj)*.

satisfaction *(n)*
a feeling of contentment, because you
have done something that you wanted
to do or have done something well.

satisfactory *(adj)*
good enough. **satisfactorily** *(adv)*.

satisfy satisfies
satisfying satisfied *(v)*
1 to please someone by doing
enough or giving them enough.
*The pizzas soon satisifed the
hungry children.* **satisfied** *(adj)*.
2 to convince someone that
something is true. *Jackson's
alibi satisfied the police.*

saturate saturating saturated *(v)*
1 to make something very wet.
saturated *(adj)*.
2 to fill something so full that
there is no room for anything else.
saturation *(n)*, **saturated** *(adj)*.

sauce *(n)*
a thick liquid served with food.

saucepan *(n)* a metal cooking pot
with a handle and sometimes a lid.

saucer *(n)* a small, curved plate
that is placed under a cup.

sauna *(sor-nah)* *(n)* a very hot
room where people sit and relax.

sausage *(n)* minced meat, bread,
herbs, etc. in a tube of thin skin.

savage savaging savaged
1 *(adj)* wild and vicious. *A savage
dog.* **savagery** *(n)*, **savagely** *(adv)*.
2 *(v)* to attack a person or an animal
by biting or scratching them.
3 *(n)* an uncivilized person.

3 to keep money to use in
the future rather than spending
it now. **savings** *(plural n)*.
4 to stop a ball from going
into the goal. **save** *(n)*.
5 If you **save** a document or a game,
you back it up to your computer so
that you don't lose it.

savoury *(adj)* having a salty or
spicy flavour, not a sweet one.

saw *(n)* a tool with a toothed
blade, used for cutting wood.
saw *(v)*. *See* **tool**, **woodwork**.

sawdust *(n)* the powder that
you get when you saw wood.

saxophone *(n)* a musical
instrument made
of brass, often
played in jazz
and dance bands.
saxophonist *(n)*.

neck

ligature
(holds reed)

mouthpiece

**alto
saxophone**

keys ——————

upper stack key ——

body ——

lower stack key

lower
octave key

spatula key

bell

say saying said
1 *(v)* to speak.
What did you say?
2 *(v)* to mean
something. *What
does that sign say?*
3 If you **have a say** in
something, you are one of
the people involved in deciding it.

saying *(n)*
a well-known phrase that gives advice.

scab *(n)* the hard covering that forms
over a wound when it is healing.

scaffold *(n)*
a raised wooden platform on
which criminals were executed.

**communications
satellite**

control
antenna

Earth cover horn
(receives signals and
sends them all
over the Earth)

horn cluster
(receives and
sends signals
to and from
reflector) —————

heat pipes
(keep equipment cool) —

communications
equipment

reflector
(receives
signals and
focuses
signals back
to Earth)

fuel tank

momentum wheel
(keeps satellite stable)

rocket motor
(blasts satellite
into circular orbit)

infra-red Earth sensor
(keeps satellite
facing Earth)

mirrored
radiator wall
(keeps equipment
cool)

thruster nozzle
(adjusts position
of satellite in
orbit)

solar array drive
mechanism
(rotates solar panels
to face Sun)

solar array panel
(generates electricity
from Sun)

solar sailing flap
(helps control
satellite's
position)

thermal
blanket cover
(layers of
protective foil)

satellite dish satellite dishes *(n)*
a dish-shaped receiver for signals
sent by satellite. Satellite dishes are
usually attached to outside walls.

satellite television *(n)*
television programmes that
are transmitted by satellite
and received by a satellite dish.

save saving
saved *(v)*
1 to rescue
someone or
something from danger.
2 If something **saves**
time, space, energy, etc.,
it does not waste it.

scaffolding *(n)* the structure of metal poles and wooden planks that workers stand on when they are working on a building.

scald scalding scalded *(v)* to burn yourself with very hot liquid. **scald** *(n)*, **scalding** *(adj)*.

scale scaling scaled
1 *(n)* one of the small, hard pieces of skin that cover the body of a fish, snake, or other reptile. **scaly** *(adj)*.
2 *(n)* a series of numbers, units, etc. that are used to measure something. *The Richter scale measures the energy released during an earthquake.*
3 *(n)* a series of musical notes going up or down in order.
4 *(n)* the relationship between the measurements on a map or model and the actual measurements.
5 **scales** *(plural n)* an instrument used for weighing things.
6 *(v)* to climb up something. *Joel scaled the mountain.*

scallop *(n)* a shellfish with two hinged shells or valves. *Scallops move around by opening and closing their valves rapidly.*

queen scallop

eye

gill

tentacles

shell or valve

adductor muscle
(holds shells together
when closed)

barnacle
growing
on shell

scalp *(n)*
the skin on the top of your head where your hair grows. *See* **brain**.

scalpel *(n)*
a small, sharp knife used by surgeons.

scamper scampering scampered *(v)* to run with short, quick steps. *The squirrel scampered along the branch.*

scan scanning scanned *(v)*
1 to look through a book or piece of writing because you are searching for something. *Mick scanned the email for news of his brother.*
2 to look carefully along something. *We scanned the horizon for ships.*
3 When a machine **scans** something, it copies pictures or text from paper onto a computer. **scan** *(n)*.

scanner *(n)*
1 a machine used by medical staff to view inside a patient's body. **scan** *(n)*, **scan** *(v)*.
2 a machine used to copy pictures or text from paper onto a computer.

scandal *(n)*
1 gossip about someone's dishonest or immoral behaviour.
2 something that you think is disgraceful. **scandalous** *(adj)*.

scanty scantier scantiest *(adj)* not enough or not big enough. *We had only scanty information.*

scapegoat *(n)*
someone who is made to take all the blame for something.

scar *(n)* a mark left on your skin by an old cut or wound. **scar** *(v)*.

scarce *(adj)*
Something that is **scarce** is hard to find because there is so little of it. *Fresh water is scarce on the island.* **scarcity** *(n)*.

scarcely *(adv)*
hardly. *I've scarcely seen Shaun today.*

scare scaring scared *(v)*
to frighten a person or an animal. **scare** *(n)*, **scared** *(adj)*, **scary** *(adj)*.

scarecrow *(n)*
a model of a person, put in a field to frighten birds away from crops.

scarf scarfs *or* scarves *(n)*
a strip of material worn round your neck or head.

scarlet *(n)*
a bright red colour. **scarlet** *(adj)*.

scatter scattering scattered *(v)*
1 to throw things over a wide area. *We scattered the seed over the earth.*
2 to run off in different directions.

scatterbrained *(adj)*
If you are **scatterbrained**, you are always forgetting things.

scavenge scavenging scavenged *(v)*
to search among rubbish for food or something useful. **scavenger** *(n)*.

scene *(seen)* *(n)*
1 a view or a picture. *Fleur paints country scenes.*
2 a part of a play or film where the events all happen in the same place.
3 the place where something happens. *The ambulance rushed to the scene of the accident.*
4 If you **make a scene**, you get very angry with someone in public.

scenery *(seen-er-ee)* *(singular n)*
1 the natural countryside of an area, such as trees, hills, and lakes.
2 the painted boards and curtains that are used on stage as the background to a play, opera, or ballet.

scenic *(seen-ik)* *(adj)*
A **scenic** place has beautiful surrounding countryside.

scent *(sent)* scenting scented
1 *(n)* a pleasant smell. *The scent of roses.* **scented** *(adj)*.
2 *(n)* a liquid that you can put on your skin to make yourself smell pleasant.
3 *(n)* an animal's smell.
4 *(v)* If you **scent** danger or victory, you start to feel that it will happen.

sceptical *(adj)* If you are **sceptical** about something, you doubt whether it is really true. **sceptic** *(n)*, **scepticism** *(n)*, **sceptically** *(adv)*.

schedule *(shed-yool)* scheduling scheduled
1 *(n)* a plan, programme, or timetable.
2 *(v)* If you **schedule** an event, you plan it for a particular time.

scheme *(skeem)* scheming schemed
1 *(n)* a plan or an arrangement.
2 *(v)* to plan or plot something, especially something secret or dishonest. **schemer** *(n)*, **scheming** *(adj)*.

scholar *(skol-er)* *(n)*
1 a student who has won a scholarship.
2 a very clever and learned person.

scholarship *(n)* a prize that pays for you to go to a school or university.

school *(n)*
1 a place where children go to be taught.
2 a group of fish or other sea creatures. *A school of porpoises.*

science *(n)* the study of nature and the physical world by testing, experimenting, and measuring. Biology, physics, and chemistry are all types of science. **scientist** *(n)*, **scientific** *(adj)*, **scientifically** *(adv)*.

science fiction *(n)* stories about life in the future, or life on other planets.

scissors *(plural n)*
a sharp tool with two blades, used for cutting paper, material, etc.

scoff scoffing scoffed *(v)*
1 to be scornful and mocking about someone or something. *Belle scoffed at the idea of ballet lessons.*
2 *(informal)* to eat very fast and greedily. *Spencer scoffed his lunch.*

scold scolding scolded *(v)*
to tell someone off.

scone *(n)*
a round bun, often eaten with butter.

scoop scooping scooped
1 *(v)* to lift or pick up something. *Zack scooped up a handful of snow.*
2 *(n)* a serving utensil used to pick things up. *An ice cream scoop.*
3 *(n)* a story in a newspaper that other papers do not have.

scooter (n)
1 a type of vehicle, with two wheels and a flat board, which you stand on with one foot, while pushing on the ground with the other foot.
2 a small motorcycle.

scope (n) the range of opportunity that something gives. *There is plenty of scope for improving this garden.*

scorch scorches scorching scorched (v)
1 to burn slightly. **scorch** (n).
2 to dry something up. *The blazing sun scorched the earth.*

scorching (adj) extremely hot. *The weather is scorching today!*

score scoring scored
1 (v) to get a goal or win a point in a game.
2 (n) the number of points or goals that each team wins in a game.
3 (n) a written piece of music.
4 (v) to cut a line or lines in a surface.
5 (n) (old-fashioned) twenty. *Seth lived for four score years.*
6 scores (plural n) a large number. *I've received scores of letters.*

scorn (n) a strong feeling of contempt and superiority. *Gaby poured scorn on my idea of becoming a doctor.* **scornful** (adj).

scorpion (n) a creature with eight legs and a venomous stinger in its tail.

tail
Sahara scorpion
pedipalp (sensitive pincer)
stinger
abdomen
walking leg

scoundrel (n) someone who cheats and lies.

scour (scow-er) scouring scoured (v)
1 to clean something by rubbing it hard. **scourer** (n).
2 to search an area thoroughly. *Police scoured the building for clues.*

scourge (skurj) (n) a cause of great harm and suffering.

scout scouting scouted
1 (n) a soldier sent ahead of the main army to find the enemy.
2 (v) to look for something. *We scouted around for firewood.*
3 (n) a member of the Scout Association.

scowl scowling scowled (v) to make an angry face. **scowl** (n).

scrabble scrabbling scrabbled (v) to dig or scratch in something with your hands or feet, usually in order to find something.

scraggy scraggier scraggiest (adj) skinny and lean. **scragginess** (n).

scramble scrambling scrambled
1 (v) to climb over rocks or hills.
2 (v) to rush or struggle to get somewhere. **scramble** (n).
3 (v) to mix up sounds or words.
4 scrambled eggs (plural n) a mixture of eggs and milk, cooked in a pan.

scrap scrapping scrapped
1 (n) a small piece of paper, food, etc.
2 (n) metal from old cars or machines.
3 (v) to get rid of something. *We had to scrap our plans due to the weather.*
4 (v) (informal) to fight or to quarrel. **scrap** (n).

scrapbook (n) a book in which you stick pictures, cuttings, etc.

scrape scraping scraped
1 (v) to clean, peel, or scratch something with a sharp object. **scrape** (n).
2 (n) (informal) an awkward situation. *Miranda's always getting into scrapes.*
3 (v) If you **scrape through** an examination, you only just pass it.

scratch scratches scratching scratched
1 (v) to make a mark or a cut. **scratch** (n).
2 (v) to rub your nails against a part of you that itches. **scratch** (n), **scratchy** (adj).
3 (informal) If you do something **from scratch**, you start from the beginning.
4 (informal) If something is **not up to scratch**, it is not good enough.

scrawl scrawling scrawled (v) to write in a quick, careless way. *Neil scrawled his name.* **scrawl** (n).

scream screaming screamed
1 (v) to cry out loudly or to shriek. **scream** (n).
2 (n) (informal) a very funny thing or person. *Jay's such a scream!*

screech screeches screeching screeched (v) to make a high, unpleasant sound. *The car screeched to a halt.* **screech** (n).

screen screening screened
1 (n) a wall or a barrier. **screen** (v).
2 (n) a television or computer monitor, or the white surface that films are shown on.
3 (v) to show something on a screen. *The film will be screened tonight.*
4 (v) to test someone, to see if they have a disease. **screening** (n).

screw screwing screwed
1 (n) a metal fastener like a nail, with a groove or cross in its head and a spiral thread.
2 (v) to fasten something with screws.
3 (v) If you **screw up** paper or material, you make it into a ball, ready to be thrown away.

screwdriver (n) a tool with a tip that fits into the head of a screw, in order to turn it. *See* **tool**, **woodwork**.

scribble scribbling scribbled (v)
1 to write carelessly or quickly. **scribble** (n).
2 to make meaningless marks with a pencil, pen, or crayon. **scribble** (n).

scribe (n) a person who copied books by hand, before printing was invented. *The picture shows a statue of an Ancient Egyptian scribe.*

Egyptian scribe

script (n)
1 an alphabet. *There are several different Indian scripts.*
2 the written version of what an actor or broadcaster says.
3 a series of instructions for a computer program.

scripture (n) religious writing, especially the Bible.

scroll

scroll scrolling scrolled
1 (n) a rolled-up piece of paper or parchment with writing on it. *The picture shows a Hebrew scroll made of parchment.*
2 (v) to move the text on a screen up and down so that you can see more of it.

scrounge scrounging scrounged (v) (informal) to get things free from people by asking for them. *Can I scrounge a sandwich from you?*

scrub scrubbing scrubbed
1 (v) to clean something by rubbing it hard with a brush.
2 (n) low bushes or short trees that cover a piece of ground.

scruffy scruffier scruffiest (adj) shabby and untidy. **scruffily** (adv).

scrum (n) a group of rugby players pushing to get the ball.

scrupulous (screw-pyoo-luss) (adj) careful and exact. *Lydia is scrupulous about money.* **scrupulously** (adv).

scrutinize or **scrutinise** scrutinizing scrutinized (v) to examine something closely. **scrutiny** (n).

seaweed

scuba diver

snorkel · mask · supply hose · torch · glove · regulator (controls air supply) · mouthpiece

air tank · buoyancy compensator jacket · weight belt · boot · rubber fin · foot pocket · knife in strap-on holder · wet suit · spare regulator · dive console · diving watch

scuba diving (n)
underwater swimming, with an air tank
on your back that is connected to your
mouth by a hose. **scuba diver** (n).

scuffle (n) a small fight. **scuffle** (v).

scull sculling sculled
1 (v) to row a boat using oars
on both sides of the boat.
2 (n) a small, light boat that is
propelled by oars, also called sculls.

sculpture (n)
1 something carved or shaped out of
stone, wood, metal, etc. *This stone
sculpture, created in 1938 by Henry
Moore, is called "Recumbent Figure".*
2 the art or work of making
sculptures. **sculptor** (n),
sculpt (v).

sculpture

scum (n)
1 a layer of dirty froth
on top of a liquid.
2 a worthless, evil person.

scurry scurries scurrying
scurried (v) to hurry, or to
run with short, quick steps.

scuttle scuttling scuttled
1 (v) to dash.
2 (n) a coal bucket.
3 (v) to make a hole
in a ship so
that it sinks.

scythe

handle · blade · grass nail (prevents grass from sticking to blade)

scythe
(sythe) (n)
a tool with a
large, curved
blade, used
for cutting
grass or crops.
scythe (v).

sea (n) a large area of salt water.

seafarer (n) a sailor, or someone
who travels by sea. **seafaring** (adj).

seafood (n)
fish or shellfish that are eaten as food.

seagull (n) a large grey or white bird
that is commonly seen near the sea.

sea horse (n)
a fish with a head shaped
like a horse's head and
a long, curling tail.

sea horse

seal sealing sealed
1 (n) a sea mammal
with small flippers
that breeds on land.
See **polar**.
2 (v) to close something
up. *We've sealed up
the old well.* **seal** (n).
3 (n) a stamp, pressed
into wax, used to make
a document official, or to
close up a letter or an envelope.

sea level (n) the average level of
the surface of the sea, which is used
to measure land heights. *Mount
Diablo is 3,800ft above sea level.*

sea lion (n) a sea mammal, similar
to a seal, but with sticking-
out ears and large
flippers.

sea lion

flipper

seam (n)
1 a line of sewing that joins
two pieces of material.
2 a band of a different kind
of rock between layers of
other rock. *A coal seam.*

seaplane (n) an aircraft that
can take off and land on water.

search searches searching
searched (v) to explore or examine
something closely. **search** (n).

search engine (n)
a software system on the internet that
finds items containing or showing
particular words that you type in.

searching (adj) deep and
thorough. *Searching questions.*

searchlight (n)
a large, powerful light that can
be turned in a particular direction.

search warrant (n) an order from a
court that allows the police to go into
a building to look for things or people.

seashell (n) the shell of a sea
creature, such as a mussel or cockle.

seashore (n) the sandy or
rocky land next to the sea.

seasick (adj) If you are **seasick**,
you feel ill because of the rolling
movement of a boat or ship.
seasickness (n).

seaside (n) the coast,
especially at a holiday resort.

season seasoning seasoned
1 (n) a time of the year. *The four
seasons are spring, summer,
autumn, and winter.* **seasonal** (adj).
2 (v) to add flavour to food
with salt, spices, etc.
3 If a food is **in season**, it is
fresh and easily available.

seasoning (n)
herbs and spices that are added
to food to give it more flavour.

seat seating seated
1 (n) a place where you can sit.
2 (v) to sit. *Jasper seated
himself on the arm of the sofa.*
3 (v) to have room for people
to sit down. *This table seats six.*

seat belt (n) a belt that you wear
across your lap and chest in a car
or plane to make you safer. See **car**.

seaweed (n) a type of algae that
grows in the sea. *The picture shows
examples of brown, green, and red
seaweed growing underwater.*

seaweed

serrated wrack · sugar kelp · thongweed · sea lettuce · dulse

secateurs *(sek-uh-terz) (plural n)* strong scissors that you use in the garden for cutting and pruning.

secluded *(adj)* quiet and private. *The farm is in a secluded valley.* **seclusion** *(n).*

second seconding seconded
1 *(adj)* next, or after the first. **second** *(adv),* **secondly** *(adv).*
2 *(v)* If you **second** a proposal at a meeting, you support it. **seconder** *(n).*
3 *(n)* a sixtieth of a minute.

secondary *(adj)*
1 to do with the second stage of something. *Secondary education.*
2 less important. *A secondary problem.* **secondarily** *(adv).*

secondary school *(n)* In Britain, a **secondary school** is a school for pupils aged 11 or 13 upwards.

second-hand *(adj)* If something is **second-hand**, it has belonged to another person first.

second-rate *(adj)* not very good.

secret
1 *(n)* a mystery, or something that only a few people know.
2 *(adj)* not known by many people. **secrecy** *(n),* **secretly** *(adv).*
3 in secret *(adv)* privately.

secret agent *(n)* a spy, or someone who obtains secret information.

secretary secretaries *(n)*
1 someone whose job is to write emails, make appointments, keep records, and do other office work for an employer. **secretarial** *(adj).*
2 a government minister or representative. *The Home Secretary.*

secrete *(sek-reet)* secreting secreted *(v)*
1 to produce a liquid. *Some snakes secrete venom.* **secretion** *(n).*
2 to hide. *The spy secreted the message in the heel of his shoe.*

section *(n)*
1 a part or division of something. *The tail section of an aeroplane.*
2 a drawing or plan that shows a slice through an object.

sector *(n)*
1 a part of a circle made by drawing two straight lines from the centre to different places on the circumference. *See* **circle**.
2 a part of a business, or an area of trade. *The marketing sector.*

secure securing secured
1 *(adj)* If you feel **secure**, you feel safe and sure of yourself. **security** *(n).*
2 *(adj)* safe, firmly closed, or well-protected. **security** *(n),* **securely** *(adv).*

3 *(v)* If you **secure** something, you make it safe, especially by closing it tightly.

sedate sedating sedated
1 *(adj)* calm and unhurried. *We strolled along at a sedate pace.* **sedately** *(adv).*
2 *(v)* to make someone calm or sleepy, especially by giving them medicine. **sedation** *(n).*

sedative *(n)* a drug that makes you quiet and calm.

sediment *(n)* solid pieces that settle at the bottom of a liquid.

sedimentary *(adj)* Sedimentary rock is formed by layers of material in the ground being pressed together. **sedimentation** *(n).*

seduce seducing seduced *(v)* If you **seduce** someone, you tempt or persuade them to do something, especially to have sex. **seduction** *(n),* **seductive** *(adj),* **seductively** *(adv).*

see seeing saw seen *(v)*
1 to use your eyes to look at or to notice someone or something.
2 to understand or to recognize. *I see what you mean.*
3 to visit or spend time with someone. *I'm seeing Peter this afternoon.*
4 If you **see through** someone or something, you are not deceived or tricked by them.
5 If you **see a job through**, you continue doing it right to the end.

seed *(n)* a small, hard object that grows into a plant. *See* **germinate**.

seedling *(n)* a young plant that has been grown from a seed.

seek seeking sought *(v)* to look for something, or search for something.

seem seeming seemed *(v)* to appear to be, or to give the impression of being. *They seem to be happy.*

seep seeping seeped *(v)* to flow or trickle slowly. *Some water has seeped through the ceiling.* **seepage** *(n).*

seethe seething seethed *(v)*
1 If a liquid **seethes**, it bubbles or boils.
2 to be very angry or excited. **seething** *(adj).*

segment *(n)*
1 a piece of something. *Eliza divided the orange into segments.*
2 a part of a circle made by drawing a straight line across it.

segregate segregating segregated *(v)* to keep groups of people apart from each other. **segregation** *(n),* segregated *(adj).*

seize *(seez)* seizing seized *(v)*
1 to take something quickly or by force. *Molly seized a rolling pin.*
2 If a machine **seizes up**, it jams or stops working.

seizure *(seez-yur)* *(n)* a sudden attack of illness.

seldom *(adv)* rarely. *We seldom see our neighbours.*

select selecting selected
1 *(v)* to pick or choose. **selector** *(n).*
2 *(adj)* carefully chosen and exclusive. *Sir Walter has a house in the select part of town.*

selective *(adj)* If you are **selective**, you choose carefully.

self selves *(n)* your individual nature or personality.

self-catering *(adj)* If you go on a **self-catering** holiday, you do your own cooking.

self-centred *(adj)* thinking only about yourself.

self-confident *(adj)* If you are **self-confident**, you know that you are all right, and that you can do things well. **self-confidence** *(n),* **self-confidently** *(adv).*

self-conscious *(adj)* If you are **self-conscious**, you think that people are looking at you, and you worry about what they are thinking. **self-consciously** *(adv).*

self-control *(n)* control of yourself and your feelings. **self-controlled** *(adj).*

self-defence *(n)* the act of protecting yourself against an attacker.

self-employed *(adj)* If you are **self-employed**, you work for yourself, not an employer.

self-explanatory *(adj)* If something is **self-explanatory**, it does not need any further explanation. *These instructions are self-explanatory.*

selfie *(n) (informal)* a photograph of yourself, taken by you.

selfish *(adj)* Someone who is **selfish** puts their own feelings and needs first. **selfishness** *(n),* **selfishly** *(adv).*

self-raising flour *(n)* flour containing baking powder, that makes cakes or bread rise.

self-respect *(n)* reasonable pride in yourself and your abilities. **self-respecting** *(adj).*

self-service *(adj)* If a shop or garage is **self-service**, you help yourself to what you want, and then pay for it at the check-out.

self-sufficient (adj) If a family or community is **self-sufficient**, they grow or make everything that they need themselves. **self-sufficiency** (n).

sell selling sold (v)
1 to give something in exchange for money. **seller** (n).
2 to offer for sale. *This shop sells fruit and vegetables.*
3 to make someone believe or want something. *Martha tried to sell us the idea of a Caribbean holiday.*
4 If a person **sells out**, they abandon their principles for money. **sellout** (n).
5 If a show **sells out**, all the tickets are sold. **sellout** (n).

semaphore (n) a way of sending a message by signalling with your arms or with flags. *The picture shows the message SOS in semaphore.*

semaphore

S   O   S

semen (*see*-men) (n) the liquid produced by males, that carries sperm to fertilize the female's egg.

semibreve (n) a musical note representing four beats. *See* **notation**.

semicircle (n) half a circle. **semicircular** (adj). *See* **circle**.

semicolon (n) the punctuation mark (;) used to separate parts of a sentence.

semidetached (adj) A **semidetached** house is joined to another house on one side.

semifinal (n) a match to decide who will play in the final. **semifinalist** (n).

semitone (n) the smallest possible space, or interval, between two musical notes.

senate (*sen*-it) (n) a governing group or council. *The American Senate.* **senator** (*sen*-at-or) (n).

send sending sent (v)
1 to make someone or something go somewhere. *Send Tamara to the shop for a paper.* **sender** (n).
2 If you **send for** someone or something, you make them come to you. *Let's send for some tea.*
3 **send up** (informal) to copy and laugh at someone or something. *David hates it when his friends send up his accent.* **send-up** (n).

send off sending off sent off
1 (v) to make a player leave the sports field as a punishment.
2 (v) to write to ask for something. *We sent off for the free offer.*
3 **sendoff** (n) (informal) If you are given a **sendoff**, people gather to wish you well for a journey, new job, etc.

senile (adj) weak in mind and body because of old age. **senility** (n).

senior (adj) Someone who is **senior** to you is older or more important than you are. **seniority** (n).

senior citizen (n) an old person, especially a pensioner.

sensation (n)
1 a feeling. *Donna was so cold, she had no sensation in her toes.*
2 something that causes a lot of excitement and interest. **sensational** (adj), **sensationally** (adv).

sense sensing sensed
1 (n) good judgement or understanding. *Rose has no sense.*
2 (n) the ability to feel or be aware of something. *A sense of direction.*
3 (n) Your five **senses** are sight, hearing, touch, taste, and smell.
4 (n) meaning. *I can't make sense of this story.*
5 (v) to feel or be aware of something. *I sensed that Noah was angry.*

senseless (adj)
1 pointless or without meaning. *What a senseless attack on an old man!* **senselessly** (adv).
2 unconscious.

sensible (adj)
If you are **sensible**, you think carefully and do not do stupid or dangerous things. **sensibly** (adv).

sensitive (adj)
1 easily offended or easily hurt. **sensitivity** (n), **sensitively** (adv).
2 aware of other people's feelings. **sensitivity** (n), **sensitively** (adv).
3 able to react to the slightest change. *Sensitive measuring equipment.* **sensitivity** (n), **sensitively** (adv).

sensor (n) an instrument that can detect changes in heat, sound, etc.

sentence (n)
1 a group of words that make sense. A sentence starts with a capital letter and ends with a full stop.
2 a punishment given to a criminal in court. *A prison sentence.* **sentence** (v).

sentimental (adj) to do with emotion, romance, or feelings. *This ring has sentimental value: it was my mother's.* **sentimentally** (adv).

sentry sentries (n)
a soldier who stands guard.

separate separating separated
1 (*sep*-er-ate) (v) to part or divide something or some people. **separation** (n).
2 (*sep*-er-rut) (adj) different, individual, or not together. *The three children have separate bedrooms.* **separately** (adv).
3 (*sep*-er-ate) (v) If a husband and wife **separate**, they stop living together. **separation** (n).
4 **separates** (*sep*-er-ruts) (plural n) clothes, such as a skirt and blouse, that you can wear together or on their own.

septic (adj) infected with bacteria. *Violet's cut finger went septic.*

septic tank (n) a tank where sewage is treated outside homes not connected to the sewage system.

sequel (*see*-kwell) (n) a second book or film that continues the story from the first.

sequence (*see*-kwence) (n) a series of things that follow in order. *My life is a sequence of disasters.*

serene (adj) calm and peaceful. **serenity** (n), **serenely** (adv).

serf (n) a farm worker in medieval times who worked for the lord of the manor. **serfdom** (n). *See* **feudalism**.

sergeant (*sar*-jent) (n) an officer in the armed forces or police force.

serial
1 (n) a story that is told in several instalments. *A television serial.* **serialization** (n), **serialize** (v).
2 (adj) Something that is **serial** happens in a row or in order.
3 (n) A **serial number** is a number that identifies a machine or other product.

series series
1 (n) a group of related things, that follow in order. *A series of lessons.*
2 (n) a number of television or radio programmes that are linked in some way. *A detective series.*
3 Electrical parts that are connected **in series** allow electricity to pass through them one after the other.

serious (adj)
1 solemn and thoughtful. **seriousness** (n), **seriously** (adv).
2 sincere or not joking. *Are you serious about leaving school?* **seriousness** (n), **seriously** (adv).
3 very bad or worrying. *A serious illness.* **seriousness** (n), **seriously** (adv).
4 important. *Stop messing about, this match is serious!* **seriousness** (n), **seriously** (adv).

a
b
c
d
e
f
g
h
i
j
k
l
m
n
o
p
q
r
S
t
u
v
w
x
y
z

sermon

sermon (n) a religious talk given during a church service.

serpent (n) (poetic) a snake. Serpents often represent evil in pictures and stories. *This Aztec pendant is made in the shape of a two-headed serpent.*

serpent pendant

serrated (adj) A **serrated** knife has teeth like a saw.

servant (n) someone who works in someone else's house, doing housework, cooking, etc.

serve serving served (v)
1 to work for someone.
2 to give someone food or help them in a shop.
3 to begin play in games such as tennis, by hitting the ball. **serve** (n).

server (n)
a computer that provides a service for other computers in a network. The server may run the network, or provide a link to a printer or some other piece of equipment.

service
1 (n) The **service** in a shop, café, etc. is the way that you are looked after.
2 (n) a business or organization that provides you with something. *The police service.*
3 (n) a religious ceremony or meeting.
4 (v) to check a car or machine to make sure that it is working properly. **service** (n).
5 services (plural n) an area next to a motorway where you can eat, rest, and fill up your vehicle with fuel.
6 services (plural n) the armed forces, such as the army, air force, or navy. **serviceman** (n), **servicewoman** (n).

serviette (n) a napkin.

session (n)
1 a period of time used for an activity. *A training session.*
2 a formal meeting. *A court session.*

set setting set
1 (n) a group of things that go together. *A chess set.*
2 (n) the scenery for a play or film.
3 (adj) ready. *Are we all set to leave?*
4 (adj) fixed. *We eat at set times.*
5 (v) to put, fix, or arrange. *Set the alarm for 6 a.m.*
6 (v) If a liquid **sets**, it becomes solid.
7 (v) When the sun **sets**, it goes below the horizon.

setback (n) something that delays you or stops you making progress.

set square (n) a flat, triangular plastic shape that you use to draw angles. See **geometry**.

settee (n)
a long, soft seat with arms and a back, and room for two or more people.

settle settling settled (v)
1 to sort out, decide, or agree on something. *We settled the argument by tossing a coin.*
2 to make yourself comfortable. *Wes settled down with a good book.*
3 to go and live somewhere. **settler** (n).
4 If you **settle in**, you get used to your new house, school, etc.
5 If you **settle up**, you pay a bill or an account.

set up setting up set up
1 (v) to get something ready for use, or to arrange it. *The film crew set up their cameras.*
2 (n) (informal) the way that something is organized or arranged.

sever severing severed (v) to cut or break something. *The two countries have severed all ties.*

several (adj) a small number of people, things, etc. *We have several umbrellas at home.* **several** (pronoun).

severe severer severest (adj) strict, harsh, or demanding. *Sammy's dad is very severe on him.* **severity** (n), **severely** (adv).

sew (so) sewing sewed sewn (v) to stitch using a needle and thread. **sewing** (n).

sewage (n) liquid and solid waste that is carried away in sewers and drains.

sewer (n) an underground pipe that carries away liquid and solid waste.

sewing machine (n) a machine for sewing very fast, worked by hand, foot, or electric motor.

sex sexes (n)
1 A person's **sex** is their identity as male or female. *The symbols used for the male and female sexes are shown here.*
2 the instinct which causes two people to be physically attracted to each other. **sexual** (adj).
3 the act of sexual intercourse.

sexist (adj) Someone who is **sexist** discriminates against members of one or the other sex. *It is sexist to assume that girls can't play football.* **sexism** (n), **sexist** (n).

sexual intercourse (n) an intimate physical act between a man and a woman, in which a man's penis enters a woman's vagina.

sexy sexier sexiest (adj) attractive in a sexual way. **sexily** (adv).

shabby shabbier shabbiest (adj)
1 worn, neglected, or in need of repair. *Shabby clothes.* **shabbiness** (n), **shabbily** (adv).
2 unfair or mean. *That was a shabby trick Kit played on you.* **shabbily** (adv).

shack (n) a small, roughly built hut.

shackles (plural n) a pair of linked metal rings put around the wrists or ankles of a prisoner.

shade shading shaded
1 (v) to shelter something from the light. *A large hat shaded her face.* **shade** (n).
2 (n) an area that is sheltered from the light. *Come and sit in the shade.* **shady** (adj).
3 (n) a level of colour or meaning. *A lighter shade of blue. This poem has several shades of meaning.*
4 (v) to make part of a drawing darker than the rest. **shading** (n).

shadow shadowing shadowed
1 (n) a dark shape made by something blocking out light. **shadowy** (adj).
2 (v) to follow someone closely and watch them carefully, and usually secretly. *We shadowed the thieves all the way back to their den.*

shaft (n)
1 the long, narrow bar of a spear, arrow, or paddle. See **car**, **kayak**.
2 a rotating bar that transmits power to wheels or a propeller.
3 a thin beam of light.
4 a hole in the ground through which you enter a mine.
5 the central stem of a feather. See **feather**.

shaggy shaggier shaggiest (adj) Shaggy hair or fur is long, rough, and uncombed.

shake shaking shook shaken (v)
1 to tremble or to quiver.
2 to take hold of something and move it quickly up and down. *Shake the bottle before opening.*

shaky shakier shakiest (adj)
1 unsteady and wobbly. *The calf stood up on shaky legs.*
2 not very good or not very strong. *Alastair's spelling is rather shaky.*

male

female

shelf

shallow shallower shallowest *(adj)*
not deep. *Shallow water.*

sham *(n)*
something that is not what
it seems to be. **sham** *(adj).*

shambles *(singular n)*
If something is a **shambles**, it is
very badly organized and chaotic.
*The match turned into a shambles
after the crowd invaded the pitch.*

shame *(n)*
1 a feeling of guilt and sadness about
something that you have done.
2 a pity, or a sad thing to have
happened. *It's a shame
that Alexandra can't
come tonight.*

shampoo *(n)*
a soapy liquid used for
washing hair, carpets,
etc. **shampoo** *(v).*

shamrock *(n)*
a small, green plant
whose leaves are
divided into three
parts. *The shamrock
is the national
emblem of Ireland.*

shanty shanties *(n)*
a song with a strong rhythm that
was sung by sailors as they worked.

shantytown *(n)* an area of
very poor, temporary housing.

shape shaping shaped
1 *(n)* the form or outline of
something. *The picture shows
a range of flat and solid shapes.*
2 *(v)* to mould something into a shape.
3 **shape up** *(v)* (informal) to develop.
The new team is shaping up well.

share sharing shared
1 *(v)* to divide what you have
between two or more people.
2 *(n)* the portion of something
that you receive.

shares *(plural n)* the equal portions
into which the overall value of a
business is divided. People can pay
money for shares in many companies,
receiving in return regular, smaller
amounts of money, based on how
profitable the company is.

shark *(n)*
1 a fierce sea fish with rows
of very sharp teeth.
2 someone who
cheats people.

tiger
shark

sharp sharper sharpest
1 *(adj)* A **sharp** edge is fine or
pointed, and is likely to prick or cut.
2 *(adj)* quick-witted or clever.
3 *(adj)* sudden and dramatic.
A sharp turn in the road.
4 *(adj)* slightly sour.
Lemon juice tastes sharp.
5 *(adj)* clearly detailed and
in focus. *A sharp picture.*
6 *(adv)* exactly. *Be here
at three o'clock sharp.*
7 *(adj)* In music, a **sharp** note is
higher in pitch than the usual note.
C sharp is a semitone higher than C.
8 *(adj)* cross and abrupt. **sharply** *(adv).*

shatter shattering shattered *(v)*
to break into tiny pieces.

shattered *(adj)*
1 shocked and upset. *I was shattered
by Bryony's news.* **shattering** *(adj).*
2 (informal) extremely tired.

shave shaving shaved *(v)*
to remove hair with a razor.

shawl *(n)*
a piece of soft material, sometimes
wrapped around a baby or worn
by women over their shoulders.

sheaf sheaves *(n)* a bundle.
A sheaf of corn. A sheaf of papers.

shear shearing sheared shorn
1 *(v)* to cut the fleece off
a sheep. *The picture
shows a farmer
shearing a sheep
with electric clippers.*
2 **shears** *(plural n)*
a large cutting
tool with two
blades, used for
cutting hedges,
trimming grass, etc.

sheepshearing

sheath *(n)* a holder
for a knife or dagger. *See **dagger**.*

shed shedding shed
1 *(n)* a small hut used
for storing things.
2 *(v)* to let something fall or
drop off. *Some reptiles shed
their skin. Some trees shed
their leaves. People shed tears.*

sheen *(n)* a shine on a surface.

sheep sheep *(n)* a farm animal
kept for its wool and meat.

sheepdog *(n)* a working farm
dog that rounds up sheep.

sheepish *(adj)*
If someone looks **sheepish**, they
look embarrassed or ashamed,
often because they have done
something foolish. **sheepishly** *(adv).*

sheer sheerer sheerest *(adj)*
1 extremely steep. *There was
a sheer drop to the rocks below.*
2 total and complete.
Our holiday was sheer bliss.
3 extremely thin and transparent.
Sheer stockings.

sheet *(n)*
1 a large, thin, rectangular piece
of cloth used to cover a bed.
2 a thin, flat piece of
paper, glass, metal, etc.

sheik *or* **sheikh** *(shake) (n)* the head
of an Arab tribe, village, or family.

shelf shelves *(n)*
a horizontal board on a wall or in
a cupboard, used for storing things.

flat shapes

circle

square

rectangle

equilateral triangle

isosceles triangle

right-angled triangle

parallelogram

trapezium

rhombus

octagon

pentagon

hexagon

solid shapes

cube

tetrahedron

pyramid

octahedron

cone

cylinder

prism

dodecahedron

shell

shell *(n)*
1 a protective outer case. *Nuts, tortoises, shellfish, and eggs all have shells.*
2 a type of bomb that is fired from a gun.

fighting conch

court cone

cowrie shell

seashells

scorpion spider conch

screw shell

shellfish shellfish *(n)* a sea creature with a shell, such as a crab, lobster, or mussel. Many shellfish are edible.

shelter *(n)* a place where you can keep dry in wet weather, or stay safe from danger. **shelter** *(v)*.

shelve shelving shelved *(v)*
1 to put something off for a while.
2 to put something on a shelf or on shelves.

shepherd *(n)* someone whose job is to look after sheep. **shepherd** *(v)*.

sherbet *(n)* fruit-flavoured powder that is eaten or used to make sweets. *Lemon sherbet.*

sheriff *(n)* the chief person in charge of enforcing the law in an American county.

sherry sherries *(n)* a strong wine.

shield shielding shielded
1 *(n)* a piece of armour, carried to protect your body from attack.
2 *(n)* a protective barrier. *A heat shield.*
3 *(v)* to protect someone or something. *Theo shielded me from the bullies. The parasol shielded us from the sun.*

shift shifting shifted
1 *(v)* to move something heavy.
2 *(n)* a set period of several hours' continuous work. *A night shift.*

shimmer shimmering shimmered *(v)* to shine with a flickering light.

shin *(n)* the front part of your leg between your knee and ankle.

shine shining shone *(v)*
1 to give off a bright light.
2 If someone **shines** at something, they are very good at it.

shingle *(n)* small, rounded pebbles.

Shinto *(n)* a Japanese religion which involves the worship of ancestors and the spirits of nature. See **architecture**.

ship *(n)* a large boat used for sea travel. *The two pictures below show HMS Victory, the ship on which Admiral Nelson was killed in 1805, during the battle of Trafalgar. The cutaway view shows a reconstruction of life on board the Victory.*

HMS Victory

main topgallant sail

main mast

mizzen topgallant sail

mizzen topsail

mizzen mast

mizzen sail

yard (supports sail)

main topsail

fore topgallant sail

foremast

fore topsail

flying jib

jib

sprit topsail

mainsail — rigging — foresail — spritsail

hammock netting

stern lantern

stern lights (windows)

captain's dining cabin

poop deck

admiral's dining cabin

mizzen mast

helmsman at ship's wheel

binnacle (case for ship's compasses)

poop rail

admiral's sleeping cabin

main capstan (for raising anchor)

main mast

upper gun deck (with lightest guns)

middle gun deck

chain pump (pumps out water)

ship's boat

quarter deck

captain's cabin

admiral's day cabin

officers' cabins

wardroom (officers' quarters)

lower gun deck (with heaviest guns)

orlop deck

rudder

hold

pintle strap

gudgeon strap

surgeon's cabin

elm keel

water casks

officers' stores

gunpowder store

hanging magazine

light room

powder monkey (fetches explosives)

shot locker

coiled anchor cable

cable tier

stores

shipshape *(adj)*
clean, tidy, and in good order.

shipwreck *(n)*
1 the wrecking or
destruction of a ship.
2 the remains of a wrecked ship.

shipyard *(n)* a place where
ships are built or repaired.

shirk shirking shirked *(v)* to avoid
doing much work. **shirker** *(n)*.

shirt *(n)* a piece of clothing that you
wear on the top half of your body.
Shirts usually have a collar, sleeves,
and buttons down the front.

shirty shirtier shirtiest *(adj) (slang)*
cross or annoyed. **shirtily** *(adv)*.

shiver shivering shivered *(v)*
to shake with cold or fear.
shiver *(n)*, shivery *(adj)*.

shoal *(n)*
1 a large group of fish
swimming together.
2 a stretch of shallow water.

shock shocking shocked
1 *(n)* a sudden, violent fright.
2 *(v)* to give someone a fright.
3 *(v)* to horrify and disgust someone.
*The news of the motorway crash
shocked us all.* **shocking** *(adj)*.
4 *(n)* the violent effect of
an electric current passing
through someone's body.
5 *(n)* a thick, untidy mass.
Jason has a shock of golden curls.

shoddy shoddier shoddiest *(adj)*
carelessly produced and of
poor quality. **shoddiness** *(n)*.

shoe *(n)* an outer covering for
the foot, often made of leather.

shoehorn *(n)* a narrow piece of
plastic or metal that you use to help
your heel slip easily into a shoe.

shoelace *(n)*
a cord used for lacing up shoes.

shoot shooting shot
1 *(v)* to fire a gun. **shot** *(n)*.
2 *(v)* to make a film or video.
3 *(v)* to move very fast.
4 *(v)* to throw or kick a ball at a goal.
5 *(n)* a young plant that has just
appeared above the surface, or a new
part of a plant that is just beginning
to grow. *See* **germinate**, **plant**.

shooting star *(n)* a meteoroid, or
piece of rock from space, which burns
up as it enters the Earth's atmosphere.

shop
1 *(n)* a place where goods
are displayed and sold.
2 *(v)* to go to the shops in order to buy
goods. **shopper** *(n)*, **shopping** *(n)*.

shop floor *(n)*
1 the area of a factory where
the machines are operated.
2 a general name for the
workers in a factory.

shopkeeper *(n)*
someone who runs a small shop.

shoplifter *(n)* someone who steals
goods from a shop. **shoplifting** *(n)*.

shopsoiled *(adj)*
Goods that are **shopsoiled** are dirty
or slightly damaged because they
have been on display in a shop.

shore *(n)* the edge of the land
where it meets a sea, river, or lake.

short shorter shortest *(adj)*
1 less than the average length, distance,
time, etc. **shortness** *(n)*, **short** *(adv)*.
2 If you are **short** of something, you
have less of it than you need. *Henry is
very short of money at the moment.*

shortage *(n)* When there is a
shortage of something, there is
not enough of it. *A food shortage.*

shortbread *(n)* a rich, buttery biscuit.

shortcoming *(n)*
a failing, or a weak point in
someone or something. *One of Ben's
shortcomings is that he is always late.*

shortening *(n)* butter, lard,
or other fat used in baking.

shorthand *(n)* a system of
writing symbols instead of words,
used for very quick note-taking.

short-handed *(adj)*
If you are **short-handed**, you do
not have enough people to do a job.

shortly *(adv)* soon or presently.
The train will be arriving shortly.

short-range *(adj)* small in time
or distance. *A short-range shot.*

shorts *(plural n)* short trousers, often
worn for sports or as leisure wear.

short-sighted *(adj)*
1 If you are **short-sighted**, you
cannot see things clearly when they
are far away. **short-sightedness** *(n)*.
2 not aware of future consequences.
A short-sighted decision.
short-sightedness *(n)*.

short-tempered *(adj)*
Someone who is **short-tempered**
becomes angry very quickly and easily.

shot *(n)*
1 the firing of a gun.
2 a photograph.
3 a heavy metal ball thrown
in an athletics event.
4 an attempt to get a ball in a goal.
5 *(informal)* an injection.
6 *(informal)* an attempt. *Faith
had a shot at beating the record.*

shotgun *(n)* a gun with a long barrel
that fires cartridges full of tiny pellets.

shot put *(n)*
an athletics event in which you throw
a heavy metal ball as far as possible.
shot-putter *(n)*. *See* **track and field**.

sheet anchor
(for emergencies)

foremast

boarding pikes
(to repel boarders)

belfry
(contains
ship's bell)

bower
anchor

cathead
(secures anchor)

marine's walk

toilets

bowsprit

figurehead

bobstay

trail board

beakhead deck

water line

sick-bay port

oak hull   cannon   gunport   anchor cable

HMS Victory
(hull cutaway)

shoulder (n) the part of your body between your neck and your arm.

shout shouting shouted (v) to call out loudly. **shout** (n).

shove (shuv) shoving shoved (v) to push roughly. **shove** (n).

shovel shovelling shovelled
1 (n) a spade with a flattened scoop.
2 (v) to move things with a shovel. *Maggie shovelled snow off the path.*

show showing showed shown
1 (v) to let something be seen. *Show me the picture!*
2 (v) to explain or to demonstrate. *Show me how to do it!*
3 (v) to guide or lead someone. *Let me show you to your seat.*
4 (v) to be visible. *The stain won't show.*
5 (n) a public performance or an exhibition. *An art show.*

show business (n) the world of theatre, films, television, and other entertainments.

shower showering showered
1 (n) a brief fall of rain. **showery** (adj).
2 (n) a piece of equipment that produces a fine spray of water for washing your body. **shower** (v).
3 (v) to fall in large numbers. *Leaves showered from the tree.*
4 (v) to give someone lots of things. *Rosa showered me with presents.*

showjumping (n) a sport in which horses and riders jump over fences. **show-jumper** (n).

show-off (n) someone who behaves in a boastful way in order to impress people. **show off** (v).

showroom (n) a large room used to display goods that are for sale. *A car showroom.*

shrapnel (n) small pieces of metal scattered by an exploding shell or bomb.

shred (n)
1 a long, thin strip of something that has been torn off. **shred** (v).
2 a small amount of something. *He doesn't have a shred of decency.*

shredder (n) a machine for cutting used documents into tiny pieces so that no one can read them.

shrew (n) a small, insect-eating mammal with a long nose and small eyes. *The picture shows a white-toothed shrew with her young.*

shrewd shrewder shrewdest (adj) clever, experienced, and cunning in dealing with practical situations. **shrewdly** (adv).

shriek shrieking shrieked (v) to cry out or scream in a shrill, piercing way. **shriek** (n).

shrill shriller shrillest (adj) harsh, high-pitched, and piercing. *The shrill blast of a whistle.*

shrimp (n) a small, edible shellfish with a pair of claws and a long tail.

shrine (n) a holy place that often contains sacred relics. See **architecture**.

shrink shrinking shrank shrunk (v)
1 If something **shrinks**, it becomes smaller, often after being wet. *My shirt has shrunk in the wash.*
2 to move away because you are frightened. *The children shrank closer to the wall as the creature approached.*

shrivel shrivelling shrivelled (v) If something **shrivels**, it becomes smaller, often after drying in heat. **shrivelled** (adj).

shrub (n) a small plant or bush with woody stems.

shrubbery shrubberies (n) an area where shrubs are planted.

shrug shrugging shrugged (v) to raise your shoulders to show doubt or lack of interest. **shrug** (n).

shudder shuddering shuddered (v) to shake violently from cold, fear, etc.

shuffle shuffling shuffled (v)
1 to walk slowly, hardly raising your feet from the floor.
2 to mix together playing cards, papers, etc.

shun shunning shunned (v) to avoid someone or something. *Mo shunned any contact with the outside world.*

shunt shunting shunted (v) to move something from one place to another. *The engine shunted the carriages into a siding.*

shut shutting shut (v)
1 to block an opening, or close something with a door, lid, cover, etc. *Shut the door behind you.* **shut** (adj).
2 **shut down** to stop or to close down. *The local factory has shut down.*

shutter (n) a cover that protects the outside of a window and keeps out the light.

shuttle (n)
1 a bus or other form of transport that travels frequently between two places. **shuttle** (v).
2 the part of a loom that carries threads from side to side.

shy shies shying shied; shier shiest
1 (adj) If someone is **shy**, they are timid and do not enjoy meeting new people. **shyness** (n).
2 (adj) lacking or short. *Benny is ten pounds shy of the amount he needs to buy the computer game.*
3 (v) If a horse **shies**, it moves backwards or sideways suddenly, because it is frightened.

sibling (n) a brother or a sister.

sick sicker sickest
1 (adj) unwell or suffering from a disease. **sickness** (n).
2 If you are **sick**, you vomit.
3 (adj) (informal) If you are **sick of** something, you have had too much of it. *I'm sick of your crazy ideas, Len.*
4 (adj) (informal) A **sick** joke makes fun of other people's suffering.

sicken sickening sickened (v) If something **sickens** you, it makes you feel shocked and disgusted. **sickening** (adj).

sickly sicklier sickliest (adj)
1 weak and often ill.
2 If food is **sickly**, it is very sweet.

side siding sided
1 (n) a surface of a shape or an object.
2 (n) an outer part of something that is not the front or the back. **side** (adj).
3 (n) a team. *Please play on our side.*
4 (v) If you **side** with someone, you support them in an argument.

sideboard (n) a piece of furniture with a large, flat surface and drawers or cupboards below. Sideboards are usually found in dining rooms.

sideburns (plural n) the hair that grows down the sides of a man's face.

side effect (n) an effect of taking a medicine besides the intended effect.

sideshow (n) a small entertainment at a fair.

sidetrack sidetracking sidetracked (v) to distract someone from what they are doing or saying.

sideways (adv) moving towards the side. **sideways** (adj).

siding (n) a section of railway track used for storing or shunting carriages.

shrew with young

Some words that begin with a "si" sound are spelt "ci", "cy", "psy", "sci", or "sy".

siege *(seej) (n)*
the military action of surrounding
a place, such as a castle or city, and
waiting for its defenders to surrender.

siesta *(see-est-a) (n)* an afternoon
rest, taken in hot countries.

sieve *(siv) (n)* a container with lots
of very small holes in it, used for
separating large from small pieces,
or liquids from solids. **sieve** *(v).*

sift sifting sifted *(v)*
1 to put substances through
a sieve to get rid of lumps.
2 to examine something carefully.
*Police sifted through
the evidence for clues.*

sigh *(rhymes with lie)*
sighing sighed *(v)*
to breathe out deeply, often to
express sadness or relief. **sigh** *(n).*

sight *(n)*
1 the ability to see. *Lily lost
her sight in an accident.*
2 a view or a scene. *The New
York skyline is a marvellous sight.*

sightseer *(n)*
someone who travels to see interesting
places for pleasure. **sightseeing** *(n).*

sign signing signed
1 *(n)* a symbol that stands for
something. *A dollar sign. A minus sign.*
2 *(n)* a public notice giving information.
A road sign. A shop sign.
3 *(v)* to write your name in
your own way. *Please sign here.*
4 **sign language** *(n)*
a way of communicating by using
your hands, not speech, used
especially by deaf people. **sign** *(v).*

signal *(n)*
1 a form of communication
that does not use speech.
A railway signal. **signal** *(v).*
2 Television and radio **signals** are
pictures and sounds sent through
the air by electrical pulses.

signature *(n)* the individual
way that you write your name.

William Shakespeare's signature

Shakespeare's signature

signature tune *(n)* the music that
is always played at the beginning and
end of a television or radio series.

significant *(adj)*
important, or meaning a great deal.
significance *(n)*, **significantly** *(adv).*

signpost *(n)*
a roadside sign giving directions.

Sikh *(seek) (n)* a member of an
Indian religious sect that believes
in a single god. **Sikhism** *(n).*

silage *(n)* cut grass or hay that is
stored in a large sealed container,
called a silo, and used as animal feed.

silencer *(n)* an attachment that
reduces noise from a vehicle
exhaust or gun. *See* **motorcycle.**

silent *(adj)* absolutely quiet.
silence *(n)*, **silently** *(adv).*

silhouette *(sil-oo-ett) (n)*
a dark outline seen against
a light background.

silicon *(n)*
a very common chemical element used
to make microchips, transistors, etc.

silk *(n)*
a soft, smooth fabric made from fibres
produced by a silkworm. **silky** *(adj).*

silkworm *(n)* a caterpillar that spins
a cocoon of silk threads and then
turns into a moth.

**life cycle of
a silkworm**

1 silkworm
hatches

2 silkworm
feeds and grows

3 silkworm spins
silk cocoon
4 silkworm
moth emerges
from cocoon

silly sillier silliest *(adj)*
foolish or not sensible. **silliness** *(n).*

silo *(n)*
1 a tower or pit for storing
grain, grass for silage, etc.
2 an underground shelter
for a guided missile.

silt *(n)*
the fine particles that are carried by
running water and settle on river beds.

silver *(n)*
1 a shiny, grey, precious metal used
in jewellery and coins. *See* **mineral.**
2 coins made from silver
or silver-coloured metal.
3 the colour of silver.
silver *(adj)*, **silvery** *(adj).*

similar *(adj)* alike, or of the same
type. **similarity** *(n)*, **similarly** *(adv).*

simile *(sim-ill-ee) (n)*
a way of describing something by
comparing it with something else,
for example, "Her eyes are like
stars and her lips are like roses".

simmer simmering simmered *(v)*
1 to boil very gently.
2 **simmer down** *(informal)*
to calm down.

simple simpler simplest *(adj)*
1 easy or not hard to understand
or do. **simplicity** *(n)*, **simply** *(adv).*
2 plain and not elaborate. *A simple
meal.* **simplicity** *(n)*, **simply** *(adv).*

simplify simplifies
simplifying simplified *(v)*
to make something easier or less
complicated. **simplification** *(n).*

simply *(adv)*
1 in a simple way.
2 absolutely. *Simply marvellous.*

simulator *(n)* a machine that allows
you to experience what it is like to
fly a plane, drive a speedboat, etc.
by using computer technology and
mechanical movement.

simultaneous *(adj)* happening at
the same time. **simultaneously** *(adv).*

sin *(n)* bad behaviour that goes
against moral and religious laws.
sin *(v)*, **sinful** *(adj)*, **sinfully** *(adv).*

since *(conj)*
1 from the time that.
I've lived here since I was three.
2 as, or because. *Since you've been
so helpful, we'll give you a treat.*

sincere *(sin-seer)*
sincerer sincerest *(adj)*
If you are **sincere**, you are honest
and truthful in what you say and
do. **sincerity** *(n)*, **sincerely** *(adv).*

sinew *(sin-yoo) (n)* a tough fibre
that connects a muscle to a bone.

sing singing sang sung *(v)*
to make a musical noise with
your voice. **singer** *(n).*

singe singeing singed *(v)*
to scorch or burn something
at the tip or the surface.

single
1 *(adj)* individual, or only one.
2 *(adj)* not in a romantic relationship.
3 *(adj)* one-way. *A single ticket to Hull.*
4 *(n)* a recording of one song
that you can buy.

single-minded *(adj)*
If you are **single-minded**, you
concentrate on achieving one aim.

singular *(adj)*
to do with one thing or one person.

sinister *(adj)* If something is **sinister**,
it seems evil and threatening.

Some words that begin with a "si" sound are spelt "ci", "cy", "psy", "sci", or "sy".

a b c d e f g h i j k l m n o p q r **s** t u v w x y z

sink

sink sinking sank sunk
1 (n) a basin with taps and
a plughole, used for washing.
2 (v) to go down slowly. *The ship
sank. Stacey sank to her knees.*
3 (v) to make a ship sink. **sinking** (n).

sinus (sy-nuss) **sinuses** (n)
one of the hollow spaces in your skull
at the top of your nose. See **brain**.

sip sipping sipped (v) to drink
slowly in small amounts. **sip** (n).

siphon or **syphon** (sy-fun) (n)
a tube through which liquid is
drained upwards and then down
to a lower level. **siphon** (v).

sir (n)
1 a formal name for a man,
used in speaking and writing.
Can I help you, sir? Dear Sir.
2 the title given to
a knight. *Sir Lancelot.*

sister (n) a girl or woman who has
the same parents as you. **sisterly** (adj).

sit sitting sat (v)
1 to rest on your buttocks.
2 If you **sit** an exam, you
answer the questions in it.

site (n)
the place where something is or
happens. *A battle site. A building site.*

sitting room (n) a room in
which people can sit and relax.

situation (n)
1 the circumstances which exist at a
particular time. *A difficult situation.*
2 the position of something. *The
house is in a pleasant situation
overlooking the sea.* **situate** (v).

size (n) the measurement of how
large or small something is.

sizeable (adj) quite large.

sizzle sizzling sizzled (v) to make
a hissing noise, like sausages frying.

skate skating skated (v)
1 (n) a boot with a blade on the
bottom, used for moving across ice.
2 (v) to move smoothly
across ice, wearing skates.

ski boot
and ski
upper shell
manual
release for
binding
velcro
adjustment
strap
adjusting catch
buckle
lower shell
ski
binding
(fixes boot to ski)

skateboard (n) a small board with
wheels, that you stand on and ride.

skeleton (n)
the framework of bones in a body.

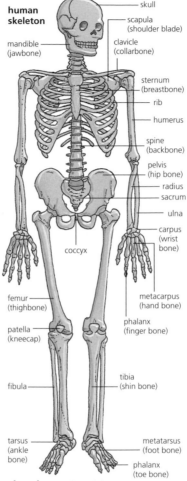

human
skeleton
skull
scapula
(shoulder blade)
mandible
(jawbone)
clavicle
(collarbone)
sternum
(breastbone)
rib
humerus
spine
(backbone)
pelvis
(hip bone)
radius
sacrum
ulna
carpus
(wrist
bone)
coccyx
metacarpus
(hand bone)
phalanx
(finger bone)
femur
(thighbone)
patella
(kneecap)
tibia
(shin bone)
fibula
tarsus
(ankle
bone)
metatarsus
(foot bone)
phalanx
(toe bone)

sketch sketches (n)
1 a quick, rough drawing
of something. **sketch** (v).
2 a short piece of acting
that is usually humorous.

skewer (n)
a long, metal pin for holding meat
or vegetables while they are cooking.

ski (n) one of a pair of
long, narrow runners
which you fasten to boots,
and use for travelling over
snow. **ski** (v), **skiing** (n).

skid skidding skidded
1 (v) to slide on a slippery surface.
2 (n) a runner on the bottom
of a helicopter. See **helicopter**.

skill (n) an ability to do something
well. **skilful** (adj), **skilled** (adj).

skim skimming skimmed (v)
1 to take something off the
top of a liquid. **skimmed** (adj).
2 to glide across a surface.

skin (n)
1 the outer covering of tissue on
the bodies of humans and animals.
2 the outer layer of a fruit or
vegetable. *A banana skin.*

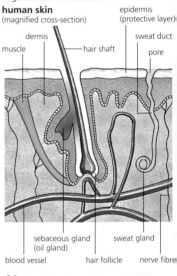

human skin
(magnified cross-section)
epidermis
(protective layer)
dermis
sweat duct
muscle
hair shaft
pore
sebaceous gland
(oil gland)
sweat gland
blood vessel
hair follicle
nerve fibre

skinny skinnier skinniest (adj)
very thin.

skip skipping skipped (v)
1 to jump over a turning rope.
2 to move along in a bouncy way,
hopping on each foot in turn.
3 (informal) to leave something
out deliberately. *I skipped the
gory scenes in my book.*

skirt (n)
a piece of clothing, worn by women
and girls, that hangs from the waist.

skittles (singular n) a game in which
you bowl a ball at bottle-shaped
pieces of wood, called skittles.

ski
(top view)
waist
sidecut
(inward curve)
tip
ski
(side view)
shovel
tail
camber
(upward curve)
steel edge

Some words that begin with a "si" sound are spelt "ci", "cy", "psy", "sy", or "sci".

skive skiving skived (v) (informal) to avoid doing any work. **skiver** (n).

skull (n) the bony framework of your head. *See* **skeleton**.

skunk (n) a black and white mammal with a bushy tail. Skunks give off a foul smell when they are threatened.

skunk

sky skies (n) the upper atmosphere as seen from the Earth.

skydiving (n) parachute-jumping that involves stunts or formation work. *This picture of skydiving shows a formation called a star.* **skydiver** (n), **skydive** (v).

skydiving

skylight (n) a window in a roof.

skyscraper (n) a very tall building with many storeys. *See* **architecture**.

slab (n) a large, flat block of stone, wood, or other heavy material.

slack slacker slackest (adj)
1 loose or not tight. **slacken** (v).
2 not busy. *In a recession, trade is slack for many shops.*
3 If you are **slack** in your work, you do not try very hard at it.

slalom (slah-lum) (n) an event in which competitors ski downhill, between poles.

slalom skier

slam slamming slammed (v) to close something heavily and loudly. *Jessie slammed the book shut.*

slander (n) an untrue, spoken statement that damages someone's name or reputation. **slander** (v).

slang (n) words and expressions used by particular groups of people, but not in formal speech or writing.

slant slanting slanted
1 (v) to slope or to be at an angle. *My handwriting slants to the right.*
2 (n) a point of view. *These new facts give a very different slant to the story.*

slap slapping slapped (v) to hit someone or something with the palm of your hand. **slap** (n).

slapdash (adj) Slapdash work is done carelessly and hurriedly.

slapstick (n) rough and noisy comedy, often performed by clowns.

slash slashes slashing slashed (v)
1 to make a sharp, sweeping cut in something with a knife or blade.
2 to reduce something dramatically. *The shop has slashed all its prices.*

slate (n)
1 a blue-grey rock that can be split into thin pieces, and is often used for roofing.
2 a roofing or flooring tile made from slate.

slaughter (slaw-ter) slaughtering slaughtered
1 (v) to kill animals for their meat.
2 (n) the brutal killing of large numbers of people. **slaughter** (v).

slave slaving slaved
1 (n) someone who is forced to work for someone else, without being paid. **slavery** (n).
2 (v) to work very hard. *I've slaved all day over my homework.*

slay slaying slayed *or* slew slain (v) (poetic) to kill someone in a violent way. *The knight slew the dragon.*

sled *or* **sledge** (n) a vehicle with wooden or metal runners, used for travelling over snow and ice.

sledgehammer (n) a heavy hammer.

sleek sleeker sleekest (adj) smooth and shiny.

sleep sleeping slept (v) to rest in an unconscious state. **sleep** (n).

sleeper (n) one of the thick concrete or wooden cross-pieces that support a railway track.

sleeping bag (n) a padded bag in which you sleep, especially when you are camping.

sleepwalker (n) someone who walks in their sleep. **sleepwalk** (v).

sleepy sleepier sleepiest (adj) tired or drowsy. **sleepiness** (n).

sleet (n) partly melted falling snow, or partly frozen rain.

sleeve (n) the part of a garment that covers your arm.

sleigh (slay) (n) a sledge, usually pulled by horses or other animals. *The picture shows a reindeer pulling a sleigh in Lapland.*

sleigh

slender slenderer slenderest (adj)
1 slim or thin.
2 small and inadequate in amount. *A slender income.*

slice (n) a thin piece or wedge of food cut from a larger piece. **slice** (v).

slick slicker slickest
1 (adj) very fast, efficient, and professional. *A slick performance.*
2 (n) a pool of oil covering an area of water or road.

slide sliding slid
1 (v) to move smoothly over a surface. *Olive is sliding down the banister.*
2 (n) a smooth surface for sliding on, especially in a playground.
3 (n) a small piece of glass on which you place a specimen, in order to view it under a microscope. *See* **microscope**.

slight slightest (adj) small or not very important. *A slight delay.* **slightly** (adv).

slim slimmer slimmest (adj)
1 very thin or narrow. **slim** (v).
2 very small. *A slim chance.*

slime (n) a slippery substance, such as that produced by a slug. **slimy** (adj).

sling slinging slung
1 (n) a piece of cloth used to support an injured arm.
2 (v) (informal) to throw something in a rough way. *Sling your bag on the top bunk.*

slip slipping slipped
1 (v) to lose your balance on a slippery surface.
2 (v) to move quickly and easily. *Ruby slipped away silently.*
3 (n) a small mistake.
4 (n) a light garment worn under a skirt or dress.

slipper *(n)* a soft, light shoe that you wear indoors.

slippery *(adj)* smooth, oily, or wet, and very hard to grip on to.

slipshod *(adj)* careless and untidy.

slit slitting slit *(v)* to make a long, narrow cut in something. **slit** *(n)*.

slither slithering slithered *(v)* to slip and slide along like a snake.

sliver *(n)* a very thin piece or slice of something.

slog slogging slogged
1 *(v)* to work hard. **slog** *(n)*.
2 *(n)* a long, hard walk. **slog** *(v)*.
3 *(v)* to hit a ball hard.

slogan *(n)* an easily-remembered word or phrase used in advertising.

slop slopping slopped *(v)* to splash or spill liquid.

slope sloping sloped *(v)* to be at an angle. *The wall slopes to the left.* **slope** *(n)*.

sloppy sloppier sloppiest *(adj)*
1 wet or slushy. **sloppiness** *(n)*.
2 *(informal)* careless and untidy. *Sloppy work.*
sloppiness *(n)*, **sloppily** *(adv)*.

slot *(n)*
1 a small, narrow space or groove in which something is fitted.
2 **slot machine** a machine that provides amusement when a coin is put in its slot.

sloth *(rhymes with cloth)* *(n)*
1 a very slow-moving South American mammal with a shaggy coat.
2 laziness. **slothful** *(adj)*.

three-toed sloth with baby

slouch slouches slouching slouched
1 *(v)* to sit, stand, or walk in a lazy way, with your shoulders and head drooping.
2 *(n)* *(slang)* a slow and lazy person. *Dan's no slouch at football.*

slovenly *(adj)* careless, untidy, and dirty. **slovenliness** *(n)*.

slow slower slowest *(adj)*
1 not fast. **slowness** *(n)*, **slowly** *(adv)*.
2 behind the right time. *My watch is five minutes slow.*

sludge *(n)* soft, thick mud.

slug *(n)*
1 a soft, slimy creature that is similar to a snail, but has no shell. *A slug moves in a series of waves in which it lifts part of its foot and then puts it down further forward. The foot is covered with mucus for protection and to help it cling to surfaces.*
2 *(slang)* a bullet.

great black slug

mantle (contains organs)

breathing hole

foot (ripples to produce movement)

eye

tentacle

sluggish *(adj)* slow-moving and lacking in energy. **sluggishly** *(adv)*.

slum *(n)* an overcrowded, poor, and neglected area of housing in a town or city.

slump slumping slumped
1 *(v)* to fall in a heavy or uncontrolled way. *Martin slumped to the ground.*
2 *(n)* a time of decline in industry and trade, when demand for products is greatly reduced.

slur slurring slurred
1 *(v)* to pronounce words unclearly by running different sounds into one another.
2 *(n)* If something is a **slur** on your character, it is insulting or damaging.

slush *(n)* snow that has partly melted. **slushy** *(adj)*.

sly slier sliest *(adj)* crafty, cunning, and secretive. **slyly** *(adv)*.

smack smacking smacked *(v)* to hit someone with the palm of your hand as a punishment. **smack** *(n)*.

small smaller smallest
1 *(adj)* little or tiny.
2 **small talk** *(n)* conversation about unimportant things.

smart smarting smarted; smarter smartest
1 *(adj)* well-dressed, tidy, and clean. **smartness** *(n)*, **smartly** *(adv)*.
2 *(adj)* clever or quick-thinking. **smartness** *(n)*.
3 *(v)* to sting or to hurt.

smash smashes smashing smashed
1 *(v)* to break something into a lot of pieces by hitting or dropping it.
2 *(n)* a car crash.
3 *(n)* a tennis stroke in which you hit the ball downwards very hard.

smear smearing smeared *(v)*
1 to rub something sticky or greasy over a surface. **smear** *(n)*.
2 to try to damage someone's reputation by telling untrue stories about them.

smell smelling smelled *or* smelt
1 *(v)* to sense through your nose. *I can smell dinner cooking.*
2 *(n)* an odour or a scent.
3 *(v)* to give off a smell, especially an unpleasant one. *Your socks smell!*
4 *(n)* the ability to notice smells. *Dogs have an excellent sense of smell.*

smelt smelting smelted *(v)* to heat rock containing metal so that the metal melts and can be removed.

smile smiling smiled *(v)* When you smile, your mouth widens and turns up at the corners to show that you are happy or amused. **smile** *(n)*.

smirk smirking smirked *(v)* to smile in an unpleasant way. **smirk** *(n)*.

smog *(n)* a mixture of fog and smoke that sometimes hangs in the air over cities and industrial areas.

smoke smoking smoked
1 *(n)* the mixture of gas and tiny particles that is given off when something burns. **smoky** *(adj)*.
2 *(v)* to give off smoke. *The bonfire was still smoking.*
3 *(v)* to hold a cigarette, cigar, or pipe in your mouth and breathe in its smoke. **smoker** *(n)*, **smoking** *(n)*.
4 *(v)* to treat food by hanging it in smoke. **smoked** *(adj)*.

smooth smoothing smoothed; smoother smoothest
1 *(adj)* A **smooth** surface is even and flat, not rough or bumpy. *A smooth road.* **smoothness** *(n)*, **smooth** *(v)*.
2 *(adj)* happening easily, with no problems or difficulties. **smoothness** *(n)*, **smoothly** *(adv)*.
3 *(v)* to make things more even and flat. *Gemma smoothed down her hair.*
4 *(adj)* Someone who is **smooth** seems too pleasant and confident.

smother *(smuth-er)* smothering smothered *(v)*
1 to cover someone's nose and mouth so that they cannot breathe.
2 to cover something completely. *Art smothered his pudding with cream.*
3 to protect someone too closely.

snort

smoulder
smouldering smouldered *(v)*
If something **smoulders**, it
burns slowly, with no flames.

SMS message *(n)*
a message that you type into
your mobile phone and send to
another person who reads it on
the screen of their mobile phone.
SMS stands for Short Messaging
Service. Often called a text message.

smudge smudging smudged *(v)*
to make a messy mark by rubbing
ink, paint, etc. **smudge** *(n)*.

smug smugger smuggest *(adj)*
If you are **smug**, you are
too pleased with yourself.
smugness *(n)*, **smugly** *(adv)*.

smuggle smuggling smuggled *(v)*
1 to take goods into a country
illegally. **smuggler** *(n)*.
2 to take something into
or out of a place secretly.

snack *(n)* a small, light meal.

snag *(n)* a small
problem or difficulty.

snail *(n)*
a small creature
with no legs, a
soft, slimy body,
and a shell on
its back.

garden snail

snake *(n)*
a long, thin reptile that has no legs
and slithers along the ground. Some
snakes have venomous bites. *The
diagram shows the internal organs of
a snake. Also see* **adder**, **venom**.

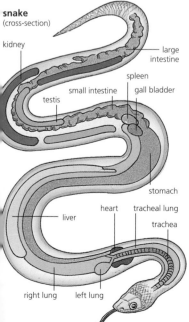
snake
(cross-section)
kidney
large
intestine
spleen
small intestine   gall bladder
testis
stomach
heart   tracheal lung
liver
trachea
right lung   left lung

snap snapping snapped
1 *(v)* to break with a sudden,
loud, cracking sound. *The twigs
snapped beneath our feet.* **snap** *(n)*.
2 *(v)* to try to bite someone.
The dog snapped at me.
3 *(v)* to speak sharply and angrily
to someone. **snappy** *(adj)*.
4 *(n)* a card game.
5 *(n)* *(informal)* a photograph.
6 *(n)* A **snap decision** is a decision
that is made very quickly.

snapshot *(n)* a photograph
taken with a simple camera.

snare snaring snared
1 *(n)* a trap for birds or animals.
2 *(v)* to catch a bird or
other animal in a snare.
3 snare drum *(n)* a small drum,
with strings or wires stretched
across its base, that produces a
rattling sound when hit. *See* **drum**.

snarl snarling snarled *(v)*
1 If an animal **snarls**, it shows its
teeth and makes a growling sound.
2 to say something angrily.

snatch snatches
snatching snatched
1 *(v)* to take or grab
something roughly.
2 *(n)* a small part. *I overheard
snatches of their conversation.*

sneak sneaking sneaked
1 *(v)* to move quietly and secretly.
Mel sneaked up on me from behind.
sneaky *(adj)*, **sneakily** *(adv)*.
2 *(v)* to bring someone or
something in where it is not
supposed to be. *Emily sneaked
the cat into her bedroom when
her mum wasn't looking.*
3 *(adj)* done secretly. *A sneak attack.*
4 *(n)* *(informal)* someone who
is tricky and dishonest.
5 *(v)* *(informal)* If someone
sneaks on you, they tell a
person in charge that you have
done something wrong. **sneak** *(n)*.

sneer sneering sneered *(v)*
to smile in an unpleasant,
mocking way. **sneer** *(n)*.

sneeze sneezing sneezed *(v)*
to push out air through your nose
and mouth suddenly, often because
you have a cold. **sneeze** *(n)*.

sniff sniffing sniffed *(v)*
1 to breathe in strongly and often
noisily, through your nose. **sniff** *(n)*.
2 to smell something. **sniff** *(n)*.

sniffle
sniffling sniffled *(v)* *(informal)*
to breathe noisily through your nose,
usually because you have a cold.

snigger sniggering sniggered *(v)*
to laugh quietly or secretly.

snip snipping snipped *(v)*
to cut something using small,
quick scissor cuts. **snip** *(n)*.

snipe sniping sniped *(v)*
1 to shoot at people from
a hidden place. **sniper** *(n)*.
2 to criticize someone in a position
where they can't criticize you back.

snivel snivelling snivelled *(v)*
to cry or complain in
a noisy, whining way.

snob *(n)*
1 someone who looks down
on people who are not rich
and powerful. **snobbery** *(n)*.
2 a person who thinks that they
are better than or superior to others.

snooker *(n)*
a game in which players use
long cues to knock coloured balls
across a table and into pockets.

snoop snooping snooped
1 *(v)* *(informal)* to look around
somewhere secretly. **snooper** *(n)*.
2 *(n)* a nosy person who pries
into other people's business.

snooty
snootier snootiest *(adj)* *(informal)*
If someone is **snooty**, they look
down on people who are not as
rich and powerful as they are.

snooze
snoozing snoozed *(v)* *(informal)*
to sleep lightly for a short time,
usually during the day. **snooze** *(n)*.

snore snoring snored *(v)*
to breathe noisily through your mouth
while you are asleep. **snore** *(n)*.

snorkel *(n)*
a tube that you
use to breathe
through when you are
swimming underwater.
snorkelling *(n)*. *Also
see* **scuba diving**.

snorkel
and
mask

snorkel   mask   adjustable
strap

snort
snorting snorted *(v)*
to breathe out air noisily through
your nose. *Janice was laughing
so hard that she suddenly
snorted loudly.* **snort** *(n)*.

snout

snout (n) the nose and mouth of a pig or similar animal.

snow snowing snowed
1 (n) light flakes of ice that fall from the sky when it is very cold.
2 (v) When it snows, snow falls from the sky. **snowy** (adj).

snowflake (magnified)

snowball snowballing snowballed
1 (n) snow pressed into a ball.
2 (v) If something **snowballs**, it grows rapidly. *Once we started inviting friends, the party snowballed.*

snowplough snowploughing snowploughed
1 (n) a vehicle used to push snow off a road or railway line.
2 (v) When you **snowplough** in skiing, you go down the slope slowly with the tips of your skis pointing inwards and the ends pointing out.

snub snubbing snubbed
1 (v) to behave in a rude, unfriendly way towards someone. **snub** (n).
2 (n) A **snub** nose is a small, turned-up nose.

snuff (n) powdered tobacco used for sniffing. *Snuff was very popular in the 18th century.*

snuffle snuffling snuffled (v) to breathe noisily and with difficulty.

snug snugger snuggest (adj) warm, cosy, and comfortable. **snugly** (adv).

snuggle snuggling snuggled (v) to sit or lie close to someone or something, so that you are warm and comfortable.

soak soaking soaked (v)
1 to put something in water and leave it there.
2 to make someone or something very wet. *The sudden rain soaked me.*
3 When something **soaks up** liquid, it absorbs it or takes it in.
soaking (adj) very wet.

soap (n) a substance that you rub on to your skin when you wash yourself. **soapy** (adj).

soap opera (n) a television series about the everyday lives of a group of people.

soar soaring soared (v)
1 to fly very high in the air.
2 to rise or increase very quickly.

sob sobbing sobbed (v) to breathe in short bursts because you are crying. **sob** (n).

sober soberer soberest (adj)
1 not drunk.
2 solemn and serious. **soberly** (adv).
3 Sober colours are dark and dull.

sob story sob stories (n) a sad tale about yourself, intended to make people feel sorry for you.

soccer (n) a game, also called football, played by two teams of eleven players who try to score goals by kicking a ball into a net at each end of a pitch. *The picture shows half a soccer pitch with a team in 4-4-2 formation.*

sociable (adj) Someone who is **sociable** enjoys talking to people and spending time with them. **sociability** (n), **sociably** (adv).

social (adj)
1 to do with the way that people live together. *This neighbourhood has many social problems.* **socially** (adv).
2 to do with activities that you take part in with other people in your spare time. *Joss has an exciting social life.* **social** (n), **socially** (adv).
3 Social animals or insects live in groups rather than on their own.

socialism (n) a way of organizing a country, with the main industries owned by the government so that everyone can benefit from the money made by them. **socialist** (n), **socialist** (adj).

social network (n)
1 a group of friends and acquaintances that you maintain online or through your phone. **social networking** (n).
2 a website where people can share information, pictures, etc. about themselves.

social security (n) money paid by the government to people who are unemployed, ill, or poorly paid.

social services (plural n) services provided by the government for people who have problems with health, childcare, housing, etc.

society societies (n)
1 all the people who live in the same country or area and share the same laws and customs.
2 an organization for people who share the same interests.

sociology (n) the study of the ways in which people live together in different societies. **sociologist** (n), **sociological** (adj).

sock socking socked
1 (n) a piece of clothing that you wear on your foot.
2 (v) (slang) to hit someone very hard.

socket (n)
1 a hole or set of holes into which an electrical plug or bulb fits.
2 a bone with a hole into which another bone fits. See **joint**.

soda (n) a kind of fizzy water that can be mixed with alcoholic drinks or fruit juice.

sodden (adj) extremely wet. *Flora fell in a pond and her clothes are sodden.*

sodium (n) a chemical found in salt.

sodium bicarbonate (n) a chemical substance used in baking to help cakes rise. Also called baking soda.

soccer pitch and players

penalty area · goal area · goal · goal line · corner flag

touchline

goalkeeper

penalty spot

right-back · central defender · central defender · left-back

linesman

penalty arc

right midfielder · central midfielder · ball on centre spot · central midfielder · left midfielder

halfway line · centre circle

referee

striker · striker

sofa *(n)* a long, soft seat with arms, a back, and room for two or more people.

soft softer softest *(adj)*
1 Something that is **soft** is not stiff or hard, and is easily pressed or bent into a different shape. *A soft cushion.* **softness** *(n)*, **soften** *(v)*.
2 smooth and gentle to touch. *Babies have very soft skin.*
3 pleasantly quiet and gentle. *Soft music.* **softly** *(adv)*.
4 not strict or tough enough. *My dad's so soft, he'll let me do anything.*
5 A **soft** drink is a cold drink that does not contain alcohol.

softball *(n)*
a game similar to baseball but played with a larger, lighter ball.

softhearted *(adj)* very kind, sympathetic, and generous to others.

software *(n)* a general name for computer programs or the disks on which the programs are stored.

soggy soggier soggiest *(adj)* very wet and heavy.

soil soiling soiled
1 *(n)* earth in which plants grow.
2 *(v)* If you **soil** something, you make it dirty or stained.

solar *(adj)*
to do with the Sun. *A solar eclipse.*

solar energy *(n)* energy from the Sun that can be used for heating, lighting, etc. *Solar panels use solar energy to produce hot water.*

solar panel (cutaway)
Sun's rays
glass or plastic cover
casing
black absorber plate
collector circuit pipe
water and anti-freeze solution flows through collector circuit pipes into heat store

solar system *(n)*
a sun and the planets that move around it. In our solar system there are eight planets, many moons, and also asteroids and comets, all of which move around the Sun. *See* **planet**.

solder soldering soldered *(v)*
to join pieces of metal together by putting a small amount of hot, liquid metal between them, which hardens as it cools.

soldier soldiering soldiered
1 *(n)* someone who is in the army. **soldierly** *(adj)*.
2 *(v)* If you **soldier on**, you keep doing something difficult.

soldiers

Roman legionnaire | 11th-century European knight | 15th-century European knight | 17th-century British cavalryman | 18th-century Prussian musketeer | 19th-century US private

sole
1 *(n)* the underneath part of the foot.
2 *(n)* a kind of flat sea fish.
3 *(adj)* only. *I was the sole survivor.* **solely** *(adv)*.

solemn *(adj)* very serious. **solemnity** *(n)*, **solemnly** *(adv)*.

solicitor *(n)* someone who is trained to give people advice about the law, and to prepare legal documents.

solid
1 *(adj)* hard and firm. *The water had frozen solid.* **solidity** *(n)*.
2 *(adj)* not hollow. *A solid chocolate egg.*
3 *(adj)* not mixed with anything else. *It was made of solid gold.*
4 *(adj)* dependable. *Solid citizens.*
5 *(n)* a three-dimensional geometric figure. *See* **shape**.

solidarity *(n)* an agreement between a group of people that they will work or fight together to achieve something.

solidify solidifies solidifying solidified *(v)*
to become hard and firm.

solidly *(adv)*
1 firmly and strongly. *This house is very solidly built.*
2 without interruption. *Aimee worked solidly for two hours.*

solitary
1 *(adj)* If someone is **solitary**, they spend a lot of time alone.
2 *(adj)* single. *There was not one solitary person on the beach.*
3 **solitary confinement** *(n)* a punishment in which a prisoner is put in a cell alone and is not allowed to see or talk to anyone.

solo *(n)*
a piece of music played or sung by one person. **soloist** *(n)*, **solo** *(adj)*.

soluble *(adj)* A substance that is **soluble** can be dissolved in liquid.

solution *(n)*
1 the answer to a problem.
2 a liquid that has something dissolved in it.

solve solving solved *(v)*
to find the answer to a problem.

solvent
1 *(n)* a liquid that makes other substances dissolve.
2 *(adj)* If you are **solvent**, you have enough money to pay your bills and pay back debts.

sombre *(som-bur) (adj)* dark and gloomy. *Karl is in a sombre mood.*

some
1 *(adj)* a number of things, or an amount of something. *Would you like some cake?*
2 *(pronoun)* a certain number of people or things. *Some of us are going abroad.*

somebody *(pronoun)* someone.

somehow *(adv)* in some way. *Somehow, the rabbit escaped.*

someone *(pronoun)* a person. *Someone has taken my pen!*

somersault *(n)* a movement where you tuck your head into your chest and roll over forwards on the ground or in the air. **somersault** *(v)*.

something *(pronoun)* a thing. *There's something in the bushes.*

sometime *(adv)* at some time in the past or future. *I'll do my homework sometime tomorrow.*

sometimes *(adv)*
at some times but not at others.

somewhere *(adv)*
to or in some place. *My aunt lives somewhere in Oxfordshire.*

son *(n)*
Someone's **son** is their male child.

sonar *(n)* a piece of equipment that is used on ships to calculate how deep the water is, or where underwater objects are. It works by sending sound waves through the water and listening for when they bounce back off something. Sonar stands for SOund Navigation And Ranging.

sonar

sound waves from ship

sound waves from submarine

sonata *(n)* a piece of music for one or two instruments.

song *(n)*
1 a piece of music with words for singing. *She loves writing songs.*
2 the musical sounds made by a bird. *The song of the nightingale.*

sonic
1 *(adj)* to do with sound waves.
2 **sonic boom** *(n)* the loud noise produced by an aeroplane when it breaks through the sound barrier and flies faster than the speed of sound. *This picture shows where the sonic boom caused by a plane can be heard.*

sonic boom

shock wave   plane

area where boom is heard

sonnet *(n)* a poem with fourteen lines and a fixed pattern of rhymes.

soon sooner soonest
1 *(adv)* in a short time. *I'll visit you soon.*
2 If you would **sooner** do something, you would prefer to do that thing.

soot *(n)*
black powder that is produced when something is burnt, and that often collects in chimneys. **sooty** *(adj)*.

soothe soothing soothed *(v)*
1 to make someone less angry or upset. *Sofia tried to soothe the screaming baby.* **soothing** *(adj)*.
2 to make something less painful or itchy. *This cream should soothe your rash.* **soothing** *(adj)*.

sophisticated *(sof-iss-tik-ate-id)* *(adj)*
1 People who are **sophisticated** have a lot of knowledge and experience of social life, fashion, and culture. **sophistication** *(n)*.
2 A **sophisticated** machine is cleverly designed and able to do difficult or complicated things. **sophistication** *(n)*.

sopping *(adj)* extremely wet.

soppy soppier soppiest *(adj)* *(informal)* overly sentimental.

soprano *(n)*
1 a high singing voice. **soprano** *(adj)*.
2 a woman or young boy with a soprano voice.

sorbet *(sor-bay)* *(n)*
a frozen dessert, rather like ice cream, made with fruit, sugar, and sometimes beaten egg whites. *Lemon sorbet.*

sorcerer *(sor-ser-er)* *(n)*
a man who performs magic by calling up evil spirits. **sorcery** *(n)*.

sorceress *(sor-ser-ess)* *(n)*
a woman who performs magic by calling up evil spirits. **sorcery** *(n)*.

sordid *(adj)*
1 dishonest and shameful.
2 dirty and messy. *A sordid room.*

sore sorer sorest
1 *(adj)* painful. **soreness** *(n)*.
2 *(n)* an area of infected, painful skin on your body. *A cold sore.*

sorrow *(n)* great sadness. **sorrowful** *(adj)*, **sorrowfully** *(adv)*.

sorry sorrier sorriest
1 *(interject)* a word that you say when you feel unhappy or upset because you have done something wrong or someone is suffering. **sorry** *(adj)*.
2 *(adj)* If you feel **sorry** for someone, you have sympathy and compassion for them.
3 If someone or something is **in a sorry state**, they are in a bad condition.

sort sorting sorted
1 *(n)* a type or a kind. *What sort of dog is that?*
2 *(v)* to arrange things into groups.
3 *(v)* If you **sort out** a problem, you deal with it and solve it.

SOS *(n)* a signal sent out by a ship or plane in need of urgent help. The initials SOS stand for Save Our Souls. *See* **semaphore**.

soul *(n)*
1 your spirit, which many people believe lives on after you have died.
2 a person. *You mustn't tell another soul.*

sound sounding sounded; sounder soundest
1 *(n)* something that you hear.
2 *(v)* If a horn or bell **sounds**, it makes a noise.
3 *(v)* to give an impression. *Your holiday sounds wonderful.*
4 *(adj)* reliable, practical, or strong. *A sound idea.* **soundly** *(adv)*.

sound barrier *(n)*
When a vehicle goes through the **sound barrier**, it meets a sudden increase in the force of the air against it because it has passed the speed of sound. *See* **sonic**.

sound effects *(plural n)*
noises that accompany a play or film to make it more realistic.

soundproof *(adj)*
If something, such as a room, is **soundproof**, it does not let any sound in or out of it. **soundproof** *(v)*.

soundtrack *(n)*
the recorded sound for a film.

soup *(n)* a liquid food made with vegetables, meat, fish, etc.

sour *(adj)*
1 Something that is **sour** has a bitter taste. **sourness** *(n)*.
2 bad-tempered. *Owen has a very sour expression.* **sourness** *(n)*, **sourly** *(adv)*.

source *(n)*
1 the place, person, or thing from which something comes. *We must find the source of the problem.*
2 the place where a stream or river starts. *See* **river**.
3 someone or something that provides information.

south
1 *(n)* one of the four main points of the compass, the direction to your left when you face the setting sun, in the Northern Hemisphere. **south** *(adj)*, **southern** *(adj)*, **south** *(adv)*.
2 *(adj)* A **south** wind blows from the south. **southerly** *(adj)*.
3 **South Pole** *(n)*
the most southerly part of the Earth, located at the bottom tip of the Earth's axis. *See* **polar**.

souvenir *(soo-ven-ear)* *(n)*
an object that you keep to remind you of a place, event, etc.

sovereign *(sov-rin)* *(n)*
a king or queen.

sow sowing sowed sown *or* sowed
1 *(rhymes with go)* (v) to put seeds into the ground so that they will grow.
2 *(rhymes with how)* (n) a female pig.

soya *(n)*
a kind of bean that can be cooked and eaten, or made into milk, oil, or flour to be used in cooking.

space *(n)*
1 an empty or available area. *We'll need lots of space for dancing.*
2 the universe beyond the Earth's atmosphere.

spacecraft *(n)*
a vehicle that travels in space.

space shuttle *(n)*
a spacecraft designed to carry passengers and spacecraft into space and back to Earth.

space station *(n)* a spacecraft large enough to house crew for long periods of time. Space stations are placed in orbit and are used for making scientific observations and as launching sites for other spacecraft.

spacesuit *(n)* the protective clothing that an astronaut wears in space. *See* **astronaut**.

spacious *(adj)*
very large. *A spacious kitchen.*

spade
1 *(n)* a tool with a flat blade and a long handle, used for digging.
2 **spades** *(plural n)* one of the four suits in a pack of cards, with a black symbol like a heart with a stalk.

the seven of spades

spaghetti *(n)*
long, thin strings of pasta. *See* **pasta**.

span *(n)*
1 Your **span** is the distance between your little finger and thumb when your hand is outstretched.
2 The **span** of something is its length from one end to the other. *This bridge has a span of over a kilometre.* **span** *(v)*.
3 a length of time. **span** *(v)*.

spank spanking spanked *(v)*
to smack someone as a punishment.

spanner *(n)*
a tool used for tightening and loosening nuts. *See* **tool**.

spare sparing spared
1 *(adj)* free for extra use. *Spare time. A spare tyre.*
2 *(v)* to make something available. *Can you spare me a few minutes?*
3 *(v)* to let someone live instead of killing them. *Thankfully, the hostages were spared.*

spark sparking sparked
1 *(n)* a red-hot speck caused by fire, electricity, or friction. **spark** *(v)*.
2 *(v)* to make something happen. *The concert sparked my interest in music.*

sparkle
sparkling sparkled *(v)*
to shine with lots of flashing points of light. **sparkle** *(n)*.

spark plug

ceramic insulator (prevents electrical current from escaping)

plug thread (screws into cylinder head)

side electrode

terminal nut (attached to lead from distributor)

plug body

centre electrode (spark crosses from here to side electrode)

spark plug *(n)*
one of the parts of a petrol engine that supplies an electrical spark to ignite the petrol and air mixture in a cylinder. Spark plugs are screwed into the cylinders and connected to the distributor, which supplies the current to create the spark. *Also see* **engine**.

sparrow *(n)*
a small, brownish-grey bird.

sparse sparser sparsest *(adj)*
1 thinly distributed. *A sparse population.* **sparsely** *(adv)*.
2 not enough. *A sparse meal.*

spasm *(n)* a short, sudden attack of pain or emotion. *A spasm of laughter.*

spatula *(n)*
1 a kitchen utensil with a broad, flat blade, used for lifting and stirring food.
2 an instrument with a flat blade, used by doctors and scientists. *See* **apparatus**.

spawn *(n)* the eggs produced by fish and amphibians. *See* **frog**.

speak speaking spoke spoken *(v)*
to talk, or to say words.

speaker *(n)*
1 someone who gives a speech in public.

2 a piece of equipment that turns electrical signals into sound, usually attached to a music system. Speaker is short for loudspeaker.

speaker
(cutaway)

protective mesh

tweeter (high range speaker)

magnet

coil of wire

woofer (low range speaker)

speaker cone (made from paper or plastic)

cabinet

spear *(n)*
a long, pointed weapon that used to be thrown in battle.

spear

Spartan warrior

This picture shows a warrior from ancient Sparta wielding a spear.

special *(adj)*
1 extraordinary and important. *A special day.* **specially** *(adv)*.
2 particular. *You need a special badge to get into the exhibition.*

special effects *(plural n)* visual and sound effects, added digitally to films to make them more exciting.

specialist *(n)* an expert at one particular job. **specialism** *(n)*.

speciality specialities *(n)*
the thing that you are particularly good at. *Jerome's speciality is cooking.*

specialize

specialize *or* **specialise**
specializing specialized (v)
to concentrate on one thing that you are good at or interested in. *Becky specializes in medieval art.*

species (spee-sheez) **species** (n)
one of the groups into which animals and plants are divided, according to their characteristics. *The domestic dog is a species of mammal.*

specific (adj) particular, definite, or individually named. *Hilda insists on a specific type of tea.* **specifically** (adv).

specification (n) detailed information and instructions about something that is to be built or made.

specify specifies specifying specified (v) to mention something in an exact way. *Please specify which course you would like to attend.*

specimen (n) a sample or an example. *Please supply a specimen of your signature.* **specimen** (adj).

speck (n) a minute piece of something, like dust or dirt.

speckled (adj) covered with small, irregular marks. *A speckled egg.*

spectacle (n)
a remarkable and dramatic sight. *The firework show was quite a spectacle.*

spectacles (plural n)
lenses set in frames which are worn to improve your eyesight.

spectacular
1 (adj) remarkable and dramatic to look at. *A spectacular waterfall.*
2 (n) a show that contains dramatic effects and acts.

spectator (n) someone who watches an event. **spectate** (v).

spectre (spek-tur) (n)
a ghost. **spectral** (adj).

spectrum spectra (n)
1 a wide range of things or ideas.
2 the range of colours that is revealed when light shines through a prism or through drops of water. *In the picture below, the white light is bent, or refracted, as it travels through the prism. Since each of the colours in light travels at a slightly different speed, they each bend at a different angle and spread out in a spectrum.*

spectrum   red   yellow green
            orange   blue
            indigo violet
glass prism
ray of white light

speculate
speculating speculated (v)
1 to wonder or guess about something when you do not know all the facts. **speculation** (n).
2 to buy shares on the stock market or to put money into other projects that carry some risk. **speculation** (n).

speech speeches (n)
1 the ability to speak.
2 a talk given to a group of people.

speechless (adj) unable to speak. *Dad was speechless with rage.*

speed speeding sped *or* speeded
1 (n) the rate at which something moves.
2 (v) to travel very fast, or to travel faster than is allowed.
3 (n) quickness of movement.

speedometer (n)
an instrument in a vehicle that shows you how fast you are travelling.

spell spelling spelt *or* spelled
1 (v) to write or say the letters of a word in their correct order.
2 (n) a period of time, usually a short one. *A spell of silence.*
3 (n) words that are believed to have magical powers.

spend spending spent (v)
1 to use money to buy things.
2 If you **spend** time or energy, you use it.

sperm sperm *or* sperms (n)
one of the reproductive cells from a male that is capable of fertilizing eggs in a female.

sphere (sfear) (n)
a ball or globe shape.
spherical (sfe-rik-al) (adj).

sphinx

sphinx (sfinks) **sphinxes** (n)
a mythical monster with the head of a human and the body of a lion. *The picture above shows a statue of a sphinx at Giza, in Egypt.*

spice (n)
a substance with a distinctive smell or taste, used to flavour foods. *The picture shows a range of spices.*

spices
cloves
powdered turmeric
paprika
caraway seeds
nutmeg
cinnamon sticks
allspice   cumin seeds

spider (n) a small creature with eight legs and no wings. Some spiders spin webs to trap insects for food. *The picture below shows a selection of spiders from around the world.*

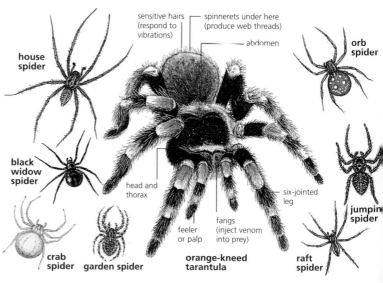
sensitive hairs (respond to vibrations)
spinnerets under here (produce web threads)
abdomen
orb spider
house spider
black widow spider
head and thorax
six-jointed leg
jumping spider
feeler or palp
fangs (inject venom into prey)
crab spider   garden spider   orange-kneed tarantula   raft spider

spike (n) a sharp point. **spiky** (adj).

spill spilling spilt or spilled (v) If you spill something, you let the contents of a container fall out accidentally.

spin spinning spun (v)
1 to turn round quickly on the spot.
2 to create a thread by twisting fine fibres together. *The picture shows a spinning jenny, a machine invented in the 18th century, that could spin up to eight threads at once.*

spinning jenny

spinach (n) a dark green, leafy vegetable. *See* **vegetable**.

spindly spindlier spindliest (adj) long, thin, and rather weak.

spin-dryer (n) a machine which extracts moisture from clothes by spinning them round very fast.

spine (n)
1 the backbone. **spinal** (adj). *See* **skeleton**.
2 part of a book's cover that joins the front and the back. *See* **book**.

spinster (n) a woman who has never been married.

spiral (adj)
A **spiral** pattern winds around in circles like a spring. *The chambers inside a nautilus shell are arranged in a spiral pattern.* **spiral** (n), **spiral** (v).

nautilus shell (cutaway)

spire (n) the pointed cone on top of some church towers. *See* **cathedral**.

spirit (n)
1 the part of a person that is not physical and is expressed in their deepest thoughts and feelings.
2 enthusiasm and determination in a person or group of people. *We shared a spirit of hope.* **spirited** (adj).
3 a ghost, or a being with no physical form.
4 a strong alcoholic drink such as whisky, gin, or vodka.
5 spirit level an instrument used for checking whether a surface is level. *See* **woodwork**.

spiritual (adj) to do with beliefs, thoughts, and feelings, and not physical things. **spiritually** (adv).

spiritualism (n) communication with the spirits of dead people. **spiritualist** (n).

spit spitting spat or spit (v) to force saliva out of your mouth.

spite
1 (n) deliberate nastiness. **spiteful** (adj), **spitefully** (adv).
2 in spite of without taking any notice of. *Ingrid went swimming in spite of the rain.*

splash splashes splashing splashed (v) to scatter liquid. **splash** (n).

splendid (adj) impressive, excellent, or very good. **splendidly** (adv).

splint (n) a piece of wood, plastic, or metal, used to support a broken or damaged limb.

splinter (n) a thin, sharp piece of wood, glass, metal, etc. **splinter** (v).

split splitting split
1 (v) to break something into separate pieces.
2 (n) a crack.
3 (v) If a couple **splits up**, they stop going out together or living together.

splutter spluttering spluttered (v)
1 to speak with difficulty, usually because you are upset.
2 If an engine **splutters**, it makes choking and spitting noises because it is not working properly.

spoil spoiling spoilt or spoiled
1 (v) to ruin or wreck something.
2 (adj) If children are **spoilt**, their parents have allowed them to have their own way too often.

sponge (n)
1 a sea animal with a rubbery, absorbent skeleton. The skeletons of sponges can be used for washing.
2 soft, man-made material, filled with holes, used for washing and cleaning. **sponge** (v), **spongy** (adj).
3 a light cake.

sponsor sponsoring sponsored
1 (v) to give money to people who are doing something worthwhile, often for charity. **sponsorship** (n).
2 (n) an organization that gives money to a sports team or television show in return for advertising.

spontaneous (adj) without previous thought or planning. **spontaneity** (n), **spontaneously** (adv).

spool (n) a reel on which yarn, thread, etc. is wound. *See* **angling**.

spoon (n) a piece of cutlery, used for eating desserts, soups, etc.

spoor (n) the trail left behind by an animal.

moss spore cases

spore (n) a cell produced by non-flowering plants such as fungi, mosses, and ferns, which develops into a new plant. *The picture shows some moss spore cases. When the cases open, the spores are spread by the wind. Also see* **fern**.

sporran (n) a small, leather pouch, worn in front of the kilt as part of the traditional Scottish highland dress.

sport (n) a general name for games involving physical activity. Sports can be played professionally, or for pleasure.

spot spotting spotted
1 (n) a small mark that is usually round. **spotted** (adj).
2 (n) a sore, red place on the skin. **spotty** (adj).
3 (n) a place or a location. *This looks like a good spot for a picnic.*
4 (v) to notice something. *Angelina has spotted a friend.*

spotless (adj) absolutely clean. **spotlessly** (adv).

spotlight (n) a powerful light used to light up a small area.

spouse (n) a husband or a wife.

spout spouting spouted
1 (n) a tube through which liquid is poured, such as the spout of a kettle.
2 (v) (informal) to talk about something in a boring, pompous way. *Bella was spouting complete nonsense.*

sprain spraining sprained (v) to injure a joint by twisting it.

sprawl sprawling sprawled (v)
1 to sit or lie with your arms and legs spread out carelessly.
2 to spread out in all directions. *The city sprawled for miles.*

spray spraying sprayed (v) to scatter liquid in very fine drops. **spray** (n).

spread spreading spread (v)
1 to unfold or to stretch out. *Hilary spread out the map on the table. Joel spread his arms wide.*
2 to cover a surface with something. *We spread the bread with peanut butter.* **spread** (n).
3 to scatter or to make known. *Spread the news.*

sprightly sprightlier sprightliest (adj) lively and energetic.

spring springing sprang sprung
1 *(n)* the season between winter and summer, when it becomes warmer and leaves grow on the trees.
2 *(v)* to jump suddenly.
The lion sprang at the antelope.
3 *(n)* a coil of metal which moves back to its original position after being compressed or pushed down.
4 *(n)* a place where water rises up from underground and becomes a stream.

springboard *(n)* a flexible board that people jump on in order to increase their height or force in diving or gymnastics. *The picture shows a diver using a springboard.*

springboard jump

spring-clean spring-cleaning spring-cleaned *(v)* to clean a house thoroughly, concentrating on the places that do not get cleaned often. **spring-cleaning** *(n)*.

sprinkle sprinkling sprinkled *(v)* to scatter liquid, powder, etc. in small amounts. *Sprinkle the top of the dish with grated cheese.*

sprint sprinting sprinted
1 *(v)* to run fast. *Gerry sprinted to the shops.*
2 *(n)* a very fast race run over a short distance.
sprinter *(n)*, **sprint** *(adj)*.

sprint start

sprocket *(n)* a wheel with a toothed edge, usually driven by a chain. *See* **bicycle**.

sprout sprouting sprouted
1 *(v)* When a plant **sprouts**, it starts to grow and produce shoots or buds.
2 *(n)* a round, green vegetable, or a plant shoot. *See* **vegetable**.

spur spurring spurred
1 *(n)* a spike or spiked wheel on the heel of a rider's boot, used to make a horse go more quickly.
2 *(v)* If something **spurs you on**, it encourages or motivates you.
3 *(n)* a hill that sticks out from a mountain range, often into a river valley. *See* **river**.

spurt spurting spurted *(v)* When something **spurts**, it moves or flows suddenly. **spurt** *(n)*.

spy spies spying spied
1 *(v)* to watch something closely from a hidden place.
2 *(n)* someone who secretly collects information about an enemy. **spy** *(v)*.

squabble *(n)* a childish argument or quarrel. **squabble** *(v)*.

squad *(n)* a small group of people involved in the same activity, such as soldiers or football players.

squalid *(adj)* dirty and unpleasant.

squander squandering squandered *(v)* to spend money wastefully.

square squaring squared
1 *(n)* a shape with four equal sides and four right angles. *See* **shape**.
2 *(v)* to multiply a number by itself. *4 squared equals 16.*
3 square root *(n)* the number that, when multiplied by itself, gives a particular number.
5 is the square root of 25.

squash squashes squashing squashed
1 *(v)* to crush or flatten something.
2 *(n)* a racket game played by two people who hit a small rubber ball against the walls of an enclosed court.
3 *(n)* a concentrated fruit drink.
4 *(n)* a fleshy kind of vegetable, such as a marrow or pumpkin.

squash court

side wall line

front wall line

service line

tin

back wall line

half court line

short line

service box

squat squatting squatted
1 *(v)* to crouch with your knees bent.
2 *(v)* to live, without permission, in a place that does not belong to you. **squat** *(n)*, **squatter** *(n)*.
3 *(adj)* short and broad.

squawk squawking squawked *(v)* to make a loud, harsh cry like the noise of a parrot. **squawk** *(n)*.

squeak squeaking squeaked *(v)* to make a short, high-pitched sound like the noise of a mouse. **squeak** *(n)*.

squeal squealing squealed *(v)* to make a shrill, high-pitched sound, usually because you are frightened or in pain. **squeal** *(n)*.

squeamish *(adj)* easily sickened or shocked. **squeamishly** *(adv)*.

squeeze squeezing squeezed *(v)*
1 to press something firmly together from opposite sides. **squeeze** *(n)*.
2 to force something into or through a space. *We squeezed into the bus.* **squeeze** *(n)*.

squid *(n)* a sea creature with a long, soft body and ten tentacles. *Squids swim by squirting water out of their bodies with great force.*

lateral fin

mantle (body)

eye (adapted for underwater light)

light-sensitive skin (changes colour for camouflage)

arm

squid

long tentacle for grasping prey

claw with suckers

squint squinting squinted
1 *(v)* If you **squint** at something, you nearly close your eyes in order to see it more clearly.
2 *(n)* Someone who has a **squint** has eyes which look in different directions from one another.

squire *(n)*
1 the chief landowner in a country district.
2 In medieval times, a **squire** was a young nobleman who accompanied and helped a knight.

squirm squirming squirmed *(v)*
1 to wriggle about uncomfortably.
2 to feel uncomfortable because you are embarrassed or ashamed.

a b c d e f g h i j k l m n o p q r s t u v w x y z

squirrel (n) a tree-climbing rodent with a bushy tail. *The grey squirrel shown here is found in Europe and North America.* **grey squirrel**

squirt squirting squirted (v) to send out a stream of liquid. *Misha turned on the hose and squirted her brothers.* **squirt** (n).

squishy squishier squishiest (adj) (informal) soft and soggy.

St. *see* **saint**.

stab stabbing stabbed
1 (v) to wound someone by piercing their skin with a knife or other sharp instrument. **stab** (n).
2 (informal) If you **make a stab** at something, you try to do it.

stable
1 (n) a building or a part of a building where a horse is kept.
2 **stables** (plural n) a place where horses are kept for use in riding lessons.
3 (adj) firm and steady. *Before you climb the ladder, check that it is stable.* **stability** (n), **stabilize** (v).
4 (adj) safe and secure. *The children had a stable upbringing.* **stability** (n).

staccato (sta-kah-toh) (adv) When you play notes **staccato**, you make them short and separate.

stack stacking stacked (v) to pile things on top of each other. **stack** (n).

stadium stadiums or stadia (n) a large building, which is often open air, in which sports events and concerts are held.

staff
1 (plural n) the people who work in an organization. *The school staff.*
2 (n) (old-fashioned) a thick, wooden stick.

stag (n) an adult male deer. *The picture shows a stag roaring. Stags roar to one another in the mating season to compete for females.*

red deer stag

stage staging staged
1 (n) a period of development. *Our plans are still at an early stage.*
2 (n) a level of progress. *You have done so well that you can move to the next stage.*
3 (n) an area where plays and concerts are performed.
4 (v) to organize a public performance or event. *Our school is staging a play.*
5 If you **go on the stage**, you become an actor.

stagecoach stagecoaches (n) a horse-drawn vehicle, used in the past to carry passengers and mail for long distances. *Stagecoaches travelled in stages and were supplied with fresh horses at each stage.*

stagecoach

stage-manage stage-managing stage-managed (v) to organize a play, concert, or other event. **stage manager** (n).

stage-struck (adj) Someone who is **stage-struck** thinks that the theatre is very glamorous, and wants to become an actor.

stagger staggering staggered
1 (v) to walk or stand unsteadily.
2 (adj) If you are **staggered** by something, you are astonished.
3 (v) When you **stagger** events, you time them so that they do not happen at the same time. *The guards staggered their breaks.*

staggering (adj) amazing or astonishing. *Ivan bought the house for a staggering amount of money.*

stagnant (adj) **Stagnant** water cannot flow and is dirty and smelly.

stagnate stagnating stagnated (v)
1 When water **stagnates**, it goes stale, often changing colour and becoming smelly.
2 If a situation or person **stagnates**, they remain the same for a long time, when they should be changing. **stagnation** (n).

staid (adj) If someone is **staid**, they are not lively and do not like change.

stain staining stained
1 (n) a mark on something that is hard to remove.
2 (v) to make a mark that is hard to remove from something. *The paint stained my coat.*
3 (n) colouring used on wood.

stained glass (n) coloured pieces of glass, held together by lead strips. Stained glass is often used in church windows. *The picture shows a stained glass window from Chartres Cathedral in France.*

stainless steel (n) a type of steel that does not rust or tarnish.

stairs (plural n) steps that allow you to walk from one level of a building to another. **staircase** (n).

stake staking staked
1 (n) a thick, pointed post that can be driven into the ground.
2 (v) to bet. *Jim staked his money on the race.*
3 (n) If you have a **stake** in something, you are involved in it or you have put money into it.
4 If something is **at stake**, it is at risk.

stained glass

stalactite (n) a thin piece of rock, shaped like an icicle, which hangs from the roof of a cave. Stalactites are made from calcium minerals, dissolved in dripping water, which have slowly solidified. *The picture below shows stalactites in a cave.*

cave
(cross-section)   soil   crack
(allows water to seep
limestone rock   stalactite   through limestone)

stalagmite   cave   pillar
(joined-up stalactite
and stalagmite)
underground river

stalagmite (n) a piece of rock which sticks up from the floor of a cave. Stalagmites are made from calcium minerals, dissolved in dripping water, which have slowly solidified. *The picture above shows stalagmites in a cave.*

stale staler stalest (adj) no longer fresh. *Stale cake.*

stalemate (n) a situation in an argument or game, in which neither side can win.

a b c d e f g h i j k l m n o p q r **s** t u v w x y z

stalk

stalk (stawk) stalking stalked
1 (n) the long, main part of
a plant from which the leaves,
flowers, and fruit grow.
2 (n) a thin branch that
holds a leaf, flower, or fruit.
3 (v) to hunt, track, or follow someone
or something in a quiet, secretive way.
The leopard stalked its prey. **stalker** (n).
4 (v) to walk in a proud, stiff way.
Emily stalked out of the room.

stall stalling stalled
1 (v) When a car **stalls**,
its engine stops suddenly.
2 (n) a table or booth from which things
are sold in a market, jumble sale, etc.
3 (n) a section in a stable or
barn where one animal is kept.
4 (v) to delay doing
something until later.
5 (plural n) In a theatre, the **stalls**
are the seats on the ground floor.

stallion (n) a male horse.

stamina (n) the energy to keep doing
something for a long while. *You need
stamina for long-distance running.*

stammer stammering stammered
(v) If you **stammer** when you
speak, you repeat the first sound
of a word before you manage to
say the whole word. **stammer** (n).

stamp
stamping stamped
1 (n) a small piece of
paper that you stick on
a letter or parcel to show
that you have paid for it
to be sent. **stamp** (v).
2 (n) an object used to
print a mark on paper.
You press the stamp
first onto an ink
pad and then onto
paper. **stamp** (v).
3 (v) to bang your
foot down.

penny black,
Britain, 1840

stamps
Japan, 1956
USA, 1969
USSR, 1959
Australia 1994

stampede stampeding stampeded
(v) When people or animals
stampede, they suddenly rush
somewhere wildly. **stampede** (n).

stand standing stood
1 (v) to be on your feet
with your body upright.
2 (v) to put something somewhere.
Stand the vase on the table.
3 (v) to continue unchanged.
My offer still stands.
4 (n) an object on which you
put things. *A music stand.*
5 (n) a covered area in a sports ground.
6 (n) a small, outdoor shop.
A hot dog stand.
7 **stand for** (v) to represent.
US stands for United States.
8 (v) If you **cannot stand**
something, you hate it.
9 (v) If you **stand by** someone, you
support them when they are in trouble.
10 (v) If something **stands out**,
it can be seen or noticed easily.

standard
1 (adj) usual or average.
What is the standard fare?
2 (n) a rule or model for judging
or measuring how good
something is. *Standards of
achievement seem to be falling.*
3 **standard lamp** (n) a lamp on
a tall base that stands on the floor.

stand-by (n)
1 someone or something that
is ready to be used if needed.
2 If a computer is **on standby mode**,
it has power running through
it and can be activated quickly.

stand-in (n) someone who takes the
place of another person when that
person cannot be there. **stand in** (v).

standstill (n) If something comes
to a **standstill**, it stops completely.

stanza (n) one of the groups of
lines into which a poem is divided.
Another name for stanza is verse.

staple
1 (n) a small piece of wire which is
punched through sheets of paper
to hold them together. **staple** (v).
2 (adj) A **staple** food is the main
food eaten as part of a person's diet.

star starring starred
1 (n) a ball of burning gases in space,
seen from the Earth as a tiny point of
light in the sky at night. **starry** (adj).
2 (n) a shape with several
points, usually five or six.
3 (n) a well-known actor or entertainer
in a film, television programme, or play.
4 (v) to take the main part in a film,
television programme, or play.

starboard (n) the right-hand side
of a ship or aircraft. **starboard** (adj).

starch starches (n)
1 a substance found in foods
such as potatoes, bread, and rice.
2 a substance used for making
cloth stiff. **starch** (v).

stare staring stared (v) to look at
someone or something for a long time
without moving your eyes. **stare** (n).

starfish starfish (n) a star-shaped
sea animal with five or more arms.

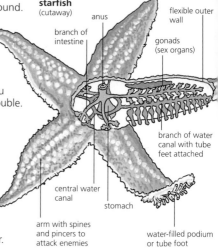
starfish (cutaway)
anus
flexible outer wall
branch of intestine
gonads (sex organs)
branch of water canal with tube feet attached
central water canal
stomach
arm with spines and pincers to attack enemies
water-filled podium or tube foot

stark starker starkest (adj)
1 bare and plain. *A stark
landscape. The stark truth.*
2 complete or total.
Stark poverty.

start starting started
1 (v) to begin to act, move, happen,
etc., or to make something begin
to act, move, happen, etc.
2 (n) the beginning of something.
3 (v) to jump in surprise.
4 (n) an advantage at the beginning
of a race. *You can have a 20m start.*

startle startling startled (v)
to surprise someone and make them
jump. **startled** (adj), **startling** (adj).

starve starving starved (v) to suffer
or die from hunger. **starvation** (n).

starving (adj)
1 suffering or dying from hunger.
2 (informal) very hungry.

state stating stated
1 (v) to say something clearly.
Please state your name.
2 (n) the government of
a country. *Affairs of state.*
3 (n) an area within a country that
makes its own laws. *The State of Texas.*
4 (n) the way that something is, or the
condition that someone or something
is in. *Your room is in a terrible state.
Betty is in a state of confusion.*
5 (informal) If someone is
in a state, they are upset.
6 **state-of-the-art** (adj)
very advanced and up to date.
A state-of-the-art computer system.

statement (n)
1 something that is said formally.
2 a list of all the amounts paid into and out of a bank account.

stay staying stayed
1 (v) to remain where you are.
2 (v) to spend time somewhere. *We didn't stay long at the party.*
3 (n) a period of time spent somewhere as a visitor. *Did you enjoy your stay?*

steam locomotive (n)
an engine powered by steam and used for pulling trains. *The steam produced by this steam locomotive forces the pistons to move. The pistons drive the connecting rods and crank rods which are connected to the driving wheels.*

Flying Scotsman

lamp bracket
chimney
smokebox
steam collector dome
boiler casing
handrail
firebox
safety valve
whistle
smokebox door handle
brake pipe
outside steam pipe
engine main frame
buffer
coupling (joins the locomotive to the carriages)
guard iron
bogie wheel
bogie frame
cylinder cover
crosshead
piston rod
sandpipe
front driving wheel
connecting rod
return crank rod
crank arm
middle driving wheel
brake rods
coupling rod
back driving wheel
axlebox
trailing wheel
driving cab
tender (carriage for fuel and water)
4472

static
1 (adj) not moving or not changing. *A static caravan. A static situation.*
2 (n) electricity that is produced by friction. Static is short for static electricity.
3 (n) the crackling noises that you hear when static electricity in the air causes interference to a radio signal.

station (n)
1 a place where trains or buses stop. *A bus station.*
2 a building used as the base for a police force, ambulance service, or fire brigade.
3 a radio or television channel.

stationary (adj)
at rest or not moving.

stationery (n) writing materials, such as paper, envelopes, and pens.

statistic (n)
a fact or a piece of information, expressed as a number or percentage. **statistical** (adj), **statistically** (adv).

statue (n) a model of a person or animal made from metal, stone, etc.

status statuses (n)
a person's rank or position in society.

statute (n) a rule or a law.

stave staving staved *or* stove
1 (n) the set of five lines on which music is written. *See* **notation**.
2 **stave off** (v) If you **stave something off**, you manage to keep it away.

steady steadies steadying steadied; steadier steadiest
1 (adj) continuous and not changing much. *Steady progress.* **steadily** (adv).
2 (adj) not moving about or not shaking. *A steady hand.* **steadily** (adv).
3 (v) to stop something moving about or shaking.
4 (adj) sensible and dependable.

steak (n) a thick slice of meat or fish.

steal stealing stole stolen (v)
1 to take and keep something that does not belong to you.
2 **steal away** to leave quietly.

stealthy (rhymes with healthy) stealthier stealthiest (adj) secret and quiet. *We crept away with stealthy steps.* **stealth** (n), **stealthily** (adv).

steam steaming steamed
1 (n) the vapour formed when water boils.
2 (v) When glass **steams up**, it gets covered with condensation.
3 (informal) If you **let off steam**, you release your stored-up energy or feelings.
4 (informal) If you **run out of steam**, you have no more energy left.

steam-engine (n)
an engine powered by steam. Coal or wood burnt in a boiler produces hot air that travels in pipes through a water tank. As the water in the tank boils, it creates steam. Steam is forced into cylinders where it pushes pistons to operate machinery. *See* **steam locomotive**.

steamroller (n) a steam-driven vehicle used to flatten road surfaces.

steel (n)
1 a hard, strong metal made mainly from iron.
2 **steel band** a group that plays music on drums, called steel pans, made from oil barrels. *See* **instrument**.

steep steeping steeped; steeper steepest
1 (adj) sharply sloping up or down. *A steep hill.* **steeply** (adv).
2 (adj) sharp or rapid. *A steep drop in student numbers.* **steeply** (adv)
3 (v) to soak something in a liquid.
4 (v) If something is **steeped** in something, it is full of it.

steeple (n)
a church tower with a spire.

steeplechase (n)
a race over obstacles such as fences, water jumps, ditches, etc.

steer steering steered (v) to make a vehicle go in a particular direction.

steering wheel (n) the wheel in a vehicle used to control its direction.

stem stemming stemmed
1 (n) the long, main part of a plant, from which the leaves, flowers, and fruit grow. *See* **plant**.
2 (v) If something **stems from** a place or thing, it comes from it. *The quarrel stemmed from a misunderstanding.*
3 (v) to stop something from flowing or spreading. *The rescue team tried to stem the flow of oil from the tanker.*

a b c d e f
k l m n o p q r s t u v w x y z

stench stenches *(n)*
a strong, unpleasant smell.

stencil *(n)* a piece of card, plastic, or metal with a design cut out of it, which can be painted over to transfer the design onto a surface. **stencil** *(v)*.

stencilling equipment

stencil brush

oiled stencil card

stencilled design

step stepping stepped
1 *(v)* to move your foot forward and put it down. **step** *(n)*.
2 *(n)* the sound of someone walking. *Can you hear steps behind you?*
3 *(n)* one of the flat surfaces on a staircase. *The bottom step.*
4 *(n)* one of the things that you need to do in order to make or achieve something. *This recipe has six steps.*
5 *(informal)* If someone says that you should **watch your step**, they are telling you to be careful.

stepfamily stepfamilies *(n)*
the family of your stepfather or stepmother.

stepfather *(n)*
the man who is married to your mother, but is not your father.

stepmother *(n)*
the woman who is married to your father, but is not your mother.

stereo *(n)*
1 sound that comes from two or more directions at the same time. Stereo is short for stereophonic.
2 a CD player or radio with stereo speakers.

stereotype *(n)* a simplified idea of a person or thing. *We've created a teenage stereotype for this advertising campaign.* **stereotypical** *(adj)*.

sterile *(adj)*
1 free from germs.
2 unable to have babies.

sterilize *or* **sterilise** sterilizing sterilized *(v)* to clean something so thoroughly that you make it free from germs. **sterilization** *(n)*.

sterling *(n)* the currency of the UK.

stern sterner sternest
1 *(adj)* serious and severe. *Paula gave me a stern look.*
2 *(n)* the back end of a ship.

steroid *(n)*
a chemical substance found naturally in your body. *Steroids are sometimes taken as a drug by athletes to build up their strength, but their use is usually banned.*

stethoscope *(n)*
a Y-shaped tube connected to two earpieces, used by a doctor to listen to a patient's heartbeat or their breathing.

eartip

ear tube

non-chill rim

double leaf spring

stainless steel chest piece

plastic tubing   **stethoscope**

stew
1 *(n)* meat and vegetables, cooked slowly in liquid. **stew** *(v)*.
2 If you are **in a stew** about something, you are upset and worried about it. **stew** *(v)*.

steward *(n)*
1 someone who looks after passengers on an aeroplane or ship.
2 someone who helps to direct people at a large public event, such as a race or concert. **steward** *(v)*.

stewardess stewardesses *(n)*
a woman who looks after passengers on an aeroplane or ship.

stick sticking stuck
1 *(n)* a long, thin piece of wood.
2 *(n)* a long, thin piece of something. *A stick of seaside rock.*
3 *(v)* to glue or fasten one thing to another. **sticky** *(adj)*.
4 *(v)* to push something with a point into something else. *Bethan stuck a pin into the pincushion.*
5 *(v)* If something **sticks**, it becomes fixed in a particular position. *This door keeps sticking.*
6 *(v)* If someone **sticks** to an idea, friend, etc. they support them and do not give them up.
7 *(v)* *(informal)* If you **stick up** for someone, you support them.

sticker *(n)* a sticky paper or plastic badge that you can attach to things.

stick insect *(n)* an insect with a long body that looks like a twig.

stiff stiffer stiffest *(adj)*
1 difficult to bend or turn. **stiffen** *(v)*, **stiffly** *(adv)*.
2 If you feel **stiff**, your muscles hurt because you have overworked them.

3 difficult or severe. *A stiff exam.*
4 formal and distant.

stifle stifling stifled
1 *(v)* If you **stifle** a cough, sneeze, or yawn, you cover your mouth to prevent it from being noticed.
2 *(n)* a knee joint in some animals. *See* **dog**.

stigma *(n)*
1 a mark of shame or embarrassment.
2 the part of a flower which receives the pollen when the flower is pollinated. *See* **flower**.

stile *(n)* a wooden step used to climb over a wall or fence.

still stiller stillest
1 *(adj)* not moving. *Stand still!*
2 *(adj)* quiet or silent. *A still night.*
3 *(adv)* even now. *Are you still here?*
4 *(adj)* not fizzy. *Still orange drink.*
5 *(adv)* however.

stimulate stimulating stimulated *(v)*
1 If someone or something **stimulates** you, they fill you with exciting new ideas. **stimulating** *(adj)*.
2 to encourage something to grow or develop.

sting stinging stung
1 *(n)* the sharp part of an insect, animal, or plant that can pierce your skin and leave some venom in it. **sting** *(v)*. *See* **scorpion**.
2 *(v)* to hurt with a sharp or throbbing pain. *My eyes are stinging.*

stingray *(n)* a flat-bodied fish that has large, wing-like fins and a long tail with venomous spines.

stingray

stingy *(stin-jee)* stingier stingiest *(adj)* very mean. **stingily** *(adv)*.

stink stinking stank stunk *(v)*
1 to have an unpleasant smell. **stink** *(n)*.
2 *(slang)* to be very bad. *Angela's plan stinks!*

stint stinting stinted
1 *(n)* a period of time. *He's just come back from a two-year stint in the army.*
2 *(v)* to get by with very little money.

stir stirring stirred
1 *(v)* to mix a liquid by moving a spoon or stick round and round in it.
2 *(v)* to move slightly.
3 If you **cause a stir**, you make people excited about something.

stitch stitches stitching stitched
1 (v) to make loops of thread
or wool in sewing or knitting.
stitch (n). See **embroidery**.
2 (v) to close up a wound by
sewing with thread. stitch (n).
3 (n) a sudden, sharp pain in
your side, caused by exercise.
4 (informal) If you are **in stitches**,
you cannot stop laughing.

stock stocking stocked
1 (v) If a shop **stocks** a product, it
keeps a supply of the product to sell.
2 (n) all the products that a factory,
warehouse, or shop has to sell.
3 (n) a liquid used in cooking, made
from the juices of meat or vegetables.
4 (v) If you **stock up** on something,
you buy a large supply of it.

stockbroker (n) someone whose
job is buying and selling stocks and
shares in companies for other people.

stock car (n) a car driven in rough
races in which the cars crash into
one another on purpose.

stocking (n) a close-fitting piece of
clothing that covers your leg and foot.

stockpile stockpiling stockpiled (v)
to build up a large supply of food or
weapons that you can use in the future.

stocks (plural n)
1 a heavy, wooden frame with
holes in it, used in the past to hold
criminals by their legs. *The picture
below shows some medieval stocks.*
2 If you have **stocks** in a company, you
have invested money in it, and receive
regular small amounts in return, based
on the company's profits.

medieval stocks

stocky stockier stockiest (adj)
short, broad, and strong. **stockily** (adv).

stodgy stodgier stodgiest (adj)
Stodgy food is very heavy and filling.

stoke stoking stoked (v)
to put more fuel on a fire
in order to keep it burning.

stomach (n)
1 the part of the body where food
is digested. See **digestion**, **organ**.
2 the front part of your body,
just below your waist.

stone stoning stoned
1 (n) a small piece of rock, usually
found on the ground. **stony** (adj).
2 (n) a valuable jewel or gem.

3 (n) a hard material used for
building, making sculptures, etc.
4 (n) a hard seed found in the middle
of a fruit, such as a cherry or peach.
5 (v) to hit someone or
something with a stone.
6 (n) a unit of weight equal to
14lbs, or 6.35kg. See page 284.

Stone Age (n) a very early period
in human history, when people used
stone to make tools and weapons.

stone circle (n) a circle of large,
tall stones put up in prehistoric times.
*The picture shows Stonehenge,
a stone circle in Wiltshire, England.*

Stonehenge

lintel stone
sarsen stone

stoned (adj) (slang)
If you are **stoned**, you are
very drunk or drugged.

stool (n)
a small seat with no back or
arms, and often only three legs.

stoop stooping stooped (v)
1 to bend down low.
2 to walk, sit, stand, etc. with your
head and shoulders bent forwards.
stoop (n), stooped (adj).

stop stopping stopped
1 (v) When something **stops**, it
comes to an end. *The music stopped.*
2 (v) If you **stop** something, you put
an end to it or do not do it anymore.
3 (v) to be no longer moving or
working. *My watch has stopped.*
4 (n) one of the places on
a route where a bus or
train picks up passengers.
5 (v) If you **stop** or **stop up**
a hole, you fill it or plug it.

stopper (n)
a piece of cork or plastic that
fits into the top of a test tube,
jar, or bottle, to close it.

stopwatch (n)
a watch that you can start and stop
at any time, used for timing races.

storage (n)
If you put something **in storage**, you
put it in a place where it can be kept
until it is needed. **storage** (adj).

store storing stored
1 (v) to put things away
until they are needed.
2 (v) to keep information on
a computer, by saving it as a file.
3 (n) a place where things are kept.
4 (n) a large shop with
many departments.

storey storeys or stories (n)
one layer or floor of a building.

stork (n) a large bird with
long, thin legs and a long bill.

storm storming stormed
1 (n) a period of bad weather with
strong wind and rain, and sometimes
thunder and lightning. **stormy** (adj).
2 (n) a show of strong and
angry feelings. *A storm of
protest.* **stormy** (adj).
3 (v) to attack somewhere suddenly.
The army stormed the castle.
4 (v) If you **storm out**, you
rush out of a place angrily.

story stories (n)
1 a spoken or written account
of someone's life or adventures.
2 a tale made up by an author.
3 a lie. *Are you telling stories?*

stout stouter stoutest (adj)
1 quite fat.
2 strong and thick. *Stout boots.*

stove (n) a piece of equipment used
for cooking or for heating a room.

stowaway (n) someone who hides
illegally in an aeroplane, ship, etc.

straggle straggling straggled (v)
to follow slowly behind a group
of people. **straggler** (n).

straight straighter straightest
1 (adj) not bent or not curved.
straighten (v).
2 (adj) level or neat. straighten (v).
3 (adj) honest or correct.
4 (adv) immediately.
May went straight home.

straightaway (adv) at once.

straightforward (adj)
1 simple and uncomplicated.
The operation was straightforward.
2 honest or to the point. *Christian
gave a straightforward answer.*

strain straining strained
1 (n) stress or tension. **strained** (adj).
2 (v) If you **strain** a muscle in your
body, you damage it by pulling
it or overusing it. strain (n).
3 (v) If you **strain** to do something,
you try very hard to do it.
4 (v) If you **strain** a mixture, you
pour it through a sieve or colander,
to separate the solids from the
liquids. **strainer** (n), **strained** (adj).

strait

strait
1 (n) a narrow strip of water between two seas or two countries. *The picture shows the Strait of Gibraltar between Spain and Morocco.*
2 If you are in **dire straits**, you are in trouble.

strait

strand (n)
1 one of the threads or wires that are twisted together to form a rope.
2 a single length of hair, yarn, etc.

stranded (adj)
1 washed up on a shore. *A stranded whale.*
2 If you are **stranded** somewhere, you are stuck there and cannot get away.

strange stranger strangest (adj) odd, unusual, or unfamiliar. strangeness (n), strangely (adv).

stranger (n)
1 someone you do not know.
2 someone who is in a place where they have not been before. *I am a stranger in this city.*

strangle strangling strangled (v) to kill someone by squeezing their throat so that they cannot breathe. strangler (n), strangulation (n).

strap strapping strapped
1 (n) a strip of leather or material, used to fasten things together.
2 (v) to fasten things, or hold things in place with straps.

strategy strategies (n) a clever plan for winning or achieving something. strategic (adj), strategically (adv).

straw (n)
1 dried stalks of barley, wheat, etc.
2 a thin, hollow tube through which you can drink.

strawberry strawberries (n) a soft, red fruit. *See* **fruit**.

stray straying strayed
1 (v) to wander away or to get lost. stray (adj).
2 (n) a lost or homeless cat or dog.

streak streaking streaked
1 (n) a stripe of colour. streaky (adj).
2 (v) to move very fast. *The sprinter streaked past us.*

stream streaming streamed
1 (n) a small river.
2 (n) a long line of moving people, cars, etc.
3 (n) a class of schoolchildren who are at the same level in their work.
4 (v) to move or flow quickly.

streamer (n) a long, thin strip of coloured paper, used as a decoration.

streamlined (adj)
If a car, aeroplane, or other vehicle is **streamlined**, it is designed so that it can cut through air or water very quickly and easily. *See* **aerodynamic**.

street (n)
1 a road with houses or other buildings along it.
2 (informal) If you have **street cred**, you are fashionable and popular. Cred is short for credibility.

streetwise (adj)
If you are **streetwise**, you know how to survive in towns or cities without getting into trouble.

strength (n)
1 If you have **strength**, you are physically strong. strengthen (v).
2 Someone's **strengths** are their good points, or the things that they can do well.

strenuous (stren-yoo-uss) (adj) Something that is **strenuous** needs a lot of energy or effort. strenuously (adv).

stress stresses stressing stressed
1 (n) worry, strain, or pressure. stressful (adj).
2 (v) If you **stress** something, you show that it is important. stress (n).

stressed (adj) If you are **stressed**, you feel anxious and under pressure.

stretch stretches stretching stretched
1 (v) to make something bigger, longer, or greater.
2 (v) to reach out or up with your arms. stretch (n).
3 (v) to extend or to spread out.
4 (n) a period of time, especially time spent in a prison.
5 **stretch out** (v) to lie full length.

stretcher (n) a narrow bed stretched between two poles, and used for carrying an injured or sick person.

strict stricter strictest (adj)
1 If someone is **strict**, they make you obey the rules and behave properly. strictness (n), strictly (adv).
2 complete or total. *This trick needs strict concentration.* strictly (adv).

stride striding strode stridden (v) to walk with long steps. stride (n).

strife (n) trouble or arguing.

strike striking struck (v)
1 to hit or attack someone or something. strike (n).
2 When a clock **strikes**, it chimes to show the time.

3 to make an impression on someone. *Bess struck me as silly.*
4 If you **strike** a match, you light it.
5 When people **strike**, they refuse to work because of a disagreement with their employer. strike (n).

striker (n)
1 a football player who plays in an attacking position. *See* **soccer**.
2 someone who is on strike.

striking (adj) unusual or noticeable in some way. strikingly (adv).

string stringing strung
1 (n) a thin cord or rope.
2 (n) a thin wire on a musical instrument such as a guitar. string (v).
3 (n) a number of things of a similar kind all in a row. *A string of pearls. A string of thefts.*
4 **string out** (v) If you **string** something out, you stretch or lengthen something. *We strung out the game until bedtime.*

strings (plural n) the section of an orchestra that is made up of stringed instruments, such as violins and cellos. *The picture shows the main parts of a violin, and other instruments in the string section of an orchestra.*

violin
scroll
tuning peg
fingerboard
horse hair
neck
wooden stick
string
double bass
viola
cello
purfling (curved band)
f hole (sound hole)
bridge
table or belly
bow
chin rest
tailpiece

subconscious

strip stripping stripped
1 (v) to take something off. *Joey stripped the wallpaper off the wall.*
2 (v) to undress. **stripper** (n).
3 (n) a narrow piece of paper, material, etc.
4 (n) the clothes that a football team wears. *Our team has a new strip.*

stripe (n) a band of colour. **striped** (adj), **stripy** (adj).

strive striving strove striven (v) to make a great effort to do something. *Strive to do your best.*

strobe (n) a light that keeps flashing on and off very quickly.

stroke stroking stroked
1 (n) a hit. *A backhand stroke. A stroke of lightning.*
2 (v) to pass your hand gently over something. *Do you want to stroke the kitten?* **stroke** (n).
3 (n) When someone has a **stroke**, the blood supply to their brain is disturbed, which sometimes causes part of their body to be paralysed.
4 (n) a line drawn by a pen or brush.
5 (n) a method of moving in swimming or rowing.

stroll (n)
a short, relaxed walk. **stroll** (v).

strong stronger strongest (adj)
1 powerful or having great force. *A strong wind.* **strongly** (adv).
2 hard to break. *A strong shelf.* **strongly** (adv).
3 full of taste, spices, alcohol, etc. *A strong curry.* **strongly** (adv).

stronghold (n) a fortress or a place that is well defended.

stroppy stroppier stroppiest (adj) (informal) quarrelsome and unhelpful. **stroppiness** (n), **stroppily** (adv).

structure (n)
1 the organization of something, or the way that it is made up. **structure** (v), **structural** (adj).
2 a building, or something that has been put together. **structural** (adj).

struggle struggling struggled (v)
1 If you **struggle** with someone, you fight or wrestle with them. **struggle** (n).
2 If you **struggle** with something, you find it difficult to do. **struggle** (n).

strum strumming strummed (v) to play a guitar, banjo, etc. by brushing the tips of your fingers over the strings.

strut strutting strutted
1 (v) to walk proudly and stiffly with your chest pushed out.
2 (n) a wooden or metal supporting bar. *See* **acoustic guitar**, **hydrofoil**.

stub stubbing stubbed
1 (n) a short end of something, such as a pencil or cigarette. **stubby** (adj).
2 (v) to hurt your toe by banging it against something.
3 **stub out** (v) to put a cigarette out.

stubble (n)
1 short, spiky pieces of barley, wheat, etc., left in a field after harvesting. **stubbly** (adj).
2 the short hair that grows back after it has been shaved. **stubbly** (adj).

stubborn (adj) obstinate, or determined not to give way. **stubbornness** (n), **stubbornly** (adv).

stuck-up (adj) (informal) conceited and snobbish.

stud (n)
1 a small, round piece of metal, such as a fastener or an earring.
2 one of the short pegs on the bottom of football or hockey boots, which give extra grip.

student (n)
someone who is studying, especially in a college or university.

studio (n)
1 a room in which an artist or a photographer works.
2 a place where films, music albums, etc. are made.

studious (stew-dee-us) (adj)
If you are **studious**, you like to study, and work carefully. **studiousness** (n), **studiously** (adv).

study studies studying studied
1 (n) an office or room where someone works.
2 (v) to spend time learning a subject or skill. **study** (n).
3 (v) to examine something carefully. *Amanda studied the football results.*

stuff stuffing stuffed
1 (n) a substance or a material.
2 (n) (informal) belongings.
3 (v) to fill something tightly. *Jon stuffed his pockets with conkers.*
4 (v) to put something into something else. *Don't forget to stuff the turkey.*
5 (v) If you **stuff yourself**, you eat so much that you are very full.
6 If you are **stuffed up**, you have a cold and it is difficult to breathe.

stuffing (n)
a filling, especially a mixture of chopped food that you cook inside a chicken, pepper, etc.

stuffy stuffier stuffiest (adj)
1 A **stuffy** room has stale air in it. **stuffiness** (n).
2 A **stuffy** person is prim and easily shocked. **stuffily** (adv).

stumble stumbling stumbled (v)
1 to trip up, or to walk in an unsteady way.
2 to make mistakes when you are talking or reading aloud.

stump (n)
1 the part that is left when a tree is cut down.
2 one of the three upright wooden sticks of a cricket wicket.

stumpy stumpier stumpiest (adj) short and thick. *A stumpy crayon.*

stun stunning stunned (v)
If you are **stunned**, you are shocked, dazed, or knocked out.

stunning (adj)
beautiful or amazing. **stunningly** (adv).

stunt stunting stunted
1 (n) a dangerous trick or act.
2 (v) to stop the proper growth of something. **stunted** (adj).
3 **publicity stunt** (n)
a trick to get public attention for a company, organization, event, etc.
4 (n) A **stunt man** or **stunt woman** takes the place of an actor to perform the dangerous actions in a film.

stupendous (adj) very good or very big. **stupendously** (adv).

stupid stupider stupidest (adj)
silly or unintelligent. **stupidity** (n), **stupidly** (adv).

sturdy sturdier sturdiest (adj)
strong and firm. *A sturdy tree.* **sturdiness** (n), **sturdily** (adv).

sturgeon (n)
a large fish covered with rows of bony, pointed scales. Its eggs are made into the luxury food, caviar.

stutter stuttering stuttered (v)
If you **stutter** when you speak, you repeat the first sound of a word before you manage to say the whole word. **stutter** (n).

sty sties (n)
1 a pen in which pigs live.
2 **sty** or **stye** a red, painful swelling on your eyelid.

style styling styled
1 (n) a way of doing something, such as writing, dressing, building, etc.
2 (n) If you do something with **style**, you do it smartly or elegantly. **stylish** (adj), **stylishly** (adv).
3 (v) to arrange or design something. *Her hair was styled by me.* **style** (n).
4 (n) the part of a flower which extends from the ovary and supports the stigma. *See* **flower**.

subconscious (n) part of your mind that influences you without your being aware of it. **subconsciously** (adv).

a b c d e f g h i j k l m n o p q r **s** t u v w x y z

subcontinent *(n)* a large area of land that is smaller than a continent. *The Indian subcontinent.*

subdivide subdividing subdivided *(v)* to divide something into smaller, even parts. *I cut the apple in half, then subdivided each half into quarters.* **subdivision** *(n).*

subdued *(adj)*
1 unusually quiet and restrained.
2 not bright. *Subdued lighting.*

subject subjecting subjected
1 *(sub-jekt)* *(n)* the topic of a book, article, conversation, etc.
2 *(sub-jekt)* *(n)* an area of study, such as geography or mathematics.
3 *(sub-jekt)* *(n)* A **subject** of a ruler is someone who lives in their country.
4 *(sub-jekt)* If you are **subject to** something, you are likely to be affected by it. *Leah is subject to terrible colds.*
5 *(sub-jekt)* *(v)* If you **subject** someone to something, you force them to suffer it. *Our neighbours subjected us to loud music all night.*

subjective *(adj)* to do with opinions rather than actual facts. *Delilah's essay on animal rights was purely subjective.* **subjectively** *(adv).*

submarine *(n)* a ship that can travel under the water for long periods.

submerge submerging submerged *(v)* to put something under water.

submit submitting submitted *(v)*
1 to hand in, or put something forward. *Have you submitted your proposal? Can I submit a plan to the committee?* **submission** *(n).*
2 to agree to obey something. *I submitted to their decision.* **submission** *(n).*

subordinate
1 *(adj)* less important.
2 *(n)* someone who is low in rank, and can be told what to do.

subscribe subscribing subscribed *(v)*
1 to pay money regularly for a website, magazine, television channel, etc. **subscriber** *(n)*, **subscription** *(n).*
2 to give money to a charity or an appeal.

subsequent *(adj)* coming after, or following. *Lucas lost the first match, but played better in subsequent ones.* **subsequently** *(adv).*

subside subsiding subsided *(v)*
1 If the ground **subsides**, it caves in or sinks down. **subsidence** *(n).*
2 to become less. *Gradually, the noise subsided.*

subsidiary *(adj)* minor, or less important. *A subsidiary role.*

subsidy subsidies *(n)* money that a government or organization contributes in order to make goods cheaper. **subsidize** *(v).*

substance *(n)*
1 a material. Objects, powders, and liquids are all substances.
2 the important part of something. *The substance of an argument.*

substantial *(adj)* solid, large, or important. **substantially** *(adv).*

substitute *(n)* someone or something used instead of another, such as a footballer who plays when another player is injured. **substitution** *(n)*, **substitute** *(v).*

subtitle *(n)*
1 the second, less important title of a book, film, etc.
2 **subtitles** *(plural n)* the translated words that appear on the screen when a foreign film is shown.

subtle *(sut-ul)* subtler subtlest *(adj)*
1 delicate, or not easy to notice. *A subtle flavour.* **subtly** *(adv).*
2 using clever or disguised methods. *A subtle plan.* **subtlety** *(n)*, **subtly** *(adv).*

subtract subtracting subtracted *(v)* to take one number away from another. *If you subtract four from six, you are left with two.* **subtraction** *(n).*

suburb *(n)* an area of housing at the edge of a large town or city. **suburbia** *(n)*, **suburban** *(adj).*

subway *(n)* a covered path for pedestrians under a road or railway.

succeed *(suk-seed)* succeeding succeeded *(v)*
1 to manage to do something. *Nick succeeded in fixing the car.*
2 to take over from someone in an important position. *Mitch succeeded his father as company director.*
3 to do well, or to get what you want. **success** *(n)*, **successful** *(adj).*

succulent *(suk-yu-lent)* *(adj)* juicy. *A succulent peach.* **succulence** *(n).*

suck sucking sucked *(v)*
1 to draw something into your mouth, using your tongue and lips. *Gale still sucks his thumb.* **suck** *(n).*
2 to pull strongly. *The vacuum cleaner sucked up my ring.*

suction *(n)* the creation of a vacuum, so that air or liquid is sucked in, or so that two surfaces stick together.

sudden *(adj)* quick or unexpected. **suddenness** *(n)*, **suddenly** *(adv).*

sue suing sued *(v)* If you **sue** someone, you take them to court to make them pay for the harm that they have done to you.

suede *(swayd)* *(n)* soft leather with a smooth, velvet-like surface.

suet *(n)* a dry fat used in cooking.

suffer suffering suffered *(v)*
1 to experience something bad, such as unhappiness or pain. **sufferer** *(n)*, **suffering** *(n).*
2 If you **suffer** from an illness, you get it often, or have it for a long time. *Jemma suffers from hay fever.*

sufficient *(suf-ish-unt)* *(adj)* If something is **sufficient**, it is enough or adequate. *We left sufficient food for the cats while we were away.* **sufficiently** *(adv).*

suffix suffixes *(n)* a group of letters added at the end of a word, to create a new but related word. For example, "ness", "ly", and "ful" are all suffixes. *The suffix "ness" is used in "sadness" and "happiness".*

suffocate suffocating suffocated *(v)*
1 If someone **suffocates**, they die because they cannot breathe. **suffocation** *(n).*
2 to stop someone breathing, so that they die.

sugar *(n)*
1 a sweet substance that comes from plants and is used in foods and drinks. **sugary** *(adj).*
2 **sugar beet** a root vegetable from which sugar is produced.
3 **sugar cane** a tall, tropical plant that has sugar in its stems.

sugar beet

suggest suggesting suggested *(v)* to put something forward as an idea or a possibility. *I suggested going to China for our next holiday.* **suggestion** *(n).*

suicide *(soo-iss-ide)* *(n)* If someone commits **suicide**, they kill themselves. **suicidal** *(adj)*, **suicidally** *(adv).*

suit suiting suited
1 *(n)* a set of smart, matching clothes, usually a man's jacket and trousers.
2 *(n)* one of the four types of playing card in a pack of cards. *The four suits are clubs, diamonds, hearts, and spades.*
3 *(v)* to be acceptable and convenient. *Does Wednesday suit you?*
4 *(v)* If a hairstyle or an outfit **suits** you, it makes you look good.

suitable *(adj)*
If something is **suitable**, it is right for a particular purpose. **suitability** *(n)*, **suitably** *(adv)*.

suitcase *(n)*
a container used for carrying clothes when you travel.

suite *(sweet) (n)*
1 a set of matching furniture.
2 a set of rooms in a hotel.

sulk sulking sulked *(v)*
If you **sulk**, you are angry and silent. **sulk** *(n)*, **sulky** *(adj)*.

sullen *(adj)* gloomy, silent, and bad-tempered. **sullenly** *(adv)*.

sulphur or **sulfur** *(sul-fur) (n)*
1 a yellow chemical element, used in gunpowder and fertilizers. See **mineral**.
2 sulphur dioxide a poisonous gas found in some industrial waste, that causes air pollution.

sultan *(n)* an emperor or ruler of an Islamic country.

sultana *(n)*
1 a small, brown, dried fruit, made from a grape.
2 the wife or daughter of a sultan.

sultry sultrier sultriest *(adj)*
1 If the weather is **sultry**, it is hot and humid. **sultriness** *(n)*.
2 If a person is **sultry**, they are passionate or sexy. **sultriness** *(n)*.

sum summing summed
1 *(n)* an amount of money.
2 *(n)* an arithmetic problem.
3 *(v)* If you **sum up**, you go through the main points of what has been said, in order to reach a conclusion.
4 sum total *(n)* the whole or the final amount.

summary summaries *(n)*
a short statement of the main points of something that has been said or written. **summarize** *(v)*.

summer *(n)* the season between spring and autumn, when the weather is warmest. **summery** *(adj)*.

summit *(n)*
1 the top of a mountain.
2 a meeting of leaders from different countries.

summon
summoning summoned *(v)*
1 to call or request someone to come. *Summon the next witness.*
2 If you **summon up** courage, you make a great effort to be brave.

summons summonses
(singular n) an order to appear in court. **summons** *(v)*.

sun sunning sunned
1 Sun *(n)* the star that the Earth moves around, and that gives us light and warmth. *See* **planet**.
2 *(n)* light and warmth from the Sun. *Don't stay too long in the sun.*
3 *(v)* If you **sun** yourself, you sit or lie in the sunlight.

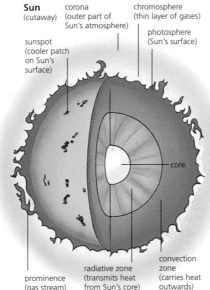

Sun *(cutaway)*
corona (outer part of Sun's atmosphere)
chromosphere (thin layer of gases)
photosphere (Sun's surface)
sunspot (cooler patch on Sun's surface)
core
convection zone (carries heat outwards)
radiative zone (transmits heat from Sun's core)
prominence (gas stream)

sunbathe sunbathing sunbathed *(v)*
to sit or lie in sunlight to make your body suntanned.

sunburn *(n)* sore, red skin caused by staying in sunlight too long. **sunburnt** *(adj)*.

sundial *(n)*
an instrument that shows the time by using the Sun's light. A pointer casts a shadow that moves around a flat, marked dial.

sundial

sunglasses *(plural n)*
dark glasses that protect your eyes from sunlight.

sunrise *(n)*
the time in the morning when the Sun appears above the horizon.

sunset *(n)* the time in the evening when the Sun sinks below the horizon.

sunshine *(n)* the light from the Sun.

sunstroke *(n)* an illness, caused by staying in hot sunlight for too long, that gives you a fever and a headache.

suntan *(n)* If you have a **suntan**, your skin is darker because you have been in sunlight. **suntanned** *(adj)*.

super *(adj)* very good.

superb *(adj)* excellent or magnificent. **superbly** *(adv)*.

superficial *(soo-per-fish-ul) (adj)*
1 on the surface. *A superficial cut.* **superficially** *(adv)*.
2 not deep or not thorough. *My interest in music is only superficial.* **superficially** *(adv)*.

superfluous *(soo-per-floo-uss) (adj)*
more than is needed or wanted.

superhero superheroes *(n)*
In stories, a **superhero** is a person with supernatural powers, who often fights crime.

superintendent *(n)*
1 someone in charge of something.
2 a senior police officer.

superior
1 *(adj)* better. *Daisy thinks that butter is superior to margarine.*
2 *(n)* someone who is in a more important position than you.
3 *(adj)* If someone acts in a **superior** way, they behave as if they were better than other people. **superiority** *(n)*.

superlative *(soo-per-la-tiv) (adj)*
1 Superlative adjectives and adverbs are used to describe the greatest or highest degree of things or actions. *"Biggest" is the superlative of "big", and "most quickly" is the superlative of "quickly".* **superlative** *(n)*.
2 very good. **superlatively** *(adv)*.

supermarket *(n)* a large shop that sells food and other household items.

supernatural *(adj)* If something is **supernatural**, it involves things that natural laws cannot explain, such as ghosts. **supernaturally** *(adv)*.

supersonic *(adj)*
faster than the speed of sound. *The picture shows Concorde, which flew at supersonic speeds.*

Concorde

superstitious *(adj)*
People who are **superstitious** are afraid that something bad will happen if they do not follow certain rules. **superstition** *(n)*.

superstore *(n)* a very large shop.

supervise supervising supervised *(v)* to watch over and be in charge of someone while they do something. **supervisor** *(n)*, **supervision** *(n)*.

supper *(n)*
1 an evening meal.
2 a snack that you eat before you go to bed.

a b c d e f g h i j k l m n o p q r s t u v w x y z

supple

supple suppler supplest *(adj)*
If you are **supple**, you can move or bend your body easily. **suppleness** *(n)*.

supplement *(n)*
an additional item. *A dietary supplement. This newspaper has a colour supplement.*
supplement *(v)*, **supplementary** *(adj)*.

supplies *(plural n)* food and equipment taken on an expedition.

supply supplies
supplying supplied *(v)*
to provide someone with what they want or need. *Bev supplies me with magazines.* **supply** *(n)*, **supplier** *(n)*.

support supporting supported *(v)*
1 to hold something up to keep it from falling. **support** *(n)*.
2 to help and encourage someone. **support** *(n)*, **supportive** *(adj)*.
3 to believe in someone or something. *Georgia supports the Green Party.* **support** *(n)*, **supporter** *(n)*.

suppose supposing supposed *(v)*
to think that something is true, or to expect something. *I suppose you're right. I suppose that Leslie will be late.*

suppress suppresses
suppressing suppressed *(v)*
1 to stop something happening. *The dictator suppressed the revolution.* **suppression** *(n)*.
2 to hide or control something. *Carly tried to suppress her giggles.*

supreme *(adj)*
the greatest, best, or most powerful. **supremacy** *(n)*, **supremely** *(adv)*.

sure surer surest *(adj)*
certain and definite. *Are you sure that he's here?* **surely** *(adv)*.

surf surfing surfed
1 *(n)* the spray produced by waves as they break on the shore.
2 *(v)* to ride on breaking waves, using a surfboard. **surfer** *(n)*, **surfing** *(n)*.
3 *(v)* to move from website to website on the internet. **surfing** *(n)*.

surfing

surface surfacing surfaced
1 *(n)* the outer face or top of something.
2 *(v)* to come to the surface or to appear. *The submarine surfaced when it was hit. The lost coins surfaced after several years.*

surfboard *(n)* a light, narrow board which surfers stand on to ride breaking waves. *See* **surf**.

surge surging surged *(v)*
to rush forward or upward. *The crowd surged forward as the gate was opened.* **surge** *(n)*.

surgeon *(sur-jun)* *(n)*
a doctor who performs operations.

surgery *(sur-jer-ee)* surgeries *(n)*
1 a place where you go to see a doctor, dentist, vet, etc.
2 medical treatment that involves cutting the patient open and repairing, removing, or replacing body parts. **surgical** *(adj)*.

surly surlier surliest *(adj)*
If someone is **surly**, they are bad-tempered and unfriendly.

surname *(n)*
a person's last name or family name.

surpass surpasses surpassing
surpassed *(v)* to do better than you have done before. *Today, Christina surpassed her previous record.*

surplus *(adj)* spare, or more than what is needed. *The charity shop is asking for any surplus clothes.*

surprise surprising surprised *(v)*
to do or say something unexpected. *Belinda's outburst surprised us all.* **surprise** *(n)*, **surprising** *(adj)*.

surrender surrendering
surrendered *(v)* to give up, or to admit that you are beaten in a fight or battle. **surrender** *(n)*.

surround surrounding surrounded *(v)*
to be on every side of something. *Robin Hood and his men surrounded Nottingham Castle.*

surroundings *(plural n)* the things around someone or something. *People work better in cheerful surroundings.*

survey surveying surveyed
1 *(sur-vay)* *(n)* a report on what people think about something. *We are producing a survey of reactions to the new shopping centre.*
2 *(sur-vay)* *(v)* to look at the whole of a scene or situation. *Mum surveyed the mess with horror.*
3 *(sur-vay)* *(v)* to measure an area in order to make a map or plan. **survey** *(sur-vay)* *(n)*, **surveyor** *(n)*.

survive surviving
survived *(v)* to stay alive, especially after some dangerous event. *Only one passenger survived the car crash.* **survival** *(n)*, **survivor** *(n)*.

sushi

sushi *(soo-shee)* *(n)*
a Japanese food made from vinegared rice mixed with other ingredients, such as raw fish or vegetables. *The picture shows sushi packed in bamboo leaves.*

suspect suspecting suspected
1 *(suss-pekt)* *(v)* to think that someone should not be trusted. **suspicion** *(n)*.
2 *(suss-pekt)* *(v)* to think that something is wrong with a situation. *The doctor suspected something more serious than flu.* **suspicion** *(n)*, **suspect** *(suss-pekt)* *(adj)*.
3 *(suss-pekt)* *(n)* someone thought to be responsible for a crime.

suspend suspending suspended *(v)*
1 to hang something downwards. *Pamela suspended a banner from her bedroom window.*
2 to stop something for a short time. *Work was suspended for the holidays.*
3 to punish someone by stopping them taking part in an activity for a short while. *Melanie was suspended from school for a week.* **suspension** *(n)*.

suspenders *(plural n)* elastic straps attached to a belt and worn to hold up women's stockings.

suspense *(n)* an anxious and uncertain feeling, caused by having to wait to see what happens.

suspicious *(adj)*
1 If you feel **suspicious**, you think that something is wrong, but have no firm proof. **suspicion** *(n)*.
2 If something is or looks **suspicious**, it makes people think that something is wrong.

sustain sustaining sustained *(v)*
1 to keep something going. *Calvin sustained a conversation with his cat for over ten minutes.*
2 If something **sustains** you, it gives you energy. *The hot soup sustained the walkers for hours.*
3 to suffer something. *Tracey sustained some nasty bruises.*

swagger swaggering swaggered *(v)* to walk or act in a conceited way.

swallow swallowing swallowed
1 *(v)* to make food or drink pass down your throat.
2 *(n)* a migrating bird with long wings and a forked tail.

swallow

symmetrical

swamp (n) an area of wet, marshy ground.

swan (n) a large water bird with webbed feet and a long neck. *The picture shows a female swan with her young.*

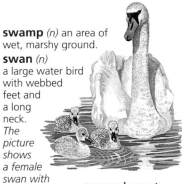

swan and cygnets

swank swanking swanked (v) (informal) to show off. *Shona was swanking about her new bike.* **swanky** (adj).

swap or **swop** swapping swapped (v) to exchange one thing for another. **swap** (n).

swarm swarming swarmed
1 (v) When bees or other insects **swarm**, they fly together in a thick mass. **swarm** (n).
2 (adj) If a place is **swarming** with people, it is very crowded.

swarthy swarthier swarthiest (adj) A **swarthy** person has dark skin.

swastika (n) the emblem of the Nazi party during Hitler's rule in Germany.

swat swatting swatted (v) to kill a fly with a quick blow.

sway swaying swayed (v)
1 to move or swing from side to side. *The corn swayed in the wind.*
2 to move or influence the way that someone else thinks.

swear swearing swore sworn (v)
1 to use rude words.
2 to make a formal, solemn promise. *I swear to tell the truth.*

sweat sweating sweated (v) When you **sweat,** you let out moisture through the pores in your skin, because you are hot or anxious. **sweat** (n).

sweater (n) a knitted piece of clothing that you wear on the top half of your body.

sweatshirt (n) a collarless, casual top with long sleeves.

sweep sweeping swept
1 (v) to clean up somewhere, using a brush.
2 (v) to move rapidly and forcefully. *The duchess swept into the room.*
3 (n) someone whose job is to sweep chimneys.

sweeping (adj) Something that is **sweeping** affects many things or people. *Sweeping changes in the firm have resulted in many job losses.*

sweet sweeter sweetest
1 (n) a small piece of food, made with sugar or chocolate.
2 (adj) Food that is **sweet** has a sugary flavour, not a savoury one.
3 (adj) pleasant or cute. *It was sweet of you to bring a gift.* **sweetly** (adv).

sweetcorn (n) the juicy, yellow seeds of the maize plant, that are eaten as a vegetable.

swell swelling swelled swollen (v) to grow larger or fatter. *Teddy's knee swelled where he had knocked it.* **swollen** (adj).

sweltering (adj) When the weather is **sweltering**, it is very hot indeed. **swelter** (v).

swerve swerving swerved (v) to change direction quickly, usually to avoid something.

swift swifter swiftest
1 (adj) fast or rapid. **swiftness** (n), **swiftly** (adv).
2 (n) a migrating bird with long, narrow wings, similar to a swallow. *See* **bird**.

swig swigging swigged (v) (informal) to drink in large gulps, usually from a bottle, flask, etc.

swim swimming swam swum (v) to propel yourself through water using your arms and legs. **swimmer** (n).

swimsuit (n) a costume worn by a woman or girl when she goes swimming.

swindle swindling swindled (v) to cheat someone out of something, especially money. **swindle** (n), **swindler** (n).

swine swine (n)
1 (old-fashioned) a pig.
2 a very unpleasant person.

swing swinging swung
1 (v) to move from side to side.
2 (n) a piece of play equipment that you sit on and move backwards and forwards.
3 (n) the amount by which votes move from one party to another. *There was a swing of 20% against the government.*
4 If something is **in full swing**, it is very busy and active. *The party was in full swing when we arrived.*

swipe swiping swiped (v)
1 (informal) to hit something or someone hard. **swipe** (n).
2 to run a plastic credit card through the groove of a machine which reads it.
3 (slang) to steal something. *Elsie swiped my chocolate!*

swirl swirling swirled (v) to move in circles. *The water swirled around the plughole.*

swish swishing swished (v) to move through the air with a hissing sound. **swish** (n).

switch switches switching switched (v)
1 to exchange one thing for another.
2 to change from one thing to another. *Miguel switched courses.*
3 If you **switch on** a piece of electrical equipment, you turn it on. **switch** (n).

switchboard (n) a control centre for a telephone system, where calls are connected.

swivel swivelling swivelled (v) to turn or rotate on the spot.

swoop swooping swooped (v) When a bird **swoops**, it flies down suddenly, often to grab its prey.

swop see **swap**.

sword (sord) (n) a weapon with a handle and a long, sharp blade. Swords were used in the past for man-to-man fighting and are still used in ceremonies such as coronations.

Viking sword
double-edged blade
hilt or grip
pommel
guard

swot swotting swotted
1 (v) (informal) to study very hard, often for an examination.
2 (n) (informal) a name that other people give to someone who studies extremely hard.

syllable (n) one of the sounds in a word. *The word America has four syllables: A-me-ri-ca.*

syllabus syllabuses or syllabi (n) a programme of work that must be covered for a particular course of study.

symbol (n) a design or object that represents something else. *A dove is a symbol of peace.* **symbolic** (adj), **symbolically** (adv).

symmetrical (adj) One half of a **symmetrical** shape exactly mirrors the other. **symmetry** (n), **symmetrically** (adv).

symmetrical shapes

sympathy

sympathy sympathies
1 *(n)* the understanding and sharing of other people's troubles. *After her accident, Polly's friends gave her lots of sympathy.* **sympathize** *(v)*, **sympathetic** *(adj)*, **sympathetically** *(adv)*.
2 If you are **in sympathy** with someone's aims or actions, you agree with them and support them.

symphony symphonies *(n)* a long piece of music for an orchestra, usually in four parts, called movements. **symphonic** *(adj)*.

symptom *(n)* something that shows that you have an illness. *A rash is one of the symptoms of measles.*

synagogue *(sin-a-gog)* *(n)* a building used by Jews for worship.

synchronize or **synchronise** *(sin-kron-ize)* synchronizing synchronized *(v)* to make things happen at exactly the same time. *Let's synchronize our watches before we arrange a meeting time.* **synchronization** *(n)*.

syncopate syncopating syncopated *(v)* to stress beats in a piece of music that are not normally stressed. **syncopation** *(n)*.

synonym *(sin-oh-nim)* *(n)* a word that means the same, or nearly the same, as another word. *"Rapid" is a synonym of "quick".*

synopsis synopses *(n)* a brief summary of a longer piece of writing.

syntax *(n)* the rules of grammar that govern the way that words are put together to make phrases and sentences.

synthesizer or **synthesiser** *(n)* an electronic keyboard instrument that can make a variety of sounds, and can imitate other musical instruments.

synthetic *(adj)* Something that is **synthetic** is man-made or artificial. **synthetically** *(adv)*.

syphon *see* **siphon**.

syringe *(n)* a tube with a plunger and a hollow needle, used for giving injections and taking blood samples.

syrup *(n)* a sweet, sticky substance made from sugar. *Maple syrup.* **syrupy** *(adj)*.

system *(n)*
1 a group of things which exist or work together in an organized way. *The Solar System. A heating system.*
2 a way of organizing or arranging things. *The education system.* **systematic** *(adj)*, **systematically** *(adv)*.

Tt

tab
1 *(n)* a small piece of paper, metal, etc. that you can hold or pull. *Most drink cans have ring tabs.*
2 *(informal)* If you **keep tabs** on someone, you watch them closely to see what they are doing.
3 *(informal)* If you **pick up the tab**, you pay the bill in a café or restaurant.

tabby tabbies *(n)* a cat with a grey or brownish-yellow striped coat. *See* **cat**.

tabernacle *(tab-er-nak-ul)* *(n)*
1 a building used for worship.
2 a container or shrine for holy objects.

table *(n)*
1 a piece of furniture with a flat top resting on legs.
2 a chart showing figures or information.
3 **tables** *(plural n)* lists of numbers multiplied by other numbers.

tablecloth *(n)* a piece of material used to protect or decorate a table.

table manners *(plural n)* the way you behave when you are eating.

tablespoon *(n)* a large spoon that you use as a measure in cooking, or to serve food. **tablespoonful** *(n)*.

tablet *(n)*
1 a small, solid piece of medicine that you swallow.
2 a small, portable computer that you operate by touching the screen.
3 a piece of stone with writing carved on it.

table tennis *(n)* a game for two or four players, who hit a small, light ball over a low net on a table, using round bats.

tabloid *(n)* a newspaper printed on small pages, with large headlines and lots of pictures. **tabloid** *(adj)*.

taboo *(adj)* If a subject is **taboo**, you may upset or offend people if you talk about it. *Death is a taboo subject in some societies.* **taboo** *(n)*.

tacit *(tass-it)* *(adj)* If something is **tacit**, it is understood or agreed without being stated. *My parents have given their tacit agreement to my staying up late.* **tacitly** *(adv)*.

taciturn *(adj)* If someone is **taciturn**, they are quiet and shy, and do not talk much. **taciturnly** *(adv)*.

tack tacking tacked
1 *(n)* a small, sharp nail.
2 *(v)* to attach or fix something using tacks. *We tacked a picture to the wall.*
3 *(v)* If you **tack** material, you sew it loosely before doing it neatly. **tack** *(n)*.
4 *(v)* to sail in a zig-zag course against the wind. **tack** *(n)*.
5 *(n)* equipment that you need to ride a horse, such as a saddle and bridle. *The picture shows the main parts of a bridle and saddle. The horse on the right wears western-style tack, which is popular in the USA.*

riding tack
western saddle with pommel
saddle blanket
western bridle
over-reach boot
martingale

bridle
headpiece
browband
cheekpiece
noseband
reins
throatlash
snaffle bit

saddle
pommel
cantle
skirt
seat
numnah (saddle cloth)
surcingle loop
panel
stirrup iron
saddle flap
stirrup leather
girth

tape

tackle tackling tackled
1 *(v)* If you **tackle** someone in a ball game, you try to get the ball away from them. **tackle** *(n)*.
2 *(v)* to deal with a problem or difficulty. *We must tackle the litter problem.*
3 *(n)* the equipment that you need to do something. *Fishing tackle.*

tacky tackier tackiest *(adj)*
1 slightly sticky. *The paint is still tacky on this door.*
2 *(informal)* If something is **tacky**, it looks cheap and tasteless. *The shop was full of tacky ornaments.*

tact *(n)* If you handle a person or situation with **tact**, you are sensitive and do not upset anyone. **tactful** *(adj)*, **tactfully** *(adv)*.

tactics *(plural n)* plans or methods to win a game or battle. **tactical** *(adj)*, **tactically** *(adv)*.

tag tagging tagged
1 *(n)* a label. *A price tag.*
2 *(n)* a children's chasing game.
3 *(v)* If you **tag along** with someone, you go with them. *Henry wasn't part of the group; he just tagged along.*

tail tailing tailed
1 *(n)* the long part at the end of an animal's body. See **bird**, **dog**, **horse**.
2 *(n)* something that is like a tail. *We joined the tail of the procession.*
3 *(v)* *(informal)* If you **tail** someone, you follow them closely. **tail** *(n)*.
4 *(v)* If something **tails off**, it gets less or weakens. *Misha's enthusiasm for the project has started to tail off.*

tailor tailoring tailored
1 *(n)* someone who makes or alters clothes, especially men's suits.
2 *(v)* to design or alter something so that it suits someone perfectly.

take taking took taken *(v)*
1 to move or carry something. *Take your plate into the kitchen.*
2 to get, seize, or capture something. *Ken's taken my pen!*
3 to accept something. *Do you take credit cards?*
4 to use something. *Does your camera take batteries?*
5 If you **take after** someone in your family, you look like them or have the same characteristics as them.
6 **take in** *(informal)* If someone **takes you in**, you believe the lies that they tell you.

takeaway *(n)*
1 a restaurant selling meals that you take and eat somewhere else.
2 a meal that you buy from a takeaway restaurant.

takeoff *(n)* the beginning of a flight, when the aircraft leaves the ground. **take off** *(v)*.

takeover *(n)* If there is a **takeover** of a company, another company buys enough shares in it to control the company. **take over** *(v)*.

takings *(plural n)* money received from customers in a shop, café, etc.

talcum powder *(n)* a fine, white powder that you can use to dry your body or to make yourself smell nice.

tale *(n)*
1 *(old-fashioned)* a story.
2 a lie or a complaint about someone. *Don't tell tales!*

talent *(n)* an ability or a skill. **talented** *(adj)*.

talk talking talked
1 *(v)* to speak.
2 *(n)* a conversation.
3 *(n)* a speech or a lecture.

talkative *(adj)* If you are **talkative**, you talk a lot.

tall taller tallest *(adj)*
1 high, or higher than usual. *A tall tree. A tall woman.*
2 having a certain height. *He was six feet tall.*
3 hard to believe. *A tall story.*

tally tallies tallying tallied
1 *(n)* a count or a record. *Keep a tally of what I owe you.*
2 *(v)* to add up or match. *These figures don't quite tally.*

Talmud *(n)* the collection of Jewish civil and religious laws.

talon *(n)* a sharp claw.

tambourine *(n)* a small round musical instrument, similar to a drum, that you play by shaking or hitting it with your hand. See **percussion**.

tame tamer tamest *(adj)*
1 A **tame** animal is not wild, and can live with people. **tame** *(v)*.
2 not very exciting. **tamely** *(adv)*.

tamper tampering tampered *(v)* to interfere with something, so that it becomes damaged or broken.

tampon *(n)* a plug of soft material that some women and girls wear inside their vaginas to absorb the flow of blood during their periods.

tan tanning tanned
1 *(n)* a light, yellow-brown colour.
2 *(n)* If you have a **tan**, your skin has become darker because you have been out in the sun a lot. **tan** *(v)*.
3 *(v)* Animal skin is **tanned** to make it into leather. **tanner** *(n)*, **tannery** *(n)*.

tandoori *(n)* an Indian method of cooking meat, bread, etc. by baking it in a clay oven.

tangent
1 *(n)* a straight line that touches the edge of a curve in one place. See **circle**.
2 If you **go off at a tangent**, you start talking about something else.

tangerine *(n)* a small, sweet orange, that you can peel easily.

tangible *(adj)*
1 able to be touched.
2 actual. *Exercise has tangible benefits.*

tangle tangling tangled *(v)* to make things twisted and muddled. **tangle** *(n)*.

tank *(n)*
1 a large container for liquid or gas. See **aquarium**.
2 an armoured vehicle used by soldiers. See **armoured vehicle**.

tanker *(n)* a ship or lorry that carries gas or liquid. *This picture shows an oil tanker.*

pipes for cleaning cargo tanks — bridge
helipad
lifeboat
living accommodation, engine room, and control rooms
anchor — pipes for loading ballast water
oil tanker

tantrum *(n)* a fit of temper.

tap tapping tapped
1 *(n)* a piece of equipment used to control the flow of a liquid.
2 *(v)* to hit or knock something gently. **tap** *(n)*.
3 *(v)* to listen to a telephone conversation, using a secret device. **tap** *(n)*.
4 *(v)* to make a hole to draw off liquid. See **rubber**.
5 **tap-dancing** *(n)* dancing with shoes that have metal plates on their soles, that make a clicking noise. **tap-dancer** *(n)*, **tap-dance** *(v)*.

tape taping taped
1 *(n)* a thin strip of material, paper, plastic, etc. *Adhesive tape.*
2 *(v)* to fasten together, wrap, or bind with tape.
3 *(n)* a long piece of magnetic ribbon used for recording sound or pictures, usually contained in a plastic case or cassette.
4 *(v)* to record sound or pictures on audio or video tape.

a b c d e f g h i j k l m n o p q r s **t** u v w x y z

tape measure (n) a long, thin strip of material or steel, marked in centimetres or inches so that you can measure things with it.

taper tapering tapered
1 (v) to become narrower at one end.
2 **taper off** (v) to become gradually smaller.
3 (n) a wooden strip or thin candle used for carrying a flame. *We lit the candles with a taper.*

tape recorder (n) an electrical machine that you use to play or record music or sound. **tape-record** (v).

tapestry tapestries (n) a heavy piece of cloth with pictures or patterns woven into it. *The picture shows a tapestry being sewn.*

tapestry

single canvas
(made from hemp
or linen thread)

tapestry wool

tapestry
needle with
rounded head

tar (n) a thick, black, sticky substance, used for making roads.

tarantula (n) a large, hairy, venomous spider. See **spider**.

target targeting targeted
1 (n) something that you aim at or attack. **target** (v).
2 (n) a round object marked with circles, at which archers often aim their arrows.
3 (v) If you **target** something, you concentrate on it. *The publicity campaign is targeting young people.*

tariff (n)
1 a tax on imports and exports.
2 a list of prices in a hotel or restaurant.

tarmac (n) a mixture of tar and small stones that is used on road surfaces. Tarmac is short for Tarmacadam. **tarmac** (v).

tarnish tarnishes tarnishing tarnished (v) If something **tarnishes**, it becomes duller or less bright.

tarpaulin (n) a heavy, waterproof sheet.

tart tarter tartest
1 (n) an open fruit pie or pastry. *An apple tart.*
2 (adj) If food is **tart**, it tastes sour or sharp. **tartness** (n).
3 (adj) A **tart** reply is unkind or sarcastic. **tartly** (adv).

tartan (n) woollen cloth patterned with squares of different colours. Tartan is used especially for Scottish kilts.

task (n) a job or a duty.

task force (n) a team, especially of soldiers, formed to deal with a problem.

tassel (n) a bunch of threads tied at one end, used as a decoration on clothing, furniture, etc. **tasselled** (adj).

taste tasting tasted
1 (n) Your sense of **taste** tells you what food you are eating.
2 (n) The **taste** of a food is whether it is sweet, sour, bitter, salty, etc. **taste** (v), **tasty** (adj).
3 (n) If you have good **taste**, you make good choices of furnishings, clothes, etc. **tasteful** (adj).
4 (v) to try a bit of food or drink to see if you like it. **taste** (n).

tattered (adj) old and torn, or scruffy. *Tattered jeans.*

tattoo (n) a picture or words that have been permanently printed on someone's skin, using ink and needles. **tattooist** (n), **tattoo** (v).

tatty tattier tattiest (adj) shabby and worn out. **tattily** (adv).

taunt taunting taunted (v) to try to make someone angry or upset by teasing them. **taunt** (n).

taut (adj) stretched tight. *A taut rope.*

tavern (n) (old-fashioned) a pub or an inn.

tawny (n) a light, sandy brown colour. **tawny** (adj).

tax taxes (n) money that has to be paid to the government for public services. **taxation** (n), **tax** (v).

taxi taxiing taxied
1 (n) a car with a driver whom you pay to take you where you want to go.
2 (v) When planes **taxi**, they move along the ground.

taxing (adj) If something is **taxing**, it is demanding and puts a strain on you.

tea (tee) (n)
1 a drink made from the leaves of a tea plant. *The picture shows tea leaves being picked on a hillside plantation in Southern India.*

tea-picking

2 a light afternoon meal.
3 an evening meal, or supper.
4 **tea bag** a thin bag of tea leaves, which is added to water to make tea.
5 **tea cosy** a soft, insulating cover for a teapot, to keep the tea warm.
6 **tea light** a small, round candle.

teach teaches teaching taught (v) to give a lesson, or show someone how to do something. *Joel taught me how to swim.* **teacher** (n).

teal (n) a dark colour between green and blue. **teal** (adj).

team teaming teamed
1 (n) a group of people who work together or play a sport together. *A hockey team.* **teamwork** (n).
2 (v) If two people **team up**, they join together to do something.

team-mate (n) a fellow member of a team.

teapot (n) a container with a spout, lid, and handle, in which tea in made.

tear tearing tore torn
1 (rhymes with dear) (n) a drop of liquid that comes from your eye. **tearful** (adj).
2 (rhymes with dare) (n) a rip in a piece of paper or material.
3 (rhymes with dare) (v) to pull one part of something away from the rest. *Ben has torn his trousers.*
4 (rhymes with dare) (v) to move very quickly. *Louise tore down the street.*

tease teasing teased (v) to mock someone by saying unkind things to them.

teaspoon (n) a small spoon that you use for stirring drinks, or as a measure in cooking. **teaspoonful** (n).

teat (n)
1 a nipple of an animal, from which its babies can suck milk.
2 a rubber top for a baby's bottle, with a small hole in the top of it.

technical (adj)
1 to do with science, machines, industry, etc. **technically** (adv).
2 using words that only experts understand. *Once we started to talk about computers, the conversation became very technical.*

technician (tek-nish-un) (n) someone who looks after scientific equipment, or does practical laboratory work.

technique (tek-neek) (n) a skilful way of doing something.

technology technologies (n) the use of science to do practical things. **technological** (adj).

temper

teddy bear (n) a stuffed toy bear made from soft, furry material. *The teddy bear shown here was made in the Steiff factory in Germany.*

teddy bear

tedious (*tee-dee-us*) (adj) long and boring. **tediously** (adv).

teeming (adj) If a place is **teeming**, it is full of people or animals.

teenager (n) someone who is between the ages of 13 and 19. **teenage** or **teenaged** (adj).

teens (plural n) the years between 13 and 19. *Tanya is in her teens.*

teepee see **tepee**.

tee shirt see **T-shirt**.

teeth (plural n) the white, bone-like structures in your mouth that you use for biting and chewing food. *The diagram shows a lower set of adult teeth.*

human adult teeth
(lower jaw)

central incisor   lateral incisor

canine

first premolar

second premolar

first molar

second molar

third molar

teething
1 (adj) If a baby is **teething**, new teeth are coming through its gums.
2 **teething troubles** (plural n) the temporary problems that you may experience when you start a new job or activity.

teetotal (adj) If a person is **teetotal**, they do not drink alcohol. **teetotaller** (n).

telecommunication (n)
1 the science that deals with the sending of messages by telephone, satellite, radio, etc. See **satellite**.
2 a message sent in this way.

telegram (n) a message that is written down and sent by radio or electrical signals. Telegrams were used to give urgent news or congratulations.

telegraph (n) a way of sending messages using radio or electrical signals. **telegraph** (v).

telekinesis (*tel-ee-ken-ee-sis*) (n) the ability to move objects just with the power of the mind. **telekinetic** (*tel-ee-ken-et-ik*) (adj).

telemetry (n) the use of radio waves to transmit and record information from a measuring instrument.

telepathy (*tel-ep-ath-ee*) (n) If you use **telepathy**, you send your thoughts to someone else without speaking, writing, or making signs. **telepathic** (*tel-uh-path-ik*) (adj).

telephone (n) a machine which uses electrical wires and radio waves to enable you to speak to someone far away. *The image above shows a selection of early telephones. In each mechanism, the sound of a voice makes the mouthpiece vibrate, sending a signal along a wire. The earpiece picks up the vibrations and reproduces the sound.* **telephone** (v).

telephoto lens (n) a camera lens that makes things that are far away look closer and larger.

telescope (n) a tube-shaped instrument which makes things that are far away look closer and larger. Telescopes are used especially for looking at stars. *The picture shows a refractor telescope and a diagram of how the light travels through it.* **telescopic** (adj).

A 'candlestick' design from 1905.

An early experimental telephone made by Bell in 1875.

earpiece

mouthpiece

number dial

A plastic telephone from the 1930s.

early telephones

television (n)
1 a piece of equipment with a screen, that receives and shows moving pictures with sound.
2 the sending of sounds and moving pictures along radio waves to be picked up by a television.

tell telling told (v)
1 to speak to someone.
2 to show something. *The red light tells you to stop.*
3 to recognize or be certain. *It was hard to tell who it was in the dark.*
4 If you **tell someone off**, you scold them because they have done something wrong.

temper (n) an angry or impatient mood.

refractor telescope

objective lens   main telescope body   eyepiece lenses

incoming light

adjustable tube (controlled by focusing knob)

main telescope body

star diagonal prism

finderscope

protective ring (prevents glare on lens)

altazimuth mount (allows horizontal and vertical movement)

objective lens inside here

wingnut (holds telescope body steady)

focusing knob

eyepiece

star diagonal prism inside here

tripod leg

temperament (n)
your nature or your personality.
Laura has a very calm temperament.

temperamental (adj)
1 excited, unpredictable, or
moody. *A temperamental artist.*
2 caused by your temperament.
temperamentally (adv).

temperate (adj) If an area has a
temperate climate, it has neither
very high nor very low temperatures.

temperature (n)
1 a measure of how cold
or hot something is.
2 If you have a **temperature**,
your body is hotter than normal
because you are ill.

tempest (n) (poetic) a violent storm.

template (n) a shape or pattern
that you draw or cut around to
make the same shape in paper,
metal, material, etc. See **geometry**.

temple (n) a building used for
worship. *This reconstruction of the
Parthenon, a temple dedicated to the
Goddess Athena, shows how it would
have looked in the 5th century BC.*

2 If you are **tempted**, you are
attracted to doing something wrong.

temptation (n)
1 the act of being tempted.
Try to resist temptation.
2 something that you want to have
or do, although you know it is wrong.
That cake is such a temptation!

tenant (n) someone who rents
a room, house, office, etc.

tend tending tended (v)
1 If something **tends** to happen,
it often or usually happens.
It tends to rain this time of year.
2 If you **tend** a person, animal,
or plant, you take care of it.

tendency tendencies (n)
If you have a **tendency** to do
something, you often or usually do it.

tender (adj)
1 sore or sensitive. *Sal's bruises
were still tender.* **tenderness** (n).
2 soft. *A tender steak.* **tenderness** (n).
3 gentle and kind. *A tender kiss.*
tenderness (n), **tenderly** (adv).

tendon (n) a strong, thick cord that
joins a muscle to a bone. See **muscle**.

tenor (n)
1 a male singing voice that
is quite high. **tenor** (adj).
2 a singer with a tenor voice.

tenpin bowling (n)
an indoor game in which you roll
a large, heavy ball at a group of
wooden objects, called pins, in order
to try to knock them all down.

tense tenser tensest
1 (adj) If you are **tense**, you are
nervous or worried. *Miriam is
always tense before an exam.*
tenseness (n), **tensely** (adv).
2 (adj) stretched tight and stiff.
*Your muscles will be tense if you
don't warm up before a game.*
tenseness (n), **tense** (v).
3 (n) a form of a verb that shows
whether an action happened in the
past, is happening in the present,
or will happen in the future.

tension (n)
1 the tightness or stiffness of a rope,
wire, etc. *After you've put up your
tent, you should test the tension
of all the guy ropes.*
2 a feeling of worry, nervousness,
or suspense. *Tension mounted as
the boxers entered the ring.*
3 If there is **tension** between two
people, there is difficulty or strain
in their relationship.

tent (n) a shelter made of polyester or
canvas, supported by poles and ropes.

ridge tent

ridge pole
under here

adjuster

pole
spindle

upright
pole

guy
rope

door

peg

sewn-in
groundsheet

inner tent   hooded flysheet

The Parthenon,
Athens,
Greece
(cutaway)

cult statue of Athena,
goddess of war
and wisdom

cella
(inner
room)

terracotta
roof tiles

carved
and painted
frieze

acroterion

water
spout

marble column

peristyle
(row of columns)

treasury containing
jewellery, vases, and statues

statue of
Nike, goddess of
victory, on pillar

pronaos
(porch)

tempo (n) the speed or
timing of a piece of music.

temporary (adj) If something
is temporary, it lasts for only
a short time. **temporarily** (adv).

tempt tempting tempted (v)
1 If you **tempt** someone,
you make them want
something by telling
them how good it is
tempting (adj).

tennis (n) a game played on a
court by two or four players who
use rackets to hit a ball over a net.

**tennis
court**

baseline

centre mark

doubles
sideline

centre line

service line

right service
court

left service
court

singles
sideline

net

tentacle (n) one of the long,
flexible limbs of some animals such
as octopuses and squids. Tentacles
are used for moving and feeling.
See **jellyfish, octopus, slug, squid**.

tentative (adj) hesitant or unsure.
*Giles made a tentative attempt to
join in the game.* **tentatively** (adv).

tenterhooks (n) If you are on
tenterhooks, you are in suspense,
waiting for something to happen.

tenuous (ten-yoo-uss) (adj)
not very important or not very
significant. **tenuously** (adv).

tepee *or* **teepee**
(n) a round tent made from animal skins or canvas, used by Native Americans.

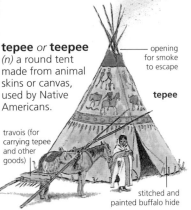

opening for smoke to escape

tepee

travois (for carrying tepee and other goods)

stitched and painted buffalo hide

tepid *(adj)* slightly warm.

term *(n)*
1 a part of the school year. **termly** *(adv)*.
2 a length of time. *The job is for a limited term of eight months.*
3 a word. *Musical terms.*
4 **terms** *(plural n)* the conditions of an agreement.

terminal
1 *(n)* a building where passengers arrive and leave. *An airport terminal.*
2 *(n)* a computer keyboard and screen linked to a network.
3 *(adj)* If someone has a **terminal** illness, they cannot be cured and will die from it. **terminally** *(adv)*.

terminate terminating terminated *(v)* to stop or to end. *The train terminates here.*

termite *(n)* an ant-like insect that destroys wood. Termites live together in colonies inside large mounds that they build themselves. *The picture shows a mound made by Nigerian termites.*

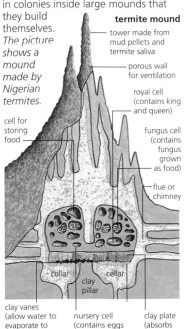

termite mound

tower made from mud pellets and termite saliva

porous wall for ventilation

royal cell (contains king and queen)

cell for storing food

fungus cell (contains fungus grown as food)

flue or chimney

cellar

clay pillar

cellar

clay vanes (allow water to evaporate to cool the cellar)

nursery cell (contains eggs and larvae)

clay plate (absorbs water)

terrace *(n)*
1 a row of houses joined together. **terraced** *(adj)*.
2 a flat area next to a house, café, etc. where you can sit.
3 **terraces** *(plural n)* wide steps where you stand to watch a match.

terracotta *(n)* a type of clay used for ornaments, pots, or roofs. *See* **temple**.

terrain *(n)* ground or land.

terrapin *(n)*
1 a water reptile with webbed feet and a shell.
2 a portable classroom, added to a school to create more space.

terrestrial *(adj)* to do with the Earth, or living on the Earth.

terrible *(adj)* very bad, shocking, or awful. *Thomas has a terrible sense of direction.* **terribly** *(adv)*.

terrific *(adj)*
1 very good or wonderful.
2 very great. *Rod set off at terrific speed.* **terrifically** *(adv)*.

terrify terrifies terrifying terrified *(v)* to frighten someone very much. *Ruth was terrified when she saw the spider.* **terrifying** *(adj)*, **terrifyingly** *(adv)*.

territory territories *(n)* an area of land, especially land that belongs to someone. **territorial** *(adj)*.

terror
1 *(n)* great fear. *His eyes were filled with terror.*
2 *(adj)* If you are **terror-struck**, you are so frightened that you cannot do anything.

terrorist *(n)* someone who uses violence, for example, bombing or hijacking, for political reasons. **terrorism** *(n)*.

terrorize *or* **terrorise** terrorizing terrorized *(v)* to frighten someone very much.

terse terser tersest *(n)* brief and abrupt. *When I asked Aunt Agatha her age, she gave a very terse reply.*

tertiary *(adj)* third in order.

tessellate tessellating tessellated *(v)* When shapes tessellate, they fit together exactly, without leaving gaps. *The picture below shows how hexagons tessellate.* **tessellated** *(adj)*.

tessellating shapes

test testing tested
1 *(n)* a set of questions or actions that check your knowledge or skill. **test** *(v)*.
2 *(n)* a medical examination or check-up. *A blood test.* **test** *(v)*.
3 *(v)* to try something out. *Esther tested the new recipe.* **test** *(n)*.

testicle *(test-ik-ul) (n)* one of the two glands behind a man's penis that produce sperm.

testify testifies testifying testified *(v)* to state the truth, or to give evidence in a court of law.

testimony testimonies *(n)* a statement given by a witness who is under oath, in a court of law.

test pilot *(n)* a pilot who flies new aeroplanes in order to test them.

test tube *(n)*
1 a small, thin, glass tube used in a science laboratory. *See* **apparatus**.
2 **test-tube baby** a baby that develops from an egg which has been fertilized outside the mother's body, but which then grows normally inside her womb.

tetanus *(n)* a serious disease caused by bacteria getting into a cut or wound. Tetanus makes your muscles, and especially your jaw, become stiff.

tether tethering tethered
1 *(v)* to tie up an animal so that it cannot move far. **tether** *(n)*.
2 If you are **at the end of your tether**, you have run out of patience.

text texting texted
1 *(n)* the main section of writing in a book, rather than the pictures or index.
2 *(n)* a text message.
3 *(v)* to write or send a text message.

textbook *(n)* a book used at school or college as part of a course.

text message *(n)* a message that you type into your phone and send to another person who reads it on their phone.

textile *(n)* a fabric or cloth.

texture *(n)* the feel of something, such as its roughness or smoothness.

thank thanking thanked
1 *(v)* to tell someone that you are grateful for what they have done.
2 **thanks** *(plural n)* spoken or written words showing that you are grateful.
3 **thank you** *(interject)* a phrase used to show that you are grateful for something that someone has done for you.

thankful *(adj)* glad or grateful. **thankfully** *(adv)*.

thatch

thatch thatches *(n)* straw or reeds used for making roofs. *The picture shows some features of a roof made of thatch.* **thatch** *(v)*, **thatched** *(adj)*.

straw ornament · ridge · **thatched cottage** · hip · block-cut pattern · thatch made from reeds or straw

thaw thawing thawed
1 *(v)* to defrost something after it has been frozen. *Leave the turkey to thaw overnight.*
2 *(n)* a time when snow and ice melt because the weather has become warmer.

theatre *(n)*
1 a place where you go to watch plays, shows, etc.
2 a part of a hospital where surgeons operate.

theatrical *(adj)*
1 to do with the theatre. *Theatrical costumes.*
2 If something is **theatrical**, it is intended to create a dramatic effect.

theft *(n)* the crime of stealing. *David is being punished for theft.*

their *(pronoun)* belonging to them. *Have the girls brought their books?* **theirs** *(pronoun)*.

them *(pronoun)* the things, people, etc. that have just been mentioned. *Owen and Aled will be here soon, so look out for them.*

theme *(theem) (n)*
1 the subject of a speech, book, film, etc.
2 a melody or a tune.
3 **theme park** a park with rides and attractions, based on a subject, such as the Wild West.

themselves *(pronoun)* them and no one else. *The children dressed themselves.*

then *(adv)*
1 at that time. *I didn't know Olivia then.*
2 afterwards. *Eat first, then talk.*
3 as a result. *If you stay up late, then you'll be tired tomorrow.*

theology theologies *(n)* the study of religion and religious beliefs. **theological** *(adj)*.

theorem *(n)* a statement, especially in maths, that can be proved to be true. *Pythagoras' theorem.*

theory *(rhymes with weary)* theories
1 *(n)* an idea that is intended to explain something.
2 *(n)* the rules and principles of a subject, rather than its practice. **theoretical** *(adj)*.
3 If something should happen in **theory**, you expect it to happen, but it may not. **theoretically** *(adv)*.

therapy therapies *(n)* a treatment for an illness, injury, or disability, for example, art therapy, or speech therapy. **therapist** *(n)*.

there
1 *(adv)* to, in, or at that place. *Let's not go there again!*
2 *(pronoun)* The word **there** is often used as a subject in sentences. *There is a man outside. There has been some mistake.*

therefore *(adv)* as a result. *Stanley is ill, therefore Joe must take his place.*

therm *(n)* a unit for measuring heat, especially heat from burning gas.

thermal
1 *(adj)* to do with heat, or holding in heat. *Thermal underwear.*
2 *(n)* a rising current of warm air.

thermometer *(n)* an instrument used to measure temperature. *The picture shows a clinical thermometer, which was used to measure body temperature. The bulb was usually placed under the tongue and, as the mercury heated up, it expanded and rose up the capillary tube.*

clinical thermometer

glass capillary tube · scale in Celsius and Fahrenheit · triangular glass stem (acts as a magnifying glass) · mercury · constriction in tube (prevents mercury returning to bulb) · thin-walled glass bulb

thermostat *(n)* a device connected to a radiator, iron, etc. that controls the temperature. *See* **refrigerator**.

thesaurus *(theh-saw-russ)* thesauruses *or* thesauri *(n)* a book containing lists of words with similar or related meanings.

these *(plural pronoun)* the things here, or the things being talked about. **these** *(adj)*.

thesis theses *(n)* an idea to be debated or proved.

they *(pronoun)*
1 the people, animals, or things being talked about.
2 people in general. *They say that it will snow.*

thick thicker thickest *(adj)*
1 wide, fat, or dense. *Thick walls. Thick soup.* **thickness** *(n)*, **thicken** *(v)*, **thickly** *(adv)*.
2 *(informal)* stupid.

thicket *(n)* a thick growth of plants, bushes, or small trees.

thief thieves *(n)* someone who steals things. **thieve** *(v)*, **thieving** *(adj)*.

thigh *(n)* Your **thigh** is the top part of your leg, between your knee and your hip.

thin thinner thinnest *(adj)* not fat, not thick, or not dense. *A thin cat. A thin sauce.* **thinness** *(n)*, **thin** *(v)*, **thinly** *(adv)*.

thing *(n)*
1 an object, idea, or event.
2 **things** *(plural n)* belongings. *Don't leave your things here.*

think thinking thought *(v)*
1 to use your mind. *Try to think of the answer.* **thinker** *(n)*.
2 to have an idea or opinion. *Sophie thinks boys are silly.*

third
1 *(n)* one of three equal parts.
2 *(adj)* If you come **third** in a race, you finish behind two other people. **thirdly** *(adv)*.

Third World *(n)* the poorer, developing countries of the world.

thirst *(n)*
1 a need for liquid. **thirst** *(v)*.
2 a longing for something. *Jesse has a great thirst for adventure.* **thirst** *(v)*.

thirsty thirstier thirstiest *(adj)* If you are **thirsty**, you want to drink something. **thirstily** *(adv)*.

this *(pronoun)* the thing here, or the thing being talked about. **this** *(adj)*.

thistle *(n)* a wild plant with prickly leaves and purple flowers.

spear thistle

thorax thoraxes *(n)*
1 the part of your body between your neck and your stomach.
2 the part of an insect's body between its head and its abdomen. *See* **beetle**.

thorn *(n)* a sharp point on the stem of a plant, such as a rose.

thorny thornier thorniest *(adj)*
1 covered with thorns.
2 difficult. *A thorny problem.*

thorough *(thuh-ruh) (adj)*
If you are **thorough**, you do
a job carefully and completely.
thoroughness *(n)*, **thoroughly** *(adv)*.

thoroughfare *(n)* a road or path
which is open at both ends. *Is there
a thoroughfare through the woods?*

those *(plural pronoun)*
the people or things there. *I don't
like those shoes.* **those** *(adj)*.

though *(thoh)*
1 *(conj)* even if, or despite the
fact that. *I'm still hungry, though
I've just had breakfast.*
2 *(adv)* nevertheless. *He's quite
friendly; I don't like him, though.*

thought *(thort) (n)*
1 an idea or opinion.
2 the act of thinking.
3 If you are **deep in thought**, you
are thinking hard about something.

thoughtful *(adj)*
1 serious or involving a lot of
thought. *A thoughtful essay.*
2 A **thoughtful** person considers
other people's feelings and needs.
thoughtfully *(adv)*.

thoughtless *(adj)*
A **thoughtless** person does not
consider other people's feelings
and needs. **thoughtlessly** *(adv)*.

thrash thrashes
thrashing thrashed *(v)*
1 to beat with a stick or a whip.
2 to beat someone thoroughly
in a game. **thrashing** *(n)*.
3 If you **thrash out** an idea
or a problem, you talk about
it until something is decided.

thread threading threaded
1 *(n)* a strand of cotton,
silk, etc. used for sewing.
2 *(v)* to pass a thread through
something, such as the eye
of a needle, or a set of beads.
3 *(n)* the raised, spiral ridge
around a screw.

threadbare *(adj)*
If your clothes are **threadbare**,
they are old and worn out.

threaten threatening
threatened *(v)* If someone
or something **threatens**
you, they frighten you or put
you in danger. **threat** *(n)*.

three-dimensional or **3-D**
(adj) solid, or not flat.
Cubes and spheres are
three-dimensional shapes.

thresh threshes threshing
threshed *(v)* to separate the
grain of a crop, such as wheat,
from the chaff and straw. *The
picture shows 19th-century farmers
threshing by hand, by beating the
corn with flails. Nowadays, most
farmers use combine
harvesters to thresh
their crops. Also
see **harvest**.*

straw
storage
bay

flagstone
threshing floor

ventilation slit

threshing barn
(cutaway)

sheaf storage bay

threshold *(n)*
1 the base of a doorway.
2 the beginning of something.
*We are on the threshold of
a great adventure!*

thrifty thriftier thriftiest *(adj)*
Someone who is **thrifty**
does not waste money,
food, supplies, etc. **thrift** *(n)*.

thrill *(n)*
a feeling of excitement and
pleasure. **thrill** *(v)*, **thrilling** *(adj)*.

thriller *(n)* an exciting story
about mystery, danger, or crime.

thrive thriving thrived *(v)*
to do well and flourish. *Roses thrive
in our garden. Yasmin is thriving
at her new school.* **thriving** *(adj)*.

throat *(n)*
1 the front of your neck.
2 the passage that runs from your
mouth into your stomach or lungs.

throb throbbing throbbed *(v)*
to beat in a regular way.
*The drumbeat throbbed
in my ears.* **throb** *(n)*.

throne
1 *(n)* an elaborate chair
for a king or queen.
*This picture from the
Bayeux Tapestry shows
Harold Godwinson
seated on his throne,
as King of England.*
2 If someone **comes
to the throne**, they
become king or queen.

throne

throng *(n)* a large crowd
of people. **throng** *(v)*.

throttle throttling throttled
1 *(v)* If you **throttle** someone,
you squeeze their throat so
that they cannot breathe.
2 *(n)* a valve in a vehicle's
engine that opens to let fuel,
or fuel and air, flow into it.

through *(throo)*
1 *(prep)* from one end or side to
the other. *Lily squeezed through
the crowd.* **through** *(adv)*.
2 *(prep)* by way of, or because of.
Elsa got the job through a friend.
3 *(adv)* completely. *Jacques was
wet through.* **through** *(adj)*.

throughout *(prep)*
all the way through. *Chickenpox
spread throughout the school.*
throughout *(adv)*.

throw throwing threw thrown *(v)*
1 to make something move,
especially through the air.
Dean threw the ball. **throw** *(n)*.
2 *(informal)* If something
throws you, it confuses you.
3 **throw away**
to get rid of
something.
4 **throw up** *(informal)*
to vomit.

thrush thrushes *(n)*
a garden bird, often
with a brown back
and a spotted breast.

song
thrush

thrust
thrusting thrust
1 *(v)* to push
something suddenly
and hard. **thrust** *(n)*.
2 *(n)* The **thrust** of an
argument is its main point.

thud *(n)*
a noise like the sound of a heavy
object falling on the ground. **thud** *(v)*.

thug *(n)* a violent person.

thumb thumbing thumbed
1 *(n)* the short, thick digit
that you have on each hand.
2 *(v)* to turn over the pages of a book.
3 *(v) (informal)* If you **thumb**
a lift, you hitchhike.

thump thumping thumped
1 *(v)* to hit someone or something
with your fist. **thump** *(n)*.
2 *(n)* a dull sound. *The paper landed
on the mat with a thump.* **thump** *(v)*.

thunder thundering thundered
1 *(n)* the loud, rumbling sound
that you hear during a storm.
2 *(v)* to make a loud noise like
thunder. *The trucks thundered past.*

a b c d e f g h i j k l m n o p q r s **t** u v w x y z

thwart thwarting thwarted *(v)*
If you **thwart** someone's plans, you prevent those plans from happening.

tiara *(n)*
a piece of jewellery like a small crown.

tick ticking ticked
1 *(n)* the sound that a clock or watch makes. **tick** *(v)*.
2 *(n)* a mark that someone makes to show that an answer is correct or that something has been done. **tick** *(v)*.
3 *(n)* a very small insect that lives on the skin of some animals.
4 **tick off** *(v)* *(informal)* If you **tick someone off**, you make them angry.

ticket *(n)* a printed piece of paper or card that proves that you have paid to do something. *A train ticket.*

tickle tickling tickled *(v)*
to keep touching or poking someone gently, often causing them to laugh or feel irritated. **ticklish** *(adj)*.

tiddlywinks *(plural n)*
a game in which each player tries to flick plastic counters into a cup.

tide *(n)* the constant change in sea level, caused by the pull of the Sun and the Moon. **tidal** *(adj)*.

tidings *(plural n)* *(poetic)* news.

tidy tidier tidiest *(adj)* neat, or in proper order. **tidiness** *(n)*, **tidy** *(v)*.

tie ties tying tied
1 *(v)* to join two pieces of string, cord, etc. together with a knot.
2 *(n)* a long piece of fabric which is worn knotted around the collar of a shirt.
3 *(n)* a situation in which two people finish level in a competition. *There was a tie for second place.* **tie** *(v)*.

tie-break or **tie-breaker** *(n)*
a special game played or question asked to decide the result of a match or competition when the players have won the same number of points.

tier *(teer) (n)*
one of several levels, placed one above the other, for example, a row of seats in a theatre or a layer of a wedding cake. **tiered** *(adj)*.

tiger *(n)* a large, striped, wild cat found in Asia.

tiger and cubs

tight tighter tightest
1 fitting closely, or fastened closely. *Tight jeans.* **tighten** *(v)*, **tightly** *(adv)*.
2 fully stretched. **tighten** *(v)*.
3 *(informal)* mean with money.
4 *(informal)* drunk.

tightrope *(n)*
a stretched, high wire on which circus performers balance.

tights *(plural n)*
a close-fitting garment that covers your hips, legs, and feet.

tile *(n)*
a small, flat piece of baked clay, cork, slate, etc., often used for covering floors, roofs, or walls. *The picture shows a baked clay, or ceramic, tile.* **tile** *(v)*.

Dutch ceramic tile

till tilling tilled
1 *(prep)* until. *Wait till I call for you.*
2 *(n)* a drawer or box in a shop, used to hold money, and often part of a cash register.
3 *(v)* to plough the soil ready for planting crops.

tilt tilting tilted *(v)*
to lean to one side. **tilt** *(n)*.

timber *(n)* cut wood used for furniture making, building, etc.

time timing timed
1 *(n)* the passing of seconds, minutes, hours, etc.
2 *(n)* a particular moment shown on a clock or watch. *What is the time now?*
3 *(n)* a particular period. *A time of great happiness.*
4 *(v)* to measure how long something takes. *I'll time you while you run.*
5 *(v)* to choose the moment for something. *Harry timed his entrance perfectly.*

timetable *(n)* a chart of the times when events, lessons, travel departures, etc. are planned to happen. **timetable** *(v)*.

timid *(adj)* shy and easily frightened. **timidly** *(adv)*.

tin *(n)*
1 a silvery metal used to make alloys and food cans.
2 a food can.

tinge *(tinj) (n)*
1 a very small amount of added colour. *White with a tinge of pink.*
2 a slight feeling. *Indra's smile had a tinge of sadness to it.*

tingle tingling tingled *(v)*
to sting, prick, or tickle. **tingle** *(n)*.

tinker tinkering tinkered *(v)*
to work at or fiddle with something, with the aim of repairing it or improving it.

tint *(n)* a small amount of added colour. **tint** *(v)*, **tinted** *(adj)*.

tiny tinier tiniest *(adj)* very small.

tip tipping tipped
1 *(v)* to make something lean or fall over.
2 *(v)* to lean or to fall over.
3 *(n)* the thin end of something. *The tip of a snooker cue.*
4 *(n)* a useful hint.
5 *(n)* a sum of money given, in addition to the bill, to a waitress, taxi driver, etc. as thanks for their services.
6 *(n)* a rubbish dump.

tiptoe tiptoeing tiptoed *(v)*
to walk quietly, without putting your heels down.

tire tiring tired *(v)*
1 to make someone tired, or to become tired and weak. **tiredness** *(n)*, **tired** *(adj)*, **tiring** *(adj)*.
2 to become bored. *I soon tired of Terry's chatter.*

tiresome *(adj)* boring, irritating, or annoying. **tiresomely** *(adv)*.

tissue *(tish-yoo* or *tiss-yoo) (n)*
1 soft, thin paper used for wiping, wrapping, etc.
2 a mass of cells which form the flesh and muscle of a living creature.

title *(n)*
1 the name of a book, film, etc.
2 the very first part of a person's name, for example, Ms, Mrs, Mr.
3 a special name, showing a high position in society, for example, Sir, Dame, Lord, Lady. **titled** *(adj)*.

toad *(n)* an amphibian similar to a frog, but with rougher skin, that lives mainly on land. *The male midwife toad carries strands of eggs wrapped around its back legs for several weeks before depositing them in a pond to hatch.*

midwife toad

toadstool *(n)* a fungus with a rounded top on a stalk. Most toadstools are poisonous.

toast toasting toasted
1 *(n)* grilled bread. **toast** *(v)*.
2 *(v)* to drink in honour of someone. **toast** *(n)*.

tobacco *(n)* the chopped, dried leaves of the tobacco plant, smoked in pipes, cigars, and cigarettes.

Some words that begin with a "ti" sound are spelt "ty".

toboggan
tobogganing tobogganed
1 *(n)* a small sledge.
2 *(v)* to travel by toboggan, especially downhill.

today
1 *(n)* this day. *Today's weather is good.* **today** *(adv)*.
2 *(adv)* nowadays, or at the present time. *Today, most adults can read and write.*

toddler *(n)*
a young child who has just learned to walk.

toe *(n)*
one of the five digits at the end of your foot.

toffee *(n)*
a chewy sweet made from boiled sugar and butter.

toga *(n)* a piece of clothing worn by Ancient Romans. It was wrapped around the body and over the left shoulder.

toga

together *(adv)* with another person or thing. *The boys arrived together.*

toil **toiling toiled** *(v)* to work very hard and continuously. **toil** *(n)*.

toilet *(n)*
1 a large bowl with flushing water, used for disposing of urine and faeces.
2 a room or building with toilets.

token *(n)*
1 a small, physical object used to represent something larger, or to show someone's feelings. *Rob gave Sue a ring as a token of his love.*
2 a card or piece of paper that can be exchanged for goods or services. *A book token.*

tolerate **tolerating tolerated** *(v)* If you **tolerate** something, you put up with it or endure it. *It is difficult to tolerate rude people.* **tolerant** *(adj)*.

toll **tolling tolled**
1 *(v)* If you **toll** a bell, you ring it, usually in a slow, solemn way.
2 *(n)* a charge for using a private road or bridge. **toll** *(adj)*.
3 If something **takes its toll**, it results in serious damage or suffering. *Years of hard labour have taken their toll on his health.*

tomahawk *(n)* a war axe used by Native Americans. *This decorated tomahawk was used by the Shawnee people.*

tomahawk

tomato **tomatoes** *(n)*
a red fruit, often eaten in salads.

tomb *(n)* a grave, usually for an important person. *The picture shows the tomb of Robert Curthose, Duke of Normandy, in Gloucester Cathedral, England.*

tomb

tomboy *(n)*
a girl who enjoys activities more often associated with boys, such as climbing trees or playing football.

tombstone *(n)*
a carved block of stone which marks the place where someone is buried.

household tools

mole wrench

side cutting nippers

screwdrivers

electrician's pliers

adjustable spanner

cross head screwdriver

hammer

stanley knife

chisel

mains tester

files

soldering iron

open-ended spanner

spirit level

hacksaws

tomorrow *(n)*
the day after today. **tomorrow** *(adv)*.

tone *(n)*
1 the way that something sounds.
2 the general atmosphere of a place or situation. *A cheerful tone.*
3 In music, a **tone** is an interval between two notes that is equal to two semitones.
4 a shade of a colour. *A pink tone.*

tongs *(plural n)*
a tool with two connected arms, used for picking up things.

tongue *(tung)* *(n)*
1 a flap of muscle in your mouth, used for tasting, eating, and talking.
2 a language. *Native tongue.*

tongue twister *(n)* a sentence or verse that is very hard to say fast, for example, "Red lorry, yellow lorry".

tonic *(n)*
1 something that makes you feel better. *Our holiday was a real tonic.*
2 a slightly bitter-tasting mineral water, that is often mixed with alcoholic drinks.

tonight *(n)*
this evening or night. **tonight** *(adv)*.

tonsillitis *(n)* a disease that makes your tonsils infected and painful.

tonsils *(plural n)*
two flaps of soft tissue in your throat at the back of your mouth.

too *(adv)*
1 as well, or in addition. *Is Janey coming too?*
2 very, extremely, or more than enough. *The heavy metal band was too noisy for Granny.*

tool *(n)* a piece of equipment that you use to do a particular job.

tooth **teeth** *(n)*
1 one of the white, bone-like structures in your mouth, used for biting and chewing food. *Also see* **teeth**.
2 one of a row of sticking out parts on a saw, comb, cogwheel, etc. *See* **gear**.

enamel — crown

gum — neck

pulp cavity (contains blood vessels and nerve endings) — root

dentine (bone-like substance) — cement

— root canal

human molar (cutaway)

nerve

blood vessels

a b c d e f g h i j k l m n o p q r s t u v w x y z

top

top topping topped
1 (n) the highest point of something.
2 (adj) very good or best. *A top singer.*
3 (n) a covering or a lid. *A bottle top.*
4 (n) a piece of clothing for the upper part of your body.
5 (v) to be the best, or to lead. *Fred topped the class in spelling.*

top-heavy (adj) If something is top-heavy, it is heavier towards the top, and therefore likely to fall over.

topic (n)
1 the subject of a discussion, study, lesson, etc.
2 an extended study on a particular subject, usually in a primary school.

topical (adj) relevant now, or in the news at present.

topple toppling toppled (v) to fall over, usually from a height.

Torah (n) the sacred scroll in a Jewish synagogue, on which the books of Genesis, Exodus, Leviticus, Numbers, and Deuteronomy are written in Hebrew.

torch torches (n)
1 a battery-powered light that you can carry with you.
2 a piece of wood dipped in wax or fat, used to light buildings in medieval times.

toreador (toh-ree-a-dor) (n) a bullfighter mounted on a horse.

torment tormenting tormented
1 (tor-ment) (v) to upset or annoy someone deliberately.
2 (tor-ment) (n) great pain.

tornado tornados *or* tornadoes (n) a windstorm that swirls in a circle.

torpedo torpedoes (n) an underwater missile that explodes when it hits something.

torrent (n) a large mass of flowing or falling water. **torrential** (adj).

torso (n) the part of your body between your neck and your waist.

tortoise (n)
a slow-moving reptile with a shell and thick, scaly skin. *The giant tortoise in the picture is allowing finches to crawl over its body in search of parasites.*

giant tortoise

torture
torturing tortured (v) to cause someone extreme pain. **torture** (n).

Tory Tories (n) a nickname for a member of the British Conservative Party. **Tory** (adj).

toss tosses
tossing tossed (v)
1 to throw something up.
2 to throw something away casually.

total
1 (n) the result of an addition or multiplication calculation. *Add up these figures and give me the total.* **total** (v).
2 (adj) complete and utter. *The party was a total surprise.* **totally** (adv).

totem pole (n) a carved pole that acts as a sacred emblem for a tribe or family of Native Americans. *The painted totem pole shown here is in Stanley Park, Vancouver, Canada.* **totem pole**

totter tottering tottered (v) to sway and stagger.

toucan (too-kan) (n) a brightly-coloured tropical bird which has a huge beak.

toucan

touch touches touching touched
1 (v) to make contact with something, using your hands or other areas of your body. **touch** (n).
2 (v) to make gentle contact with another object. *The ship touched the quay as it docked.* **touch** (n).
3 (n) Your **sense of touch** is your ability to feel things with your fingers, or with other parts of your body.
4 If you **keep in touch** with someone, you contact them regularly, by text, email, etc.

touchdown (n) the moment when an aircraft or a spacecraft lands.

touching (adj) appealing to the emotions. **touchingly** (adv).

touchline (n) the line marking the side of a pitch in sports such as soccer and rugby. *See* **soccer**.

touchscreen (n) a computer or phone that is operated by touching the screen. **touchscreen** (adj).

touchy touchier touchiest (adj) irritable and easily annoyed. **touchiness** (n).

tough (tuff) tougher toughest (adj)
1 strong and difficult to damage, either physically or mentally. *Tough boots. A tough personality.*
2 difficult. *A tough decision.*

toupee (too-pay) (n) a piece of false hair, usually used to disguise a man's baldness.

tour
1 (n) a journey around a set route, often for sightseeing. **tour** (v).
2 When a band or team go **on tour**, they go to different places to play.

tourist (n) someone who travels and visits places for pleasure. **tourism** (n).

tournament (n)
1 a competition for players of sports, chess, cards, etc. *A tennis tournament.*
2 In the Middle Ages, **tournaments** were events where knights jousted against each other. *See* **joust**.

tourniquet (tor-nik-ay) (n) a very tight bandage or band put around a wounded limb to stop the flow of blood.

tow towing towed (v) to pull something behind you, usually with a rope, chain, etc. *The breakdown truck towed the car away.* **tow** (n).

towards *or* **toward** (prep) in the direction of. *Oswin marched towards the door.*

towel (n) a thick, soft, absorbent cloth for drying yourself.

tower
towering towered
1 (n) a tall structure that is thin in relation to its height. *The picture shows the Leaning Tower of Pisa in Italy.*
2 (v) to be very tall and dominant. *The skyscraper towered over the houses.*

tower

town (n)
a place with houses, shops, offices, schools, etc. where many people live.

towpath (n)
a path beside a canal or river.

toxic (adj) poisonous. **toxin** (n).

toy toying toyed
1 (n) an object that people play with.
2 (v) If you **toy with** something, you play with it in a half-hearted, unenthusiastic way.

trace tracing traced
1 (v) to find out where someone or something is.
2 (v) to draw over the outline of a shape. **tracing** (n).
3 (n) a visible sign that something has happened or that someone has been somewhere. *Traces of blood.*

tracks

brown hare

pigeon

reindeer

fox

brown bear

track tracking tracked
1 (n) the marks left behind by a moving animal or person.
2 (n) a path or route.
3 (n) a course used for races. *A greyhound racing track.*
4 (v) to follow someone or something. **tracking** (n).

track and field (n)
competitive athletic sports that involve running, jumping, or throwing. *The picture shows the standard layout of a stadium used for track and field.* **track-and-field** (adj).

track-and-field stadium

pole vault runway

landing area

high jump fan

running lane

back straight

eight lane track

hammer and discus cage

finish line

home straight

infield

javelin runway

shot-putting circle

triple jump runway

long jump runway

landing area

tracksuit (n) loose trousers and a top, usually worn for sports.

traction (n)
the friction or gripping power that stops something from slipping on a surface as it moves.

tractor (n) a powerful vehicle used on farms. Tractors are often used to pull farm machinery or heavy loads. *Also see* **farm**.

tractor
(cutaway)

radio aerial
access panel
front work light
rear-view mirror
exhaust pipe
steering wheel on telescoping column
radiator
engine air filter
air pre-cleaner
front drawbar
front linkage (connects tractor to other machinery)
headlight
battery
control panel
driver's swivel seat
sunroof and escape hatch
air-conditioned driver's cab
control buttons
step
passenger seat
chevron tread tyre
side light
tool box
rear wheel with disk brakes

trade trading traded
1 (n) the business of buying and selling things. **trader** (n), **trade** (v).
2 (n) a particular job or craft. *Bob's trade is plumbing.*

3 (v) to exchange one thing for another. *We've started a club to trade computer games.*

trademark (n) a name, sign, or design that shows that a product is made by a particular company.

trade union or **trades union** (n) an organized group of workers, set up to help improve working conditions and pay. **trade unionist** (n).

tradition (n) a custom that has been passed down from generation to generation. **traditional** (adj).

traffic trafficking trafficked
1 (n) moving vehicles. *Heavy traffic.*
2 (v) to buy and sell drugs or other goods illegally. **trafficking** (n).

traffic jam (n) a line of vehicles that can hardly move because there are so many cars on the road.

traffic lights (plural n) a set of lights that controls traffic on roads.

traffic warden (n)
someone whose job is to check that vehicles are parked legally.

tragedy tragedies (n)
1 a serious play with a sad ending.
2 a very sad event. **tragic** (adj), **tragically** (adj).

trail trailing trailed
1 (n) a track or path to follow.
2 (v) to follow someone or something, to check up on or catch them.
3 (v) to follow slowly behind others.

trailer (n)
1 a vehicle that is towed by a car or truck and used to carry things.
2 a short piece of film used to advertise a film or programme to be shown in the future.

train training trained
1 (n) a string of railway carriages pulled by an engine. *The train shown below is a French TGV Atlantic, which is powered by electricity from overhead wires.*
2 (v) to learn how to do something, such as a job. **training** (n).
3 (v) to teach a person or animal how to do something. *You need to potty train your new puppy.*
4 (v) to practise and prepare for a sports event. **training** (n).
5 (n) the long piece of fabric that trails behind a bride's dress.

train (cutaway)

pantograph (carries electric current to train from overhead wires)

motor ventilation system

brake rheostat (controls braking)

driver's cab

windscreen wiper

light

passenger carriage

motor ventilator

main transformer (changes high voltage from overhead wires to lower working voltage)

freon tank (stores gas to cool motor)

traction motor (drives wheels)

auxiliary energy supply unit (alternative energy source)

bogie (wheeled support for traction motor)

railway track

trainer (n)
1 someone who helps a person or an animal become good enough to compete in a sport or competition.
2 a light shoe with a thick sole, designed to be used for sport.

traitor (n) someone who betrays their country or friends by working for an enemy. **traitorous** (adj).

tram (n) a large vehicle that carries passengers. Trams run on rails laid in roads and are usually powered by electricity from overhead wires.

tramp tramping tramped
1 (v) to go for a long walk. *We tramped through the countryside.* **tramp** (n).
2 (v) to walk or tread with heavy steps. **tramp** (n).
3 (n) someone who does not have a permanent home.

trample trampling trampled (v) to damage something by walking all over it. *My phone has been trampled.*

trampoline (n) a piece of thick, stretchy material attached to a frame by elastic ropes or springs. Trampolines are used for jumping on, for sport or pleasure. **trampolining** (n).

trance (n) If you are in a trance, you are conscious, but not really aware of what is happening around you.

tranquil (tran-kwil) (adj) calm and peaceful. **tranquillity** (n).

transaction (n) a business deal. **transact** (v).

transatlantic (adj)
1 crossing the Atlantic Ocean. *A transatlantic telephone call.*
2 on or from the other side of the Atlantic. *A transatlantic trend.*

transfer transferring transferred
1 (trans-fur) (v) to move a person or thing from one place to another. *I transferred the ball to my right hand.* **transfer** (trans-fur) (n).
2 (trans-fur) (n) a small picture or design that can be stuck to another surface by rubbing or ironing.

transform transforming transformed (v) to make a great change in something. *Meeting Alphonso has transformed my life.* **transformation** (n).

transformer (n) a piece of equipment that changes the voltage of an electric current.

transfusion (n) the injection of blood from another person into the body of someone who is injured or ill.

transient (adj) lasting for a short time only. **transience** (n).

transistor (n) a small electrical component that controls the flow of a current.

transit (n) If goods are in transit, they are being moved from one place to another.

transition (n) a change from one situation to another.

transitive (adj) A transitive verb usually needs a direct object to make sense. *The verbs "to hit", "to pull", and "to cut" are all transitive.*

translate translating translated (v) to put something into another language. **translation** (n), **translator** (n).

translucent (adj) A translucent substance is not clear, like glass, but will still let the light through. *Frosted glass is translucent.* **translucency** (n).

transmit transmitting transmitted (v)
1 to send something from one place or person to another. **transmission** (n).
2 to send out radio or television signals. *The programme will be transmitted next Friday.* **transmission** (n), **transmitter** (n).

transparency (singular n) If you work with **transparency**, you operate in a way that makes it easy for others to see and understand what is being done, especially in business, finance, and government.

transparent (adj)
1 A transparent substance is clear, like glass, and lets light through.
2 obvious or clear. *The woman was a transparent liar.* **transparency** (n).

transpiration (n) the process by which plants lose moisture into the atmosphere. **transpire** (v).

transplant transplanting transplanted
1 (trans-plant) (v) to remove something, like a plant, and put it somewhere else.
2 (trans-plant) (n) a surgical operation in which a diseased organ, such as a kidney, is replaced by a healthy one.

transport transporting transported
1 (trans-port) (v) to move people and goods from one place to another.
2 (trans-port) (singular n) all types of vehicles that carry people or goods.

trap trapping trapped (v) to capture a person or an animal by using some sort of trick or bait. **trap** (n).

trap door (n) a horizontal door in a floor or ceiling.

trapeze *(trap-eez)* *(n)*
a bar hanging from two ropes, used
by circus performers and gymnasts.

trapezium
trapeziums *or* **trapezia** *(n)*
a four-sided shape with one pair of
opposite parallel sides. *See* **shape**.

trash
1 *(n)* rubbish or nonsense.
2 *(v)* to damage or destroy.

traumatic *(adj)* If something
is **traumatic**, it is shocking and
very upsetting. **trauma** *(n)*.

travel **travelling** **travelled** *(v)* to go
from one place to another. **travel** *(n)*.

travel agent *(n)*
a person or company that organizes
travel and holidays for its customers.
travel agency *(n)*.

traveller *(n)*
1 someone who is travelling
or who travels regularly.
2 a travelling sales representative.
3 someone who lives in a van
or mobile home and travels
around, often in a group.

trawler *(n)* a fishing boat that
drags a large, bag-shaped net
through the water. **trawl** *(v)*.

tray *(n)* a flat board used
for carrying food and drinks.

treacherous *(tretch-er-uss)* *(adj)*
dangerous or not to be trusted.
*A treacherous character. A treacherous
path.* **treacherously** *(adv)*.

treacle *(n)*
a sweet, sticky syrup made from sugar.

tread **treading** **trod** **trodden**
1 *(v)* to put your foot
down on the ground.
I have trodden in some mud.
2 *(n)* the ridges on a tyre
or on the sole of a shoe
that help to prevent slipping.

treason *(n)* the crime of betraying
your country, for example, by spying
for another country.

treasure **treasuring** **treasured**
1 *(n)* very precious and valuable
objects, such as gold and jewels.
2 *(v)* to love and value very highly
something that you have or own.
I treasure my independence.
treasure *(n)*, **treasured** *(adj)*.

treasurer *(n)*
the person who looks after the
money for an organization, club, etc.

treasury **treasuries** *(n)*
1 a place where treasure
is stored. *See* **temple**.
2 the funds of an organization,
government, etc.

treat **treating** **treated** *(v)*
1 to deal with people or things
in a certain way. *In China, old
people are treated with great
respect.* **treatment** *(n)*.
2 Doctors **treat** people to try to
cure them of illness. **treatment** *(n)*.
3 to process something in order to
change it in some way. *Sewage is
treated with chemicals to make it
harmless.* **treatment** *(n)*.
4 to give someone a special gift, or
take someone somewhere special.
*Uncle Bonzo treated us to tea at
a smart hotel.* **treat** *(n)*.

treaty **treaties** *(n)*
a formal agreement between
two or more countries.

treble
1 *(adj)* three times as big, or
three times as many. **treble** *(v)*.
2 *(adj)* high-pitched. *A treble recorder.*
3 *(n)* a boy's singing voice
that is very high.

tree *(n)* a large, woody plant
with a trunk, roots, branches,
and leaves. *See* **trunk**.

trek **trekking** **trekked** *(v)*
to walk a long way, often in
difficult conditions. **trek** *(n)*.

trellis **trellises** *(n)* a criss-cross
framework of thin strips of wood,
used to support growing plants.

tremble **trembling** **trembled** *(v)*
to shake, especially from fear
or excitement.

tremendous *(adj)*
1 huge or enormous. *A tremendous
explosion.* **tremendously** *(adv)*.
2 very good or excellent.
We had a tremendous time.

tremor *(n)* a shaking movement.
*Earth tremors are very common
in the earthquake belt.*

trench **trenches** *(n)*
a long, thin channel dug in the ground.

trend *(n)*
1 the general direction in which things
are changing. *Recently, there has been
a trend towards smaller families.*
2 the latest fashion. *The trend
this season is for shorter skirts.*
trendy *(adj)*.

trespass **trespasses**
trespassing **trespassed** *(v)*
1 to enter someone's
private property without
permission. **trespasser** *(n)*.
2 *(n)* *(old-fashioned)*
to commit a sin. **trespass** *(n)*.

tress **tresses** *(n)* *(poetic)*
a lock of hair.

trial *(n)*
1 a test. *Athletes have to do a trial if
they want to join the team.* **trial** *(adj)*.
2 the examination of someone
who appears in court accused
of a criminal offence.

trial bike *(n)*
a light, strong motorcycle built for
cross-country racing and riding.

triangle *(n)*
1 a three-sided shape.
triangular *(adj)*. *See* **shape**.
2 a triangular percussion instrument.
You play the triangle by striking it
with a metal rod. *See* **percussion**.

tribe *(n)*
a group of people who share
the same ancestors, customs,
and laws. **tribal** *(n)*.

tribunal *(n)* a law court.

tributary **tributaries** *(n)*
a stream or river that flows into
a larger stream or river. *See* **river**.

tribute
If you **pay tribute to** someone
or something, you praise them.

trick **tricking** **tricked**
1 *(v)* If you **trick** someone, you
make them believe something
that is not true. *Kevin tricked
me into believing that he was
related to the Queen.* **trick** *(n)*.
2 *(n)* a clever and entertaining act.
A magic trick.

trickle **trickling** **trickled** *(v)*
to flow very slowly in small
quantities. *Water constantly
trickled from the tap.* **trickle** *(n)*.

tricky **trickier** **trickiest** *(adj)*
difficult or awkward. *A tricky situation.*

tricycle *(n)* a three-wheeled cycle.

trident *(n)* a spear with
three prongs. *See* **gladiator**.

trifle *(n)*
1 a dessert made from
layers of sponge cake,
fruit, jelly, custard and cream.
2 something that is not very
important. **trifling** *(adj)*.

trigger **triggering** **triggered**
1 *(n)* the lever on a gun that you
pull to fire it. *See* **blunderbuss**.
2 *(v)* to cause something to happen,
as a reaction. *The man's arrest
triggered riots in the streets.*

trim **trimming** **trimmed**;
trimmer **trimmest**
1 *(v)* to cut small pieces off
something in order to improve
its shape. **trim** *(n)*.
2 *(adj)* slim and shapely.
A trim waistline.

trimming (n)
1 something used as a decoration.
2 **trimmings** (plural n) the things that go with something. *Roast turkey and all the trimmings.*

spotted grouper

■ French angelfish

trio (n)
1 a group of three things or people.
2 a piece of music that is played or sung by three people.

trip tripping tripped
1 (v) to stumble or to fall over.
2 (n) a journey or a visit. *A trip to the zoo.* **tripper** (n).

■ longnose filefish

triple tripling tripled
1 (v) to make something three times as big or three times as many. **triple** (adj).
2 (adj) made up of three parts. *The triple jump involves a hop, a step, and a jump.*

■ common clownfish

yellow longnose butterflyfish

triplet (n) one of three children born to the same mother at almost the same time.

tripod (n) a three-legged stand used to support a camera or other piece of equipment. See **apparatus**.

trireme (try-reem) (n) an Ancient Greek warship, propelled by oars.

triumph (n) a victory or a great achievement. **triumph** (v), **triumphant** (adj).

trivial (adj) If something is **trivial**, it is not very important. *Don't bother me with such trivial questions.* **trivia** (plural n), **trivialize** (v).

trolley (n)
1 a two or four-wheeled cart used for carrying things. *A shopping trolley.*
2 a table on wheels.

troop trooping trooped
1 (n) an organized group of soldiers, scouts, etc.
2 (v) to move in a group. *Sid and his friends trooped through the house.*

trophy (troh-fee) trophies (n) a prize or award, especially a cup.

tropic (n)
1 one of the lines of latitude that are 23.5° north and south of the equator, and are called the Tropic of Cancer and the Tropic of Capricorn.
2 **the tropics** (plural n) the extremely hot area between the Tropic of Cancer and the Tropic of Capricorn.

tropical (adj) to do with, or living in the hot, rainy area of the tropics.

tropical fish tropical fish (n) fish that originally come from the tropics. *This picture shows a range of tropical fish.*

tropical fish
■ freshwater
■ saltwater

■ swordtail

■ Siamese fighting fish

■ neon tetra

■ multispotted catfish

trot trotting trotted (v) When a horse **trots**, it moves briskly at a pace between a walk and a canter. **trot** (n).

trouble troubling troubled
1 (n) a difficult or dangerous situation. **troublesome** (adj).
2 (v) to disturb or worry someone. *The letter troubled Amelia.*
3 If you **take the trouble** to do something, you make an effort to do it.
4 (v) to bother someone by asking them for help.

trough (troff) (n) a long, narrow container from which animals can drink or feed.

trousers (plural n) a piece of clothing with two legs that covers the lower part of your body.

trout trout (n) an edible, freshwater fish.

trowel (n)
1 a tool with a small, curved blade used for planting and other light garden work.
2 a tool with a flat, diamond-shaped blade, used for laying cement, filling holes in plaster, etc.

truant (n)
1 (n) a pupil who stays away from school without permission. **truancy** (n).
2 If pupils **play truant,** they stay away from school without permission.

truce (n) a temporary agreement to stop fighting.

truck (n)
1 a large motor vehicle used for carrying goods by road. *The picture shows an articulated truck, which is made up of a cab and a trailer, linked by a flexible joint.*
2 a large container used for carrying goods by rail.

articulated truck (cutaway) — ladder — hydraulic lift for tipping semi-trailer — air deflector — rear view mirrors — anti-glar shield

semi-trailer

tractor unit

bunk bed

folding seat

tri-axle bogie (wheel and axle unit)

handle for landing leg

fuel tank

exhaust pipe

hydraulic cab tilt pump

step

driver's cab

raised landing leg

rear wheel of tractor unit

susie connectors (pipes and wires for air and electricity)

wheel arch

tunnel

trudge trudging trudged (v)
to walk slowly and heavily.
We trudged through the mud.

true truer truest (adj)
accurate or correct. **truly** (adv).

trumpet (n) a brass wind instrument
that makes a loud, clear sound.
See **brass**, **orchestra**.

truncheon (n)
a thick, rounded stick used by
the police in violent situations.

trundle trundling trundled (v)
1 to move along on wheels or rollers.
The bus trundled up the hill.
2 (informal) to walk slowly.

trunk (n)
1 the main stem of a tree. Tree
trunks contain xylem and phloem
vessels which transport fluids up and
down the tree. *In the picture below,
you can see the rings of xylem, or
sapwood, that are created each year.*
2 a large case or box, used
for storage or for carrying
clothes on a long journey.
3 the upper part of your body,
not including your head and arms.
4 the long nose of an elephant.
5 **trunks** (plural n) close-fitting shorts
worn by men or boys for swimming.

tree trunk (section)
annual ring
bark covering
layers of phloem
heartwood or hardened xylem
sapwood or xylem

trust trusting trusted (v)
If you **trust** someone, you believe that
they are honest and reliable. **trust** (n).

trustworthy (adj)
honest, reliable, and able to be
trusted. **trustworthiness** (n).

truth (n) the real facts.
truthful (adj), **truthfully** (adv).

try tries trying tried
1 (v) to attempt to do something,
or to do the best you can. **try** (n).
2 (v) to examine someone accused of
a criminal offence in a court of law.
3 (n) If you score a **try** in rugby,
you touch the ball down behind
your opponent's try line.

trying (adj) If a person is **trying**, they
make you feel annoyed and impatient.

tsar see **czar**.

T-shirt or **tee shirt** (n)
a light, cotton top, usually with
short sleeves and a round neck.

tsunami (n) a very large,
destructive wave caused by an
underwater volcano or earthquake.

tub (n)
1 a plastic container used for
storing foods. *A tub of ice cream.*
2 (old-fashioned) a large, wide
container, used for bathing in,
or for washing clothes.

tubby tubbier tubbiest (adj)
Tubby people are slightly fat.
tubbiness (n).

tuba (n)
a large, low-pitched brass instrument.

tube (n)
1 a long, hollow cylinder.
The poster came rolled in a tube.
2 **The Tube** the nickname for
London's underground railway system.

tubular (adj) shaped like a tube.

tuck tucking tucked
1 (v) to fold or push something into
a restricted space. *Tuck the sheets in.*
2 (n) a small fold sewn in material.
3 (v) (informal) If you **tuck in** to your
food, you eat it enthusiastically.
4 **tuck shop** (n) a shop in a school
where sweets, crisps, etc. are sold.

tuft (n)
an upright bunch of hair, grass,
feathers, etc. **tufted** (adj).

tug tugging tugged
1 (v) to pull hard. *Josh tugged the
loose thread on his jumper.* **tug** (n).
2 **tug** or **tugboat** (n) a small,
powerful boat that tows large ships.
3 **tug of war** (n)
a contest between two teams, each
at one end of a rope, who try to
pull each other over a centre line.

Channel Tunnel (cutaway)
sea bed
cliff
sea
chalk
chalk marl
clay
running tunnel
service tunnel
running tunnel

running tunnel (cross-section)
overhead line equipment
main lighting
double-decker shuttle train
cooling water pipes
maintenance walkway
rails
drains
evacuation walkway

---

tuition (tew-ish-un) (n)
training or teaching, often given to
a single person or to a small group.

tumble tumbling tumbled
1 (v) to fall, often with
a rolling motion.
2 **tumble dryer** (n)
a machine which dries clothes by
tossing them around in hot air.

tumbler (n)
a tall glass with straight sides.

tummy tummies (n) (informal)
your stomach.

tumour (n) a swelling or lump
caused by the abnormal growth
of a mass of new cells.

tumult (n) loud noise and confusion.
*There was tumult when the fire
alarm went off.* **tumultuous** (adj).

tuna tuna or tunas (n)
a large, edible sea fish.

tundra (n) the cold areas of
northern Europe and Asia where
there are no trees and the soil under
the surface is permanently frozen.

tune tuning tuned
1 (n) a series of musical notes,
arranged in a pattern. **tuneful** (adj).
2 (v) to adjust a radio, the pitch
of a musical instrument, etc.
3 **in tune** producing the right
notes. *Can you sing in tune?*

tunic (n) a loose, sleeveless garment.

tuning fork (n)
a piece of metal with two prongs,
used for tuning musical instruments.

tunnel (n)
an underground passage. *The picture
below shows cutaway sections of
the Channel Tunnel. The tunnel runs
under the sea bed between Cheriton,
near Folkestone, in England, and
Coquelles, near Calais, in France.*

a b c d e f g h i j k l m n o p q r s t u v w x y z

turban (n) a headdress, made from a long cloth wound round the head. Some Muslims, Hindus, and Sikhs wear turbans.

turbine (n) an engine driven by water, steam, or gas which passes through the blades of a wheel and makes it revolve. See **jet engine**.

turbo (adj) A **turbo** or **turbo-charged** engine has high-pressure air forced into its cylinders by a turbine to produce extra power.

turbofan (n) a type of aircraft engine in which a large fan, driven by a turbine, pushes air into the hot exhaust at the rear of the engine, giving extra power. See **jet engine**.

turbulent (adj) wild, confused, or unpredictable. *Turbulent waters.*

turf (n) the surface layer of grass and earth on a lawn or sports pitch.

turkey (n)
1 a large, flightless bird, usually reared for its meat. *The picture shows a North American wild turkey.*
2 (slang) a hopeless or useless person or thing.

wild turkey

turmoil (n) violent confusion. *The class was in turmoil.*

turn turning turned
1 (v) to change direction. *Turn left at the junction.* **turn** (n).
2 (v) to spin or to revolve. *Turn the wheel.*
3 (v) to change appearance or state. *The liquid turns into a vapour when heated.*
4 (v) to move a switch, tap, etc. in order to control the supply of something. *Turn down the volume.*
5 (n) If it is your **turn** to do something, it is your chance or duty to do it.
6 (n) A **good turn** is a helpful action.
7 (v) If you **turn something down**, you refuse it.
8 (v) If someone **turns up**, they appear or arrive.
9 (v) (slang) If something **turns you on**, it makes you enthusiastic and excited. **turn-on** (n).

turnip (n) a round, white root vegetable.

turnstile (n) a revolving gate that only goes one way round, and controls admission to a sports ground, theme park, etc.

turntable (n) a circular, revolving surface. Turntables of different sizes can be used for playing records or turning engines.

turpentine (n) a mixture of tree resin and oil, used in paint and medicines. See **artist**.

turquoise (tur-kwoyz) (n)
1 a bluish-green, semiprecious stone. See **mineral**.
2 a bluish-green colour. **turquoise** (adj).

turtle (n) a water reptile with flippers and a large shell. *The shell of the mata mata turtle looks like a dead leaf.*

mata mata turtle

tusk (n) one of the pair of long, curved, pointed teeth of an elephant, walrus, etc.

tussle tussling tussled (v) to fight or wrestle vigorously. **tussle** (n).

tutor (n) a teacher, usually one who teaches people individually or in small groups. **tutorial** (n).

tutu (n) a short ballet skirt made of several stiff layers of net.

tuxedo (n) (US) a man's dinner jacket with silk lapels, worn with a bow tie for formal occasions. Tuxedo is often shortened to tux.

TV short for **television**.

tweezers (plural n) small pincers used for pulling out hairs or for picking up very small objects.

twice (adv) two times.

twig twigging twigged
1 (n) a small, thin branch.
2 (v) (informal) to realize or understand something.

twilight (n) the time of day when the Sun has just set and it is beginning to get dark.

twin twinning twinned
1 (n) one of two children born to the same mother at almost the same time.
2 (adj) belonging to a matching pair. *Twin beds.*
3 If a town is **twinned** with a town in another country, the two towns exchange visits and organize events together.

twinge (twinj) (n) a sudden pain or unpleasant feeling.

twinkle twinkling twinkled (v) to shine and sparkle. **twinkle** (n).

twirl twirling twirled (v) to turn or spin round and round. **twirl** (n).

twist twisting twisted (v)
1 to turn or to bend.
2 to wind two strands of something together.

twitch twitches twitching twitched (v) to make small, jerky movements. **twitch** (n), **twitchy** (adj).

type typing typed
1 (n) a kind or a sort of thing. *What type of car do you have?*
2 (v) to write something using a keyboard on a computer, phone, etc.
3 (n) printed letters and numbers. *This picture shows two kinds of type. Serif has a small line, or serif, at the end of each letter's main strokes. Sans serif has no serifs.*

type

serif

type

sans serif

typewriter (n) an old-fashioned machine that could print letters and numbers when you pressed keys with your fingers.

typhoid (ty-foyd) (n) a serious, infectious disease that causes fever, diarrhoea, and sometimes death. It is caused by germs in food or water.

typhoon (ty-foon) (n) a violent, tropical storm.

typical (adj)
1 Something that is **typical** has the usual features that you associate with that kind of thing. *A typical English village.* **typically** (adv).
2 If someone does something that is **typical**, they behave in their usual way. *It's typical of Toby to forget my birthday!* **typically** (adv).

typist (n) someone who uses a computer to write things.

tyrant (n) someone who rules other people in a cruel and unkind way. **tyranny** (n), **tyrannical** (adj).

tyre (n) a circle of rubber around the rim of a wheel. Tyres are usually filled with air.

a b c d e f g h i j k l m n o p q r s t u v w x y z

Uu

udder *(n)* the bag-like part of a cow, sheep, etc. that hangs down near its back legs and produces milk.

UFO *(n)* a strange object seen flying in the sky, that is believed by some people to be a spaceship from another planet. UFO is short for unidentified flying object.

ugly uglier ugliest *(adj)*
1 If someone or something is ugly, they are unattractive and unpleasant to look at.
2 dangerous and violent. *There were ugly scenes as police and demonstrators clashed.*

ulcer *(ul-ser) (n)* a sore area, either on your skin or inside your mouth or stomach.

ultimate
1 *(adj)* last or final. **ultimately** *(adv)*.
2 *(adj)* original or basic. *The Sun is the ultimate source of most of our energy.* **ultimately** *(adv)*.
3 *(n)* the greatest or the best. *This car is the ultimate in speed and luxury.*

ultimatum *(n)* a final warning.

ultrasound *(n)* sound that is of too high frequency for the human ear to hear it. *Ultrasound waves are used in medical scans.*

ultraviolet light *(n)* light that cannot be seen by the human eye, which is given off by the Sun and causes your skin to tan.

umbilical cord *(n)* the tube that connects an unborn baby to its mother's body and through which it gets oxygen and food. *See* **pregnant**.

umbrella *(n)* a frame with a circular cloth stretched over it that you hold over your head to protect you from the rain.

umpire *(n)* someone who makes sure that a cricket or tennis match is played according to the rules.

unable *(adj)* If you are **unable** to do something, you cannot do it.

unacceptable *(adj)* If something is **unacceptable**, it is not good enough to be allowed or accepted.

unaccustomed *(adj)* If you are **unaccustomed** to something, you are not used to it.

unadulterated *(adj)* If a substance is **unadulterated**, it has not had anything extra added to it.

unaided *(adj)* If you do something **unaided**, you do it on your own without any help.

unanimous *(yoo-nan-im-uss) (adj)* agreed by everyone. *A unanimous decision.* **unanimously** *(adv)*.

unapproachable *(adj)* Someone who is **unapproachable** is not friendly, or is not easy to get to know.

unarmed *(adj)* Someone who is **unarmed** is not carrying any weapons.

unauthorized *or* **unauthorised** *(adj)* If something is **unauthorized**, it is done without official permission.

unavoidable *(adj)* If something is **unavoidable**, it is impossible to prevent. **unavoidably** *(adv)*.

unaware *(adj)* If you are **unaware** of something, you do not know that it exists or is happening.

unbalanced *(adj)*
1 Something that is **unbalanced** cannot balance and falls over.
2 Someone who is **unbalanced** has mental health problems.
3 A piece of writing or a speech that is **unbalanced** puts forward only one side of an argument.

unbearable *(adj)* If something is **unbearable**, it is so bad or unpleasant that you cannot stand it.

unbelievable *(adj)* If something is **unbelievable**, it is so strange, surprising, or wonderful that you find it hard to accept that it is true.

unbending *(adj)* If someone is **unbending**, they are very firm and will not change their mind.

unburden
unburdening unburdened *(v)* If you **unburden yourself**, you get rid of a load or a worry. *James unburdened himself by confessing what he had done.*

uncanny *(adj)* very strange and difficult to explain or understand. **uncannily** *(adv)*.

uncertain *(adj)* If you are **uncertain** about something, you are not sure about it. **uncertainty** *(n)*.

uncivilized *or* **uncivilised** *(adj)*
1 not yet civilized or educated. *An uncivilized country.*
2 Uncivilized behaviour is rude and rough.

uncle *(n)* the brother of your father or mother, or the husband of your aunt

uncomfortable *(adj)*
1 If you are **uncomfortable**, you do not feel relaxed in your body or your mind. **uncomfortably** *(adv)*.
2 Something that is **uncomfortable** makes you feel uneasy or unhappy. *An uncomfortable situation.*

uncomplimentary *(adj)* insulting or rude.

uncompromising *(adj)* If you are **uncompromising**, you refuse to change your mind. **uncompromisingly** *(adv)*.

unconditional *(adj)* not depending on anything else. *Maxine has an unconditional college place.* **unconditionally** *(adv)*.

unconfirmed *(adj)* not yet known to be true. *Unconfirmed rumours.*

unconscious *(adj)*
1 not awake, or unable to see, hear, think, etc. because you have fainted or been knocked out.
2 unaware of something. *George was unconscious of the fact that the bus was leaving.*

uncontrollable *(adj)* Something that is **uncontrollable** cannot be stopped or controlled. **uncontrollably** *(adv)*.

uncooperative *(adj)* If you are **uncooperative**, you refuse to help people or do things for them.

uncouth *(adj)* rough and rude.

uncover uncovering uncovered *(v)*
1 to take a cover off something.
2 to reveal something. *The police investigation uncovered a major fraud.*

undaunted *(adj)* If you are **undaunted**, you are not put off by dangers or difficulties.

undecided *(adj)* If you are **undecided** about something, you have not made up your mind about it.

undeniable *(adj)* Something that is **undeniable** is certainly true. **undeniably** *(adv)*.

under *(prep)*
1 below or beneath something. *The key is under the doormat.*
2 less than a number or amount. *Children under 12 will not be admitted.*
3 If you have people **under** you, you give them orders.

underarm *(adv)* throwing with your arm swinging under your shoulder. **underarm** *(adj)*.

undercarriage *(n)* the part of an aircraft, including the wheels, which supports it when it is on the ground. *See* **aircraft**.

a b c d e f g h i j k l m n o p q r s t **u** v w x y z

underclothes

underclothes *(plural n)*
clothes that you wear under your other clothes. *The picture shows European underclothes from four centuries.*

underclothes

| 1580s: bodice and farthingale | 1600s: stays and petticoat | 1800s: crinoline, petticoat, and drawers | 1900s: united garment | 1950s: long bra and corset |

underdog *(n)* a person or team that is expected to be the loser in a situation or competition.

underestimate
underestimating underestimated *(v)*
1 to think that something is not as good or as great as it really is. *Freddie feels that his mother underestimates his talents.*
2 to make a guess which is too low. *Kevin underestimated the amount of food we would need.*

underfoot *(adv)* under your feet, or on the ground. *It's slippery underfoot.*

undergo undergoes undergoing underwent undergone *(v)*
to experience or suffer something. *Dan underwent a serious operation.*

underground
1 *(adj)* below the ground. *An underground stream.* **underground** *(adv)*.
2 *(adj)* secret and often illegal. *An underground organization.*

3 *(n)* a railway system in which the trains travel through tunnels below the ground. *The London Underground.*

undergrowth *(n)* bushes and plants that grow in a thick mass under trees, usually in a wood or forest.

underline
underlining underlined *(v)*
1 to draw a line under a word or sentence.
2 to stress how important something is.

undermine
undermining undermined *(v)*
to weaken something gradually.

underneath *(prep)* under or below something. **underneath** *(adj)*.

undernourished *(adj)* Someone who is **undernourished** is weak and unhealthy through lack of food.

underpants *(plural n)*
underclothes worn by men or boys.

underpass underpasses *(n)*
a road or path that passes underneath another road.

underprivileged *(adj)*
Someone who is **underprivileged** is poor and does not have the opportunities that most people have.

understand
understanding understood *(v)*
1 to know what something means or how something works. *Luke understands engines.*
2 to know what someone is like or why they behave in the way that they do. *I can understand why you're so happy.* **understanding** *(adj)*.
3 to believe that something is true. *I understand that Simon's family is moving to Melbourne.*

understandable *(adj)*
1 easy to grasp or understand.
2 easy to sympathize with. *It's understandable that Jack's upset.* **understandably** *(adv)*.

undertake undertaking undertook undertaken *(v)* If you **undertake** something, you agree to do a particular job. **undertaking** *(n)*.

undertaker *(n)* someone whose job is to arrange funerals and prepare dead bodies to be buried or cremated.

underwater *(adj)* living or happening under the surface of water. *The picture shows a submersible and a remote operated vehicle (ROV), which are both used for underwater exploration.* **underwater** *(adv)*.

submersible
(cutaway)

sail or conning tower

crew cabin

floodlight

light

strobe light

camera

ALVIN

telephone and radio equipment (for contact with mother ship)

vertical thruster

pressurized air tank

horizontal thruster

crew hatch

porthole

umbilical (attached to pilot vehicle on surface)

thruster (propels ROV)

video camera

light

remote operated vehicle (ROV)

light

pilot's view port

robotic arm

rechargeable batteries

pressurized air tank

water sample bottle

basket (for samples)

underwear *(singular n)* clothes that you wear next to your skin, under your other clothes. *See* **underclothes.**

underworld *(n)*
1 the secret world of criminals.
2 In legends, **the Underworld** is the place under the ground where the spirits of dead people live.

undesirable *(adj)* unpleasant.

undeveloped *(adj)*
1 An **undeveloped** country is poor and does not have many modern industries.
2 Undeveloped land does not have buildings on it.

undo undoes undoing undid undone *(v)*
1 to untie or unfasten something.
2 to remove or destroy the effects of something.

undress undresses undressing undressed *(v)* to take off your clothes.

unearth unearthing unearthed *(v)*
1 to dig something up.
2 to find something after searching for it. *At last, I unearthed my pen.*

uneasy *(adj)* If you feel **uneasy** about something, you feel slightly worried or unhappy about it. uneasiness *(n)*, uneasily *(adv)*.

unemployed *(adj)* Someone who is **unemployed** does not have a paid job. unemployment *(n)*.

unequal *(adj)* not the same as something else in size, value, or amount. unequally *(adv)*.

uneven *(adj)*
1 not flat or not smooth.
2 not regular or not consistent. *An uneven essay.* unevenly *(adj)*.

uneventful *(adj)* not interesting or not exciting.

unexpected *(adj)* Something that is **unexpected** is surprising because you did not think it would happen. unexpectedly *(adv)*.

unfair unfairer unfairest *(adj)* not reasonable or not right. unfairly *(adv)*.

unfaithful *(adj)*
1 not loyal or not trustworthy. unfaithfully *(adv)*.
2 Someone who is **unfaithful** to their partner has a sexual relationship with someone else.

unfamiliar *(adj)*
1 not well-known or not easily recognized. *The room was full of unfamiliar people.*
2 If you are **unfamiliar with** something, you do not know it well.

unfit *(adj)*
1 not healthy or not strong.
2 not suitable or not good enough. *The king was unfit to rule.*

unfold unfolding unfolded *(v)*
1 to open something that was folded. *I unfolded the letter.*
2 When a story or plan **unfolds**, more of it becomes known.

unforgettable *(adj)* so good, bad, etc. that you will never forget it.

unforgivable *(adj)* If someone does something **unforgivable**, they do something so bad that you cannot forgive them. unforgivably *(adv)*.

unfortunate *(adj)*
1 unlucky. *An unfortunate accident.* unfortunately *(adv)*.
2 If you say that something was **unfortunate**, you mean that you wish it had never happened.

unfriendly unfriendlier unfriendliest *(adj)* unkind or unhelpful. unfriendliness *(n)*.

ungrateful *(adj)* If you are **ungrateful** for something, you are not thankful for it and do not appreciate it. ungratefully *(adv)*.

unhappy unhappier unhappiest *(adj)* miserable or upset. unhappiness *(n)*, unhappily *(adv)*.

unhealthy unhealthier unhealthiest *(adj)*
1 unfit or not well.
2 Something that is **unhealthy** makes you unfit. *An unhealthy diet.*

unhygienic *(adj)* unclean and not free from germs. *It's unhygienic to prepare food without washing your hands first.*

unicorn *(n)* an imaginary animal like a horse with one straight horn growing from its forehead. *This unicorn comes from a series of tapestries called "The Lady and the Unicorn", made in about 1500.*

unicorn

unicycle *(n)* a bicycle with only one wheel.

unidentified *(adj)* If something is **unidentified**, no one knows what it is. unidentifiable *(adj)*.

uniform
1 *(n)* a special set of clothes worn by all the members of a school, army, or organization. uniformed *(adj)*.
2 *(adj)* Things that are **uniform** are all the same, and not different or changing in any way. uniformity *(n)*, uniformly *(adv)*.

unify unifies unifying unified *(v)* to bring together different people or groups in order to form a larger group. unification *(n)*.

unimportant *(adj)* Something that is **unimportant** will not have a great effect and does not need to be taken seriously.

uninhabited *(adj)* If a place is **uninhabited**, no one lives there.

unintelligible *(adj)* If something is **unintelligible**, it cannot be understood. unintelligibly *(adv)*.

unintentional *(adj)* done by accident, not deliberately. unintentionally *(adv)*.

uninterested *(adj)* If you are **uninterested** in something, you do not want to know about it.

union *(n)*
1 an organized group of workers set up to help improve work conditions and pay.
2 the joining together of two or more things or people.

unique *(yoo-neek) (adj)* If something is **unique**, it is the only one of its kind. uniquely *(adv)*.

unisex *(adj)* able to be used by both men and women. *Unisex clothing.*

unison *(n)* If people say or do something in **unison**, they say or do it together.

unit *(n)*
1 a single, complete thing.
2 a group of people who work together to do a job. *An army unit.*
3 a piece of furniture that fits together with similar ones. *Kitchen units.*
4 an amount used as a standard of measurement. *A gram is a unit of weight.*

unite uniting united *(v)* If people **unite**, they join together or work together to achieve something. unity *(n)*.

universal
1 *(adj)* Something that is **universal** applies to everyone or everything. universally *(adv)*.
2 **universal indicator** *(n)* a solution or a piece of paper that turns a different colour to show how acidic or alkaline a substance or solution is. *See* **pH.**

universe (n)
everything in space, including
the Earth, Sun, Moon, and stars.

university universities (n)
a place where people can study
for degrees or do research.

unjust (adj)
not fair or not right. **unjustly** (adv).

unkempt (adj) untidy and neglected.

unkind unkinder unkindest (adj)
unfriendly, unhelpful, and
not generous. **unkindly** (adv).

unknown (adj) unfamiliar or not
known about. *An unknown planet.*

unless (conj) except or if not. *I can't
come unless someone gives me a lift.*

unlike (prep)
If one thing is **unlike** another,
the two things are very different.

unlikely unlikelier unlikeliest (adj)
not probable.

unlimited (adj)
If there is an **unlimited** amount
of something, you can have or
use as much of it as you want.

unload unloading unloaded (v)
to remove things from
a container or vehicle.

unlock unlocking unlocked (v)
to unfasten something with a key.

unlucky unluckier unluckiest (adj)
1 Someone who is **unlucky**
is unfortunate and bad things
seem to happen to them.
2 Something that is **unlucky**
happens by chance and is
unfortunate. **unluckily** (adv).
3 An **unlucky** number, date,
etc. is one that you think will
bring you bad luck.

unmistakable (adj) If someone
or something is **unmistakable**,
they are very individual and cannot
be confused with someone or
something else. **unmistakably** (adv).

unnatural (adj)
1 unusual or not normal.
An unnatural sound.
unnaturally (adv).
2 false, or not sincere. *Stan
sounded nervous and unnatural.*
unnaturally (adv).

unnecessary (adj) If something is
unnecessary, you do not need to do
it or have it. **unnecessarily** (adv).

unobserved (adj)
unseen or unnoticed.

unofficial (adj)
1 not approved by someone in
authority. *An unofficial report.*
2 informal. *An unofficial visit.*

unpack unpacking unpacked (v)
to take objects out of a box, case, etc.

unpleasant (adj) horrible or
not likeable. **unpleasantly** (adv).

unplug unplugging unplugged (v)
to remove a plug from
an electric socket.

unpopular (adj)
not liked or enjoyed by many people.

unpredictable (adj) If something
or someone is **unpredictable**, you
do not know what they will do or
say next. **unpredictably** (adv).

unprepared (adj)
not ready for something.

unprovoked (adj) If an action
is **unprovoked**, no one has done
anything to cause it or encourage it.

unravel unravelling unravelled (v)
1 to unwind a tangled
mass of string, wool, etc.
2 to search for and discover the
truth about a complex situation.
The detectives unravelled the mystery.

unreasonable (adj) not fair.
*The film star's demands were totally
unreasonable.* **unreasonably** (adv).

unrecognizable or
unrecognisable (adj) If someone
or something is **unrecognizable**
they have totally changed so that
you do not immediately know
who or what they are.

unreliable (adj) Someone or
something who is **unreliable**
cannot be depended on or trusted.

unrest (n) disturbance and trouble.

unrestricted (adj) without rules
or restrictions. *This ticket gives you
unrestricted use of the pool.*

unripe (adj) not yet ready to
be harvested, picked, or eaten.

unrivalled (adj)
better than anything else.

unroll unrolling unrolled (v)
to open out something that is rolled
up. *We unrolled our sleeping bags.*

unruly unrulier unruliest (adj)
badly behaved and disobedient.

unscathed (adj) not hurt. *The
driver survived the crash unscathed.*

unscrupulous (adj)
Unscrupulous people have few
principles and are not concerned
about whether their actions are right
or wrong. **unscrupulously** (adv).

unseen (adj)
hidden or not able to be seen.

unsettle unsettling unsettled (v)
to disturb someone, or to
make someone feel uneasy.

unsightly (adj)
ugly and unpleasant to look at.

unskilled (adj) An **unskilled** worker
has no particular skill or training.

unstable (adj)
1 not firm or not steady.
2 An **unstable** person has rapid
changes of mood and behaviour.

unsteady (adj)
shaky or wobbly. **unsteadily** (adv).

unstuck
1 (adj) If something has
come **unstuck**, it is not
glued together any more.
2 (informal) If your plans
come **unstuck**, you are
not able to carry them out.

unsuccessful (adj)
If you are **unsuccessful**, you do
not do well, or do not get what
you want. **unsuccessfully** (adv).

unsuitable (adj) not right for a
particular purpose. *Clive was wearing
unsuitable clothes for the expedition.*
unsuitability (n), **unsuitably** (adv).

unsure (adj)
not certain or not definite.
Katie is unsure about the future.

unthinkable (adj) If something is
unthinkable it is out of the question
and cannot be considered.

untidy untidier untidiest (adj)
not neat. **untidiness** (n), **untidily** (adv).

untie untying untied (v)
to undo knots or bows.

until (conj) up to the time that.
You can stay until tomorrow.

unto (prep) (old-fashioned) to.

untold (adj) too great to be counted
or worked out. *Untold damage.*

untouched (adj)
1 not handled by anyone.
2 left alone or ignored. *The
thieves took the money, but
left the jewellery untouched.*

untrue (adj) false or incorrect.

unused (adj) An **unused**
item has never been used.

unusual (adj) strange, abnormal,
or odd. **unusually** (adv).

unwaged (adj) without a paid job.

unwanted (adj)
If something is **unwanted**,
you do not need or want it.

unwelcome (adj) If someone or
something is **unwelcome**, they are
not gladly received or accepted.

unwell (adj) ill or poorly.

unwieldy (adj) difficult to hold or
hard to manage. *An unwieldy parcel.*

U-turn

unwilling *(adj)*
reluctant or not keen to do something. **unwillingly** *(adv).*

unwind unwinding unwound *(v)*
1 to undo something that has been wound up. *Tina unwound the hose.*
2 to relax and become less worried or tense. *Ann plays sport to unwind.*

unworthy *(adj)* not deserving, or below standard. *The beer crate made an unworthy seat for the President.*

unwrap unwrapping unwrapped *(v)* to take the packaging or outer layer off something.

up *(prep)* from a lower to a higher place. **upward** *(adj),* **up** *(adv).*

upbeat *(adj) (informal)* optimistic and cheerful.

upbringing *(n)* the way that a child is raised or brought up.

update updating updated *(v)*
1 to give someone the latest information. *Please update us on your plans.* **update** *(n).*
2 to change something in order to include the latest style or information. *We are updating our catalogue.*

upgrade upgrading upgraded *(v)*
1 to improve something. *Jamal upgraded his computer by adding extra memory.*
2 to promote someone to a better or more important job.

upheaval *(n)* a big change or disturbance. *Moving house was a great upheaval for us all.*

uphill *(adj)* sloping upwards.

upholstery *(n)*
the stuffing, covering, etc. that is put in or on furniture.

upkeep *(n)* the work or cost of looking after something or someone.

up-market *(adj)*
Goods that are **up-market** are expensive and of high quality.

upon *(prep)* on.

upper *(adj)* higher. *An upper window.*

upper case *(adj)*
Upper case letters are capital letters.

upright
1 *(adj)* standing up or standing straight. **upright** *(adv).*
2 *(adj)* honest and fair. *An upright citizen.*
3 *(n)* a vertical post.

uprising *(n)*
a rebellion or a revolt.

uproar *(n)* shouting, noise, and confusion. *The lesson ended in uproar.* **uproarious** *(adj).*

uproot uprooting uprooted *(v)*
1 to take a plant out of the earth.
2 to move someone from where they are settled in their home or work.

upset upsetting upset *(v)*
1 to make someone unhappy or distressed. **upset** *(adj).*
2 to overturn something. *Sinead upset the milk.*
3 to make someone feel ill. *Oysters always upset me.*

upside down
1 *(adj)* the wrong way up.
2 *(adv)* in a confused or untidy condition. *The thieves turned the place upside down.*

upstairs *(adv)* to or on a higher floor.

uptight *(adj) (informal)*
1 tense or anxious.
2 unable to express your feelings easily.

up-to-date *(adj)*
If something is **up-to-date**, it contains the most recent information or is in the latest style.

urban *(adj)* to do with or living in towns or cities. *Urban wildlife.*

Urdu *(n)* a language spoken in Pakistan and India.

urge urging urged
1 *(v)* to encourage or persuade someone strongly. *Dad urged me to try harder.*
2 *(n)* a strong wish or need to do something. *Tom felt a sudden urge to throw something.*

urgent *(adj)* If something is **urgent**, it needs very quick or immediate action. **urgency** *(n),* **urgently** *(adv).*

urinate *(yoor-in-ate)*
urinating urinated *(v)* to pass urine from your body. **urination** *(n).*

urine *(yoor-in) (n)*
the liquid waste that people and animals pass out of their bodies.

URL *(n)* the series of letters (and sometimes numbers) that you type into your computer to enable a browser to find a particular website or page. URL stands for Uniform Resource Locator. Another name for URL is web address.

urn *(n)*
1 a vase used as an ornament or as a container for the ashes of a dead person. *The picture shows an urn made in Ancient Greece.*
2 a large insulated container, used for serving tea or coffee and for keeping them hot.

urn

usage *(n)*
1 the way that something is used or treated. *Careless usage.*
2 the way that a language is spoken and written. *English usage.*

use using used
1 *(yooz) (v)* to do a job with something. *I used a penknife to cut through the wrapping.*
2 *(yooce) (n)* the action of using something. *I'm sure I can find a use for your present. Put away the tools after use.*
3 *(yooz) (v)* If you **use** someone, you take advantage of them in order to get something that you want.
4 **use up** *(yooz) (v)* If you **use** something up, you finish it.

used
1 *(yoozed) (adj)* already made use of. *A used car.*
2 *(yoost)* If you are **used to** something, you know it well. *I'm used to driving this way to work.*
3 *(yoost)* If you **used to do** something, you did it in the past.

useful *(yooce-ful) (adj)* Something that is **useful** is helpful and can be used a lot. **usefulness** *(n).*

useless *(yooce-less) (adj)*
1 Something that is **useless** cannot be used or is not helpful. *The instruction manual was completely useless.*
2 *(informal)* not very good. *I'm useless at French.*

user-friendly *(adj)* If a machine is **user-friendly**, it is easy to use.

usher *(n)* someone who shows people to their seats in a court, at a wedding, etc. **usher** *(v).*

usual *(adj)*
normal or regular. *Annie ordered her usual drink at the café.* **usually** *(adv).*

utensil *(n)* a tool or container, often one used in the kitchen.

utmost *(n)* the most or the greatest possible. *The government said they would do their utmost to help the refugees.* **utmost** *(adj).*

utter uttering uttered
1 *(v)* to speak or to make some sort of sound from your mouth. *Erica uttered a low moan.* **utterance** *(n).*
2 *(adj)* complete, total, or absolute. *The play was an utter disaster.* **utterly** *(adv).*

U-turn *(n)*
1 a U-shaped turn made by a vehicle, in order to change its direction.
2 a complete reversal of policy or attitude. *A government U-turn.*

vacant

Vv

vacant *(adj)*
1 empty or not occupied.
A vacant house.
2 available. *This job is vacant.*
vacancy *(n)*.
3 If someone looks **vacant**, they have
a blank expression on their face.

vacate vacating vacated *(v)*
to leave or to make somewhere
empty. *Hotel guests should vacate
their rooms by 10 a.m.*

vacation *(n)*
a break between university
or college terms.

vaccinate vaccinating vaccinated
(v) to protect someone against
a disease, usually by giving them
an injection. **vaccination** *(n)*.

vaccine *(vak-seen)* *(n)*
a substance injected or given
by mouth to protect someone
from disease.

vacuum *(vak-yoom)* *(n)*
a sealed space from which all
air or gas has been emptied.

vacuum cleaner *(n)*
a machine that sucks up dirt
from carpets, furniture, etc.

vacuum flask *(n)*
a container that keeps liquids
hot or cold. The vacuum between
its two glass walls prevents heat
or cold escaping.

vagina *(vaj-eye-na)* *(n)*
the passage leading from the womb,
through which babies are born.

vague *(vayg)* vaguer vaguest *(adj)*
not clear or not definite. *I have
only vague memories of Miranda.*

vain vainer vainest *(adj)*
1 If you are **vain**, you are too
proud of yourself, especially
of the way that you look.
2 unsuccessful or futile.
*Beatrice made a vain
attempt to stop the bus.*

valentine *(n)*
1 a gift or greeting card that you
send to a friend, relative or loved one
on Valentine's Day (February 14th).
2 a sweetheart or loved one
chosen on Valentine's Day.

valiant *(adj)*
brave or courageous. *Greek
myths describe Achilles
as a valiant warrior.*
valiantly *(adv)*.

valid *(adj)*
1 sensible and acceptable. *You
can leave early only if you have
a valid reason.* **validity** *(n)*.
2 acceptable or legal. *To travel on
the train, you need a valid ticket.*

valley *(n)*
an area of low ground between two
hills, usually containing a river.

valour *(n)* *(poetic)* bravery or courage.

valuable
1 *(adj)* Something that is **valuable**
is worth a lot of money, or is very
important in some other way. *A
valuable jewel. Valuable information.*
2 **valuables** *(plural n)* possessions
that are worth a lot of money.

value valuing valued
1 *(n)* what something is worth.
What is the value of this watch?
2 *(v)* to think that something
is important. *I value Posy's
friendship greatly.*
3 *(v)* to assess how much something
is worth. *The auctioneer valued
the paintings before the sale.*
4 *(plural n)* People's **values**
are their beliefs and
ideas about what is
most important in life.

valve *(n)* a type of tap that
controls the flow of fluid,
air, etc. *See* **engine**, **heart**.

vampire *(n)*
In folk tales and horror
stories, a **vampire** is a
corpse with fangs that rises
from its grave to drink the
blood of human victims.

van *(n)* a closed vehicle for
carrying goods. *A delivery van.*

vandal *(n)* someone who
needlessly damages or destroys
other people's property.
vandalism *(n)*, **vandalize** *(v)*.

vane *(n)*
1 A **weather vane** is a pointer
that swings around to show
the direction of the wind.
2 the flat part of a bird's
feather. *See* **feather**.

vanilla *(n)* the pod or bean
of a tropical orchid, used for
flavouring ice cream, cakes, etc.

vanish
vanishes
vanishing
vanished *(v)* to
disappear suddenly.

vanilla

vanilla
orchid

vanilla
pods

vanity *(n)*
a feeling of extreme pride and conceit.

vapour *(n)* a gas, usually one
that has been changed from a
liquid or solid. *Water vapour is
visible as clouds, mist, or steam.*

variable
1 *(adj)* likely to change. *Variable
weather.* **variability** *(n)*.
2 *(n)* In maths, a **variable**
is a value, given to a symbol,
such as x or y, that may change.

variation *(n)* a change in something.

variety varieties *(n)*
1 a selection of different things.
2 a different type of the same
thing. *A new variety of rose.*

various *(adj)*
1 several. *I have various hobbies.*
2 different. *The cakes were many
and various.*

varnish varnishes *(n)* a clear coating
that you paint on wood to protect it
and give it a shiny finish. **varnish** *(v)*.

vary varies varying varied *(v)*
1 to change or be different.
*Mimi's handwriting varies
depending on her mood.*
2 If you **vary** something,
you make changes to it.

vase *(n)* an ornamental
container, often used for
flowers. *The picture shows
an Art Deco style enamelled
vase, made in the 1930s.*

vase

vast vaster vastest *(adj)*
huge in area or extent. *The vast
Sahara Desert. Polly has a vast fund
of jokes.* **vastness** *(n)*, **vastly** *(adv)*.

VAT *(n)*
a tax added to the cost of many
types of goods. The initials VAT
stand for Value-Added Tax.

vault vaulting vaulted
1 *(v)* to leap over something,
using your hands or other
support. **vault** *(n)*.
2 *(n)* an underground burial chamber.

VDU *(n)*
the screen of a computer and
the keyboard connected to
it. The initials VDU stand for
Visual Display Unit.

veal *(n)* the meat from a calf.

veer veering veered *(v)*
to change direction. *The car veered
dangerously across the road.*

vegan *(vee-gan)* *(n)*
someone who does not use
or eat any animal products.
veganism *(n)*, **vegan** *(adj)*.

vegetable (n) a plant grown to be used as food. Vegetables are usually eaten with savoury foods. *The picture shows a variety of different vegetables.*

vegetables

lettuce
onion
spinach
red cabbage
cabbage
leeks
cauliflower
Brussels sprouts
artichoke
mangetout
runner beans
broccoli
green peas
corn on the cob
pumpkin
marrow
aubergine
courgettes
sweet pepper
cucumber
beetroot
carrots
okra
celery
parsnips
radishes
potato
sweet potato
chilli peppers
asparagus

vegetarian (n) someone who does not eat meat or fish **vegetarianism** (n), **vegetarian** (adj).

vegetation (n) plant life of all types.

vehement (*vee-uh-ment*) (adj) If you are **vehement** about something, you express your feelings about it very strongly. **vehemence** (n), **vehemently** (adv).

vehicle (*vee-ik-ul*) (n) something in which people or goods are carried from one place to another. Vehicles can range in size and power from a sledge to an express train.

veil (*vale*) (n) a fine piece of material worn by women to hide their faces.

vein (*vane*) (n) one of the tubes through which blood is carried back to the heart from other parts of the body. *See* **circulation**.

vellum (n)
1 fine parchment made from the skin of a calf, lamb, etc.
2 very high quality writing paper.

velocity (*vel-oss-it-ee*) **velocities** (n) speed. *The velocity of the rocket is 3,000mph.*

velvet (n)
1 a soft, thick fabric made from cotton or silk. **velvety** (adj).

2 the soft skin on the growing antler of a deer. *See* **antler**.

vendetta (n) a long-running feud between two families, gangs, etc.

vending machine (n) a coin-operated machine from which you can buy food, drink, or other products.

venetian blind (n) an indoor blind made from thin strips that can be raised or tilted to alter the amount of light coming in.

vengeance (n) action that you take to pay someone back for harm that they have done to you or to your friends or family.

venom (n) poison produced by some snakes and spiders and injected through their fangs into their victims' bodies. *This diagram of a snake's jaws shows where its venom is stored.*

snake's jaws

fang
upper jaw
flexible muscle (allows jaw bones to separate)
venom sac
lower jaw

vent venting vented
1 (n) an opening through which waste can escape.
2 (n) the shaft of a volcano through which smoke and lava escape. *See* **volcano**.

3 (v) If you **vent** your feelings, you show them in an obvious way.

ventilate ventilating ventilated (v) to let fresh air into a place and to let stale air out. **ventilation** (n).

ventriloquism (n) the art of speaking without moving your lips so that your words seem to come from somewhere else, for example, from a dummy's mouth. **ventriloquist** (n).

venture venturing ventured
1 (v) to put yourself at risk by doing something daring or dangerous. *The explorers ventured bravely into the dense jungle.*
2 (n) a project which is rather risky.

venue (*ven-yoo*) (n) a place where an event is held.

veranda or **verandah** (n) a raised platform around the outside of a house, often with a roof.

verb (n) a word that describes what someone or something does, thinks, or feels. "Sing", "have" and "come" are all verbs. *See page 3.*

verbal (adj)
1 to do with words. *A verbal reasoning test.*
2 spoken. *Verbal abuse.*
3 to do with verbs.

verdict (n)
1 the decision of a judge or jury on whether someone is guilty or not guilty.
2 a decision or an opinion. *What's your verdict on my chicken casserole?*

verge verging verged
1 (n) land at the side of a road, often with grass on it.
2 If you are **on the verge** of doing something, you will do it soon. *Harry is on the verge of leaving.*
3 (v) to be very near to something. *Christina's behaviour was verging on madness.*

verify verifies verifying verified (v) to confirm or to back up something. *Roberta verified that what the witness said was true.* **verification** (n), **verifiable** (adj).

verruca (*ver-oo-kuh*) **verrucae** or **verrucas** (n) a small, hard, and sometimes painful growth, usually on the sole of the foot.

versatile (adj) talented or useful in many ways. *A versatile entertainer. A versatile tool.* **versatility** (n).

verse (n)
1 one part of a poem or song, made up of several lines.
2 a general name for poetry.

version (n)
1 one way of expressing
something. *Holly gave her
version of the day's events.*
2 a revised form or model of a
book, car, piece of software, etc.

versus (prep) against. *Today's
match is England versus France.*

vertebra vertebrae (n) one of
the bones that make up your spine.

vertebrate (n) a creature with
a backbone. *Humans, elephants,
and snakes are all vertebrates.*
vertebrate (adj).

vertex vertexes or vertices (n)
1 the highest point of something.
2 the point where two lines meet
to form an angle.

vertical (adj) upright and
perpendicular to the ground.
A vertical post. **vertically** (adv).

very
1 (adv) to a great extent,
much, or most. *I am very
pleased to see you.*
2 (adj) exact. *You're the very
person I wanted to see.*

vessel (n)
1 a general name for a ship.
2 (old-fashioned) a container
for liquids.

vest (n)
a piece of underwear worn
on the top half of your body.

vestige (vest-ij) (n)
a trace of something. *There's a
vestige of truth in what Ian says.*

vet vetting vetted
1 (n) someone who is trained
to treat sick animals. Vet is
short for veterinary surgeon.
2 (v) to check that someone can
be trusted. *We have vetted every
member of our gang.*

veteran (n)
1 someone with a lot of
experience of something.
2 a soldier who has returned
from war.
3 veteran car a car made
before 1919, especially one
made before 1905.

veterinary
1 (adj) to do with the
treatment of animals.
2 veterinary surgeon (n) see **vet**.

veto (vee-toe)
vetoes vetoing vetoed (v)
If someone **vetoes** something,
they use their power to put a stop
to a plan. *The minister vetoed
the proposition.* **veto** (n).

vex vexes vexing vexed (v)
to annoy or irritate somebody.
vexation (n), vexatious (adj).

VHF (n)
a waveband that can be used for
high-frequency reception of radio
and TV signals. The initials VHF
stand for Very High Frequency.

via (prep) by way of. *This train
goes to Edinburgh via York.*

viable (adj)
workable or capable of succeeding.
A viable plan. viability (n).

viaduct (n) a large bridge that carries
a railway or road across a valley.

vibrant (adj) bright or lively.
Vibrant colours. A vibrant personality.
vibrancy (n), vibrantly (adv).

vibrate vibrating vibrated (v)
to shake rapidly. vibration (n).

vicar (n)
a priest in the Church of England.

vicarage (n) a vicar's house.

vice (n)
1 immoral or criminal behaviour.
2 a tool that holds an object between
two jaws so that you can work on it.

vice-captain (n) a deputy who helps
the captain and takes over duties
when the captain is unable to act.

vice president (n)
a deputy who helps the president
and takes over duties when the
president is unable to act.

vice versa (adv) a Latin phrase
meaning "the other way round".
You help me and vice versa.

vicinity (vis-in-it-ee) vicinities (n)
the area near a particular place.
*After the robbery, the police sealed
off all the roads in the vicinity.*

vicious (adj) bad-tempered,
aggressive, and violent.
viciousness (n), viciously (adv).

victim (n) someone who suffers
or is killed because of something
or someone else. *There were
many victims of the air crash.*

victimize or **victimise**
victimizing victimized (v)
to pick someone out for unfair
treatment. victimization (n).

victor (n)
the winner in a battle or contest.

victory victories (n)
a win in a battle or contest.
victorious (adj), victoriously (adv).

video videoing videoed
1 (v) to record sound and pictures.
video (adj).
2 (n) a recording of sound and pictures.

video tape (n)
a strip of magnetic tape once used to
hold recordings of sound and pictures.

vie vying vied (v) If you **vie** with
someone, you compete with them.
The brothers vied for attention.

view viewing viewed
1 (n) what you can see from a certain
place. *The view from my window.*
2 (v) to look at something to see if
you want to buy it. *May we view the
house next weekend?* viewing (n).
3 (n) what you think about something.
What are your views on whaling?

vigilant (adj) watchful and alert.
vigilance (n), vigilantly (adv).

vigorous (adj) energetic, lively, or
forceful. *Vigorous exercise. A vigorous
speech.* vigour (n), vigorously (adv).

Viking (n) one of the Scandinavian
peoples who invaded England and
parts of northern Europe between the
8th and 11th centuries. See **longship**.

vile viler vilest (adj)
horrible and disgusting. vileness (n).

villa (n)
1 In Ancient Roman times, a **villa**
was a country house, usually built
around a courtyard and including
farm buildings.
2 a large house set in a garden,
usually in Mediterranean countries.

village (n)
a small group of houses
and other buildings in the
countryside. villager (n).

villain (vill-un) (n)
a wicked person, often an evil
character in a film. villainous (adj).

villein (vill-ayn) (n) a farm worker
in medieval times who belonged to
the lord of the manor. See **feudalism**.

vindictive (adj)
Someone who is **vindictive**
is unforgiving and wants
revenge. vindictiveness (n),
vindictively (adv).

vine (n) a climbing plant on which
grapes and some other fruits grow.

vinegar (n) a sour-tasting liquid
made from fermented wine, cider,
etc. and used to flavour food.

vineyard (vin-yard) (n) an area of
farmland where grapes are grown.

vintage (vin-tij)
1 (n) the wine produced in
a particular year.
2 (adj) very good or the best
of its kind. *Jodie gave a
vintage performance.*
3 (adj) to do with the past.
Vintage clothing.

volcano

violate violating violated (v)
1 to break a promise, a rule, or a law. *Marcus had to pay a fine for violating parking laws.* violation (n).
2 to treat a person or place with no respect. violation (n).

violence (n)
the use of physical force to hurt or kill. violent (adj), violently (adv).

violet (n)
a blue-purple colour. violet (adj).

violin (n)
a musical instrument with four strings, played with a bow. See **strings**.

VIP (n) a famous or important person. The initials VIP stand for Very Important Person.

viper (n) an adder. See **adder**.

virgin
1 (n) someone who has never had sexual intercourse.
2 (adj) untouched or in its natural state. *Virgin snow.*

virile (adj) Someone who is virile has qualities that are supposed to be typical of men. virility (n).

virtually (adv)
nearly or almost. *We have virtually finished.* virtual (adj).

virtual reality (n) an environment created by a computer which seems real to the person who experiences it.

virtue (n)
a good quality. *Patience is a virtue.* virtuous (adj), virtuously (adv).

virtuoso (n) a highly skilled performer, especially a musician.

virulent (adj)
1 If a disease is virulent, it is very severe or harmful. virulence (n), virulently (adv).
2 Virulent criticism is very severe or bitter. virulence (n), virulently (adv).

virus viruses (n)
1 an organism that multiplies in body cells, often causing disease. See **AIDS**.
2 the disease caused by a virus.
3 hidden instructions within a computer program, designed to damage data or destroy a computer system.

visa (vee-zer) (n)
a document giving permission for someone to enter a foreign country.

visible (adj)
Something that is visible is able to be seen. *The island was visible on the horizon.* visibility (n), visibly (adv).

vision (n)
1 sight. *Eagles have excellent vision.*
2 something that you see in a dream or trance, which is often strange or beautiful.
3 the ability to think ahead.

visit visiting visited (v)
to go to see people or places. visit (n), visitor (n).

visual
1 (adj) to do with seeing. *A visual guide.* visually (adv).
2 (n) an image or a picture.

visualize or **visualise**
visualizing visualized (v)
to picture something or to see something in your mind. visualization (n).

vital (adj)
essential or absolutely necessary. vitally (adv).

vitality (n) energy and liveliness. *Puppies are usually full of vitality.*

vitamin (n) one of the substances in food that is necessary for good health.

vivacious (adj) A vivacious person has a lively personality. vivacity (n), vivaciously (adv).

vivid (adj) very bright, clear, or realistic. *A vivid dream. Vivid colours.* vividness (n), vividly (adv).

vivisection (n)
the use of live animals for scientific and medical research.

vocabulary vocabularies (n)
the range of words that a person uses and understands. *Karen has a very wide vocabulary.*

vocal
1 (adj) to do with the voice.
2 (adj) If someone is vocal they are outspoken and often express their opinions. vocally (adv).
3 (plural n) In music, the vocals are the parts that are sung.

vocalist (n) a singer.

vocation (n)
1 a strong feeling that you want to do a particular job.
2 a job or profession, especially one that needs special training. vocational (adj).

vociferous
(vo-sif-er-us) (adj)
If someone is vociferous, they are noisy and talkative and insist on being heard. vociferously (adv).

vodka (n) a strong alcoholic drink made from grain or potatoes.

vogue (vohg) (n) If something is in vogue, it is the current fashion.

voice voicing voiced
1 (n) the power to speak and sing. *Lois has lost her voice.*
2 (n) the sound produced when you speak or sing. *Minnie has a high voice.*
3 (v) When you voice an opinion, you express it. voice (n).

void
1 (n) an empty space. *The spaceship careered into the void.*
2 (adj) If a result is declared void, it does not count any more.

volatile (adj)
1 A volatile chemical evaporates very easily or is unstable in some other way. volatility (n).
2 Someone who is volatile has rapid mood changes.

volcano volcanoes (n)
a mountain with vents through which molten lava, ash, cinders, and gas erupt, sometimes violently. Volcanoes occur along the boundaries of the Earth's plates, where molten rock is forced upwards from magma reservoirs. Some volcanoes are extinct, others are dormant, and a few are active. *This picture shows a cutaway view of an erupting volcano.*

cone volcano (cutaway)

pyroclast (lump of solidified lava)

volcanic ash and gas

molten lava

volcanic bomb (large pyroclast)

crater

branch pipe

vent

layers of solidified ash and lava

main pipe

lava flow

reservoir of magma (molten rock)

volley

volley (n) a shot in games, such as tennis and football, where the ball is hit or kicked before it can bounce.

volleyball (n) a six-a-side game in which teams use their hands to hit a large ball over the net and try to make it hit the ground on their opponent's side.

volt (n) a unit of electrical force. Volts are used to measure voltage.

voltage (n) the force of an electrical supply, expressed in volts. *12 volts is the voltage of most car batteries.*

volume (n)
1 the amount of space taken up by a three-dimensional shape, such as a box or room. To work out the volume of an object, you multiply its length by its width by its height.
2 the degree of sound produced by a radio, a pop group, etc.
3 a large book, often one of a series. *This encyclopedia has 12 volumes.*

voluntary
1 (adj) willing and unforced. *A voluntary decision.*
2 **voluntary work** (n) unpaid work, usually done to help others.

volunteer
volunteering volunteered (v) to offer to do a job. **volunteer** (n).

vomit vomiting vomited (v) When you **vomit**, you bring up food from your stomach through your mouth. **vomit** (n).

vote voting voted (v) to make a choice in an election or other poll, usually by marking a paper or raising your hand. **vote** (n).

voucher (n) a piece of paper which can be exchanged for goods or services. *A gift voucher.*

vow vowing vowed (v) to make a serious and important promise.

vowel (n) one of the letters a, e, i, o, and u. Y is also a vowel in words such as gymnastics, but a consonant in words such as yo-yo.

voyage (n) a sea journey. **voyager** (n).

vulgar (adj) rude or coarse. **vulgarity** (n).

vulnerable (adj) If someone or something is **vulnerable**, they are in a weak position and likely to be hurt or damaged in some way. **vulnerability** (n), **vulnerably** (adv).

vulture (n)
1 a large bird of prey.
2 someone or something that preys on the vulnerable.

Ww

wad (wod) (n) a thick pad or a bundle. *A wad of banknotes.*

waddle waddling waddled (v) to walk awkwardly, swaying from side to side. *The geese waddled into the farmyard.*

wade wading waded (v) to walk through water.

wader (n)
1 a wading bird.
2 a thigh-high waterproof boot, used for fishing in deep water.

wafer (n) a thin, light, crispy type of biscuit.

waffle waffling waffled
1 (n) a type of square pancake, sometimes eaten with syrup.
2 (v) (informal) to speak in a long-winded, rambling way. **waffle** (n).

wag wagging wagged (v) to move something from side to side. *Fido wagged his tail.*

wage waging waged
1 **wage** or **wages** (n) the money someone is paid for their work.
2 (v) If you **wage** a campaign or a war, you start it and carry on with it.

waggle waggling waggled (v) to move from side to side. *Geri waggled her finger at me.*

wagon (n)
1 a horse-drawn cart.
2 a railway truck.

wail wailing wailed (v) to let out a long cry of sadness or distress. **wail** (n).

waist (n) the middle part of your body, between your hips and your ribs, where your body narrows.

waistcoat (n) a short, light, sleeveless jacket, often worn under the jacket of a suit.

wait waiting waited (v)
1 to pause, or to stop doing something for a period of time.
2 If you **wait on** someone, you serve them food and drink in a restaurant.

waiter (n) a man who serves people with food and drink in a restaurant or bar.

waiting room (n) a room where people sit and wait for something, such as a train or an appointment.

waitress waitresses (n) a woman who serves people with food and drink in a restaurant or bar.

wake waking woke woken
1 (v) to become fully conscious after being asleep. *Dora always wakes at dawn.*
2 (v) to rouse someone from sleep.
3 (n) the trail left by something. *He left chaos in his wake.*

walk walking walked
1 (v) to move along on your feet. **walker** (n).
2 (n) a journey on foot.
3 (v) (informal) If you **walk all over** someone, you take advantage of them.

walking stick (n) a stick held by someone to help them to walk.

walkover (n) (informal) a very easy victory in a sports match, especially one gained because an opponent is unfit to play.

wall (n) a solid structure that separates two areas or supports a roof.

wallaby wallabies (n) a plant-eating animal similar to a kangaroo.

red-necked wallaby

wallet (n) a pouch for holding money, usually made of leather.

wallop walloping walloped (v) (informal) to hit someone very hard, usually as a punishment. **wallop** (n).

wallow wallowing wallowed (v)
1 to roll about in mud or water.
2 If you **wallow in** something, you enjoy it greatly.

wallpaper (n) patterned or coloured paper that is stuck in strips to a wall in order to decorate a room.

walrus walruses (n) a large sea animal from the Arctic with long tusks and flippers.

waltz waltzes (n) a ballroom dance with a regular 1-2-3 beat. **waltz** (v).

wand (rhymes with pond) (n) a thin stick that is supposed to have magical powers.

walruses

Some words that begin with a "w" sound are spelt "wh".

waterlogged

wander wandering wandered *(v)*
1 to walk around without going in
any particular direction. **wander** *(n)*.
2 to move around. *Don't let your
thoughts wander.*

wane waning waned *(v)*
1 to get smaller or less. *As the job
progressed, Mel's enthusiasm waned.*
2 When the Moon **wanes**, it appears
to get smaller. *See* **Moon**.

wangle wangling wangled *(v)*
(informal) to gain something by crafty
or dishonest methods. *I managed
to wangle a front row seat.*

want wanting wanted *(v)*
1 to feel that you would like
something. *I want a chocolate.*
want *(n)*.
2 to need something. *What Victoria
wants is a good meal.* **want** *(n)*.

war *(n)*
1 fighting between opposing forces.
2 a struggle against something.
A war against hunger.

ward warding warded
1 *(n)* a large room in a hospital
where patients are looked after.
2 *(n)* a young person who is
under the care of a guardian.
3 **ward off** *(v)* to prevent something
from attacking or hurting you.
I'm trying to ward off a cold.

warden *(n)* someone in charge of
a building where people stay, such as
a youth hostel or old people's home.

warder *(n)* someone who works
in a prison, dealing with prisoners
and maintaining security.

wardrobe *(n)*
1 a tall cupboard used for
storing clothes.
2 a collection of clothes or
theatrical costumes.

warehouse *(n)* a large building
used for storing goods.

warfare *(n)* a general term for the
fighting of wars. *Jungle warfare.*

warlike *(adj)* hostile, aggressive,
or likely to start a war.

warm warming warmed;
warmer warmest
1 *(adj)* fairly hot. **warmth** *(n)*.
2 *(v)* to increase the temperature
of something.
3 *(adj)* very friendly. *We were
given a warm welcome.*
warmth *(n)*, **warmly** *(adv)*.
4 *(v)* If you **warm up** before a sports
match, you exercise gently to prepare
yourself for it. **warm-up** *(n)*.
5 *(v)* When an engine **warms up**,
it starts to run smoothly.

warm-blooded *(adj)*
Warm-blooded animals have
a body temperature that remains
approximately the same, whatever
their surroundings.

warn warning warned *(v)*
If you **warn** someone, you tell them
about a danger or a bad thing that
might happen. **warning** *(n)*.

warp warping warped *(v)*
If an object **warps**, it gets twisted
or bent by heat or dampness.

warrant *(n)* an official piece of
paper that gives permission for
something. *A search warrant.*

warren *(n)* a group of underground
tunnels where rabbits live.

warrior *(n)* a soldier or someone
who fights. *See* **samurai**.

warship *(n)* a ship with guns
on it, used in war. *See* **ship**.

wart *(rhymes with port)* *(n)* a small
hard lump on your skin. **warty** *(adj)*.

wary warier wariest *(adj)*
cautious and careful. *Emma
is always very wary of dogs.*
wariness *(n)*, **warily** *(adv)*.

wash washes washing washed
1 *(v)* to clean something with
water, soap, etc. **wash** *(n)*.
2 *(n)* the trail of disturbed water
behind a moving boat.
3 *(v)* When you **wash up**, you clean
the plates, cutlery, etc. after a meal.
4 *(v)* If the sea **washes up** something,
it leaves it on the shore.

washable *(adj)*
If a material is **washable**, you can
wash it without damaging it.

washer *(n)* a plastic or metal ring
that fits under a bolt or screw to give
a tighter fit or to prevent a leak.

washing *(n)*
1 clothes that are going to be
washed, or have been washed.
2 **washing-up** the plates, cutlery,
etc. that need cleaning after a meal.

washing machine *(n)*
a machine that washes clothes.

wasp *(n)* a flying insect that has
black and yellow stripes and can
sting. *See* **insect**, **nest**.

wastage *(n)* loss. *There was
a lot of food wastage.*

waste wasting wasted
1 *(v)* If you **waste** something, you
use it wrongly or throw it away
when you do not need to. *Don't
waste your time.* **waste** *(n)*.
2 *(n)* rubbish or something left
over and not needed. **waste** *(adj)*.

3 *(v)* If someone **wastes away**,
they get thinner and weaker
because of illness or starvation.

wasteful *(adj)* If you are **wasteful**,
you use things up needlessly and
do not think about saving them.
wastefulness *(n)*, **wastefully** *(adv)*.

wasteland *(n)*
land that is not used for anything.

watch watches watching watched
1 *(n)* a small clock, usually worn
on your wrist.
2 *(v)* to look at something. *Lauren
was watching the television news.*
3 *(v)* to notice or to be careful about
something. *Watch what you're doing
with those scissors!*

water watering watered
1 *(n)* a colourless liquid that
you can drink.
2 *(v)* to pour water on something.
Can you water the plants?
3 *(v)* If your mouth **waters**, you
see or smell food and feel hungry.
4 *(v)* If your eyes **water**, tears
come from them.
5 **water down** *(v)* If you **water**
something down, you make it
weaker, usually by adding water.
*The cordial was too strong
until I watered it down.*

watercolours *(plural n)*
paints that are mixed with
water, not oil. *See* **artist**.

water cycle *(n)*
the constant movement of the
Earth's water. Water from rivers
and oceans evaporates, and plants
transpire, making water vapour.
This vapour rises, forms clouds and
then falls as rain, hail, or snow. Some
water enters plants and soil and the
rest runs off into rivers and oceans.

water cycle

rain, hail, or snow
water
vapour
cloud
river

waterfall *(n)* water from a stream
or river that falls down over rocks.

watering can *(n)* a metal or plastic
container with a handle and a long
spout, used for watering plants.

waterlogged *(adj)*
If something is **waterlogged**, it
is completely flooded or filled with
water. *A waterlogged football pitch.*

Some words that begin with a "w" sound are spelt "wh".

water main (n) a large supply pipe that carries water under the ground.

watermark (n)
a mark in paper that you can see when you hold it up to the light.

waterproof (adj) If something is **waterproof**, it keeps water out.

water-ski
water-skiing water-skied (v) to travel on skis over water, towed by a boat. water-skier (n), water-skiing (n).

watertight (adj) If something is **watertight**, it is completely sealed so that water cannot enter.

water vapour (n) the gas produced when water evaporates.

watt (n)
a unit of electrical power. **wattage** (n).

wave waving waved
1 (v) to move your hand, for example when you are saying hello or goodbye to someone. wave (n).
2 (v) to move something from side to side in the air. The fairy godmother waved her magic wand. wave (n).
3 (n) a moving ridge on the surface of water, especially the sea.
4 (n) a curl in your hair. wavy (adj).
5 (n) a vibration of energy that travels through air or water, for example, sound waves or radio waves.

wavelength (n)
1 the distance between one wave of light, sound, etc. and another.
2 the size of wavelength that a radio station uses to transmit its programmes.
3 (informal) If you are **on the same wavelength** as someone, you think in the same way as they do.

waver wavering wavered (v) to be uncertain or unsteady. Nadia never wavered in her determination to win.

wax waxes waxing waxed
1 (n) a substance made from fats or oils and used to make crayons, polish, and candles. waxy (adj).
2 (v) to put wax polish on something, such as a car.
3 (v) When the Moon **waxes**, it appears to get larger. See **Moon**.

way (n)
1 a direction. Which way is north?
2 a road or route. Do you know the way home?
3 a method or style of doing something. Is this the right way to spell your name?
4 ways (plural n) habits or customs.

WC (n) a toilet. The initials WC stand for Water Closet.

weak weaker weakest
1 (adj) not powerful or not having much force. weakness (n), weaken (v), weakly (adv).
2 (adj) easy to break.
3 (adj) lacking taste. Weak tea.
4 Your **weak points** are the things that you are not very good at.

weakling (n)
a weak person or animal.

wealthy wealthier wealthiest (adj)
Someone who is **wealthy** has a lot of money or property. wealth (n).

wean weaning weaned (v)
1 When you **wean** babies, you start giving them food instead of just milk.
2 If you **wean someone off** something, you help them to give it up gradually.

weapon (n) something that can be used for fighting, such as a sword or a gun. weaponry (n).

wear (wair) wearing wore worn
1 (v) to be dressed in something or to have something attached to you. Rosie wore a red brooch. wearer (n).
2 (n) clothes. Boys' wear.
3 (n) the gradual damage done to something by constant use. My coat is showing signs of wear.
4 wear out (v) If an activity **wears you out**, it makes you very tired.
5 (v) If you **wear out** your clothes, you make them ragged and useless.
6 wear away (v) to destroy something slowly, bit by bit.
7 wear off (v) to become less. The effects of the painkiller have worn off.

weary wearier weariest (adj)
very tired or exhausted. weariness (n), wearily (adv).

weather weathering weathered
1 (n) the state of the atmosphere, for example, how hot or cold it is and whether it is raining, snowing, etc.
2 (informal) If you are **under the weather**, you feel unwell.
3 (v) If you **weather** a storm or a crisis, you get through it.

weather-beaten (adj)
Something that is **weather-beaten** is damaged or worn by the weather.

weather forecast (n)
a prediction about the weather for the next few days.

weave weaving wove or weaved woven or weaved (v)
1 to make cloth, baskets, etc. by passing threads, strips, or canes over and under each other. weaver (n).
2 to move from side to side in order to get through something. Dan wove his way through the crowd.

web (n)
1 the web a collection of linked pages stored on computers all over the world that people can look at by using the internet. The web is short for the World Wide Web.
2 a very fine net of sticky threads made by a spider to catch flies and other insects.
3 webcam a camera that records video footage directly onto a website.
4 web page a computer document on the web.
5 website a collection of linked web pages, set up by an individual or organization.

webbed (adj) Animals with **webbed** feet have skin connecting their toes, which helps them to swim.

wedding (n) a marriage ceremony.

wedge wedging wedged
1 (n) a piece of food, wood, etc. that is thin at one end and thick at the other. A wedge of cheese.
2 (v) If you **wedge** something, you fix it tightly, or force it into a space. Wedge open the door.

wee (adj) very small or tiny.

weed weeding weeded
1 (n) a wild plant growing in a garden or a field.
2 (v) If you **weed** your garden, you pull the weeds out.

week (n)
a period of seven days, usually from Sunday to Saturday. weekly (adj).

weekday (n)
one of the five working days of the week, from Monday to Friday.

weekend (n) Saturday and Sunday.

weep weeping wept (v)
to cry because you feel very sad or very emotional. weepy (adj).

weigh weighing weighed (v)
1 to measure how heavy or light someone or something is, on scales or on a weighing machine.
2 If you **weigh up** an idea or a situation, you think about it carefully.
3 If you are **weighed down**, you have too much to carry.

weight (n)
1 Someone or something's **weight** is how heavy they are.
2 a heavy object. This backpack is a weight!
3 a heavy object that people lift as an exercise to make their muscles stronger.

Some words that begin with a "w" sound are spelt "wh".

a b c d e f g h i j k l m n o p q r s t u v **w** x y z

weightlifting *(n)* a sport in which people lift weights to show how strong they are. **weightlifter** *(n)*.

weir *(rhymes with fear) (n)* a wall built across a river to control the flow of water.

weird *(adj)* strange or mysterious. **weirdness** *(n)*, **weirdly** *(adv)*.

welcome welcoming welcomed
1 *(v)* If you **welcome** someone, you greet them in a friendly way. **welcome** *(n)*, **welcoming** *(adj)*, **welcome** *(interject)*.
2 *(adj)* If something is **welcome**, you like it or are glad to have it. **welcome** *(v)*.

weld welding welded *(v)* to join two pieces of metal by heating them and then fixing them together. **welder** *(n)*.

welfare *(n)* Someone's **welfare** is their state of health, happiness, and comfort.

welfare state *(n)* a system in which the government uses money from taxes to pay for education, health care, and social services.

well
1 *(adv)* If you do something **well**, you do it successfully.
2 *(adv)* thoroughly. *Wash your hands well.*
3 *(adj)* healthy. *You're looking well.*
4 *(n)* a hole from which you can draw water or oil from under the ground.
5 *(interject)* You say **well** at the start of a sentence to show surprise or doubt. *Well, look who's here!*

wellbeing *(n)* health and happiness.

wellington *(n)* a rubber boot that you wear in the rain.

well-known *(adj)* known by many people. *A well-known fact.*

well-off *(adj)* If someone is **well-off**, they are wealthy or rich.

west
1 *(n)* one of the four main points of the compass; the direction in which the Sun sets. **west** *(adj)*, **west** *(adv)*.
2 *(adj)* A **west** wind blows from the west. **westerly** *(adv, adj or n)*.

western
1 *(adj)* to do with the west of a country or the west of the world. *Western Australia. Western civilization.*
2 *(n)* a cowboy film, set in the western part of the USA.

wet wetting wet *or* wetted; wetter wettest
1 *(adj)* covered with or full of liquid.
2 *(v)* to make something wet. *Wet the cloth before you wipe those shelves.*

wetland *(n)* marshy land.

whack *(n)* a hard hit. **whack** *(v)*.

whale
1 *(n)* a large sea mammal, shaped like a fish. Whales take air into their lungs but live in water.
2 *(informal)* When you have a **whale of a time**, you really enjoy yourself.

orca or killer whale

dorsal fin

flipper

tail fluke

whaler *(n)*
1 someone who hunts whales for their meat and oil. **whaling** *(n)*.
2 a boat used to catch whales.

wharf *(worf)* wharfs *or* wharves *(n)* a place where boats and ships can be loaded or unloaded.

what
1 *(adj)* The word **what** is used in questions to discover more about something. *What music do you like?*
2 *(pronoun)* the thing or things that. *I heard what you said.*
3 *(adj)* The word **what** is used to emphasize how great, small, strange, etc. someone or something is. *What a surprise! What an idiot!*

whatever *(pronoun)*
1 anything that. *Wear whatever you like.*
2 what. *Whatever have you done that for?*

wheat *(n)* a cereal plant whose grain is used for making flour. *See* **grain**.

wheel wheeling wheeled
1 *(n)* a circular object which turns on an axle, used to work machinery or move a vehicle.
2 *(v)* to push something on wheels. *Wheel your bicycle up the hill.*

wheelbarrow *(n)* a small cart with one wheel at the front, often used in gardens.

wheelchair *(n)* a chair on wheels for people who are ill, injured, or disabled.

wheelie *(n) (informal)* If you do a **wheelie** on a bicycle or motorcycle, you ride with the front wheel off the ground.

wheeze wheezing wheezed *(v)* to breathe with difficulty, making a whistling noise in your chest. **wheeziness** *(n)*, **wheezy** *(adj)*.

when
1 *(conj)* at the time that. *I told Jake the news when I saw him yesterday.*
2 *(adv)* The word **when** is used to ask about the time that something happened. *When was Dickens born?*

whenever *(conj)* at any time. *We'll eat whenever you're hungry.*

where
1 *(conj)* at the place that. *I visited the house where my friend lives.*
2 *(adv)* The word **where** is used to ask about the place or position of something. *Where is Cheryl?*

whereabouts
1 *(adv)* roughly where. *Whereabouts in New York did you stay?*
2 *(n)* the place where someone or something is. *I'm afraid we don't know Kimberley's whereabouts.*

whereas *(conj)* but. *My parents eat meat, whereas I am a vegetarian.*

wherever *(conj)* to any place. *We'll go wherever you suggest.* **wherever** *(adv)*.

whether *(conj)* if. *I wonder whether it will rain.*

whey *(n)* When you separate milk to make cheese, the watery part is **whey**.

which
1 *(adj)* The word **which** is used to ask about a choice of things. *Which dress shall I wear?*
2 *(pronoun)* You use **which** to show what you mean. *It's the house which has a red door.*

whichever *(pronoun)* any or no matter which. *You can have whichever you want.*

whiff *(n)* a smell in the air.

while
1 *(n)* a period of time. *It was a long while before I ate noodles again.*
2 **while** *or* **whilst** *(conj)* during the time that. *Can you feed my gerbil while I am away?*
3 *(conj)* in contrast to. *Hannah likes skating while I prefer swimming.*

a b c d e f g h i j k l m n o p q r s t u v **w** x y z

whim (n) a sudden idea or wish, which is often rather silly.

whimper
whimpering whimpered (v) to make weak, crying noises. whimper (n).

whine whining whined (v)
1 to make a long, drawn-out sound that is sad or unpleasant.
2 to complain or moan about something in an irritating way.

whinge whingeing whinged (v) (informal) to whine or to complain.

whip whipping whipped
1 (n) a long piece of leather used for hitting people or animals. whip (v).
2 (v) to move something suddenly.
3 (v) to beat cream, eggs, etc. until they are stiff.

whirl whirling whirled
1 (v) If something whirls, it moves around quickly. Leaves were whirling across the playground.
2 (n) a fast or confused movement. A whirl of activity.
3 (informal) If you give something a whirl, you try it out.

whirlwind
1 (n) a wind similar to a cyclone, that moves in a tall column and goes round and round very fast.
2 (adj) very quick or sudden. A whirlwind tour of Europe.

whisk whisking whisked
1 (n) a metal tool that you use for beating eggs or cream. whisk (v).
2 (v) to move something quickly or suddenly. Our plates were whisked away before we finished eating.

whisker (n) one of the long, stiff hairs near the mouth of some animals.

whisky whiskies (n) a strong alcoholic drink made from barley or rye.

whisper whispering whispered (v) to talk very quietly or to make a soft sound. whisper (n).

whistle whistling whistled
1 (n) an instrument that makes a high, loud sound when you blow it.
2 (v) to blow air through your lips to make a sound or a tune. whistle (n).
3 (v) to move very fast with a whistling sound. The train whistled past.

white whiter whitest
1 (n) the colour of snow. white (adj).
2 (adj) White people have naturally light skin, or are descended from people with light skin.
3 (adj) If coffee or tea is white, it has milk in it.
4 (n) The white of an egg is the part around the yolk. See **egg**.

whitewash
1 (n) a mixture of lime, chalk, and water, used for painting things white. whitewash (v).
2 (v) to cover up someone's mistakes or wrongdoings.

whizz
whizzes whizzing whizzed (v) to move very fast, often with a buzzing sound.

who (hoo) (pronoun)
1 The word **who** is used to ask questions about people. Who is that man?
2 The word **who** is used to show which person you are talking about, or to give more information about someone. The woman who lives next door. I visited my granny, who wasn't very well.

whoever (hoo-ev-er) (pronoun)
1 anyone at all or no matter who. Whoever made this mess will have to tidy it up.
2 who. Whoever could that be at the door?

whole (hole)
1 (adj) the total amount of something. I've eaten a whole loaf of bread.
2 (adj) complete or not broken. I'd rather have a whole biscuit than a broken one.
3 (n) the entire thing or all the parts of something. Two halves make a whole.

wholefood (hole food) (n) food that has been processed as little as possible, such as brown rice.

wholemeal (hole-meel) (adj) Wholemeal flour has all the grain left in it.

wholesale (hole-sayl) (adv) When shopkeepers buy things wholesale, they buy them cheaply in large quantities, in order to sell them in their shops. wholesaler (n).

wholesome (hole-sum) (adj) healthy or good for you. A wholesome diet.

wholly (hoe-lee) (adv) completely. I am wholly to blame for the mess.

whooping cough (hoo-ping koff) (n) an infectious disease that makes you cough violently and breathe in a noisy way.

whose (hooz) (pronoun)
1 The word **whose** is used to ask who something belongs to. Whose skateboard is this?
2 The word **whose** is used to indicate the person or thing that you are talking about. That's the girl whose party I've been invited to.

why (adv) The word **why** is used to ask about the reason for something. Why did you leave? why (conj).

wick (n) the twisted cord running through a candle, which you light.

wicked (adj)
1 very bad, cruel, or evil. wickedness (n), wickedly (adv).
2 (slang) very good.

wicket (n)
1 a set of three stumps, with two bails resting on them, used in cricket. The batsman stands in front of the wicket and the bowler aims at it.
2 the strip of ground between two wickets.
3 the act of a batsman being got out. The bowler took six wickets.

wide wider widest (adj)
1 from one side to the other or from edge to edge. This room is seven metres wide.
2 large from side to side. A wide tunnel. widen (v).
3 covering a large number of things. We stock a wide range of magazines. widely (adv).

widespread (adj) happening in many places or among many people. Widespread panic.

widow (n) a woman whose husband has died and who has not married again. widowed (adj).

widower (n) a man whose wife has died and who has not married again. widowed (adj).

width (n) the distance from one side of something to the other.

widthways (adv) in the direction of the widest side. Fold the paper widthways.

wife (n) a female partner in a marriage.

wig (n) a covering of artificial or real hair made to fit someone's head.

wiggle wiggling wiggled (v) to make small movements from side to side or up and down. wiggly (adj).

wild wilder wildest (adj)
1 natural and not tamed by humans. Wild animals. wildness (n).
2 uncontrolled, often in an angry way. wildly (adv).

wilderness wildernesses (n) an area of wild, uninhabited land, such as a desert.

wildlife (n) wild animals and plants.

wilful (adj)
1 deliberate. wilfully (adv).
2 Someone who is wilful is determined to have their own way. wilfulness (n).

will *(n)*
1 written instructions stating what should happen to someone's property and money when they die.
2 Your **will** is your determination to do something. *Ruth has an amazing will to succeed.*

willing *(adj)* People who are **willing** are eager and pleased to offer their help. **willingness** *(n)*, **willingly** *(adv)*.

willow *(n)* a tree with thin, narrow leaves and branches, often near water.

wilt wilting wilted *(v)*
1 If a plant **wilts**, it begins to droop.
2 If a person **wilts**, they become tired through lack of energy or food.

wimp *(n)* *(informal)* a feeble or cowardly person. **wimpish** *(adj)*.

win winning won *(v)*
1 to come first in a contest. **win** *(n)*, **winner** *(n)*.
2 to gain or deserve something. *James won his brother's respect.*

wince wincing winced *(v)* to twitch or flinch because you are in pain. **wince** *(n)*.

winch winches *(n)* a cable wound around a rotating drum that you use for pulling or hoisting things. **winch** *(v)*. See **portcullis**, **rescue**.

wind winding wound
1 *(rhymes with pinned)* *(n)* moving air. **windy** *(adj)*.
2 *(rhymes with kind)* *(v)* to wrap something round something else. *Verity wound her scarf several times around her neck.*
3 *(rhymes with kind)* *(v)* to twist and turn. *The road winds up the mountainside.*
4 *(rhymes with kind)* *(v)* to turn the key of a clock.
5 **wind up** *(rhymes with kind)* *(v)* *(slang)* If you **wind someone up**, you deliberately make them more and more annoyed. **wind-up** *(n)*.

winded *(adj)* If you are **winded**, you are out of breath because of exercise or a sudden hit in the stomach.

windfall *(n)*
1 fruit that has been blown off a tree.
2 a sudden piece of good fortune, usually an unexpected gain of money.

wind instrument *(n)* an instrument played by blowing, for example, the trombone, harmonica, and clarinet. See **brass**, **harmonica**, **woodwind**.

19th-century windmill *(cutaway)*

sail — brake — brake wheel — wallower — striking rod — shutter — miller's boy loading grain into bin — stone nut (turns upper millstone) — great spur wheel (turns stone nut) — reefing stage

cap — grain bin

fantail (turns sails into the wind) — chain wheel (controls angle of sail shutters) — wheel for turning cap by hand — sack hoist — vertical shaft — grain sack — sack trap — grain hopper — millstone (grinds grain between upper and lower stones) — endless chain (attached to chain wheel) — weight (controls angle of shutters) — meal chute — miller checking meal — grain sacks

wing

windmill *(n)*
a machine for grinding grain to make flour, worked by the wind turning a set of sails. *The picture shows a 19th-century windmill. Its sails turn the wallower which is connected by a series of shafts and cogwheels to the greater spur wheel, which turns the millstones to grind grain into flour.*

window *(n)* a transparent piece of glass within a wall.

window-shopping *(n)* If you go **window-shopping**, you look in shop windows but do not buy anything.

windpipe *(n)*
the tube that links the lungs with the nose and mouth. See **respiration**.

windscreen *(n)* the window of strengthened glass in front of the driver of a vehicle. See **car**.

windsurfing *(n)* the sport of sailing by standing on a board with a flexible mast and a sail, and holding on to a curved boom. **windsurfer** *(n)*.

windswept *(adj)* exposed and blown by the wind.

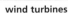
windsurfing

wind turbine *(n)*
a machine with blades shaped like propellers that uses energy from the wind to make electricity.

wine *(n)* an alcoholic drink made from the juice of grapes.

wind turbines

wing *(n)*
1 one of the feather-covered limbs of a bird, which the bird flaps in order to fly. See **bird**.
2 an outer part or extension of something. *The new wing of the hospital will be opened next month.*
3 a wing-like structure on an aircraft that makes it able to fly.
4 **wings** *(plural n)* the side of a theatre stage which cannot be seen by the audience.

Some words that begin with a "w" sound are spelt "wh".

a b c d e f g h i j k l m n o p q r s t u v w x y z

wingspan *(n)*
the distance between the outer tips of the wings of a bird or an aircraft.

wink winking winked *(v)*
to close one eye briefly as a signal or a friendly gesture. **wink** *(n)*.

winner *(n)*
1 a person or team that wins a contest.
2 *(informal)* an excellent idea or plan. *Caroline knew she was on to a winner.*

winter *(n)* the season between autumn and spring, when the weather is coldest. **wintry** *(adj)*.

wipe wiping wiped *(v)*
1 to clear or clean a surface with your hand or a cloth, using a sweeping motion.
2 to rub something in order to clean it. *Wipe your feet.*
3 to remove something. *Wipe that smile off your face!*
4 **wipe out** to destroy totally.

wire wiring wired
1 *(n)* a long, thin, flexible piece of metal. Wire can be used to pull or support things or to conduct an electrical current.
2 **wire up** *(v)* to connect electrical wires to equipment. *Russell wired up the new cooker.*

wireless *(adj)* communicating without connecting wires. *A wireless network. A wireless printer.*

wiry wirier wiriest *(adj)*
1 tough and stiff. *Wiry hair.*
2 A **wiry** person is thin but tough.

wisdom *(n)* knowledge, experience, and understanding.

wise wiser wisest *(adj)*
Wise people have good judgement and know what is right to say and do in different situations. **wisely** *(adv)*.

wish wishes wishing wished *(v)*
1 to think or say that you would like something. **wish** *(n)*.
2 to hope for something for somebody else. *I wish you a happy New Year!*

wisp *(n)* a small and delicate piece of something. *A wisp of hair. A wisp of smoke.* **wispy** *(adj)*.

wit *(n)*
1 the ability to say clever and funny things.
2 someone who can say clever and funny things.
3 the ability to think quickly and clearly. *Steven had the wit to find an escape route.*

witch witches *(n)*
a woman with magical powers.

with *(prep)* attached to or accompanying. *Chicken with fried noodles.*

withdraw withdrawing withdrew withdrawn *(v)*
1 to remove or to take away something. *Sadie withdrew the cash from her bank. Alex withdrew his support for the project.* **withdrawal** *(n)*.
2 to drop out or to go away. *Lee withdrew from the team because of injury.*

withdrawn *(adj)* A withdrawn person is very shy and quiet.

wither withering withered
1 *(v)* When something **withers**, it shrivels up because it has lost moisture.
2 *(adj)* A **withering** look or remark is a very scornful one.

withhold withholding withheld *(v)*
to keep something back, or to refuse to give something. *My parents withheld their permission for a party.*

within *(prep)* inside.
Within the cave was a dragon.
within *(adv)*.

without *(prep)* If you are **without** something, you do not have it.

withstand withstanding withstood *(v)* to bear or to stand something. *The sea wall withstood the pounding of the waves.*

witness witnesses *(n)*
someone who sees something happen and who may be called to give evidence in court. **witness** *(v)*.

witty wittier wittiest *(adj)*
Someone who is **witty** says or writes humorous things. **wittily** *(adv)*.

wizard *(n)*
a man with magical powers.

wobble
wobbling wobbled *(v)* to move from side to side in an unsteady manner. *The cups wobbled on the tray.* **wobbly** *(adj)*.

woe *(n)* great sadness or grief. **woeful** *(adj)*, **woefully** *(adv)*.

wolf wolves *(n)*
a wild mammal that looks like a large dog and hunts in a pack.

Asiatic wolf

woman *(n)*
an adult female human being. **womanhood** *(n)*, **womanly** *(adj)*.

womb *(woom) (n)*
the part of a woman in which a baby develops before it is born. *See* **pregnant**.

wombat *(n)*
a short-legged marsupial that makes burrows.

wombat

wonder wondering wondered
1 *(v)* to think about something in a casual or curious way. *I wonder whether it is time for tea.*
2 *(v)* to be amazed at something.
3 *(n)* someone or something that is amazing or impressive.

wonderful *(adj)*
1 amazing, splendid, or magnificent. *The Himalayas were a wonderful sight.*
2 extremely pleasant. *It was wonderful to see Hugh again.* **wonderfully** *(adv)*.

wood *(n)*
1 the substance that forms the trunk and branches of a tree. **wooden** *(adj)*.
2 an area of trees that is smaller than a forest. **wooded** *(adj)*.

woodland *(n)*
land covered mainly by trees.

woodlice *(plural n)*
small, insect-like creatures which feed on rotten wood and are found in damp, shaded places. The singular of woodlice is woodlouse.

great spotted woodpecker

woodpecker *(n)* a bird that can drill through bark and wood with its bill. Most woodpeckers live in forests.

Some words that begin with a "w" sound are spelt "wh".

worm

oboe flute piccolo bassoon

cor anglais

clarinet

barrel

ligature

mouthpiece
containing reed

top or
upper joint

key

fingerhole

lower joint

bell

woodwind *(n)*
The **woodwind**
section of an orchestra
is made up of instruments
that you blow into and that
were originally made of wood.
*The illustration above shows a
clarinet, with its main parts labelled,
and five other instruments from the
woodwind section of an orchestra.*

woodwork *(n)*
1 things made out of wood.
An exhibition of woodwork.
2 the craft of making things
from wood. *The picture shows
a range of tools used for woodwork.*
woodworking *(adj)*.

wool *(n)* the
hair of a sheep,
spun into a thread
for knitting, weaving,
etc. **woollen** *(adj)*.

word
1 *(n)* a group of spoken sounds or
written letters that has a meaning.
2 *(n)* an order. *Jump when I
give the word!*

3 *(n)* news or a message.
Is there any word from London?
4 If you **give your word**,
you promise something.

word processing *(n)*
the use of a computer and software
to type and print documents. Words
are viewed on screen and can easily
be changed, copied, and stored.
word processor *(n)*.

work working worked
1 *(v)* to study, or to do a job.
work *(n)*.
2 *(v)* to function properly.
Does your laptop work?
3 *(n)* a piece of music, painting,
sculpture, etc. *A work of art.*
4 *(v)* If you **work out** a puzzle,
you solve it by thinking hard.
5 *(v)* When you **work out** in a gym,
you do physical exercise. **workout** *(n)*.

workable *(adj)* If a plan is
workable, it can be carried out.

worker *(n)* someone who
is employed to do a job.

workman workmen *(n)*
a man who does manual work.

workshop *(n)*
1 a room, shed, or other building
where things are made or mended.
2 a group of people who meet to
discuss, learn about, or practise a
particular skill. *A writer's workshop.*

world *(n)*
1 the planet Earth.
2 an area of activity.
The world of sport.

worldly worldlier worldliest *(adj)*
1 concerned with the world
of money and material things,
rather than with spiritual or
religious matters. **worldliness** *(n)*.
2 used to the way that people behave.

worldwide *(adj)* to do with or
reaching most parts of the world.

World Wide Web *(n)*
a collection of
linked pages
stored on
computers all
over the world,
which people can
look at by using
the internet.

worm *(n)*
a small
creature that
lives in the
soil. Worms
have long,
thin, soft
bodies and
no backbones.

woodworking
tools

steel rule

files

tenon saw

mallet

bradawl screwdriver

hand
drill

coping saw

junior
hacksaw

smoothing
plane

mitre box

sandpaper
and block

bench hook

g-cramp

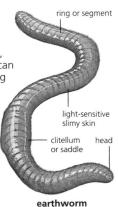

ring or segment

light-sensitive
slimy skin

clitellum
or saddle

head

earthworm

Some words that begin with a "w" sound are spelled "wh".

worn

worn *(adj)* Something that is **worn** is old and less useful because it has been used a lot. *Worn tyres can be very dangerous.*

worry worries worrying worried
1 *(v)* to be anxious or uneasy about something. **worrier** *(n)*, **worrying** *(adj)*, **worryingly** *(adv)*.
2 *(n)* something that makes you anxious. *Neil is a worry to his mum.*

worse *(adj)* less good. *Your spelling is worse than mine.*

worship worshipping worshipped
1 *(v)* to express your love and devotion to God or a god. **worship** *(n)*.
2 *(n)* a church service.
3 *(v)* If you **worship** someone, you think that they are wonderful.

worst *(adj)* worse than anything else. *Hugo's handwriting is the worst I've ever seen.*

worth *(adj)*
1 having a certain value. *This painting is worth a fortune.* **worth** *(n)*.
2 deserving, or good enough for. *It's worth going to the sale for the bargains.*

worthless *(adj)* If something is **worthless**, it has no value or is useless. **worthlessness** *(n)*.

worthwhile *(adj)* useful and valuable. *Learning French is a worthwhile activity.*

worthy worthier worthiest *(adj)* deserving. *I'm happy to give money to a worthy cause.*

wound *(n)* an injury in which the skin is cut, usually caused by an accident, violence, etc. **wound** *(v)*.

wraith *(rayth)* *(n)* a ghost or ghostlike figure.

wrangle wrangling wrangled *(v)* to argue or debate in a noisy or angry way. *The government wrangled over the budget.* **wrangle** *(n)*.

wrap wrapping wrapped *(v)* to cover something in paper, material, etc. to protect it.

wrapper *(n)* the protective material in which something is wrapped. *A sweet wrapper.*

wrath *(roth)* *(n)* anger.

wreak *(reek)* wreaking wreaked *(v)* to cause or to inflict. *The children wreaked havoc in the toy shop.*

wreath *(reeth)* *(n)*
1 a circle of flowers or leaves worn on the head. *A laurel wreath.*
2 an arrangement of flowers, leaves, etc. in memory of the dead.

wreck wrecking wrecked
1 *(v)* to destroy or ruin something completely.
2 *(n)* something that has been ruined, for example, a ship.

wreckage *(n)* the broken remains at the site of a crash or explosion.

wrench wrenches wrenching wrenched
1 *(v)* to pull something suddenly and forcefully. *I wrenched open the door.*
2 *(n)* an adjustable tool for gripping and pulling nuts, bolts, etc. *See* **tool**.

wrestle wrestling wrestled *(v)*
1 to fight by gripping an opponent and trying to throw them to the floor.
2 If you **wrestle** with a problem, you try to solve it by thinking very hard.

wrestling *(n)* a sport in which you fight according to rules. *The picture shows the ancient Japanese sport of Sumo wrestling.* **wrestler** *(n)*.

Sumo wrestling

wretch wretches *(n)*
1 a miserable and unfortunate person. **wretched** *(adj)*.
2 a mean and unpleasant person.

wriggle wriggling wriggled *(v)* to twist and turn.

wring wringing wrung *(v)* to squeeze the moisture from wet material by twisting it with both hands.

wrinkle *(n)* a crease or line in someone's skin or in material.

wrist *(n)* the joint that connects your hand and your arm.

write writing wrote written *(v)*
1 to put down letters, words, or numbers on paper or another surface, using a pen, pencil, etc.
2 to compose poetry, prose, music, etc. **writer** *(n)*.
3 If someone **writes** off a car in a crash, it is a total wreck and cannot be repaired. **write-off** *(n)*.

writhe writhing writhed *(v)* to twist about. *Lou writhed in agony.*

writing *(n)*
1 anything that has been written. *Who did this writing on the wall?*
2 literature, stories, poems, etc.

wrong *(adj)*
1 incorrect or not right. *Wrong answers.* **wrongly** *(adv)*.
2 bad and sinful. *It is wrong to steal.* **wrong** *(n)*, **wrongful** *(adj)*.

WWW *(n)* The initials **WWW** are short for World Wide Web.

Xx

Xmas *see* **Christmas**.

x-ray *(n)*
1 a beam of energy that can pass through solid things. **x-ray** *(adj)*.
2 a photograph of the inside of a person's body, taken using x-rays. *The picture shows an x-ray of a hand.* **x-ray** *(v)*.

x-ray

xylophone *(zy-luh-fone)* *(n)* a musical instrument with wooden bars of different sizes, which are struck to give different notes.

Yy

yacht *(rhymes with dot)* *(n)*
1 a large sailing boat, used for pleasure or for racing. **yachting** *(n)*.
2 a large, luxury motor cruiser.

yak *(n)* a long-haired ox from Tibet and central Asia.

yaks

yank yanking yanked *(v)* to pull something sharply and strongly. **yank** *(n)*.

yap yapping yapped *(v)* to bark repeatedly, with short, high-pitched sounds.

yard *(n)*
1 an enclosed area with a hard surface, usually next to a building.
2 a unit of measurement. *See page 284.*

yardstick *(n)* a standard used to judge things or people. *I judge comedians by the yardstick of whether they make me laugh.*

yarn
1 *(n)* a very long strand of wool or cotton, used for sewing, knitting, etc.
2 *(informal)* If someone **spins a yarn**, they tell a long and exaggerated story.

zoom

yashmak (n) a veil worn by some Muslim women to cover all of their face except for their eyes.

yawn yawning yawned (v)
1 to open your mouth wide and breathe in, often because you are tired or bored. **yawn** (n).
2 to make a wide opening or gap. *A huge gulf yawned between the two rocks.*

year (n)
a period of 365 days, or 366 days in a leap year, which is the time that it takes the Earth to circle the Sun once.

yearn (rhymes with burn)
yearning yearned (v)
to wish or long for something very strongly. **yearning** (n).

yeast (n)
a yellow fungus used to make bread and to ferment alcoholic drinks.

yell yelling yelled (v) to shout or scream very loudly. **yell** (n).

yellow (n) the colour of lemons or butter. **yellow** (adj).

yelp yelping yelped (v) When a dog yelps, it makes a sharp, high-pitched cry, showing that it is in pain. **yelp** (n).

yen (n)
1 the main unit of money in Japan.
2 (informal) If you have a **yen** for something, you want it very much.

yes (interject)
a word used to show agreement.

yesterday (n) the day before today.

yet
1 (adv) so far. *I haven't received an answer yet.*
2 (adv) up to now. *You're not allowed out yet.*
3 (adv) still or even. *There were yet more surprises in store.*
4 (conj) but. *Celia passed all her exams yet couldn't find a job.*

yield yielding yielded (v)
1 to produce something. *The field yielded 90 tons of potatoes.* **yield** (n).
2 to surrender. *Yield, Sir Jasper!*

yodel yodelling yodelled (v)
to sing in a voice that changes rapidly between high and low sounds. Yodelling is popular in Switzerland. **yodeller** (n).

yoga (n)
a system of exercises and meditation that helps people to become mentally relaxed and physically fit. Yoga originally came from Hindu teachings.

yogurt or **yoghurt** (n)
a slightly sour-tasting food prepared from milk curdled by bacteria.

yoke (n) a wooden frame attached to the necks of oxen to link them together for ploughing. *See* **plough**.

yolk (rhymes with poke) (n)
the yellow part of an egg. *If the egg is fertilized, the protein and fat from the yolk nourish the developing embryo. See* **egg**.

Yom Kippur (n)
the most important Jewish holy day of the year, when Jews fast all day. It is also known as the Day of Atonement.

yonder (adj) (old-fashioned)
over there. **yonder** (adv).

you (pronoun)
1 the person or people that someone is talking to.
2 anyone, or people in general. *You never know.*

young younger youngest
1 (adj) Someone who is **young** has lived for a short time.
2 (adj) Something that is **young** has existed for a short time. *A young country.*
3 (plural n) the offspring of an animal.

youngster (n) a young person.

your (pronoun) belonging to you.

yours (pronoun) the one or ones belonging or having to do with you.

yourself yourselves (pronoun)
you and nobody else.
Help yourself to some food.

youth (n)
1 the time of life when a person is young.
2 a young person, usually aged between 13 and 18.
3 (plural n) young people in general. *The youth of today.*
4 **youth hostel** a place where people can stay very cheaply while on holiday. Youth hostels are usually used by young people.

yo-yo (n) a toy consisting of a string wound around a flat reel. You loop the string over your finger and flick the reel up and down on the string.

yuletide (n) (old-fashioned)
the Christmas season.

Zz

zany zanier zaniest (adj) humorous in an unusual, crazy way. **zanily** (adv).

zap zapping zapped (v) (slang)
to shoot someone, usually in a game.

zeal (zeel) (n) enthusiasm and eagerness. **zealous** (zel-uss) (adj).

zebra (n) an African wild animal, similar to a horse, with black and white stripes on its body.

zebras

zebra crossing (n)
a pedestrian crossing marked by flashing orange lights and broad white stripes painted on the road.

zero (n) nothing, nought, or nil.

zest (n)
1 enthusiasm and liveliness.
2 the outer skin of a citrus fruit.

zigzag (n) a line with sharp, diagonal turns. **zigzag** (v).

zimmer frame (n)
a light, metal frame with four legs, used to support people as they walk.

zinc (n) a bluish-white metal that is used in some alloys and for coating metals so that they will not rust.

zip zipping zipped
1 (n) a fastener for fabrics. A zip consists of two strips of metal or plastic teeth which link when pulled together. **zip** (v).
2 (v) to move fast.

zodiac (n)
a circular, imaginary belt in the sky which includes the path of the Sun, the Moon, and the planets. The zodiac is divided into twelve equal parts whose names are the names of constellations. The names or signs of the zodiac are used in astrology.

zombie (n)
1 a dead body brought back to life by supernatural power.
2 (informal) someone who seems lifeless or dull.

zone (n)
an area that is separate from other areas and used for a special purpose. *A conservation zone.*

zoo (n)
a place where animals are kept for people to see or study them.

zoology (n)
the study of animals.
zoologist (n), **zoological** (adj).

zoom zooming zoomed (v) to move very fast. *Anne zoomed off on her bike.*

a b c d e f g h i j k l m n o p q r s t u v w x y z

COUNTRIES AND NATIONALITIES

If a nationality is not given with the country, you refer to people from that country as a citizen of .....

Afghanistan - *Afghan*
Albania - *Albanian*
Algeria - *Algerian*
Andorra - *Andorran*
Angola - *Angolan*
Antigua and Barbuda
Argentina - *Argentine*
Armenia - *Armenian*
Australia - *Australian*
Austria - *Austrian*
Azerbaijan - *Azerbaijani*
Bahamas - *Bahamian*
Bahrain - *Bahraini*
Bangladesh - *Bangladeshi*
Barbados - *Barbadian*
Belarus - *Belarussian*
Belgium - *Belgian*
Belize - *Belizean*
Benin - *Beninese*
Bhutan - *Bhutanese*
Bolivia - *Bolivian*
Bosnia-Herzegovina
Botswana - *Batswana/Motswana*
Brazil - *Brazilian*
Brunei
Bulgaria - *Bulgarian*
Burkina Faso - *Burkinian*
Burma - *Burmese*
Burundi
Cambodia - *Cambodian*
Cameroon - *Cameroonian*
Canada - *Canadian*
Cape Verde - *Cape Verdean*
Central African Republic
Chad - *Chadian*
Chile - *Chilean*
China - *Chinese*
China (Taiwan) - *Nationalist Chinese*
Colombia - *Colombian*
Comoros - *Comoran*
Congo - *Congolese*
Congo (Democratic Republic)
Costa Rica - *Costa Rican*
Croatia - *Croat*
Cuba - *Cuban*
Cyprus - *Cypriot*
Czech Republic - *Czech*
Denmark - *Dane*
Djibouti - *Djiboutian*
Dominica - *Dominican*
Dominican Republic
East Timor
Ecuador - *Ecuadorian*
Egypt - *Egyptian*
El Salvador - *Salvadorean*
Equatorial Guinea - *Equatorial Guinean*
Eritrea - *Eritrean*
Estonia - *Estonian*
Ethiopia - *Ethiopian*
Fiji
Finland - *Finn*
France - *Frenchman, Frenchwoman*
Gabon - *Gabonese*
Gambia, The - *Gambian*
Georgia - *Georgian*
Germany - *German*

Ghana - *Ghanaian*
Greece - *Greek*
Grenada - *Grenadian*
Guatemala - *Guatemalan*
Guinea - *Guinean*
Guinea-Bissau
Guyana - *Guyanese*
Haiti - *Haitian*
Honduras - *Honduran*
Hungary - *Hungarian*
Iceland - *Icelander*
India - *Indian*
Indonesia - *Indonesian*
Iran - *Iranian*
Iraq - *Iraqi*
Ireland, Republic of
Israel - *Israeli*
Italy - *Italian*
Ivory Coast
Jamaica - *Jamaican*
Japan - *Japanese*
Jordan - *Jordanian*
Kazakhstan - *Kazakh*
Kenya - *Kenyan*
Kiribati
Korea, North - *North Korean*
Korea, South - *South Korean*
Kosovo - *Kosovan*
Kuwait - *Kuwaiti*
Kyrgyzstan - *Kyrgyz*
Laos - *Laotian*
Latvia - *Latvian*
Lebanon - *Lebanese*
Lesotho
Liberia - *Liberian*
Libya - *Libyan*
Liechtenstein
Lithuania - *Lithuanian*
Luxembourg - *Luxembourger*
Macedonia - *Macedonian*
Madagascar - *Malagsy*
Malawi - *Malawian*
Malaysia
Maldives - *Maldivian*
Mali - *Malian*
Malta - *Maltese*
Marshall Islands - *Marshall Islander*
Mauritania - *Mauritanian*
Mauritius - *Mauritian*
Mexico - *Mexican*
Micronesia - *Micronesian*
Moldova - *Moldovan*
Monaco - *Monegasque*
Mongolia - *Mongolian*
Montenegro
Morocco - *Moroccan*
Mozambique - *Mozambican*
Namibia - *Namibian*
Nauru - *Nauruan*
Nepal - *Nepalese*
Netherlands - *Dutchman, Dutchwoman*
New Zealand - *New Zealander*
Nicaragua - *Nicaraguan*
Niger
Nigeria - *Nigerian*
Norway - *Norwegian*
Oman - *Omani*
Pakistan - *Pakistani*
Palau - *Palauan*
Palestine - *Palestinian*
Panama - *Panamanian*

Papua New Guinea - *Papua New Guinean*
Paraguay - *Paraguayan*
Peru - *Peruvian*
Philippines, The - *Filipino, Filipina*
Poland - *Pole*
Portugal - *Portuguese*
Qatar - *Qatari*
Romania - *Romanian*
Russia - *Russian*
Rwanda
St. Kitts and Nevis
St. Lucia - *St Lucian*
St. Vincent and the Grenadines
Samoa - *Samoan*
San Marino
São Tomé and Príncipe
Saudi Arabia - *Saudi Arabian*
Senegal - *Senegalese*
Seychelles
Sierra Leone - *Sierra Leonean*
Serbia - *Serbian*
Singapore - *Singaporean*
Slovakia - *Slovak*
Slovenia - *Slovene*
Solomon Islands - *Solomon Islander*
Somalia - *Somali*
South Africa - *South African*
South Sudan - *South Sudanese*
Spain - *Spaniard*
Sri Lanka
Sudan - *Sudanese*
Surinam - *Surinamer*
Swaziland - *Swazi*
Sweden - *Swede*
Switzerland - *Swiss*
Syria - *Syrian*
Tajikistan - *Tajik*
Tanzania - *Tanzanian*
Thailand - *Thai*
Togo - *Togolese*
Tonga -*Tongan*
Trinidad and Tobago
Tunisia - *Tunisian*
Turkey - *Turk*
Turkmenistan - *Turkmen*
Tuvalu - *Tuvaluan*
Uganda - *Ugandan*
Ukraine - *Ukrainian*
United Arab Emirates
United Kingdom
United States - *American*
Uruguay - *Uruguayan*
Uzbekistan - *Uzbek*
Vanuatu
Vatican City
Venezuela - *Venezuelan*
Vietnam - *Vietnamese*
Yemen - *Yemeni*
Zambia - *Zambian*
Zimbabwe - *Zimbabwean*

MONTHS OF THE YEAR

January	July
February	August
March	September
April	October
May	November
June	December

MEASUREMENTS

Length

METRIC
1 millimetre (mm)
1 centimetre (cm) = 10mm
1 metre (m) = 100cm
1 kilometre (km) = 1,000m

IMPERIAL
1 inch (in)
1 foot (ft) = 12in
1 yard (yd) = 3ft
1 mile = 1,760yd

Volume

METRIC
1 millilitre (ml)
1 centilitre (cl) = 10ml
1 litre (l) = 100cl
1 kilolitre (kl) = 1,000l

IMPERIAL
1 fluid ounce (fl oz)
1 pint (pt) = 20fl oz
1 quart = 2pt
1 gallon (gal) = 8pt

Weight

METRIC
1 milligram (mg)
1 gram (g) = 1,000mg
1 kilogram (kg) = 1,000g
1 tonne (t) = 1,000kg

IMPERIAL
1 ounce (oz)
1 pound (lb) = 16oz
1 stone = 14lb
1 hundredweight (cwt) = 112lb
1 ton = 20cwt

Area

METRIC
1 square cm (cm^2)
1 square m (m^2) = 10,000cm^2
1 hectare = 10,000m^2
1 square kilometre (km^2) = 100 hectares

IMPERIAL
1 square inch (in^2)
1 square foot (ft^2) = 144in^2
1 square yard (yd^2) = 9ft^2
1 acre = 4,840yd^2
1 square mile = 640 acres

NUMBERS

1 - one		16 - sixteen	
2 - two		17 - seventeen	
3 - three		18 - eighteen	
4 - four		19 - nineteen	
5 - five		20 - twenty	
6 - six		21 - twenty-one	
7 - seven		30 - thirty	
8 - eight		40 - forty	
9 - nine		50 - fifty	
10 - ten		60 - sixty	
11 - eleven		70 - seventy	
12 - twelve		80 - eighty	
13 - thirteen		90 - ninety	
14 - fourteen		100 - hundred	
15 - fifteen		1000 - thousand	

INDEX OF PICTURE LABELS

Usborne
Illustrated English Thesaurus

Contents

What is a thesaurus?

A thesaurus is a book which gives lists of words with similar meanings. This thesaurus will help you choose the best words for your writing.

Is there a more exciting word for "new"?

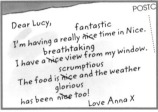

If you know the word that you need, but want to say it in a more interesting way, your thesaurus will provide you with a list of alternative words, or "synonyms", for that word.

Your thesaurus can help you avoid using the same word over and over again. Really overused words, such as "nice" and "good", have panels with synonyms arranged in lists to help you make the right choices.

Dear Lucy,
I'm having a really ~~nice~~ fantastic time in Nice.
I have a ~~nice~~ breathtaking view from my window.
The food is ~~nice~~ scrumptious and the weather ~~has been nice too!~~ glorious
Love Anna X

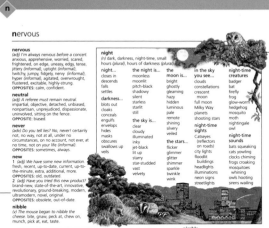

nervous

nervous
(adj) I'm always nervous before a concert. anxious, apprehensive, nervy, scared, frightened, on edge, uneasy, edgy, tense, jittery (informal), uptight (informal), twitchy, jumpy, fidgety, nervy (informal), hyper (informal), agitated, overwrought, flustered, excitable, highly-strung.
OPPOSITES: calm, confident.

neutral
(adj) A referee must remain neutral. impartial, objective, detached, unbiased, nonpartisan, unprejudiced, dispassionate, uninvolved, sitting on the fence.
OPPOSITE: biased.

never
(adv) Do you tell lies? No, never! certainly not, no way, not at all, under no circumstances, on no account, not ever, at no time, not on your life (informal).
OPPOSITES: sometimes, always.

new
1 (adj) We have some new information. fresh, recent, up-to-date, current, up-to-the-minute, extra, additional, more.
OPPOSITES: old, outdated.
2 (adj) Have you tried this new product? brand-new, state-of-the-art, innovative, revolutionary, ground-breaking, modern, ultramodern, novel, original.
OPPOSITES: obsolete, out-of-date.

nibble
(v) The mouse began to nibble the cheese. bite, gnaw, peck at, chew on, munch, pick at, eat, taste.

nice
a nice person	a nice meal	a nice view	I had a nice time.	You look nice.
agreeable	appetizing	beautiful	agreeable	attractive
amiable	delectable	breathtaking	amusing	beautiful
caring	delicious	glorious	brilliant	divine (informal)
charming	lovely	gorgeous	enjoyable	gorgeous
considerate	luscious	impressive	entertaining	handsome
delightful	mouthwatering	lovely	excellent	lovely
friendly	scrumptious	magnificent	fabulous	pretty
generous	(informal)	picturesque	fantastic	ravishing
gentle	tasty	spectacular	(informal)	stunning
good-natured	yummy (slang)	splendid	fun	(informal)
helpful	**nice weather**	superb	good	wonderful
kind	beautiful	wonderful	great	**Nice people don't swear.**
likable	bright	**a nice piece of work**	(informal)	courteous
lovely	dry	accurate	interesting	genteel
obliging	fair	careful	lovely	gentlemanly
pleasant	fine	methodical	marvellous	ladylike
sweet	glorious	meticulous	pleasant	polite
sympathetic	gorgeous	neat	super	refined
thoughtful	lovely	painstaking	(informal)	respectable
understanding	mild	pleasing	terrific	well-bred
unselfish	pleasant	well-presented	(informal)	
warm-hearted	sunny	well-written	wonderful	
	warm			

night
(n) dark, darkness, night-time, small hours (plural), hours of darkness (plural).

night...	the night is...	the moon is...	in the sky you see...	night-time creatures
closes in	moonless	bright	clouds	badger
descends	moonlit	ghostly	constellations	bat
falls	pitch-black	gleaming	crescent	firefly
settles	shadowy	hazy	moon	frog
darkness...	silent	hidden	full moon	glow-worm
blots out	starless	luminous	Milky Way	hedgehog
cloaks	starlit	pale	planets	mosquito
conceals	still	remote	shooting stars	moth
engulfs	**the sky is...**	shining	**night-time sights**	nightingale
envelops	clear	silvery	Catseyes	owl
hides	cloudy	veiled	(reflectors	**night-time sounds**
masks	illuminated	**the stars...**	on roads)	bats squeaking
obscures	inky	flicker	city lights	cats yowling
swallows up	jet-black	glimmer	floodlit	clocks chiming
veils	starry	glitter	buildings	frogs croaking
	star-studded	shimmer	headlights	mosquitoes
	vast	sparkle	illuminations	whining
	velvety	twinkle	neon signs	owls hooting
		wink	streetlights	sirens wailing

nimble
(adj) You must be nimble to be a good footballer. light on your feet, agile, lithe, nippy (informal), speedy, quick, swift, supple, acrobatic, deft, skilful, proficient.

noise
1 (n) I heard a faint noise. sound.
2 (n) The noise in the classroom was unbelievable. din, racket, row, clamour, uproar, hullabaloo, tumult, rumpus, hubbub, commotion, pandemonium.

noisy
1 (adj) A noisy aeroplane. See loud 1.
2 (adj) A noisy gang of kids. boisterous, riotous, rowdy, uproarious, raucous, clamorous, rackety, talkative, vociferous.
OPPOSITES: quiet, subdued.

nonsense
1 (n) Don't talk nonsense. rubbish, drivel, garbage, rot, guff (informal), baloney (informal), twaddle, balderdash, piffle, claptrap (informal), codswallop (slang), poppycock (informal), gibberish.
OPPOSITE: sense.
2 (n) Mrs Badger won't stand for any nonsense. silliness, foolishness, stupidity, tomfoolery, monkey business (informal), mischief, antics (plural), high jinks (plural).

104

This thesaurus contains illustrated panels on lots of different subjects to give you ideas for writing and to help get your imagination working. You can see a list of panels on the page opposite.

A night in the forest

Slowly darkness enveloped the ... The sky was star-studded and v... I stood still and listened carefull... hedgehog snuffled about in the ... an owl hooted and in the di...nce siren began to wail. Shadowy shapes of bat...ter silvery in the moonlig...

You can also use your thesaurus to find a word that you know, but just can't remember.

What's that word that means "noise" and begins with "d"?

Looking at an entry

headword All headwords are arranged in alphabetical order.

part of speech shows the part that the word plays in a sentence. Look at the **Guide to parts of speech** on the page facing this one.

opposite gives an opposite word or words.

number introduces each new meaning of the word.

list of synonyms gives you a choice of alternative words, with the most suitable ones first. Most of the synonyms fit exactly into the example sentence, so you can try out each one until you find the word you like.

frantic
(adj) You'll be frantic when you hear the news. beside yourself, at your wits' end, desperate, panic-stricken, distraught, hysterical, overwrought, worked up, frenzied.
OPPOSITE: calm.

fraud
1 (n) Dodgy Dave is guilty of fraud. swindling, cheating, deception, sharp practice, double-dealing, embezzlement, trickery.
2 (n) (informal) That man is a fraud. impostor, phoney (informal), fake, cheat, con man (informal), swindler, double-dealer, charlatan, quack (doctor).

You may not recognize all the synonyms in a list. Always use a dictionary to check unfamiliar words.

example sentence or **phrase** demonstrates how the word is used and helps you to find the meaning that you want.

word-use label shows that a word is informal, slang or old-fashioned. Informal words are not normally used in formal or official writing.

Word-use labels also show when a word is plural or if it should only be used in a certain situation.

What's in your thesaurus?

chameleon

leaping goalkeeper

List of panels

staring eyes

treasure island

spicy stir-fry

jester

perplexed

sorcerer's castle

Other helpful features

word lists give groups of related words for you to choose from. Some of these lists are illustrated.

song
(n) **TYPES OF SONG:** anthem, aria, ballad, calypso, canon, carol, chant, folk song, hymn, jingle, love song, lullaby, madrigal, nursery rhyme, pop song, psalm, round, sea shanty, serenade, spiritual.

cross-references point you to the headword where you will find the list of words you want. The number shows you which meaning you need to look for.

> **prod** *see* **poke** 2.

cross-references to panels direct you to a range of related words in an illustrated panel.

castle
(n) fortress, fort, stronghold, citadel, palace, chateau.
❖ *Also see* **medieval life**.

> If you can't find the word you want, look for a similar word. For example, for "slowly", look up "slow".

Guide to parts of speech

noun *(n)* Nouns give the name of a person, animal or thing. They tell you who or what a sentence is about. "Sofa" and "happiness" are nouns.
Some nouns, such as "ruins", which are normally used in the plural form, have a label *(plural n)*.

pronoun *(pronoun)* Pronouns refer to a person or thing without naming it. They act like nouns. "We" and "it" are pronouns.

adjective *(adj)* Adjectives are descriptive words which tell you more about a person or thing. They are used with nouns and pronouns. "Huge" and "busy" are adjectives.

verb *(v)* Verbs are action words. They tell you what someone or something does, thinks or feels. "Destroy" and "imagine" are verbs.

adverb *(adv)* Adverbs tell you how, when, where or why something happens. They are used with verbs. "Suddenly" and "sadly" are adverbs.

preposition *(prep)* Prepositions show where people or things are, or what relation they have to each other. "Under" and "near" are prepositions.

phrase *(phrase)* This thesaurus also contains phrases which are made up of several parts of speech. "Fall in love with" and "take advantage of" are phrases.

noun —— Chloë
and
pronoun —— I
verb —— clambered
adverb —— cautiously
preposition —— up
the
adjective —— craggy
noun —— cliff.

Choosing and using words

You can transform your writing by choosing interesting words. Try to avoid repeating the same words and use your thesaurus to find exciting alternatives.

Before you start to write, think carefully about the effect you want to create. The examples on this page will give you ideas for using words in different ways.

Creating atmosphere

To make a scene really come to life, try to use all your senses to describe what you see, hear, smell and feel.

Fire swept through the forest, devouring everything in its path. Flames licked around the blackened trees and lit up the night sky with a weird orange glow. Branches snapped and crackled in the blaze and the air was thick with the acrid smell of smoke.

Conveying action and excitement

Lots of verbs (action words) and short sentences will give your writing a sense of speed and drama.

Buzz dived for the ball, grabbed it and raced off. Bouncing the ball in front of him, he dodged and swerved up the court. Suddenly he stopped, took aim and shot. It was a goal! The crowd roared with delight. Buzz had saved the match.

Describing people

Make your characters interesting and convincing by describing their features, their expressions, their build and the way they move. Details of hair and clothing will help to create a realistic picture.

A burly figure strode along the quay, his crimson frockcoat flapping in the breeze. Where his left hand should have been, a silver hook gleamed from under a lacy cuff. One eye was hidden by a black patch, but the other glittered greedily. Beneath his tangled beard, his mouth looked thin and cruel and a deep scar ran across his weather-beaten cheek.

WANTED
DEAD OR ALIVE

Writing conversation

To make a conversation sound natural, think about the way people talk in real life. Try to find different ways of saying "said" (see panel on page 127) and begin a new line whenever a different person starts to speak.

Poppy inquired

Is that a love letter?

It's none of your business!

Ben snapped

"Is that a love letter?" inquired Poppy, nosily, leaning over Ben's shoulder.
"It's none of your business!" snapped Ben, blushing furiously. "Now clear off and leave me alone!"
"Is it to Sophie?" she continued. Ben was silent. "Because, if so, I'm sure she'll be very happy..." Poppy tailed off, miserably.
"Sophie? No way!" Ben retorted. He took a deep breath. "It's actually to you."

Starting a story

There are lots of different ways to begin a story. You can introduce a character, or set a scene, or even jump straight in with an exciting piece of action or an intriguing conversation. A really dramatic opening will grab your readers' attention and make them want to read on.

Thump!
A large, scaly, orange dragon landed at Todd's feet.
"Excuse me," said Todd, stepping carefully over its tail. "You're blocking the pavement."
"Not for long!" cried the dragon. "Come on, there isn't a moment to lose. We might already be too late !"

Ending a story

You can finish a story by tidying everything up, but sometimes it's fun to leave a mystery unsolved.

It was time to leave Netherfield Manor. Of course it wasn't haunted, it was just a creaky, draughty old house. As I fumbled for my key, I glanced in the hall mirror. Was it just the reflection of the candle flame or was there someone there, calling to me? I locked the door behind me and walked away for ever.

Aa

abandon
1 *(v) When the river flooded, we had to abandon our homes.* leave, desert, leave behind, vacate, quit, evacuate.
2 *(v) Rain forced us to abandon the match.* discontinue, stop, scrap, give up.

ability
1 *(n) I know I have the ability to do better.* potential, capacity, power, capability.
2 *(n) Pablo has great ability in art.* skill, talent, expertise, flair, aptitude.

able
(adj) Vikram is an able tennis player. capable, competent, proficient, accomplished, practised, skilled, skilful, expert, gifted, talented, clever.

abnormal *see* **strange** 1.

abolish
(v) The government wants to abolish smoking in public places. stamp out, put an end to, do away with, eradicate, wipe out, get rid of, eliminate, stop.

about
(adv) Jo has about 20 hats! approximately, roughly, around, more or less, close to, nearly, approaching, nearing.
OPPOSITE: exactly.

abroad
(adv) Mum is abroad this week. overseas, out of the country, in a foreign country.

abrupt
1 *(adj) My ride came to an abrupt end.* sudden, rapid, swift, hasty, unexpected, surprising, unanticipated, unforeseen.
OPPOSITES: gradual, slow.
2 *(adj) Alice gave an abrupt reply.* curt, blunt, brusque, brisk, terse, snappy, direct.

absent *see* **away** 1.

absent-minded
(adj) Professor Peabody is so absent-minded. forgetful, scatterbrained, vague, dreamy, distracted, preoccupied, inattentive, lost in thought.

absolute
(adj) That goal was absolute magic! pure, sheer, complete, total, utter, perfect.

absolutely
(adv) This is absolutely ridiculous! completely, totally, altogether, utterly, perfectly, positively, thoroughly, entirely.

absorb
1 *(v) Use a cloth to absorb the water.* soak up, mop up, suck up, drink up.
2 *(v) I can't absorb all this information at once. See* **take in**.
3 *(v) This book will absorb you for hours.* enthral, captivate, engross, fascinate, rivet.

absorbing *see* **fascinating**.
absurd *see* **ridiculous**.
abuse
1 *(v) Don't abuse your computer.* misuse, ill-treat, damage, harm, manhandle.
2 *(v) It's wrong to abuse animals.* ill-treat, maltreat, be cruel to, harm, hurt, injure, beat, batter, molest.
3 *(n) I've had enough of this abuse.* rudeness, insults *(plural)*, attacks *(plural)*, character assassination, invective, ridicule, derision, slander *(spoken)*, libel *(written)*, cursing, swearing.

accelerate *see* **speed up** 1.
accept
1 *(v) I hope you will accept this gift.* take, receive, welcome.
OPPOSITES: reject, refuse.
2 *(v) I can't accept this behaviour!* allow, tolerate, put up with *(informal)*, take, stand, bear.
3 *(v) I hope you can accept our plan.* agree to, approve, consent to, go along with, resign yourself to, submit to.
OPPOSITE: reject.

accident
1 *(n) Our holiday consisted of one accident after another.* mishap, disaster, misfortune, calamity, catastrophe, blow.
2 *(n) There's been an accident on the motorway. See* **crash** 2.
3 *(n) I broke the plate by accident.* mistake, bad luck.
4 *(n) We met by accident.* chance, coincidence, luck, fluke, serendipity.

accidental
(adj) An accidental meeting. chance, unexpected, unintentional, unplanned, unforeseen, casual, fluky *(informal)*.

accompany *see* **go with** 1.
accomplish *see* **achieve**.
account
(n) A written account. report, record, description, narrative, explanation, statement, diary, journal, log, history.

accurate
1 *(adj) Accurate measurements.* exact, precise, correct, spot-on *(informal)*, strict, unerring, faultless, careful, meticulous.
OPPOSITES: approximate, rough.
2 *(adj) An accurate newspaper report.* correct, factual, true, truthful, faithful.
OPPOSITES: inaccurate, false.

accuse
(v) I don't want to accuse you of stealing. blame you for, charge you with, denounce you for, take you to task for.

ache
(v) My knee is starting to ache. hurt, throb, pound, be painful, be sore, smart.

achieve
(v) See what you can achieve in an hour. accomplish, manage, bring about, do, complete, finish, carry out.

achievement
(n) Climbing the mountain was a great achievement. accomplishment, attainment, feat, triumph, exploit, success.

act
1 *(v) Hugh loves to act in his own plays.* perform, appear, take part, star, play.
2 *(v) Act your age!* behave.
3 *(v) This medicine should act quickly.* work, take effect, react, function.
4 *(n) Saving Fido was a courageous act.* deed, feat, action, undertaking, enterprise, exploit, effort, move, step, operation, accomplishment, achievement.
5 *(n) Rosie's shyness is just an act.* pose, pretence, show, sham, front, façade, mask, cover-up, fake, counterfeit.

action
1 *(n) That was a brave action. See* **act** 4.
2 *(n) The film was packed with action.* activity, drama, excitement, adventure, movement, energy, incident.

active
1 *(adj) Gran is very active.* lively, sprightly, energetic, sporty, vigorous, nimble, spry.
OPPOSITES: sluggish, slow.
2 *(adj) Sally has an active life.* busy, full, energetic, bustling, action-packed.
OPPOSITES: sedentary, idle.
3 *(adj) Marco is an active member of the group.* enthusiastic, hard-working, energetic, involved, committed, dedicated.

activity
1 *(n) The classroom was full of activity.* action, movement, bustle, hustle and bustle, life, commotion.
2 *(n) Football is my favourite leisure activity.* pursuit, occupation, pastime, interest, hobby, project, undertaking.

actor, actress
(n) performer, player, film star, star, lead, supporting actor, character actor, bit player, extra, starlet, dramatic artist.

adapt
1 *(v) I want to adapt my bike so it can go faster.* modify, alter, adjust, convert, remodel, reconstruct, rebuild, change.
2 *(v) Dan plans to adapt his book for TV.* alter, change, modify, tailor, edit, rewrite.
3 *(v) It's hard to adapt to life in a new country.* acclimatize, adjust, get used, accustom yourself, fit in.

adaptable *see* **flexible** 3.
add
1 *(v) Add one more name to the list.* append, attach, tack on *(informal)*, include, insert, affix.
2 *(v) Add these figures together. See* **add up** 1.

addict
1 *(n) A drug addict.* user *(informal)*, junkie *(informal)*, crack-head *(slang)*.
2 *(n) A computer addict.* enthusiast, fanatic, devotee, freak *(informal)*, buff *(informal)*, nut *(slang)*, fiend *(informal)*.

addicted
1 *(adj) Alice is addicted to computer games.* hooked on, obsessed by, crazy about, devoted to.
2 *(adj) Ziggy is addicted to drugs.* hooked on, dependent on.

additional *see* **extra**.

add up
1 *(v) Add up these figures.* add, count up, tot up, total, reckon up, find the sum of.
2 *(v) How much does my bill add up to?* amount to, come to, total.
3 *(v) I'm not sure that our story will add up.* make sense, sound convincing, ring true, hold water, be plausible.

adequate
1 *(adj) Do you have adequate supplies for your voyage?* sufficient, enough, ample.
OPPOSITES: inadequate, insufficient.
2 *(adj) Your work is adequate, but nothing more.* satisfactory, fair, passable, acceptable, tolerable, good enough, O.K. *(informal),* all right, so-so *(informal).*
OPPOSITE: unsatisfactory.

adjust
1 *(v) Are you starting to adjust to your new life?* adapt, acclimatize, get used, accustom yourself, reconcile yourself.
2 *(v) We need to adjust our TV.* tune, retune, regulate, fix, fiddle with *(informal).*
3 *(v) Adjust the straps until they fit tightly.* alter, change, move, fiddle with *(informal).*

admire
1 *(v) I do admire Uncle Jim.* respect, look up to, think highly of, rate *(slang),* approve of, idolize, revere, appreciate, value.
OPPOSITE: despise.
2 *(v) Let's all admire Gary's new car.* praise, marvel at, wonder at, delight in.

admirer
(n) Do you have an admirer? fan, follower, devotee, supporter, disciple, suitor, lover, wooer, worshipper.

admiring
(adj) An admiring glance. appreciative, adoring, approving, delighted, devoted.
OPPOSITES: scornful, disdainful.

admission
1 *(n) Admission to the concert is free.* entrance, entry, admittance, access.
2 *(n) Burglar Beryl made an admission of guilt. See* **confession**.

admit
1 *(v) How many pupils will the school admit?* accept, take in, give a place to, allow in, receive, welcome.
OPPOSITE: exclude.
2 *(v) You must admit that you're lying.* confess, own up, acknowledge, concede, accept, recognize, grant.
OPPOSITE: deny.

adolescence
(n) Dad remembers his adolescence with affection. teenage years *(plural),* teens *(plural),* youth, puberty.

adolescent
(n) teenager, youngster, youth, juvenile.

adopt
1 *(v) Let's adopt Fran's idea.* take up, follow, accept, go in for, support, endorse.
OPPOSITE: reject.
2 *(v) Will you adopt this injured duck?* take in, befriend, foster, parent, take under your wing.

adorable
(adj) An adorable little kitten. lovable, appealing, endearing, charming, delightful, sweet, cute, cuddly, winsome.
OPPOSITES: revolting, repellent.

adore
1 *(v) Juliet, I adore you. See* **love** 1.
2 *(v) (informal) I adore fudge. See* **like** 1.

adult
1 *(n) Wait until you're an adult.* grown-up.
OPPOSITE: child.
2 *(adj) Rosie seems very adult.* mature, grown-up, experienced, sensible.
OPPOSITES: immature, childish.

advance
1 *(v) The army began to advance.* move forward, move onward, press on, proceed, progress, approach, come near, bear down.
OPPOSITES: retreat, withdraw.
2 *(v) I hope to advance rapidly this term. See* **improve** 1.
3 *(v) The money will help to advance research.* promote, further, develop, boost, accelerate.
OPPOSITES: hinder, obstruct.
4 *(v) Please advance me some money.* lend, loan.
5 *(n) This is a major advance in space technology.* development, step, improvement, breakthrough.
OPPOSITE: setback.

advanced
1 *(adj) An advanced new computer system.* modern, up-to-date, state-of-the-art, progressive, sophisticated.
OPPOSITES: out of date, obsolete.
2 *(adj) Advanced maths.* complicated, complex, higher, difficult, hard.
OPPOSITES: elementary, basic.

advantage
1 *(n) A good memory is an advantage if you want to learn a language.* asset, help, benefit, bonus, boon, blessing.
OPPOSITES: disadvantage, handicap.
2 **take advantage of** *see* **take advantage of**.

adventure
1 *(n) Crossing the rapids was a great adventure.* feat, escapade, experience, exploit, enterprise, undertaking, venture.
2 *(n) Amanda longed for adventure.* excitement, drama, thrills *(plural),* thrills and spills *(plural),* danger.

adventure words

adventures can be...

action-packed	incredible
amazing	intriguing
astonishing	nail-biting
baffling	nerve-racking
dangerous	perilous
exciting	perplexing
exhilarating	puzzling
extraordinary	remarkable
fascinating	scary *(informal)*
frightening	strange
hair-raising	terrifying
hazardous	thrilling

adventure clues

ancient manuscript	last will and testament
chart	map
cryptic message (message in code)	newspaper cutting
cypher (code)	parchment scroll
diary	photograph
footprints	riddle
inscription	sealed letter
	secret symbols
	tape recording

cryptic message

penknife

equipment for adventures

binoculars	rope ladder
camera	rucksack
codebook	survival kit
compass	torch
magnifying glass	vine cutters
map	water bottle
notebook	
penknife	

compass

binoculars

LOST CITY

in the city you see...
- bridge
- canal
- city walls
- courtyard
- lake
- market place
- mosaic pavement
- palace
- pyramid
- river
- temple
- tombs
- winding streets

courtyard

temple

the city is...
- ancient
- beautiful
- deserted
- fabled
- forbidding
- forgotten
- hidden
- legendary
- magnificent
- mysterious
- remote
- ruined
- sinister
- undiscovered
- unexplored

plan of labyrinth

under the lost city
- cavern
- dead end
- labyrinth
  (network of tunnels)
- maze
- pillar
- sealed passage
- secret entrance
- stone steps
- tunnel
- underground chamber
- underground passage
- underground waterway

the tunnels under the city are...
- airless
- bewildering
- claustrophobic
- confusing
- creepy (informal)
- crooked
- dark
- disorientating
- endless
- meandering
- musty
- narrow
- shadowy
- silent
- stuffy
- tortuous
- twisting
- winding

underground passage

TEMPLES AND TOMBS

in the temples and tombs you see...
- burial chamber
- carved symbols
- coffin
- corridor
- engravings
- flaming torch
- gilded shrine
- gilded throne
- hidden entrance
- hieroglyphics
  (picture writing)
- mummy
  (embalmed body)
- pillar
- sacrificial altar
- sarcophagus
  (stone coffin)
- shrine
- skull rack
- staircase
- statue
- stone slab
- stone tablet
- treasure chamber
- tunnel
- wall painting

hieroglyphics

sarcophagus

statue

the temple is...
- awe-inspiring
- colossal
- crumbling
- immense
- imposing
- magnificent
- majestic
- massive
- monumental
- towering
- vast

inside the temple it is...
- cool
- dim
- dingy
- eerie
- gloomy
- menacing
- murky
- mysterious
- sinister
- smoky

treasures of the tombs
- amulet (lucky charm)
- armlet
- bowl
- bracelet
- chalice
  (drinking cup)
- coin
- dagger
- diadem
  (light crown)
- flagon (jug)
- goblet
- golden casket
- golden mask
- helmet
- idol
- jewelled collar
- medallion
- necklace
- pendant
- shield
- sword

golden mask

goblet

dagger

necklace

coins

shield

Also see **fantasy words, ghosts & hauntings, jungle, pirates & shipwrecks, space adventure, treasure words**.

adventurous

adventurous
1 *(adj) Gerry is an adventurous climber.*
See **daring**.
2 *(adj) Kit loves adventurous holidays.*
exciting, challenging, dangerous, risky.

advertise
(v) Let's advertise our play in the paper.
publicize, announce, draw attention to,
plug *(informal)*, promote, push.

advertisement
(n) advert *(informal)*, ad *(informal)*, plug
(informal), announcement.
TYPES OF ADVERTISEMENT: blurb *(book
jacket)*, brochure, classified advertisement
(newspaper), commercial *(TV and radio)*,
display, flier, hand-out, leaflet, notice,
placard, poster, promotion, publicity stunt,
sandwich board, small ad *(newspaper)*
(informal).

advice
*(n) I need some advice on how to mend
my bicycle.* suggestions *(plural)*, hints
(plural), tips *(plural)*, guidance, help.

advise
(v) I advise that you try again. suggest,
recommend, urge, counsel, encourage.

affair
1 *(n) I'll handle this; it's my affair.*
business, concern, problem, responsibility.
2 *(n) Kurt's disappearance was a strange
affair.* business, occurrence, event,
incident, episode, matter, case.
3 *(n) Romeo and Juliet had a passionate
affair.* love affair, romance, relationship,
attachment, involvement, liaison.
4 *(n) The party was a grand affair.*
occasion, event, do *(informal)*, function.

affect
(v) The weather can affect my mood.
influence, have an effect on, have an
impact on, sway, alter, change, transform.

affection
(n) Kate looked at her mum with affection.
fondness, tenderness, warmth, devotion,
love, liking, friendship.

affectionate see **loving**.

afford
(v) I can't afford a new pair of jeans. pay
for, spare the money for, meet the cost of,
find the cash for, bear the expense of.

afraid see **scared** 1, 2.

age
1 *(n) We're studying the Elizabethan age.*
period, era, days *(plural)*, time, epoch.
2 *(v) We all age as time passes.* grow old,
decline, deteriorate, fade, grow older,
grow up, mature, come of age.
3 *(n) ages (plural n) I haven't seen Hugo for
ages.* a long time, a long while, weeks
(plural), months *(plural)*, years *(plural)*,
aeons *(plural)*, yonks *(plural)* *(informal)*.

aggravate
1 *(v) Complaining will only aggravate the
problem.* make worse, worsen, magnify,
intensify, heighten, exacerbate.

2 *(v) (informal) Practical jokes aggravate
Mrs Badger.* See **annoy** 1.

aggressive
*(adj) Roger is so aggressive; he's always
starting fights.* quarrelsome, belligerent,
pugnacious, argumentative, antagonistic,
provocative, hostile, violent.
OPPOSITES: submissive, friendly.

agile
*(adj) Monkeys are agile in their
movements.* nimble, lithe, sprightly,
acrobatic, lively, supple, limber, flexible.
OPPOSITES: awkward, stiff.

agitated
(adj) The long wait made me feel agitated.
uneasy, edgy, restless, fidgety, nervous,
worked up, anxious, perturbed, unnerved,
disconcerted, troubled, worried.
OPPOSITES: calm, serene.

agonizing
(adj) An agonizing pain. excruciating,
racking, stabbing, shooting, piercing,
searing, acute, intense, unbearable.

agony
1 *(n) When he broke his ankle, Marvin
was in agony.* pain, torment, distress,
paroxysms *(plural)*.
2 *(n) Parting from Peter was agony.*
misery, torture, torment, anguish.

agree
1 *(v) Do you agree that this is a good film?*
acknowledge, admit, accept, recognize.
OPPOSITE: deny.
2 *(v) Let's agree a date to play tennis.* fix,
decide on, arrange, settle on, arrive at.
3 *(v) I wish you two would agree!*
get on, see eye to eye, be united, concur.
OPPOSITES: disagree, quarrel.
4 **agree with** *(v) I agree with animal
rights.* See **support** 3.
5 **agree with** *(v) Does your version of
events agree with mine?* correspond to,
coincide with, match, fit, conform to, tally
with, square with.
OPPOSITE: differ from.
6 **agree to** *(v) I hope that Nat will agree
to our plan.* consent to, accept, go along
with, comply with, assent to, approve.

agreement
(n) The two sides reached an agreement.
understanding, consensus, settlement,
arrangement, deal *(informal)*, bargain,
contract, pact, truce, treaty.

aid
1 *(n) Many countries offered aid to victims
of the earthquake.* help, assistance, relief,
support, backing, a helping hand.
2 *(v) The money we raise will aid starving
children.* See **help** 3.

aim
1 *(n) My aim is to become a pilot.*
ambition, goal, target, intention, plan,
objective, wish, dream, hope, aspiration.
2 *(v) I aim to be famous one day.* intend,
plan, mean, want, wish, aspire, propose.

3 *(v) Aim the arrow at the bull's-eye.*
point, direct, line up with, zero in on.

aimless
*(adj) Amy wandered around in an aimless
way.* pointless, purposeless, futile,
haphazard, random, rambling, desultory.
OPPOSITE: purposeful.

air
1 *(n) The kite soared high into the air.* sky,
atmosphere, heavens *(plural)*, ether.
2 *(n) The air felt cool on my face.* fresh air,
breeze, wind, draught, breath of air.
3 *(n) The house had an air of mystery.*
appearance, look, atmosphere, feeling,
sense, aura, mood, impression.

aircraft
(n) plane, aeroplane,
flying machine
(old-fashioned).
TYPES OF AIRCRAFT:
airliner, airship,
biplane, bomber, cargo
plane, executive jet,
fighter, glider, hang-
glider, helicopter, hot-air
balloon, jet, jumbo jet, jump
jet, microlight, reconnaissance
plane, rescue helicopter,
seaplane, stealth bomber,
supersonic jet, tanker, triplane.
❖ *Also see* **journey words**.

*hot-air
balloon*

airport
(n) aerodrome, airfield, heliport.

airy
(adj) The room was light and airy. fresh,
well-ventilated, draughty, spacious, open.
OPPOSITE: stuffy.

alarm
1 *(n) If you hear the alarm, run for cover!*
siren, bell, buzzer, signal, warning, alert.
2 *(n) Seb shrank back in alarm.* dismay,
panic, consternation, fear, fright, terror.
3 *(v) This news may alarm you.* startle,
frighten, scare, worry, panic, unnerve, put
the wind up *(informal)*, upset, disturb,
distress, shock, dismay.
OPPOSITE: reassure.

alert
1 *(adj) You seem very alert this morning.*
wide-awake, sharp, quick, perceptive,
attentive, on the ball *(informal)*, on your
toes, lively, quick off the mark *(informal)*.
OPPOSITES: lethargic, slow.
2 *(adj) The guards stayed alert all night.*
See **awake**.
3 *(v) Alert the police!* See **warn** 1.

alien
1 *(n) An alien stepped from the
spacecraft.* extraterrestrial, space creature.
2 *(adj) The new school seemed alien to
me.* See **strange** 3.

alike
(adj) The twins look alike. identical, the
same, similar, like peas in a pod *(informal)*.
OPPOSITE: different.

alive
1 *(adj) Our rabbits are still alive.* living, breathing, alive and kicking, in the land of the living *(informal)*, surviving, flourishing. OPPOSITE: dead.
2 *(adj) There are no dinosaurs alive today.* living, existing, in existence. OPPOSITE: extinct.

alley
(n) alleyway, backstreet, passage, lane.

allow
1 *(v) Will your dad allow you to go?* give you permission, permit, let, authorize, give you leave, give you the green light, give you the go-ahead *(informal)*. OPPOSITE: forbid.
2 *(v) Mrs Badger will not allow talking in class.* permit, tolerate, stand for *(informal)*, put up with *(informal)*, endure, sanction. OPPOSITES: forbid, prohibit.

allowance
1 *(n) Each refugee had an allowance of food.* share, portion, ration, measure, amount, quota, allocation.
2 *(n) A clothes allowance.* grant, subsidy.

all right
1 *(adj) Is it all right to come in?* O.K. *(informal)*, permitted, in order, acceptable.
2 *(adj) I had an accident but I'm all right.* O.K. *(informal)*, unharmed, uninjured, safe, safe and sound, healthy, well.
3 *(adj) The food was all right.* adequate, acceptable, satisfactory, average, fair, O.K. *(informal)*, reasonable, tolerable, passable.

ally
(n) America was an ally of Britain in World War II. partner, associate, colleague, friend, helper.
OPPOSITE: enemy.

almost see **nearly**.
alone
1 *(adj) Are you alone in the house?* on your own, by yourself, unaccompanied, unattended, solitary, solo.
2 *(adj) After my friends left, I felt alone.* lonely, solitary, isolated, friendless, forlorn, abandoned, forsaken, deserted, desolate.

aloof see **cold 4**.
a lot see **many**.

wing · jet

tail rotor · rotor blade · helicopter

propeller · biplane · landing gear · nose cone

tail cone · supersonic jet

thruster · rudder · tail fin · fuselage (body)

tail plane · jump jet · parachute

cargo · cargo door · military cargo plane

seaplane · float · hull · stealth bomber · cockpit

also
(adv) too, as well, besides, in addition, additionally, furthermore, on top of that.

alter
1 *(v) Let's alter our plans. See* **change 1**.
2 *(v) I need to alter my trousers.* adjust, take in, take up, let out, let down, shorten, lengthen, remodel, revamp, transform.

alternative
1 *(adj) Let's try an alternative plan.* different, other, substitute, back-up.
2 *(n) Do I have an alternative?* choice, option, fall-back.

always
1 *(adv) Fifi is always late.* consistently, invariably, without exception, regularly, repeatedly, unfailingly, constantly, continually, perpetually, forever.
OPPOSITES: never, rarely.
2 *(adv) I will love you always.* forever, forever and ever, evermore, eternally, unceasingly, until the end of time.

amaze see **astonish**.
amazed see **astonished**.
amazement
(adj) Tiggy looked at me in amazement. astonishment, surprise, shock, confusion, bewilderment, wonder, admiration.

amazing
(adj) Arthur made an amazing discovery. astonishing, incredible, remarkable, extraordinary, unusual, startling, astounding, staggering, stunning, breathtaking, miraculous, phenomenal, electrifying, sensational *(informal)*.

ambition
1 *(n) My ambition is to become a pilot.* See **aim 1**.
2 *(n) Joel has plenty of ambition.* drive, enthusiasm, eagerness, enterprise, get-up-and-go *(informal)*, oomph *(informal)*.

ambitious
(adj) An ambitious businessman. go-getting *(informal)*, pushy *(informal)*, go-ahead, forceful, purposeful, enterprising.
OPPOSITE: unambitious.

ammunition
(n) TYPES OF AMMUNITION: blank cartridge, bullet, cannonball, cartridge, grenade, missile, rocket, rubber bullet, shell, shot, shrapnel.

amount
1 *(n) We bought a large amount of jelly babies.* quantity, number, supply.
2 *(n) The reservoir holds a large amount of water.* quantity, volume, mass, expanse.
3 *(n) What was the final amount that you raised?* sum, total, grand total, sum total.
4 **amount to** *(v) Lord Lucre's savings amount to millions. See* **add up 2**.

amuse
1 *(v) I think this joke will amuse you.* make you laugh, tickle you *(informal)*, cheer you up, raise a smile.
2 *(v) This game will amuse you for hours.* entertain, keep you amused, occupy, absorb, engross, interest, fascinate.
OPPOSITE: bore.

amusement
1 *(n) The joke caused much amusement.* laughter, hilarity, mirth, merriment.
OPPOSITES: boredom, sadness.
2 *(n) What do you do for amusement?* fun, pleasure, entertainment, enjoyment, interest, recreation, leisure, pastime, sport.

amusing
1 *(adj) An amusing joke. See* **funny 1**.
2 *(adj) An amusing game of cards. See* **entertaining**.

analyse
(v) Let's analyse the situation. examine, think through, investigate, study, consider, review, inquire into, scrutinize, evaluate.

ancient
1 *(adj) How did people live in ancient times?* early, past, bygone, olden *(old-fashioned)*, primeval, prehistoric, primitive.
OPPOSITES: modern, recent.
2 *(adj) Our school buildings are ancient.* old, aged, archaic, antiquated, timeworn, out of date, old-fashioned, outmoded, antediluvian, out of the ark *(informal)*.
OPPOSITES: modern, state-of-the-art.

Ancient Egypt

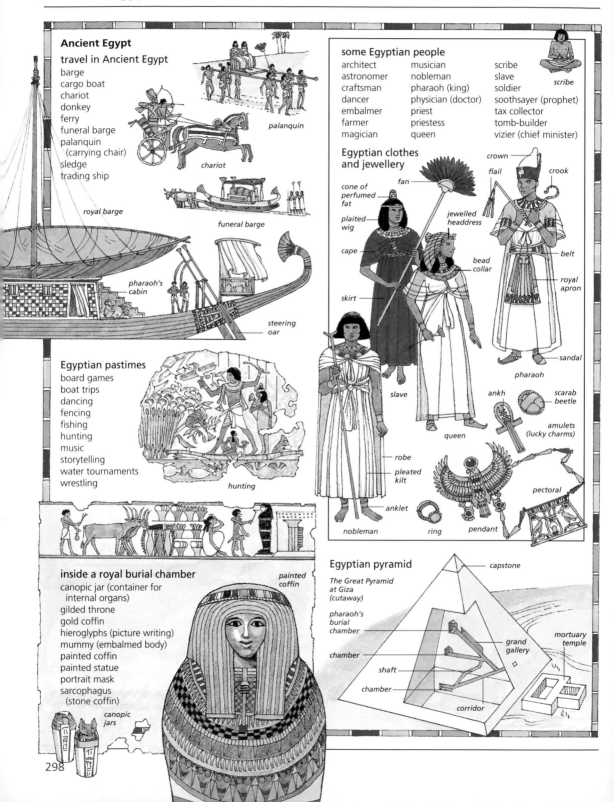

Ancient Egypt

travel in Ancient Egypt
barge
cargo boat
chariot
donkey
ferry
funeral barge
palanquin
  (carrying chair)
sledge
trading ship

palanquin

chariot

royal barge

funeral barge

pharaoh's cabin

steering oar

Egyptian pastimes
board games
boat trips
dancing
fencing
fishing
hunting
music
storytelling
water tournaments
wrestling

hunting

some Egyptian people
architect	musician	scribe
astronomer	nobleman	slave
craftsman	pharaoh (king)	soldier
dancer	physician (doctor)	soothsayer (prophet)
embalmer	priest	tax collector
farmer	priestess	tomb-builder
magician	queen	vizier (chief minister)

scribe

Egyptian clothes and jewellery

crown

flail   *crook*

cone of perfumed fat

fan

plaited wig

jewelled headdress

cape

bead collar

belt

skirt

royal apron

slave

sandal

pharaoh

ankh   *scarab beetle*

queen

amulets (lucky charms)

robe

pleated kilt

pectoral

anklet

nobleman   *ring*   *pendant*

inside a royal burial chamber
canopic jar (container for
  internal organs)
gilded throne
gold coffin
hieroglyphs (picture writing)
mummy (embalmed body)
painted coffin
painted statue
portrait mask
sarcophagus
  (stone coffin)

painted coffin

canopic jars

Egyptian pyramid

The Great Pyramid at Giza (cutaway)

capstone

pharaoh's burial chamber

chamber

grand gallery

mortuary temple

shaft

chamber

corridor

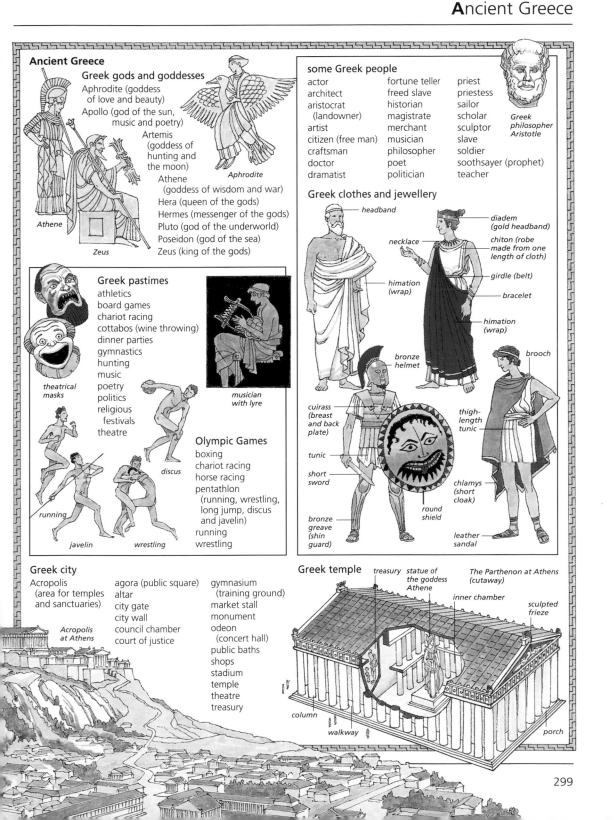

Ancient Greece

Greek gods and goddesses

Aphrodite (goddess of love and beauty)

Apollo (god of the sun, music and poetry)

Artemis (goddess of hunting and the moon)

Athene (goddess of wisdom and war)

Hera (queen of the gods)

Hermes (messenger of the gods)

Pluto (god of the underworld)

Poseidon (god of the sea)

Zeus (king of the gods)

Athene

Zeus

Aphrodite

some Greek people

actor
architect
aristocrat (landowner)
artist
citizen (free man)
craftsman
doctor
dramatist
fortune teller
freed slave
historian
magistrate
merchant
musician
philosopher
poet
politician
priest
priestess
sailor
scholar
sculptor
slave
soldier
soothsayer (prophet)
teacher

Greek philosopher Aristotle

Greek pastimes

athletics
board games
chariot racing
cottabos (wine throwing)
dinner parties
gymnastics
hunting
music
poetry
politics
religious festivals
theatre

theatrical masks

musician with lyre

Olympic Games

boxing
chariot racing
horse racing
pentathlon (running, wrestling, long jump, discus and javelin)
running
wrestling

running

discus

javelin

wrestling

Greek clothes and jewellery

headband

diadem (gold headband)

necklace

chiton (robe made from one length of cloth)

himation (wrap)

girdle (belt)

bracelet

himation (wrap)

bronze helmet

brooch

cuirass (breast and back plate)

thigh-length tunic

tunic

short sword

bronze greave (shin guard)

round shield

chlamys (short cloak)

leather sandal

Greek city

Acropolis (area for temples and sanctuaries)

agora (public square)
altar
city gate
city wall
council chamber
court of justice

gymnasium (training ground)
market stall
monument
odeon (concert hall)
public baths
shops
stadium
temple
theatre
treasury

Acropolis at Athens

Greek temple

treasury

statue of the goddess Athene

The Parthenon at Athens (cutaway)

inner chamber

sculpted frieze

column

walkway

porch

anger
1 *(n) Mum turned purple with anger.* rage, fury, wrath, indignation, annoyance, exasperation, irritation, outrage.
2 *(v) Your giggles will anger Mrs Badger.* infuriate, enrage, madden, incense, rile, annoy, exasperate, irritate, provoke.
OPPOSITES: pacify, placate.

angry
(adj) Dad was angry that I hadn't told the truth. furious, livid, irate, incensed, fuming, seething, raging, enraged, mad *(informal)*, apoplectic, cross, annoyed, indignant.

animal
(n) A wild animal. creature, beast.

announce
1 *(v) I heard the head announce that the trip was cancelled.* state, declare, give out, reveal, disclose, make known, make public.
2 *(v) Will you announce the next act in the talent show?* introduce, present, lead into.

announcement
(n) Did you hear the announcement? notice, statement, message, bulletin, communication, advertisement, report, declaration, disclosure.

announcer
(n) presenter, broadcaster, anchorman, newsreader, newscaster, commentator, master of ceremonies, town crier.

annoy
1 *(v) Doesn't your brother annoy you?* irritate, exasperate, infuriate, get on your nerves *(informal)*, madden, provoke, rile, bug *(informal)*, rub you up the wrong way, aggravate *(informal)*, needle *(informal)*, get to *(informal)*, get up your nose *(slang)*, nark *(slang)*, get on your wick *(slang)*.
2 *(v) Don't annoy Dad when he's busy.* disturb, bother, trouble, pester, hassle *(informal)*, badger, harass, worry.

annoyed
(adj) Kim was annoyed that she hadn't got her own way. irritated, exasperated, cross, indignant, displeased, vexed, riled, miffed *(informal)*, peeved *(informal)*, piqued.
OPPOSITE: pleased.

annoying
(adj) Are you being deliberately annoying? irritating, infuriating, maddening, exasperating, aggravating *(informal)*, tiresome, trying, irksome, troublesome.

anonymous
1 *(adj) The writer wishes to remain anonymous.* nameless, unnamed, unidentified, unknown, unacknowledged, uncredited, incognito.
2 *(adj) An anonymous letter.* unsigned.

answer
1 *(v) You didn't answer my question.* reply to, respond to, react to, acknowledge.
OPPOSITE: ask.
2 *(v) "Never!" I heard Luke answer.* reply, respond, retort, return, rejoin, retaliate.
OPPOSITES: ask, inquire.

3 *(n) Kay gave no answer to my question.* reply, response, reaction, comeback *(informal)*, acknowledgment, rejoinder.
OPPOSITE: question.
4 *(n) What is the answer to this problem?* solution, explanation, key.

answer back
(v) Don't answer back! talk back, argue, contradict, be cheeky, be impertinent.

anticlimax *see* **letdown**.

antisocial
(adj) Antisocial behaviour. disruptive, anarchic, rebellious, uncooperative, offensive, disagreeable, hostile, disorderly, unruly, antagonistic.

anxiety *see* **worry** 3.

anxious
1 *(adj) Sally is anxious about her exams.* worried, apprehensive, concerned, nervous, tense, uneasy, edgy, on edge, uptight *(informal)*, jittery *(informal)*, troubled, agitated, perturbed, fretful, fearful, distressed, overwrought.
OPPOSITES: calm, confident.
2 *(adj) We are anxious to get started. See* **eager** 2.

apathetic *see* **indifferent**.

apologetic *see* **sorry** 1.

apologize
(v) You ought to apologize for breaking the window. say sorry, say you are sorry, make an apology, express regret, be penitent about, ask forgiveness, beg pardon, eat humble pie.

apology
(n) Mum accepted my apology. expression of regret, confession, explanation, excuse, plea, defence, justification.

appalling *see* **dreadful** 1, 2, 3.

apparent *see* **obvious**.

appeal
1 *(n) A charity appeal.* campaign.
2 *(n) Burglar Beryl made an appeal for mercy.* plea, request, cry, call, petition.
3 *(v) We will have to appeal for more volunteers.* ask, put in a plea, beg, plead, call, request, petition, canvass.
4 **appeal to** *(v) This film will appeal to young children.* interest, delight, attract, fascinate, captivate, enthral, enchant, charm, please.
OPPOSITES: bore, repulse, alienate.

appealing *see* **charming**.

appear
1 *(v) We watched the ship appear over the horizon.* come into view, come into sight, emerge, loom, materialize, surface.
OPPOSITES: disappear, vanish.
2 *(v) What time did you appear at the party?* arrive, turn up, show up *(informal)*, roll up *(informal)*, come.
OPPOSITES: leave, depart.
3 *(v) Do you appear in the play?* feature, figure, perform, act, take part, play a part.

4 *(v) You appear fit and well.* look, seem, give the impression of being.
5 *(v) The next issue of "Rap Weekly" will appear on Monday.* come out, be published, become available, come on the market, hit the shops *(informal)*.

appearance
1 *(n) Can you describe Samantha's appearance?* looks *(plural)*, bearing, demeanour, figure, image, expression, air.
2 *(n) Ed gives the appearance of being confident.* impression, illusion, outward appearance, show, semblance, pretence.
OPPOSITE: reality.
3 *(n) The sudden appearance of rain spoiled the barbecue.* arrival, advent, coming, presence.
OPPOSITE: disappearance.

---

appearance words

tall	thin	strong
lanky	bony	athletic
leggy	emaciated	beefy
towering	gaunt	*(informal)*
	lanky	brawny
short	lean	broad-
diminutive	scraggy	shouldered
dumpy	scrawny	burly
little	skeletal	hulking
petite	skinny	muscular
pint-sized	spare	powerful
(informal)	spindly	sinewy
small	waiflike	stocky
squat		strapping
tiny	**slim**	sturdy
	dainty	thickset
fat	elfin	well-built
chubby	lithe	wiry
corpulent	slender	
flabby	slight	**weak**
heavy	svelte	anaemic
hefty	sylphlike	delicate
obese	trim	feeble
overweight	willowy	fragile
paunchy		frail
plump	**curvy**	puny
podgy	bosomy	sickly
portly	busty	weedy
potbellied	buxom	*(informal)*
stout	curvaceous	wimpish
tubby	shapely	*(informal)*
weighty	voluptuous	
		upright
		erect
		straight
		straight-
		backed
		unbending

hulking sumo wrestler

appetite
(n) *Indiana has an appetite for adventure.* taste, thirst, hunger, need, desire, passion, liking, longing, craving, yearning, hankering, eagerness, zest.
OPPOSITES: dislike, aversion.

appetizing *see* **delicious**.

applaud
(v) *The audience are sure to applaud.* clap, cheer, whistle, give you a standing ovation, give you a big hand *(informal)*, put their hands together, ask for an encore.
OPPOSITES: boo, heckle.

apply
1 (v) *Apply the lotion twice a day.* use, smear on, put on, rub in, spread on, administer, cover with.

hunched	smart
bent	dapper
bowed	neat
crooked	spruce
drooping	tidy
slouching	well-dressed
stooping	well-groomed
young	messy
boyish	bedraggled
girlish	dishevelled
youthful	scruffy
	shabby
old	tatty
aged	unkempt
elderly	untidy
graceful	fashionable
agile	chic
dignified	trendy *(informal)*
elegant	smart
lithe	stylish
poised	up-to-date
clumsy	unfashionable
awkward	dowdy
blundering	old-fashioned
bumbling	
gangling	sophisticated
gauche	classy *(slang)*
gawky	debonair
lumbering	elegant
shambling	glamorous
uncoordinated	refined
ungainly	suave

sylphlike ballerina

wiry gymnast

Also see **faces & features, hair & hairstyles**.

2 (v) *This comment could apply to you.* refer, relate, be relevant, be applicable, be pertinent, have a bearing on, pertain.
3 **apply for** (v) *Did you apply for the job?* make an application for, put in for, try for, inquire after, request.
4 **apply yourself** (v) *You need to apply yourself to your work. See* **concentrate** 2.

appointment
(n) *I have an appointment at four o'clock.* engagement, meeting, date, rendezvous, interview, consultation *(medical)*.

appreciate
1 (v) *I will always appreciate your help.* value, be grateful for, be thankful for, be appreciative of, be obliged to you for, be indebted to you for, welcome.
OPPOSITE: be ungrateful for.
2 (v) *Aunt Bertha will never appreciate pop music.* enjoy, approve of, admire, think much of, think highly of, rate *(slang)*, understand.
OPPOSITE: despise.
3 (v) *Do you appreciate how long it took to make this meal? See* **realize**.

apprehensive *see* **anxious** 1.

approach
1 (v) *The army began to approach.* draw near, come closer, move nearer, edge nearer, bear down, near, advance, push forward, catch up.
OPPOSITES: move away, back off.
2 (v) *I intend to approach Dad about my pocket money.* speak to, talk to, tackle, sound out, appeal to, make a proposal to.
3 (v) *I'm not sure how to approach this essay.* tackle, set about, go about, start, begin, embark on, make a start on.

approachable *see* **friendly**.
appropriate *see* **suitable** 1, 2.

approve
1 (v) *The chairman must approve the plan first.* accept, agree to, authorize, pass, endorse, consent to, give the go-ahead to *(informal)*, rubber-stamp *(informal)*.
2 **approve of** (v) *I hope you'll approve of what I've done.* be pleased with, like, applaud, admire, think highly of, have a good opinion of, appreciate, respect.
OPPOSITE: disapprove of.

approximately *see* **about**.

area
1 (n) *I have a lot of friends in this area.* district, neighbourhood, locality, part of the world, region, vicinity.
2 (n) *The fire destroyed a large area of forest.* expanse, stretch, patch, tract.

arena
(n) *A sports arena.* stadium, ground, field, ring, pitch, bowl, oval, rink.

argue
1 (v) *My brothers argue all the time.* quarrel, squabble, bicker, row, fight, fall out *(informal)*, disagree, wrangle.
OPPOSITES: agree, get on.

2 (v) *My cousins argue that eating animals is wrong.* claim, assert, declare, maintain, insist, reason, hold, contend.

argument
1 (n) *We had an argument over who should pay.* row, quarrel, squabble, disagreement, dispute, difference of opinion, clash, fight, tiff *(informal)*, bust-up *(informal)*, set-to *(informal)*.
OPPOSITE: agreement.
2 (n) *The argument about violence on TV continues.* debate, discussion, controversy.
3 (n) *Your argument is very convincing.* reasoning, logic, evidence, defence, justification, case, reasons *(plural)*, grounds *(plural)*.

armed
1 (adj) *The robber is armed.* carrying weapons, armed to the teeth.
OPPOSITES: unarmed, defenceless.
2 (adj) *The soldiers were armed with swords.* equipped, fitted out, supplied, provided, issued.

armour
(n) protection.
TYPES OF ARMOUR: body armour, bulletproof vest, chain mail, flak jacket, plate armour, riot shield, suit of armour.

helmet
visor
cuirass *(breast and back plate)*
gauntlet
cuisse *(thigh guard)*
greave *(shin guard)*
suit of armour

aroma *see* **smell** 1.

arrange
1 (v) *Would you arrange these ornaments for me?* display, set out, put out, tidy, position, line up, align, put in order.
2 (v) *Can you arrange these words in alphabetical order?* sort, group, organize, set out, rank, classify, categorize, collate.
3 (v) *Let's arrange a party.* organize, plan, fix up, set up, prepare, schedule.

arrangement
1 (n) *The arrangement is that we use the gym on Tuesdays.* agreement, understanding, deal *(informal)*, set-up *(informal)*, system, plan, scheme.
2 (n) *What a beautiful arrangement of flowers!* display, array, show.

arrest
(v) *The police decided to arrest Burglar Beryl.* take into custody, detain, apprehend, catch, capture, seize, haul in, collar *(informal)*, run in *(informal)*, pick up *(informal)*, nab *(informal)*, nick *(slang)*.

arrive
1 (v) *When do you think Tracy will arrive?* appear, turn up, show up (informal), come, roll up (informal), get here, put in an appearance, show (informal).
OPPOSITES: leave, depart.
2 (v) *When will we arrive in New York?* land, touch down, dock, berth, disembark.
OPPOSITES: leave, take off, set sail.

arrogant *see* **proud** 2.

art
1 (n) *Lysander is studying art.* the visual arts (plural), design, fine art, art history.
TYPES OF ART: architecture, carving, computer art, drawing, engraving, etching, graphics, illustration, installation art, mosaic making, painting, photography, printing, sculpture, stained glass, tapestry.
Also see **drawing, painting**.
2 (n) *We admired the potter's art.*
See **skill**.

article
1 (n) *There's an interesting article in the newspaper.* item, feature, story, report, write-up, piece, column, exclusive, scoop (informal), editorial, leader.
2 (n) *What's that odd-looking article on the table?* object, thing, item.

artificial
1 (adj) *Lycra is an artificial fibre.* synthetic, man-made, manufactured.
OPPOSITE: natural.
2 (adj) *Artificial pearls are cheaper than real ones.* imitation, fake, simulated, synthetic, sham, mock, pseudo (informal).
OPPOSITES: genuine, natural.
3 (adj) *Araminta gave me an artificial smile.* insincere, forced, false, feigned, affected, phoney (informal), put-on.
OPPOSITES: genuine, sincere.

ascend *see* **rise** 1.

ash
(n) *The ash from the volcano glowed red-hot.* cinders (plural), embers (plural).

ashamed
(adj) *Ben looked ashamed that he'd lost his temper.* guilty, conscience-stricken, sorry, mortified, embarrassed, shamefaced, sheepish, red-faced, repentant, remorseful, rueful, abashed, chastened, humiliated.
OPPOSITE: unrepentant.

ask
1 (v) *Jon wants to ask if his answer is right.* inquire, enquire, query, question.
OPPOSITES: reply, answer.
2 (v) *The police want to ask Burglar Beryl about the robbery.* question, interrogate, cross-examine, quiz, grill (informal), pump, give the third degree to.
3 (v) *Wait for the doctor to ask you into the surgery.* invite, summon, order, bid.
4 **ask for** (v) *Jo decided to ask for more pocket money.* request, appeal for, beg for, plead for, demand, call for, claim, press for, petition for, apply for.

5 **ask for** (v) *You did rather ask for that punch on the nose!* deserve, bring on yourself, provoke, cause, encourage.

asleep
(adj) *Dad's asleep on the sofa.* sleeping, fast asleep, sound asleep, dozing, snoozing (informal), napping, having a kip (slang), slumbering (old-fashioned), crashed out (slang), dead to the world (informal).
OPPOSITE: awake.

assault *see* **attack** 2, 4, 5.

assemble
1 (v) *Mrs Badger told us to assemble in the hall.* See **meet** 3.
2 (v) *The workers began to assemble the car.* construct, build, put together, manufacture, piece together.
OPPOSITES: dismantle, take apart.

assembly *see* **meeting** 2.

assertive
1 (adj) *You should try to be more assertive.* confident, self-assured, firm, decisive, positive, emphatic, forceful.
OPPOSITE: passive.
2 (adj) *Pat is becoming too assertive.* domineering, overbearing, aggressive, opinionated, dogmatic, forceful, strong-willed, pushy (informal).
OPPOSITE: submissive.

assistance *see* **help** 5.

assistant
(n) helper, deputy, second-in-command, right-hand man or woman, henchman (informal), subordinate.

associate
1 (v) *Don't associate with those boys! See* **mix** 3.
2 (v) *I always associate that smell with school dinners.* connect, identify, link, lump together, relate to.

assorted *see* **mixed** 1.

assortment *see* **mixture** 1.

assume
(v) *I assume you like chocolate.* presume, take it for granted, expect, suppose, imagine, suspect, believe, guess (informal).

assure
(v) *Can you assure me that I won't be in danger?* promise, give your word, swear, guarantee, reassure, convince, persuade.

astonish
(v) *Marvello the Magician will astonish you with his tricks.* amaze, astound, stun, stagger, leave you speechless, startle, surprise, dazzle, take your breath away, leave you open-mouthed, wow (slang).

astonished
(adj) *I was astonished to hear the news.* amazed, astounded, stunned, staggered, surprised, startled, taken aback, shocked, flabbergasted (informal), dumbfounded, gobsmacked (slang), thunderstruck.

astonishing *see* **amazing**.

astound *see* **astonish**.

astronaut
(n) spaceman, spacewoman, cosmonaut (Russian), space traveller, shuttle crew member. ❖ *Also see* **space adventure**.

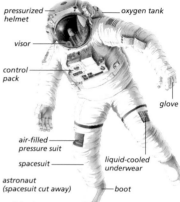

pressurized helmet
oxygen tank
visor
control pack
glove
air-filled pressure suit
spacesuit
liquid-cooled underwear
boot
astronaut (spacesuit cut away)

athletics
(n) track and field events (plural), games (plural).
TYPES OF ATHLETICS EVENT: cross-country, decathlon, discus, hammer throw, heptathlon, high jump, hurdles, javelin, long jump, marathon, pentathlon, pole vault, relay, running, shot put, sprint, steeplechase, triple jump, walking.
❖ *Also see* **sport words**.

atmosphere
1 (n) *The spaceship blasted into the atmosphere.* air, sky, heavens (plural), space, ether.
2 (n) *There was a strange atmosphere at the party.* feeling, mood, ambience, air, aura, vibrations (plural) (informal), vibes (plural) (slang).

atrocious *see* **dreadful** 1, 2, 3.

attach
(v) *Attach the pieces together.* fasten, join, fix, link, connect, stick, pin, tie, secure.
OPPOSITES: detach, separate.

attack
1 (v) *The soldiers will attack the city by night.* invade, storm, charge, strike, fall upon, descend on, bombard, raid, rush.
OPPOSITES: defend, protect.
2 (v) *The robbers threatened to attack the guard.* assault, beat up (informal), mug (informal), jump on, set on, set about, lay into (informal), put the boot in (slang).
3 (v) *The newspapers often attack the government.* criticize, find fault with, blame, slate (informal), have a go at (informal), lay into (informal), snipe at, get at, harangue, censure, berate.
OPPOSITE: defend.
4 (n) *The commanders planned their attack.* assault, charge, invasion, offensive, strike, raid, sortie, foray, onslaught, bombardment, blitz (air raid).
OPPOSITE: defence.

5 *(n) We were shocked by the attack on the old lady.* assault, mugging *(informal)*.
6 *(n) Lord Lucre was upset by the newspaper's attack.* criticism, slating *(informal)*, censure, tirade, onslaught, character assassination, denigration.
7 *(n) Joseph had an attack of coughing.* fit, bout, spell, outbreak.

attempt *see* **try** 1, 2.

attend
1 *(v) Are you planning to attend the club meeting?* go to, be present at, be at, turn up for, put in an appearance at, show up at *(informal)*.
2 attend to *(v) Please attend to your work. See* **concentrate** 2.
3 attend to *(v) The doctor will attend to you now. See* **see to**.

attic
(n) loft, roof space, garret *(old-fashioned)*.

attitude
1 *(n) What's your attitude towards fox-hunting?* opinion of, view on, reaction to, position on, point of view on, perspective on, stance on, thoughts on *(plural)*.
2 *(n) I don't like your attitude.* approach, outlook, manner, behaviour, disposition, frame of mind, mood, air, demeanour.

attract
(v) This window display is bound to attract customers. draw, pull *(informal)*, bring in, entice, lure, seduce, tempt, appeal to, interest, fascinate, captivate, enchant.
OPPOSITES: repel, drive away, put off.

attractive
(adj) Sam is really attractive. good-looking, handsome, pretty, striking, stunning *(informal)*, beautiful, gorgeous, fetching *(informal)*, charming, enchanting, alluring.
OPPOSITES: unattractive, ugly.

audible
(adj) Jon's yells were audible all over the school. easy to hear, clear, loud, distinct, detectable, perceptible.
OPPOSITE: inaudible.

audience
(n) crowd, spectators *(plural) (sport)*, viewers *(plural) (TV)*, listeners *(plural) (radio)*, congregation *(religious meeting)*.

author *see* **writer**.

authority
1 *(n) Do you have authority to use this computer? See* **permission**.
2 *(n) The headteacher has authority over us.* power, control, command, influence.

authorize *see* **approve** 1.

automatic
1 *(adj) An automatic machine.* automated, mechanized, mechanical, computerized, programmable, push-button, robotic.
OPPOSITES: manual, hand-operated.
2 *(adj) An automatic gesture.* instinctive, involuntary, unconscious, spontaneous, unthinking, mechanical, reflex.
OPPOSITES: conscious, deliberate.

available
1 *(adj) There are still some seats available. See* **free** 3.
2 *(adj) There is lots more food available.* to hand, on tap, at your disposal, obtainable, ready, handy, convenient, accessible.
OPPOSITE: unavailable.

avenue *see* **road**.

average
1 *(adj) Brownchester is an average small town.* ordinary, typical, everyday, normal, standard, run-of-the-mill, commonplace, unremarkable, unexceptional.
OPPOSITES: unusual, extraordinary.
2 *(adj) The meal was average.* mediocre, middling, so-so *(informal)*, not bad, tolerable, passable, fair, indifferent.
OPPOSITES: outstanding, exceptional.

avoid
1 *(v) I think that Sasha is trying to avoid me.* keep away from, steer clear of, hide from, evade, elude, shun, ignore.
2 *(v) Josh managed to avoid doing the washing-up.* get out of, escape, evade, dodge, wriggle out of, duck out of *(informal)*, shirk, sidestep.

awake
(adj) The guards stayed awake all night. wide-awake, alert, aware, conscious, wakeful, watchful, vigilant, attentive, on the lookout, on guard, on the alert.
OPPOSITE: asleep.

award
1 *(v) Who will award the prizes on Sports Day? See* **present** 5.
2 *(n) Finn won an award for his poem. See* **prize** 1.

aware of
1 *(adj) Patsy was aware of the danger.* conscious of, mindful of, sensitive to, heedful of, alive to, wise to *(slang)*.
OPPOSITES: unaware of, oblivious to.
2 *(adj) Are you aware of the rules about school uniform?* familiar with, acquainted with, conversant with, knowledgeable about, clued-up on *(informal)*.
OPPOSITES: unaware of, ignorant of.

away
1 *(adj) Nathan is away today.* absent, not here, not present, off.
2 *(adj) Our neighbours are away.* not here, not at home, on holiday, abroad.

awe
1 *(n) I looked at the painting with awe.* wonder, amazement, astonishment, admiration, reverence, respect.
2 *(n) We gazed at the monster with awe.* dread, fear, horror, terror, alarm.

awful *see* **dreadful** 1, 2, 3.

awkward
1 *(adj) Penny is so awkward; she's always dropping things.* clumsy, uncoordinated, butter-fingered *(informal)*, ham-fisted *(informal)*, inept, bungling, all thumbs.
OPPOSITE: dexterous.

2 *(adj) The robot moved with awkward steps.* clumsy, uncoordinated, ungainly, stiff, jerky, gawky, lumbering, blundering, ungraceful, inelegant, gauche.
OPPOSITE: graceful.
3 *(adj) This parcel is a really awkward shape.* inconvenient, difficult, unwieldy, unmanageable, cumbersome, bulky, troublesome.
OPPOSITES: convenient, handy.
4 *(adj) Nina is being deliberately awkward.* difficult, uncooperative, unhelpful, perverse, obstinate, stubborn, stroppy *(informal)*, bolshie *(informal)*, bloody-minded *(informal)*, impossible *(informal)*.
OPPOSITES: cooperative, obliging.
5 *(adj) This is a really awkward problem to solve.* difficult, tricky, perplexing, baffling, thorny, troublesome, problematic.
OPPOSITE: straightforward.
6 *(adj) Gus found himself in an awkward situation.* difficult, tricky, delicate, embarrassing, uncomfortable, unpleasant, ticklish, problematic, sticky *(informal)*, cringe-making *(informal)*, compromising.

babble *see* **prattle**.

baby
(n) infant, child, newborn child, babe *(old-fashioned)*, sprog *(slang)*, rug rat *(slang)*.

babyish *see* **childish**.

back
1 *(n) Jed has hurt his back.* spine, spinal column, backbone, vertebrae *(plural)*.
2 *(n) I sat at the back of the bus.* rear, rear end, far end, tail end, end, stern *(ship)*.
OPPOSITE: front.
3 *(adj) The horse kicked its back legs in the air.* hind, rear.
OPPOSITES: fore, front.
4 *(v) Jack began to back along the ledge.* retreat, move back, reverse, backtrack.
OPPOSITE: advance.
5 *(v) Jo will back my idea. See* **support** 3.

background
1 *(n) Tell me a bit about your background.* upbringing, education, family history, family circumstances *(plural)*, experience, qualifications *(plural)*, credentials *(plural)*.
2 *(n) Choose a dramatic background for your picture.* backdrop, setting, backcloth, scene, surroundings *(plural)*, context.

back out
(v) You can't back out now - I need you! drop out, pull out, resign, withdraw, get cold feet, chicken out *(informal)*.

back up
(v) Will you back me up if I tell the truth? support, side with, stand by, stand up for, stick up for *(informal)*, vouch for.

bad

bad

a bad person	a bad accident	a bad smell	bad work	bad weather	Smoking is bad for you.	I feel bad about what I have done.
corrupt	appalling	disgusting	abysmal	awful	damaging	ashamed
criminal	catastrophic	foul	awful	dismal	dangerous	awful
crooked	disastrous	horrible	diabolical	dreadful	detrimental	conscience-
(informal)	dreadful	loathsome	*(informal)*	dreary	harmful	stricken
depraved	horrendous	nasty	dreadful	filthy	risky	contrite
dishonest	horrific	nauseating	inadequate	foul	unhealthy	dreadful
evil	nasty	offensive	inferior	murky		embarrassed
immoral	serious	repulsive	poor	nasty	**Overeating makes you feel bad.**	guilty
sinful	terrible	revolting	substandard			mortified
villainous	tragic	sickening	unacceptable	dreadful	**After you left I felt bad.**	red-faced
wicked		unpleasant	unsatisfactory	ill		regretful
	a bad film	vile		nauseous	awful	remorseful
a bad child	abysmal		**a bad mood**	off colour	blue	rueful
badly behaved	appalling	**bad food**	angry	poorly	depressed	sad
cheeky	atrocious	decayed	bad-tempered	*(informal)*	down	shamefaced
difficult	diabolical	mildewed	cross	queasy	dreadful	sheepish
disobedient	*(informal)*	mouldy	grouchy	rotten *(informal)*	glum	sorry
mischievous	dire *(informal)*	off	*(informal)*	sick	low	terrible
naughty	lousy *(slang)*	putrid	grumpy	terrible	melancholy	uncomfortable
rebellious	pathetic	rancid	irritable	unwell	miserable	uneasy
rude	*(informal)*	rotten	peevish		sad	upset
uncooperative	rotten *(informal)*	sour	ratty *(informal)*		unhappy	
unruly	terrible	spoiled	sulky		wretched	

badge
(n) I sewed the badge on to my sweater. emblem, crest, logo, symbol, insignia.

badger *see* **pester**.

bad-tempered
(adj) Dad gets bad-tempered when we're late. irritable, cross, short-tempered, grumpy, grouchy *(informal)*, ratty *(informal)*, crabby, crotchety *(informal)*, cantankerous, snappy, touchy, fractious, peevish, testy, morose, surly.
OPPOSITE: good-humoured.

baffle *see* **puzzle** 2.

bag
(n) TYPES OF BAG: backpack, basket, briefcase, carrier bag, handbag, holdall, knapsack, rucksack, sack, satchel, shopping bag, shoulder bag, sports bag, suitcase.

baggy *see* **loose** 1.

baking *see* **hot** 1.

balance
1 *(v) Can you balance a ball on your nose?* support, keep steady, steady, poise.
2 *(v) Try to make the scales balance.* even up, be equal, be level, counterbalance, reach equilibrium, be steady, stabilize.

ball
1 *(n) A ball of fire.* sphere, globe, orb.
2 *(n) A masked ball.* dance, party.

ban
(v) The judge decided to ban Dave from driving. prohibit, bar, prevent, stop, disqualify.
OPPOSITES: permit, authorize.

band
1 *(n) My skirt has a blue band round the bottom.* stripe, strip, line, ribbon.
2 *(n) Fasten the bundle with a leather band.* strap, strip, thong, belt, hoop.
3 *(n) William has a large band of friends.* See **group** 3.
4 *(n) Let's listen to the band.* group, ensemble, orchestra.

jazz band   sousaphone   piano   trumpet

drums

trombone   banjo   clarinet

bang
1 *(n) I heard a loud bang from the science lab.* explosion, blast, crash, thud, thump, boom, pop, report.
2 *(v) Don't bang your head on that shelf!* See **hit** 2.

banish
(v) The king decided to banish the magician. exile, send away, expel, cast out, outlaw, throw out, deport.
OPPOSITES: admit, welcome.

bank
1 *(n) We walked along the river bank.* side, shore, edge, embankment, brink.
2 *(n) We climbed a grassy bank.* mound, slope, embankment, knoll, ridge, rise, hill.

bankrupt
(adj) Flash Frank is bankrupt. ruined, insolvent, broke *(informal)*.
OPPOSITE: solvent.

banquet
(n) The king laid on a magnificent banquet. feast, dinner, spread *(informal)*, meal.

bar
1 *(n) A metal bar.* rod, pole, post, stake, railing, girder, crowbar, jemmy.
2 *(n) A bar of chocolate.* slab, block, piece, hunk, chunk.
3 *(n) We had drinks in a local bar.* pub, inn, wine bar, public house, tavern *(old-fashioned)*, boozer *(informal)*.
4 *(v) Don't bar my way!* block, obstruct.

bare
1 *(adj) The boys were bare to the waist.* naked, stripped, undressed, unclothed, uncovered, nude, exposed.
OPPOSITES: dressed, clothed.
2 *(adj) The room was completely bare.* unfurnished, empty, vacant, stripped.
OPPOSITES: full, cluttered.
3 *(adj) We climbed the bare hillside.* bleak, barren, desolate, windswept, exposed.
4 *(adj) Give me a bare outline of what happened.* basic, simple, straightforward, plain, stark, bald, unembellished, unvarnished, unadorned.
OPPOSITE: elaborate.

barely *see* **hardly**.

bargain
1 *(n) Ann has found a bargain.* good deal, good buy, special offer, reduction, discount, steal *(informal)*, snip *(informal)*.

2 *(n) The two sides made a bargain.* deal *(informal)*, agreement, arrangement, pact, contract, settlement, treaty.
3 *(v) You have to bargain for food in the market.* haggle, barter, negotiate.

bark
(v) The dog began to bark. yap, woof, growl, snarl, howl, yelp, bay, bow-wow.

barrel
(n) cask, keg, tub, vat, drum.

base
1 *(n) The base of the statue is cracked.* bottom, foot, foundation, plinth, stand, pedestal, support.
OPPOSITE: top.
2 *(n) All troops must return to their base.* headquarters *(plural)*, camp, station, quarters *(plural)*, billet, garrison, base camp, starting point.
3 *(v) Base your essay on your own experience.* model, ground, construct, build, develop from, derive from.

bash *(informal) see* **hit** 1, 2, 4.

basic
1 *(adj) What are the basic points in your essay?* fundamental, key, central, underlying, main, chief, essential.
2 *(adj) I'm learning basic Italian.* elementary, simple, easy, rudimentary.
OPPOSITE: advanced.

bath
1 *(n) Fill the bath with water.* tub.
2 *(n) Matt had a bath after the match.* soak, wash, scrub, sponge down, shower.

bathe
1 *(v) Is it safe to bathe here? See* **swim** 2.
2 *(v) Bathe your feet in warm water.* soak, immerse, douse, dip, wash, cleanse.

batter
(v) Don't batter the door like that! pound, hammer, thump, bash *(informal)*, beat, pummel, thrash, smash, buffet.

battered
1 *(adj) A battered old suitcase.* worn-out, beaten-up, scruffy, damaged, squashed, scarred, dilapidated, weather-beaten.
2 *(adj) Claude emerged battered from the fight.* bruised, beaten, hurt, injured, bleeding, wounded, scarred.

battle
1 *(n) The battle was long and bloody.* fight, conflict, struggle, skirmish, confrontation, clash, combat, campaign, siege, dogfight, shoot-out, rebellion.
2 *(v) Carl had to battle to win the game.* struggle, fight, strive.

bay
(n) The yacht sheltered in the bay. cove, estuary, inlet, natural harbour.

beach
1 *(n) Let's go to the beach today.* seaside, coast, seashore, shore. ❖ *Also see* **sea & seashore**, **seaside words**.
2 *(n) We played tennis on the beach.* sand, sands *(plural)*, shingle.

beam
1 *(v) The sight of his new bike made Ben beam.* grin, smile, grin from ear to ear.
2 *(n) A beam of sunlight shone through the curtains.* ray, shaft, streak, stream, gleam, glimmer, glow.
3 *(n) Don't remove that beam or the ceiling will collapse.* plank, support, joist, girder, rafter, timber, prop, brace, spar.

bear
1 *(v) Can you bear my weight?* take, support, carry, shoulder.
2 *(v) I can't bear the noise! See* **stand** 4.

beast
1 *(n) A wild beast.* animal, creature.
2 *(n) A beast with two heads. See* **monster** 1.

beastly *(informal) see* **mean** 6.

beat
1 *(v) Teachers used to beat their pupils.* hit, strike, thrash, cane, whip, flog, belt *(slang)*, clout *(informal)*, wallop *(informal)*, thump, batter, birch.
2 *(v) I'm bound to beat you at chess.* defeat, thrash, get the better of, hammer *(informal)*, slaughter *(informal)*, clobber *(informal)*, wipe the floor with *(informal)*, lick *(informal)*, blow you out of the water *(informal)*, run rings round *(informal)*, triumph over.
3 *(v) The suspense made my heart beat fast.* pound, thump, hammer, bang, palpitate, pulsate, pulse.
4 *(v) Beat the egg whites until they are stiff.* whisk, whip, stir, mix, blend.
5 *(n) This song has a very strong beat.* rhythm, pulse, stress, accent.

beat up
(v) (informal) Don't let Bozo beat you up. assault, attack, batter, lay into *(informal)*, knock you about, rough you up *(informal)*, beat the living daylights out of *(informal)*, work you over *(slang)*, duff you up *(slang)*, put the boot in *(slang)*.

beckon *see* **signal** 2.

become
(v) This caterpillar will become a butterfly. turn into, change into, develop into, grow into, be transformed into.

bed
(n) TYPES OF BED: air bed, berth, bunk bed, camp bed, cot, cradle, divan, double bed, four-poster bed, futon, hammock, single bed, sofa bed, water bed.

beg
1 *(v) The poor woman had to beg for food.* scrounge *(informal)*, ask, cadge.
2 *(v) I'll beg Dad to let us go.* plead with, implore, entreat, beseech *(old-fashioned)*.

begin
1 *(v) Let's begin!* start, get started, get going, get moving, get the show on the road *(informal)*, take the plunge *(informal)*, start the ball rolling, kick off *(informal)*.
OPPOSITE: stop.
2 *(v) It's time to begin our work.* start, set about, commence, embark on.
OPPOSITE: finish.
3 *(v) Don't begin an argument.* start, provoke, initiate, trigger off, spark off, cause, instigate, incite.
OPPOSITE: end.
4 *(v) When did life on earth begin?* start, appear, originate, come into being, come into existence, emerge, arise, burst forth.
OPPOSITES: cease, end.

beginner
(n) I'm just a beginner. novice, learner, fledgling, greenhorn, new recruit.

beginning
1 *(n) I was there at the beginning of the project.* start, birth, outset, onset, starting point, commencement, inception, origin.
OPPOSITES: end, conclusion.
2 *(n) We've missed the beginning of the film.* start, opening, introduction, kickoff *(informal)*, prologue *(play)*, preface *(book)*.
OPPOSITES: end, conclusion.

beautiful a beautiful woman	beautiful weather	beautiful music	beautiful scenery
alluring	brilliant	bewitching	awe-inspiring
attractive	delightful	captivating	breathtaking
dazzling	fabulous	enchanting	glorious
fetching	*(informal)*	entrancing	impressive
(informal)	fair	exquisite	incredible
good-looking	fine	glorious	magnificent
gorgeous	glorious	haunting	marvellous
lovely	gorgeous	heavenly	picturesque
pretty	lovely	*(informal)*	spectacular
radiant	magnificent	inspiring	striking
ravishing	marvellous	lovely	stunning
striking	perfect	magnificent	*(informal)*
stunning	superb	poignant	superb
(informal)	wonderful	sublime	wonderful

behave

behave
1 (v) I'm sure you'll behave sensibly. act, conduct yourself, acquit yourself.
2 (v) When will you learn to behave? be polite, remember your manners, mind your manners, control yourself.
OPPOSITES: misbehave, be rude.

behind
(adv) Nat is behind with his project. late, behind schedule, overdue.
OPPOSITE: ahead.

believable
(adj) Your story is not believable. credible, plausible, convincing, possible, probable, likely, conceivable, trustworthy.
OPPOSITES: unbelievable, implausible.

believe
1 (v) It's hard to believe your story. trust, accept, credit, feel convinced by, have faith in, be certain of, be sure of, swallow (informal), buy (informal), count on, fall for.
2 (v) I used to believe that girls were stupid. think, be convinced, feel, consider, be of the opinion, be certain.
3 (v) I believe this is for me. think, assume, guess (informal), presume, suppose, imagine, reckon, gather, suspect.

bellow see **shout**.

belongings see **things**.

bend
1 (v) The road should bend just here. turn, curve, twist, wind, swerve, veer.
2 (v) Can you bend this metal rod? twist, flex, curve, shape, wind, loop, contort, buckle, warp.
3 (v) Bend down to get through the tunnel. stoop, crouch, bow, lean, squat.
4 (n) Watch out for the bend! curve, turn, corner, twist, hairpin bend, loop, zigzag.

bendy see **flexible** 1.

bent
1 (adj) A bent bicycle wheel. twisted, buckled, crooked, warped, contorted.
OPPOSITE: straight.
2 (adj) (slang) A bent cop. See **corrupt** 1.

best
1 (adj) Jon is the best runner in the team. finest, top, foremost, leading, outstanding, unrivalled, unsurpassed, supreme.
OPPOSITE: worst.
2 (adj) What's the best thing to do? right, correct, most appropriate, most suitable, most fitting.
OPPOSITE: worst.

bet see **gamble** 1,2.

betray
1 (v) I hope your friend won't betray you. deceive, be disloyal to, stab you in the back (informal), inform on, give you away, double-cross, sell you out (informal), sell you down the river (informal).
2 (v) Don't betray the one you love. deceive, be unfaithful to, cheat on (informal), two-time (informal).
3 (v) Try not to betray your true feelings. reveal, show, give away, expose, lay bare, let slip, blurt out, indicate.

better
1 (adj) There's a better way of doing that. preferable, easier, more effective, more appropriate, more acceptable.
OPPOSITE: worse.
2 (adj) Are you better now? fully recovered, well, fit, cured, on the mend, fitter, stronger, back on your feet.
OPPOSITE: worse.

beware of
(v) Beware of falling rocks. watch out for, look out for, be careful of, keep clear of, steer clear of, be on your guard against.

bewildered see **confused**.

biased
(adj) A biased magazine article. one-sided, unfair, prejudiced, distorted, slanted.
OPPOSITES: impartial, unbiased.

bicycle
(n) bike, cycle, pushbike, two-wheeler, mountain bike, racing bike, touring bike, BMX (motocross bicycle), tandem.

bill
(n) Send me the bill. account, invoice, statement, reckoning, charge.

billow
1 (v) We watched the sails billow in the wind. swell, bulge, fill out, balloon, puff out.
2 (v) As the storm approached, the waves began to billow. swell, rise, surge, roll, heave.

bind see **tie** 1.

bird
(n) fowl, feathered friend (informal), cock (male), hen (female), chick, nestling, fledgling.
TYPES OF BIRD: bird of paradise, blackbird, budgerigar, canary, chaffinch, chicken, cockatoo, crane, crow, cuckoo, dove, duck, eagle, emu, falcon, finch, flamingo, goose, grouse, gull, hawk, heron, hummingbird, jackdaw, jay, kingfisher, kiwi, kookaburra, lark, macaw, magpie, mina bird, moorhen, nightingale, ostrich, owl, parakeet, parrot, partridge, peacock, pelican, penguin, pheasant, pigeon, puffin, quail, raven, robin, rook, seagull, sparrow, starling, stork, swallow, swift, thrush, tit, toucan, turkey, turtledove, vulture, woodpecker, wren.

big

a big person	a big building	a big mountain	a big bag	a big bang
beefy (informal)	enormous	enormous	bulky	almighty (informal)
burly	huge	high	capacious	colossal
fat	immense	huge	enormous	deafening
heavy	large	lofty	heavy	ear-splitting
hefty	massive	massive	huge	enormous
obese	roomy	towering	large	loud
overweight	spacious		mammoth	mighty
stout	tall	a big helping of pudding	voluminous	resounding
strapping	towering			terrific
tall	vast	ample	a big wardrobe	tremendous
towering		enormous	capacious	
	a big monster	generous	enormous	a big decision
a big desert	colossal	huge	huge	critical
enormous	elephantine	jumbo (informal)	immense	crucial
extensive	enormous	large	large	grave
huge	gigantic	liberal	massive	important
immense	ginormous (informal)	mammoth	sizable	major
vast	hulking	mega (informal)	a big sister	momentous
	humongous (informal)	mountainous	elder	serious
		substantial	grown-up	significant
			older	weighty

gigantic blue whale

blue

bird words

claw
dazzling
bird of
paradise

bird moves
circle	plummet
dart	plunge
dive	pounce
drop	preen
flit	rise
float	roost
flutter	sail
fly	skim
glide	soar
hop	splash
hover	strut
land	swim
paddle	swoop
peck	take off
perch	waddle

hovering
tern

tail feathers

crown

beak

diving
kingfisher

bird sounds
cackle	honk
call	hoot
caw	peep
chatter	pipe
cheep	quack
chirp	screech
chirrup	shriek
coo	sing
crow	squawk
cry	trill
gabble	tweet
gaggle	twitter
gobble	warble
hiss	whistle

a bird's feathers can be...
bedraggled	gleaming
colourful	iridescent
dazzling	ruffled
downy	smooth
dull	speckled

wing

throat

breast

warbling
blackbird

bit
1 (n) I'd love a bit of cheese. piece, lump, chunk, hunk, block, slab, wedge, slice, morsel, scrap, fragment, crumb.
2 (n) Would you like a bit of my orange? piece, share, segment, section, part, portion, slice.
3 (n) I'll be there in a bit. See **moment** 1.

bitchy (informal) see **spiteful**.

bite
1 (v) Bite on this apple. chew, nibble, gnaw, chomp, crunch.
2 (v) That insect might bite. sting, nip.
3 (n) Can I have a bite of your biscuit? nibble, taste, bit, piece, mouthful, morsel.

biting see **cold** 2.

bitter
1 (adj) This drink has a bitter taste. sour, sharp, tart, acid, vinegary, pungent, acrid.
OPPOSITES: sweet.
2 (adj) Does Jo's success make you feel bitter? resentful, sore, embittered, begrudging, aggrieved, sour, jealous, envious, put out, wounded, hurt.
OPPOSITES: glad, grateful.
3 (adj) The girls had a bitter row. fierce, angry, violent, heated, acrimonious, vicious, savage.
4 (adj) I have bitter memories of that time. painful, agonizing, unhappy, distressing, heartbreaking, poignant, bittersweet.
OPPOSITES: happy, pleasant.
5 (adj) The wind was bitter. See **cold** 2.

bizarre see **strange** 1.

black
(adj) Count Dracula wore a black cloak. coal-black, jet-black, pitch-black, inky, sable, ebony, raven (hair).

blame
1 (v) I blame you for starting this row. hold you responsible, accuse you of, charge you with, condemn, reproach, criticize, find fault with, censure.

2 (n) Max accepted the blame for the incident. responsibility, liability, censure, criticism, rap (slang), stick (informal).

bland
1 (adj) A bland sauce. mild, tasteless, flavourless, insipid, weak, nondescript.
OPPOSITES: tasty, spicy.
2 (adj) A bland speech. dull, boring, uninspiring, uninteresting, unexciting, humdrum, flat, monotonous, tedious.
OPPOSITES: exciting, stimulating.

blank
1 (adj) Take a blank sheet of paper. clean, empty, new, unused, unmarked, bare.
2 (adj) Marcus looked blank when I questioned him. vacant, glazed, at a loss, uncomprehending, flummoxed, puzzled, bewildered, confused, at sea.

blaze see **burn** 1, 2.

bleak
1 (adj) We surveyed the bleak landscape. bare, barren, exposed, windswept, desolate, deserted.
2 (adj) The future looks bleak. grim, depressing, gloomy, dismal, hopeless, dreary, forbidding, sombre.
OPPOSITES: hopeful, bright.

blend see **mix** 1.

blind
1 (adj) Great Grandma is blind. unable to see, sightless, visually impaired.
2 (adj) How could I be so blind? unaware, blinkered, unobservant, unsuspecting, insensitive, inattentive, heedless, dim, stupid, inconsiderate, thoughtless.
OPPOSITES: aware, sensitive.

blissful see **heavenly** 2.

blizzard
(n) snowstorm. ❖ Also see **ice, frost & snow**.

blob
(n) A blob of cream. drop, spot, dollop (informal), splodge.

block
1 (n) Please will you move this block of stone? slab, lump, piece, chunk, hunk, mass, brick, cube, wedge.
2 (v) Leaves sometimes block our drainpipe. clog, stop up, obstruct, choke, fill, bung up.
3 (v) Don't try to block my progress. bar, obstruct, impede, interfere with, check, hinder, thwart, prevent, halt, stop.

bloke (informal) see **man** 1, 2.

blond, blonde
1 (adj) James is blond; Jenny is blonde too. fair-haired, golden-haired, fair, tow-headed, flaxen-haired (old-fashioned).
2 (adj) Millie has blonde hair. fair, golden, ash-blonde, platinum-blonde, strawberry-blonde, honey-coloured, straw-coloured, sandy, yellow, peroxide-blonde, bleached, flaxen (old-fashioned).

bloodthirsty see **savage** 2.

bloody
1 (adj) A bloody wound. bleeding, gory.
2 (adj) A bloody shirt. bloodstained, blood-soaked, blood-spattered.
3 (adj) A bloody fight. gory, fierce, ferocious, savage, violent, vicious.

bloom see **flower** 1, 2.

blot
1 (n) My work was spoilt by a large blot of ink. spot, blotch, smear, smudge, blob, splodge, splotch, patch.
2 (n) That shed is a blot on the landscape. blemish, eyesore, flaw, scar.

blotchy
(adj) Nancy's face looks blotchy. mottled, spotty, patchy, blemished.

blow
1 (v) Blow on the paint to make it dry. breathe, puff, huff, breathe out, exhale.
2 (v) The leaves began to blow around. whirl, flutter, waft, swirl, flap, whisk.
3 (n) Bozo is recovering from a blow on the head. bang, knock, bump, hit, smack, whack, bash (informal), thump, punch, wallop (informal), belt (informal).
4 (n) Losing the match was a real blow. disappointment, disaster, catastrophe, calamity, setback, upset, misfortune, bombshell, shock, tragedy.

blow up
1 (v) This bomb may blow up without any warning. explode, detonate, go off.
2 (v) The soldiers were ordered to blow up the bridge. bomb, dynamite, destroy, blast.
3 (n) You need to blow up your bicycle tyres. inflate, pump up.
4 (v) (informal) Please don't blow up when you see the mess. See **lose your temper**.

blue
1 (n) SHADES OF BLUE: aquamarine, azure, cobalt, cornflower, cyan, forget-me-not, indigo, navy, powder blue, royal blue, sapphire, sky blue, turquoise, ultramarine.
2 (adj) Kim is feeling blue. See **depressed**.

blunt
1 *(adj) This blade is blunt.* not sharp, unsharpened, dull, rounded.
OPPOSITE: sharp.
2 *(adj) Carl's blunt comment upset me.* frank, candid, forthright, direct, tactless, insensitive, outspoken, curt, brusque, rude.
OPPOSITES: tactful, polite.

blurred
(adj) Without my glasses, everything is blurred. out of focus, fuzzy, hazy, misty, foggy, unclear, indistinct, faint.
OPPOSITES: clear, sharp, in focus.

blush
(v) I wish I wouldn't blush whenever I'm embarrassed. go red, go pink, redden, colour, turn scarlet, turn crimson, flush.

boast
(v) Don't boast about your success. brag, show off *(informal)*, crow, swank *(informal)*, swagger, exaggerate, blow your own trumpet, sing your own praises.

boastful
(adj) Leah is so boastful; she's always showing off. conceited, bigheaded *(informal)*, swollen-headed *(informal)*, cocky, vain, puffed up, arrogant.
OPPOSITES: modest, self-effacing.

boat
(n) ship, vessel, craft.
TYPES OF BOAT: aircraft carrier, barge, battleship, cabin cruiser, canoe, catamaran, clipper, coracle, cruise liner, cruiser, destroyer, dhow, dugout, ferry, fishing boat, freighter, frigate, galleon, galley, gondola, houseboat, hovercraft, hydrofoil, hydroplane, inflatable dinghy, junk, kayak, launch, lifeboat, liner, man o' war, minesweeper, motorboat, narrow boat, paddle steamer, powerboat, punt, raft, rowing boat, sailing boat, sailing dinghy, schooner, skiff, speedboat, steamship, supertanker, tanker, trawler, trireme, tug, warship, yacht.
❖ *Also see*
journey words.

Ancient Greek galley

pennant *yard* *15th-century galleon*
topsail
mast
mizzen sail
foresail *mainsail*
bowsprit *poop deck*
stern
prow *rudder*
deck *hull*

paddle wheel *19th-century paddle steamer*
radio aerial
radar antenna
bridge
passenger area
hull
funnel *strut*
bridge
lifeboat *helipad*
tanker *foil* *hydrofoil*

body
1 *(n) Jason has a muscular body.* build, physique, figure, frame, form, torso, trunk.
PARTS OF THE BODY: OUTSIDE: Adam's apple, ankle, arm, armpit, back, breast, buttock, calf, cheek, chest, chin, ear, elbow, eye, face, finger, foot, forehead, genitals *(plural)*, groin, hand, head, heel, hip, jaw, knee, knuckle, leg, limb, lip, midriff, mouth, navel, neck, nipple, nose, nostril, scalp, shin, shoulder, stomach, thigh, thumb, toe, waist, wrist. INSIDE: abdomen, adenoid, anus, aorta, appendix, artery, bladder, bone, bowel, brain, cartilage, colon, diaphragm, duodenum, eardrum, epiglottis, gall bladder, gland, gum, heart, intestine, kidney, larynx (voice box), ligament, liver, lung, muscle, nerve, oesophagus (gullet), ovary, pancreas, rectum, rib, sinew, spine, spleen, stomach, tendon, throat, tongue, tonsil, trachea (windpipe), uterus (womb), vein, vocal cords *(plural)*. Also see **bone**.
2 *(n) The police found a body in the woods.* dead body, corpse, remains *(plural)*, stiff *(slang)*.

bog
(n) marsh, marshland, peat bog, fen, swamp, quagmire, wetlands *(plural)*.

boil
(v) Wait for the water to boil. come to the boil, bubble, simmer, seethe, steam.
OPPOSITE: freeze.

boiling *see* **hot 1, 2, 3.**
boisterous *see* **rowdy.**

bold
1 *(adj) A bold knight.* intrepid, daring, audacious, brave, courageous, fearless, adventurous, heroic, valiant *(old-fashioned)*, gallant *(old-fashioned)*.
OPPOSITES: cowardly, fearful.
2 *(adj) A bold reply. See* **cheeky.**
3 *(adj) Bold colours.* bright, strong, vivid, striking, loud, eye-catching, conspicuous.
OPPOSITES: pale, unobtrusive.

bolshie *(informal) see* **awkward 4.**

bolt
1 *(v) Please bolt the door. See* **lock 1.**
2 *(v) Burglar Beryl tried to bolt when she saw the police. See* **run away.**

bomb
1 *(n) The soldiers made the bomb safe.* explosive, device.
TYPES OF BOMB: atom bomb, car bomb, depth charge, grenade, H-bomb (hydrogen bomb), incendiary device (firebomb), land mine, letter bomb, mine, napalm bomb, nuclear bomb, petrol bomb, time bomb.
2 *(v) Terrorists tried to bomb the building. See* **blow up 2.**

bone
(n) TYPES OF BONE: backbone, clavicle (collarbone), cranium (skull), femur (thighbone), mandible (jawbone), patella (kneecap), pelvis (hipbone), rib, scapula (shoulder blade), sternum (breastbone), tibia (shinbone), vertebra.

bony *see* **thin 1.**

boo
(v) When the villain appeared, we all began to boo. jeer, heckle, catcall, hiss.
OPPOSITES: cheer, applaud.

book
1 *(n) A best-selling book.* title, publication, work, paperback, hardback, volume.
2 *(n) Write your ideas in your book.* jotter, notebook, notepad, pad, exercise book.
3 *(v) We need to book a room in advance.* reserve, organize, arrange, order, secure.

booty *see* **loot 1.**

border
1 *(n) We crossed the border into Germany.* frontier, boundary, borderline.
2 *(n) My writing paper has a blue border.* edge, margin, surround, frame.
3 *(n) Susie's skirt has a red border.* edging, hem, trimming, frill, fringe.

bore
1 *(v) This film will bore you.* send you to sleep, bore you to death, bore you to tears, bore you out of your mind, leave you cold *(informal)*, turn you off *(informal)*, pall on, tire, weary.
OPPOSITES: interest, fascinate.
2 *(v) The miners had to bore deep into the rock.* drill, penetrate, tunnel, mine.
3 *(n) Shopping can be a bore.* drag *(informal)*, yawn *(informal)*, turn-off *(informal)*, nuisance, bother, pain *(informal)*, pain in the neck *(informal)*.

bored
(adj) Learning endless facts can make you feel bored. bored to death, bored to tears, bored out of your mind, fed up (informal), switched off (informal), indifferent, apathetic, weary, listless, jaded, restless.
OPPOSITES: interested, fascinated.

boring
(adj) A boring job. dull, tedious, uninteresting, monotonous, repetitive, routine, humdrum, unvaried, mind-numbing, unexciting, uninspiring, dreary.
OPPOSITES: interesting, fascinating.

borrow
(v) Can I borrow some paper? have, use, scrounge (informal), cadge, have the loan of, touch you for (slang).
OPPOSITE: lend.

boss
(n) (informal) employer, manager, supervisor, director, gaffer (informal).

bossy
(adj) My sister is so bossy; she's always ordering me around. domineering, overbearing, dictatorial, high-handed, imperious, autocratic, tyrannical, bullying.
OPPOSITES: meek, submissive.

bother
1 (v) I don't want to bother you, but I need a lift. trouble, disturb, put you out, impose on, inconvenience, pester, hassle (informal), harass, nag.
2 (v) Doesn't it bother you that someone's been in your room? worry, concern, upset, annoy, irritate, trouble, disturb, perturb, distress, alarm, dismay.
3 (v) Dad didn't seem to bother about the mess. mind, care, be bothered, be concerned, be worried, object to.
4 (n) Our new car has given us a lot of bother. See **trouble** 1.

bottom
1 (n) The bottom of the statue was set in concrete. foot, base, foundation, pedestal, plinth, support.
OPPOSITE: top.
2 (n) What's that muck on the bottom of your shoe? sole, underside, underneath.
3 (n) Joe slipped and fell on his bottom. behind (informal), backside (informal), bum (slang), rear, rear end, posterior, rump.
4 (n) The submarine sank to the bottom of the sea. depths (plural), bed, floor.

boulder see **rock** 1.

bounce
1 (v) We watched the kangaroos bounce across the plain. bound, spring, leap, jump.
2 (v) Can you make this ball bounce off the wall? rebound, ricochet.

bouncy
1 (adj) A bouncy diving board. springy, flexible, bendy, elastic, resilient, rubbery.
OPPOSITES: rigid, stiff.
2 (adj) A bouncy girl. See **lively** 1.

bound see **leap** 1, 3.

box
(n) TYPES OF BOX: carton, case, casket, chest, coffer, coffin, crate, jewellery box, lunch box, matchbox, shoe box, trunk.

boy
(n) lad, youth, schoolboy, young man.

brain
(n) Crosswords exercise your brain. mind, intellect, brains (plural) (informal), powers of reasoning (plural), brainpower, grey matter (informal), intelligence.

brainy (informal) see **clever** 1.

branch
1 (n) A branch of a tree. bough, limb, twig, stem, sprig.
2 (n) A branch of a bank. division, local office, department, section, subdivision.

brash
(adj) A brash salesman. over-confident, cocky, assertive, aggressive, pushy (informal), bumptious, swaggering, self-important, boastful, bigheaded (informal).
OPPOSITES: timid, retiring.

brave
(adj) A brave knight. courageous, fearless, intrepid, plucky, gutsy (informal), heroic, valiant (old-fashioned), gallant (old-fashioned), daring, bold, lion-hearted.
OPPOSITES: cowardly, fearful.

bravery see **courage**.

break
1 (v) Don't break that plate! smash, shatter, smash to smithereens, crack, splinter, chip, fracture (bone).
2 (v) That branch could break at any moment. crack, snap, split, splinter, give way, come away, disintegrate, fragment.
3 (v) Don't break my radio! damage, ruin, wreck, destroy, bust (informal).
4 (v) If you break the rules, you'll be in trouble. disobey, disregard, defy, flout, infringe, violate.
OPPOSITES: obey, abide by.
5 (n) The break from revision will do you good. rest, breather (informal), time off, time out, breathing space, respite.
6 (n) Cross when there's a break in the traffic. lull, gap, let-up (informal), interval, pause, interruption.

breakable see **fragile**.

break down
1 (v) I hope the car doesn't break down. stop, stop working, conk out (informal), die, seize up, go kaput (informal).
2 (v) Anji will break down when she hears the news. go to pieces, collapse, lose control, be overcome, crack up (informal), fall apart (informal).

break-in
(n) Police are investigating the break-in. burglary, forced entry, robbery, theft, raid.

break up
1 (v) The yacht hit the rocks and began to break up. disintegrate, break into pieces, break apart, smash up, splinter, shatter.

2 (v) When will school break up? See **end** 6.
3 (v) Justin thinks his parents may break up. See **separate** 3.

breasts
(plural n) Pam has large breasts. bust, bosom, chest, boobs (plural) (slang).

breathe
(v) Don't forget to breathe! take a breath, inhale, exhale, take a gulp of air.

breathless
(adj) Giles was breathless after his run. out of breath, out of puff, panting, gasping, wheezing, winded.

breed
1 (v) Jamie's rabbits have started to breed. reproduce, multiply, produce young.
2 (n) What breed of cat do you like best? See **kind** 3.

breezy see **windy** 1.

bribe
1 (v) Burglar Beryl tried to bribe the police. buy off, influence, corrupt, pay off (informal), grease the palm of (slang).
2 (n) Beryl offered the judge a bribe. incentive, tip, pay-off (informal), backhander (slang), sweetener (slang).

bridge
(n) footbridge, flyover, overpass, viaduct, aqueduct, ropebridge, drawbridge.

brief
1 (adj) Dad gave a brief account of the accident. See **short** 2.
2 (adj) We paid a brief visit to Aunt Bertha. See **short** 3.
3 (v) The coach will brief you before the match. instruct, give you the facts, inform, fill you in (informal), put you in the picture (informal), give you the lowdown (informal), prepare, prime, advise.

bright
1 (adj) A bright light. dazzling, blinding, glaring, shining, blazing, beaming, intense, brilliant, radiant, incandescent.
OPPOSITES: dull, dim.
2 (adj) Bright colours. vivid, bold, vibrant, intense, rich, brilliant, glowing, luminous, fluorescent, loud, glaring, gaudy, garish.
OPPOSITES: dull, pale.
3 (adj) Bright weather. sunny, clear, fair, cloudless, pleasant.
OPPOSITES: dull, cloudy.
4 (adj) A bright student. See **clever** 1.
5 (adj) A bright future. See **hopeful** 2.

brilliant
1 (adj) A brilliant diamond. dazzling, sparkling, glittering, scintillating, flashing, shining, glistening, shimmering, gleaming, lustrous, bright, flashy, showy.
OPPOSITE: dull.
2 (adj) A brilliant child. gifted, talented, accomplished, bright, clever, intelligent, brainy (informal), precocious, exceptional.
OPPOSITES: stupid, slow.
3 (adj) A brilliant party. See **fantastic** 3.

bring
1 *(v) A boat will bring supplies from the mainland.* fetch, carry, take, deliver, transport, ferry, convey, transfer.
2 *(v) Did someone bring you home?* See **take** 3.
3 *(v) Hooligans bring trouble.* cause, create, produce, provoke, give rise to, lead to, result in, generate, attract.

bring up
1 *(v) It's hard to bring up children on your own.* raise, rear, look after, support, care for, nurture, educate, train.
2 *(v) Stop leaping about or you'll bring up your lunch.* See **vomit**.
3 *(v) Don't bring up the subject of homework.* See **mention** 2.

brisk
1 *(adj) Will walked at a brisk pace.* quick, fast, swift, rapid, spanking *(informal)*, speedy, energetic, vigorous, sprightly.
OPPOSITES: leisurely, sluggish.
2 *(adj) Mrs Badger has a brisk manner.* businesslike, no-nonsense, crisp, decisive, bustling, lively, bright.
OPPOSITE: lethargic.

bristly *see* **hairy** 2.

brittle *see* **fragile**.

broad
1 *(adj) Lawrence surveyed the broad stretch of desert.* wide, vast, large, extensive, expansive, sweeping, boundless.
OPPOSITE: narrow.
2 *(adj) This shop sells a broad range of magazines.* wide, extensive, large, varied, comprehensive, wide-ranging, all-embracing, unlimited, encyclopedic.
OPPOSITES: narrow, limited.
3 *(adj) Chloë gave a broad description of the thief.* See **general** 2.

broad-minded *see* **tolerant** 1.

broke
(adj) (informal) Flash Frank will be broke if his business fails. penniless, bankrupt, ruined, insolvent, poverty-stricken, impoverished, destitute, stony-broke *(slang)*, skint *(slang)*, strapped for cash *(slang)*, cleaned out *(slang)*.
OPPOSITES: solvent, flush *(informal)*.

broken
1 *(adj) This bone is broken.* fractured, cracked, chipped, shattered, smashed, crushed, splintered, snapped, severed.
2 *(adj) Our washing machine is broken.* out of order, faulty, defective, broken-down, inoperative, damaged, on the blink *(slang)*, clapped out *(informal)*, bust *(informal)*, kaput *(informal)*.
3 *(adj) Since his business failed, Frank is a broken man.* demoralized, dispirited, discouraged, humbled, humiliated, crushed, ruined, beaten, defeated.
4 *(adj) The tourist spoke in broken English.* halting, faltering, disjointed, hesitating, stammering, imperfect.

broken-down *see* **broken** 2.

brown
1 *(n)* SHADES OF BROWN: beige, bronze, buff, chocolate, cinnamon, cocoa, coffee, copper, donkey brown, dun, fawn, ginger, hazel, khaki, russet, rust, sepia, tan, terracotta, umber.
2 *(adj) Brown hair.* dark, brunette, mousy, sandy, tawny, chestnut, auburn, coppery.
3 *(adj) Brown skin.* See **tanned**.

bruise
1 *(n) Darren has a bruise on his forehead.* black mark, shiner *(informal)*, bump, swelling, lump, contusion.
2 *(v) Be careful not to bruise your shins.* bump, bang, bash *(informal)*, knock, hit, injure, hurt, mark, make black and blue.

brush
1 *(n) Where's the brush?* broom, floor brush, scrubbing brush, clothes brush.
2 *(v) I must brush my hair.* comb, tidy, straighten, neaten, untangle, smooth.
3 *(v) Please brush the floor.* sweep, clean.

brutal *see* **savage** 2.

bubble
1 *(v) The sauce began to bubble.* See **boil**.
2 *(v) Look at the lemonade bubble.* fizz, sparkle, effervesce, foam, froth.
3 *(n) A bubble of paint ran down the tin.* bead, globule, drop, droplet, blob, blister.
4 **bubbles** *(plural n) Soap bubbles.* suds *(plural)*, lather, foam, froth.

bubbly
1 *(adj) Bubbly lemonade.* See **fizzy**.
2 *(adj) A bubbly personality.* See **lively** 1.

buckle
1 *(v) Buckle the straps on your rucksack.* fasten, do up, secure, close, clip, clasp.
2 *(v) The collision made my bicycle wheel buckle.* crumple, warp, twist, fold, bend, bulge, become contorted, collapse.

budge
(v) Rick found a good seat and wouldn't budge. move, shift, stir, give way.

bug
1 *(n) There's a bug hiding under that stone.* insect, creepy-crawly *(informal)*.
2 *(n) (informal) This bug is making me feel sick.* virus, infection, germ.
3 *(n) (informal) There's a bug in my computer program.* error, fault, defect, failing, flaw, virus, gremlin, malfunction, snarl-up *(informal)*.
4 *(v) (informal) The detectives decided to bug Beryl's phone calls.* tap, listen in on, monitor, eavesdrop on.
5 *(v) (informal) Rodney's jokes really bug me.* See **annoy** 1.

build
1 *(v) It took Dad ages to build the shed.* construct, put up, erect, assemble, put together, make, knock together *(informal)*.
OPPOSITES: demolish, dismantle.
2 *(n) Ed has a muscular build.* frame, body, physique, figure, form, shape.

building
(n) structure, edifice, construction, premises *(plural)*, pile *(informal)*.

buildings can be...

austere	graceful	outlandish
awe-inspiring	hideous	plain
	historic	rambling
beautiful	imposing	ruined
crumbling	impressive	simple
dazzling	lofty	solemn
elaborate	magical	stark
exotic	magnificent	striking
flamboyant	majestic	sumptuous
futuristic	massive	towering
gleaming	monstrous	ugly
glittering	ornate	vast

MOSQUE

outside a mosque
cupola (small dome)
dome
onion dome
minaret
outer wall

mosaic design

inside a mosque

ablution fountain (washing fountain)	kiblah (wall facing Mecca)
arcade (row of arches)	mihrab (niche showing direction of Mecca)
calligraphy (decorative writing)	minbar (pulpit)
carpets	mosaics
courtyard	pointed arch
enamel tiles	prayer hall
jali (latticed screen)	women's section

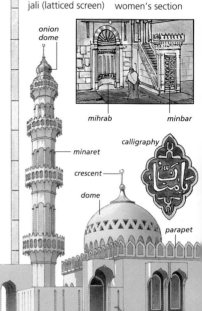

onion dome

mihrab   minbar

calligraphy

minaret

crescent

dome

parapet

column

colonnade

hall of mirrors

PALACE

outside a palace

balcony
balustrade
 (ornamental railing)
colonnade
 (row of columns)
courtyard
parapet (low wall
 along roof)

portico
 (covered
 entrance)
terrace
tower
turret
wing

inside a palace

ballroom
banqueting hall
bedroom
boudoir
 (lady's bedroom
 or sitting room)
chapel

corridor
drawing room
dressing room
entrance hall
grand staircase
great hall
hall of mirrors
kitchens
laundry
library
long gallery
music room
nursery
portrait gallery
servants' quarters
spiral staircase
state apartment
stateroom
throne room

inside the palace rooms

carved frieze
chandelier
gilt stucco
 (gold plasterwork)
marble floor
painted ceiling
panelled wall
parquet floor
 (polished
 wooden floor)
sculpture
tapestry
wall hanging

parapet

ornamental pool

gilt
stucco

painted ceiling

CHURCH

outside a church

belfry (bell tower)
buttress (support)
carving
flying buttress
gargoyle
lancet window
 (narrow, pointed
 window)
lead roof
pinnacle
porch
rose window
 (large, round window)
spire
stained-glass window
steeple
tower
weather vane

inside a church

aisle
altar
arch
carving
chancel
 (area for
 altar and
 choir)

choir screen
choir stalls
 (seats for choir)
column
crypt
 (underground
 burial
 chamber)

effigy (statue)
font
lectern (stand
 for Bible)
nave
 (main area)
organ loft
pew
pillar
pulpit
side chapel
tiled floor
tomb
transept
 (side wing)

painted
carving

pinnacle

lead
roof

belfry

stained-glass
window

organ

altar

choir
stalls

pulpit

lectern

pew

aisle

font

buttress

transept

SKYSCRAPER

outside a skyscraper

balcony
bronze glass
fire escape
helipad
navigation light
plaza
 (paved forecourt)
radio mast
reflective glass
roof garden
scenic lift
tinted glass

inside a skyscraper

atrium (central hall)
entrance lobby
escalator
express lift
fountain
mezzanine floor
 (halfway level
 between ground
 and first floor)
observation platform
open-plan office
penthouse suite
revolving restaurant
shopping mall
underground
 car park

plaza

atrium

Also see **Ancient Egypt, Ancient Greece, houses & homes, medieval life, Roman life**.

build-up
(n) After all the build-up, the concert was disappointing. hype, publicity, promotion, advertising, ballyhoo (informal), fuss.

build up
1 (v) Jet has managed to build up a huge collection of CDs. amass, assemble, accumulate, collect, put together, construct, create, establish.
2 (v) Jet aims to build up her collection even further. See **increase** 3.
3 (v) Don't let the noise build up any more. See **increase** 2.

bulging
1 (adj) The monster had bulging eyes. protruding, sticking out, popping out, bug.
2 (adj) My bag is bulging. bursting at the seams, straining at the seams, overstuffed, swollen, distended.

bulky
(adj) A bulky parcel. large, enormous, massive, unwieldy, unmanageable, cumbersome, hulking, heavy, weighty.

bullet
(n) shot, slug, pellet, rubber bullet.

bully
1 (v) I didn't mean to bully you. intimidate, frighten, terrorize, torment, persecute, tyrannize, bulldoze (informal), bludgeon.
2 (n) I tried to escape from the bully. bully boy, tormentor, persecutor, tyrant, tough, thug, heavy (slang).

bump
1 (n) Guy has a bump on his knee. lump, swelling, bulge.
2 (n) Ed fell out of bed with a bump. thud, thump, crash, bang, jolt, smack, clunk.
3 (v) Don't bump your head! See **hit** 2.
4 (v) We watched the jeep bump across the field. bounce, jolt, rattle, jerk.

bump into see **crash into**.

bumpy
1 (adj) A bumpy track. rough, uneven, potholed, rutted, pitted, lumpy.
OPPOSITES: smooth, even.
2 (adj) A bumpy ride. rough, bouncy, bone-breaking, jolting, jerky, jarring.
OPPOSITE: smooth.
3 (adj) A bumpy sea crossing. rough, choppy, stormy, turbulent.
OPPOSITE: smooth.

bunch
1 (n) Romeo clutched a bunch of flowers. bouquet, posy, spray, arrangement.
2 (n) I've lost a bunch of papers. set, bundle, collection, sheaf, batch, stack, heap, pile, group, number, quantity, mass, clump, cluster, assortment.
3 (n) (informal) A bunch of people watched the juggler. See **crowd** 1.

bundle
1 (n) A bundle of papers. sheaf, bunch, batch, pile, bale, heap, stack, group, collection, mass, package, packet.

2 (v) Please bundle these newspapers together. tie, bind, fasten, pack, roll, heap.
3 (v) Did you see the kidnappers bundle a man into their car? shove, push, hustle, hurry, rush, thrust, throw.

bung
(v) (slang) Bung your trainers in the wardrobe. throw, shove (informal), sling (informal), dump, stick (informal), put, plonk, drop, stuff.

bungle see **make a mess of**.

burglar
(n) housebreaker, robber, thief, cat burglar, intruder, ram raider (informal).

burglary
1 (n) Beryl was arrested for burglary. housebreaking, robbery, stealing, theft, breaking and entering, ram raiding (informal).
2 (n) Police are investigating the burglary. See **break-in**.

burn
1 (v) The forest could burn for days. blaze, be on fire, be in flames, be alight, be ablaze, smoulder, glow, smoke.
2 (v) Matilda watched the candle burn. flicker, glow, blaze, flare, flash.
3 (v) We need to burn this garden rubbish. set fire to, incinerate, set alight, set on fire, reduce to ashes, ignite, kindle.
4 (v) If the iron is too hot it will burn your top. singe, scorch, char, sear, scald (liquid).
5 (v) My skin is starting to burn. go red, go pink, redden, blister, peel, sting, smart, tingle, prickle.

burning
1 (adj) We watched the burning coals. blazing, flaming, glowing, fiery, red-hot, smouldering, sizzling, smoking.
2 (adj) A burning smell came from the science lab. smoky, pungent, acrid.
3 (adj) Jan has a burning desire to change the world. passionate, intense, ardent, fervent, all-consuming, deep, sincere, earnest, raging, frenzied, frantic.

burp
(v) (informal) belch, bring up wind.

burst
1 (v) Our pipes might burst. crack, split, break, break open, rupture, fracture, explode, shatter, disintegrate, tear apart.
2 (v) Shall I burst this balloon? pop, puncture, prick, pierce, stab.
3 (v) Don't burst into the room like that! rush, charge, barge (informal), crash, dash.
4 (v) Dan had a sudden burst of energy. spurt, surge, rush.

bury
(v) Pirate Peg plans to bury the treasure in her garden. conceal, hide, stow away, stash (informal), secrete, cover up.

bus
(n) We travelled by bus. coach, double-decker, minibus, charabanc (old-fashioned), omnibus (old-fashioned).

bush
(n) Hide behind this bush! shrub, hedge, shrubbery, plant.

bushy
(adj) Bushy hair. thick, shaggy, wiry, bristly, fuzzy, frizzy, tangled, unruly, luxuriant.

business
1 (n) A computer business. See **firm** 6.
2 (n) This company has a lot of business with Japan. trade, commerce, trading, buying and selling, dealings (plural), transactions (plural).
3 (n) It's my business how I spend my money. See **affair** 1.

businessman, businesswoman
(n) executive, tycoon, financier, industrialist, trader, entrepreneur, manager, director.

bust
1 (n) This T-shirt is too tight round the bust. chest, bosom, breasts (plural).
2 (adj) (informal) My radio is bust. See **broken** 2.

busy
1 (adj) You always seem to be busy. occupied, fully occupied, active, bustling about, on the go (informal), up to your eyes (informal), working, hard at work, slaving away, on duty.
OPPOSITES: idle, at a loose end.
2 (adj) Jem is busy doing her homework. hard at work, involved in, engaged in, occupied with, absorbed in, engrossed in, preoccupied with.
3 (adj) We stayed in a busy seaside resort. bustling, lively, buzzing, humming (informal), crowded, swarming, teeming, hectic, frenetic.
OPPOSITES: quiet, sleepy.

butt in see **interrupt** 1.

buy
(v) Let's buy a TV. purchase, get, acquire, invest in (informal), obtain, pay for.
OPPOSITE: sell.

by accident
(phrase) Timmy hit me by accident. accidentally, by mistake, by chance, unintentionally, inadvertently, unwittingly.

cadge see **scrounge**.

café
(n) snack bar, coffee shop, tea shop, restaurant, buffet, cafeteria.

cake
(n) gateau, sponge cake, layer cake, fruitcake, swiss roll, gingerbread, cupcake, bun, pastry, éclair, doughnut.

calamity see **disaster**.

calculate see **figure out** 1.

call
1 (v) *Did you call for help?* shout, yell, cry, cry out, scream, holler (informal), bellow.
2 (v) *Call the boys to come in for tea.* summon, order, instruct, invite, assemble, rally, gather, collect, muster.
3 (v) *What shall we call our gang? See* **name** 1.
4 (v) *I'll call you later. See* **phone** 1.
5 (v) *Can I call this morning?* drop in (informal), come round, visit, pop in (informal), look in (informal), stop by, pay you a visit, look you up.
6 **call for** (v) *Did Ali call for the parcel?* come for, collect, fetch, pick up.

callous
(adj) *Bozo is so callous about other people's feelings.* uncaring, unfeeling, heartless, hardhearted, cold, cruel, unsympathetic, insensitive, thick-skinned.
OPPOSITES: caring, sympathetic.

calm
1 (adj) *The sea was calm.* still, smooth, motionless, tranquil, unruffled, glassy.
OPPOSITES: rough, choppy.
2 (adj) *Claire always seems so calm.* serene, peaceful, untroubled, placid, tranquil, unflustered, relaxed, laid-back (informal), self-possessed, cool, composed, level-headed, unflappable (informal).
OPPOSITES: agitated, frantic.
3 (v) *Heather tried to calm the crying baby.* soothe, settle, quieten, pacify, hush.

camouflage see **disguise** 1, 3.

cancel
(v) *Let's cancel the match.* call off, scrap, drop, ditch (slang), abandon, write off.

capable see **able**.

capture see **catch** 2.

car
(n) motorcar, motor, vehicle, automobile (old-fashioned), wheels (plural) (informal), banger (informal).
TYPES OF CAR: classic car, convertible, estate, family car, hatchback, limousine, off-road vehicle, people carrier, racing car, rally car, saloon, sports car, stretch limo (informal), veteran car, vintage car.

care
1 (v) *You should care about the future.* mind, be concerned, concern yourself, be bothered, be interested in, worry.
2 (n) *Act with care. See* **caution**.
3 **care for** (v) *Can you care for my rat while I'm away? See* **look after**.

career see **job** 2.

careful
1 (adj) *Neesha always does careful work.* painstaking, meticulous, methodical, well-organized, neat, accurate, thoughtful.
OPPOSITES: careless, slapdash.
2 (adj) *Be careful crossing the road.* wary, attentive, alert, cautious, on your guard, observant, watchful.

careless
1 (adj) *Careless work.* slapdash, sloppy (informal), scrappy, untidy, shoddy, slipshod, rushed, disorganized, inaccurate.
OPPOSITES: careful, meticulous.
2 (adj) *Careless actions.* thoughtless, inconsiderate, negligent, irresponsible.
OPPOSITES: careful, considerate.

carry
1 (v) *Carry your luggage to the car.* take, bring, transfer, move, shift, cart, lug, haul, hump (informal), ferry, transport, deliver.
2 (v) *Can you carry my weight?* support, bear, take, hold, shoulder, sustain.

carry on see **continue** 1, 2, 3.

carry out
(v) *We must carry out our plan.* execute, accomplish, complete, carry through, fulfil.

carve
(v) *Try to carve a figure.* sculpt, hew, chisel, whittle, form, shape, engrave, etch.

case
1 (n) *I'll carry your case.* suitcase, bag, holdall, trunk, luggage, baggage.
2 (n) *Put that away in its case.* container, holder, wrapper, cover, box, cabinet.

castle
(n) fortress, fort, stronghold, citadel, palace, chateau. ❖ *Also see* **medieval life**.

casual
1 (adj) *A casual manner.* nonchalant, blasé, informal, free and easy, offhand, careless, relaxed, laid-back (informal).
2 (adj) *Casual clothes.* informal, leisure, comfortable, ordinary, everyday, sporty.

cat
(n) pussy (informal), pussycat (informal), puss (informal), moggy (informal), kitten, tomcat (male), tom (male), mouser.
TYPES OF CAT: Burmese, chinchilla, long-haired cat, Manx, Persian, short-haired cat, Siamese, tabby, tortoiseshell.

catastrophe see **disaster**.

catch
1 (v) *Catch the ball.* grab, seize, grasp, clutch, snatch, get, intercept.
2 (v) *The police are trying to catch a thief.* capture, seize, trap, snare, arrest, nick (slang), nab (informal), collar (informal).
3 (v) *I don't want to catch another cold.* get, contract, pick up, develop, go down with, succumb to, get infected with.
4 (n) *What's the catch?* snag, drawback, disadvantage, hitch, trap, trick.

catching
(adj) *Is this disease catching?* infectious, contagious.

catty (informal) see **spiteful**.

cause
1 (v) *This decision may cause problems.* create, produce, lead to, bring about, give rise to, generate, start, trigger off, spark off, stir up, provoke, make.
2 (n) *What was the cause of the problem?* root, source, reason for, origin.
3 (n) *Please support this cause.* campaign, movement, project, enterprise, charity.

caution
(n) *Act with caution.* care, attention, watchfulness, vigilance, forethought.

cautious
1 (adj) *A cautious swimmer.* careful, wary, unadventurous.
OPPOSITES: careless, reckless.
2 (adj) *A cautious reply.* guarded, careful, cagey (informal), noncommittal, discreet, circumspect.
OPPOSITES: careless, unguarded.

pouncing Siamese

---

cat words

cat moves

claw	paw
creep	pounce
crouch	prowl
curl up	scratch
dash	slink
dive	sprawl
drop	spring
leap	stalk
nuzzle	stretch
pad	

playful kittens

cat sounds
caterwaul
cough
hiss
mew
miaow
purr
screech
spit
squeak
yelp
yowl

a cat's coat can be...
bedraggled
flea-bitten
fluffy
mangy
matted
shaggy
shiny
silky
sleek
smooth
soft

a cat can seem...

adventurous	independent
affectionate	inquisitive
alert	lazy
aloof	mischievous
contented	playful
crazy	quizzical
curious	supercilious
dignified	timid
friendly	wild

— muzzle

— chest

sleek
tabby

ruff —

frill —

fluffy long-haired cat

cave

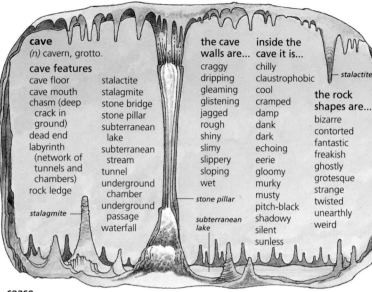

cave
(n) cavern, grotto.

cave features

cave floor	stalactite
cave mouth	stalagmite
chasm (deep	stone bridge
crack in	stone pillar
ground)	subterranean
dead end	lake
labyrinth	subterranean
(network of	stream
tunnels and	tunnel
chambers)	underground
rock ledge	chamber
	underground
stalagmite	passage
	waterfall

the cave walls are...
craggy
dripping
gleaming
glistening
jagged
rough
shiny
slimy
slippery
sloping
wet

stone pillar

subterranean lake

inside the cave it is...
chilly
claustrophobic
cool
cramped
damp
dank
dark
echoing
eerie
gloomy
murky
musty
pitch-black
shadowy
silent
sunless

stalactite

the rock shapes are...
bizarre
contorted
fantastic
freakish
ghostly
grotesque
strange
twisted
unearthly
weird

cease
see **stop** 3.

ceaseless
(adj) I can't stand this ceaseless noise. constant, continual, incessant, never-ending, nonstop, continuous, everlasting, endless, unending, unceasing, perpetual, relentless, persistent, interminable.
OPPOSITES: occasional, intermittent.

celebrate
1 *(v) Do you celebrate St Patrick's Day?* observe, commemorate, keep, mark.
2 *(v) You should celebrate on your birthday.* enjoy yourself, party *(informal)*, whoop it up *(informal)*, live it up *(informal)*, make merry, paint the town red *(informal)*.

celebration
(n) The celebration lasted all weekend. festivity, merrymaking, revelry, jollification, festivities *(plural)*, party, shindig *(informal)*, bash *(informal)*, rave *(slang)*, feast, carnival, gala, jubilee, festival.

celebrity
(n) Jason has become a TV celebrity. star, personality, idol, superstar, VIP (very important person), big name, big shot *(informal)*, megastar.

cellar
(n) basement, vault, crypt *(church)*.

cemetery
(n) graveyard, burial ground, churchyard.

central
1 *(adj) The central part of the city.* inner, middle, innermost, interior, core, focal.
OPPOSITE: outer.
2 *(adj) The central point of an argument.* main, key, focal, pivotal, principal, major, dominant, leading, most important, chief, basic, fundamental, essential.

centre
1 *(n) Drive to the centre of the city.* middle, heart, midpoint.
OPPOSITES: edge, outskirts *(plural)*.
2 *(n) This office is the centre of our operation.* hub, heart, focal point, nerve centre, core, focus, nucleus, crux.

ceremony
(n) Is there a ceremony to mark the end of term? event, function, gathering, celebration, do *(informal)*, service, ritual.

certain
1 *(adj) Chas was certain he had seen a ghost.* sure, positive, in no doubt, confident, convinced, satisfied, assured, persuaded, definite.
2 *(adj) The detectives need certain proof.* definite, absolute, conclusive, undeniable, unquestionable, indisputable, irrefutable, clear, unmistakable, reliable.
3 *(adj) Is it certain that Dad will lose his job?* definite, guaranteed, inevitable, unavoidable, inescapable, inexorable, sure, fixed, destined, fated.
4 *(adj) The shop is closed on certain days.* specific, particular, special, individual, established, fixed, set.

chain
1 *(n) A chain of disasters. See* **series**.
2 **chains** *(plural n) The prisoners were kept in chains.* irons *(plural)*, shackles *(plural)*, fetters *(plural)*, handcuffs *(plural)*, manacles *(plural)*, leg irons *(plural)*.

chair
(n) seat.
TYPES OF CHAIR: armchair, deck chair, dining chair, easy chair, office chair, reclining chair, rocking chair, sun lounger, swivel chair, throne.

challenge
1 *(v) Is it safe to challenge the burglars?* confront, accost, tackle, take on, have a go at *(informal)*.
2 *(v) Who will challenge me to jump?* dare, defy, invite, provoke, goad, taunt, throw down the gauntlet.
3 *(v) Don't challenge what I say!* question, query, dispute, doubt, take issue with, argue with, object to.

challenging
(adj) A challenging job. demanding, testing, taxing, stimulating, hard, difficult, stretching, worthwhile.
OPPOSITES: easy, soft *(informal)*.

champion
(n) winner, victor, prizewinner, titleholder, conqueror.

chance
1 *(n) We met by chance.* accident, coincidence, luck, fluke, destiny, fate, providence, good fortune, serendipity.
2 *(n) There's a chance of snow.* possibility, prospect, probability, likelihood, risk, danger, threat.
3 *(n) Will you take a chance?* risk, gamble, leap in the dark.
4 *(n) You will have another chance to win soon.* opportunity, occasion, time, turn.
5 *(adj) It was a chance meeting.* accidental, coincidental, unexpected, unintentional, unplanned, unforeseen, random, casual, fluke, fortuitous.

change
1 *(v) We must change our plans.* alter, revise, amend, modify, adapt, vary, reform.
2 *(v) I want to change my room.* alter, rearrange, transform, make over, redo, reorganize, remodel, revamp.
3 *(v) The frog began to change into a prince.* turn, be transformed, morph *(informal)*, mutate, metamorphose, transmute, become.
4 *(v) Can I change this jumper for a smaller one?* exchange, swap, switch, trade, substitute, replace with.
5 *(v) Let's change our direction.* switch, alter, shift, reverse.
6 *(n) There's been a change in Guy's attitude.* shift, switch, alteration, transformation, turnaround, sea change, reversal, metamorphosis.
7 *(n) This is a pleasant change.* variation, departure, diversion, break, novelty.
8 *(n) I need some change for the bus.* coins *(plural)*, small change, loose change, cash, coppers *(plural)*, silver.

change your mind
(phrase) Why don't you change your mind and stay? revise your opinion, think better of it, think twice, reconsider, rethink.

chaos
(n) There was chaos in the classroom. confusion, disorder, pandemonium, bedlam, turmoil, uproar, tumult, anarchy.

chaotic
(adj) The office was chaotic. disorganized, jumbled, muddled, topsy-turvy, shambolic *(informal)*, out of control, riotous, anarchic.

character
1 *(n) Marie has a very gentle character.* personality, nature, temperament, disposition, make-up.
2 *(n) Yves is a strange character.* person, individual, type *(informal)*, sort *(informal)*.
3 *(n) (informal) Eddie's a real character!* individual, eccentric, clown, comic, case *(informal)*, oddball *(informal)*.
4 *(n) This village has a special character.* quality, atmosphere, feel, personality.

characteristic
(n) Untidiness is a characteristic of many teenagers. quality, attribute, trait, feature, peculiarity, idiosyncrasy, mark, property.

charge
1 *(n) What is the charge for entering the museum?* cost, fee, price, rate, payment.
2 *(v) The troops began to charge the enemy.* attack, storm, assault, rush at.
3 *(v) The police will charge Beryl with burglary.* accuse of, indict, prosecute for.

charm
1 *(n) Oz has a mysterious charm.* appeal, charisma, allure, magnetism, fascination.
2 *(n) A wizard's charm. See* **spell**.
3 *(n) A lucky charm.* amulet, talisman.
4 *(v) Kamala will charm you with her singing.* delight, captivate, enchant, bewitch, beguile, fascinate, mesmerize.

charming
(adj) A charming smile. appealing, attractive, enchanting, captivating, winning, bewitching, engaging, irresistible, disarming, fetching *(informal)*.

chart
(n) Study this chart. plan, map, table, diagram, graph, blueprint.

chase
(v) Fido loves to chase Pickles. run after, pursue, follow, tail, hunt, stalk, trail.

chat *see* **talk** 1, 5, 6.

chatter *see* **prattle**.

chatterbox
(n) (informal) Sophie is a real chatterbox! gossip, chatterer, prattler, motormouth *(slang)*, windbag *(slang)*.

chatty
(adj) (informal) Zoë sent me a chatty letter. gossipy, newsy, friendly, informal.

cheap
1 *(adj) This CD is cheap.* inexpensive, reasonable, moderately priced, good value, economical, cut-price, reduced.
OPPOSITE: expensive.
2 *(adj) This cheap furniture won't last.* poor-quality, inferior, shoddy, trashy, tacky *(informal)*, tawdry, rubbishy, crappy *(slang)*, crummy *(slang)*, worthless.
OPPOSITES: high-quality, superior.
3 *(adj) What a cheap trick! See* **mean** 6.

cheat
1 *(v) Watch out for Dodgy Dave or he'll cheat you.* trick, swindle, con *(informal)*, screw *(informal)*, sting *(informal)*, bamboozle *(informal)*, dupe, do *(informal)*, fleece, rip you off *(slang)*, take you for a ride *(informal)*, pull a fast one on *(slang)*, hoodwink, defraud.
2 *(v) Don't cheat in this test.* break the rules, bend the rules, copy, crib *(informal)*.
3 *(n) That man's a cheat.* swindler, con man *(informal)*, rogue, shark *(informal)*, double-dealer, double-crosser, fraud *(informal)*, crook *(informal)*, impostor.

check
(v) Check your bike carefully before you set off. examine, inspect, check out, test, try out, give it the once-over *(informal)*, look over, scrutinize.

checkup
(n) A medical checkup. examination, medical *(informal)*, physical *(informal)*.

cheeky
(adj) I've had enough of your cheeky comments! impertinent, impudent, rude, saucy, bold, insolent, disrespectful, insulting, pert, fresh *(informal)*, forward.
OPPOSITES: polite, respectful.

cheer
(v) When we heard the score, we all began to cheer. applaud, clap, whoop, whistle, yell, stamp, give a standing ovation.

cheerful
(adj) Sally is always cheerful. happy, good-humoured, cheery, light-hearted, jolly, sunny, chirpy *(informal)*, perky, merry, bright, breezy, buoyant, optimistic.
OPPOSITES: miserable, depressed.

cheer up
1 *(v) Try to cheer up.* perk up *(informal)*, buck up *(informal)*, take heart, rally, brighten, snap out of it.
2 *(v) How can I cheer you up?* encourage, comfort, buck you up *(informal)*, give you new heart, buoy you up, jolly you along *(informal)*, gladden, hearten.

chest
1 *(n) A person's chest.* ribcage, breast *(old-fashioned)*.
2 *(n) A storage chest.* trunk, box, crate, container, case, strongbox, coffer, casket.

chew
(v) Chew your food thoroughly. munch, crunch, chomp, gnaw, grind up, nibble.

chief
1 *(adj) Amy was the chief bridesmaid.* principal, senior, head, leading, main.
2 *(adj) What is your chief reason for leaving? See* **main**.

child
(n) kid *(informal)*, youngster, young person, boy, girl, little one, nipper *(informal)*, brat, kiddywink *(informal)*, sprog *(slang)*, infant, toddler, tot, tiny tot, adolescent, teenager, juvenile, minor.

childish
(adj) Childish behaviour. infantile, juvenile, immature, babyish, puerile, foolish, silly.

chilly
1 *(adj) A chilly morning.* cold, icy, frosty, crisp, cool, nippy, fresh, raw, wintry.
OPPOSITE: warm.
2 *(adj) A chilly response.* cool, frosty, unfriendly, aloof, standoffish, cold, hostile.
OPPOSITES: friendly, warm.

chip
1 *(n) My mug has a chip in it.* nick, crack, split, flaw, notch, scratch, dent, gash.
2 *(n) I knocked a chip off the table.* splinter, sliver, shaving, flake, piece, fragment, chunk, wedge.

choice
1 *(n) Do I have a choice?* option, alternative, vote, say, voice.
2 *(n) There was a wide choice of desserts.* selection, range, variety, array, assortment.
3 *(n) Have you made your choice?* selection, pick, decision, preference.

choke
1 *(v) The thick smoke made us choke.* gasp, gag, retch, cough, suffocate.
2 *(v) The villain tried to choke his victim.* strangle, throttle, garrotte, suffocate, smother, stifle, overwhelm, overpower.
3 *(v) Leaves often choke the stream.* block, clog, stop up, obstruct, dam, bung up, constrict, congest.

choose
1 *(v) I think we should choose Bill as our captain.* select, pick, elect, appoint, decide on, opt for, settle on, fix upon.
2 *(v) You may choose to walk alone.* decide, prefer, opt, elect, see fit, wish, resolve, make up your mind, determine.

choosy *(informal) see* **fussy**.

chop
1 *(v) Can you chop this log in two?* split, cut, cleave, hew, hack, slice, divide, sever.
2 *(v) Chop the carrots finely.* chop up, cut up, slice, dice, cube, mince.

choppy
(adj) A choppy sea. rough, ruffled, stormy, squally, turbulent, heaving.
OPPOSITES: smooth, calm.

chore *see* **task**.

chubby *see* **plump**.

chuck *(informal) see* **throw** 1.

chuckle *see* **giggle**.

chuffed *(slang) see* **pleased**.

chunk
(n) A chunk of cheese. block, hunk, slab, lump, wedge, slice, wodge *(informal)*.

circle
1 *(n) Draw a circle.* ring, loop, disc, hoop, band, round shape, circular shape.
2 *(v) The road will circle the city.* surround, enclose, encircle, ring, skirt, hem in, orbit.
3 *(v) Watch the dancers circle round the room. See* **whirl**.

city

city	on the pavement	people may...	the traffic may be...	you can shop at...	the city may be...
(n) metropolis, town.	you can see...	brush past	at a standstill	boutique	bewildering
	beggar	crowd	bumper-to-	chain store	bustling
city sights **city streets**	busker	dawdle	bumper	covered market	busy
art gallery alley	bus stop	hurry	chock-a-block	department	buzzing
bridge avenue	entertainer	jostle	crawling	store	congested
cathedral backstreet	flower seller	loiter	slow-moving	kiosk	crowded
cinema boulevard	fruit stall	mill about	snarled up	open-air	dirty
city hall crescent	lamppost	rush	solid	market	dynamic
concert hall cul-de-sac	litter	wander	tailed back	shopping mall	exciting
fountain flyover	newspaper	window-shop		supermarket	grimy
hotel lane	vendor				high-tech
ice rink one-way street	pedestrian	**city transport**	**traffic sounds**	**you can eat**	historic
leisure complex passage	police officer	bicycle	beep	**and drink at...**	lively
library plaza	road sweeper	bus	chug	bistro	noisy
mosque ring road	shopper	car	growl	burger bar	overwhelming
museum square	street artist	open-topped	honk	café	packed
nightclub subway	tourist	bus	hum	coffee shop	polluted
opera house (underground		taxi	purr	pavement café	pulsing
park passage)		tram	roar	pub	run-down
skyscraper		tube	screech	restaurant	shabby
sports stadium	*city skyline*	underground	squeal	snack bar	smart
temple			toot	tea shop	smoggy
theatre			wail	wine bar	smoky
tower					spectacular
block					throbbing

Also see **building**.

claim
1 (v) *I've come to claim my money.* demand, ask for, collect, pick up, request.
2 (v) *I still claim that I was right.* insist, maintain, argue, assert, affirm, declare.

clammy *see* **damp** 3.

clap *see* **applaud**.

class
(n) *Which class are you in at school?* form, group, set, stream, year, level.

clean
1 (v) *I must clean everything in my room.* wash, wipe, mop, scrub, scour, sponge, dust, soap, sweep, vacuum, cleanse, launder, rinse, disinfect.
2 (adj) *Everything in my room is clean.* spotless, immaculate, squeaky-clean, fresh, sanitary, hygienic, unsoiled, unstained, washed, laundered, swept, scrubbed, scoured, dusted, disinfected.
OPPOSITES: dirty, soiled.
3 (adj) *You must only drink clean water.* pure, uncontaminated, unpolluted, purified, sterile, clear, unadulterated.
OPPOSITES: polluted, contaminated.
4 (adj) *Use a clean sheet of paper.* blank, new, empty, unused, unmarked, fresh.

clear
1 (adj) *A clear stream.* transparent, limpid, pure, crystal clear, crystalline.
OPPOSITES: muddy, cloudy.

2 (adj) *A clear signal.* definite, plain, distinct, recognizable, unmistakable.
OPPOSITES: unclear, confusing.
3 (adj) *Clear writing.* legible, bold, neat.
OPPOSITE: illegible.
4 (adj) *A clear day.* See **fine** 3.
5 (adj) *A clear outline.* clean, clear-cut, definite, distinct, sharp, well-defined.
OPPOSITE: fuzzy.
6 (adj) *A clear voice.* audible, distinct, penetrating, piercing.
OPPOSITES: indistinct, muffled.
7 (adj) *A clear argument.* clear-cut, coherent, simple, straightforward, easy to follow, unambiguous, lucid.
OPPOSITES: confusing, complicated.
8 (adj) *A clear space.* See **empty** 1.
9 (v) *I must clear this rubbish from my room.* get rid of, remove, empty, strip, unload, unpack, disentangle.
10 (v) *I wish the mist would clear.* disappear, evaporate, melt away, lift.

clear up
1 (v) *Clear up the kitchen.* See **tidy** 3.
2 (v) *Let's clear up this problem.* sort out, settle, resolve, clarify, unravel, put right.
3 (v) *I hope your cold will clear up soon.* go away, disappear, get better.

clever
1 (adj) *A clever student.* intelligent, bright, able, quick, brainy (informal), smart, gifted, talented, capable, knowledgeable.

2 (adj) *A clever trick.* cunning, crafty, ingenious, shrewd, smart, slick, inventive.

cliff
(n) precipice, rockface, crag, escarpment.
❖ *Also see* **sea & seashore**.

climax
(n) *The climax of Jackson's career was winning the gold medal.* high point, high spot, highlight, culmination, crowning point, pinnacle, peak.

climb
1 (v) *We tried to climb the mountain.* scale, clamber up, go up, ascend, shin up.
OPPOSITES: descend, go down.
2 (v) *I think prices will climb.* See **rise** 2.
3 (v) *The road began to climb.* See **rise** 4.

cling on to *see* **hold on to**.

clip *see* **fasten** 2.

clog *see* **block** 2.

close
1 (v) *Close the gate.* See **shut** 1.
2 (adj) *Bill and Ben are close friends.* See **intimate** 1.
3 (adj) *The match was close.* evenly matched, well-matched, hard-fought, neck and neck.
4 **close to** (adj) *I live close to the park.* See **near** 1.

cloth *see* **material**.

clothes (*plural n*) clothing, garments (*plural*), gear (*informal*), togs (*plural*) (*informal*), get-up (*informal*), dress, costume, attire (*old-fashioned*).

suits
boiler suit
dress suit
lounge suit
morning suit
overalls
pinstripe suit
safari suit
sailor suit
shell suit
three-piece suit
tracksuit
trouser suit

three-piece suit

safari suit

skirts
flared skirt
gathered skirt
kilt
miniskirt
pleated skirt
puffball skirt
sarong
split skirt
straight skirt
tiered skirt
wrapover skirt

puffball skirt

wrapover skirt

trousers and shorts
bermuda shorts
chinos
corduroys
culottes
cut-offs
cycling shorts
drainpipes
dungarees
flannels
flares
jeans
jodhpurs
knickerbockers
leggings
palazzo pants
pedal pushers
plus fours
ski pants

waistband

chinos

culottes

palazzo pants

pinafore dress

shift dress

dresses
ball gown
cocktail dress
gym slip
kimono
maternity dress
minidress
pinafore
sari
shift dress
sundress

tops
blouse
body
camisole top
cardigan
crew-neck jumper
cropped top
lumberjack shirt
polo-neck jumper
polo shirt
pullover
rugby shirt
smock
sweater
sweatshirt
tanktop
T-shirt
turtleneck jumper
vest top
V-neck jumper
waistcoat

blouse

cropped top

camisole top

fabrics
acrylic
cashmere
chiffon
corduroy
cotton
crushed velvet
denim
fur
jersey
lamé
leather
lycra
satin
silk
suede
taffeta
tweed
velvet
wool

patterns
checked
floral
gingham
paisley
polka dot
striped
tartan

gingham

floral

tartan

some clothes have...
beads
embroidery
flounces
frills
fringes
ruffles
sequins
tassels
tiers

sequin

bead

coats and jackets
anorak
blazer
bomber jacket
cagoule
cape
cloak
combat jacket
dinner jacket
double-breasted jacket
duffle coat
fleece
fur coat
greatcoat
mackintosh
overcoat
raincoat
shawl
sports jacket
tail coat
trench coat
waxed jacket

double-breasted jacket

collar

lapel

trench coat

accessories
bag
belt
bow tie
braces
cravat
cummerbund
gloves
jewellery
sash
scarf
shoes
tie

clothes can look...
baggy
casual
chic
clingy
comfortable
daring
dashing
drab
elegant
fashionable
feminine
figure-hugging
flamboyant
flattering
floating
flowing
formal
frilly
frumpy
fun
fussy
glamorous
glittering
neat
old-fashioned
outrageous
practical
revealing
roomy
scruffy
see-through
severe
skintight
slinky
smart
sophisticated
sporty
tight-fitting

clothes can be...
backless
cropped
fitted
flared
gathered
padded
pleated
ribbed
sleeveless
strapless
tailored
tapered

Also see **hat, jewellery, shoe**.

cloudy

cloudy
1 *(adj) A cloudy sky.* overcast, hazy, grey, dull, gloomy, dismal, dark, leaden, heavy, thundery, threatening, sunless, starless.
OPPOSITES: clear, cloudless.
2 *(adj) Cloudy water.* murky, muddy, milky, opaque.
OPPOSITES: clear, transparent.

club
(n) Please join our club! group, society, organization, association, circle, clique, company, league, union, federation.

clue
(n) This clue may help solve the crime. lead, pointer, information, evidence, tip-off, suggestion, hint, sign, key, idea.

clumsy *see* **awkward** 1, 2.

clutch *see* **grip**.

clutter
1 *(n) Tidy up this clutter! See* **mess** 1.
2 *(v) Don't clutter the lounge with your comics.* litter, mess up, strew, make untidy.

coach
1 *(n) We travelled by coach. See* **bus**.
2 *(n) We've got a new tennis coach.* instructor, trainer, teacher, tutor, mentor.
3 *(v) Who'll coach the team? See* **train** 4.

coarse
1 *(adj) Coarse material.* rough, scratchy, bristly, prickly, hairy, thick, homespun.
OPPOSITES: fine, soft.
2 *(adj) Coarse jokes. See* **crude**.

coast *see* **shore**.

coat
1 *(n) Put on your coat.* ❖ *See* **clothes**.
2 *(n) An animal's coat keeps it warm in winter.* fur, hair, fleece, wool, pelt, hide.
3 *(n) Apply a coat of varnish. See* **layer** 1.

coax *see* **persuade**.

cocky *see* **conceited**.

coil *see* **loop** 1, 2

cold
1 *(adj) It was a cold winter's day.* chilly, freezing, frosty, icy, crisp, nippy, raw, bitter, bleak, perishing *(informal)*, wintry.
OPPOSITES: warm, hot.
2 *(adj) A cold wind blew in off the sea.* chill, icy, freezing, bitter, keen, biting, cutting, piercing, penetrating, arctic.
OPPOSITES: warm, balmy.
3 *(adj) I'm cold!* chilly, freezing, frozen, frozen stiff, perishing *(informal)*, chilled to the bone, shivering, numbed.
OPPOSITES: warm, hot.
4 *(adj) Mr Steel is a rather cold person.* distant, remote, aloof, reserved, unfriendly, standoffish, impersonal, unemotional, unfeeling, unsympathetic, uncaring.
OPPOSITES: warm, friendly.

collapse
1 *(v) Let's hope the roof doesn't collapse.* fall in, cave in, give way, subside, tumble down, crumble, disintegrate, fall to pieces, fall apart, crumple, buckle.

2 *(v) Jenny may collapse when she hears the bad news.* faint, pass out, lose consciousness, keel over, swoon *(old-fashioned)*, break down, go to pieces.
3 *(n) The collapse of Communism.* fall, ruin, downfall, destruction, break-up.

collect
1 *(v) Fran has started to collect old comics.* save, keep, accumulate, amass, pile up, gather together, stockpile, hoard.
2 *(v) We'll collect you from the station.* fetch, come and get, pick you up, call for.
3 *(v) A crowd began to collect around the juggler.* gather, assemble, congregate, converge, cluster, flock, concentrate, mass.
OPPOSITES: disperse, scatter.

collection
(n) Melissa has a collection of stamps. set, assortment, array, hoard, mass, pile, stack.

collision *see* **crash** 2.

colossal *see* **huge**.

colour
1 *(n) That colour of blue suits you.* shade, tone, tint, tinge, hue.
2 *(v) Colour the background green.* paint, shade, tint, dye, stain, tinge, colourwash.

colourful
(adj) A colourful shirt. brightly coloured, bright, vivid, vibrant, multicoloured, gaudy, jazzy *(informal)*, psychedelic.
OPPOSITES: dull, colourless.

column
1 *(n) A stone column. See* **pillar**.
2 *(n) A column of people. See* **line** 3.
3 *(n) A newspaper column. See* **article** 1.

combine
(v) Let's combine the teams to create a winning side. merge, put together, pool, mix, unite, join, integrate, amalgamate.
OPPOSITES: separate, divide.

come
1 *(v) The enemy will come under cover of darkness.* approach, advance, move closer, draw near, close in, bear down.
OPPOSITE: go.
2 *(v) Please come on time. See* **arrive** 1.
3 **come to** *(v) Stop when you come to the lights.* reach, get to, arrive at, get as far as.

comedy
(n) light entertainment, humour, fun.
TYPES OF COMEDY: black comedy, clowning, farce, improvisation, pantomime, parody, revue, satire, sitcom (situation comedy), sketch, skit, slapstick, spoof *(informal)*, stand-up comedy.

come in *see* **enter** 1.

come round
1 *(v) Please come round soon. See* **call** 5.
2 *(v) We waited anxiously for Jo to come round after her fall.* come to, regain consciousness, revive, recover, wake up.

come up
(v) Did any problems come up? crop up *(informal)*, arise, occur, emerge, happen.

comfort
1 *(v) Gina tried to comfort her sobbing sister.* console, soothe, calm, reassure, encourage, cheer up, sympathize with.
2 *(n) Lord Lucre enjoys a life of comfort.* ease, contentment, wellbeing, cosiness, luxury, affluence, opulence.
OPPOSITE: hardship.

comfortable
1 *(adj) A comfortable sofa.* comfy *(informal)*, soft, squashy, well-padded, well-cushioned, cosy, snug, roomy.
OPPOSITE: uncomfortable.
2 *(adj) Comfortable clothes.* comfy *(informal)*, loose-fitting, roomy, baggy, sloppy, stretchy, snug, casual, sporty.
OPPOSITES: uncomfortable, tight-fitting.

command *see* **order** 1, 3.

comment
1 *(v) Beth was quick to comment that I looked better.* remark, point out, mention, observe, note, say.
2 *(n) Ben made a nasty comment about my hair.* remark, observation, statement.

commit
(v) Beryl may commit another crime. carry out, perpetrate, execute, be guilty of.

common
1 *(adj) Red buses are a common sight in London.* normal, familiar, usual, everyday, frequent, regular, daily, ordinary, routine, commonplace, run-of-the-mill, standard.
OPPOSITES: rare, uncommon.
2 *(adj) There's a common theory that chocolate gives you spots. See* **popular** 3.
3 *(adj) Araminta says I'm common.* coarse, uncouth, vulgar, crude, rough, yobbish *(informal)*, loutish, ill-bred, inferior.
OPPOSITES: refined, well-bred.

communicate
1 *(v) Please communicate this message.* convey, pass on, relay, spread, transmit.
2 *(v) We try to communicate regularly.* be in touch, make contact, talk, converse, speak, correspond, write, e-mail.

company
1 *(n) I enjoy Orlando's company.* friendship, companionship.
2 *(n) We have company for dinner.* guests *(plural)*, visitors *(plural)*, callers *(plural)*.
3 *(n) An electronics company. See* **firm** 6.

compare
1 *(v) Compare your results with mine.* check against, contrast, set against.
2 **compare with** *(v) This restaurant can compare with any in the area.* equal, rival, match, measure up to, bear comparison with, hold a candle to *(informal)*.

compete
1 *(v) Are you going to compete on Sports Day?* take part, participate, join in, enter, be a contestant, be in the running.
2 *(v) Six teams will compete for the cup.* contend, vie, battle, fight, rival each other.

competent *see* **able**.

competition
1 *(n) Who won the competition?* contest, championship, tournament, match, game, race, event, challenge, rally, quiz.
2 *(n) There's a lot of competition for places at the school.* rivalry, one-upmanship *(informal)*, opposition.

competitive
1 *(adj) Tony is so competitive.* ambitious, pushy *(informal)*, aggressive, combative.
2 *(adj) We live in a competitive society.* dog-eat-dog, cutthroat, aggressive.

competitor
(n) Are you a competitor in this race? contestant, contender, challenger, participant, entrant, runner, candidate.

complain
(v) I'm tired of hearing you complain. criticize, find fault, make a fuss, protest, grumble, moan, grouse, whine, whinge *(informal)*, gripe *(informal)*, carp, groan *(informal)*, beef *(slang)*, bellyache *(slang)*.

complaint
(n) Please see the manager with your complaint. grievance, criticism, objection, protest, grouse, gripe *(informal)*.

complete
1 *(adj) Do you have the complete set?* See **whole**.
2 *(adj) The match was a complete disaster.* absolute, total, utter, unqualified, out-and-out, outright, thoroughgoing, perfect.
3 *(v) We must complete our project today.* See **finish 1**.

completely see **absolutely**.

complex
(n) Nathan has a complex about being short. obsession, fixation, phobia, preoccupation, hang-up *(informal)*.

complicated
(adj) Complicated directions. complex, involved, elaborate, convoluted, intricate, difficult, perplexing, puzzling.
OPPOSITES: simple, straightforward.

compliment
(n) Freddie's compliment made me blush. flattering remark, praise, admiration, tribute, flattery, congratulations *(plural)*.

compose see **write 2**.

compromise
(v) We couldn't agree, so we had to compromise. make concessions, meet halfway, make a deal *(informal)*, strike a balance, find the middle ground, give and take, find a solution.

compulsory
(adj) At my school, wearing uniform is compulsory. obligatory, required, mandatory, necessary, stipulated.
OPPOSITE: optional.

computer
(n) TYPES OF COMPUTER: hand-held, laptop, mainframe, notebook, palmtop, PC (personal computer), server, word processor, work station.

(n) PARTS OF A COMPUTER: CD-ROM (compact disc with read-only memory), CD-ROM drive, CD-writer, CPU (central processing unit), disk drive, floppy disk, hard disk, keyboard, memory expansion card, modem, monitor, mouse, printer, scanner, screen, sound card, speaker, VDU (visual display unit).

con
1 *(n) (informal) This offer is a real con!* swindle, cheat, con trick *(informal)*, rip-off *(slang)*, swiz *(informal)*, scam *(slang)*.
2 *(v) (informal) Dodgy Dave will con you out of your money.* See **cheat 1**.

conceal see **hide 1, 2, 3**.

conceited
(adj) Jack is so conceited; he's always boasting. vain, bigheaded *(informal)*, swollen-headed *(informal)*, puffed up, proud, arrogant, self-important, self-satisfied, boastful, cocky, bumptious.
OPPOSITES: modest, self-effacing.

concentrate
1 *(v) Do you find it hard to concentrate?* focus your thoughts, focus your attention, pay attention, stop your mind wandering.
2 **concentrate on** *(v) Concentrate on your work.* keep your mind on, focus on, give your full attention to, apply yourself to, attend to.

concern
1 *(v) This decision will concern you all.* affect, involve, apply to, relate to, be relevant to, be of interest to, matter to.
2 *(v) Don't let this problem concern you.* See **worry 2**.
3 *(n) Granny's illness has caused us a lot of concern.* See **worry 3**.
4 *(n) Show some concern for your sister!* consideration, care, sympathy, regard.
5 *(n) This mess is not my concern.* affair, business, responsibility, problem.

conclusion
1 *(n) We had to leave before the conclusion.* See **end 1**.
2 *(n) After all that thinking, what's your conclusion?* decision, judgment, verdict, opinion, deduction, answer, solution.

condemn
1 *(v) Don't condemn Ziggy for being different.* criticize, blame, denounce, censure, reproach, damn, slam *(slang)*.
2 *(v) The judge decided to condemn Burglar Beryl.* See **convict 1**.

condescending
(adj) Araminta is so condescending; she looks down on everyone. patronizing, superior, supercilious, disdainful, snobbish, snooty *(informal)*, toffee-nosed *(slang)*.

condition
1 *(n) Are you in good condition?* health, shape, trim, nick *(informal)*, form.
2 *(n) Our school is in a dreadful condition.* state, state of repair, order, situation, position, predicament, plight.

3 **conditions** *(plural n) The conditions in the prison were terrible.* circumstances *(plural)*, surroundings *(plural)*, environment, situation, way of life.

confess
1 *(v) Did Beryl confess that she was guilty?* admit, own up, acknowledge, concede, declare, reveal, disclose, blurt out, confide.
2 *(v) If you broke the window you should confess.* own up, accept responsibility, plead guilty, come clean *(informal)*, make a clean breast of it, spill the beans *(informal)*.

confession
(n) A confession of guilt. admission, acknowledgment, declaration, profession.

confide in
(v) You can confide in me; I won't tell a soul. open your heart to, unburden yourself to, tell your secrets to, tell all to *(informal)*, trust, have confidence in.

confident
1 *(adj) Izzy is confident in new situations.* self-confident, self-assured, poised, self-possessed, composed, assertive, fearless.
OPPOSITES: diffident, insecure.
2 *(adj) I'm confident that it will be sunny.* certain, sure, convinced, positive, optimistic, hopeful.
OPPOSITE: doubtful.

confidential see **private 2**.

confirm
(v) Sid's actions confirm my suspicions about him. bear out, verify, prove, substantiate, corroborate, validate, back up, support, strengthen, reinforce.

confiscate
(v) Mrs Badger will confiscate that comic. seize, remove, take away, impound.

confront
(v) Are you brave enough to confront Bozo? face, face up to, stand up to, resist, oppose, defy, challenge, tackle, accost.

confuse
1 *(v) Complicated instructions confuse me.* bewilder, perplex, baffle, puzzle, muddle, flummox, faze, mystify, bemuse.
2 **confuse with** *(v) I often confuse you with your twin brother.* mistake you for, mix you up with, take you for.

confused
(adj) Don't speak so fast; it makes me feel confused. bewildered, dazed, muddled, disorientated, befuddled, at sixes and sevens, at sea, perplexed, baffled, flummoxed, nonplussed, puzzled.

confusing
(adj) These instructions are confusing. baffling, bewildering, perplexing, mystifying, puzzling, misleading, ambiguous, unclear, complicated.
OPPOSITES: clear, straightforward.

confusion
(n) A scene of total confusion met my eyes. chaos, turmoil, muddle, disorder, disarray, disorganization, jumble, clutter, shambles.

congratulate

congratulate
(v) I'll be the first to congratulate you if you win. shake your hand, pat you on the back *(informal)*, compliment, praise, offer you good wishes, wish you joy.
OPPOSITE: commiserate with.

conjurer *see* **magician** 2.

connect
1 *(v) Connect the cable to the television.* join, attach, link up, fix, fasten, secure.
OPPOSITE: disconnect.
2 *(v) I always connect that smell with school dinners. See* **associate** 2.

connection
(n) Is there a connection between air pollution and asthma? link, correlation, relationship, association, tie-in, parallel.

conquer
1 *(v) The army managed to conquer their enemy.* defeat, beat, overcome, subdue, overthrow, overpower, triumph over, crush, thrash, rout, vanquish, subjugate.
2 *(v) I'm trying to conquer my fear of flying.* overcome, get the better of, quell, subdue, master, rise above.

conscience
(n) Dodgy Dave has no conscience when it comes to lying. scruples *(plural)*, misgivings *(plural)*, qualms *(plural)*, principles *(plural)*, standards *(plural)*, morals *(plural)*, ethics *(plural)*, sense of right and wrong.

conscientious
(adj) Oliver is conscientious about his work. diligent, careful, meticulous, thorough, painstaking, dedicated, hard-working.
OPPOSITES: careless, slack.

conscious
1 *(adj) Fergus bumped his head, but remained conscious.* aware, awake, alert, compos mentis, with it *(informal)*.
OPPOSITES: unconscious, out cold.
2 *(adj) Annie made a conscious decision to stay out late. See* **deliberate**.

consequence *see* **result** 1.

consider
1 *(v) Consider the consequences before you take action.* think about, weigh up, give thought to, reflect on, examine, contemplate, ponder, mull over, chew over, turn over in your mind.
2 *(v) I consider fox-hunting to be wrong.* believe, regard, judge, deem, hold, think.

considerate *see* **thoughtful** 1.

consistent
1 *(adj) Toby is a consistent worker.* steady, dependable, reliable, predictable, stable, unchanging, unvarying, unfailing.
2 *(adj) The reports are consistent on this point.* compatible, in agreement, the same, matching, all of a piece.

consist of
(v) The new maths course will consist of ten different modules. be made up of, be composed of, comprise, include, contain, involve, incorporate.

console *see* **comfort** 1.

conspicuous *see* **noticeable**.

conspiracy *see* **plot** 1.

constant
1 *(adj) I can't stand this constant noise.* continuous, continual, incessant, never-ending, nonstop, ceaseless, perpetual, relentless, unremitting, interminable, unending, unceasing, persistent.
OPPOSITES: intermittent, occasional.
2 *(adj) Mum drove at a constant speed.* steady, even, consistent, uniform, fixed, unchanging, unvarying, invariable.
OPPOSITES: erratic, varying.

constantly
(adv) Fifi talks constantly. all the time, nonstop, continuously, continually, incessantly, without stopping, night and day, endlessly, unceasingly, relentlessly, perpetually, interminably, always.
OPPOSITES: occasionally, now and then.

construct *see* **build** 1.

consult
(v) I'd like to consult you before I make up my mind. ask, ask your advice, speak to, confer with, discuss something with, compare notes with, refer to, turn to.

contact
(v) I must contact Mandy. get in touch with, get hold of, communicate with, reach, ring, call, phone, speak to, write to, e-mail, text, fax.

contain
1 *(v) What does this file contain?* hold, include, consist of, comprise, incorporate.
2 *(v) I couldn't contain my laughter.* control, restrain, hold in, keep in, keep back, suppress, stifle, curb, check.

contaminate
(v) Industrial waste can contaminate the water supply. pollute, make impure, poison, infect, taint, dirty, foul, blight.
OPPOSITES: purify, decontaminate.

contemplate
1 *(v) This is a good spot to contemplate the view. See* **look at** 3.
2 *(v) I need to contemplate what I should do next. See* **consider** 1.
3 *(v) Ziggy loves to sit cross-legged and contemplate. See* **think** 4.

contemporary *see* **modern**.

contempt *see* **scorn** 2.

contented
(adj) I feel quite contented about how things have turned out. content, pleased, satisfied, gratified, glad, happy, cheerful, relaxed, at ease, comfortable, serene.
OPPOSITES: discontented, dissatisfied.

contents
(plural n) The contents of a book. content, subject matter, subject, theme, topic, sections *(plural)*, chapters *(plural)*.

contest *see* **competition** 1.

contestant *see* **competitor**.

continual *see* **constant** 1.

continually *see* **constantly**.

continue
1 *(v) We must continue walking.* keep, keep on, carry on, go on, persevere with, stick at, persist in.
2 *(v) This storm could continue for hours.* last, carry on, drag on, go on, persist.
3 *(v) You can continue your painting next week.* carry on with, return to, resume, proceed with, take up, pick up where you left off, start again, recommence.

continuous *see* **constant** 1.

continuously *see* **constantly**.

contract
1 *(v) This metal pipe will contract if you cool it.* get smaller, get shorter, get narrower, shrink, reduce, narrow, tighten, compress, draw in, close up.
OPPOSITE: expand.
2 *(n) Be sure you understand the contract before you sign.* agreement, settlement, arrangement, deal *(informal)*, bargain, transaction, commitment, pact, lease.

contradict
(v) Don't contradict what I say! argue with, dispute, disagree with, deny, challenge, oppose, object to.
OPPOSITES: agree with, support.

contrast
1 *(v) Contrast these two photos to see how Jack has changed.* compare, set side by side, set one against the other.
2 *(v) Your explanations contrast radically. See* **differ** 1.
3 *(n) Notice the contrast between the two pictures. See* **difference**.

contribute
1 *(v) Please contribute generously to the school fund. See* **give** 2.
2 **contribute to** *(v) Fine weather will contribute to a successful barbecue.* lead to, play a part in, add to, be conducive to, be partly responsible for, help.
OPPOSITE: detract from.

control
1 *(v) It's the headteacher's job to control the school's affairs.* manage, be in charge of, be in control of, direct, govern, run, administer, supervise, oversee, preside over, look after, deal with, handle, be in the driver's seat, hold the purse strings.
2 *(v) Try to control your giggles.* keep under control, keep in check, hold back, contain, restrain, curb, suppress, subdue.
3 *(n) Who has control over these men?* command, charge, authority, power, management, supervision, supremacy.

controversial
(adj) The referee's decision was controversial. contentious, open to question, questionable, debatable, arguable, disputed, widely discussed.
OPPOSITE: noncontroversial.

convalesce *see* **recover** 1.

convenient
1 *(adj) A convenient shop. See* **handy** 2.
2 *(adj) A convenient date. See* **suitable** 2.

conventional
1 *(adj) Black is the conventional colour to wear to a funeral.* standard, customary, usual, normal, correct, proper, orthodox.
OPPOSITES: unconventional, unorthodox.
2 *(adj) Jet thinks her parents are too conventional.* conservative, traditional, conformist, unadventurous, stuffy, strait-laced, rigid, bourgeois.
OPPOSITE: unconventional.

conversation *see* **talk** 5, 6.

convert
1 *(v) I want to convert my bike so it can take a passenger. See* **adapt** 1.
2 *(v) Don't worry; I'm not trying to convert you.* change your mind, persuade, convince, reform, re-educate.

convict
1 *(v) The judge decided to convict Burglar Beryl.* find guilty, declare guilty, condemn, sentence.
OPPOSITE: acquit.
2 *(n) A convict has escaped from prison.* prisoner, jailbird, con *(slang)*, criminal, offender, felon.

convince
(v) How can I convince you that I'm right? prove to, satisfy, assure, persuade, talk you round, bring you round, win you over.

convincing
1 *(adj) That's quite a convincing argument.* powerful, persuasive, plausible, credible, telling, cogent, conclusive.
OPPOSITES: unconvincing, weak.
2 *(adj) Our team had a convincing win* decisive, conclusive, impressive, definite.
OPPOSITES: unconvincing, inconclusive.
3 *(adj) Ella gave a convincing impression of Mrs Badger. See* **realistic** 2.

cook
(v) Dad offered to cook lunch. make, prepare, rustle up *(informal)*, concoct, put together, heat up, warm up.
WAYS TO COOK: bake, barbecue, boil, braise, broil, casserole, deep-fry, fry, grill, microwave, poach, roast, sauté, scramble, simmer, steam, stew, stir-fry, toast.

cool
1 *(adj) A cool breeze blew in off the sea.* fresh, refreshing, chilly, cold, nippy.
OPPOSITE: warm.
2 *(adj) Stay cool in a crisis. See* **calm** 2.
3 *(adj) Araminta gave us a cool welcome.* lukewarm, unenthusiastic, offhand, half-hearted, unemotional, apathetic, indifferent, reserved, chilly, aloof, distant, standoffish, unfriendly, unwelcoming.
OPPOSITES: warm, friendly.
4 *(adj) (informal) Jet looks cool in those clothes. See* **fashionable**.
5 *(adj) (informal) What a cool idea! See* **great** 9.

6 *(v) Cool the mixture.* chill, refrigerate.
OPPOSITES: warm up, heat.

cooperate
(v) Let's all cooperate to get the job done fast. work together, pull together, join forces, help each other, collaborate, work as a team, pitch in, pool resources, unite.
OPPOSITE: compete.

cooperative
(adj) Oscar was very cooperative about the move. obliging, accommodating, helpful, supportive, willing.

cope
1 *(v) Life is hard but I'm sure you'll cope.* manage, survive, get by *(informal)*, muddle through, struggle through, win through, hold your own, rise to the occasion.
2 **cope with** *(v) Alex has a lot to cope with.* deal with, handle, contend with, bear, endure, grapple with, wrestle with.

copy
1 *(n) Pirate Peg made a copy of the map.* duplicate, replica, photocopy, carbon copy, facsimile, transcript, tracing.
2 *(n) This painting is a copy; the original is in Paris.* reproduction, replica, print, imitation, fake, forgery, counterfeit, sham.
3 *(v) Selena decided to copy her friend's work.* duplicate, reproduce, photocopy, print, crib *(informal)*, forge, counterfeit.
4 *(v) Donna can copy Aunt Bertha's voice.* imitate, mimic, impersonate, ape, echo.

cord
(n) string, rope, twine, cable, line.

core *see* **centre** 2.

corner
1 *(n) The car took the corner too fast.* bend, turn, curve, hairpin bend, turning, junction, intersection.
2 *(n) Find a dark corner to hide.* nook, niche, recess, cranny, crevice, hole, hideaway, hide-out, hidey-hole *(informal)*.
3 *(v) The police managed to corner the thieves. See* **trap** 2.

corny
1 *(adj) (slang) A corny joke.* unfunny, old, familiar, tired, stale, clichéd, hackneyed.
2 *(adj) (slang) A corny love song. See* **sentimental** 2.

corpse *see* **body** 2.

correct
1 *(adj) Is this the correct answer? See* **right** 1.
2 *(adj) What's the correct way to address a king?* right, proper, conventional, standard, acceptable, appropriate, fitting.
OPPOSITES: wrong, inappropriate.
3 *(v) Please correct your spelling mistakes.* put right, rectify, amend, remedy, improve.
4 *(v) Mrs Badger will correct your work. See* **mark** 7.

correspond
1 *(v) Our stories must correspond or no one will believe us.* match, agree, tally, be consistent, coincide, square.

2 *(v) My cousin and I try to correspond regularly.* write, exchange letters, communicate, be in touch, be in contact.

corridor
(n) passage, passageway, hallway, aisle.

corrode *see* **wear away**.

corrupt
1 *(adj) A corrupt official.* dishonest, crooked *(informal)*, bent *(slang)*, bribable, fraudulent, unscrupulous, untrustworthy.
2 *(v) Can violence on television corrupt children?* lead astray, be a bad influence on, warp, brutalize, deprave, pervert.

cost
1 *(v) How much will a new TV cost?* come to, set you back *(informal)*, sell for, fetch, go for, be worth.
2 *(n) Can we afford the cost of a room in this hotel? See* **price** 1.

costume
(n) Your costume is perfect for the fancy-dress party. outfit, get-up *(informal)*, garb, gear *(informal)*, clothes *(plural)*, dress, attire *(old-fashioned)*, period costume, national costume, uniform, livery.

cosy
(adj) A cosy cottage. snug, comfortable, comfy *(informal)*, homely, warm, secure.

cough
(n) Have you taken anything for that cough? tickle in your throat, hacking cough, bark, frog in your throat.

count
1 *(v) Let's count how much money we've made.* count up, add up, tot up, calculate, reckon up, total, tally.
2 *(v) Your result won't count if you're disqualified.* matter, mean anything, count for anything, amount to anything, signify, be taken into consideration, carry weight.

count on *see* **depend on** 1, 2.

country
1 *(n) A European country.* nation, state, land, kingdom, realm *(old-fashioned)*, republic, principality, people *(plural)*.
2 *(n) A house in the country.* countryside, rural area, green belt, farmland, outback *(Australia)*, bush *(Australia)*, backwoods *(plural)*, wilds *(plural)*, sticks *(informal)*, back of beyond.

couple
1 *(n) We're a couple now.* twosome, pair, item *(informal)*, duo, married couple, husband and wife, girlfriend and boyfriend, partners *(plural)*.
2 **a couple of** *(phrase) I need a couple of nails.* two, two or three, a few, several.

courage
(n) The rescuers showed great courage. bravery, fearlessness, guts *(plural) (informal)*, heroism, valour *(old-fashioned)*, gallantry, nerve, pluck, spirit, grit, bottle *(slang)*, boldness, daring, audacity.
OPPOSITE: cowardice.

courageous *see* **brave**.

course

1 (n) I'm having a course of tennis lessons. series, sequence, programme.
2 (n) Are you taking the new maths course? syllabus, programme, module, curriculum, classes (plural), lessons (plural), lectures (plural).
3 (n) We worked out the ship's course. route, path, bearings (plural), direction.

court

(n) Beryl's case will be tried in a court. law court, high court, crown court, magistrates' court, county court.

cover

1 (v) Cover the statue with a cloth. drape, wrap, cloak, veil, swathe, shroud, envelop, curtain, clothe, spread over, lay over.
OPPOSITE: uncover.
2 (v) Use this scarf to cover your face. shield, protect, hide, conceal, veil, shade, screen, obscure, mask, disguise.
OPPOSITE: expose.
3 (v) A sprinkling of snow began to cover the ground. carpet, blanket, cloak, coat.
4 (v) This book should cover all you need to know. contain, include, incorporate, encompass, embrace, deal with, examine, consider, describe, survey.
5 (v) This should cover your train fare. pay for, be enough for, be sufficient for, meet.
6 (n) Is there a cover for this? See **top** 2.
7 (n) Do you need a cover for your bed? duvet, bedspread, quilt, blanket, rug, sheet, eiderdown, coverlet (old-fashioned).
8 (n) We ran for cover. shelter, protection, refuge, safety, sanctuary.
9 (n) The troops need some cover. protection, support, covering fire.
10 (n) Beryl dropped her cover to reveal her true identity. disguise, front, mask, pretence, façade, cover-up, smoke screen.

cover up

(v) It's no use trying to cover up your mistake. conceal, hide, hush up, keep secret, suppress, cover your tracks, keep it under your hat.

cowardly

(adj) Sir Lancelittle was too cowardly to attack the dragon. timid, fearful, scared, afraid, spineless, faint-hearted, chicken (informal), yellow (informal), weak-kneed (informal), nervous, anxious.
OPPOSITES: brave, courageous.

cower

(v) Don't cower in the corner! cringe, grovel, skulk, crouch, shrink, quail, tremble, shiver, flinch.

crack

1 (n) This plate has a crack in it. split, chip, break, fracture, flaw.
2 (n) The explorers squeezed through a crack in the rock. chink, cleft, slit, crevice, cranny, fissure, rift, split, rent, gash.
3 (n) I heard a loud crack. snap, bang, crackle, smack, pop.
4 (v) Don't crack the plate. See **break** 1.

5 (v) Let's crack this problem. See **solve**.
6 (v) Mel may crack under pressure. crack up (informal), break down, go to pieces, fall apart (informal), collapse, lose control.

cracked

(adj) A cracked mug. chipped, split, broken, crazed, flawed, damaged.

crackle see **crack** 3.

crack up (informal) see **crack** 6.

craft

(n) A craft exhibition. handicraft, art.

crafty see **cunning**.

cram

1 (v) Don't cram so many chocolates into your mouth! stuff, jam, ram, shove, force, pack, squash, squeeze, press, crowd.
2 (v) (informal) Celia is trying to cram for her exams. See **study** 1.

cramped

(adj) This room is so cramped! tiny, small, narrow, confined, constricting, oppressive, claustrophobic, crowded, overcrowded.
OPPOSITES: spacious, roomy.

crash

1 (n) The tray landed with a tremendous crash. bang, clatter, thump, thud, clang, clash, clunk, boom, din, racket.
2 (n) There's been a crash in the high street. collision, accident, smash, smash-up (informal), pile-up (informal), multiple pile-up (informal), prang (informal).
3 (v) We watched the tower crash to the ground. fall, topple, plunge, collapse, hurtle, clatter, overbalance.
4 (v) Dad is scared that Leo will crash his car. smash, smash up (informal), bump, prang (informal), write off (informal), total (slang), wreck, trash (slang).
5 (v) Frank's firm may crash. See **fail** 4.

crash into

(v) Don't crash into me. bump into, collide with, career into, barge into (informal).

crave see **long** 3.

crawl

1 (v) You'll have to crawl along this ledge. go on all fours, go on your hands and knees, worm your way, edge, inch, creep, slither, wriggle, drag yourself, squirm.
2 (v) The car began to crawl forwards. creep, edge, inch, move at a snail's pace.
3 (v) Trust Calvin to crawl to the teacher. grovel, toady, suck up (informal), butter up, flatter, fawn, pander.

craze

(n) What's the latest craze? trend, fashion, fad, thing (informal), novelty, mania, passion, enthusiasm, excitement.

crazy see **mad** 2, 3, 5.

creak

(v) Listen to the gate creak! squeak, grind, grate, scrape, screech, squeal, rasp.

cream

(n) SHADES OF CREAM: buttermilk, ivory, off-white, oyster, pearl.

creamy

(adj) A creamy sauce. smooth, rich, thick, velvety, buttery.

crease

1 (v) Don't crease your dress! crumple, crush, rumple, wrinkle, pucker, ruck up, scrunch up, screw up.
2 (n) There's a crease in this material. fold, tuck, pleat, wrinkle, pucker, crumple.

create

1 (v) Callum plans to create a model village. make, build, construct, produce, devise, design, develop, dream up, invent, concoct, fabricate, form, bring into being.
2 (v) This decision may create problems. See **cause** 1.

creation

(n) We're learning about the creation of the universe. origin, birth, dawning, beginning, formation, shaping, genesis.

creative

(adj) Ben's written work is very creative. imaginative, inventive, inspired, original.

creature

(n) An odd creature. animal, beast, being.

credible see **believable**.

creep

1 (v) The snail began to creep along the path. crawl, slither, inch, wriggle, worm, squirm, glide, dawdle, go at a snail's pace.
2 (v) Emma tried to creep past her sleeping sister. slip, sneak, steal, tiptoe, sidle, edge, inch, slink.
3 (n) (slang) Calvin is such a creep! toady, groveller, bootlicker (informal), sneak, telltale.

creepy (informal) see **spooky**.

crest

1 (n) Our pet cockatoo has a scarlet crest. plume, tuft, comb, topknot.
2 (n) We climbed to the crest of the hill. summit, top, peak, brow, ridge, crown.

crime

1 (n) Crime is increasing. lawbreaking, misconduct, delinquency, corruption, villainy, wrongdoing, foul play, vice.
2 (n) What crime did Beryl commit? offence, misdeed, misdemeanour, violation, wrong, atrocity, outrage, trespass, felony (old-fashioned).
TYPES OF CRIME: abduction, armed robbery, arson, assassination, assault, attempted murder, blackmail, breaking and entering, bribery and corruption, burglary, conspiracy to murder, criminal damage, drink-driving, drug pushing, drug trafficking, extortion, forgery, fraud, GBH (grievous bodily harm), hijacking, hit and run, hold-up, indecent assault, joyriding, kidnapping, looting, manslaughter, money laundering, mugging (informal), murder, poaching, racial attack, ram raiding (informal), shoplifting, smuggling, speeding, trespassing, rape, robbery, terrorism, theft, vandalism.

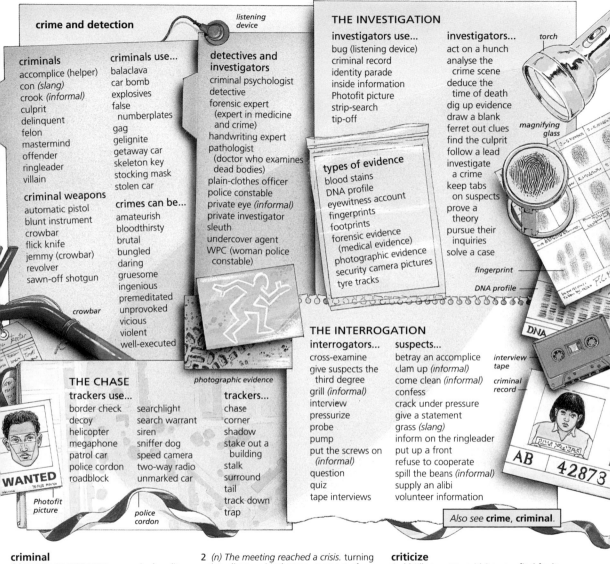

crime and detection

listening device

criminals
accomplice (helper)
con *(slang)*
crook *(informal)*
culprit
delinquent
felon
mastermind
offender
ringleader
villain

criminal weapons
automatic pistol
blunt instrument
crowbar
flick knife
jemmy (crowbar)
revolver
sawn-off shotgun

crowbar

criminals use...
balaclava
car bomb
explosives
false
  numberplates
gag
gelignite
getaway car
skeleton key
stocking mask
stolen car

crimes can be...
amateurish
bloodthirsty
brutal
bungled
daring
gruesome
ingenious
premeditated
unprovoked
vicious
violent
well-executed

detectives and investigators
criminal psychologist
detective
forensic expert
  (expert in medicine
  and crime)
handwriting expert
pathologist
  (doctor who examines
  dead bodies)
plain-clothes officer
police constable
private eye *(informal)*
private investigator
sleuth
undercover agent
WPC (woman police
  constable)

THE INVESTIGATION

investigators use...
bug (listening device)
criminal record
identity parade
inside information
Photofit picture
strip-search
tip-off

types of evidence
blood stains
DNA profile
eyewitness account
fingerprints
footprints
forensic evidence
  (medical evidence)
photographic evidence
security camera pictures
tyre tracks

investigators...
act on a hunch
analyse the
  crime scene
deduce the
  time of death
dig up evidence
draw a blank
ferret out clues
find the culprit
follow a lead
investigate
  a crime
keep tabs
  on suspects
prove a
  theory
pursue their
  inquiries
solve a case

torch

magnifying glass

fingerprint

DNA profile

THE INTERROGATION

interrogators...
cross-examine
give suspects the
  third degree
grill *(informal)*
interview
pressurize
probe
pump
put the screws on
  (informal)
question
quiz
tape interviews

suspects...
betray an accomplice
clam up *(informal)*
come clean *(informal)*
confess
crack under pressure
give a statement
grass *(slang)*
inform on the ringleader
put up a front
refuse to cooperate
spill the beans *(informal)*
supply an alibi
volunteer information

interview tape

criminal record

DNA

THE CHASE

trackers use...
border check
decoy
helicopter
megaphone
patrol car
police cordon
roadblock

searchlight
search warrant
siren
sniffer dog
speed camera
two-way radio
unmarked car

photographic evidence

trackers...
chase
corner
shadow
stake out a
  building
stalk
surround
tail
track down
trap

WANTED

Photofit picture

police cordon

AB 42873

Also see **crime**, **criminal**.

---

criminal
(n) TYPES OF CRIMINAL: assassin, bandit, blackmailer, bomber, burglar, computer hacker, drug dealer, forger, gangster, gunman, hijacker, hit man *(slang)*, joyrider, kidnapper, mugger *(informal)*, murderer, pickpocket, poacher, rapist, robber, shoplifter, swindler, terrorist, thief, vandal.

cringe
(v) Dad's jokes make me cringe. wince, flinch, shudder, quail, blush, blench, recoil.

crisis
1 *(n) If this pipe bursts, we'll have a crisis.* problem, emergency, disaster, catastrophe, panic, alarm, predicament, mess.

2 *(n) The meeting reached a crisis.* turning point, climax, critical stage, moment of truth, crunch *(informal)*, culmination, crux.

crisp
1 *(adj) A crisp cracker.* crispy, crunchy, brittle, hard, dry, crumbly.
OPPOSITES: soft, soggy.

2 *(adj) A crisp winter's day. See* **cold 1**.

critical
1 *(adj) Critical remarks.* scathing, derogatory, disapproving, disparaging, censorious, nit-picking *(informal)*, nagging, niggling, uncomplimentary, hypercritical.
OPPOSITES: complimentary, flattering.

2 *(adj) A critical decision. See* **vital**.

criticize
1 *(v) I'll try not to criticize you.* find fault with, knock *(informal)*, snipe at, pick on, censure, denigrate, disparage, pick holes in, nitpick *(informal)*, cast aspersions on, slate *(informal)*, pan *(informal)*, bad-mouth *(slang)*, slag you off *(slang)*.
OPPOSITES: praise, compliment.

2 *(v) Please criticize this poem.* analyse, review, evaluate, discuss, assess, comment on, give your opinion of.

croak
(v) Your cold is making you croak. speak huskily, speak hoarsely, have a frog in your throat, rasp, wheeze, squawk, caw *(bird)*.

crooked

1 *(adj) A crooked path.* winding, twisting, curving, zigzag, meandering, tortuous. OPPOSITE: straight.

2 *(adj) A crooked branch. See* **twisted** 1.

3 *(adj) That poster is crooked.* tilted, at an angle, slanting, sloping, askew, skewwhiff *(informal)*, lopsided, off-centre. OPPOSITES: straight, level.

4 *(adj) (informal) Don't get involved in Dave's crooked deals.* dishonest, criminal, illegal, corrupt, fraudulent, unscrupulous, dodgy *(informal)*, dubious, questionable, shady *(informal)*, underhand, deceitful. OPPOSITES: honest, legal.

cross

1 *(adj) Liz is cross that she wasn't invited.* annoyed, indignant, put out, disgruntled, upset, offended, peeved *(informal)*, miffed *(informal)*, irritated, piqued, vexed, cheesed off *(slang)*, hacked off *(slang)*, in a bad mood, sulky, in a huff. OPPOSITES: pleased, contented.

2 *(adj) Dad was really cross when I broke the CD player. See* **angry**.

3 *(adj) Aunt Bertha always seems so cross. See* **bad-tempered**.

4 *(v) How will we cross the desert?* get across, travel across, journey across, traverse, cut across, ford *(river)*.

5 *(v) The new bridge will cross the railway line.* span, pass over, stretch across, bridge.

6 *(v) Where do the two streets cross?* intersect, meet, join, converge, crisscross.

cross out

(v) Cross out my name from the list. strike out, delete, rub out, scratch out, erase.

crouch

(v) Let's crouch behind this bush. squat, bend down, hunker down, duck, kneel, stoop, hunch over, cower.

crowd

1 *(n) A crowd of people gathered in the square.* group, bunch *(informal)*, gang, cluster, knot, throng, horde, mass, flock, swarm, mob, pack, army, crush, rabble, multitude, collection, company, assembly.

2 *(v) We watched the fans crowd into the stadium.* swarm, flock, throng, stream, surge, pile, push, shove, jostle, elbow, pack, squeeze, squash, press, cram, jam.

crowded

(adj) The stadium was crowded. packed, jam-packed, full, overcrowded, congested, overflowing, swarming, thronging, cramped, full to bursting.

crown

(n) The queen wore a glittering golden crown. coronet, diadem, tiara, circlet.

crucial *see* **vital**.

crude

(adj) Crude jokes. coarse, vulgar, rude, uncouth, crass, tasteless, indecent, dirty, smutty, bawdy, lewd, obscene, offensive. OPPOSITES: polite, sophisticated.

cruel

1 *(adj) A cruel murder.* brutal, vicious, savage, barbaric, bloodthirsty, sadistic, cold-blooded, callous, heartless, ruthless, pitiless, inhuman, diabolical, fiendish. OPPOSITES: kind, gentle.

2 *(adj) A cruel remark.* hurtful, unkind, spiteful, malicious, vicious, cutting, heartless, callous, hardhearted, unfeeling. OPPOSITE: kind.

crumb

(n) A crumb of food. morsel, bit, fragment, scrap, shred, speck, grain, particle, atom.

crumble

(v) The old castle will crumble if it isn't repaired. disintegrate, collapse, fall apart, fall to pieces, break up, fall into decay, go to rack and ruin.

crumple *see* **crease** 1, 2.

crunch

(v) Don't crunch your carrot so noisily! munch, chomp, chew, gnaw, champ.

crush

1 *(v) Try not to crush the strawberries.* squash, squeeze, bruise, flatten, pulp, mash, mangle, pulverize.

2 *(v) Crush the biscuits into little pieces.* grind, pound, smash, crumble, pulverize, shatter, crunch, break.

3 *(v) Don't crush your skirt. See* **crease** 1.

cry

1 *(v) Todd began to cry when he heard the news.* weep, sob, shed tears, blubber, snivel, whimper, wail, howl, bawl.

2 *(v) Gina tried to cry for help. See* **call** 1.

3 *(n) I heard a cry.* call, shout, scream, shriek, yell, screech, squeal, yelp, howl.

cuddle

(v) Henry loves to cuddle his bunny. hug, snuggle up to, fondle, caress, embrace, nestle against, hold, clasp.

cunning

(adj) A cunning plan. crafty, wily, devious, sneaky, artful, tricky, deceitful, sly, shrewd, clever, ingenious, subtle.

cup

(n) TYPES OF CUP: beaker, chalice, coffee cup, goblet, mug, tankard, teacup, trophy.

cure

(v) Will this ointment cure my rash? heal, make better, clear up, put right, help, treat, ease, relieve, alleviate, remedy. OPPOSITES: aggravate, make worse.

curious

1 *(adj) I'm curious to know what really happened.* interested, intrigued, puzzled, burning with curiosity, inquisitive. OPPOSITES: incurious, indifferent.

2 *(adj) Curious neighbours. See* **nosy**.

3 *(adj) A curious hat. See* **strange** 1.

curl

1 *(n) A curl of hair.* wave, coil, kink, ringlet, corkscrew, twist, spiral, lock.

2 *(v) Did you curl your hair yourself?* crimp, kink, coil, wave, perm, frizz.

3 *(v) The snake began to curl round my leg.* coil, wind, loop, spiral, twist, twine, twirl, writhe, snake, curve, bend.

curly

(adj) Curly hair. curling, wavy, frizzy, fuzzy, curled, crimped, permed, corkscrew. OPPOSITE: straight.

current

(adj) Marcie likes to keep up with current fashions. present-day, contemporary, modern, up-to-date, up-to-the-minute, popular, fashionable, happening *(informal)*, existing, prevailing. OPPOSITES: past, out of date.

curse

1 *(v) Please don't curse! See* **swear** 1.

2 *(n) Duncan let out a curse.* oath, swearword, obscenity, expletive, profanity.

3 *(n) The wizard put a curse on the village.* jinx, spell, malediction, the evil eye.

curt *see* **abrupt** 2.

curve *see* **bend** 1, 2, 4.

curved

(adj) A curved surface. bent, rounded, arched, bowed, bulging, convex, concave. OPPOSITES: flat, level.

custom

(n) Kissing under the mistletoe is a popular custom. tradition, practice, convention, institution, procedure, ritual, ceremony.

cut

1 *(v) How did you cut your finger?* gash, slash, slit, nick, graze, lacerate, wound.

2 *(v) We need to cut some wood for the fire. See* **chop** 1.

3 *(v) Will you cut my hair?* trim, clip, crop, snip, shape, layer, shave.

4 *(v) We must cut that low branch.* trim, prune, clip, lop off, hack off, mow *(grass)*.

5 *(v) Don't cut your name in the desk!* carve, gouge, score, scratch, chisel, engrave, inscribe, chip, notch, whittle.

6 *(v) You need to cut this essay.* shorten, trim, prune, abridge, condense, abbreviate, summarize, précis.

7 *(v) Is it a good idea to cut violent films for TV?* edit, censor, clean up, sanitize.

8 *(v) Supermarkets may cut their prices. See* **reduce** 1.

9 *(n) Zina has a cut on her leg.* gash, nick, slash, scratch, graze, laceration, wound.

10 *(n) We expect a cut in prices. See* **decrease** 1.

cute *see* **sweet** 3.

cutting

1 *(adj) A cutting remark.* hurtful, scathing, barbed, sarcastic, caustic, acerbic, vicious, malicious, spiteful, vitriolic, wounding.

2 *(adj) A cutting wind. See* **cold** 2.

cut up *see* **chop** 2.

cynical

(adj) Cyril has a cynical approach to life. sceptical, negative, pessimistic, mocking, ironic, sneering, suspicious, distrustful. OPPOSITES: positive, optimistic, trusting.

Dd

dab
1 *(v) Dab some lotion on that itchy bite.* pat, daub, dot, smear, stroke, wipe, tap.
2 *(n) You've got a dab of paint on your nose.* drop, spot, speck, blob, smudge.

dabble
1 *(v) If you dabble about in the stream you'll get wet.* paddle, splash, slosh *(informal)*, wade, wallow.
2 **dabble in** *(v) Sylvie likes to dabble in astrology.* dip into, play at, toy with, trifle with, tinker with, potter about with.

daft *(informal) see* **silly** 1, 2.

dainty
1 *(adj) A dainty ballerina.* graceful, petite, small-boned, trim, elegant, pretty.
OPPOSITES: clumsy, ungainly.
2 *(adj) Dainty stitching.* neat, delicate, fine, exquisite.
OPPOSITES: clumsy, coarse.

dam
(n) If the dam bursts the valley will be flooded. barrier, barrage, dyke, wall, barricade, embankment.

damage
1 *(n) The hurricane caused widespread damage.* destruction, devastation, havoc, ruin, harm, injury, suffering, loss.
2 *(v) Vandals damage other people's property.* spoil, deface, wreck, destroy, ruin, vandalize, abuse, harm, mar, tamper with, play havoc with, devastate.
3 *(v) Reading in poor light can damage your eyesight.* harm, impair, weaken, strain, injure, hurt.

damaging *see* **harmful** 1.

damp
1 *(adj) Damp ground.* moist, dewy, wet, soggy, sodden, sopping, waterlogged.
OPPOSITE: dry.
2 *(adj) A damp day on the moor.* wet, drizzly, rainy, misty, foggy, dank.
OPPOSITE: dry.
3 *(adj) A damp day in the jungle.* humid, muggy, clammy, steamy, sticky, sweaty.
OPPOSITE: dry.
4 *(adj) A damp cave. See* **dank**.

dance
1 *(n) Alexander is interested in dance.* dancing, choreography.
2 *(n) I went to the dance with Carl.* disco, discotheque, rave *(slang)*, hop *(informal)*, ball, barn dance, dinner-dance.
3 *(v) Let's dance!* bop *(informal)*, boogie *(slang)*, jive, rock, move to the music, take the floor, trip the light fantastic.
4 *(v) Mo began to dance about when she heard the news.* leap, jump, skip, prance, bounce, hop, caper, romp, frolic, cavort.

dance words

types of dance
ballet
ballroom dancing
belly dancing
break dancing
contemporary dance
country dancing
disco dancing
flamenco dancing
folk dancing
formation dancing
hip-hop
jazz dance
Latin American dancing
limbo dancing
line dancing
morris dancing
old-time dancing
rock 'n' roll
square dancing
tap

ballroom dances
cha-cha-cha
foxtrot
jive
quickstep
rumba
samba
tango
waltz

break dancing

folk dances
highland fling
hornpipe
jig
reel

other dances
cancan
conga
jitterbug
minuet
polka
salsa
twist

contemporary dance

dancers can be...
acrobatic
agile
athletic
balletic
clumsy
dainty
elegant
energetic
expressive
exuberant
graceful
lithe
lively
lumbering
nimble
poised
rhythmic
skilful
sprightly
stately
supple

dancers may...
boogie *(slang)*
bop *(informal)*
dart
glide
gyrate
hop
jiggle
jive
jump
kick
leap
pogo
prance
rock
shuffle
skip
slide
spin
spring
stomp *(informal)*
stretch
strut
sway
swing
swirl
swivel
teeter
totter
twirl
twist
whirl
wiggle

ballroom dancing

jazz dance

grand jeté

tap dancing

ballet words
arabesque
ballerina
choreographer (dance creator)
corps de ballet (group of dancers)
grand jeté (leap)
pas-de-deux (dance for two)
pirouette
prima ballerina (leading ballerina)
principal dancer
tutu (ballet dress)

arabesque

danger
1 *(n) There's a danger of snow.* risk, threat, chance, possibility.
2 *(n) Indiana encountered one danger after another.* hazard, threat, peril, risk, menace, pitfall, crisis.

dangerous
1 *(adj) Indiana set out on a dangerous expedition.* hazardous, perilous, risky, treacherous, hairy *(slang)*, dicey *(informal)*.
OPPOSITE: safe.
2 *(adj) That bridge looks dangerous.* precarious, unsafe, insecure, unstable, unreliable, dodgy *(informal)*, shaky, rickety.
OPPOSITES: safe, secure.

3 *(adj) The robber is armed and dangerous.* violent, unpredictable, ruthless, desperate, threatening, menacing.
OPPOSITE: harmless.
4 *(adj) Acid is a dangerous substance.* hazardous, harmful, poisonous, toxic, noxious, deadly, destructive.
OPPOSITES: harmless, safe.

dangle
(v) Relax and let your arms dangle by your side. hang, hang down, swing, droop, trail, fall, flop, sway, flap.

dank
(adj) A dank cave. damp, wet, chilly, clammy, dripping, slimy.

dare

dare
1 *(v) Would you dare to sleep in a haunted house?* have the nerve, have the courage, be brave enough, risk, venture.
2 *(v) If you dare me to jump into the river I will!* challenge, defy, goad, taunt, provoke, throw down the gauntlet.
3 *(n) I did it for a dare.* challenge, bet.

daring
(adj) A daring climber. fearless, intrepid, adventurous, bold, audacious, plucky, brave, undaunted, daredevil, reckless, rash.
OPPOSITES: timid, cowardly.

dark
1 *(adj) A dark dungeon.* dim, dingy, pitch-dark, unlit, shadowy, murky, gloomy, dismal, drab, cheerless, grim, sombre.
OPPOSITES: bright, cheerful.
2 *(adj) A dark sky.* black, pitch-black, inky, jet-black, moonless, starless, sunless, cloudy, overcast, leaden, ominous.
OPPOSITES: bright, light.
3 *(adj) Dark hair.* brown, brunette, black, jet-black, raven, ebony, sable.
OPPOSITES: fair, blonde.
4 *(adj) Dark skin.* brown, black, swarthy, tanned, dusky, olive, sallow.
OPPOSITE: fair.

darkness
(n) A figure vanished into the darkness. dark, blackness, night, gloom, shadows *(plural)*, shade, gathering gloom, dusk.

dart *see* **dash** 2.

dash
1 *(v) I must dash! See* **hurry** 1.
2 *(v) I saw a rabbit dash across the field.* run, race, tear, hurtle, sprint, dart, shoot, scoot, bolt, speed, flash, whiz *(informal)*.

data
(n) information, facts *(plural)*, figures *(plural)*, details *(plural)*, statistics *(plural)*, info *(informal)*, lowdown *(informal)*.

date
1 *(n) I have a date with Paula on Saturday.* meeting, rendezvous, appointment, engagement, assignation.
2 *(n) Luke and Lucy have set a date for their wedding.* day, time, specific day.

daunting
(adj) Facing the dragon was a daunting prospect for Sir Lancelittle. alarming, unnerving, frightening, terrifying, intimidating, disconcerting, off-putting *(informal)*, discouraging, disheartening.

dawdle
(v) If you dawdle we'll be late. delay, waste time, lag behind, go at a snail's pace, straggle, loiter, linger, dally, hang about.

dawn
1 *(n) We got up at dawn.* daybreak, sunrise, break of day, crack of dawn, first light, sunup, cockcrow.
OPPOSITES: dusk, sunset.
2 **dawn on** *(v) It didn't dawn on me until it was too late. See* **occur** 2.

day
1 *(n) Vampires sleep during the day.* daytime, daylight hours *(plural)*, daylight.
OPPOSITE: night.
2 *(n) Luke and Lucy have decided on a day for their wedding.* date, time, specific day.
3 *(n) In my granddad's day there were no computers.* time, era, age, period, generation, heyday.

daydream
1 *(v) Sebastian likes to sit and daydream.* dream, stargaze, fantasize, imagine, muse.
2 *(n) I was in a daydream. See* **dream** 2.

dazed
1 *(adj) The blow from the ball left Leah dazed. See* **stunned** 1.
2 *(adj) Naresh felt dazed when he heard the news. See* **stunned** 2.
3 *(adj) I felt dazed with everyone shouting at once. See* **confused**.

dazzle
1 *(v) Bright lights dazzle me.* blind, confuse, daze, disorientate.
2 *(v) Marvello will dazzle you with his magic tricks. See* **astonish**.

dazzling
1 *(adj) A dazzling jewel. See* **brilliant** 1.
2 *(adj) A dazzling display of acrobatics. See* **spectacular**.

dead
1 *(adj) Queen Victoria is dead.* deceased, dead and buried, passed away, departed, gone, no more, perished.
OPPOSITES: alive, living.
2 *(adj) The man lay dead on the ground.* lifeless, inert, cold, rigid, stiff.
3 *(adj) The dodo is a dead species.* extinct, defunct, died out.
OPPOSITES: existing, living.
4 *(adj) My fingers feel dead. See* **numb**.
5 *(adj) At night the town is dead.* lifeless, deserted, quiet, boring, dull, uninteresting.
OPPOSITES: lively, buzzing.
6 *(adj) The radio is dead.* not working, useless, out of order, inoperative.
OPPOSITES: working, operational.

deadly
1 *(adj) Deadly fumes.* lethal, poisonous, toxic, noxious, dangerous, hazardous, venomous *(snake)*, virulent *(disease)*.
2 *(adj) A deadly wound.* lethal, fatal, mortal, death-dealing, terminal *(illness)*.
3 *(adj) Deadly enemies.* mortal, bitter, hated, sworn, out-and-out, irreconcilable, remorseless, implacable, murderous.
4 *(adj) A deadly aim.* accurate, sure, true, unerring, unfailing, exact, precise.

deafening *see* **loud** 1.

deal
1 *(n) (informal) The businessmen made a deal.* arrangement, agreement, bargain, pact, contract, transaction.
2 *(v) Does Dodgy Dave still deal in second-hand cars?* trade, do business, buy and sell, stock, traffic *(drugs)*.
3 *(v) It's your turn to deal the cards.* give out, dole out, distribute, hand out, divide.
4 **deal with** *(v) Can you deal with this problem?* handle, see to, take care of, tackle, cope with, manage, sort out.
5 **deal with** *(v) What issues will your essay deal with?* be about, be concerned with, have to do with, cover, consider, discuss, examine, explore, treat.

dear
1 *(adj) Lopa is a dear friend.* close, much-loved, intimate, valued, cherished, treasured, beloved, adored, bosom.
2 *(adj) That watch is much too dear. See* **expensive**.
3 *(n) What's the matter, dear?* darling, love, honey, pet, sweetheart, dearest, beloved *(old-fashioned)*.

death
1 *(n) The death of the king saddened the nation.* passing, demise, loss, dying.
OPPOSITE: birth.
2 *(n) There's been a death in the family.* bereavement, loss.
3 *(n) The crash resulted in only one death.* fatality, casualty.

debate
1 *(n) We had a debate about the death penalty.* discussion, argument, dispute.
2 *(v) Nina was keen to debate the issue of animal rights. See* **discuss**.

debris
(n) Rescuers sifted through the debris. rubble, wreckage, remains *(plural)*, ruins *(plural)*, wreck, fragments *(plural)*, pieces *(plural)*, bits *(plural)*, rubbish, litter, waste.

decay *see* **rot** 1, 2, 3.

deceitful
(adj) A deceitful politician. untruthful, untrustworthy, dishonest, insincere, hypocritical, two-faced, double-dealing, duplicitous, devious, underhand, tricky, sneaky, slippery, shifty, crafty, cunning, sly.
OPPOSITES: honest, truthful.

deceive
1 *(v) Keep your wits about you or Dodgy Dave will deceive you.* trick, fool, mislead, delude, pull the wool over your eyes, take you in *(informal)*, dupe, hoodwink, double-cross, bamboozle *(informal)*, kid *(informal)*, cheat, swindle, con *(informal)*, diddle *(informal)*, take you for a ride *(informal)*, pull a fast one on you *(slang)*.
2 *(v) Don't deceive the one you love.* be unfaithful to, betray, cheat on *(informal)*, two-time *(informal)*.

decent
1 *(adj) Mum thinks this top is not decent.* respectable, presentable, seemly, proper, dignified, modest, fitting, appropriate, suitable, tasteful, fit to be seen.
OPPOSITES: indecent, improper.
2 *(adj) My bedroom is a decent size.* reasonable, adequate, acceptable, satisfactory, ample, sufficient, average.
OPPOSITES: inadequate, unsatisfactory.

3 *(adj) Mr Badger is a decent man.* good, kind, honest, honourable, trustworthy, thoughtful, helpful, obliging, generous, polite, courteous, respectable, upright.
4 *(adj) (informal) This band's really decent!* See **great** 9.

decide
1 *(v) Decide which book you want.* make up your mind, choose, select, pick, come to a decision about.
2 *(v) Once you decide to do something you should see it through.* make up your mind, make a decision, resolve, determine, commit yourself.
3 *(v) Let's decide the argument by tossing a coin.* settle, resolve, clinch, put an end to, clear up, sort out, end, conclude.

decipher
(v) Can you decipher this secret message? decode, work out, figure out *(informal)*, understand, read, interpret, translate, unravel, solve, crack, suss out *(slang)*.

decision
1 *(n) It's a hard decision to make.* choice.
2 *(n) The judge gave her decision.* verdict, judgment, ruling, conclusion, finding.

decisive
1 *(adj) Our team won a decisive victory.* See **convincing** 2.
2 *(adj) Jon is a decisive person.* firm, strong-minded, forceful, purposeful, resolute, determined, definite, incisive.
OPPOSITES: indecisive, hesitant.

declare
(v) Declare your loyalty to the king - or die! announce, proclaim, profess, swear, state, make known, assert, affirm, confirm.

decline
1 *(v) I'm afraid I'll have to decline your offer.* See **refuse** 1.
2 *(v) Pupil numbers are expected to decline.* See **decrease** 2.

decorate
1 *(v) It's my turn to decorate the tree.* trim, adorn, embellish, festoon, trick out.
2 *(v) I helped Dad to decorate the front room.* paint, paper, do up *(informal)*, spruce up, refurbish, renovate, revamp.

decoration
1 *(n) Hang this decoration on the Christmas tree.* ornament, bauble, trinket, streamer, tinsel, spangle, trimming.
2 *(n) Granny wore a plain dress with no decoration.* trimming, embroidery, frill, flounce, ruffle, fringe, tassel, frippery.

decorative
(adj) A decorative bow. ornamental, fancy, pretty, elaborate, ornate, nonfunctional.
OPPOSITES: functional, plain.

decrease
1 *(n) There has been a decrease in the number of crimes.* drop, fall, decline, reduction, cut, downturn, falling off, dwindling, lessening, slump, ebb.
OPPOSITE: increase.

2 *(v) Pupil numbers are expected to decrease.* fall, drop, decline, fall off, drop off, dwindle, lower, go down, tumble, slump, slide, plummet, plunge, nose-dive.
OPPOSITE: increase.
3 *(v) The wind began to decrease.* drop, subside, lessen, abate, let up, die down.
OPPOSITE: increase.
4 *(v) Decrease your speed.* See **reduce** 3.

decrepit see **dilapidated**.

dedicated
(adj) A dedicated nurse. committed, single-minded, enthusiastic, keen, devoted.

deed see **act** 4.

deep
1 *(adj) A deep crack opened up in the earth.* bottomless, yawning, gaping, fathomless, unfathomable, cavernous.
OPPOSITE: shallow.
2 *(adj) Our new carpet is a deep shade of blue.* dark, rich, strong, vivid, intense.
OPPOSITES: pale, light.
3 *(adj) The giant spoke in a deep voice.* low, low-pitched, bass, rich, booming, rumbling, resounding, resonant, sonorous.
OPPOSITES: high, high-pitched.
4 *(adj) Ned has a deep dislike of spiders.* profound, deep-seated, deep-rooted, intense, strong, extreme, heartfelt, fervent.

defeat
1 *(v) The soldiers were determined to defeat the enemy.* See **conquer** 1.
2 *(v) I hope we defeat the other team.* See **beat** 2.
3 *(n) The match ended in a defeat for our team.* beating, thrashing, pasting *(slang)*, drubbing, failure, setback, humiliation, disappointment, frustration.
OPPOSITES: victory, triumph.

defect see **fault** 1.

defence
(n) The police used shields as a defence against the rioters. protection, safeguard, guard, screen, shield, shelter, deterrent.

defenceless
(adj) Without weapons the soldiers were defenceless. vulnerable, open to attack, helpless, powerless, unprotected, unarmed, exposed, in danger.

defend
1 *(v) The soldiers did their best to defend the castle.* protect, guard, fortify, secure, safeguard, keep safe, shield, preserve, keep from harm, watch over, fight for.
2 *(v) Nathan tried to defend his point of view.* justify, explain, give reasons for, make a case for, argue for, vindicate.
3 *(v) Burglar Beryl has a lawyer to defend her.* speak for, plead for, support, back, stand up for, stick up for *(informal)*.

defiant
(adj) The defiant child refused to go to bed. disobedient, rebellious, insolent, truculent, recalcitrant, mutinous.
OPPOSITES: obedient, meek.

definite
1 *(adj) Is it definite that you can't come?* certain, sure, decided, settled, final, cut and dried *(informal)*, guaranteed, positive.
OPPOSITE: uncertain.
2 *(adj) Do you have any definite plans for the future?* specific, particular, explicit, precise, clear, clear-cut, clearly defined, set, fixed, confirmed, categorical.
OPPOSITES: vague, obscure.
3 *(adj) Your work shows a definite improvement.* marked, noticeable, obvious, distinct, unmistakable, pronounced, decided, perceptible, positive.
OPPOSITES: imperceptible, slight.

definitely
(adv) Carl is definitely the best-looking boy in the school. certainly, without doubt, undoubtedly, undeniably, unquestionably, beyond a shadow of a doubt, for certain, clearly, obviously, easily, far and away.

deformed
(adj) The monster was horribly deformed. misshapen, disfigured, contorted, bent, twisted, crooked, gnarled, maimed, mutilated, unsightly, grotesque, ugly.

defy
1 *(v) Rick doesn't dare to defy his parents.* disobey, disregard, fly in the face of, flout, challenge, confront, resist, stand up to.
OPPOSITES: obey, submit to.
2 *(v) I defy you to jump into the river.* See **dare** 2.

degrading
(adj) Living conditions in the prison were degrading. demeaning, humiliating, shameful, disgraceful, contemptible, debasing, dehumanizing, brutalizing.

dejected see **depressed**.

delay
1 *(v) If you delay any longer, you won't get a ticket.* wait, hesitate, hang around, stall, dither, pause, procrastinate, dawdle.
OPPOSITE: hurry.
2 *(v) I hope the traffic doesn't delay you.* hold you up, slow you down, keep you back, make you late, detain, keep you waiting, hamper, bog you down.
3 *(v) Mrs Badger agreed to delay the test for a week.* See **postpone**.
4 *(n) There was no delay on the journey.* hold-up, interruption, setback, stoppage.

delete
(v) Delete that word from your essay. remove, cut out, take out, omit, edit out, eradicate, scrub *(informal)*, erase, rub out, cross out, strike out, wipe.

deliberate
(adj) Anji took a deliberate risk. intentional, conscious, calculated, considered, studied, intended, planned, premeditated *(crime)*.
OPPOSITES: accidental, unintentional.

delicacy
(n) Caviar is a great delicacy. luxury, speciality, treat, gourmet food.

delicate

delicate
1 *(adj) Delicate lace curtains.* fine, dainty, exquisite, intricate, flimsy, fragile, gauzy, wispy, silky, gossamer, cobwebby.
OPPOSITES: coarse, tough.
2 *(adj) A delicate child.* frail, weak, sickly, ailing, unhealthy, feeble, peaky, unwell.
OPPOSITES: robust, healthy.
3 *(adj) A delicate shade of blue.* soft, subtle, subdued, gentle, muted, pastel.
OPPOSITES: strong, bright.
4 *(adj) A delicate flavour. See* **mild** 3.
5 *(adj) A delicate situation.* difficult, sensitive, tricky, sticky *(informal)*, ticklish, dicey *(informal)*, critical, precarious.
6 *(adj) This situation needs delicate handling.* careful, sensitive, tactful, discreet, diplomatic, kidglove.
OPPOSITES: tactless, indiscreet.

delicious
(adj) A delicious meal. tasty, appetizing, mouthwatering, scrumptious *(informal)*, yummy *(slang)*, delectable, luscious, flavoursome, moreish *(informal)*.
OPPOSITES: unappetizing, revolting.

delight
1 *(n) The birth of the baby caused great delight. See* **happiness**.
2 *(v) Gemma's singing will delight you.* captivate, charm, thrill, enchant, enthral, entrance, entertain, amuse, please, cheer.

delighted *see* **pleased**.

delightful
1 *(adj) We spent a delightful day by the river. See* **lovely** 2.
2 *(adj) Carrie is a delightful girl.* charming, lovely, pleasant, agreeable, attractive, enchanting, engaging, bewitching.
OPPOSITES: unpleasant, disagreeable.

delirious
1 *(adj) Without water, the travellers were soon delirious.* light-headed, feverish, incoherent, raving, babbling, hallucinating, demented, deranged, crazy, irrational.
OPPOSITES: rational, clear-headed.
2 *(adj) Maria was delirious about meeting Famous Fred. See* **ecstatic**.

deliver
1 *(v) A boat will deliver supplies to the island.* bring, carry, take, transport, convey.
2 *(v) Ahmed is in a hurry to deliver his invitations.* distribute, give out, hand out, dish out *(informal)*, send, post, dispatch.

demand
1 *(v) I know Dad will demand an apology.* insist on, expect, require, ask for, call for, request, press for.
2 *(v) These problems demand urgent action.* call for, require, need, necessitate, cry out for, want.

demanding
1 *(adj) A demanding job. See* **difficult** 2.
2 *(adj) A demanding child.* nagging, insistent, hard to please, fussy, impatient, fractious, clamorous.

demolish
(v) It didn't take long to demolish the building. knock down, pull down, tear down, destroy, dismantle, break down, wreck, flatten, level, raze to the ground, bulldoze, blow up, dynamite.

demonstrate
1 *(v) Can you demonstrate how to make an omelette?* show, illustrate, give an idea of, make clear, explain, describe, teach.
2 *(v) Demonstrate your loyalty by voting for me.* show, indicate, display, prove, confirm, express, testify to.
3 *(v) We decided to demonstrate against the new road.* protest, lobby, march, picket, hold a rally, hold a sit-in.

demonstration
1 *(n) A demonstration of country dancing.* display, exhibition, show, presentation, illustration, explanation, exposition.
2 *(n) A demonstration against nuclear weapons.* protest, demo *(informal)*, march, rally, mass rally, sit-in, picket, parade.

demoralized *see* **discouraged**.

den
1 *(n) The animal hid in its den. See* **hole** 4.
2 *(n) Bozo's gang has a den in the woods.* hide-out, base, hiding place, hideaway, secret place, retreat, hang-out, haunt.

dense
1 *(adj) Dense undergrowth. See* **thick** 4.
2 *(adj) Dense fog. See* **thick** 5.
3 *(adj) The crowd was so dense we couldn't move.* solid, tightly packed, jam-packed, jammed together, crammed together, compacted, close-knit.
OPPOSITES: sparse, scattered.
4 *(adj) Don't be so dense! See* **stupid** 1.

dent
(v) I didn't mean to dent the car door. knock in, make a dent in, bash in *(informal)*, push in, dint, buckle, crumple.

deny
1 *(v) Burglar Beryl was quick to deny the charges.* reject, declare untrue, dispute, contradict, disagree with, repudiate, refute, rebuff, disclaim.
2 *(v) Your parents seem to deny you nothing.* refuse, deprive you of, begrudge, forbid, withhold from you.

depart *see* **leave** 1.

department
(n) Which department does your dad work in? section, branch, division, segment.

dependable *see* **reliable** 1, 2.

depend on
1 *(v) All Bethan's friends depend on her.* rely on, count on, lean on, trust, have confidence in, turn to, confide in.
2 *(v) You can depend on Tim being early.* rely on, count on, bank on, be sure of, reckon on, calculate on, bet on.
3 *(v) Our plans must depend on the weather.* hang on, hinge on, turn on, be determined by, be subject to, rest on.

depressed
(adj) Jessica is feeling depressed. unhappy, sad, miserable, down, blue, low, glum, gloomy, down in the dumps *(informal)*, dejected, downhearted, despondent, melancholy, discouraged, disheartened, dispirited, moody, morose, suicidal.
OPPOSITES: cheerful, happy.

depressing
1 *(adj) This is such a depressing film.* sad, gloomy, dreary, dismal, bleak, black, dark, morbid, sombre, melancholy, cheerless, heartbreaking, distressing, harrowing.
OPPOSITES: cheerful, happy.
2 *(adj) It's depressing when you always lose. See* **discouraging**.

derelict
(adj) A derelict cottage. dilapidated, tumbledown, ramshackle, run-down, crumbling, ruined, rickety, broken-down, neglected, abandoned, deserted.

descend
1 *(v) The plane began to descend.* go down, come down, drop, fall, sink, plummet, plunge, nose-dive, tumble.
OPPOSITES: ascend, climb.
2 *(v) The road starts to descend here.* go down, slope, drop, dip, fall, slant, incline.
OPPOSITES: ascend, rise, climb.

describe
1 *(v) Ned was eager to describe how he caught the thief.* relate, explain, report, outline, tell, give an account of, give details of, put into words, recount, narrate.
2 *(v) How would you describe your sister?* define, characterize, portray, label, depict.

description
1 *(n) Write a description of your first day at this school.* account, report, chronicle, narration, narrative, commentary.
2 *(n) Write a detailed description of your brother.* characterization, portrayal, depiction, pen portrait, sketch.

descriptive
(adj) A descriptive piece of writing. expressive, vivid, graphic, detailed, colourful, striking, imaginative.

desert
1 *(v) Don't desert your friends.* abandon, leave, forsake, turn your back on, walk out on *(informal)*, leave in the lurch, leave high and dry, run out on *(informal)*, cast off.
2 *(v) The demoralized troops decided to desert.* run away, abscond, make off, escape, bolt, turn tail, go AWOL (absent without leave), flee, fly, decamp, defect.
3 *(n) The travellers were lost in the desert.* wilderness, wasteland, wilds *(plural)*.
4 *(adj) Few plants can survive in desert conditions.* dry, arid, moistureless, parched, hot, burning, barren, infertile.

deserted
(adj) A deserted farmhouse. abandoned, neglected, empty, vacant, uninhabited, unoccupied, isolated, desolate, lonely.

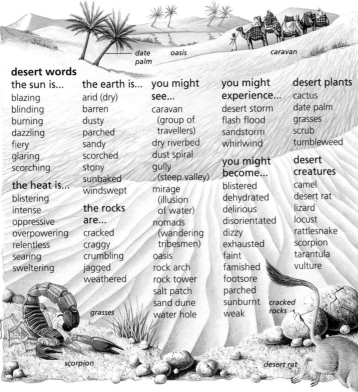

desert words

the sun is...
blazing
blinding
burning
dazzling
fiery
glaring
scorching

the heat is...
blistering
intense
oppressive
overpowering
relentless
searing
sweltering

the earth is...
arid (dry)
barren
dusty
parched
sandy
scorched
stony
sunbaked
windswept

the rocks are...
cracked
craggy
crumbling
jagged
weathered

you might see...
caravan
 (group of
 travellers)
dry riverbed
dust spiral
gully
 (steep valley)
mirage
 (illusion
 of water)
nomads
 (wandering
 tribesmen)
oasis
rock arch
rock tower
salt patch
sand dune
water hole

you might experience...
desert storm
flash flood
sandstorm
whirlwind

you might become...
blistered
dehydrated
delirious
disorientated
dizzy
exhausted
faint
famished
footsore
parched
sunburnt
weak

desert plants
cactus
date palm
grasses
scrub
tumbleweed

desert creatures
camel
desert rat
lizard
locust
rattlesnake
scorpion
tarantula
vulture

date palm
oasis
caravan
grasses
scorpion
cracked rocks
desert rat

deserve
1 *(v) Your painting must surely deserve a prize.* warrant, merit, be worthy of, justify, be qualified for, be entitled to, win.
2 *(v) You've worked hard enough to deserve a holiday.* be entitled to, have a right to, earn.

design
1 *(n) Rajesh is working on a design for a toy plane.* drawing, sketch, plan, blueprint, draft, outline, diagram, model, prototype.
2 *(n) I don't like the design on that wallpaper.* pattern, motif, decoration.
3 *(n) The design of this book cover is striking.* layout, composition, format, style, arrangement, organization.
4 *(n) Our car is the latest design. See* **model** 2.
5 *(v) Mel was asked to design a cover for the school magazine.* draw up, devise, create, think up, dream up, conceive, originate, plan, draft, map out, sketch, outline, draw.

desirable
1 *(adj) This house is in a desirable neighbourhood.* attractive, popular, sought-after, fashionable, enviable, pleasant, appealing, agreeable, excellent, good, advantageous, in demand.
2 *(adj) A desirable person. See* **sexy** 1.

desire
1 *(v) The genie will bring you anything you desire.* wish for, want, fancy, set your heart on, long for, yearn for, hunger for, thirst for, hanker after, crave, covet, need.
2 *(n) Sir Lancelittle had no desire for adventure.* wish, appetite, thirst, hunger, craving, longing, hankering, yearning, urge, need.
3 *(n) Cinderella's beauty filled the prince with desire.* passion, ardour, love, lust, the hots *(plural) (slang).*
4 *(n) The sight of the gold filled Pirate Peg with desire. See* **greed** 2.

desolate
(adj) The wind howled across the desolate moor. bleak, barren, bare, windswept, wild, inhospitable, lonely, remote, isolated, empty, deserted, uninhabited.

despair
1 *(v) The marooned sailors began to despair.* lose hope, give up hope, lose heart, be discouraged, be despondent.
2 *(n) Mirza tried to conquer her feelings of despair.* desperation, hopelessness, dejection, despondency, depression, gloom, pessimism, misery, wretchedness, distress, anguish.
OPPOSITES: hope, optimism.

despairing *see* **desperate** 4.

desperate
1 *(adj) The travellers were desperate for water.* in urgent need of, in want of.
2 *(adj) Indiana made a desperate bid to escape.* frantic, daring, death-defying, bold, audacious, determined, risky, dangerous, hazardous, reckless, rash, hasty, foolhardy, harebrained, madcap.
3 *(adj) The climbers found themselves in a desperate situation.* hopeless, impossible, perilous, precarious, dangerous, life-threatening, serious, critical, dire, drastic, appalling, dreadful, terrible, awful.
4 *(adj) Juliet felt desperate when she saw that Romeo was dead.* despairing, hopeless, distraught, grief-stricken, brokenhearted, heartbroken, inconsolable, distressed, wretched, anguished, suicidal.
OPPOSITES: hopeful, optimistic.

despise *see* **scorn** 1.

dessert
(n) What's for dessert? sweet, pudding, afters *(plural) (informal).*

destined
1 *(adj) The expedition was destined to fail.* doomed, bound, certain, meant, fated.
2 *(adj) It was destined that we should fall in love.* inevitable, unavoidable, inescapable, ordained, written in the stars, predestined, meant.

destiny *see* **fate** 1, 2.

destroy
1 *(v) Earthquakes can destroy whole cities.* wreck, devastate, demolish, ruin, flatten, level, wipe out, lay waste to, raze to the ground, wreak havoc on, ravage, smash, shatter.
2 *(v) The soldiers were ordered to destroy the enemy.* annihilate, wipe out, obliterate, exterminate, liquidate, kill, slay, slaughter, massacre, decimate, waste *(informal).*

destruction
(n) The earthquake caused widespread destruction. devastation, desolation, havoc, ruin, wreckage, damage.

detached
(adj) Try to remain detached; don't take sides. objective, disinterested, impartial, unbiased, unprejudiced, dispassionate, aloof, unemotional, unconcerned.

detail
1 *(n) Check every detail of the plan.* aspect, element, part, item, point, feature, particular, component.
2 **details** *(plural n) Samir asked Mrs Badger for details about the French trip.* information, particulars *(plural)*, facts *(plural)*, specifics *(plural).*

detailed
(adj) Bart gave a detailed account of the match. full, thorough, comprehensive, in-depth, exhaustive, complete, meticulous, precise, blow-by-blow, elaborate.
OPPOSITES: brief, general.

detective

(n) investigator, sleuth (informal), private detective, private investigator, private eye (informal). ❖ Also see **crime & detection**.

deteriorate see **get worse**.

determination

(n) Chris showed great determination in finishing the race. perseverance, tenacity, persistence, willpower, drive, resolve, single-mindedness, dedication, guts (plural) (informal), grit, spirit.

determined

1 (adj) Patsy is a very determined person. persistent, tenacious, single-minded, strong-willed, assertive, firm, gutsy (informal), obstinate, stubborn, dogged.
OPPOSITES: indecisive, weak-willed.
2 (adj) I don't want to go, but Nat is determined. resolved, immovable, insistent, set on it, bent on it, intent on it.
OPPOSITES: unsure, wavering.

detest see **hate** 1.

detour

(n) We took a detour to get home. diversion, indirect route, roundabout route, long way round, scenic route.

develop

1 (v) Nadia should develop once she starts her new school. mature, blossom, flourish, grow up, make progress, progress, grow, fill out, shoot up.
2 (v) Dad wants to develop his grocery business. See **expand** 2.
3 (v) Tom may develop a taste for modern art. acquire, pick up, cultivate, form.
4 (v) I might develop mumps. See **catch** 3.
5 (v) It's a good idea, but you need to develop it. enlarge on, elaborate on, expand, flesh out, pad out, fill out.

development

(n) We're studying the development of modern medicine. progress, advance, evolution, growth, improvement, spread, expansion, history, course.

devious see **cunning**.

devoted

1 (adj) Mo is a devoted friend. See **loyal**.
2 (adj) Sally is devoted to caring for sick animals. dedicated, committed.

devour see **eat** 2.

diagram

(n) Study this diagram. representation, figure, sketch, drawing, line drawing, outline, chart, plan, map, graph, table.

diarrhoea

(n) the runs (plural) (informal), the trots (plural) (informal), holiday tummy (informal), Delhi belly (informal), dysentery.

diary

1 (n) Jo keeps a diary to record her secret thoughts. journal, record, chronicle, log.
2 (n) Priscilla entered the meeting in her diary. personal organizer, appointments book, engagement book, calendar.

dictate

1 (v) You dictate and I'll take notes. read aloud, speak slowly, recite.
2 (v) I can't dictate what you should think. tell you, lay down the law about, decree, impose, direct, order, determine, ordain.

die

1 (v) Everyone must die eventually. expire, pass away, pass on, decease, snuff it (informal), kick the bucket (informal), bite the dust (informal), give up the ghost (informal), croak (slang).
2 (v) Soldiers sometimes die in battle. perish, fall, lose their lives, give their lives.
3 (v) Those flowers will die without water. wither, wilt, shrivel up, droop, fade.

diet

1 (v) I must diet to fit into this skirt. lose weight, slim, eat sparingly, fast.
2 (n) You need to go on a special diet. programme, regimen, regime, fast.
3 (n) Is this your usual diet? food, nutrition, nourishment, fare.

differ

1 (v) Our tastes in music tend to differ. be different, contrast, vary, conflict, diverge.
2 (v) Matt and I differ about which team is best. See **disagree** 1.

difference

(n) Note the difference in price between the two items. contrast, disparity, divergence, discrepancy, inconsistency.
OPPOSITE: similarity.

different

1 (adj) Mum and I have different opinions on clothes. differing, dissimilar, contrasting, conflicting, opposing, contradictory, clashing, incompatible.
OPPOSITES: similar, identical.
2 (adj) We stock a range of different chocolates. various, assorted, mixed, varied, miscellaneous, multifarious.
3 (adj) Try a different approach. new, fresh, other, original, changed, altered.
4 (adj) Every fingerprint is different. individual, distinct, unique, special, distinctive, separate, unrelated, personal.
5 (adj) With his purple hair, Ziggy is certainly different. See **unusual** 2.

difficult

1 (adj) A difficult maths problem. hard, tough, knotty (informal), advanced, complicated, complex, challenging, testing, baffling, thorny, puzzling.
OPPOSITES: easy, straightforward.
2 (adj) A difficult assault course. hard, challenging, demanding, testing, taxing, strenuous, tough, gruelling, exhausting, killing (informal), backbreaking, arduous.
OPPOSITES: easy, undemanding.
3 (adj) A difficult child. demanding, hard to please, fussy, fractious, unmanageable, uncooperative, unruly, obstreperous, bolshie (informal), stroppy (informal), wilful, awkward, obstinate, stubborn.
OPPOSITES: cooperative, undemanding.

4 (adj) A difficult situation. See **awkward** 6.

difficulty

1 (n) Gran has had a life full of difficulty. See **trouble** 2.
2 (n) Don't let this little difficulty put you off. problem, complication, obstacle, snag, stumbling block, hurdle, pitfall, hiccup (informal), hassle (informal), hindrance.

dig

1 (v) The climbers tried to dig a hole in the snow. scoop out, gouge out, hollow out, excavate, shovel, burrow, tunnel.
2 (v) Mum asked me to dig the flowerbed. turn over, fork over.
3 **dig up** (v) Pirate Peg began to dig up the treasure. unearth, excavate, uncover.

dignified

1 (adj) The duchess has a dignified manner. stately, solemn, formal, proud, lofty, majestic, upright, elegant, refined.
OPPOSITES: undignified, coarse.
2 (adj) Hetty gave a dignified reply. calm, composed, restrained, solemn, grave.
OPPOSITES: rude, unrestrained.

dilapidated

(adj) A dilapidated farmhouse. run-down, decaying, decrepit, ramshackle, tumbledown, neglected, crumbling, broken-down, rickety, shabby, uncared-for.
OPPOSITE: well-maintained.

dilute

(v) You need to dilute this sauce. water down, weaken, thin, add water to.
OPPOSITES: condense, thicken.

dim

1 (adj) A dim cave. dark, gloomy, murky, dingy, dull, poorly lit, ill-lit, shadowy.
OPPOSITES: bright, well-lit, sunny.
2 (adj) A dim figure in the mist. faint, indistinct, shadowy, pale, vague, hazy, fuzzy, bleary, blurred, ill-defined, misty.
OPPOSITES: clear, distinct.
3 (adj) Don't be so dim! See **stupid** 1.

din see **noise** 2.

dingy

(adj) A dingy attic. drab, dreary, dark, gloomy, ill-lit, shabby, grimy, cheerless.
OPPOSITES: bright, clean, cheerful.

dip

1 (n) Do you want a dip in the river? swim, bathe, dunk, splash, plunge, soaking, ducking.
2 (n) Watch out for that dip in the ground. hollow, depression, dent, hole, pit, incline, slope.
3 (v) Dip your mug in the stream. plunge, dunk, submerge, immerse, lower, rinse.
4 (v) The plane began to dip. See **drop** 2.

direct

1 (adj) Take the direct road. straight, shortest, undeviating, unswerving.
OPPOSITES: indirect, winding.
2 (adj) Take the direct train. nonstop, express, through.

3 *(adj)* You can rely on Nat to give a direct answer. See **frank**.
4 *(adj)* We need a direct response. See **immediate**.
5 *(v)* Greg will direct operations. supervise, oversee, take charge of, control, run, manage, handle, lead, mastermind.
6 *(v)* Let me direct you to the school. show you the way, guide, point, lead, steer.

direction
(n) Which direction should we take? way, route, path, track, course, bearing.

directions
(plural n) Follow the directions carefully. instructions *(plural)*, guidelines *(plural)*, rules *(plural)*, recommendations *(plural)*, suggestions *(plural)*.

dirt
(n) We must get rid of all this dirt. grime, filth, muck, sludge, slime, mud, dust, crud *(informal)*, gunge *(informal)*, gunk *(informal)*, grot *(slang)*, mess, pollution.

dirty
1 *(adj)* This room is really dirty. filthy, grimy, mucky, grubby, squalid, sordid, foul, grotty *(slang)*, grungy *(slang)*, dusty, muddy, sooty, smoky, black, stained, soiled, spattered, streaked, insanitary.
OPPOSITES: clean, spotless.
2 *(adj)* Don't tell dirty jokes. blue, risqué, smutty, rude, filthy, indecent, crude, vulgar, obscene, pornographic.
OPPOSITES: clean, decent.
3 *(adj)* George was sent off the pitch for dirty play. See **foul 5**.
4 *(v)* Try not to dirty your clothes. soil, stain, muddy, mess up, make a mess of, muck up *(slang)*, smear, spatter, spot.

disabled
(adj) handicapped, incapacitated, infirm, paralysed, paraplegic, quadriplegic.
OPPOSITE: able-bodied.

disadvantage
(n) It's a disadvantage to live a long way from school. handicap, drawback, inconvenience, hindrance, nuisance, pain *(informal)*, hardship, fly in the ointment.
OPPOSITES: advantage, benefit.

disagree
1 *(v)* We often disagree about which team is best. argue, quarrel, row, squabble, bicker, fall out *(informal)*, clash, differ.
OPPOSITE: agree.
2 disagree with *(v)* Why do you disagree with everything I say? object to, take issue with, quarrel with, argue with, dispute, oppose, contradict.
OPPOSITE: agree with.
3 disagree with *(v)* Do spicy meals disagree with you? upset, make you ill, give you indigestion, cause you problems, bother, nauseate.

disagreement
1 *(n)* We had a disagreement over who should pay. See **argument 1**.

2 *(n)* There's been a lot of disagreement about this matter. conflict, dissent, division, difference of opinion, debate.
OPPOSITES: harmony, agreement.

disappear
(v) Slowly, the figure began to disappear. vanish, fade away, melt away, become invisible, vanish into thin air, leave no trace, dissolve, evaporate, dematerialize.
OPPOSITES: appear, materialize.

disappoint
(v) I'm sorry to disappoint you. let you down, dash your hopes, disillusion, disenchant, fail, fail to live up to your expectations, dishearten, sadden, dismay, displease, upset, frustrate, thwart.

disappointed
(adj) I felt disappointed when I learnt the truth. let down, dejected, despondent, crestfallen, downcast, disenchanted, disillusioned, saddened, discouraged, downhearted, miffed *(informal)*, fed up *(informal)*, disgruntled, dissatisfied.
OPPOSITES: satisfied, gratified.

disapprove
1 *(v)* My parents disapprove when I play loud music. object, protest, take exception.
OPPOSITE: approve.
2 disapprove of *(v)* I disapprove of fox-hunting. object to, take exception to, have a low opinion of, take a dim view of *(informal)*, frown on, condemn, deplore.
OPPOSITE: approve of.

disapproving see **critical 1**.

disaster
(n) We must try to avoid another disaster. catastrophe, calamity, tragedy, misfortune, mishap, accident, fiasco, cataclysm.

disastrous
(adj) The pilot made a disastrous mistake. catastrophic, fatal, tragic, terrible, devastating, horrendous, calamitous, grievous, ill-fated, unlucky, cataclysmic.
OPPOSITES: fortunate, lucky.

discipline
1 *(v)* The coach will discipline the players. train, instruct, school, drill, control.
2 *(v)* If you break the rules, I will have to discipline you. punish, penalize, reprimand, teach you a lesson, bring you into line, rebuke, chastise, chasten, correct, scold.
3 *(n)* Good athletes need discipline. self-discipline, self-control, strictness, firmness, routine, order, training.

discourage
(v) What can I do to discourage you from going? dissuade, deter, prevent, stop, talk you out of, put you off, advise you against.
OPPOSITE: encourage.

discouraged
(adj) We were discouraged by the bad news. disheartened, demoralized, dismayed, daunted, depressed, crushed, deterred, cowed, put off, unnerved.
OPPOSITES: encouraged, reassured.

discouraging
(adj) It's discouraging when you always lose. demoralizing, disheartening, depressing, disappointing, demotivating, dispiriting, daunting, off-putting *(informal)*.
OPPOSITES: encouraging, heartening.

discover
1 *(v)* It didn't take me long to discover that Oz was lying. find out, learn, become aware, realize, detect, spot, discern, work out, deduce, suss out *(slang)*, ascertain.
2 *(v)* The explorers were lucky to discover the treasure. See **find 1**.
3 *(v)* The journalist was determined to discover the truth. find out, uncover, bring to light, ferret out, dig up, expose, reveal.

discovery
(n) This is an amazing discovery. invention, find, revelation, innovation, breakthrough.

discreet
(adj) You can trust Tony; he's always discreet. careful, guarded, reserved, cautious, tactful, diplomatic, prudent.
OPPOSITES: indiscreet, rash.

discrimination
(n) I hate discrimination of all kinds. prejudice, bigotry, unfairness, favouritism, bias, racism, sexism, chauvinism, ageism.
OPPOSITE: tolerance.

discuss
(v) Can we discuss this later? talk about, consider, debate, examine, exchange views on, argue about, confer about, go into, thrash out, argue the toss on *(informal)*.

discussion
(n) We had a discussion about where to go on holiday. conversation, debate, exchange of views, argument, talk, powwow, dialogue, conference.

disease see **illness 1, 2**.

disgrace
(n) Burglar Beryl has brought disgrace to her family. shame, embarrassment, humiliation, dishonour, scandal, ignominy.
OPPOSITES: honour, credit.

disgraceful
1 *(adj)* Disgraceful behaviour. appalling, shameful, scandalous, shocking, outrageous, disgusting, deplorable, despicable, contemptible, disreputable.
2 *(adj)* A disgraceful defeat. See **humiliating**.

disguise
1 *(n)* I'll need a good disguise to get into the house. cover, front, screen, façade, camouflage, alias.
2 *(n)* Sally looks wonderful in her disguise. fancy dress, costume, outfit, get-up *(informal)*, mask, veil, make-up, face paint.
3 *(v)* The soldiers used bushes to disguise the tank. camouflage, hide, cover up, conceal, screen, mask, shroud, veil.
4 *(v)* Burglar Beryl decided to disguise herself as the milkman. dress up as, pretend to be, impersonate, imitate.

disgust

1 *(n) The details of the crime filled me with disgust.* loathing, distaste, revulsion, repugnance, contempt, hatred, antipathy.
OPPOSITES: delight, approval.
2 *(v) Doesn't bad language disgust you?* sicken, revolt, appal, nauseate, turn your stomach, repel, offend, put you off.
OPPOSITES: delight, attract.

disgusted

(adj) Gran was disgusted by Mark's jokes. appalled, sickened, outraged, offended, scandalized, shocked, nauseated, repelled.
OPPOSITE: delighted.

disgusting

1 *(adj) A disgusting smell.* revolting, repulsive, nauseating, sickening, loathsome, offensive, obnoxious, foul, vile.
OPPOSITES: delightful, lovely.
2 *(adj) Disgusting behaviour.* appalling, obnoxious, offensive, odious, detestable, abominable, shocking, scandalous.
OPPOSITES: delightful, pleasing.

dishonest

(adj) A dishonest businessman. deceitful, fraudulent, lying, crooked *(informal)*, bent *(slang)*, immoral, untrustworthy, unscrupulous, corrupt, double-dealing, treacherous, slippery, shady *(informal)*, tricky, wily, two-faced, hypocritical.
OPPOSITES: honest, truthful.

dishonesty

(n) Dad cannot stand dishonesty. deceit, deceitfulness, untruthfulness, insincerity, deviousness, lies *(plural)*, cheating, double-dealing, sharp practice, fraud, hypocrisy.
OPPOSITES: honesty, truthfulness.

dish up

(v) Dad will dish up the vegetables. serve, serve up, dole out, give out, hand out.

disillusioned see disappointed.

disintegrate

1 *(v) The yacht hit the rocks and began to disintegrate. See* **break up** 1.
2 *(v) The wallpaper is starting to disintegrate.* crumble, rot, moulder away, decay, decompose, fall apart, fall to pieces.

dislike

1 *(v) I dislike bullies. See* **hate** 1.
2 *(n) George surveyed his broccoli with dislike.* distaste, displeasure, disgust, loathing, revulsion, repugnance, hatred, hostility, detestation, animosity.
OPPOSITES: liking, delight.

disloyal

(adj) A disloyal friend. false, unfaithful, two-faced, untrustworthy, treacherous.
OPPOSITES: loyal, faithful.

dismal

1 *(adj) Dismal weather. See* **dull** 1.
2 *(adj) A dismal story. See* **depressing** 1.

dismay

(n) I gazed at the mountain with dismay. alarm, apprehension, anxiety, trepidation, consternation, dread, distress, fear, horror.

dismiss

1 *(v) The boss may have to dismiss you.* give you notice, sack *(informal)*, fire *(informal)*, let you go, release, make you redundant, lay you off, give you your cards *(informal)*, show you the door *(informal)*.
2 *(v) Don't dismiss my idea without thinking about it first.* reject, discount, spurn, pooh-pooh *(informal)*, disregard.

disobedient

(adj) A disobedient child. rebellious, uncooperative, defiant, badly behaved, disruptive, naughty, wilful, wayward, unruly, uncontrollable, unmanageable.
OPPOSITE: obedient.

disobey

1 *(v) Mum will be angry if you disobey her.* defy, refuse to obey, resist, rebel against, revolt against, go your own way.
OPPOSITE: obey.
2 *(v) Don't disobey the school rules.* break, flout, disregard, ignore, infringe, overstep.
OPPOSITE: obey.

disorganized

1 *(adj) Daisy is such a disorganized person.* scatterbrained, undisciplined, scatty *(informal)*, muddleheaded, untogether *(slang)*, shambolic *(informal)*, chaotic.
OPPOSITE: well-organized.
2 *(adj) This essay is very disorganized.* jumbled, muddled, confused, chaotic, unstructured, unplanned, illogical, haphazard, unsystematic, unmethodical.
OPPOSITES: well-organized, clear.

display

1 *(n) We went to see the display.* demonstration, exhibition, presentation, show, array, pageant, spectacle, parade.
2 *(v) The makers were keen to display their products.* show, demonstrate, exhibit, present, unveil, reveal, show off, flaunt.

disprove

(v) Burglar Beryl's lawyer set out to disprove the charges. refute, prove false, discredit, invalidate, contradict.
OPPOSITE: prove.

disqualified

(adj) Our team is disqualified from the competition. banned, eliminated, debarred, out of the running, knocked out.

disrespectful

(adj) Don't be so disrespectful to your father! rude, impertinent, insolent, cheeky, impolite, impudent, irreverent, insulting.
OPPOSITE: respectful.

dissatisfied

(adj) I feel dissatisfied with the way I've been treated. displeased, unhappy, disgruntled, disappointed, discontented, fed up *(informal)*, cheesed off *(slang)*.
OPPOSITES: satisfied, contented.

dissolve

(v) Wait for the stock cube to dissolve. melt, break up, disintegrate, disperse, liquefy, soften, thaw, disappear.

distance

1 *(n) A short distance.* space, span, gap, interval, length, breadth, width.
2 *(n) A long distance.* stretch, extent, range, length, breadth, width.

distant

(adj) Distant lands. faraway, far-flung, far-off, remote, out-of-the-way, outlying.
OPPOSITES: nearby, neighbouring.

distinct

1 *(adj) A distinct signal. See* **clear** 2.
2 *(adj) A distinct outline. See* **clear** 5.
3 *(adj) A distinct voice. See* **clear** 6.
4 *(adj) The two companies are quite distinct.* different, separate, unconnected, dissimilar, distinguishable, detached.

distinguish

(v) Can you distinguish between frogs and toads? tell the difference, differentiate, discriminate, tell apart.

distort see twist 5.

distract

(v) Will it distract you if I watch television? put you off, disturb, bother, ruin your concentration, faze, disconcert, sidetrack, unsettle, worry, confuse, annoy.

distress

1 *(n) Your news caused me much distress.* pain, heartache, misery, anguish, torment, worry, anxiety, grief, agony, upset.
OPPOSITE: comfort.
2 *(v) This film might distress you. See* **disturb** 2.

distressing see disturbing.

distribute see give out.

distrust see suspect 1.

disturb

1 *(v) I don't want to disturb you while you're working.* bother, interrupt, distract, put you off, pester, hassle *(informal)*, butt in on, annoy, trouble, disrupt.
2 *(v) It might disturb you to know the truth.* upset, alarm, distress, unsettle, worry, trouble, perturb, fluster, disconcert.

disturbed

1 *(adj) When I read your letter, I felt disturbed.* uneasy, worried, troubled, concerned, upset, distressed, alarmed, anxious, apprehensive, agitated, nervous.
2 *(adj) A disturbed teenager.* troubled, confused, unbalanced, neurotic, maladjusted, screwed up *(informal)*.
OPPOSITE: well-adjusted.

disturbing

(adj) I found the film really disturbing. upsetting, distressing, worrying, unsettling, disquieting, troubling, perturbing, harrowing, alarming, frightening.

ditch

1 *(n) Henry fell into a ditch.* gully, trench, dyke, channel, hollow, pit, moat, drain.
2 *(v) (slang) Jason wants to ditch his girlfriend. See* **drop** 6.

dither see hesitate.

dive
1 (v) *We watched Alexis dive into the river.* plunge, jump, leap, fall, belly-flop, plummet, go under.
2 (v) *Suddenly, the plane began to dive.* drop, sink, plunge, plummet, fall, descend, swoop, dip, nose-dive, tumble, submerge (*submarine*).
OPPOSITE: rise.
3 (v) *The goalkeeper prepared to dive for the ball.* lunge, pounce on, swoop on, fall upon, leap, jump.

diver
(n) frogman, scuba diver.

divide
1 (v) *Where does the path divide?* branch, fork, split, separate, diverge, subdivide.
2 (v) *Can you divide this apple for me?* cut up, halve, split, bisect.
3 (v) *Let's divide the money between us.* share, share out, split, distribute, dole out, deal out, allocate, allot, apportion, go halves, go fifty-fifty (*informal*).
4 (v) *Please divide these papers into groups. See* **sort** 3.

divine
(adj) *A divine being.* heavenly, celestial, holy, sacred, godlike, angelic, spiritual, supernatural, immortal, superhuman.

divorce
(v) *Joe's parents have decided to divorce.* split up, separate, part, break up.

dizzy
(adj) *After her fall, Fran felt dizzy.* giddy, faint, light-headed, woozy (*informal*), groggy (*informal*), reeling, weak at the knees, shaky, dazed, wobbly, unsteady.

do
1 (v) *I have lots of things to do.* undertake, carry out, get on with, achieve, accomplish, perform, complete, finish.
2 (v) *Let's ask Mrs Bunn to do the teas.* make, prepare, organize, handle, deal with, take care of, see to, manage, look after, arrange, be responsible for.
3 (v) *This will do for our needs.* be good enough, be adequate, be sufficient, suffice, be useful, be acceptable.
4 (v) *Can you do this puzzle?* solve, answer, complete, work out, figure out (*informal*), crack, find the solution to.
5 (v) *You may do as you please.* behave, act, live, lead your life, carry on.
6 (v) *This may do some good.* result in, cause, bring about, give rise to, lead to.
7 (v) *William should do better at his new school.* manage, get on, get along, cope, progress, advance, make out, fare.
8 (v) *I must do my room.* tidy, straighten up, sort out, organize, arrange, neaten.
9 (v) *Sunita hopes to do drama at college.* study, learn, take up, go in for.
10 (v) *This car will do 130 miles per hour.* travel at, go at, reach.
11 (v) (informal) *Watch out for Dodgy Dave or he'll do you! See* **cheat** 1.

dock
1 (n) *We moored our boat at the dock.* quay, wharf, jetty, harbour, landing stage.
2 (v) *When will the boat dock?* berth, moor, tie up, anchor, drop anchor.

doctor
(n) medical practitioner, medic (*informal*), doc (*informal*), quack (*informal*).
TYPES OF DOCTOR: anaesthetist, brain surgeon, consultant, GP (general practitioner), gynaecologist, homeopath, neurologist, obstetrician, orthopaedic surgeon, osteopath, paediatrician, plastic surgeon, psychiatrist, specialist, surgeon.

dodge
1 (v) *I threw a pillow at Kevin, but he managed to dodge it.* avoid, evade, escape, sidestep, swerve, duck, turn aside.
2 (v) *Oz tries to dodge work. See* **avoid** 2.

dodgy
1 (adj) (informal) *Dave made a dodgy deal. See* **crooked** 4.
2 (adj) (informal) *That bridge looks dodgy. See* **dangerous** 2.

dog
(n) hound, bitch (*female*), pup, puppy, mutt (*informal*), pooch (*slang*), mongrel, cur, canine, man's best friend.
TYPES OF DOG: Afghan hound, Alsatian, beagle, bloodhound, boxer, bulldog, Chihuahua, collie, corgi, dachshund, Dalmatian, Doberman, foxhound, Great Dane, greyhound, gundog, husky, Labrador, Pekingese, pointer, poodle, pug, retriever, Rottweiler, St Bernard, setter, sheepdog, spaniel, terrier, whippet, wolfhound.

dominate
1 (v) *Do your big brothers dominate you?* tyrannize, keep you under their thumb, rule, domineer over, boss you around (*informal*), take you over, have the whip hand over, take control of, monopolize.
2 (v) *The skyscrapers dominate the city.* tower over, overshadow, dwarf, look down on, loom over, soar above.

domineering *see* **bossy**.

donate *see* **give** 2.

done for
(adj) (informal) *After the fight, Lee felt he was done for.* finished, ruined, defeated, destroyed, dead, doomed, lost.

done in (informal) *see* **exhausted**.

doodle *see* **scribble** 2.

doomed
(adj) *I'm afraid our love is doomed.* cursed, ill-fated, fated, luckless, condemned, star-crossed, ill-omened, hopeless.

door
(n) doorway, entrance, entry, exit, gate, gateway, opening.

dope *see* **drug** 2, 3.

dopey
1 (adj) (informal) *I felt dopey after my operation.* groggy (*informal*), drowsy, woozy (*informal*), dazed, sleepy, muzzy, sluggish, lethargic, drugged.
2 (adj) (slang) *Don't be so dopey! See* **stupid** 1.

dot
(n) *Remove that dot.* spot, speck, fleck, mark, dab, blob, full stop, decimal point.

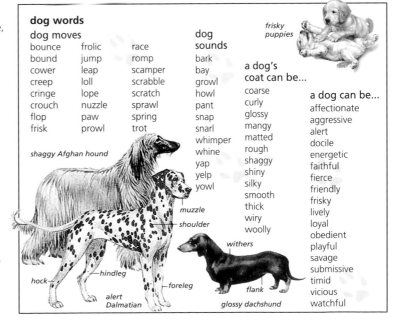

dog words

dog moves

bounce	frolic	race
bound	jump	romp
cower	leap	scamper
creep	loll	scrabble
cringe	lope	scratch
crouch	nuzzle	sprawl
flop	paw	spring
frisk	prowl	trot

shaggy Afghan hound

dog sounds

bark
bay
growl
howl
pant
snap
snarl
whimper
whine
yap
yelp
yowl

frisky puppies

a dog's coat can be...

coarse
curly
glossy
mangy
matted
rough
shaggy
shiny
silky
smooth
thick
wiry
woolly

a dog can be...

affectionate
aggressive
alert
docile
energetic
faithful
fierce
friendly
frisky
lively
loyal
obedient
playful
savage
submissive
timid
vicious
watchful

muzzle
shoulder
withers
hock
hindleg
foreleg
flank
alert Dalmatian
glossy dachshund

double

double
1 *(adj) Double railway tracks.* dual, twin, paired.
2 *(n) I've just seen your double.* twin, spitting image *(informal)*, lookalike, clone, counterpart.
3 *(v) We aim to double our numbers.* increase, multiply, expand, duplicate.

doubt
1 *(v) I'm starting to doubt if Oz will come.* be uncertain, be unsure, have doubts about, be dubious, wonder, question.
OPPOSITES: be sure, be certain.
2 *(v) I have reason to doubt your motives.* See **suspect** 1.
3 *(n) There's no doubt about Beryl's guilt.* uncertainty, question, debate, ambiguity.
OPPOSITE: certainty.
4 *(n) I have some doubt about your story.* suspicions *(plural)*, misgivings *(plural)*, reservations *(plural)*, qualms *(plural)*, scepticism, distrust, disbelief, incredulity.

doubtful
1 *(adj) It's doubtful whether the story is true.* uncertain, unclear, arguable, debatable, questionable, iffy *(informal)*.
OPPOSITES: certain, definite.
2 *(adj) Ellen was doubtful about her chances.* uncertain, dubious, unsure, unconvinced, hesitant, tentative.
OPPOSITES: confident, certain.

do up *(informal)* see **decorate** 2.

dowdy
(adj) Aunt Bertha wears such dowdy clothes. frumpy, drab, dreary, unattractive, unfashionable, old-fashioned, dull, dingy.
OPPOSITES: smart, fashionable.

down see **depressed**.

down-and-out see **homeless**.

down-to-earth
(adj) Roger has a down-to-earth approach. realistic, practical, hard-headed, nononsense, matter-of-fact, common-sense, sensible, sane, pragmatic.
OPPOSITES: unrealistic, impractical.

doze
(v) Granny likes to doze after lunch. snooze *(informal)*, catnap, sleep, take a nap, have forty winks *(informal)*, nod off *(informal)*, drop off *(informal)*, get some shuteye *(informal)*, have a kip *(slang)*.

drab
(adj) A drab bedsit. dreary, dingy, dismal, cheerless, gloomy, shabby, dull.
OPPOSITES: bright, cheerful.

drag
1 *(v) Drag that carpet over here.* pull, haul, tow, lug, tug, yank, trail, draw.
2 *(n) (informal) Shopping can be such a drag.* See **bore** 3.
3 **drag behind** *(v) Don't drag behind the others.* See **drop behind**.

drain
1 *(n) A drain for waste water.* ditch, pipe, sewer, trench, channel, gutter, drainpipe.

2 *(v) We watched the water drain away.* seep, ooze, trickle, ebb, leak, flow, escape.
3 *(v) Drain the water from the pond.* empty, draw off, siphon off, bleed, tap.

drama
1 *(n) We are staging a new drama.* See **play** 5.
2 *(n) Melissa wants to study drama.* acting, stagecraft, the theatre, the dramatic arts *(plural)*.
3 *(n) There was some drama in town.* crisis, incident, excitement, commotion, fuss, scene, turmoil, histrionics *(plural)*.

dramatic see **exciting**.

drastic
(adj) Drastic action is needed. radical, extreme, forceful, strong, serious, severe, desperate, rigorous, harsh, far-reaching.

draw
1 *(v) I want to draw a cat.* sketch, depict, portray, trace, outline, design, pen, pencil.
2 *(v) Draw a number from the bag.* pick, select, take out, pull out, choose, extract.
3 *(v) Horses draw carts.* See **pull**.
4 *(v) I think the teams will draw.* tie, finish equal, be neck and neck, be even, be level.
5 *(v) This game should draw a big crowd.* See **attract**.
6 *(n) The match ended in a draw.* tie, dead heat, stalemate, deadlock, impasse.
7 *(n) Are you entering the draw?* lottery, raffle, sweepstake, competition.

drawback see **disadvantage**.

drawing
(n) picture, study, design.
TYPES OF DRAWING: caricature, cartoon, charcoal drawing, comic strip, doodle, illustration, line drawing, pen-and-ink drawing, portrait, sketch, still life.

drawn see **haggard**.

draw on
(v) You can draw on your own experience for this story. make use of, use, employ, rely on, utilize, exploit, fall back on.

dread
1 *(v) There's no need to dread visiting the dentist.* fear, be afraid of, be apprehensive about, be scared of, shrink from, cringe at, shudder at, tremble at, flinch from, have cold feet, have butterflies in your stomach.
2 *(n) The sight of the monster filled Cedric with dread.* See **fear** 1.

dreadful
1 *(adj) A dreadful crime.* appalling, terrible, horrible, horrific, horrifying, horrendous, shocking, frightful, atrocious, awful, ghastly, vile, foul, hideous, gruesome, grisly, monstrous, sickening, harrowing, distressing, despicable, deplorable, unspeakable, tragic.
2 *(adj) A dreadful essay.* awful, terrible, atrocious, appalling, abysmal, abominable, diabolical *(informal)*, disgraceful, dire *(informal)*, deplorable, bad, lousy *(slang)*.
OPPOSITES: wonderful, excellent.

3 *(adj) Dreadful weather.* awful, terrible, horrible, atrocious, appalling, bad, foul, filthy, dirty, rough, miserable, dismal, murky, bleak, wet, rainy, stormy, wild.
OPPOSITES: wonderful, brilliant.

dream
1 *(n) I thought I could fly, but it was only a dream.* nightmare, daydream, fantasy, illusion, delusion, hallucination, speculation, vision.
2 *(n) You're in a dream again.* daydream, trance, daze, world of your own, reverie.
3 *(n) Eddie's dream is to be a star.* fantasy, hope, wish, desire, ideal, aspiration, ambition, goal, vision.
4 *(adj) This is my dream house.* ideal, perfect, fantasy.
5 *(v) Do you ever dream that you can fly?* imagine, fancy, fantasize, envisage, visualize, daydream, muse.
6 **dream up** *(v) Gita loves to dream up new recipes.* See **think up**.

dreamy
(adj) Daisy is so dreamy, she never knows where she is. absent-minded, airy-fairy, vague, faraway, abstracted, distracted.

dreary
1 *(adj) Dreary weather.* dull, depressing, dismal, gloomy, murky, bleak, grey, wet.
OPPOSITES: cheerful, bright.
2 *(adj) A dreary lesson.* See **boring**.

drenched see **soaking**.

dress
1 *(v) It's time to dress for the party.* get dressed, get changed, change, put your clothes on, dress up.
2 *(n) Poppy wore a red dress.* frock, gown, robe. ❖ *Also see* **clothes**.
3 *(n) Formal dress is required.* clothes *(plural)*, clothing, wear, gear *(informal)*, attire *(old-fashioned)*, costume, get-up *(informal)*, garments *(plural)*, togs *(plural)* *(informal)*, kit.

dress up
(v) It's time to dress up and go out. dress up to the nines *(informal)*, dress for dinner, put on your glad rags *(informal)*, tart yourself up *(slang)*, doll yourself up *(slang)*.

dribble
1 *(v) Look at Fido dribble!* drool, slobber, slaver, salivate, water at the mouth.
2 *(v) Don't let the syrup dribble out of the bottle.* trickle, drip, leak, ooze, seep, run.

drift
1 *(v) The boat began to drift downstream.* float, glide, sail, be carried, coast.
2 *(v) I love to drift around town.* See **wander** 1.
3 *(n) Zak fell into a drift of snow.* bank, mound, ridge, heap, pile, mass.

drill
1 *(v) Can you drill through this wood?* bore, pierce, penetrate, punch, puncture.
2 *(v) Our coach will drill us every day.* See **train** 4.

drink
1 *(v) Drink your milk.* sip, swallow, down, swig *(informal)*, gulp, guzzle, drain, knock back *(informal)*, quaff *(old-fashioned)*.
2 *(n) Bring some drink for the journey.* liquid, refreshment, beverage.
3 *(n) Supermarkets sell alcoholic drink.* liquor, spirits *(plural)*, booze *(informal)*, plonk *(informal)*, grog *(informal)*.
4 *(n) Take a drink from the bottle.* sip, swig *(informal)*, slug, swallow, gulp, suck.
5 *(n) Dodgy Dave went out for a drink.* tipple, tot, dram, booze-up *(slang)*.

drip
1 *(v) Look at the water drip from the ceiling!* trickle, splash, dribble, fall in drops, plop, leak, drop, seep, sprinkle, drizzle.
2 *(n) Clem could hear the steady drip of water.* dripping, trickle, dribble, splash.
3 *(n) (informal) Cyril is a real drip!* wimp *(informal)*, weed *(informal)*, wet *(informal)*, softy *(informal)*, mummy's boy *(informal)*, nerd *(slang)*, weakling.

drive
1 *(v) Let's drive home.* motor, travel, journey, go by car, ride.
2 *(v) Do you know how to drive this car?* handle, steer, control, operate.
3 *(v) How can I drive you to work harder?* force, spur you on, goad, push, compel, motivate, prompt, prod, incite, coerce, dragoon, oblige, urge, press.
4 *(n) We went for a drive in the car.* run, ride, spin *(informal)*, whirl *(informal)*, trip, journey, jaunt, outing, excursion.
5 *(n) Jacob has lots of drive.* ambition, determination, energy, push *(informal)*, motivation, enthusiasm, oomph *(informal)*.

drive out
(v) The king tried to drive out the sorcerer. banish, send away, send packing, cast out, throw out, expel, exile, evict, turf out *(informal)*, drum out, kick out *(informal)*.

droop
1 *(v) Don't let the scarf droop over your face.* hang down, sag, dangle, flop, trail.
2 *(v) The tulips are starting to droop.* wilt, go limp, sag, go floppy, hang down, flag, slump, wither, shrivel.

droopy *see* **floppy**.

drop
1 *(v) Don't drop that vase!* let go of, lose your grip on, let fall, let slip.
2 *(v) Suddenly the plane began to drop.* fall, sink, descend, dip, dive, plunge, plummet, tumble, nose-dive.
OPPOSITE: rise.
3 *(v) Prices may drop. See* **decrease** 2.
4 *(v) Can I drop my flute lessons?* give up, stop, discontinue, abandon, finish with.
5 *(v) We'll have to drop you from the team.* exclude, eliminate, leave you out of, kick you off *(informal)*, axe *(informal)*.
6 *(v) Holly decided to drop her boyfriend.* finish with, leave, dump *(informal)*, chuck *(informal)*, ditch *(slang)*, jilt.

7 *(n) A drop of paint ran down the tin.* droplet, bubble, globule, drip, bead, blob.
8 *(n) Add just a drop of sauce.* dash, spot, trace, dribble, bit, little, sprinkle, trickle, taste, pinch, soupçon, smidgen *(informal)*.
9 *(n) There's been a drop in crime. See* **decrease** 1.
10 *(n) The path led to a steep drop.* chasm, precipice, abyss, cliff, slope.

drop behind
(v) Try not to drop behind! fall behind, lag behind, straggle behind, trail behind, drag behind, dawdle, linger, loiter, dally, bring up the rear *(informal)*.

drop in *(informal) see* **call** 5.

drop off
1 *(v) Dad will drop you off at school.* set you down, let you off, leave, deposit.
2 *(v) (informal) Gran tends to drop off in front of the TV.* fall asleep, doze off, nod off *(informal)*, snooze *(informal)*, catnap, drowse, have forty winks *(informal)*.

drown
1 *(v) The pirates may drown if their ship sinks.* go under, go down, go to a watery grave, go to Davy Jones's locker.
2 *(v) The new reservoir will drown the village. See* **flood** 2.

drowsy *see* **sleepy** 1.

drug
1 *(n) Dr Dose wasn't sure which drug to prescribe.* medication, medicine, remedy, treatment, tonic, painkiller, antibiotic, tranquillizer, sedative, stimulant, antidepressant.
2 *(n) Cannabis is a type of drug.* narcotic, dope *(informal)*.
3 *(v) The vet had to drug the wild tiger.* dope, tranquillize, sedate, knock out, anaesthetize, put to sleep, inject.

drum
(v) Listen to the rain drum on the roof. beat, rap, tap, pound, thrum, reverberate.

drunk
1 *(adj) Dad said Dodgy Dave was drunk.* intoxicated, inebriated, tipsy, under the influence *(informal)*, tiddly *(informal)*, merry *(informal)*, legless *(informal)*, sozzled *(informal)*, paralytic *(informal)*, plastered *(slang)*, smashed *(slang)*, sloshed *(slang)*.
OPPOSITE: sober.
2 *(n) Dodgy Dave is a real drunk.* drunkard, alcoholic, hard drinker, heavy drinker, boozer *(informal)*, wino *(informal)*.
OPPOSITE: teetotaller.

dry
1 *(adj) The travellers crossed the dry desert.* arid, parched, dried up, barren, torrid, waterless, moistureless, scorched.
OPPOSITES: wet, humid.
2 *(adj) Lauren's dad has a dry sense of humour.* keen, sharp, shrewd, wry, ironic, laconic, sarcastic, deadpan, droll.
3 **dry up** *(v) Don't let the plants dry up.* wither, shrivel up, wilt, dehydrate, dry out.

duck
1 *(n) A duck paddled across the pond.* drake *(male)*, duckling.
2 *(v) You'll have to duck to avoid that beam.* stoop, bend down, lower your head, bob down, crouch down, dodge.
3 *(v) I'll duck you in the deep end!* dunk, push you under, submerge, plunge, dip, douse, immerse.

dull
1 *(adj) The sky has been dull all day.* cloudy, overcast, grey, gloomy, murky, leaden, dark, dismal, dreary, sunless.
OPPOSITES: bright, clear.
2 *(adj) Mrs Badger's lessons are never dull. See* **boring**.
3 *(adj) Aunt Bertha wears such dull colours.* drab, dreary, sombre, muted, subdued, dark, faded, colourless.
OPPOSITE: bright.
4 *(adj) Are you being deliberately dull? See* **stupid** 1.
5 *(adj) The prisoner stared with dull eyes.* lifeless, listless, expressionless, indifferent, apathetic, dead, blank, lacklustre.
OPPOSITES: bright, lively.

dumb
1 *(adj) I was dumb with fear.* speechless, unable to speak, tongue-tied, at a loss for words, silent, mute, mum.
2 *(adj) (informal) Don't be dumb! See* **stupid** 1.

dump
1 *(n) Take your rubbish to the dump.* tip, rubbish dump, rubbish tip, scrapheap, refuse centre, waste disposal site, junkyard, scrap yard, recycling centre.
2 *(n) (informal) This place is a dump.* hole *(informal)*, dive *(informal)*, tip *(informal)*, slum, pigsty, hovel, the pits *(informal)*.
3 *(v) Don't dump your bag on the floor.* drop, throw, plonk, sling *(informal)*, fling, toss, deposit, park *(informal)*.
4 *(v) (informal) You should dump that rubbish. See* **throw away** 1.
5 *(v) (informal) Holly decided to dump her boyfriend. See* **drop** 6.

dumpy
(adj) Mrs Bunn is a dumpy woman. squat, short, tubby, stubby, chubby, plump, stout, chunky, roly-poly, podgy, pudgy.
OPPOSITE: lanky.

dungeon
(n) The traitors were thrown into a dark dungeon. prison, cell, underground chamber, vault, lockup, pit.

dusk
(n) I must be home before dusk. nightfall, twilight, evening, sunset, sundown.
OPPOSITES: dawn, sunrise.

dust
1 *(n) The floor is covered in dust.* grime, dirt, grit, powder.
2 *(v) Dust the table.* wipe, clean, polish.
3 *(v) Dust the cake with icing sugar.* sprinkle, powder, cover, scatter.

dusty

1 *(adj)* *The attic was dusty.* dirty, grimy, grubby, filthy, mucky, sooty, unswept.
2 *(adj)* *The earth was dry and dusty.* crumbly, powdery, sandy, chalky, fine.

duty

1 *(n)* *It's my duty to tidy up.* responsibility, obligation, job, task, business, role, function, mission, vocation, calling.
2 *(n)* *Nigel worked late out of a sense of duty.* responsibility, loyalty, obligation, allegiance, obedience, respect, service.

dwindle

(v) *Seth's strength began to dwindle.* diminish, decline, weaken, decrease, lessen, shrink, wane, fade, peter out, ebb, sink, subside, abate, wither, disappear.
OPPOSITES: increase, strengthen.

dye

(v) *Let's dye this shirt.* colour, tint, stain.

dying

1 *(adj)* *The old man was dying.* declining, sinking, failing, fading fast, at death's door, breathing his last, expiring.
2 *(adj)* *(informal)* *I'm dying to know who won. See* **eager** 2.

dynamic

(adj) *A dynamic salesperson.* energetic, lively, vigorous, active, forceful, driving, go-getting *(informal)*, high-powered, go-ahead, zappy *(slang)*, aggressive.

Ee

eager

1 *(adj)* *An eager student.* enthusiastic, keen, interested, motivated, committed, zealous, diligent, hard-working.
OPPOSITES: apathetic, indifferent.
2 *(adj)* *Jade was eager to open her presents.* keen, impatient, bursting, dying *(informal)*, itching *(informal)*, anxious, longing, yearning, hungry, raring.
OPPOSITE: reluctant.

early

1 *(adv)* *I bet Kit will arrive early.* in good time, ahead of time, in advance, too soon.
OPPOSITE: late.
2 *(adj)* *An early manuscript.* old, ancient, primitive.
3 *(adj)* *Early humans hunted for food.* primitive, prehistoric, primeval, primordial.

earn

1 *(v)* *Nic is hoping to earn a lot of money.* make, bring in, obtain, gain, take home, rake in *(informal)*, collect, clear, gross, net.
2 *(v)* *You've worked hard enough to earn a holiday. See* **deserve** 2.
3 *(v)* *I want to earn a medal. See* **win** 2.

earnest *see* **serious** 1, 2.

earth

1 *(n)* *The earth is round.* world, globe, planet.
2 *(n)* *Dan dug up the earth.* ground, soil, land, clay, loam, topsoil, dirt, dust, turf.

---

earthquake

(n) earth tremor, quake *(informal)*.

earthquakes...	you might see...
destroy	
devastate	chasms
flatten	cracks
ravage	crushed cars
shatter	debris
smash	dust
wreck	fallen trees
	flames
the earth may...	rubble
cave in	ruins
crack	smoke
gape	trapped victims
jolt	wreckage
judder *(informal)*	
open up	**earthquake dangers**
quake	broken cables
quiver	burst dam
shake	burst water main
shift	collapsed bridge
subside	cracked pipes
tremble	falling masonry
vibrate	fire
yawn	flying glass
	gas explosion
buildings may...	landslide
buckle	tidal wave
collapse	
crack	
crumble	**earthquake words**
crumple	aftershock
disintegrate	epicentre
lurch	(earthquake
rock	centre)
shake	seismic wave
shudder	(shock wave)
sway	
tilt	
topple	
totter	water
tumble	gushing
wobble	from burst
	water main
rubble	
	chasm crack

---

easy

1 *(adj)* *The test was easy!* simple, straightforward, uncomplicated, a doddle *(informal)*, a piece of cake *(informal)*, child's play *(informal)*, a pushover *(slang)*.
OPPOSITES: hard, difficult.
2 *(adj)* *Declan thinks his new job is really easy.* undemanding, cushy *(informal)*, effortless, painless, light, soft *(informal)*.
OPPOSITES: hard, demanding.
3 *(adj)* *Lord Lucre has an easy life.* comfortable, carefree, untroubled, pleasant, relaxed, leisurely, contented, calm, tranquil, secure, affluent.
OPPOSITES: harsh, difficult, stressful.
4 *(adj)* *Dom's parents are too easy on him.* lenient with, lax with, indulgent towards, liberal with, tolerant towards.
OPPOSITES: hard, strict.

easy-going

(adj) *Omar is so easy-going; nothing ever bothers him.* even-tempered, placid, calm, relaxed, laid-back *(informal)*, carefree, happy-go-lucky, nonchalant, flexible, amenable, undemanding, tolerant.
OPPOSITES: uptight *(informal)*, intolerant.

eat

1 *(v)* *I need to eat.* have a meal, feed, dine, take food, take nourishment.
2 *(v)* *I can eat a huge amount.* consume, devour, swallow, put away, demolish.
WAYS TO EAT: bite, bolt, champ, chew, chomp, crunch, gnaw, gobble, gorge, grind, gulp, guzzle, lick, make a pig of yourself *(informal)*, munch, nibble, overeat, peck at, pick at, pig out *(slang)*, scoff *(informal)*, slurp *(informal)*, stuff yourself, suck, tuck into *(informal)*, wolf down.
3 eat away *(v)* *Eventually the sea will eat away the rocks. See* **wear away**.

eavesdrop

(v) *I didn't mean to eavesdrop on your conversation.* listen in, snoop, overhear, bug *(informal)*, tap.

eccentric

1 *(adj)* *Ziggy's behaviour is quite eccentric.* bizarre, peculiar, weird, strange, odd, unconventional, outlandish, quirky, idiosyncratic, cranky *(informal)*, wacky *(slang)*, off-the-wall *(slang)*, abnormal.
2 *(n)* *Professor Peabody is a real eccentric.* oddity, character *(informal)*, oddball *(informal)*, crank *(informal)*, crackpot *(informal)*, weirdo *(informal)*, nut *(slang)*.

echo

1 *(v)* *We heard the screams echo round the cave.* reverberate, ring, resound, sound, repeat.
2 *(v)* *Don't echo what I say. See* **repeat** 2.

ecstatic

(adj) *I was ecstatic when I won.* delighted, overjoyed, thrilled, elated, thrilled to bits *(informal)*, over the moon *(informal)*, on cloud nine *(informal)*, delirious, euphoric, in raptures, frenzied, hysterical.
OPPOSITES: wretched, dejected.

edge
1 *(n) Go to the edge of the field.* end, side, boundary, limit, perimeter, border, margin, kerb *(street)*, verge *(road)*, outskirts *(town) (plural)*.
OPPOSITES: centre, middle.
2 *(n) Theo filled the jug up to the edge.* rim, brim, lip.
3 *(n) Lucy caught the edge of her skirt on a nail.* hem, border, fringe, edging, trimming, bottom.
4 *(n) The expedition is on the edge of disaster.* brink, threshold, verge, point.
5 *(v) Try to edge forwards.* inch, creep, ease, crawl, sidle, worm your way, work your way, steal, sneak, slink.

edgy see nervous.

education
(n) Your education must come first. schooling, teaching, tuition, training, instruction, coaching, drilling.

educational
(adj) An educational film. informative, instructive, edifying, enlightening, improving, cultural.

eerie see spooky.

effect
1 *(n) One effect of the fire was to make us more careful.* result, consequence, outcome, upshot, aftereffect, side effect, knock-on effect, aftermath.
2 *(n) Going to France had a great effect on me.* influence, impact, impression.

efficient
1 *(adj) An efficient worker.* capable, competent, well-organized, businesslike, proficient, productive, effective, skilful.
OPPOSITES: inefficient, incompetent.
2 *(adj) An efficient business.* productive, cost-effective, streamlined, well-run, well-organized, economical, cost-cutting, energy-saving, timesaving.
OPPOSITES: inefficient, wasteful.

effort
1 *(n) Let's make an effort to break the record.* attempt, bid, try, endeavour, stab *(informal)*, shot *(informal)*, crack *(informal)*.
2 *(n) You must have put lots of effort into making this.* exertion, work, energy, power, force, muscle, labour, toil, trouble.

elaborate
1 *(adj) An elaborate ballgown.* extravagant, ornate, fancy, decorative, fussy, showy, ostentatious.
OPPOSITES: plain, simple.
2 *(adj) Elaborate plans. See complicated.*

elect see choose 1, 2.

elegant
1 *(adj) Mel looks elegant in that suit.* smart, sophisticated, stylish, chic *(female)*, debonair *(male)*, suave *(male)*, dashing, fashionable, handsome *(male)*, poised.
2 *(adj) What an elegant room!* tasteful, stylish, exquisite, classical, beautiful, splendid, luxurious, sumptuous, stately.

embarrass
(v) Would it embarrass you if Dad wore his tank top? humiliate, make you uncomfortable, make you self-conscious, make you blush, mortify, shame, upset, distress, show you up *(informal)*.

embarrassed
(adj) Mr Plod felt embarrassed when his wig fell off. self-conscious, uncomfortable, humiliated, mortified, ashamed, red in the face *(informal)*, flustered, disconcerted.

embarrassing
(adj) This is such an embarrassing situation. awkward, humiliating, uncomfortable, mortifying, cringe-making *(informal)*, upsetting, distressing, compromising.

embrace see hug.

embroidery
(n) needlework, sewing, tapestry.

emerge
(v) Wait for the train to emerge from the tunnel. come out, appear, come into view, become visible, surface.

emergency
(n) If there's an emergency, ring for help. crisis, danger, difficulty, predicament, panic stations *(plural) (informal)*.

emotion see feeling 3.

emotional
1 *(adj) Letty is such an emotional person.* excitable, highly strung, temperamental, sensitive, sentimental, passionate, hot-blooded, intense, melodramatic.
OPPOSITE: unemotional.
2 *(adj) An emotional film. See moving 2.*

emphasize
(v) I must emphasize the importance of safety. stress, underline, highlight, play up, point out, lay emphasis on, lay stress on, insist on, press home, accentuate.
OPPOSITE: play down.

empty
1 *(adj) This cupboard is completely empty.* bare, clear, free.
OPPOSITES: full, stuffed.
2 *(adj) Dustin handed in an empty page. See blank 1.*
3 *(adj) The house next door is empty.* vacant, unoccupied, uninhabited, deserted, unfurnished, bare, free.
OPPOSITES: occupied, furnished.
4 *(adj) I wasted the day in empty pursuits.* meaningless, pointless, futile, purposeless, aimless, hollow, frivolous, worthless, trivial.
OPPOSITES: worthwhile, valuable.
5 *(v) Empty the rubbish into the bin.* tip, dump, unload, pour, clear, drain.

enchant
1 *(v) Erica will enchant you with her singing. See delight 2.*
2 *(v) The magician planned to enchant the princess.* bewitch, cast a spell on, charm, hypnotize, mesmerize.

enchanting see delightful 2.

encourage
1 *(v) I think this result will encourage you.* reassure, cheer you up, inspire, give you confidence, give you hope, spur you on, comfort, console, hearten, buoy you up.
OPPOSITES: discourage, demoralize.
2 *(v) We all turned out to encourage the team.* support, spur on, urge on, cheer, applaud, rally, rouse, egg on.
3 *(v) Parents should encourage their children to read.* urge, persuade, prompt, help, assist, aid.
OPPOSITES: discourage, dissuade.

encouraging
(adj) This is an encouraging result. reassuring, heartening, comforting, promising, favourable, satisfactory.
OPPOSITES: discouraging, demoralizing.

end
1 *(n) Let's wait until the end of the show.* finish, conclusion, completion, ending, close, finale, climax, final curtain *(theatre)*.
OPPOSITES: start, beginning, opening.
2 *(n) This is the end of the school grounds.* limit, boundary, edge, border, perimeter, margin.
3 *(n) Our expedition reached its end.* destination, goal, target, journey's end.
OPPOSITE: starting point.
4 *(n) Get to the end of the queue.* back, rear, tail, tail end.
OPPOSITES: front, head.
5 *(n) What caused the end of the Roman Empire?* fall, ruin, demise, destruction, collapse, death, dissolution, extinction.
OPPOSITES: birth, beginning.
6 *(v) When does school end for the summer?* stop, finish, close, break up, come to an end, cease, wind up.
OPPOSITES: start, open.
7 *(v) Mrs Badger decided to end the lesson early.* finish, stop, bring to an end, conclude, wind up, break off, discontinue.
OPPOSITES: start, begin.

ending
(n) What a sad ending! end, conclusion, finish, resolution, finale, climax, outcome, upshot, result.
OPPOSITES: beginning, opening.

endless
1 *(adj) The desert seemed endless.* unending, never-ending, limitless, infinite, boundless, measureless.
2 *(adj) The city was invaded by an endless stream of tourists.* constant, continuous, never-ending, perpetual, nonstop, uninterrupted, incessant, interminable.

endure
1 *(v) I can't endure any more suffering.* bear, stand, put up with *(informal)*, tolerate, take, cope with, handle, suffer, go through, undergo, experience, stomach, swallow, brave, withstand, stick *(slang)*.
2 *(v) The poet's fame will endure for ever. See live 4.*

enemy
1 *(n) Japan was Britain's enemy in World War II.* opponent, foe, adversary, rival.
OPPOSITES: ally, friend.
2 **the enemy** *(n) Sir Blackheart has joined the enemy.* the other side, the opposition.

energetic
1 *(adj) Emma always seems so energetic.* lively, dynamic, active, full of life, full of beans *(informal)*, spirited, animated, vibrant, zippy *(informal)*, tireless.
OPPOSITES: lethargic, listless.
2 *(adj) Squash is an energetic sport.* strenuous, vigorous, fast-moving, active.

energy
1 *(n) I admire Marco's energy.* vitality, stamina, strength, vigour, drive, get-up-and-go *(informal)*, enthusiasm, liveliness, spirit, verve, zest, sparkle, exuberance, oomph *(informal)*.
2 *(n) Are you in favour of nuclear energy?* power, fuel.

enjoy
1 *(v) I enjoy cycling. See* **like** 2.
2 *(v) My parents enjoy good food.* love, appreciate, relish, take pleasure in, have a taste for, delight in, revel in, savour.
OPPOSITES: dislike, hate.
3 **enjoy yourself** *(v) Enjoy yourself at the party!* have a good time, have fun, have a laugh *(informal)*, have a ball *(informal)*, let your hair down, have the time of your life.

enjoyable
(adj) An enjoyable holiday. pleasant, delightful, fun, amusing, entertaining, pleasurable, lovely, great *(informal)*.

enlarge
(v) The council plans to enlarge the local sports field. extend, expand, make bigger, make larger, widen, lengthen, add to, develop, supplement, augment, blow up *(photograph) (informal)*, magnify *(image)*.
OPPOSITE: reduce.

enormous
(adj) Marcie eats an enormous amount of chocolate. huge, vast, massive, immense, colossal, gigantic, tremendous, prodigious, monstrous, mountainous, astronomic, stupendous, humongous *(informal)*, mammoth, monster.
OPPOSITES: tiny, minute.

enough
(adj) I think we have enough supplies for the journey. sufficient, adequate, ample, abundant, plenty of.
OPPOSITES: insufficient, inadequate.

enquire *see* **ask** 1.

enter
1 *(v) I let Mrs Badger enter in front of me.* go in, come in, move in, pass in.
OPPOSITE: leave.
2 *(v) Will you enter the competition?* take part in, participate in, sign up for, put your name down for, go in for, volunteer for, enrol in, be a competitor in.

3 *(v) Enter the results of the experiment in your notebook.* record, note down, write, take down, jot down, log, list, insert.

entertain
1 *(v) This game will entertain you while you're ill.* amuse, keep you amused, occupy, keep you occupied, cheer you up, divert, distract, delight, please, interest.
2 *(v) My parents like to entertain guests.* receive, invite, welcome, show hospitality to, play host to, wine and dine, put up.

entertaining
(adj) An entertaining novel. amusing, interesting, enjoyable, light-hearted, witty, funny, humorous, comical, hilarious, delightful, charming, enchanting.

entertainment *see* **amusement** 2.

enthralling *see* **fascinating**.

enthusiasm
(n) Tristan approaches his work with enthusiasm. eagerness, interest, relish, zest, excitement, keenness, passion, fervour, zeal, devotion, delight.
OPPOSITES: apathy, indifference.

enthusiastic
1 *(adj) Alice is an enthusiastic football fan.* keen, avid, eager, ardent, fervent, passionate, fanatical, zealous, mad keen *(informal)*, devoted, committed, earnest.
OPPOSITES: apathetic, half-hearted.
2 *(adj) Halim is always so enthusiastic.* positive, optimistic, exuberant, spirited, ebullient, lively, willing.
OPPOSITES: apathetic, indifferent.

entire *see* **whole**.

entrance
1 *(n) Don't block the entrance.* way in, entry, gateway, gate, doorway, door, drive, opening, access, approach.
OPPOSITE: exit.
2 *(n) Entrance to the museum is free.* admission, admittance, entry, access.
3 *(n) Famous Fred made a dramatic entrance.* entry, appearance, arrival.
OPPOSITE: exit.

envious
(adj) Toby looked envious when he saw my new bike. jealous, green with envy, green-eyed, resentful, grudging, covetous.

environment
1 *(n) I like to see animals in their natural environment.* surroundings *(plural)*, setting, habitat, location, territory, domain.
2 *(n) I can't work in this environment.* surroundings *(plural)*, situation, conditions *(plural)*, atmosphere.

envy
1 *(n) Toby was filled with envy when he saw my new bike.* jealousy, covetousness, desire, resentment, bitterness, discontent, the green-eyed monster *(informal)*.
2 *(v) It's pointless to envy other people's success.* be envious of, be jealous of, resent, begrudge, covet.

episode
1 *(n) Did you see the last episode of "WestEnders"?* instalment, part, section, scene, chapter.
2 *(n) I'd rather forget that embarrassing episode. See* **event** 1.

equal
1 *(adj) The boys are equal in their ability.* identical, alike, the same, comparable, evenly matched, evenly balanced, level, neck and neck, at level pegging *(informal)*.
2 *(adj) Two dozen is equal to 24.* equivalent, identical, the same as.
3 *(v) Two plus two will always equal four.* be equal to, make, add up to, total, amount to, correspond to, equate to.
4 *(v) We managed to equal the scores by half-time.* level, even up, balance, equalize.
5 *(v) Nothing can equal a steaming hot bath.* compare with, match, be as good as, match up to, touch, rival, measure up to, come near, hold a candle to *(informal)*.

equipment
(n) Do you have all your equipment for the expedition? gear, tackle, stuff, apparatus, tools *(plural)*, baggage, supplies *(plural)*.

erase
(v) Erase that word from your essay. remove, delete, rub out, wipe out, scratch out, cross out, strike out, cancel, expunge.

erode *see* **wear away**.

errand
(n) Mum gave me an errand to do in town. job, task, message, assignment, mission.

error *see* **mistake** 1.

escape
1 *(v) Burglar Beryl longs to escape from prison.* get away, run away, break loose, break free, break out of, bolt, abscond, scarper *(slang)*, do a bunk *(slang)*, do a runner *(slang)*, flit *(informal)*, flee, fly.
2 *(v) Don't let the oil escape from the barrel. See* **leak** 2.
3 *(v) Sid always tries to escape the washing-up.* avoid, evade, shirk, dodge, get out of, wriggle out of, duck *(informal)*.
4 *(n) Burglar Beryl plans to make her escape tonight.* getaway, break-out, flight.

essay
(n) I have to write an essay for homework. composition, piece, story, report, paper, extended essay, dissertation, review.

essential
(adj) Essential instructions. necessary, vital, crucial, indispensable, important, basic, fundamental, key.
OPPOSITES: inessential, unnecessary.

establish
1 *(v) Mum aims to establish a successful business.* set up, start, begin, found, get going, get off the ground *(informal)*, create, form, build, construct, originate.
2 *(v) I need to establish exactly what happened.* find out, ascertain, determine, confirm, prove, verify, authenticate.

estimate
1 *(v) Try to estimate the cost of this dress.* assess, evaluate, guess, judge, work out, calculate, reckon, weigh up, gauge.
2 *(n) Annie supplied an estimate for her work.* quotation, price, costing, valuation.

eternal
(adj) Eternal life. everlasting, endless, never-ending, without end, immortal, infinite, limitless, undying, timeless.
OPPOSITES: ephemeral, transitory.

even
1 *(adj) An even surface.* level, flat, smooth, horizontal, straight, flush.
OPPOSITES: uneven, rough, sloping.
2 *(adj) An even flow of water.* steady, regular, consistent, constant, unvarying, smooth, continuous, uninterrupted.
OPPOSITES: erratic, irregular.
3 *(adj) The scores are even.* level, equal, identical, all square, at level pegging *(informal)*, tied, drawn, neck and neck.
OPPOSITE: unequal.

evening
(n) dusk, nightfall, twilight, sunset, sundown, gloaming *(old-fashioned)*.

event
1 *(n) I'd rather forget that unfortunate event.* incident, episode, affair, business, matter, occasion, occurrence, experience.
2 *(n) We've been planning this event for months.* activity, do *(informal)*, function, occasion, ceremony, entertainment.
3 *(n) A sports event. See* **competition** 1.

eventually *see* **finally** 1.

evidence
1 *(n) The detectives need evidence.* proof, confirmation, documentation, data.
2 *(n) Is there any evidence of damage?* indication, sign, trace, symptoms *(plural)*.

evident *see* **obvious**.

evil
1 *(adj) This evil deed must be punished.* wicked, sinful, bad, diabolical, fiendish, villainous, vile, depraved, immoral, corrupt, atrocious, vicious, malicious, wrong.
OPPOSITES: good, virtuous.
2 *(n) We must overcome evil.* wickedness, sin, sinfulness, depravity, corruption, vice, immorality, villainy, wrongdoing, malice.
OPPOSITE: good.

exact
1 *(adj) Are these measurements exact? See* **accurate** 1.
2 *(adj) At that exact moment, I sneezed.* very, precise, specific, particular, actual.
3 *(adj) An exact copy.* faithful, identical, perfect, precise, strict, true, flawless.
OPPOSITE: rough.

exaggerate
(v) Jo tends to exaggerate her problems. overstate, overemphasize, magnify, overplay, dramatize, embellish, embroider, make too much of, play up, inflate.
OPPOSITES: play down, understate.

examination
1 *(n) A school examination.* exam, test, assessment, oral, practical.
2 *(n) A medical examination.* checkup, investigation, observation, inspection, test, scan, probe, once-over *(informal)*.

examine
(v) Detectives will examine the evidence. look at, inspect, study, look into, go over, go through, sift through, scrutinize, survey, check, consider, weigh up, analyse, check out, investigate, explore, probe, test.

example
1 *(n) This is an example of Finn's bad behaviour.* instance, illustration, case, case in point, sample, specimen.
2 *(n) Rosa has set an example for you to follow.* model, pattern, standard, ideal.

exasperate *see* **annoy** 1.

excellent
(adj) An excellent film. superb, brilliant, fantastic *(informal)*, wonderful, terrific *(informal)*, marvellous, outstanding, great, first-class, first-rate, impressive, magnificent, splendid, fine, exceptional, superlative, remarkable, extraordinary, tremendous *(informal)*, sensational *(informal)*, stunning *(informal)*.
OPPOSITES: terrible, inferior.

exception
(n) It's usually warm in July; this snow is an exception. rarity, freak, oddity, peculiarity, special case, quirk, anomaly, irregularity.

exceptional
1 *(adj) This hot weather is exceptional for March. See* **unusual** 1.
2 *(adj) Your work is exceptional. See* **excellent**.

exchange
(v) May I exchange this shirt for a bigger one? swap, change, switch, replace with, trade.

excited
(adj) Everyone was excited before the party. animated, worked up, wound up *(informal)*, agitated, overwrought, high *(informal)*, hyper *(informal)*, restless, wild, feverish, frantic, frenzied, hysterical.

excitement
1 *(n) Gemma was beside herself with excitement.* eagerness, anticipation, exhilaration, enthusiasm, elation, agitation.
2 *(n) I like films that are full of excitement.* tension, suspense, thrills *(plural)*, action, adventure, drama, kicks *(plural)* *(informal)*.
3 *(n) What's all the excitement about?* commotion, fuss, activity, confusion, furore, hubbub, kerfuffle *(informal)*.

exciting
(adj) An exciting film. thrilling, dramatic, exhilarating, electrifying, fast-moving, action-packed, cliffhanging, nail-biting, heart-stopping, spine-tingling, stirring, gripping, compelling, riveting.
OPPOSITES: boring, dull.

exclude
(v) If you try to spoil the game we'll exclude you. leave you out, ostracize, ignore, pass you over, leave you out in the cold *(informal)*, shut you out, bar, ban, throw you out, kick you out *(informal)*.

excruciating *see* **agonizing**.

excuse
1 *(v) I can't excuse your behaviour.* forgive, pardon, condone, make allowances for, overlook, ignore, tolerate.
2 *(v) Dodgy Dave tried to excuse his actions.* defend, justify, explain, vindicate, give reasons for.
3 *(n) What's your excuse for arriving so late?* reason, justification, grounds *(plural)*, defence, alibi *(legal)*, pretext.

exercise
1 *(v) You'll get fat if you don't exercise.* keep fit, work out, train, play sport, exert yourself, pump iron *(slang)*.
2 *(n) Exercise is good for you.* activity, training, exertion, sport, games *(plural)*, working out, pumping iron *(slang)*, physical jerks *(plural)* *(informal)*.

exhausted
(adj) After the race I was exhausted. tired out, worn out, ready to drop, shattered *(informal)*, dead tired, weary, drained, dead beat *(informal)*, done in *(informal)*, whacked *(informal)*, zonked *(slang)*.

exhausting
(adj) An exhausting job. tiring, gruelling, arduous, strenuous, draining, punishing, backbreaking, killing *(informal)*, difficult, hard, laborious, taxing, testing.

exhibition *see* **display** 1.

exhilarating *see* **exciting**.

expand
1 *(v) Pipes expand when water freezes in them.* swell, enlarge, increase in size, widen, thicken, lengthen, dilate, fill out.
OPPOSITES: contract, shrink.
2 *(v) Dad wants to expand his business.* develop, build up, extend, enlarge.
3 *(v) It's a good idea, but you need to expand it. See* **develop** 5.

expect
1 *(v) I expect that Danni will arrive late.* assume, presume, suppose, imagine, reckon, guess *(informal)*, think, believe, envisage, anticipate, predict, foretell.
2 *(v) Can we expect some improvement?* look forward to, anticipate, look for, hope for, reckon on, bank on.
3 *(v) Dad will expect an apology.* insist on, demand, require, look for, call for, want.

expedition
(n) The explorers set out on an expedition. journey, voyage, trip, mission, quest, exploration, trek, safari, hike, tramp, tour.

expel
(v) The head may expel you from school. exclude, dismiss, ban, send you away, throw you out, turf you out *(informal)*.

expensive
(adj) An expensive holiday. dear, pricey *(informal),* costly, overpriced, exorbitant, extortionate, extravagant, steep *(informal).*
OPPOSITES: cheap, inexpensive.

experience
1 *(n) What an amazing experience!* incident, occurrence, adventure, episode, affair, happening, event, ordeal.
2 *(n) For this job, you need the right experience.* skill, know-how *(informal),* practical knowledge, training, background.
3 *(n) You will learn by experience.* doing, taking part, practice, participation, involvement, familiarity.
4 *(v) You may have to experience hardship.* undergo, suffer, endure, face, go through, live through, encounter, meet.

experienced
(adj) Bo is an experienced cook. practised, seasoned, skilled, accomplished, expert, proficient, competent, trained, qualified.
OPPOSITE: inexperienced.

experiment
1 *(n) Write up the results of your experiment.* investigation, practical, inquiry, test, trial, demonstration, research.
2 *(v) I love to experiment when I cook.* try things out, improvise, explore.

expert
1 *(n) We need an expert to mend our computer.* specialist, professional, consultant, authority, pro *(informal),* pundit, boffin *(informal),* anorak *(slang).*
OPPOSITE: novice.
2 *(n) Dean is an expert at juggling.* master, genius, wizard, ace *(informal),* virtuoso, past master, maestro, whiz *(informal),* whiz kid *(informal),* dab hand *(informal).*
3 *(adj) An expert footballer. See* **skilful**.

explain
1 *(v) Can you explain what this means?* make clear, clarify, spell out, throw light on, elucidate, interpret, define, describe.
2 *(v) Please explain why you are late.* give an explanation for, give a reason for, account for, justify.

explode
(v) This bomb may explode without any warning. blow up, go off, detonate, erupt.

exploit *see* **take advantage of**.

explore
(v) Let's explore the castle. investigate, scout around, take a look around, check out *(informal),* survey, reconnoitre, tour.

explorer
(n) discoverer, traveller, voyager.

explosion
(n) The explosion made the windows shake. blast, bang, boom, rumble, crash, detonation, report.

expose
1 *(v) Dad rolled up his trousers to expose his hairy legs. See* **reveal** 1.

2 *(v) The journalist was determined to expose the truth.* uncover, bring to light, make known, lay bare, unmask, reveal, disclose, divulge, leak, blow wide open *(slang),* blow the whistle on *(informal).*

express
1 *(v) Nasim was keen to express his views.* state, put into words, voice, make known, air, put across, communicate, point out, give vent to, articulate, verbalize.
2 *(adj) Take the express train.* high-speed, fast, nonstop, direct, through.

expression
1 *(n) Sim's face wore a strange expression.* look, appearance, aspect, air.
2 *(n) Where did you hear that expression?* word, phrase, saying, turn of phrase, idiom, term, choice of words, remark.

extend
1 *(v) Extend the elastic. See* **stretch** 1.
2 *(v) The desert seemed to extend for miles. See* **stretch** 4.
3 *(v) We plan to extend our house.* enlarge, build on to, add on to, make bigger, make larger, expand.

extinct
(adj) That species is extinct. dead, defunct, vanished, lost, died out, wiped out, gone.
OPPOSITES: surviving, extant.

extra
(adj) This extension will give us extra space. more, additional, further, added, spare, surplus, excess, leftover, superfluous.

extraordinary
1 *(adj) Carl's artistic talent is extraordinary.* exceptional, outstanding, unique, out of the ordinary, unprecedented, remarkable, amazing, phenomenal, unusual, rare.
OPPOSITES: unexceptional, ordinary.
2 *(adj) Ziggy wears some extraordinary clothes. See* **strange** 1.

extravagant
1 *(adj) Letty is so extravagant; she's always wasting money.* wasteful, careless with money, self-indulgent, lavish, imprudent.
OPPOSITES: thrifty, economical.
2 *(adj) What an extravagant gift!* lavish, costly, expensive, flashy, showy, over the top, overgenerous, excessive, immoderate, outrageous, OTT *(slang).*

extreme
1 *(adj) Extreme pain.* severe, intense, acute, great.
2 *(adj) Extreme measures. See* **drastic**.
3 *(adj) Extreme political views.* fanatical, radical, uncompromising, unreasonable, hardline, way-out *(informal),* outrageous, exaggerated, excessive, immoderate.
OPPOSITE: moderate.

extrovert
(adj) Kylie is so extrovert; she's the life and soul of the party. outgoing, lively, vivacious, bubbly, sociable, gregarious, friendly, confident, exuberant, animated.
OPPOSITES: introverted, withdrawn.

Ff

fabric *see* **material**.
fabulous *(informal) see* **fantastic** 3.
face
1 *(n) Burglar Beryl has a distinctive face.* features *(plural),* appearance, countenance *(old-fashioned),* mug *(slang),* kisser *(slang).*
2 *(n) Lisa made a horrible face.* scowl, grimace, frown, smirk, pout.
3 *(v) Our new house will face the sea.* overlook, look onto, look towards, front onto, be opposite.
4 *(v) The explorers will face many dangers.* encounter, experience, come up against, come across, meet, be confronted by.
5 *(v) I can't face this problem on my own.* deal with, cope with, face up to, tackle, confront, meet head-on, brave, get to grips with, come to terms with.

faces and features		
faces	**complexions**	
angular	ashen	pasty
babyish	black	peaches-
chubby	blotchy	and-cream
craggy	bronzed	pimply
flabby	brown	pitted
fleshy	clear	radiant
gaunt	coarse	rosy
haggard	dark	rough
heart-shaped	delicate	ruddy
long	dusky	sallow
oval	fair	scarred
pinched	florid	shiny
plump	flushed	sickly
podgy	freckled	smooth
round	fresh	spotty
square	glowing	stubbly
strong-jawed	greasy	swarthy
triangular	healthy	tanned
	ivory	unshaven
	oily	wan
	olive	white
	pale	wrinkled
	pallid	

heart-shaped face

stubbly complexion

haggard face

fact

1 *(n) The fact is that pigs can't fly.* truth, reality, naked truth, actuality, certainty. OPPOSITE: fiction.

2 **facts** *(plural n) Give me the facts.* details *(plural)*, particulars *(plural)*, information, data, whole story, lowdown *(informal)*, info *(informal)*, gen *(informal)*.

factual

(adj) Write a factual account of your holiday. true, accurate, true-to-life, truthful, honest, faithful, authentic, realistic, matter-of-fact, exact, precise, objective, unbiased, unvarnished. OPPOSITES: fictional, imaginary.

fade

1 *(v) I hope my shirt doesn't fade in the wash.* lose colour, become pale, become bleached, become washed out, whiten.

2 *(v) Bright sunlight will fade the carpet.* bleach, discolour, dull, whiten.

3 *(v) The light began to fade.* die away, wane, dwindle, fail, diminish, weaken, grow faint, dim, disappear, vanish.

fail

1 *(v) I bet I'll fail in the exam.* be unsuccessful, not pass, not make the grade *(informal)*, not come up to scratch *(informal)*, come to grief, come a cropper *(informal)*, flunk *(informal)*. OPPOSITES: succeed, pass.

2 *(v) Henry's plan is bound to fail.* fall through, be unsuccessful, fall flat, misfire, miscarry, come to nothing, be frustrated, founder, flop *(informal)*, fizzle out. OPPOSITES: succeed, prosper.

3 *(v) I hope the engine doesn't fail.* cut out, give out, stop working, break down, die, conk out *(informal)*, cease to function.

4 *(v) Flash Frank is afraid his business will fail.* collapse, crash, go bankrupt, go under, go to the wall, close down, go out of business, fold *(informal)*, flop *(informal)*, go bust *(informal)*, go broke *(informal)*. OPPOSITES: succeed, prosper, thrive.

5 *(v) Aunt Bertha's eyesight is starting to fail.* deteriorate, weaken, decline, get worse, degenerate, go. OPPOSITES: improve, strengthen.

6 *(v) I won't fail you.* let you down, disappoint, abandon, desert, forsake.

failing see **weakness** 1.

failure

1 *(n) The match ended in failure.* defeat, disaster, disappointment, frustration. OPPOSITE: success.

2 *(n) The play was a failure.* disaster, fiasco, flop *(informal)*, catastrophe, nonstarter, washout *(informal)*. OPPOSITE: success.

3 *(n) Cyril thinks he's a failure.* loser, no-hoper *(informal)*, ne'er-do-well, non-achiever, disappointment, incompetent. OPPOSITE: success.

4 *(n) The storm caused a power failure.* cut, loss, breakdown, stoppage, outage.

faint

1 *(v) Simone will faint when she sees all this blood.* pass out, black out, lose consciousness, keel over *(informal)*, collapse, swoon *(old-fashioned)*.

2 *(adj) Anjali felt faint after her run.* dizzy, giddy, light-headed, muzzy, woozy *(informal)*, unsteady, weak, exhausted.

3 *(adj) There's a faint pink glow in the sky.* pale, soft, delicate, hazy, misty, vague. OPPOSITES: bright, distinct.

4 *(adj) Sarah spoke in a faint voice.* weak, feeble, low, soft, scarcely audible, hushed, whispered, subdued, muffled, muted. OPPOSITES: loud, clear.

fair

1 *(adj) Jenny has fair hair.* See **blonde** 2.

2 *(adj) Mrs Badger may be strict, but she is always fair.* just, impartial, even-handed, fair-minded, unbiased, unprejudiced, objective, open-minded. OPPOSITES: unfair, unjust.

3 *(adj) I hope the weather will be fair tomorrow.* fine, dry, clear, bright, sunny, cloudless, favourable, clement. OPPOSITE: foul.

4 *(adj) Your work is fair.* adequate, satisfactory, acceptable, passable, reasonable, respectable, decent, not bad, all right, pretty good, average, middling, mediocre, tolerable, so-so *(informal)*.

5 *(n) We went on lots of rides at the fair.* See **funfair**.

6 *(n) The school fair was a success.* fête, bazaar, sale, gala, carnival, festival.

7 *(n) Our village is putting on a craft fair.* exhibition, show, display, exhibit.

fairly see **quite** 1.

fairy

(n) pixie, elf, sprite, imp, brownie, leprechaun. ❖ *Also see* **fantasy words**.

faithful

1 *(adj) A faithful friend.* loyal, devoted, true, reliable, dependable, trustworthy, trusty, constant, staunch, unwavering. OPPOSITES: disloyal, faithless.

2 *(adj) Is this a faithful account of the accident?* See **true** 2.

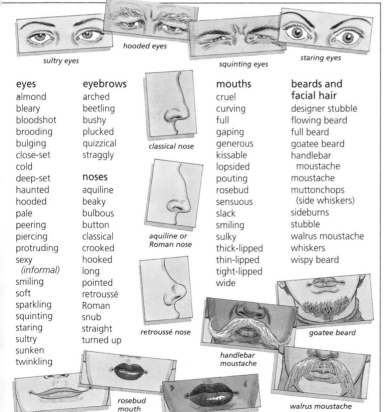

sultry eyes

hooded eyes

squinting eyes

staring eyes

eyes
almond
bleary
bloodshot
brooding
bulging
close-set
cold
deep-set
haunted
hooded
pale
peering
piercing
protruding
sexy
(informal)
smiling
soft
sparkling
squinting
staring
sultry
sunken
twinkling

eyebrows
arched
beetling
bushy
plucked
quizzical
straggly

noses
aquiline
beaky
bulbous
button
classical
crooked
hooked
long
pointed
retroussé
Roman
snub
straight
turned up

classical nose

aquiline or Roman nose

retroussé nose

handlebar moustache

rosebud mouth

curving mouth

full mouth

mouths
cruel
curving
full
gaping
generous
kissable
lopsided
pouting
rosebud
sensuous
slack
smiling
sulky
thick-lipped
thin-lipped
tight-lipped
wide

beards and facial hair
designer stubble
flowing beard
full beard
goatee beard
handlebar
  moustache
moustache
muttonchops
  (side whiskers)
sideburns
stubble
walrus moustache
whiskers
wispy beard

goatee beard

walrus moustache

Also see **hair & hairstyles**.

fake

fake

1 *(n)* *This painting is a fake.* copy, forgery, imitation, reproduction, sham, counterfeit.
OPPOSITE: original.
2 *(n)* *That man is a fake.* impostor, fraud *(informal)*, phoney *(informal)*, charlatan.
3 *(adj)* *Dodgy Dave deals in fake money.* counterfeit, forged, false, bogus, sham, phoney *(informal)*, imitation.
OPPOSITES: genuine, authentic.
4 *(v)* *Carol tried to fake an attack of flu.* feign, put on, sham, simulate, counterfeit.

fall

1 *(v)* *Be careful you don't fall.* trip, slip, fall over, trip over, overbalance, stumble, go head over heels, come a cropper *(informal)*, tumble, collapse, fall in a heap.
2 *(v)* *The plane began to fall.* See **drop** 2.
3 *(v)* *Watch the leaves fall to the ground.* drift, float, waft, flutter, swirl, tumble.
4 *(v)* *The flood water started to fall.* sink, subside, recede, ebb, abate, lower.
OPPOSITE: rise.
5 *(v)* *Pupil numbers are expected to fall.* See **decrease** 2.
6 *(n)* *Nat had a bad fall.* tumble, spill.
7 *(n)* *There has been a fall in the number of crimes* See **decrease** 1.
8 *(n)* *We're studying the fall of the Roman Empire.* See **collapse** 3.

fall apart *see* **disintegrate** 2.

fall asleep

(v) *Gran tends to fall asleep in front of the TV.* go to sleep, doze off, nod off *(informal)*, drop off *(informal)*.
OPPOSITE: wake up.

fall in love with

(phrase) *Could you ever fall in love with me?* fall for, become fond of, lose your heart to, take a fancy to, become infatuated with, be smitten by, be bowled over by *(informal)*, become attached to.

fall out *(informal)* *see* **argue** 1.

fall over *see* **fall** 1.

fall through *see* **fail** 2.

false

1 *(adj)* *It's false to say that pigs can fly.* incorrect, untrue, wrong, inaccurate, mistaken, erroneous, misleading.
OPPOSITES: true, correct.
2 *(adj)* *Dodgy Dave has a false passport.* See **fake** 3.
3 *(adj)* *Burglar Beryl uses a false name.* made-up, assumed, fictitious, invented, phoney *(informal)*, spurious, unreal.
OPPOSITES: real, genuine.

familiar

1 *(adj)* *That's a familiar sight.* well-known, common, recognizable, everyday, normal, commonplace, routine, frequent, ordinary.
OPPOSITES: unfamiliar, strange.
2 **familiar with** *(adj)* *Are you familiar with the rules of football?* acquainted with, knowledgeable about, conversant with, well up on, versed in, informed about.

family

1 *(n)* *Dad stayed at home to look after the family.* children *(plural)*, offspring, brood.
2 *(n)* *When did you last see your family?* relatives *(plural)*, relations *(plural)*, nearest and dearest, people *(plural)*, flesh and blood, kin, kith and kin.
3 *(n)* *Hugh comes from a noble family.* dynasty, clan, line, tribe, ancestors *(plural)*.

famous

(adj) *A famous musician.* well-known, world-famous, prominent, renowned, celebrated, legendary, notable, eminent, distinguished, leading, illustrious.
OPPOSITES: unknown, obscure.

fan

1 *(n)* *Hanif is a computer fan.* fanatic, addict, enthusiast, buff *(informal)*, freak *(informal)*, fiend *(informal)*, nut *(slang)*.
2 *(n)* *Maisie is a fan of Famous Fred.* supporter, admirer, follower, groupie *(slang)*, devotee.

fanatical

1 *(adj)* *Sonia is a fanatical football supporter.* See **enthusiastic** 1.
2 *(adj)* *Dan holds fanatical views.* extreme, irrational, extremist, dogmatic, obsessive, radical, militant, bigoted, narrow-minded.

fancy

1 *(adj)* *A fancy vase.* See **decorative**.
2 *(v)* *I fancy a night out.* feel like, would like, could do with, feel the need for, want, long for, hanker after, yearn for.
3 *(v)* *(informal)* *Mel will really fancy you in that shirt.* go for, fall for, like the look of, be attracted to, take to, take a liking to, be captivated by, be crazy about *(informal)*, desire, lust after.

fantastic

1 *(adj)* *I saw a fantastic creature with two heads.* strange, peculiar, weird, odd, grotesque, outlandish, freakish, exotic, fabulous, fantastical, fairy-tale.
2 *(adj)* *(informal)* *I've put a fantastic amount of work into this project.* huge, enormous, massive, great, tremendous, terrific, overwhelming.
3 *(adj)* *(informal)* *I had a fantastic time.* great *(informal)*, wonderful, brilliant, excellent, terrific *(informal)*, marvellous, amazing *(informal)*, incredible *(informal)*, fabulous *(informal)*, superb, tremendous *(informal)*, smashing *(informal)*, sensational *(informal)*, mega *(slang)*, wicked *(slang)*.
OPPOSITES: awful, terrible.

fantasy

1 *(n)* *I love reading tales of fantasy.* make-believe, imagination, invention, fiction.
2 *(n)* *It's just a fantasy; it isn't real.* dream, daydream, flight of fancy, figment of the imagination, illusion, hallucination, vision, delusion, apparition, invention, fabrication.
3 *(adj)* *Miranda lives in a fantasy world.* dream, imaginary, make-believe, pretend, unreal, fairy-tale.

fantasy words

fantasy characters
dwarf
elf
enchanter
enchantress
giant
gnome
goblin
healer
hobgoblin
king
knight
magician
maiden
mermaid
ogre
pixie
prince
princess
queen
seer (prophet)
sorcerer
sorceress
troll
warrior
witch
wizard
wood nymph

fantasy creatures
dragon
sea monster
serpent
unicorn
winged horse

wood nymph

ogre

unicorn

hobgoblin

serpent

dragon's lair

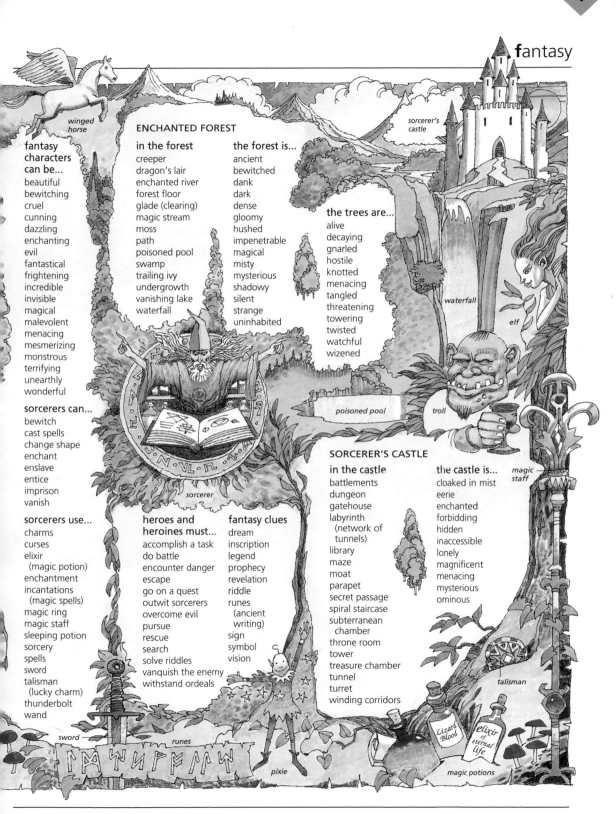

winged horse

ENCHANTED FOREST

fantasy characters can be...
beautiful
bewitching
cruel
cunning
dazzling
enchanting
evil
fantastical
frightening
incredible
invisible
magical
malevolent
menacing
mesmerizing
monstrous
terrifying
unearthly
wonderful

sorcerers can...
bewitch
cast spells
change shape
enchant
enslave
entice
imprison
vanish

sorcerers use...
charms
curses
elixir
  (magic potion)
enchantment
incantations
  (magic spells)
magic ring
magic staff
sleeping potion
sorcery
spells
sword
talisman
  (lucky charm)
thunderbolt
wand

in the forest
creeper
dragon's lair
enchanted river
forest floor
glade (clearing)
magic stream
moss
path
poisoned pool
swamp
trailing ivy
undergrowth
vanishing lake
waterfall

heroes and heroines must...
accomplish a task
do battle
encounter danger
escape
go on a quest
outwit sorcerers
overcome evil
pursue
rescue
search
solve riddles
vanquish the enemy
withstand ordeals

the forest is...
ancient
bewitched
dank
dark
dense
gloomy
hushed
impenetrable
magical
misty
mysterious
shadowy
silent
strange
uninhabited

fantasy clues
dream
inscription
legend
prophecy
revelation
riddle
runes
  (ancient
  writing)
sign
symbol
vision

the trees are...
alive
decaying
gnarled
hostile
knotted
menacing
tangled
threatening
towering
twisted
watchful
wizened

sorcerer's castle

waterfall

elf

poisoned pool

troll

sorcerer

SORCERER'S CASTLE

in the castle
battlements
dungeon
gatehouse
labyrinth
  (network of
  tunnels)
library
maze
moat
parapet
secret passage
spiral staircase
subterranean
  chamber
throne room
tower
treasure chamber
tunnel
turret
winding corridors

the castle is...
cloaked in mist
eerie
enchanted
forbidding
hidden
inaccessible
lonely
magnificent
menacing
mysterious
ominous

magic staff

talisman

sword

runes

pixie

Lizard Blood

elixir of eternal life

magic potions

far

far
(adv) Have you travelled far? a long way, a great distance, a good way, miles.

faraway *see* **distant**.

far-fetched *see* **incredible 1**.

farm
(n) TYPES OF FARM: arable farm, croft *(Scotland)*, dairy farm, fish farm, fruit farm, hill farm, hop garden, livestock farm, market garden, organic farm, pig farm, plantation *(tropical countries)*, poultry farm, ranch *(North America)*, sheep station *(Australia, New Zealand)*, smallholding, stud farm *(horse-breeding farm)*, vineyard.

farming
(n) agriculture.

fascinate
(v) This film will fascinate you. intrigue, enthral, engross, hold you spellbound, mesmerize, transfix, rivet, entrance, captivate, bewitch, tantalize.

fascinating
(adj) A fascinating story. intriguing, enthralling, compelling, gripping, riveting, engrossing, absorbing, spellbinding, mesmerizing, captivating, tantalizing.

fashion
1 *(n) These new jeans are the latest fashion.* style, trend, thing, look, cut, craze, fad, vogue, rage.
2 *(n) Jake is interested in fashion.* clothes *(plural)*, clothes design, the rag trade *(informal)*, the clothing industry, couture.

fashionable
(adj) Minty always wears fashionable clothes. the latest, up-to-date, trendy *(informal)*, stylish, chic, smart, up-to-the-minute, modern, in, happening *(informal)*, cool *(informal)*, hip *(slang)*.
OPPOSITES: unfashionable, frumpy.

fast
1 *(adj) We had a fast tour of the castle.* quick, rapid, swift, brisk, speedy, hasty, hurried, flying, breakneck.
OPPOSITES: slow, leisurely.
2 *(adj) Flash Frank drives a fast car.* speedy, nippy *(informal)*, express *(train)*, high-speed *(train)*, supersonic *(plane)*.
OPPOSITE: slow.
3 *(adv) Rory finished his homework fast.* quickly, rapidly, in no time, swiftly, speedily, hurriedly, hastily, in a flash, like a shot *(informal)*, posthaste, pdq *(slang)*.

fasten
1 *(v) Fasten your bike to the railings.* secure, attach, chain, lock, padlock, bolt, tie, lash, fix, clamp, screw.
OPPOSITES: unfasten, detach.
2 *(v) Fasten these papers together.* attach, secure, clip, clasp, staple, pin, tack, tie, bind, tape, fix, stick, paste.
OPPOSITES: unfasten, detach.
3 *(v) Phil bent down to fasten his shoe.* do up, tie, lace, knot, buckle, strap.
OPPOSITE: undo.

4 *(v) My jeans won't fasten.* close, button, zip up, meet.

fat
1 *(adj) A fat man.* overweight, obese, flabby, stout, large, corpulent, paunchy, portly, plump, podgy, pudgy, chubby, tubby, potbellied, beefy *(informal)*.
OPPOSITE: thin.
2 *(adj) A fat book.* thick, weighty, bulky.
OPPOSITE: slim.

fatal
1 *(adj) A fatal disease.* deadly, lethal, terminal, killer, incurable, inoperable, malignant, mortal *(wound)*.
OPPOSITES: harmless, minor.
2 *(adj) The pilot made a fatal mistake.* See **disastrous**.

fate
1 *(n) Fate brought us together.* destiny, providence, the stars *(plural)*, fortune.
2 *(n) Sir Lancelittle accepted his fate.* destiny, doom, lot, future, end.

father
(n) dad *(informal)*, daddy *(informal)*, pop *(informal)*, pa *(informal)*, papa *(informal)*, old man *(informal)*, old boy *(informal)*.

fatty
(adj) Chips are a fatty food. greasy, oily.

fault
1 *(n) There's a fault in this computer program.* flaw, defect, bug *(informal)*, malfunction, mistake, error, inaccuracy, weakness, failing, shortcoming, snag.
2 *(n) It's all my fault.* responsibility.

faulty
(adj) Our new toaster is faulty. broken, not working, defective, out of order, inoperative, on the blink *(informal)*, damaged, unusable, useless.

favourite
1 *(adj) Who is your favourite singer?* preferred, best-loved, most-liked, ideal.
2 *(n) Benji is Mrs Badger's favourite.* pet, darling, blue-eyed boy *(informal)*.

fear
1 *(n) Sir Lancelittle shrank back in fear.* terror, dread, horror, fright, panic, trepidation, alarm, dismay, consternation, fear and trembling, awe.
2 *(n) Paul has a fear of heights.* horror, dread, terror, phobia about, thing about *(informal)*, hang-up about *(informal)*.
3 *(n) My greatest fear is that I might fail.* worry, concern, anxiety, doubt, suspicion.
4 *(v) There's no need to fear going to the dentist.* See **dread 1**.

fearless *see* **brave**.

feast
(n) banquet, dinner, slap-up meal *(informal)*, spread *(informal)*, nosh-up *(slang)*, blowout *(slang)*.

feat
(n) Crossing the rapids was an amazing feat. achievement, exploit, deed, act, stunt, accomplishment, performance.

feathers
(plural n) Birds' feathers. plumage, down.

feathery
(adj) The clouds looked feathery. wispy, fluffy, fleecy, downy.

feature
1 *(n) Which feature of this book do you like best?* aspect, detail, facet, side, characteristic, quality, attribute, point.
2 *(n) Amit wrote a feature for the school magazine.* See **article 1**.
3 *(v) The film will feature an unknown actress.* star, present, highlight, turn the spotlight on, give prominence to, promote.
4 **features** *(plural n) Can you describe Beryl's features?* See **face 1**.

fed up with
(adj) (informal) I'm fed up with your constant complaining. tired of, sick of *(informal)*, sick and tired of *(informal)*, weary of, bored with, browned off with *(informal)*, cheesed off with *(slang)*, hacked off with *(slang)*, irritated by, irked by.

feeble
1 *(adj) Hattie felt feeble after her illness.* See **weak 1**.
2 *(adj) Don't be so feeble!* See **weak 3**.
3 *(adj) That's a feeble excuse.* weak, poor, lame, flimsy, unconvincing, implausible, pathetic, inadequate.
OPPOSITE: convincing.

feed
(v) It costs a lot to feed a family of four. provide for, cater for, give food to, nourish, sustain.

feel
1 *(v) Feel the kitten's fur!* touch, stroke, run your hands over, fondle, caress, handle, finger, paw *(informal)*.
2 *(v) You won't feel any pain.* sense, be aware of, be conscious of, notice, perceive, experience, suffer, go through, undergo.
3 *(v) Do my hands feel cold?* seem, appear, strike you as.
4 *(v) Dom tried to feel for the light switch.* fumble, grope, feel around, explore.
5 *(v) What do you feel about fox-hunting?* See **think 1**.
6 **feel like** *(v) I feel like a night out.* See **fancy 2**.

feeling
1 *(n) Veronica lost all feeling in her fingers.* sensation, sense of touch, sensitivity, awareness.
2 *(n) I have a feeling I've been here before.* idea, funny feeling, hunch, notion, gut feeling *(informal)*, suspicion, sneaking suspicion, inkling, sense, impression.
3 *(n) Celia spoke with great feeling.* emotion, passion, fervour, warmth, enthusiasm, sentiment, affection.
4 *(n) There's a strange feeling in this room.* See **atmosphere 2**.
5 **feelings** *(plural n) It hurts my feelings when people laugh at me.* self-esteem, ego, sensibilities *(plural)*.

feelings

happy	sad	excited	annoyed	upset	surprised	worried
blissful	blue	eager	cross	dismayed	amazed	agitated
cheerful	dejected	enthusiastic	disgruntled	distraught	astonished	anxious
chirpy *(informal)*	depressed	feverish	exasperated	distressed	astounded	apprehensive
contented	despairing	frenzied	indignant	disturbed	dumbfounded	concerned
delighted	despondent	high *(informal)*	irritated	grieved	dumbstruck	distracted
ecstatic	doleful	hyper *(informal)*	miffed *(informal)*	hurt	flabbergasted	frantic
elated	down	hysterical	needled	pained	*(informal)*	fretful
euphoric	forlorn	overwrought	*(informal)*	shaken	gobsmacked	nervous
glad	gloomy	restless	vexed	shattered	*(slang)*	on edge
gleeful	glum	thrilled			incredulous	perturbed
jolly	grief-stricken	worked up	**angry**	**scared**	open-mouthed	tense
joyful	heartbroken		enraged	afraid	shocked	troubled
jubilant	low	**bored**	fuming	alarmed	speechless	uneasy
light-hearted	melancholy	apathetic	furious	frightened	staggered	
optimistic	miserable	fed up	incensed	horrified	startled	**confused**
overjoyed	mournful	*(informal)*	infuriated	panicky	stunned	baffled
perky	sorrowful	indifferent	irate	panic-stricken	stupefied	bewildered
pleased	tearful	jaded	livid	petrified	taken aback	dazed
rapturous	unhappy	listless	outraged	terrified	thunderstruck	disorientated
thrilled	wistful	weary	seething			fazed
						flummoxed
						flustered
						muddled
						mystified
						nonplussed
						perplexed
						puzzled

jubilant   despondent   listless   livid   petrified   perplexed

---

ferocious *see* **fierce** 1, 2.

fertile
(adj) A fertile field. fruitful, productive, rich, lush, well-manured, flourishing.
OPPOSITE: barren.

festival
(n) Our town is planning a festival to mark the end of the war. celebration, carnival, festivities *(plural),* jamboree, fête, gala day, feast, holiday, jubilee, commemoration.

fetch
1 *(v) Would you fetch Dad's suit from the cleaner's?* go and get, get, collect, pick up, call for, go for, bring, carry, retrieve.
2 *(v) This painting will fetch a fortune.* sell for, go for, bring in, make, yield, earn.

feud *see* **quarrel** 3.

feverish
1 *(adj) You seem feverish; have you got a temperature?* hot, flushed, fevered, burning, shivery, trembling.
2 *(adj) The classroom was filled with feverish activity.* frenzied, frenetic, frantic, hectic, excited, agitated, restless.

few
(adj) Few people have walked on the moon. not many, hardly any, scarcely any, one or two, a handful of, a small number of, a couple of *(informal).*
OPPOSITES: many, lots of.

fiasco *see* **failure** 2.

fictional *see* **imaginary** 1.

fiddle with
(v) Don't fiddle with your pencil case! fidget with, play with, toy with, finger, tinker with, tamper with, interfere with.

fidget
(v) Sit still and don't fidget! wriggle, squirm, jiggle, fiddle, jerk about, twitch, jitter *(informal),* mess about.

fidgety
(adj) Waiting makes me fidgety. restless, nervous, nervy, on edge, edgy, jumpy, twitchy, jittery *(informal),* uneasy, impatient, agitated, restive.

field
1 *(n) The cows are grazing in the field.* meadow, pasture, paddock, enclosure.
2 *(n) The players gathered on the sports field.* pitch, playing field, ground, arena.
3 *(n) Professor Peabody is an expert in the field of physics.* area, subject, sphere, discipline, department, domain.

fierce
1 *(adj) A fierce tiger.* ferocious, vicious, savage, wild, dangerous, fearsome, angry.
OPPOSITES: docile, tame.
2 *(adj) A fierce warrior.* ferocious, brutal, savage, violent, fearsome, cruel, ruthless, grim, bloodthirsty, menacing, threatening, barbaric, murderous, tigerish, wolfish.
OPPOSITES: gentle, kind.

3 *(adj) A fierce storm. See* **violent** 3.
4 *(adj) Fierce competition.* strong, intense, keen, cutthroat, relentless, furious.

fiery
1 *(adj) Fiery coals. See* **burning** 1.
2 *(adj) A fiery personality.* hot-headed, passionate, impetuous, excitable, irritable, irascible, peppery, choleric, violent.
OPPOSITES: even-tempered, docile.

fight
1 *(v) The two armies prepared to fight.* do battle, take up arms, go to war, wage war, attack, mount an attack, cross swords, engage in hostilities, clash, struggle.
2 *(v) The boys began to fight in the playground.* brawl, scuffle, tussle, scrap *(informal),* grapple, spar, wrestle, box.
3 *(v) We fight all the time. See* **argue** 1.
4 *(v) We will fight the decision to close our school.* oppose, contest, resist, campaign against, protest against, take a stand against, dispute, defy, object to.
5 *(n) Many soldiers were wounded in the fight.* conflict, battle, skirmish, encounter, confrontation, struggle, clash, combat, action, raid, war, hostilities *(plural).*
6 *(n) There was a fight in the playground.* brawl, scuffle, tussle, punch-up *(informal),* scrap *(informal),* set-to *(informal),* free-for-all *(informal),* riot.
7 *(n) I've had a fight with my sister. See* **argument** 1.

fight back
(v) *Should you fight back if someone punches you?* defend yourself, hit back, put up a fight, retaliate, give tit for tat.

figure
1 (n) *Our phone number starts with the figure 8.* number, digit, numeral, symbol.
2 (n) *Sasha has a slim figure.* build, frame, shape, physique, body.
3 (n) *I saw a dim figure in the mist.* shape, shadow, form, outline, silhouette.
4 (n) *Queen Victoria is a famous historical figure.* personality, character, person, personage, celebrity.

figure out
1 (v) (informal) *Can you figure out the cost?* work out, calculate, count up, add up, tot up, compute, reckon up.
2 (v) (informal) *I can't figure out these instructions. See* **understand** 2.

fill
1 (v) *Don't fill your bag with rubbish.* pack, stuff, cram, load, overload.
OPPOSITE: empty.
2 (v) *Can I fill your glass?* fill up, fill to the brim, replenish, refill, top up (informal).
OPPOSITES: empty, drain.
3 (v) *Fill the hole with earth.* close up, block up, bung up, plug, stop up, seal.
4 (v) *The scent of roses seemed to fill the air.* pervade, permeate, suffuse, saturate.

fill in
1 (v) *Please fill in this questionnaire.* complete, answer, fill out.
2 **fill in for** (v) *Can you fill in for James while he's ill? See* **stand in for**.
3 **fill you in on** (phrase) (informal) *Can I fill you in on what's happened?* update you on, bring you up to date with, give you the facts about, brief you about, inform you about, acquaint you with.

filling
(adj) *A filling meal.* satisfying, substantial, hearty, ample, heavy, stodgy, square.

film
1 (v) *A camera crew are going to film the wedding.* record on film, capture on film, photograph, take pictures of, make a film of, video, televise, shoot.
2 (n) *This book has been made into a film.* motion picture, movie (informal), picture.
TYPES OF FILM: action film, adventure film, animated film, black-and-white film, blockbuster, cartoon, comedy, detective film, disaster film, drama, epic, fantasy film, feature film, gangster film, horror film, martial arts film, musical, romantic film, sci-fi (science fiction) film, silent film, spoof (informal), 3-D film, thriller, war film, weepy (informal), Western. ❖ *Also see* **television & film**.
3 (n) *A film of dust. See* **layer** 1.

filthy *see* **dirty** 1, 2.

final
1 (adj) *The final episode. See* **last** 1.

2 (adj) *The referee's decision is final.* absolute, conclusive, decisive, indisputable, unalterable, irrevocable, definitive, definite.

finally
1 (adv) *Finally, the bus arrived.* eventually, at last, at long last, at length, at the last minute, in the end, ultimately.
2 (adv) *Finally, I'd like to thank you all for coming.* lastly, in conclusion, to conclude, to sum up, in summary.

find
1 (v) *Pirate Peg was lucky to find the treasure.* discover, come across, stumble upon, hit upon, spot, catch sight of, locate, uncover, unearth, turn up, chance upon.
2 (v) *Did you manage to find your pencil case?* locate, track down, trace, get back, recover, retrieve, regain.
OPPOSITES: lose, mislay.

find out *see* **discover** 1, 3.

fine
1 (adj) *That's a fine painting.* great, magnificent, splendid, superb, excellent, first-class, exceptional, outstanding, exquisite, beautiful, admirable, masterly, superior.
OPPOSITES: poor, second-rate.
2 (adj) *It's fine for you to come on Saturday.* all right, O.K. (informal), convenient, acceptable, satisfactory.
3 (adj) *The weather will be fine tomorrow.* dry, bright, sunny, fair, pleasant, clear, cloudless, clement.
OPPOSITES: bad, unpleasant.
4 (adj) *A fine crack appeared in the wall.* thin, narrow, hairline, threadlike.
OPPOSITES: wide, thick.
5 (adj) *The bride wore a veil of fine silk.* delicate, sheer, thin, lightweight, light, flimsy, floaty, translucent, transparent, gauzy, gossamer, chiffony, filmy, cobwebby, diaphanous.
OPPOSITES: heavy, thick.
6 (adj) *Granny collects fine china.* dainty, delicate, exquisite, elegant, fragile.
OPPOSITE: coarse.
7 (n) *Mum had to pay a fine for speeding.* penalty, charge.

finish
1 (v) *You must finish your project today.* complete, finalize, conclude, get done, round off, put the finishing touches to, bring to a close, end, wind up, wrap up (informal), sew up (informal).
OPPOSITES: start, begin.
2 (v) *When does school finish for the summer? See* **end** 6.
3 (v) *How quickly can you finish your dinner?* eat up, get through, polish off (informal), dispose of, consume, devour.
4 (n) *We waited to see the finish of the match. See* **end** 1.

finished
(adj) *I'm glad that job is finally finished.* completed, done, accomplished, wrapped up (informal), sewn up (informal), ended, over and done with, in the past.

fire
1 (n) *The fire could be seen for miles around.* blaze, flames (plural), inferno, conflagration.
2 (n) *The troops came under heavy fire.* gunfire, shelling, bombardment, sniping.
3 (v) *Watch the soldiers fire the rocket.* launch, let off, set off, trigger, discharge.
4 (v) (informal) *I hope the boss doesn't fire you. See* **dismiss** 1.
5 **on fire** (phrase) *Look! The forest is on fire!* blazing, burning, in flames, flaming, alight, ablaze, aflame.

fire words

fires...	flames...	you hear...
blaze	dance	crack
burn	dart	crackle
consume	flash	hiss
damage	flare	murmur
destroy	flicker	pop
devastate	gleam	roar
devour	glitter	rustle
dwindle	glow	snap
engulf	leap	whisper
glow	lick	
grow	play	**after the fire you see...**
ignite	shimmer	
kindle		ashes
rage	**smoke...**	blackened walls
rampage	belches	blistered paint
ravage	billows	buckled iron
raze to the ground	blinds	charred wood
scorch	chokes	debris
singe	coils	embers
smoke	curls	gutted buildings
smoulder	envelops	rubble
sweep	obscures	scorched earth
	spirals	smouldering ruins
	suffocates	
	swirls	
	twists	
	wreathes	
	smoke smells...	
	acrid	
	bitter	
	pungent	
	sooty	

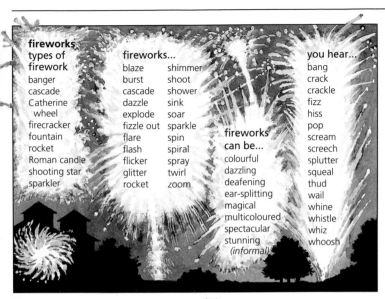

fireworks
types of
firework

banger	blaze	shimmer
cascade	burst	shoot
Catherine	cascade	shower
wheel	dazzle	sink
firecracker	explode	soar
fountain	fizzle out	sparkle
rocket	flare	spin
Roman candle	flash	spiral
shooting star	flicker	spray
sparkler	glitter	twirl
	rocket	zoom

fireworks...

blaze shimmer
burst shoot
cascade shower
dazzle sink
explode soar
fizzle out sparkle
flare spin
flash spiral
flicker spray
glitter twirl
rocket zoom

fireworks
can be...
colourful
dazzling
deafening
ear-splitting
magical
multicoloured
spectacular
stunning
(informal)

you hear...
bang
crack
crackle
fizz
hiss
pop
scream
screech
splutter
squeal
thud
wail
whine
whistle
whiz
whoosh

firm
1 *(adj) The ground felt firm underfoot.* hard, solid, unyielding, resistant, rigid, compacted, compressed, frozen, stony. OPPOSITE: soft.
2 *(adj) Make sure the ladder is firm.* steady, stable, secure, fixed, anchored, fastened, immovable, unshakable. OPPOSITES: unsteady, wobbly.
3 *(adj) Do you have any firm plans for the future?* definite, fixed, settled, established, unalterable, unchangeable, inflexible. OPPOSITES: vague, flexible.
4 *(adj) Ed and I are firm friends.* See **loyal**.
5 *(adj) Jess is firm in her ideas about animal rights.* adamant, resolute, inflexible, unbending, obstinate, unshakable, unfaltering, unwavering, unswerving. OPPOSITES: wavering, irresolute.
6 *(n) Mum works for a big electronics firm.* company, business, organization, concern, corporation, conglomerate, multinational, outfit *(informal)*.

first
1 *(adj) The first computers seem very basic now.* earliest, original, initial, primitive. OPPOSITE: latest.
2 *(adj) Read the first chapter for homework.* opening, introductory, initial. OPPOSITES: last, closing.
3 *(adj) United play in the first division.* top, premier, highest, foremost, leading, main. OPPOSITES: lowest, bottom.
4 *(adj) Rudi has mastered the first steps in ballet.* basic, elementary, rudimentary, primary, fundamental, key, cardinal.
5 *(adv) First, think of a title for your story.* firstly, first of all, to start with, to begin with, before anything else, in the first place, at the outset, beforehand. OPPOSITES: last, lastly.

fish
(n) TYPES OF FISH: angelfish, brill, carp, catfish, clown fish, cod, eel, flounder, flying fish, goldfish, guppy, haddock, hake, halibut, herring, lamprey, mackerel, minnow, mullet, perch, pike, pilchard, piranha, plaice, ray, roach, salmon, sardine, sea horse, shark, skate, sole, sprat, stickleback, sturgeon, swordfish, tiddler *(informal)*, trout, tuna, whitebait, whiting.

fishy *(informal) see* **suspicious** 2.

fit
1 *(v) Do you think these jeans will fit?* be the right size, be big enough, be small enough, be the right shape.
2 *(v) Fit the parts of the puzzle together.* piece, put, join, connect, fix, place, lay, position, arrange.
3 *(v) The punishment should fit the crime.* suit, correspond to, match, be fitting for.
4 *(adj) Swimming keeps me fit.* healthy, in shape, in good shape, in good condition, in trim, toned up, strong, in good health. OPPOSITES: unfit, out of shape.
5 *(adj) This video isn't fit for children.* See **suitable** 1.
6 *(n) Fido had a fit and died.* seizure, convulsion, attack, turn *(informal)*.
7 *(n) Den had a fit of coughing.* attack, bout, spell, outbreak, outburst.

fix
1 *(v) I need to fix my bike.* See **repair** 1.
2 *(v) Did you fix a date for the party?* agree on, decide on, set, settle, arrange, arrive at, establish, name, specify.
3 *(v) Fix the pieces together.* attach, join, link, fasten, connect, secure, stick, glue, paste, pin, nail, screw, bolt, tie, cement.
4 *(v) I must fix my hair.* tidy, neaten, arrange, see to, sort out, put in order.

5 *(v) (informal) The goalie tried to fix the result of the match.* rig, fiddle *(informal)*, manipulate, influence, set up *(informal)*.

fixed
1 *(adj) We have our meals at fixed times.* See **set** 7.
2 *(adj) Ed has very fixed views.* See **set** 8.
3 *(adj) Is my bike fixed yet?* mended, repaired, sorted, in working order, going.

fizzy
(adj) A fizzy drink. sparkling, bubbly, gassy, carbonated, effervescent, frothy, foaming. OPPOSITES: still, flat.

flabby
(adj) Flabby thighs. flaccid, slack, fleshy, sagging, soft, unfirm, out of shape.

flag
(n) banner, standard, pennant, ensign.

flake
1 *(n) A flake of paint peeled off.* chip, sliver, shaving, peeling, wafer, fragment.
2 *(v) This paint is beginning to flake.* peel, peel off, blister, chip, fall off.

flame
(n) A flame of fire. tongue, flicker, blaze.

flaming *see* **burning** 1.

flap
1 *(v) Watch the bird flap its wings.* beat, flutter, flail, thrash, waggle, shake.
2 *(v) The sail began to flap in the breeze.* flutter, sway, wave, swish, swing, thrash about, flail about, whip around.
3 *(n) (informal) The chef was in a flap.* panic, state *(informal)*, tizzy *(informal)*, fluster, flutter, stew *(informal)*, sweat *(informal)*, dither.

flash
1 *(n) A flash of light lit up the sky.* blaze, flare, burst, streak, shaft, ray, glare, glint, gleam, flicker, sparkle, shimmer, glimmer.
2 *(n) Mehmet had a flash of inspiration.* burst, rush, surge, touch, sudden show.
3 *(v) I saw a light flash on the horizon.* flicker, flare, wink, blink, blaze, beam, gleam, glint, sparkle, twinkle, shimmer.
4 *(v) I saw a car flash past.* See **shoot** 3.

flashy *see* **vulgar** 2.

flat
1 *(adj) Find a flat surface to work on.* level, horizontal, even, smooth. OPPOSITES: uneven, sloping, vertical.
2 *(adj) Oz lay flat on the ground.* stretched out, full length, prostrate, outstretched, prone, spread-eagled, reclining.
3 *(adj) You can't cycle with a flat tyre.* deflated, burst, punctured, blown out.
4 *(adj) After the show, the actors felt flat.* deflated, let down, low, down, dejected, despondent, depressed, dispirited. OPPOSITES: high *(informal)*, elated.
5 *(adj) Cyril has a flat voice.* monotonous, boring, lifeless, unvarying, dull, lacklustre.
6 *(n) We live in a flat on the fifth floor.* apartment, bedsit, studio, penthouse, set of rooms, rooms *(plural)*, pad *(slang)*.

flatten
1 (v) *Please flatten this cloth.* smooth out, make flat, level, iron out, even out, press.
2 (v) *Someone should flatten those tower blocks. See* **demolish**.
3 (v) *Don't flatten the roses.* trample, squash, crush, compress, press down.

flatter
1 (v) *I always flatter you when I want something.* compliment, butter you up, praise, cajole, soft-soap (informal), sweet-talk (informal), play up to, suck up to (informal), toady to, fawn on.
2 (v) *Those jeans really flatter your figure.* suit, set off, enhance, do something for, show to advantage.

flavour
1 (v) *You need to flavour this soup.* season, spice, ginger up, pep up.
2 (n) *This soup needs more flavour.* taste, zest, zing (informal), seasoning, flavouring, savour, relish, piquancy.

flawless *see* **perfect** 1, 2.

fleck *see* **speck** 1.

flexible
1 (adj) *This rod is quite flexible.* pliable, bendy, supple, springy, pliant.
OPPOSITE: rigid.
2 (adj) *Our plans must be flexible.* open, fluid, adaptable, adjustable, elastic.
OPPOSITES: fixed, settled.
3 (adj) *Karen won't mind; she's very flexible.* adaptable, accommodating, amenable, open-minded, compliant.
OPPOSITE: inflexible.

flicker
(v) *The flame began to flicker.* blink, gutter, tremble, quiver, waver, glimmer, shimmer, flutter, glitter, sparkle, flash.

flimsy
1 (adj) *A flimsy chair.* weak, insubstantial, fragile, rickety, shaky, tottery, jerry-built.
OPPOSITES: sturdy, strong.
2 (adj) *Flimsy fabric. See* **fine** 5.
3 (adj) *A flimsy excuse. See* **feeble** 3.

flinch
(v) *I always flinch at the sight of a needle.* cringe, wince, draw back, recoil, cower, quail, shrink, baulk, shy away, start, jump.

fling *see* **throw** 1.

flippant
(adj) *Don't make flippant remarks.* cheeky, impertinent, glib, pert, offhand, frivolous, flip (informal), disrespectful, irreverent.
OPPOSITES: serious, respectful.

flirt with
(v) *Did Lydia flirt with you at the party?* tease, chat you up (informal), make eyes at, lead you on, make advances to, ogle.

float
1 (v) *The bottle started to float down the stream.* sail, drift, glide, slip, bob, swim.
2 (v) *I watched the balloon float through the air.* waft, sail, glide, drift, hover.

flood
1 (v) *I hope the river doesn't flood.* overflow, burst its banks, brim over.
2 (v) *The river may flood the valley.* engulf, swamp, submerge, drown, deluge, immerse, cover, fill.
3 (v) *I'll try not to flood you with letters.* swamp, overwhelm, inundate, deluge, shower, bog you down, snow you under.
4 (n) *Our village was cut off by the flood.* torrent, deluge, tide, flood water.
5 (n) *We received a flood of complaints.* torrent, stream, deluge, rush, mass, spate.

floor
(n) *Our flat is on the second floor.* storey, level, landing.

flop
1 (v) *Don't let your hood flop over your face.* fall, droop, hang, sag, dangle, flap, drop, collapse, slump, tumble, topple.
2 (n) (informal) *The play was a flop. See* **failure** 2.

floppy
(adj) *Fido has floppy ears.* droopy, sagging, dangling, limp, pendulous, flapping, soft, loose, flaccid, flabby.

flow
1 (v) *Watch the water flow over the rocks.* glide, stream, gush, rush, surge, pour, run, swirl, spill, cascade, sweep, course, trickle, ripple, drift, spurt, seep, ooze, leak.
2 (v) *Complaints have started to flow in.* flood, pour, stream, trickle.
3 (n) *There was a steady flow of water from the roof.* stream, cascade, flood, torrent, spurt, gush, surge, trickle, leak.

flower
1 (n) *What's your favourite flower?* bloom, blossom, plant.
TYPES OF FLOWER: bluebell, buttercup, carnation, chrysanthemum, cowslip, crocus, cyclamen, daffodil, dahlia, daisy, dandelion, forget-me-not, foxglove, freesia, geranium, hollyhock, hyacinth, iris, lily, lupin, marigold, nasturtium, orchid, pansy, passionflower, poppy, primrose, rose, snowdrop, sunflower, sweet pea, tulip, violet, wallflower, water lily.
2 (v) *Our tree will flower soon.* blossom, bloom, be in flower, produce flowers, burst into bloom.

flowing
(adj) *A flowing robe.* loose, swirling, floating, sweeping, trailing, cascading.

fluent
(adj) *Max is a fluent public speaker.* articulate, eloquent, polished, confident, natural, self-assured, glib, smooth-talking.
OPPOSITES: tongue-tied, hesitant.

fluffy
(adj) *Fluffy baby animals.* furry, fuzzy, woolly, fleecy, downy, feathery, soft.

fluid *see* **liquid** 1, 2.

fluke *see* **chance** 1, 5.

flushed
(adj) *You look flushed.* red, crimson, hot, red in the face, hot and bothered, feverish, flustered, burning, glowing, rosy.

flustered
(adj) *All this attention makes me feel flustered.* agitated, hot and bothered, disconcerted, rattled (informal), ruffled, confused, fazed, unnerved, upset.

flutter *see* **flap** 1, 2, 3.

fly
1 (v) *Watch those birds fly!* soar, swoop, glide, flit, hover, circle, sail, coast, flutter, take to the air, take wing, take off.
2 (v) *See how the flags fly in the breeze.* flutter, wave, flap, swirl, stream, float.
3 (v) *The time seemed to fly by.* rush, race, whiz (informal), zoom, hurtle, slip, roll.
4 (v) *Elliot is learning to fly a plane.* pilot, operate, control, navigate.
5 (v) *I must fly or I'll be late! See* **hurry** 1.

foam
1 (n) *The bowl was full of foam.* bubbles (plural), froth, suds (plural), lather, scum.
2 (n) *Fill the cushion with foam.* sponge.
3 (v) *The potion began to foam.* bubble, froth, fizz, effervesce, seethe, lather.

foggy
(adj) *A foggy night.* misty, smoggy, murky, hazy, cloudy, shadowy, soupy.

fold
1 (v) *Fold the cloth.* double over, turn over, bend, crease, pleat, tuck, gather.
2 (n) *There's a fold in this material.* pleat, gather, tuck, crease, wrinkle, crinkle.

follow
1 (v) *The detectives decided to follow Burglar Beryl.* pursue, go after, tail, trail, shadow, stalk, chase, track, hunt, hound.
2 (v) *Who will follow Lisa as captain?* come after, go after, succeed, take over from, take the place of, replace, supplant, supersede, step into the shoes of.
3 (v) *Follow these instructions.* obey, observe, pay attention to, comply with, be guided by, attend to, keep to, heed.
4 (v) *The lecture was hard to follow.* understand, keep up with, take in, comprehend, grasp, catch on to (informal).

follower *see* **fan** 2.

fond
1 (adj) *A fond mother. See* **loving**.
2 fond of (adj) *Efra is fond of her boyfriend.* attached to, keen on, devoted to, in love with, stuck on (slang), crazy about (informal), mad about, besotted by.
3 fond of (adj) *Gus is fond of sweets.* keen on, partial to, crazy about (informal), mad about, hooked on, addicted to.

food
(n) *I need food.* nourishment, sustenance, refreshment, provisions (plural), rations (plural), grub (informal), nosh (informal), tuck (informal), victuals (plural), fodder.

food and flavours

nice food is...
appetizing
delicious
luscious
moreish
  (informal)
mouthwatering
scrumptious
  (informal)
tasty
yummy *(slang)*

**nasty
food is...**
disgusting
foul
inedible
nauseating
revolting
unappetizing
vile
yucky *(slang)*

**food
can be...**
burnt
charred
dry
fatty
filling
fresh
healthy
indigestible
juicy
lukewarm
mouldy
nourishing
piping hot
raw
rich
satisfying
scalding
sizzling
stale
steaming
stodgy
succulent
tepid
undercooked
unhealthy
unsatisfying
well-cooked
wholesome

**food
can feel...**
chewy
creamy
crisp
crumbly
crunchy
glutinous
  (gluey)
gooey
  (informal)
greasy
leathery
lumpy
mushy
oily
rubbery
runny
slimy
sloppy
smooth
soggy
spongy
squashy
squidgy
sticky
stringy
tender
tough
wobbly

**food
can taste...**
acid
bitter
bland
fiery
fruity
hot
insipid
  (tasteless)
peppery
salty
savoury
sharp
sickly
sour
spicy
sugary
sweet
syrupy
tangy
tart
vinegary

*juicy
grapes*

*gooey
gateau*

*sticky
jam
tart*

*squidgy
pizza*

*crisp
lettuce*

crunchy carrots

fool
1 *(v)* You can't fool me. See **deceive** 1.
2 *(n)* Dwayne's such a fool! See **idiot**.

fool around
(v) (informal) Don't fool around in class.
clown around, act the fool, mess about
(informal), muck about *(slang)*, waste time.

foolish see **silly** 1, 2.

forbid
(v) I love skating; please don't forbid it!
ban, prohibit, rule out, veto, block.
OPPOSITES: allow, permit.

forbidden
(adj) Smoking is forbidden. not allowed,
banned, prohibited, outlawed, taboo.
OPPOSITES: permitted, allowed.

force
1 *(v)* If you don't want to go, I won't force
you. make, compel, pressurize, push,
coerce, oblige, bring pressure to bear on,
put the squeeze on *(informal)*, dragoon.
2 *(v)* We had to force the lock. prise open,
break open, wrench open, smash.
3 *(n)* You'll need lots of force to open this
door. See **strength** 1.

foreign
1 *(adj)* Indy often travels to foreign lands.
remote, distant, exotic, faraway, far-flung,
unfamiliar, unknown, strange, alien.
OPPOSITE: native.
2 *(adj)* We have some foreign visitors.
overseas, international.

foresee see **predict**.

forever see **always** 1, 2.

forgery see **fake** 1.

forget
1 *(v)* How could you forget my birthday?
fail to remember, overlook, be oblivious to,
lose track of, neglect, ignore.
OPPOSITE: remember.
2 *(v)* Try to forget this unfortunate
incident. put out of your mind, pay no
attention to, dismiss, discount, disregard.
OPPOSITES: remember, recall.
3 *(v)* Don't forget your lunch. go without,
leave behind, fail to take, abandon.
OPPOSITE: remember.

forgetful
(adj) Professor Peabody is so forgetful!
absent-minded, scatterbrained, vague,
abstracted, dreamy, inattentive.

forgive
(v) I will forgive you for what you did.
pardon, excuse, let you off, accept your
apologies, exonerate, absolve.

forgiveness
(n) I need your forgiveness. pardon, mercy.

forlorn see **sad** 1.

form
1 *(n)* What form of music do you like?
kind, type, sort, style, variety, manner.
2 *(n)* The enchanter took on the form of a
serpent. See **shape** 3.
3 *(n)* What form are you in at school?
See **class**.
4 *(n)* Please fill in this form. document,
paper, sheet, questionnaire, application.
5 *(n)* I hope Linford is in good form.
condition, shape, health, spirits *(plural)*.
6 *(v)* It takes centuries for stalactites to
form. develop, take shape, grow, come
into existence, appear, materialize.
7 *(v)* Let's form a computer club. create,
establish, set up, start, found, organize.

formal
1 *(adj)* The banquet will be a formal affair.
dignified, stately, ceremonial, solemn,
correct, proper, posh *(informal)*, stiff.
OPPOSITES: informal, casual.
2 *(adj)* Please wear formal clothes. smart,
dressed-up *(informal)*, posh *(informal)*,
proper, correct, conventional.
OPPOSITE: casual.
3 *(adj)* You'll need formal permission to
emigrate. official, lawful, proper, legal.

fortunate see **lucky** 1, 2.

fortune
1 *(n)* Lord Lucre's fortune is phenomenal.
wealth, riches *(plural)*, possessions *(plural)*,
assets *(plural)*, inheritance, estate.
2 *(n)* Giles has won a fortune. huge
amount, pile *(informal)*, packet *(informal)*,
bundle *(informal)*, millions *(plural)*.
3 *(n)* We found the house by good
fortune. See **luck** 1.

foul
1 *(adj)* A foul heap of rubbish. filthy,
squalid, disgusting, revolting, nauseating,
loathsome, repulsive, rotten, putrid,
stinking, vile, sordid, grotty *(slang)*.
2 *(adj)* Foul language. indecent, obscene,
profane, blasphemous, filthy, offensive,
smutty, lewd, crude, coarse, vulgar.
OPPOSITES: polite, decent, clean.
3 *(adj)* A foul crime. vile, horrible,
monstrous, shocking, revolting, odious,
sordid, despicable, contemptible,
detestable, atrocious, abominable, wicked,
villainous, evil, heinous, infamous.
4 *(adj)* Foul weather. rough, dirty, stormy,
squally, rainy, foggy, drizzly, murky.
OPPOSITES: fair, fine.
5 *(adj)* Callum was sent off for foul play.
unfair, rough, dirty, unsporting, violent,
sneaky, unscrupulous, prohibited, illegal.
OPPOSITE: fair.

fragile

fragile
(adj) Fragile china. delicate, breakable, brittle, thin, weak, flimsy, insubstantial, frail, dainty.
OPPOSITES: strong, durable.

fragment see **piece** 2, 3.

frail
(adj) A frail old lady. delicate, weak, feeble, infirm, unsteady, vulnerable, puny.
OPPOSITES: strong, robust.

frank
(adj) A frank answer. plain, straight, direct, candid, forthright, honest, truthful, blunt, no-nonsense, upfront *(informal)*, sincere, open, outspoken, unreserved.
OPPOSITES: evasive, insincere.

frantic
1 *(adj) You'll be frantic when you hear the news.* beside yourself, at your wits' end, desperate, panic-stricken, distraught, hysterical, overwrought, worked up.
OPPOSITE: calm.
2 *(adj) The classroom was filled with frantic activity. See* **feverish** 2.

fraud
1 *(n) Dodgy Dave was sentenced for fraud.* swindling, cheating, deception, sharp practice, double-dealing, embezzlement, trickery, chicanery.
2 *(n) (informal) That man is a fraud.* impostor, phoney *(informal)*, fake, cheat, hoaxer, con man *(informal)*, swindler, double-dealer, charlatan, quack *(doctor)*.

freak
1 *(adj) Freak weather. See* **unusual** 1.
2 *(n) (informal) Nathan is a computer freak. See* **fan** 1.

free
1 *(adj) I'd like to go out tonight. Are you free?* available, uncommitted, footloose, fancy-free, off the leash *(informal)*, off the hook *(informal)*, at liberty.
OPPOSITES: busy, tied up.
2 *(adj) The prisoners longed to be free.* released, set free, set loose, unconfined, at liberty, unrestrained, on the loose.
OPPOSITES: imprisoned, confined.
3 *(adj) Is this seat free?* vacant, empty, unoccupied, unused, spare, available.
OPPOSITES: occupied, reserved, engaged.
4 *(adj) These tickets are free.* free of charge, complimentary, cost-free, gratis, on the house.
5 *(v) Let's campaign to free the hostages. See* **release** 1.
6 *(v) The judge decided to free Burglar Beryl. See* **release** 2.
7 *(v) Can you free the boot from your fishing line?* untangle, untie, extricate, undo, disentangle, disengage, clear.

freedom
(n) Pandora's parents allow her lots of freedom. independence, liberty, autonomy, leeway, licence, latitude, personal space, privileges *(plural)*.

freeze
1 *(v) I think the pond will freeze tonight.* ice up, ice over, go solid, harden, solidify.
2 *(v) Don't go outside; you'll freeze!* die of cold *(informal)*, be chilled to the bone, perish *(informal)*, go numb.
3 *(v) "Freeze, or I'll shoot!" said Arnie.* keep still, stay where you are, stand still, don't move a muscle, stand stock-still.

freezing see **cold** 1, 2, 3.

frenzied see **feverish** 2.

frenzy
(n) The news sent us into a frenzy. turmoil, uproar, furore, confusion, passion, rage, fury, fit, paroxysm, hysteria.

frequent
1 *(adj) A frequent problem.* persistent, recurrent, regular, repeated, continual, constant, incessant, oft-repeated.
2 *(adj) A frequent sight. See* **familiar** 1.

fresh
1 *(adj) This magazine needs some fresh ideas.* new, original, novel, innovative, creative, inventive, untried, unfamiliar, up-to-date, up-to-the-minute, modern.
OPPOSITES: stale, outdated.
2 *(adj) You should eat lots of fresh food.* natural, unprocessed, untreated, uncontaminated, uncooked, raw *(fruit, vegetables)*, freshly picked, freshly cooked.
OPPOSITES: processed, cooked, stale.
3 *(adj) Is this water fresh?* pure, drinkable, unpolluted, uncontaminated, running.
OPPOSITES: polluted, salty, stagnant.
4 *(adj) Start on a fresh sheet of paper.* clean, new, blank, empty, unused, spare.
OPPOSITES: used, full.
5 *(adj) Can you feel that fresh sea breeze?* cool, refreshing, brisk, bracing, invigorating, keen, chilly, nippy.

friend
(n) It's great to have a friend to talk to. mate *(informal)*, pal *(informal)*, chum *(informal)*, buddy *(informal)*, companion, comrade, soul mate, bosom friend, kindred spirit, confidant *(male)*, confidante *(female)*, crony, ally, well-wisher.
OPPOSITE: enemy.

friendly
(adj) Sasha is a friendly girl. warm, outgoing, sociable, chummy *(informal)*, matey *(informal)*, pally *(informal)*, companionable, hospitable, neighbourly, welcoming, open, approachable, warm-hearted, affectionate, sympathetic, kind-hearted, considerate, understanding, supportive, generous, helpful, convivial.
OPPOSITES: unfriendly, cold.

fright
1 *(n) I shrank back in fright. See* **fear** 1.
2 *(n) You gave me a fright. See* **scare** 3.
3 *(n) (informal) What a fright you look! See* **sight** 4.

frighten see **scare** 1, 2.

frightened see **scared** 1, 2.

frightening
(adj) What a frightening experience! scary *(informal)*, terrifying, petrifying, spine-chilling, hair-raising, bloodcurdling, horrifying, fearsome, ghastly, creepy *(informal)*, eerie, spooky *(informal)*, alarming, daunting, unnerving, sinister.
OPPOSITES: comforting, reassuring.

frilly
(adj) A frilly dress. flouncy, ruffled, ruched, flounced, lacy, frothy, fancy.

frisky
(adj) A frisky puppy. lively, playful, high-spirited, sprightly, bouncy, skittish, active.

frivolous
(adj) Frivolous remarks. empty-headed, foolish, fatuous, superficial, shallow, flippant, flip *(informal)*, silly, trivial, puerile, childish, inane, dizzy, giddy, pointless, worthless, insignificant, idle, trifling.
OPPOSITES: serious, sensible.

front
1 *(n) Put some people in the front of your painting.* foreground, forefront.
OPPOSITES: background, back.
2 *(n) Ivy grew up the front of the house.* face, façade, frontage.
OPPOSITES: rear, back.
3 *(n) Go to the front of the queue.* top, head, beginning.
OPPOSITES: end, back.
4 *(n) Dean's self-confidence is just a front.* pretence, show, mask, façade, cover, disguise, cover-up, sham, blind, screen.

frosty
1 *(adj) It's frosty this morning.* icy, freezing, hoary, crisp, wintry, keen, chilly, nippy, cold. ❖ *Also see* **ice**, **frost & snow**.
2 *(adj) Aunt Bertha gave a frosty reply.* cold, icy, chilly, glacial, unfriendly, cool, standoffish, stiff, aloof, discouraging.
OPPOSITES: warm, friendly.

frown
(v) Mum will frown at you if you snigger. scowl, glare, glower, grimace, look daggers, give you a dirty look, look stern.

frozen
1 *(adj) The roads are frozen.* icy, frosty, icebound, ice-covered, frozen solid.
2 *(adj) My nose is frozen.* freezing, numb, icy, chilled, dead, frostbitten, frozen solid.

fruit
(n) TYPES OF FRUIT: apple, apricot, avocado, banana, bilberry, blackberry, blackcurrant, blueberry, cherry, clementine, crab apple, cranberry, damson, date, elderberry, fig, gooseberry, grape, grapefruit, greengage, guava, kiwi fruit, kumquat, lemon, lime, loganberry, lychee, mandarin, mango, melon, nectarine, olive, orange, papaya, passion fruit, peach, pear, pineapple, plum, pomegranate, prickly pear, quince, raspberry, redcurrant, rhubarb, satsuma, star fruit, strawberry, tangerine, tomato, ugli fruit.

Gg

frustrated
(adj) I felt frustrated that I couldn't go to the party. disgruntled, vexed, annoyed, peeved *(informal)*, miffed *(informal)*, resentful, thwarted, foiled, disappointed, embittered, sick as a parrot *(informal)*.

full
1 *(adj) The box is full.* full up, filled, full to the brim, overflowing, packed, crammed, stuffed, jam-packed, chock-a-block, full to bursting, bursting at the seams, brimming over, chock-full, jammed, crowded, laden, loaded, teeming, swarming, well-stocked. OPPOSITE: empty.
2 *(adj) I want a full explanation.* thorough, complete, detailed, comprehensive, exhaustive, unabridged, uncut, unedited. OPPOSITES: incomplete, partial.
3 *(adj) Charlotte felt full after her lunch.* satisfied, well-fed, sated, satiated, gorged, stuffed *(informal)*, replete. OPPOSITES: empty, hungry.

fun
1 *(n) Let's have some fun!* amusement, enjoyment, entertainment, fun and games *(plural)*, pleasure, recreation, diversion, distraction, high jinks *(plural)*, sport.
2 *(n) Oz is full of fun.* merriment, laughter, sparkle, high spirits *(plural)*, verve, zest, mirth, jollity, hilarity.
3 *(adj) The party was fun.* See **enjoyable**.

funny
1 *(adj) A funny comedian.* amusing, comical, witty, humorous, hilarious, entertaining, satirical, ironic, droll, sarcastic, facetious, hysterical *(informal)*, side-splitting, absurd, ludicrous, laughable, farcical, ridiculous, riotous.
2 *(adj) A funny habit.* See **strange** 1.
3 *(adj) A funny noise.* See **strange** 2.

furious see **angry**.

furry
(adj) A furry creature. fluffy, fuzzy, hairy, woolly, fleecy.

fuss
(v) Don't fuss about petty details. worry, fret, get worked up, flap *(informal)*, be agitated, be in a stew *(informal)*, niggle.

fussy
(adj) Di is fussy about her food. particular, choosy *(informal)*, fastidious, hard to please, difficult, picky *(informal)*, finicky, pernickety *(informal)*, faddy *(informal)*.

future
(n) Your future looks bright. prospects *(plural)*, expectations *(plural)*, outlook.

fuzzy
1 *(adj) It's hard to control my fuzzy hair.* frizzy, fluffy, woolly, wiry, bushy.
2 *(adj) Without my glasses, everything looks fuzzy.* See **blurred**.

gabble
(v) Don't gabble! I can't understand you. jabber, babble, rabbit on *(informal)*, rattle on, prattle, spout *(informal)*, blabber, gush.

gadget
(n) This gadget slices apples. device, tool, instrument, utensil, contraption, appliance, widget *(informal)*, gizmo *(slang)*, invention.

gaffe see **mistake** 2.

gain see **win** 2.

gale see **storm** 1.

gamble
1 *(v) If you gamble, you may lose.* bet, place a bet, have a flutter *(informal)*, speculate, take a risk, take a chance, try your luck, stick your neck out *(informal)*. OPPOSITE: play safe.
2 **gamble on** *(v) Flash Frank loves to gamble on the horses.* bet on, put money on, back, have a flutter on *(informal)*.

game
1 *(n) Don't take it so seriously; it's only a game.* amusement, diversion, distraction, entertainment, romp, lark *(informal)*, prank, jest, joke, bit of fun.
2 *(n) Football is a popular game.* sport, pastime, recreation, entertainment, amusement, leisure activity.
3 *(n) When does the rugby game start?* match, competition, tournament, contest.

gang
(n) Can I join your gang? group, crowd, club, set, bunch *(informal)*, circle, crew *(informal)*, clique, posse *(informal)*, mob, team, squad.

gap
1 *(n) We found a gap in the wall.* hole, crack, opening, space, chink, crevice, cranny.
2 *(n) There will be a gap between each act.* interval, pause, break, rest, breathing space, lull, interlude, intermission.
3 *(n) Measure the gap between the two houses.* space, distance, interval.

gape see **stare** 1.

gaping
(adj) Beneath us stretched a gaping hole. yawning, cavernous, vast, wide, wide-open, enormous.

garden
(n) patch, plot, lawn, grounds *(plural)*, back yard, yard.

garish see **gaudy**.

gash see **cut** 1, 9.

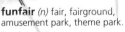

funfair *(n)* fair, fairground, amusement park, theme park.

funfair rides
big dipper
big wheel
bumper cars
carousel
Dodgems
Ferris wheel

ghost train
helter-skelter
merry-go-round
roller coaster
simulator
swingboat

on a ride you...
bounce
bump
climb
crash
dive
drop
hang
hurtle
jerk
jolt
lurch
plummet
plunge

revolve
rock
slide
speed
spin
sway
swerve
swing
swoop
tilt
twist
whirl
zoom

rides can be...
exciting
exhilarating
hair-raising
nail-biting
scary *(informal)*
spine-tingling
stomach-churning
terrifying
thrilling

other amusements
amusement arcade
bouncy castle
coconut shy
fortune-teller
hall of mirrors
laser show
shooting gallery
skittles
slot machine
stall

people at a funfair...
gape
gasp
gaze
jostle
mill about
push
queue
scream
screech
shove
shriek
squeal
yell

funfair lights can be...
blazing
colourful
dazzling
flashing
glittering
magical
whirling

funfair music can be...
blaring
booming
jangling
pounding
rhythmic
strident
tinny

gasp

gasp
1 *(v) This icy water will make you gasp.* catch your breath, gulp, splutter, choke.
2 *(v) Jogging makes me gasp. See* **pant**.

gate
(n) entrance, exit, gateway, doorway, way in, way out, door, opening, turnstile, stile.

gather
1 *(v) A crowd began to gather at the end of the pitch. See* **collect** 3.
2 *(v) I gather I'm next. See* **understand** 3.

gaudy
(adj) A gaudy tie. garish, loud, lurid, bright, glaring, flashy, vulgar, showy, tasteless.

gaunt
(adj) After their ordeal, the prisoners looked gaunt. haggard, wasted, scrawny, emaciated, sunken-cheeked, hollow-eyed, drawn, pinched, skeletal, cadaverous.

gaze *see* **stare** 1.

gear
1 *(n) Climbing gear. See* **equipment**.
2 *(n) (informal) Oz looks great in his party gear.* clothes *(plural)*, outfit, things *(plural)*, togs *(plural) (informal)*, strip *(sport)*.

general
1 *(adj) Untidiness is a general problem among teenagers.* common, widespread, normal, typical, everyday, usual, universal.
OPPOSITES: individual, unusual.
2 *(adj) Chloë gave a general outline of the story.* broad, rough, vague, loose, approximate, imprecise, sweeping.
OPPOSITES: precise, detailed.

generation
1 *(n) I get on best with people of my own generation.* age, age group, peer group.
2 *(n) Steam trains belong to a different generation.* era, age, time, period, epoch.

generous
(adj) Lord Lucre is generous with his money. open-handed, liberal, ungrudging, unstinting, free, lavish, magnanimous, kind, charitable, bountiful.
OPPOSITES: mean, stingy.

genius
(n) Imran is a genius at maths. mastermind, marvel, ace *(informal)*, whiz *(informal)*, brainbox *(slang)*, whiz kid *(informal)*, hotshot *(informal)*, prodigy *(child)*.

gentle
1 *(adj) Neesha has a gentle nature.* mild, sweet-tempered, peaceful, placid, tender, meek, docile, unassertive, kind.
OPPOSITES: violent, aggressive.
2 *(adj) The leaves stirred in the gentle breeze.* light, soft, faint, slight, mild, balmy, caressing.
OPPOSITES: strong, violent.
3 *(adj) Dad spoke to me in a gentle voice.* soft, soothing, quiet, low, reassuring.
OPPOSITES: harsh, loud.
4 *(adj) We cycled down a gentle slope.* gradual, slight, imperceptible, easy, steady.
OPPOSITES: steep, sudden.

5 *(adj) A gentle hint. See* **subtle** 2.

genuine
1 *(adj) Is that a genuine gold nugget?* real, actual, authentic, bona fide, true, veritable, solid, pure, natural, original *(art)*.
OPPOSITES: fake, imitation, artificial.
2 *(adj) Sophie's enthusiasm seems to be genuine. See* **sincere** 1.

gesture
1 *(n) I don't know what Sam's gesture means.* sign, signal, action, gesticulation.
2 *(v) I tried to gesture to you that the branch wasn't safe. See* **signal** 2.

get
1 *(v) Where did you get those jeans?* buy, get hold of, obtain, acquire, come by.
2 *(v) Please get me a chair. See* **fetch** 1.
3 *(v) When will we get our exam results?* receive, be given, hear, be told, be sent.
4 *(v) Oz hopes to get first prize.* win, gain, take, obtain, earn, achieve, attain, pick up.
5 *(v) It should get warmer in the afternoon.* become, grow, turn.
6 *(v) When did you finally get home?* arrive, come, reach, make it *(informal)*.
7 *(v) Shall I get supper?* make, prepare, fix *(informal)*, get ready, organize, cook.
8 *(v) I wish I could get you to go out with me.* persuade, convince, induce, coax, talk you into, wheedle you into, make, force.
9 *(v) I mustn't get a cold. See* **catch** 3.
10 *(v) I don't get what you mean. See* **understand** 1.
11 *(v) (informal) I'm going to get you for stealing my hat! See* **pay back** 2.

get across
1 *(v) How will we get across the desert? See* **cross** 4.
2 *(v) It's important to get your message across.* get over, put over, communicate, make clear, get through, bring home.

get at
1 *(v) I can't get at that shelf. See* **reach** 1.
2 *(v) Can you see what I'm trying to get at?* suggest, imply, lead up to, insinuate, convey, indicate, mean.
3 *(v) Why does everyone always get at me? See* **pick on**.

getaway *see* **escape** 4.

get away
1 *(v) Burglar Beryl tried to get away from the police. See* **escape** 1.
2 **get away with** *(v) Don't try to cheat; you won't get away with it.* get off scot-free, go unpunished, pull it off.

get back
1 *(v) What time did you get back? See* **return** 1.
2 *(v) Did you manage to get your pencil case back? See* **retrieve**.

get better
1 *(v) You must take your medicine if you want to get better. See* **recover** 1.
2 *(v) The situation can only get better. See* **improve** 2.

get even *(informal) see* **get your own back**.

get off
1 *(v) Don't get off until the bus stops.* get out, alight, disembark, dismount, exit.
2 *(v) (informal) Did you get off with Jo at the party?* make a date, get together, get lucky *(informal)*, make out *(informal)*.

get on
1 *(v) I wonder how I'll get on at my new school. See* **manage** 1.
2 *(v) The driver told us to get on.* get in, board, climb aboard, embark, enter.
3 *(v) Did you and Sarah get on?* get along, hit it off *(informal)*, become friends, make friends, see eye to eye, agree.

get out
(v) If there's a fire, get out as fast as you can! leave, clear out *(informal)*, escape, make your escape, exit, evacuate, free yourself, extricate yourself, break out.

get out of *see* **avoid** 2.

get over
1 *(v) It didn't take long for Alice to get over her illness.* recover from, get better from, shake off, convalesce, recuperate.
2 *(v) It can be hard to get over losing a friend.* recover from, survive, bounce back from, put behind you, forget.

get rid of
(v) Please get rid of that mouldy sandwich. throw away, dispose of, remove, bin, chuck *(slang)*, dump *(informal)*, ditch *(slang)*, do away with, discard.

get together *see* **meet** 3.

get up
(v) It's time to get up! get out of bed, rise and shine *(informal)*, wake up, surface *(informal)*, get dressed, rise, stand up.

get worse
(v) Your marks will get worse if you don't work harder. deteriorate, worsen, go downhill *(informal)*, take a turn for the worse, slip, slide, fall, slump, decline, lapse.
OPPOSITES: get better, improve.

get your own back
(phrase) (informal) Don't try to get your own back. take revenge, get your revenge, retaliate, get even *(informal)*, settle the score, be avenged, give tit for tat.

ghastly
1 *(adj) A ghastly crime. See* **horrible** 1.
2 *(adj) I saw a ghastly face in the moonlight.* deathly pale, ashen, spectral, deathlike, cadaverous, gruesome.

ghost
(n) Max says he saw a ghost on the stairs. spirit, spook *(informal)*, spectre, phantom, apparition, wraith, poltergeist, ghoul.

ghostly
1 *(adj) A ghostly sound. See* **spooky** 1.
2 *(adj) A ghostly figure.* ghostlike, spectral, phantom, wraithlike, shadowy, supernatural, unearthly, ghoulish.

ghosts and hauntings

ghosts and ghouls

apparition
banshee
bogeyman
ghost
ghoul
gremlin
phantom
poltergeist
(mischievous spirit)
spectre
spirit
spook *(informal)*
vampire
werewolf
wraith
zombie

haunted house

panelled room

grand staircase

in a haunted house

attic
bats
candelabra
cellar
chains
cobwebs
fluttering curtains
four-poster bed
grandfather clock
grand staircase
guttering candles
library
locked door
looking glass
manacles
(handcuffs)
mice
oak chest
panelled room
portrait
secret door
secret passageway
shadows
sliding panel
spiral staircase
stone steps
study
suit of armour
sword
tapestry
trap door
turret
west wing
winding corridor

ghosts and ghouls may...

appear
avenge (take
revenge for)
beckon
creep
disappear
drift
flit
float
flutter
glide
glow
haunt
hover
loom
lurk
materialize
pace
pester
plague
possess
shimmer
skim
slide
slink
slither
stalk
sway
torment
trouble
vanish into
thin air
waft
wander

ghostly sounds

bang
bump
cackle
chime
clank
clatter
clink
crash
creak
cry
grate
grind
groan
hammer
hoot
howl
knock
moan
murmur
mutter
rattle
rustle
scream
screech
shriek
sigh
sob
thud
wail
whisper

ghostly sounds can be...

bloodcurdling
chilling
creepy *(informal)*
disturbing
echoing
eerie
hair-raising
haunting
heart-stopping
high-pitched
lingering
long-drawn-out
melancholy
petrifying
piercing
reverberating
spine-chilling
uncanny
unearthly
unnerving
weird

ghosts and ghouls may be...

anguished
ghastly
ghostly
ghoulish
grisly
grotesque
gruesome
horrifying
invisible
luminous
malevolent
mournful
restless
scary *(informal)*
shadowy
sinister
slimy
spectral
supernatural
tormented

haunted houses can be...

bleak
creepy *(informal)*
crumbling
cursed
derelict
deserted
dilapidated
forbidding
gloomy
grim
isolated
lonely
menacing
moonlit
mysterious
neglected
rambling
ramshackle
remote
spooky
(informal)
swathed in mist
tumbledown
uninhabited

guttering candle

candelabra

manacle

giant
1 (n) Jack dreamt about a fearsome giant. ogre, monster, hulk, titan.
2 (adj) Giant sale now on. See **huge**.

gibberish see **nonsense** 1.

giddy see **dizzy**.

gift
1 (n) Dad gave me this book as a gift. See **present** 1.
2 (n) Lord Lucre gave the school a generous gift. donation, contribution, grant, hand-out, offering, bequest, legacy.
3 (n) Mark has a gift for languages. talent, aptitude, flair, ability, facility, knack, bent, genius, skill, expertise.

gifted see **talented** 1, 2.

gigantic see **huge**.

giggle
(v) You'll giggle when you see Dad in his tank top. titter, snigger, chuckle, chortle, laugh, cackle, snicker.

gimmick
(n) This toy is just a gimmick to make you buy the cereal. novelty, ploy, trick, stunt, publicity device, dodge, wheeze (slang).

girl
(n) schoolgirl, lass, young woman, maiden (old-fashioned), damsel (old-fashioned).

gist
(n) Do you get the gist of what I'm saying? idea, general sense, drift, point, meaning, essence, substance, significance.

give
1 (v) Give your ticket to the driver. hand, pass, hand over, present, submit, deliver.
2 (v) Lord Lucre offered to give some money to our fund. donate, contribute, grant, award, present, allocate, make over, fork out (slang), provide, supply, entrust, bestow, bequeath (after death).
OPPOSITES: take away, receive.
3 (v) A graph is a good way to give information. communicate, convey, put across, display, show, set out, deliver, express, explain, demonstrate, impart.
4 (v) Let's give a party! throw, have, organize, arrange, put on, host, stage.
5 (v) Please let me come; I won't give any trouble. cause, make, create, produce.

give away see **betray** 1, 3.

give in
(v) Why don't you just give in and end the argument? give up, admit defeat, back down, climb down, throw in the towel, concede defeat, capitulate, surrender.

give out
(v) Mrs Badger asked me to give out the books. hand out, hand round, pass round, dish out (informal), distribute, dole out, share out, circulate.
OPPOSITES: collect, take in.

give up
1 (v) I'm determined to give up biting my nails. See **stop** 3.

2 (v) This assault course is tough, but I'm not going to give up. give in, admit defeat, quit, lose heart, despair, drop out, throw in the towel, throw in the sponge, pack it in (informal), call it a day (informal).
3 (v) Would you give up your pocket money for a good cause? sacrifice, forfeit, relinquish, forgo, surrender, offer.

give way see **collapse** 1.

glad see **pleased**.

glamorous
1 (adj) Helen looks glamorous in her ballgown. dazzling, alluring, stunning (informal), smart, elegant, sophisticated, snazzy (informal), charming, enchanting, bewitching, entrancing, irresistible, captivating, sexy (informal), seductive.
OPPOSITES: dull, dowdy.
2 (adj) The party was a glamorous affair. glittering, dazzling, glitzy (slang), ritzy (slang), colourful, fascinating, exciting.
OPPOSITES: humdrum, mundane.

glamour
(n) The glamour of Hollywood. glitter, dazzle, razzmatazz (slang), razzle-dazzle (slang), glitz (slang), magic, fascination, allure, appeal, attraction, charm, elegance.

glance
1 (n) Take a quick glance. See **look** 4.
2 (v) Would you glance at my homework? See **look at** 2.

glare
(v) Aunt Bertha will glare at you if you interrupt. give you a hard stare, glower, look daggers, give you a dirty look, frown, scowl, give you a black look.

glaring
1 (adj) Glaring headlights. See **bright** 1.
2 (adj) A glaring mistake. See **obvious**.

glass
(n) Fill the glass to the brim. tumbler, wineglass, goblet, flute (champagne).

gleam
1 (v) As Aladdin rubbed the lamp, it began to gleam. shine, glisten, glint, shimmer, glimmer, glow, sparkle, glitter, twinkle.
2 (n) A gleam of light. See **flash** 1.

gleaming see **shiny** 1, 2.

glide
1 (v) I'd like to glide through the air like a bird. float, drift, sail, soar, fly, coast, hover.
2 (v) Watch me glide across the ice! skate, slide, skim, sail, slip, skid.

glimmer see **gleam** 1.

glimpse
(n) I got a glimpse of something shiny in the grass. quick look, brief view, glance, peep, peek, sight, squint.

glint see **gleam** 1.

glisten see **gleam** 1.

glitter
1 (v) The light made the diamonds glitter. sparkle, shimmer, twinkle, glisten, shine, glint, gleam, glimmer, flash.

2 (n) The glitter of the treasure dazzled me. sparkle, brilliance, lustre, brightness.
3 (n) Jodie is fascinated by the glitter of Hollywood. See **glamour**.

gloat
(v) Don't gloat if you win. crow, brag, rub it in (informal), boast, show off (informal).

globe
1 (n) The sun is a globe of fire. See **ball** 1.
2 (n) Indiana has travelled round the globe. See **world** 1.

gloom
(n) When she heard the news, Emma was filled with gloom. melancholy, sorrow, sadness, unhappiness, despondency, dejection, misery, depression, despair, desolation, hopelessness, woe, pessimism.
OPPOSITES: happiness, delight.

gloomy
1 (adj) It was a gloomy winter's day. dismal, dreary, dull, dark, murky, cheerless, overcast, cloudy, sunless, dim, sombre.
OPPOSITES: bright, sunny.
2 (adj) Wet weather makes me feel gloomy. See **depressed**.

glorious
1 (adj) A glorious victory. magnificent, splendid, triumphant, heroic, honourable, famous, celebrated, renowned, illustrious.
OPPOSITES: shameful, humiliating.
2 (adj) Glorious weather. See **gorgeous** 3.

glossy
1 (adj) Glossy paintwork. shiny, shining, gleaming, bright, sparkling, shimmering, brilliant, smooth, polished, glazed.
OPPOSITES: dull, matt.
2 (adj) Glossy hair. shiny, shining, gleaming, sleek, silky, smooth, lustrous.
OPPOSITE: dull.

glow
1 (n) I saw a strange glow in the sky. light, gleam, glimmer, brightness, burning.
2 (n) The wind will bring a glow to your cheeks. bloom, blush, rosiness, pinkness, redness, flush.
3 (v) We watched the coals glow in the hearth. glimmer, burn, redden, smoulder.
4 (v) These stickers glow in the dark. shine, shimmer, gleam, glimmer, show up.

glowing
1 (adj) Glowing coals. See **burning** 1.
2 (adj) Glowing colours. See **bright** 2.
3 (adj) A glowing complexion. rosy, pink, healthy, radiant, reddish, ruddy, florid.
OPPOSITES: pale, wan.
4 (adj) A glowing report. complimentary, enthusiastic, ecstatic, rave (informal).
OPPOSITES: critical, scathing.

glue see **stick** 5.

glum see **depressed**.

gnarled
(adj) Gnarled hands. twisted, misshapen, knobbly, knotted, distorted, contorted, weather-beaten, leathery, wrinkled.

gnash see **grind** 2.

gnaw
(v) *Carrots are nice to gnaw.* chew, bite, nibble, munch, crunch.

go
1 (v) *Do you want to go to London?* travel, journey, make your way, drive, fly, take the train, cycle, walk, motor, ride, sail, cruise, voyage, move.
2 (v) *It's time to go. See* **leave** 1.
3 (v) *The time seemed to go so quickly. See* **pass** 2.
4 (v) *Wind up the toy to make it go. See* **work** 4.
5 (v) *Where do these books go?* belong, stay, live (informal), fit in, have a place.
6 (v) *Will this belt go round my waist?* reach, extend, stretch, fit.
7 (v) *Let's wait and see how things go.* work out, turn out, develop, unfold, progress, end up, pan out (informal).
8 (v) *This cake will go mouldy if you don't eat it.* become, grow, turn, get.
9 (v) *If you use this cream, your rash will soon go. See* **go away** 3.
10 (v) *That chair will have to go.* be thrown away, be got rid of, be disposed of, be discarded, be chucked out (informal), be dumped (informal).
OPPOSITE: stay.
11 (v) *Granny's eyesight is beginning to go. See* **fail** 5.
12 (v) *Do these shorts and socks go?* match, go together, coordinate, complement each other, blend, harmonize.
13 (n) (informal) *Have a go! See* **try** 1.
14 (n) (informal) *Matty has lots of go.* energy, drive, vitality, get-up-and-go (informal), oomph (informal), push (informal), vigour, life, spirit, verve.

go about
(v) *I'm not sure how to go about this task.* approach, tackle, begin, set about.

go after *see* **follow** 1, 2.

go-ahead (informal) *see* **permission**.

go ahead
(v) *We decided to go ahead without you.* start, begin, proceed, go on, continue.

goal *see* **aim** 1.

go along with
1 (v) *David asked me to go along with him. See* **go with** 1.
2 (v) *Let's hope Nat will go along with our plan. See* **agree** 6.

go away
1 (v) *Go away and leave me alone!* clear off (informal), shove off (informal), push off (informal), get lost (informal), scram (informal), beat it (slang), hop it (slang).
OPPOSITES: come here, stay.
2 (v) *Do you have to go away so soon? See* **leave** 1.
3 (v) *I wish these spots would go away.* go, clear up, disappear, vanish, fade away, die down, melt away.
OPPOSITES: stay, appear.

go back *see* **return** 1, 2.

gobble
(v) *Don't gobble your food.* bolt, guzzle, gulp, scoff (informal), wolf down, shovel down, devour, pig out on (slang).

gobsmacked (slang) *see* **astonished**.

god
(n) deity, divine being, divinity, Creator.

go down
1 (v) *As we approached land, the plane began to go down. See* **descend** 1.
2 (v) *Prices are expected to go down. See* **decrease** 2.
3 (v) *I watched the sun go down over the sea. See* **set** 5.

go for
1 (v) *Did you see our goalie go for the ball?* reach for, stretch for, lunge for, dive for, clutch at, grab at, fetch, go and get.
2 (v) *I'm scared the dog might go for me.* attack, set upon, rush at, spring at.
3 (v) *Mel will really go for you in that shirt. See* **fancy** 3.

go in *see* **enter** 1.

golden
1 (adj) *Golden treasure.* gilded, gilt, shining, gleaming, brilliant.
2 (adj) *Golden hair. See* **blonde** 2.

gone
(adj) *All the food's gone.* finished, eaten, consumed, used up, done, missing, disappeared, vanished, lost.

good-looking *see* **attractive**.

gooey
(adj) (informal) *A gooey mixture.* sticky, squidgy, gluey, glutinous, tacky, syrupy.

go off
1 (v) *This bomb could go off at any moment. See* **explode**.
2 (v) *Don't go off without saying goodbye. See* **leave** 1.
3 (v) (informal) *This cheese will go off soon.* go mouldy, go bad, rot, decay, decompose, putrefy, go stale, go sour.
4 (v) (informal) *At present Tom likes the Howlers, but he'll soon go off them.* get bored with, tire of, get sick of (informal), take a dislike to, turn against.

go on *see* **continue** 1, 2.

go out
1 (v) *I just saw Samantha go out.* leave, walk out, walk off, depart, exit.
OPPOSITES: come in, enter.
2 (v) *It took ages for the fire to go out.* die down, be extinguished, be quenched.
OPPOSITES: kindle, ignite.

go out with
(v) *I don't want to go out with you any more.* see, go with, go steady with (informal), date (informal).

go over
(v) *Go over this topic carefully before the test.* look over, revise, review, read through, work through, study, examine, check, scan, skim.

good				
a good person	**a good deed**	**a good footballer**	**good work**	**a good excuse**
blameless	altruistic	accomplished	admirable	adequate
decent	(unselfish)	capable	careful	genuine
honest	caring	competent	commendable	legitimate
honourable	charitable	expert	competent	proper
just	considerate	fine	excellent	reasonable
kind	generous	first-class	first-rate	satisfactory
law-abiding	helpful	gifted	pleasing	valid
moral	humane	proficient	satisfactory	
righteous	kind	skilful	sound	**good food**
saintly	thoughtful	skilled	splendid	appetizing
trustworthy		talented	thorough	delicious
upright	**a good film**			mouthwatering
virtuous	brilliant	**good weather**	**a good mood**	scrumptious (informal)
a good child	excellent	bright	buoyant	tasty
angelic	fantastic (informal)	calm	carefree	well-cooked
cooperative	great	clear	cheerful	yummy (informal)
docile	impressive	cloudless	cheery	
helpful	marvellous	fabulous (informal)	chirpy (informal)	**Fruit is good for you.**
obedient	outstanding	fair	contented	beneficial
obliging	sensational (informal)	fine	happy	healthy
polite	superb	glorious	jolly	nourishing
well-behaved	terrific (informal)	mild	jovial	nutritious
well-mannered	wonderful	sunny	light-hearted	wholesome
willing			optimistic	
			positive	

gorgeous
1 *(adj) The queen wore a gorgeous diamond necklace.* magnificent, beautiful, splendid, superb, dazzling, glittering, stunning *(informal)*, brilliant, breathtaking, resplendent, opulent, sumptuous, showy.
OPPOSITES: plain, ugly.
2 *(adj) You look gorgeous in that dress.* beautiful, lovely, stunning *(informal)*, dazzling, ravishing, attractive, sexy *(informal)*, drop-dead gorgeous *(slang)*.
OPPOSITES: plain, unattractive.
3 *(adj) The weather was gorgeous.* glorious, wonderful, lovely, beautiful, marvellous, terrific *(informal)*, fantastic *(informal)*, superb, excellent, fine.
OPPOSITE: awful.

go round
(v) Take the new road, if you want to go round the town. bypass, skirt, avoid, steer clear of, get round, make a detour round.

gory
(adj) This film contains some gory scenes. bloody, bloodthirsty, grisly, gruesome, brutal, violent, horrific, sickening, savage.

gossip
1 *(v) It's unkind to gossip about other people.* spread rumours, spread gossip, circulate rumours, spread stories, spread scandal, tittle-tattle, bad-mouth *(slang)*.
2 *(v) Don't gossip in class. See* **talk** 1.
3 *(n) Have you heard the gossip?* rumours *(plural)*, latest *(informal)*, scandal, tittle-tattle, hearsay, idle talk, dirt *(slang)*.
4 *(n) Mrs Bunn is a real gossip.* scandalmonger, gossipmonger, busybody, telltale, tattler, chatterbox *(informal)*.

go through
1 *(v) This arrow will never go through the dragon's skin. See* **pierce**.
2 *(v) I can't go through another day of this misery. See* **suffer** 3.
3 *(v) Try not to go through your pocket money so quickly.* spend, use up, exhaust, squander, fritter away, consume.

go under
1 *(v) Pirate Peg was scared her ship would go under.* sink, go down, be submerged.
2 *(v) Dad's firm may go under. See* **fail** 4.

go up see **rise** 1, 2.

govern
(v) Who will govern the country after the next election? rule, run, be in charge of, lead, control, administer, manage, conduct the affairs of, be in power over, direct, steer, command, preside over, reign over.

go with
1 *(v) Oz asked me to go with him to the party.* accompany, escort, go along with.
2 *(v) Does this top go with my skirt? See* **match** 2.

go without
(v) Could you go without chocolate, if you had to? do without, survive without, abstain from, deny yourself, go short of.

go wrong
1 *(v) Where did I go wrong in this maths question?* make a mistake, miscalculate, slip up *(informal)*, go astray, blunder.
2 *(v) Why do my brilliant ideas always go wrong?* turn out badly, end in disaster, come to grief, come to nothing, fail, misfire, fall flat, flop *(informal)*.

grab
1 *(v) I felt someone grab my arm.* clutch, seize, grip, clasp, grasp, catch hold of.
2 *(v) Burglar Beryl managed to grab the jewels. See* **snatch**.

graceful
1 *(adj) A graceful ballerina.* elegant, poised, supple, lithe, agile, nimble.
OPPOSITES: clumsy, awkward.
2 *(adj) Graceful dance steps.* smooth, elegant, flowing, fluid, balletic.
OPPOSITES: clumsy, awkward.

grade
1 *(n) I hope I get a good grade for my homework. See* **mark** 4.
2 *(n) Mum was promoted to a higher grade in the company. See* **level** 6.
3 *(v) Mrs Badger didn't have time to grade our tests.* assess, evaluate, classify, rate.

gradual
1 *(adj) There's been a gradual improvement in your work.* steady, continuous, progressive, systematic, step-by-step, slow, moderate, unspectacular.
OPPOSITE: sudden.
2 *(adj) There's a gradual slope down to the river. See* **gentle** 4.

grand
1 *(adj) Lord Lucre lives in a grand mansion.* magnificent, imposing, impressive, splendid, superb, palatial, stately, sumptuous, opulent, luxurious.
OPPOSITE: modest.
2 *(adj) The king made a grand entrance.* dignified, stately, majestic, regal.
3 *(adj) Our new neighbours seem very grand.* posh *(informal)*, upper class, upper crust *(informal)*, distinguished, aristocratic, haughty, high and mighty *(informal)*, lordly, imperious, pompous, pretentious.
OPPOSITES: ordinary, common.

grapple
1 *(v) Indiana had to grapple with the monster. See* **struggle** 2.
2 *(v) I'm too tired to grapple with this problem now. See* **tackle** 2.

grasp
1 *(v) Grasp my hand so you don't fall! See* **grip**.
2 *(v) I don't quite grasp what you're saying. See* **understand** 1.
3 *(n) Winter held the country in its icy grasp.* grip, embrace, clasp, clutches *(plural)*, hold.
4 *(n) Rick has a good grasp of the subject.* understanding, comprehension, awareness, knowledge, mastery, grip, appreciation, perception, insight.

grass
1 *(n) Don't walk on the grass!* lawn, turf, green, pitch, playing field.
2 *(n) The cows roamed through the grass.* meadow, pasture, field.
3 *(v) (slang) Burglar Beryl didn't want to grass on her friends. See* **inform** 2.

grate
1 *(v) Please grate this carrot.* shred, mince.
2 *(v) I heard the door grate across the tiles.* scrape, grind, rasp, scratch, rub, creak, squeak.

grateful
(adj) I'm grateful for your help. thankful, appreciative of, obliged to you, indebted to you.
OPPOSITE: ungrateful.

grave
1 *(n) We visited the grave of Queen Victoria.* burial place, tomb, sepulchre, burial chamber, mausoleum, crypt, vault.
2 *(adj) Mrs Badger looked grave as she gave us the news. See* **serious** 1.
3 *(adj) A grave problem. See* **serious** 3.
4 *(adj) A grave illness. See* **serious** 4.

graveyard
(n) cemetery, burial ground, churchyard.

graze
1 *(v) How did you graze your knee?* scrape, scratch, cut, skin, chafe.
2 *(v) Cows graze in fields.* feed, browse.

greasy
1 *(adj) I hate greasy chips.* fatty, oily.
2 *(adj) The mud made the path greasy. See* **slippery** 1.
3 *(adj) Flash Frank is such a greasy character. See* **slimy** 2.

great
1 *(adj) The explorers crossed a great stretch of desert.* immense, vast, large, huge, extensive, boundless, unlimited.
OPPOSITES: small, short.
2 *(adj) A great boulder blocked the cave entrance.* large, huge, enormous, massive, immense, gigantic, colossal, stupendous, tremendous, mammoth, gargantuan.
OPPOSITE: small.
3 *(adj) Clare's broken leg caused her great pain.* extreme, intense, considerable, acute, excessive, exceptional, inordinate.
OPPOSITES: slight, little.
4 *(adj) This is a great day for the school.* important, significant, momentous, historic, red-letter.
OPPOSITES: unimportant, insignificant.
5 *(adj) Anji is a great tennis player.* skilful, skilled, expert, first-class, ace *(informal)*, capable, proficient, able, talented, gifted, outstanding, impressive, crack *(slang)*.
OPPOSITES: poor, terrible.
6 *(adj) Charles Dickens was a great writer.* remarkable, outstanding, exceptional, talented, gifted, superb, excellent, distinguished, illustrious, eminent, famous, celebrated, renowned, notable.
OPPOSITES: second-rate, insignificant.

7 *(adj) Zoë is a great fan of Famous Fred.* devoted, enthusiastic, keen, zealous.
8 *(adj) Paris is one of the world's great cities. See* **major** 1.
9 *(adj) (informal) The party was really great.* excellent, superb, fantastic *(informal),* terrific *(informal),* tremendous *(informal),* marvellous, decent *(informal),* cool *(informal),* mega *(slang),* crucial *(slang),* wicked *(slang),* neat *(slang).*

greed
1 *(n) Kevin's tummyache was the result of his greed.* greediness, gluttony, overeating, self-indulgence, piggishness, insatiability.
OPPOSITE: self-restraint.
2 *(n) The sight of the gold filled Pirate Peg with greed.* avarice, covetousness, desire, hunger, longing, craving, eagerness.
OPPOSITE: generosity.

greedy
1 *(adj) Don't be so greedy! Leave some ice cream for me!* gluttonous, self-indulgent, piggish, hoggish, insatiable, voracious.
OPPOSITES: self-restrained, abstemious.
2 *(adj) The greedy miser wouldn't share his money.* selfish, avaricious, grasping, covetous, rapacious, miserly, tightfisted, niggardly, money-grubbing *(informal).*
OPPOSITES: generous, unselfish.

green
1 *(n)* SHADES OF GREEN: acid green, apple green, bottle green, emerald, grass green, jade, khaki, lime green, Lincoln green, moss green, olive green, pea green, racing green, sage green, sea green.
2 *(adj) Daniel is interested in green issues.* environmental, ecological, conservationist.
3 *(adj) Unleaded petrol is supposed to be green.* environmentally friendly, non-polluting, eco-friendly, ecologically sound.
OPPOSITE: environmentally harmful.
4 *(adj) The cottage nestled in a green valley.* grassy, verdant, leafy, flourishing.
5 *(adj) Sîan looked green when she saw my new bike. See* **envious.**

greet
(v) Mrs Badger was waiting to greet us as we arrived. welcome, say hello to, meet, receive, shake hands with, acknowledge, give a greeting to, salute, hail *(old-fashioned),* nod to, wave to.

grey
1 *(n)* SHADES OF GREY: charcoal grey, dove grey, gunmetal, iron grey, pearl grey, pewter, silver, slate grey, smoke grey, steel grey.
2 *(adj) Winter days are often grey.* dull, cloudy, overcast, foggy, misty, murky, dark, dim, sunless, dreary, dismal, gloomy, drab, depressing, cheerless.
OPPOSITES: bright, sunny.
3 *(adj) Granddad's hair is grey.* silver, silvery, grizzled, greying, hoary, white.
4 *(adj) Cyril has such a grey personality.* colourless, anonymous, nondescript, dull, characterless, uninteresting.

5 *(adj) Natasha's face turned grey. See* **pale** 2.

grief
(n) Alice couldn't hide her grief when her dog died. sorrow, sadness, unhappiness, misery, dejection, distress, anguish, despair, heartache, pain, agony, suffering, regret, mourning, woe.
OPPOSITES: joy, delight.

grieve
(v) It's natural to grieve when someone dies. be sad, mourn, sorrow, weep, cry, sob, be heartbroken, pine, ache, mope, lament *(old-fashioned),* go into mourning.
OPPOSITE: rejoice.

grim
1 *(adj) Mrs Badger looked grim as she gave us our test results.* serious, stern, sombre, severe, forbidding, formidable, fierce, cross, implacable, merciless.
OPPOSITES: cheerful, sympathetic.
2 *(adj) The witch's castle looked grim in the moonlight.* forbidding, menacing, ominous, sinister, bleak, gloomy.
OPPOSITES: pleasant, welcoming.
3 *(adj) This film contains some grim battle scenes.* grisly, gruesome, ghastly, shocking, harrowing, horrible, horrendous, hideous, frightful, appalling, unspeakable.
OPPOSITE: pleasant.

grimy *see* **dirty** 1.

grin *see* **smile** 1, 2.

grind
1 *(v) We need to grind some coffee.* crush, mill, pulverize, pound, powder, crumble, granulate, mash, smash, grate.
2 *(v) I hate it when you grind your teeth.* gnash, grate, rub together, scrape, grit.
3 *(n) (informal) I'm dreading the grind of revising.* hard work, slog, drudgery, chore, toil, sweat *(informal),* exertion.

grip
(v) Grip my hand so you don't fall. grab, clutch, grasp, clasp, hold, hold on to, hang on to, seize, take hold of, clench.

gripe *(informal) see* **complaint.**

gripping *see* **fascinating.**

grisly *see* **gruesome.**

groan
1 *(v) I heard Bruno groan with pain.* moan, cry, murmur, whimper, sigh, whine.
2 *(v) (informal) My parents groan about the mess in my room. See* **complain.**

groggy *(informal) see* **dizzy.**

groom
1 *(n) I work as a groom at the local stables.* stableboy, stablegirl, stable lad, ostler *(old-fashioned).*
2 *(v) Groom your pony regularly.* rub down, curry, brush, clean.

groove
(n) Make a groove in the wood. channel, cut, score, slot, track, scratch, hollow, trench, rut, trough, furrow, indentation.

grope
(v) I had to grope around in the dark for my key. fumble, feel, scrabble, pick, fish, search, hunt.

gross
(adj) (slang) That pink shirt is really gross. disgusting, revolting, vile, repulsive, foul, tasteless, tacky *(informal),* naff *(slang),* yucky *(slang).*

grotesque
(adj) hideous, repulsive, ugly, misshapen, deformed, strange, bizarre, weird, outlandish, freakish, unnatural, monstrous.

a grotesque gargoyle

grotty
1 *(adj) (slang) Ziggy lives in a grotty flat.* horrible, disgusting, dingy, shabby, tatty, scruffy, run-down, dilapidated, seedy, dirty, filthy, grubby, squalid, sordid, stinking, crummy *(slang),* scuzzy *(slang).*
OPPOSITES: smart, attractive.
2 *(adj) (slang) I feel really grotty this morning. See* **rotten** 3.

ground
1 *(n) Lie flat on the ground!* floor, deck *(informal),* earth.
2 *(n) Plant the seeds in the ground. See* **earth** 2.
3 *(n) The council is building a new football ground.* pitch, field, stadium, arena, park.
4 *(v) This storm could ground the ship.* run ashore, beach, wreck, shipwreck, strand.
5 *(v) (informal) Dad will ground you if you misbehave.* keep you in, forbid you to go out, confine you to the house, restrict.
6 **grounds** *(plural n) Lord Lucre's house is set in extensive grounds.* gardens *(plural),* parkland, surroundings *(plural),* estate, land, property, acres *(plural),* fields *(plural).*
7 **grounds** *(plural n) Bella has good grounds for complaint. See* **reason** 1.

group
1 *(v) Group round your team leaders.* gather, collect, get together, congregate, assemble, come together, cluster, crowd, get into groups.
OPPOSITES: split up, disperse.
2 *(v) Group the photos according to size. See* **sort** 3.
3 *(n) You're welcome to join our group.* gang, band, clique, posse *(informal),* circle, set, bunch *(informal),* crowd, crew *(informal),* mob, club, community, party, company, meeting, gathering, assembly, society, association, organization.
4 *(n) A group of animals.* herd, horde, brood *(chicks),* colony *(ants, rabbits),* flock *(birds, sheep),* gaggle *(geese),* litter *(kittens, piglets, puppies),* pack *(hounds, wolves),* pride *(lions),* school *(dolphins, whales),* shoal *(fish),* swarm *(insects).*
5 *(n) A group of things.* bunch, bundle, cluster, clump, set, batch, assortment, collection, array, arrangement.

grovel
(v) There's no need to grovel to Lord Lucre. crawl, creep, toady, kowtow, bow and scrape, bootlick (informal), fawn, suck up (informal), curry favour with, ingratiate yourself with, humble yourself before.

grow
1 (v) I hope I'll grow this year. get bigger, get taller, fill out, shoot up.
OPPOSITES: shrink, get smaller.
2 (v) Before our eyes, the puddle began to grow. expand, get bigger, get larger, spread, swell, enlarge, increase, extend, stretch, fill out, widen, lengthen, deepen.
OPPOSITES: contract, decline.
3 (v) Mum hopes that her business will grow. expand, develop, progress, advance, increase, prosper, flourish, boom, thrive.
OPPOSITES: contract, decline.
4 (v) These seeds will grow in the spring. germinate, sprout, bud, develop, spring up, shoot up, flourish, thrive.
5 (v) We grow orchids in our greenhouse. cultivate, produce, propagate, breed, raise, nurture, farm.
6 (v) Eventually, Luke will grow more sensible. become, get, come to be, turn.

grown-up see **adult** 1, 2.

growth
1 (n) The rapid growth in technology has changed the world. expansion, rise, increase, development, evolution, progress, advance, improvement.
OPPOSITE: decline.
2 (n) There has been a marked growth in crime. See **increase** 4.

grow up
(v) The prince waited for the princess to grow up. mature, develop, come of age, become an adult, reach adulthood.

grub
1 (n) It's cruel to keep that grub in a jam jar. caterpillar, maggot, larva.
2 (n) (informal) I'm desperate for some grub. See **food**.

grubby see **dirty** 1.

grudge
(n) This grudge of yours will eat you up inside. resentment, bitterness, grievance, hard feelings (plural), spite, malice, ill will, envy, hatred, malevolence, venom, hostility, animosity, antipathy, dislike.

grudging
(adj) Ellie gave me a grudging smile when I won. reluctant, half-hearted, unenthusiastic, lukewarm, unwilling, ungracious, resentful, envious.
OPPOSITES: enthusiastic, wholehearted.

gruelling see **exhausting**.

gruesome
(adj) A gruesome monster. grisly, ghastly, ghoulish, horrible, hideous, loathsome, repulsive, monstrous, horrifying, frightful, fearful, terrible, dreadful, spine-chilling, hair-raising, macabre, grim.

gruff
1 (adj) Uncle Arthur has a gruff voice. husky, low, hoarse, croaky, rough, gravelly, harsh, rasping, throaty, guttural.
2 (adj) Aunt Bertha has a gruff manner. blunt, brusque, curt, abrupt, ungracious, crusty, crabby, grumpy, grouchy (informal), crotchety (informal), surly, bad-tempered.
OPPOSITES: gracious, pleasant.

grumble see **complain**.

grumpy
(adj) Max gets grumpy when he's tired. irritable, bad-tempered, grouchy (informal), cross, ratty (informal), crabby, crotchety (informal), tetchy, peevish, surly, sullen, sulky, huffy, cantankerous.
OPPOSITES: good-humoured, cheerful.

grungy (slang) see **scruffy** 2.

guarantee see **promise** 1, 2.

guard
1 (v) We must guard the house. protect, keep watch over, safeguard, defend, patrol, police, mind, secure, shield.
2 (n) A guard is on patrol. watchman, lookout, sentinel, sentry (army), warder (prison), jailer (prison), bodyguard, escort.

guess
1 (v) Try to guess the weight of the doll. estimate, hazard a guess at, have a stab at (informal), work out, calculate, speculate about, predict, second-guess (informal).
2 (v) (informal) I guess I should go now. See **think** 2.
3 (n) Your guess was quite right. estimate, conjecture, speculation, guesswork, guesstimate (informal), prediction, shot in the dark, supposition, theory, hypothesis.

guest
(n) Try to be polite in front of our guest. visitor, caller, company.

guidance
(n) You need guidance when choosing a career. advice, counselling, direction, help, briefing, instruction, guidelines (plural), pointers (plural), tips (plural), hints (plural).

guide
1 (v) Guide me to the nearest shelter. lead, take, show, escort, accompany, direct, conduct, steer, shepherd.
2 (v) Try to guide the ship into harbour. steer, pilot, navigate, manoeuvre, direct.
3 (v) You need someone to guide you as you choose a career. advise, give you advice, counsel, give you direction, give you pointers, help, inform, instruct.
4 (n) We followed the guide through the mountains. leader, scout, escort, courier.
5 (n) Use this as a guide when you do your drawing. model, example, pattern, master, standard, benchmark, yardstick.

guilt
1 (n) Gregory was tormented by guilt. feelings of guilt (plural), remorse, regret, shame, self-reproach, self-condemnation, guilty conscience, bad conscience.

2 (n) The fingerprints proved Burglar Beryl's guilt. culpability, responsibility, wrongdoing, misconduct, criminality.
OPPOSITE: innocence.

guilty
1 (adj) Burglar Beryl was guilty. to blame, at fault, responsible, culpable, convicted.
OPPOSITES: innocent, guiltless.
2 (adj) Gregory felt guilty. ashamed, conscience-stricken, guilt-ridden, filled with regret, remorseful, repentant, rueful, sheepish, shamefaced, hangdog.
OPPOSITES: unrepentant, unashamed.

gullible
(adj) Letty is so gullible, she'd believe anything. naive, trusting, easily taken in, unsuspecting, credulous, innocent, green.
OPPOSITES: suspicious, cynical.

gulp
1 (v) Don't gulp your cola so quickly. swallow, swig (informal), knock back (informal), down (informal), swill, slurp (informal), guzzle, toss off.
2 (v) Don't gulp your food. See **gobble**.
3 (v) The icy water made me gulp. See **gasp** 1.
4 (n) A gulp of water might cure your hiccups. mouthful, swallow, swig (informal), slurp (informal), draught.

gun
(n) firearm, artillery (heavy military guns).
TYPES OF GUN: airgun, automatic pistol, blunderbuss, cannon, handgun, howitzer, machine gun, mortar, musket, pistol, revolver, rifle, sawn-off shotgun, shotgun, stun gun, sub-machine-gun.

gunman
(n) armed robber, sniper, assassin, hit man (slang), terrorist, gangster, killer, murderer.

gurgle
1 (v) Can you hear the baby gurgle? burble, crow, chuckle, laugh.
2 (v) Listen to the stream gurgle over the stones. babble, bubble, burble, splash, murmur, tinkle, ripple, lap, plash.

gush
(v) Water began to gush from the pipe. pour, cascade, stream, flow, flood, spurt, spout, squirt, splash, surge, overflow.

gust
(n) A gust of wind blew my hat off. puff, blast, flurry, rush, squall, gale, breeze.

gusty see **windy** 1.

gut
1 (n) I have a pain in my gut. stomach, belly, tummy (informal), guts (plural), insides (plural) (informal), intestines (plural), innards (plural) (informal).
2 (adj) (informal) I didn't think about it; it was a gut reaction. instinctive, intuitive, spontaneous, involuntary, unthinking, natural, emotional, deep-seated.
3 **guts** (plural n) (informal) It takes guts to face up to a bully. See **courage**.

guzzle see **gobble**.

habit
1 (n) Cindy has a habit of biting her nails. practice, way, tendency, quirk, mannerism.
2 (n) It's our habit to spend Christmas with Grandma. custom, practice, tradition, routine, convention, procedure, rule.
3 (n) Mum wants to kick her habit of smoking. addiction to, dependence on, craving for, weakness for, obsession with, fixation with.

haggard
(adj) The rescued sailors looked haggard. drawn, drained, exhausted, worn out, tired out, thin, gaunt, hollow-cheeked, hollow-eyed, pinched, wasted, emaciated, all skin and bone (informal), cadaverous.

haggle see **bargain** 3.

hair
1 (n) Sharmila's hair reaches her waist. locks (plural), tresses (plural), curls (plural), mop (informal), mane, shock, head of hair.
2 (n) Craig is starting to get some hair on his chin. whiskers (plural), bristles (plural), stubble, down, fuzz (informal).
3 (n) The animal's hair was matted. fur, coat, wool, fleece (sheep), mane (horse).

hair-raising see **frightening**.
hairy
1 (adj) A hairy animal. furry, shaggy, long-haired, fleecy, woolly, fuzzy.
OPPOSITE: hairless.
2 (adj) A hairy face. bearded, whiskery, bristly, stubbly, unshaven, fuzzy.
OPPOSITE: clean-shaven.

half-hearted
1 (adj) I feel half-hearted about this plan. lukewarm, unenthusiastic, apathetic, indifferent, unconcerned, unemotional, neutral, passive, uncommitted.
OPPOSITE: enthusiastic.
2 (adj) The goalie made a half-hearted attempt to reach the ball. listless, lacklustre, perfunctory, cursory, superficial.
OPPOSITES: wholehearted, determined.

hall
1 (n) The dining room is at the far end of the hall. hallway, entrance hall, lobby, foyer (hotel, theatre), passage, corridor.
2 (n) Over a hundred people gathered in the hall. meeting hall, assembly hall, village hall, church hall, concert hall, auditorium, conference hall, exhibition hall.

halt see **stop** 1, 4, 9.
hammer
1 (n) Len dropped the hammer on his foot. mallet, sledgehammer, gavel.
2 (v) Hammer this nail into the wood. bang, drive, hit, knock, tap.

hamper see **hinder** 1.
hand
1 (n) Raise your hand if you disagree. fist, palm, paw (informal), mitt (slang).
2 (n) I need a hand to move this table. helping hand, help, assistance, aid.
3 (n) The audience gave me a big hand. clap, round of applause, ovation.
4 (v) Hand your ticket to the bus driver. give, hand over, pass, present, submit, offer, deliver, reach (informal).

handcuffs
(plural n) cuffs (plural) (informal), bracelets (plural) (slang), manacles (plural) (old-fashioned), fetters (plural) (old-fashioned), shackles (plural) (old-fashioned).

hand down
1 (v) I hand down my clothes to my younger sister. pass on, pass down, give.
2 (v) Lord Lucre plans to hand down his fortune to his children. leave, pass on, bequeath, will, transfer, give.

handicap
1 (n) Deafness is a physical handicap. disability, impairment.
2 (n) It's a handicap to live a long way from school. disadvantage, drawback, inconvenience, nuisance, obstacle, hindrance, impediment, stumbling block.
OPPOSITE: advantage.

hair and hairstyles

hair colours	hairstyles	you can have your hair...	hair can be...	
auburn	Afro	backcombed	bouncy	unkempt
black	beehive	bleached	bushy	wavy
blonde	bob	braided	coarse	wild
brown	braids	crimped	curly	windswept
carroty	bun	cropped	dishevelled	wiry
chestnut	bunches	dyed	fine	wispy
coppery	chignon	flicked back	floppy	
dark	cornrows	gelled	flowing	
fair	crew cut	hennaed	frizzy	**other hair**
flaxen	dreadlocks	highlighted	glossy	**words**
(golden)	flat-top	layered	greasy	bald patch
ginger	French plait	permed	lank	blue rinse
grey	hippy braids	plaited	limp	fringe
greying	mohican	scraped back	matted	hair band
mousy	pageboy	shaved	neat	hair extension
platinum	perm	slicked back	receding	hairline
blonde	pigtail	streaked	shaggy	hairnet
raven (black)	plaits	tinted	shining	hairpiece
red	ponytail	undercut	sleek	hair ribbon
sandy	pudding-bowl		smooth	hair slide
silver	quiff		spiky	parting
snowy	ringlets		straggly	sideburns
strawberry	short back		straight	toupee (man's
blonde	and sides		tangled	hairpiece)
white	skinhead		thinning	wig
	wedge		tousled	

beehive

braids

cornrows

chignon

quiff

bob

dreadlocks

mohican

beads

hairpin

hairgrip

gel

handicapped *see* **disabled**.

handle
1 *(v) Be careful how you handle your guinea pig.* hold, pick up, touch, stroke, fondle, caress, feel, finger, paw *(informal)*.
2 *(v) This machine is easy to handle.* control, operate, manage, work, use, run, manoeuvre, drive, steer, manipulate.
3 *(v) Mrs Badger can handle our class.* deal with, manage, control, cope with.

hand out *see* **give out**.

handsome
(adj) Ryan is so handsome! attractive, good-looking, gorgeous, hunky *(informal)*.
OPPOSITES: ugly, unattractive.

handwriting *see* **writing**.

handy
1 *(adj) This gadget is really handy.* useful, practical, helpful, easy to use, user-friendly, convenient, well-designed, neat *(slang)*.
OPPOSITES: awkward, impractical.
2 *(adj) Do you have your ruler handy?* within easy reach, close at hand, nearby, accessible, convenient, available, ready.
OPPOSITES: inaccessible, out-of-the-way.

hang
1 *(v) I'd like the streamers to hang from the ceiling.* hang down, be suspended, dangle, swing, trail, drape, sway.
2 *(v) Look how the trees hang over the pond.* lean, bend, bow, droop, sag, loll.
3 *(v) Is this a good place to hang the picture?* put up, fix, pin up, nail, stick, hook, suspend, fasten, attach.
4 *(v) The eagle seemed to hang in the air.* See **hover**.

hang around
1 *(v) Is this where you like to hang around?* hang about, hang out *(informal)*, spend your time, loiter, linger, hang loose *(informal)*, frequent, haunt.
2 *(v) Don't hang around - we'll be late!* See **delay** 1.

hang on *see* **hold on** 1, 2.

hang-up
(n) (informal) I have a hang-up about flying. phobia, fear of, problem with, thing *(informal)*, mental block, inhibition.

happen
1 *(v) Anything could happen if you make a wish.* occur, take place, come about, come to pass *(old-fashioned)*, follow, result, transpire, come up, crop up *(informal)*.
2 *(v) Did you happen to see Vanessa?* chance, have the good fortune, have the luck, have the misfortune.
3 **happen to** *(v) What will happen to me if I fail my exams?* become of, befall.

happiness
(n) The thought of his holiday filled Mac with happiness. joy, delight, pleasure, contentment, bliss, glee, elation, ecstasy, jubilation, rejoicing, exuberance, euphoria, high spirits *(plural)*, rapture, merriment.
OPPOSITES: sadness, sorrow.

happy
1 *(adj) I feel happy.* cheerful, contented, in good spirits, light-hearted, jolly, joyful, jubilant, elated, ecstatic, euphoric, on cloud nine *(informal)*, over the moon *(informal)*, in seventh heaven, walking on air *(informal)*.
OPPOSITES: sad, miserable.
2 *(adj) I'm so happy you could come.* See **pleased**.
3 *(adj) We had a happy holiday.* blissful, heavenly, idyllic, jolly, merry, enjoyable.
OPPOSITE: miserable.

harass *see* **pester**.

harbour *see* **port**.

hard
1 *(adj) We tried to dig a hole, but the ground was too hard.* firm, solid, stony, rocky, unyielding, impenetrable, resistant, rigid, dense, compacted, frozen.
OPPOSITE: soft.
2 *(adj) This sum is hard!* See **difficult** 1.
3 *(adj) Gardening is such hard work.* exhausting, gruelling, strenuous, backbreaking, tough, killing *(informal)*, demanding, laborious, uphill, heavy.
OPPOSITES: easy, light.
4 *(adj) Barney has had a hard year.* difficult, tough, rough *(informal)*, unpleasant, painful, distressing, grim, unbearable, intolerable, disastrous, calamitous, dark, black.
OPPOSITES: easy, pleasant.
5 *(adj) The boxer suffered a hard blow to the head.* heavy, violent, powerful, driving, forceful, severe, strong, fierce, sharp.
OPPOSITES: gentle, light.
6 *(adj) Miss Blackheart is a hard woman.* hardhearted, heartless, unsympathetic, unfeeling, cold, callous, cruel, ruthless, pitiless, merciless, inflexible, unrelenting, stern, strict, brutal.
OPPOSITES: kind, softhearted.
7 *(adv) Greg works hard.* diligently, industriously, conscientiously, energetically, strenuously, vigorously, untiringly, persistently, doggedly, unceasingly, steadily, resolutely, furiously.

harden
(v) Wait for the mixture to harden. set, solidify, go hard, stiffen, freeze, jell, congeal, cake.
OPPOSITE: soften.

hardly
(adv) I hardly recognized you in that hat! scarcely, only just, barely, with difficulty.
OPPOSITE: easily.

hard-wearing
(adj) Hard-wearing fabric. tough, strong, sturdy, durable, long-lasting, rugged, resilient, stout.

hard-working
(adj) Libby is so hard-working! industrious, diligent, conscientious, energetic, tireless, productive, busy, indefatigable, keen.
OPPOSITES: lazy, workshy.

harm
1 *(v) Casper wouldn't harm anyone.* hurt, injure, ill-treat, abuse, wound, inflict pain on, inflict suffering on.
2 *(v) Reading in poor light can harm your eyesight.* See **damage** 3.
3 *(n) The fire caused a lot of harm.* See **damage** 1.
4 *(n) The rumours caused a lot of harm.* damage, distress, suffering, pain, ill feeling, mischief, upset, trauma.
OPPOSITE: benefit.

harmful
1 *(adj) Smoking is harmful.* damaging, bad for you, dangerous, detrimental, injurious.
OPPOSITES: beneficial, healthy.
2 *(adj) Bleach contains harmful substances.* See **dangerous** 4.

harmless
1 *(adj) This mixture is harmless.* safe, innocuous, nontoxic, nonpoisonous.
OPPOSITES: dangerous, deadly.
2 *(adj) It was just a bit of harmless fun.* gentle, innocent, inoffensive, innocuous, blameless, unobjectionable.
OPPOSITES: hurtful, offensive.

harrowing *see* **disturbing**.

harsh
1 *(adj) The commander spoke in a harsh voice.* grating, rasping, rough, strident, raucous, jarring, guttural, gruff, hoarse.
OPPOSITES: soft, gentle.
2 *(adj) Life in the prison was harsh.* hard, tough, austere, grim, Spartan, bleak, comfortless, brutal.
OPPOSITES: easy, comfortable.
3 *(adj) Aunt Bertha's criticisms were harsh.* severe, stern, unsparing, unkind, caustic, abrasive, stringent, ruthless, cruel.
OPPOSITES: gentle, compassionate.
4 *(adj) The station lights were harsh.* glaring, dazzling, garish, over-bright.
OPPOSITES: restful, subdued.

hassle
1 *(n) (informal) I got my ticket without any hassle.* bother, trouble, difficulty, fuss, inconvenience, problem, struggle.
2 *(v) (informal) I wish you wouldn't hassle me!* See **pester**.

hassled
(adj) (informal) After the shopping trip, Mum looked hassled. harassed, stressed, strained, uptight *(informal)*, worried, careworn, troubled, distraught, harried.
OPPOSITES: carefree, relaxed.

hasty
1 *(adj) You'll make mistakes if you're too hasty.* rash, impetuous, impulsive, impatient, hot-headed, reckless, foolhardy.
OPPOSITES: cautious, careful.
2 *(adj) The robbers made a hasty getaway.* See **fast** 1.
3 *(adj) I had a hasty glance at the paper.* quick, brief, rapid, hurried, fleeting, passing, cursory, perfunctory.
OPPOSITES: leisurely, thorough.

hat
(n) headdress, headgear, head covering.

stetson

TYPES OF HAT: balaclava, baseball cap, beanie, bearskin *(soldier)*, beret, boater, bobble hat, bonnet, bowler, cap, cloche, coronet, crash helmet, crown, deerstalker, fez, hard hat, homburg, hunting cap, jockey cap, mitre *(bishop)*, nightcap, Panama hat, peaked cap, pillbox, pith helmet, skullcap, sombrero, sou'wester, stetson, sunhat, tiara, top hat, trilby, turban, wimple *(nun)*.

deerstalker

boater

pillbox

Panama hat

pith helmet

fez

trilby

cloche

hate
1 *(v) I hate bad language.* detest, loathe, despise, cannot stand, cannot bear, have an aversion to, dislike, abhor, abominate. OPPOSITES: love, adore.
2 *(n) Miss Blackheart is full of hate.* hatred, hostility, loathing, dislike, ill will, malice, venom, animosity, antagonism, vindictiveness, antipathy, enmity, rancour. OPPOSITE: love.

haughty *see* **proud** 2.

haul *see* **pull**.

haunted
1 *(adj) Do you think that Greystone Grange is haunted?* visited by spirits, cursed, jinxed, ghostly, spooky *(informal)*, eerie. ❖ *Also see* **ghosts & hauntings**.
2 *(adj) I was haunted by the memory of Samantha's smile.* obsessed, preoccupied, plagued, tormented, troubled, worried.

have
1 *(v) I have six pets.* own, possess, keep.
2 *(v) How many chapters does your book have?* contain, consist of, include, comprise, incorporate.
3 *(v) You will have good and bad times in your life.* experience, go through, live through, undergo, encounter, meet with, endure, enjoy, suffer.
4 *(v) Everyone will have a prize.* get, receive, be given, win, gain, obtain, acquire, secure, take.
5 *(v) Let's have a party! See* **give** 4.
6 *(v) Let's have tea.* eat, take, consume.
7 *(v) Mum's going to have another baby.* give birth to, produce, bring into the world, bear, deliver, bring up, raise.

have to
1 *(v) I have to do my homework.* must, should, ought to, have got to, need to.
2 *(v) There's no escaping. You'll have to pay.* be forced to, be compelled to, be made to, be obliged to, be required to.

havoc
(n) (informal) The pigs caused havoc in the pantry. chaos, confusion, mayhem, turmoil, upheaval, disruption, disorder.

haze
(n) I can hardly see you through the haze. mist, fog, murk, fumes *(plural)*, clouds *(plural)*, smog, smoke, dust.

hazy
1 *(adj) It's so hazy I can hardly see.* misty, foggy, smoky, cloudy, dim, smoggy. OPPOSITES: clear, bright.
2 *(adj) Without my glasses, everything looks hazy. See* **blurred**.
3 *(adj) I have a hazy memory of that weekend. See* **vague** 2.

head
1 *(n) I bumped my head.* forehead, temple, skull, pate, cranium, crown, nut *(slang)*, bonce *(slang)*, block *(slang)*.
2 *(n) Why don't you use your head!* brain, brains *(plural) (informal)*, intelligence, intellect, common sense, wits *(plural)*, reason, loaf *(slang)*, noddle *(informal)*.
3 *(n) Our school has a new head.* headteacher, principal, headmaster, headmistress.
4 *(n) Dad is the head of his company.* boss *(informal)*, chief executive, director, president, chairman, MD (managing director), manager, chief, leader.
5 *(n) The problem came to a head at the end of the week.* climax, crisis, critical point, turning point, crossroads, culmination.
6 *(v) Who will head the team? See* **lead** 2.

headache
(n) I've got a headache. splitting headache, migraine, sick headache, sore head.

head for
(v) Let's head for home. make for, aim for, go towards, make a beeline for, set off for.

heal
1 *(v) Will this heal my rash? See* **cure**.
2 *(v) I hope your broken arm will heal soon.* get better, mend, recover, improve, be cured, knit *(bones)*.

health
(n) Exercise is good for your health. wellbeing, fitness, strength, constitution.

healthy
1 *(adj) My parents have always been healthy.* fit, well, in good shape, hale and hearty, strong, active, vigorous, bursting with health, blooming. OPPOSITES: sickly, unwell.
2 *(adj) Try to eat foods that are healthy.* nutritious, wholesome, nourishing, good for you, healthgiving, beneficial. OPPOSITES: unhealthy, harmful.

heap
1 *(v) Heap the leaves together. See* **pile** 2.
2 *(n) A heap of papers. See* **pile** 1.
3 **heaps** *(plural n) (informal) Lord Lucre has heaps of money. See* **plenty**.

hear
1 *(v) Did you hear what I said?* catch, pick up, listen to, pay attention to, take in, overhear, eavesdrop on, listen in on.
2 *(v) I hear that you're leaving. See* **understand** 3.

heart
1 *(n) I like living in the heart of the city. See* **centre** 1, 2.
2 *(n) Andrew has a kind heart.* nature, temperament, character, disposition.

heartbreaking
(adj) A heartbreaking story. heart-rending, tragic, distressing, harrowing, poignant, pitiful, agonizing, tear-jerking *(informal)*.

heartless *see* **cruel** 1, 2.

hearty
1 *(adj) We gave the explorers a hearty welcome.* enthusiastic, effusive, friendly, warm, cordial, sincere, genuine, heartfelt, genial, unreserved, back-slapping. OPPOSITES: cool, lukewarm.
2 *(adj) After our walk, we'll need a hearty meal.* substantial, filling, satisfying, sizable, nourishing, solid, square. OPPOSITES: meagre, modest.

heat
1 *(n) This heat is making me ill.* warmth, high temperature, sultriness, hot weather, warm weather, heatwave, hot spell. OPPOSITE: cold.
2 *(v) I'll heat some soup for lunch.* heat up, warm up, reheat, cook, make hot. OPPOSITES: chill, cool.

heated *see* **passionate** 1.

heath *see* **moor** 1.

heave
1 *(v) Heave the chest onto the deck.* haul, lug, pull, lift, raise, hoist, tug.
2 *(v) Heave the rubbish overboard. See* **throw** 1.
3 *(v) I'm going to heave! See* **vomit**.

heaven
1 *(n) Do you believe that there is a heaven?* paradise, afterlife, hereafter, next world, life to come, life everlasting. OPPOSITE: hell.
2 *(n) Our holiday was pure heaven!* bliss, delight, joy, ecstasy, paradise, happiness, seventh heaven. OPPOSITES: hell *(informal)*, misery.

heavenly
1 *(adj) A heavenly messenger.* divine, angelic, celestial, holy, blessed. OPPOSITE: earthly.
2 *(adj) (informal) A heavenly scent.* glorious, exquisite, delightful, sublime, out of this world, blissful, divine *(informal)*, gorgeous, wonderful. OPPOSITES: vile, disgusting.

heavy
1 *(adj) I struggled with the heavy suitcase.* weighty, bulky, unwieldy, cumbersome, hefty, massive, top-heavy, immovable. OPPOSITE: light.
2 *(adj) Ed is heavy for his age.* overweight, hefty, large, beefy *(informal)*, stout, portly. OPPOSITES: light, slight.
3 *(adj) Mrs Badger has a heavy workload.* demanding, exhausting, gruelling, killing *(informal)*, taxing, onerous, tough, backbreaking, arduous, intolerable. OPPOSITES: light, undemanding.
4 *(adj) Heavy rain forced us to stay indoors.* torrential, continuous, nonstop, steady, unremitting, severe, penetrating. OPPOSITE: light.
5 *(adj) The bush was heavy with berries.* laden, weighed down, loaded, burdened.
6 *(adj) This film is too heavy for me.* serious, deep, difficult, profound, dry. OPPOSITES: lightweight, light-hearted.
7 *(adj) The sky was heavy before the snowstorm.* leaden, louring, gloomy, dull, overcast, threatening, oppressive.

hectic
(adj) The shops are hectic. busy, bustling, chaotic, frenzied, frantic, frenetic.

heir, heiress
(n) Who is the heir to the throne? next in line, successor, inheritor of.

hell
1 *(n) Do you believe that there is a hell?* underworld, nether world, lower world, infernal regions *(plural)*, inferno. OPPOSITE: heaven.
2 *(n) (informal) Mum went through hell worrying about Alice. See* **torture** 2.

help
1 *(v) I'd like to help you.* give you a hand, assist, lend you a hand, be of use to, be of assistance to, be helpful to, cooperate with, collaborate with, support, advise, give you moral support, back, stand by. OPPOSITES: obstruct, hinder.
2 *(v) I'll help you if you get into trouble.* rescue, save, come to your rescue, come to your aid, save you from danger.
3 *(v) We raised money to help starving children.* support, aid, assist, benefit.
4 *(v) Will this help my toothache?* cure, relieve, ease, soothe, calm, make better, alleviate, do a world of good for.
5 *(n) I'm grateful for my parents' help.* support, assistance, backing, guidance, advice, cooperation, friendship, aid, encouragement, helping hand.

helpful
1 *(adj) Yusuf is always helpful.* obliging, cooperative, supportive, kind, friendly, considerate, caring, neighbourly. OPPOSITES: unhelpful, uncooperative.
2 *(adj) Cam had some helpful suggestions.* useful, constructive, practical, handy, valuable, worthwhile, beneficial, positive. OPPOSITES: useless, unhelpful.

helping
(n) Mo wants another helping of pudding. portion, serving, plate, bowl, plateful, bowlful, dollop *(informal)*, share, ration.

helpless
1 *(adj) Jon's injuries left him helpless.* weak, feeble, incapacitated, disabled, debilitated, paralysed, incapable, bedridden, laid up *(informal)*, dependent.
2 *(adj) Without weapons the soldiers were helpless.* powerless, impotent, useless, ineffective, defenceless, unprotected, vulnerable, exposed to danger.

herb
(n) TYPES OF HERB: basil, bay leaf, chives *(plural)*, coriander, dill, fennel, fenugreek, marjoram, mint, oregano, parsley, rosemary, sage, tarragon, thyme.

hero
1 *(n) Write about a sporting hero.* champion, celebrity, star, superstar, megastar, great man, great woman.
2 *(n) Famous Fred is my hero.* idol, role model, ideal, shining example, heart-throb.
3 *(n) I'm playing the hero in the school play.* lead, leading man, good guy *(informal)*, protagonist. OPPOSITE: villain.

heroic
(adj) Indiana has performed many heroic deeds. brave, courageous, daring, adventurous, fearless, bold, intrepid, death-defying, swashbuckling, gallant, chivalrous, valiant *(old-fashioned)*. OPPOSITES: cowardly, faint-hearted.

heroine
1 *(n) Miranda is my heroine.* idol, role model, ideal, shining example.
2 *(n) I'm playing the heroine in the school play.* lead, leading lady, protagonist. OPPOSITE: villain.

hesitant
(adj) Judd was hesitant at first, but in the end he joined in. tentative, cautious, wary, unsure, uncertain, diffident, reluctant, indecisive, half-hearted, wavering, timid. OPPOSITES: decisive, resolute.

hesitate
(v) Don't hesitate; just do it! falter, dither, delay, think twice, waver, hang back.

hidden
1 *(adj) Make sure that Mum's present is hidden.* concealed, out of sight, covered up, invisible, unseen, shrouded, veiled. OPPOSITES: visible, exposed.
2 *(adj) Can you find the hidden message?* secret, obscure, cryptic, coded, mysterious.

hide
1 *(v) Quick! It's time to hide!* take cover, lie low, go into hiding, hole up *(informal)*, go to ground, keep out of sight, find a hiding place, conceal yourself, hide out.
2 *(v) Let's hide the present under these clothes.* conceal, put out of sight, cover up, bury, secrete, stow, stash *(informal)*.

3 *(v) It's hard to hide your feelings.* conceal, disguise, cover up, mask, keep secret, suppress, keep under your hat. OPPOSITES: reveal, show.
4 *(v) The soldiers used bushes to hide the tank. See* **disguise** 3.

hideous
1 *(adj) A hideous monster. See* **ugly** 1.
2 *(adj) A hideous crime. See* **horrible** 1.

high
1 *(adj) A high tower. See* **tall** 2.
2 *(adj) Your work is of high quality.* excellent, outstanding, exceptional, top, first-class, superior. OPPOSITES: low, poor.
3 *(adj) Jo has a high voice.* high-pitched, shrill, piercing, piping, soprano, treble. OPPOSITES: low, deep.
4 *(adj) The price of the meal was rather high.* excessive, steep *(informal)*, exorbitant, extortionate, unreasonable. OPPOSITES: low, reasonable.
5 *(adj) Lord Lucre moves in high society.* distinguished, exalted, aristocratic, upper class, eminent, leading, influential. OPPOSITES: humble, lower class.
6 *(adj) (informal) We were all high after the concert. See* **excited**.
7 *(adj) (informal) Ziggy was high after taking drugs.* stoned *(slang)*, spaced out *(slang)*, on a trip *(informal)*, delirious.

highlight
1 *(n) Leonora's solo was the highlight of the show.* high spot, climax, high point. OPPOSITE: low point.
2 *(v) Use make-up to highlight your best features.* emphasize, play up, draw attention to, accentuate, set off, spotlight. OPPOSITES: conceal, disguise.
3 *(v) The report will highlight the importance of safety. See* **emphasize**.

highly strung
(adj) Try not to upset Bo; she's very highly strung. nervous, excitable, temperamental, easily upset, sensitive, twitchy, nervy *(informal)*, uptight *(informal)*, tense, hypersensitive, neurotic, wired *(slang)*.

hijack
(v) Terrorists have threatened to hijack the plane. seize, skyjack, take over, commandeer, hold up, divert, waylay.

hike
1 *(v) We had to hike all the way home.* walk, trek, tramp, backpack, trudge, slog, march, ramble, plod, hoof it *(slang)*.
2 *(n) It's a short hike home. See* **walk** 3.

hilarious
(adj) The clowns were hilarious. side-splitting, hysterical *(informal)*, uproarious, riotous, funny, entertaining.

hill
1 *(n) Let's run to the top of the hill.* hillside, mound, hillock, hummock, knoll, dune, bank, peak, ridge, tor, fell.
2 *(n) This hill is too steep for our old van.* slope, incline, rise, gradient.

hinder
1 *(v) That suitcase will hinder you terribly.* hamper, get in your way, slow you down, hold you up, delay, handicap, encumber.
2 *(v) If you want to go, I won't hinder you.* deter, stand in your way, hold you back, prevent, thwart, oppose, obstruct, curb.

hint
1 *(n) There was no hint that Megan was planning to leave.* clue, indication, suggestion, inkling, whisper, tip-off, intimation, insinuation, innuendo, allusion.
2 *(n) I've picked up a handy hint from this book.* tip, suggestion, piece of advice.
3 *(n) Is there a hint of garlic in the sauce?* trace, suggestion, touch, suspicion, whiff, tinge, dash, soupçon, taste.
4 *(v) I did hint that I wanted a bike.* imply, suggest, indicate, insinuate, let it be known, mention, signal, give you a tip-off.

hit
1 *(v) I hope Bozo won't hit you.* punch, thump, strike, belt *(slang)*, clobber *(slang)*, biff *(slang)*, whop *(informal)*, deck *(slang)*, clout *(informal)*, bash *(informal)*, wallop *(informal)*, sock *(slang)*, take a swipe at *(informal)*, beat you up *(informal)*, kick, knee, slap, smack, spank, beat, club, cosh, batter, pummel, hammer, jab, prod, poke.
2 *(v) Don't hit your head!* bump, bang, bash *(informal)*, knock, strike, whack, thump, smash, hurt.
3 *(v) Hit the ball hard.* strike, slam, wham, whack, drive, smash, sock *(slang)*, knock, swat, swipe at *(informal)*, kick, head, punch, tap, volley, lob, putt *(golf)*.
4 *(v) I hope our car doesn't hit anything.* bump into, crash into, run into, collide with, smash into, bash into *(informal)*, knock, strike, bang into, meet head-on.
5 *(v) The bad weather will hit tourism this summer.* damage, affect, have an impact on, influence, make an impression on, leave its mark on, knock for six *(informal)*.
6 *(n) (informal) This film will be a hit. See* **success** 1.

hitch
(n) I'm sorry I'm late; there's been a hitch. problem, snag, complication, difficulty, hold-up, setback, hiccup *(informal)*, delay.

hoard
(v) Jamal loves to hoard his sweets. save, keep, hold on to, hang on to, save up, stockpile, store up, accumulate, amass, stack up, stash away *(informal)*, stow away, set aside, set by, squirrel away.

hoarse
(adj) My voice is hoarse from shouting. croaky, husky, rough, gruff, rasping, cracked, throaty, raucous, gravelly, harsh.

hobble
(v) These new shoes make me hobble. limp, shuffle, stumble, totter, stagger.

hobby
(n) Do you have a hobby? pastime, leisure activity, interest, pursuit, sideline.

hoist *see* **heave** 1.

hold
1 *(v) I want to hold the baby.* cuddle, embrace, hug, cradle, carry.
2 *(v) Hold my hand. See* **hold on to**.
3 *(v) I can't hold your weight.* carry, take, support, bear, shoulder.
4 *(v) The police will hold the suspect.* detain, confine, keep, remand in custody.
OPPOSITES: release, let go.
5 *(v) We decided to hold a meeting.* call, organize, arrange, convene.
6 *(v) The hall will hold six hundred people.* seat, take, accommodate, contain, sit.
7 *(v) I hope this weather will hold until the weekend.* last, hold out, continue, hang on, carry on, stay, persist, keep up, endure.
8 *(n) Leya couldn't get a hold on the rock.* grip, foothold, footing, purchase.
9 *(n) Polly's parents have no hold over her.* control, authority, influence, power, clout.

hold back
(v) Try to hold back your giggles. keep back, control, check, suppress, stifle, smother, restrain, bite back.

hold on
1 *(v) Try to hold on until help comes.* hang on, hold out, keep going, persevere, stick it out *(informal)*, hang in there *(informal)*.
2 *(v) (informal) Hold on! I'm coming.* hang on *(informal)*, wait a minute, stay there, don't go away, hold the line *(telephone)*.

hold on to
(v) Hold on to my hand. hold, take, hang on to, grip, grasp, clasp, clutch, seize, cling on to, clench.

hold-up *see* **delay** 4.

hold up
1 *(v) I hope the traffic doesn't hold you up. See* **delay** 2.
2 *(v) These pillars hold up the roof. See* **support** 1.
3 *(v) The robbers planned to hold up the train.* rob, hijack, stick up *(slang)*, waylay.

hole
1 *(n) Don't fall into that hole!* pit, crater, trench, hollow, dip, depression, burrow, tunnel, pothole, abyss, shaft, excavation.
2 *(n) We found a hole in the wall.* gap, opening, cavity *(wall, tooth)*, crack, crevice, cranny, chink, fissure, slit, space.
3 *(n) There's a hole in my tyre.* puncture, slit, tear, split, cut, gash, rent, pinprick.
4 *(n) The creature returned to its hole.* lair, den, burrow *(rabbit)*, warren *(rabbit)*, earth *(fox)*, sett *(badger)*, cave, tunnel, nest.

holiday
1 *(n) You deserve a holiday.* break, rest, vacation, time off, leave.
2 *(n) Let's plan a holiday.* vacation, trip, tour, cruise, package holiday, self-catering holiday, camping holiday, beach holiday, skiing trip, adventure holiday, safari.
❖ *Also see* **journey words**, **mountain words**, **sea & seashore**, **seaside words**.

hollow
1 *(n) We found a hollow in the ground.* dip, depression, indentation, dent, recess, hole, crater, pit, cavity, trough, basin.
OPPOSITES: rise, hill.
2 *(adj) The tube was hollow.* empty, unfilled, void, hollowed out, vacant.
OPPOSITES: solid, filled.
3 *(adj) The drum made a hollow sound.* deep, low, echoing, reverberating, rumbling, muffled, muted, dull, dead.
4 *(adj) The prisoner had hollow cheeks.* sunken, caved-in, concave, deep-set *(eyes)*.
5 *(adj) I can't trust your hollow promises.* empty, meaningless, false, insincere.
OPPOSITES: genuine, sincere.

holy
1 *(adj) A holy person.* saintly, pious, devout, God-fearing, religious, spiritual, virtuous, pure, godly.
2 *(adj) A holy place.* sacred, blessed, consecrated, sanctifed, divine, hallowed *(old-fashioned)*.

home
(n) Is this your home? house, residence, pad *(slang)*, dwelling, dwelling place, domicile, abode *(old-fashioned)*, home town, birthplace, native land.
TYPES OF HOME: apartment, bedsit, bungalow, cabin, caravan, castle, chalet, chateau, cottage, council house, detached house, farmhouse, flat, high-rise flat, hostel, houseboat, hut, lodge, log cabin, maisonette, manor house, mansion, mill, mobile home, palace, prefabricated house, ranch, semi-detached house, shack, stately home, studio flat, tenement building, tent, terraced house, tower block, villa, windmill. ❖ *Also see* **houses & homes**.

homeless
(adj) You can't imagine what it's like to be homeless. destitute, down-and-out, outcast, abandoned, without a roof over your head, on the streets.

homely
(adj) Granny's cottage has a homely feel. cosy, comfortable, friendly, welcoming, snug, modest, unassuming, unpretentious, plain, simple.
OPPOSITES: grand, pretentious.

honest
1 *(adj) I want an honest answer to my question.* truthful, sincere, straight, frank, candid, plain, direct, open, forthright, straightforward, upfront *(informal)*.
OPPOSITES: false, insincere.
2 *(adj) Mr Badger wouldn't cheat; he's an honest man.* truthful, honourable, trustworthy, upright, moral, scrupulous, virtuous, law-abiding, principled.
OPPOSITE: dishonest.
3 *(adj) I must find an honest way to earn money.* above board, legitimate, on the level *(informal)*, ethical, moral, legal, lawful, genuine, bona fide.
OPPOSITES: dishonest, fraudulent.

honour

honour
1 (n) *Mr Badger wouldn't cheat; he's a man of honour.* integrity, principle, high principles *(plural)*, honesty, morality, scruples *(plural)*, decency, virtue.
2 (n) *I will fight to defend my honour. See* **reputation**.
3 (n) *It's an honour to be chosen for the team.* privilege, credit, achievement, source of pride, compliment.

honourable *see* **honest** 2.

hooked *see* **addicted** 1, 2.

hooligan
(n) vandal, delinquent, yob *(informal)*, yobbo *(informal)*, thug, ruffian, roughneck *(slang)*, tough, rowdy, lout, lager lout.

hop *see* **skip** 1.

hope
1 (v) *We hope that we will arrive on time.* expect, anticipate, believe, trust.
2 (v) *I hope to be a star.* long, want, wish, yearn, aspire, intend, plan, expect, dream.
3 (n) *This result should give you some hope.* confidence, faith, optimism, belief, trust, assurance, expectations *(plural)*.
4 (n) *Cassandra's hope is to be a star. See* **wish** 1.
5 (n) *Try this door; it's our only hope.* chance, opportunity, prospect, possibility.

hopeful
1 (adj) *We are hopeful that we will win.* optimistic, confident, expectant.
OPPOSITES: pessimistic, despairing.
2 (adj) *The future looks hopeful.* promising, encouraging, heartening, reassuring, bright, rosy, favourable.
OPPOSITES: hopeless, grim.

hopeless
1 (adj) *The situation is hopeless.* beyond hope, beyond repair, beyond remedy, impossible, irredeemable, irreparable.
OPPOSITES: promising, hopeful.
2 (adj) *All our efforts proved to be hopeless.* futile, useless, pointless, worthless, in vain, worth nothing.
OPPOSITES: worthwhile, useful.
3 (adj) *The bad news made us feel hopeless. See* **pessimistic**.
4 (adj) (informal) *I'm hopeless at French.* useless *(informal)*, no good, clueless *(slang)*, incompetent, pathetic *(informal)*, rotten *(informal)*, lousy *(slang)*.
OPPOSITES: expert, proficient.

horrible
1 (adj) *We were shocked by the horrible crime.* dreadful, appalling, horrifying, horrific, horrendous, terrible, shocking, ghastly, vile, gruesome, grisly, monstrous, sickening, harrowing, awful, frightful, atrocious, hideous, loathsome, despicable.
2 (adj) *What a horrible meal!* revolting, disgusting, foul, nasty, awful, terrible, dreadful, horrid, vile, yucky *(slang)*, nauseating, stomach-turning, inedible.
OPPOSITES: lovely, delicious.

3 (adj) *Don't be so horrible to me!* mean, nasty, beastly *(informal)*, horrid *(informal)*, unkind, disagreeable, unpleasant, hateful, cruel, spiteful, vicious, offensive, hostile.
OPPOSITES: kind, considerate.

horrific *see* **horrible** 1.

horrified
(adj) *Mum will be horrified when she hears the news.* shocked, appalled, aghast, outraged, scandalized, disgusted, revolted, sickened, nauseated, offended.

horrify
1 (v) *The sight of the monster will horrify you. See* **scare** 1.
2 (v) *Your jokes will horrify Aunt Bertha. See* **shock** 2.

horror
(n) *Ellie gazed at the scene in horror.* shock, alarm, dismay, dread, fear, terror, fright, fear and trembling, disgust, loathing, revulsion, consternation, panic.

horse
(n) pony, stallion (male), mare (female), foal (baby), colt (young male), filly (young female), gelding (castrated male), mount, steed, nag *(informal)*, charger.
TYPES OF HORSE: carthorse, cob, dressage horse, driving horse, event horse, hunter, polo pony, racehorse, show horse.
COLOURS OF HORSE: bay, chestnut, dapple-grey, dun, grey, palomino, piebald, roan, skewbald.

hostile
(adj) *Why are you so hostile?* antagonistic, aggressive, anti *(informal)*, belligerent, unsympathetic, unfriendly, unwelcoming.
OPPOSITES: friendly, peaceable.

hot
1 (adj) *I can't stand this hot weather.* sweltering, baking, boiling, scorching, roasting, blistering, burning, blazing, searing, sultry, humid, steamy, torrid.
OPPOSITES: cold, freezing, icy.
2 (adj) *Be careful! This food is hot.* boiling, boiling hot, scalding, piping hot, steaming, sizzling, red-hot, bubbling.
OPPOSITES: cold, chilled.
3 (adj) *I feel hot.* flushed, feverish, sweaty, perspiring, boiling, boiling hot, overheated.
OPPOSITES: cold, freezing.
4 (adj) *Bozo has a hot temper.* fiery, violent, fierce, savage, flaming, impetuous.
OPPOSITES: mild, sweet.
5 (adj) *This curry has a hot taste.* spicy, peppery, fiery, piquant, sharp, strong, pungent, biting.
OPPOSITE: mild.

house
1 (n) *Is this your house?* home, residence, pad *(slang)*, dwelling, dwelling place, domicile, abode *(old-fashioned)*.
2 (v) *You need someone to house you.* take you in, put you up, give you a roof over your head, shelter, accommodate.

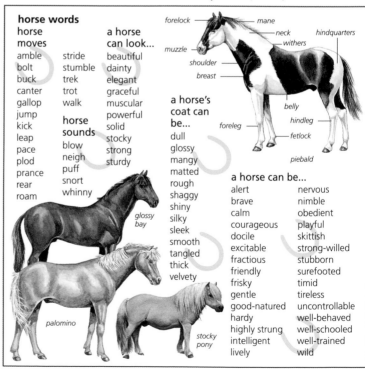

horse words

horse moves
amble
bolt
buck
canter
gallop
jump
kick
leap
pace
plod
prance
rear
roam

stride
stumble
trek
trot
walk

horse sounds
blow
neigh
puff
snort
whinny

a horse can look...
beautiful
dainty
elegant
graceful
muscular
powerful
solid
stocky
strong
sturdy

a horse's coat can be...
dull
glossy
mangy
matted
rough
shaggy
shiny
silky
sleek
smooth
tangled
thick
velvety

forelock
mane
neck
hindquarters
muzzle
withers
shoulder
breast
belly
foreleg
hindleg
fetlock
piebald

glossy bay

palomino

stocky pony

a horse can be...
alert
brave
calm
courageous
docile
excitable
fractious
friendly
frisky
gentle
good-natured
hardy
highly strung
intelligent
lively

nervous
nimble
obedient
playful
skittish
strong-willed
stubborn
surefooted
timid
tireless
uncontrollable
well-behaved
well-schooled
well-trained
wild

houses and homes

half-timbered cottage

high-rise flats

futuristic house

types of home
apartment
bedsit
bungalow
caravan
castle
cottage
council house
detached house
farmhouse
high-rise flat
hostel
houseboat
maisonette
mansion
mill
mobile home
semi-detached
  house
stately home
tenement
  building
terraced house
tower block
villa

homes can be made of...
brick
concrete
glass
slate
steel
stone
timber

homes can be...
half-timbered
ivy-covered
painted
pebble-dashed
plastered
thatched
timber-framed
whitewashed

OUTSIDE THE HOME
homes may have...
balcony
bay window
casement window
  (hinged window)
chimney pots
dormer window
  (window in roof)
French windows
picture window
sash window
  (push-up
  window)
satellite dish
shutters
skylight
sliding doors
solar panel
TV aerial
window box

outside you may see...
crazy paving
creeper
drive
dustbin
fence
fire escape
flowerbed
flower tub
garage
garden
gate
graffiti
hedge
lawn
parking spaces
patio
railings
trellis
washing line

mobile home

INSIDE THE HOME
at the windows
bamboo blinds
faded curtains
floor-length
  curtains
net curtains
roller blinds
ruched curtains
tattered curtains
Venetian blinds
vertical blinds

homes can look...
dilapidated
drab
dreary
elegant
futuristic
gloomy
grand
imposing
modern
neat
neglected
palatial
pretty
quaint
rambling
ramshackle
shabby
tumbledown

on the floors
bare boards
carpet
cork tiles
flagstones
lino
marble floor
parquet floor
quarry tiles
rugs
rush matting
wooden floor

on the walls
bare plaster
ceramic tiles
damp patch
fancy border
flaking paint
gleaming
  paintwork
mould
peeling wallpaper
picture rail
wood panelling

homes can feel...
airy
chilly
cluttered
cosy
cramped
damp
dank
draughty
homely
lived-in
luxurious
musty
roomy
snug
spacious
stuffy
sunny
warm
welcoming

sash window   dormer window   casement window

---

hover
(v) The eagle seemed to hover in the air. hang, be suspended, float, drift, be poised, flutter.

howl
1 (v) The baby began to howl. bawl, wail, cry, scream, yell, shriek, caterwaul, bellow.
2 (v) Can you hear the wolves howl? bay, yelp, yowl.

huddle
1 (v) Let's huddle together to stay warm. bunch, cluster, squeeze, snuggle, nestle, cuddle, press, pack, crowd, herd, throng. OPPOSITES: scatter, disperse.
2 (n) The players formed a huddle in the centre of the pitch. cluster, group, mass, crowd, pack, throng, jumble, heap.

huff see **mood** 2.

hug
(v) I long to hug you. take you in my arms, hold you close, cuddle, embrace, squeeze, hold, enfold, clasp, cling to.

huge
(adj) A huge building. enormous, immense, massive, vast, extensive, colossal, gigantic, monumental, mighty, lofty, towering, mammoth, giant, monstrous, monster, gargantuan, stupendous, ginormous (informal), humongous (informal). OPPOSITES: tiny, minute.

hum
(n) Can you hear the hum of the engine? buzz, drone, murmur, purr, whir, throb, thrum, pulsing, vibration.

humble
1 (adj) Carl was humble about his success. See **modest** 1.
2 (adj) The emperor expects his subjects to be humble. meek, submissive, docile, respectful, polite, courteous, deferential, servile, slavish, subservient, obsequious. OPPOSITES: proud, arrogant.
3 (adj) The woodcutter lived in a humble cottage. poor, simple, modest, ordinary, plain, unpretentious, lowly (old-fashioned), small, insignificant, unremarkable. OPPOSITES: grand, ostentatious.

humid
(adj) It was humid in the jungle. sultry, muggy, steamy, sticky, clammy, close, sweltering, sweaty, damp, dank, misty. OPPOSITES: dry, arid.

humiliate
(v) Your mum would never humiliate you in public. degrade, demean, put you down, make you feel small, take you down a peg (informal), make you eat humble pie, debase, deflate, disgrace, discredit, shame, make you ashamed, embarrass.

humiliating
(adj) A humiliating defeat. crushing, degrading, demeaning, ignominious, shameful, disgraceful, discreditable, embarrassing, mortifying, undignified.

humorous see **funny** 1.

hunger

(n) *The refugees were dying of hunger.* starvation, malnutrition, lack of food.

hungry

1 (adj) *After the match, we were all hungry.* ravenous, famished, starving (informal), peckish (informal), in need of food, half-starved, empty (informal).
OPPOSITES: full, satisfied.
2 (adj) *Fred is hungry for success.* eager, longing, yearning, desperate, greedy.

hunt

1 (v) *Foxes hunt small animals.* prey on, stalk, track, trail, chase, pursue, hunt down, hound, capture, kill.
2 (v) *I must hunt for my tie.* See **search** 2.
3 (n) *The police organized a hunt for the escaped prisoner.* See **search** 3.

hurl *see* **throw** 1.

hurricane *see* **storm** 1.

hurry

1 (v) *We must hurry or we'll be late.* rush, be quick, get a move on (informal), hurry up, lose no time, dash, fly, run, step on it (informal), make haste (old-fashioned).
OPPOSITES: dawdle, delay.
2 (v) *You can't hurry this process.* rush, hasten, speed up, accelerate, quicken.
OPPOSITES: slow down, delay.
3 (n) *Jessica left in a hurry.* rush, flurry, flap (informal), commotion, bustle.

hurt

1 (v) *How did you hurt your arm?* injure, wound, bruise, cut, scratch, graze, scrape, burn, scald, sprain, break, damage.
2 (v) *My comment wasn't meant to hurt you.* hurt your feelings, upset, wound, distress, cause you pain, offend, grieve, sadden, sting, cut you to the quick.
3 (v) *This won't hurt.* be painful, be sore, sting, smart, burn, ache, throb, be tender.
4 (adj) *I felt hurt when Ben ignored me.* upset, wounded, saddened, distressed, cut to the quick, aggrieved, offended, put out.

hurtful

(adj) *A hurtful remark.* upsetting, distressing, offensive, unkind, cruel, nasty, spiteful, malicious, vicious, cutting, biting, scathing, wounding, sarcastic, withering.

hurtle *see* **speed** 4.

husky *see* **hoarse**.

hut

(n) *The refugees lived in a tiny hut.* shack, shelter, shed, cabin, hovel, shanty, den.

hype

1 (n) *After all the hype, the film was disappointing.* See **build-up**.
2 (v) *Famous Fred is trying to hype his new release.* See **promote** 2.

hypocritical

(adj) *It's hypocritical of Burglar Beryl to condemn stealing.* two-faced, insincere, deceitful, dishonest, duplicitous, phoney (informal), inconsistent, self-righteous, sanctimonious, holier-than-thou.

hysterical

1 (adj) *You'll be hysterical when you hear the news.* frantic, frenzied, in a frenzy, berserk, beside yourself, distraught, overwrought, in a panic, out of control, wild, out of your mind, crazed.
2 (adj) (informal) *The comedy act was hysterical.* See **hilarious**.

icy

1 (adj) *The weather was icy.* See **cold** 1, 2.
2 (adj) *The pavement was icy.* slippery, like glass, frosty, frozen over, treacherous, glassy, slippy (informal).
3 (adj) *Aunt Bertha gave me an icy stare.* cold, chilly, frosty, glacial, frigid, stony, steely, hard, disapproving, withering, forbidding, hostile, unfriendly.
OPPOSITES: warm, friendly.

idea

1 (n) *The idea came to me in the bath.* thought, notion, inspiration, brainwave, plan, scheme, design, concept, theory, hypothesis, solution.

ice, frost and snow

ice, frost and snow words

black ice
blizzard
hail
hailstones
hoarfrost
icicles
Jack Frost
sheet ice
sleet
snowdrift
snowflakes
snowstorm
sub-zero temperatures

the wind is...

arctic
biting
bitter
chilling
freezing
glacial
icy
numbing
piercing
polar
raw
Siberian
stinging

the air feels...

bracing
chilly
crisp
fresh
frosty
invigorating
nippy

the ground is...

blanketed with snow
carpeted with snow
dusted with snow
frost-bound
frozen solid
hard
icy
slippery
slushy
sprinkled with snow
treacherous

the trees are...

bare
encrusted with ice
frost-covered
hoary
snow-covered
snow-laden

snow-laden trees

hoary leaves

snowflakes...

drift
eddy
float
settle
swirl
tumble
waft
whirl

snow...

blankets
buries
camouflages
drifts
envelops
muffles
shrouds
transforms

the snow is...

blinding
crisp
crunchy
dazzling
deep
fresh
frozen
glistening
glittering
melting
packed
powdery
slushy
soft
sparkling
thawing
untrodden

snowdrift

blizzard

in the snow you...

flounder
plod
sink in
slog
stomp (informal)
struggle
stumble
tramp
trudge
wade
wallow

frost...

coats
etches patterns
glistens
glitters
sparkles

the ice is...

brittle
cracked
crazed
glassy
gleaming
glinting
shiny
slippery
smooth

on the ice you...

glide
skate
skid
skim
slide
slip
slither

2 *(n) I had an idea that Aunt Bertha was angry.* feeling, notion, suspicion, hunch, inkling, sense, impression.
3 *(n) Give me an idea about what you'd like for your birthday.* clue, hint, indication, suggestion, inkling, intimation.
4 *(n) What was the idea of running off like that?* point, purpose, aim, object, intention, meaning, sense, use.
5 *(n) We all had the same idea about the film.* opinion, thoughts *(plural)*, view, viewpoint, feeling, attitude, impression, judgment, interpretation, conclusion.

ideal
1 *(adj) Edward is an ideal pupil.* model, perfect, faultless, exemplary, dream.
2 *(adj) This is the ideal time to buy a house.* best, perfect, right, most suitable, correct, most advantageous, optimum.
3 *(adj) In my ideal world it would always be summer.* imaginary, dream, fantasy, hypothetical, perfect, Utopian.

idealistic
(adj) Jamie has an idealistic view of life. unrealistic, romantic, over-optimistic, impractical, starry-eyed, perfectionist.
OPPOSITES: realistic, down-to-earth.

identical
(adj) These socks are identical. the same, matching, indistinguishable, similar, alike.
OPPOSITE: different.

identify
1 *(v) Can you identify these flowers?* recognize, name, put a name to, classify, catalogue, label.
2 *(v) Try to identify the differences between the two pictures.* See **spot** 1.
3 **identify with** *(v) Can you identify with the hero in the film?* relate to, sympathize with, feel for, empathize with, put yourself in the shoes of, see through the eyes of.

idiot
(n) Don't be such an idiot! fool, imbecile *(informal)*, nincompoop, twit *(informal)*, nitwit *(informal)*, numskull, dimwit *(informal)*, twerp *(informal)*, wally *(slang)*, prat *(slang)*, plonker *(slang)*, nerd *(slang)*, jerk *(slang)*, dork *(slang)*, airhead *(slang)*.

idiotic see **stupid** 1, 2.

idle see **lazy** 1.

idol
1 *(n) Who is your idol at the moment?* hero, heroine, heart-throb, pin-up *(slang)*, favourite, darling, ideal, star.
2 *(n) Indiana found a golden idol in the tomb.* image, statue, effigy, god.

idolize
(v) I idolize Famous Fred. adore, worship, hero-worship, look up to, admire, revere.

ignorant
1 *(adj) I'm totally ignorant about politics.* uninformed, unaware, unknowledgeable, clueless *(slang)*, unenlightened, naive, green, uneducated, unlearned, illiterate.
OPPOSITES: well-informed, educated.

2 *(adj) That was a very ignorant remark.* stupid, thoughtless, insensitive, shallow, superficial, crass, rude, crude, coarse.
OPPOSITES: intelligent, astute.
3 **ignorant of** *(adj) Ziggy is ignorant of the dangers of taking drugs.* unaware of, oblivious to, blind to, unfamiliar with, unacquainted with, in the dark about, unconscious of, ill-informed about.
OPPOSITES: aware of, conscious of.

ignore
1 *(v) Try to ignore Theo's nasty remarks.* take no notice of, pay no attention to, disregard, overlook, pass over, turn a deaf ear to, turn a blind eye to, be oblivious to.
OPPOSITES: pay attention to, heed.
2 *(v) If you try to spoil our game, we'll ignore you.* take no notice of, pay no attention to, send you to Coventry, shut you out, ostracize, shun, reject, snub, give you the cold shoulder *(informal)*, freeze you out *(informal)*, cut you dead *(informal)*.
OPPOSITE: pay attention to.

ill
1 *(adj) Are you ill?* sick, unwell, poorly *(informal)*, off colour, ailing, indisposed, under the weather *(informal)*, out of sorts.
OPPOSITES: well, healthy.
2 *(adj) I came off the boat feeling ill.* sick, queasy, groggy *(informal)*, nauseous, green around the gills *(informal)*, peculiar, funny *(informal)*, queer, rough *(informal)*, grotty *(slang)*, weak, faint, delicate, fragile, frail.
OPPOSITES: well, strong.

illegal
1 *(adj) Have you ever done anything illegal?* unlawful, criminal, against the law, illicit, forbidden, outlawed, banned, prohibited, proscribed.
OPPOSITES: legal, above board.
2 *(adj) Dodgy Dave sells illegal whisky.* unlicensed, black market, bootleg, under-the-counter *(informal)*, contraband.
OPPOSITE: legal.

illegible
(adj) Mrs Badger says my handwriting is illegible. impossible to read, hard to make out, indecipherable, unreadable, unclear, unintelligible, scribbled, scrawled, squiggly.
OPPOSITES: legible, clear.

illness
1 *(n) Araminta is absent with a mysterious illness.* ailment, complaint, disorder, sickness, disease, infection, virus, bug *(informal)*, lurgy *(slang)*, malady, indisposition, affliction, attack.
2 *(n) Our family has been plagued by illness.* ill health, poor health, sickness, disease, disability, infirmity.
OPPOSITES: good health, fitness.

illusion
1 *(n) That white lady you saw was just an illusion.* hallucination, apparition, figment of your imagination, phantom, spectre, fantasy, dream, mirage (illusion of water).
OPPOSITE: reality.

2 *(n) One line looks longer than the other, but that's an illusion.* trick, optical illusion, false impression, deception, misperception.

illustrate
(v) Write out your poem and illustrate it. add pictures to, add drawings to, provide artwork for, depict, decorate, adorn, embellish, ornament.

illustration
1 *(n) Look at the illustration on page 14.* picture, drawing, sketch, artwork, graphics *(plural)*, figure, plate, diagram, graph.
2 *(n) Give me an illustration of what you mean.* See **example** 1.

image
1 *(n) Can you see an image on your computer screen?* picture, symbol, figure, icon, photograph, reflection.
2 *(n) You're the image of your dad.* double, living image, spitting image *(informal)*, twin, clone, dead ringer for *(slang)*, chip off the old block *(informal)*.
3 *(n) People have the wrong image of me.* idea, impression, picture, perception.
4 *(n) Flash Frank is worried about his image.* public persona, reputation, public perception, outward appearance, aura.

imaginary
1 *(adj) Dragons aren't real; they're imaginary.* make-believe, fictional, nonexistent, unreal, fantastic, legendary, mythical, mythological, fairy-tale.
OPPOSITE: real.
2 *(adj) Justin has an imaginary illness.* made-up, pretend, invented, imagined, notional, nonexistent.
OPPOSITES: real, actual.

imagination
1 *(n) Designers need imagination.* creativity, inventiveness, originality, inspiration, vision, flair, ingenuity, insight.
2 *(n) The monster only exists in your imagination.* mind, fantasies *(plural)*, dreams *(plural)*, head.

imaginative
(adj) Jabir is full of imaginative ideas. creative, original, inspired, inventive, innovative, ingenious, resourceful.
OPPOSITES: unimaginative, unoriginal.

imagine
1 *(v) Can you imagine a world without flowers?* picture, envisage, visualize, see in your mind's eye, conceive of, think of, conjure up, dream up.
2 *(v) I imagine you'd like some lunch.* See **assume**.

imitate
1 *(v) Felix can imitate Elvis Presley.* do an impression of, impersonate, mimic, do *(informal)*, take off *(informal)*, send up *(informal)*, parody, ape, caricature.
2 *(v) Try to imitate the style of this poem.* copy, match, duplicate, emulate, follow, take as a model, follow the example of.
3 *(v) Do soaps on TV imitate real life?* reflect, mirror, echo, parallel, simulate.

imitation
1 (n) Is this painting real or is it an imitation? See **copy** 2.
2 (n) Bobby does a good imitation of Elvis Presley. See **impression** 4.
3 (adj) My bag is made of imitation leather. synthetic, artificial, mock, fake, man-made, simulated, sham.
OPPOSITES: real, genuine.

immature
(adj) Act your age and don't be so immature! childish, babyish, juvenile, infantile, puerile, adolescent, callow, unsophisticated, inexperienced, green.
OPPOSITES: mature, grown-up.

immediate
(adj) I received an immediate reply. instant, instantaneous, prompt, quick, speedy, swift, direct, punctual.

immediately
(adv) Come here immediately! at once, straightaway, right away, instantly, without delay, promptly, directly, now, right now, this minute, this instant, in the twinkling of an eye.

immense see **huge**.

immerse see **dip** 3.

immoral
1 (adj) How could anyone be so immoral? unprincipled, dishonest, unscrupulous, amoral, unethical, depraved, perverted, corrupt, debauched, degenerate, dissolute, promiscuous, evil, wicked, sinful, bad.
OPPOSITES: moral, upright, virtuous.
2 (adj) It's immoral to show violent films to young children. See **wrong** 2.

immortal
(adj) An immortal being. eternal, undying, everlasting, indestructible, timeless, ageless, deathless, divine.
OPPOSITE: mortal.

impact
1 (n) The car headlights were shattered by the impact. blow, collision, crash, bump, bang, jolt, smash, knock, clash.
2 (n) What sort of impact did the book have? effect, influence, significance, consequences (plural), repercussions (plural), impression, splash (informal).

impartial see **neutral**.

impatient
1 (adj) Waiting makes me feel impatient. restless, fidgety, edgy, on edge, irritable, agitated, fretful, anxious, nervous, tense, wound up (informal), jittery (informal), excited, like a caged lion.
OPPOSITES: patient, calm.
2 (adj) Aunt Bertha was very impatient with me. abrupt, brusque, curt, snappy, short, intolerant, short-tempered, peevish.
OPPOSITES: patient, tolerant.
3 (adj) I was impatient to open my presents. See **eager** 2.

impersonate see **imitate** 1.

impertinent see **cheeky**.

imply see **hint** 4.

importance
(n) Mrs Badger stressed the importance of the situation. significance, seriousness, gravity, momentousness, urgency.

important
1 (adj) This is an important decision. significant, major, serious, momentous, vital, critical, crucial, key, grave, weighty, far-reaching, historic, once-in-a-lifetime, earthshaking (informal).
OPPOSITES: insignificant, trivial.
2 (adj) It's important that you come on time. essential, vital, necessary, crucial.
OPPOSITES: unimportant, unnecessary.
3 (adj) Underline the important points in your notes. See **main**.
4 (adj) I'd like to be an important person. influential, powerful, prominent, high-ranking, leading, eminent, distinguished, outstanding, notable, famous.
OPPOSITES: unimportant, insignificant.

impose on
(v) I don't want to impose on you. be a nuisance to, take advantage of, inconvenience, put you out, make you go out of your way, abuse your hospitality, exploit, burden, saddle (informal).

imposing see **impressive** 1.

impossible
1 (adj) Pigs can't fly - it's impossible! out of the question, beyond the bounds of possibility, unthinkable, inconceivable, unimaginable, not to be thought of.
OPPOSITE: possible.
2 (adj) Don't set yourself impossible goals. unrealistic, unreasonable, unachievable, unattainable, impractical, unworkable, ridiculous, ludicrous, preposterous, crazy.
OPPOSITES: reasonable, realistic.
3 (adj) I'm in an impossible situation. hopeless, intolerable, unbearable, unacceptable, catch-22, no-win (slang).
4 (adj) (informal) Evie is being impossible again! See **awkward** 4.

impractical
1 (adj) An impractical plan. unworkable, impossible, unrealistic, useless, wild, crazy.
OPPOSITES: practical, viable.
2 (adj) Daisy is so impractical. unrealistic, unbusinesslike, up in the clouds, idealistic, romantic, starry-eyed.
OPPOSITES: sensible, down-to-earth.

impress
1 (v) Did the film impress you? make an impression on, affect, inspire, move, touch, excite, stir, leave its mark on, stick in your mind (informal), grab (informal), influence.
2 (v) Justin wore a smart suit in order to impress. make an impact, stand out, cause a stir, be conspicuous, arouse comment, attract attention, make a hit (informal).

impression
1 (n) This book made a big impression on me. impact, effect, influence, mark.

2 (n) What was your impression of the film? opinion, view, memory, recollection.
3 (n) I got the impression something was wrong. See **feeling** 2.
4 (n) Do your impression of Elvis Presley. impersonation, imitation, takeoff (informal), send-up (informal), parody.

impressive
1 (adj) An impressive view of the mountains. striking, imposing, magnificent, splendid, majestic, awe-inspiring, breathtaking, remarkable, grand.
2 (adj) An impressive film. powerful, inspiring, remarkable, memorable, magnificent, great, stunning (informal), stirring, moving, touching, thrilling.

imprison see **jail** 2.

improbable see **unlikely**.

improve
1 (v) Jamal has begun to improve this term. make progress, get better, develop, make strides, make headway, progress, come on, advance, shape up (informal).
OPPOSITES: get worse, fall behind.
2 (v) Mum hopes that business will improve soon. get better, pick up, perk up, look up, recover, rally, take a turn for the better (informal).
OPPOSITES: worsen, fall off.
3 (v) I'm doing my best to improve the situation. make better, put right, rectify, correct, help, mend, ameliorate.
OPPOSITES: make worse, aggravate.
4 (v) The patient is starting to improve. get better, recover, be on the mend, be on the road to recovery, recuperate, rally, convalesce, heal, turn the corner.
OPPOSITES: get worse, deteriorate.

improvement
1 (n) I've seen some improvement in your work. progress, development, advance.
OPPOSITE: deterioration.
2 (n) Our flat needs some improvement. renovation, refurbishment, redecoration, modernization, alterations (plural).

improvise
(v) If you haven't prepared a speech, you'll have to improvise. ad-lib, make it up as you go along, wing it (informal), speak off the cuff (informal), extemporize.

impudent see **cheeky**.

impulsive
1 (adj) Letty is such an impulsive person. impetuous, unpredictable, spontaneous, hot-headed, rash, reckless, capricious.
OPPOSITES: cautious, prudent.
2 (adj) Jen took an impulsive decision to become a vegetarian. See **sudden** 2.

inaccessible see **remote**.

inaccurate
(adj) This account is inaccurate. incorrect, inexact, imprecise, untrue, false, wrong, flawed, unreliable, unsound, misleading, vague, full of errors, wide of the mark.
OPPOSITES: accurate, exact.

inadequate

1 *(adj) Our supplies are inadequate.*
insufficient, not enough, meagre, scanty,
sparse, in short supply, low.
OPPOSITES: adequate, sufficient.
2 *(adj) Mrs Badger said my essay was
inadequate.* unsatisfactory, unacceptable,
not good enough, not up to scratch
(informal), incomplete, deficient, sketchy.
OPPOSITES: adequate, satisfactory.
3 *(adj) My older sister makes me feel
inadequate. See* **inferior** 2.

incessant *see* **constant** 1.

in charge *see* **responsible** 3.

incident

1 *(n) That was a memorable incident! See*
event 1.
2 *(n) I hope there won't be an incident at
the match.* disturbance, clash, skirmish,
confrontation, scene, commotion, row,
fracas, fight, contretemps.

include

1 *(v) This kit should include everything you
need.* contain, incorporate, hold, consist
of, comprise, involve, take in, encompass,
embrace.
OPPOSITES: exclude, leave out.
2 *(v) Try to include this point in your essay.*
incorporate, bring in, build in, cover, take
into account, deal with, introduce, put in,
insert, slip in, add, enter.
OPPOSITES: leave out, omit.

incompetent

*(adj) Mum thinks her boss is totally
incompetent.* incapable, inept, inadequate,
ineffectual, inexpert, useless *(informal)*,
hopeless *(informal)*, inefficient, unqualified.
OPPOSITES: competent, capable.

inconsiderate *see* **thoughtless**.

inconvenient

1 *(adj) You've picked an inconvenient
moment to arrive.* awkward, inopportune,
ill-timed, untimely, unfortunate,
unsuitable, embarrassing, bad.
OPPOSITES: convenient, suitable.
2 *(adj) It's inconvenient when the water is
cut off.* awkward, tiresome, annoying,
irritating, troublesome, a nuisance, a bore.
OPPOSITES: convenient, handy.
3 *(adj) This parcel is an inconvenient
shape. See* **awkward** 3.

increase

1 *(v) Pupil numbers should increase.* rise,
grow, multiply, escalate, climb, soar, shoot
up, rocket, snowball, spiral, mushroom.
OPPOSITES: decrease, decline.
2 *(v) The noise began to increase when
Mrs Badger left the room.* grow, rise, build
up, intensify, mount, escalate, heighten.
OPPOSITES: decrease, diminish.
3 *(v) Jet wants to increase her CD
collection.* expand, extend, enlarge, build
up, widen, broaden, develop, add to,
boost, swell, enhance, augment.
OPPOSITES: reduce, decrease.

4 *(n) There has been an increase in crime.*
rise, growth, explosion, escalation,
upsurge, upturn, leap.
OPPOSITES: decrease, fall.

incredible

1 *(adj) Jojo told an incredible tale about
meeting an alien.* unbelievable, far-
fetched, unlikely, implausible, improbable,
impossible, unconvincing, amazing,
extraordinary, absurd, preposterous.
2 *(adj) (informal) I had an incredible time
at the party. See* **fantastic** 3.

indecent

1 *(adj) An indecent joke. See* **rude** 2.
2 *(adj) Indecent clothes.* immodest,
improper, unseemly, revealing, titillating,
outrageous, shocking, tasteless, vulgar.
OPPOSITES: decent, respectable.

indecisive

*(adj) Bart is so indecisive, he just can't
make up his mind.* irresolute, dithery,
tentative, hesitant, undecided, uncertain,
vacillating, in two minds.
OPPOSITES: decisive, certain.

independent

1 *(adj) Europe is made up of many
independent countries.* separate, distinct,
unconnected, individual, self-governing,
autonomous, sovereign, non-aligned.
2 *(adj) Fenella is too independent to work
well in a team.* self-reliant, self-sufficient,
self-contained, individualistic,
unconventional, free-thinking, liberated.

indicate *see* **show** 2, 5.

indifferent

*(adj) How can you be so indifferent when
people are suffering?* unconcerned,
unfeeling, apathetic, unsympathetic,
uncaring, unmoved, impassive, heedless,
blasé, detached, unemotional, cold.
OPPOSITES: caring, concerned.

indignant *see* **annoyed**.

indirect

(adj) I took an indirect route home.
roundabout, circuitous, winding,
meandering, rambling, tortuous, long.
OPPOSITES: direct, straight.

individual

1 *(adj) You can buy individual portions of
butter.* single, separate, personal.
2 *(adj) Maisie has an individual style.*
unique, distinctive, personal, idiosyncratic,
particular, characteristic, special, singular.

indulge

1 *(v) Gran loves to indulge us. See* **spoil** 3.
2 **indulge in** *(v) Why don't you indulge in
a relaxing bath?* treat yourself to, wallow
in, luxuriate in, revel in, bask in.

indulgent

*(adj) I wish my parents were as indulgent
as yours.* lenient, permissive, tolerant,
liberal, easy-going, understanding,
sympathetic, forbearing, generous, doting,
fond, overindulgent, soft.
OPPOSITE: strict.

inevitable

(adj) This disaster was inevitable.
unavoidable, unpreventable, inescapable,
bound to happen, certain, fated, destined,
ordained, decreed, out of your hands.

inexperienced

(adj) An inexperienced team member. new,
untried, untrained, untutored, unpractised,
unseasoned, unqualified, green, raw.
OPPOSITE: experienced.

infatuated *see* **in love with**.

infect

(v) This virus could infect our water supply.
contaminate, poison, pollute, blight, taint.

infectious *see* **catching**.

inferior

1 *(adj) This is inferior work. See* **poor** 2.
2 *(adj) My older sister makes me feel
inferior.* inadequate, useless *(informal)*,
worthless, ineffectual, small, no good.

infinite

1 *(adj) Infinite time.* unlimited, endless,
never-ending, eternal, everlasting.
2 *(adj) Infinite space.* boundless, limitless,
bottomless, immeasurable, fathomless.
3 *(adj) There are an infinite number of
stars in the sky.* countless, incalculable,
untold, numberless, unimaginable.

inflate *see* **blow up** 3.

influence

1 *(n) Jak has a lot of influence in my life.*
control, clout, pull, sway, impact, effect,
authority, dominance, mastery.
2 *(v) I don't want to influence your
decision.* affect, sway, control, bring
pressure to bear on, prejudice, guide,
determine, direct, manipulate, alter.

inform

1 *(v) We need to inform everyone of the
new arrangements. See* **tell** 1.
2 **inform on** *(v) Burglar Beryl doesn't
want to inform on her friends.* betray,
denounce, incriminate, accuse, tell on
(informal), blow the whistle on *(informal)*,
grass on *(slang)*, shop *(slang)*, squeal on
(slang), snitch on *(slang)*, rat on *(informal)*.

informal

1 *(adj) The party will be quite informal.*
casual, relaxed, simple, unpretentious,
cosy, unceremonious, unofficial, easy.
OPPOSITES: formal, official.
2 *(adj) Sanjay has an informal manner. See*
casual 1.
3 *(adj) Don't use informal language in
your essay.* colloquial, slangy, chatty.
OPPOSITE: formal.

information

1 *(n) Computers store information.* data,
facts *(plural)*, statistics *(plural)*, details
(plural), material, knowledge.
2 *(n) I'd like some information about
camping.* details *(plural)*, advice, info
(informal), bumf *(informal)*, gen *(informal)*,
inside knowledge, lowdown *(informal)*.

infuriating *see* **annoying**.

initiative
(n) You need lots of initiative to set up a theatre company. resourcefulness, enterprise, get-up-and-go (informal), dynamism, drive, ambition, push (informal), leadership, inventiveness, originality, creativity.

injection
(n) My arm was sore after the injection. jab (informal), inoculation, vaccination, shot (informal), booster.

injure
(v) Did the terrorists injure many people? hurt, harm, wound, maim, stab, shoot, beat up (informal), bruise, cripple, disable, mutilate, mangle, damage.

injustice
(n) Todd wants to fight against injustice. unfairness, discrimination, prejudice, inequality, oppression, partisanship, bias. OPPOSITES: justice, fairness.

in love with
(phrase) Maisie is in love with Famous Fred. attracted to, infatuated with, head over heels in love with, besotted with, passionate about, crazy about (informal), smitten with, devoted to, enamoured of.

innocent
1 (adj) Burglar Beryl insists that she is innocent. not guilty, in the clear (informal), free from blame, blameless, guiltless, above suspicion, clean (slang).
OPPOSITE: guilty.
2 (adj) It was just an innocent remark. See **harmless** 2.
3 (adj) When Jet left home she was still very innocent. naive, inexperienced, childlike, gullible, credulous, trusting, unworldly, wet behind the ears (informal).
OPPOSITES: sophisticated, worldly.

inquire see **ask** 1.

inquisitive
1 (adj) Don't you hate inquisitive neighbours? See **nosy**.
2 (adj) Lara has an inquisitive approach to life. inquiring, questioning, interested, curious, lively, alert, probing, sceptical.

insane see **mad** 1, 2, 3.

inscription
(n) Can you read the inscription on this stone? writing, lettering, words (plural), engraving, carving, etching.

insect
(n) creepy-crawly (informal), bug.

insensitive see **thoughtless**.

inside
1 (n) We cleaned the inside of the car. interior, contents (plural).
OPPOSITES: outside, exterior.
2 (adv) Stay inside! indoors, under cover.
OPPOSITE: outside.
3 (adj) The inside walls are flimsy. interior, internal, indoor, inner, innermost.
OPPOSITE: outside.

insignificant see **unimportant**.

insincere
1 (adj) I despise insincere politicians. hypocritical, two-faced, deceitful, devious, evasive, untruthful, dishonest, shifty.
OPPOSITES: sincere, honest.
2 (adj) Jessie gave me an insincere smile. false, artificial, feigned, affected, put-on, phoney (informal), flattering.
OPPOSITES: sincere, genuine.

insist
1 (v) I insist that you tidy your room. demand, require, command, urge, order.
2 (v) If anyone objects, you must insist. stand firm, stand your ground, make a stand, put your foot down, be resolute, be determined, not take no for an answer.
OPPOSITES: back down, give way.
3 (v) Beryl continues to insist that she is innocent. claim, assert, maintain, affirm, emphasize, stress, swear, vow.

inspect
(v) Experts came to inspect our school. examine, check, monitor, look over, check out, scrutinize, investigate, study, survey, view, observe, appraise.

inspiration
1 (n) What was the inspiration for your poem? stimulus, idea, spur, motivation, starting point, influence, encouragement.
2 (n) I've had an inspiration! See **idea** 1.

inspire
(v) This book should inspire you. stimulate, fire your imagination, motivate, spark you off, spur you on, encourage, enthuse, energize, galvanize, stir, hearten.

instant
1 (n) I'll go in an instant. See **moment** 1.
2 (adj) An instant reply. See **immediate** 1.

instinct
1 (n) Oscar has an instinct for saying the right thing. knack, gift, talent, genius, intuition, aptitude, capacity, predisposition.
2 (n) I had an instinct that someone was following me. feeling, hunch, sense, gut feeling (informal), presentiment, intuition, sixth sense, gut reaction (informal).

instructions
(plural n) Follow the instructions carefully. directions (plural), rules (plural), guidelines (plural), recommendations (plural), advice.

instrument see **musical instrument**.

insult
1 (v) I hope the boys won't insult you. be rude to, call you names, slag you off (slang), put you down, sneer at, abuse, offend, snub, slight, hurt your feelings, mortify, humiliate, wound, revile, slander.
2 (n) Your insult really hurt me. abuse, taunt, gibe, put-down, snub, slur, slight.

insulting
(adj) Insulting comments. rude, abusive, hurtful, wounding, offensive, snide, disparaging, patronizing, scornful, humiliating, slanderous, scurrilous.

intelligent
1 (adj) An intelligent pupil. See **clever** 1.
2 (adj) An intelligent comment. astute, perceptive, discerning, sensible, shrewd, apt, well-informed, profound, wise, clever.
OPPOSITES: stupid, ignorant.

intend see **mean** 3.

intense
1 (adj) I felt an intense pain in my leg. sharp, agonizing, excruciating, severe, acute, violent, extreme, great, fierce.
OPPOSITES: slight, mild.
2 (adj) Jan was seized by an intense desire to win. See **strong** 6.

intentional see **deliberate**.

interest
1 (n) The poster has attracted lots of interest. attention, curiosity, notice, concern, suspicion, scrutiny, awareness, response, reaction, sympathy.
2 (n) The lecture was of no interest to me. relevance, concern, importance, significance, consequence, value, note.
3 (n) Taking up a new interest is a good way to meet people. See **hobby**.
4 (v) I think this game should interest you. appeal to, arouse your curiosity, capture your imagination, hold your attention, amuse, attract, intrigue, turn you on (slang), grab (informal), fascinate, captivate, enthral, absorb, engross, rivet.
OPPOSITE: bore.

interested
1 (adj) I'm interested to know how the story ends. curious, fascinated, intrigued, keen, eager, excited, concerned.
2 (adj) Benji is an interested pupil. enthusiastic, keen, attentive, responsive.
OPPOSITES: apathetic, bored.
3 interested in (adj) Yoko is interested in science fiction. into (informal), keen on, fascinated by, enthusiastic about, fond of.

interesting
1 (adj) This TV programme is really interesting. fascinating, intriguing, compelling, enthralling, absorbing, gripping, riveting, engrossing, thought-provoking, stimulating, entertaining, spell-binding, captivating, compulsive.
OPPOSITES: boring, dull.
2 (adj) Barney has an interesting job. fascinating, varied, stimulating, exciting, challenging, unpredictable, unusual.
OPPOSITES: boring, tedious.

interfere
1 (v) It's best not to interfere. get involved, poke your nose in (informal), stick your oar in (informal), intervene, be a busybody, meddle, tamper, intrude, pry, butt in.
2 interfere with (v) Bad weather will interfere with our plans. See **upset** 2.

international
(adj) Pollution is an international problem. global, worldwide, universal.
OPPOSITES: national, regional, local.

interrogate *see* **question** 5.

interrupt
1 *(v) Don't interrupt when I'm talking.* butt in, barge in *(informal)*, cut in, chip in *(informal)*, chime in *(informal)*, heckle, muscle in *(informal)*, disturb, intrude.
2 *(v) We must interrupt this programme to bring you a newsflash.* break off, break into, suspend, cut short, discontinue.

interview
1 *(v) We will interview six candidates for the job.* talk to, sound out, question, quiz.
2 *(v) The detective was keen to interview Burglar Beryl. See* **question** 5.
3 *(n) I had an interview with the careers teacher. See* **talk** 6.

intimate
1 *(adj) Jade is an intimate friend of mine.* close, dear, bosom, treasured, special.
2 *(adj) My diary contains my most intimate secrets. See* **private** 2.
3 *(adj) This cottage has an intimate feel.* cosy, friendly, warm, welcoming, inviting.

intimidate *see* **scare** 2.

intolerable *see* **unbearable**.

intolerant
(adj) Why is Aunt Bertha so intolerant? critical, disapproving, narrow-minded, small-minded, bigoted, prejudiced, illiberal, racist, sexist, ageist, homophobic, chauvinist, xenophobic.
OPPOSITES: tolerant, broad-minded.

intriguing *see* **fascinating**.

introduce
1 *(v) May I introduce you to Jon?* present, make you known, acquaint you with.
2 *(v) Simon will introduce the magic act. See* **announce** 2.
3 *(v) Mrs Badger wants to introduce a new system of rewards.* bring in, set up, start, establish, initiate, launch, inaugurate, institute, set in motion, pioneer.

introduction
(n) Listen to this introduction. opening, intro *(informal)*, lead-in, preamble, opening remarks *(plural)*, foreword *(book)*, preface *(book)*, overture *(music)*, opening bars *(plural)* *(music)*, prologue *(play)*.
OPPOSITE: conclusion.

invade
(v) The soldiers will invade the city. attack, storm, march into, enter, descend on, take over, overrun, occupy, raid, plunder.

invasion *see* **attack** 4.

invent
(v) Gita loves to invent new recipes. make up, think up, devise, create, concoct, dream up, come up with, improvise, formulate, design.

invention
(n) Professor Peabody has come up with a new invention. creation, discovery, innovation, design, brainchild *(informal)*, gadget, contraption, contrivance, device.

investigate
(v) We need to investigate the causes of the accident. inquire into, look into, go into, make inquiries about, gather evidence about, study, examine, consider, explore, research, probe, scrutinize, analyse, inspect, check out.

investigation
1 *(n) Please work on this investigation for homework.* study, exploration, research, analysis, survey, review, examination.
2 *(n) The police are conducting an investigation.* inquiry, postmortem (examination of a dead body), hearing, inquest, fact-finding exercise, review.

invisible
(adj) The camouflaged soldiers were invisible in the bushes. hidden, concealed, disguised, undetectable, indiscernible, inconspicuous, out of sight.
OPPOSITES: visible, conspicuous.

invite
(v) The king and queen invite you to the ball. ask, request the pleasure of your company at, summon, bid *(old-fashioned)*.

inviting *see* **tempting**.

involve
1 *(v) The pantomime will involve everyone.* affect, concern, draw in, include, touch.
OPPOSITE: exclude.
2 *(v) I won't involve you in this crazy plan.* include, mix you up, implicate, embroil.
3 *(v) What will the job involve?* entail, require, demand, necessitate, mean, imply.

involved
1 *(adj) I don't like story lines that are too involved. See* **complicated**.
2 *(adj) Do you know who was involved in the robbery?* mixed up, implicated, caught up, in on *(informal)*, included, associated, concerned, taking part, participating.

irrelevant
(adj) Your comments are irrelevant to the subject. unrelated, unconnected, beside the point, neither here nor there, inappropriate, unnecessary, inessential, immaterial, pointless, extraneous.
OPPOSITES: relevant, pertinent.

irresistible
(adj) I felt an irresistible urge to laugh. powerful, overpowering, overwhelming, compelling, uncontrollable, urgent.

irresponsible
(adj) You're too irresponsible to be trusted. unreliable, untrustworthy, reckless, careless, immature, harebrained, wild, scatterbrained, erratic, flighty, feckless.
OPPOSITES: responsible, reliable.

irritable *see* **bad-tempered**.

irritate
1 *(v) Seb's jokes irritate me. See* **annoy** 1.
2 *(v) Will this cardigan irritate the baby's skin?* chafe, rub, scratch, itch *(informal)*, hurt, tickle, inflame, redden, make itchy.

irritated *see* **annoyed**.

irritating *see* **annoying**.

isolated
1 *(adj) The cottage was very isolated.* remote, out-of-the-way, inaccessible, lonely, in the middle of nowhere, secluded, off the beaten track, cut off.
2 *(adj) Imogen felt isolated in her new school. See* **alone** 2.

issue
1 *(n) Gus feels strongly about the issue of whaling. See* **subject**.
2 *(n) Have you read the November issue of "Rap Weekly"?* edition, copy, instalment, publication, number.
3 *(v) The police will issue a description of Burglar Beryl. See* **release** 3.
4 *(v) The prison will issue you with a uniform.* supply, provide, furnish, equip.

itch
1 *(n) I've got an itch on my back.* tickle, prickle, tingling, itchiness, irritation.
2 *(v) Chickenpox makes your skin itch.* tickle, prickle, tingle, crawl, burn.

itchy
(adj) The nettles gave me an itchy rash. prickly, tickly, irritating, maddening, uncomfortable, painful, burning.

item
1 *(n) Jen added another item to her list.* object, article, thing, point, detail, entry.
2 *(n) I saw an interesting item in the newspaper. See* **article** 1.

jab
1 *(v) Jo began to jab at the paper with her brush.* stab, poke, lunge, thrust, punch.
2 *(v) Andy gave me a jab in the ribs.* dig, poke, prod, nudge, stab, punch.
3 *(n) (informal) Did the doctor give you a jab? See* **injection**.

jacket *see* **clothes**.

jagged
1 *(adj) The knife had a jagged edge.* uneven, serrated, ragged, notched, barbed, toothed, irregular, zigzag, spiky.
2 *(adj) I walked carefully over the jagged rocks.* craggy, sharp, uneven, spiky, pointed, ridged, rough, angular.

jail
1 *(n) Burglar Beryl spent a month in the local jail.* gaol, prison, detention centre, cells *(plural)*, nick *(slang)*, can *(slang)*, slammer *(slang)*, clink *(slang)*.
2 *(v) The judge decided to jail Burglar Beryl.* send to prison, lock up, send down *(informal)*, imprison, put away, put behind bars, detain, incarcerate, confine.
OPPOSITES: free, release.

jam

jam
1 (n) *The accident caused a jam on the bypass.* traffic jam, hold-up, snarl-up (informal), tailback, bottleneck, blockage, obstruction, gridlock, congestion.
2 (v) *I tried to jam all my clothes into the case.* See **cram** 1.
3 (v) *All these cars will jam the town centre.* clog, congest, block, obstruct, overcrowd, bung up.

jangle
(v) *I heard the keys jangle in the lock.* clink, clank, clang, rattle, clatter, chime (bell).

jealous
1 (adj) *I was jealous when I saw Liam's new bike.* See **envious**.
2 (adj) *Clarissa's boyfriend is so jealous.* possessive, suspicious, distrustful, doubting, insecure, clingy, overprotective.

jealousy
1 (n) *I was filled with jealousy when I saw Carl's new bike.* See **envy** 1.
2 (n) *Jon's jealousy drove his girlfriend away.* suspicion, suspiciousness, distrust, possessiveness, insecurity.

jeer
1 (v) *Let's jeer at the villain!* See **boo**.
2 jeer at (v) *I'm scared Bozo will jeer at me.* See **make fun of**.

jerk
1 (v) *Jerk the rope when you're ready.* tug, yank, pull, twitch, tweak, jiggle, wrench.
2 (v) *I felt the train jerk.* See **jolt** 1.

jerky
(adj) *The robot moved with jerky steps.* jumpy, twitchy, shaky, jolting, lurching, fitful, spasmodic, convulsive.
OPPOSITES: smooth, gliding.

jet
(n) *A jet of water gushed from the pipe.* spurt, fountain, stream, spout, spray, gush.

jewel
(n) gem, precious stone, gemstone, stone, rock (slang), sparkler (informal).
TYPES OF JEWEL: amethyst, aquamarine, diamond, emerald, garnet, jade, jasper, jet, lapis lazuli, moonstone, onyx, opal, pearl, ruby, sapphire, topaz, turquoise, zircon.
❖ Also see **treasure words**.

jewellery
(n) *Shall I wear my jewellery?* jewels (plural), trinkets (plural), finery, gems (plural), regalia, costume jewellery.
TYPES OF JEWELLERY: anklet, bangle, beads (plural), bracelet, brooch, chain, charm bracelet, choker, crucifix, cuff links (plural), earring, engagement ring, eternity ring, locket, medallion, necklace, nose ring, pendant, pin, signet ring, tiara, tiepin, watch, wedding ring.

jingle
1 (v) *Can you hear the sleigh bells jingle?* ring, tinkle, jangle, chime, clink, clank.
2 (n) *I can't get that jingle out of my head.* song, tune, melody, ditty, chorus.

jittery (informal) see **nervous**.

job
1 (n) *It's my job to keep the classroom tidy.* responsibility, duty, task, chore, role, function, contribution.
2 (n) *What type of job are you interested in?* work, career, employment, occupation, profession, trade, business, line of work.
3 (n) *Mum is looking for a new job.* post, position, situation, appointment.

jog
1 (v) *I jog every day.* run, go running, go jogging, exercise.
2 (v) *Don't jog me when I'm writing.* nudge, prod, poke, push, knock, tap, elbow, jiggle, jolt, jerk, jar, jostle.
3 (v) *This picture should jog your memory.* refresh, jolt, prompt, stir, stimulate, prod.

join
1 (v) *Join the pieces together.* attach, fasten, fix, fit, link, connect, stick, glue, tie, bind, pin, nail, fuse, weld, solder, cement.
OPPOSITES: detach, separate.
2 (v) *Do you want to join our club?* become a member of, enrol in, sign up for, register with, enlist in, affiliate with.
3 (v) *Where do the two roads join?* meet, come together, converge, cross, intersect.
OPPOSITES: fork, divide.

join in
(v) *I want you all to join in.* take part, participate, contribute, pitch in, pull your weight, do your bit, lend a hand.

joint
(adj) *The garden is our joint responsibility.* shared, mutual, common, collective, combined, united, communal, cooperative.
OPPOSITE: individual.

joke
1 (n) *Have you heard the joke about the purple cat?* gag (informal), wisecrack (informal), one-liner (informal), quip, pun.
2 (n) *Let's play a joke on Joel.* See **trick** 2.
3 (v) *It's a serious matter; don't joke.* make jokes, crack jokes, jest, fool around (informal), tease, mock, be facetious.

jolly see **merry**.

jolt
1 (v) *I felt the train jolt as it moved off.* lurch, jerk, jar, start, bump, shake, jounce.
2 (v) *Don't jolt me!* See **jog** 2.

jostle
(v) *Don't let the others jostle you out of the way.* push, shove, elbow, crowd, hustle, press, squeeze, force, knock, bump.

journalist see **reporter**.

journey
1 (n) *The explorers set out on their journey.* voyage, travels (plural), expedition, trek, safari, adventure, odyssey.
2 (n) *Write about your journey to France.* trip, excursion, outing, jaunt, tour, flight, crossing, cruise, drive, voyage.
3 (v) *I must journey home.* See **travel** 1.

journey words

for your journey you may need...
boarding pass
foreign currency
hand luggage
luggage
map
passport
phrasebook
travel games
traveller's cheques
travel tickets
visa

journeys can be...
boring
bumpy
dramatic
eventful
exhilarating
fascinating
nerve-racking
relaxing
rough
smooth
tedious
thrilling
tiring
turbulent (air)

luggage sticker

on a journey you may feel...
airsick
bored
excited
exhausted
expectant
fed up (informal)
fidgety
hot
jet-lagged
jittery (informal)

nervous
queasy
restless
seasick
sticky
sweaty
tired
travel-sick
worn out

AIR
at the airport
air-traffic control tower
arrivals hall
bureau de change
check-in desk
customs
departure lounge
duty-free shop
flight indicator board
information desk
luggage carousel
luggage trolley
observation terrace
passenger bus
passenger terminal
passport control
restaurant
runway
X-ray machine

you can travel by...
aeroplane
airliner
executive jet
helicopter
jumbo jet (informal)
light aircraft

planes...
ascend
bank
circle
climb
cruise
descend
drop
glide
land
mount
nose-dive
rise
soar
take off
taxi

hovering helicopter

network map

high-speed train

RAIL

at the station
arrivals and
  departures board
concourse
  (large central area)
left-luggage office
luggage locker
luggage trolley
platform
railway track
snack bar
station
  announcement
taxi rank
ticket machine
ticket office
waiting room

you can travel by...
commuter train
express train
high-speed train
locomotive
monorail
overnight train
steam train
tube
underground
  train

luggage label

trains...
glide
grind to a halt
hurtle
jerk
jolt
judder
  (informal)
lurch
pull away
pull in
rock
shake
shudder
sway
trundle

train sounds
clank
clatter
click
creak
grind
hum
rattle
squeal
swish
whistle
whoosh

rail tickets

trains can be...
airless
comfortable
cramped
crowded
draughty
jam-packed
shabby
stuffy

rail problems
cancellation
derailment
obstruction on
  the line
points failure
rail strike
signal failure

SEA

you can travel by...
catamaran
cruise ship
ferry
hovercraft
hydrofoil
liner

ships...
berth
cruise
dock
glide
list
pitch
plough through
  the waves
put to sea
roll
sail
set sail
skim
steam
tilt
toss
wallow

on the ship
bridge
cabin
cafeteria
car deck
cinema
control room
deck
duty-free shop
engine room
funnel
lifeboat
lookout tower
passenger lounge
porthole
restaurant
snack bar
sun deck

problems at sea
cancelled crossing
choppy seas
delayed crossing
engine failure
running aground
stormy seas

cruising catamaran

airliner leaving the runway

plane sounds
drone
hum
roar
shriek
throb
vibrate
whine

on the plane
air steward
aisle
captain
emergency exit
flight deck
foldaway table
galley (kitchen)
in-flight
  entertainment
life jacket
overhead
  compartment
safety
  demonstration
seat belt
window seat

foreign coins

air travel problems
air pockets
bad weather
cancelled flight
delayed flight
lost luggage
turbulence

hire car key

ROAD

you can travel by...
bicycle
bus
camper van
car
coach
hire car
minibus
moped
motorcycle
scooter
taxi

vehicles...
accelerate
brake
crawl
cruise
nose forward
overtake
park
pass
reverse
skid
speed
stall
swerve

traffic sounds
beep
chug
cough
growl
honk
hum
purr
rev
roar
screech
splutter
toot
vroom

roads can be...
bumpy
busy
chock-a-block
congested
empty
endless
hazardous
narrow
scenic
single-track
smooth
steep
straight
treacherous
tree-lined
twisting
wide
winding

problems on the road
accident
bad weather
breakdown
hold-up
pile-up (informal)
roadworks
tailback
traffic diversion
traffic jam

camper van

*Also see **aircraft**, **boat**.*

joy

joy *see* **happiness**.
joyful *see* **happy** 1.

judge
1 *(v) Who will judge Burglar Beryl's case?* try, hear, examine, give a verdict on, pass sentence on.
2 *(v) Mrs Badger will judge the competition entries.* assess, evaluate, appraise, size up, examine, weigh up, review, criticize.
3 *(v) It was hard to judge if Seb was lying.* gauge, decide, work out, guess, determine, discern, ascertain.
4 *(n) I like this painting, but I'm not much of a judge.* expert, authority, critic, connoisseur.

judgment
1 *(n) What was the court's judgment?* verdict, ruling, decision, conclusion, finding, decree, sentence.
2 *(n) Sam showed a complete lack of judgment.* common sense, good sense, intelligence, discernment, understanding, wisdom, shrewdness, discretion, taste.

jug
(n) A jug of water. pitcher, ewer, carafe, decanter, flagon, crock, urn.

juicy
1 *(adj) Juicy plums.* succulent, luscious, moist, squelchy, soft.
OPPOSITES: dry, shrivelled.
2 *(adj) Juicy gossip.* sensational, spicy *(informal)*, tasty *(informal)*, racy, hot *(informal)*, scandalous, risqué, fascinating, exciting, colourful.

jumble
1 *(v) Don't jumble my papers!* muddle, muddle up, mix up, mess up, make a mess of, shuffle, tangle, disturb, disorganize.
2 *(n) Tidy up this jumble!* mess, chaos, confusion, muddle, clutter, litter, shambles, hotchpotch, hodgepodge, mishmash.

jump
1 *(v) Look at the frog jump!* leap, bound, spring, bounce, hop, skip.
2 *(v) Watch me jump that fence!* clear, vault, hurdle, leap over, sail over.
3 *(v) The noise of the fireworks made me jump.* flinch, start, jerk, recoil, wince, twitch, quiver.
4 *(v) I could jump for joy! See* **dance** 4.
5 *(n) The horse cleared the final jump.* hurdle, fence, gate, rail, hedge, obstacle, barrier, ditch, gap.
6 *(n) I woke with a jump.* jolt, start, jerk, twitch, shudder, shake, quiver.
7 *(n) We predict a jump in prices.* See **rise** 5.

jumper
(n) Put on your jumper. sweater, jersey, pullover, woolly. ❖ *Also see* **clothes**.

jumpy *see* **nervous**.

---

jungle
(n) rainforest, tropical forest, equatorial forest.

jungle words
clearing
 (open space)
foliage
forest floor
leaf canopy
quagmire
river
stream
swamp
undergrowth

jungles can be...
airless
claustrophobic
damp
dank
dark
dim
gloomy
humid
misty
muddy
muggy
murky
rainy
shady
slimy
squelchy
steamy
sticky
stifling
swampy
treacherous
unexplored

tree snake

jungle trees and plants
avocado tree
banana tree
cacao tree
ebony tree
fern
liana (creeper)
mahogany tree
mangrove
 (shrub growing
 in a swamp)
moss
orchid
palm tree
pineapple tree
rubber tree
teak tree

jungle foliage can be...
bushy
dense
impenetrable
knotted
lush
luxuriant
rotting
tangled

tree frog

chameleon

jungle creatures
alligator
ant
anteater
armadillo
beetle
bird of paradise
butterfly
chameleon
crocodile
gorilla
hummingbird
jaguar
leech
 (bloodsucker)
leopard
macaw
monkey
mosquito
parrot
piranha
 (flesh-eating fish)
porcupine
snake
spider
termite
tiger
toucan
tree frog
tree snake

orchid

jungle creatures may...
attack
bite
crawl
creep
dart
flit
flutter
hover
hunt
lie in wait
pad
pounce
prey on other
 creatures
prowl
scamper
scuttle
slither
spring
stalk
sting
suck blood
swarm
swoop

jungle sounds
burble
buzz
croak
growl
grunt
gurgle
hiss
rustle
screech
shriek
splash
squawk
squeak
squeal
squelch

macaw

toucan

in the jungle you might...
become
 disorientated
be eaten alive
break into a run
develop a fever
climb
creep
crouch
faint
forage
 (search
 for food)
get stuck in a
 swamp
hack through the
 undergrowth
hide
itch
lose your way
panic
pant
scrabble
scramble
scratch
slither
slog
splash through
 streams
squirm
stagger
stumble
sweat
swim
swing from
 creepers
trek
trip
trudge
wade through
 mud

hummingbird

liana

armadillo

forest floor

jaguar

junk
(n) Please throw out this junk. rubbish, trash, garbage, litter, scrap, clutter, odds and ends (plural), bric-a-brac.

just
1 (adj) Mrs Badger is strict but she's always just. See **fair** 2.
2 (adj) Burglar Beryl received a just sentence. fitting, appropriate, suitable, proper, apt, rightful, well-deserved.
OPPOSITES: unjust, inappropriate.

justify see **excuse** 2.

keen
1 (adj) Tejal is a keen student. committed, motivated, enthusiastic, eager, interested, willing, conscientious, diligent, ambitious.
OPPOSITES: unenthusiastic, apathetic.
2 (adj) Kate is keen to open her birthday presents. See **eager** 2.
3 keen on (adj) Jenny is keen on football. See **interested** 3.

keep
1 (v) Keep the champagne for a special occasion. hold on to, keep hold of, hang on to, save, put aside, reserve, put away, store, stash away (informal)
OPPOSITES: get rid of, use.
2 (v) Oil the wood to help it keep its shine. retain, maintain, hold, preserve, conserve, keep intact, prolong.
OPPOSITE: lose.
3 (v) Just keep walking. See **continue** 1.
4 (v) Keep off the grass! stay, remain.
5 (v) It costs a lot to keep a family. provide for, feed, support, maintain, nourish.
6 (v) Does your dad keep pigeons? have, own, care for, look after, tend, mind.

keep on see **continue** 1.

keep up with
(v) I'm doing my best to keep up with the others. keep pace with, keep abreast of, compete with, rival, match, vie with.

key
1 (n) This key will open the door. latchkey, master key, pass key, skeleton key.
2 (n) Detectives are looking for a key to the mystery. See **clue**.
3 (adj) Select the key facts. See **main**.

kick
1 (v) Kick the ball. boot, dribble, pass.
2 (v) (informal) Mum is trying to kick smoking. See **stop** 3.

kid
1 (n) (informal) Stop acting like a kid! See **child**.
2 (v) (informal) Who are you trying to kid? See **deceive** 1.

kidnap
(v) In fairy tales, elves sometimes kidnap babies. snatch, seize, abduct, carry off, steal, hold to ransom, hold hostage.

kill
1 (v) A hit man was paid to kill the President. murder, assassinate, take the life of, do away with, bump off (slang), do in (slang), take out (slang), top (slang).
2 (v) The soldiers were ordered to kill the enemy troops. put to death, slaughter, massacre, butcher, slay, wipe out, destroy, annihilate, obliterate, eradicate, exterminate, liquidate, decimate, waste (informal), execute, hang, behead.
3 (v) (informal) Don't run the marathon - it'll kill you! tire you out, exhaust, wear you out, overtire, overtax, strain.

killer see **murderer**.

killing
1 (n) Police are investigating the killing. murder, assassination, homicide, manslaughter, massacre, slaying.
2 (n) The killing must stop. bloodshed, slaughter, carnage, butchery, genocide.
3 (adj) (informal) The runners set off at a killing pace. See **exhausting**.

kind
1 (adj) Mr Badger is a kind person. kind-hearted, kindly, caring, thoughtful, considerate, sympathetic, understanding, unselfish, compassionate, warm-hearted, softhearted, generous, charitable, hospitable, helpful, obliging, neighbourly, friendly, gentle, patient, well-meaning.
OPPOSITES: unkind, cruel.
2 (n) What kind of food do you like? sort, type, style, variety, make, brand.
3 (n) What kind of bird is that? sort, type, breed, species, family, class, category.

kindness
(n) I appreciate your kindness. helpfulness, thoughtfulness, consideration, generosity, hospitality, sympathy, compassion, understanding, patience, tolerance.

king
(n) monarch, sovereign, ruler.

kingdom see **country** 1.

kiss
1 (v) I don't mind if people kiss in public. embrace, exchange kisses, blow a kiss, smooch (informal), neck (informal), snog (slang), canoodle (slang).
2 (n) Ned gave me a kiss on the cheek. peck (informal), smacker (slang).

kit
1 (n) The explorers packed their kit into rucksacks. gear, equipment, tackle, stuff, paraphernalia, apparatus, instruments (plural), tools (plural), supplies (plural), provisions (plural), baggage, luggage.
2 (n) I like your new sports kit. gear, strip, rigout (informal), outfit, colours (plural), clothes (plural), uniform.

knack
(n) I'd love to be able to juggle, but I don't have the knack. skill, ability, talent, aptitude, expertise, capability, gift, flair.

kneel
(v) Kneel before the king! get down on your knees, fall to your knees, bow down.

knock
1 (v) Knock the nails into the wood. tap, hammer, bang, drive, rap, pound, hit.
2 (v) Don't knock your head on that shelf. See **hit** 2.
3 (n) I heard a loud knock on the door. tap, rap, bang, thud, ratatat-tat.

knock down
1 (v) The builders were told to knock down this house. See **demolish**.
2 (v) If you insult me again, I'll knock you down! knock you to the floor, throw you to the ground, floor, deck (slang).
3 (v) Be careful that bus doesn't knock you down! See **run over**.

knock out
(v) A blow on the head could knock you out. make you unconscious, knock you out cold, floor, knock you for six (informal), put you out for the count, KO (slang).

knot
1 (n) I can't undo this knot in my shoelace. loop, twist, bow, tangle.
2 (v) Knot the two ropes together. tie, loop, bind, twist, weave, braid, secure.

know
1 (v) You need to know these facts for the test. be familiar with, be acquainted with, be conversant with, have a knowledge of, be aware of, have memorized, have learnt by heart, understand.
OPPOSITE: be ignorant of.
2 (v) How can you know that ghosts exist? know for certain, be sure, be certain, be positive, be confident.
3 (v) You can't possibly know what I'm going through. realize, understand, comprehend, tell, be aware of, be conscious of, sense, have experience of.
4 (v) I used to know Famous Fred. be acquainted with, have dealings with, socialize with, associate with, be friends with, be on good terms with, be close to.

knowledge
1 (n) Books are a great source of knowledge. information, facts (plural), data, learning, wisdom, enlightenment.
2 (n) Penny's knowledge of the subject is good. understanding, grasp, awareness, comprehension, expertise in.
OPPOSITE: ignorance.

knowledgeable
1 (adj) The professor is a knowledgeable person. well-informed, educated, well-read, learned, scholarly, erudite, intelligent.
2 knowledgeable about (adj) Are you knowledgeable about the rules of football? See **familiar** 2.

Ll

label
1 *(n) The price is on the label.* tag, tab, sticker, ticket, docket, marker.
2 *(v) Label your luggage.* attach a label to, put a sticker on, name, mark, tag, stamp.
3 *(v) It's unfair to label a child as "difficult".* identify, describe, define, brand, class, categorize, classify, call, term, dub.

lack
1 *(n) There's a distinct lack of books in our school. See* **shortage**.
2 *(v) The refugees seem to lack basic medicines.* be without, be lacking, be short of, be missing, need, require, want.
OPPOSITES: have, possess.

lacy
(adj) Lacy material. gauzy, cobwebby, wispy, gossamer, delicate, frilly, meshy.

lag behind *see* **drop behind**.

laid-back *(informal) see* **relaxed** 1, 2.

lair
(n) The creature returned to its lair. den, hole, haunt, cave, tunnel, burrow *(rabbit)*, warren *(rabbit)*, earth *(fox)*, sett *(badger)*.

lake
(n) We paddled in the lake. loch *(Scottish)*, lough *(Irish)*, lagoon, tarn *(mountain lake)*, reservoir, boating lake, pool, pond.

land
1 *(n) The sailors were glad to be back on land.* dry land, solid ground, terra firma.
2 *(n) This land is very fertile.* ground, soil, earth, clay, loam, farmland, countryside.
3 *(n) Lord Lucre's wealth comes from his land.* property, real estate, estate, grounds *(plural)*, acres *(plural)*, farmland.
4 *(n) Indiana is visiting a distant land. See* **country** 1.
5 *(v) When will the plane land?* touch down, come in to land, arrive.
OPPOSITE: take off.

landscape
(n) We admired the landscape. countryside, scenery, view, panorama, scene, vista, outlook.

lane
(n) Our garden opens on to a narrow lane. path, pathway, footpath, track, passageway, passage, alley, alleyway.

lank
(adj) Lank hair. limp, straggly, straight, long, dull, lifeless, lustreless, drooping.
OPPOSITES: bouncy, shiny.

lanky
(adj) A lanky youth. tall, long-legged, rangy, gangling, thin, skinny, scrawny, bony, spindly, weedy *(informal)*.
OPPOSITES: dumpy, squat.

lap
1 *(n) Pickles settled on my lap.* knee.
2 *(n) I ran a lap of the track.* circuit, circle.
3 *(v) Look at Pickles lap his milk.* drink, lick up, sip, slurp *(informal)*, sup.
4 *(v) Listen to the water lap against the boat.* wash, slap, splash, slosh, plash, swish, ripple, gurgle.

large
1 *(adj) Mum gave me a large helping of chips.* big, huge, enormous, substantial, generous, liberal, sizable, ample, massive, immense, colossal, gigantic, giant, mammoth, mountainous, prodigious, outsize, king-size, whopping *(informal)*.
OPPOSITES: small, modest.
2 *(adj) Aunt Bertha is a large woman.* big, well-built, big-boned, stout, hefty, thickset, heavy, burly, strapping, fat, corpulent.
OPPOSITES: small, slight.
3 *(adj) Lord Lucre lives in a large mansion.* great, huge, enormous, spacious, roomy, vast, immense, massive, extensive, sizable, palatial, towering, monumental.
OPPOSITES: small, poky.

last
1 *(adj) Read the last chapter of the book.* final, concluding, closing, ultimate.
OPPOSITES: first, opening.
2 *(adj) Why am I always last?* at the end, at the back, at the rear, last in line.
OPPOSITE: first.
3 *(adj) What was the last film you saw?* most recent, latest.
4 *(v) That plant won't last much longer.* live, survive, hold out, hold on, live on, linger, endure, continue.
5 *(v) The rain could last for hours. See* **continue** 2.

lasting *see* **permanent** 2.

lastly *see* **finally** 2.

late
1 *(adj) Why was the train late?* behind schedule, not on time, delayed.
OPPOSITES: early, on time.
2 *(adj) Minty is always late.* unpunctual, behind time, behind, tardy, slow.
OPPOSITES: early, punctual.
3 *(adj) I'm sorry about your late birthday present.* belated, overdue.
OPPOSITE: early.
4 *(adj) The funeral of the late Mr Ray was held yesterday.* deceased, departed, dead.

later
(adv) I'll come over later. later on, in a while, afterwards, in a bit, by and by, at a later date, at some point in the future.

lather *see* **foam** 1, 3.

laugh
1 *(v) This joke will make you laugh.* chuckle, giggle, chortle, titter, snigger, roar with laughter, guffaw, split your sides, crack up *(informal)*, fall about *(informal)*, crease up *(informal)*, have hysterics *(informal)*, be in stitches *(informal)*.

2 *(n) Bruce is such a laugh!* clown, joker, comedian, comic, scream *(informal)*, hoot *(informal)*, card *(informal)*, wit.
3 **laugh at** *(v) Don't laugh at me. See* **make fun of**.

laughable *see* **ridiculous**.

laughter
1 *(n) The sound of laughter filled the air.* laughing, giggling, chuckling, chortling, tittering, sniggering, guffawing.
2 *(n) Dom's jokes are a great source of laughter.* amusement, hilarity, mirth, merriment, entertainment.

lavatory *see* **toilet**.

lavish
1 *(adj) Lord Lucre is lavish with his money. See* **generous**.
2 *(adj) Posy spooned on a lavish amount of cream.* copious, abundant, plentiful, profuse, generous, liberal, extravagant, excessive, immoderate, wasteful.
OPPOSITES: meagre, frugal.

law
(n) This new law prohibits smoking in public places. rule, regulation, order, directive, command, decree, edict, pronouncement, bill, statute, act.

lawful *see* **legal**.

lay
1 *(v) Lay the photos on the table.* put, place, spread, leave, arrange, set out, set, set down, position, deposit.
2 *(v) Hens don't normally lay golden eggs.* produce, bring forth, bear, deposit.
3 *(v) Please lay the table. See* **set** 3.

layer
1 *(n) A layer of snow settled on the ground.* covering, coating, sheet, film, blanket, mantle, sprinkling, dusting, coat.
2 *(n) Each layer of rock was a different colour.* stratum, seam, vein, bed, thickness, level, row, tier.

lay into *(informal) see* **attack** 2, 3.

layout *see* **design** 3.

lay out *see* **set out** 2.

laze
(v) I'm going to laze on the beach all day. sit about, lie about, lounge, loll about, loaf about, do nothing, relax, unwind, rest, veg out *(slang)*.

lazy
1 *(adj) Mrs Badger says I'm lazy.* idle, slothful, workshy, indolent, slack, lax.
OPPOSITES: industrious, hard-working.
2 *(adj) I feel really lazy today.* sluggish, listless, lethargic, languid, inactive, drowsy.
OPPOSITE: energetic.

lead
1 *(v) I can lead you to the treasure.* take, show you the way, lead the way, guide, conduct, escort, steer, usher, pilot.
2 *(v) Will you lead the team?* be in charge of, head, direct, command, manage, supervise, oversee, head up *(informal)*.

3 (v) *Sally managed to lead until the last lap.* be in the lead, head the field, be in front, be out in front, be ahead, come first, blaze a trail.
4 (v) *Rob seems to lead a lonely life.* live, have, spend, pass, experience, undergo.
5 (v) *Your behaviour might lead me to change my mind.* cause, persuade, influence, prompt, induce, incline, move, dispose, sway, make.
6 (n) *Follow Amanda's lead.* example, direction, guidance, leadership, model.
7 (n) *After the first lap, Harry was in the lead.* first place, leading position, front.
8 (n) *Sally has quite a lead over the others.* advantage, edge, margin, start, head start.
9 (n) *I was desperate to play the lead in the school play.* leading role, starring role, title role, principal character, main part, male lead, female lead, hero, heroine.
10 (n) *The police need a lead. See* **clue.**
11 (n) *Connect this lead to the television.* wire, flex, cable.
12 (n) *Fasten the lead to your dog's collar.* leash, strap, chain, rope, cord, tether, rein.

leader
1 (n) *The country needs a strong leader.* ruler, premier, prime minister, president, governor, chancellor, dictator, figurehead.
2 (n) *Take me to your leader!* chief, boss (informal), skipper, captain, commander, superior, director, manager, supervisor, number one (informal), ringleader.
OPPOSITE: follower.

lead to *see* **cause 1.**

leaflet
(n) *Someone pushed a leaflet through the door.* hand-out, circular, flyer, pamphlet, booklet, brochure, handbill, mailshot.

leak
1 (n) *There's a leak in this pipe.* hole, crack, chink, break, fissure, puncture, cut, gash, slit, crevice, opening.
2 (v) *Water began to leak from the pipe.* escape, drip, dribble, seep, trickle, ooze, spill, gush, percolate.
3 (v) *Someone is bound to leak this story to the press.* tell, reveal, disclose, divulge, pass on, make known, make public, let slip, let the cat out of the bag, spill the beans (informal), blow wide open (slang).

leaky
(adj) *We must fix this leaky pipe.* leaking, dripping, cracked, split, broken, punctured, perforated, holey.

lean
1 (v) *The tower began to lean.* tilt, tip, heel over, slant, slope, incline, list (ship).
2 (v) *Lean against the wall if you feel tired.* support yourself, prop yourself up, rest, recline, steady yourself.
3 (adj) *The gymnast had a lean, muscular body. See* **thin 1.**
4 (adj) *I prefer lean meat.* low-fat, unfatty.
OPPOSITE: fatty.

lean on *see* **depend on 1.**

leaping frog

leap
1 (v) *Watch that frog leap!* jump, hop, bound, bounce, skip, spring.
2 (v) *Sita began to leap about when she heard the news. See* **dance 4.**
3 (n) *With one giant leap, I cleared the fence.* jump, bound, spring, vault, hop.
4 (n) *We'll see a leap in prices. See* **rise 5.**

learn
1 (v) *Chinese is a hard language to learn.* study, grasp, master, become competent in, take in, absorb, pick up, acquire.
2 (v) *Try to learn the words of the song.* memorize, learn by heart, remember, commit to memory, get off pat, get word-perfect, swot up on (informal).
3 (v) *I was sorry to learn that Tom was leaving.* hear, discover, find out, be told, get word, gather, become aware.

learner
(n) beginner, novice, pupil, student, trainee, apprentice, greenhorn, L-driver.

leave
1 (v) *Do you have to leave so soon?* go, set off, set out, depart, make tracks, get going, start, be on your way, be off, disappear, say goodbye, go away, go off.
OPPOSITES: arrive, come.
2 (v) *The demoralized soldiers decided to leave.* run away, abscond, desert, make off, clear off (informal), take off (informal), slope off, pull out, disappear, split (informal), flit (informal), scarper (slang), do a bunk (slang), hook it (slang).
OPPOSITE: come.
3 (v) *If you don't like your job you should leave. See* **resign 1.**
4 (v) *Don't leave me! See* **desert 1.**
5 (v) *Leave your bag in the hall. See* **put 1.**
6 (v) *Did you leave your umbrella on the train?* leave behind, forget, lose, mislay.
7 (v) *The sauce will leave a stain on your skirt.* leave behind, produce, cause, make.
8 (v) *You can leave this job to Mr Badger.* entrust, assign, hand over, consign, refer.
9 (v) *Did your grandma leave you any money?* bequeath, hand down, will.
10 (n) *How much leave do you have?* holiday, vacation, time off, leave of absence, furlough, sabbatical.

leave out
1 (v) *Leave out chapter three. See* **omit.**
2 (v) *Don't leave me out! See* **exclude.**

lecture
1 (n) *I went to an interesting lecture on astronomy.* talk, speech, address.
2 (n) *I got a real lecture when I stayed out late.* scolding, reprimand, telling-off (informal), talking-to (informal), going-over (informal), dressing-down (informal).
3 (v) *Please don't lecture me. See* **tell off.**

ledge
(n) *The climbers sheltered under a rocky ledge.* overhang, shelf, sill, ridge.

leftover
(adj) *What will we do with the leftover food?* remaining, extra, surplus, excess, spare, uneaten, unused, unwanted.

leftovers *see* **scraps.**

legal
(adj) *Are Dodgy Dave's activities legal?* lawful, legitimate, above board, permissible, allowed, permitted, acceptable, authorized, valid, legit (slang).
OPPOSITES: illegal, unlawful.

legalize
(v) *Should the government legalize the use of cannabis?* make legal, permit, allow, decriminalize, ratify, authorize, sanction.
OPPOSITES: ban, outlaw.

legend
(n) *Do you know the legend of the glass mountain?* story, tale, myth, folk tale, saga, fairy tale, fable, epic.

leisure
(n) *Everyone needs some leisure.* free time, spare time, time off, relaxation, recreation, rest, breathing space, holiday, vacation.
OPPOSITE: work.

leisurely
(adj) *A leisurely walk.* relaxed, unhurried, gentle, easy, laid-back (informal), restful, comfortable, slow, lazy, lingering.
OPPOSITES: brisk, hasty, rushed.

lend
(v) *I'd be happy to lend you my bike.* loan, let you use, give you the loan of, let you have the use of, advance (money).
OPPOSITE: borrow.

length
1 (n) *Work out the length of the bridge from end to end.* extent, span, distance, reach, measurement.
2 (n) *Burglar Beryl spent a length of time in jail.* period, stretch, spell, term, space, span, duration.

lengthen
1 (v) *I asked Mum to lengthen my skirt.* let down, make longer.
OPPOSITES: shorten, take up.
2 (v) *This detour will lengthen our journey.* make longer, increase, extend, add to, prolong, stretch out, draw out, protract.
OPPOSITES: shorten, cut down.

lengthy *see* **long 1, 2.**

lenient
(adj) *Pandora's parents are really lenient.* easy-going, tolerant, indulgent, soft, gentle, kind, forgiving, forbearing, compassionate, merciful.
OPPOSITE: strict.

lesson
1 (n) *When does the next lesson start?* period, class, lecture, tutorial, seminar.
2 (n) *This story contains a lesson for us all.* message, moral, warning, rebuke, deterrent, example, model.

let

(v) Will your parents let you go to the disco? allow, give you permission, permit, give you the go-ahead *(informal)*, give you the green light, give you the thumbs up, authorize, agree to, consent to.
OPPOSITE: forbid.

letdown

(n) After all the hype, the concert was a letdown. anticlimax, disappointment, comedown *(informal)*, fiasco, washout *(informal)*.

let down

1 *(v) If you trust me, I won't let you down.* disappoint, fail, leave you in the lurch, leave you stranded, desert, forsake.
2 *(adj) I felt let down when I learnt the truth about Mark. See* **disappointed**.

let go *see* **release** 1, 2.

lethal *see* **deadly** 1, 2.

lethargic

(adj) This heat makes me feel lethargic. listless, sluggish, languid, lazy, weary, slow, drowsy, sleepy, heavy, torpid, slothful, apathetic, passive, unenthusiastic.
OPPOSITES: lively, energetic.

let in

(v) We can't let you in without a ticket. allow you to enter, admit, give you access, take you in, receive, welcome.

let off

1 *(v) It's your turn to wash up, but I'll let you off.* excuse, spare, exempt.
2 *(v) The judge may let Burglar Beryl off. See* **release** 2.
3 *(v) Don't let off the fireworks yet.* set off, detonate, light, ignite, explode.

let on

(v) (informal) Don't let on that you know Justin's secret. let slip, give away, let out, reveal, divulge, disclose, tell, admit, let the cat out of the bag.

letter

1 *(n) What's the last letter in the alphabet?* character, symbol.
2 *(n) Thank you for your letter.* note, message, reply, answer, epistle, communication.

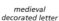
medieval decorated letter

level

1 *(adj) The football pitch should be level.* flat, even, smooth, horizontal.
OPPOSITES: uneven, sloping.
2 *(adj) Is this picture level?* straight, horizontal, flush, square, in line, aligned.
OPPOSITES: crooked, tilted.
3 *(adj) The two teams are level.* equal, evenly balanced, well-matched, all square, on a level, neck and neck, at level pegging *(informal)*, on a par, the same.
OPPOSITE: unequal.
4 *(v) Level the icing on the cake.* level out, even out, smooth out, smooth, flatten.

5 *(n) The river rose to an alarming level.* height, depth, altitude.
6 *(n) Mr Badger has reached a senior level at work.* position, grade, rank, status.

lick

1 *(v) Can I lick your ice cream?* taste, suck.
2 *(v) The flames began to lick around the curtains.* flicker, dart, flick, ripple, play.

lid

(n) Put the lid on the toothpaste. cap, top, stopper, cover, plug, cork *(bottle)*.

lie

1 *(v) I love to lie in front of the fire.* stretch out, recline, sprawl, loll, lounge, relax, rest, be prostrate, be horizontal.
2 *(v) Where is the treasure supposed to lie?* be, be situated, be located, be found.
3 *(v) Don't lie, if you want to be trusted.* tell lies, tell untruths, fib, falsify the facts, make up stories, bluff, perjure yourself, be economical with the truth.
OPPOSITE: tell the truth.
4 *(n) Bo told a lie.* fib, untruth, falsehood, barefaced lie, white lie, whopper *(informal)*, porky *(slang)*, cock-and-bull story *(informal)*, tall tale *(informal)*.
5 **lies** *(plural n) That rumour is pure lies.* fabrication, fiction, invention, deceit.
OPPOSITE: truth.

life

1 *(n) There's no life in a stone statue.* animation, vitality, breath, growth.
2 *(n) You will have many adventures in your life.* lifetime, career, the course of your life, lifespan, time on earth, existence.
3 *(n) Could there be life on Mars?* living things *(plural)*, living creatures *(plural)*, living beings *(plural)*, flora, fauna, wildlife.
4 *(n) What do you know about the life of the Vikings?* way of life, lifestyle, daily life, everyday life, activities *(plural)*, behaviour, habits *(plural)*, customs *(plural)*.
5 *(n) Aisha is so full of life.* energy, vitality, enthusiasm, get-up-and-go *(informal)*, vigour, verve, dynamism, exuberance, high spirits *(plural)*, sparkle, pizzazz *(informal)*, oomph *(informal)*, zip *(informal)*.

lifelike *see* **realistic** 2.

lift

1 *(v) Can you lift this case?* pick up, carry, lift up, raise, hoist.
2 *(v) The balloon began to lift off the ground. See* **rise** 1.
3 *(v) Wait for the fog to lift. See* **clear** 10.
4 *(v) Can I have a lift in your car?* ride, run, drive, trip, spin *(informal)*.

light

1 *(v) We waited for Mum to light the bonfire.* set light to, set fire to, set alight, put a match to, kindle, ignite.
OPPOSITES: put out, extinguish.
2 *(n) I saw a strange light in the sky.* flash, flare, glare, blaze, glow, gleam, glimmer, shimmer, glint, sparkle, twinkle, glitter, ray of light, beam of light, shaft of light, brightness, illumination, radiance.

3 *(n) You need a light to see at night.* lamp, bulb, torch, flashlight, lantern, candle, taper, flare, beacon.
4 *(n) I woke as soon as it was light.* day, daylight, daytime, daybreak, morning, sunrise, dawn, first light.
OPPOSITES: dark, dusk.
5 *(adj) Big windows make a room really light.* bright, full of light, sunny, well-lit.
OPPOSITES: dark, gloomy.
6 *(adj) My shirt is light blue. See* **pale** 3.
7 *(adj) This box is really light.* lightweight, insubstantial, flimsy, easy to carry, portable, underweight *(person)*.
OPPOSITES: heavy, weighty.
8 *(adj) I just had a light lunch.* small, modest, frugal, scanty, snack, digestible.
OPPOSITES: heavy, rich.
9 *(adj) The dancer moved with light steps.* agile, graceful, nimble, lithe, deft, sprightly, light-footed, airy, sylphlike.
OPPOSITES: heavy, clumsy.
10 *(adj) A light breeze. See* **gentle** 2.
11 *(adj) A light workload. See* **easy** 2.

light up

(v) Those lamps light up the street beautifully. illuminate, lighten, brighten, shed light on, flood with light, floodlight.

likable *see* **pleasant** 3.

like

1 *(v) I used to like mushy peas.* love, be partial to, have a taste for, enjoy, be keen on, be fond of, adore *(informal)*, relish.
OPPOSITES: hate, loathe.
2 *(v) I'm sure Robbie will like badminton.* enjoy, be keen on, be interested in, go in for, be into *(informal)*, love, take pleasure in, get a kick out of *(informal)*.
OPPOSITES: dislike, hate.
3 *(v) I used to like Melissa.* be fond of, have a soft spot for, admire, think a lot of, think highly of, respect, have a high regard for, love, be attracted to, fancy *(informal)*.
OPPOSITES: dislike, detest.
4 *(v) Choose whichever cake you like.* want, wish, fancy, please, prefer, desire.
5 *(adj) Our house is like yours.* similar to, much the same as, not unlike, identical to, comparable to, equivalent to, resembling.
OPPOSITES: unlike, different from.

likely

1 *(adj) It's likely that we'll win.* probable, to be expected, anticipated, on the cards, odds-on, possible, plausible, feasible.
OPPOSITE: unlikely.
2 *(adj) Jon is likely to lose his temper if we are late.* liable, apt, inclined, prone.
OPPOSITE: unlikely.

limit

1 *(n) This fence marks the limit of our property.* boundary, border, edge, end, furthest extent, cut-off point, frontier, perimeter, periphery, confines *(plural)*.
2 *(n) There's a limit on how fast you can drive.* limitation, restriction, constraint, check, curb, ceiling, maximum.

3 *(v) Mum is going to limit my TV viewing.* restrict, ration, curb, keep within bounds, hold in check, control, regulate, reduce.

limited
(adj) Our time at the pool is limited. restricted, rationed, fixed, controlled, finite, insufficient, inadequate, minimal.
OPPOSITES: unlimited, unrestricted.

limp
1 *(v) I hurt my leg and had to limp.* hobble, shuffle, shamble, hop.
2 *(adj) Let your arms go limp.* floppy, relaxed, slack, loose, droopy, soft, flexible, flabby, flaccid.
OPPOSITES: stiff, firm, tense.

line
1 *(n) Draw a line on the page.* rule, stroke, underline, slash, dash, hyphen.
2 *(n) My shirt has a red line on the collar.* stripe, band, strip, bar, streak, mark.
3 *(n) The pupils formed a line.* queue, column, row, crocodile *(informal)*, file, procession, cordon, chain, string.
4 *(n) Copy this line of figures.* row, column, list, series, sequence.
5 *(n) Don't step over the line.* boundary, borderline, demarcation line, mark, limit, edge, border, frontier.
6 *(n) Mum spotted a new line on her face.* wrinkle, crease, furrow, crow's foot, groove, scar.
7 *(n) Throw me a line. See* **rope**.

linger
1 *(v) The smell of garlic tends to linger.* hang around, stay around, stick around *(informal)*, persist, endure, last, remain.
OPPOSITES: go, disappear.
2 *(v) Don't linger on your way to school. See* **dawdle**.

link
1 *(n) Our town has a close link with yours.* connection, association, relationship, tie, attachment, affiliation, liaison, bond.
2 *(v) The police will link Burglar Beryl with the robbery. See* **associate** 2.
3 *(v) Link the two ends of the chain. See* **join** 1.

liquid
1 *(n) Drink this liquid.* fluid, juice, solution.
OPPOSITE: solid.
2 *(adj) Liquid gold.* liquified, fluid, runny, flowing, molten, wet, watery, sloppy.
OPPOSITES: solid, solidified.

list
1 *(n) Is there a list of items for sale?* listing, record, inventory, catalogue, register, directory, file, index, schedule.
2 *(v) List everything that you will need.* write down, note down, jot down, itemize, record, log, enter, set down, catalogue.

listen
1 *(v) The music is about to start, so please listen.* pay attention, prick up your ears, keep your ears open, pin back your ears *(informal)*, be all ears, lend an ear, concentrate, attend, be attentive.

2 *(v) Listen when I tell you what to do!* pay attention, take notice, take heed, obey, do as you are told.
3 listen to *(v) Did you listen to what I said? See* **hear** 1.

listless *see* **lethargic**.

litter
1 *(n) Don't drop litter. See* **rubbish** 1.
2 *(v) Don't litter the room with your magazines. See* **mess up** 3.

little
1 *(adj) A little speck of dust.* small, tiny, minute, minuscule, microscopic, infinitesimal, wee, titchy *(slang)*, teeny.
OPPOSITE: large.
2 *(adj) A little dancer.* petite, diminutive, dainty, small-boned, slight, slender, elfin, short, pint-sized *(informal)*, Lilliputian.
OPPOSITE: large.
3 *(adj) Little kittens.* young, baby, infant, immature, undeveloped.
OPPOSITES: adult, mature.
4 *(adj) A little helping of ice cream.* small, modest, meagre, measly *(informal)*, inadequate, insufficient, mean, stingy, mingy *(informal)*, scant, skimpy.
OPPOSITES: large, generous.
5 *(adj) A little problem.* trivial, minor, unimportant, insignificant, trifling, paltry.
OPPOSITES: major, important.
6 *(n) There's only a little left.* small amount, bit, spot, scrap, trace, dash, smidgen *(informal)*, pinch, taste, touch, dab, tad *(informal)*, speck, grain.
OPPOSITES: lot, plenty.

live
1 *(v) I will love you for as long as I live.* have life, draw breath, breathe, exist, have being, walk the earth.
OPPOSITE: die.
2 *(v) Where will you live when you grow up?* have your home, reside, dwell *(old-fashioned)*, settle, stay, hang out *(informal)*, lodge, hang your hat *(informal)*.
3 *(v) Can you live on your salary?* survive, support yourself, make a living, make ends meet, get by *(informal)*, pay the bills.
4 *(v) The memory of this will live for ever.* last, endure, survive, persist, stay alive, be remembered, abide *(old-fashioned)*.
OPPOSITES: die, fade.
5 *(adj) I saw a live snake.* living, alive.
OPPOSITE: dead.

lively
1 *(adj) Mo is so lively.* full of life, vivacious, high-spirited, energetic, bubbly, bouncy, feisty *(informal)*, animated, enthusiastic, exuberant, cheerful, chirpy *(informal)*.
OPPOSITES: lifeless, listless.
2 *(adj) Our puppies are really lively.* frisky, active, energetic, boisterous, playful, alert.
OPPOSITES: inactive, sluggish.
3 *(adj) The film provoked a lively discussion.* animated, heated, enthusiastic, excited, spirited, interesting, stimulating.
OPPOSITES: dull, apathetic.

4 *(adj) This café looks lively.* buzzing, bustling, jumping *(slang)*, busy, crowded, swarming, thronging, hectic, astir.
OPPOSITES: dull, quiet.

livid *see* **angry**.

living *see* **alive** 1, 2.

load
1 *(n) Customs officers inspected the load.* cargo, consignment, shipment, vanload, lorryload, containerload, freight.
2 *(n) You've taken a load off my mind.* weight, burden, worry, millstone, strain.
3 *(v) Load the car with shopping.* fill, fill up, pack, cram, stuff, pile, heap, stack.
OPPOSITE: unload.

loathe *see* **hate** 1.

loathing *see* **disgust** 1.

local
(adj) Let's meet in the local hall. nearby, neighbourhood, community, municipal, district, regional, village, parish, town, city.

lock
1 *(v) Make sure you lock the gate.* bolt, bar, padlock, secure, chain up, fasten.
OPPOSITE: unlock.
2 *(n) I'd love to have a lock of Famous Fred's hair.* strand, tuft, curl, ringlet.

logical
(adj) Try to think in a logical way. rational, systematic, methodical, clear, coherent, consistent, well-organized, reasonable, sensible, intelligent.
OPPOSITES: illogical, unsystematic.

loiter *see* **hang around** 1.

lonely
1 *(adj) A lonely person.* friendless, solitary, lonesome, alone, neglected, abandoned, outcast, rejected, forsaken, forlorn.
2 *(adj) A lonely cottage. See* **isolated** 1.

loner
(n) Don't expect Nicholas to join in; he's a loner. outsider, individualist, lone wolf, recluse, hermit.

long
1 *(adj) Nasim crawled down a long tunnel.* lengthy, extensive, endless, never-ending.
OPPOSITE: short.
2 *(adj) Aunt Bertha is recovering from a long illness.* lengthy, prolonged, long-drawn-out, lingering, protracted, seemingly endless, interminable.
OPPOSITES: short, brief.
3 long for *(v) It's pointless to long for something you can't have.* yearn for, wish for, hanker after, eat your heart out over, pine for, dream of, crave, hunger for, thirst for, ache for, hope for, want, desire.

longing *see* **desire** 2.

long-winded
(adj) A long-winded speech. long, lengthy, overlong, rambling, wordy, verbose, long-drawn-out, repetitious, boring, tedious.
OPPOSITES: brief, concise.

loo *(informal) see* **toilet**.

look

look
1 (v) *Please don't look!* watch, stare, peep, peek, gape, gawp *(slang)*, ogle.
2 (v) *Do I look tired?* seem, appear, strike you as, give the impression of being.
3 (v) *Let's look for clues.* See **search** 2.
4 (n) *Take a look over here!* glance, peek, peep, glimpse, squint *(informal)*, look-see *(slang)*, butcher's *(slang)*, shufti *(slang)*.
5 (n) *Famous Fred has the look of a film star.* appearance, air, manner, bearing, demeanour, face, expression.
6 (n) *What a sad look!* See **expression** 1.

look after
(v) *Please look after my rat while I'm away.* take care of, care for, mind, keep an eye on, watch, guard, protect, attend to.

lookalike
(n) *Sidney is a lookalike of Elvis Presley.* double, living image, clone, twin, spitting image *(informal)*, dead ringer for *(slang)*.

look at
1 (v) *Look at those acrobats!* take a look at, watch, see, check out *(informal)*, get a load of *(informal)*, clock *(slang)*.
2 (v) *Could you look at my homework?* take a look at, glance at, cast your eye over, run your eyes over, skim through, scan, check, read, scrutinize, examine.
3 (v) *I love to look at the waves crashing on the shore.* watch, gaze at, stare at, contemplate, study, survey, observe, view.

look down on see **scorn** 1.

look forward to
(v) *I look forward to your next letter.* long for, count the days until, await, anticipate, wait for, hope for.

look like
(v) *Don't the girls look like their mum?* resemble, take after, remind you of, bear a resemblance to, look similar to, put you in mind of, have a look of, favour *(informal)*.

look out
(v) *Look out or you'll get hurt!* watch out, pay attention, keep your eyes open, be careful, beware, be alert, keep an eye out.

look up to see **admire** 1.

loop
1 (n) *Make a loop in the rope.* coil, circle, hoop, ring, spiral, twist, kink, curl, curve.
2 (v) *Loop the rope round this post.* coil, wind, twist, knot, entwine, circle, spiral, curl, bend.

loose
1 (adj) *Wear loose clothing on the plane.* loose-fitting, baggy, sloppy, loosened, unbuttoned, slack, flowing.
OPPOSITES: tight, close-fitting.
2 (adj) *Don't let the leads become loose.* free, unattached, unfastened, untied, detached, disconnected, insecure, wobbly.
OPPOSITES: secure, firm.
3 (adj) *Tighten the rope so it isn't loose.* slack, floppy, dangling, hanging, free.
OPPOSITES: taut, tight.

4 (adj) *My hamster is loose in the kitchen!* on the loose, free, at large, at liberty, roaming, unconfined, unrestricted.

loosen
(v) *Uncle Walter had to loosen his belt.* let out, slacken, undo, release, unfasten, unbutton, unhook, untie.
OPPOSITE: tighten.

loot
1 (n) *Burglar Beryl ran home with the loot.* booty, spoils *(plural)*, swag *(slang)*, haul, plunder, stolen goods *(plural)*, takings *(plural)*, ill-gotten gains *(plural)*.
2 (v) *The rioters began to loot the shops.* raid, steal from, ransack, rob, plunder, burgle, pillage.

lopsided
(adj) *That clay pot looks lopsided.* off-balance, crooked, uneven, cockeyed *(informal)*, skewwhiff *(informal)*, askew, asymmetrical, warped, out of true.
OPPOSITES: symmetrical, straight.

lorry
(n) *Tim's dad drives a lorry.* truck, HGV (heavy goods vehicle), articulated lorry, artic *(informal)*, van, juggernaut, tanker.

lose
1 (v) *I'm scared I might lose my bus fare.* mislay, misplace, drop, be unable to find.
OPPOSITE: find.
2 (v) *I knew I would lose.* be beaten, be defeated, be the loser, be thrashed, lose out *(informal)*, suffer defeat, take a licking *(informal)*, come a cropper *(informal)*.
OPPOSITE: win.
3 (v) *Don't lose your chance to go on the outing.* See **miss** 3.

lose your temper
(phrase) *There's no need to lose your temper!* fly into a rage, blow up *(informal)*, blow your top *(informal)*, throw a fit *(informal)*, fly off the handle *(informal)*, go off the deep end *(informal)*, go berserk, blow a fuse *(informal)*, go mad *(informal)*, go crazy *(informal)*, see red *(informal)*, lose your cool *(slang)*, lose it *(slang)*.

loss
1 (n) *You may notice a loss of sound.* lack, absence, disappearance, failure.
2 (n) *Granny never recovered from the loss of her home.* ruin, destruction, wrecking, demolition, eradication.
3 (n) *I sent my friend a card consoling her on her loss.* bereavement, misfortune.
4 (n) *The company made a loss last year.* deficit, shortfall.
OPPOSITES: profit, gain.

lost
1 (adj) *I'm sad because my kitten's lost.* missing, disappeared, vanished, gone, strayed, untraceable.
OPPOSITE: found.
2 (adj) *We keep lost items in this cupboard.* mislaid, misplaced, missing, forgotten, unclaimed, abandoned.
OPPOSITE: found.

3 (adj) *The explorers realized they were lost.* off-course, off-track, adrift, astray, disoriented, going round in circles, at sea.
4 (adj) *You may feel lost when you start at your new school.* confused, bewildered, baffled, at a loss, out of your depth, at sea, helpless, mystified, perplexed.
5 (adj) *Joel was lost in his own thoughts.* absorbed, engrossed, deep, rapt, preoccupied, distracted, spellbound.
6 (adj) *Think of those lost opportunities.* wasted, missed, squandered, frittered away, misspent, misused.

lots (informal) see **many**.

loud
1 (adj) *Loud music came from the disco.* noisy, deafening, ear-splitting, booming, blaring, piercing, ear-piercing, thunderous, resounding, clamorous, strident.
OPPOSITES: quiet, soft.
2 (adj) *I hate loud shirts.* See **gaudy**.
3 (adj) *Barry can't help being loud.* brash, vulgar, loudmouthed *(informal)*, rowdy, boisterous, raucous, offensive, brazen, coarse, crude, crass, pushy *(informal)*.
OPPOSITES: quiet, retiring.

lovable see **adorable**.

love
1 (v) *I will always love you.* adore, be devoted to, be in love with, think the world of, dote on, worship, idolize, be infatuated with, care for, have a soft spot for, be fond of, be attached to, treasure, cherish, desire, fancy *(informal)*.
OPPOSITES: hate, loathe.
2 (v) *I used to love fudge.* See **like** 1.
3 (n) *My love for you will never die.* affection, passion, fondness, tenderness, desire, devotion to, infatuation with, adoration, yearning, adulation, regard.
OPPOSITES: hatred, loathing.
4 (n) *Pirate Peg's love for adventure is well known.* fondness, liking, taste, relish, soft spot, weakness, enjoyment of.
5 fall in love with see **fall in love with**.
6 in love with see **in love with**.

lovely
1 (adj) *Laura looks lovely.* beautiful, gorgeous, stunning *(informal)*, enchanting, ravishing, bewitching, captivating, appealing, adorable, alluring, charming, pretty, elegant, attractive, glamorous.
OPPOSITES: unattractive, hideous.
2 (adj) *We had a lovely day at the seaside.* delightful, blissful, enjoyable, wonderful, fabulous *(informal)*, fantastic *(informal)*, marvellous, brilliant, glorious, pleasant.
OPPOSITES: awful, terrible.
3 (adj) *Mrs Honey is a lovely person.* delightful, engaging, warm, charming, sweet, agreeable, pleasant, amiable.
OPPOSITES: obnoxious, disagreeable.

loving
(adj) *Loving parents.* affectionate, caring, devoted, fond, adoring, doting, kind, warm-hearted, tender, demonstrative.

Mm

low

1 *(adj) A low hedge.* small, little, short, stumpy, stubby, squat, stunted, knee-high. OPPOSITES: high, tall.

2 *(adj) A low salary.* small, meagre, paltry, inadequate, pathetic *(informal)*, poor. OPPOSITE: high.

3 *(adj) A low rank.* junior, inferior, humble, menial, lowly *(old-fashioned)*. OPPOSITES: high, senior.

4 *(adj) This work is of a low standard.* inferior, poor, mediocre, second-rate, unacceptable, substandard. OPPOSITE: high.

5 *(adj) Supplies are low.* meagre, scanty, inadequate, sparse, few, depleted, reduced, diminished, wanting, deficient. OPPOSITE: ample.

6 *(adj) A low whisper. See* **quiet** 1.

7 *(adj) Low prices.* reasonable, cheap, modest, inexpensive, economical. OPPOSITES: high, exorbitant.

8 *(adj) Low notes. See* **deep** 3.

9 *(adj) I'm feeling low. See* **miserable** 1.

lower

1 *(adj) We offer lower prices.* reduced, decreased, slashed, pruned, cut, diminished, pared down. OPPOSITES: higher, increased.

2 *(adj) These soldiers are in the lower ranks.* junior, subordinate, inferior, minor. OPPOSITES: higher, senior.

3 *(v) Lower your speed. See* **reduce** 3.

4 *(v) Lower your voice.* tone down, soften, quieten, moderate, hush, muffle. OPPOSITE: raise.

5 *(v) Lower the sail.* take down, let down, pull down, haul down, drop, let fall. OPPOSITE: raise.

lower yourself

(v) Don't lower yourself by answering back. demean yourself, degrade yourself, humiliate yourself, debase yourself, belittle yourself, humble yourself, discredit yourself, stoop, sink, condescend.

loyal

(adj) A loyal friend. faithful, devoted, firm, true, steadfast, staunch, trustworthy, constant, dependable, unwavering. OPPOSITES: disloyal, fickle.

lucid *see* **clear** 7.

luck

1 *(n) We found the right path by luck.* chance, accident, coincidence, fluke, good fortune, a stroke of luck, serendipity.

2 *(n) I wish you luck.* good luck, good fortune, success, happiness, prosperity.

lucky

1 *(adj) Who are the lucky winners?* fortunate, favoured, jammy *(slang)*, successful, happy.

2 *(adj) This book was a lucky find.* fortunate, happy, fluky *(informal)*, chance, accidental, fortuitous, providential, opportune, timely.

ludicrous *see* **ridiculous**.

luggage

(n) Don't forget your luggage! baggage, bags *(plural)*, cases *(plural)*, belongings *(plural)*, things *(plural)*, gear.

lukewarm

1 *(adj) This water is lukewarm.* tepid, warm, at room temperature.

2 *(adj) I feel lukewarm about this plan. See* **half-hearted** 1.

lump

1 *(n) A lump of cheese.* piece, wedge, slab, chunk, hunk, block, bit, nugget, wodge *(informal)*, mass.

2 *(n) Robyn has a lump on her knee.* bump, bruise, bulge, swelling, growth, cyst, tumour, hump.

lumpy

1 *(adj) This custard is lumpy.* full of lumps, granular, clotted, curdled. OPPOSITE: smooth.

2 *(adj) My mattress is lumpy.* bumpy, uneven, knobbly, bulging. OPPOSITES: flat, even.

lunge

(n) Bozo made a lunge at me. charge, rush, dive, swipe *(informal)*, swing, jab, stab.

lurch

1 *(v) The drunk began to lurch towards us.* stagger, totter, teeter, stumble, sway, reel, weave, lunge, jerk.

2 *(v) The storm made the ship lurch.* wallow, roll, pitch, tilt, list, lean, heel.

lure

(v) The wizard tried to lure the princess into his castle. entice, tempt, ensnare, inveigle, draw, seduce, cajole, attract.

lurid *see* **sensational** 1.

lurk

(v) Wolves lurk in this forest. skulk, lie in wait, lie low, hide, crouch, wait, prowl, slink, steal, take cover.

luscious *see* **delicious**.

lush

(adj) We pushed our way through the lush vegetation. luxuriant, flourishing, overgrown, dense, thick, verdant, green, profuse, abundant, teeming, riotous. OPPOSITE: sparse.

luxurious

(adj) A luxurious hotel. comfortable, sumptuous, plush *(informal)*, lavish, opulent, ritzy *(slang)*, de luxe, grand, magnificent, posh *(informal)*, swish *(informal)*, swanky *(informal)*, up-market. OPPOSITES: basic, Spartan.

luxury

1 *(n) Let's have a day of luxury.* comfort, pleasure, indulgence, ease, enjoyment, bliss, self-indulgence, opulence, affluence, high living, splendour, hedonism. OPPOSITES: discomfort, self-denial.

2 *(n) Caviar is a luxury.* treat, extravagance, indulgence, extra, frill, nonessential. OPPOSITE: essential.

machine

(n) Is there a machine to do this job? appliance, contraption, device, gadget, instrument, tool, mechanism, apparatus.

machinery

(n) Do you have the machinery for this job? machines *(plural)*, apparatus, equipment, gear, tackle, mechanism, tools *(plural)*.

macho

(adj) Bozo thinks it's good to be macho. virile, manly, butch *(slang)*, hard, tough, masculine, muscular, Ramboesque, strong, strapping, chauvinist, sexist.

mad

1 *(adj) The doctor thought her patient might be mad.* insane, deranged, psychotic, manic, of unsound mind, unbalanced, mentally ill. OPPOSITES: sane, rational.

2 *(adj) You must be mad to dress up as a gorilla.* crazy, insane, demented, out of your mind, raving mad *(informal)*, unhinged, barmy *(slang)*, bonkers *(slang)*, batty *(slang)*, screwy *(slang)*, loopy *(informal)*, nuts *(slang)*, bananas *(slang)*, off your head *(slang)*, off your trolley *(slang)*, round the twist *(slang)*, nutty as a fruitcake *(slang)*, out to lunch *(slang)*.

3 *(adj) Bathing in baked beans is a mad thing to do.* crazy, absurd, ridiculous, insane, daft *(informal)*, ludicrous, nonsensical, preposterous, wild.

4 *(adj) (informal) Mum was mad that I'd broken her best vase. See* **angry**.

5 *(adj) Kevin is mad about football.* crazy *(informal)*, fanatical, passionate, wild, nuts *(slang)*, bonkers *(slang)*, hooked on, devoted to, keen on, into *(informal)*.

made-up

1 *(adj) Is that a made-up story?* invented, fictional, make-believe, imaginary, fantasy, mythical, fairy-tale. OPPOSITES: true, real-life.

2 *(adj) I don't want to hear any of your made-up excuses.* fabricated, invented, trumped up, concocted, manufactured, false, untrue, spurious. OPPOSITES: true, genuine.

magazine

(n) journal, weekly, monthly, quarterly, glossy, fanzine, mag *(informal)*, paper, comic, colour supplement, periodical.

magic

1 *(n) The witch was an expert in magic.* sorcery, enchantment, witchcraft, wizardry, black magic, the black arts *(plural)*, voodoo, spell-making.

2 *(n) Miraculous Marvello produced a rabbit by magic.* conjuring, hocus-pocus, illusion, sleight of hand, trickery, wizardry.

magician

1 *(n) The magician cast a spell.* sorcerer, wizard, enchanter, sorceress, enchantress.
2 *(n) The magician did an amazing trick.* conjurer, illusionist.

magnificent

1 *(adj) What a magnificent palace!* splendid, impressive, imposing, majestic, superb, grand, noble, stately, regal, resplendent, sumptuous, opulent, ornate, lavish, elegant, awe-inspiring, stunning *(informal)*, striking.
2 *(adj) Maggie gave a magnificent performance.* splendid, superb, stunning *(informal)*, masterly, excellent, accomplished, skilful, brilliant, terrific *(informal)*, wonderful, virtuoso.

magnify

(v) The scientist used a microscope to magnify the cells. enlarge, make larger, expand, increase, blow up *(informal)*.

mail *see* **post** 2, 4.

main

(adj) What are the main arguments in your essay? major, central, principal, chief, leading, important, key, basic, essential, fundamental, critical, pivotal, vital, prime, primary, foremost.

mainly *see* **mostly** 1, 2.

maintain

1 *(v) I can't maintain this effort for long.* keep up, sustain, continue, uphold, prolong, keep alive, perpetuate.
2 *(v) Oil the wood to help it maintain its shine. See* **keep** 2.
3 *(v) Do you know how to maintain your bike?* look after, take care of, service, keep in good repair, keep in good condition.
4 *(v) Burglar Beryl continues to maintain that she is innocent. See* **insist** 3.

major

1 *(adj) New York is one of the world's major cities.* largest, biggest, great, most important, main, principal, leading, chief.
OPPOSITE: minor.
2 *(adj) We're making some major changes.* great, significant, wide-ranging, extensive, drastic, radical, serious, important, crucial, large-scale, wholesale.
OPPOSITES: minor, insignificant.
3 *(adj) The play was a major success.* great, outstanding, huge, enormous, phenomenal, notable, mega *(informal)*.

make

1 *(v) Kim loves to make things.* construct, put together, assemble, build, produce, create, fashion, shape, model, mould, devise, form, manufacture, mass-produce.
2 *(v) I don't want to go, so don't make me! See* **force** 1.
3 *(v) Can you make this sheet into a ghost costume? See* **turn** 3.
4 *(v) Let's make some money. See* **earn** 1.
5 *(v) Five and five make ten.* add up to, come to, amount to, total.

6 *(v) We want to make you captain.* appoint, elect, nominate, name, create.
7 *(v) We must make some new rules.* draw up, decide on, agree on, formulate, put together, frame, introduce, bring in.
8 *(v) Joe may make trouble. See* **cause** 1.
9 *(v) Anne will make a good doctor.* be, become, grow into, develop into.
10 *(v) You might make the train if you run.* catch, get, arrive in time for.
OPPOSITE: miss.
11 *(v) I make the total to be 65.* calculate, estimate, reckon, work out, judge, gauge.
12 *(n) Which make of chocolate do you prefer?* brand, type, sort, kind, variety.

make a mess of

(phrase) I hope I don't make a mess of this. muff, botch, mess up, bungle, fudge, make a hash of *(informal)*, screw up *(informal)*, muck up *(slang)*, cock up *(slang)*, make a pig's ear of *(slang)*.

make-believe

1 *(n) Josephine lives in a world of make-believe.* fantasy, imagination, invention, romance, pretence, play-acting, illusion, unreality, dreams *(plural)*.
OPPOSITE: reality.
2 *(adj) A dragon is a make-believe animal. See* **imaginary** 1.

make believe *see* **pretend** 1.

make better

1 *(v) How can we make the situation better? See* **improve** 3.
2 *(v) This ointment will make your rash better. See* **cure**.

make fun of

(phrase) Don't make fun of me because I'm small. laugh at, poke fun at, tease, take the mickey out of *(informal)*, taunt, scoff at, jeer at, sneer at, mock, ridicule.

make love

(phrase) have sex, sleep together, go to bed together, have sexual intercourse, copulate.

make out

1 *(v) I could just make out a figure coming through the fog.* distinguish, recognize, see, perceive, discern, detect, pick out.
2 *(v) Can you make out what this means? See* **understand** 2.
3 *(v) Edwin tried to make out that he was 18.* pretend, bluff, claim, suggest, give the impression, let on *(informal)*, imply.
4 *(v) I wonder how Marco will make out as an actor.* fare, get on, shape up *(informal)*, manage, cope, succeed.

make-up

(n) Put on your make-up and let's go out! cosmetics *(plural)*, war paint *(informal)*, greasepaint *(theatre)*, face paint.

make up

1 *(v) Oz will make up a silly excuse.* invent, fabricate, manufacture, cook up *(informal)*, trump up, concoct, dream up, hatch, come up with, conjure up.

2 *(v) Ruby loves to make up new songs.* compose, invent, write, originate, devise, create, think up, dream up.
3 *(v) How many players make up a team?* form, constitute, comprise, compose.
4 *(v) I'm sick of fighting; let's make up.* be friends, shake hands, call it quits, bury the hatchet, forgive and forget, make peace.

make up for

(v) How can I make up for forgetting your birthday? compensate for, make amends for, atone for, recompense you for.

make up your mind

(phrase) You'll have to make up your mind soon. decide, make a decision, come to a decision, reach a decision, choose.

make worse

(v) Arguing will only make the situation worse. worsen, exacerbate, aggravate.

malicious *see* **spiteful**.

man

1 *(n) Who's that man over there?* guy *(informal)*, bloke *(informal)*, chap *(informal)*, gentleman, fellow.
2 *(n) Sonia joined a dating agency to find herself a man.* boyfriend, partner, husband, lover, spouse, bloke *(informal)*.
3 *(n) Man is descended from the apes.* human beings *(plural)*, people *(plural)*, mankind, the human race, humankind.

manage

1 *(v) I wonder how I'll manage at my new school?* cope, get on, get along, survive, make out, fare.
2 *(v) Mum has always wanted to manage her own business.* run, be in charge of, be in control of, be the manager of, preside over, direct, administer, organize, oversee, supervise, head up *(informal)*.
3 *(v) See what you can manage in an hour. See* **achieve**.
4 *(v) A large family can be hard to manage.* look after, cope with, deal with, handle, organize, control.

man-made *see* **artificial** 1.

manners

1 *(plural n) Haven't you learnt any manners?* etiquette, good manners *(plural)*, social graces *(plural)*, politeness, courtesy, civility, refinement, decorum.
2 *(plural n) Pip's manners are terrible.* behaviour, conduct.

manufacture *see* **make** 1.

many

(adj) Nadya received many presents. lots of *(informal)*, a lot of, masses of *(informal)*, a great many, loads of *(informal)*, scores of, tons of *(informal)*, heaps of *(informal)*, stacks of *(informal)*, piles of *(informal)*, oodles of *(informal)*, countless, innumerable, numerous.

map

(n) We need a map to find the way. plan, guide, street map, town plan, road atlas, route map, atlas, chart *(sea, air)*.

march

1 *(v) We watched the soldiers march past.* file, troop, parade, strut.
2 *(v) Dan loves to march across the moors.* stride, pace, stomp *(informal)*, walk, hike, trek, tramp, slog, stalk.
3 *(n) Please join our march against war.* demonstration, demo *(informal)*, protest march, protest, parade, procession.

banner

protest march

mark

1 *(n) What's that mark on the wall?* spot, blot, blotch, smear, smudge, streak, splotch, speck, dot, stain, scribble, line, scratch, dent, nick, chip, notch, pit, pock, score, gash, cut, blemish, flaw, impression.
2 *(n) Ed has a mark on his face.* blemish, birthmark, scar, scratch, bruise, tattoo.
3 *(n) Did the thief leave any mark?* trace, sign, trail, tracks *(plural)*, footprints *(plural)*, fingerprints *(plural)*, vestige.
4 *(n) Zanzi got a good mark for her test.* grade, percentage, rating, valuation.
5 *(n) Did the experience leave a mark on you?* lasting impression, scar, impression, effect, impact, influence, imprint.
6 *(v) Don't mark the paintwork!* damage, make a mark on, dirty, stain, smear, smudge, scratch, dent, chip, nick, score, cut, scribble on, spoil, blemish, deface.
7 *(v) Mrs Badger will mark our tests fairly.* correct, assess, grade, evaluate, appraise.
8 *(v) Mark the spot clearly.* identify, label, show, tag, signpost, flag, highlight, name, initial, stamp.

market

(n) You'll find great bargains in the market. open-air market, covered market, flea market, bazaar, fair, marketplace.

marooned *see* **stranded**.

marriage

1 *(n) My parents are celebrating 15 years of marriage.* matrimony, wedlock, union.
2 *(n) We've been invited to Simon's marriage.* wedding, wedding ceremony, marriage ceremony, nuptials *(plural)*.

marry

(v) Luke and Lucy are planning to marry. get married, become man and wife, wed, tie the knot *(informal)*, walk down the aisle *(informal)*, get hitched *(slang)*, get spliced *(informal)*, take the plunge *(informal)*.
OPPOSITES: stay single, divorce.

marsh

(n) We squelched through the marsh. bog, swamp, marshland, fen, wetland, morass, quagmire, mire, mud flats *(plural)*.

marshy

(adj) Marshy ground. swampy, boggy, soggy, waterlogged, squelchy, spongy, muddy, wet.

marvel

1 *(n) The pyramids were a marvel of the Ancient World. See* **wonder** 2.
2 *(n) Oz is a marvel at art. See* **genius**.
3 **marvel at** *(v) You'll marvel at the skill of the acrobats.* be amazed by, be astonished by, be filled with amazement at, wonder at, gape at, goggle at, admire, applaud, not believe your eyes.

marvellous *see* **wonderful** 1, 2.

mash

(v) Did you mash the vegetables? purée, pulp, crush, pound, pulverize, squash, smash, beat, reduce to a pulp.

mask

1 *(n) Ben wore a gruesome mask to the Hallowe'en party.* false face, disguise.
2 *(n) Wear this mask to protect your face.* protective mask, visor, shield, safety goggles *(plural)*.
3 *(n) Dean's charming manner is just a mask. See* **front** 4.
4 *(v) The soldiers used bushes to mask the tank. See* **disguise** 3.

mass

1 *(n) A mass of papers covered the desk.* load, lot, quantity, heap, mound, pile, stack, bundle, bunch, collection.
2 *(n) A mass of people packed the stadium. See* **crowd** 1.
3 *(n) The statue was carved from a mass of rock.* block, lump, piece, chunk, hunk.
4 *(v) A crowd began to mass in the square. See* **collect** 3.
5 *(adj) There was mass rioting after the match.* widespread, general, large-scale, wholesale, extensive, indiscriminate.
6 **masses** *(plural n) (informal) Gita has masses of CDs. See* **many**.

massive *see* **huge**.

master

1 *(v) Greek is hard to master. See* **learn** 1.
2 *(v) Indy will master the situation.* take command of, gain control of, take charge of, get the better of, manage, control, handle, get the upper hand.
3 *(n) Jan is a master at golf. See* **expert** 2.

match

1 *(n) When does the match start?* game, contest, competition, tournament, event, trial, head-to-head, tie, bout *(boxing, wrestling)*, test match *(cricket)*.
2 *(v) This top should match my leggings.* go with, coordinate with, tone in with, be the same colour as, complement, blend with, team with, harmonize with.
3 *(v) The coach will match you with a suitable partner.* link you up, pair, put you together, team you up, join you up.
4 *(v) Nothing can match a steaming hot bath. See* **equal** 5.

matching

(adj) The twins wore matching clothes. identical, similar, the same, coordinating, corresponding, toning, harmonizing.

material

(n) What sort of material is your shirt made of? fabric, cloth, stuff, textile.
TYPES OF MATERIAL: acrylic, calico, canvas, cashmere, chambray, cheesecloth, chiffon, chintz, corduroy, cotton, crêpe de chine, damask, denim, felt, flannel, gauze, gingham, hessian, jersey, lace, lamé, linen, lycra, muslin, net, nylon, oilcloth, polyester, rayon, satin, seersucker, silk, taffeta, tulle, tweed, velours, velvet, viscose, wool.

matter

1 *(v) Will the way I dress matter?* make a difference, be important, carry weight, count, be relevant, signify, be of any consequence, make any odds.
2 *(n) What's the matter, Kirsty?* trouble, problem, difficulty, worry, wrong.
3 *(n) Mrs Badger dealt with the matter quickly.* situation, incident, episode, affair, occurrence, subject, issue, question.

matter-of-fact

(adj) Guy gave a matter-of-fact account of the accident. factual, straightforward, down-to-earth, sober, unemotional, prosaic, mundane, unimaginative, plain, unvarnished, unsentimental, humdrum.
OPPOSITES: emotional, imaginative.

mature

(adj) Carl is mature for his age. grown-up, advanced, well-developed, adult, sensible, responsible, sophisticated, wise, shrewd.
OPPOSITES: immature, childish.

meadow *see* **field** 1.

meal

(n) What a delicious meal! spread *(informal)*, feast, banquet, snack, picnic, barbecue, blowout *(slang)*, nosh-up *(slang)*, tuck-in *(informal)*, beanfeast *(informal)*, repast *(old-fashioned)*. ❖ *Also see* **food & flavours**.

mean

1 *(v) What do those initials mean?* stand for, indicate, represent, signify, symbolize, denote, convey, communicate, spell, say.
2 *(v) What does Hamlet mean in this speech?* suggest, imply, hint at, drive at, insinuate, indicate, allude to, say, convey.
3 *(v) Did you mean to break the record?* intend, plan, set out, want, resolve, determine, have plans, aim, wish, hope, aspire, have in mind, have the intention.
4 *(v) Being in the team will mean a lot of work.* involve, entail, necessitate, require, lead to, result in, give rise to.
5 *(adj) Scrooge was too mean to share his money.* miserly, stingy, tightfisted, niggardly, tight, mingy *(informal)*, selfish, grasping, penny-pinching *(informal)*.
OPPOSITE: generous.
6 *(adj) That was a mean thing to do.* nasty, horrible, spiteful, malicious, cruel, unkind, shabby, cheap, sneaky, shameful, despicable, contemptible, lousy *(slang)*, rotten *(informal)*, beastly *(informal)*, low-down *(informal)*.

meaning
1 *(n) Use a dictionary to find the meaning of this word.* definition, sense, explanation.
2 *(n) Did you grasp the meaning of my poem?* sense, gist, drift, message, thrust, implication, significance, import.
3 *(n) What's the meaning of your awful behaviour?* reason for, explanation for, point, purpose, aim, objective, intention.

meaningless
1 *(adj) I can't understand Ziggy's meaningless babble.* unintelligible, incomprehensible, incoherent, senseless.
2 *(adj) I wasted the day in meaningless pursuits. See* **empty 4**.

meant
1 *(adj) You're not meant to walk here.* supposed, allowed, permitted, authorized.
2 *(adj) I don't know what we're meant to do.* supposed, expected, required.
3 *(adj) We seem to be meant for each other.* made, destined, intended, fated, suited to, cut out, designed.

measure
(v) Can you measure the amount of sugar in this cup? determine, find out, quantify, calculate, work out, compute, gauge, estimate, assess, judge, evaluate, weigh, calibrate, mark off, pace off, time.

measurement
1 *(n) Your measurement must be accurate.* calculation, estimation, assessment, reckoning, computation, calibration, timing, survey.
2 **measurements** *(plural n) Work out the measurements of this box.* dimensions *(plural)*, size, length, width, height, depth, area, volume, capacity, mass, weight.

meat
(n) flesh, red meat, white meat.
TYPES OF MEAT: bacon, beef, beefburger, chicken, chop, corned beef, cutlet, duck, escalope, game, gammon, goose, ham, hamburger, joint, kebab, kidney, lamb, liver, meatloaf, mince, mutton, offal, pâté, pheasant, pork, poultry, rissole, roast, salami, sausage, smoked ham, sparerib, steak, tripe, turkey, veal, venison.

mechanical
1 *(adj) Ken's dad drives a mechanical digger.* automatic, automated, motor-driven, power-driven, machine-driven.
OPPOSITE: manual.
2 *(adj) Blinking is a mechanical response. See* **automatic 2**.

meddle *see* **interfere 1**.

medicine
(n) Take your medicine! medication, medicament, drug, remedy, cure.
TYPES OF MEDICINE: antibiotic, antiseptic, capsule, cream, decongestant, drops *(plural)*, herbal remedy, linctus, lotion, lozenge, ointment, over-the-counter drug, painkiller, pill, powder, prescription drug, spray, syrup, tablet, tonic, tranquillizer.

medieval life

some medieval people

baker	dog handler	knight	minstrel	pilgrim
baron	falconer	lady	(musician)	priest
beggar	(falcon handler)	lady-in-waiting	monk	queen
bishop	foot soldier	lord	nun	serf (slave)
blacksmith	friar	man-at-arms	ostler	servant
candlemaker	(travelling priest)	(mounted	(groom)	squire
carpenter	goldsmith	soldier)	page	(trainee
cook	jester	merchant	peasant	knight)
craftsman	king	miller	pedlar	stonemason

jester

medieval clothes and jewellery

chaperon hat
scarf
undertunic
gold necklet
houppeland gown
fur-lined sleeve
hose (tights)
long-toed shoe
embroidered gown
undergown
lord

hennin
veil
pouch
jewelled necklace
hose (tights)
lady

hood
shoulder cape with dagged edge
hood
liripipe
short tunic
peasant
apron
overgown
undergown
servant

medieval pastimes
archery
chess
dancing
embroidery
fairs
  (with acrobats,
  jugglers and
  dancing bears)
falconry
  (hunting
  with falcons)
feasting
hunting
jousting
music
singing
storytelling
tournaments

falconry

chess

fair

medieval castle (cutaway)

- turret
- arrow loop
- lord's bedchamber
- solar (private room for lord's family)
- parapet
- battlements
- spiral staircase
- tower
- keep
- inner bailey
- moat
- drawbridge
- gatehouse
- outer bailey
- barbican (watchtower)
- stables
- garderobe (toilet)
- forge
- great hall
- kitchen
- chapel
- oven
- guard room
- well
- storeroom
- dungeon
- dovecote

medieval weapons

battering ram	lance
battleaxe	longbow
boiling oil	mace
broadsword	mangonel (catapult)
crossbow	morning star (spiked ball on a chain)
dagger	
great sword (two-handed sword)	pike staff
	siege tower
halberd (long-handled axe)	slingshot
	catapult

- crossbow
- mace
- battleaxe
- longbow and arrows
- mangonel
- battering ram

medieval knights

- broadsword
- plume
- gauntlet
- helm (fancy helmet)
- morning star
- chain mail
- tunic
- shield with coat of arms
- caparison

mediocre

mediocre see **average** 2.

medium
(adj) Susie is of medium height. average, moderate, middling, normal, middle.

meek
(adj) A meek tone of voice. timid, humble, mild, submissive, docile, quiet, soft, gentle, unassuming, deferential, resigned.
OPPOSITES: arrogant, assertive.

meet
1 *(v) I didn't expect to meet you here!* bump into *(informal)*, run into, come across, run across, find, see, come upon, encounter, come face to face with.
2 *(v) Is anyone coming to meet you?* fetch, pick you up, greet, welcome.
3 *(v) On Fridays all the pupils meet in the hall.* gather, assemble, congregate, come together, get together, collect, convene.
OPPOSITES: disperse, scatter.
4 *(v) The two paths meet here. See* **join** 3.

meeting
1 *(n) Al's parents arranged a meeting with his teacher.* appointment, get-together *(informal)*, interview, chat, rendezvous.
2 *(n) We all attended the meeting about animal rights.* discussion group, gathering, seminar, rally, conference, convention, forum, assembly, council, congress.
3 *(n) Tim had an unexpected meeting with a bull.* encounter, confrontation, brush.

melancholy
1 *(adj) Melancholy music makes me feel low.* mournful, sombre, sad, depressing, gloomy, dismal, doleful, lugubrious.
OPPOSITES: cheerful, lively.
2 *(adj) I feel melancholy. See* **depressed**.

melt
1 *(v) The ice will melt soon.* thaw, defrost.
OPPOSITE: freeze.
2 *(v) If you heat the butter it will melt.* soften, dissolve, liquefy, run.
OPPOSITES: harden, solidify.

memorize see **learn** 2.

menace
(n) That driver is a menace to other motorists. threat, danger, hazard, risk.

menacing
(adj) Bozo gave me a menacing look. threatening, intimidating, ominous, forbidding, grim, sinister, frightening, dark.

mend
1 *(v) I must mend my bike. See* **repair** 1.
2 *(v) Can you mend my trousers?* sew up, stitch, darn, patch, repair.
3 *(v) Broken bones mend slowly. See* **heal** 2.

mention
1 *(v) Mrs Badger happened to mention that she was leaving.* say, remark, observe, let slip, let on *(informal)*, reveal, divulge, disclose, make known, declare, state.
2 *(v) Don't mention this subject again!* bring up, raise, broach, refer to, speak about, allude to, touch upon, hint at.

merciful
(adj) Burglar Beryl hoped the judge would be merciful. compassionate, lenient, forgiving, pitying, forbearing, sympathetic, humane, tenderhearted, generous, kind.
OPPOSITES: merciless, hardhearted.

merciless see **ruthless**.

mercy
(n) The judge showed no mercy. pity, compassion, leniency, forgiveness, sympathy, understanding, feeling, kindness, charity, clemency.
OPPOSITES: severity, harshness.

merge
1 *(v) The two schools are going to merge.* amalgamate, join together, unite, link up, combine, integrate, join forces, team up.
OPPOSITES: separate, split up.
2 *(v) The trees seemed to merge into the background.* blend, melt, mingle, fuse, mix, become lost in, be swallowed up by.

merry
(adj) A merry smile. happy, cheerful, cheery, chirpy *(informal)*, carefree, bright, jolly, jovial, joyful, gleeful.
OPPOSITES: sad, serious.

mess
1 *(n) Clear up this mess!* clutter, rubbish, jumble, litter, dirt, muck, gunge *(informal)*, gunk *(informal)*, grot *(slang)*.
2 *(n) My room is in a total mess.* muddle, shambles, jumble, state *(informal)*, chaos, confusion, disarray, disorder, turmoil.
3 *(n) You got me into this mess!* predicament, difficulty, quandary, dilemma, muddle, mix-up, fix *(informal)*, jam *(informal)*, pickle *(informal)*, stew *(informal)*, tight spot, hot water *(informal)*.
4 **make a mess of** see **make a mess of**.

mess about
1 *(v) I like to mess about on the beach.* potter about, play about, footle about *(informal)*, muck about *(slang)*, loaf about, lounge about, fiddle about *(informal)*.
2 *(v) Don't mess about with my computer!* interfere, tamper, meddle, tinker, fiddle *(informal)*, play about, muck about *(slang)*.
3 *(v) (informal) Don't mess about in class. See* **fool around**.

message
1 *(n) I sent you a message.* note, memo, communication, letter, fax, e-mail, text message, bulletin, dispatch, communiqué, report, statement, announcement, news.
2 *(n) The message of this story is clear.* meaning, moral, point, theme, thrust, idea.

messenger
(n) A messenger delivered the parcel. courier, carrier, dispatch rider, runner, delivery boy *(old-fashioned)*, go-between.

mess up
1 *(v) I hope I don't mess up this exam. See* **make a mess of**.
2 *(v) Don't mess up my papers. See* **jumble** 1.

3 *(v) Don't mess up the room with your comics.* clutter, litter, strew, make untidy, throw into disorder, dirty.
OPPOSITES: tidy up, clean up.

messy
1 *(adj) Josie's room always looks messy.* untidy, cluttered, chaotic, in a muddle, shambolic *(informal)*, in disarray, littered, dirty, grubby, filthy, mucky.
OPPOSITES: neat, tidy.
2 *(adj) Why do you always look so messy?* untidy, scruffy, unkempt, dishevelled, rumpled, crumpled, slovenly, shambolic *(informal)*, tousled *(hair)*, windswept.
OPPOSITES: neat, tidy.
3 *(adj) Mrs Badger criticized my messy work.* untidy, careless, slapdash, sloppy *(informal)*, slipshod, disorganized.
OPPOSITES: neat, meticulous.

metal
(n) TYPES OF METAL: aluminium, brass, bronze, chrome, copper, gold, iron, lead, mercury, nickel, pewter, platinum, silver, steel, tin, zinc.

method
(n) What method did you use in your experiment? procedure, process, approach, technique, system, practice, scheme, plan.

methodical
(adj) Jo has a methodical approach to her work. orderly, well-organized, systematic, structured, logical, disciplined, businesslike, efficient, careful, painstaking, meticulous.
OPPOSITES: haphazard, chaotic.

middle
1 *(n) We ate our picnic in the middle of the wood.* centre, heart, thick, depths *(plural)*, midst *(old-fashioned)*, core.
2 *(n) Tie this scarf around your middle.* waist, midriff, tummy *(informal)*, waistline.
3 *(adj) The middle window is smaller than the others.* central, inner, inside.
4 *(adj) Find the middle point of the line.* mid, halfway, midway, central, median.

miffed *(informal)* see **annoyed**.

mighty see **strong** 1.

mild
1 *(adj) Mr Badger has a mild manner.* gentle, placid, meek, docile, calm, easy-going, peaceable, serene, amiable, affable.
OPPOSITES: aggressive, violent.
2 *(adj) It was a mild evening.* warm, balmy, pleasant, temperate *(climate)*.
OPPOSITES: cool, cold.
3 *(adj) This soup has a mild flavour.* delicate, subtle, faint, bland, insipid.
OPPOSITE: strong.

mime
(v) Can you mime the title of the film? act out, use gestures to indicate, gesture.

mimic
1 *(v) Dominic can mimic Elvis Presley. See* **imitate** 1.
2 *(n) Tony is an excellent mimic.* impressionist, impersonator, imitator.

mind
1 *(n) Use your mind to work out the answer.* brain, head, intelligence, intellect, brains *(plural) (informal)*, brainpower, powers of reasoning *(plural)*, wits *(plural)*, judgment, grey matter *(informal)*.
2 *(n) Don't let your mind wander.* attention, thoughts *(plural)*, concentration.
3 *(n) I must be losing my mind!* sanity, wits *(plural)*, senses *(plural)*, judgment, reason, marbles *(plural) (informal)*.
4 *(v) I won't mind if you go without me.* object, take offence, be upset, care, worry, be bothered, be resentful, disapprove.
5 *(v) Mind the cars!* watch out for, look out for, be careful of, beware of, be wary of, remember, pay attention to.
6 *(v) Please mind my rat while I'm away.* See **look after**.
7 change your mind *see* **change your mind**.
8 make up your mind *see* **make up your mind**.

mingle
1 *(v) Trina likes to mingle with people of her own age.* See **mix** 3.
2 *(v) Let the paints mingle together on the page.* See **merge** 2.

minor
(adj) Don't worry about such a minor mistake. small, slight, trivial, insignificant, unimportant, negligible, trifling, petty.
OPPOSITE: major.

minute
1 *(n) I'll be with you in a minute.* See **moment** 1.
2 *(adj) A minute speck of dust.* See **tiny** 2.

miracle
(n) It's a miracle how I passed my exams! wonder, mystery, marvel, phenomenon.

miraculous *see* **wonderful** 2.

mischievous
1 *(adj) A mischievous child.* See **naughty** 1.
2 *(adj) A mischievous smile.* impish, playful, teasing, roguish, wicked, arch.

miserable
1 *(adj) Carl is feeling miserable.* depressed, unhappy, low, down, blue, glum, gloomy, down in the dumps *(informal)*, down in the mouth *(informal)*, dejected, despondent, melancholy, tearful, mournful, downcast, forlorn, doleful, wretched, heartbroken, grief-stricken, brokenhearted.
OPPOSITES: cheerful, happy.
2 *(adj) It was a miserable day.* dismal, dreary, depressing, gloomy, grey, dull.
OPPOSITES: fine, bright.
3 *(adj) Conditions in the prison were miserable.* grim, hard, harsh, cheerless, filthy, squalid, sordid, desperate, wretched, inhuman, unbearable, distressing, pitiful, disgraceful, shameful, deplorable.
OPPOSITES: comfortable, pleasant.

miserly *see* **mean** 5.

misery
1 *(n) Gemma couldn't hide her misery when her dog died.* sadness, sorrow, unhappiness, grief, anguish, pain, agony, despair, heartache, distress, suffering, torment, torture, desolation, depression.
OPPOSITES: joy, happiness.
2 *(n) The film showed the misery of the refugees' lives.* hardship, wretchedness, poverty, squalor, deprivation, discomfort, trials *(plural)*, tribulations *(plural)*.
OPPOSITES: ease, comfort.
3 *(n) (informal) Don't be such a misery!* wet blanket *(informal)*, misery guts *(informal)*, moaner, spoilsport *(informal)*, killjoy, grouch *(informal)*, pessimist.

misfortune
(n) I had the misfortune to be ill on my birthday. bad luck, hard luck.
OPPOSITES: good fortune, good luck.

misjudge
1 *(v) It's easy to misjudge how fast traffic is moving.* miscalculate, underestimate, overestimate, make a mistake about, be wrong about, guess wrongly.
2 *(v) People misjudge Ziggy because of how he looks.* get the wrong idea about, jump to the wrong conclusion about, underrate, undervalue, overrate.

mislead *see* **deceive** 1.

misleading
1 *(adj) A misleading signpost.* confusing, ambiguous, muddling, puzzling, deceptive.
OPPOSITE: clear.
2 *(adj) A misleading answer.* deceitful, deceptive, ambiguous, evasive, tricky, dishonest, false, wrong.
OPPOSITES: straightforward, honest.

miss
1 *(v) That shot will miss the dartboard by a mile.* be wide of, fall short of, fail to hit.
OPPOSITE: hit.
2 *(v) Hurry up or you'll miss the train.* be too late for, fail to catch.
OPPOSITE: catch.
3 *(v) You mustn't miss the chance to go skiing.* miss out on, pass up *(informal)*, forgo, let slip, lose, let go, fail to grasp.
OPPOSITES: take, seize.
4 *(v) I hope you won't miss school tomorrow.* be away from, be absent from, play truant from, skip *(informal)*, skive off *(informal)*, bunk off *(slang)*, dodge, avoid.
OPPOSITE: attend.
5 *(v) I know I'll miss my mum when I'm away.* be homesick for, want, need, long to see, long for, pine for, yearn for.

missing *see* **lost** 1, 2.

miss out
1 *(v) Don't miss out any questions in the exam.* leave out, omit, skip, overlook, pass over, fail to notice, forget, ignore.
2 miss out on *(v) If you go now, you'll miss out on all the fun.* miss, be deprived of, lose out on *(informal)*, be left out of, forgo, pass up *(informal)*.

mist
(n) I couldn't see through the mist. fog, haze, spray, steam, vapour, condensation.

mistake
1 *(n) Rani spotted a mistake in her maths homework.* error, inaccuracy, slip, fault, miscalculation, slip-up *(informal)*, boob *(informal)*, blunder, howler *(informal)*, bloomer *(informal)*, oversight, flaw, lapse.
2 *(n) It was a mistake to invite Stan to the party.* error of judgment, faux pas, gaffe, misjudgment, blunder, clanger *(informal)*.
3 mistake for *(v) I often mistake you for your sister.* See **confuse** 2.

misty
1 *(adj) A misty day.* hazy, foggy, murky.
OPPOSITE: clear.
2 *(adj) Misty glass.* steamy, cloudy, opaque, frosted.
OPPOSITE: clear.

mix
1 *(v) Mix the sugar and butter in a bowl.* combine, blend, stir together, mingle.
OPPOSITE: separate.
2 *(v) Mix the two packs of cards.* shuffle, jumble, combine, join, merge, mingle.
OPPOSITE: separate.
3 *(v) Zoë prefers to mix with people of her own age.* socialize, associate, go around, hang out *(informal)*, mingle, hobnob, rub shoulders *(informal)*, circulate, meet.

mixed
1 *(adj) I'd like a bag of mixed sweets.* assorted, different, various, miscellaneous.
2 *(adj) I have mixed feelings about moving house.* confused, ambivalent, uncertain.
3 *(adj) Do you go to to a mixed school?* coeducational, co-ed.
OPPOSITE: single-sex.

mixed-up
(adj) After her parents' divorce, Lucy was really mixed-up. confused, disturbed, screwed up *(informal)*, bewildered, upset, untogether *(slang)*, maladjusted.

mixture
1 *(n) This box contains a mixture of chocolates.* assortment, selection, variety, range, choice, collection.
2 *(n) The house was a mixture of styles.* blend, combination, fusion, amalgamation, mix, jumble, hotchpotch, mishmash, mixed bag, potpourri, hybrid, conglomeration.
3 *(n) We created a horrible mixture.* concoction, brew, potion, compound.
4 *(n) Drink up your cough mixture.* medicine, syrup, linctus.

mix-up
(n) We need to sort out this mix-up. mistake, misunderstanding, confusion, muddle, mess, snarl-up *(informal)*.

moan
1 *(v) Tom began to moan with pain.* groan, whimper, whine, sob, wail, sigh.
2 *(v) Samantha will moan if we're late.* See **complain**.

mob
1 *(n) The police tried to control the angry mob.* crowd, rabble, throng, horde, swarm, pack, mass, gang.
2 *(v) The fans will mob Famous Fred when he appears.* crowd around, swarm around, surround, besiege, jostle, converge on.

mock *see* **make fun of**.

mocking
(adj) Jacinta gave me a mocking smile. sneering, scornful, disdainful, contemptuous, disparaging, sardonic, ironic, sarcastic, taunting, teasing.

model
1 *(n) This dinosaur is only a model.* copy, imitation, replica, dummy, mock-up.
2 *(n) Our car is the latest model.* version, type, design, style, shape, mark.
3 *(adj) Helen collects model aeroplanes.* miniature, toy, scaled down, imitation. OPPOSITES: real, full-size.
4 *(adj) Jason is a model pupil.* perfect, ideal, exemplary, dream.
5 *(v) Can you model a hippo out of clay?* mould, shape, form, make, create, fashion *(old-fashioned)*, sculpt, carve, chisel, cast.
6 *(v) Claudia will model the latest style in beachwear.* wear, display, show off, sport *(informal)*.

moderate
1 *(adj) I have a moderate amount of homework.* fair, average, middling, reasonable, normal, ordinary, unexceptional, modest, limited, adequate. OPPOSITE: excessive.
2 *(adj) My parents have moderate views.* middle-of-the-road, reasonable, restrained, rational, fair, sensible, temperate, mild. OPPOSITE: extreme.

modern
(adj) Do you like modern music? contemporary, current, present-day, recent, new, up-to-date, up-to-the-minute, the latest, fashionable, trendy *(informal)*. OPPOSITES: ancient, old-fashioned.

modernize
(v) The editor wants to modernize the magazine. bring up to date, update, revamp, remodel, give a face-lift to, make over, refresh, renovate *(building)*.

modest
1 *(adj) Akin was modest about his success.* humble, self-effacing, self-deprecating, unassuming, unpretentious, reticent, quiet. OPPOSITES: conceited, boastful.
2 *(adj) Di is too modest to get undressed with the others.* self-conscious, shy, embarrassed, bashful, diffident, demure, coy, reserved, prudish, prim and proper.
3 *(adj) I've saved a modest sum of money.* See **moderate** 1.

moist
1 *(adj) The cave walls felt moist.* damp, dank, dripping, wettish, wet. OPPOSITE: dry.

2 *(adj) The air feels moist.* humid, clammy, muggy, steamy, sticky, damp, dank, misty. OPPOSITES: dry, arid.

moisten *see* **wet** 5.

moisture
1 *(n) I could feel the moisture in the air.* humidity, dampness, dankness, wetness, condensation, steam, vapour.
2 *(n) Drops of moisture ran down Garth's face.* perspiration, sweat, water, liquid.

moment
1 *(n) I'll be with you in a moment.* minute, second, bit, tick *(informal)*, instant, jiffy *(informal)*, two shakes of a lamb's tail *(informal)*, flash, trice, the twinkling of an eye, no time.
2 *(n) At that moment, the clock struck midnight.* minute, second, instant, point, point in time, juncture, stage.

money
1 *(n) Lord Lucre may leave his money to the dogs' home.* cash, wealth, riches *(plural)*, funds *(plural)*, capital, hard cash, gold, silver, dosh *(slang)*, lolly *(slang)*, dough *(slang)*, readies *(plural)* *(informal)*.
2 *(n) Take some foreign money with you.* currency, coins *(plural)*, notes *(plural)*.

monotonous
1 *(adj) Harvey has such a monotonous voice.* boring, dull, flat, droning, toneless, colourless, unvarying, samey *(informal)*. OPPOSITES: animated, lively.
2 *(adj) A monotonous job. See* **boring**.

monster
1 *(n) I dreamt about a big green monster.* creature, beast, dragon, sea monster, giant, ogre, troll, goblin, ghoul, werewolf, zombie, vampire, gremlin, mutant.
2 *(n) Heidi's brother is a little monster.* terror, horror, devil, demon, fiend, brute.
3 *(adj) I had a monster portion of ice cream. See* **enormous**.

monstrous
1 *(adj) I dreamt of a monstrous creature with two heads.* hideous, gruesome, grotesque, repulsive, horrible, frightful, fiendish, hellish, freakish, mutant.
2 *(adj) A monstrous crime. See* **horrible** 1.
3 *(adj) A monstrous amount of chocolate. See* **enormous**.

monument
(n) This monument is dedicated to those who died in battle. memorial, statue, column, pillar, shrine, cenotaph, obelisk, cairn, mausoleum, sepulchre, tombstone.

mood
1 *(n) What sort of mood are you in?* frame of mind, state of mind, humour, temper.
2 *(n) I wish you'd snap out of this mood.* bad mood, bad temper, sulk, huff, grumps *(plural)* *(informal)*, depression, blues *(plural)*, doldrums *(plural)*, melancholy.
3 *(n) How would you describe the mood of the film?* atmosphere, feel, tone, flavour, character, ambience.

moody
1 *(adj) Tricia gets moody if she doesn't have her own way.* cross, grumpy, bad-tempered, irritable, ratty *(informal)*, sulky, in a huff, peevish, touchy, snappy, crotchety *(informal)*, crabby, sullen, miserable, depressed, down in the dumps *(informal)*, down in the mouth *(informal)*, in the doldrums, glum, gloomy. OPPOSITES: cheerful, contented.
2 *(adj) Jason is so moody, you can't tell how he'll react.* unpredictable, erratic, temperamental, volatile, mercurial, impulsive, capricious, unstable. OPPOSITES: steady, predictable.

moor
1 *(n) We hiked across the moor.* heath, moorland, fell.
2 *(v) Moor the dinghy or it will drift away.* tie up, secure, make fast, anchor, berth.

mope
1 *(v) Don't mope; it will all come right in the end.* be miserable, be despondent, be dejected, fret, pine, be down in the mouth *(informal)*, eat your heart out, brood, sulk.
2 **mope about** *(v) Barney tends to mope about on his own.* drift about, mooch about *(slang)*, hang around, knock around, wander about, languish, idle.

moral
(n) What is the moral of this story? lesson, teaching, message, meaning, point.

morbid
1 *(adj) Don't be so morbid!* pessimistic, gloomy, glum, melancholy, morose, obsessed with death, preoccupied with death, fixated with death. OPPOSITE: cheerful.
2 *(adj) Carla has a morbid fascination with graveyards.* unhealthy, unwholesome, grim, ghoulish, macabre, grisly, gruesome, horrible, sick *(informal)*, brooding. OPPOSITE: healthy.

more
(adj) This extension will give us more space. extra, additional, added, further, supplementary, spare, fresh, new. OPPOSITE: less.

morning
(n) dawn, daybreak, break of day, sunrise, morn *(old-fashioned)*, forenoon *(old-fashioned)*.

mostly
1 *(adv) Mostly I shop at the supermarket.* usually, normally, generally, as a rule, mainly, in general, on the whole, typically, most often, for the most part, in the main.
2 *(adv) Miranda's bedroom is mostly blue.* mainly, almost entirely, predominantly, largely, primarily, for the most part, chiefly.

mother
1 *(n) Jemima lives with her mother.* mum *(informal)*, mummy *(informal)*, ma *(informal)*, mamma *(informal)*, old woman *(informal)*, old lady *(informal)*.

2 *(v) Alexander likes to mother his little sister.* look after, care for, protect, comfort, nurse, fuss over, baby, pamper, indulge, spoil.

motionless *see* **still** 1, 2.

motivate
1 *(v) Maybe this news will motivate you to take some action. See* **prompt** 1.
2 *(v) A good teacher should be able to motivate you.* inspire, get you going, spur you on, give you some incentive, stimulate.

motive
(n) There seemed to be no motive for the murder. reason, cause, motivation, rationale, grounds *(plural)*, purpose, stimulus, spur, incentive.

mould
1 *(n) The damp walls were covered in mould.* fungus, mildew.
2 *(n) Pour the jelly into a mould.* cast, form, shape.
3 *(v) Can you mould a hippo out of clay? See* **model** 5.

mouldy
1 *(adj) This plum is mouldy.* bad, rotten, mildewed, spoiled, decaying, putrefying.
OPPOSITE: fresh.
2 *(adj) I hate the smell of mouldy clothes.* mildewed, musty, fusty.

mound
1 *(n) A mound of dirty clothes. See* **pile** 1.
2 *(n) A grassy mound.* bank, hill, hillock, hummock, knoll, embankment, dune.

mountain
1 *(n) The mountain was hidden by clouds.* peak, hill, fell, pinnacle, alp.
2 *(n) Please move this mountain of rubbish. See* **pile** 1.

mountainous
(adj) The picture shows a mountainous landscape. alpine, highland, hilly, rugged, craggy, rocky.
OPPOSITE: flat.

mourn *see* **grieve**.

move
1 *(v) Stay there and don't move!* budge, stir, shift, fidget, change position.
2 *(v) Please move your things into the spare room.* shift, take, carry, bring, transfer, switch, transport.
3 *(v) Try to move steadily through the forest.* advance, proceed, walk, make your way, go, march, journey, pass.
4 *(v) I may have to move to Spain.* move house, relocate, move away, emigrate.
5 *(v) It's time to move!* go, set off, get moving, make tracks, get started, get going, make a move, take action, act.
6 *(v) This film will really move you.* touch, affect, upset, make you cry, reduce you to tears, tug at your heartstrings, get to *(informal)*, disturb, have an effect on, make an impression on, stir, inspire.
7 *(v) I hope this news will move you to take some action. See* **prompt** 1.
8 *(n) One move and I'll shoot!* movement, motion, gesture, change of position.
9 *(n) Taking the train was a good move.* step, thing to do, manoeuvre, tack, plan, stratagem, tactic, ploy, trick.
10 *(n) It's your move now.* go, turn.

movement
(n) I saw some movement in the bushes. activity, motion, action, moving, stirring.

moving
1 *(adj) This model car has moving parts.* movable, mobile, working.
OPPOSITES: fixed, immovable.
2 *(adj) The film was so moving it made me cry.* touching, emotional, poignant, heart-rending, inspiring, stirring, heart-warming, tear-jerking *(informal)*, sentimental.

muck
(n) Clean that muck off your shoes! dirt, filth, mud, grime, slime, sludge, gunge *(informal)*, gunk *(informal)*, manure, dung.

mucky *see* **dirty** 1.

mud
(n) My boots are covered in mud. clay, dirt, soil, silt, muck, sludge, slime, slurry, ooze.

muddle
1 *(v) Please don't muddle my papers. See* **jumble** 1.
2 *(v) Complex instructions muddle me. See* **confuse** 1.
3 *(n) Tabitha's room is in a total muddle. See* **mess** 2.

muddled
1 *(adj) All these instructions make me feel muddled. See* **confused**.
2 *(adj) Your essay is very muddled.* disorganized, confused, jumbled, chaotic, incoherent, woolly, unclear, mixed-up, scrambled, higgledy-piggledy *(informal)*.
OPPOSITES: clear, well-organized.

muddy
1 *(adj) How did your boots get so muddy?* dirty, mucky, filthy, grubby, grimy, caked with mud, mud-spattered.
OPPOSITE: clean.
2 *(adj) We squelched across a muddy field.* marshy, mucky, soggy, waterlogged, swampy, boggy, miry, sodden, slimy.
OPPOSITES: dry, firm.
3 *(adj) The water in our pond is muddy.* cloudy, murky, dirty, opaque.
OPPOSITES: clear, clean.

muffled
(adj) I heard a muffled cry from the cellar. faint, indistinct, dull, smothered, stifled, muted, suppressed, strangled.

mug
1 *(n) Wash up your mug.* cup, beaker, tankard, jug, flagon *(old-fashioned)*.
2 *(v) (informal) Someone tried to mug Dodgy Dave.* attack, rob, set upon, beat up *(informal)*, assault, lay into *(informal)*, rough up *(informal)*, duff up *(slang)*, do over *(slang)*, work over *(slang)*.

---

mountain words

mountains can be...
awe-inspiring
bare
barren
breathtaking
craggy
forbidding
jagged
lofty
looming
majestic
massive
rocky
rugged
shrouded in mist
snowcapped
soaring
spectacular
towering
treacherous

glacier

in the mountains
alpine flowers
alpine meadow
avalanche
boulder
cable car
cave
chair lift
chalet
conifers
crevasse (crack in glacier)
crevice (crack in rock face)
glacier (river of ice)
gorge
ice field
ledge
log cabin
mountain pass
mountain range
peak
precipice
ridge
scree (loose stones)
slope
stream
summit
tunnel
waterfall

in the mountains you may feel...
alone
awestruck
breathless
chilled to the bone
daunted
dazzled
dizzy
dwarfed
exhilarated
insignificant
overawed

mountain activities
abseiling
bobsleighing
climbing
hang-gliding
hiking
mountain biking
mountaineering
paragliding
skiing
snowblading
snowboarding
tobogganing
walking
white-water rafting

snowboarding

muggy

muggy
(adj) This muggy weather makes me sweat. sticky, sultry, humid, steamy, clammy, oppressive, close, stuffy, airless.

mumble
(v) Speak up and don't mumble! mutter, murmur, stutter, stammer, hem and haw.

munch *see* **chew**.

murder
1 *(n) The police are investigating the murder. See* **killing** 1.
2 *(v) A hit man was paid to murder the President. See* **kill** 1.

murderer
(n) killer, assassin, hit man *(slang)*, cutthroat, butcher, slayer, slaughterer.

murky
1 *(adj) It was a murky Autumn day.* dark, dull, foggy, misty, grey, cloudy, overcast, gloomy, dismal, dreary, cheerless.
OPPOSITES: bright, clear.
2 *(adj) I won't swim in such murky water.* cloudy, muddy, dirty, opaque.
OPPOSITE: clear.

murmur
1 *(v) Did you murmur something?* mutter, mumble, whisper, say under your breath.
2 *(n) The hall was filled with the murmur of voices.* hum, buzzing, whispering, muttering, drone, mumble, babble, burble.

muscular *see* **strong** 1.

mushy
1 *(adj) Mushy peas.* pulpy, squashy, squelchy, slushy, squidgy, soft.
2 *(adj) (informal) A mushy love story. See* **sentimental** 2.

music
(n) melody, harmony, rhythm.

musical
(adj) The bells made a musical sound. tuneful, melodious, melodic, harmonious, lilting, sweet-sounding, dulcet.
OPPOSITES: discordant, cacophonous.

musical instrument
(n) TYPES OF MUSICAL INSTRUMENT:
BRASS: bugle, cornet, euphonium, French horn, sousaphone, trombone, trumpet, tuba. KEYBOARD: accordion, harpsichord, organ, piano, synthesizer. PERCUSSION: bass drum, bongos, cabasa, castanets, chime bars, claves, cymbals, finger cymbals, glockenspiel, guiro *(West Indies)*, maracas, rattle, side drum, sleigh bells, steel drum *(West Indies)*, tabla *(India)*, tambourine, tam-tam *(gong)*, timpani *(kettle drums)*, triangle, tubular bells, vibraphone, wood block, xylophone. STRINGS: balalaika *(Russia)*, banjo, cello, double bass, guitar, harp, lute, lyre, mandolin, sitar *(India)*, ukulele, viola, violin, zither. WIND: bagpipes, bassoon, clarinet, cor anglais, didgeridoo *(Australia)*, fife, flute, harmonica *(mouth organ)*, oboe, panpipes *(South America)*, penny whistle, piccolo, recorder, saxophone.

musician
(n) performer, player, instrumentalist, minstrel *(old-fashioned)*, singer.
TYPES OF MUSICIAN: accompanist, bandsman, bassoonist, bugler, busker, cellist, clarinettist, composer, conductor, cornetist, drummer, fiddler, flautist, guitarist, harpist, oboist, organist, percussionist, pianist, piper, soloist, timpanist, trombonist, trumpeter, violinist.
Also see **singer**.

must
1 *(v) I must go now. See* **have to** 1.
2 *(n) Sensible shoes are a must if you want to go hiking.* necessity, essential, requirement, prerequisite.
OPPOSITE: option.

musty
(adj) The cellar smells musty. mouldy, mildewy, fusty, damp, dank, stale, stuffy, airless, frowsty.
OPPOSITES: fresh, airy.

music words

kinds of music
ballad
ballet
calypso
carol
concerto
  (music for an orchestra
  and one or more
  solo instruments)
folk song
hornpipe
hymn
lullaby
madrigal
march
minuet
musical
opera
overture
  (music at
  the start of a
  performance)
polka
round
sea shanty
serenade
spiritual
symphony
  (music in
  several
  sections for
  an orchestra)
theme tune
waltz

panpipes

sitar

mandolin

violin

tuba

music can be...
choral
  (sung by
  a choir)
classical
contemporary
electronic
ethnic
improvised
instrumental
orchestral
traditional
unaccompanied
vocal

music is made up of...
chords
harmony
  (notes
  accompanying
  the melody)
melody (tune)
notes
pauses
rests
rhythm
themes
variations

other music words
accent
bar
beat
key
octave
pitch
scale
tempo
  (speed)

the melody may be...
catchy
cheerful
enchanting
flowing
haunting
intricate
jaunty
lilting
monotonous
mournful
plaintive
repetitive
rousing
simple
solemn
stirring
tuneful

the rhythm may be...
erratic
irregular
jazzy
lively
pounding
precise
pronounced
regular
stately
steady
syncopated
  (with the
  accent not
  on the
  first beat
  of the bar)

music can sound...
atmospheric
cacophonous
depressing
dignified
discordant
dramatic
dreary
eerie
ethereal
evocative
exuberant
graceful
joyful
majestic
melancholy
mysterious
poignant
restful
rhythmic
shrill
spirited
strident
wild

maracas

accordion

steel drums

Also see **musical instrument**, **musician** *and* **pop, rock & jazz**.

mutter
(v) *Did I hear you mutter that you weren't satisfied?* mumble, murmur, say under your breath, grumble, complain, grouse.

mysterious
(adj) *A mysterious crime.* baffling, puzzling, perplexing, mystifying, unexplained, inexplicable, insoluble, cryptic, enigmatic, strange, curious, bizarre, weird, uncanny.

mystery
1 (n) *Can you solve the mystery of the green cat?* enigma, puzzle, riddle, conundrum, problem, secret.
2 (n) *Nadia reads one mystery after another.* detective story, crime story, whodunit (informal), thriller.

Nn

nag
(v) *Don't nag me!* scold, keep on at, go on at (informal), harp on at, find fault with, badger, pester, hassle (informal), henpeck.

naive
(adj) *Emily is so naive, she trusts everybody.* gullible, unsuspecting, trusting, credulous, innocent, green, inexperienced, unworldly, unsophisticated, childlike.
OPPOSITES: experienced, cynical.

naked
(adj) *It's normal to be naked in the bath.* nude, bare, in the nude, undressed, stark naked, starkers (informal), in your birthday suit (informal), in the altogether (informal), without a stitch on.
OPPOSITES: dressed, fully clothed.

name
1 (v) *What shall we name our gang?* call, entitle, label, term, style, tag, dub.
2 (v) *Can you name all the European capitals?* identify, list, cite, reel off, recite.
3 (n) *What is your name?* first name, given name, Christian name, surname, family name, middle name, maiden name, married name, nickname, alias, pseudonym (pen name), handle (informal).

nap see **sleep** 3.

narrow
1 (adj) *What a narrow space!* tight, confined, cramped, restricted, limited.
OPPOSITES: wide, ample.
2 (adj) *This chair has narrow legs.* thin, slim, slender, tapering, fine.
OPPOSITES: wide, broad.

nasty
1 (adj) *What a nasty smell!* disgusting, revolting, horrible, unpleasant, foul, repulsive, nauseating, sickening, vile, loathsome, odious, obnoxious, offensive, repugnant, repellent, yucky (slang).
OPPOSITES: pleasant, nice.

2 (adj) *Don't be nasty!* See **horrible** 3.
3 (adj) *Ria has a nasty illness.* unpleasant, serious, bad, severe, major, critical, painful.
4 (adj) *Should nasty videos be banned?* pornographic, obscene, blue, dirty, smutty, indecent, off colour, violent, offensive.

national
(adj) *Tomorrow will be a national holiday.* public, state, nationwide, countrywide, general, widespread, coast-to-coast.

natter see **talk** 1, 5.

natural
1 (adj) *It's natural to grieve when someone dies.* normal, healthy, understandable, usual, common, typical.
OPPOSITES: abnormal, unnatural.
2 (adj) *Dom has a natural musical ability.* innate, inborn, instinctive, intuitive, intrinsic, inherent, inherited.
3 (adj) *I prefer to eat natural foods.* unprocessed, pure, organic, additive-free, chemical-free, unrefined, uncoloured, unbleached, whole, plain, wholesome.
OPPOSITES: processed, synthetic.
4 (adj) *Jenny has a natural manner.* unaffected, artless, genuine, open, frank, spontaneous, easy, unselfconscious, unsophisticated, unpretentious, unstudied.
OPPOSITES: affected, artificial.

nature
(n) *I enjoy learning about nature.* the environment, the countryside, natural history, wildlife, the living world, the natural world, the earth.

naughty
1 (adj) *A naughty child.* disobedient, badly behaved, mischievous, unruly, defiant, unmanageable, wild, wilful, wayward, undisciplined, cheeky, exasperating.
OPPOSITES: well-behaved, obedient.
2 (adj) *A naughty joke.* See **rude** 2.

near
1 (prep) *I live near the shops.* close to, not far from, next to, adjacent to, handy for, within sniffing distance of (informal).
OPPOSITE: far from.
2 (adj) *Winter is near.* coming, approaching, looming, just around the corner, close at hand, imminent.
OPPOSITES: far off, distant.

nearly
(adv) *I've nearly finished.* almost, just about, practically, virtually, as good as, to all intents and purposes, not quite.

neat
1 (adj) *Ned's room looks neat.* See **tidy** 2.
2 (adj) *The carpenter did a neat job.* careful, precise, meticulous, skilful, deft, expert, competent, accurate, efficient.
OPPOSITES: clumsy, messy.

necessary
(adj) *A hard hat is necessary for riding.* essential, vital, compulsory, obligatory, needed, indispensable, mandatory.
OPPOSITES: unnecessary, optional.

need
1 (v) *This project will need a lot of work.* require, demand, call for, necessitate, entail, want.
2 (v) *Come back - I need you!* want, miss, rely on, depend on, yearn for, pine for.
3 (n) *There's a need for qualified teachers.* demand, call, lack of, shortage of, want of.
4 **needs** (plural n) *Will this money satisfy your needs?* requirements (plural), demands (plural), wants (plural), wishes (plural), desires (plural).
5 **need to** (v) *I need to revise for the test.* See **have to** 1.

neglect
1 (v) *Don't neglect your dog.* fail to look after, fail to care for, abandon, leave alone, forsake.
OPPOSITES: look after, care for.
2 (v) *If you neglect your studies, you'll fail the exam.* let slide, pay no attention to, skimp on, leave undone, shirk, avoid.
OPPOSITES: pay attention to, attend to.

neglected
1 (adj) *A neglected animal.* abandoned, uncared-for, unfed, mistreated, unloved.
2 (adj) *A neglected flowerbed.* untended, overgrown, unweeded, uncared-for, derelict (building), run-down (building).

neighbourhood see **area** 1.

nervous
(adj) *I'm always nervous before a concert.* anxious, apprehensive, worried, scared, frightened, on edge, uneasy, edgy, tense, jittery (informal), uptight (informal), twitchy, jumpy, fidgety, nervy (informal), hyper (informal), agitated, overwrought, flustered, highly strung, excitable.
OPPOSITES: calm, confident.

neutral
(adj) *A referee must remain neutral.* impartial, objective, detached, unbiased, nonpartisan, unprejudiced, dispassionate, uninvolved, sitting on the fence.
OPPOSITE: biased.

never
(adv) *Do you tell lies? No, never!* certainly not, no way, not at all, under no circumstances, on no account, not ever, at no time, not on your life (informal).
OPPOSITES: sometimes, always.

new
1 (adj) *We have some new information.* fresh, recent, up-to-date, current, up-to-the-minute, extra, additional, more.
OPPOSITES: old, outdated.
2 (adj) *Have you tried this new product?* brand-new, state-of-the-art, revolutionary, innovative, ground-breaking, advanced, modern, ultramodern, novel, original.
OPPOSITES: obsolete, out of date.
3 (adj) *Start on a new page.* See **fresh** 4.
4 (adj) *Let's explore a new path.* different, unfamiliar, unknown, untried, unexplored, uncharted, untouched, untrodden, fresh.
OPPOSITE: familiar.

news

1 *(n) The news from the war zone shocked the nation.* report, bulletin, news item, newsflash, story, press release, announcement, communiqué, dispatch, message, account, statement, information, facts *(plural)*, intelligence, info *(informal)*, update, leak, disclosure, revelation.
2 *(n) Have you heard the news about Jason?* latest *(informal)*, rumours *(plural)*, gossip, lowdown *(informal)*, word, talk, stories *(plural)*, tittle-tattle, gen *(informal)*, scandal, dirt *(slang)*.
3 **the news** *(n) I like to keep up with the news.* current affairs *(plural)*, world events *(plural)*.

newspaper

(n) paper, daily, weekly, Sunday paper, national paper, local paper, tabloid, broadsheet, rag *(informal)*.

next

1 *(adj) We planned our work for the next four weeks.* following, succeeding, ensuing, subsequent, coming.
OPPOSITES: previous, past.
2 *(adj) Can you hear voices in the next room?* adjacent, adjoining, neighbouring, nearest, closest.
3 *(adv) Next add the sugar.* then, after that, afterwards, later, subsequently.

nibble

1 *(v) The mouse began to nibble the cheese.* bite, gnaw, peck at, chew on, munch, pick at, eat, taste.
2 *(n) I've only had a nibble of my sandwich.* See **bite 3**.

night

(n) dark, darkness, night-time, small hours *(plural)*, hours of darkness *(plural)*.

night...	the night is...	the moon is...	in the sky you see...	night-time creatures
closes in	moonless	bright	clouds	badger
descends	moonlit	ghostly	constellations	bat
falls	pitch-black	gleaming	crescent	firefly
settles	shadowy	hazy	moon	frog
	silent	hidden	full moon	glow-worm
darkness...	starless	luminous	Milky Way	hedgehog
blots out	starlit	pale	planets	mosquito
cloaks	still	remote	shooting stars	moth
conceals		shining		nightingale
engulfs	**the sky is...**	silvery	**night-time sights**	owl
envelops	clear	veiled	Catseyes	
hides	cloudy		(reflectors	**night-time sounds**
masks	illuminated	**the stars...**	on roads)	bats squeaking
obscures	inky	flicker	city lights	cats yowling
swallows up	jet-black	glimmer	floodlit	clocks chiming
veils	lit up	glitter	buildings	frogs croaking
	starry	shimmer	headlights	mosquitoes
	star-studded	sparkle	illuminations	whining
	vast	twinkle	neon signs	owls hooting
	velvety	wink	streetlights	sirens wailing

nice

a nice person	a nice meal	a nice view	I had a nice time.	You look nice.
agreeable	appetizing	beautiful	agreeable	attractive
amiable	delectable	breathtaking	amusing	beautiful
caring	delicious	glorious	brilliant	divine
charming	lovely	gorgeous	enjoyable	*(informal)*
considerate	luscious	impressive	entertaining	gorgeous
delightful	mouthwatering	lovely	excellent	handsome
friendly	scrumptious	magnificent	fabulous	lovely
generous	*(informal)*	picturesque	*(informal)*	pretty
gentle	tasty	spectacular	fantastic	ravishing
good-natured	yummy *(slang)*	splendid	*(informal)*	stunning
helpful		superb	fun	*(informal)*
kind	**nice weather**	wonderful	good	wonderful
likable	beautiful		great	
lovely	bright	**a nice piece of work**	*(informal)*	**Nice people don't swear.**
obliging	dry	accurate	interesting	courteous
pleasant	fair	careful	lovely	genteel
sweet	fine	methodical	marvellous	gentlemanly
sympathetic	glorious	meticulous	pleasant	ladylike
thoughtful	gorgeous	neat	super	polite
understanding	lovely	painstaking	*(informal)*	refined
unselfish	mild	pleasing	terrific	respectable
warm-hearted	pleasant	well-presented	*(informal)*	well-bred
	sunny	well-written	wonderful	
	warm			

nightmare

1 *(n) You've had a nightmare.* bad dream.
2 *(n) The test was a nightmare.* ordeal, torment, torture, agony, horror, trial.

nimble

(adj) You must be nimble to be a good footballer. light on your feet, agile, lithe, nippy *(informal)*, speedy, quick, swift, supple, acrobatic, deft, skilful, proficient.

noble

(adj) Many noble lords attended the banquet. aristocratic, titled, highborn, blue-blooded, distinguished.

nod

(v) Nod your head if you agree. incline, bow, bob, dip, duck, shake up and down.

noise

1 *(n) I heard a faint noise.* sound.
2 *(n) The noise in the classroom was unbelievable.* din, racket, row, clamour, uproar, hullabaloo, tumult, rumpus, hubbub, commotion, pandemonium.

noisy

1 *(adj) A noisy aeroplane.* See **loud 1**.
2 *(adj) A noisy gang of kids.* boisterous, riotous, rowdy, uproarious, raucous, clamorous, rackety, talkative, vociferous.
OPPOSITES: quiet, subdued.

nonsense
1 *(n) Don't talk nonsense.* rubbish, drivel, garbage, rot, guff *(informal)*, baloney *(informal)*, twaddle, balderdash, piffle, claptrap *(informal)*, codswallop *(slang)*, poppycock *(informal)*, gibberish, double Dutch *(informal)*, gobbledegook *(informal)*.
OPPOSITE: sense.
2 *(n) Mum won't stand for any nonsense.* silliness, foolishness, stupidity, tomfoolery, monkey business *(informal)*, misbehaviour, mischief, antics *(plural)*, high jinks *(plural)*.

normal
1 *(adj) It's normal for babies to cry.* common, usual, commonplace, natural, typical, standard, accepted, expected.
OPPOSITES: unusual, unnatural.
2 *(adj) Our normal routine was disrupted.* See **usual**.
3 *(adj) A normal person wouldn't behave like that.* sane, well-adjusted, rational, well-balanced, reasonable.
OPPOSITES: abnormal, insane.

nosy
(adj) (informal) Nosy neighbours. inquisitive, prying, snooping *(informal)*, eavesdropping, curious, overcurious, interfering, meddlesome, intrusive.

note
1 *(n) I must send Henry a note.* message, letter, reminder, memo, memorandum, line *(informal)*, communication.
2 *(v) Note down this date.* See **write** 1.

nothing
1 *(pronoun) There's nothing in the box.* not a thing, nothing at all, zilch *(slang)*, not a sausage *(informal)*.
2 *(pronoun) We scored nothing.* nought, zero, nil, love *(tennis)*, a duck *(cricket)*.

notice
1 *(v) Did you notice Burglar Beryl's new brooch?* see, spot, observe, catch sight of, note, take in, take note of, spy, detect, discern, perceive, get a load of *(informal)*.
2 *(n) Have you seen the notice about the sale?* announcement, poster, sign, advertisement, circular, leaflet, pamphlet, brochure, bulletin, communication.

noticeable
(adj) There has been a noticeable change in Toni's behaviour. distinct, perceptible, discernible, unmistakable, obvious, clear, marked, visible, pronounced, striking, conspicuous, definite, significant, evident.
OPPOSITE: imperceptible.

now
1 *(adv) I must go now.* See **immediately**.
2 *(adv) Most families now have a TV.* nowadays, these days, today, in this day and age, at the moment, at present.

nude *see* **naked**.

nudge
(v) Don't nudge me when I'm writing. poke, prod, jog, jolt, bump, knock, jab, push, shove, touch, elbow.

nuisance
1 *(n) It's a nuisance when you miss the bus.* inconvenience, problem, pain *(informal)*, pain in the neck *(informal)*, hassle *(informal)*, drag *(informal)*, headache *(informal)*, bore, disadvantage.
2 *(n) Jemima is such a nuisance.* pest, pain *(informal)*, pain in the neck *(informal)*, problem, bother, plague, bore.

numb
(adj) My fingers feel numb. dead, paralysed, frozen, chilled, anaesthetized, without feeling, asleep, desensitized.

number
1 *(n) Think of a number between one and ten.* figure, digit, numeral, integer, unit.
2 *(n) Count the number of sweets in the bag.* amount, quantity, total, sum, tally.
3 *(n) A large number of people gathered in the hall.* group, crowd, throng, horde, mass, collection, company, multitude.

obedient
(adj) An obedient child. well-behaved, dutiful, respectful, biddable, submissive, compliant, manageable, amenable, docile, meek, well-trained *(animal)*.
OPPOSITES: disobedient, rebellious.

obey
1 *(v) You must obey the school rules.* observe, follow, keep to, stick to, abide by, comply with, adhere to, respect, submit to, conform to, be ruled by, heed.
OPPOSITES: disobey, defy.
2 *(v) You'll get into trouble if you don't obey.* do as you are told, follow orders, toe the line, knuckle under *(informal)*.
OPPOSITES: rebel, revolt.

object
1 *(n) What's that red object?* See **thing** 1.
2 *(v) My parents object when I play loud music.* See **disapprove** 1.

obscene
(adj) An obscene film. indecent, pornographic, blue, immoral, corrupting, offensive, shocking, sickening, vile, lewd, vulgar, smutty, suggestive, raunchy *(slang)*, dirty, filthy, kinky *(slang)*, sick *(informal)*.
OPPOSITE: decent.

observant
(adj) Spies need to be observant. watchful, alert, eagle-eyed, sharp-eyed, perceptive, attentive, vigilant, wide-awake, aware.
OPPOSITES: unobservant, oblivious.

observe
1 *(v) The police will observe Beryl's actions.* watch, keep an eye on, monitor, keep under observation, keep tabs on *(informal)*, keep under surveillance, spy on.

2 *(v) Did you observe that the clock was five minutes fast?* See **notice** 1.

obsessed
(adj) Leo is obsessed by the fear of failing. consumed, gripped, possessed, haunted, tormented, plagued, preoccupied with.

obstacle
(n) Mum's disapproval could be a major obstacle. difficulty, problem, stumbling block, hurdle, impediment, drawback, disadvantage, snag, deterrent, barrier.

obstinate *see* **stubborn**.

obstruct *see* **block** 2, 3.

obtain *see* **get** 1, 4.

obvious
(adj) Ziggy's boredom is obvious. plain, clear, evident, self-evident, easy to see, crystal clear, visible, apparent, noticeable, conspicuous, striking, unmistakable, undisguised, unconcealed, undeniable, transparent, blatant, glaring, flagrant.
OPPOSITES: imperceptible, hidden.

occasion *see* **event** 1, 2.

occasional
(adj) I heard an occasional rumble of thunder. intermittent, periodic, infrequent, sporadic, irregular, odd, rare.
OPPOSITES: frequent, continuous.

occupation *see* **job** 2.

occupy
1 *(v) This puzzle will occupy you for hours.* See **amuse** 2.
2 *(v) Does sport occupy a lot of your time?* take up, fill, use up, eat up, consume.
3 *(v) The Smiths occupy a small house.* live in, inhabit, dwell in, reside in, rent, own.

occur
1 *(v) When did this occur?* See **happen** 1.
2 occur to *(v) When did the idea occur to you?* come to, dawn on, enter your head, cross your mind, spring to mind, strike.

ocean *see* **sea** 1.

odd
1 *(adj) Odd behaviour.* See **strange** 1.
2 *(adj) An odd noise.* See **strange** 2.
3 *(adj) Why is there always one odd sock in the wash?* spare, unmatched, leftover, remaining, single, solitary, lone.

off
1 *(adj) Mrs Badger says the trip is off.* cancelled, called off, postponed, shelved.
2 *(adj) Tom is off today.* See **away** 1.
3 *(adj) This yoghurt is off.* bad, mouldy, sour, rancid, turned, curdled, rotten.
4 *(adj) (informal) That comment was really off.* out of order, uncalled-for, unjustified, unwarranted, unacceptable, in bad taste, objectionable, non-pc *(informal)*.

offend
(v) I didn't mean to offend you. upset, hurt your feelings, put your back up, give offence, insult, slight, snub, tread on your toes *(informal)*, put your nose out of joint *(informal)*, annoy, anger, provoke, rile.

offended

(adj) Dad looked offended when I criticized his cooking. hurt, upset, wounded, put out, piqued, affronted, miffed (informal), insulted, resentful, disgruntled, in a huff, annoyed, incensed, outraged.

offensive

1 (adj) An offensive smell. See **nasty** 1.
2 (adj) Offensive remarks. See **rude** 1, 2.

offer

1 (v) Most schools offer a good education. provide, supply, give, give the opportunity of, place at your disposal, make available.
2 (v) Did Jo offer to help? See **volunteer**.
3 (v) Did you offer Grandma some cake? give, hand, proffer, pass, present with.

official

1 (adj) Is that an official certificate? authorized, approved, recognized, valid, bona fide, authentic, legitimate, legal.
2 (adj) The mayor attends many official functions. formal, ceremonial, solemn.

often

(adv) Fifi is often late. frequently, regularly, usually, generally, repeatedly, constantly, habitually, again and again, time after time, over and over again, time and again.
OPPOSITES: rarely, seldom.

O.K. (informal) see **all right** 1, 2, 3.

old

1 (adj) I'll look after you when you're old. older, elderly, getting on, advanced in years, grey-haired, aged, past your prime, over the hill (informal), past it (informal), doddery (informal), decrepit.
OPPOSITE: young.
2 (adj) Our school buildings are old. ancient, historic, antiquated, dilapidated, crumbling, decaying, run-down.
OPPOSITES: new, modern.
3 (adj) Do you have to wear those old clothes? ancient, worn-out, shabby, scruffy, moth-eaten, ragged, tattered, cast-off, second-hand.
OPPOSITE: new.
4 (adj) Flash Frank collects old cars. vintage, veteran, antique.
OPPOSITES: new, modern.
5 (adj) Life was harder in the old days. bygone, former, olden (old-fashioned), early, past, forgotten, of old, of yore.
OPPOSITES: recent, modern.
6 (adj) Kissing under the mistletoe is an old custom. ancient, age-old, long-established, long-standing, time-honoured, traditional, enduring, antiquated.
OPPOSITES: modern, recent.

old-fashioned

(adj) Aunt Bertha's ideas are really old-fashioned. out of date, behind the times, dated, outdated, outmoded, out of fashion, unfashionable, backward-looking, reactionary, old-fogyish, square (informal), ancient, archaic, antiquated, quaint, medieval, out of the ark (informal).
OPPOSITES: up-to-date, modern.

ominous

(adj) An ominous silence. forbidding, menacing, threatening, grim, sinister, dark, unpromising, inauspicious, baleful, fateful.
OPPOSITES: encouraging, promising.

omit

(v) We'll sing the song, but omit verse three. leave out, miss out, skip, pass over, exclude, drop, forget about, cut.

on purpose

(phrase) You did that on purpose! deliberately, intentionally, purposely, wilfully, knowingly, consciously, wittingly.
OPPOSITES: accidentally, by accident.

ooze

(v) Fat began to ooze from the sausage. seep, dribble, trickle, drip, escape, leak.

open

1 (v) Could you open this for me? undo, unfasten, untie, unwrap, unlock, unbolt, unbar, unseal, uncork, unroll, unfold.
OPPOSITES: close, shut.
2 (v) Will you open the discussion? See **start** 4.
3 (adj) The door was left open. ajar, wide-open, unlocked, unfastened, unbolted, unbarred, unlatched, gaping, yawning.
OPPOSITES: closed, locked.
4 (adj) When are the tennis courts open? available, free, accessible, usable, public.
OPPOSITES: unavailable.
5 (adj) We reached some open country. wide-open, empty, clear, undeveloped, unbuilt-up, uncrowded, spacious, unenclosed, unfenced, exposed, wild.
OPPOSITES: enclosed, built-up.
6 (adj) Please be open with me. See **honest** 1.

opinion see **view** 2.

opportunity

1 (n) Take every opportunity that you're offered. chance, opening, break (informal).
2 (n) Is this a good opportunity to talk? moment, time, occasion.

oppose

(v) No one dares to oppose Aunt Bertha. defy, challenge, resist, stand up to, take a stand against, cross, contradict, disagree with, take issue with, confront, quarrel with, argue with, gainsay, thwart.

opposite

1 (adj) I sat opposite Sandy. facing, face-to-face with, across from.
2 (adj) We have opposite views. opposing, conflicting, contradictory, incompatible, differing, different, diametrically opposed.
OPPOSITES: identical, similar.

optimistic

(adj) Ryan is optimistic about the future. positive, confident, hopeful, cheerful, sanguine, buoyant, upbeat (informal).
OPPOSITES: pessimistic, cynical.

orange

(n) SHADES OF ORANGE: amber, apricot, ginger, ochre, peach, tangerine.

ordeal

(n) I never want to go through this ordeal again. torture, torment, agony, nightmare, distress, anguish, suffering, hardship, trial, tribulation, struggle, difficulty, trouble.

order

1 (v) Didn't I order you to go home? tell, command, instruct, direct, bid, charge.
2 (v) Did you order tickets for the concert? apply for, send away for, book, reserve, request, ring for, place an order for.
3 (n) The general gave the order to advance. command, instruction, direction.
4 (n) Can you see any order in this group of numbers? pattern, structure, sequence, progression, system, plan, organization, regularity, grouping, arrangement.
OPPOSITES: chaos, muddle.
5 (n) Mrs Badger quickly restored order. discipline, control, peace and quiet, calm, tranquillity, harmony, neatness, tidiness, obedience, law and order.
OPPOSITES: disorder, pandemonium.
6 (n) Try to keep your bicycle in good order. condition, shape, nick (informal).

ordinary

1 (adj) Guitar practice is part of my ordinary routine. See **usual**.
2 (adj) I live in an ordinary terraced house. typical, standard, conventional, run-of-the-mill, common or garden (informal), commonplace, simple, modest, humble.
OPPOSITES: unusual, extraordinary.
3 (adj) This is a rather ordinary piece of work. average, mediocre, indifferent, nondescript, unexceptional, unremarkable, unimpressive, unimaginative, uninspired, dull, run-of-the-mill, banal, pedestrian.
OPPOSITES: exceptional, outstanding.

organize

1 (v) Let's organize a trip. See **arrange** 3.
2 (v) Mrs Badger asked me to organize the cake stall. take charge of, be responsible for, set up, run, manage, coordinate, look after, see to, take care of.
3 (v) Try to organize your essay more clearly. structure, plan, construct, put together, shape.
4 (v) I must organize my CDs. See **sort** 3.

original

1 (adj) Who were the original inhabitants of Australia? first, earliest, initial, native, indigenous, aboriginal, primitive, primeval.
2 (adj) Your essay contains lots of original ideas. new, fresh, unique, individual, innovative, novel, ground-breaking, imaginative, ingenious, inspired, inventive, creative, unusual, unconventional.
OPPOSITES: old, familiar.
3 (adj) Is this an original painting? genuine, authentic, real, unique.
OPPOSITES: copied, fake.

ornament

(n) Hang the ornament on the tree. trinket, knick-knack, bauble, decoration, trimming.

outgoing see **extrovert**.

outing see **trip** 1.

outline
1 *(n) Show me an outline of your design.* rough draft, sketch, drawing, tracing, plan, diagram, layout.
2 *(n) Give me an outline of the story.* rough idea, quick rundown, summary, shortened version, résumé, synopsis, main points *(plural)*, bare bones *(plural)*.
3 *(n) I saw the outline of a man through the mist.* shape, silhouette, figure, profile.

outrageous
1 *(adj) Conditions in the prison were outrageous.* shocking, scandalous, atrocious, barbaric, monstrous, disgraceful, intolerable, unbearable, abominable, vile.
2 *(adj) Dodgy Dave sells his cars at outrageous prices.* exorbitant, excessive, preposterous, scandalous, unreasonable, over the top, extravagant, OTT *(slang)*.
OPPOSITES: reasonable, fair.

outside
1 *(n) We need to paint the outside of our house.* exterior, façade, front, surface.
OPPOSITE: inside.
2 *(adv) Let's play outside.* outdoors, out-of-doors, in the open air, in the fresh air.
OPPOSITE: inside.
3 *(adj) The outside walls look damp.* external, exterior, outer, outermost.
OPPOSITE: inside.

outspoken see **blunt** 2.

outstanding
(adj) An outstanding writer. exceptional, great, first-class, superlative, excellent, remarkable, impressive, distinguished, notable, important, celebrated, eminent.
OPPOSITES: unremarkable, insignificant.

over
1 *(adj) I'm glad that unpleasant affair is over.* over and done with, at an end, finished, ended, past, closed, concluded, settled, ancient history *(informal)*.
2 *(prep) We've invited over 20 people.* more than, in excess of, above.

overcome see **conquer** 1, 2.

overhear
(v) Did you overhear our conversation? listen in on, eavesdrop on, pick up, catch.

overpowering
1 *(adj) I felt an overpowering urge to laugh.* See **irresistible**.
2 *(adj) The smell of Wayne's aftershave is overpowering.* suffocating, sickening, nauseating, stifling, unbearable.

overtake
(v) Let's try to overtake that car. pass, get past, get by, go past, outdistance, outstrip, outdo, go faster than, leave behind.

overweight
(adj) Dad is getting overweight. heavy, chubby, tubby, plump, podgy, stout, portly, paunchy, fleshy, hefty, corpulent, fat, obese, huge, massive, outsize, gross.
OPPOSITE: underweight.

own
1 *(v) I hope to own a pony one day.* have, be the owner of, possess, keep, be in possession of, be responsible for.
2 *(adj) Everyone needs their own space.* personal, individual, private, particular.

own up see **confess** 1, 2.

pace
1 *(n) Take one pace forwards.* See **step** 2.
2 *(v) Don't pace about; it makes me nervous.* march, walk, stride, tramp, pad.

pack
(v) Can you pack all your books in this box? put, place, load, stow, fit, stuff, cram, bundle, squeeze, jam, wedge, ram.

paddle
(v) Let's paddle in the sea. wade, splash about, slosh about, dabble.

page
(n) Take a new page for each question. side, sheet, piece of paper, leaf, folio.

pain
1 *(n) You may feel a little pain.* soreness, discomfort, tenderness, irritation, twinge, pang, spasm, throbbing, ache, cramp.
2 *(n) This behaviour will cause your parents great pain.* See **distress** 1.

painful
1 *(adj) Is your arm painful?* See **sore**.
2 *(adj) Splitting up with your boyfriend can be painful.* upsetting, distressing, unpleasant, hard, tough, heartbreaking, traumatic, agonizing, harrowing.

paint
1 *(n) This paint will hide the dirt.* colour, pigment, dye, tint, stain, emulsion, gloss, whitewash, undercoat, primer.
2 *(v) Can you paint the sunset?* depict, portray, represent.
3 *(v) Dad plans to paint the house himself.* decorate, redecorate, do up *(informal)*.

painting
(n) TYPES OF PAINTING: abstract painting, altarpiece, fresco, landscape, miniature, mural, oil painting, portrait, seascape, self-portrait, still life, watercolour.

pair
(n) Sam and Seb are a good pair. couple, match, combination, partnership, double act, twosome, duo, team.

palace
(n) chateau, stately home, mansion, castle, official residence. ❖ *Also see* **building**.

pale
1 *(adj) Megan has a pale complexion.* fair, light, creamy, ivory, pallid, waxen, pasty.
OPPOSITES: rosy, ruddy.

2 *(adj) You look pale.* peaky *(informal)*, washed out *(informal)*, drained, white, ashen, anaemic, sickly, grey, green, like death warmed up *(informal)*.
OPPOSITES: flushed, blooming.
3 *(adj) Claire's room is decorated in pale shades of blue.* light, soft, subtle, pastel, muted, subdued, faint, faded, bleached.
OPPOSITES: dark, bright, strong.

pamper see **spoil** 3.

panic
1 *(n) The sight of the fire filled us with panic.* alarm, horror, fear, terror, dread, consternation, hysteria, confusion, dismay.
2 *(v) Don't panic!* be alarmed, be scared, become hysterical, overreact, go to pieces, lose your head, lose your nerve, freak out, get into a tizzy *(informal)*, lose your cool *(slang)*, throw a wobbly *(slang)*.

pant
(v) Exercise makes me pant. gasp, wheeze, breathe heavily, puff, huff and puff.

paper
1 *(n) I need some more paper.* writing paper, notepaper, stationery, file paper, rough paper, scrap paper, cartridge paper, graph paper, tracing paper.
2 *(n) Which paper do your parents read?* See **newspaper**.
3 **papers** *(plural n) These papers prove that Dodgy Dave is guilty.* documents *(plural)*, records *(plural)*, files *(plural)*, certificates *(plural)*, forms *(plural)*, deeds *(plural)*, diaries *(plural)*, archives *(plural)*.

parade
(n) Crowds lined the street to watch the parade. procession, cavalcade, march past *(troops)*, motorcade, cortege *(funeral procession)*, display, spectacle, pageant.

paradise see **heaven** 1, 2.

parcel
(n) Is this parcel for me? package, packet, box, carton, pack, bundle.

pardon see **forgive**.

park
(n) Let's walk around the park. public park, recreation ground, gardens *(plural)*, botanical gardens *(plural)*, green, common, woodland, parkland, grounds *(plural)*.

part
1 *(n) Have a part of my orange.* See **bit** 2.
2 *(n) Which part of the course do you prefer?* bit, section, element, unit, module, component, constituent.
3 *(n) Which part of the company interests you?* bit, area, branch, division, section, department, sector, segment.
4 *(n) Which part of the country are you from?* bit, area, region, district, neck of the woods *(informal)*, neighbourhood.
5 *(n) I'd love to play a part in the pantomime.* role, character, starring role, lead, supporting role, speaking part, bit part, walk-on part, extra, cameo role.
6 **take part** see **take part**.

participate

participate see **take part**.

particular
1 *(adj) This sauce has a particular flavour.* distinct, unique, special, unmistakable, specific, definite, individual, certain.
OPPOSITES: vague, general.
2 *(adj) Aunt Bertha is particular about her food. See* **fussy**.

partner
1 *(n) Bring your partner to the dance.* boyfriend, girlfriend, wife, husband, spouse, other half *(informal)*, mate.
2 *(n) Dad had a business lunch with his partner.* associate, colleague, collaborator, ally, sidekick *(informal)*, accomplice.

party
1 *(n) Let's have a party!* celebration, gathering, get-together *(informal)*, bash *(informal)*, thrash *(informal)*, do *(informal)*, rave-up *(slang)*, shindig *(informal)*, knees-up *(informal)*, function, reception.
2 *(n) Which party do you belong to?* group, faction, alliance, association, camp, side, team, gang, crew *(informal)*, band.

pass
1 *(v) The guard let us pass.* go by, go past, pass by, move past, move on, proceed, go on, go ahead, go through, enter.
2 *(v) The time seemed to pass so quickly.* go, go by, go past, pass by, elapse, slip by, tick away, fly by, glide by, flow by, roll by.
3 *(v) Can we pass that car? See* **overtake**.
4 *(v) Your anger will pass.* blow over, run its course, come to an end, die away, fade away, disappear, evaporate, peter out.
5 *(v) How do you pass the time?* occupy, fill, spend, while away, fritter away, kill.
6 *(v) Pass me your plate. See* **hand** 4.
7 *(v) This exam is so hard; I hope I'll pass.* succeed, get through, come up to scratch *(informal)*, pass muster, qualify, graduate.
OPPOSITE: fail.

passage
1 *(n) The thieves escaped down a narrow passage.* passageway, alley, alleyway, lane, path, track, corridor, tunnel.
2 *(n) Listen to this passage from "Oliver Twist".* excerpt, extract, quotation, piece, section, episode, scene, paragraph, verse.

passion
1 *(n) The actor played his part with passion.* feeling, emotion, intensity, fervour, zeal, warmth, fire, zest, gusto, enthusiasm, energy, animation.
2 *(n) Jason is consumed with passion for Jodie.* love, adoration, desire, lust, longing, yearning, hunger, the hots *(plural) (slang)*.

passionate
1 *(adj) A passionate argument.* heated, emotional, impassioned, intense, fierce, vehement, furious, violent, fiery, stormy.
OPPOSITES: cool, dispassionate.
2 *(adj) A passionate embrace.* loving, ardent, amorous, steamy *(informal)*, sensual, lustful, urgent, burning, frenzied.
OPPOSITE: cool.

past
1 *(adj) Those times are past. See* **over** 1.
2 *(adj) You can learn a lot from past events.* former, bygone, earlier, previous, prior, recent, historical, ancient.
OPPOSITE: future.
3 **the past** *(n) I like learning about the past.* history, past times, former times, days gone by, the olden days, the good old days, yesteryear *(old-fashioned)*, recent history, ancient history, prehistory.
OPPOSITE: the future.

pastel see **pale** 3.

pastime see **hobby**.

pat
1 *(v) Come and pat Fido.* stroke, pet.
2 *(v) Pat Joe on the back; he's coughing!* slap, thump, hit, smack, bang, clap, tap.

patch
1 *(v) I must patch my jeans.* mend, sew up, stitch up, reinforce, darn, repair, fix.
2 *(n) We grow turnips on this patch.* plot, piece of land, spot, bed, lot, allotment, ground, area, stretch, tract, clearing.

path
(n) footpath, pathway, pavement, towpath, bridle path, track, trail, lane.

pathetic
1 *(adj) Fido gave a pathetic whimper.* pitiful, plaintive, forlorn, doleful, mournful, woeful, touching, moving, poignant, heart-rending, heartbreaking, distressing.
2 *(adj) Dad made a pathetic attempt to be trendy.* feeble, unsuccessful, unconvincing, pitiful, dismal, woeful, sorry, sad *(slang)*.
3 *(adj) (informal) I'm pathetic at maths. See* **hopeless** 4.

patient
1 *(adj) Mrs Badger is always patient with us.* tolerant, long-suffering, forbearing, understanding, sympathetic, calm, even-tempered, accommodating, indulgent.
OPPOSITES: impatient, short-tempered.
2 *(adj) Try to be patient; you'll get there in the end.* persistent, persevering, steady, unhurried, resolute, determined, dogged, resigned, philosophical, stoical.
OPPOSITES: impatient, restless.

patronizing see **condescending**.

pattern
1 *(n) Use this as a pattern for your sketch.* guide, model, example, master, blueprint, template, stencil, standard.
2 *(n) A floral pattern. See* **design** 2.

pause
1 *(v) Don't pause at the end of every sentence.* stop, break off, hesitate, wait, delay, rest, take a break, have a rest, halt.
2 *(n) There will be a pause between each act. See* **gap** 2.

pay
1 *(v) Who will pay for the party?* foot the bill, pay up, settle the bill, meet the cost, shell out *(informal)*, cough up *(informal)*, stump up *(informal)*, fork out *(slang)*.

2 *(v) I didn't pay much. See* **spend** 1.
3 *(v) Mum said she'd pay me if I washed the car.* reward, reimburse, compensate.
4 *(v) You'll pay for this!* suffer, be punished, answer, pay the price, make amends, get your comeuppance *(informal)*.
5 *(n) At your interview, ask about the pay.* salary, wages *(plural)*, earnings *(plural)*, fee, payment, remuneration.

pay attention
(v) Pay attention or you won't know what to do. listen, watch, concentrate, take notice, listen up *(slang)*.

pay back
1 *(v) You must pay back the money.* repay, return, refund, reimburse.
2 *(v) I'll pay you back for taking my pen!* repay, get revenge on, get even with *(informal)*, get *(informal)*, settle the score with, retaliate against, hit back at.

peace
1 *(n) I wish there could be peace all over the world.* harmony, goodwill, agreement, accord, friendship, reconciliation.
2 *(n) The two armies agreed to a permanent peace.* truce, ceasefire, armistice, cessation of hostilities, reconciliation, alliance, treaty, pact.
3 *(n) I love the peace of the countryside.* peace and quiet, tranquillity, peacefulness, calm, stillness, quietness, silence, hush.

peaceful
1 *(adj) It's so peaceful here.* tranquil, restful, quiet, still, calm, relaxing, soothing.
OPPOSITES: noisy, bustling.
2 *(adj) Alice looks so peaceful.* tranquil, serene, at peace, relaxed, untroubled, unruffled, unworried, calm, placid.

peak
1 *(n) A snowy mountain peak. See* **top** 1.
2 *(n) Famous Fred is at the peak of his career.* height, high point, climax, zenith.

peculiar
1 *(adj) Peculiar behaviour. See* **strange** 1.
2 *(adj) A peculiar noise. See* **strange** 2.
3 *(adj) I feel peculiar. See* **ill** 2.

peep
(v) Did you peep at your presents? peek, steal a look, sneak a look, take a sly look.

peer
(v) I saw you peer through the window. spy, peek, peep, squint, snoop, try to see, look closely, screw up your eyes.

people
1 *(plural n) What makes people different from animals?* humans *(plural)*, human beings *(plural)*, the human race, mankind.
2 *(plural n) How many people were hurt?* men and women *(plural)*, children *(plural)*, individuals *(plural)*, persons *(plural)*.
3 *(plural n) The king addressed the people.* nation, citizens *(plural)*, populace, general public, community, population, crowd, masses *(plural)*, multitude, mob, rabble, rank and file, hoi polloi.

perceptive
(adj) Perceptive comments. shrewd, discerning, astute, penetrating, incisive, observant, sensitive, understanding.

perfect
1 (adj) If you buy something new, you expect it to be perfect. flawless, in mint condition, undamaged, unblemished, unscratched, unbroken, clean, spotless, immaculate, intact, complete, whole.
OPPOSITES: imperfect, faulty.
2 (adj) Ali gave a perfect performance. flawless, faultless, exemplary, unerring, impeccable, consummate, unrivalled, matchless, unequalled, ideal, definitive.
OPPOSITES: flawed, poor.
3 (adj) A perfect copy. See **exact** 3.
4 (adj) A perfect choice. See **ideal** 2.

perform
1 (v) Will you perform in the concert? take part, appear, play, act, dance, sing, star.
2 (v) Let's perform a play. See **stage** 3.

performance
(n) I'm sure you'll enjoy the performance. show, production, play, concert, recital, gig (informal), act, presentation, display, spectacle, entertainment, matinée, debut, premiere, preview, dress rehearsal.

perfume see **scent** 1, 2.

period
1 (n) I spent a period in Spain. See **time** 1.
2 (n) We're studying the medieval period. See **age** 1.

permanent
1 (adj) Billy has a permanent cough. constant, continual, perpetual, persistent.
2 (adj) Is this a permanent arrangement? fixed, firm, definite, unalterable, unchangeable, irreversible, immutable, binding, lasting, enduring, stable.
OPPOSITES: short-lived, temporary.

permission
(n) We need police permission to hold a street party. authorization, approval, authority, consent, leave, go-ahead (informal), rubber stamp, green light.

permit see **allow** 1, 2.

perplexing see **puzzling**.

persecute
(v) The refugees feared the officials would persecute them. hound, plague, pursue, harass, harry, bully, terrorize, victimize, oppress, ill-treat, torment, molest, torture.

persevere
(v) Try to persevere when life gets hard. keep going, carry on, soldier on, stick at it, keep at it, hang in there (informal), be resolute, persist, plug away (informal).

person
(n) Each person is different. human being, individual, character, living being, soul.

personal
1 (adj) Cynthia has her own personal style. See **individual** 2.

2 (adj) Don't open that letter; it's personal! See **private** 2.
3 (adj) Don't make personal comments. insulting, offensive, rude, nasty, critical, negative, hurtful, disparaging, derogatory.

personality see **character** 1.

perspire see **sweat** 2.

persuade
(v) Can I persuade you to try some squid? coax, tempt, entice, induce, cajole, urge, prompt, prevail on, convince, talk you into, wheedle you into, sweet-talk you into (informal), win you over, bring you round.
OPPOSITES: dissuade, deter.

persuasive
(adj) The salesman was very persuasive. convincing, compelling, forceful, plausible, credible, believable, eloquent, silver-tongued, seductive, coaxing, winning.
OPPOSITES: unconvincing, implausible.

pessimistic
(adj) I feel pessimistic about the future. gloomy, hopeless, negative, despondent, despairing, depressed, glum, melancholy, fatalistic, defeatist, resigned, cynical.
OPPOSITES: optimistic, positive.

pester
(v) Answer my question and I won't pester you anymore. badger, bother, plague, torment, hound, harass, harry, hassle (informal), disturb, annoy, nag, be on your back (slang), get in your hair (informal).

petrified see **scared** 1.

phase see **stage** 2.

phone
1 (v) Did Sid phone you? call, telephone, ring you up, give you a call, give you a bell (slang), give you a tinkle (informal), give you a buzz (informal), get on the blower to you (informal).
2 (n) We've bought a new phone. telephone, mobile phone, cordless phone, car phone, cellphone, answerphone, videophone, handset, blower (informal).

photograph
1 (n) Look at this photograph of Granddad. photo (informal), picture, print, snap (informal), snapshot, shot, slide, transparency, enlargement, likeness.
2 (v) I want to photograph you in your clown suit. take a photograph of, take a picture of, capture you on film, get a shot of, shoot, film, snap (informal), record.

phrase see **expression** 2.

pick
1 (v) Pick a number. See **choose** 1.
2 (v) Shall I pick some flowers? gather, cut, collect, pluck, harvest (fruit).

pick on
(v) Pick on someone else for a change! criticize, find fault with, blame, nag, get at, tease, torment, badger, bully.

pick up
1 (v) Pick up that box. See **lift** 1.

2 (v) I'll pick you up at two o'clock. call for, come for, collect, give you a lift, fetch.
3 (v) Did you pick up any French on holiday? acquire, learn, get the hang of (informal), grasp, master.

picture
1 (n) That's a good picture of your dad. likeness, portrayal, depiction, representation, study, portrait, photograph, drawing, sketch, painting, caricature, cartoon, silhouette, etching, engraving, print, poster.
2 (v) I can't picture Aunt Bertha as a teenager. See **imagine** 1.

picturesque see **pretty** 2.

piece
1 (n) I'd like a piece of cheese. See **bit** 1.
2 (n) I dropped a piece of food on the floor. bit, scrap, morsel, mouthful, fragment, crumb, speck, particle.
3 (n) I cut my foot on a piece of glass. bit, fragment, sliver, splinter, shard, chip.
4 (n) Do you need that piece of material? bit, scrap, snippet, shred, remnant, length.
5 (n) Have a piece of my apple. See **bit** 2.
6 (n) This kit has a piece missing. bit, part, section, element, component.
7 (n) I'm learning a new piece for the concert. work, composition, item.
8 (v) Piece the parts together. See **fit** 2.

pierce
(v) Did the spear pierce the dragon's skin? puncture, penetrate, make a hole in, enter, go through, pass through, perforate, prick, wound, stab, spike, skewer.

pile
1 (n) Matt has a huge pile of magazines in his room. stack, heap, mound, mountain, mass, bundle, load, hoard, store, stockpile.
2 (v) Pile the papers here. stack, heap, gather, collect, amass, assemble, store.

pill
(n) tablet, capsule, lozenge.

pillar
(n) That pillar holds up the roof. column, post, pole, support, upright, prop, shaft.

pinch
1 (v) Don't pinch my leg. nip, squeeze.
2 (v) These shoes pinch my feet. hurt, cramp, squeeze, crush, confine, chafe.
3 (v) Add a pinch of salt. bit, taste, touch, dash, smidgen (informal), soupçon, small amount, trace, tad (informal), speck.

pink
(adj) Pink cheeks. rosy, flushed.
SHADES OF PINK: cerise, coral, flesh-colour, rose, salmon, shell pink, shocking pink.

pipe
(n) Water flowed through the pipe. tube, hose, duct, water main, pipeline, drainpipe, channel, conduit.

pirate
(n) buccaneer, raider, marauder, freebooter, cutthroat. ❖ Also see **pirates & shipwrecks**.

pirates

pirates and shipwrecks

pirates may be...

barbaric
black-hearted
bloodthirsty
bold
brutal
daring
dastardly
drunken
grasping
greedy

heartless
infamous
lawless
murderous
notorious
remorseless
ruthless
swashbuckling
vengeful
villainous

cutlass

pirates may...

board ships
bury treasure
drop anchor
keelhaul
  mutineers (drag
  rebels by a rope
  under the ship)
lie in wait
loot
make prisoners
  walk the plank
mutiny (rebel)
pillage

plunder
pursue
raid
ransack
rob
sail the high seas
seek revenge
sink ships
slit throats
take prisoners
weigh anchor
  (raise the
  anchor)

whale

pirates may have...

booty
bottle of rum
breeches
cockatoo
cocked hat
cutlass
doubloons
  (gold coins)
ducats (gold or
  silver coins)
eye patch
gold earrings
grog
  (diluted rum)
hook

kerchief
  (headscarf)
logbook
parrot
peg leg
  (wooden leg)
pieces of eight
  (coins)
pigtail
pistol
scar
sea chart
tattoo
telescope
treasure map

sea battle

on board a pirate ship

bow (front)
cabin
cannon
crow's nest
deck
fo'c'sle
  or forecastle
hammock
hull (main
  body of ship)
Jolly Roger
  (flag with
  skull and
  crossbones)

keel
  (ship's bottom)
mast
poop deck
port
  (left side)
rigging
rudder
sail
ship's lantern
starboard
  (right side)
stern (back)
wheel

Jolly Roger
crow's nest
rigging
bow
hull
mast
poop deck
stern
rudder
fo'c'sle

in a storm, a ship may...

break up on the rocks
capsize
creak
disintegrate
founder (sink)
groan
list
lurch
pitch
run aground
shatter
shudder
sink beneath the waves
splinter
split apart

jagged rocks

message in a bottle

shipwreck

after a shipwreck you might...

be marooned
be the sole survivor
be washed ashore
cling to the wreckage
encounter sharks
go down with the ship
go to a watery grave
swim for the shore

treasure island

pieces of eight

on a desert island you might find...

buried treasure
coral reef
dense jungle
driftwood
footprints
lagoon
palm trees
pirates' hide-out
silver sand
volcano

footprints

on the island you might...

build a shelter
climb trees
collect berries
dive down to the wreck
drink coconut milk
explore the island
fish
forage for food
hunt
light a fire
make a raft
search through the wreckage
send a message in a bottle
send smoke signals

quicksand

volcano

jellyfish

survivors

shark

raft

telescope

desert island dangers

contaminated water
jellyfish
poisonous berries
quicksand (sinking sand)
shark-infested waters
swamps
treacherous currents
venomous snakes
wild beasts

Also see **sea & seashore, storm words, treasure words.**

cocked hat
eye patch
pigtail
pistol

WANTED
Dead or Alive

planets in the solar system — Jupiter — Jupiter's rings — Saturn — Saturn's rings — Uranus — Neptune — Mercury — Earth — Venus — Mars

pity
1 *(n) The judge showed no pity.* sympathy, compassion, understanding, fellow feeling, mercy, charity, kindness, emotion, feeling.
2 *(n) It's a pity you can't come.* shame, crying shame, stroke of bad luck, bummer *(slang)*, misfortune, tragedy, sin.
3 *(v) I pity anyone out in this blizzard.* feel sorry for, sympathize with, feel for, commiserate with, feel pity for, have compassion for, weep for, grieve for.

place
1 *(n) What a good place for a picnic!* spot, position, site, location, situation, setting.
2 *(n) Riverdale is an interesting place to visit.* village, town, city, neighbourhood, district, area, region, spot, locality.
3 *(n) Save me a place!* seat, chair, space.
4 *(v) Place the fruit in the bowl. See* **put** 1.

placid
(adj) Anna is a placid child. calm, even-tempered, docile, easy-going, peaceable, serene, self-possessed, composed, level-headed, unexcitable, steady.
OPPOSITES: excitable, temperamental.

plain
1 *(adj) The room was decorated in a plain style.* simple, basic, restrained, subdued, unpretentious, austere, stark, severe, Spartan, unadorned, unembellished, undecorated, unpatterned.
OPPOSITES: fancy, ornate.
2 *(adj) Aunt Bertha likes plain food.* simple, basic, ordinary, homely, everyday, unsophisticated, unexciting, frugal.
OPPOSITES: fancy, elaborate.
3 *(adj) Martha is a plain child.* ordinary-looking, unattractive, unprepossessing.
OPPOSITES: attractive, good-looking.
4 *(adj) Mrs Badger's feelings were plain. See* **obvious**.

plan
1 *(n) That sounds like a sensible plan.* idea, scheme, plan of action, suggestion, proposal, proposition, strategy, procedure, system, method, tactic.
2 *(n) Look at this plan of our new house.* drawing, scale drawing, blueprint, layout, diagram, sketch, outline, representation, illustration, map, chart, bird's-eye view.
3 *(v) I didn't plan to cheat. See* **mean** 3.
4 *(v) Plan your project before you start.* think out, sketch out, map out, outline, organize, prepare, draft, design, formulate, devise, shape, frame.

plane *see* **aircraft**.

planet
(n) The planet floated in space. sphere, orb, globe, satellite, heavenly body.
PLANETS IN THE SOLAR SYSTEM: Earth, Jupiter, Mars, Mercury, Neptune, Saturn, Uranus, Venus. ❖ *Also see* **space adventure**.

plant
(n) What's that unusual plant? flower, bloom, seedling, weed, shrub, bush, climber, creeper, herb, vegetable, grass, fern, cactus, moss, lichen.

plaster *see* **smear** 1.

play
1 *(v) You have all day to play.* amuse yourself, entertain yourself, enjoy yourself, have fun, play games, mess about.
2 *(v) The others won't let me play.* join in, take part, participate, be in the game.
3 *(v) Rangers will play United.* play against, take on, challenge, compete against, rival, vie with, contend with.
4 *(v) Gill will play Cinderella.* act, be, take the part of, take the role of, portray.
5 *(n) Did you enjoy the play?* show, production, performance, drama.
TYPES OF PLAY: comedy, farce, historical play, melodrama, mime, musical, nativity play, pageant, pantomime, puppet show, radio play, satire, tragedy, TV play.

play about *see* **mess about** 1, 2.

playful
1 *(adj) Playful puppies. See* **lively** 2.
2 *(adj) A playful grin. See* **mischievous** 2.

plead with *see* **beg** 2.

pleasant
1 *(adj) A pleasant day out. See* **enjoyable**.
2 *(adj) What pleasant weather!* lovely, beautiful, glorious, delightful, fine, mild, warm, sunny, balmy.
OPPOSITES: unpleasant, nasty.
3 *(adj) Mrs Honey is a pleasant person.* likable, lovely, good-natured, amiable, delightful, charming, agreeable, friendly.
OPPOSITES: unpleasant, obnoxious.
4 *(adj) This makes a pleasant change.* agreeable, welcome, refreshing, pleasing, satisfying, appreciated.
OPPOSITES: unwelcome, unpleasant.

please
1 *(v) I'm doing my best to please you.* make you happy, give you pleasure, satisfy, cheer you up, delight, charm, entertain, amuse, indulge, gratify, humour, suit.
2 *(v) Do as you please. See* **like** 4.

pleased
(adj) Kim was pleased when she passed her exams. happy, delighted, glad, contented, satisfied, thrilled, overjoyed, jubilant, elated, euphoric, over the moon *(informal)*, thrilled to bits *(informal)*, chuffed *(slang)*.

pleasure
(n) Lord Lucre leads a life of pleasure. enjoyment, contentment, satisfaction, comfort, ease, gratification, entertainment, amusement, bliss, delight.
OPPOSITES: misery, suffering.

plenty
(n) Lord Lucre has plenty of money. a great deal, a lot, lots *(plural) (informal)*, a large amount, more than enough, enough, sufficient, a fund, heaps *(plural) (informal)*, loads *(plural) (informal)*, masses *(plural) (informal)*, oodles *(plural) (informal)*, piles *(plural) (informal)*, stacks *(plural) (informal)*.

plot
1 *(n) The pirates hatched a plot.* scheme, conspiracy, plan, stratagem, intrigue.
2 *(n) Can you follow the plot of this play?* storyline, story, narrative, thread, structure.
3 *(v) Let's plot to get our revenge.* plan, scheme, conspire, intrigue, manoeuvre.

plough
1 *(v) Farmer Phyllis plans to plough this field.* cultivate, till, turn over, dig up.
2 *(v) We tried to plough through the mud.* plunge, push, wallow, wade, cut, drive.

plump
(adj) Mrs Honey is rather plump. chubby, tubby, podgy, dumpy, pudgy, roly-poly, well-rounded, stout, portly, corpulent, fat, well-padded, fleshy, buxom, matronly.
OPPOSITES: slim, slender.

plunge *see* **dive** 1, 2.

plush *(informal) see* **luxurious**.

poem
(n) rhyme, verse, ditty, ballad, ode, sonnet, limerick, haiku, elegy, epic, jingle.

poetic
(adj) This story is written in a poetic style. lyrical, imaginative, creative, artistic, flowing, lilting, graceful, songlike, flowery.

poignant *see* **sad** 2.

point
1 *(n) This is the point where we started.* spot, place, position, site, location.
2 *(n) At that point, Zak left.* moment, very moment, instant, second, stage, juncture.
3 *(n) This spear has a sharp point.* tip, end, spike, prong, sharp end.
4 *(n) What is the point of this game?* purpose, aim, objective, object, use.
5 *(n) I don't understand the point of this story.* meaning, significance, relevance, thrust, drift, theme, main idea, substance.
6 *(n) I covered that point in my talk.* detail, aspect, item, feature, particular, facet.
7 *(v) Point me to the station. See* **direct** 6.
8 *(v) Point your arrow at the bull's-eye. See* **aim** 3.

pointless *see* **useless** 1.

point out
(v) *Why didn't you point out this problem earlier?* draw attention to, mention, bring up, allude to, refer to, indicate, identify.

poisonous
(adj) *Bleach is a poisonous substance.* toxic, noxious, lethal, deadly, harmful, venomous *(snakes, spiders).*
OPPOSITES: harmless, nontoxic.

poke
1 *(v)* *Don't poke your finger in the trifle!* See **stick** 6.
2 *(v)* *Poke me if I start to snore.* prod, jab, nudge, elbow, butt, hit.

poky
(adj) *This room is so poky.* cramped, small, tiny, narrow, confined, cell-like.
OPPOSITES: spacious, large.

pole
(n) rod, bar, post, stake, stick, staff, spar.

polish
1 *(n)* *Look at the polish on that table!* See **shine** 4.
2 *(v)* *Polish your shoes.* shine, buff up, rub, wax, brush, clean, burnish *(metal).*

polite
1 *(adj)* *Cyril is always polite.* courteous, well-behaved, well-mannered, civil, tactful, diplomatic, respectful, deferential, obliging, considerate, thoughtful.
OPPOSITES: rude, discourteous.
2 *(adj)* *It's not polite to gobble your food.* acceptable, done, proper, seemly, nice, genteel, civilized, ladylike, gentlemanly.
OPPOSITES: rude, ignorant.

pollute
(v) *Cars pollute the air.* contaminate, poison, dirty, foul up, taint, blight, infect.

pool
(n) puddle, pond, fish pond, duck pond, millpond, oasis, water hole, lake, tarn, swimming pool, paddling pool.

poor
1 *(adj)* *I hate being poor.* short of money, badly off, hard up *(informal)*, penniless, poverty-stricken, destitute, down-and-out, on the rocks, impoverished, broke *(informal)*, flat broke *(informal)*, stony-broke *(slang)*, skint *(slang).*
OPPOSITES: rich, wealthy.
2 *(adj)* *This is a poor piece of work.* inadequate, unsatisfactory, second-rate, mediocre, inferior, substandard, below average, disappointing, feeble, worthless, dismal, rubbishy, shoddy, rotten *(informal).*
OPPOSITES: good, excellent.
3 *(adj)* *The poor kitten was soaked!* unfortunate, unlucky, wretched, luckless, hapless, miserable, pathetic, pitiable.
4 *(adj)* *Eva earns a poor salary.* See **low** 2.

pop
(v) *Can you hear the firecrackers pop?* bang, crack, snap, go bang, explode, go off, go off with a bang, detonate, burst.

pop, rock and jazz

musical styles

acid jazz	dub	hip-hop	rave
beat	easy listening	house	reggae
bebop	folk	indie	rhythm
big band	funk	jazz	and blues
blues	garage	jungle	rock 'n' roll
country and	glam rock	pop	salsa
western	gospel	psychedelia	ska
dance	hardcore	punk	soul
disco	hard rock	ragga	swing
doo-wop	heavy metal	rap	techno

jazz musician

volume control — tempo control (changes speed) — display screen — sound editing buttons — pitch blend (changes pitch) — vibrato — synthesizer — keyboard

a band may use...

acoustic guitar
amplifier
bass guitar
drum kit
drum machine
electric guitar
headphones
keyboard
microphone
mixing desk
multitrack tape machine
PA system
record deck
sampler (equipment to mix in sounds)
sequencer (equipment to memorize a sequence of notes)
speakers
synthesizer

drummer

you might listen to...

acoustic version	live recording
album	new release
chart music	remix
compilation album	single
concept album	soundtrack
cover version	track
hit single	unplugged
live performance	version

crash cymbal — ride cymbal — tom-toms — hi-hat cymbal — snare drum — floor tom — pedal — bass drum — pedal
drum kit

vocalist

punk

on a track you might hear...

backing vocals	key change
bass line	lyrics
beat	melody
bridge (link)	refrain (chorus)
chords	rhythm
drum break (drum solo)	riff (repeated chord sequence)
echo effects	sample
fade	(mixed-in extract from another record)
harmony	scratching
hook (catchy phrase)	sound effects
improvisation	theme
instrumental section	vocals (singing)
intro *(informal)*	

a track may sound...

bland	original
catchy	polished
dreamy	raucous
fresh	repetitive
funky *(informal)*	rhythmic
futuristic	sexy *(informal)*
haunting	slick
laid-back *(informal)*	smooth
manic	soulful
melancholy	tinny
mellow	tribal
melodic (tuneful)	tuneless
monotonous	unoriginal
	upbeat *(informal)*
	weird

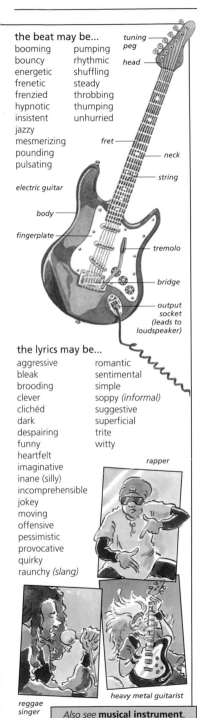

the beat may be...

booming	pumping
bouncy	rhythmic
energetic	shuffling
frenetic	steady
frenzied	throbbing
hypnotic	thumping
insistent	unhurried
jazzy	
mesmerizing	
pounding	
pulsating	

electric guitar

tuning peg

head

fret

neck

string

tremolo

bridge

output socket (leads to loudspeaker)

body

fingerplate

the lyrics may be...

aggressive	romantic
bleak	sentimental
brooding	simple
clever	soppy *(informal)*
clichéd	suggestive
dark	superficial
despairing	trite
funny	witty
heartfelt	
imaginative	
inane (silly)	
incomprehensible	
jokey	
moving	
offensive	
pessimistic	
provocative	
quirky	
raunchy *(slang)*	

rapper

reggae singer

heavy metal guitarist

Also see **musical instrument, musician, music words, singer.**

popular
1 *(adj) Josie has always been popular.* well-liked, admired, in demand, in favour, sought-after, accepted, loved, idolized. OPPOSITE: unpopular.
2 *(adj) Short hair is popular at the moment.* fashionable, in fashion, in, in favour, trendy *(informal)*, hip *(slang)*. OPPOSITES: unfashionable, out.
3 *(adj) There's a popular theory that chocolate gives you spots.* common, widespread, general, well-known, current, prevailing, prevalent.

port
(n) The ship approached the port. harbour, dock, seaport, marina, anchorage, wharf, quay, landing stage, dockyard, dry dock.

portion see **helping.**

portrait
(n) Do you like this portrait of Fergus? picture, self-portrait, painting, drawing, sketch, photograph, study, likeness, portrayal, image, depiction, impression.

posh
1 *(adj) (informal) We stayed in a posh hotel.* grand, luxurious, plush *(informal)*, up-market, classy *(slang)*, swish *(informal)*, swanky *(informal)*, ritzy *(slang)*, high-class. OPPOSITES: modest, humble.
2 *(adj) (informal) Araminta is much too posh to talk to us.* grand, superior, swanky *(informal)*, upper class, refined, genteel, snooty *(informal)*, toffee-nosed *(slang)*, stuck-up *(informal)*, la-di-da *(informal)*.

position
1 *(n) What a perfect position for a house!* See **place 1.**
2 *(n) Ben's request put me in a difficult position.* situation, predicament, spot, plight, dilemma, state.
3 *(n) What's your mum's position in the company?* See **rank.**
4 *(n) Mrs Badger applied for the position of deputy head.* See **job 3.**
5 *(n) I can't hold this position for much longer.* pose, stance, posture, attitude.

positive
1 *(adj) Are you positive that you saw a ghost?* See **certain 1.**
2 *(adj) Do you have any positive proof?* real, actual, definite, clear-cut, firm, concrete, categorical, absolute, conclusive, indisputable, undeniable, irrefutable.
3 *(adj) Mrs Badger made some positive suggestions.* helpful, constructive, encouraging, useful, practical, beneficial. OPPOSITES: negative, unhelpful.

possible
1 *(adj) Anything is possible if you try.* achievable, attainable, feasible, within reach, practicable, workable, doable. OPPOSITES: impossible, unattainable.
2 *(adj) This story has only one possible ending.* conceivable, imaginable, plausible, credible, likely, probable, potential. OPPOSITES: inconceivable, unthinkable.

post
1 *(n) Stick the post in the ground.* stake, pole, upright, support, pillar, gatepost.
2 *(n) Don't open my post.* mail, letters *(plural)*, correspondence.
3 *(n) May I apply for this post? See **job 3.**
4 *(v) I must post this parcel.* mail, send, send off, dispatch.

postpone
(v) We'll have to postpone the match. put off, put back, defer, hold over, delay, shelve, suspend, adjourn, put on the back burner *(informal)*, take a rain check on *(informal)*, put on ice *(informal)*.

potion
(n) A magic potion. brew, concoction, mixture, drink, draught, elixir, drug.

potter about see **mess about 1.**

pounce
1 *(v) The eagle will pounce when it sees its prey.* strike, attack, swoop down, drop down, descend.
2 **pounce on** *(v) Ed is waiting to pounce on you.* jump on, leap out at, spring on, swoop on, lunge at, make a grab for, ambush, attack, take you by surprise.

pour
1 *(v) Water began to pour from the pipe.* See **flow 1.**
2 *(v) Please pour the tea.* pour out, serve.
3 *(v) It's going to pour.* See **rain 1.**

powdery
(adj) Powdery earth. crumbly, fine, dry, loose, dusty, sandy, chalky, grainy.

power
1 *(n) You'll need all your power to lift that sack.* See **strength 1.**
2 *(n) I wish I had the power to fly.* ability, capacity, capability, potential.
3 *(n) The king has power over his people.* control, authority, command, mastery, supremacy, dominance, sovereignty, influence, sway, clout.
4 *(n) Nuclear power.* energy, fuel.

powerful
1 *(adj) A powerful leader.* strong, forceful, influential, dominant, commanding, high-powered, authoritative, mighty, supreme, invincible, all-powerful, omnipotent. OPPOSITES: weak, powerless.
2 *(adj) A powerful wrestler.* See **strong 1.**
3 *(adj) A powerful film.* compelling, effective, impressive, convincing, forceful, inspiring, stirring, moving, disturbing.

powerless see **helpless 2.**

practical
1 *(adj) Mandy is a practical person.* sensible, down-to-earth, matter-of-fact, no-nonsense, hard-headed, businesslike, efficient, realistic, pragmatic. OPPOSITES: impractical, idealistic.
2 *(adj) Your idea isn't really practical.* practicable, workable, feasible, viable, doable, possible, realistic, sensible, sound. OPPOSITES: impractical, unworkable.

practice

practice
1 (n) *To be a good pianist you must do lots of practice.* training, exercises (plural), drill, repetition, preparation.
2 (n) *This is the last practice before the concert. See* **rehearsal**.

practise
1 (v) *Let's practise our performance.* rehearse, work at, go over, run through, go through, prepare, polish, fine-tune.
2 (v) *Dancers practise daily. See* **train** 3.

praise
1 (n) *Neesha would flourish if you gave her more praise.* compliments (plural), approval, appreciation, congratulations (plural), acclaim, applause, admiration.
OPPOSITES: criticism, censure.
2 (v) *I'm sure the critics will praise your performance.* compliment you on, congratulate you on, commend, acclaim, rave about (informal), sing the praises of, eulogize about, admire, applaud, cheer.
OPPOSITES: criticize, revile.

prance
(v) *Look how the ponies prance about!* leap, jump, skip, caper, cavort, romp, frisk, dance, gambol.

prank *see* **trick** 2.

prattle
(v) *Sophie can prattle for hours.* chatter, natter, gossip, gabble, jabber, twitter, babble, rattle on, rabbit on (informal), waffle, witter on (informal), go on (informal), yak (slang), jaw (slang).

precarious
(adj) *Indy is in a precarious position.* dangerous, risky, hazardous, perilous, tricky, dicey, dodgy (informal), hairy (slang), vulnerable, insecure, unstable, uncertain, touch and go.
OPPOSITES: safe, secure.

precious
1 (adj) *Precious jewels. See* **valuable** 1.
2 (adj) *Don't hurt my precious child.* beloved, adored, cherished, treasured, darling, dearest, idolized, valued, prized.

precise
1 (adj) *Please take precise measurements. See* **accurate** 1.
2 (adj) *At that precise moment, Eve burst in.* very, exact, specific, particular, actual.
3 (adj) *Jo is so precise; she even keeps her CDs in alphabetical order.* particular, methodical, meticulous, careful, exact, finicky, fastidious, fussy, prim.
OPPOSITES: sloppy (informal), careless.

predicament *see* **mess** 3.

predict
(v) *It's hard to predict what problems may arise.* foresee, foretell, anticipate, forecast, prophesy, guess, second-guess (informal).

prefer
(v) *Which team do you prefer?* like better, favour, fancy, incline towards, support, back, go for, opt for, recommend.

pregnant
(adj) *Auntie Penny is pregnant.* expecting (informal), having a baby, in the family way (informal), in the club (slang), in the pudding club (slang), preggers (informal).

prejudiced
(adj) *Don't be so prejudiced; try to keep an open mind.* bigoted, biased, intolerant, narrow-minded, opinionated, partisan, one-sided, unfair, racist, sexist, chauvinist, ageist, homophobic, xenophobic.
OPPOSITES: open-minded, tolerant.

prepare
1 (v) *We must prepare for the play.* get ready, plan, make arrangements, gear up, practise, rehearse, train, get into shape.
2 (v) *Let's prepare this room for our visitors.* get ready, make ready, arrange, sort out, organize, fix up, set up.
3 **prepare yourself** (v) *Prepare yourself for a shock.* get ready, be prepared, brace yourself, steel yourself, gear yourself up, psych yourself up (informal).

present
1 (n) *Thank you for the present.* gift, pressie (informal), offering, contribution, donation, hand-out, freebie (informal).
2 (n) *Try to live for the present.* here and now, present day, today, this day and age.
OPPOSITES: past, future.
3 (adj) *Let's consider the present situation.* current, existing, immediate.
OPPOSITES: past, future.
4 (adj) *Is everyone present?* here, there, on the spot, at hand, ready, in attendance, available, accounted for.
OPPOSITES: absent, away.
5 (v) *Lord Lucre will present the prizes.* give, hand out, distribute, give out, hand over, award, bestow, donate, grant.

press
1 (v) *Press the mixture into the tin.* push down, squeeze, compress, force down, cram, jam, crush, flatten, smooth out.
2 (v) *Look how the fans press round their team.* push, crowd, surge, swarm, cluster, throng, flock, mill, huddle, squeeze.
3 **the press** (n) *What does the press say?* papers (plural), newspapers (plural), media, journalists (plural), reporters (plural).

pressure
1 (n) *The ice will break under the pressure.* weight, force, load, burden, stress, strain.
2 (n) *I can't stand all this pressure!* stress, strain, tension, anxiety, worry, hassle (informal), demands (plural).
3 (n) *I only came here under pressure.* duress, obligation, constraint, compulsion, coercion, force.

pressurize
(v) *I don't want to go, so don't pressurize me.* push, pressure, put pressure on, press, browbeat, bully, force, drive, compel, coerce, bulldoze (informal), dragoon, try to persuade, lean on (informal).

presume *see* **assume**.

pretence *see* **front** 4.

pretend
1 (v) *Let's pretend we're space aliens.* imagine, make believe, suppose, fantasize.
2 (v) *I don't know how to speak Chinese, but I could pretend.* bluff, fake it, put on an act, play-act, put it on, sham, feign.

pretentious
(adj) *Araminta is so pretentious; she's always putting on airs.* affected, phoney (informal), false, unnatural, pseudo (informal), showy, ostentatious, stagy.
OPPOSITES: unpretentious, unassuming.

pretty
1 (adj) *Yasmin is really pretty.* attractive, good-looking, cute, beautiful, lovely, fetching (informal), striking, appealing.
OPPOSITES: plain, ugly.
2 (adj) *What a pretty village!* picturesque, quaint, charming, beautiful, old-world, scenic, chocolate-box (informal).
OPPOSITES: ugly, unattractive.
3 (adv) (informal) *I did pretty well. See* **quite** 1.

prevent
1 (v) *Try to prevent any accidents.* avoid, avert, ward off, head off, stave off, pre-empt, forestall, nip in the bud (informal).
OPPOSITE: cause.
2 (v) *We must prevent Joel from leaving.* stop, deter, hinder, hamper, impede, obstruct, thwart, deflect, foil, hold back.

price
1 (n) *I can't afford such a high price.* cost, charge, amount, figure, sum, rate, payment, fee, outlay, expenditure.
2 (n) *Fred has discovered the price of being famous.* cost, consequence, result, outcome, penalty, sacrifice, punishment.

priceless
(adj) *Don't break that vase; it's priceless.* beyond price, irreplaceable, precious, valuable, expensive, costly, worth a king's ransom, worth its weight in gold, rare, treasured, cherished, prized.
OPPOSITE: worthless.

prick
(v) *Prick the balloon with a pin.* jab, stab, puncture, pierce, put a hole in, perforate, spike, nick, jag (informal).

prickly
1 (adj) *Ned scratched himself on a prickly branch.* thorny, spiky, spiny, brambly, barbed, bristly, briery.
2 (adj) *This rash gives me a prickly feeling.* itchy, scratchy, tingly, stinging, crawling.

pride
1 (n) *It hurts my pride when people laugh at me.* self-esteem, self-respect, self-worth, dignity, self-image, ego, feelings (plural).
2 (n) *Pride is one of the seven deadly sins.* conceit, vanity, arrogance, haughtiness, self-importance, bigheadedness (informal), self-love, egotism.
OPPOSITE: humility.

3 *(n) You can take pride in a job well done.* pleasure, satisfaction, delight, joy.
OPPOSITES: shame, dissatisfaction.

prim
(adj) Aunt Bertha is too prim to join in the fun. strait-laced, starchy, stuffy, proper, prissy, priggish, prudish, stiff, formal.

prison *see* **jail** 1.

prisoner
1 *(n) Burglar Beryl shared a cell with another prisoner.* convict, jailbird, con *(slang)*, lifer *(informal)*.
2 *(n) Granddad was a prisoner during the war.* captive, hostage, POW (prisoner of war), detainee.

private
1 *(adj) Flash Frank has his own private jet.* personal, individual, special, exclusive, particular, privately owned.
OPPOSITE: public.
2 *(adj) This letter contains private information.* confidential, personal, intimate, secret, restricted, classified, unofficial, off the record, hush-hush *(informal)*, inside.
OPPOSITE: public.
3 *(adj) This beach seems very private.* secluded, solitary, remote, isolated, secret, quiet, sequestered, unknown, hidden.

prize
1 *(n) Kirsty won a prize on Sports Day.* award, trophy, cup, medal, shield, badge, rosette, certificate, reward, accolade.
2 *(n) How did you spend your prize from the lottery?* winnings *(plural)*, jackpot, windfall, haul.

probable *see* **likely** 1.

problem
1 *(n) I can't cope with this problem alone.* difficulty, dilemma, predicament, mess, setback, snag, complication, worry, burden, trouble, quandary.
2 *(n) Mrs Badger gave us a problem to solve.* question, puzzle, riddle, brain-teaser *(informal)*, conundrum, poser, mystery.

procession *see* **parade**.

prod *see* **poke** 2.

produce
1 *(v) How many cars can the factory produce in a week?* turn out, manufacture, make, put together, build, assemble, construct, supply, churn out *(informal)*.
2 *(v) We produce all our own vegetables.* grow, cultivate, supply.
3 *(v) The police can't produce any evidence.* supply, provide, furnish, offer, put forward, reveal, show, present, display.
4 *(v) This decision will produce a lot of ill feeling.* cause, give rise to, result in, lead to, provoke, generate, bring about, make for, engender, spark off, trigger.

programme
1 *(n) What's the programme for today?* plan, schedule, timetable, order of events, agenda, line-up, order of the day.

2 *(n) Would you like to buy a programme?* brochure, leaflet, guide, list of events, list of performers, list of players.
3 *(n) What's your favourite TV programme?* show, broadcast, production.
❖ *Also see* **television & film**.

progress
1 *(n) Have you made any progress on your project?* headway, advance, improvement, steps forward *(plural)*, progression, development, breakthrough.
2 *(v) You've really begun to progress this term. See* **improve** 1.

prohibit *see* **forbid**.

project
1 *(n) Have you finished your science project?* assignment, topic, task, activity, investigation, research, piece of work.
2 *(n) I'm involved in a project to clean up the pond.* scheme, campaign, venture, operation, programme, plan, undertaking.

promise
1 *(v) Promise you'll love me always!* vow, swear, give your word, pledge, guarantee, take an oath, undertake, cross your heart.
2 *(n) I give you my promise.* word, word of honour, assurance, guarantee, pledge, vow, oath, commitment, undertaking.
3 *(n) Your work shows promise.* potential, ability, aptitude, talent, flair.

promising
1 *(adj) The future looks promising. See* **hopeful** 2.
2 *(adj) Benji is a promising young actor.* talented, gifted, up-and-coming, budding.

promote
1 *(v) If you work hard the company may promote you.* give you promotion, upgrade, advance, move you up, move you up the ladder, give you a rise.
OPPOSITES: demote, downgrade.
2 *(v) Famous Fred is keen to promote his new album.* publicize, advertise, push, plug *(informal)*, hype, market, sell.

prompt
1 *(v) This news may prompt Judd to take some action.* motivate, induce, lead, cause, move, persuade, influence, encourage, inspire, rouse, stir, stimulate, provoke.
2 *(v) I'll prompt you if you forget your lines. See* **remind** 1.
3 *(adj) I need a prompt reply. See* **quick** 2.

proof
(n) Is there any proof that Burglar Beryl is guilty? evidence, confirmation, verification, corroboration, testimony.

proper
1 *(adj) I need the proper equipment for diving.* right, correct, appropriate, suitable.
OPPOSITES: inappropriate, unsuitable.
2 *(adj) This is the proper way to use chopsticks.* right, correct, usual, normal, conventional, accepted, established, acceptable, orthodox.
OPPOSITES: wrong, unconventional.

3 *(adj) Aunt Bertha expects proper behaviour.* decent, seemly, respectable, polite, fitting, genteel, refined, ladylike, gentlemanly, sedate, decorous, dignified.
OPPOSITES: improper, unseemly.

property
(n) Keep your hands off my property! possessions *(plural)*, belongings *(plural)*, things *(plural)*, personal effects *(plural)*, land, ground, estate, house, money, wealth, riches *(plural)*, assets *(plural)*.

protect
1 *(v) Don't worry; I'll protect you.* look after, watch over, keep you safe, take care of, shield, shelter, guard, defend, save, stick up for *(informal)*, cover up for.
OPPOSITES: expose to danger, betray.
2 *(v) The soldiers did their best to protect the city. See* **defend** 1.
3 *(v) These goggles will protect your eyes.* shield, cover, safeguard, save, preserve, screen, mask, conceal.
OPPOSITES: expose, endanger.

protest
1 *(n) If there's any protest we'll go home.* objection, opposition, complaint, dissent, disagreement, disapproval, outcry, fuss.
2 *(n) Mel took part in a protest against fox-hunting. See* **demonstration** 2.
3 protest against *(v) We will protest against the education cuts.* oppose, fight, take a stand against, object to, say no to, speak out against, raise objections to, put up a fight against, kick up a fuss about *(informal)*, complain about, grumble about, demonstrate against.
OPPOSITES: accept, go along with.

proud
1 *(adj) I felt proud to be chosen.* pleased, gratified, full of pride, honoured, chuffed *(slang)*, satisfied, contented, happy.
OPPOSITE: ashamed.
2 *(adj) Araminta is so proud; she looks down on everyone.* arrogant, haughty, high and mighty *(informal)*, supercilious, disdainful, conceited, vain, self-satisfied, self-important, overbearing, snobbish, stuck-up *(informal)*, snooty *(informal)*, toffee-nosed *(slang)*, uppity *(informal)*.
OPPOSITES: humble, unassuming.

prove
(v) This letter will prove that I am right. demonstrate, show, establish, confirm, provide evidence, give proof, bear out.
OPPOSITES: disprove, refute.

provide
1 *(v) Can you provide enough food for everyone?* supply, lay on, offer, produce, contribute, deliver, donate, grant.
2 provide for *(v) Uncle Pete works hard to provide for his family. See* **support** 2.

provoke
1 *(v) Don't provoke me! See* **annoy** 1.
2 *(v) This news may provoke a riot.* cause, start, spark off, trigger, incite, give rise to, lead to, produce, prompt, precipitate.

public

public
1 *(adj) I think education should be a public service.* state, national, social, civic, nationwide, countrywide, universal. OPPOSITE: private.
2 *(adj) Is this road public?* open to the public, free to all, accessible to all, unrestricted, communal. OPPOSITES: private, restricted.
3 *(adj) Charles's secret soon became public.* widely known, well-known, publicized, famous, notorious, obvious, apparent, evident, plain, exposed, visible. OPPOSITES: secret, unknown.
4 *(n) What will the public say about this?* people *(plural)*, country, nation, society, community, citizens *(plural)*, populace, voters *(plural)*, electorate, masses *(plural)*, hoi polloi, rank and file, Joe Public *(slang)*.

pudding *see* **dessert**.

puff
1 *(n) Did you feel that puff of wind?* gust, breath, blast, whiff, flurry, draught.
2 *(v) Running makes me puff. See* **pant**.

puffy *see* **swollen**.

puke *(slang) see* **vomit**.

pull
(v) Pull the sledge up the hill. drag, haul, tug, heave, lug, tow, trail, draw, yank, jerk. OPPOSITE: push.

pull through *see* **recover** 1.

pull yourself together
(phrase) get a grip on yourself, control yourself, snap out of it *(informal)*.

pump
1 *(v) Pump the water through the pipe.* siphon, force, push, drive, send, drain.
2 **pump up** *(v) You need to pump up your tyres.* inflate, blow up.

punch
(v) Let me past or I'll punch you! hit, thump, sock *(slang)*, bash *(informal)*, belt *(slang)*, biff *(slang)*, whack, thwack, slug, clout *(informal)*, strike, clobber *(slang)*, wallop *(informal)*, hammer, pummel.

punctual
(adj) Carly is always punctual. on time, prompt, early, in good time, on the dot. OPPOSITES: unpunctual, late.

punish
(v) The head will punish you if you cheat in exams. penalize, discipline, teach you a lesson, correct, scold, chastise, slap your wrists, rap your knuckles, sentence.

pure
1 *(adj) Is this water pure?* clean, fresh, uncontaminated, unpolluted, clear, untainted, natural, germ-free, uninfected, sterilized, pasteurized *(milk)*, undiluted. OPPOSITES: contaminated, polluted.
2 *(adj) Despite temptations, Eve remained pure.* chaste, virtuous, uncorrupted, undefiled, unstained, blameless, innocent, true, upright, squeaky-clean *(informal)*. OPPOSITES: impure, corrupt.

3 *(adj) That goal was pure magic! See* **absolute**.

purple
(n) SHADES OF PURPLE: aubergine, burgundy, grape, lavender, lilac, maroon, mauve, mulberry, plum, puce, violet.

purpose
1 *(n) What was your purpose in cycling to Rome?* aim, object, goal, objective, target, motive, intention, plan, reason, rationale.
2 *(n) What is the purpose of this machine?* use, function, point, value, advantage.
3 **on purpose** *see* **on purpose**.

pursue *see* **follow** 1.

push
1 *(n) Give the door a push.* shove, nudge, prod, jolt, thrust. OPPOSITE: pull.
2 *(v) Push this button.* press, press down, push down, depress, put pressure on.
3 *(v) Buzo tried to push me into the pool.* shove, propel, force, drive, thrust, ram.
4 *(v) Can you push through the crowd?* force your way, squeeze, press, shove, barge *(informal)*, elbow, shoulder, jostle.
5 *(v) Mum has to push me to do my piano practice. See* **pressurize**.
6 *(v) Famous Fred is keen to push his new album. See* **promote** 2.

pushy
(adj) (informal) Jemima is so pushy; she's invited herself to the party! assertive, forceful, forward, aggressive, bumptious, brash, loud, bold, cocksure, ambitious. OPPOSITES: timid, retiring.

put
1 *(v) Put the files on the desk.* place, lay, leave, set, stand, rest, plonk, dump, park *(informal)*, set down, deposit.
2 *(v) Don't put your finger in the trifle! See* **stick** 6.
3 *(v) I bet Mrs Badger will put you in the top stream.* place, assign you to, consign you to, allocate you to, rank, grade.

put away
(v) Put away your clothes. tidy away, clear away, tidy up, put back, replace.

put down
1 *(v) The vet had to put down the sick animal.* put to sleep, put out of its misery, destroy, do away with, put away.
2 *(v) My friends never put me down.* belittle, humiliate, disparage, denigrate, sneer at, deflate, crush.

put off
1 *(v) We'll have to put off the match until next week. See* **postpone**.
2 *(v) Don't let the spectators put you off. See* **distract**.
3 *(v) Don't let this one setback put you off.* discourage, dissuade, deter, dishearten, dismay, daunt, perturb, faze, throw *(informal)*, rattle *(informal)*.
4 *(v) Doesn't lumpy custard really put you off? See* **disgust** 2.

put on
1 *(v) Why don't you put on your jeans?* slip into, change into, don, get dressed in. OPPOSITE: take off.
2 *(v) It doesn't matter if you put on a bit of weight.* gain, add. OPPOSITES: take off, lose.
3 *(v) Araminta likes to put on a posh accent.* affect, fake, feign, assume.
4 *(v) We're hoping to put on a pantomime. See* **stage** 3.

put out
1 *(v) Put out the flames!* extinguish, quench, douse, smother, stifle, stamp out, blow out, snuff out *(candle)*.
2 *(adj) Kim felt put out that she hadn't been invited. See* **offended**.

put up
1 *(v) Dad plans to put up a new garage. See* **build** 1.
2 *(v) We can easily put you up for the night.* take you in, give you a bed, give you a room, accommodate, give you lodging.

put up with *(informal) see* **stand** 4.

puzzle
1 *(n) I can't get my head round this puzzle.* problem, question, brain-teaser *(informal)*, poser, riddle, conundrum, mystery, enigma, paradox, crossword.
2 *(v) The crime seemed to puzzle the police.* baffle, mystify, perplex, flummox, floor *(informal)*, stump, bewilder, confuse, confound, defeat, nonplus.

puzzling
(adj) A puzzling code. baffling, perplexing, mystifying, cryptic, bewildering, confusing, mindboggling *(informal)*, insoluble, incomprehensible, mysterious, strange. OPPOSITES: simple, straightforward.

Qq

quaint
(adj) Tourists think our village is quaint. old-fashioned, picturesque, charming, old-world, antiquated, twee *(informal)*.

quality
1 *(n) This work is of a poor quality.* standard, level, grade, class.
2 *(n) Aren't you impressed by the quality of the acting?* high standard, calibre, excellence, superiority, distinction, merit.
3 *(n) Honesty is a quality I value in a friend. See* **characteristic**.

quantity *see* **amount** 1, 2.

quarrel
1 *(v) My sisters quarrel all the time. See* **argue** 1.
2 *(n) We had a quarrel about who should pay. See* **argument** 1.

3 (n) *The quarrel between the two families lasted for years.* feud, dispute, disagreement, misunderstanding, argument, hostility, enmity, conflict, vendetta, bad blood, rivalry.

quarrelsome
(adj) *Andy is so quarrelsome; he's always fighting with someone.* argumentative, belligerent, aggressive, pugnacious, cantankerous, irritable, irascible.
OPPOSITES: easy-going, even-tempered.

quay
(n) *We tied up our boat at the quay.* jetty, wharf, landing stage, dock, harbour.

queasy see **sick** 2.

queen
(n) monarch, sovereign, ruler.

quest
(n) *The white knight set out on a perilous quest.* mission, search, hunt, expedition, adventure, voyage, journey, crusade.

question
1 (n) *Do you have a question?* query, inquiry.
OPPOSITES: answer, reply.
2 (n) *Mrs Badger set us a difficult question. See* **problem** 2.
3 (n) *There's some question about who won the race.* doubt, uncertainty, dispute, debate, argument, controversy, confusion.
4 (n) *That's an interesting question for a debate. See* **subject**.
5 (v) *Detectives want to question Burglar Beryl.* interview, interrogate, cross-examine, cross-question, quiz, grill (informal), pump, give the third degree to.
6 (v) *Why do you question everything I say?* query, call into question, challenge, dispute, raise objections to, oppose, throw doubt on, suspect.
OPPOSITES: accept, believe.

queue
1 (n) *There was a long queue of traffic at the lights.* line, string, column, row, tailback, chain, file.
2 (v) *You must queue for tickets.* line up, wait in line, stand in line, form a queue.

quick
1 (adj) *The sprinter ran at a quick pace.* fast, swift, rapid, brisk, speedy, spanking (informal), breakneck, headlong.
OPPOSITES: slow, sluggish.
2 (adj) *I need a quick response.* instant, immediate, instantaneous, prompt, early, swift, rapid, speedy.
OPPOSITES: slow, delayed.
3 (adj) *We paid a quick visit to Aunt Bertha. See* **short** 3.
4 (adj) *Let's go home the quick way. See* **short** 4.
5 (adj) *Ed will see the problem right away; he's very quick.* bright, sharp, astute, quick on the uptake (informal), quick-witted, shrewd, clever, perceptive, discerning, intelligent, able, all there (informal).
OPPOSITES: slow, stupid.

6 (adj) *Sharmeen is always quick to help. See* **willing**.

quiet
1 (adj) *Ellen spoke in a quiet voice.* soft, low, hushed, scarcely audible, muted.
OPPOSITE: loud.
2 (adj) *Toni crept past with quiet steps.* silent, soundless, noiseless, inaudible.
OPPOSITES: noisy, loud.
3 (adj) *Frances is a quiet member of the class.* reserved, uncommunicative, unforthcoming, taciturn, silent, shy, retiring, diffident, unassertive, introverted, unobtrusive, subdued, restrained.
OPPOSITES: noisy, talkative.
4 (adj) *Everything was quiet before the storm.* still, calm, peaceful, tranquil.
OPPOSITES: restless, agitated.
5 (adj) *The cottage stood in a quiet valley.* peaceful, sleepy, secluded, isolated, lonely, remote, out-of-the-way, private.
OPPOSITES: bustling, crowded.
6 be quiet (phrase) *Be quiet and listen!* stop talking, shut up (informal), shush, quieten down, don't say a word, don't make a sound, hush, hold your tongue, put a sock in it (slang), belt up (slang), shut your trap (slang), pipe down (slang).

quite
1 (adv) *It's quite windy today.* rather, fairly, pretty (informal), moderately, reasonably, relatively, a bit, somewhat.
OPPOSITE: very.
2 (adv) *Your answer is quite correct.* absolutely, completely, totally, perfectly, entirely, wholly, utterly.
OPPOSITES: partly, more or less.

quiver see **shiver**.

quote
1 (v) *Try to quote plenty of examples in your essay.* give, mention, cite, refer to, allude to, name.
2 (v) *Can you quote any lines from Shakespeare?* recite, repeat, recall, recollect, reel off.

Rr

race
1 (n) *Lateefah took part in the race.* competition, contest, heat, final, relay race, sprint, marathon, cross-country, steeplechase, hurdles.
2 (n) *The Ancient Greeks were a civilized race.* people, nation, tribe, ethnic group.
3 (v) *I must race for my bus. See* **run** 1.
4 (v) *I'll race you to the corner.* have a race with, try to beat, compete with, take you on, run faster than.

racket see **noise** 2.

rage see **anger** 1.

ragged
1 (adj) *The little boy's trousers were ragged.* tattered, torn, frayed, worn-out, in tatters, in holes, in shreds, in ribbons, threadbare, patched, shabby, tatty.
2 (adj) *The torn page had a ragged edge.* uneven, rough, jagged, irregular, serrated.
OPPOSITES: smooth, even.

raid
1 (n) *There's been a raid at the bank.* robbery, hold-up, heist (slang), smash-and-grab (informal), stick-up (slang), break-in, ram raid (informal).
2 (n) *We hid underground during the raid. See* **attack** 4.
3 (v) *Pirate Peg planned to raid the enemy's hide-out.* attack, invade, break into, storm, charge, rush, swoop on, rob, loot, plunder, pillage, ransack, rifle.

rain
1 (v) *Suddenly it began to rain.* pour, pelt down, bucket down, lash down, teem, rain cats and dogs (informal), come down in torrents, spit, drizzle, sleet, hail.
2 (n) *I wish this rain would stop.* shower, drizzle, downpour, deluge, thunderstorm, cloudburst, torrential rain, driving rain, rainfall, raindrops (plural), sleet, hail.

rainforest see **jungle**.

rainy
(adj) *I like to stay inside on rainy days.* wet, drizzly, showery, damp.
OPPOSITES: dry, fine, sunny.

raise
1 (v) *We'll need a crane to raise those girders.* lift, hoist, pick up, heave up, jack up, put up, elevate, set upright.
OPPOSITE: lower.
2 (v) *Supermarkets may raise their prices.* put up, increase, hike (informal), inflate.
OPPOSITES: lower, reduce, cut.
3 (v) *We need to raise a lot of money for our new computer.* make, collect, get together, gather together, scrape together, pull in, drum up, obtain.
4 (v) *This campaign will raise awareness about drugs.* heighten, increase, promote, boost, strengthen, improve, enhance.
5 (v) *How can we raise some enthusiasm for the campaign?* arouse, awaken, stimulate, stir up, whip up, drum up, summon up, excite, kindle, foster.
6 (v) *It's hard to raise a family on your own. See* **bring up** 1.
7 (v) *Please don't raise that subject again. See* **mention** 2.

ram
1 (v) *Saul tried to ram my Dodgem car.* crash into, slam into, smash into, bump into, drive into, run into, collide with, hit.
2 (v) *Ram your stuff in here. See* **cram** 1.

ramshackle
(adj) *A ramshackle cottage.* tumbledown, dilapidated, run-down, derelict, neglected, decrepit, crumbling, rickety, unsafe, falling to pieces, gone to rack and ruin.

random

(adj) I jotted down my ideas in a random way. haphazard, arbitrary, indiscriminate, casual, unplanned, unsystematic, unmethodical, aimless, desultory.
OPPOSITES: deliberate, orderly.

range

1 *(n) This shop stocks a wide range of CDs.* variety, assortment, selection, choice, collection, array.
2 *(n) The ship is outside the range of our radar.* reach, scope, field, span, sweep, radius, limits *(plural),* bounds *(plural).*
3 *(v) Your marks range from good to excellent.* vary, fluctuate, stretch, extend.

rank

(n) Mum has a high rank in the company. grade, status, position, level, standing.

rapid *see* **fast** 1.

rare

(adj) Vases like this one are rare. unusual, out of the ordinary, scarce, few and far between, uncommon, exceptional, remarkable, thin on the ground, sparse, irreplaceable, unique, valuable, precious.
OPPOSITES: common, plentiful.

rarely

(adv) We rarely see Lucy. hardly ever, seldom, scarcely ever, almost never, once in a while, once in a blue moon *(informal),* on rare occasions, infrequently.
OPPOSITES: often, frequently.

rash

1 *(n) Your rash should soon clear up.* spots *(plural),* allergy, itch, hives *(plural).*
2 *(adj) Don't make any rash decisions.* reckless, impetuous, impulsive, hasty, sudden, hurried, foolhardy, harebrained, madcap, imprudent, ill-considered, ill-advised, risky, careless, thoughtless.
OPPOSITES: careful, considered.

rate

1 *(n) Gus raced off at a tremendous rate.* speed, pace, velocity.
2 *(n) What's the rate for a single room?* charge, cost, price, fee, tariff, payment, damage *(informal),* figure.
3 *(v) Would you rate my performance as good?* regard, consider, judge, count, evaluate, assess, appraise, classify, rank.
4 *(v) (slang) I don't rate our new teacher at all. See* **admire** 1.

rather *see* **quite** 1.

rattle

(v) The wind made the shutters rattle. clatter, bang, clank, clink, clunk, clack, shake, vibrate, jiggle.

rave

1 *(adj) (informal) Our play got rave reviews.* rapturous, enthusiastic, ecstatic, excellent, favourable.
OPPOSITES: lukewarm, critical.
2 *(n) (slang) I hear there was a rave last night.* party, warehouse party, disco, rave-up *(slang),* bash *(informal).*

ravenous *see* **hungry** 1.

raw

1 *(adj) Raw meat.* uncooked, unprepared, bloody, underdone, rare, fresh *(vegetables, fruit).*
OPPOSITES: cooked, well-done.
2 *(adj) Raw materials.* unprocessed, unrefined, untreated, natural, basic, crude, unfinished, coarse, rough.
OPPOSITES: refined, processed.
3 *(adj) Raw skin.* chafed, grazed, scraped, scratched, red, inflamed, sensitive, sore.
4 *(adj) A raw winter's day. See* **cold** 1.

ray

(n) A ray of sunlight. beam, shaft, stream, gleam, streak, flash, glimmer, glint, flicker.

reach

1 *(v) Can you reach that book on the top shelf?* get at, get hold of, touch, grab, grasp, catch at, clutch at, seize.
2 *(v) Did the explorers reach the North Pole?* get to, make, make it to *(informal),* get as far as, arrive at, set foot on, land at.
3 *(v) The mountains seemed to reach the sky.* touch, stretch to, extend to.
4 *(v) (informal) Please reach me that book.* pass, hand, give, hand over.
5 *(v) I tried to reach you yesterday, but you were out. See* **contact**.

reach out

(v) Reach out and grab the railing. stretch out, hold out your hand, stick out your hand, lean out, lean over.

react

(v) How did Zak react when he heard the news? respond, behave, act, cope, reply.

reaction

(n) Did you get any reaction to your suggestion? response, reply, answer, feedback, comeback *(informal),* backlash.

read

1 *(v) Did you read the paper yesterday?* look at, study, browse through, scan, skim through, glance at, run your eye over, dip into, pore over, wade through, peruse.
2 *(v) I have to read a poem in assembly.* read out, read aloud, recite, say, deliver.
3 *(v) Your writing is hard to read.* make out, decipher, understand, interpret, comprehend, decode.

ready

1 *(adj) Is everything ready?* prepared, arranged, organized, set up, finished, completed, finalized, ready and waiting, in readiness, primed, all set, fitted out.
OPPOSITES: unprepared, unfinished.
2 *(adj) Grandma is always ready to babysit. See* **willing**.
3 *(adj) Have you got your bus fare ready? See* **handy** 2.
4 *(adj) Louise looked ready to cry.* about, likely, liable, close, in danger of, on the brink of, on the point of, on the verge of.

real

1 *(adj) Is that real gold? See* **genuine** 1.

2 *(adj) These are the real facts.* true, actual, veritable, unquestionable, correct, certain, positive, tangible, truthful, factual.
OPPOSITES: false, imaginary.
3 *(adj) I can't hide my real feelings.* true, genuine, sincere, honest, heartfelt.
OPPOSITES: feigned, insincere.

realistic

1 *(adj) You must be realistic about your job prospects.* practical, sensible, level-headed, clear-sighted, rational, objective, pragmatic, down-to-earth, businesslike, hard-headed, unromantic, unsentimental.
OPPOSITES: unrealistic, idealistic.
2 *(adj) What a realistic model!* lifelike, convincing, true-to-life, naturalistic, authentic, faithful, accurate, precise.
OPPOSITES: unrealistic, unconvincing.

realize

(v) I didn't realize what had happened. understand, appreciate, grasp, comprehend, take in, absorb, twig *(informal),* catch on to *(informal),* cotton on to *(informal),* notice, recognize.

really

1 *(adv) This film is really gruesome.* totally, utterly, absolutely, truly, extremely, thoroughly, completely, positively, very.
2 *(adv) Archie says that he's nine, but he's really only seven.* actually, in fact, in reality, in truth, as a matter of fact.

reason

1 *(n) Do you have any reason for being late?* grounds *(plural),* cause, explanation, excuse, justification, pretext, rationale.
2 *(n) What is the reason behind your visit? See* **purpose** 1.
3 **reason with** *(v) It's a waste of time trying to reason with you.* argue with, persuade, dissuade, talk you round, win you over, bring you round, plead with, show you the error of your ways.

reasonable

1 *(adj) That sounds like a reasonable explanation.* sensible, logical, rational, credible, plausible, believable, intelligent, well-thought-out, reasoned, sound.
OPPOSITES: irrational, incredible.
2 *(adj) Mr Badger is a reasonable man.* moderate, fair, just, sensible, rational, wise, open to reason.
OPPOSITE: unreasonable.
3 *(adj) Your exam results are reasonable. See* **all right** 3.
4 *(adj) Reasonable prices. See* **low** 7.

reassure

(v) Did Mrs Badger's comments reassure you? put your mind at rest, comfort, calm, soothe your fears, encourage, give you confidence, cheer you up, hearten, bolster.
OPPOSITES: discourage, worry.

reassuring

(adj) Dad gave me a reassuring smile. encouraging, supportive, comforting, heartening, sympathetic, soothing.
OPPOSITES: discouraging, disturbing.

rebel

1 (v) *The citizens threatened to rebel.* revolt, riot, rise up, mutiny, take to the streets, take up arms, man the barricades, take a stand, resist.

2 **rebel against** (v) *Teenagers sometimes rebel against their parents.* See **disobey** 1.

rebellion *see* **revolution** 1.

rebellious

1 (adj) *A rebellious teenager.* defiant, disobedient, unruly, difficult, stroppy (informal), obstinate, uncontrollable, wild. OPPOSITES: obedient, compliant.

2 (adj) *Rebellious soldiers.* mutinous, insubordinate, rioting, disloyal, disaffected, rebel, revolutionary, insurgent. OPPOSITES: loyal, obedient.

receive

1 (v) *I was thrilled to receive a prize.* be given, be awarded, get, accept, collect, pick up, obtain, gain, come by. OPPOSITE: give.

2 (v) *I hope to receive some good news.* hear, be given, be told, be informed of.

recent

(adj) *A recent invention.* new, modern, present-day, contemporary, fresh, novel, up-to-the-minute, current, up-to-date. OPPOSITES: old, early.

recite

(v) *Can you recite the alphabet backwards?* say, repeat, reel off, read aloud, run through, go through, perform, deliver.

reckless *see* **rash** 2.

reckon *see* **think** 1, 2.

recognize

1 (v) *I didn't recognize you with short hair.* know, spot, identify, notice, pick you out, remember, recall, place.

2 (v) *Do you recognize what you've done wrong?* realize, see, understand, know, accept, acknowledge, appreciate, admit to.

recommend

1 (v) *What did the doctor recommend?* advise, suggest, propose, advocate, urge.

2 (v) *All my friends recommend this film.* speak highly of, praise, rave about (informal), approve of, commend, vouch for, put in a good word for, applaud.

record

1 (n) *Is there a record of this trip?* account, report, chronicle, diary, log, journal, note, memo, file, dossier, document, archives (plural).

2 (n) *Have you heard Famous Fred's new record?* See **release** 4.

3 (n) *Leo has a good record of punctuality.* track record (informal), history, background, past performance, reputation.

4 (v) *Record your progress every day.* document, log, note, write down, set down, enter, chronicle, put on record, put in writing, jot down, tape, video.

5 (v) *The band hope to record a single.* cut, make a recording of, lay down (slang).

recover

1 (v) *I'm sure you'll soon recover.* get better, get well, improve, get back on your feet, bounce back, rally, pull through, recuperate, convalesce, heal, mend. OPPOSITES: deteriorate, get worse.

2 (v) *I tried to recover my lost suitcase.* See **retrieve**.

red

1 (n) SHADES OF RED: beetroot red, blood red, brick red, burgundy, cardinal red, cherry red, crimson, flame red, magenta, maroon, pillar-box red, poppy red, puce, ruby, scarlet, tomato, vermilion.

2 (adj) *Red hair.* ginger, auburn, carroty, chestnut, coppery, sandy, reddish, flame-coloured, rust-coloured, russet, Titian.

3 (adj) *A red face.* flushed, flaming, burning, rosy, glowing, ruddy, florid, sunburnt, rosy-cheeked, apple-cheeked.

4 (adj) *Red eyes.* bloodshot, red-rimmed.

reduce

1 (v) *We will reduce our prices.* lower, bring down, cut, slash, discount, trim, halve, mark down, knock down (informal). OPPOSITES: raise, increase.

2 (v) *Earplugs will reduce the sound.* cut down, decrease, lessen, lower, diminish, minimize, tone down, muffle, dull. OPPOSITES: increase, amplify.

3 (v) *Please reduce your speed.* lower, decrease, cut down, cut, lessen, ease off. OPPOSITE: increase.

refer to

1 (v) *Who could this rude note refer to?* apply to, relate to, concern, be aimed at, be directed at, be relevant to, pertain to.

2 (v) *Did the letter refer to our visit?* mention, make reference to, speak about, touch on, allude to, comment on, hint at.

3 (v) *Refer to your textbooks.* consult, look at, turn to, look up.

reflect

1 (v) *The lakes reflect the trees.* mirror.

2 (v) *Do soaps on TV reflect real life?* See **imitate** 3.

3 (v) *Your marks reflect your ability.* do justice to, demonstrate, display, reveal, indicate, bear out, speak volumes about.

refreshing

1 (adj) *This drink is very refreshing.* thirst-quenching, cooling, reviving, revitalizing, rejuvenating, fortifying, restorative.

2 (adj) *I've just had a refreshing swim.* bracing, invigorating, cooling, freshening, exhilarating, revitalizing.

refuse

1 (v) *Here's an offer you can't refuse.* turn down, say no to, decline, reject, pass up (informal), resist, spurn, rebuff, dismiss. OPPOSITE: accept.

2 (v) *Damian's parents refuse him nothing.* See **deny** 2.

region

(n) *A mountainous region.* area, place, district, land, country, province, territory.

regret

1 (v) *Don't you regret that you lied to me?* feel sorry, feel ashamed, feel remorse, reproach yourself, have qualms, repent.

2 (v) *When you're older you'll regret this lost opportunity.* feel sorry about, pine over, fret over, bemoan, weep over.

3 (n) *Amir was filled with regret.* remorse, shame, guilt, self-reproach, contrition, repentance, sadness, sorrow, grief. OPPOSITES: satisfaction, pleasure.

regular

1 (adj) *Guitar practice is part of my regular routine.* See **usual**.

2 (adj) *You'll receive a regular progress report.* periodic, frequent, yearly, quarterly, termly, monthly, weekly, daily, hourly. OPPOSITES: occasional, infrequent.

3 (adj) *The trees were planted at regular intervals.* constant, fixed, set, equal, even, uniform, unvarying, consistent, measured. OPPOSITES: irregular, erratic.

rehearsal

(n) *We need another rehearsal before the performance.* practice, practice session, run-through, trial run, dress rehearsal, dummy run, dry run (informal).

reign

(v) *Who will reign when the king dies?* be king, be queen, sit on the throne, wear the crown, rule, govern, hold power.

reinforce *see* **strengthen** 2, 3.

reject

1 (v) *I bet the head will reject our plans.* say no to, veto, disallow, give the thumbs down to, throw out, scrap, discard, bin. OPPOSITES: accept, approve.

2 (v) *How could you reject your best friend?* disown, turn your back on, spurn, abandon, cast aside, forsake, drop (informal), dump (informal), ditch (slang).

3 (v) *Don't reject my offer.* See **refuse** 1.

rejoice

(v) *The whole school will rejoice if we win.* be happy, be pleased, be glad, be delighted, be jubilant, be overjoyed, jump for joy, celebrate, triumph, exult. OPPOSITES: mourn, grieve.

related

(adj) *The two crimes seem to be related.* connected, linked, interconnected, associated, similar, comparable, parallel.

relation

(n) *Aunt Bertha is a close relation.* relative, member of the family, family member, blood relative, relative by marriage.

relax

1 (v) *Relax your grip.* loosen, slacken, ease, weaken, unclench, lessen, reduce, release. OPPOSITE: tighten.

2 (v) *You can relax after the exams.* unwind, take it easy, rest, ease up, put your feet up, laze about, chill out (slang), hang loose (informal), let your hair down, lighten up (slang).

relaxed

1 (adj) Bianca has a relaxed attitude to her work. easy-going, laid-back (informal), casual, free and easy, leisurely, nonchalant, blasé, unconcerned, slack.
OPPOSITES: uptight (informal), serious.
2 (adj) We had a relaxed lunch. leisurely, unhurried, restful, informal, laid-back (informal), cosy, comfortable.
OPPOSITES: formal, tense.

relaxing

(adj) We spent a relaxing day on the beach. restful, peaceful, quiet, leisurely, unhurried, lazy, languid, soothing.
OPPOSITE: stressful.

release

1 (v) Let's campaign to release the hostages. free, set free, liberate, deliver, emancipate, let go, let out, turn loose.
OPPOSITE: imprison.
2 (v) The judge decided to release Burglar Beryl. free, let go, let off, spare, excuse, acquit, discharge, pardon, absolve.
OPPOSITE: detain.
3 (v) The police will release a description of the criminal. issue, put out, publish, broadcast, circulate, distribute, make public, make known, reveal, disclose.
OPPOSITES: withhold, suppress.
4 (n) Listen to this new release. recording, record, disc, tape, CD, single, album, EP (extended play), 12-inch, remix, rerelease.

relevant

(adj) Is that remark relevant to the discussion? related, pertinent, connected, linked, applicable, essential, significant.
OPPOSITES: irrelevant, beside the point.

reliable

1 (adj) Lateefah is a reliable friend. dependable, trustworthy, trusty, staunch, faithful, loyal, devoted, unfailing, constant, steady, true, responsible, honest.
OPPOSITES: unreliable, fickle.
2 (adj) Is your information reliable? dependable, well-founded, sound, tried and tested, trustworthy, credible, true.
OPPOSITES: unreliable, dodgy (informal).

relieve

1 (v) This ointment will relieve the pain. ease, alleviate, soothe, lessen, reduce, deaden, dull, numb, blunt.
OPPOSITES: increase, intensify.
2 (v) A substitute will relieve you at half-time. take over from, replace, stand in for, take your place, give you a break.

religion

(n) What is your religion? faith, belief, creed, denomination, sect.

religious

1 (adj) Religious books. theological, devotional, spiritual, sacred, holy, divine.
OPPOSITE: secular.
2 (adj) A religious woman. pious, devout, God-fearing, godly, churchgoing.

reluctant see **unwilling**.

rely on see **depend on** 1, 2.
remain see **stay** 1, 4.
remains

1 (plural n) What shall we do with the remains of this meal? leftovers (plural), scraps (plural), remnants (plural), crumbs (plural), dregs (plural) (drink), rest, residue.
2 (plural n) Experts sifted through the remains. rubble, debris, wreckage, ruins (plural), ashes (plural), bones (plural).

remark see **comment** 1, 2.
remarkable

(adj) What a remarkable painting! amazing, astonishing, incredible, extraordinary, astounding, surprising, startling, striking, distinctive, unusual, strange, outstanding, exceptional.
OPPOSITES: ordinary, unremarkable.

remember

1 (v) Can you remember my name? think of, recall, recollect, call to mind, place.
OPPOSITE: forget.
2 (v) It took me ages to remember my lines. See **learn** 2.
3 (v) Granny likes to remember her youth. reminisce about, think about, think back on, look back on, hark back to, recall, recollect, talk about, be nostalgic about.
OPPOSITE: forget about.

remind

1 (v) I'll remind you when it's time to go. prompt, jog your memory, refresh your memory, give you a reminder, prod.
2 **remind you of** (v) This song will remind you of our holiday. make you think of, bring back memories of, take you back to, awaken memories of, put you in mind of.

remote

(adj) Pirate Peg landed on a remote island. faraway, far-off, distant, far-flung, outlying, out-of-the-way, isolated, lonely, inaccessible, secluded, godforsaken.
OPPOSITES: accessible, nearby.

remove

1 (v) Please do not remove these books. take, take away, take out, carry away, move, shift, dislodge, withdraw, borrow, throw out, steal.
2 (v) This liquid will remove stains. get rid of, eradicate, eliminate, dislodge, shift, move, budge, erase, wipe out, root out.
3 (v) Remove your hat. See **take off** 1.

repair

1 (v) Can you repair my radio? fix, mend, put right, restore to working order, patch up, sort out, overhaul, rebuild, recondition.
2 (v) I must repair my jeans. See **mend** 2.

repay see **pay back** 1, 2.
repeat

1 (v) Don't repeat this story to anyone! tell, pass on, quote, relate, recount, reiterate, retell, restate, recite.
2 (v) Listen to the violins repeat the tune. echo, reiterate, re-echo, restate, replay, play back, copy, duplicate, reproduce.

replace

1 (v) Please replace the knives and forks. put back, put away, return.
2 (v) You must replace those worn tyres. change, renew, exchange, swap, switch.
3 (v) Who will replace Jodie on the team? take the place of, stand in for, substitute for, deputize for, cover for, take over from, succeed, follow, supplant, supersede.

reply see **answer** 1, 2, 3.
report

1 (n) Have you read this report? account, description, statement, write-up, article, news story, piece, message, communiqué, communication, note, summary, narrative.
2 (v) The committee will report their findings. present, state, announce, declare, publish, make public, communicate, outline, document, detail, give an account of, put in writing, broadcast, circulate.
3 (v) I'm going to report you to the head. complain about, denounce, tell on (informal), inform on, blow the whistle on (informal), shop (slang), snitch on (slang).

reporter

(n) journalist, correspondent, hack, newshound (informal), writer, investigator, commentator, broadcaster, feature writer, columnist, member of the press.

represent

1 (v) What do the letters "PC" represent? See **stand for**.
2 (v) Rose will represent our class on the school council. speak for, act on behalf of, be the voice of, be the spokesperson for.

repulsive see **disgusting** 1.
reputation

(n) This rumour could damage Famous Fred's reputation. name, good name, character, honour, respectability, standing, status, position, prestige, fame, renown.

request

1 (n) The police issued a request for information. appeal, call, plea, demand.
2 (v) The genie will do anything you request. See **ask** 4.

require

1 (v) This project will require a lot of work. See **need** 1.
2 (v) I expect Dad will require an apology. See **demand** 1.

rescue

1 (v) Don't panic; I'll rescue you! save, save your life, help, come to your rescue, free, release, set you free, get you out, deliver you from danger, liberate.
2 (v) Pirate Peg managed to rescue her map from the wreck. recover, retrieve, salvage, save, extricate, fish out.
3 (n) We watched the rescue on television. rescue operation, rescue attempt, air-sea rescue, recovery, salvage operation, relief operation.
4 (n) Please come to my rescue. aid, help, assistance.

rescue words

rescue situations

avalanche	climbing	road accident
boating	accident	shipwreck
accident	earthquake	train crash
bomb	fire	underground
explosion	flood	collapse
caving	hurricane	volcanic
accident	plane crash	eruption

rescuers

air ambulance	helicopter
crew	pilot
ambulance	lifeboat crew
crew	lifeguard
cave rescue	mountain
team	rescue
coastguard	team
diver	paramedic
doctor	police officer
firefighter	winchman

rescuers may...

airlift casualties	maintain radio
cut through	contact
wreckage	reassure
dig out	victims
survivors	respond to
enter a	a Mayday
burning	signal
building	risk their
give mouth-	lives
to-mouth	sift through
resuscitation	rubble
launch a	winch up
lifeboat	survivors

rescuers may use...

breathing	loud-hailer
apparatus	medical kit
climbing	protective
equipment	clothing
cutting	radar
equipment	ropes
heat-seeking	searchlight
camera	sniffer dog
life belt	two-way
life jacket	radio

survivors may suffer from...

broken bones	frostbite
burns	heatstroke
concussion	hypothermia
cuts and bruises	(low body
dehydration	temperature)
(lack of water)	shock
exposure	spinal injuries

survivors may be...

bleeding	marooned
choking	overcome
critically ill	by fumes
cut off by	panicky
the tide	shivering
dazed	stranded
delirious	struggling
disorientated	for breath
drowning	suffocating
exhausted	terrified
injured	trapped
level-headed	unconscious

Labels: pilot, cockpit, rescue helicopter, rotor blade, rescue winch, winch operator, tail rotor, viewing window, searchlight, lifeline, stretcher, winchman, undercarriage, tail plane

---

research
1 *(n) I need to do some research for my project.* reading, background reading, groundwork, fact-finding, investigation, study, experiments *(plural),* tests *(plural).*
2 *(v) I've decided to research my family history. See* **investigate**.

resent
1 *(v) Aunt Bertha will resent not being invited.* feel bitter about, feel aggrieved at, be offended at, take offence at, take umbrage at, bear a grudge about, have hard feelings about, take exception to.
2 *(v) Try not to resent your sister's success.* begrudge, feel bitter about, envy, be jealous of, feel aggrieved at.

resentful *see* **bitter** 2.

reserve
1 *(v) Please reserve a room. See* **book** 3.
2 *(n) Who will be the reserve?* substitute, replacement, stand-in *(informal),* deputy.

resign
1 *(v) If you don't like your job, why don't you resign?* leave, hand in your notice, give notice, quit, stand down, step down *(informal),* give up, pack it in *(informal).*

2 **resign yourself to** *(phrase) Revising is dull, but you'll have to resign yourself to it.* reconcile yourself to, accept, come to terms with, put up with *(informal),* grin and bear *(informal),* make the best of.

resigned
(adj) How can Dad be so resigned about losing his job? accepting, philosophical, stoical, patient, long-suffering, calm, reasonable, unresisting, passive, defeatist.

resist
1 *(v) How can you resist eating that cake?* prevent yourself from, keep from, avoid, refrain from, abstain from, stop.
2 *(v) I can't resist your offer. See* **refuse** 1.
3 *(v) We will resist any attempt to close our school. See* **fight** 4.

respect
1 *(n) You should have more respect for people's feelings.* consideration, concern, regard, deference, appreciation, reverence. OPPOSITES: contempt, disdain.
2 *(v) People respect Mr Badger.* think highly of, think well of, have a high opinion of, admire, look up to, revere. OPPOSITES: look down on, scorn.

respectable
1 *(adj) Mr Badger is a respectable citizen.* respected, upstanding, decent, law-abiding, upright, honest, well-regarded. OPPOSITE: disreputable.
2 *(adj) Put on your dressing gown; you're not respectable! See* **decent** 1.

respond
1 *(v) Didn't Ed respond when you tickled him?* react, retaliate, hit back, reciprocate.
2 *(v) I heard Kate respond. See* **answer** 2.
3 **respond to** *(v) I must respond to this letter. See* **answer** 1.

response *see* **answer** 3.

responsible
1 *(adj) We need a responsible babysitter.* reliable, dependable, trustworthy, sensible, level-headed, conscientious, mature. OPPOSITES: irresponsible, unreliable.
2 *(adj) What a mess! Who is responsible?* guilty, to blame, at fault, culpable.
3 **be responsible for** *(phrase) Who will be responsible for the team's actions?* take responsibility for, be in charge of, take control of, be accountable for, be answerable for, take the blame for.

rest

rest
1 (n) Granny is having a rest. See **sleep** 3.
2 (n) You deserve a rest after your hard work. break, breather (informal), holiday, vacation, time off, leave, breathing space.
3 (n) What shall I do with the rest? remainder, surplus, excess, balance, residue, remains (plural), remnants (plural), leftovers (plural) (food), others (plural).
4 (v) You should rest for a while. take a break, have a rest, take a breather (informal), relax, take it easy, sit down, lie down, put your feet up, take a nap, have forty winks (informal).
5 (v) Rest your bike against the wall. lean, prop, support, stand, balance, steady.

restaurant
(n) TYPES OF RESTAURANT: bistro, brasserie, burger bar, café, cafeteria, canteen, carvery, diner, grill, pizzeria, snack bar, steakhouse, takeaway.

restful see **relaxing**.

restless
1 (adj) Before the show, all the cast were restless. unsettled, agitated, fidgety, jittery (informal), excitable, impatient, edgy, nervous, on edge, jumpy, anxious, fretful.
OPPOSITES: calm, composed.
2 (adj) I had a restless night. sleepless, wakeful, disturbed, unsettled, troubled.
OPPOSITES: peaceful, undisturbed.

restrict see **limit** 3.

result
1 (n) The meeting had an unexpected result. outcome, consequence, effect, upshot, aftermath, sequel, legacy, end product, repercussion, side effect, spin-off.
2 (v) If the two countries can't agree, war may result. follow, ensue, develop, come about, take place, happen, occur, arise.
3 result in (v) These talks could result in a solution. lead to, bring about, give rise to, produce, create, culminate in, end in, finish in, conclude in, terminate in.

retreat
(v) The soldiers were forced to retreat. withdraw, draw back, back off, back away, pull back, pull out, give ground, flee, take flight, turn tail, bolt, retire, depart.
OPPOSITE: advance.

retrieve
(v) I tried to retrieve my lost suitcase. get back, reclaim, recover, track down, find, salvage, rescue, regain, recapture.

return
1 (v) Dad said he would return after tea. come back, be back, get back, go back, reappear, come home.
2 (v) If you return the same way you may find your keys. go back, walk back, retrace your steps, double back, backtrack, retreat.
3 (v) I asked Shelley to return my pen. give back, put back, replace, send back.
4 (n) I couldn't wait for Dad's return. homecoming, reappearance, arrival.

reveal
1 (v) Does this skirt reveal too much leg? expose, show, display, bare, uncover.
OPPOSITES: cover up, conceal.
2 (v) Will Melissa reveal her true feelings? give away, betray, let out, let slip, disclose, divulge, declare, make known, make public, broadcast, display, lay bare, unveil.
OPPOSITES: hide, conceal.

revenge
1 (n) We think the attack was an act of revenge. vengeance, retaliation, reprisal, retribution, vindictiveness, tit for tat.
2 take revenge for (phrase) You must take revenge for this injustice. avenge, wreak your revenge for, get your own back for (informal), even the score for, repay, retaliate against, hit back at.

reverse
1 (v) You'll have to reverse up the drive. back, go backwards, drive backwards, go into reverse, back away, retreat, backtrack.
2 (v) The head won't reverse her decision. overturn, go back on, revoke, change, alter, undo, overrule, retract, repeal.
3 (n) The instructions are on the reverse. other side, back, rear, opposite side, flip side, underside, underneath.

review
1 (n) Write a review of this book. criticism, critique, appreciation, evaluation, assessment, appraisal, report, write-up.
2 (v) Will you review the school play for our magazine? give your opinion of, comment on, discuss, write a critique of, evaluate, assess, appraise, criticize.

revise
(v) I must revise these facts before the test. go over, run through, memorize, learn, swot up on (informal), mug up on (slang), reread, study.

revive
1 (v) Doctors tried to revive the patient. resuscitate, bring back to life, breathe life into, save, bring round, rouse, awaken.
2 (v) The patient began to revive. come round, regain consciousness, rally, recover.

revolt
1 (n) An armed revolt. See **revolution** 1.
2 (v) The citizens will revolt. See **rebel** 1.

revolting see **disgusting** 1.

revolution
1 (n) Troops were brought in to crush the revolution. uprising, rebellion, revolt, coup, coup d'état, mutiny, riot, insurrection, insurgency, armed struggle, civil war.
2 (n) Computers have caused a revolution in the way we work. complete change, radical change, transformation, sea change, turnaround, shift, upheaval.

revolve
1 (v) Watch the cogs revolve. See **turn** 1.
2 revolve around (v) Satellites revolve around the earth. circle, orbit, travel round, spin round, rotate around.

reward
1 (n) Do we get a reward for effort? prize, payment, remuneration, recompense, bonus, tip, compensation, award.
OPPOSITES: penalty, punishment.
2 (v) The leader will reward you if you succeed. repay, pay, compensate, make it worth your while, recompense, honour.
OPPOSITES: penalize, punish.

rhythm
(n) Listen to the rhythm of the music. beat, pulse, throbbing, pounding, tempo, phrasing, pattern, lilt, swing, syncopation.

rich
1 (adj) Lord Lucre is rich. wealthy, well-off, affluent, prosperous, well-to-do, well-heeled (informal), made of money (informal), stinking rich (informal), loaded (slang), rolling in it (slang).
OPPOSITE: poor.
2 (adj) The walls were hung with rich tapestries. costly, expensive, valuable, priceless, sumptuous, luxurious, opulent, lavish, ornate, elaborate, fine, exquisite, magnificent, splendid, gorgeous.
OPPOSITES: worthless, shabby.
3 (adj) Red is a rich colour. strong, deep, warm, vibrant, vivid, bright, intense.
OPPOSITES: pale, insipid.
4 (adj) This sauce is too rich for me. heavy, fatty, creamy, spicy, highly flavoured, indigestible, full-bodied (wine).
OPPOSITES: light, bland.

rickety
(adj) A rickety bridge. broken-down, wobbly, tumbledown, ramshackle, flimsy, unstable, unsafe, weak, decrepit.
OPPOSITES: strong, stable.

riddle see **puzzle** 1.

ride
1 (v) Rod's moped is hard to ride. control, handle, manage, steer, pedal, drive.
2 (v) I love to ride on the bus. travel, go, take a trip on, journey, sit, stand.
3 (n) Come for a ride in our new car! See **drive** 4.

ridiculous
(adj) The idea of a flying pig is ridiculous. absurd, ludicrous, crazy, mad, incredible, preposterous, outrageous, unbelievable, laughable, farcical, comical, hilarious, daft (informal), foolish, silly, nonsensical, zany.
OPPOSITE: sensible.

right
1 (adj) Is this the right answer? correct, proper, true, exact, precise, perfect, most accurate, valid, spot-on (informal).
OPPOSITES: wrong, incorrect.
2 (adj) I try to do what's right. just, fair, honourable, good, honest, decent, ethical, moral, proper, legal, above board.
OPPOSITES: wrong, immoral.
3 (adj) Is this outfit right for a funeral? suitable, appropriate, fitting, fit, proper, seemly, sensible.
OPPOSITES: inappropriate, unsuitable.

4 *(n) Do you have the right to do that?* authority, power, entitlement, prerogative, privilege, permission, authorization, justification, licence, freedom, liberty.

rigid
1 *(adj) Rigid plastic. See* **stiff** 1.
2 *(adj) Rigid rules. See* **strict** 2.

ring
1 *(n) Make a paper ring.* circle, disc, hoop, loop, band, cordon.
2 *(n) The police are investigating a drugs ring.* circle, gang, group, organization, band, syndicate, cartel, cell, mob.
3 *(v) Listen to the bells ring.* chime, peal, toll, tinkle, jingle, jangle, clang, ding, ping, sound, resound, reverberate, fill the air.
4 *(v) Please ring me tonight. See* **phone** 1.

riot
1 *(n) This news may cause a riot.* uprising, revolt, breach of the peace, insurrection, rebellion, upheaval, disturbance, street fight, brawl, scuffle, free-for-all *(informal)*, violence, unrest, fighting, uproar, anarchy.
2 *(v) The people will riot when they hear the news.* run riot, rise up, take to the streets, revolt, rebel, take the law into their own hands, run amok, go on the rampage.

rip *see* **tear** 1, 2, 4.

ripe
(adj) Wait until the fruit is ripe. matured, mellow, ready to eat, fully developed, seasoned, perfect, fully grown.

rise
1 *(v) Watch the plane rise into the air.* lift, climb, ascend, soar, go up, fly up, shoot up, rocket, mount, spiral, take off.
OPPOSITES: fall, descend.
2 *(v) House prices may rise.* increase, go up, climb, escalate, spiral, soar, shoot up, rocket, surge, jump, leap, grow.
OPPOSITES: fall, drop.
3 *(v) Can you see the mountain rise above us?* tower, loom, soar, rear up, stand out.
4 *(v) The path began to rise.* get steeper, climb, incline, go uphill, slope upwards.
OPPOSITE: fall.
5 *(n) I predict a rise in prices.* jump, increase, leap, surge, escalation, upturn.
OPPOSITES: drop, fall.

risk
1 *(n) There's a risk of snow. See* **chance** 2.
2 *(n) Dodgy Dave took a risk.* gamble, chance, leap in the dark, speculation.
3 *(n) There's some risk involved in motor racing.* danger, hazard, peril, uncertainty.
4 *(v) Don't risk all your money on a bet.* gamble, hazard, chance, speculate with.
5 *(v) Would you risk your life to save me?* endanger, put at risk, put in jeopardy, imperil, jeopardize, gamble with.

risky
(adj) Skating on thin ice is risky. dangerous, hazardous, fraught with danger, perilous, unsafe, precarious, dicey *(informal)*, chancy *(informal)*, dodgy *(informal)*, iffy *(informal)*.
OPPOSITE: safe.

river
(n) stream, brook, creek, rivulet, tributary, waterway, torrent.

along a river you might see...
estuary (river mouth)
ford (crossing)
gorge (deep river valley)
island
lock
meander (loop)
pool
rapids (fast-moving water)
reeds
river bank
river bed
rushes
stepping stones
towpath
waterfall
weeds
weir

rivers may be...
choked up
clean
contaminated
crystal clear
dark
deep
fast-flowing
foaming
frothing
glassy
glittering
icy
muddy
polluted
shallow
shimmering
silted up
silvery
slow-moving
sluggish
sparkling
turbulent
wide

rivers may...
babble
bubble
burble
cascade
eddy
flood
flow
glide
gurgle
gush
meander
murmur
plunge
race
ripple
roar
rush
snake
splash
stream
surge
sweep
swirl
thunder
trickle
tumble
twist
wind

river activities
angling
canoeing
cruising
fishing
paddling
punting
rowing
sailing
swimming
wading
white-water rafting

river source

tributary (river joining larger river)

rapids

waterfall

gorge

pool

meander (loop)

island

flood plain

estuary (river mouth)

road
(n) Which road do we take? route, way, direction, course.
TYPES OF ROAD: alley, avenue, backstreet, boulevard, bypass, close, crescent, cul-de-sac, drive, dual carriageway, high street, highway, lane, main road, minor road, motorway, one-way street, ring road, side street, single-track road, street, track.

roar
1 *(v) The giant began to roar.* bellow, thunder, shout, yell, bawl, howl, shriek.
2 *(v) Listen to the thunder roar.* boom, rumble, roll, growl, crash, thunder.

rob
1 *(v) Someone tried to rob the post office.* burgle, break into, hold up, raid, loot, steal from, ransack, ram raid *(informal)*.
2 *(v) Don't let anyone rob you.* steal from, pick your pocket, mug *(informal)*, swindle, con *(informal)*, defraud, cheat, diddle *(informal)*, rip you off *(slang)*.

robber
(n) thief, burglar, pickpocket, shoplifter, housebreaker, looter, mugger *(informal)*, bandit, brigand, highwayman, pirate.

robbery
1 *(n) Beryl was found guilty of robbery.* burglary, theft, stealing, housebreaking, ram raiding *(informal)*, shoplifting, pilfering, swindling, fraud, embezzlement.

2 *(n) There's been a robbery in town.* burglary, break-in, smash-and-grab *(informal)*, hold-up, raid, heist *(slang)*, stick-up *(slang)*, ram raid *(informal)*.

robot
(n) android, automaton, machine.

rock
1 *(n) Crispin sat on a rock.* boulder, stone, crag, rocky outcrop.
2 *(v) The waves made the boat rock.* sway, roll, toss, pitch, lurch, wobble, swing.

rocky
(adj) We scrambled over the rocky ground. stony, boulder-strewn, pebbly, rough, hard, rugged, craggy, jagged, barren.

rod
(n) A wooden rod. stick, pole, switch, cane, birch, wand, baton, staff, crook, bar.

roll
1 *(v) Look at the coin roll across the floor.* trundle, travel, spin, wheel, twirl, whirl.
2 *(v) Let's roll in the snow!* tumble, somersault, go head over heels.
3 *(v) The wheels roll smoothly. See* **turn** 1.
4 *(v) Roll your hair around your fingers.* curl, coil, wind, wrap, twist, entwine, bind.
5 *(v) Use a rolling pin to roll the dough.* roll out, flatten, smooth, even out, level, spread out, press down.
6 *(n) I need another roll of paper.* spool, reel, cylinder, drum, scroll, tube, bobbin.

Roman life

Roman life

Roman gods and goddesses

Apollo (god of the sun, music and healing)
Diana (goddess of hunting and the moon)
Juno (goddess of women and childbirth)
Jupiter (king of the gods)
Mars (god of war)

Mercury (messenger of the gods)
Minerva (goddess of wisdom and war)
Neptune (god of the sea)
Venus (goddess of love and beauty)

Mercury

Neptune

Venus

some Roman people

architect
astrologer
centurion (army officer)
citizen (man with the right to vote)
consul (senior government official)
emperor
engineer
farmer
freed man (former slave)

gladiator
lawyer
legionary (foot soldier)
merchant
paedagogus (slave who supervised a child's education)
patrician (nobleman or noblewoman)
plebeian (commoner)

Roman emperor Nero

poet
politician
priest
scribe
senator (statesman)
slave
teacher

Roman town house
(cutaway)

tiled roof

mosaic

atrium (central room)

mosaic floor

impluvium (pool for catching rainwater)

kitchen

triclinium (dining room)

tablinum (study)

shrine of the household gods

peristylium (walled garden)

Roman clothes and jewellery

tunic
belt
slave
hairpin

fibula (cloak pin)
tunic
belt
cloak
sandal
farmer

tunic
toga (robe made from one length of cloth)
senator
gold chain
palla (wrap)
stola (robe)
sandal
patrician

gold earring
garnet ring
cameo
ivory hairpins
snake bracelets

Roman town

amphitheatre (sports arena)
apartment block
aqueduct (bridge for carrying water)
arch

basilica (public building used as law court)
circus (racetrack)
curia (town hall)
domus (town house)
forum (main square)

fountain
gate
inn
library
market stall
monument
public baths
shops
temple
theatre
town wall
viaduct (bridge)
villa (country house)

gate
temple
public baths
apartment block
town wall
amphitheatre

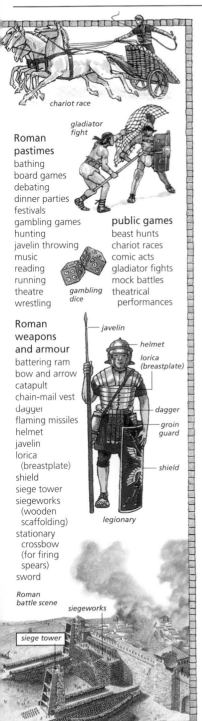

chariot race

gladiator fight

Roman pastimes

bathing
board games
debating
dinner parties
festivals
gambling games
hunting
javelin throwing
music
reading
running
theatre
wrestling

gambling dice

public games

beast hunts
chariot races
comic acts
gladiator fights
mock battles
theatrical performances

Roman weapons and armour

battering ram
bow and arrow
catapult
chain-mail vest
dagger
flaming missiles
helmet
javelin
lorica
  (breastplate)
shield
siege tower
siegeworks
  (wooden
  scaffolding)
stationary
crossbow
(for firing
spears)
sword

javelin

helmet

lorica (breastplate)

dagger

groin guard

shield

legionary

Roman battle scene

siegeworks

siege tower

romantic

1 *(adj) Romantic films make me cry.* sentimental, lovey-dovey, emotional, heart-warming, soppy *(informal)*, slushy *(informal)*, schmaltzy, mushy *(informal)*.
2 *(adj) Ed held Eve in a romantic embrace.* loving, tender, fond, amorous, passionate.
3 *(adj) Daisy is hopelessly romantic.* dreamy, starry-eyed, unrealistic, idealistic, optimistic, impractical.
OPPOSITES: down-to-earth, realistic.
4 *(adj) Paris is a romantic city.* colourful, fascinating, glamorous, exciting, exotic, charming, picturesque, idyllic, inspiring.
OPPOSITES: unromantic, banal.

room

1 *(n) I need more room. See* **space** 2.
2 *(n) A secret room.* chamber.
TYPES OF ROOM: attic, ballroom, basement, bathroom, bedroom, boudoir *(old-fashioned)*, breakfast room, cellar, cloakroom, conservatory, den, dining room, drawing room, dressing room, gallery, games room, guest room, hall, kitchen, landing, larder, lavatory, library, living room, loft, loo *(informal)*, lounge, music room, nursery, office, pantry, parlour, playroom, scullery *(old-fashioned)*, sitting room, spare room, store room, studio, study, toilet, utility room, WC (water closet). ❖ *Also see* **building**.

rope

(n) Pull the rope tight. cord, cable, line, string, twine, guy rope, lasso.

rot

1 *(v) These tomatoes will rot if we don't eat them soon.* go bad, go mouldy, spoil, deteriorate, go off *(informal)*, decay, perish, decompose, fester, putrefy.
2 *(v) The wallpaper had started to rot.* fall apart, disintegrate, crumble, perish, decay.
3 *(v) Sweets can rot your teeth.* eat away, eat into, decay, erode, corrode *(metal)*.

rotten

1 *(adj) These tomatoes are rotten.* bad, mouldy, spoiled, off, sour *(milk)*, putrid, festering, foul, fetid, decomposing.
OPPOSITE: fresh.
2 *(adj) Be careful! The floorboards are rotten.* decayed, decaying, crumbling, disintegrating, unsound, corroded *(metal)*.
OPPOSITE: sound.
3 *(adj) (informal) I feel rotten.* ill, unwell, sick, off colour, ghastly, rough *(informal)*, under the weather *(informal)*, poorly *(informal)*, grotty *(slang)*, lousy *(slang)*.
OPPOSITE: well.
4 *(adj) (informal) That was a rotten trick! See* **mean** 6.
5 *(adj) (informal) This is a rotten piece of homework. See* **poor** 2.

rough

1 *(adj) The cave walls felt rough.* uneven, bumpy, irregular, jagged, craggy, pitted, ridged, lumpy, rugged, rocky, stony.
OPPOSITE: smooth.

2 *(adj) The sea is rough today.* choppy, stormy, turbulent, tempestuous, wild.
OPPOSITES: calm, smooth.
3 *(adj) Granddad's skin feels rough.* scratchy, bristly, unshaven, leathery, callused, chapped, wrinkled.
OPPOSITES: smooth, soft.
4 *(adj) My dog has a rough coat.* coarse, bristly, wiry, fuzzy, shaggy, tangled.
OPPOSITES: smooth, silky.
5 *(adj) Peg has a rough voice. See* **gruff** 1.
6 *(adj) Cynthia hates rough games.* rowdy, boisterous, violent, tough, unruly, wild.
OPPOSITES: gentle, quiet.
7 *(adj) Nat made a rough drawing.* basic, quick, sketchy, crude, clumsy, rough-and-ready, hasty, incomplete, unfinished.
OPPOSITES: detailed, precise.
8 *(adj) I only have a rough idea of what to do. See* **vague** 2.

round

1 *(adj) I saw a round object in the sky.* circular, spherical, ball-shaped, balloon-like, curved, globular, bulbous, cylindrical.
2 *(adj) Augustus has a round face.* rounded, full, chubby, plump, podgy, fat, fleshy, moon-shaped, babyish.
3 *(n) I got to the last round of the contest.* stage, phase, level, heat, game, lap.

routine

1 *(n) My normal routine was disrupted.* procedure, schedule, pattern, programme, system, practice, custom, habit.
2 *(adj) This is just a routine checkup.* normal, ordinary, standard, typical, regular, everyday, usual, customary, conventional.
OPPOSITES: unusual, special.

row

1 *(v) I hate it when we row. See* **argue** 1.
2 *(n) Anita and Alice are having a row. See* **argument** 1.
3 *(n) What's that awful row? See* **noise** 2.
4 *(n) Look at that long row of cars.* line, queue, string, column, file, chain.
5 *(v) Let's row down the river.* paddle, scull, canoe, punt, boat.

rowdy

(adj) A rowdy class. unruly, noisy, boisterous, loud, riotous, obstreperous, disorderly, rough, loutish, wild.
OPPOSITES: quiet, subdued.

rub

1 *(v) Rub the lamp until it gleams.* polish, buff up, scrub, clean, shine, burnish, scour.
2 *(v) I knew the label would rub my neck.* chafe, irritate, scratch, scrape, graze.
3 *(v) Shall I rub suntan lotion on to your back?* smear, smooth, massage, spread, stroke, apply, work in.

rubbish

1 *(n) Put the rubbish in the bin.* litter, waste, refuse, garbage, trash, junk *(informal)*, scraps *(plural)*, leftovers *(plural)*, dregs *(plural)*, debris.
2 *(n) Don't talk rubbish! See* **nonsense** 1.

rub out *see* **erase**.

rude

rude
1 *(adj) That was a rude remark.* insolent, impertinent, cheeky, impudent, impolite, insulting, offensive, abusive, discourteous, disrespectful, inconsiderate, tactless.
OPPOSITES: polite, civil.
2 *(adj) Bozo told a rude joke.* dirty, smutty, crude, coarse, vulgar, filthy, indecent, obscene, blue, lewd, suggestive, risqué, naughty, saucy, tasteless, offensive.
OPPOSITES: clean, decent.

rugged
(adj) A rugged coastline. rocky, craggy, jagged, rough, stony, irregular, uneven.

ruin
1 *(v) This haircut could ruin my image.* wreck, destroy, shatter, spoil, damage, play havoc with, harm, mar, undermine, screw up *(informal)*, blow *(slang)*.
2 *(v) Earthquakes can ruin whole cities.* See **destroy** 1.
3 *(v) If your business fails, it could ruin you.* bankrupt, break, destroy, crush, make you a pauper, impoverish, bring you down.
4 *(n) This mistake could lead to ruin.* disaster, defeat, failure, collapse, breakdown, destruction, devastation, bankruptcy, insolvency, destitution.

ruined
(adj) The ruined castle looked ghostly in the moonlight. crumbling, derelict, dilapidated, ramshackle, tumbledown.

ruins
(plural n) Rescuers searched the ruins. rubble, wreckage, debris, remains *(plural)*.

rule
1 *(n) You must obey this rule.* regulation, ruling, guideline, directive, order, commandment, law, decree, statute.
2 *(v) Who will rule the country?* See **govern**.

rumble
1 *(v) I felt the ground rumble under my feet.* thunder, reverberate, boom, roar, murmur, groan, shake.
2 *(v) My tummy began to rumble.* gurgle, grumble, growl, murmur.

rumour
(n) Have you heard the rumour about Famous Fred? gossip, talk, word, news, story, buzz, hearsay, scandal, dirt *(slang)*.

run
1 *(v) You'll have to run to catch the bus.* race, sprint, jog, dash, hurry, rush, hotfoot it, leg it *(informal)*, get a move on *(informal)*, tear along, speed along, charge along, hare along *(informal)*, career along, scoot, scurry, scamper, gallop.
2 *(v) Does this car run on unleaded petrol?* go, work, function, operate, perform.
3 *(v) Water began to run down the walls.* trickle, dribble, drip, pour, flow, stream, cascade, course, spill, gush, spout.
4 *(v) These skis run smoothly over the snow.* glide, skim, slide, move, go.

5 *(v) I hope to run a music shop one day.* See **manage** 2.
6 *(v) I hope the colours don't run.* bleed, mix, spread, wash out.
7 *(n) Let's go for a run around the park.* jog, sprint, race, trot, gallop, marathon.

run after see **chase**.

run away
(v) Run away or you'll get caught! run off, take off *(informal)*, make a run for it, take to your heels, bolt, escape, flee, scram *(informal)*, scarper *(slang)*, beat it *(slang)*, do a runner *(slang)*, do a bunk *(slang)*.

runny
1 *(adj) This paint is too runny.* thin, watery, liquid, fluid, diluted, flowing.
OPPOSITES: thick, solid.
2 *(adj) I've got a runny nose.* streaming.

run out
1 *(v) When does your season ticket run out?* expire, lapse, finish, end, terminate.
2 *(v) Our supplies will soon run out.* be finished, be used up, dry up, be exhausted, give out, peter out.

run over
(v) Watch out or that bus will run you over. knock you down, run you down, knock you over, hit, bump into.

rush
1 *(v) We must rush or we'll be late.* See **hurry** 1.
2 *(v) You can't rush such an important decision.* See **hurry** 2.
3 *(n) It was a rush to get there on time.* race, scramble, struggle, mad dash.
4 *(n) Take your time; there's no rush.* hurry, urgency, pressure.

rustle
(v) The wind made the leaves rustle. swish, whisper, crackle, crinkle.

ruthless
(adj) The king was ruthless in his revenge. merciless, pitiless, heartless, remorseless, relentless, without pity, cruel, hardhearted, callous, unfeeling, unrelenting, implacable, inhuman, ferocious.
OPPOSITES: merciful, compassionate.

Ss

sack *(informal)* see **dismiss** 1.

sad
1 *(adj) Leah felt sad.* unhappy, miserable, depressed, down, blue, low, glum, gloomy, down in the dumps *(informal)*, dejected, melancholy, mournful, sorrowful, forlorn, wistful, despondent, upset, tearful, heartbroken, brokenhearted, grief-stricken, sick at heart, wretched, despairing.
OPPOSITES: happy, cheerful.

2 *(adj) This film has a sad ending.* unhappy, poignant, tear-jerking *(informal)*, heartbreaking, heart-rending, touching, moving, tragic, depressing, sombre, dark.
OPPOSITE: happy.
3 *(adj) I have some sad news for you.* bad, serious, grave, unfortunate, upsetting, painful, regrettable, distressing, tragic, heartbreaking, grim, harrowing.
OPPOSITES: happy, good.
4 *(adj) (slang) Dad made a sad attempt to be trendy.* See **pathetic** 2.

sadden
(v) It will sadden you to hear this tragic news. upset, grieve, distress, break your heart, pain, dismay, make you cry, bring tears to your eyes, make your heart bleed.
OPPOSITES: cheer, comfort.

sadness see **sorrow**.

safe
1 *(adj) All the explorers are safe.* unharmed, unhurt, uninjured, unscathed, safe and sound, alive and well, in one piece *(informal)*, out of danger, all right.
OPPOSITES: hurt, injured.
2 *(adj) The villagers were safe inside the castle.* secure, protected, out of harm's way, sheltered, defended, shielded, guarded, invulnerable, unassailable, out of danger, free from harm.
OPPOSITES: in danger, at risk.
3 *(adj) Mum is a safe driver.* careful, prudent, sensible, responsible, reliable, dependable, cautious, unadventurous.
OPPOSITES: dangerous, reckless.
4 *(adj) This snake is quite safe.* harmless, docile, tame, nonpoisonous, innocuous.
OPPOSITE: dangerous.
5 *(adj) Is the tap water safe?* pure, uncontaminated, unpolluted, drinkable, nontoxic, wholesome, edible *(food)*.
OPPOSITES: unsafe, harmful.
6 *(n) Put your valuables in the safe.* safe-deposit box, cash box, deposit box, strongbox, coffer, strongroom, vault.

sag
(v) My bed is starting to sag in the middle. sink, slump, droop, dip, cave in, give way, subside, hang down, drop, fall.

sail
1 *(v) Pirate Peg is ready to sail.* set sail, put to sea, leave port, weigh anchor, hoist sail, get under way, embark.
2 *(v) Did you sail to France?* go by boat, cruise, go by sea, steam, ride the waves, voyage.
3 *(v) Watch the balloon sail through the air.* See **glide** 1.

same
1 *(adj) That's the same tune I heard before.* selfsame, very same, very, identical.
OPPOSITE: different.
2 **the same** *(adj) Our hats are the same.* identical, alike, matching, like peas in a pod *(informal)*, indistinguishable.
OPPOSITES: different, dissimilar.

3 the same *(adj) These two experiments should give the same results.* identical, matching, corresponding, equivalent, parallel, comparable, similar.
OPPOSITES: different, dissimilar.
4 the same *(adj) At the North Pole, the weather is always the same.* unchanging, unvarying, consistent, constant, uniform.
OPPOSITES: variable, changeable.

sarcastic
(adj) Sarcastic comments. cutting, scathing, caustic, biting, withering, acerbic, sharp-tongued, disparaging, contemptuous, scornful, mocking, sneering, taunting, jeering, sarky *(informal)*, ironic, sardonic.

satisfactory *see* all right 3.

satisfied
1 *(adj) After his enormous tea, Augustus felt satisfied. See* **full** 3.
2 *(adj) Once she's won the prize, Lucy will feel satisfied.* content, contented, pleased, gratified, happy, glad, at ease, self-satisfied, complacent, smug, like the cat that swallowed the cream *(informal)*.
OPPOSITES: dissatisfied, discontented.

savage
1 *(adj) Savage animals.* wild, ferocious, fierce, vicious, untamed, undomesticated.
OPPOSITES: tame, gentle.
2 *(adj) A savage attack.* brutal, vicious, ferocious, violent, bloody, bloodthirsty, barbaric, murderous, sadistic, cruel, callous, cold-blooded, merciless, pitiless, ruthless, inhuman, diabolical, bestial.

save
1 *(v) Don't panic; I'm coming to save you! See* **rescue** 1.
2 *(v) Try to save your money.* hold on to, hang on to, be sparing with, be thrifty with, be frugal with, economize, set aside, put aside, put away, stash away *(informal)*, keep for a rainy day, hoard, accumulate, amass, bank, deposit, invest.
OPPOSITES: squander, waste.
3 *(v) Let's campaign to save the whales.* protect, preserve, conserve, safeguard, defend, guard, keep safe, look after.
OPPOSITES: endanger, imperil.

say
1 *(v) Sam couldn't say what was bothering her.* put into words, articulate, express, communicate, give voice to, convey, put across, mention, tell, relate, reveal, disclose, divulge, come out with.
2 *(v) Say your lines out loud.* recite, repeat, speak, deliver, perform, rehearse, declaim, read.
3 *(v) What does the recipe say?* specify, state, indicate.
4 *(v) I would say it's about four o'clock. See* **think** 2.
5 *(v) People say Dodgy Dave is a crook.* claim, allege, suggest, put about, report.
6 *(n) Do I have any say in this decision?* input, voice, share, part, vote, influence, clout, sway, weight.

say words

"I'm leaving home," Ziggy...
announced
declared
exclaimed
proclaimed
pronounced
stated

I'm leaving home.
Ziggy declared

"It's a lovely day," Kamal...
commented
mentioned
noted
observed
pointed out
reflected
remarked

"I'm innocent," Melissa...
affirmed
asserted
claimed
emphasized
insisted
maintained
professed
protested
stressed

"I broke the window," Sam...
acknowledged
admitted
blurted out
confessed
confirmed
disclosed
divulged
revealed

"What are you doing?" Poppy...
asked
demanded
inquired
queried
questioned

"It's none of your business," Ben...
answered
rejoined
replied
responded
retorted

What are you doing?
Poppy inquired

It's none of your business!

Ben retorted

"I'm bored," Josh...
complained
drawled
groaned
grumbled
moaned
sighed
wailed
whined
whinged

Please may I go to the party?

I'm bored.

"I can't find my kitten," Shama...
babbled
cried
gabbled
gasped
gulped
sobbed
spluttered
stammered
stuttered
whimpered

"I'm sorry," Matt...
mumbled
murmured
muttered
whispered

"You look funny in that hat," Jemima...
chortled
chuckled
giggled
laughed
sneered
sniggered
tittered

Lopa pleaded

whined

"Please may I go to the party?" Lopa...
begged
beseeched
entreated
implored
pleaded
wheedled

"Keep out of my room!" Edwin...
barked
bawled
bellowed
commanded
growled
ordered
roared
screamed
shouted
shrieked
snapped
snarled
yelled

KEEP OUT

Keep out of my room!

KEEP OUT

snarled

You look funny in that hat.

chuckled

scalding *see* hot 2.

scamper
1 *(v) Watch the mouse scamper across the floor.* scurry, scuttle, scoot, scramble, dart, dash, run, sprint, race, beetle *(informal)*.
2 scamper about *(v) My rabbit loves to scamper about in the grass.* run about, romp, frisk, frolic, gambol, cavort.

scan
1 *(v) Scan the front page. See* **look at** 2.
2 *(v) Beryl stopped to scan the street for police.* survey, search, scrutinize, scour, inspect, take stock of, check out *(informal)*, recce *(informal)*, look up and down.

scandal
1 *(n) Don't believe the scandal you read in the papers.* gossip, rumours *(plural)*, dirt *(slang)*, tittle-tattle, libel *(written)*, slander *(spoken)*, muckraking, smear campaign.
2 *(n) It's a scandal that so many people are homeless.* disgrace, outrage, crime, sin, shame, crying shame.

scandalous
1 *(adj) Dodgy Dave's behaviour is scandalous. See* **disgraceful** 1.
2 *(adj) Who started that scandalous rumour?* slanderous *(spoken)*, libellous *(written)*, scurrilous, malicious, untrue.

scarce

scarce
(adj) Bananas were scarce during the war.
in short supply, few and far between,
seldom seen, hard to find, thin on the
ground, rare, uncommon.
OPPOSITES: plentiful, common.

scarcely *see* **hardly**.

scare
1 *(v) This film will scare you.* frighten,
scare you out of your wits, scare you stiff,
terrify, horrify, petrify, make your hair
stand on end, send shivers down your
spine, make your blood run cold, make
your flesh creep, unnerve, alarm, startle.
2 *(v) Don't let Bozo scare you.* intimidate,
frighten, terrorize, bully, threaten, menace,
put the wind up *(informal)*, cow, daunt.
3 *(n) The news gave me a real scare.*
fright, shock, panic, start, jolt.
4 *(n) The shops are closed because of a
bomb scare.* alert, alarm, hoax.

scared
1 *(adj) Weren't you scared when the lights
went out?* afraid, frightened, terrified,
petrified, scared stiff, scared out of your
wits, panic-stricken, terror-stricken,
panicky, apprehensive, alarmed, anxious,
fearful, startled, horrified, horrorstruck.
2 **be scared of** *(phrase) There's no need
to be scared of spiders.* be afraid of, be
frightened of, fear, have a phobia about,
have a horror of, dread, shudder at,
tremble at, live in fear of, shake in your
shoes, be in a blue funk *(informal)*.

scarred
(adj) A scarred face. disfigured, blemished,
marked, pockmarked, pitted.

scary *(informal) see* **frightening**.

scatter
1 *(v) Don't scatter your magazines over
the floor.* strew, spread, throw, fling, toss,
drop, shower, sprinkle, distribute.
2 *(v) The crowd began to scatter.* break
up, disperse, disband, separate, dissolve.

scatterbrained
*(adj) Don't rely on Kylie; she's much too
scatterbrained!* absent-minded, forgetful,
muddleheaded, disorganized, vague, scatty
(informal), featherbrained, bird-brained
(informal), empty-headed, giddy, dizzy,
flighty, unreliable, not with it *(informal)*.

scene
1 *(n) We admired the scene. See* **view** 1.
2 *(n) Let's investigate the scene of the
crime.* site, location, setting, place, area,
spot, position, whereabouts, locality,
locale, neighbourhood, region.
3 *(n) In this scene the hero dies.* act,
episode, sequence, shot, clip, take.
4 *(n) The curtain rose on a stunning scene.*
set, stage, setting, tableau, backdrop.

scenery
1 *(n) Isn't the scenery beautiful!*
landscape, countryside, surroundings
(plural), terrain, view, vista, panorama.

2 *(n) Natalie designed the scenery for our
school play.* set, stage set, staging, setting,
backdrop, backcloth, décor.

scent
1 *(n) Don't these roses have a wonderful
scent!* perfume, fragrance, smell, bouquet,
aroma *(food, drink)*.
2 *(n) Do you like my new scent?* perfume,
fragrance, eau de Cologne, cologne, body
spray, toilet water, aftershave.

schedule
(n) Try to keep to the schedule. plan,
programme, timetable, agenda, itinerary.

scheme
1 *(n) The government announced a
scheme to cut crime. See* **plan** 1.
2 *(n) Dodgy Dave has a new scheme to
make money.* plan, idea, stratagem, ploy,
plot, ruse, intrigue, dodge, manoeuvre,
subterfuge, conspiracy, racket *(informal)*.
3 *(v) Let's scheme to get our revenge. See*
plot 3.

school
(n) college, academy.
TYPES OF SCHOOL: boarding school,
co-ed (coeducational school),
comprehensive school, day school,
grammar school, grant-maintained school,
high school, independent school, infant
school, junior school, kindergarten, middle
school, mixed school, nursery school, prep
school (preparatory school), primary
school, private school, public school,
secondary school, selective school, single-
sex school, sixth-form college, state school,
technology college.

scold *see* **tell off**.

scorch
(v) Don't scorch the paintwork! burn,
singe, char, blacken, blister, sear, roast.

scorching *see* **hot** 1.

score
1 *(n) What was the score at half-time?*
tally, result, number of points, total, mark.
2 *(v) We need to score ten points.* win,
earn, gain, achieve, make, total, chalk up
(informal), notch up *(informal)*, amass.
3 *(v) Don't score your name in the desk!
See* **cut** 5.

scorn
1 *(v) Don't scorn my efforts at sewing.*
sneer at, scoff at, jeer at, look down on,
despise, be contemptuous of, turn up your
nose at *(informal)*, mock, deride.
OPPOSITES: admire, respect.
2 *(n) Hilda viewed my painting with scorn.*
contempt, derision, disdain, disgust,
mockery, ridicule, sarcasm.
OPPOSITES: admiration, respect.

scornful
*(adj) Maddy gave her brother a scornful
look.* disdainful, contemptuous, scathing,
withering, condescending, supercilious,
sneering, derisive, sarcastic, mocking.
OPPOSITES: admiring, respectful.

scowl
(v) Mum will scowl at you if you snigger.
frown, grimace, glower, glare, look
daggers, give you a dirty look.

scramble
1 *(v) Can you scramble up this cliff?*
clamber, scrabble, climb, crawl, struggle,
swarm, scale, scurry.
2 *(v) Watch the fans scramble for a seat.*
jostle, scrabble, fight, scuffle, struggle,
jockey, battle, vie, rush, dash, scurry.

scrap
1 *(n) Pick up that last scrap.* piece, bit,
fragment, crumb, morsel, speck, grain,
snippet, sliver, remnant, mouthful, drop.
2 *(n) (informal) The boys had a scrap in
the playground. See* **fight** 6.
3 *(v) Don't scrap that paper! See* **throw
away** 1.
4 *(v) Let's scrap the match. See* **cancel**.

scrape
1 *(v) How did you scrape your knee?*
graze, scratch, skin, scuff.
2 *(v) Scrape the food off the floor.* scoop,
shovel, scrub, scour, clean.
3 *(v) Can you hear my fingernails scrape
against the blackboard?* grate, scratch,
rasp, squeak, grind, screech.

scraps
(plural n) Leave the scraps for the birds.
leftovers *(plural)*, remains *(plural)*, leavings
(plural), pickings *(plural)*, scrapings *(plural)*,
crumbs *(plural)*, remnants *(plural)*.

scratch
1 *(v) Don't scratch the table.* score, mark,
scrape, cut, gouge, claw at, damage.
2 *(n) I have a scratch on my leg.* cut,
graze, scrape, gash, nick, abrasion, mark.

scrawl *see* **scribble** 1, 2.

scrawny *see* **thin** 1.

scream
*(v) I'll scream if you put that spider down
my neck.* shriek, screech, squeal, squawk,
cry out, yell, howl, yelp, yowl, wail, holler
(informal), bawl, bellow, shout.

scribble
1 *(v) I just had time to scribble a message.*
scrawl, dash off, jot down, write, pen.
2 *(v) Don't scribble on the walls!* doodle,
scrawl, write, draw, write graffiti.

scrounge
*(v) (informal) Let's scrounge some money
off Dad.* cadge, sponge, beg for, wheedle.

scrub
*(v) We'll have to scrub the floor to get the
dirt off.* scour, wash, clean, rub, swab.

scruffy
1 *(adj) Barney always looks scruffy.*
dishevelled, unkempt, untidy, messy,
down-at-heel, bedraggled, shabby.
OPPOSITES: smart, neat.
2 *(adj) I like wearing scruffy jeans.* tatty,
shabby, worn, tattered, ragged, holey,
sloppy, grungy *(slang)*.
OPPOSITE: smart.

3 *(adj) Ziggy lives in a scruffy part of town.* shabby, tatty, run-down, dilapidated, seedy, disreputable, squalid, dirty, dingy, grotty *(slang)*, rough.
OPPOSITE: smart.

scrumptious *(informal) see* **delicious**.

scuffle *see* **fight** 2, 6.

sea
1 *(n) Pirate Peg sailed across the sea.* ocean, waves *(plural)*, high seas *(plural)*, briny *(informal)*, deep, drink *(informal)*.
2 *(adj) An octopus is a sea creature.* saltwater, aquatic, marine.

seal
1 *(v) Seal the bottle.* stop up, plug, cork, make airtight, make waterproof, bung.
2 *(v) The police decided to seal the room.* close up, shut up, lock, secure, seal off, close off, board up, wall up, cordon off.

search
1 *(v) Rescuers had to search the wreckage.* hunt through, look through, comb, scour, sift through, rummage through, rifle through, examine, scrutinize, investigate, go over with a fine-tooth comb, turn upside down, turn inside out, ransack.

2 *(v) The police began to search for clues.* look, hunt, poke about, nose about, ferret around, scout around, cast around, look high and low, seek, probe, pry, leave no stone unturned.
3 *(n) Hundreds of people joined in the search.* hunt, pursuit, quest, investigation, inquiry, exploration, chase.

seaside
(n) We spent our holiday at the seaside. beach, coast, shore, seashore, sands *(plural)*, seaside resort, coastal resort.
❖ *Also see* **seaside words**.

sea and seashore

sea words

breaker	spume (foam)
crest (top	surf
of wave)	swell
current	tidal wave
high tide	white horses
low tide	(waves with
spray	white crests)

the sea may be...

aquamarine	rough
billowing	sapphire blue
calm	shimmering
choppy	silvery
crystal clear	sparkling
emerald	stormy
green	tempestuous
glassy	tranquil
grey	turbulent
heaving	turquoise
raging	wild

raging sea

the waves may...

billow	plash	spill
break	plunge	splash
churn	pound	surge
crash	race	swirl
curl	ripple	swish
foam	roar	thunder
froth	roll	tumble
lap	rush	wash

stack   *rock arch*

shore words

bay	inlet
beach	mud flat
boulder	pebble
cave	rock arch
cliff	rock pool
coast	sand dune
cove	seaweed
(small bay)	shell
driftwood	shingle
estuary	spit (ridge of
(place	sand jutting
where river	into sea)
meets sea)	stack
headland	(rock pillar)

the cliffs may be...

bare	precipitous
chalky	rocky
craggy	rugged
crumbling	sheer
dramatic	spectacular
jagged	towering
jutting	treacherous
overhanging	vertical

the beach may be...

crowded	remote
deserted	sandy
exposed	secluded
golden	sheltered
idyllic	shelving
inaccessible	(sloping)
isolated	shingly
jam-packed	stony
lonely	sun-
muddy	drenched
pebbly	unspoilt
polluted	windswept

sea birds

albatross	penguin
auk	petrel
booby	puffin
cormorant	razorbill
fulmar	shag
gannet	skua
guillemot	tern
gull	
kittiwake	
pelican	

booby

puffin

octopus

squid

whale

shark

sea creatures

dolphin	shark
eel	squid
octopus	stingray
porpoise	turtle
sea horse	whale
seal	
sea lion	
sea otter	
sea snake	

seashore wildlife

barnacle	sandhopper
clam	(sand flea)
coral	sea anemone
crab	sea snail
cuttlefish	sea urchin
jellyfish	shrimp
limpet	sponge
lobster	starfish
mussel	whelk
oyster	worm
prawn	

sea urchin

jellyfish

coral reef

Also see **seaside words**.

seaside

seaside words

at a seaside resort
amusement arcade
aquarium
boating lake
campsite
caravan park
disco
fairy lights
funfair
guesthouse
harbour
hotel
ice cream kiosk
jetty
marina
nightclub
pier
promenade
souvenir shop

on the beach
beach ball
beach café
beach hut
breakwater
bucket and spade
deckchair
parasol
Punch and Judy show
sandcastle
sun-lounger
volleyball net
windbreak

seaside food
candyfloss
fish and chips
ice cream
ice lolly *(informal)*
seafood
seaside rock
shellfish

a resort may be...
bustling
busy
buzzing
crowded
elegant
fashionable
jumping *(slang)*
lively
noisy
packed
peaceful
picturesque
quiet
shabby
sleepy
smart
tacky *(informal)*
tatty
touristy *(informal)*
up-market

mask
snorkel

seaside activities
beachcombing
boat trips
collecting shells
donkey rides
exploring caves
fishing trips
jet skiing
paddling
parasailing
sailing
sandsailing
scuba diving
shrimping
snorkelling
sunbathing
surfing
swimming
volleyball
water-skiing
windsurfing

candy floss

Also see **sea & seashore**.

---

seat
(n) Find yourself a seat. chair, stool, bench, place. Also see **chair**, **sofa**.

second
1 (adj) I asked for a second helping of pudding. extra, additional, further, other.
2 (n) The butterfly was gone in a second. See **moment** 1.

secret
1 (adj) This information must remain secret. hidden, concealed, under wraps, unpublished, undisclosed, private, confidential, restricted, classified, off the record, hush-hush (informal).
OPPOSITES: public, well-known.
2 (adj) Agent Arthur was sent on a secret mission. undercover, covert, cloak-and-dagger, underground, clandestine, hush-hush (informal), furtive, surreptitious.
OPPOSITES: open, well-known.
3 (adj) The treasure chamber had a secret entrance. concealed, hidden, camouflaged, disguised, invisible.
OPPOSITES: obvious, visible.
4 (adj) Can you read this secret message? cryptic, encoded, mysterious, hidden.
OPPOSITE: straightforward.
5 (n) Don't tell Mum - it's a secret! private matter, confidential matter, confidence.
6 (n) What is the secret of eternal youth? formula, recipe, key, solution, answer.

section
1 (n) Have a section of my pear. See **bit** 2.
2 (n) What section of the company do you work in? See **part** 3.
3 (n) Read the next section for homework. bit, part, passage, paragraph, chapter, unit, module, page, instalment.

secure
1 (adj) I feel secure at my new school. safe, confident, at ease, unworried, relaxed, comfortable, reassured.
OPPOSITES: insecure, uneasy.
2 (adj) Is that ladder secure? firm, steady, stable, fixed, immovable, safe, strong.
OPPOSITES: unsafe, precarious.
3 (adj) Make sure the windows are secure. fastened, locked, shut, closed, barred.
4 (adj) The villagers were secure inside the castle. See **safe** 2.
5 (v) Secure your bike to the railings. See **fasten** 1.

see
1 (v) Did you see the comet? catch sight of, catch a glimpse of, spot, notice, glimpse, make out, identify, observe, sight, note, spy, witness, clap eyes on (informal).
2 (v) It was hard to see what Alice meant. understand, grasp, follow, take in, make out, know, make sense of, comprehend, get the drift of, get the hang of (informal), catch on to (informal), get, twig (informal).

3 (v) Mrs Badger wants to see my parents. talk to, speak to, meet, consult, confer with, interview, visit.
4 (v) Can you see when the film starts? find out, have a look, ask, discover, ascertain, determine, investigate.
5 (v) See that Tommy doesn't hurt himself. make sure, mind, see to it, take care, make certain, ensure.
6 (v) "Can I go to the disco?" "I'll see." think about it, give it some thought, think it over, consider it, mull it over.
7 (v) I'll see you to your car. show, walk, accompany, escort, lead, usher.
8 (v) I can't quite see you as a film star. picture, imagine, visualize, envisage.
9 (v) I see problems ahead. foresee, envisage, anticipate, predict, foretell.

seem
(v) Do I seem sad? appear, look, strike you as, give the impression of being, sound.

see-through see **transparent**.

see to
(v) Can you see to the baby? attend to, check up on, look after, take care of, be responsible for, manage, take charge of.

seize
1 (v) I felt someone seize me by the arm. See **grab** 1.
2 (v) Customs officials were quick to seize the drugs. See **confiscate**.

seldom see **rarely**.

select see **choose** 1.

selection
1 (n) This shop stocks a wide selection of CDs. See **choice** 2.
2 (n) This book contains a selection of poems. collection, anthology, miscellany, choice, variety, range, medley, potpourri.

self-centred see **selfish**.

self-confident see **confident** 1.

self-conscious
(adj) Zoë feels self-conscious when she has to sing in public. awkward, embarrassed, uncomfortable, ill at ease, shy, diffident, nervous, insecure, bashful, mortified.

self-control
(n) It took great self-control not to shout at my brother. self-discipline, self-restraint, restraint, willpower, strength of mind, patience, composure, coolness, calmness.

selfish
(adj) Nev is so selfish; he never thinks of others. self-centred, egocentric, egotistical, self-absorbed, demanding, greedy, mean.
OPPOSITES: unselfish, generous.

self-satisfied see **smug**.

sell
1 (v) We're planning to sell our house. put up for sale, put on the market, auction off.
OPPOSITE: buy.
2 (v) Dodgy Dave is trying to sell stolen goods. sell off, dispose of, peddle, hawk, tout, exchange, deal in, traffic in, handle.

3 (v) Does this shop sell balloons? stock, keep (informal), supply, carry, trade in, deal in, offer for sale, retail.
4 (v) Famous Fred is keen to sell his new single. See **promote** 2.

send
1 (v) Don't forget to send your card to Granny. See **post** 4.
2 (v) Can you send this message for me? convey, relay, forward, transmit, dispatch, radio, fax, e-mail, broadcast.
3 (v) Will your parents send you to boarding school? pack you off, ship you off, farm you out, dispatch, consign.

send for see **summon**.

sensational
1 (adj) A sensational newspaper article. dramatic, melodramatic, lurid, shocking, scandalous, electrifying, startling, staggering, spectacular, astounding, horrifying, alarmist, shock-horror.
2 (adj) (informal) A sensational party. See **fantastic** 3.

sense
1 (n) I had a sense that something was wrong. feeling, impression, hunch, sensation, awareness, instinct, intuition, premonition, presentiment.
2 (n) I can't work out the sense of this poem. See **meaning** 2.
3 (n) Adrian has no sense. common sense, brains (plural) (informal), wit, judgment, understanding, intelligence, nous (slang).
4 (v) Didn't you sense that Mrs Badger was annoyed? feel, get the impression, get the feeling, have a hunch, suspect, notice, pick up, perceive, observe, realize.

sensible
1 (adj) A sensible girl. level-headed, down-to-earth, practical, matter-of-fact, serious-minded, thoughtful, mature, steady.
OPPOSITES: silly, foolish.
2 (adj) A sensible choice. wise, prudent, intelligent, logical, rational, reasonable, sound, realistic, shrewd, well-thought-out.
OPPOSITES: foolish, stupid.
3 (adj) Sensible shoes. practical, comfortable, functional, suitable, hard-wearing, serviceable.
OPPOSITES: impractical, unsuitable.

sensitive
1 (adj) Don't tease Mary; she's very sensitive. thin-skinned, touchy, easily upset, oversensitive, hypersensitive.
OPPOSITES: thick-skinned, tough.
2 (adj) My skin is sensitive. easily irritated, delicate, soft, tender, painful, sore, raw.
OPPOSITE: tough.
3 (adj) Karen will notice if you're unhappy; she's very sensitive. perceptive, discerning, receptive, responsive, impressionable.
OPPOSITES: obtuse, insensitive.
4 (adj) Try to deal with this situation in a sensitive way. discreet, diplomatic, tactful, sympathetic, thoughtful, understanding.
OPPOSITES: insensitive, heavy-handed.

5 (adj) This is a sensitive issue. delicate, difficult, awkward, controversial, contentious, problematic, thorny, ticklish.

sentimental
1 (adj) Old love songs make Granny feel sentimental. emotional, nostalgic, tearful, weepy (informal), dewy-eyed, maudlin, softhearted, tenderhearted, warm.
2 (adj) I hate sentimental poetry. romantic, lovey-dovey, mawkish, soppy (informal), slushy (informal), corny (slang), mushy (informal), schmaltzy, sugary, syrupy, weepy (informal), tear-jerking (informal).

separate
1 (v) The police tried to separate the fighting fans. split up, break up, part, disentangle, divide, come between, keep apart, segregate, isolate, scatter, disperse.
2 (v) Be careful! The pieces could separate in your hands. come apart, fall apart, break apart, come away, detach, split, divide, disconnect, disintegrate, scatter.
3 (v) I'm sorry that you and Jason have decided to separate. split up, break up, part, part company, go your separate ways, live apart, divorce.
4 (v) At the big tree, the two paths separate. See **divide** 1.
5 (adj) The two schools are quite separate. unconnected, unrelated, distinct, different, independent, autonomous, detached.

series
(n) A series of disasters. sequence, string, chain, run, row, succession, train, procession, progression, set, cycle.

serious
1 (adj) Edwin is a serious boy. solemn, earnest, sober, grave, pensive, thoughtful, sedate, staid, humourless, sombre.
OPPOSITES: frivolous, cheerful.
2 (adj) We had a serious discussion. earnest, grave, weighty, heavy, deep, profound, sincere, important, significant.
OPPOSITES: frivolous, trivial.
3 (adj) Pollution is a serious problem. grave, major, urgent, pressing, acute, critical, far-reaching, worrying, alarming.
OPPOSITES: minor, insignificant.
4 (adj) Aunt Bertha has a serious illness. major, severe, grave, critical, dangerous, acute, incapacitating, crippling, incurable, inoperable, fatal, terminal, malignant.
OPPOSITES: mild, minor.
5 (adj) A serious accident occurred. major, catastrophic, calamitous, tragic, fatal.
OPPOSITE: minor.
6 (adj) You must be serious if you want to learn ballet. committed, determined, in earnest, sincere, resolved, resolute, dedicated, single-minded, unwavering, conscientious, hard-working, diligent.
OPPOSITES: half-hearted, casual.

servant
(n) attendant, helper, assistant, help, hired help, retainer, hireling, domestic, dogsbody (informal), skivvy, drudge, slave.

serve
1 (v) The genie will serve the owner of the lamp. work for, obey, assist, help, be of use to, wait on, attend to, minister to.
2 (v) Shall I serve tea? put out, set out, dish up, give out, hand round, pass round.
3 (v) Do you serve refreshments? supply, provide, offer, sell, lay on.

service
(n) We all joined in the service. ceremony, act of worship, worship, prayers (plural), celebration, assembly, meeting.

serving see **helping**.

set
1 (v) Set the dish on the table. See **put** 1.
2 (v) Let's set a date. See **fix** 2.
3 (v) Please set the table for tea. lay, spread, prepare, arrange, make ready.
OPPOSITE: clear.
4 (v) Wait for the jelly to set. jell, harden, solidify, thicken, stiffen, take shape, congeal, crystallize, cake, coagulate.
5 (v) The sun began to set. go down, sink, drop below the horizon, disappear, vanish.
OPPOSITE: rise.
6 (v) Can you set the video timer? adjust, regulate, fix, programme, synchronize.
7 (adj) We have our meals at set times. fixed, established, agreed, definite, appointed, arranged, scheduled, regular.
OPPOSITES: flexible, varying.
8 (adj) Aunt Bertha has set views. fixed, definite, hard and fast, inflexible, unbending, firm, strict, entrenched, deep-seated, hidebound, narrow-minded.
OPPOSITES: flexible, open-minded.
9 (adj) The story is set in India. located, supposed to take place, situated, placed.
10 (n) I'm collecting the whole set. series, range, collection, group, batch, class, kit.
11 (n) Tanya designed the set for our play. See **scenery** 2.
12 (n) Which set are you in for English? See **class**.

setback
(n) Don't let this setback discourage you. hitch, difficulty, problem, snag, hiccup (informal), complication, obstacle, disappointment, misfortune, blow, relapse.

set fire to see **light** 1.

set free see **release** 1.

set off
1 (v) It's time to set off. See **leave** 1.
2 (v) Don't set off the fireworks. let off, detonate, light, ignite, trigger off, explode.

set out
1 (v) It's time to set out. See **leave** 1.
2 (v) Set out your work neatly. lay out, present, arrange, organize, display, exhibit.
3 (v) I didn't set out to cheat. See **mean** 3.

setting
(n) Paris is the ideal setting for a romantic weekend. place, location, situation, venue, backdrop, scene, background, environment, surroundings (plural).

settle

settle
1 (v) Do you plan to settle in Australia? stay, set up home, make your home, put down roots, take up residence, become established, move to, emigrate to, live.
2 (v) The moth may settle on your hand. come to rest, stop, rest, stay, land, alight.
3 (v) We need to settle this dispute. sort out, resolve, clear up, put an end to, end, patch up, decide, deal with.
4 (v) Wait for the dust to settle. die down, subside, sink, clear.
5 settle on (v) Let's settle on a date. See **agree** 2.

settle down
1 (v) Settle down and get on with your work. calm down, quieten down, be quiet.
2 (v) Settle down and enjoy the film. sit down, relax, make yourself comfortable, snuggle down, curl up.

set up see **start** 5.

severe
1 (adj) Aunt Bertha always looks so severe. See **stern** 1.
2 (adj) Jamie is recovering from a severe illness. See **serious** 4.
3 (adj) We should expect severe weather conditions. bad, extreme, harsh, rough, violent, fierce, drastic, dangerous, freezing. OPPOSITES: mild, moderate.

sew
1 (v) Can you teach me how to sew? stitch, tack, embroider, do needlework, make clothes, do dressmaking.
2 sew up (v) I need to sew up this hole in my shirt. See **mend** 2.

sex
1 (n) What sex is your kitten? gender.
2 (n) Should children be taught about sex at school? the facts of life (plural), sexual intercourse, sexuality, reproduction.
3 have sex see **make love**.

sexy
1 (adj) (informal) Sam is really sexy. desirable, sexually attractive, seductive, sultry, sensuous, voluptuous (female), shapely, kissable, fit (slang).
2 (adj) (informal) Mum thinks my dress is too sexy. slinky, seductive, titillating, provocative, revealing.
3 (adj) (informal) This song has very sexy lyrics. suggestive, raunchy (slang), erotic, risqué, pornographic, obscene.

shabby
1 (adj) Your jeans are looking shabby. worn, faded, threadbare, tatty, scruffy, worn-out, frayed, ragged, tattered. OPPOSITES: smart, new.
2 (adj) Ziggy lives in a shabby part of town. See **scruffy** 3.

shade
1 (n) Those trees will provide some shade. shadow, shelter, protection, coolness.
2 (n) That shade of green suits you. colour, tone, hue, tint, tinge.

shadow
1 (n) Emma sat in the shadow of a tree. See **shade** 1.
2 (n) I saw a shadow on the wall. shape, silhouette, outline, figure, image.
3 shadows (plural n) I saw a figure lurking in the shadows. dark, darkness, gloom, dimness, blackness, dusk, semi-darkness.
4 (v) The detectives decided to shadow Burglar Beryl. See **follow** 1.

shadowy see **dim** 2.

shady
1 (adj) We walked through a shady wood. shadowy, shaded, dim, dark, cool, leafy, sunless, gloomy, sun-dappled. OPPOSITES: sunny, sunlit.
2 (adj) (informal) Dodgy Dave is a shady character. See **suspicious** 2.

shaggy
(adj) Shaggy hair. bushy, thick, tousled, tangled, unkempt, untidy, rough, woolly.

shake
1 (v) The earthquake made the buildings shake. vibrate, quake, shudder, judder (informal), tremble, totter, sway, wobble, quiver, shiver, jiggle, joggle, convulse.
2 (v) Shake the mixture. shake up, stir up, churn up, agitate, swirl, jiggle, joggle.
3 (v) Don't shake that stick at me. brandish, flourish, wave, waggle, jiggle.

shaky
1 (adj) Don't stand on that shaky chair. wobbly, rickety, unsteady, rocky, flimsy, unsafe, unstable, tottery, teetering, weak. OPPOSITES: steady, firm.
2 (adj) I answered the questions in a shaky voice. faltering, tremulous, trembling, quavering, quivery, quivering, unsteady, wavering, wobbly, weak, nervous. OPPOSITES: steady, firm.
3 (adj) I felt shaky when I got up this morning. See **dizzy**.

shallow
(adj) Mrs Badger said my essay was too shallow. superficial, trivial, empty, flimsy, slight, lightweight, insubstantial, glib, frivolous, facile, unconvincing, skin-deep. OPPOSITES: thoughtful, thorough.

shame
1 (n) Casper was filled with shame for what he had done. remorse, self-reproach, guilt, guilty conscience, disgust, self-loathing, mortification, chagrin. OPPOSITE: pride.
2 (n) I can't bear the shame of losing. humiliation, disgrace, ignominy, degradation, indignity, embarrassment, dishonour, scandal, stigma, stain, infamy. OPPOSITES: honour, glory.
3 (n) It's a shame that Dad is so strict. pity, crying shame, hard luck, disgrace, outrage, scandal, tragedy, sin.
4 (v) Your mum would never shame you in public. See **humiliate**.

shameful see **humiliating**.

shape
1 (n) TYPES OF SHAPE: circle, cone, cube, cylinder, diamond, hexagon, oblong, octagon, oval, parallelogram, pentagon, prism, pyramid, rectangle, rhombus, sphere, square, trapezium, triangle.
2 (n) Can you recognize the shape of France on a map? outline, form, contours (plural), profile, silhouette, lines (plural).
3 (n) The enchanter took on the shape of a serpent. form, guise, likeness, look, semblance, aspect.
4 (n) I try to keep in good shape. See **condition** 1.
5 (v) Can you shape a hippo out of clay? See **model** 5.

shapeless
1 (adj) A shapeless cloud. nebulous, formless, vague, undefined, unformed, ill-defined, amorphous, indeterminate.
2 (adj) A shapeless dress. loose, baggy, sack-like, sloppy, unfitted, ill-fitting.

share
1 (n) We all had a share of the profits. portion, part, fraction, proportion, percentage, quota, ration, cut (informal), helping, whack (informal), piece, slice.
2 (v) Share the sweets between you. share out, divide, split, distribute, deal out, dole out, allocate, apportion, measure out, go halves, go fifty-fifty (informal).

sharp
1 (adj) Don't cut yourself on that sharp knife. razor-sharp, pointed, keen-edged, serrated, sharpened, jagged, barbed. OPPOSITE: blunt.
2 (adj) The rocks are sharp. See **jagged** 2.
3 (adj) I felt a sharp pain. piercing, stabbing, shooting, violent, excruciating, agonizing, intense, severe, acute. OPPOSITE: dull.
4 (adj) Aunt Bertha gave a sharp reply. cutting, stinging, caustic, scathing, sarcastic, barbed, curt, tart, acid, acerbic. OPPOSITE: gentle.
5 (adj) Lemons taste sharp. See **sour** 1.
6 (adj) We came to a sharp bend. tight, sudden, abrupt, unexpected, hairpin. OPPOSITES: gentle, gradual.
7 (adj) In front of us was a sharp drop. See **steep** 1.
8 (adj) Try to get a sharp picture on the TV. See **clear** 5.

shatter see **smash** 2.

shattered
1 (adj) Kim was shattered by the news. devastated, stunned, dazed, crushed, heartbroken, destroyed, upset, shocked.
2 (adj) (informal) I was shattered after the race. See **exhausted**.

shed
(n) garden shed, tool shed, potting shed, woodshed, hut, shack, shelter, outhouse.

sheer
1 (adj) That goal was sheer magic! See **absolute**.

2 *(adj) In front of us was a sheer drop.*
See **steep** 1.
3 *(adj) The bride wore a veil of sheer silk.*
See **fine** 5.

sheet
1 *(n) Start each question on a new sheet.*
piece of paper, page, side, leaf, folio.
2 *(n) A metal sheet covered the window.*
panel, plate, piece, slab, pane *(glass).*
3 *(n) A sheet of snow covered the ground.*
See **layer** 1.

shelf
(n) Put the clock on that shelf. ledge,
mantelpiece, windowsill, bracket.

shell
(n) Some seeds are protected by a hard
shell. casing, covering, case, pod, husk,
exterior, outside, outer layer.

shelter
1 *(v) The trees will shelter us from the*
rain. protect, shield, screen, provide cover
for, provide protection for, provide refuge
for, safeguard.
2 *(v) Where can we shelter from the*
storm? take cover, take shelter, take
refuge, seek refuge, seek protection.
3 *(n) The refugees looked for shelter.*
cover, protection, refuge, safety, asylum,
sanctuary, safe haven.

sheltered
1 *(adj) Our garden is sheltered because of*
the trees. protected, shielded, shaded,
screened, secluded, snug, windless.
OPPOSITES: exposed, open.
2 *(adj) Mary had a sheltered childhood.*
quiet, protected, cloistered,
unadventurous, unexciting, secluded,
isolated, reclusive.

shield *see* **protect** 1, 3.

shift
1 *(v) Shift your things into the spare room.*
See **move** 2.
2 *(v) You'll need hot water to shift that*
stain. See **remove** 2.

shimmer *see* **shine** 2.

shine
1 *(v) Light bulbs are supposed to shine.*
give out light, shed light, emit light, be
bright, be luminous.
2 *(v) I saw something shine in the sky.*
gleam, glow, shimmer, glimmer, twinkle,
sparkle, glint, glitter, glisten, blaze, flash,
flicker, beam, glare.
3 *(v) Jo manages to shine at everything*
she does. excel, do well, stand out, be
brilliant, be expert, show talent, star.
4 *(n) Look at the shine on that table!*
polish, sheen, gloss, gleam, sparkle, lustre,
finish, patina.

shining
(adj) I saw a shining light in the sky. bright,
brilliant, dazzling, blazing, radiant,
luminous, glowing, beaming, gleaming,
shimmering, sparkling, glittering,
glistening, glaring, fluorescent.

shiny
1 *(adj) A shiny golden goblet.* gleaming,
shining, sparkling, glistening, glittering,
dazzling, bright, polished, burnished.
OPPOSITES: dull, matt.
2 *(adj) Shiny hair.* glossy, shining,
gleaming, sleek, lustrous, silky, satiny.
OPPOSITE: dull.

ship *see* **boat**.

shiver
(v) Ghost stories make me shiver. shudder,
shake, tremble, quiver, quake.

shock
1 *(v) This news may shock you.* stun,
stagger, startle, take your breath away,
amaze, astonish, astound, surprise, alarm,
dismay, shake, shake you up *(informal),*
shatter, devastate, disturb, distress,
traumatize, perturb, daze, numb, stupefy.
2 *(v) Rude jokes shock Aunt Bertha.*
horrify, disgust, offend, scandalize, appal,
outrage, revolt, sicken, nauseate.
3 *(n) You gave me a shock! See* **scare** 3.
4 *(n) The news came as a shock.* surprise,
blow, bombshell, bolt from the blue,
revelation, eye-opener *(informal).*

shocking
1 *(adj) Have you heard the shocking news*
about Mrs Badger? astonishing, surprising,
startling, staggering, stunning, stupefying,
unexpected, disturbing, perturbing,
upsetting, disquieting, unsettling.
2 *(adj) Bozo's behaviour is shocking.*
outrageous, disgusting, scandalous,
appalling, disgraceful, offensive, revolting,
repugnant, sickening, nauseating,
atrocious, monstrous, indecent.
3 *(adj) There has been a shocking*
accident. horrific, horrendous, horrifying,
appalling, ghastly, harrowing, grisly,
gruesome, terrible, dreadful, frightening.

shoddy
(adj) Mrs Badger criticized my shoddy
work. second-rate, poor-quality, inferior,
careless, messy, slapdash, sloppy
(informal), slovenly, slipshod, untidy, tatty.
OPPOSITES: careful, meticulous.

shoe
(n) footwear.
TYPES OF SHOE: ballet shoe, boot,
bootee, brogue, clog, court shoe, deck
shoe, dolly shoe, espadrille, flip-flop, gym
shoe, high-heeled shoe, lace-up, loafer,
moccasin, mule, patent shoe, peep-toe,
platform shoe, plimsoll, pump, running
shoe, sandal, slingback, slip-on, slipper,
sneaker, stiletto, suede shoe, tennis shoe,
trainer, winklepicker.

shoot
1 *(v) "Don't move or I'll shoot you!" Arnie*
said. fire at, open fire on, gun you down,
snipe at, blow your brains out, take a pot
shot at, pump you full of lead *(slang),*
riddle you with bullets, zap *(slang),* shell.
2 *(v) Shoot the arrows at the target.* fire,
aim, launch, propel, let fly.
3 *(v) Watch the comet shoot through the*
sky. fly, hurtle, streak, flash, speed, whiz
(informal), zoom, zip, tear, race, dash.
4 *(n) A shoot will grow.* bud, offshoot,
tendril, sprout, new growth, stem, twig.

shop
(n) corner shop, supermarket, store,
department store, superstore, megastore,
hypermarket, boutique, market, cash-and-
carry, emporium *(old-fashioned).*

shore
(n) We walked along the shore. seashore,
beach, coast, sand, sands *(plural),* water's
edge, waterside, waterfront, lakeside,
seafront, foreshore, shingle, strand. ❖ *Also*
see **sea & seashore**, **seaside words**.

short
1 *(adj) Dil is rather short.* small, squat,
little, tiny, petite, diminutive, dumpy,
stubby, stumpy, pint-sized *(informal).*
OPPOSITE: tall.
2 *(adj) Write a short account of your trip.*
brief, concise, succinct, pithy, compressed,
to the point, abridged, abbreviated.
OPPOSITES: long, long-winded.
3 *(adj) We paid a short visit to Aunt*
Bertha. brief, quick, fleeting, hurried,
hasty, short-lived, cursory.
OPPOSITES: long, leisurely.
4 *(adj) Shall we go home the short way?*
quick, direct, straight, obvious.
OPPOSITES: long, indirect.

shortage
(n) There's a noticeable shortage of books
in our school. lack, scarcity, shortfall,
absence, dearth, deficiency.
OPPOSITES: abundance, surplus.

shorts *see* **clothes**.

shot
1 *(n) Did you hear that shot?* gunshot,
crack, bang, pop, report, explosion, blast.
2 *(n) That was a great shot!* hit, stroke,
volley, lob, smash, throw, pass, kick,
header, drive, putt, pot, pot shot.
3 *(n) (informal) Have a shot! See* **try** 1.

shout
(v) Please don't shout. yell, raise your voice,
bawl, bellow, holler *(informal),* scream,
shriek, screech, roar, call out, cry out.

deck shoe *loafer* *slingback*

brogue *winklepicker*

espadrille *mule* *stiletto*

shove

shove *see* **push** 1, 3, 4.

show

1 *(v)* *Will this mark show?* show up, be visible, be seen, stand out, be noticeable, catch the eye, attract attention.
2 *(v)* *Todd tried not to show his true feelings.* display, make obvious, make plain, make known, indicate, express, betray, reveal, expose, disclose, divulge.
3 *(v)* *I want to show an alien in my painting.* depict, portray, illustrate, represent, feature.
4 *(v)* *Delia will show you how to make an omelette. See* **demonstrate** 1.
5 *(v)* *This letter will show that I am telling the truth.* indicate, demonstrate, make clear, prove, establish, confirm, clarify.
6 *(n)* *Enjoy the show! See* **performance**.
7 *(n)* *You'll see all kinds of cars at the show.* exhibition, fair, expo *(informal)*, display, demonstration, presentation.
8 *(n)* *Nina put on a show of affection for Aunt Bertha.* display, appearance, pretence, pose, affectation, illusion.

shower

1 *(n)* *The sudden shower surprised us.* downpour, cloudburst, deluge, rainfall.
2 *(v)* *Be careful the elephants don't shower you with water! See* **spray** 1.

show-off

(n) *(informal)* *Jeremy is such a show-off.* bighead *(informal)*, boaster, poser *(informal)*, exhibitionist, braggart.

show off

1 *(v)* *Al is keen to show off his computer.* flaunt, parade, display, demonstrate.
2 *(v)* *(informal)* *Don't show off about all your prizes. See* **boast**.

show up

1 *(v)* *This orange shirt will certainly show up.* be visible, stand out, be conspicuous, catch the eye, leap out at you.
2 *(v)* *Bright light will show up my spots.* accentuate, draw attention to, highlight, expose, reveal.
3 *(v)* *(informal)* *Don't you hate it when your parents show you up!* let you down, embarrass, humiliate, disgrace, shame, mortify, show you in a bad light.

shred

1 *(n)* *The detectives found a shred of cloth.* scrap, snippet, strip, bit, piece, fragment, ribbon, rag, tatter, wisp.
2 *(n)* *There isn't a shred of evidence against Burglar Beryl.* scrap, bit, jot, iota, trace, grain, speck, crumb, atom, particle.

shriek *see* **scream**.

shrill

(adj) *A shrill sound.* high-pitched, piercing, ear-piercing, ear-splitting, penetrating, strident, screeching, piping, sharp.

shrink

1 *(v)* *This balloon is starting to shrink.* grow smaller, deflate, contract, shrivel up.
OPPOSITES: expand, swell.

2 *(v)* *Famous Fred's record sales may shrink.* decrease, decline, dwindle, drop off, fall off, diminish, contract, reduce.
OPPOSITES: expand, increase.
3 *(v)* *Don't shrink away from me. See* **cower**.

shrivel

(v) *The flowers will shrivel in the sun.* wither, dry up, wilt, droop, dry out, dehydrate, shrink, wrinkle up, pucker up.

shudder *see* **shiver**.

shuffle

1 *(v)* *Shuffle the cards.* mix, mix up, jumble up, rearrange, reorganize.
2 *(v)* *I hate the way you shuffle around in those shoes.* shamble, drag your feet, paddle, pad, hobble, stumble, limp.

shut

1 *(v)* *Shut the door.* close, slam, lock, bolt, bar, secure, fasten, latch, pull to, push to.
OPPOSITE: open.
2 *(v)* *Shut the curtains.* close, draw, pull.
OPPOSITE: open.
3 *(v)* *Why did the king shut the princes in the tower?* lock, imprison, incarcerate, shut up, keep, confine, detain, enclose, coop up, wall up, cage, box.
4 *(adj)* *Is the shop shut?* closed, locked up, shut up, bolted and barred, closed down.
OPPOSITE: open.

shut down

(v) *The car factory may have to shut down.* close down, cease operating, cease production, cease trading *(shop, business)*.

shut out *see* **exclude**.

shut up

(v) *(informal)* *Shut up and listen!* be quiet, stop talking, keep quiet, shush, hush, hold your tongue, put a sock in it *(slang)*, belt up *(slang)*, shut your trap *(slang)*.

shy

(adj) *Amy is too shy to come to the party.* timid, diffident, reserved, retiring, mousy, bashful, self-conscious, inhibited, reticent, introverted, wary, coy.
OPPOSITES: self-assured, assertive.

sick

1 *(adj)* *Kamilah can't come to school because she's sick. See* **ill** 1.
2 *(adj)* *I feel sick.* nauseous, queasy, bilious, green around the gills *(informal)*.
3 *(adj)* *Bozo's behaviour makes me sick.* disgusted, sickened, appalled, revolted, nauseated, upset, distressed, outraged, repelled, offended, horrified.
4 *(adj)* *(informal)* *Harriet has a sick sense of humour.* twisted, black, perverted, morbid, macabre, ghoulish, sadistic.
5 **sick of** *(adj)* *(informal)* *I'm sick of staying at home. See* **fed up with**.
6 **be sick** *(v)* *I'm going to be sick! See* **vomit**.

sickening

1 *(adj)* *The smell from the drains was sickening. See* **disgusting** 1.

2 *(adj)* *The way Araminta sucks up to Mrs Badger is sickening.* loathsome, disgusting, nauseating, distasteful, cringe-making *(informal)*, repellent, repulsive, obnoxious, odious, objectionable, stomach-turning.

sickly

1 *(adj)* *A sickly baby. See* **delicate** 2.
2 *(adj)* *A sickly dessert.* sugary, syrupy, treacly, cloying, nauseating, saccharine.

side

1 *(n)* *Paint one side of the box.* face, surface, facet, flank, elevation *(building)*.
2 *(n)* *Stand at the side of the pool.* edge, rim, brink, perimeter, periphery, boundary, verge *(road)*, kerb *(pavement)*.
3 *(n)* *The side of the page was covered with notes.* edge, margin, border.
4 *(n)* *Start each question on a new side. See* **page**.
5 *(n)* *Which side won?* team, group, faction, camp, party, army, sect, cause.
6 *(n)* *Try to look at the problem from every side.* angle, aspect, perspective, point of view, viewpoint, standpoint, position.
7 **side with** *(v)* *Did you side with Dalal in the argument?* agree with, support, back, take the part of, go along with, team up with, ally with, champion, second.

sieve

1 *(v)* *Sieve the mixture.* strain, sift, filter, separate, pan *(gold)*.
2 *(n)* *Pass me the sieve.* strainer, colander.

sigh

1 *(v)* *Did I hear you sigh?* exhale, let out your breath, moan, groan.
2 *(v)* *The wind began to sigh through the branches.* whisper, rustle, moan.

sight

1 *(n)* *I'm worried about Matty's sight.* eyesight, vision, eyes *(plural)*, short-sightedness, long-sightedness.
2 *(n)* *We watched the balloon until it was out of sight.* view, range, eyeshot, range of vision, field of vision.
3 *(n)* *What a beautiful sight!* scene, vision, spectacle, picture, image, view, vista, panorama, display, prospect, outlook.
4 *(n)* *(informal)* *You look a sight!* fright *(informal)*, mess *(informal)*, wreck, eyesore.

sign

1 *(n)* *Is there any sign that Burglar Beryl has been here?* indication, hint, suggestion, clue, evidence, proof, pointer, trace, vestige, giveaway, telltale sign.
2 *(n)* *Did you read the sign?* notice, poster, placard, board, signpost.
3 *(n)* *Let's design a secret sign for our gang.* symbol, badge, emblem, identification mark, logo, insignia.
4 *(n)* *Give me a sign when it's time to begin.* signal, indication, tip-off, cue, message, hint, reminder, warning, wave, nod, wink, gesture, go-ahead *(informal)*.
5 *(n)* *Arthur knew the pile of bones was a sign.* warning, omen, portent, forewarning, message, token, pointer.

6 *(v) Please sign this postcard.* write your name on, autograph, initial, inscribe, put your name to, put your mark on.

signal
1 *(n) Give me a signal when it's time to begin.* See **sign 4**.
2 *(v) I'll signal to you when it's safe.* indicate, make a sign, gesture, sign, motion, wave, nod, beckon, gesticulate.

significant *see* **important 1**.

silence
1 *(n) I love the silence of evening.* quietness, stillness, calm, tranquillity, peacefulness, peace, quiet, hush.
OPPOSITE: noise.
2 *(n) Sarah's silence puzzled us.* lack of speech, dumbness, muteness, reticence, uncommunicativeness.
3 *(v) How can we silence the sound of Paula's trumpet?* quieten, muffle, stifle, smother, deaden, suppress, subdue.

silent
1 *(adj) Ravi approached with silent steps.* soundless, noiseless, inaudible, muffled.
OPPOSITES: noisy, loud.
2 *(adj) The shock made me silent for a while.* speechless, tongue-tied, dumbstruck, unable to get a word out, mute, dumb, mum.
3 *(adj) Edward is a rather silent member of the class.* See **quiet 3**.
4 *(adj) Everything was silent before the storm.* See **still 3**.
5 *(adj) We watched with silent approval.* unspoken, unvoiced, unexpressed, wordless, tacit, implied, implicit.

silhouette *see* **outline 3**.

silky
(adj) I stroked the horse's silky coat. sleek, smooth, velvety, satiny, shiny, glossy, soft.
OPPOSITES: rough, matted.

silly
1 *(adj) What a silly idea!* stupid, foolish, daft *(informal)*, idiotic, crazy, absurd, ridiculous, preposterous, ludicrous, senseless, nonsensical, brainless, irrational, illogical, misguided, half-baked *(informal)*, inane, harebrained, foolhardy, reckless.
OPPOSITES: sensible, clever.
2 *(adj) Daisy can be so silly.* idiotic, brainless, daft *(informal)*, foolish, stupid, senseless, dotty *(slang)*, dippy *(slang)*, dopey *(slang)*, goofy *(informal)*, immature, childish, infantile, puerile, irresponsible, featherbrained, giddy, flighty, frivolous.
OPPOSITES: sensible, mature.

silver
(adj) A silver moon. silvery, pearly, ivory.

similar
(adj) Our answers are similar. alike, comparable, much the same, close, in agreement, corresponding, matching.
OPPOSITES: different, dissimilar.

simple
1 *(adj) The test was simple!* See **easy 1**.

2 *(adj) The instructions are written in simple language.* clear, straightforward, uncomplicated, plain, intelligible, understandable, comprehensible, easy to follow, foolproof, uninvolved.
OPPOSITES: complicated, complex.
3 *(adj) The peasants lived in a simple cottage.* modest, ordinary, humble, plain, basic, unpretentious, undecorated, austere, stark, Spartan, poor, lowly, rustic.
OPPOSITES: grand, fancy.
4 *(adj) I like simple meals.* See **plain 2**.
5 *(adj) Give me the simple truth.* plain, honest, naked, stark, bald, basic, unvarnished, unembellished, unadorned.

sincere
1 *(adj) Peter's sympathy seems to be sincere.* genuine, real, wholehearted, heartfelt, in earnest, unfeigned, bona fide.
OPPOSITES: insincere, feigned.
2 *(adj) Mr Badger is a sincere person.* truthful, honest, frank, candid, open, straightforward, genuine, artless, guileless, upfront *(informal)*, plain-dealing.
OPPOSITES: insincere, deceitful.

sing
1 *(v) Dad likes to sing in the shower.* warble, croon, carol, yodel, chant, serenade, hum, whistle.
2 *(v) The nightingale began to sing.* trill, warble, twitter, chirrup, cheep, chirp, whistle, pipe, peep, squawk.

singer
(n) vocalist, songster, songstress.
TYPES OF SINGER: alto, backing singer, baritone, bass, choirboy, choirgirl, chorister, contralto, countertenor, crooner, folk singer, jazz singer, lead singer, mezzo-soprano, opera singer, pop singer, prima donna (leading female opera singer), rapper, rock singer, soloist, soprano, tenor, treble, troubadour *(old-fashioned)*.

single
1 *(adj) Do you have single rooms?* individual, separate, personal, unshared.
OPPOSITES: shared, double.
2 *(adj) A single tree stood on the hill.* lone, solitary, isolated, unique, individual, unaccompanied, on its own, solo.
3 *(adj) Do you think you'll stay single?* unattached, unmarried, celibate, on your own, unwed, partnerless, not tied down, free, fancy-free, footloose.
OPPOSITES: attached, married.

sinister
(adj) The shadows looked sinister. threatening, menacing, ominous, forbidding, frightening, disturbing, spooky *(informal)*, malevolent, evil, malign.

sink
1 *(v) The ship is going to sink!* go down, go under, founder, submerge, go to the bottom, go to Davy Jones's locker, drown.
OPPOSITE: float.
2 *(v) The plane began to sink.* See **drop 2**.
3 *(v) We watched the sun sink.* See **set 5**.

4 *(v) Oliver tried to sink his toy boat.* submerge, scupper, scuttle, capsize, drown, swamp, flood, immerse, engulf, dunk, duck, torpedo.
5 *(v) How could you sink to that level of meanness?* lower yourself, stoop, be reduced, debase yourself, succumb, yield.
OPPOSITES: aspire, rise.
6 *(n) Fill the sink.* washbasin, basin.

sit
(v) You can sit here. sit down, be seated, seat yourself, take a seat, settle down, perch, squat, rest, take the weight off your feet, loll, sprawl, flop, collapse.

situation *see* **position 2**.

sketch
1 *(v) Why don't you sketch your cat?* See **draw 1**.
2 *(n) We admired Meg's sketch.* drawing, picture, study, design, outline, diagram, plan, representation, rough drawing.

skid
(v) The car began to skid. slide, slip, spin, go into a skid, go into a spin, go out of control, sideslip, veer, glide, aquaplane.

skilful
(adj) Ryan is a skilful footballer. skilled, accomplished, talented, expert, capable, proficient, deft, versatile, ace *(informal)*.
OPPOSITES: inept, incompetent.

skill
(n) We admired the potter's skill. expertise, technique, prowess, talent, ability, artistry, craftsmanship, workmanship, art, craft, deftness, dexterity, versatility, finesse.

skim
1 *(v) Watch me skim over the ice!* glide, slide, skate, sail, fly, float, coast.
2 *(v) See how the dragonflies skim the surface of the pond.* brush, graze, touch.
3 skim through *(v) Skim through this booklet.* glance through, look through, run your eye over, leaf through, scan, flip through, skip through, thumb through.

skin
1 *(n) With your fair skin you should avoid the sun.* complexion, colouring, skin tone.
2 *(n) This fruit has a tough skin.* rind, peel, outer layer, exterior, surface, casing, covering, shell, husk, pod.
3 *(n) Is this jacket made from an animal's skin?* hide, pelt, coat, fleece, fur.
4 *(n) I hate custard with a skin on top.* film, coating, layer, crust, scum.

skinny *see* **thin 1**.

skip
1 *(v) I love to see the children skip around the garden!* prance, dance, bounce, frolic, gambol, cavort, bound, jump, leap, hop.
2 *(v) Let's skip this page.* See **miss out 1**.
3 *(v) (informal) You mustn't skip school.* miss, play truant from, dodge, skive off *(informal)*, bunk off *(slang)*, cut *(informal)*, play hooky from *(informal)*.

skirt *see* **clothes**.

skulk

skulk *see* **lurk**.

sky
(n) My balloon floated up into the sky. air, atmosphere, skies *(plural),* space, heavens *(plural),* stratosphere, blue, firmament.

slab *see* **block** 1.

slag off *(slang) see* **criticize** 1.

slant
1 *(v) That chimney seems to slant to one side. See* **lean** 1.
2 *(n) Look at the slant of that table top! See* **slope** 1.
3 *(n) Veena gave the story a new slant.* angle, emphasis, twist, perspective, bias.

slap
1 *(v) Don't slap Caroline! See* **smack**.
2 *(v) Sam started to slap paint on the walls.* slop, splash, slosh *(informal),* daub, dollop *(informal),* plaster, spread.

slapdash *see* **careless** 1.

slash
1 *(v) The vandals began to slash the furniture.* cut, slit, gash, rip, tear, lacerate, score, knife, hack at.
2 *(v) Supermarkets may slash their prices. See* **reduce** 1.

slaughter
1 *(n) The slaughter must be stopped. See* **killing** 2.
2 *(v) The farmers had to slaughter their sick cattle. See* **kill** 2.
3 *(v) (informal) We'll slaughter the other team. See* **beat** 2.

sleazy
(adj) The street was full of sleazy bars. sordid, seedy, disreputable, squalid, run-down, tacky *(informal),* crummy *(slang).*
OPPOSITES: respectable, up-market.

sleek *see* **silky**.

sleep
1 *(v) You can sleep at my house.* spend the night, stay, sleep over, kip *(slang),* doss down *(slang),* crash out *(slang).*
2 *(v) Aunt Bertha likes to sleep after lunch.* doze, take a nap, snooze *(informal),* catnap, drowse, have forty winks *(informal),* get some shuteye *(informal),* drop off *(informal),* nod off *(informal),* rest.
3 *(n) Granny is having a sleep.* nap, rest, siesta, snooze *(informal),* doze, catnap, lie-down, forty winks *(plural) (informal),* kip *(slang),* shuteye *(informal),* zizz *(informal).*

sleeping *see* **asleep**.

sleepy
1 *(adj) Do you feel sleepy?* tired, drowsy, half-asleep, weary, exhausted, unable to keep your eyes open, lethargic, sluggish, dozy, dopey *(informal),* ready for bed.
OPPOSITES: wide-awake, alert.
2 *(adj) Nothing ever happens in this sleepy town.* quiet, peaceful, dozy, unexciting, boring, dull, dreary, dead.
OPPOSITES: lively, bustling.

slender *see* **slim** 1, 2.

slice
1 *(n) Have a slice of cake.* piece, segment, slab, wedge, sliver, doorstep *(informal),* chunk, portion, helping, wodge *(informal).*
2 *(v) Will you slice the pineapple?* cut up, divide, carve, segment, dissect.

slide
(v) Felix began to slide across the ice. slip, slither, skid, glide, skate, skim, sideslip, veer, toboggan, ski.

slight
(adj) There's been a slight improvement in your work. small, minor, modest, negligible, imperceptible, insignificant, trivial, tiny, trifling, measly *(informal).*
OPPOSITES: great, considerable.

slim
1 *(adj) Natasha has a slim figure.* slender, trim, slight, lean, thin, willowy, sylphlike, svelte, graceful.
OPPOSITES: chubby, fat.
2 *(adj) There's a slim chance that we might survive.* slight, small, slender, faint, remote, outside.

slimy
1 *(adj) We squelched through a slimy swamp.* slippery, sludgy, oozy, gooey *(informal),* sticky, muddy, mucky.
2 *(adj) Flash Frank is a slimy character.* smooth, smarmy *(informal),* oily, greasy, obsequious, ingratiating, grovelling, fawning, toadying, sycophantic, unctuous.

sling *see* **throw** 1.

slink
(v) The thieves tried to slink through the bushes. creep, sneak, steal, slip, sidle, prowl, skulk, tiptoe, pussyfoot *(informal).*

slinky
(adj) Naomi wore a slinky black dress. clinging, figure-hugging, skintight, close-fitting, sleek, sexy *(informal).*

slip
1 *(v) It's easy to slip if the pavement is icy.* skid, lose your balance, lose your footing, fall, trip, slide, slither, glide, skate.
2 *(v) Try to slip out of the house unnoticed. See* **creep** 2.
3 *(n) I made a slip in my calculations. See* **mistake** 1.
4 *(n) Write your phone number on this slip of paper.* scrap, piece, bit, strip, snippet.
5 *(n) Your slip is showing.* petticoat, underskirt.

slippery
1 *(adj) The path is slippery.* icy, greasy, oily, slimy, slithery, slippy *(informal),* skiddy *(informal),* glassy, treacherous.
2 *(adj) Dodgy Dave is a slippery character. See* **deceitful**.

slip up *(informal) see* **go wrong** 1.

slit
1 *(n) Jamie has a slit in his trousers.* cut, split, slash, tear, rip, gash.
2 *(n) I peeped through a slit in the rock. See* **crack** 2.

slither
(v) Watch the snake slither over the sand! slide, glide, slip, wriggle, squirm, skitter, slink, writhe, twist, snake, worm, creep.

slobber
(v) Look at Fido slobber over his bone. drool, slaver, dribble, salivate.

slope
1 *(n) Look at the slope of that roof!* slant, angle, tilt, rake, pitch, skew, incline, gradient, camber *(road).*
2 *(n) Our house is built on a slope.* hill, hillside, bank, rise, incline, ramp.
3 *(v) The path began to slope steeply.* rise, fall, drop, descend, ascend, incline, shelve.
4 *(v) That chimney seems to slope to one side. See* **lean** 1.

sloppy
1 *(adj) A sloppy trifle.* runny, slushy, watery, soggy, squidgy, oozy, liquid.
OPPOSITES: firm, solid.
2 *(adj) (informal) Sloppy work. See* **careless** 1.
3 *(adj) A sloppy jumper. See* **loose** 1.

slot
(n) Insert a knife in the slot. slit, crack, opening, hole, groove, notch, channel.

slouch
(v) Sit up and don't slouch! slump, stoop, droop, hunch, loll, lounge, sprawl, sag.

slow
1 *(adj) Tortoises move at a slow pace.* unhurried, steady, plodding, sluggish, ponderous, snail-like, dawdling, crawling, leisurely, easy, lazy, measured, deliberate.
OPPOSITES: fast, quick.
2 *(adj) Aunt Bertha's recovery was slow.* gradual, long-drawn-out, protracted, prolonged, lingering, interminable.
OPPOSITES: fast, rapid.
3 *(adj) Rory was slow in handing in his project.* late, delayed, unpunctual, tardy, behind, dilatory.
OPPOSITE: prompt.
4 *(adj) This film is so slow!* slow-moving, uneventful, tedious, monotonous, dull, boring, tiresome, wearisome.
OPPOSITES: fast-moving, action-packed.

slow down
1 *(v) Slow down; you're going too fast!* reduce your speed, slacken your speed, decelerate, put the brakes on, brake.
OPPOSITES: speed up, accelerate.
2 *(v) Don't slow me down. See* **delay** 2.

sly
(adj) That was a sly trick you played. crafty, sneaky, cunning, wily, artful, devious, deceitful, underhand, stealthy, furtive, insidious, scheming, clever, smart, shrewd.
OPPOSITES: straightforward, honest.

smack
(v) Should parents smack their children? slap, hit, strike, whack, spank, wallop *(informal),* belt *(slang),* thump, cuff, clout *(informal),* biff *(slang),* beat.

small

a small person	a small child	a small helping of pudding	a small space	a small mistake
dainty	little	inadequate	confined	insignificant
diminutive	teeny	insubstantial	cramped	minor
elfin	tiny	meagre	limited	negligible
Lilliputian	wee	mean	narrow	slight
little	young	measly	poky	trifling
petite		*(informal)*	restricted	trivial
pint-sized	**a small radio**	mingy		unimportant
(informal)	compact	*(informal)*	**a small speck**	
puny	dinky	moderate	infinitesimal	**Don't make me feel small!**
short	*(informal)*	modest	microscopic	foolish
slender	mini	scanty	minuscule	humiliated
slight	miniature	skimpy	minute	ridiculous
squat	pocket-sized	stingy	teeny	sheepish
tiny	tiny	tiny	teeny-weeny	silly
titchy *(slang)*	toy	titchy *(slang)*	tiny	stupid
undersized				

smart
1 *(adj) Ellie always looks smart.* elegant, stylish, chic, well-dressed, well-groomed, presentable, spruce, neat, tidy, dashing, dapper, natty *(informal),* snazzy *(informal).*
OPPOSITES: scruffy, dowdy.
2 *(adj) That was a smart move.* clever, intelligent, shrewd, crafty, astute, quick-witted, bright, ingenious, wise, sensible.
OPPOSITES: stupid, idiotic.
3 *(adj) Oliver loves to make smart remarks.* clever, witty, facetious, impertinent, cheeky, saucy, smart-alecky *(informal),* clever-clever *(informal),* clever-Dick *(informal),* droll, waggish.
4 *(v) If you get soap in your eyes it will smart.* See **sting**.

smash
1 *(n) Was anyone injured in the smash?* See **crash** 2.
2 *(v) If you drop that bowl it will smash.* shatter, splinter, smash to smithereens, break, break into pieces, crack, split, fracture, disintegrate.
3 **smash into** *(v) Try not to smash into that tree.* See **hit** 4.

smear
1 *(v) Don't smear paint on the walls!* spread, daub, plaster, smudge, wipe, rub.
2 *(n) You've got a smear of paint on your nose.* streak, smudge, splodge, blotch, splotch, daub, spot, mark.

smell
1 *(n) What a wonderful smell!* fragrance, scent, perfume, aroma, bouquet, odour.
2 *(n) What a horrible smell!* stink, stench, pong *(informal),* odour, whiff, reek.
3 *(v) Your feet smell!* See **stink** 1.
4 *(v) A fox can smell chickens from miles away.* scent, sniff out, nose out, sense, detect, track down, get wind of *(informal).*
5 *(v) Smell that lovely aroma!* inhale, breathe in, take in, sniff, get a whiff of.

smelly
(adj) Throw away that smelly cheese. stinking, reeking, pongy *(informal),* whiffy *(slang),* stinky *(informal),* pungent, strong-smelling, foul-smelling, evil-smelling, malodorous, high, putrid, fetid.
OPPOSITES: sweet-smelling, fragrant.

smile
1 *(v) Smile for the camera!* grin, beam, look happy, smirk, simper, say cheese.
2 *(n) The witch gave a horrible smile.* grin, smirk, leer, grimace, sneer.

smoke
1 *(v) Please don't smoke.* light up, chain-smoke, puff away, have a drag *(informal),* have a fag *(slang),* inhale.
2 *(v) The fire started to smoke.* smoulder, give off smoke, emit smoke, billow.
3 *(n) The air was filled with smoke.* clouds of smoke *(plural),* exhaust fumes *(plural),* pollution, smog, haze.

smooth
1 *(adj) You need a smooth lawn for bowls.* level, flat, even, horizontal, flush.
OPPOSITES: bumpy, uneven.
2 *(adj) Clare has smooth skin.* soft, velvety, silky, downy, flawless, unlined, unwrinkled.
OPPOSITES: rough, coarse.
3 *(adj) This table has a smooth surface.* polished, shiny, glossy, satiny, sleek, even.
OPPOSITES: rough, bumpy.
4 *(adj) Nothing disturbed the smooth surface of the lake.* calm, still, unruffled, glassy, mirror-like, tranquil, placid, flat.
OPPOSITES: choppy, rough.
5 *(adj) You'll love the smooth taste of this sauce.* mild, mellow, creamy, velvety, pleasant, agreeable, bland.
6 *(adj) I hope you have a smooth journey.* easy, comfortable, straightforward, effortless, peaceful, uneventful, uninterrupted, trouble-free, stress-free.
OPPOSITES: difficult, stressful.

7 *(adj) Ballet dancers should have smooth movements.* easy, effortless, flowing, fluid, graceful, steady, rhythmic, regular.
OPPOSITES: jerky, erratic.
8 *(adj) Flash Frank has a smooth manner.* suave, polished, glib, charming, persuasive, flattering, ingratiating, sophisticated, urbane, slick, smarmy *(informal),* slimy.
OPPOSITES: rough, abrasive.
9 *(v) Smooth the sheets before you fold them.* smooth out, flatten, iron, press.
OPPOSITES: crumple, crease.
10 *(v) I must smooth the edges of this box.* file, sand, plane, even, level off.

smother
1 *(v) Don't smother me with that pillow!* suffocate, stifle, asphyxiate, choke.
2 *(v) Try to smother your giggles.* stifle, suppress, hold back, keep in, muffle, hide.
3 *(v) Let's smother the cake with cream.* cover, plaster, heap, pile, envelop, drown, swamp, engulf, surround, blanket.

smudge
1 *(n) There's a smudge on the front of this book.* smear, streak, dirty mark, blotch, splotch, blot, spot, stain, smut.
2 *(v) Try not to smudge the glass.* smear, streak, blur, dirty, mark, blotch, stain.

smug
(adj) Don't look so smug when you get the answer right. self-satisfied, pleased with yourself, complacent, superior, conceited, self-righteous, holier-than-thou, priggish.

snake
1 *(n) I saw a snake in the grass.* serpent.
TYPES OF SNAKE: adder, boa constrictor, cobra, grass snake, python, rattlesnake, sea snake, sidewinder, tree snake, viper.
2 *(v) The path began to snake up the mountain.* See **wind** 2.

snap
1 *(v) I hope this rope doesn't snap!* break, break in two, give way, split, come apart.
2 *(v) Can you hear the twigs snap under your feet?* crack, crackle, pop, crunch.
3 **snap at** *(v) Did the dog snap at you?* bite, nip, go for, have a go at *(informal),* snarl, yap at, bark at, growl at.

snarl
1 *(v) Don't snarl, Fido!* growl, show your teeth, bare your teeth.
2 *(n) "Clear off!" the man said with a snarl.* growl, scowl, sneer, grimace.

snatch
(v) A thief tried to snatch my bag. grab, seize, take, wrench away, make off with, run off with, steal, nick *(slang),* nab *(informal),* swipe *(slang).*

sneak
1 *(v) Try to sneak past the guard.* See **creep** 2.
2 *(v) I tried to sneak the kitten into my bedroom.* smuggle, slip, spirit.
3 **sneak on** *(v) (informal) Will your sister sneak on us?* See **tell on**.

sneaky

sneaky see **sly**.

sneer
1 *(n)* *"It's your own fault," said Edwin with a sneer.* smirk, snigger, curl of the lip.
2 **sneer at** *(v)* *Don't sneer at my efforts.* See **scorn** 1.

sniff
(v) *Don't sniff!* sniffle, snuffle, snort, snivel.

snigger see **giggle**.

snobbish
(adj) *Araminta is so snobbish; she looks down on everyone.* condescending, snooty *(informal),* stuck-up *(informal),* superior, haughty, arrogant, disdainful, patronizing, hoity-toity *(informal),* toffee-nosed *(slang).*

snooze *(informal)* see **sleep** 2, 3.

snub
(v) *Did Araminta snub you at the party?* ignore, cut, cut you dead *(informal),* give you the cold shoulder, give you the brush-off *(slang),* put you down, humiliate, slight.

snug see **cosy**.

snuggle
(v) *Watch the piglets snuggle against their mother.* cuddle, nestle, nuzzle, curl up.

soak
1 *(v)* *Soak the fruit in the liquid.* immerse, steep, saturate, marinate, submerge, wet.
2 *(v)* *This rain will soak my shoes.* saturate, drench, seep through, penetrate.
3 **soak up** *(v)* *This cloth will soak up the water.* absorb, mop up, take in, take up.

soaking
(adj) *My shoes are soaking.* wet through, sopping wet, dripping wet, wringing wet, sodden, saturated, drenched, dripping, soggy, waterlogged *(ground).*
OPPOSITES: dry, bone-dry *(informal).*

soar see **rise** 1, 2, 3.

sob see **cry** 1.

sofa
(n) settee, couch, sofa bed, divan, chaise longue, futon, ottoman.

soft
1 *(adj)* *Clare's skin is so soft.* smooth, delicate, tender, silky, velvety, downy.
OPPOSITES: rough, tough.
2 *(adj)* *The baby animals felt soft.* fluffy, furry, fleecy, silky, downy, feathery, velvety, satiny, sleek, smooth.
OPPOSITES: rough, coarse.
3 *(adj)* *This sofa is really soft.* comfortable, well-padded, well-cushioned, squashy, bouncy, springy, yielding.
OPPOSITES: hard, uncomfortable.
4 *(adj)* *Uri rubbed the spoon until it was soft.* bendy, pliable, flexible, supple, malleable, bendable, limp, floppy.
OPPOSITES: hard, rigid.
5 *(adj)* *This biscuit is soft.* See **soggy** 2.
6 *(adj)* *Be careful! The ground is soft.* spongy, soggy, boggy, swampy, marshy, waterlogged, muddy, crumbly, yielding.
OPPOSITES: hard, firm.

7 *(adj)* *Mum spoke in a soft voice.* quiet, low, gentle, soothing, hushed, faint, scarcely audible, whispered, murmured.
OPPOSITES: loud, harsh.
8 *(adj)* *The room was bathed in a soft light.* gentle, dim, subdued, faint, low, pale, subtle, muted, restful, diffuse.
OPPOSITES: harsh, glaring.

soggy
1 *(adj)* *The rain has made my shoes soggy.* See **soaking**.
2 *(adj)* *These biscuits are soggy.* soft, mushy, spongy, squashy, pulpy, doughy.
OPPOSITES: crisp, crunchy.

soil see **earth** 2.

soldier
(n) fighter, trooper, serviceman, warrior *(old-fashioned),* marine, paratrooper, commando, guardsman, sentry, gunner, rifleman, cavalryman, infantryman, mercenary, conscript.

solemn
1 *(adj)* *Sara looks solemn.* See **serious** 1.
2 *(adj)* *The coronation was a solemn occasion.* stately, ceremonial, formal, grand, dignified, majestic, imposing, awe-inspiring, momentous, impressive.
OPPOSITES: frivolous, informal.

solid
1 *(adj)* *Cement becomes solid when it sets.* hard, firm, rigid, set, unyielding, thick, dense, compact.
OPPOSITES: liquid, powdery.
2 *(adj)* *The castle walls are solid.* thick, strong, sturdy, firm, substantial, stout, sound, unshakable, well-built, well-made.
OPPOSITES: flimsy, shaky.
3 *(adj)* *My ring is solid silver.* pure, real, genuine, unalloyed, unadulterated.
4 *(adj)* *The traffic formed a solid line.* continuous, unbroken, uninterrupted.

solve
(v) *Can you solve this mystery?* work out, figure out *(informal),* unravel, clear up, decipher, get to the bottom of, find the answer to, resolve, crack, find the key to, find the solution to, suss out *(slang).*

song
(n) *Listen to this song.* tune, ditty, air, melody, number, chorus.
TYPES OF SONG: anthem, aria, ballad, calypso, canon, carol, chant, folk song, hymn, jingle, love song, lullaby, madrigal, nursery rhyme, pop song, psalm, round, sea shanty, serenade, spiritual. ❖ *Also see* **music words** *and* **pop**, **rock & jazz**.

soothing
(adj) *Let's listen to some soothing music.* restful, relaxing, peaceful, calming, gentle.

sophisticated
(adj) *Eva has become quite sophisticated since she went to Paris.* stylish, poised, cultured, cultivated, urbane, refined, cosmopolitan, worldly, worldly-wise, blasé.
OPPOSITES: unsophisticated, naive.

soppy *(informal)* see **sentimental** 2.

sore
(adj) *My knee is sore where I scraped it.* painful, tender, raw, hurting, smarting, stinging, throbbing, aching, bruised, burning, inflamed, chafed, irritated.

sorrow
(n) *Demi's sorrow was unbearable.* sadness, grief, misery, anguish, despair, distress, unhappiness, heartache, heartbreak, wretchedness, woe, melancholy, gloom, despondency.
OPPOSITES: happiness, joy.

sorry
1 *(adj)* *I hope you're sorry about breaking that window!* repentant, remorseful, regretful, conscience-stricken, penitent, contrite, apologetic, ashamed, guilt-ridden.
OPPOSITES: unrepentant, unapologetic.
2 *(adj)* *I was sorry when I heard that your cat had died.* sad, upset, distressed, unhappy, miserable, sorrowful, grieved, concerned, disconsolate, crestfallen.
OPPOSITES: unconcerned, unmoved.
3 **feel sorry for** *(phrase)* *You should feel sorry for the losing team.* feel for, feel pity for, feel compassion for, sympathize with, commiserate with, condole with.

sort
1 *(n)* *What sort of bread shall I buy?* See **kind** 2.
2 *(n)* *What sort of dog is that?* See **kind** 3.
3 *(v)* *Sort your books according to subject.* organize, group, put in order, order, arrange, file, separate, divide, subdivide, classify, categorize, grade, rank, catalogue.

sound
1 *(n)* *Can you hear a sound?* noise.
2 *(adj)* *Are these old floorboards sound?* solid, sturdy, strong, substantial, intact, whole, undamaged, in good condition.
OPPOSITES: flimsy, weak.
3 *(adj)* *Nadia gave me some sound advice.* See **sensible** 2.

sour
1 *(adj)* *Lemons taste sour.* sharp, tangy, acid, tart, bitter, vinegary, piquant, unripe.
OPPOSITE: sweet.
2 *(adj)* *This milk is sour.* curdled, rancid, off, turned, bad, spoiled, fermented.
OPPOSITE: fresh.

space
1 *(n)* *How can we fill this space?* gap, hole, opening, blank, blank space, interval, area, expanse, stretch, vacuum.
2 *(n)* *We need more space for our activities.* room, scope, capacity, freedom, elbow room, room to manoeuvre, leeway.
3 *(n)* *Vijay stared into space.* infinity, emptiness, nothingness, the distance, thin air, the void, the blue.
4 *(n)* *I'm reading a book about space.* the universe, outer space, interplanetary space, interstellar space, intergalactic space, the galaxy, the solar system, the stars *(plural),* the planets *(plural),* astronomy.

space adventure

space adventure

space characters
alien
android or droid
astronaut
cyborg (half-human robot)
hologram
mutant
robot
shape-shifter
space pirate
space traveller

you might live in...
space city
space colony
spacelab
space station
star base

you might travel by...
rocket
rocket pack
space buggy
spacecraft
spaceship
space shuttle
starship
teleporter

in space you might see...
asteroid (rock that orbits the sun)
asteroid belt
comet
galaxy
man-made satellite
moon
nebula (cloud of gases)
planet
probe (unmanned spacecraft)
pulsar (very small spinning star)
red dwarf (small cool star)
red giant (old swollen star)
space debris
star cluster
supernova (exploding star)
white dwarf (dying star)

on a spaceship
booster rocket
bridge
cargo bay
deflector shield
docking bay
escape pod
heat shield
instrument panel
laboratory
life-support system
navigation system
on-board computer
scanner
sensor
sickbay
video screen
weapon system

a spaceship may...
blast off
break out of orbit
burn up
crash-land
cruise
drift
hurtle
jolt
lift off
lurch
malfunction
orbit
re-enter earth's atmosphere
self-destruct
spin out of control
travel at warp speed
vibrate
zoom

on a mission you might...
answer a distress call
be hurled into a parallel universe
be lost in deep space
be stranded on a remote planet
be sucked into a black hole
board an alien vessel
conduct experiments
discover new life forms
enter a time warp
experience zero gravity
explore distant galaxies
go spacewalking
hit a force field
jump into hyperspace
launch a satellite
prevent an intergalactic war
seek out new solar systems
slip through a wormhole (take a short cut through space)

on a planet you might see...
alien life forms
canyon
coloured sky
crater
desert
domed city
dust storm
gas clouds
ice cliff
lush vegetation
meteor storm
mining installation
molten rock
ocean
poisonous clouds
signs of civilization
streaks of lightning
swirling clouds
volcano

planets may be...
airless
arid
baking
barren
desolate
dusty
fertile
fiery
frozen
gaseous
glowing
humid
icy
idyllic
inhabited
inhospitable
radioactive
rocky
teeming with life
uninhabitable
volcanic
windless
windy

aliens may be...
aggressive
friendly
grotesque
harmless
hideous
hostile
humanoid (like a human)
inquisitive
insect-like
intelligent
peaceful
reptilian (like a reptile)
silent
sinister
technologically advanced
telepathic
threatening
unintelligible
weird

Labels (illustrations)
telescope
docking port
antenna
space station
solar panel
accommodation module

rudder
main engine
fuel tank
observation window
video camera
manipulator arm
cargo bay
radiator panel (stops shuttle overheating)
flight deck
wing
spacelab
cargo bay door
space shuttle
tunnel linking crew compartment to spacelab
heat shield

poisonous clouds
volcano
molten rock
domed city
ringed planet
mining installation
rock arch
crater

*Also see **astronaut, planet**.*

spank

spank *see* **smack**.

spare
1 *(adj) Take some spare socks.* extra, additional, supplementary, reserve.
2 *(adj) Is that sandwich spare?* left over, going begging, unwanted, unneeded, superfluous, surplus to requirements.
3 *(adj) In my spare time I play tennis.* free, leisure, unoccupied, remaining, available.
4 *(v) I can spare a few pounds for a good cause.* afford, part with, donate, give up, sacrifice, let you have, give, provide.
5 *(v) I can spare this piece of cake.* let you have, do without, manage without, get along without, dispense with.
6 *(v) The judge decided to spare Burglar Beryl.* have mercy on, be lenient towards, go easy on *(informal)*, pardon, let off, reprieve, release, free, let go.
OPPOSITES: punish, condemn.

spark
(n) The firework sent out a spark of light. flash, flicker, flare, glint, gleam, glimmer.

sparkle
(v) Look how the stars sparkle in the sky. twinkle, flicker, shimmer, flash, glitter, glisten, glint, glimmer, gleam, shine, glow.

speak
1 *(v) Why didn't you speak earlier?* say something, speak out, speak up, make yourself heard, open your mouth, have your say, express yourself, pipe up.
2 *(v) Can you speak Chinese?* talk, communicate in, express yourself in, hold a conversation in, get by in *(informal)*.
3 *(v) Please speak your words more clearly.* pronounce, enunciate, articulate.
4 *(v) Dad can speak for hours on any subject.* talk, hold forth, lecture, spout *(informal)*, sermonize, spiel, speechify, give a talk, give a speech, deliver an address.

speak to
(v) Mrs Badger would like to speak to you. talk to, have a word with, chat to, have words with, have a discussion with, converse with, bend your ear *(informal)*.

special
1 *(adj) Eliza has a special talent for drawing.* extraordinary, exceptional, remarkable, unusual, rare, outstanding, notable, unique, singular.
OPPOSITES: unexceptional, commonplace.
2 *(adj) This is a special day for our school.* important, momentous, significant, noteworthy, memorable, red-letter, gala.
OPPOSITES: normal, ordinary.
3 *(adj) Soy sauce has a special flavour.* distinctive, unique, unmistakable, characteristic, distinct, definite, specific, particular, individual, peculiar.
OPPOSITES: unremarkable, undistinctive.

speck
1 *(n) I've got a speck of paint on my shirt.* spot, fleck, speckle, dot, smudge, mark.
2 *(n) There isn't a speck of food left.* bit, crumb, grain, shred, trace, jot, iota, atom.

speckled
(adj) A speckled egg. flecked, freckled, spotted, spotty, stippled, mottled, dappled.

spectacular
(adj) The acrobats gave a spectacular display. breathtaking, dazzling, eye-catching, dramatic, daring, extraordinary, remarkable, staggering, striking, stunning *(informal)*, sensational, magnificent, impressive, astonishing, amazing.

spectator
(n) onlooker, viewer, observer, looker-on, bystander, passer-by, witness, eyewitness.

speech
1 *(n) The speech lasted for hours.* talk, address, lecture, sermon, oration, spiel.
2 *(n) Mum says my speech isn't clear.* pronunciation, diction, enunciation, articulation, accent, voice, dialect.

speechless
(adj) Your news left me speechless. dumbstruck, dumbfounded, thunderstruck, stunned, at a loss for words, tongue-tied, silent, mute.

speed
1 *(n) The speed of the car amazed us.* pace, swiftness, rapidity, quickness, velocity, acceleration, momentum.
OPPOSITES: sluggishness, slowness.
2 *(n) Jo walks at a great speed.* rate, pace.
3 *(v) You may be fined if you speed.* break the speed limit, exceed the speed limit, go over the speed limit, drive too fast.
4 *(v) I saw you speed past on your bike.* race, zoom, flash, fly, whiz *(informal)*, whoosh *(informal)*, zip, hurtle, tear, bomb, belt *(slang)*, streak, career, dash, go like the wind, go like a bat out of hell *(slang)*.
OPPOSITES: dawdle, crawl.

speed up
1 *(v) The train began to speed up.* accelerate, pick up speed, gather speed, go faster, quicken, gain momentum, put on a spurt, get a move on *(informal)*.
OPPOSITES: slow down, decelerate.
2 *(v) We need to speed up the wedding preparations. See* **hurry** 2.

speedy *see* **fast** 1, 2.

spell
(n) The witch used a spell to turn the prince into a frog. charm, incantation, magic formula, magic words *(plural)*, curse.

spend
1 *(v) How much money did you spend?* pay, pay out, get through, part with, lay out *(informal)*, shell out *(informal)*, fork out *(slang)*, cough up *(informal)*, lash out *(informal)*, splurge, blow *(slang)*, squander, waste, fritter away.
OPPOSITE: save.
2 *(v) How shall we spend the day?* occupy, fill, pass, while away, use up.
3 *(v) You should spend more time on your homework.* put in, concentrate, invest, lavish, devote.

spice
(n) This curry needs more spice. flavouring, seasoning, taste, flavour, bite, piquancy.
TYPES OF SPICE: allspice, caraway seed, cardamom, cayenne, chilli, cinnamon, clove, coriander, cumin, curry powder, ginger, mace, nutmeg, paprika, pepper, pimento, saffron, star anise, turmeric.

spicy
1 *(adj) A spicy curry.* hot, peppery, fiery, piquant, aromatic, highly seasoned.
OPPOSITES: bland, mild.
2 *(adj) (informal) Spicy gossip. See* **juicy** 2.

spike
(n) Be careful of that spike! point, prong, barb, stake, nail, thorn, prickle, needle.

spiky *see* **prickly** 1.

spill
1 *(v) Try not to spill your drink.* knock over, overturn, tip over, upset.
2 *(v) Lift the bucket slowly so the water doesn't spill.* spill out, slop over, run over, brim over, overflow, pour out, flow out.

spin
(v) Open the music box and watch the ballerina spin. go round, turn, twirl, whirl, pirouette, revolve, rotate, gyrate, wheel.

spine *see* **back** 1.

spine-chilling *see* **frightening**.

spirit
1 *(n) Do you think your spirit will live on after you die?* soul, inner self, psyche.
2 *(n) The castle was haunted by a spirit. See* **ghost**.
3 *(n) The explorers showed great spirit in the face of danger. See* **courage**.
4 *(n) It's hard to suppress Lydia; she's got so much spirit.* energy, life, enthusiasm, sparkle, fire, vigour, zest, verve, zip *(informal)*, willpower, determination.

spit
1 *(v) Don't spit on the floor!* gob *(informal)*, spew, expectorate, hawk.
2 *(v) Graham tends to spit when he talks.* splutter, sputter, spray, hiss.

spiteful
(adj) Tania's spiteful comments upset me. malicious, snide, hurtful, cruel, nasty, unkind, catty *(informal)*, bitchy *(informal)*, vicious, vindictive, poisonous, venomous.

splash
1 *(v) Marcus began to splash paint on the walls.* slap, slop, slosh *(informal)*, spatter, splatter, sprinkle, squirt, spray, shower, spill, daub, splodge.
2 *(v) Can you hear the waves splash against the rocks?* break, dash, wash, surge, smack, swish, swash, plash, plop.
3 *(v) I love to splash in the river.* paddle, wallow, wade, dabble, bathe, plunge.

splendid
1 *(adj) Splendid tapestries.* magnificent, gorgeous, impressive, rich, costly, sumptuous, opulent, ornate, dazzling, glittering, resplendent, lavish, luxurious.

2 *(adj) A splendid essay.* See **excellent**.

splinter
1 *(n) A small splinter broke off the table.*
See **chip** 2.
2 *(v) The explosion made the glass
splinter.* See **smash** 2.

split
1 *(v) I hope this bag doesn't split.* burst,
tear, rip, come apart, break, give way.
2 *(v) The ground seemed to split beneath
my feet.* open, crack, gape, yawn, part.
3 *(v) Where does the path split in two?*
See **divide** 1.
4 *(v) Let's split the money between us.*
See **divide** 3.
5 *(n) I have a split in my jeans.* See **tear** 4.

split up see **separate** 1, 3.

spoil
1 *(v) One mistake could spoil your chances
of winning.* See **ruin** 1.
2 *(v) I didn't mean to spoil your painting.*
damage, ruin, wreck, deface, mess up,
smudge, blemish, mark, stain, botch.
3 *(v) I wish Granny wouldn't spoil you.*
indulge, overindulge, pamper,
mollycoddle, wait on you hand and foot,
cosset, spoon-feed, baby, pander to.

spoilsport
(n) Don't be such a spoilsport! killjoy, wet
blanket *(informal)*, party pooper *(informal)*,
misery *(informal)*, dog in the manger.

spoof
*(n) (informal) This film is a spoof of a
disaster movie.* takeoff *(informal)*, send-up
(informal), parody, pastiche, satire.

spooky
*(adj) (informal) The castle looks spooky in
the moonlight.* eerie, creepy *(informal)*,
mysterious, ghostly, uncanny, unearthly,
weird, frightening, spine-chilling, haunted.
❖ *Also see* **ghosts & hauntings**.

sport
(n) Sport is good for you. exercise, games
(plural), physical activity, PE (physical
education), physical recreation.
TYPES OF SPORT: aikido, American
football, angling, archery, athletics,
badminton, baseball, basketball, beach
volleyball, billiards, bobsleighing, bowls,
boxing, canoeing, cricket, croquet, curling,
cycling, darts, diving, dressage, eventing,
fencing, Gaelic football, golf, greyhound
racing, gymnastics, handball, hockey,
horse racing, hurling, ice hockey, judo,
jujitsu, karate, lacrosse, luge, motorcycle
racing, motor racing, mountaineering,
netball, orienteering, polo, pool, rallycross,
rock climbing, rounders, rowing, rugby
league, rugby union, sailing, shooting,
show jumping, skating, skiing, snooker,
soccer, softball, squash, surfing,
swimming, synchronized swimming, table
tennis, tae kwon do, tennis, trampolining,
volleyball, water polo, water-skiing,
weightlifting, windsurfing, wrestling,
yachting. *Also see* **athletics**.

sport words

types of sporting event

challenge	play-off
championship	preliminary
competition	round
contest	qualifying
final	round
fixture	quarterfinal
friendly match	race
game	regatta
head-to-head	replay
heat	semifinal
match	test match
Olympic Games	time trial
Paralympics	tournament

sport moves

attack	evade	pass	speed
block	field	pitch	spin
bowl	glide	punch	sprint
catch	hurtle	race	stretch
chase	intercept	reach	strike
corner	jump	retrieve	swerve
dart	kick	save	swing
defend	leap	score	tackle
deflect	lob	shoot	throw
dive	lunge	skim	tumble
dodge	mark	slam	twist
dribble	overtake	slide	vault
duck	parry	smash	volley

competitors may...

be disqualified	go flat out	storm ahead
be stretchered off	miss a shot	take a penalty
break a record	play safe	take evasive
cheat	put on a spurt	action
clinch the match	reach a new	take the lead
commit a foul	personal best	use tactics
draw level	run out of steam	work as a
equalize	score a hat-trick	team
fend off a tackle	set the pace	
follow a game plan		

sporting events can be...

dangerous	hotly
demanding	contested
draining	nail-biting
dramatic	nerve-racking
dull	punishing
electrifying	strenuous
emotional	tedious
exhausting	tense
exhilarating	testing
frustrating	thrilling
gruelling	uneventful

sporting events can end in...

celebration	humiliation
controversy	injury time
dead heat	photo finish
defeat	riot
disaster	success
draw	tie
extra time	triumph
failure	victory

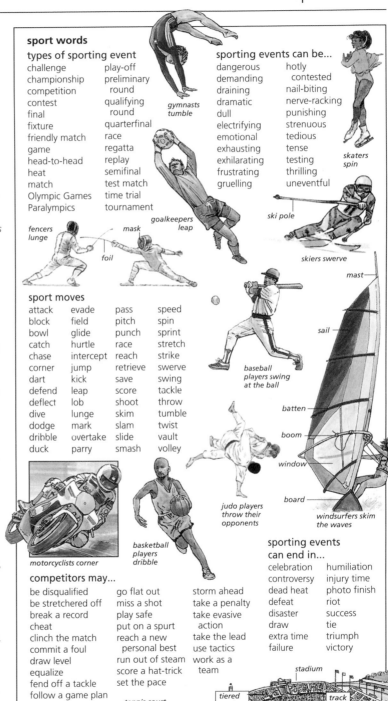

*gymnasts
tumble*

*skaters
spin*

ski pole

skiers swerve

*fencers
lunge*

mask

foil

*goalkeepers
leap*

*baseball
players swing
at the ball*

mast

sail

batten

boom

window

board

*judo players
throw their
opponents*

*windsurfers skim
the waves*

motorcyclists corner

*basketball
players
dribble*

stadium

*tiered
seating*

track

tennis court

field

sports complex

sports hall

swimming pool

sporty
(adj) Tabby is very sporty. athletic, active, energetic, fit, hearty, outdoorsy *(informal)*.

spot
1 *(v) Did you spot the difference between the pictures?* notice, detect, identify, pinpoint, discover, pick out, single out, observe, put your finger on *(informal)*.
2 *(v) Did you spot my note? See* **notice** 1.
3 *(n) Try to rub that spot off the wall.* mark, stain, speck, fleck, smudge, blotch, blob, blot, splotch, patch, blemish.
4 *(n) Jilly has a spot on her chin.* pimple, zit *(slang)*, blackhead, boil, pustule, mole.
5 *(n) We found a perfect spot to camp. See* **place** 1.
6 **spots** *(plural) Our curtains are blue with yellow spots.* dots *(plural)*, polka dots *(plural)*, circles *(plural)*, blobs *(plural)*.

spotless *see* **clean** 2.

spotty
(adj) Spike has a spotty face. pimply, acne-covered, blotchy, blemished, freckled.

sprawl
(v) I love to sprawl in front of the telly. stretch out, lie around, lounge, loll, flop, slouch, slump, spread-eagle.

spray
1 *(v) Don't spray water over me!* sprinkle, shower, spatter, splash, scatter, squirt.
2 *(n) The fountain sent out a spray of water.* jet, shower, sprinkling, mist, drizzle, squirt, droplets *(plural)*, vapour.

spread
1 *(v) Spread the rug on the ground.* spread out, stretch out, open out, lay out, unroll, unfold, arrange, display.
2 *(v) Spread the glue thickly.* apply, smear on, plaster on, lay on, daub, coat.
3 *(v) See the puddle spread! See* **grow** 2.
4 *(v) The violence may spread.* increase, escalate, mushroom, grow, proliferate.
5 *(v) Spread the news!* pass on, circulate, broadcast, publicize, make known, make public, proclaim, disseminate, transmit.

spring *see* **jump** 1.

springy *see* **bouncy** 1.

sprinkle
1 *(v) Sprinkle sugar over the cake.* scatter, strew, shower, spread, dust, pepper.
2 *(v) Don't sprinkle water everywhere! See* **spray** 1.

sprint *see* **run** 1.

spurt
1 *(v) Water began to spurt from the pipe. See* **squirt**.
2 *(n) I felt a spurt of speed as the car accelerated.* burst, surge, rush, explosion.

spy
1 *(n) Could Stanley be a spy?* secret agent, undercover agent, enemy agent, mole *(informal)*, double agent, infiltrator.
2 **spy on** *(v) Let's spy on Leo!* keep watch on, keep an eye on, follow, shadow, tail, trail, snoop on, eavesdrop on.

squabble *see* **argue** 1.

squash
1 *(v) Don't squash the strawberries!* crush, squeeze, squish, flatten, pulp, pulverize, smash, mash, mangle, compress, pound, stamp on, tread on, trample on, crumple.
2 *(v) I can't squash any more food into the fridge. See* **squeeze** 1.

squashy
(adj) I hate squashy bananas. soft, squishy, squidgy, mushy, pulpy, spongy, soggy.

squat
1 *(v) Squat behind this bush! See* **crouch**.
2 *(adj) Angus has a squat figure.* dumpy, stocky, chunky, stubby, thickset, short.
OPPOSITE: lanky.

squawk
(v) The parrot began to squawk. screech, shriek, squeal, cackle, crow, cheep, hoot.

squeak
(v) Can you hear my brakes squeak? squeal, screech, creak, scrape, grate, peep.

squeal *see* **scream**.

squeeze
1 *(v) I can't squeeze any more food into the fridge.* squash, cram, stuff, pack, crowd, jam, ram, force, wedge.
2 *(v) Try to squeeze the water out of the cloth.* wring, force, twist, screw, extract.
3 *(v) Don't squeeze my hand like that!* grip, clasp, clutch, pinch, nip, press, crush, squash, compress.
4 *(v) Try to squeeze your way through the crowd.* edge, shoulder, worm, wriggle, squirm, wiggle, elbow, jostle, push, shove.
5 *(n) I gave Anna a friendly squeeze.* hug, embrace, cuddle, clasp, grasp, bear hug.

squirm
1 *(v) Don't squirm about! See* **wriggle** 1.
2 *(v) Dad's jokes make me squirm.* cringe, wince, die of shame *(informal)*, curl up and die *(informal)*, flinch, blench, writhe.

squirt
(v) Watch the water squirt out of the hose. spurt, shoot, gush, spout, jet, spray, splash, spatter, pour, spit, spew, shower.

stab
(v) Stab the dragon through the heart! pierce, spear, knife, spike, lance, skewer, impale, run through, gore, transfix.

stack *see* **pile** 1, 2.

stage
1 *(n) Stand on the stage to recite your poem.* platform, dais, rostrum, podium.
2 *(n) We completed the final stage of our journey.* phase, leg, section, step, lap.
3 *(v) Let's stage a play next term.* perform, put on, produce, present, mount.

stagger
1 *(v) The weight of the parcel made me stagger.* totter, teeter, reel, lurch, stumble, wobble, sway, falter.
2 *(v) The height of the skyscrapers will stagger you. See* **astonish**.

stagnant
(adj) A pool of stagnant water. motionless, still, stale, foul, dirty, filthy, polluted.
OPPOSITES: flowing, fresh.

stain
1 *(n) I must get this stain off my shirt.* mark, spot, blotch, smudge, smear, blot.
2 *(n) The rumour left a stain on my reputation.* smear, slur, blot, blemish, taint.
3 *(v) Those sweets will stain your tongue blue.* dye, colour, tinge, tint, discolour.

stairs
(plural n) steps (plural), flight of stairs, staircase, stairway.

stale
1 *(adj) This bread is stale.* old, dry, dried up, dried out, hard, mouldy.
OPPOSITE: fresh.
2 *(adj) The air in the cellar smelt stale.* musty, fusty, frowsty, stuffy, foul, damp.
OPPOSITE: fresh.

stammer
(v) I always stammer when I'm nervous. stutter, splutter, falter, hesitate, stumble.

stamp
1 *(n) Look for the maker's stamp on the vase.* mark, imprint, hallmark, seal, label, logo, signature, impression, brand.
2 *(v) Please don't stamp around the house.* stomp *(informal)*, clump, clomp, tramp, pound, thump, thud.
3 **stamp on** *(v) Don't stamp on the flowers! See* **trample on**.

stand
1 *(v) Stand when the judge comes in.* stand up, rise, get to your feet, get up.
OPPOSITES: sit, sit down.
2 *(v) Don't stand on my toes! See* **step** 5.
3 *(v) Stand the photograph on the shelf.* put, place, set, position, set upright, prop.
4 *(v) I can't stand the sight of blood!* bear, stick *(slang)*, endure, abide, tolerate, stomach, take, handle, cope with, put up with *(informal)*.

standard
1 *(n) Are you pleased with the standard of my work? See* **quality** 1, 2.
2 *(n) Steve's tennis is below standard.* average, the norm, par.
3 *(adj) It's standard practice to brush your teeth in the morning. See* **normal** 1.

stand by
1 *(v) I'll stand by you whatever happens.* support, be loyal to, stay with, stick with *(informal)*, back, take your side, defend.
2 *(v) Stand by for takeoff!* be prepared, be ready, wait, wait in the wings.

stand for
(v) What does "PC" stand for? represent, mean, indicate, denote, signify, symbolize.

stand in for
(v) I'll stand in for you if you're ill. take your place, fill in for, cover for, deputize for, take over from, substitute for, replace, represent, understudy *(theatre)*.

stand out
(v) *You'll certainly stand out in that orange shirt!* stick out, be noticed, attract attention, be conspicuous, be eye-catching, stand out from the crowd.

stand up for
(v) *I'll stand up for you.* stick up for (informal), defend, come to your defence, back, support, take your side, stand by.

star
1 (n) *Astronomers have sighted a new star.* ❖ See **space adventure**.
2 (n) *Jodie longs to be a star.* celebrity, superstar, megastar, big name, top draw, idol, screen goddess, starlet, celeb (informal), VIP (very important person).
3 (v) *Who will star in this film?* take the lead, play the starring role, head the cast, top the bill, co-star, feature.

stare
1 (v) *When I met Famous Fred, all I could do was stare.* gape, gaze, look, gawp (slang), gawk, goggle, be open-mouthed, ogle, rubberneck (slang).
2 (n) *A hard stare.* glare, look, dirty look.

start
1 (v) *You've got lots to do, so you'd better start soon.* get started, make a start, make a beginning, begin, get going, get moving, get weaving (informal), take the plunge (informal), get the show on the road (informal), pull your finger out (informal).
OPPOSITE: stop.
2 (v) *When did life on earth first start?* See **begin** 4.
3 (v) *Are you packed and ready to start?* See **leave** 1.
4 (v) *Who will start the discussion?* begin, commence, open, initiate, kick off (informal), set in motion, kick-start, get going, get under way, start the ball rolling.
OPPOSITES: end, finish.
5 (v) *Mum wants to start her own business.* set up, establish, launch, create, found, form, pioneer, get off the ground (informal), get going, get set in motion.
OPPOSITES: wind up, close down.
6 (n) *Danni missed the start of the show.* beginning, opening, commencement, kickoff (informal), introduction.
OPPOSITE: end.
7 (n) *Greg got a start on the others at the beginning of the race.* head start, lead, advantage, edge, margin.
8 (n) *Bo woke with a start.* See **jump** 6.

startle
(v) *Did the firecracker startle you?* alarm, scare, frighten, make you jump, give you a start, catch you unawares, shock, surprise, unnerve, unsettle, disturb, disconcert.

starving
1 (adj) *The refugees were starving.* hungry, starved, famished, underfed, malnourished, dying of starvation.
2 (adj) (informal) *I'm starving!* ravenous, famished, hungry.

state
1 (v) *Did Beryl state that she was innocent?* declare, say, assert, affirm, announce, proclaim, profess, reveal.
2 (v) *You'll have a chance to state your opinion.* put, express, voice, present, put across, explain, communicate, submit.
3 (n) *The castle is owned by the state.* nation, country, government, people (plural), citizens (plural), republic, kingdom, realm (old-fashioned), commonwealth.
4 (n) *What sort of state are the survivors in?* condition, shape, frame of mind, mood, spirits (plural), form, health.

stay
1 (v) *Don't stay in town too long.* remain, hang around, linger, loiter, delay, stop, wait around, dally.
2 (v) *We're hoping to stay in a luxury hotel.* spend the night, stop over, take a room, put up, lodge, board.
3 (v) *If we like Australia we might stay there.* See **settle** 1.
4 (v) *Please stay standing.* remain, keep, continue, carry on, go on.
5 (n) *Enjoy your stay in London!* holiday, break, stopover, visit, vacation.

steady
1 (adj) *This chair isn't very steady.* firm, stable, safe, secure, solid.
OPPOSITES: unsteady, wobbly.
2 (adj) *The steady rain kept us indoors.* continuous, constant, incessant, nonstop, endless, persistent, ceaseless, unremitting.
OPPOSITES: intermittent, sporadic.
3 (adj) *The drummer kept up a steady beat.* regular, rhythmic, even, constant, repeated, unvarying, uniform, unhurried.
OPPOSITES: irregular, uneven.

steal
1 (v) *It's wrong to steal.* thieve, pilfer, shoplift, pick pockets, commit a theft.
2 (v) *Someone tried to steal my purse.* take, make off with, walk off with, pocket, filch, misappropriate, pinch (informal), nick (slang), lift (informal), swipe (slang).

steep
1 (adj) *There's a steep drop down to the beach.* sheer, precipitous, sharp, sudden, abrupt, vertical, perpendicular.
OPPOSITES: gentle, gradual.
2 (v) *Steep your shirt in water.* See **soak** 1.

steer
(v) *The car was hard to steer.* control, handle, drive, direct, navigate, pilot.

step
1 (n) *My foot slipped off the step.* stair, rung (ladder), doorstep, tread (staircase).
2 (n) *Take one step forwards.* pace, stride.
3 (n) *We must plan our next step carefully.* move, manoeuvre, course of action, act.
4 (n) *Learning to read is an important step for a child.* step forward, advance, development, progression, stage, phase.
5 (v) *Don't step on my toes!* tread, stand, tramp, trample, walk, stamp.

stern
1 (adj) *A stern look.* severe, grim, forbidding, serious, disapproving, tight-lipped, steely-eyed, frowning, unsmiling, unsympathetic, sombre, sober, austere.
2 (adj) *A stern teacher.* See **strict** 1.

stick
1 (n) *Throw another stick on the bonfire.* branch, twig, switch, piece of wood.
2 (n) *Grandpa uses a stick when he walks.* walking stick, cane, crutch, staff, crook.
3 (n) *Don't hit me with that stick!* rod, cane, switch, birch, truncheon, baton, club, cudgel, cosh.
4 (n) *Tie the ivy to a stick so it won't droop.* cane, pole, stake, post.
5 (v) *Stick the pieces together.* glue, tape, paste, gum, fix, fasten, attach, join, bond.
6 (v) *Don't stick your finger in the trifle!* put, poke, jab, stab, dig, thrust, insert.
7 (v) *Let's hope the car doesn't stick in the mud.* get stuck, get bogged down, get embedded, get lodged, get clogged up.
8 (v) *I felt a bone stick in my throat.* catch, lodge, wedge, jam, get trapped, snag.
9 (v) (informal) *Stick your trainers in the wardrobe.* See **bung**.
10 (v) (slang) *I can't stick this noise any longer!* See **stand** 4.

stick at *see* **persevere**.

stick out
1 (v) *How far does the ledge stick out?* jut out, extend, project, protrude, overhang.
2 (v) *You'll certainly stick out in that orange shirt!* See **stand out**.

sticky
1 (adj) *A sticky label.* gummed, adhesive.
2 (adj) *A sticky mixture.* gluey, gooey (informal), tacky, glutinous, viscous.
3 (adj) *A sticky bun.* gooey (informal), syrupy, treacly, sugary, creamy, jammy.
4 (adj) *Sticky weather.* See **muggy**.

stiff
1 (adj) *I can't bend this plastic; it's too stiff.* rigid, hard, firm, inflexible, unbending, unyielding, inelastic, brittle.
OPPOSITES: flexible, pliable.
2 (adj) *After the climb my muscles felt stiff.* tight, tense, taut, unsupple, painful, aching, sore, creaky (informal), arthritic.
OPPOSITE: supple.
3 (adj) *The robot's movements looked stiff.* See **awkward** 2.

stifle *see* **smother** 1, 2.

still
1 (adj) *Andy stood still and stared.* motionless, stock-still, rooted to the spot, without moving, immobile, stationary, paralysed, transfixed, spellbound, frozen.
2 (adj) *The clouds were reflected in the still water.* calm, motionless, smooth, unruffled, undisturbed, stagnant.
OPPOSITE: turbulent.
3 (adj) *What a still evening!* quiet, silent, calm, tranquil, peaceful, windless, airless.
OPPOSITES: stormy, noisy.

sting
(v) *If you get soap in your eyes it will sting.* smart, burn, prick, hurt, tingle, irritate.

stingy see **mean 5.**

stink
1 (v) *Those rotten eggs really stink.* smell, reek, pong (informal), stink to high heaven (informal), hum (slang), whiff (slang).
2 (n) *What's making that stink?* stench, bad smell, foul odour, pong (informal).

stir
1 (v) *Stir the ingredients together.* mix, blend, whisk, beat, whip.
2 (v) *The leaves began to stir in the breeze.* move, quiver, tremble, flutter, rustle, shake, twitch.
3 **stir up** (v) *Oscar loves to stir up trouble.* make, cause, start, provoke, spark off, trigger off, incite, instigate, inflame.

stomach
1 (n) *Tabitha has a pain in her stomach.* tummy (informal), belly, abdomen, insides (plural) (informal), guts (plural).
2 (n) *Trevor has a huge stomach.* tummy (informal), paunch, gut (slang), beer belly (slang), spare tyre (informal), potbelly.

stone
1 (n) *I found a smooth stone on the beach.* pebble, rock, boulder.
2 (n) *Flash Frank wears a ring with a huge stone in it.* See **jewel**.
3 (n) *Don't eat the stone in the middle of the fruit.* pip, seed, kernel, nut.
4 (n) *The grave was marked by a stone.* gravestone, headstone, tombstone, monument, memorial stone, tablet.
5 **stones** (plural n) *Don't slip on the stones!* gravel, scree, shingle, pebbles (plural), cobbles (plural).

stony
(adj) *We struggled over the stony ground.* rocky, rough, pebbly, gravelly, shingly (beach), boulder-strewn, hard, flinty.

stoop
1 (v) *You'll have to stoop to get into the cave.* duck, crouch, bend down, lean down, bow down, bend your head, lower your head, hunch your shoulders, squat.
2 (v) *How could you stoop to playing such a mean trick?* See **lower yourself**.

stop
1 (v) *Wait for the bus to stop before you get off.* come to a stop, come to a halt, come to a standstill, pull up, draw up, halt, come to rest, grind to a halt.
OPPOSITES: go, start.
2 (v) *Let's stop now; I'm tired.* pause, have a break, rest, finish, call it a day (informal), knock off (informal), down tools.
OPPOSITES: keep going, carry on.
3 (v) *Dad has decided to stop smoking.* finish, cease, quit, give up, desist from, refrain from, leave off, cut out (informal), pack in (informal), kick (informal).
OPPOSITES: start, take up.

4 (v) *The college may stop our pottery classes.* put an end to, call a halt to, end, finish, wind up, shut down, discontinue, cut short, break off, axe (informal), drop.
OPPOSITES: start, set up.
5 (v) *You can't stop me from going to the disco.* See **prevent 2.**
6 (v) *Stop that man!* catch, seize, restrain, hold, capture, intercept, arrest, detain.
7 (v) *We must stop the bleeding.* stem, staunch, check, hold back, control.
8 (v) *Will you stop anywhere on your way to Paris?* break your journey, spend time, stay, spend a night, stay over, put up, visit.
9 (n) *Is this your stop?* bus stop, station, halt, terminus, destination, depot.

store
1 (v) *Farmers have to store hay for the winter.* stock up on, set aside, put by, lay in, save, reserve, stash away (informal), salt away, accumulate, amass, hoard, stockpile.
2 (n) *Pirate Peg has a huge store of gold.* hoard, stock, stockpile, quantity, supply, fund, reserve, cache, accumulation.

storm
1 (n) *The storm wrecked our garden.* gale, squall, tempest, thunderstorm, blizzard, hurricane, typhoon, cyclone, tornado, whirlwind, twister (informal), monsoon.
2 (v) *Why did Josie storm out of the room like that?* flounce, stamp, stomp (informal), rush, charge, fly, stalk, march, stride.

stormy
1 (adj) *Stormy weather.* rough, windy, squally, blustery, gusty, thundery, rainy, foul, dirty, wild, violent.
OPPOSITES: calm, fine.
2 (adj) *Stormy seas.* See **rough 2.**

story
1 (n) *Tell me the story of the giant octopus!* tale, yarn (informal), anecdote, account, history, narrative.
TYPES OF STORY: adventure story, allegory, crime story, detective story, fable, fairy tale, fantasy story, folk tale, ghost story, historical romance, horror story, legend, love story, mystery, myth, novel, parable, romance, saga, science fiction story, spy story, thriller, whodunit (informal).
2 (n) *Clark wrote a good story for "Rap Weekly".* See **article 1.**

stout see **plump.**

straight
1 (adj) *This wall isn't straight.* level, even, horizontal, perpendicular, vertical, upright, true, flush, plumb, square, aligned, in line.
OPPOSITES: crooked, bent.
2 (adj) *We took the straight route to the coast.* direct, short, undeviating, quick.
OPPOSITES: indirect, circuitous.
3 (adj) *Our team has had five straight wins.* consecutive, successive, unbroken, uninterrupted, continuous, in a row.
4 (adj) *A straight answer.* See **honest 1.**

---

storm words

in a storm	thunder may...	the rain may...	storms can...	storms can be...
billowing clouds	boom	beat down	block roads	awe-inspiring
cloudburst	crack	bucket down	bring down power lines	cataclysmic
deluge	crash	lash down	cut off villages	catastrophic
downpour	echo	pelt down	damage crops	deafening
driving rain	growl	pour down	destroy buildings	destructive
forked lightning	resound	teem down	flatten fences	devastating
gale	reverberate		flood homes	dramatic
gust of wind	roar	**the wind may...**	mangle cars	ear-splitting
hailstones	roll	batter	maroon motorists	fierce
inky sky	rumble	blast	rip off roof tiles	frightening
lashing rain		blow	smash windows	furious
leaden sky	**lightning may...**	buffet	start fires	powerful
peal of thunder	flare	gust	swell rivers	raging
sheet of lightning	flash	howl	topple chimneys	savage
streak of lightning	flicker	moan	uproot trees	short-lived
thunderbolt	light up the sky	rage	wreck ships	spectacular
thunderclap	streak across the sky	roar		squally
torrential rain	strike	shriek		tempestuous
	zigzag	swirl		turbulent
		wail		unrelenting
		whirl		violent
				wild

5 (adv) Go straight to school. directly, immediately, at once, instantly, without delay, by the shortest route.

straightaway see **immediately**.

strain
1 (n) I can't take the strain any longer! See **pressure** 2.
2 (v) Did you strain a muscle? pull, sprain, injure, damage, hurt, twist, tear, wrench.
3 (v) Reading in the dark can strain your eyes. tire, weaken, tax, fatigue, damage.
4 (v) Strain the mixture. sieve, sift, filter, separate, percolate (coffee).

stranded
(adj) Pirate Peg was stranded on a desert island. marooned, shipwrecked, cast away, left high and dry, stuck, abandoned.

strange
1 (adj) Ziggy wears some really strange clothes. unusual, extraordinary, remarkable, funny, odd, peculiar, curious, queer, weird, bizarre, outlandish, eccentric, way-out (informal), wacky (slang), off-the-wall (slang), uncommon, abnormal.
OPPOSITES: normal, standard.
2 (adj) I heard a strange noise outside the window. odd, peculiar, funny, weird, mysterious, eerie, spooky (informal), uncanny, unnatural, unearthly, puzzling, perplexing, mystifying, inexplicable.
OPPOSITES: ordinary, unremarkable.
3 (adj) The new school seemed strange to me. unfamiliar, alien, foreign, different, new, novel, unknown.
OPPOSITES: familiar, well-known.
4 (adj) Indiana was alone in a strange land. unfamiliar, foreign, alien, exotic, remote, little-known, unexplored.
OPPOSITES: familiar, well-known.
5 (adj) I felt strange being the only girl in the class. odd, awkward, ill at ease, uncomfortable, out of place, lost.
OPPOSITES: at ease, comfortable.

strangle
(v) Don't strangle yourself with that scarf! choke, throttle, strangulate, garrotte.

strap
(v) Strap the parcel to your bicycle rack. buckle, lash, fasten, attach, secure, tie.

stray
1 (adj) We're looking after a stray dog. abandoned, lost, homeless, unclaimed.
2 (v) Don't stray too far from the path. wander, roam, ramble, drift, straggle, rove, range, deviate, go off course, go astray.

streak
1 (n) Our car has a black streak down the side. stripe, strip, line, band, slash, zigzag, smear, smudge, mark.
2 (n) Look at that streak of lightning! flash, bolt, fork, stroke, sheet.

stream
1 (n) Gregory paddled in the stream. brook, river, spring, beck, burn, creek, rivulet, tributary. ❖ Also see **river**.

2 (n) A stream of water poured from the washing machine. flood, torrent, cascade, jet, gush, rush, surge, flow, outpouring.
3 (v) Tears began to stream down Anji's face. See **run** 3.

street see **road**.

strength
1 (n) Wilf hasn't the strength to lift a paper bag! power, might, muscle, brawn, force, energy, stamina, vigour.
OPPOSITES: weakness, frailty.
2 (n) Jade showed great strength under pressure. courage, bravery, fortitude, strength of character, spirit, grit, determination, firmness, backbone.
OPPOSITE: weakness.
3 (n) Don't underestimate the strength of my feelings. intensity, depth, force, vehemence, ardour.

strengthen
1 (v) Fluoride can strengthen your teeth. harden, toughen, make stronger, build up.
OPPOSITE: weaken.
2 (v) The soldiers tried to strengthen the castle walls. reinforce, fortify, make stronger, support, brace up, buttress.
OPPOSITE: weaken.
3 (v) This success should strengthen your desire to do well. reinforce, increase, heighten, deepen, intensify, confirm.
OPPOSITES: weaken, undermine.

strenuous see **exhausting**.

stress
1 (n) Too much stress can make you ill. pressure, strain, tension, anxiety, worry, hassle (informal), nervous tension.
2 (n) Put the stress on the first word. emphasis, accent, weight, beat.
3 (v) I must stress the importance of safety. See **emphasize**.

stressed
(adj) I always feel stressed at exam time. under pressure, pressurized, hassled (informal), tense, anxious, overworked, overstretched, pushed to the limit.
OPPOSITE: relaxed.

stressful
1 (adj) The exam period can be a stressful time. tense, worrying, anxious, nerve-racking, nail-biting, agonizing, traumatic.
2 (adj) Teaching is a stressful job. pressurized, high-pressure, demanding, tough, taxing, challenging, difficult, trying.

stretch
1 (v) Stretch the elastic. pull, extend, draw out, tighten, tauten, lengthen, elongate.
2 (v) Balloons stretch when you blow them up. expand, inflate, swell, distend.
3 (v) I hope this jumper doesn't stretch. pull out of shape, get larger, get bigger, widen, lengthen.
OPPOSITE: shrink.
4 (v) How far does the desert stretch? extend, spread, reach, continue, range.
5 (v) This test will stretch you. challenge, push you to the limit, tax, extend.

stretchy
(adj) Rubber bands are stretchy. elastic, stretchable, rubbery, springy.

strict
1 (adj) Jason's dad is really strict. stern, firm, severe, harsh, hard, tough, inflexible, uncompromising, authoritarian, autocratic, iron-handed, iron-fisted, tyrannical.
OPPOSITES: lenient, lax.
2 (adj) Our school has strict rules about uniform. stringent, rigid, hard and fast, rigorous, exacting, inflexible, tight, set.
OPPOSITES: flexible, lax.

stride
1 (v) We watched the sentry stride up and down. pace, march, pound, parade, strut.
2 (n) With one stride the giant crossed the river. step, pace, bound, leap.

strike
1 (v) Should parents ever strike their children? See **hit** 1.
2 (v) Strike the ball hard. See **hit** 3.
3 (v) I saw the car strike a tree. See **hit** 4.
4 (v) When did it strike you that you'd forgotten your key? See **occur** 2.
5 (v) The workers decided to strike. go on strike, walk out, take industrial action, stop work, down tools, come out.
6 (n) Do you support the teachers' strike? industrial action, walkout, stoppage, sit-in.

striking
1 (adj) The similarity between the sisters is striking. obvious, unmistakable, evident, noticeable, conspicuous, visible, remarkable, extraordinary, incredible.
2 (adj) That's a striking painting. eye-catching, distinctive, unusual, arresting, dazzling, stunning (informal), memorable.

string
1 (n) Tie the parcel up with string. cord, twine, yarn, rope.
2 (n) Sasha is wearing a string of pearls. row, strand, rope, necklace.
3 (n) I had a string of disasters. See **series**.

strip
1 (v) You have to strip before you shower. take your clothes off, get undressed, undress, strip off (slang), peel off (slang), remove your clothes, strip naked.
OPPOSITES: get dressed, dress.
2 (v) Strip the paper off the walls. peel, scrape, tear, rip, flake, remove, clear.
3 (n) My sweatshirt has a red strip round the bottom. stripe, band, line, bar.
4 (n) Cut off a strip of material. band, piece, bit, ribbon, swathe, slip, shred.

stripe see **strip** 3.

stroke
1 (v) Fido loves it when you stroke his ears. rub, pat, fondle, caress, pet.
2 (n) What a brilliant stroke! See **shot** 2.

stroll
(v) Why don't you stroll into town? amble, wander, saunter, walk, make your way, mooch (slang), mosey (informal), ramble.

strong

strong
1 *(adj) A strong giant has uprooted the trees!* powerful, mighty, muscular, brawny, hefty, strapping, athletic, sinewy, wiry, sturdy, burly, Ramboesque.
OPPOSITES: weak, puny.
2 *(adj) Clint is a strong character who always gets his way.* forceful, strong-willed, assertive, aggressive, tough, determined, tenacious, unyielding.
OPPOSITES: weak, spineless.
3 *(adj) Ellie has been very strong since her mum fell ill.* brave, courageous, plucky, resilient, gutsy *(informal)*, resourceful.
OPPOSITES: feeble, pathetic.
4 *(adj) The walls are strong. See* **solid** 2.
5 *(adj) Farmer Phyllis wears strong boots.* stout, sturdy, hard-wearing, heavy, heavy-duty, durable, indestructible, robust.
OPPOSITES: lightweight, flimsy.
6 *(adj) Karen has a strong desire to win.* deep, deep-seated, passionate, fervent, intense, keen, fierce, heartfelt, ardent.
OPPOSITES: superficial, half-hearted.
7 *(adj) There are strong arguments against smoking.* compelling, convincing, persuasive, forceful, cogent, potent.
OPPOSITES: unconvincing, weak.
8 *(adj) Ziggy's room is painted in strong colours.* bright, bold, vivid, loud, glaring, dazzling, brilliant, stark, clear, intense.
OPPOSITES: pale, muted.
9 *(adj) This soup has a strong flavour.* intense, concentrated, overpowering, spicy, tangy, piquant, pungent, sharp, biting, fiery, highly flavoured.
OPPOSITES: bland, delicate.
10 *(adj) This drink is too strong for me.* concentrated, overpowering, alcoholic, intoxicating, potent, heady.
OPPOSITES: weak, nonalcoholic.
11 *(adj) A strong wind blew in off the sea.* stiff, high, brisk, fresh, gusting, gale-force.
OPPOSITES: light, gentle.

stroppy *(informal) see* **awkward** 4.

struggle
1 *(v) You will have to struggle to stay in the race.* work hard, strain every muscle, exert yourself, do your utmost, make a huge effort, go all out *(informal)*, bust a gut *(informal)*, break your neck *(informal)*.
2 *(v) Indiana had to struggle with the monster.* grapple, wrestle, tussle, fight, scuffle, skirmish, brawl, scrap *(informal)*, clash, do battle, slog it out, spar, vie.
3 *(v) The puppy will struggle when you put him on the lead.* strain, wriggle, squirm, writhe, flail about.
4 *(n) It was a struggle to complete the assault course.* effort, grind *(informal)*, battle, challenge, slog, long haul.

strut *see* **swagger**.

stubborn
(adj) Don't be so stubborn! obstinate, pig-headed, headstrong, wilful, self-willed, inflexible, defiant, determined.

stuck
1 *(adj) Should the pieces be stuck together?* fixed, fastened, joined, attached, glued, taped, pasted, gummed, cemented.
2 *(adj) I'm stuck in a hole!* stuck fast, stuck tight, wedged, jammed, stranded.
3 *(adj) (informal) Ask Mrs Badger to help you if you're stuck.* stumped, baffled, at a loss, at a standstill, bogged down, beaten, up against a brick wall, at your wits' end.

stuck-up *(informal) see* **snobbish**.

study
1 *(v) Study this chapter for the test.* work on, look at, revise, read up on, swot up on *(informal)*, mug up on *(slang)*, cram *(informal)*, burn the midnight oil.
2 *(v) Dustin wants to study Spanish at college.* learn, take, read, master.
3 *(v) The detectives will study the evidence. See* **examine**.
4 *(n) We're doing a study of local traffic problems. See* **survey**.

stuff
1 *(n) Pick up all your stuff! See* **things**.
2 *(n) The alien's clothes were made of some odd green stuff.* substance, material, fabric, cloth, textile, fibres *(plural)*.
3 *(v) I can't stuff anything more into this case. See* **squeeze** 1.

stuffy
(adj) It was stuffy in the attic. airless, fusty, musty, stale-smelling, frowsty, fuggy, stifling, suffocating, oppressive, poorly ventilated, close, muggy.
OPPOSITES: airy, well-ventilated.

stumble *see* **trip** 2.

stunned
1 *(adj) The blow from the cricket ball left Ian stunned.* dazed, semiconscious, reeling, seeing stars, dizzy, groggy *(informal)*, senseless, in a stupor, unconscious, knocked out, out for the count *(informal)*.
2 *(adj) The news left us stunned.* amazed, astonished, staggered, dazed, shocked, numb, dumbstruck, flabbergasted *(informal)*, dumbfounded, thunderstruck, stupefied, gobsmacked *(slang)*, devastated.

stupid
1 *(adj) Andy isn't usually so stupid!* dim, dense, idiotic, brainless, thick, slow, clueless *(slang)*, gormless *(informal)*, dopey *(slang)*, dumb *(informal)*, dull, obtuse.
OPPOSITES: clever, intelligent.
2 *(adj) What a stupid idea!* idiotic, foolish, daft *(informal)*, crackbrained, ludicrous, silly, senseless, pointless, irresponsible, foolhardy, rash, half-baked *(informal)*.
OPPOSITES: sensible, clever.

sturdy *see* **strong** 1, 5.

stutter *see* **stammer**.

style
1 *(n) I love the style of this skirt.* cut, design, shape, lines *(plural)*.
2 *(n) These jeans are the latest style. See* **fashion** 1.

subject
(n) Choose a subject to debate. topic, issue, question, theme, point, motion.

subtle
1 *(adj) A subtle shade of green.* delicate, understated, gentle, pale, muted, unobtrusive, low-key, tasteful.
2 *(adj) A subtle hint.* gentle, indirect, veiled, implied, tactful, insinuated, crafty.

succeed
1 *(v) I'm sure you'll succeed.* do well, be successful, prosper, thrive, flourish, get on, get to the top, make it *(informal)*, make good, arrive *(informal)*, triumph.
OPPOSITES: fail, be unsuccessful.
2 *(v) My scheme didn't succeed.* work, work out, turn out well, produce results, come off *(informal)*, bear fruit.
OPPOSITES: fail, fall flat.

success
1 *(n) I hope our play will be a success.* hit *(informal)*, smash hit *(informal)*, sensation, triumph, winner, crowd puller *(informal)*, sellout *(informal)*, blockbuster *(informal)*.
OPPOSITES: failure, flop *(informal)*.
2 *(n) Success hasn't spoiled Famous Fred.* stardom, fame, good fortune, glory, honour, acclaim, recognition, prosperity.
OPPOSITE: failure.

successful
1 *(adj) Mum runs a successful business.* profitable, thriving, flourishing, booming, lucrative, fruitful, productive, profit-making, moneymaking, rewarding.
OPPOSITES: failing, unsuccessful.
2 *(adj) Mr Mustafa is a successful businessman.* wealthy, prosperous, well-off, high-earning, high-flying, high-powered, top, best-selling *(writer)*.
OPPOSITES: unsuccessful, failed.
3 *(adj) Our team has been successful all year.* victorious, unbeaten, on a winning streak, out in front *(informal)*, triumphant.
OPPOSITES: unsuccessful, defeated.

suck
(v) Suck your drink through a straw. drink, suck up, slurp *(informal)*, draw up, take in.

suck up *(informal) see* **crawl** 3.

sudden
1 *(adj) A sudden noise.* unexpected, startling, surprising, unforeseen.
OPPOSITES: expected, anticipated.
2 *(adj) A sudden decision.* instant, quick, speedy, hasty, snap, spur-of-the-moment, immediate, hurried, impetuous, impulsive, spontaneous, rash, unconsidered.
OPPOSITES: considered, careful.
3 *(adj) Sudden movements.* abrupt, jerky, rapid, quick, unpredictable, unexpected.
OPPOSITES: slow, gradual.

suddenly
(adv) Suddenly the car swerved. all of a sudden, all at once, without warning, unexpectedly, out of the blue *(informal)*, on the spur of the moment, abruptly.

suffer
1 (v) *The vet made sure that Fido wouldn't suffer.* be in pain, feel any pain, be hurt, be in agony, be racked with pain, be sore.
2 (v) *If parents fight, their children will suffer.* be distressed, be upset, be hurt, feel miserable, feel wretched, have a bad time, go through hell (informal), grieve.
3 (v) *I can't suffer another day of this misery.* go through, endure, tolerate, put up with (informal), bear, stand, take, stick (slang), cope with, handle.

suffocate *see* **smother** 1.

suggest
1 (v) *What did Dr Honey suggest?* propose, advise, recommend, advocate, put forward, counsel, urge, prescribe.
2 (v) *The pictures suggest that the hotel has a pool.* give the impression, give the idea, lead you to believe, make you think, indicate, show, imply, hint, insinuate.

suit
1 (n) *That's a very smart suit.* outfit, ensemble. ❖ *Also see* **clothes**.
2 (v) *Those jeans suit you.* look good on, look right on, do something for, flatter, suit your image, become (old-fashioned).
3 (v) *Would three o'clock tomorrow suit you?* be convenient for, be good for, be acceptable to, do for, meet your requirements, please, satisfy.

suitable
1 (adj) *This video isn't suitable for children.* appropriate, fit, acceptable, meant, cut out, right, fitting, relevant to.
OPPOSITES: unsuitable, inappropriate.
2 (adj) *Is this a suitable moment to talk?* convenient, appropriate, opportune, good.
OPPOSITES: inappropriate, awkward.

sulky
(adj) *There's no need to be sulky just because you lost.* in a sulk, in a huff, resentful, disgruntled, put out, piqued, grumpy, cross, petulant, peevish, grouchy (informal), sullen, moody, bad-tempered, in a strop (slang), morose, surly, sour.

summary
(n) *Write a summary of what happened in the first chapter.* outline, résumé, précis, synopsis, overview, rundown, survey, analysis, review, summing-up.

summon
(v) *Summon the king's musicians!* send for, call for, call, fetch, call together, assemble, gather, muster, demand the presence of.

sum up
(v) *Can you sum up what happened in the last chapter?* summarize, give a summary of, outline, give a rundown of, give the main points of, put in a nutshell, encapsulate, précis, review.

sunburnt
(adj) *Dad looks sunburnt.* red, scarlet, like a lobster, burnt, blistered, peeling, tanned, suntanned, brown as a berry, bronzed.

sunny
(adj) *Sunny weather.* sunshiny, fine, summery, bright, clear, cloudless, brilliant.
OPPOSITES: cloudy, dull.

sunrise *see* **dawn** 1.

sunset *see* **dusk**.

sunshine
(n) *Open the curtains and let in the sunshine.* sun, sunlight, sunbeams (plural), sun's rays (plural), daylight, light.

supple
(adj) *A supple gymnast.* lithe, agile, loose-limbed, nimble, flexible, lissom, limber.
OPPOSITES: stiff, awkward.

supply
1 (v) *Can you supply some backing for our project?* provide, contribute, produce, give, offer, donate, come up with, fork out (slang), grant, pass on.
2 (v) *The school will supply you with books.* provide, equip, furnish, kit you out.
3 (n) *Anjali keeps a supply of chocolate in her bedroom.* hoard, store, stock, stockpile, quantity, fund, reserve, cache.
4 **supplies** (plural n) *Do we have enough supplies for the trip?* food, rations (plural), provisions (plural), stores (plural), equipment, materials (plural).

support
1 (v) *These pillars support the ceiling.* hold up, keep up, prop up, carry, bear, underpin, shore up, strengthen, reinforce.
2 (v) *Uncle Pete works hard to support his family.* provide for, keep, take care of, look after, finance, maintain, sustain, nourish.
3 (v) *Do you support animal rights?* agree with, go along with, back, defend, uphold, stand up for, stick up for (informal), speak out for, argue for, promote, champion.
OPPOSITE: oppose.
4 (n) *I'm grateful for the support of my parents.* encouragement, moral support, backing, backup, help, assistance, approval, reassurance, loyalty, friendship.

suppose
1 (v) *I suppose Tom is ill. See* **assume**.
2 (v) *Let's suppose that pigs could fly!* imagine, pretend, make believe, fantasize.

sure *see* **certain** 1, 3.

surface
1 (n) *This fruit has a knobbly surface.* exterior, covering, outside, skin, outer face, wall, crust, coat.
2 (n) *The table has a shiny surface.* top, coating, finish, veneer, sheen, polish, patina, appearance, texture.
3 (n) *Paint each surface of the box a different colour. See* **side** 1.

surge
1 (v) *We watched the waves surge around the rocks.* gush, rush, swirl, eddy, billow, seethe, stream, well up, heave, roll.
2 (v) *Did you see the fans surge on to the pitch?* rush, charge, stampede, swarm, stream, throng, flood, sweep, push.

surprise
1 (v) *This news will surprise you.* amaze, astonish, astound, stun, stagger, shock, take your breath away, bowl you over (informal), leave you open-mouthed, throw (informal), wow (slang).
2 (v) *Did Mum surprise you as you were raiding the fridge?* burst in on, catch you out, catch you unawares, take you by surprise, catch you in the act, catch you red-handed, startle, ambush.
3 (n) *Kate's eyes opened wide with surprise.* amazement, astonishment, incredulity, wonder, shock, bewilderment.
4 (n) *What a surprise! See* **shock** 4.

surprised
(adj) *I bet you're surprised to see me!* amazed, astonished, astounded, startled, taken aback, taken by surprise, shocked, stunned, staggered, thunderstruck, flabbergasted (informal), gobsmacked (slang), bowled over (informal).

surprising
(adj) *A surprising result.* amazing, astonishing, astounding, incredible, staggering, startling, extraordinary, unexpected, unforeseen, unpredicted, unusual, remarkable, shocking.
OPPOSITES: predictable, unsurprising.

surrender
(v) *Will you surrender?* give in, admit defeat, give yourself up, submit, yield, cave in (informal), lay down your arms, show the white flag, throw in the towel, quit.

surround
(v) *The soldiers planned to surround the castle.* circle, ring, close in on, encircle, hem in, fence in, hedge in, encompass, enclose, envelop, besiege, lay siege to.

surroundings
(plural n) *The hotel is situated in pleasant surroundings.* environment, location, neighbourhood, setting, vicinity, locality.

survey
(n) *Show the results of your survey in a graph.* study, investigation, inquiry, examination, analysis, research, review, poll, questionnaire, ballot, count, census.

survive
1 (v) *The explorers managed to survive.* stay alive, hold out, get by (informal), cling to life, keep body and soul together (informal), pull through, live, exist.
2 (v) *Did the daffodils survive the storm?* come through, withstand, weather, live through, outlast, outlive.

suspect
1 (v) *Why should Oz suspect you?* distrust, doubt, have suspicions about, have doubts about, have misgivings about, have qualms about, be sceptical about, disbelieve, mistrust, think you are guilty, smell a rat.
2 (v) *I suspect we'll lose.* have a feeling, have a hunch, have a sneaking suspicion, think, guess (informal), imagine, suppose.

suspense

(n) *The suspense is killing me!* tension, uncertainty, anticipation, expectation, excitement, anxiety.

suspicious

1 (adj) *Don't be so suspicious; you can trust me.* distrustful, wary, doubtful, uneasy, apprehensive, sceptical, jealous.
OPPOSITES: trusting, unsuspecting.
2 (adj) *That man in the dark glasses looks suspicious.* questionable, suspect, dubious, shifty, dodgy (informal), shady (informal), fishy (informal), disreputable, slippery.
OPPOSITES: above board, respectable.

swagger

(v) *Look at Bozo swagger about in his leather jacket!* strut, parade, prance, swank (informal), show off (informal).

swallow

1 (v) *Swallow your bun.* See **eat** 2.
2 (v) *Swallow your juice.* See **drink** 1.

swamp

(n) bog, marsh, marshland, morass, mire, quagmire, fen, quicksand.

swap see **exchange**.

swarm see **crowd** 1, 2.

sway

(v) *The wind made the trees sway.* bend, lean, wave, move to and fro, rock, swing.

swear

1 (v) *Don't swear!* use bad language, curse, be foul-mouthed, blaspheme, turn the air blue (informal), cuss (informal).
2 (v) *Swear you'll always love me!* See **promise** 1.

sweat

1 (n) *I'm covered in sweat.* perspiration.
2 (v) *The runners began to sweat.* perspire, break out in a sweat, drip with perspiration, swelter, glow, steam.

sweaty

(adj) *I was sweaty after the match.* sweating, perspiring, dripping with perspiration, drenched in sweat, sticky, clammy, glowing.

sweep

1 (v) *Sweep the crumbs off the table.* brush, clear, clean, dust, remove, push.
2 (v) *Fire began to sweep through the building.* spread, race, tear, rip, whip, whoosh (informal), fly, streak, course.

sweet

1 (adj) *This pudding tastes really sweet.* sugary, syrupy, sickly, cloying, treacly, sweetened, saccharine.
OPPOSITES: bitter, sour, savoury.
2 (adj) *The sweet smell of roses filled the air.* fragrant, sweet-smelling, aromatic, balmy, fresh, cloying, sickly.
OPPOSITES: foul, acrid.
3 (adj) *What a sweet child!* cute, appealing, lovable, charming, endearing, winsome, engaging, delightful, sweet-tempered, pretty, lovely, attractive.
OPPOSITES: nasty, obnoxious.

4 (adj) *I love the sweet sound of the lark's song.* tuneful, melodious, musical, dulcet, harmonious, mellow, soft, soothing.
OPPOSITES: harsh, discordant.
5 (n) *What's for sweet?* See **dessert**.
6 **sweets** (plural n) *Inga spends all her money on sweets.* confectionery, sweeties (plural) (informal), candy, bonbons (plural).

swell

1 (v) *My ankle started to swell.* puff up, balloon, bulge, blow up, become bloated.
2 (v) *The sails began to swell.* fill out, billow, inflate, expand, balloon, bulge.

swerve

(v) *The car had to swerve.* veer, turn aside, change direction, take evasive action, go off course, dodge, weave, swing, wheel.

swift see **fast** 1.

swim

1 (v) *I can't swim.* float, doggy-paddle, do breaststroke, do the crawl, do backstroke, do butterfly, tread water.
OPPOSITE: sink.
2 (v) *Let's swim in the lake.* go for a swim, go swimming, take a dip, bathe, splash about, go skinny-dipping, dive, plunge.

swing

1 (v) *Monkeys like to swing by their tails.* hang, dangle, move back and forth, rock, sway, be suspended.
2 (v) *Nola's mood can swing from one extreme to the other.* shift, fluctuate, veer, waver, seesaw, change, vary, alter.

swirl see **whirl**.

switch see **change** 4, 5, 6.

swivel

(v) *Press the button to make the robot's head swivel.* pivot, rotate, revolve, spin, turn, swing round, gyrate, twirl, wheel.

swollen

(adj) *After the fight, Rocky had a swollen nose.* puffy, inflamed, bulbous, enlarged, bulging, distended, bloated, puffed up.

swoop

(v) *Watch the eagles swoop.* dive, plunge, sweep down, drop, plummet, descend, fly down, nose-dive, pounce, lunge.

sword

(n) blade, steel.
TYPES OF SWORD: broadsword, cutlass, dagger, dirk, foil, machete, rapier, sabre, samurai sword, scimitar.

symbol

1 (n) *A horseshoe is a symbol of good luck.* sign, token, emblem, mark, image.
2 (n) *The school symbol is a swan.* badge, emblem, insignia, logo, sign, motif.

sympathetic

(adj) *Mum was sympathetic when I had to change schools.* understanding, supportive, caring, concerned, kind, comforting, considerate, consoling, sorry, compassionate, encouraging, approving.
OPPOSITES: unsympathetic, callous.

Tt

tackle

1 (v) *Try to tackle Simon before he scores.* challenge, intercept, block, take on, bring down, grab, seize, stop.
2 (v) *I'm ready to tackle the next question.* get to work on, embark on, set about, get stuck into (informal), wade into, attempt, try, have a go at (informal), have a stab at (informal), deal with, get to grips with, grapple with.
3 (v) *Who will tackle Dad about bedtimes?* confront, challenge, talk to, speak to, take on, have a go at (informal), face up to.

tactful

(adj) *It's not tactful of you to laugh at my hair.* diplomatic, discreet, polite, subtle, sensitive, considerate, thoughtful.
OPPOSITES: tactless, insensitive.

tactless

(adj) *Dom made a tactless remark about Dad's bald patch.* indiscreet, undiplomatic, unsubtle, indelicate, blundering, clumsy, heavy-handed, insensitive, thoughtless, inconsiderate, impolite, rude, hurtful.
OPPOSITES: tactful, diplomatic.

take

1 (v) *Take your suitcase upstairs.* carry, bring, move, cart, lift, haul.
2 (v) *Take my hand!* take hold of, hold on to, grab, grasp, grip, clutch, hang on to.
3 (v) *Dad will take you to school.* bring, drive, run, give you a lift, accompany, walk, escort, ferry, transport, convey.
4 (v) *Please take a piece of cake.* have, help yourself to, pick out, choose, select.
5 (v) *Did the burglars take anything valuable?* See **steal** 2.
6 (v) *Did the terrorists take any hostages?* capture, seize, abduct, kidnap, snatch, carry off, detain, arrest.
7 (v) *Take your medicine.* swallow, gulp down, get down, drink, consume, inhale.
8 (v) *Do you take the bus?* catch, travel by, go by, come by, use.
9 (v) *Card tricks take a lot of practice.* need, require, call for, demand.
10 (v) *I can't take this noise.* See **stand** 4.

take advantage of

(phrase) *Don't take advantage of your friends.* exploit, use, walk all over (informal), impose on, manipulate, milk, squeeze dry, rip off (slang).

take away

(v) *Take away three from eight.* subtract, take, deduct, minus, remove.
OPPOSITE: add.

take in

(v) *I can't take in all this information at once.* absorb, digest, assimilate, make sense of, grasp, understand, comprehend.

take off
1 (v) *Take off your clothes.* remove, strip off, peel off, throw off, drop, discard. OPPOSITE: put on.
2 (v) *We watched the plane take off.* leave the ground, take to the air, rise into the air, become airborne, lift off, climb. OPPOSITE: land.

take part
(phrase) *Do you want to take part?* join in, participate, be involved, contribute, play a part, be included, enter (competition).

talented
1 (adj) *I really envy Jemima; she's so talented.* gifted, accomplished, versatile, clever, able, brilliant, artistic, musical.
2 (adj) *Gary is a talented footballer.* accomplished, skilful, brilliant, gifted, skilled, expert, proficient, capable, deft.

talk
1 (v) *Mum can talk for hours.* speak, chat, chatter, converse, hold forth, spout (informal), natter, gossip, rattle on, prattle on, rabbit on (informal), witter on (informal), jabber on, go on (informal), yak (slang), jaw (slang), spiel, gabble, babble.
2 (v) *Can you talk Italian?* See **speak** 2.
3 (v) *If you're upset it helps to talk.* express your feelings, discuss things, share your thoughts, get things off your chest (informal), put things into words.
4 (v) *The police quizzed Burglar Beryl but she wouldn't talk.* blab, let the cat out of the bag, give the game away, speak out, confess, tell, tell tales, spill the beans (informal), squeal (slang), grass (slang).
5 (n) *Sophie and I had a talk on the phone.* chat, conversation, word, gossip, natter, chinwag (informal), confab (informal), heart-to-heart, tête-à-tête.
6 (n) *I had a long talk with the careers teacher.* chat, conversation, discussion, meeting, interview, consultation.
7 (n) *Dad gave a talk.* See **speech** 1.

talkative
(adj) *Zoë is so talkative, it's hard to shut her up.* chatty, gossipy, garrulous, loquacious, voluble, gushing, effusive.

tall
1 (adj) *Fran is quite tall.* big, lanky, rangy, long-legged, leggy, gangling, statuesque. OPPOSITES: short, small.
2 (adj) *Tall towers loomed over us.* high, lofty, giant, towering, soaring, sky-high. OPPOSITES: small, low.

tame
(adj) *Is your pet tame?* domesticated, used to humans, safe, docile, gentle, manageable, obedient, trained, house-trained, broken in (horse). OPPOSITES: wild, untamed.

tamper
(v) *Don't tamper with my computer!* interfere, meddle, tinker, fiddle (informal), mess about, muck about (slang), monkey around, fool around (informal), damage.

tangle
1 (n) *Can you sort out this tangle of threads?* jumble, muddle, mass, mess, knot, snarl, coil, mesh, web, confusion.
2 (v) *Don't tangle yourself in that wire.* entangle, ensnare, enmesh, get tangled up, get snarled up, get muddled up, trap. OPPOSITES: untangle, extricate, free.

tangled
(adj) *I can't straighten out these tangled threads.* snarled, twisted, knotted, jumbled, scrambled, messy, matted, tousled (hair), dishevelled (hair).

tanned
(adj) *Kit looks tanned.* suntanned, brown, bronzed, sunburnt, weather-beaten.

tantrum see **temper** 1.

tap
1 (n) *Water gushed out of the tap.* spout, valve, stopcock, mixer tap.
2 (n) *I heard a tap.* See **knock** 3.
3 (v) *Did you hear something tap against the window?* knock, rap, thud, bang, beat, drum, hammer, strike, hit.
4 (v) *Tap Ed on the back.* touch, pat, slap.

tape
1 (n) *Wrap some tape round the parcel.* sticky tape, adhesive tape, ribbon, string.
2 (n) *What's on this tape?* cassette, video, video tape, video cassette, audiocassette.
3 (v) *Tape the pieces together.* stick, fasten, fix, attach, tie, bind, secure.
4 (v) *Did you tape the concert?* record, video, tape-record.

target
1 (n) *Aim at the target.* bull's-eye, mark.
2 (n) *My target is to run a mile.* See **aim** 1.

task
(n) *I have a task to complete.* job, chore, duty, assignment, activity, undertaking, piece of work, exercise, challenge, mission.

taste
1 (n) *This dish doesn't have much taste.* flavour, tang, flavouring, savour, relish, character, zest, aftertaste. ❖ *Also see* **food & flavours**.
2 (n) *Give me a taste of your supper.* mouthful, spoonful, bite, nibble, sip, drop, morsel, titbit, nip, swallow.
3 (n) *Kylie has no taste!* style, flair, class, fashion sense, judgment, discernment, colour sense, design sense.
4 (n) *Flash Frank has a taste for fast cars.* liking, penchant, fondness, preference, appetite, desire, fancy, relish, weakness.
5 (v) *Taste this snack.* try, sample, try out, test, nibble, sip, relish, savour.
6 (v) *The sauce should taste of orange.* have a flavour, smack, savour, have a tang.
7 (v) *Can you taste the garlic in this dish?* make out, distinguish, identify, recognize.

tasteless
1 (adj) *Tasteless soup.* flavourless, bland, insipid, unexciting, uninteresting, boring, weak, watery, mild, dull, watered down.

2 (adj) *A tasteless comment.* crude, vulgar, crass, uncouth, coarse, cheap, offensive, distasteful, insensitive, tactless.
3 (adj) *Tasteless clothes.* See **vulgar** 2.

tasty see **delicious**.

taunt see **make fun of**.

taut see **tight** 1.

teach
1 (v) *Dan wants to teach photography.* be a teacher of, give lessons in, give classes in, give instruction in, lecture in, demonstrate.
2 (v) *Mrs Badger aims to teach her students thoroughly.* educate, instruct, tutor, coach, train, drill, inform, enlighten.
3 (v) *Can you teach Daisy how to tie her shoelaces?* show, explain to, demonstrate to, train, instruct.

teacher
(n) TYPES OF TEACHER: coach, don, governess, guide, guru, headteacher, instructor, lecturer, mentor, professor, schoolteacher, trainer, tutor.

team
(n) *Please join our team.* side, crew, squad, troupe, line-up, club, gang, band, group, company, unit, staff, alliance, party.

tear
1 (v) *The brambles will tear your dress.* rip, cut, rip to shreds, slit, slash, split, pull to pieces, snag, pierce, mangle, claw at.
2 (v) *Louis started to tear the paper off his present.* rip, pull, yank, wrench, peel.
3 (v) *I saw Jim tear past.* See **speed** 4.
4 (n) *There's a tear in my shorts.* rip, split, slit, slash, cut, hole, gash, snag, run.

tease
(v) *Does your brother tease you?* pull your leg (informal), wind you up (informal), have you on (informal), kid (informal), make fun of, laugh at, taunt, mock, goad, torment, pester, annoy, provoke.

teenager
(n) adolescent, young person, youngster, youth, juvenile.

telephone see **phone** 1, 2.

television
(n) *What's on the television tonight?* TV, telly (informal), box (informal), gogglebox (slang), small screen (informal).
TYPES OF TELEVISION PROGRAMME: arts programme, cartoon, chat show, children's programme, classic drama, comedy, costume drama, courtroom drama, current affairs programme, debate, detective series, discussion programme, docudrama, documentary, drama, film, game show, hospital drama, live show, magazine programme, miniseries, murder mystery, natural history programme, news broadcast, newsflash, play, police drama, quiz, real-life drama, serial, series, sitcom (situation comedy), soap (soap opera), sports programme, talk show, variety show, whodunit (informal). ❖ *Also see* **television & film**.

television and film

hair-raising stunt

television and film

TV and film people

broadcaster	interviewer
camera operator	narrator
cast (actors and actresses)	newsreader
	presenter
commentator	producer
director	reporter
film crew	researcher
floor manager	scriptwriter
game show host	sound engineer
	stuntman
	stuntwoman

TV programmes and films can be...

banned
censored
cut
dubbed
edited for language
subtitled

costume

TV and film people use...

autocue	microphone
camera	props
costume	scenery
lighting	script
locations	sets
make-up	studio

films and TV dramas may contain...

action	happy ending	sound effects
car chase	humour	soundtrack
climax	incidental music	special effects
close-up shots	intrigue	stunts
computer animation	love scene	suspense
dialogue	murder hunt	sword fight
flashback	plot (storyline)	theme music
gratuitous violence	shoot-out	trick photography

swashbuckling sword fight   *romantic love scene*

TV programmes may contain...

action replay	exclusive footage
audience participation	highlights
background music	in-depth investigation
canned laughter	interview
commentary	library pictures
commercial break	live coverage
computer graphics	news report
crime reconstruction	outside broadcast
debate	phone-in
discussion	satellite link-up
	title music
	video clip
	voice-over

news report

audience participation

films and TV dramas can be...

action-packed	harrowing	slow-moving
atmospheric	heart-warming	spectacular
chilling	inspiring	spooky (informal)
cliffhanging	intriguing	stirring
compelling	melodramatic	swashbuckling
depressing	moving	tear-jerking (informal)
disturbing	nail-biting	tense
dramatic	poignant	terrifying
enthralling	predictable	thrilling
gory	realistic	touching
gripping	romantic	violent
grisly	sentimental	visually stunning
gruesome	shocking	
hair-raising		

arc lamp

TV studio

lighting

period costume

prop

microphone

boom

monitor

sound engineer

TV camera

camera operator

dolly (camera stand on wheels)

floor manager

movie camera

microphone

nail-biting car chase

comedies can be...

amusing	riotous
anarchic	satirical
entertaining	side-splitting
farcical	slapstick
frenetic	wacky (slang)
hilarious	way-out (informal)
idiotic	witty
inane (silly)	zany
offbeat	
quirky	

current affairs programmes and documentaries can be...

alarmist	hard-hitting
controversial	informative
distressing	provocative
disturbing	revealing
educational	shocking
enlightening	superficial
factual	thought-provoking
fascinating	

*Also see **comedy**, **film**, **television**.*

tell

1 (v) I'll tell you where the treasure is buried. let you know, inform, notify, reveal to, disclose to, divulge to, describe to, recount to, relate to, mention to, report to, confess to, own up to, tip you off about.
2 (v) The signs tell you that it isn't safe to swim. show, inform, advise, indicate to, warn, notify, tip you off, proclaim to.
3 (v) Didn't I tell you to be home by ten o'clock? See **order** 1.
4 (v) I'll tell the story while you act it out. relate, narrate, recount, recite, describe.
5 (v) I couldn't tell which twin it was. make out, work out, identify, recognize, distinguish, discern, discover, differentiate.

tell off

(v) (informal) Dad will tell you off if you're late. scold, reprimand, lecture, tick you off (informal), bawl you out (informal), tear you off a strip (informal), read you the riot act, give you a rocket (informal), give you a dressing-down (informal), haul you over the coals (informal), rebuke, castigate.

tell on

(v) (informal) Your secret is safe; I won't tell on you! betray, give you away, tell tales about, sneak on (informal), snitch on (slang), rat on (informal), grass on (slang), report, shop (slang), breathe a word.

temper

1 (n) Dad's in a temper. rage, fury, bad temper, foul temper, tantrum, bad mood.
2 (n) People avoid Danielle because of her temper. quick temper, hot temper, irritability, peevishness, irascibility, hot-headedness, unpredictability, volatility.
3 lose your temper see **lose your temper**.

temporary

1 (adj) Jo's bad moods are only temporary. short-lived, brief, passing, fleeting, momentary, a flash in the pan, transient, impermanent, ephemeral.
OPPOSITES: permanent, long-lasting.
2 (adj) This is a temporary arrangement. provisional, interim, stopgap, short-term.
OPPOSITES: permanent, long-term.

tempt

(v) The witch tried to tempt the princess off the path. lure, entice, draw, lead, coax, persuade, woo, inveigle, seduce, bribe.

tempting

(adj) The thought of a tropical holiday is so tempting! inviting, irresistible, enticing, attractive, alluring, tantalizing, seductive, appetizing (food), mouthwatering (food).

tender

1 (adj) Cook the meat until it's tender. soft, succulent, juicy, coming off the bone.
OPPOSITES: tough, chewy.
2 (adj) Is your finger still tender? See **sore**.
3 (adj) Max gave me a tender look. affectionate, loving, gentle, sympathetic, caring, tenderhearted, warm, kind, doting.
OPPOSITES: cold, unsympathetic.

tense

1 (adj) I feel tense. wound up (informal), worked up, keyed up, uptight (informal), stressed, under pressure, nervous, edgy, on edge, jumpy, jittery (informal), anxious.
OPPOSITE: relaxed.
2 (adj) We had some tense moments waiting for the result. See **stressful** 1.
3 (adj) My muscles were tense as I waited for the race to start. taut, tight, strained, stretched, rigid, flexed, braced, stiff.
OPPOSITE: relaxed.

tension

(n) I can't bear the tension of waiting. suspense, stress, strain, anxiety, worry, uncertainty, anticipation, excitement.

terrible

1 (adj) A terrible crime. See **dreadful** 1.
2 (adj) A terrible essay. See **dreadful** 2.
3 (adj) A terrible smell. See **horrible** 2.
4 (adj) A terrible predicament. See **desperate** 3.

terrific

1 (adj) A terrific storm. tremendous, enormous, gigantic, huge, great, mighty, fierce, violent, intense, severe, dreadful, awful, terrible, horrific, awesome.
2 (adj) (informal) A terrific party. See **great** 9.

terrified see **scared** 1.

terrifying see **frightening**.

terror see **fear** 1, 2.

test

1 (n) Did you pass the test? exam, examination, assessment, oral test, written test, practical, audition, medical (informal).
2 (v) This quiz will test your general knowledge. put to the test, assess, evaluate, check, examine, probe, appraise.
3 (v) Scientists test medicines to make sure they are safe. run tests on, investigate, analyse, experiment on, check, check out, research, inspect, scrutinize.

thank

(v) Remember to thank Granny for the present. say thank you to, show your appreciation to, express gratitude to.

thankful see **grateful**.

thaw

(v) Don't let the ice cream thaw. defrost, melt, soften, liquefy, warm up, unfreeze.
OPPOSITE: freeze.

then see **next** 3.

theory

(n) The detective's theory was proved right. idea, hypothesis, supposition, conjecture, speculation, notion, belief, assumption.

thick

1 (adj) Thick walls. broad, wide, deep, solid, substantial, sturdy, stout, chunky.
OPPOSITES: thin, flimsy.
2 (adj) A thick book. fat, chunky, bulky, heavy, weighty, big, large.
OPPOSITES: thin, slim.

3 (adj) Thick hair. abundant, luxuriant, bushy, shaggy, coarse, wiry, frizzy, woolly.
OPPOSITES: thin, sparse.
4 (adj) Thick jungle. dense, impenetrable, impassable, heavy, lush, closely packed.
OPPOSITES: sparse, thin.
5 (adj) Thick fog. dense, heavy, soupy, impenetrable, murky, smoggy, opaque.
OPPOSITES: thin, light.
6 (adj) Thick custard. condensed, concentrated, solid, viscous, gelatinous, congealed, coagulated, firm, stiff.
OPPOSITES: thin, runny.

thicken

(v) Wait for the mixture to thicken. set, jell, solidify, coagulate, congeal, cake, condense, reduce, clot (blood).

thief

(n) pickpocket, shoplifter, pilferer, poacher, burglar, housebreaker, robber, mugger (informal), swindler, embezzler, fraudster.

thin

1 (adj) A thin girl. slim, slender, slight, lean, lanky, skinny, underweight, spindly, scrawny, bony, gaunt, scraggy, flat-chested, waiflike, skeletal, emaciated, undernourished, anorexic.
OPPOSITES: plump, fat, obese.
2 (adj) A thin crack. See **fine** 4.
3 (adj) Thin curtains. light, lightweight, flimsy, fine, delicate, floaty, gauzy, filmy, gossamer, diaphanous, sheer, translucent, transparent, see-through, threadbare.
OPPOSITES: thick, heavy.
4 (adj) Thin hair. sparse, wispy, fine, straggly, thinning, scanty, scarce.
OPPOSITES: thick, luxuriant.
5 (adj) Thin gravy. runny, watery, diluted, wishy-washy (informal), weak.
OPPOSITES: thick, concentrated.

thing

1 (n) What's that thing on the table? object, article, item.
2 (n) There's a thing crawling out of the swamp! creature, being, entity.
3 (n) We have a thing for crushing cans. gadget, device, machine, contraption, appliance, tool, instrument, implement.
4 (n) A funny thing happened. incident, occurrence, happening, phenomenon.
5 (n) There's one more thing I have to do. job, task, chore.
6 (n) What made you do such a crazy thing? act, deed, exploit, feat.
7 (n) A worrying thing occurred to me. thought, idea, notion, theory.
8 (n) What's the thing you like best about this book? aspect, feature, quality, characteristic, attribute, detail, point.

things

(plural n) Put your things away. belongings (plural), stuff, paraphernalia, bits and pieces (plural), odds and ends (plural), possessions (plural), clothes (plural), gear, kit, equipment, tools (plural), tackle, junk (informal), clobber (slang), baggage.

think

1 (v) *I used to think that girls were silly.* believe, consider, reckon, be convinced, be of the opinion, maintain, feel.
2 (v) *I think it's about four o'clock.* reckon, imagine, suppose, guess (informal), would say, estimate, assume, presume, believe.
3 (v) *I didn't think that you'd come.* expect, foresee, anticipate, envisage, suppose, imagine, dream.
4 (v) *Lauren likes to sit in her room and think.* meditate, contemplate, cogitate, deliberate, reflect, ponder, muse, brood.
5 **think about** (v) *You should think about your future.* consider, give thought to, put your mind to, concentrate on, reflect on, mull over, chew over, weigh up, work out.

think up

(v) *We must think up a cunning plan.* dream up, come up with, make up, concoct, devise, invent, create, contrive.

thirsty

(adj) *The explorers were thirsty.* parched, dry (informal), dehydrated, gasping, panting, dying of thirst (informal).

thorough

(adj) *A thorough investigation.* detailed, in-depth, extensive, comprehensive, exhaustive, full, complete, wide-ranging, meticulous, painstaking, methodical.

thought

1 (n) *This plan will need a lot of thought.* consideration, reflection, deliberation, thinking, brainwork, concentration, reasoning, contemplation, meditation.
2 (n) *An interesting thought. See* **idea** 1.

thoughtful

1 (adj) *It was thoughtful of you to visit Granny.* considerate, kind, caring, unselfish, friendly, helpful, compassionate. OPPOSITES: thoughtless, selfish.
2 (adj) *Tessa wrote a thoughtful essay.* well-thought-out, perceptive, insightful, profound, penetrating, discerning. OPPOSITES: superficial, shallow.
3 (adj) *Hanif is in a thoughtful mood.* pensive, reflective, contemplative, philosphical, meditative, introspective, brooding, wistful, dreamy.

thoughtless

(adj) *A thoughtless remark.* insensitive, tactless, inconsiderate, unkind, uncaring, unsympathetic, cruel, rude, indiscreet. OPPOSITES: thoughtful, tactful.

thrash *see* beat 1, 2.

thread

(n) *Pull the thread tight.* strand, cotton, string, yarn, twine, wool, silk.

threaten

1 (v) *Did Bozo threaten you?* intimidate, bully, terrorize, make threats to, menace, browbeat, pressurize, lean on (informal).
2 (v) *Reckless drivers threaten lives.* put at risk, endanger, imperil, put in jeopardy.

threatening *see* menacing.

thrill

(n) *Luke gets a thrill out of surfing.* sense of excitement, feeling of exhilaration, kick (informal), buzz (slang), charge (slang).

thrilling *see* exciting.

throb

(v) *Loud music began to throb through the house.* pulsate, pound, thump, thud, beat, vibrate, reverberate, pulse.

throw

1 (v) *Throw the ball.* hurl, fling, chuck (informal), lob (informal), sling, toss, pitch, shy, heave, send, launch, propel, let fly.
2 (v) (informal) *Did Aunt Bertha's arrival throw you?* faze, disconcert, put you off, throw you off your stride, worry, unsettle, unnerve, upset, rattle (informal).

throw away

1 (v) *Throw away your rubbish.* get rid of, throw out, dispose of, chuck out (informal), bin, dump (informal), scrap, ditch (slang), discard, jettison.
2 (v) *Don't throw away this opportunity. See* waste.

throw out

(v) *Why did the football club throw you out?* expel, eject, kick you out (informal), turf you out (informal), oust, banish, evict.

throw up (informal) *see* vomit.

thump

1 (v) *Don't thump your brother! See* hit 1.
2 (v) *My heart began to thump loudly. See* beat 3.
3 (n) *Jack fell out of the tree with a thump.* thud, crash, bang, clunk, clonk, clump, clomp, thwack, smack, wham.

tidy

1 (adj) *Jo always looks tidy.* neat, smart, well-turned-out, well-groomed, trim, spruce, spick-and-span, presentable. OPPOSITES: untidy, messy.
2 (adj) *Adam keeps his room tidy.* neat, uncluttered, clean, well-organized, in good order, shipshape, spick-and-span, immaculate, in apple-pie order (informal). OPPOSITES: untidy, messy.
3 (v) *Please tidy your room.* sort out, tidy up, clear up, neaten up, put straight.

tie

1 (v) *Tie the boat to the post.* tie up, secure, fasten, attach, make fast, tether, lash, knot, moor, hitch, bind, rope, chain.
2 (v) *Please tie your shoelaces.* tie up, do up, knot, make a bow in, make a knot in.
3 (n) *The result was a tie. See* draw 6.
4 (n) *Dad wore a spotty tie.* necktie, bow tie, dicky bow, cravat, neckerchief.

tight

1 (adj) *Pull the rope until it's tight.* taut, rigid, stretched, strained, tense. OPPOSITES: slack, loose.
2 (adj) *Mo wore a tight skirt.* tight-fitting, close-fitting, skintight, figure-hugging, snug, clinging, straining at the seams. OPPOSITES: baggy, roomy.

3 (adj) *Screw the lid on until it's tight.* sealed, secure, airtight, watertight. OPPOSITE: loose.
4 (adv) *Hold on tight!* tightly, firmly, fast.

tilt *see* lean 1.

time

1 (n) *Burglar Beryl spent a short time in prison.* period, while, spell, interval, stretch, term, season, session, duration.
2 (n) *What did people wear in the time of Queen Victoria? See* age 1.
3 (n) *The bomb could blow up at any time.* moment, minute, second, instant, point, point in time, stage, juncture.
4 (n) *What time would suit you?* day, date, time of day, hour, week, month, season, year, decade, century, millennium.
5 (v) *Time how long the journey takes.* measure, count, clock, record, calculate.

timid *see* shy.

tingle

(v) *Can you feel your skin tingle?* prickle, prick, tickle, itch, sting, come up in goose pimples, have pins and needles (informal).

tinkle *see* jingle 1.

tiny

1 (adj) *A tiny girl.* small, slight, petite, titchy (slang), undersized, pint-sized (informal), diminutive, Lilliputian. OPPOSITES: big, tall, enormous.
2 (adj) *A tiny speck.* minute, minuscule, microscopic, infinitesimal, teeny, weeny, teeny-weeny, itsy-bitsy (informal). OPPOSITES: huge, enormous.

tip

1 (n) *The tip of an iceberg.* top, peak, pinnacle, summit, point, cap, crown, apex.
2 (n) *A pencil tip.* end, point, sharp end.
3 (n) *A useful tip.* piece of advice, hint, suggestion, pointer, tip-off, clue.
4 (v) *Tip the scraps into the bin.* pour, empty, dump, unload, slide.
5 **tip over** (v) *Don't let the desk tip over!* fall over, topple over, keel over, overturn, upend, capsize (boat).

tired

1 (adj) *You must be tired after your hard work.* worn out, exhausted, weary, sleepy, drowsy, ready to drop, dead tired, drained, shattered (informal), done in (informal), dead on your feet (informal), whacked (informal), bushed (slang), zonked (slang). OPPOSITES: wide-awake, rested.
2 **tired of** (adj) *I'm tired of your moaning. See* fed up with.

tiring

(adj) *Teaching is a tiring job.* exhausting, draining, wearing, wearying, taxing, demanding, tough, arduous, strenuous.

toilet

(n) lavatory, loo (informal), WC (water closet), public convenience, urinal, bog (slang), john (slang), khazi (slang), ladies (informal), gents (informal), cloakroom, bathroom, powder room, washroom.

tolerant
1 (adj) I try to be tolerant about other people's views. open-minded, broad-minded, unprejudiced, unbigoted, fair, liberal, understanding, sympathetic.
OPPOSITES: intolerant, narrow-minded.
2 (adj) Amy's dad is so tolerant; he lets her do anything. easy-going, permissive, free and easy, indulgent, lenient, soft, patient, long-suffering, unshockable, forgiving.
OPPOSITES: strict, authoritarian.

tolerate see endure 1.

tomb
(n) grave, burial place, sarcophagus, burial chamber, vault, crypt, sepulchre, mausoleum, catacomb, final resting place.

tool
(n) implement, instrument, device, utensil, gadget, appliance, machine, contraption.

tooth
(n) An animal's tooth. fang, tusk.

top
1 (n) I climbed to the top of the mountain. peak, summit, pinnacle, crest, tip, crown (hill), brow (hill), highest point, apex.
2 (n) Put the top back on. lid, cap, cover, stopper, cork, covering.
3 (n) Paula has a new top. ❖ See clothes.
4 (adj) The jug is on the top shelf. highest, topmost, upper, uppermost.
OPPOSITES: bottom, lowest.
5 (adj) Who got the top marks in the test? highest, best, most, maximum, winning.
OPPOSITES: lowest, bottom.
6 (adj) Professor Peabody is a top scientist. leading, eminent, outstanding, great, important, famous, celebrated, renowned, noted, high-ranking, crack (slang).
OPPOSITES: second-rate, obscure.

topic see subject.

torment see torture 1, 2.

torture
1 (v) Will the kidnappers torture their prisoners? inflict pain on, hurt, abuse, maltreat, ill-treat, be cruel to, torment, use force on, intimidate, persecute, bully.
2 (n) You can't imagine the torture I went through. agony, torment, anguish, pain, suffering, misery, distress, hell (informal).

toss
1 (v) Toss the ball to me. See throw 1.
2 (v) Bad dreams made me toss around all night. thrash, toss and turn, roll, twist and turn, writhe, wriggle, wallow, tumble.
3 (v) Look at the boats toss on the waves. bob, wallow, lurch, pitch, tumble, heave.

total
1 (n) Add up the figures and tell me the total. tally, full amount, sum total, grand total, answer, sum, aggregate, gross.
2 (adj) What's the total population of the two towns? overall, complete, sum, full, gross, entire, whole, combined.
3 (adj) A total disaster. See complete 2.

totter see stagger 1.

touch
1 (v) Don't let the wires touch! come into contact, connect, meet, come together.
2 (v) I felt the cobweb touch my face. brush, graze, tickle, rub against.
3 (v) Don't touch the animals! lay a finger on, handle, feel, stroke, pat, rub, fondle, caress, nuzzle, tickle, pick up.
4 (v) Don't touch my radio! lay a finger on, move, pick up, interfere with, fiddle with (informal), tamper with, finger.
5 (v) I only managed to touch the ball once in the match. hit, strike, kick, head, tap, knock, come into contact with.
6 (v) Never touch drugs! get involved with, have anything to do with, concern yourself with, handle, consume, use.

touchy
(adj) Treat Amy carefully; she's very touchy. sensitive, easily offended, thin-skinned, oversensitive, irritable, ratty (informal), tetchy, grouchy (informal), bad-tempered.
OPPOSITES: easy-going, thick-skinned.

tough
1 (adj) Bulletproof glass needs to be tough. strong, hard, thick, solid, durable, resilient, hard-wearing, unbreakable, indestructible, sturdy, inflexible, firm, rigid.
OPPOSITES: flimsy, fragile.
2 (adj) You must be tough to go on this expedition. fit, strong, sturdy, hardy, robust, resilient, brawny, muscular.
OPPOSITES: feeble, delicate.
3 (adj) Gangsters are pretty tough characters. rough, hard, hardened, hard-bitten, ruffianly, wild, vicious, violent, lawless, rowdy, hard as nails.
OPPOSITES: gentle, civilized.
4 (adj) This steak is tough. chewy, leathery, rubbery, stringy, gristly, sinewy.
OPPOSITES: tender, succulent.
5 (adj) A tough puzzle. See difficult 1.
6 (adj) A tough job. See difficult 2.

tower
(n) Let's climb up this tower. turret, keep, clock tower, bell tower, steeple, spire, belfry, minaret, column, pillar, obelisk.

trace
1 (n) There's just a trace of sherry in this trifle. dash, touch, spot, bit, drop, splash, smattering, hint, whiff, tinge, soupçon.
2 (n) Indy found no trace of the temple. sign, evidence, indication, record, remains (plural), remnants (plural), vestiges (plural).
3 (v) Police are trying to trace Dodgy Dave. find, locate, track down, hunt down, seek out, uncover, unearth, get in touch with.

track
1 (n) The fox left a track. trail, scent, spoor, footprints (plural), prints (plural), marks (plural), traces (plural).
2 (n) We cycled along a narrow track. path, pathway, bridle path, footpath, trail.
3 (n) The competitors sped round the track. racetrack, circuit, running track, racecourse, speedway.

tradition see custom.

tragic
1 (adj) A tragic ending. See sad 2.
2 (adj) A tragic accident. catastrophic, disastrous, calamitous, terrible, appalling, dreadful, awful, shocking, fatal, deadly.

trail
1 (n) Angus left a trail of rubbish. line, train, stream, track, path, wake, wash.
2 (n) Follow the fox's trail. See track 1.
3 (v) Let the streamers trail from the ceiling. See hang 1.
4 (v) Watch the queen's robes trail behind her. drag, sweep, fall, stream out, flow.
5 (v) Don't trail behind. See drop behind.

train
1 (n) The train pulled into the station. locomotive, engine.
TYPES OF TRAIN: boat train, bullet train (Japan), diesel train, electric train, express train, freight train, goods train, high-speed train, intercity train, maglev, monorail, steam train, tube train, underground train.
❖ Also see journey words.
2 (v) Matt wants to train to be a nurse. study, learn, qualify, prepare.
3 (v) Athletes train regularly. practise, exercise, work out, prepare, get fit.
4 (v) Who will train the team? coach, prepare, drill, instruct, guide, teach.

tramp see trudge.

trample on
(v) Don't trample on the tulips! tread on, tramp all over, step on, stamp on, walk on, squash, crush, flatten, grind under foot.

transform see change 2.

transparent
(adj) Transparent material. see-through, clear, glassy, crystal clear, translucent, sheer, filmy, gauzy, diaphanous.
OPPOSITE: opaque.

trap
1 (n) The creature was caught in a trap. snare, noose, net, pit, mousetrap, mantrap, booby trap, web.
2 (v) The police managed to trap Burglar Beryl. catch, capture, snare, ensnare, corner, cut off, ambush, smoke out.

travel
1 (v) Which way will you travel? go, journey, voyage, head, proceed, drive, walk, cycle, ride, fly, sail, cruise, motor, ramble, roam, wander, trek, commute.
❖ Also see journey words.
2 (v) Uncle Walter loves to travel. see the world, go abroad, go on trips, go on journeys, tour, go globetrotting, sightsee.

treasure
1 (n) Pirate Peg buried her treasure. riches (plural), valuables (plural), fortune, hoard, jewels (plural), coins (plural), gold, silver, money. ❖ Also see treasure words.
2 (v) Clare will treasure this gift. cherish, value, prize, appreciate, love, adore, dote on, be careful with, keep safe, look after.

treasure words

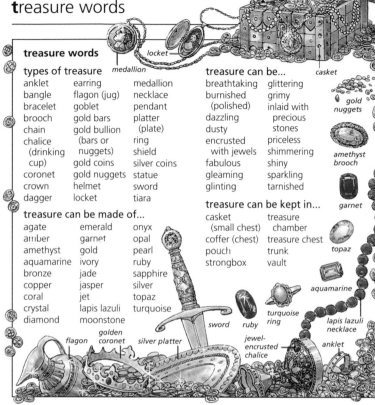

treasure words

types of treasure

anklet	earring	medallion
bangle	flagon (jug)	necklace
bracelet	goblet	pendant
brooch	gold bars	platter
chain	gold bullion	(plate)
chalice	(bars or	ring
(drinking	nuggets)	shield
cup)	gold coins	silver coins
coronet	gold nuggets	statue
crown	helmet	sword
dagger	locket	tiara

treasure can be made of...

agate	emerald	onyx
amber	garnet	opal
amethyst	gold	pearl
aquamarine	ivory	ruby
bronze	jade	sapphire
copper	jasper	silver
coral	jet	topaz
crystal	lapis lazuli	turquoise
diamond	moonstone	

treasure can be...

breathtaking	glittering
burnished	grimy
(polished)	inlaid with
dazzling	precious
dusty	stones
encrusted	priceless
with jewels	shimmering
fabulous	shiny
gleaming	sparkling
glinting	tarnished

treasure can be kept in...

casket	treasure
(small chest)	chamber
coffer (chest)	treasure chest
pouch	trunk
strongbox	vault

locket
medallion
casket
gold nuggets
amethyst brooch
garnet
topaz
aquamarine
turquoise ring
lapis lazuli necklace
sword
ruby
jewel-encrusted chalice
anklet
flagon
golden coronet
silver platter

treat

1 (n) *I enjoyed my birthday treat.* present, gift, entertainment, party, outing, surprise, celebration, fun.
2 (v) *How did your penfriend's family treat you?* behave towards, act towards, relate to, look upon, talk to, deal with, handle.
3 (v) *Does the doctor treat outpatients?* look after, take care of, give treatment to, care for, see to, attend to, patch up.

tree

(n) *Look at that tree!* conifer, evergreen, deciduous tree, fruit tree, sapling, bonsai.
TYPES OF TREE: alder, apple, apricot, ash, aspen, beech, birch, cedar, cherry, cypress, ebony, elder, elm, eucalyptus, fig, fir, hawthorn, hazel, holly, horse chestnut, juniper, laburnum, larch, lemon, lime, magnolia, mahogany, mango, maple, mimosa, monkey puzzle, oak, olive, orange, palm, peach, pear, pine, plane, plum, poplar, redwood, rowan, rubber, sequoia, spruce, sweet chestnut, sycamore, walnut, weeping willow, willow, yew.

tremble *see* shiver.

tremendous

1 (adj) *A tremendous bang.* terrific, enormous, colossal, mighty, stupendous, almighty (informal), dreadful, awful, terrible, frightful, deafening, ear-splitting.
2 (adj) (informal) *A tremendous experience.* See fantastic 3.

trick

1 (n) *We were amazed by the magician's trick.* conjuring trick, illusion, magic trick, stunt, sleight of hand.
2 (n) *Mum wasn't amused by our trick.* joke, practical joke, prank, leg-pull (informal), wind-up (slang), hoax, gag (informal), stunt, jape, April fool.
3 (v) *Don't let Ed trick you. See deceive* 1.

trickle *see* dribble 2.

tricky *see* awkward 5, 6.

trip

1 (n) *We're going on a trip to France.* outing, visit, excursion, jaunt, expedition, coach trip, day trip, field trip, tour, journey.
2 (v) *Be careful not to trip!* trip up, fall, fall over, lose your footing, lose your balance, go head over heels, stumble, take a tumble, slip, stagger, catch your foot.

trivial

(adj) *Don't waste my time with trivial details.* unimportant, insignificant, inconsequential, petty, minor, negligible, trifling, piffling, worthless, frivolous.
OPPOSITES: important, significant.

trouble

1 (n) *Our new car has caused us a lot of trouble.* bother, problems (plural), hassle (informal), inconvenience, difficulty, irritation, annoyance, worry, anxiety.
OPPOSITES: pleasure, convenience.

2 (n) *Granny has had a lot of trouble in her life.* difficulty, hardship, adversity, problems (plural), trials (plural), tribulations (plural), misfortune, bad luck, sadness, unhappiness, heartache, pain, suffering.
OPPOSITES: happiness, good fortune.
3 (v) *I didn't mean to trouble you. See bother* 1, 2.
4 in trouble (phrase) *Call me if you're in trouble.* in difficulty, having problems, in a predicament, in a mess, in hot water (informal), in dire straits, in danger.

trousers *see* clothes.

truck *see* lorry.

trudge

(v) *I watched you trudge through the snow.* plod, tramp, slog, stomp (informal), traipse (informal), trek, hike, clomp, yomp, lumber, drag your feet, shuffle.

true

1 (adj) *This is a true story.* real, real-life, factual, actual, based on real life.
OPPOSITES: fictional, made-up.
2 (adj) *Is your account true?* correct, accurate, right, truthful, faithful, exact, precise, reliable, genuine, confirmed.
OPPOSITES: false, fabricated.
3 (adj) *Tell me your true feelings. See real* 3.

trust

(v) *You can trust me; I won't let you down.* put your trust in, have confidence in, have faith in, be sure of, rely on, depend on, count on, pin your hopes on, confide in.

truthful *see* honest 1, 2.

try

1 (n) *Have a try!* attempt, go (informal), bash (informal), stab (informal), shot (informal), crack (informal), effort.
2 (v) *You should try to break the record.* attempt, make an attempt, endeavour, aim, seek, strive, make an effort, do your best, exert yourself, go all out (informal), bend over backwards (informal).
3 (v) *Let's try that new restaurant.* try out, check out (informal), sample, investigate, experience, test, give it a whirl (informal).

tug *see* pull.

tumble *see* fall 1, 3, 6.

tummy (informal) *see* stomach 1, 2.

tune

(n) *A catchy tune.* melody, song, theme, air, refrain. ❖ *Also see* music words.

tunnel

(n) passageway, passage, shaft, mine, burrow, hole, subway, underpass.

turn

1 (v) *Watch the wheels turn.* go round, spin, revolve, rotate, gyrate, roll, circle, wheel, pivot, swivel, twirl, whirl.
2 (v) *It's unlikely that this frog will turn into a prince. See change* 3.
3 (v) *Let's turn the garage into a games room.* convert, adapt, transform, change, make, remodel, alter, make over.

4 (n) We came to a turn in the road. bend, curve, twist, hairpin bend, U-turn, corner, turning, turn-off, angle, loop, zigzag.
5 (n) Everyone will have a turn on the computer. go (informal), try, chance, shot (informal), opportunity, attempt, bash (informal), stab (informal), spell, stint.

turn out
(v) How did things turn out? work out, end up, develop, pan out (informal), evolve, come about, happen, transpire (informal).

TV see **television**.

twinkle see **sparkle**.

twist
1 (v) Twist the threads together. weave, wind, entwine, intertwine, tangle, plait, braid, knot, loop, wreathe, coil, wrap.
2 (v) The noise made Posy twist round in her seat. turn, spin, swivel, swing, pivot.
3 (v) The path began to twist. See **wind** 2.
4 (v) Try not to twist your ankle. sprain, turn, wrench, strain, rick (neck).
5 (v) Reporters can twist what you say. distort, slant, warp, garble, misquote, misrepresent, falsify, change, alter.

twisted
1 (adj) A twisted tree trunk. distorted, contorted, crooked, bent, deformed, misshapen, gnarled, knotted.
2 (adj) Twisted threads. See **tangled**.

twitch
(v) Do you twitch in your sleep? jerk, fidget, wriggle, squirm, writhe, quiver, shiver, tremble, start, jump.

type see **kind** 2, 3.

typical
1 (adj) It was a typical weekend at home. normal, average, standard, ordinary, usual, commonplace, everyday, run-of-the-mill.
OPPOSITES: extraordinary, remarkable.
2 (adj) Woodchester is a typical English village. archetypal, quintessential, classic, characteristic, representative, stereotypical.
OPPOSITES: atypical, unique.
3 (adj) It's typical of Dan to be late. characteristic, in character, true to type, true to form, in keeping, unsurprising.
OPPOSITE: unusual.

Uu

ugly
1 (adj) You look ugly in that mask. hideous, grotesque, horrible, repulsive, disgusting, revolting, ghastly, monstrous, deformed, disfigured, misshapen.
OPPOSITES: beautiful, lovely.
2 (adj) What an ugly building! unsightly, unattractive, hideous, horrible, ghastly, vile, grim, inelegant, tasteless, monstrous.
OPPOSITES: beautiful, lovely.

unavoidable see **inevitable**.

unaware see **ignorant** 1, 3.

unbearable
(adj) The noise is unbearable. intolerable, unendurable, insupportable, insufferable, unacceptable, too much (informal).

unbelievable see **incredible** 1.

uncertain
1 (adj) I'm uncertain about what to do. unsure, doubtful, dubious, undecided, hesitant, in two minds, unclear, vague.
2 (adj) It's uncertain who won the race. unclear, undecided, unresolved, unconfirmed, inconclusive, arguable, open to question, ambiguous, up in the air.

unclear
(adj) This message is unclear. hard to read, illegible, hard to understand, unintelligible, indecipherable, cryptic, ambiguous, vague, confused, garbled, mystifying, puzzling.

uncomfortable
1 (adj) My new shoes are uncomfortable. tight, cramped, hard, stiff, painful.
OPPOSITE: comfortable.
2 (adj) I feel uncomfortable in this situation. awkward, ill at ease, self-conscious, embarrassed, out of place, uneasy, tense, on edge, nervous, edgy.
OPPOSITES: comfortable, at ease.

unconscious
(adj) The patient lay unconscious. senseless, comatose, out cold, knocked out, concussed, stunned, sleeping.

underground
(adj) An underground chamber. subterranean, sunken, buried, covered.

understand
1 (v) I didn't understand what you meant. realize, see, grasp, know, recognize, take in, comprehend, follow, get, catch on to (informal), cotton on to (informal), twig (informal), get the drift of.
2 (v) I can't understand this code. make sense of, make head or tail of (informal), make out, work out, figure out (informal), suss out (slang), decipher, decode.
3 (v) I understand that you're leaving. believe, hear, gather, learn.

understanding
1 (n) Samirah has a good understanding of history. See **grasp** 4.
2 (adj) My dad is very understanding. sympathetic, compassionate, tolerant, forgiving, forbearing, patient, kind, considerate, thoughtful, sensitive.

undo
(v) Can you undo this? unfasten, open, loosen, untie, unwrap, unbutton, unzip, unlace, unhook, unclip, unclasp, unscrew, unpin, unlock, unchain, disentangle, untangle, unravel, release.

undress
(v) Undress before you shower. get undressed, take your clothes off, strip, strip off (slang), peel off (slang), disrobe.

unemployed
(adj) Justin's dad is unemployed. out of work, out of a job, on the dole (informal), jobless, laid off, redundant.

uneven see **bumpy** 1.

unexpected see **surprising**.

unfair
(adj) An unfair decision. unjust, biased, prejudiced, one-sided, partisan, arbitrary, unreasonable, unjustified, uncalled-for.
OPPOSITES: fair, just.

unfamiliar see **strange** 3, 4.

unfortunate
(adj) An unfortunate accident. unlucky, regrettable, dreadful, disastrous, calamitous, tragic, lamentable.

unfriendly
(adj) Unfriendly neighbours. unsociable, aloof, distant, standoffish, cold, cool, chilly, disagreeable, unpleasant, uncivil, hostile, aggressive, antisocial.

unhappy see **sad** 1, 2.

unhealthy
1 (adj) The stray dog looked unhealthy. ill, sick, in poor health, unwell, sickly, poorly (informal), ailing, infirm, weak, feeble, frail, undernourished, unfit, out of condition.
OPPOSITES: healthy, well.
2 (adj) The refugees lived in unhealthy conditions. insanitary, unhygienic, squalid, dirty, disease-ridden, polluted, harmful.
OPPOSITES: clean, healthy.
3 (adj) A diet of chips and fizzy drinks is unhealthy. bad for you, unwholesome, unnourishing, harmful, damaging.

unimportant
(adj) Leave out anything that is unimportant. of no importance, trivial, insignificant, inessential, inconsequential, of no consequence, irrelevant, immaterial.
OPPOSITES: important, significant.

uninhabited
1 (adj) An uninhabited flat. See **empty** 3.
2 (adj) An uninhabited planet. unpopulated, unpeopled, uncolonized, unsettled, deserted, desolate, barren.

unique
(adj) Ziggy's hairstyle is unique. distinctive, in a class of its own, one-off (informal), without equal, unparalleled, unrivalled.

united
1 (adj) Let's make a united effort to win. combined, joint, concerted, cooperative, collaborative, collective, common, unified.
2 (adj) We are united in our opposition to the plan. agreed, in agreement, undivided, at one, of one mind, unanimous.
OPPOSITES: divided, at odds.

unkind
(adj) It was unkind of you to laugh at me. cruel, nasty, mean, heartless, uncaring, callous, unfriendly, inconsiderate, insensitive, thoughtless, hurtful, spiteful.
OPPOSITES: kind, considerate.

unknown
1 *(adj) The causes of the disease are unknown.* unidentified, undiscovered, undecided, unrecognized, mysterious, undisclosed, hidden, concealed, secret.
2 *(adj) This song is by an unknown band called Purple Pig.* little-known, obscure, unheard-of, unfamiliar, insignificant.
3 *(adj) Pirate Peg sailed into unknown waters.* unfamiliar, unexplored, uncharted, unmapped, undiscovered, new, strange.

unlikely
(adj) It's unlikely that there's life on Venus. improbable, not likely, doubtful, questionable, inconceivable, unimaginable.

unlucky
1 *(adj) You really are unlucky, aren't you?* unfortunate, accident-prone, jinxed, cursed, ill-fated, ill-starred, star-crossed, out of luck, down on your luck, luckless.
OPPOSITES: lucky, fortunate.
2 *(adj) Seeing a magpie is supposed to be unlucky.* bad luck, a bad sign, a bad omen, inauspicious, ominous, ill-omened.
OPPOSITES: lucky, auspicious.

unnecessary
(adj) Smart clothes are unnecessary on a cycling holiday. inessential, nonessential, uncalled-for, superfluous, surplus to requirements, redundant, dispensable.
OPPOSITES: necessary, essential.

unpleasant
1 *(adj) An unpleasant child.* disagreeable, objectionable, bad-tempered, unfriendly, unkind, nasty, spiteful, hateful, unlovable.
2 *(adj) An unpleasant smell. See* **nasty** 1.

unpopular
(adj) You'll be unpopular if you start telling tales. disliked, friendless, unwanted, unwelcome, out of favour, detested, hated, despised, avoided, ignored, rejected, shunned.
OPPOSITES: popular, well-liked.

unrealistic *see* **impractical** 1, 2.

unreasonable
(adj) Don't be so unreasonable! irrational, illogical, inconsistent, opinionated, obstinate, headstrong, biased, prejudiced.

unreliable
(adj) Don't trust Oz; he's too unreliable. undependable, irresponsible, erratic, inconsistent, unpredictable, untrustworthy.
OPPOSITES: reliable, dependable.

unselfish
(adj) It was unselfish of you to give me your last chocolate. self-sacrificing, selfless, noble, generous, magnanimous, kind, big-hearted, big, altruistic, charitable.

unsuccessful
(adj) My attempts to talk Dad round were unsuccessful. fruitless, futile, in vain, to no avail, useless, abortive, unproductive, ineffective, foiled, thwarted, frustrated.
OPPOSITES: successful, fruitful.

unsure *see* **uncertain** 1.

untidy
1 *(adj) My desk is untidy.* messy, chaotic, cluttered, disorganized, muddled, jumbled, littered, topsy-turvy, shambolic *(informal)*.
OPPOSITES: tidy, neat.
2 *(adj) You look untidy. See* **messy** 2.
3 *(adj) What untidy work! See* **messy** 3.

unusual
1 *(adj) Pat has an unusual ability to learn languages.* extraordinary, exceptional, rare, remarkable, phenomenal, singular, uncommon, abnormal, freak, atypical.
2 *(adj) Ziggy dresses in an unusual way.* strange, peculiar, odd, weird, bizarre, eccentric, unconventional, outlandish, curious, offbeat, original, different, exotic.

unwilling
(adj) Andy was unwilling to volunteer. reluctant, loath, slow, disinclined, not in the mood, ill-disposed, unenthusiastic.
OPPOSITES: willing, eager.

upset
1 *(v) I didn't mean to upset you.* hurt, distress, offend, rub you up the wrong way, annoy, irritate, worry, alarm, disturb, ruffle, fluster, faze, dismay, unsettle.
2 *(v) Don't upset our plans.* disrupt, interfere with, spoil, ruin, wreck, mess up, throw into confusion, turn upside down.
3 *(adj) I can see that you're upset.* hurt, distressed, worried, troubled, disturbed, bothered, agitated, in a state *(informal)*, put out, offended, angry.

urge
(n) I felt a sudden urge to scream. impulse, desire, compulsion, need, drive, longing, yearning, inclination, wish, whim.

urgent
(adj) I must see the doctor; it's urgent. imperative, vital, essential, critical, crucial, important, high-priority, serious, pressing.

use
1 *(v) Can you use these empty boxes?* find a use for, make use of, put to good use, utilize, do something with.
2 *(v) This whisk is easy to use.* operate, control, work, manage, handle.
3 *(v) Fenella will use you to get what she wants. See* **take advantage of**.
4 *(n) What's the use of complaining?* point, purpose, good, advantage, benefit, value, usefulness, worth.

used to
(adj) I'm used to coming last. accustomed to, resigned to, hardened to, familiar with, at home with, in the habit of, given to.

useful
1 *(adj) A useful gadget.* practical, handy, convenient, effective, helpful, valuable, functional, multipurpose, all-purpose.
OPPOSITES: useless, ineffective.
2 *(adj) Useful suggestions.* helpful, practical, worthwhile, valuable, invaluable, constructive, positive, beneficial.
OPPOSITES: useless, unhelpful.

useless
1 *(adj) The search was useless.* futile, pointless, a waste of time, in vain, fruitless, unsuccessful, hopeless, unproductive.
OPPOSITES: worthwhile, fruitful.
2 *(adj) This knife is useless.* no use, unusable, ineffective, impractical, hopeless *(informal)*, faulty, defective, broken.
OPPOSITES: useful, effective.

usual
(adj) Jogging is part of my usual routine. normal, regular, customary, accustomed, everyday, daily, ordinary, typical, standard, general, familiar, set, fixed, established.

Vv

vacant
1 *(adj) A vacant flat. See* **empty** 3.
2 *(adj) A vacant seat.* empty, available, free, unoccupied, not in use, not taken.
OPPOSITES: occupied, in use.
3 *(adj) A vacant stare.* blank, glazed, expressionless, faraway, dreamy, absent-minded, abstracted, vague, inattentive.

vague
1 *(adj) I could see a vague shape through the fog.* indistinct, hazy, shadowy, ill-defined, blurred, fuzzy, dim, faint.
OPPOSITES: clear, distinct.
2 *(adj) Justin has a vague idea of history.* hazy, woolly, foggy, inexact, imprecise, rough, broad, generalized.
OPPOSITES: clear, well-defined.
3 *(adj) Professor Peabody is terribly vague. See* **absent-minded**.

vain
(adj) Too much praise can make you vain. conceited, bigheaded *(informal)*, swollen-headed *(informal)*, self-satisfied, proud, arrogant, narcissistic, cocky, puffed up.
OPPOSITES: modest, humble.

valuable
1 *(adj) A valuable painting.* expensive, precious, costly, priceless, invaluable, dear, treasured, highly prized.
OPPOSITES: worthless, inexpensive.
2 *(adj) A valuable clue. See* **useful** 2.

vanish
(v) The figure seemed to vanish. disappear, become invisible, vanish into thin air, dematerialize, vanish off the face of the earth, fade away, melt away.
OPPOSITES: appear, materialize.

vast
1 *(adj) The universe is vast.* immense, huge, boundless, infinite, immeasurable, never-ending, limitless, unending, unbounded, sweeping, extensive.
OPPOSITES: tiny, limited.
2 *(adj) A vast appetite. See* **enormous**.

vegetable
(n) greens (plural), garden produce.
TYPES OF VEGETABLE: artichoke, asparagus, aubergine, beetroot, broad bean, broccoli, Brussels sprout, cabbage, carrot, cauliflower, celery, chicory, courgette, cucumber, fennel, garlic, haricot bean, kale, leek, lettuce, mangetout, marrow, mushroom, okra, onion, parsnip, pea, potato, pumpkin, radish, rocket, runner bean, shallot, spinach, spring greens (plural), spring onion, squash, string bean, swede, sweet corn, sweet pepper, sweet potato, turnip, watercress.

very
1 (adv) I was very sad to hear your news. extremely, really, terribly, dreadfully, deeply, truly, profoundly, intensely, acutely, awfully (informal).
2 (adv) Mrs Badger was very impressed with Oscar's work. extremely, really, tremendously, highly, greatly, most, exceedingly, enormously, hugely, mightily.

vibrate see shake 1.

vicious see fierce 1.

victory
(n) The team were excited by their victory. win, success, triumph, conquest.
OPPOSITE: defeat.

view
1 (n) What a beautiful view! vista, scene, sight, outlook, prospect, panorama, landscape, seascape, spectacle, picture.
2 (n) Kali shared my view that the film was awful. opinion, point of view, judgment, belief, conviction, assessment, way of thinking, idea, feeling, impression.

viewpoint
(n) Try to see the problem from a different viewpoint. angle, perspective, point of view, standpoint, position, side, slant.

vile see horrible 1, 2.

violent
1 (adj) A violent attack. savage, vicious, brutal, bloody, bloodthirsty, ferocious, fierce, barbaric, murderous, frenzied.
2 (adj) Violent emotions. powerful, uncontrollable, passionate, burning, intense, vehement, tempestuous, overwhelming, ungovernable, extreme.
3 (adj) A violent storm. raging, tempestuous, tumultuous, turbulent, wild, blustery, fierce, severe, devastating.
4 (adj) A violent stab of pain. See sharp 3.

visible see noticeable.

visit
1 (v) May I visit you next summer? come to see, go to see, call in on, drop in on (informal), look you up, pay you a visit, stay with, be your guest, descend on.
2 (n) Enjoy your visit to Paris! See trip 1.

vital
(adj) The doctor made a vital decision. critical, crucial, life-or-death, urgent, serious, significant, important, key, major.

vivid
1 (adj) I love vivid colours. brilliant, vibrant, glowing, bright, bold, strong, rich, deep, clear, luminous, fluorescent, dazzling.
OPPOSITES: dull, pale.
2 (adj) Gita gave a vivid account of her travels. graphic, dramatic, colourful, lively, exciting, striking, powerful, expressive, imaginative, true-to-life, realistic, lifelike.
OPPOSITES: dull, lifeless.

---

volcano
volcanoes...

belch	growl	smoulder
blow up	grumble	spew
erupt	roar	spurt
explode	rumble	steam
flare up	smoke	thunder

volcanoes send out...

burning rock	smoke
cinders	steam
lava (molten rock)	suffocating
lava flow	clouds
poisonous gas	volcanic ash

lava may...

burn	flow	solidify
bury	gush	spread
destroy	harden	stream
devastate	pour	surge
engulf	slide	sweep

lava can be..

bubbling	glimmering	runny
fiery	glowing	sticky
flaming	lumpy	viscous
fluid	red-hot	(thick)

volcanoes can be...

active
dormant
extinct
underwater

volcanic bomb (lump of solidified lava)

smoke

cone

lava fountain

crater

river of lava

---

volunteer
(v) Did you volunteer to help? offer, put yourself forward, come forward, step forward, offer your services.

vomit
(v) I think I'm going to vomit! be sick, throw up (informal), puke (slang), spew up, retch, heave, gag, bring up, do a technicolour yawn (slang).

vote
1 (n) What was the result of the vote? poll, ballot, show of hands, election.
2 vote for (v) I didn't know who to vote for. cast a vote for, choose, elect, return, nominate, opt for, select, pick, support.

voyage see journey 1, 2.

vulgar
1 (adj) Vulgar jokes. See crude.
2 (adj) Vulgar jewellery. tasteless, flashy, showy, gaudy, garish, ostentatious, tawdry, tacky (informal), cheap and nasty.
OPPOSITE: tasteful.

Ww

waffle
(v) Don't waffle! Stick to the point! ramble, witter (informal), rabbit on (informal), blather, beat about the bush.

wail
(v) Babies wail when they're hungry. cry, howl, yowl, sob, weep, bawl, shriek, caterwaul, moan, whine, complain.

wait
1 (v) Wait until it's your turn. be patient, hold on (informal), hang on (informal), sit tight, stand by, hold back, hold your horses, cool your heels, hang fire.
2 (v) Wait here until I get back. stay, stop, remain, stay put, hang around.

wake up
(v) I didn't wake up until midday. wake, stir, surface (informal), get up, rise, come to life, awaken (old-fashioned).

walk
1 (v) I usually walk to school. go on foot, travel on foot, foot it, hoof it (slang).
WAYS TO WALK: amble, crawl, creep, dodder, hike, hobble, limp, lope, march, mince, mooch (slang), pace, pad, parade, plod, prowl, ramble, saunter, scuttle, shamble, shuffle, slink, stagger, stalk, stomp (informal), stride, stroll, strut, stumble, swagger, teeter, tiptoe, toddle, totter, traipse (informal), tramp, trek, trot, trudge, waddle, wander.
2 (v) Don't walk on the tulips! tread, trample, tramp, step, stamp, walk all over.
3 (n) Let's go for a walk. stroll, saunter, wander, ramble, hike, tramp, trek, march.

wander

1 (v) *I'll just wander round town.* drift, saunter, stroll, amble, mooch (slang), traipse (informal), roam, ramble, cruise.
2 (v) *Don't wander off! See* **stray** 2.

want

(v) *The genie will give you whatever you want.* desire, wish for, fancy, like, dream of, crave, long for, yearn for, hanker after, set your heart on, covet, pine for, need.

war

(n) *Many soldiers were killed in the war.* conflict, fighting, hostilities (plural), armed conflict, struggle, confrontation, combat.

warm

1 (adj) *A warm evening.* mild, balmy, hot, sultry, sunny, summery, fine, pleasant.
OPPOSITES: cool, cold.
2 (adj) *Warm water.* lukewarm, tepid.
OPPOSITES: cool, cold.
3 (adj) *A warm coat.* thick, heavy, woolly, fleecy, cosy, snug, thermal, padded.
OPPOSITES: thin, lightweight.
4 (adj) *A warm welcome.* hearty, cordial, friendly, heartfelt, fervent, enthusiastic, emotional, effusive, ecstatic, rapturous.
OPPOSITES: cool, hostile.

warn

1 (v) *I'll warn you if anyone comes.* alert, tip you off, let you know, inform, notify, give you fair warning, raise the alarm.
2 (v) *Didn't I warn you not to hitchhike?* caution, tell, advise, counsel, urge, remind.

warning

(n) *Did you have any warning of what would happen?* advance notice, forewarning, tip-off, notification, word, sign, hint, indication, premonition, omen.

wash

1 (v) *Did you wash before you went to bed?* have a wash, wash yourself, have a bath, have a shower, bath, shower.
2 (v) *We must wash our car.* clean, shampoo, sponge down, scrub, soap, swab down, wipe, mop, launder (clothes).

waste

(v) *Don't waste all your money at the fair.* squander, fritter away, throw away, blow (slang), use up, run through, exhaust.

watch

1 (v) *I like to watch the people.* look at, observe, see, gaze at, stare at, survey, view, contemplate, check out (informal), scrutinize, inspect, peer at, peep at, gape at, gawp at (slang), ogle, clock (slang).
2 (v) *Watch what I do first.* observe, look at, notice, pay attention to, mark, note.
3 (v) *I'll watch your bike for you.* keep watch over, keep an eye on, guard, mind, take care of, look after, protect.

watch out

(v) *Watch out for signs of trouble.* look out, be on the lookout, keep a lookout, keep your eyes open, be on the alert, be on your guard, be vigilant, be watchful.

wave

1 (v) *Wave when the coast is clear.* signal, indicate, gesture, motion, sign, beckon.
2 (v) *Don't wave that stick at me!* shake, waggle, brandish, flourish, swing, twirl.
3 (v) *Watch the grass wave in the breeze.* sway, stir, ripple, quiver, shake, flutter.
4 (n) *The surfer was carried along on the wave.* breaker, roller, billow, surf, swell, white horses (plural), tidal wave.

way

1 (n) *Is this the right way home?* route, direction, road, path, street, lane, track.
2 (n) *Think of a way to solve the puzzle.* method, technique, procedure, system, means (plural), plan, approach, scheme.

weak

1 (adj) *Mia felt weak after her illness.* frail, feeble, delicate, fragile, faint, shaky, unsteady, debilitated, infirm, incapacitated, sickly, tired, exhausted, wasted, puny.
OPPOSITES: strong, energetic.
2 (adj) *The bridge is too weak to support us.* flimsy, insubstantial, rickety, unsafe, shaky, unsteady, thin, fragile, delicate.
OPPOSITES: strong, sturdy.
3 (adj) *Don't be weak!* feeble, spineless, timid, cowardly, pathetic, wet (informal), soft, wimpish (informal), weedy (informal).
OPPOSITES: assertive, brave.
4 (adj) *This drink is too weak.* watery, diluted, watered down, wishy-washy (informal), tasteless, insipid, thin.
OPPOSITES: strong, concentrated.
5 (adj) *A weak excuse. See* **feeble** 3.
6 (adj) *A weak cry. See* **faint** 4.

weakness

1 (n) *Nat's weakness is laziness.* failing, shortcoming, fault, flaw, defect, problem.
OPPOSITES: strength, asset.
2 (n) *Jo has a weakness for sweets.* liking, fondness, taste, passion, love, soft spot.

wealthy *see* **rich** 1.

weapons

(plural n) arms (plural), munitions (plural), armaments (plural), weaponry, offensive weapons (plural).
TYPES OF WEAPON: battering ram, battleaxe, bayonet, bazooka, biological weapons (plural), blowpipe, bomb, boomerang, bow and arrow, cannon, catapult, cosh, crossbow, cudgel, dagger, flame-thrower, grenade, guided missile, gun, harpoon, lance, longbow, missile, mortar, mustard gas, nerve gas, pike, rocket, shell, spear, sword, tear gas, tomahawk, torpedo, truncheon, warhead.
Also see **bomb**, **gun**, **sword**.

wear

(v) *What will you wear?* put on, dress in, be dressed in, have on, sport (informal).

wear away

(v) *The sea will slowly wear away the rocks.* erode, eat away, wear down, grind down, wash away, crumble, dissolve, corrode (metal), eat into, rot, decay.

wear out

(v) *My shirt is starting to wear out.* become worn, show signs of wear, wear thin, fray, go into holes, become threadbare.

weather

(n) climate, weather conditions (plural).

a stormy day

it is hot
baking
blistering
boiling
roasting
scorching
searing
sizzling
sweltering
torrid

a scorching day

it is cloudy
dark
dismal
dreary
dull
gloomy
grey
overcast
sunless

it is humid
clammy
close
muggy
oppressive
steamy
sticky
stifling
stuffy
suffocating
sultry

it is fine
balmy
bright
calm
clear
cloudless
dry
fair
mild
pleasant
still
summery
sunny
sunshiny
warm

it is wet
bucketing (informal)
coming down in torrents
damp
drizzly
lashing down
pelting down
pouring
rainy
showery
spitting
teeming
tipping down (informal)

it is foggy
hazy
misty
murky
smoggy

it is windy
blowy
blustery
breezy
gusty
squally
stormy

it is cold
bitter
bracing
chilly
cool
crisp
freezing
fresh
frosty
icy
nippy
numbing
parky (informal)
perishing (informal)
raw
snowy
wintry

a murky evening

a frosty morning

Also see **ice, frost & snow, storm words.**

wedding *see* **marriage** 2.

weird *see* **strange** 1, 2.

welcome
(adj) Emily's parents made me feel welcome. at home, one of the family, accepted, appreciated, wanted, included.
OPPOSITES: unwelcome, excluded.

well
1 *(adj) You look well.* healthy, fit, in good health, blooming, strong, robust, thriving.
OPPOSITES: unwell, ill.
2 *(n) The well provided water for the village.* water hole, borehole, spring, water source, oasis, artesian well, wishing well.

well-behaved
(adj) A well-behaved child. good, obedient, cooperative, amenable, compliant, docile, polite, well-mannered, dutiful.
OPPOSITES: badly behaved, naughty.

well-known *see* **famous**.

wet
1 *(adj) My clothes are wet.* damp, soaking, dripping, sopping wet, sodden, drenched, wringing wet, saturated, wet through.
OPPOSITES: dry, bone-dry *(informal)*.
2 *(adj) After the rain, the ground was wet.* damp, moist, sodden, waterlogged, saturated, soggy, spongy, muddy, dewy.
OPPOSITES: dry, parched.
3 *(adj) If it's wet we won't go out.* rainy, raining, pouring, drizzly, showery, damp, misty, dank, clammy, humid.
OPPOSITES: dry, fine.
4 *(adj) (informal) Stand up for yourself and don't be so wet! See* **weak** 3.
5 *(v) Wet the cloth.* dampen, moisten, soak, drench, saturate, steep, douse, splash, sprinkle, spray, irrigate *(ground)*.

whine
1 *(v) The toddler began to whine.* whimper, wail, cry, grizzle *(informal)*.
2 *(v) Cecil always finds something to whine about. See* **complain**.

whip *see* **beat** 1, 4.

whirl
(v) Watch the dancers whirl round the room. spin, twirl, swirl, circle, wheel, reel, pirouette, gyrate, revolve, rotate, swivel.

whisper
1 *(v) I can't hear you when you whisper.* speak under your breath, speak in hushed tones, talk quietly, speak softly, keep your voice down, murmur, mutter.
2 *(n) Sandy spoke in a whisper.* low voice, quiet voice, soft voice, murmur, stage whisper, undertone, hushed tones *(plural)*.

white
1 *(adj) The statue looked white in the moonlight.* milky, chalky, pearly, silvery, snow-white, alabaster, ivory, ghostly.
2 *(adj) Granny has white hair.* snowy, snow-white, silver, silvery, hoary.
3 *(adj) Edmund's face was white with fear.* ashen, pale, pallid, bloodless, wan, pasty, waxen, chalky, drained.

whole
(adj) Will the whole film be shown on television? entire, complete, full, total, uncut, unedited, unabridged *(book)*.

wicked
1 *(adj) A wicked criminal.* evil, bad, sinful, immoral, corrupt, depraved, villainous, vicious, vile, fiendish, diabolical, devilish, black-hearted, lawless.
OPPOSITES: good, virtuous.
2 *(adj) A wicked grin. See* **mischievous** 2.

wide *see* **broad** 1, 2.

wild
1 *(adj) That dog is quite wild.* untamed, undomesticated, savage, fierce, ferocious.
OPPOSITES: tame, domesticated.
2 *(adj) We crossed some wild country.* uncultivated, unspoilt, untamed, natural, deserted, empty, waste, barren, desolate, bleak, rough, rugged, overgrown.
OPPOSITES: cultivated, inhabited.
3 *(adj) What wild weather! See* **stormy** 1.
4 *(adj) The boys are very wild.* rowdy, boisterous, unruly, uncontrollable, undisciplined, wayward, out of control, rough, noisy, violent, rude, riotous.
5 *(adj) Ziggy had a wild idea. See* **mad** 3.
6 *(adj) Al is wild about soccer. See* **mad** 5.

willing
(adj) Helen is always willing to help. glad, happy, pleased, ready, quick, prepared, eager, keen, game *(informal)*.
OPPOSITES: unwilling, reluctant.

wilt *see* **wither**.

win
1 *(v) I hope that I will win.* come first, be the winner, get first place, take first prize, finish first, be victorious, triumph, succeed.
OPPOSITES: lose, come last.
2 *(v) Mo wants to win a medal.* gain, earn, secure, obtain, receive, collect, pick up.

wince *see* **flinch**.

wind
1 *(n) A strong wind can cause a lot of damage.* breeze, gust, blast, squall, headwind, crosswind, tailwind, gale, tornado, cyclone, whirlwind, twister *(informal)*. ❖ *Also see* **storm words**.
2 *(v) The path began to wind up the mountain.* meander, snake, twist and turn, twist, zigzag, weave, spiral, corkscrew.
3 *(v) Wind the tinsel round the tree.* loop, twist, coil, entwine, wrap, curl, thread.

window
(n) TYPES OF WINDOW: bay window, bow window, casement window, dormer window, fanlight, French window, leaded window, louvred window, oriel window, picture window, plate-glass window, porthole, rose window, sash window, skylight, stained-glass window.

windy
1 *(adj) A windy day.* breezy, blustery, blowy, gusty, squally, stormy, wild.
OPPOSITES: calm, still.

2 *(adj) A windy spot.* exposed, open, unprotected, windswept, bleak, desolate.
OPPOSITE: sheltered.

winner
(n) Who is the winner? victor, champion, prizewinner, medallist, champ *(informal)*.
OPPOSITE: loser.

wipe
(v) Wipe the surface. clean, sponge, mop, swab, wash, dust, polish, rub, brush.

wise
1 *(adj) A wise ruler.* learned, clever, knowledgeable, intelligent, astute, shrewd, perceptive, discerning, understanding, enlightened, experienced, deep-thinking.
OPPOSITE: foolish.
2 *(adj) A wise choice. See* **sensible** 2.

wish
1 *(n) Josie has a secret wish to be famous.* desire, longing, hankering, yearning, craving, hunger, ambition, aspiration, hope, dream, fancy, whim.
2 *(n) The genie will carry out your every wish.* request, desire, demand, command, order, instruction, bidding.
3 **wish for** *(v) The genie will give you whatever you wish for. See* **want**.

wistful
(adj) You look wistful; what are you thinking about? sad, forlorn, melancholy, disconsolate, thoughtful, pensive, dreamy.

witch
(n) sorceress, enchantress, crone.

wither
(v) The daffodils will wither if you don't water them. wilt, dry up, shrivel up, fade, droop, go limp, flop, sag, flag, die.
OPPOSITES: flourish, bloom.

witty
(adj) Tim's witty remarks made me laugh. funny, humorous, amusing, clever, quick-witted, sparkling, lively, droll, facetious.

wizard *see* **magician** 1.

wobble
1 *(v) Can you make the bottle wobble without knocking it over?* teeter, totter, rock, sway, waver, seesaw, oscillate.
2 *(v) Look at the jelly wobble!* quiver, tremble, shake, vibrate, quake.

woman
(n) Who's that woman? lady, girl, female, dame *(slang)*, lass, maiden *(old-fashioned)*.

wonder
1 *(n) We gazed at the magician in wonder.* amazement, astonishment, awe, wonderment, admiration, curiosity, bewilderment, surprise, disbelief.
2 *(n) The pyramids were a wonder of the Ancient World.* marvel, phenomenon, miracle, spectacle, curiosity, attraction.
3 *(v) It's pointless to wonder what might have happened.* think about, ponder, speculate about, ask yourself, puzzle over, reflect on, meditate on, query, question, be curious about, be inquisitive about.

wonderful

1 *(adj) What a wonderful party!* fantastic *(informal)*, marvellous, great *(informal)*, terrific *(informal)*, superb, excellent, fabulous *(informal)*, tremendous *(informal)*, amazing *(informal)*, sensational *(informal)*, magnificent, wicked *(slang)*, decent *(informal)*, cool *(informal)*.
OPPOSITES: terrible, dreadful.
2 *(adj) Modern medicine can do wonderful things.* amazing, astonishing, incredible, astounding, extraordinary, remarkable, staggering, marvellous, miraculous, phenomenal, awe-inspiring.
OPPOSITES: commonplace, unremarkable.

wood

1 *(n) Don't get lost in the wood.* woods *(plural)*, woodland, copse, spinney, thicket, coppice, forest, trees *(plural)*.
2 *(n) The shed was made of wood.* timber, logs *(plural)*, planks *(plural)*, boards *(plural)*.

word

1 *(n) What's the proper word for this thing?* name, term, expression.
2 *(n) Give me your word you'll be there.* See **promise** 2.

work

1 *(v) You'll have to work if you want to pass your exams.* slog away, slave, graft *(informal)*, sweat *(informal)*, labour, toil, exert yourself, beaver away *(informal)*, peg away, keep your nose to the grindstone.
2 *(v) Lord Lucre doesn't need to work.* have a job, go to work, earn a living.
3 *(v) This whisk is easy to work.* See **use** 2.
4 *(v) Our CD player doesn't work properly.* function, go, perform, run, operate, play.
5 *(v) My plan might work.* See **succeed** 2.
6 *(n) I need a rest after all that work.* hard work, effort, toil, labour, exertion, drudgery, graft *(informal)*, hard grind *(informal)*, donkey-work, slavery.
7 *(n) What work do you do?* See **job** 2.

work out

1 *(v) Can you work out the answer to this question?* figure out *(informal)*, calculate, deduce, puzzle out, suss out *(slang)*, find out, discover, solve, find the solution to.
2 *(v) We must work out a plan.* think up, come up with, concoct, devise, construct, put together, decide on, formulate.
3 *(v) Pamela likes to work out on the beach.* exercise, do exercises, train, keep fit, tone up, lift weights, pump iron *(slang)*.

world

1 *(n) Captain Stardust travelled round the world.* earth, globe, planet.
2 *(n) How did the world begin?* earth, universe, cosmos, life, existence, human life, nature, creation, everything.

worn out *see* **exhausted**.
worried *see* **anxious** 1.

worry

1 *(v) Don't worry about the exams.* fret, be anxious, be apprehensive, get in a state *(informal)*, get worked up, get in a stew *(informal)*, agonize, torment yourself.
2 *(v) Don't let this small problem worry you.* trouble, concern, bother, distress, upset, disturb, unsettle, make you anxious.
3 *(n) Ziggy has caused his parents a lot of worry.* anxiety, concern, unease, distress, bother, hassle *(informal)*, problems *(plural)*.

worthwhile

(adj) I want to do a job that's really worthwhile. useful, valuable, helpful, worth the effort, constructive, beneficial, important, rewarding, profitable.
OPPOSITES: worthless, pointless.

wound

1 *(n) The doctor examined the wound.* cut, gash, laceration, knife wound, stab wound, bullet wound, incision, injury.
2 *(v) Did the terrorists wound anyone?* See **injure**.

wrap

1 *(v) Wrap the ornament in cotton wool.* pack, cover, bundle up, surround, swathe, drape, enfold, enclose, envelop, cocoon.
2 *(v) Wrap the tape round the pole.* wind, loop, twist, roll, coil, twine, bind.

wreck

1 *(v) Don't wreck the furniture!* destroy, demolish, break, smash, trash *(slang)*, total *(slang)*, write off *(car)* *(informal)*.
2 *(v) One mistake could wreck our chances of winning.* See **ruin** 1.
3 *(n) Divers explored the wreck.* shipwreck, sunken ship, wreckage, hulk.

wreckage

(n) Rescuers sifted through the wreckage debris, remains *(plural)*, rubble, ruins *(plural)*, fragments *(plural)*.

wriggle

1 *(v) Sit still and don't wriggle!* fidget, squirm, jiggle about, twist around, writhe around, shift around, jerk about.
2 *(v) Watch the snake wriggle across the grass.* wiggle, zigzag, twist and turn, writhe, snake, worm, slither, crawl, slink.

wrinkled

1 *(adj) A wrinkled face.* lined, wrinkly, furrowed, wizened, crinkly, creased.
2 *(adj) A wrinkled shirt.* creased, crumpled, rumpled, crinkled, unironed.

write

1 *(v) I'll write your number on this pad.* write down, note down, jot down, take down, make a note of, record, scribble, scrawl, print, put in writing, copy, inscribe.
2 *(v) I have to write a story for homework.* make up, invent, create, compose, draft, pen, dash off, put together, concoct.

writer

(n) author, novelist, scriptwriter, dramatist, playwright, poet, biographer, journalist.

writing

(n) I can't read this writing. handwriting, scrawl, scribble, script, print, letters *(plural)*, characters *(plural)*, calligraphy.

wrong

1 *(adj) My theory turned out to be wrong.* incorrect, inaccurate, mistaken, off target, wide of the mark, erroneous, false, untrue, off beam *(informal)*, way out *(informal)*.
OPPOSITES: right, correct.
2 *(adj) It's wrong to sell stolen goods.* illegal, unlawful, criminal, immoral, unethical, dishonest, corrupt, deceitful, crooked *(informal)*, wicked, sinful, evil.
OPPOSITES: right, legal.
3 *(adj) It would be wrong to wear a bikini to school.* inappropriate, unsuitable, unfitting, unseemly, improper, unacceptable, not done, unconventional, funny, incongruous, incorrect.
OPPOSITES: right, proper.
4 **go wrong** *see* **go wrong** 1, 2.

Xx Yy Zz

xylophone

(n) glockenspiel, chime bars *(plural)*.

yearn *see* **long** 3.
yell *see* **shout**.

yellow

(n) SHADES OF YELLOW: amber, buttercup yellow, canary yellow, gold, lemon, mustard, ochre, primrose, saffron.

young

1 *(adj) Young children can't look after themselves.* small, little, infant, newborn.
OPPOSITES: old, grown-up.
2 *(adj) Zak is so young for his age.* childish, babyish, immature, juvenile, infantile, puerile, adolescent.
OPPOSITES: mature, grown-up.
3 *(adj) My parents still seem young.* youthful, boyish, girlish, fresh-faced, sprightly, spry, well-preserved, active.
OPPOSITES: old, elderly.
4 *(plural n) Animals try to protect their young.* babies *(plural)*, offspring *(plural)*, little ones *(plural)*, litter, brood, family.

zero *see* **nothing** 2.
zoom *see* **speed** 4.